FIRST CENSUS
OF THE UNITED STATES
1790

❧

NORTH CAROLINA

Southern Historical Press, Inc.
Greenville, South Carolina

Please direct all correspondence and book orders to:
SOUTHERN HISTORICAL PRESS, Inc.
PO Box 1267
Greenville, SC   29602-1267

DEPARTMENT OF COMMERCE AND LABOR

BUREAU OF THE CENSUS

S. N. D. NORTH, DIRECTOR

HEADS OF FAMILIES

AT THE FIRST CENSUS OF THE

UNITED STATES TAKEN

IN THE YEAR

1790

NORTH CAROLINA

WASHINGTON

GOVERNMENT PRINTING OFFICE

1908

HEADS OF FAMILIES AT THE FIRST CENSUS
1790

INTRODUCTION.

The First Census of the United States (1790) comprised an enumeration of the inhabitants of the present states of Connecticut, Delaware, Georgia, Kentucky, Maine, Maryland, Massachusetts, New Hampshire, New Jersey, New York, North Carolina, Pennsylvania, Rhode Island, South Carolina, Tennessee, Vermont, and Virginia.

A complete set of the schedules for each state, with a summary for the counties, and in many cases for towns, was filed in the State Department, but unfortunately they are not now complete, the returns for the states of Delaware, Georgia, Kentucky, New Jersey, Tennessee, and Virginia having been destroyed when the British burned the Capitol at Washington during the War of 1812. For several of the states for which schedules are lacking it is probable that the Director of the Census could obtain lists which would present the names of most of the heads of families at the date of the First Census. In Virginia, state enumerations were made in 1782, 1783, 1784, and 1785, but the lists on file in the State Library include the names for only 39 of the 78 counties into which the state was divided.

The schedules of 1790 form a unique inheritance for the Nation, since they represent for each of the states concerned a complete list of the heads of families in the United States at the time of the adoption of the Constitution. The framers were the statesmen and leaders of thought, but those whose names appear upon the schedules of the First Census were in general the plain citizens who by their conduct in war and peace made the Constitution possible and by their intelligence and self-restraint put it into successful operation.

The total population of the United States in 1790, exclusive of slaves, as derived from the schedules was 3,231,533. The only names appearing upon the schedules, however, were those of heads of families, and as at that period the families averaged 6 persons, the total number was approximately 540,000, or slightly more than half a million. The number of names which is now lacking because of the destruction of the schedules is approximately 140,000, thus leaving schedules containing about 400,000 names.

The information contained in the published report of the First Census of the United States, a small volume of 56 pages, was not uniform for the several states and territories. For New England and one or two of the other states the population was presented by counties and towns; that of New Jersey appeared partly by counties and towns and partly by counties only; in other cases the returns were given by counties only. Thus the complete transcript of the names of heads of families, with accompanying information, presents for the first time detailed information as to the number of inhabitants—males, females, etc.—for each minor civil division in all those states for which such information was not originally published.

In response to repeated requests from patriotic societies and persons interested in genealogy, or desirous of studying the early history of the United States, Congress added to the sundry civil appropriation bill for the fiscal year 1907 the following paragraph:

The Director of the Census is hereby authorized and directed to publish, in a permanent form, by counties and minor civil divisions, the names of the heads of families returned at the First Census of the United States in seventeen hundred and ninety; and the Director of the Census is authorized, in his discretion, to sell said publications, the proceeds thereof to be covered into the Treasury of the United States, to be deposited to the credit of miscellaneous receipts on account of " Proceeds of sales of Government property:"

Provided, That no expense shall be incurred hereunder additional to appropriations for the Census Office for printing therefor made for the fiscal year nineteen hundred and seven; and the Director of the Census is hereby directed to report to Congress at its next session the cost incurred hereunder and the price fixed for said publications and the total received therefor.

The amount of money appropriated by Congress for the Census printing for the fiscal year mentioned was unfortunately not sufficient to meet the current requirement of the Office and to publish the transcription of the First Census, and no provision was made in the sundry civil appropriation bill for 1908 for the continuance of authority to publish these important records. Resources, however, were available for printing a small section of the work, and the schedules of New Hampshire, Vermont, and Maryland accordingly were published.

The urgent deficiency bill, approved February 15, 1908, contained the following provision:

That the Director of the Census is hereby authorized and directed to expend so much of the appropriation for printing for the Department of Commerce and Labor allotted by law to the Census Office for the fiscal year ending June thirtieth, nineteen hundred and eight, as may be necessary to continue and complete the publication of the names of the heads of families returned at the First Census of the United States, as authorized by the sundry civil appropriation act approved June thirtieth, nineteen hundred and six.

In accordance with the authority given in the paragraph quoted above, the names returned at the First Census in the states of Connecticut, Maine, Massachusetts, New York, North Carolina, Pennsylvania, Rhode Island, and South Carolina have been published, thus completing the roster of the heads of families in 1790 so far as they can be shown from the records of the Census Office. As the Federal census schedules of the state of Virginia for 1790 are missing, the lists of the state enumerations made in 1782, 1783, 1784, and 1785 have been substituted and, while not complete, they will, undoubtedly, prove of great value.

THE FIRST CENSUS.

The First Census act was passed at the second session of the First Congress, and was signed by President Washington on March 1, 1790. The task of making the first enumeration of inhabitants was placed upon the President. Under this law the marshals of the several judicial districts were required to ascertain the number of inhabitants within their respective districts, omitting Indians not taxed, and distinguishing free persons (including those bound to service for a term of years) from all others; the sex and color of free persons; and the number of free males 16 years of age and over.

The object of the inquiry last mentioned was, undoubtedly, to obtain definite knowledge as to the military and industrial strength of the country. This fact possesses special interest, because the Constitution directs merely an enumeration of inhabitants. Thus the demand for increasingly extensive information, which has been so marked a characteristic of census legislation, began with the First Congress that dealt with the subject.

The method followed by the President in putting into operation the First Census law, although the object of extended investigation, is not definitely known. It is supposed that the President or the Secretary of State dispatched copies of the law, and perhaps of instructions also, to the marshals. There is, however, some ground for disputing this conclusion. At least one of the reports in the census volume of 1790 was furnished by a governor. This, together with the fact that there is no record of correspondence with the marshals on the subject of the census, but that there is a record of such correspondence with the governors, makes very strong the inference that the marshals re-ceived their instructions through the governors of the states. This inference is strengthened by the fact that in 1790 the state of Massachusetts furnished the printed blanks, and also by the fact that the law relating to the Second Census specifically charged the Secretary of State to superintend the enumeration and to communicate directly with the marshals.

By the terms of the First Census law nine months were allowed in which to complete the enumeration. The census taking was supervised by the marshals of the several judicial districts, who employed assistant marshals to act as enumerators. There were 17 marshals. The records showing the number of assistant marshals employed in 1790, 1800, and 1810 were destroyed by fire, but the number employed in 1790 has been estimated at 650.

The schedules which these officials prepared consist of lists of names of heads of families; each name appears in a stub, or first column, which is followed by five columns, giving details of the family. These columns are headed as follows:

Free white males of 16 years and upward, including heads of families.

Free white males under 16 years.

Free white females, including heads of families.

All other free persons.

Slaves.

The assistant marshals made two copies of the returns; in accordance with the law one copy was posted in the immediate neighborhood for the information of the public, and the other was transmitted to the marshal in charge, to be forwarded to the President. The schedules were turned over by the President to the Secretary of State. Little or no tabulation was required, and the report of the First Census, as also the reports of the Second, Third, and Fourth, was produced without the employment of any clerical force, the summaries being transmitted directly to the printer. The total population as returned in 1790 was 3,929,214, and the entire cost of the census was $44,377.

A summary of the results of the First Census, not including the returns for South Carolina, was transmitted to Congress by President Washington on October 27, 1791. The legal period for enumeration, nine months, had been extended, the longest time consumed being eighteen months in South Carolina. The report of October 27 was printed in full, and published in what is now a very rare little volume; afterwards the report for South Carolina was "tipped in." To contain the results of the Twelfth Census, ten large quarto volumes, comprising in all 10,400 pages, were required. No illustration of the expansion of census inquiry can be more striking.

The original schedules of the First Census are now contained in 26 bound volumes, preserved in the Census Office. For the most part the headings of the schedules were written in by hand. Indeed, up to and

including 1820, the assistant marshals generally used for the schedules such paper as they happened to have, ruling it, writing in the headings, and binding the sheets together themselves. In some cases merchants' account paper was used, and now and then the schedules were bound in wall paper.

As a consequence of requiring marshals to supply their own blanks, the volumes containing the schedules vary in size from about 7 inches long, 3 inches wide, and ½ inch thick to 21 inches long, 14 inches wide, and 6 inches thick. Some of the sheets in these volumes are only 4 inches long, but a few are 3 feet in length, necessitating several folds. In some cases leaves burned at the edges have been covered with transparent silk to preserve them.

THE UNITED STATES IN 1790.

In March, 1790, the Union consisted of twelve states—Rhode Island, the last of the original thirteen to enter the Union, being admitted May 29 of the same year. Vermont, the first addition, was admitted in the following year, before the results of the First Census were announced. Maine was a part of Massachusetts, Kentucky was a part of Virginia, and the present states of Alabama and Mississippi were parts of Georgia. The present states of Ohio, Indiana, Illinois, Michigan, and Wisconsin, with part of Minnesota, were known as the Northwest Territory, and the present state of Tennessee, then a part of North Carolina, was soon to be organized as the Southwest Territory.

The United States was bounded on the west by the Mississippi river, beyond which stretched that vast and unexplored wilderness belonging to the Spanish King, which was afterwards ceded to the United States by France as the Louisiana Purchase, and now comprises the great and populous states of South Dakota, Iowa, Nebraska, Missouri, Kansas, Arkansas, and Oklahoma, and portions of Minnesota, North Dakota, Montana, Wyoming, Colorado, New Mexico, Texas, and Louisiana. The Louisiana Purchase was not consummated for more than a decade after the First Census was taken. On the south was another Spanish colony known as the Floridas. The greater part of Texas, then a part of the colony of Mexico, belonged to Spain; and California, Nevada, Utah, Arizona, and a portion of New Mexico, also the property of Spain, although penetrated here and there by venturesome explorers and missionaries, were, for the most part, an undiscovered wilderness.

The gross area of the United States was 827,844 square miles, but the settled area was only 239,935 square miles, or about 29 per cent of the total. Though the area covered by the enumeration in 1790 seems very small when compared with the present area of the United States, the difficulties which confronted the census taker were vastly greater than in 1900. In many localities there were no roads, and where these did exist they were poor and frequently impassable; bridges were almost unknown. Transportation was entirely by horseback, stage, or private coach. A journey as long as that from New York to Washington was a serious undertaking, requiring eight days under the most favorable conditions. Western New York was a wilderness, Elmira and Binghamton being but detached hamlets. The territory west of the Allegheny mountains, with the exception of a portion of Kentucky, was unsettled and scarcely penetrated. Detroit and Vincennes were too small and isolated to merit consideration. Philadelphia was the capital of the United States. Washington was a mere Government project, not even named, but known as the Federal City. Indeed, by the spring of 1793, only one wall of the White House had been constructed, and the site for the Capitol had been merely surveyed. New York city in 1790 possessed a population of only 33,131, although it was the largest city in the United States; Philadelphia was second, with 28,522; and Boston third, with 18,320. Mails were transported in very irregular fashion, and correspondence was expensive and uncertain.

There were, moreover, other difficulties which were of serious moment in 1790, but which long ago ceased to be problems in census taking. The inhabitants, having no experience with census taking, imagined that some scheme for increasing taxation was involved, and were inclined to be cautious lest they should reveal too much of their own affairs. There was also opposition to enumeration on religious grounds, a count of inhabitants being regarded by many as a cause for divine displeasure. The boundaries of towns and other minor divisions, and even those of counties, were in many cases unknown or not defined at all. The hitherto semi-independent states had been under the control of the Federal Government for so short a time that the different sections had not yet been welded into an harmonious nationality in which the Federal authority should be unquestioned and instructions promptly and fully obeyed.

AN ACT PROVIDING FOR THE ENUMERATION OF THE INHABITANTS OF THE UNITED STATES

APPROVED MARCH 1, 1790

SECTION 1. Be it enacted by the Senate and House of Representatives of the United States of America in Congress assembled, That the marshals of the several districts of the United States shall be, and they are hereby authorized and required to cause the number of the inhabitants within their respective districts to be taken; omitting in such enumeration Indians not taxed, and distinguishing free persons, including those bound to service for a term of years, from all others; distinguishing also the sexes and colours of free persons, and the free males of sixteen years and upwards from those under that age; for effecting which purpose the marshals shall have power to appoint as many assistants within their respective districts as to them shall appear necessary; assigning to each assistant a certain division of his district, which division shall consist of one or more counties, cities, towns, townships, hundreds or parishes, or of a territory plainly and distinctly bounded by water courses, mountains, or public roads. The marshals and their assistants shall respectively take an oath or affirmation, before some judge or justice of the peace, resident within their respective districts, previous to their entering on the discharge of the duties by this act required. The oath or affirmation of the marshal shall be, "I, A. B., Marshal of the district of ———, do solemnly swear (or affirm) that I will well and truly cause to be made a just and perfect enumeration and description of all persons resident within my district, and return the same to the President of the United States, agreeably to the directions of an act of Congress, intituled 'An act providing for the enumeration of the inhabitants of the United States,' according to the best of my ability." The oath or affirmation of an assistant shall be "I, A. B., do solemnly swear (or affirm) that I will make a just and perfect enumeration and description of all persons resident within the division assigned to me by the marshal of the district of ———, and make due return thereof to the said marshal, agreeably to the directions of an act of Congress, intituled 'An act providing for the enumeration of the inhabitants of the United States,' according to the best of my ability." The enumeration shall commence on the first Monday in August next, and shall close within nine calendar months thereafter. The several assistants shall, within the said nine months, transmit to the marshals by whom they shall be respectively appointed, accurate returns of all persons, except Indians not taxed, within their respective divisions, which returns shall be made in a schedule, distinguishing the several families by the names of their master, mistress, steward, overseer, or other principal person therein, in manner following, that is to say:

The number of persons within my division, consisting of ———, appears in a schedule hereto annexed, subscribed by me this ——— day of ———, 179-. A. B. *Assistant to the marshal of* ———.

Schedule of the whole number of persons within the division allotted to A. B.

Names of heads of families.	Free white males of 16 years and upwards, including heads of families.	Free white males under 16 years.	Free white females, including heads of families.	All other free persons.	Slaves.

SECTION 2. And be it further enacted, That every assistant failing to make return, or making a false return of the enumeration to the marshal, within the time by this act limited, shall forfeit the sum of two hundred dollars.

SECTION 3. And be it further enacted, That the marshals shall file the several returns aforesaid, with the clerks of their respective district courts, who are hereby directed to receive and carefully preserve the same: And the marshals respectively shall, on or before the first day of September, one thousand seven hundred and ninety-one, transmit to the President of the United States, the aggregate amount of each description of persons within their respective districts. And every marshal failing to file the returns of his assistants, or any of them, with the clerks of their respective district courts, or failing to return the aggregate amount of each description of persons in their respective districts, as the same shall appear from said returns, to the President of the United States within the time limited by this act, shall, for every such offense, forfeit the sum of eight hundred dollars; all which forfeitures shall be recoverable in the courts of the districts where the offenses shall be committed, or in the circuit courts to be held within the same, by action of debt, information or indictment; the one-half thereof to the use of the United States, and the other half to the informer; but where the prosecution shall be first instituted on the behalf of the United States, the whole shall accrue to their use. And for the more effectual discovery of offenses, the judges of the several district courts, at their next sessions, to be held after the expiration of the time allowed for making the returns of the enumeration hereby directed, to the President of the United States, shall give this act in charge to the grand juries, in their respective courts, and shall cause the returns of the several assistants to be laid before them for their inspection.

SECTION 4. And be it further enacted, That every assistant shall receive at the rate of one dollar for every one hundred and fifty persons by him returned, where such persons reside in the country; and where such persons reside in a city, or town, containing more than five thousand persons, such assistants shall receive at the rate of one dollar for every three hundred persons; but where, from the dispersed situation of the inhabitants in some divisions, one dollar for every one hundred and fifty persons shall be insufficient, the marshals, with the approbation of the judges of their respective districts, may make such further allowance to the assistants in such divisions as shall be deemed an adequate compensation, provided the same does not exceed one dollar for every fifty persons by them returned. The several marshals shall receive as follows: The marshal of the district of Maine, two hundred dollars; the marshal of the district of New Hampshire, two hundred dollars; the marshal of the district of Massachusetts, three hundred dollars; the marshal of the district of Connecticut, two hundred dollars; the marshal of the district of New York, three hundred dollars; the marshal of the district of New Jersey, two hundred dollars; the marshal of the district of Pennsylvania, three hundred dollars; the marshal of the district of Delaware, one hundred dollars; the marshal of the district of Maryland, three hundred dollars; the marshal of the district of Virginia, five hundred dollars; the marshal of the district of Kentucky, two hundred and fifty dollars; the marshal of the district of North Carolina, three hundred and fifty dollars; the marshal of the district of South Carolina, three hundred dollars; the marshal of the district of Georgia, two hundred and fifty dollars. And to

obviate all doubts which may arise respecting the persons to be returned, and the manner of making the returns.

SECTION 5. Be it enacted, That every person whose usual place of abode shall be in any family on the aforesaid first Monday in August next, shall be returned as of such family; the name of every person, who shall be an inhabitant of any district, but without a settled place of residence, shall be inserted in the column of the aforesaid schedule, which is allotted for the heads of families, in that division where he or she shall be on the said first Monday in August next, and every person occasionally absent at the time of the enumeration, as belonging to that place in which he usually resides in the United States.

SECTION 6. And be it further enacted, That each and every person more than 16 years of age, whether heads of families or not, belonging to any family within any division of a district made or established within the United States, shall be, and hereby is, obliged to render to such assistant of the division, a true account, if required, to the best of his or her knowledge, of all and every person belonging to such family, respectively, according to the several descriptions aforesaid, on pain of forfeiting twenty dollars, to be sued for and recovered by such assistant, the one-half for his own use, and the other half for the use of the United States.

SECTION 7. And be it further enacted, That each assistant shall, previous to making his return to the marshal, cause a correct copy, signed by himself, of the schedule containing the number of inhabitants within his division, to be set up at two of the most public places within the same, there to remain for the inspection of all concerned; for each of which copies the said assistant shall be entitled to receive two dollars, provided proof of a copy of the schedule having been so set up and suffered to remain, shall be transmitted to the marshal, with the return of the number of persons; and in case any assistant shall fail to make such proof to the marshal, he shall forfeit the compensation by this act allowed him.

Approved March 1, 1790.

Population of the United States as returned at the First Census, by states: 1790.

DISTRICT.	Free white males of 16 years and upward, including heads of families.	Free white males under 16 years.	Free white females, including heads of families	All other free persons.	Slaves.	Total.
Vermont	22,435	22,328	40,505	255	[1] 16	[2] 85,539
New Hampshire	36,086	34,851	70,160	630	158	141,885
Maine	24,384	24,748	46,870	538	None.	96,540
Massachusetts	95,453	87,289	190,582	5,463	None.	378,787
Rhode Island	16,019	15,799	32,652	3,407	948	68,825
Connecticut	60,523	54,403	117,448	2,808	2,764	237,946
New York	83,700	78,122	152,320	4,654	21,324	340,120
New Jersey	45,251	41,416	83,287	2,762	11,423	184,139
Pennsylvania	110,788	106,948	206,363	6,537	3,737	434,373
Delaware	11,783	12,143	22,384	3,899	8,887	[3] 59,094
Maryland	55,915	51,339	101,395	8,043	103,036	319,728
Virginia	110,936	116,135	215,046	12,866	292,627	747,610
Kentucky	15,154	17,057	28,922	114	12,430	73,677
North Carolina	69,988	77,506	140,710	4,975	100,572	393,751
South Carolina	35,576	37,722	66,880	1,801	107,094	249,073
Georgia	13,103	14,044	25,739	398	29,264	82,548
Total number of inhabitants of the United States exclusive of S. Western and N. territory	807,094	791,850	1,541,263	59,150	694,280	3,893,635

	Free white males of 21 years and upward.	Free males under 21 years of age.	Free white females.	All other persons.	Slaves.	Total.
S. W. territory	6,271	10,277	15,365	361	3,417	35,691
N. "						

[1] The census of 1790, published in 1791, reports 16 slaves in Vermont. Subsequently, and up to 1860, the number is given as 17. An examination of the original manuscript returns shows that there never were any slaves in Vermont. The original error occurred in preparing the results for publication, when 16 persons, returned as "Free colored," were classified as "Slave."

[2] Corrected figures are 85,425, or 114 less than figures published in 1790, due to an error of addition in the returns for each of the towns of Fairfield, Milton, Shelburne, and Williston, in the county of Chittenden; Brookfield, Newbury, Randolph, and Strafford, in the county of Orange; Castleton, Clarendon, Hubbardton, Poultney, Rutland, Shrewsbury, and Wallingford, in the county of Rutland; Dummerston, Guilford, Halifax, and Westminster, in the county of Windham; and Woodstock, in the county of Windsor.

[3] Corrected figures are 59,096, or 2 more than figures published in 1790, due to error in addition.

Summary of population, by districts and counties: 1790.

EDENTON DISTRICT.

COUNTY.	Number of heads of families.	Free white males of 16 years and upward, including heads of families.	Free white males under 16 years.	Free white females, including heads of families.	All other free persons.	Slaves.	Total.	COUNTY.	Number of heads of families.	Free white males of 16 years and upward, including heads of families.	Free white males under 16 years.	Free white females, including heads of families.	All other free persons.	Slaves.	Total.
Bertie	1,430	1,762	1,841	3,514	348	5,141	12,606	Hertford	653	814	823	1,533	216	2,442	5,828
Camden	583	727	759	1,477	30	1,040	4,033	Pasquotank	799	951	1,034	1,810	79	1,623	5,497
Chowan, excluding Edenton town	376	460	446	876	7	1,647	3,436	Perquimans	709	885	923	1,717	37	1,878	5,440
Edenton town	180	181	113	306	34	941	1,575	Tyrrell	705	807	959	1,777	35	1,166	4,744
Currituck	794	1,017	1,024	1,960	115	1,103	5,219	Total	6,858	8,394	8,697	16,485	994	19,200	53,770
Gates	629	790	775	1,515	93	2,219	5,392								

FAYETTE DISTRICT.

COUNTY.	Number of heads of families.	Free white males of 16 years and upward, including heads of families.	Free white males under 16 years.	Free white females, including heads of families.	All other free persons.	Slaves.	Total.	COUNTY.	Number of heads of families.	Free white males of 16 years and upward, including heads of families.	Free white males under 16 years.	Free white females, including heads of families.	All other free persons.	Slaves.	Total.
Anson	790	1,034	1,183	2,047	41	828	5,133	Richmond	830	1.096	1,205	2,116	55	583	5,055
Cumberland, excluding Fayetteville town	1,067	1,397	1,362	2,661	49	1,666	7,135	Robeson	869	1.131	1,141	2,244	277	533	5,326
Fayetteville town	281	394	195	398	34	515	1,536	Sampson	935	1,145	1,281	2,316	140	1,183	6,065
Moore	639	849	968	1,570	12	371	3,770	Total	5,411	7,046	7,335	13,352	608	5,679	34,020

HALIFAX DISTRICT.

COUNTY.	Number of heads of families.	Free white males of 16 years and upward, including heads of families.	Free white males under 16 years.	Free white females, including heads of families.	All other free persons.	Slaves.	Total.	COUNTY.	Number of heads of families.	Free white males of 16 years and upward, including heads of families.	Free white males under 16 years.	Free white females, including heads of families.	All other free persons.	Slaves.	Total.
Edgecombe	1,260	1,659	1,879	3,495	70	3,152	10,255	Nash	853	1,143	1,426	2,627	188	2,009	7,393
Franklin	804	1,089	1,400	2,316	37	2,717	7,559	Northampton	1,113	1,334	1,273	2,503	462	4,409	9,981
Halifax, including Halifax town	1,442	1,835	1,778	3,403	443	6,506	13,965	Warren	800	1,070	1,319	2,220	68	4,720	9,397
Martin	798	1,064	1,009	2,022	96	1,889	6,080	Total	7,070	9,194	10,084	18,586	1,364	25,402	64,630

HILLSBOROUGH DISTRICT.

COUNTY.	Number of heads of families.	Free white males of 16 years and upward, including heads of families.	Free white males under 16 years.	Free white females, including heads of families.	All other free persons.	Slaves.	Total.	COUNTY.	Number of heads of families.	Free white males of 16 years and upward, including heads of families.	Free white males under 16 years.	Free white females, including heads of families.	All other free persons.	Slaves.	Total.
Caswell[1]	1,412	1,801	2,110	3,377	72	2,736	10,096	Granville—Continued.							
Caswell district	201							Knap of Leeds district	77						
Gloucester district	211							Oxford district	65					182	
Nash district	118							Ragland district	58						
Richmond district	253							Tabb's Creek district	57						
St. Davids district	166							Tar River district	63						
St. James district	111							Orange[1]	1,534	2,433	2,709	4,913	101	2,060	12,216
St. Lawrence district	215							Caswell district	200						
St. Lukes district	137							Chatham district	166						
Chatham	1,270	1,756	2,160	3,664	9	1,632	9,221	Hillsboro district	187						
Granville[1]	966	1,581	1,873	3,050	315	4,163	10,982	Hillsboro town	40						
Abraham's Plains district	62							Orange district	228						
Beaver Dam district	80							St. Asaph's district	199						
Dutch district	76							St. Mark's district	138						
Epping Forest district	65					74		St. Mary's district	237						
Fishing Creek district	59							St. Thomas' district	139						
Fort Creek district	70							Randolph	1,160	1.582	1,952	3,266	24	452	7,276
Goshen district	67							Wake	1,290	1.772	2,089	3,688	180	2,463	10,192
Henderson district	60							Total	7,632	10,925	12,893	21,958	701	13,506	59,983
Island Creek district	107														

MORGAN DISTRICT.

COUNTY.	Number of heads of families.	Free white males of 16 years and upward, including heads of families.	Free white males under 16 years.	Free white females, including heads of families.	All other free persons.	Slaves.	Total.	COUNTY.	Number of heads of families.	Free white males of 16 years and upward, including heads of families.	Free white males under 16 years.	Free white females, including heads of families.	All other free persons.	Slaves.	Total.
Burke	1,255	1,706	2,115	3,683	11	595	8,110	Rutherford—Continued.							
First company	114	170	219	357	.....	92	838	Fourth company	54	71	101	169	.....	24	365
Second company	80	90	148	263	.....	24	525	Fifth company	100	97	139	235	.....	22	493
Third company	84	120	156	248	7	76	607	Sixth company	103	151	216	379	.....	50	796
Fourth company	80	99	129	203	.....	10	441	Seventh company	73	111	138	230	.....	35	514
Fifth company	85	124	146	275	.....	51	596	Eighth company	75	103	154	248	2	20	527
Sixth company	98	141	169	306	2	59	677	Ninth company	98	119	167	287	.....	11	584
Seventh company	99	124	152	268	.....	87	631	Tenth company	85	114	165	259	.....	60	598
Eighth company	113	150	183	324	.....	28	685	Eleventh company	142	186	287	430	.....	51	954
Ninth company	114	147	187	317	.....	26	677	Twelfth company	105	139	209	305	.....	39	692
Tenth company	74	99	126	213	.....	21	459	Thirteenth company	62	93	93	163	.....	9	358
Eleventh company	88	133	119	269	.....	38	559	Fourteenth company	70	108	85	185	.....	8	386
Twelfth company	73	94	155	217	.....	15	481	Wilkes	1,277	1,615	2,251	3,739	2	549	8,156
Thirteenth company	153	215	226	423	2	68	934	First company	81	111	132	237	.....	55	535
Lincoln	1,409	2,053	2,294	4,037	.....	935	9,319	Second company	90	101	164	268	.....	76	609
First company	69	110	124	215	.....	43	492	Third company	78	100	131	233	2	38	504
Second company	80	114	127	229	.....	39	509	Fourth company	84	106	157	265	.....	13	541
Third company	85	118	146	221	.....	18	503	Fifth company	75	88	146	222	.....	11	467
Fourth company	113	166	180	349	.....	38	733	Sixth company	105	121	169	291	.....	20	601
Fifth company	98	130	167	289	.....	16	602	Seventh company	55	76	100	162	.....	54	392
Sixth company	187	250	261	494	.....	94	1,099	Eighth company	55	76	105	133	.....	5	319
Seventh company	95	170	174	279	.....	110	733	Ninth company	94	118	150	297	.....	66	631
Eighth company	104	148	184	303	.....	18	653	Tenth company	76	109	132	224	.....	23	488
Ninth company	215	315	309	608	.....	188	1,420	Eleventh company	85	109	149	246	.....	96	600
Tenth company	112	145	189	333	.....	51	718	Twelfth company	68	88	122	199	.....	34	443
Eleventh company	125	201	227	351	.....	230	1,009	Thirteenth company	121	152	205	332	.....	33	722
Twelfth company	126	186	206	366	.....	90	848	Fourteenth company	60	75	96	188	.....	18	377
Rutherford	1,181	1,577	2,121	3,502	2	609	7,811	Fifteenth company	63	78	114	173	.....	4	369
First company	76	105	110	218	.....	140	573	Sixteenth company	87	107	179	269	.....	3	558
Second company	84	110	147	244	.....	80	581	Total	10,244	13,902	17,562	29,922	30	5,376	66,792
Third company	54	70	110	150	.....	60	390								

[1] Names taken from county tax lists.

Summary of population, by districts and counties: 1790—Continued.

NEWBERN DISTRICT.

COUNTY	Number of heads of families.	Free white males of 16 years and upward, including heads of families.	Free white males under 16 years.	Free white females, including heads of families.	All other free persons.	Slaves.	Total.	COUNTY.	Number of heads of families.	Free white males of 16 years and upward, including heads of families.	Free white males under 16 years.	Free white females, including heads of families.	All other free persons.	Slaves.	Total.
Beaufort	780	951	926	1,824	129	1,632	5,462	Johnston	776	1,039	1,119	2,083	64	1,329	5,634
Carteret	578	718	707	1,502	92	713	3,732	Jones	583	736	794	1,541	70	1,681	4,822
Craven, including Newbern town	1,440	1,709	1,538	3,227	337	3,658	10,469	Pitt	1,095	1,461	1,507	2,915	25	2,367	8,275
Dobbs	915	1,162	1,293	2,478	45	1,915	6,893	Wayne	804	1,064	1,219	2,256	37	1,557	6,133
Hyde	625	795	718	1,522	37	1,048	4,120	Total	7,596	9,635	9,821	19,348	836	15,900	55,540

SALISBURY DISTRICT.

COUNTY	Number of heads of families.	Free white males of 16 years and upward, including heads of families.	Free white males under 16 years.	Free white females, including heads of families.	All other free persons.	Slaves.	Total.	COUNTY.	Number of heads of families.	Free white males of 16 years and upward, including heads of families.	Free white males under 16 years.	Free white females, including heads of families.	All other free persons.	Slaves.	Total.
Guilford	1,096	1,607	1,799	3,242	27	516	7,191	Stokes	1,329	1,846	2,104	3,778	13	787	8,528
Iredell	769	1,118	1,217	2,239	3	858	5,435	Surry	1,074	1,531	1,762	3,183	17	698	7,191
Mecklenburg	1,742	2,378	2,573	4,771	70	1,603	11,395	Total	9,988	13,908	15,826	28,366	242	8,138	66,480
Montgomery	703	967	1,121	1,798	5	834	4,725								
Rockingham	842	1,173	1,413	2,491	10	1,100	6,187								
Rowan, including Salisbury town	2,433	3,288	3,837	6,864	97	1,742	15,828								

WILMINGTON DISTRICT.

COUNTY	Number of heads of families.	Free white males of 16 years and upward, including heads of families.	Free white males under 16 years.	Free white females, including heads of families.	All other free persons.	Slaves.	Total.	COUNTY.	Number of heads of families.	Free white males of 16 years and upward, including heads of families.	Free white males under 16 years.	Free white females, including heads of families.	All other free persons.	Slaves.	Total.
Bladen	635	837	830	1,683	58	1,676	5,084	Onslow	721	828	939	1,788	84	1,748	3,639
Brunswick	320	380	398	779	3	1,511	3,071	Total	3,028	3,914	4,049	7,801	215	10,056	26,035
Duplin	724	1,035	1,187	2,054	3	1,383	5,662								
New Hanover, including Wilmington town	628	834	695	1,497	67	3,738	6,831								

Assistant marshals for the state: 1790.

DISTRICT.	NAME.	DISTRICT.	NAME.
Edenton district (part of) Bertie county.	Thomas Lee Harrimond.	Hillsborough district (part of) Chatham, Randolph, and Wake counties.	Ellick Sanders.
Edenton district (part of) Camden, Chowan (including Edenton town), Currituck, Pasquotank, and Perquimans counties.	Edmund Blount.	Hillsborough district (part of) Caswell, Granville, and Orange counties (missing).	
Edenton district (part of) Gates county.	James Walton.	Morgan district Burke, Lincoln, Rutherford, and Wilkes counties.	Joseph McDowell.
Edenton district (part of) Hertford county.	Amos Rayner.	Newbern district Beaufort, Carteret, Craven (including Newbern town), Dobbs, Hyde, Johnston, Jones, Pitt, and Wayne counties.	Edw. Pasteur.
Edenton district (part of) Tyrrell county.	Levi Blounts.	Salisbury district (part of) Guilford, Rockingham, Stokes, and Surry counties.	Tho. Henderson.
Fayette district Anson, Cumberland (including Fayetteville town), Moore, Richmond, Robeson, and Sampson counties.	Guilford Dudley.	Salisbury district (part of) Iredell, Mecklenburg, Montgomery, and Rowan (including Salisbury town) counties.	Lª Beard.
Halifax district (part of) Edgecombe, Halifax (including Halifax town), and Martin counties.	Hance Bond.	Wilmington district Bladen, Brunswick, Duplin, New Hanover (including Wilmington town), and Onslow counties.	James Kenan.
Halifax district (part of) Franklin, Nash, and Warren counties.	Benjamin Moss.		
Halifax district (part of) Northampton county.	Rich. W. Freear.		

EDENTON DISTRICT, BERTIE COUNTY.[1]

Column headers (repeated for each panel):
- **NAME OF HEAD OF FAMILY.**
- **Free white males of 16 years and upward, including heads of families.**
- **Free white males under 16 years.**
- **Free white females, including heads of families.**
- **All other free persons.**
- **Slaves.**

Panel 1

Name of Head of Family	Males ≥16	Males <16	Females	Other free	Slaves
Armistead, Anthony	1		1		13
Ashburn, William	3	2	5	2	12
Ashburn, Benjᵃ	3			1	7
Asben, James	3	2	4		
Arnold, Richᵈ	3	2	4		8
Archebᵉ, James	3	2	4		
Aulssbart, Alexʳ	1	2	5		
Armistead, William	4	1	4	4	33
Askew, Thomas	1	1			
Askew, James	1	1	3		2
Asbald, James	2	2	4		
Askew, Ann	1		1		
Askew, William	1	1	1		
Askew, John	1		1		2
Avis, Abraham	1	1	2		7
Asbald, Aaron	1	3	4		
Adkins, Metehill	1	4	2		1
Acru, John	1	1	3		2
Acru, William	1		1	2	
Acru, Edwᵈ	1	5	2		8
Acru, Leonard	1				
Acru, John	2	1	5		2
Andrews, John	1	4	4		3
Abbington, Littleberry	1	1			16
Ashe, James			1	6	
Andrw, Stephen	1		2		7
Andrw, John	1				3
Andrws, William	2		4		8
Askew, John	1		1		1
Asbald, Joseph	1	1	5		1
Askew, Aaron	1		2		24
Askew, David	3	3	4		17
Allen, John	1	2	2		10
Anthony, John	2	2	4		32
Appleton, Mary		1	3		
Andrws, William	1				
Adkinson, Mary			2		
Allen, John	1	2	5		10
Bailey, Sarah			1		1
Boyce, Robert	1	3	4		
Brimage, Elizabeth	1		4		14
Burn, John	1		4		29
Billups, Richᵈ	1	1	3		
Bryan, Edward	2		2		15
Brown, Hardy	2	1	2		
Byrd, John	1	3	2		3
Baker, Thomas	1	1	5	1	5
Billups, William	1		2		6
Britt, Jessee	1				
Brantly, Darby				4	
Billups, Thomas	1	1	2		
Barber, Charles	1	3	3		
Barber, Prudence	1				
Barber, Elizabeth					3
Byrom, David	1	2	2		
Barns, Thomas	1				
Bond, Thomas	3		4		25
Baker, Edward	1		4		
Butler, Tobias	1	4	3		25
Bryant, Jessee	1	1	4		
Bryant, Michᵗ	2		2		
Bryant, Elizᵃ		1	5		1
Boyce, Jessee	1	2	3		
Ditto for S. Williams					26
Barns, Cader	2	3	4		
Bryant, William	2	1	6	1	12
Bridges, Robᵗ	2	1	3		2
Bridges, Robᵗ, Junʳ	1	1	2		
Beazy, Pharoby		1	1		
Barley, Joseph	1	1	2		
Brogdon, William	1	2	2		
Brogdon, John	1		2		
Bently, John	2	1	2		1
Blacton, Henry	2		2		
Bond, John	2		1		12
Barber, Elizᵃ	1		4		
Booth, Mary			3		
Blackledge, Richᵈ	3	1	4	1	15
Britt, Thomas	1	1	4		4
Bolton, Aaron	2		4	5	
Burn, Levy	2				9
Bond, Thomas	1		1		7
Bond, Mary		3	2		18
Britt, Joel	1	4	6		
Brogdon, John	1		2		1
Bass, Thomas	1		2		
Barber, David	1		2		
Bently, William	1	2	3		
Bently, John	1		5		
Broadwell, David	1		4		
Ditto for Cullen Pollock					14
Bently, John	1				
Bazemore, James	1	5	2		1
Bench, Frederick	1		3		1
Bunch, William	2	3	2		

Panel 2

Name of Head of Family	Males ≥16	Males <16	Females	Other free	Slaves
Barrett, Jennett			3		
Bazemore, Malichia	1	2	3		1
Birch, Micajah	1	2	2	3	
Bunch, Zadok	1	1	2		4
Butler, John	1	2	3	3	
Baker, Jonaᵃ	1	3	3		
Britt, Joel	1	2	2		
Bazemore, Jessee	3	2	3		13
Bazemore, John	1	2	6		2
Boyce, John	2	2	2		
Barns, Henry	1	2	2		
Barns, Solomon	1	2	5		
Barns, Thomas	1	4	3		6
Baker, John	1		1		4
Barns, John	1	3	3		4
Brown, Jessee	1	2	3	1	4
Bunch, Nehemᵗ	2	3	4		
Bazmore, John	1	3	3	2	9
Byron, John	2	1	4		1
Bass, William	2				5
Belote, Noah	1				1
Bass, Jacob	1	2	4		1
Bass, John	2	2	2		1
Byrsell, Joseph	1				
Bazemore, James	1	5	2		
Butler, Isaac	1	3	4		
Burns, John	1	1	3		8
Burry, Jeremiah	3	5	2		3
Bowen, Benjᵃ	2	3	3		
Barrett, John	2	1	3		
Buck, Stephen	4	3	5		
Boswell, Thomas	3	4	5	1	
Billips, Ramsom	2	2	8		
Boswell, Charles	1		3		
Baker, James	1	2	1		
Bowin, Hardy	1	1	2		
Byrd, Jacob	1	2	3		
Boswell, William	1				
Butler, Jeremiah	1				
Britt, Jessee	1				
Barber, David	1	2	1		
Boswill, John	1	1	2		
Bryant, Luis	1	1	1		
Barnecaster, Richᵈ	1	1	1		
Brown, John	1	2	6		3
Bridges, Thomas	1	1	2		
Bates, Sarah			1	4	
Benton, William	1		3	1	
Bridges, James	1			3	
Buice, Jeremiah	1	3	6		
Baker, Blake	2	2	5		9
Barker, Zedckʰ	1	2	2		
Bently, John	2	2	3		
Baker, Mary			2		
Bardell, William	1				2
Bardell, Joseph	1				3
Bardell, James	1	1			4
Baker, Levi	2		4		2
Boyce, John	3	3	2		1
Baker, Mary			2	5	
Boyce, Hardy	1	1	1		
Burn, James	1	2	3		18
Bailey, Sarah			2	1	1
Bogen, Robert	1	3	4		
Brimage, Elizᵃ	4	2	4	1	16
Burns, John	1		4		20
Billups, Richᵈ	1	1	3		
Bryan, Edward	2		2		15
Bowen, Hardy	2	1	2		
Byrd, John	1	3	2		3
Baker, Thomas	1	1	5	1	5
Billups, William	1		2		6
Britt, Jessee	1				
Bromley, Darby				4	
Billups, Thomas	1	1	2		
Barber, Charles	1	3	3		
Barber, Prudence			3		
Barber, Elizᵃ			3		
Baker, Elias	1		2		
Berry, John	2	3	4		
Berry, Wright	2	2	3		
Berry, John	1	1	1		
Baker, Demcey	1	2	3		
Baker, Solᵒ	1		2		
Belch, Miles	1				
Bryan, William	1				
Berry, Miles	1				
Butler, Arther	1		1		
Boyce, Demsey	1	1	2		
Barns, William	1	6	4		
Barrett, John	1	1	4		
Brown, Benjᵃ	1		3		
Briton, John	1	1	1		3
Bay, John	3		3		
Byrd, Richᵈ	1	2	3		
Butler, John	1	1	8		

Panel 3

Name of Head of Family	Males ≥16	Males <16	Females	Other free	Slaves
Brown, William	4		9		
Briton, Michᵗ	1				
Briton, John	2	1	6		3
Brantly, Mathew	1	4	4		
Belote, John	2	2	6		10
Butler, Joseph	1	4	4		4
Barry, Thomas	2				4
Bass, Jacob	1	2	4		4
Bass, Cader	1	1	2		1
Britt, Joel	1	2	2		4
Bunch, Jeremᵗ	3	6	2		
Bunch, John	1				3
Butler, Isaac	1	2	6		
Beazley, Ambrose	1	3	2		
Butler, William	1	1	1		
Burt, William	1				
Butler, Thomas R	1				
Brantly, Mathew	2	3	4		
Bass, Augᵃ			3		5
Butler, William	1	1	1		
Butler, John	1	1	3		4
Belote, Henry	1	1	3		4
Bently, James	1	1	2		2
Byron, James	1				
Boyce, Luis	1				
Bently, James	1				
Belote, Noah	1				2
Bartlett, Hall				4	
Belote, Peleg	1				
Brogdon, Peter	1	5	1		
Bates, Henry	1	2	2		1
Burkett, William	1	1	5		
Brogdon, John	1	2	1		
Brogdon, William	2		2		
Brinkly, Ella	1		2		
Bates, Sarah		1	4		5
Byrom, John	1	2	4		
Billups, Richᵈ	1		1		
Brogdon, Thomas	1				
Brogdon, Timothy	1	1	2		
Bently, Henry	1	2	3		
Burkett, William	1	2	3		
Belote, Thoˢ	1	1	1		
Boyce, Hardy	1	1	1		
Byrom, Abner	1	1	1		
Bond, Thomas	1		2	1	8
Brogdon, John	1		2		1
Brinkly, Elijah	1	2	4		5
Brown, Jessee	1				6
Brown, Joel	3	2	2	1	3
Brown, James	1				3
Brown, Arther	1				5
Bishop, Moses					3
Brown, James	1				
Bishop, Mason	2	4	3		6
Barnacaster, Sarᵗ					9
Byrd, Elisha	1				
Barry, Miles	1				
Chery, Solomon	1	1	5		14
Collins, David	1	1	3		
Curry, James	5		2		1
Curry, Jacob	1	1	2		
Collins, Josiah	1	3	3		2
Cherry, Thomas	1		3		
Cook, Joel	1	3	2		
Cherry, John	1		3		
Cowen, John	1	1	8		
Cowen, William	1		5		
Cowen, William	2	3	1		
Cralet, Geo	1	2	3		
Cory, Benjᵃ	3	2			4
Carter, Joseph	1		1		1
Cherry, William	1	3	4	1	3
Chavis, Cezar				1	
Curry, Marry			2		
Castelow, James	1		2		
Cob, Henry	1	2	5		2
Cob, Nichoˢ	2		3		
Cook, Samᵗ	3	1	4		
Calloway, Thoˢ	2	6	3		3
Castelow, Jnᵒ	1	1	3		
Cowen, John	1	2	3		
Cowen, Willᵐ	1		3		
Cob, Edwᵈ	1				
Castelow, James	1ᵇ	3	4		
Carter, Joseph	1		2		1
Collins, Luke	4	2	1		20
Charton, Jesper	1		1		22
Christᵃ, Clark	4	2	4		26
Cullifer, Elizᵃ	3		2		
Clements, Geo	1	1	1		3
Collins, Thoˢ	2		2		13
Cooper, Cadcy	1	4	5		1
Caphart, John	1	1	2		4
Cob, James	2	3	6		
Caphart, William	1		2		9
Caphart, Geo	1				

[1] No attempt has been made in this publication to correct mistakes in spelling made by the assistant marshals, and the names have been reproduced as they appear upon the census schedule.

EDENTON DISTRICT, BERTIE COUNTY—Continued.

NAME OF HEAD OF FAMILY.	Free white males of 16 years and upward, including heads of families.	Free white males under 16 years.	Free white females, including heads of families.	All other free persons.	Slaves.
Cob, John	1	1	6		1
Cofield, Jethro	1	2	1		
Cullifer, Nathl	1		2		
Culfer, Thomas	1				
Cook, Jno	1	2	4		2
Cullifer, James	2	1	4		
Cook, Winifred		3	2		4
Cullifer, Nathl	2	2	6		
Craft, Moses	2	3	2		
Carney, Absolom	3		4		13
Clark, Thomas		1	2		
Castelow, John	2	5	3	1	3
Craft, Moses	1	2	1		
Campbell, John	1	2			1
Campbell, James	3	2	5		41
Curry, David	2	6	4		12
Cole, Rebecca		3	1		
Cole, Cudby	1	3	4		8
Cole, John	1	1	3	1	6
Cokron, Thomas	1	3	3		5
Cokhilgo, William	1		4		
Cokron, Thomas	1	4	6	2	8
Cittrell, John	4		3		31
Cowen, Geo	1				1
Cowen, William	1	3	1		
Cob, Eleaner			1		
Cole, Sarah			4		
Cob, Dolley		2	1		
Cherry, Aaron	1				
Cherry, Jno	1	1	1		
Cherry, Joshua	1		3		
Cooper, Blunt	1				
Cofield, Josiah	1	2	3		
Curry, Jacob	1				
Cooper, Jessee	1	4	3		
Curry, Jacob	1	2	2		
Colten, Saml	1	1	1		
Cartey, Joseph	1	2	2		1
Callis, Zedekiah	1				9
Callum, David	1	1	3		
Colten, Jessee	2	1	3		14
Callum, Willis	3	2	2		18
Cambell, Eliza			2		
Cox, Benjn	4	2	2		
Collins, Joseph	1	1	2		
Clifton, Ann		2	4		9
Curry, Mary			2	1	
Collins, Joseph	3	1	1	1	8
Collins, Henry	1				
Chevat, Cezer				7	
Collins, Josiah	3	2	4		2
Curry, James	1				
Cooper, Jona	1				
Curry, Ebenezr	1				
Cooper, Jno	1	1			
Canady, Alis		2	6		
Cowen, Geo	1		1		1
Curry, Jeames	2		1		
Curry, Jacob	1				
Cox, William	1	1	4		
Conner, Wright	1				
Cox, Benjn	1	3	3		
Cofield, David	1	2	2	1	
Conner, Thomas	1				
Cox, Jno	1				4
Clark, Thomas	2	1	3		4
Cittrell, Demsey	3	3	3		6
Carney, Josiah	1	1	1		4
Conner, William	1	1	3		
Cook, James	1	1	2		
Cook, Jno	1	1	4		
Cook, Reuben	3	1	5		7
Cole, Job	1		3		
Cole, Christian		1	1		
Cook, Demsey	2	3	3		2
Cob, Nathan	2	2	4		1
Churchwill, Henry	1	3	2		
Codwell, William	1	1	1	1	1
Cofield, David	1	2	2		1
Channell, Tempey			1		4
Chamberlain, Malc	1	3	2	2	2
Churchwill, Ann	1	2	5		
Cartior, Saml	1	2	4		
Cone, Thomas	1		2		
Ditto for W. Williams					21
Collins, Frederick	1	1			1
Cole, Peggy		1	3		
Conner, Edwd	1				
Demsey, Melvin	1	3	2		
Demsey, Shadrack	1	1	5		
Damont, Charles	1	3	4		4
Duning, Shadrack	1	1	5		
Davis, Geo	1	4	6		
Deville, McSteven	3	1	5		2
Davidson, Amos	1	4	3		3
Davis, James	2	1	4		
Darnes, Jacob	1				
Darnell, Uriah	1	1	2		
Davison, Amos	1	4	3		3
Dukes, Abraham	1				
Duffin, Salley			4		
Duffin, James	1				
Duning, Jeremiah	3	5	4		
Dotry, Patry	1		4		
Debun, Dennis	1				3
Doore, James	2		1		
Dawson, Richard	5		4	1	9
Darlett, Anthy	1	2	2		10
Dawson, William	1		4		5
Devenport, Joseph	1		1	1	
Doore, John	2	1	4		
Demsey, Melvin	1	4	6		
Davis, Smith	1		2		
Davis, David	1		2		
Davidson, David	1	2	1		
Davis, Geo	1	2	1		
Deane, Saml	1	1	2		
Deane, Solo	1	3	1		
Davidson, William	1	1	3		
Dunning, John	1		3		
Dunning, Saml	1		3		9
Dunning, Charles	1	2	3		2
Davis, Mary		4	6		
Davis, Nathaniel	1	1	4		
Ditto for Saml Johnston					11
Dunning, Jeremiah	2	4	4		
Deane, Samuel	1		2		
Dunning, Jeremiah	1	1	3	2	
Davis, Thomas	1	2	3		
Dryden, Isaac	1		5		
Darby, Joseph				4	
Dunark, Michel	2	5	7	4	1
Dunston, Edmond	2	2	5		12
Durgan, Ann			2		9
Dyer, Thomas	2				
Demsey, Thowegood				7	
Demsey, George				9	
Demsey, Joshua				9	
Dawson, William					
Eason, Abner	3		1		20
Edwards, Nathan	1	3	3	2	
Eason, Joseph	1	1	1	1	5
Edward, Nathan	1	3	6	2	
Eason, Abner	1	4	3		10
Eleaner, Williams	1	3	5		
Engs, Mathew	1		3		
Evarts, Luther	1		1		1
Epperson, Mary		1	3		
Evins, William	1	4	5		1
Evins, Etherald	1				
Evins, Joshua	1	3	2		
Evins, Robert	1		1		
Everite, Luther	1		1		
Edward, John	2	1	2	2	
Everite, John	1		1		12
Edward, David	1				
Engs, Mathew	1		1		
Early, John	1	1	4		2
Early, Asa	1	1	2		1
Edward, James	1		5		8
Early, Benjn	1	2	7		6
Early, Shadrack	1		2		3
Everite, Henry	1	3	2	2	13
Everite, Jessee	1		3		21
Everite, Amelia			2		10
Fryar, Willis	1	2	3		
Farmer, James	1	4	8	2	
Freeman, King	2	2	1		8
Ferguson, Alexr	1	2	2		4
Fleetwood, Edmond	1	3	4		6
Felps, Henry	1	1	3		
Fleetwood, Hardy	1	3	1		3
Fleetwood, William	2	1	5		1
Freeman, Aaron	1	1	3	2	2
Freeman, Charles	1	2	5		8
Freeman, Hardy	1			1	
Freeman, William	1				
Freeman, Joshua	4	1	4	1	30
Freeman, Jeremiah	1				
Freeman, Joshua	1				
Freeman, John	1	2	2		19
Fryer, Sian	1				
Fryar, Willis	1	1	2		
Ford, Alexr	1				
Floyd, John	1	3	4		
Fanner, William	1	2	3		
Frain, John	1	1	3		
Farmer, Joseph	2	4	6		
Freman, Moses	1	5	4		12
Fenner, James	1	2	3		
Freeman, Martha	1	1	8		11
Folk, Thomas	3	3	3		3
Felps, John	1	3	6		2
Felps, Frederick	1	2	4		2
Felps, Cudworth	1	4	7	1	3
Felps, Mary		2	4		
Frazier, Alexr	2		2		
Goff, Joney				1	
Gardner, Martin	1				1
Griffin, Abraham	1				
Gardener, Everite	1	1	4		6
Gardener, Bryom	2	2	3	2	6
Gardener, John	1	1	1	1	4
Gardner, Everite	1	1	5	1	6
Gill, Richard	1	4	4		
Green, Solo	1	2	3		
Griffin, William	1	1	6		
Griffin, William, Junr	2		5		8
Griffin, Creacy	2		3		
Griffin, Lucretia		1	3		
Goff, Rachell		1	3		
Gardener, Mary	1	2	4		7
Gardener, Salley	3		3	8	9
Gardener, Nancy		2	3	3	1
Glisten, Ann		1	5	1	
Godfrey, Ann		1	2		
Gains, Rebeca			3	1	
Gains, Sarah			3	4	
Glawhorn, Willm	1	2	3	2	1
Gardener, William	2	1	3		
Gardener, Isaac	1	1	2		1
Gardener, Thos	1	2	3		
Gaskins, Thos	1	1	3		
Garrett, David	1	2	3		16
Green, George	1	2	2		
Gillum, Moses	1		1		22
Gray, William	4	2	5	1	53
Gardner, Nathl	1				
Grandbury, John	3	1	1		10
Grover, Sir James	3		1	4	5
Glisten, Edward	1				
Gummery, Ann		2	3		
Garrett, Frederick	1		3		
Gains, Rebecca			2		1
Groudy, McHenry	1				
Gardener, John	1	2	5		3
Gardener, Jean		4	2	3	1
Gardner, Penelope	3		3		
Glisten, Henry	1				
Grimes, Eliza			1		
Garrett, Jacob	1	4	1		8
Garrett, Jessee	2	3	5		20
Green, Malichi	1	1	3		
Green, Eliza		1	3		
Green, Malichi	2	1	4		
Harman, Abraham	1	3	4		4
Harman, Stephen	1	1	1		
Holder, Elijah	1	3	1		
Holder, Elzabeth		2	3		
Harmon, Nichos	1	3	6		
Hollum, Joel	1	2	3		10
Hendrickson, Isaac	1	2	3		
Howard, Elijah	1	4	4		
Howard, Benjn	1	1	4		1
Hale, Jessee	1	3	4		
Hunter, William	1	3	2	1	4
Harramond, Henry	2	1	7		19
Harramond, Thomas	1		2		22
Harrald, David	1	2	1		
Hyman, Hugh	3		2		14
Hodder, John	1	1	1		
Hawkins, Thomas	1	2	3		
Harden, Thomas	1	4	3		1
Harrill, Davis	1	2	2		
Hardy, Lemuel	1		1		
Harris, Amos	1	1	5		8
Harramond, Margt		1	4		9
Hawkins, John	3		3		
Hopkins, Alexr	1				
Hale, John	1				
Hexstall, John	1	1	3		
Hardy, Sarah	2	1	2		12
Hopkins, Joseph	2	1	4		2
Holley, Prudence			3		
Hill, Mary		1	3		
Harrill, Noah	2				7
Harrill, John	1		2		1
Hays, Sarah			6		
Higgs, John	2	2	2		5
House, Bailess	1	3	1		6
Horten, Frederick	1		4		5
Harrill, Guin	1		1	2	4
Harrill, William	3	3			
Holland, Frederick	1	1			7
Hinton, Noah	1				28
Hinton, John	1				25
Higgs, John	2	4	3		6
House, James	1		4		14
Hodges, Mathew	4	1	2	3	3

EDENTON DISTRICT, BERTIE COUNTY—Continued.

NAME OF HEAD OF FAMILY.	Free white males of 16 years and upward, including heads of families.	Free white males under 16 years.	Free white females, including heads of families.	All other free persons.	Slaves.
Hill, Whitnall					130
Hile, Henry	2	5	2	1	37
Harrill, William	3	3			
Harmon, Nicholas	3	3	4		
Hibbls, Pithsia	1				
Hays, James	1	2	5	1	
Harrald, Nancy	3	2	5		1
Hays, Joshua	1		9		2
Howell, Thomas	2	2		1	
House, Thomas	3	1	7	3	26
Harrill, William	1	3	1		5
Hawkins, Thomas	1	2	3		7
Hyman, John	1	1	3		7
Hyman, Eliza		2	4		
Holten, Sarah			6		
Hardy, William	2		1		
Hardy, Joseph	1	1	4		
Hanes, Edwd	1				12
Hare, Penelope			1		6
How, Mary	1	1	3		16
Hubbord, Bird	2	1	7		7
Hyman, John	1	1	3		10
Hyman, Thomas	1				
Hardy, William	1	1	3		
Hunter, John	1				11
Harte, Samuel	1	4	2		
Harrill, John	1	2	5		
Harrill, Joseph	2	2	4		
Harrill, John	2	1	5		
Harrill, Isaac	3	2	5		
Harrill, Isaac	1				
Hunsford, Jenkins	1	1	2		
Hendry, William	1				
Hendry, Robert	2	3	2		2
Hunter, Timothy	1				
Hunter, Hardy	1	1	4		16
Harrill, Job	1				
Harris, John	1				
Harrill, Hughs	1				
Hallum, Judah	1	4	1		
Huggins, Humphry	1				
Holland, Chrisa	1	3	3		5
Hughs, Geo	1	3	3		1
Hugh, Solo	1	4	4		
Horsen, Reuben	1		1		
Hughs, William	1		5		
Hughs, Josiah	1				
Hughs, James	1	4	3		
Hughs, Thomas	1	1	3		
Horson, Geo	1	2	2		
Hughs, David	1	4	3		
Hughs, Geo	1		1		
Horson, King	1	1	3		
Hughs, George	1	3	3		
Hale, Jonas	1	5	4		
Horten, William	1	5	2		
Horson, Ann			1		
Hughs, Thomas	1	1	3		
Hughs, Geo	1	2	3		
Howly, James	1	5	4		8
Hawley, Sarah		1	4		
Hunter, Timothy	1	3	4		19
Hodder, William	1		1	1	
Harrill, Allen	1				
Howard, Jacob	1				
Hunter, William	1	3	2	1	4
Hudson, Sarah			3		
Hudson, Sarah		2	4		
Hollaway, Arther	2				3
Hays, Joshua	1		7	1	4
Harrill, John W	1				1
Harrill, John	1				
Hollowell, Asa	2		4		1
Howell, Josiah	1	1	2		4
Harrill, Elijah	1				
Harrill, Demsey	1	5	1	1	4
Harrill, Luis	2	3	4		2
Harrill, Demsey	2	4	2	1	13
Hollowell, William	1		2		
Harrill, Amos	1	1	3		5
Hollowell, Asa	2				1
Hambleton, Pharober		2	4		
Hollowell, Noah	1		3		2
Higgs, John	1	2	2		5
Holden, Elijah	3	1	3		
Hogart, William	3	3	3		
Hix, John	1	1	2		
Hubbord, Rachall			4		
Hunter, Robert	1				
Huff, Corna	1				
Holder, Thomas	1	3	1		
Hardy, Humphrey	3	2	4		18
Horten, William	1	4	1		
Hyman, William	1	2	6		4
Hodder, John	1	2	6		5
Hardy, John	1				
Hopkins, John	2	3	2		1

NAME OF HEAD OF FAMILY.	Free white males of 16 years and upward, including heads of families.	Free white males under 16 years.	Free white females, including heads of families.	All other free persons.	Slaves.
Hawkins, Thomas	2	1	1		
Hardy, Elza	1	1	3		
Hardy, Lemuel	1	1	1		
Harlowe, John	1	1	4		6
Holley, James	1	5	4		8
Hays, James	1	2	5	1	
Holland, Lewel	1	1	9		
Harrill, Arther	1		4		4
Hodges, Mathew	1	1	3		3
Higgs, Judith			2		1
Horn, Joseph	1	4	2	1	3
Harrill, Rachell			1		
Harrill, Eliza	1	4	4		
Harrill, Jacob	1	4	4		
Holland, John	1	1	4		
Harrill, David	1	1	2		1
Harrill, James	2	3	5		
Harrill, Henry	2	2	3		
Holland, John	1				
Hays, James	1	3	4		
Hays, Sam	1	3	4		
Hodges, William	1				2
Higgs, Reuben	1	1	6		
Hodges, John	1				
Harrill, Josiah	1				
Hiat, Elisha	1	1	6		
Higgs, William	1	4	3		6
Harrill, Benj	1	3	5		12
Harrill, Christa	1		1		
Harrill, Hodges	1				
Harrill, Nancy		4	5		1
Harte, Saml	1	4	2		
Hogard, Patrick	3	1	4		
Hogard, John	1	1	4		
Hays, Susanna			2	1	
Hawley, Prudence			2		
Homes, Shadrack	1	2	3	1	1
Jinkins, Geo	1				
Jordan, James	1				
James, Frederick					9
Johnson, Thomas	3	1	1		
Jenkins, Cader	3	1	3		3
Johnson, John	1	1	6		
Jenkins, Moore	1	3	8	4	5
Jacob, Saml	1		2		1
Jenkins, Luis	1		5		5
James, Andrew				4	
Jordan, Hannah		1	4		26
James, Nancy					3
Jones, William				9	6
Jordan, Joseph			1		10
Johnson, John	1	2	5		
Johnson, Thomas	1	1	2		
Jordan, Mary	2	2	5		13
Johnson, John	1	1	2		7
Jacocks, Jona	2		2		25
Jacocks, Charles	1				10
Johnson, Levy	1	3	3		
Jordan, James B	3	2	3		24
Jonakin, Jessee	1	1	3		
Barker, Thos, Decd					80
Jonathan, James	1		2		
James, Emmanuel	1	1	2		
Jonakin, Arther	2		3		18
Jonakin, Benja	1				6
Johnson, Byrrell	2	1	4		
Jenkins, Luis	2		5		7
Jones, Mary		1	5	1	
Jenkins, Nathan	1	1	5		1
Jenkins, Charles	1				
Johnson, Byrrell	3	2	3		
Johnson, Snoden	1		4		
Johnson, James	1				
Jones, Friddle	1		3		
Johnston, James	1				
Johnson, Jacob	3			2	3
Johnson, William	1	1	7		
James, Frederick					5
James, James					8
Job, Saml	1		2		
Jenkins, King	1				
Jones, Solo	2	2	5		
Jones, Thomas	1				6
Jones, David	1		4	2	4
Jenkins, Isum	1				
Jenkins, James	1		3		2
Jenkins, Jeames	1		2		15
Jenkins, Luis	2	1	5		7
Jonakin, Saml	1		3		4
Jenkins, Godfrey	1	1	3		
Jenkins, Abraham	1	2	4		
Jeames, Mary				3	
Jones, Mary	1		2		
Jones, Jessee	1	1	2		
Jones, William	2		3		
King, Charles	1	3	3		
Knott, Joseph	1				4

NAME OF HEAD OF FAMILY.	Free white males of 16 years and upward, including heads of families.	Free white males under 16 years.	Free white females, including heads of families.	All other free persons.	Slaves.
Kinnigan, Jacob	1				
King, Henry	1	2	3		5
King, Charles	3	3	2		11
King, Charles	1	3	3		4
King, Michael	1		2		23
King, William	1	2	3		12
Knott, Mary	1		3		
Knight, Reuben	1		1		
Kail, Josiah	1		3		4
Keaton, William	1		2		
King, Cader	1	2	1		
King, James	1				
King, Charles	1		1	1	7
King, Cader	3	2	1		
Kennady, James	1				
King, Charles	1	1	2		
King, James	1				
King, John H	1	1	2		3
Keen, Moses	1	3	5		
Kennedy, Ellis		2	4		
Knott, Thomas	1				
Kinnehorn, Jacob	1				
Lawrence, Abner	1	2	2		
Liscomb, Wilson	2	3	3		11
Lawrence, John	1		2		
Langly, Thos	1	2	1		4
Lawrence, Prudence		1	2		
Lawrence, Robt	1	1	4		2
Lawrence, Abner	1	3	4		2
Lawrence, Willim	1	2	3		4
Lee, Isaac	1		3		
Lassiter, Mary			4		
Luth, Lydia		3	1		
Liggett, Jeremiah	2	2	2		7
Lockhart, Mary	1	1	5		28
Lawrence, Fredk	1	2	4	3	13
Lawrence, Reuben	1	3	4		4
Lackey, Thomas	1		2		
Liddenham, Jno	1	1	2		
Lazy, Salley			2		
Liggett, Thomas	3	4	6		10
Liggett, Jeremiah	2	2	2		8
Liggett, Alexr	1	1	1		5
Liggett, Rachell	1	1	4		5
Liggett, Eliza			2		1
Lester, John	1		1		
Lester, John	1	1	2		
Lockhart, James	1	1	2		24
Lane, John	1				
Lassiter, Mary	1	3	4		
Lawrence, Joseph	1	1	2		
Lane, David	1				
Lane, James	3	1	5		
McLallen, Geo	2				
McLallen, Jno	1	1			
Letke, John	1		2		
McLane, Drury	1		2		2
Lully, William	1	2	4		7
Lattin, William	1		2		
Lattern, James	1	1	6		1
Lenox, John	1		3		91
Lee, Abraham	1	3	2		
Liggett, Thomas	2	1	2		10
Liggett, Rachell	1	1	6		9
Lee, Isaac	1		2		
Lloyd, James	1	1	2		
Lloyd, Jessee	1	1	1	3	
Lloyd, Josiah	1	2	2		
Lee, Stephen	1				
Lee, John	1	2	2		
Low, James	1				
Lassiter, Mary			6		
Long, Joel	1		3		
Latin, Saml	1	1	3		
Lawrence, John	1				
Lucust, Nancy	1	2	3		
Lucust, Jno	2	3	4		
Lee, Jno	1	2	2		
Lee, Henry	2	1	2		7
Lee, Joshua	1		2		2
Liggett, James	1	2	6		6
Morriss, William	2	2	4	2	5
Milburn, Henry	2	2	2	1	
Moon, John	2	3	3		4
Morriss, James	1		3		
Michel, Joseph	1	4	3		3
Mezell, John	1	3	4		
Mais, Saml	1		2		5
Mahone, James	1	3	1		
Merideth, Davis	1	1	1		
McGlawhorn, Jno	1	2	2		9
Morgan, John	1	2	2	1	
McGlawhorn, Wm	1	2	3	1	1
Miller, John	3	5	3		
Morriss, William	1	3	4		
Martin, John	1	3	7		3
Morriss, John	1		2		

EDENTON DISTRICT, BERTIE COUNTY—Continued.

NAME OF HEAD OF FAMILY.	Free white males of 16 years and upward, including heads of families.	Free white males under 16 years.	Free white females, including heads of families.	All other free persons.	Slaves.
Morriss, John	1		1		
Minard, Meniah	1	3	2		
Michl, Thomas	1	3	3		1
Manly, Moses				3	
Moore, Titus	1				17
Ditto for L. Collins					2
Moore, Moses	3		8		20
Michel, Jeremiah	1	1	1		9
Mear, Jno	1	2	4		1
Montgomery, Auga	1	1	3		
Minton, Benja	1				
Mitchell, Jerry	1	1	1		6
McClone, Hepsiber			4		7
Mahone, James	1	1	2		
Morgan, John	1	2	4		
Monk, Nottingm	1	1	1		
Monk, Nottingh	1	3	3		11
Monk, Letice	4		1		
Miller, John	1	2	2		13
McCate, —				4	
Mitchell, Sarah		1	1		
Murden, Sarah	1	4	6	3	4
Manning, Luke	1	1	3		
Madry, James	2	4	1		1
Meredith, David				20	
Megill, John	1	1	4		
Moore, John	1	1	3		9
Megill, Cader	1	3	3		
Michel, Willim	1	2	3		
Miller, Jonathan	1	3	3		
Megil, Thomas	1	2	4		
Miller, Solomon	1	3	2		
Megill, Henry	1	4	3		2
Megill, Joshua	1	1	3		
Megill, John	1		1		
Megill, Moses	1				
Megill, Aaron	1	2	2		
Morriss, Joseph	1	1	3		
Morriss, Zedeklb	1				
Murfrey, Geo	1	1	1		
Meagill, Timothy	1		5		
Mires, Benja	2	3	7		5
Moore, Agness	2		1		
Madry, John	1	1	3		
Mahone, John	2	2	6		6
Miller, Nathl	1	2	2		
Manly, Moses	1	1	1		
Mason, Willim	1	1	1		6
Mahon, John	1	2	5		
Mahon, Josiah	1	3	4		
Megill, James	1	2	3		
Madry, Thos	1	1	2		
Madry, John	1	1	3		
Morriss, Thomas	1				
Madry, Joseph	1		2		
Moore, John	1				
Morriss, Willi	1				
Moore, Joseph	1		1		
Moore, Saml	2	2	1	2	
Morriss, James	1	2	3		
Mullins, Mother			1		
Megill, James	1	2	6		
Megill, John	1		1		1
Magee, James	1				
Minton, Thomas	1	2	3		
Morriss, William	1		1		
Madry, John	1		1		
Mason, John	2	1	5		
Moore, Moses	1	2	7		24
Moore, Joseph	1	1	2		
Madry, Joseph	1		2		5
Michell, Cader	1	5	3		2
Michill, Mathew	3	3	5		1
Morriss, Abrahm	1	1	3		
Morriss, John	1		2		
Michell, Ephm	1	6	4		1
Martin, Miles	1	3	1		
Michell, Jeames	4	1	4		
Michl, Nathan	3	6	3		
Michell, William	1		4		2
Minet, Grime		3	2		
Mitchell, John	2		4		
Newben, Thos	1	1	4		2
Newben, Geo	1	3	4	1	5
Nichols, John	3	1	4		1
Nichols, John	2	1	3		9
Nichols, Peter	1				
Noel, Edgard			2		
Norflett, James					3
Norflett, Reuben	1	2	3		48
Northam, Geo	1	2	2		
Neal, John	1				
Norflett, James	1				1
Northam, George	1	2	2		
Northam, Geo	1	2	2		
North, Joseph	2	2	3		7
Outlaw, James	1				
Outhouse, Isarel	1	2	4		
Outlaw Martha	1	1	5		2
Oxley, John	2	2	5		4
Outlaw, Jacob	1		3		4
Outlaw, Geo	2	1	1		21
Outlaw, Aaron	2	3	5		7
Outlaw, Luis	2	1	5		6
Outlaw, James	1				5
Outlaw, John	1	3	8	2	10
Overton, Churton	1		2		
Outlaw, James	1				
Outlaw, Edwd	1	1	3		14
Outlaw, Thomas	1	2	4		
Oldham, George	1				
Owens, Elsi			6		
Outerbridge, Stephen	1	1	1	1	1
Outhouse, Isarel	1	2	4		
Outlaw, Edward	2		3		10
Overton, Andrew	3	2	4		21
Overton, John	3	2	3		21
Overton, John	1	1	3		
Outlaw, Amos	1	1	3		6
Overton, Asa	1		2		
Outlaw, George	1	2	6		18
Owens, Penelope		3	5		
Pierce, Willm	1	1	2		
Perry, Elthred	1				
Peal, William	1	3	3		
Perry, John	1	3	1		
Pierce, Zedekh	1				
Pierce, Reder	1	1	1		
Pierce, John	2		2		2
Pender, Patune	1	2	1		8
Perry, Isaac	1				
Perry, James	2	2	2		
Perry, Joshua	2	3	5		16
Powers, Susan	2	1	3		5
Powers, Samson	1	1	4		4
Parker, Joseph	1				
Ditto for M. King					5
Pierce, Jerry	2	1	2	2	2
Page, James				2	2
Pugh, Thos	2	2	4	1	18
Price, James	1	1	2		
Pierce, Jereh	2	1	2		2
Page, Joshua	1	2	1		
Page, Thomas	1	1	1		
Page, Nathan	2	2	1		
Peal, Joshua	1		1		1
Page, Sarah			2		
Page, Catherine		1	3		
Pugh, Francis	3	3	4		30
Prudon, David	1	1	2		
Prudon, Abm	1				
Penay, James	2	1	3		
Purvey, William	1				
Parker, Elisha	1				
Purvis, Cullin	1				
Parker, Isaac	4	3	2		
Parker, Luke	1				
Parker, James	1		3		
Parker, Isaac	1		2		
Purvis, Jean		1	2		16
Peal, Josiah	2	3	5		
Parker, Joseph	1				6
Pugh, Thos	1				45
Ditto for P. Barker	1	1	2		33
Pugh, William	2	7	1		33
Powel, Cader	2	4	7		15
Page, Nathan	4	2	1		
Page, Sole	1	1	1		4
Perry, James	1				
Purvis, Allen	3		2	3	8
Pierce, Thomas	2		1		
Purvis, James	1		3		
Pugh, John	1				5
Powell, Willis	1	3	1	1	6
Passmore, Thos	1		2		
Pierce, Jeremiah	2	1	2		2
Page, Catherine		1	2		
Parker, Isaac	3	2	3		
Parnell, Joseph	1		3		
Pender, John	2				
Pender, Patience	1	2	3		10
Pierce, John	1		3		2
Pender, William	2	1	2		3
Pace, Saml	1	5	1		
Pender, John	2		2		3
Pierce, John	2		2		
Pender, William	1	2	2		6
Parnell, Joseph	1	2	4		
Parks, John	1	1	1		
Parks, Young	1	3	7	2	3
Prichard, Chrisr	2				
Pugh, W. Thos	1	1	6		35
Prichard, James	1	1	1		
Prichard, Jona	2		4		
Parker, Joseph	3	2	3		15
Perry, Thomas	1		2		9
Parker, Richd	1	4	2		6
Perry, Geo	1		3		2
Parker, Rich'd	1		2		6
Perry, Doctor	1	1	4		3
Pridden, David	1		1		
Pridden, Abm	1				1
Rhodes, Henry	1		2		7
Rhodes, John	1				3
Rice, William	1				
Rhodes, Isaac	1	1	4		
Rhodes, Isaac, Junr	1	4	4		
Rhodes, James	2	4	5	2	3
Rhodes, Henry	1	1	3		4
Rhodes, James	2	5	5		2
Rhodes, William	1	1	3		14
Rhodes, James	1				
Ralls, Rebecca	2		3		
Reed, Christian	3	2	5		23
Ryan, Thomas	2				9
Rascoe, Thomas	1	1	2		9
Razor, Josiah	1		3		7
Ridditt, Constant	1		1		
Ridditt, Lodwick	1				
Ryan, Cornelius	4	1	4		38
Razor, Eliza	1	2	6		12
Rhodes, Mary		2	2		
Rogers, Minet	3		3		
Rowlands, Robert	1	2	2		1
Relch, Luis	2	4	3		
Roberson, John	2	4	3		4
Runner, Eliza	1		2		
Roberson, David	1				
Rants, Samuel	3				
Runner, William	1				6
Ray, William	1				3
Runner, Joshua	1				
Runner, John	1	1	3		
Ramsey, John	1	2	4		1
Rhodes, Thomas	2	1	7		1
Rhodes, Eliza	1		2		
Rhodes, Henry	3	3	2		18
Rhodes, Jacob	1				
Rhodes, James	1				
Rhodes, William	1	1	2		12
Rutland, John	1	1	2	3	6
Rhodes, Henry	2	2	5		6
Rhobbinson, Eliza		1	1		
Raba, Hester	1	3	3		
Rhodes, Thomas	3	1	7		12
Rhodes, Elza	1	2	2		6
Rutland, John	1	5	3		
Raby, Jerutha	1	1	3		
Rice, James	1	2	3		2
Ridditt, Job	1	2			
Ralls, Jonas	1	2	2		
Ralls, Josiah	1	1	2		
Ralls, Josiah	1	4	4		1
Ralls, Job	1				
Ralls, Henry	1	2	4		
Ralls, Jonas	1				
Rhodes, Robert	1				
Rutland, James	1	1	5		
Ralls, Philip	1		4		
Rhodes, Robert	1	4	3		
Rascoe, Arther	1	2	4	1	2
Ralls, Levy	1		3		
Rauns, Else			3		
Ralls, Rebecca		3	7		
Rhodes, Ephraim	1	1	2		1
Raby, Bleak	1		2		
Ditto for Thos Barkr					74
Rascoe, William	3	5	4	1	3
Ruffin, William	3	5	3		15
Robinson, Eliza	1		3		
Rodgers, Thomas	1	1	4		1
Robinson, John	1	3	5	2	
Rollins, Isaac	1				
Rigging, Thomas (for Cullen Pollock)					83
Rascoe, Thomas	1	1	2		9
Rascoe, James	3	1	4		16
Rascoe, Arther	1	1	4	1	2
Rascoe, Peter	2	1	1		2
Rhodes, Mary		2	3		
Rogers, Minett	2	4			
Rhodes, Henry	1				
Rhodes, Mary	1	2	3		
Rodah, John	3	1			1
Sowel, Charles	2	2	5	1	6
Shehan, Thomas	1				1
Simons, Joseph	2	1	6		4
Skiles, William	2				4
Sowell, Francis	2	1	4		1
Standley, Jona	3	1	3		14
Simon, Steven	1	2	3		
Sparkman, R. Willm	1		3		5

EDENTON DISTRICT, BERTIE COUNTY—Continued.

NAME OF HEAD OF FAMILY.	Free white males of 16 years and upward, including heads of families.	Free white males under 16 years.	Free white females, including heads of families.	All other free persons.	Slaves.
Sumner, Jacob	1	1	2		
Shoulders, John	1	1	1		
Standley, Edmond	3	1	5		12
Shoulder, John	2	1	1		
Shoulder, Hare	1	1	1		
Shoulder, James	1	2	5		
Shoulder, Benjⁿ	3	3	2		
Stone, Zedkʰ	5	2			25
Sutton, Thomas	1		2		19
Sutton, William	2				1
Smithwick, John	2	1	1		5
Speller, Henry	3	1	2		9
Sutton, Joshua	3	1	1		5
Stue, William	1				
Smith, Stephen	2		1		6
Sparkman, William	1	1	3		
Seal, Thomas	1		1		
Smithwick, Jnᵒ	1	5	1		1
Stone, William	1	2	2		
Sorrell, Nancy		1	2	1	2
Sorrell, Benjⁿ	1		2		
Stone, Solᵒ	1	6	2		
Sorrell, Luis	1	3	1		5
Stoughton, John	1	1	1		
Stone, Sparkman	1				
South, Andrew	1	2	4		
Sparkman, Redwᵐ	1	1	2		2
Spivy, Jonathan	1	1	5		1
Sparkman, James	1				
Sparkman, Edward	1	3	3		
Sparkman, George	1	1	2		1
Slaughter, Thomas	1		3		5
Sylivan, Martha	2		1		
Siles, John	1	3	1		
Spivy, Joshua	1				
Stanby, John	1				
Sylivan, William	1	4	4		
Smith, Josiah	1	2	2		
Sylivan, William	1				
Stanley, Jonathan	1				3
Spivy, Aaron	1	2	2		10
Sylivan, John	2	3	5		
Stanley, William	1		1		1
Shyles, William (for Cullen Pollock)					43
Stanley, William	1		4		4
Shoulder, Thomas	1		1		
Ditto for Blake B. Wiggins					15
Shyles, John	1	2	2		
Stanby, David	2	1	4		23
Spivy, Jonathan	1				
Shyles, Benjamin	1				
Sheton, Mary		1	1		
Spence, John	1	1	2		4
Seay, James	1		6		
Spivy, Aaron	2	4	2		13
Sherlock, Thoˢ	4	5	2		4
Sowel, Frances	3	1	3		2
Sumlin, Noah	1	1	3		
Simons, George	1	1	1		1
Simons, Joseph	1	2	6		
Sowel, James	1				
Sumlin, Jacob	1	1	2		
Simons, James	1	1	3		
Simons, George	1	1	1		1
Simpson, John	1				
Sowel, John	1	1	3		
Slade, John	1	1	1		4
Spivy, John	1	1	5		2
Stall, John	1	5	4		
Swain, Richᵈ	3	1	2		3
Stallions, John	1		2		2
Smith, William	1		3		
Stallions, Mary	1	4	4		
Sorrel, Matthew	1		1		
Spivy, Easter	3		2		14
Sowel, Josiah	1				
Stallions, Mary	1		4		
Smith, Silas	1	5	4		2
Staten, Stephen	1		5		1
Stall, John	1		2		
Shoulder, John	1	1	2		
Stall, John	1	4	4		
Smith, Arthur	1				1
Smith, Sally		1	2		5
Sullivan, John	2	3	5		
Shaw, Nancy	2		2		
Stanton, Andrew	2	2	4		3
Swinson, Richard	2	2	4		1
Shiles, John	1	3	2		
Swain, Henrietta		1	4		4
Swain, Elisabeth	1	2	4		12
Todd, Moses	2	5	2		
Todd, Samuel	1		3		
Todd, Jesse	1		4		
Todd, Joshua	1				
Turner, David	3	3	2		12
Todd, Hardy	1				
Todd, William	1	3	5		
Trumble, Jethro					12
Thomas, Amos	1	2	3		
Theston, Amos	3	2	4		
Taylor, David	3	1	5		5
Turner, Simon	1	3	3		28
Thompson, James	1	1	3		
Thompson, John	3		2		
Turner, William	1	4	3		
Todd, Thomas	2	4	4		
Tibner, Perry	2				5
Tannison, Matthew	1	1	3		
Taylor, John	1				
Thompson, Charles	1		2		
Thompson, William	1	3	2		
Thomas, Jordon	1				
Turner, Amos	1	1			7
Thomson, Zedekiah	1				
Thomson, John	3	3	5		
Tarrinton, Benjamin	1	2	2		
Taylor, James	1	3	5		
Taylor, David	4	1	4		5
Turner, James	1	4	5		5
Thomas, Josiah	4		2		4
Talton, Benjamin	1		2		
Tall, James	1				
Trotman, Thoˢ		1	2		4
Tart, Nathan	1	1	2		1
Tart, Thomas	1	2	4		1
Tart, Nathan	4		1	1	3
Taylor, Abraham	2	3	1		3
Thomas, Jonathan	1		5		
Thompson, Noah	1	2	3		35
Thompson, William	1				10
Turner, Matthew	1		1		7
Thompson, Zedekiah	3		2	1	21
Thompson, Lewis	3		3		20
Trotman, Thomas	1	1	1		1
Turner, James	1	4	5		5
Turner, James	1	2	2		20
Tony, Anthony				4	
Thomas, Ezakiah	1	1	4		5
Thomas, James	1	1	2		
Thompson, James	1	1	2		
Vanpelt, Peter	1	2	3		
Vanpelt, James	1				
Vanson, Thomas	2	4	2		
Ventris, Moses	2		2	1	
Ventris, Moses	1	1	3		
Vale, Thomas	3	2	7	8	5
Virgin, William	1				
William, Allen	1				
Wilkinson, Joshua	1		2		
Willson, Josiah	1	1	3		
Willson, Edward	1	4	5		
Whiteaker, Whitmill	1	1	2		
Willifred, P. Wright	1		4		
Williams, William	1				
Willfred, Archibald	1	1	3		
Weston, Willᵐ	1	5	2		
Weston, Ephraim	1	1	1		4
Weston, John	1	1	3	1	3
Weston, Ephraim	2		3		4
Weston, Solomon	1	3	5		
Williams, Joab	1	3	1		5
Wimbely, Willᵐ	1		2		
West, Penelope	1	2	2		
Winant, Winants	1	1	4		1
White, Joshua	2		1		14
Wolfin, John	1		2	1	12
Williams, Benjamin	3	2	8		26
Wharburton, Luke	2	2	2		13
William, Moses	1		3		1
Williams, John	2		1		
Whitefield, Elisabeth			1		4
Worley, Daniel	2	1	3		10
Winslow, Rebecca			3		
Wells, Sarah			1		
Whitefield, Benjamin	1	3	6		14
Ward, Mary			1		6
Warren, James	1	1	2		
Watson, Sarah			3		2
Warwick, Jane		2	8	1	1
Wimbely, Mary		3	4		
Whitefield, Elisabeth			1		3
Ward, Mary	1		1		5
White, Peter	2	2	1		3
White, Luke	1	6	2		
White, William	1	2	3		4
Whitefield, Elizabeth			1		3
Williams, Benjamin	1		3		
Williams, Sarah			4		1
White, George	1	1	4		
White, Joel	1		2		
White, Luke	1	2	5		1
Wharburton, John				4	
Watford, Jonathan	1	2	1		5
White, William	1	4	3		
White, Jesse	1	1	1		
Wyns, Jesse	2	1	3		5
Wards, Joshua	1				
Ward, Thomas	1		4		16
Williams, John	1	3	3		
Wyns, John	1	3	4		1
Ward, Samuel	1	2	3		
Watford, Joseph	1		2		13
Walter, Timothy	1	3	4	1	8
Ward, Michael	1	2	1	1	3
Ward, James	1	1	2		4
Weeler, John	1				
Willson, Isaac	1	1	2		
Wilkins, Joshua	1		2		
Wiggins, Michael				4	
Watson, John	1		6		14
Willson, William	1	1	2		
Watson, John	1	3	5	1	10
Wiggins, Samuel				13	
Wilks, James	1	2	1		5
Willifred, Sarah				14	
Wimbely, Benjamin	1		2	1	
White, Noah	1	2	4		
White, Reuben	1				
Weston, Amos	1	2	4		
Willson, Edward	2	2	2		
Willfred, Isom	1				
Warren, James	1	1	2		
Whitefield, Elisabeth			3	1	2
Whitehouse, Lydia	1	1	1		
Watson, William	1	2	5		5
Williams, Elizabeth		3	2	2	7
Walker, Edward	1		1		
Williams, John	1				
Weston, Ephraim	1	1	1		4
West, Robert	1			1	15
Ward, Samuel	1		1		
White, Reuben	1				
Western, Amos	1	3	2		
Wilford, Archibald	1		3		
Williams, John	1				
Weston, William	1	5	2		
Wilks, James	1	3	2	2	
Wilks, Micajah	1		1		2
Wimbely, William	1	5	5		
Wimbely, William	1				
Wilks, James	1	1	1		6
Wiggins, Anthony	1				
Willson, William	1	1	2		
Wimbely, Willᵐ	1		2		7
Wimbely, John	2	2	4		9
Wimbely, Benjamin	2		3	1	3
Ward, Patsy		1	4		
White, Willᵐ	2	1	3	2	
Ditto for Samuel Johnston	2				61
Ware, Jarret	1	3	5		1
Wood, Jones	1	2	2		11
Wimbely, Frederick	1	4	5		5
Wimbely, Ezekiel	2	2	6		5
Wimbely, Lewis	1	2	2	1	8
Wimbely, Levy	1	1	4		
Willson, Edward	1		3		
Williams, James	1	1	6		2
White, Thomas (for John Granbury)					21
White, Thomas	1	1	2		2
Young, John	1	1	2		5
Yeats, William	1	1	3		
Yeats, Thomas	2	2	3		1
Yeats, Peter	1		1		2
Yeats, Elizabeth			4	1	3
Yeats, Ismay	1				
Yeats, Edward	1				
Young, John	1	1	2	1	5
Umplit, Job	1		2		
Umplit, Benjamin	1		2		
Ure, Tomfry	1		3		1
Urvin, Mary	1	3	2		1
Zilano, George	3	1	2		2

EDENTON DISTRICT, CAMDEN COUNTY.

NAME OF HEAD OF FAMILY.	Free white males of 16 years and upward, including heads of families.	Free white males under 16 years.	Free white females, including heads of families.	All other free persons.	Slaves.	NAME OF HEAD OF FAMILY.	Free white males of 16 years and upward, including heads of families.	Free white males under 16 years.	Free white females, including heads of families.	All other free persons.	Slaves.	NAME OF HEAD OF FAMILY.	Free white males of 16 years and upward, including heads of families.	Free white males under 16 years.	Free white females, including heads of families.	All other free persons.	Slaves.
Mercer, Coy	3		3			Wilroy, William	3	2	4		2	Spence, Grieves	1		3		
Mercer, John	1	2	3			Sawyer, Asa	1	2	2		6	Spence, Mark	1		4		
Sanderlin, Elizabeth	1		4			Winn, Letetia			2			McCoy, Mary	1	1	2		
Sanderlin, Levi	1	1	4			Johnson, Molly			3			Riggs, Isaac, Junr	1		1		
Sanderlin, Jacob	1	2	2			Overton, Garshum	2	2	4			Riggs, Noah	1	1	4		
Upton, Christian		1	3			Sikes, Elizabeth		2	4			Spence, John	1		2		
Shanning, Lovey		3	3			Rifle, Rebecca			5			Rhodes, Newton	2	3	3		
Mercer, Coy, Junr	1		2			Will (a free negro)				2		Bright, Malachi	2	4	5		
Morrissett, Peter	2	1	1		1	Ferrell, Benjamin	2		2			Chamberlin, Sally		1	6		
Gregory, Noah	1	1	3		3	Evans, William	2		4			Bright, Hezekiah	1	2			
Lockwood, Holland	1				1	Etheridge, David	1					Overton, Anthony	1	1	1		
Williams, Leonard	1	1	1		3	Sawyer, Job	1	5	3			Chamberlin, Joshua	1	3	3		1
Gregory, David	1	2	2			Etheridge, Joshua	2	1	3		1	Powers, Caleb	1		1		
Bernard, Prissilla	1		2		1	Sawyer, Jeremiah	2		2		5	Overton, Richard	1	4	3		
Terrel, Mary	1		3		6	Cooper, Seth	2	2	1			Overton, Eli	1	3	2		
Gregory, Judith	1		4			Taylor, William	1	7	2			Bright, Jeremiah	1		3		1
Greenman, Elizabeth		2	3			Overton, Lazarus	1	1	2			McFarson, Aby	1	1	2		
Oakley, Elizabeth			3			Ketor, William	1	2	1			McFarson, Matthew	2	1	1		
Spelman, Lydia				4		Overton, James	2	1	2			Overton, David	1	2	2		
Whitehouse, Sarah	1		4			Overton, Joseph	2	3	5			Jones, Edward	1	3	3		
Lamb, Abner	1		2		11	Scaff, David	1		1			McFarson, Demsey	1	1	4		1
Kemp, Ann	2	2	4			Overton, Francis	1	2	4			Brite, Charles	1				
Morrissett, Jonathan	1		1			McCoy, Nancy			2		1	Linton, Lemuel	1				
Forbes, Isaac, Junr	1	1	4			Upton, Hilliry	1	2	2		3	Chamberlin, Joshua, Junr	1				
Snow, Dinah			2			Sawyer, Zale	1	1	1			Chamberlin, Jeremiah	1	1	2		
Overton, John	1		1			Robertson, Benjamin B	1		1			McCoy, Joshua	1	3	4		
Bell, William	2	1	2			Robertson, Fanny		1	2			Chamberlin, Elizabeth			1		
Smith, Elizabeth		1	2			Overton, Joshua	2	2	1			Overton, Aby		3	2		
Forbes, Suthy	1	1	2			McFarson, Sally		3	2			Davis, Francis	1	2	1		2
Forbes, Elib	1	1	5			Culpepper, Daniel	1	2	1			Taylor, William	1	4	4		2
Garrott, Jacob	1		1			McCoy, John	1	1	2		1	Whitehouse, Gedeon	1		3		
Sanderlin, Joseph	1					McCoy, Nathan	1	1	1			Whitehouse, Amy	1	1	2		
Gregory, Samson	1	2	5			McCoy, Kesiah			1			Conner, Asa	2	1	3		
Sawyer, Benjamin	3	3	6			Snowden, Benjamin	1		3			Prichard, Thomas	2		3		
Lambert, John	1	2	3			Ketor, John	2	2	2			Weavour, John	2		1		
Gregory, James	1	2	3		1	McCoy, Joel	1	1	2			Prichard, Mary	1	2	4		2
Morgan, Macke	3	1	6		1	McFarson, John	1	4	2			Grandy, Ann			2		7
Wilroy, Abraham	2	1	3		6	Harrison, Demsey	2	1	2			Barcoe, Willis	1	1	2		
Sawyer, Jacob	4	2	3		4	McCoy, Malachi	1	2	1			Sawyer, Enoch	2		4	1	10
Empson, Caleb	1		2			Hearring, Jonathan	3	1	3		23	Rhodes, Samuel	1		2	3	
Grandy, Thomas, Junr	1		2		9	Milford, Matthew	1		5		1	Jones, Benjamin	1	4	4	4	36
O'Daniel, Elizabeth		2	5			McCoy, William	1	1	4			Milford, Matthew	1	2	2		
Gregory, John	2	1	3			McCoy, Bridget		3	2			Kenady, John	1		2		
Humphries, John	1					Pritchard, David	2	1	5		3	Sawyer, Mary	1	1	3		
Gregory, Isaac	1	1	1			Linton, Thomas	1	3	6			Hastings, Devotion	1	1	2		
Gregory, Aby			2			McCoy, James	2	2	2			Hastings, Carter	1		4		
Gregory, Matthias	1	2	4			McFarson, Jesse	1		2			Taylor, John	1	1	2		
Spilman, Timothy				1		Kenady, Robert	1	2	3			Herrington, Matthew	1	1	1		
Sikes, William	1	3	2			Taylor, Thomas	1		2			Spence, Thomas	1				
Ackland, John	2		2			Kite, William	1	5	2			Jones, Joseph	3	2	5		15
Bell, Joseph	1	2	3		2	Ketor, Solomon	1	1	3			Burges, Thomas	1	2	3		
Bell, Thomas	1		2			Taylor, Esdars	1	1	1			Grandy, Charles	1	1	4		23
Spence, Thomas, Junr	1		1			Ketor, Elisha	1	1	1			Pugh, James	1	3	1		
Williams, Benjamin	1	3	5			Smith, Daniel	1	2	2			Norton, John	1		1		
Williams, Joseph	2		1			Smith, Hannah			1		2	Cartwright, Jesse	1				
Dauge, Caleb	1	1	5		1	Whitehouse, John	1	1				Bray, Samuel	1	4	3		
Sawyer, Demsey	1		2			Overton, Richard			1			Needham, Joseph	1		2		1
Grandy, Sarah		2	2		4	Chamberlin, Nathan	1					Willson, Caleb	2		3		7
Jackson, Thomas	1					Spence, John	1	2	1			Needham, Thomas	2	3	5		
Mansfield, John	3	1				Grandy, Caleb	2	3	5		9	Brown, Dinah			1		1
Sawyer, Caleb, Junr	1					Smith, Elizabeth		2	1			Beels, Jesse	1				
Hulett, Abraham	1	1	2			Barcoe, Coston	1	2	1		1	Jones, Britton	1		2		
Hulett, Isaac	1	1	2			Burges, John	2	2	4		4	Squires, Elizabeth	1	1	6		
Hulett, Nelly	2	3	1			Burges, Zephaniah	1	1	1		4	Read, Robert	1		3		
Sawyer, Evan	1	1	8			Forbes, Surthy	1	1	1			White, Elias	1	3	3		
Noble, Thamer			4			Gregory, William	1		3			Snow, William	1		3		
Rifle, Elizabeth		1	1			Gallop, Luke	2	1	3			Godfrey, John	2	4	3		
Dauge, James	2		1		1	Toskey, Caleb	1	1	1			Laughinghouse, John	1	1	8		
Dauge, Meriam		2	5			Griffin, John	2	3	3			Neval, William	1		6		4
Empson, John	2	2	2			Sanderlin, Eli	1	1				Dauge, Willis	1	3	2		
Jones, Joseph, Junr	1	2	1			Spelman, Aaron				1		Griffin, Elizabeth		3	5		
Cartwright, Robert	2	1	2			Williams, William		1	3			Lurry, Thomas	2	1	5		12
Spence, David	1	2	1		1	Jones, Caleb	1		1			Barcoe, William	3	1	4		2
Sawyer, Shadrach	1		4			Jones, John, Junr			1		1	Jones, John	2	3	6		
Sawyer, Hilliry	1		4			Kennady, John	1	2				Sanderlin, James	3	1	2		
Smith, James	1	2	3		1	Rhodes, Samuel	1	2	3			Forbes, Aaron	2	1	1		
Mason, John	10	4	7		10	Payne, Nathaniel	3					Sanderlin, Robert	2		2		
Smith, Darcas			2			Goodlin, Richard	1		1			Gallop, Joshua	1	2	4		
Dill, Balser	3		2			Dowdy, Dinah			3			Dauge, Peter	1		3		12
Taylor, Lydia	1	1	2			Cartwright, Samuel	1	1	3		2	Bray, Isaac	1	4	4		
Hall, David			1	2		Chamberlin, Henry	1		3			Faircloth, Edward	1		5		
Jones, Joseph (son of Evan)	1	2	5			Overton, Amos	1		4			White, Cornelius	2	1	5		
Taylor, Jacob	2	2	3			Overton, Polly		1	4			Gray, Laban	1	2	3		
Edny, Newton	5	2	4		10	Gray, John (R. B.)	1	2	3		1	Harrison, John W	2	1	3		
Cartwright, Daniel	1	1	1		2	Burnham, Ann	3	1	1		2	Wright, Thamer	1	1	2		5
McFarson, Joseph	3	2	1			Edny, Newton (son of S.)	1	2	2		2	Harrison, Elizabeth	2	1	3		
Sawyer, Pharoah	2	1	4			Sawyer, William	1	3	2			Wright, Mary		2	3		5
David, Elisha	1		4		4	Riggs, Isaac	2	1	1			Gregory, Abi	1		2		
Abbott, Mary	1		2			Sawyer, John	1		1			Garlington, James	1	2	2		
Burnham, David	1	2	4		7	Overton, Asa	1	1	1			Williams, John	1	5	5		
Etheridge, Willis	2	2	2			Cartwright, Jabez	1	1	5			Kite, Zachariah	3		2		
Richardson, Sarah		1	6			Overton, Henry	2	2				McDowel, Ann		1	1		
Jones, William	1	4	1			Overton, Joshua	1	2	2		1	Seamore, Benjamin	1	1	3		
White, Benjamin	1					Overton, Peter	2	2	3			Seamore, Adam	1	1	1		
Campbell, Josiah	1	3	3		12	Rhodes, Leven	1	2	2			Burgess, Ann		3	3		
Pritchard, Benjamin	1	1	4			Sawyer, Joel	1	2	5			Beals, Julian	2		3		
Jones, John	2	1	4		10	Chamberlin, James	1	1	3			Toxey, Sarah		3	3		
Deal, John	1	5	2			Spence, Noah	1	2	2			Cartwright, Edy		1	1		

EDENTON DISTRICT, CAMDEN COUNTY—Continued.

NAME OF HEAD OF FAMILY.	Free white males of 16 years and upward, including heads of families.	Free white males under 16 years.	Free white females, including heads of families.	All other free persons.	Slaves.
Mitchell, Kesiah	1		5		
Smith, William	1		1		1
Burgess, Hezekiah	1	5	2		
Burris, John	1		1		
Needham, Thomas Junr	1	2	2		
Gray, Joshua	1	2	3		
Bray, Daniel	1	1	1		
Wright, Barny	1	2	2		4
Beals, Micajah	2	3	3		
Oggs, Charles				4	
Seamore, David	1	1	2		
Mitchell, Mary		2	2		
Burges, Thomas	1	1	3		
Cartwright, Moses	1	2	2		
Cartwright, Elijah	1				
Faircloth, Isaac			1		
Seamore, Jarvis	3		1		1
Sharborough, Christopher	1	1	1		1
Burges, John (D. R.)	1	2	3		1
Johnston, Ann		1	4		
Cartwright, Tulle	1	1	2		
Cox, Jesse	1		1		
Burges, Zebedee	1		4		
Canady, Alexander	1				
Bell, Josiah	2	1	3		
Canady, John	1				
Poyner, John	1	3	4		5
Beals, Zephaniah	1	1	2		
Godfrey, Isaac	1		2		
Smith, Thomas	1	1	2		
Seamore, Abel	1		1		1
Mitchell, Richard	1	1	1		
Beals, Jacob	1	1	3		
Cartwright, John	1		4		
Cartwright, Ann		1	2		
Baum, Peter	1	2	3		6
Seamore, Abraham	1		2		1
Curling, Josiah	2	1	3		
Jones, Willoby	1	3	2		
Beals, Asa	1	2	5		
Seamore, John	2	2	3		
Riggs, Isaac			3		
Mercer, William	1		6		2
Needham, Gideon	1	3	3		
Dowdy, James	1	4	2		
Miller, Stephen	1	3	4		9
Cartwright, Hosea	1				
Mitchell, William	1	2			
Sanderlin, Griffith	1		1		1
Cooper, Benjamin	2	1	4		
Gray, William	2	1	2		
Morrisett, Cason	1	5	1		
Hayvard, Thomas	3	1	3		
Burges, Demsey	1	2	3		30
Divers, Francis	1	2	1		
Gail, Sarah	1	3	4		5
Gregory, Lemuel	1	1	3		
Standley, Evan	1	3	2		
Mercer, Jesse	1		4		
Lewis, William	1	1	1		1
Gregory, Caleb	2	2	3		
Nichols, Thomas	1	1	1		9
Abbott, Henry	1		1		6
Mercer, Thomas	2	3	4		2
Dayley, Thomas	1		2		
Coats, Malchia	2	1	2		9
Lewis, Ralph	1	1	4		10
Wright, Elizabeth			3		1
Taylor, John	1		3		
Bell, Nathan	1	1	4		
Sexton, Jeremiah	1		2	2	1
Upton, William	1	1	1		3
Snowden, William	2		2		6
Nash, Sally	1	5	2		6
Philips, Daniel	1	5	2		
Riggs, David	1	1	2		
Williams, Lodewick	1	1	4		1
Williams, John (N. R.)	2	4	5		
Linton, Abel	1		3		
Abbott, Joseph	1		3		
Sanderlin, Devotion	2	2	2		8
Watkins, Sarah	1	1	2		6
Grandy, William	1	1	3		18
Hughs, William, Junr	1		1		1
Barnard, Lavina		4	3		2
Barclift, Blake	1	5	1		3
Mercer, Peter	4	1	1		
Sawyer, Stephen	1	1	4		8
Grandy, Thomas	1	1	4		
Snowden, Nathan	1	1	4		14
Etheridge, Davis	1		1		
Etheridge, Grandy	4	2	4		6
Sawyer, Willis	2	1	2		5
Gray, John	1		2		13
Sawyer, Griffith	3		2		7
Sawyer, John	1	1	5		18
Godfrey, Jesse	1	3	2		
Fennel, Michael	1				1
Mercer, William	1	1	3		2
Sawyer, Elisha	4	1	5		2
Freshwater, William A	3	1	3		1
Snowden, John	1		3		4
Perkins, John	2		1		
Linton, Isaac	2	2	4		1
Etheridge, Willis	2	3	2		2
Burges, William	1	1	2	2	2
Harney, Silby	1	7	3	1	4
Forbes, Malchia	2	3	2		1
Berry, John	1	2	3		5
Berry, Solomon	1	3	2		
Dunlap, James	2	2	3		1
Bell, Samuel	1	1	2		10
Roberts, Jonathan	1	2	4		3
Nash, Thomas, Junr	1			2	
Murden, Isaac	2	1	3		8
McBride, Elisha	1	2	6		10
Sawyer, Levi	1	2	4		2
Dicks, Charles			2		
Sawyer, Thomas	1		1		
Harrison, Isaac	2	3	5		1
Wright, John	1	1	3		10
Swills, Seth	3	1	7		3
Etheridge, Grace					
Wright, Capt William	3	1	5		
Parker, James	2	1	3		
Smithson, John	1		1		2
Lerry, Evan	2	4	3		3
Sawyer, Thomas (up River)	1	1	3		2
Dailey, Enoch	2	3	2		2
Barnard, Edward	1	1	2		2
Brockett, Joel	1				4
Squires, John	1	3	4		4
Spence, James	1		2		
Toxey, Meriam	1	2	6		
Love, William	2	4	4		
Kerby, James	1	1	1		3
Sawyer, Jacob	3	3	3		2
Riggs, Abraham	1	5	2		2
Jones, Evan	1	1	2		11
Forehand, Lowis		2	3		
Richardson, Hugh	1	3	5		2
Willson, Willis	1	5	2		6
Jalot, Thomas	1	2			
Toxey, Elliott	1	1	1		
Sawyer, Tulle	1	3	4		3
Jerrell, Mary		1	1		
Jerrell, Tabitha		1	2		
Williams, James	1		4		
Macoy, William	4	2	4		1
Nash, Thomas	1	4	4		3
Whithurst, William	3	3	4		4
Grandy, Absalom			3		14
Gregory, Abner	1	2	4		
Brite, Nathan	4	3	3		
Jones, John	1		3		2
Towner, Richard	1	1	3		2
Wright, William	2	1	2		18
Grandy, Noah	1	1	4		1
Casey, Demsey	2	1	1		1
Emson, John	1		1		
Cotter, Timothy	2	2	2		8
Sawyer, Elistra (B. S.)	4	3	4		
Dauge, John	2	2	8		8
Gregory, Nathan	2	1	7		
Humphries, Isaac	1		9		
Ferrell, Samuel	1	1	6		2
Homer, John	1		1		1
Willson, Benjamin	2	1	6		6
Webster, William	1	1	2		2
Humphries, Adam	1		2		
Forbes, Matthias	1	1	2		
Cartwright, Caleb	1	3	3		3
Sawyer, David	1	2	2		
Hatch, Lizar	1				
Kelly, Meriam	2	2	3		7
Sawyer, James	1	2	1		3
Cartwright, Robert	1	1	2		5
Cartwright, James	1	3	3		1
Snowden, Edmund	1		1		10
Bray, Henry	1	2	4		2
Bray, Daniel	1		2		
Cartwright, Isaac	1	1	1		
Aydlott, Henry	1		2		
Dauge, Isaac	1		2		7
Sawyer, Lucy			2		5
Sawyer, David	2	1			
Pretman, Elijah	1		2		
Gregory, Cornelius	2	2	5		6
Sikes, John	1		1		
Herrington, Jonathan	1	3	1		
Gregory, Richard	1		1		2
Sanderlin, Ezekiel	4	2	6		
Toxey, Joseph	1		1		9
Edny, Robert	2		1		1
Forbes, Henry	2	2	3		
Sanderlin, Nancy		2	6		7
Davis, Samuel	1	1	2		1
Ferrell, James	1	3	3		1
Bell, William	1	2	3		
Brown, Benjamin	1	3	3		
Morgan, Claudias	1	2	6		
Walkup, Samuel	1		1		
Etheridge, Thomas	1	2	4		
Dunkin, David	2	4	6		
Cartwright, Jacob	1	1	4		
Forbes, Caleb	3	1	3		1
Brockett, John	1	4	2		9
Parr, Jesse	1	3	2		
Griffith, Joseph	1				3
Forbes, Adam	1	3	3		
Williams, Lodewick, Senr	1	2	5		1
Barco, Tabitha	1	1	1		
Williams, Urias	1	3	1		1
Jones, Timothy	1	3	4		2
Sawyer, Richard	1	2	4		
Gray, Cornelius	1	1	1		11
Dauge, Evan	1		1		1
Upton, Edward	2	1	5		
Coats, James	1		5		
Coats, Caleb	1		1		
Lamb, Luke	3	2	5		12
Gilford, Isaac	1	2	2		15
Gregory, James	2	1	2		
Gregory, Asael	2	1	2		
Gregory, Judy (up R.)	1	1	2		
Whithurst, Sarah (up R.)	1		4		
Harrison, Robert	4	1	4		
Harrison, Peter	1	1	4		
Harrison, Caleb	1	1	4		
Harrison, John	1	1	3		
Sanderlin, Isaac	1		2		
Bray, Christopher	1	2	4		
Tumlin, Susannah	1		4		
Kite, Zachariah	1				
Burges, Mary	1		3		
Perry, Elizabeth	1	2	4		
Upton, Willis	3	1	4		4
Gail, John	1		2		8
Sawyer, Edmund	1				11
Bright, Willis	2		2		13
McPherson, Joshua	2	2	6		9
Cartwright, Morgan	1	1	1		5
Sawyer, Mary			1		4
Bell, Robert	1	3	1		2
Herrington, Isaac	1	1			3
Williams, Robert	1	1	3		
Sanderlin, Benjamin	1	1	2		
Barco, Adron	1	1	2		
Garrott, William	1	1	4		
Garrott, James	3	2	3		
Kite, Malchia	1		2		
Mercer, Joshua	1	3	3		
Sanderlin, Thomas	1	1	3		
Barco, Evan	1				
Gregory, Silvia	1		2		2
Walston, Thomas	1	1	2		
Walston, Mary	1		1		
Staples, Thomas	1		2		
Jerroll, James	1		1		
Skilton, Christopher	1	3	4		
Forbes, James	2		2		
Forbes, Jacob	1	1	3		
Sheppard, John	1	1	1		
Adkins, Thomas	1	1	2		
Williams, Shadrach	1		2		
Forbes, Joshua, Senr	1	1	3		
Forbes, Sarah	1	1	3		
Forbes, Thomas	3		4		1
Forbes, Isaac, Senr	1	3	2		2
Bray, Thomas	1	2	3		
White, James	1	1	1		
Forbes, Aaron	1		1		
Forbes, Isabella		1	1		
Barclift, John	2	1	1		
Morris, Benjamin	1	1	1		
Gregory, James (N. River)	1	1	2		
Gray, Lodewick	1		5		
Gallop, Isaac	1	1	3		
Gregory, Genl Isaac	1	2	2		23
Gregory, Isaac, Junr	1	1	2		6
Sawyer, Demsey	1	3	5	1	18
Ballance, Joseph	1				
Bray, Henry (S. N.)	3	1	6		
Griffith, John (M. R.)	1	1	3		15
Gardner, Debby			3		7
Gregory, Abi	1		2		
Gregory, Caleb (N. R.)	1	1	2		
Gregory, Arthur	1	2	4		
Gregory, Malchia (N. R.)	1	3	4		
Mercer, John, Senr	1	1	2		

EDENTON DISTRICT, CHOWAN COUNTY (EXCLUDING EDENTON TOWN).

NAME OF HEAD OF FAMILY.	Free white males of 16 years and upward, including heads of families.	Free white males under 16 years.	Free white females, including heads of families.	All other free persons.	Slaves.
Ashley, William	2	2	3		
Ashley, Meade	1	3	3		
Ashley, Jeremiah	1	1	3		
Ashley, Joseph	1	1	1		
Ashley, William, Junr	3	2	3		
Ashley, Peggy			2		
Avery, John	1		4		1
Bartle, Anthony	4	2	4		2
Bains, George	4	5	4		
Burkett, Thomas	1				
Blount, Ann		2	2		6
Beasley, Martha		1	2		7
Beasley, Elizabeth	1	1	3		20
Barrow, John	1	1	2		5
Benbury, Richard, Esqr	1		4		15
Beasley, John	2		1		8
Beasley, George	1		6		4
Beasley, Robert	2				4
Benbury, Thomas, Esqr	2				88
Benbury, Joseph	1				14
Blount, John	1	2	1		14
Beasley, James	1	1	3		4
Boulton, Jonathan	1		4		12
Bunch, James	1				2
Bunch, Mary	1	2	3		11
Bunch, Joseph	1				1
Bonner, Henry	1	3	4		13
Bond, John, Esqr	1	4	4		9
Benbury, Ruth			5		10
Beasley, Francis	1		1		2
Bennett, William, Esqr	1	4	6		49
Boyd, Meriam			3		6
Badham, Mary	1	1	2		5
Bonner, Thomas	1				
Bains, George, Junr	1	1	4		17
Bond, Elizabeth		2	4		20
Blount, Edmund	4	2	6	2	34
Brinn, James	1	2	1		
Bunch, Solomon	1	1	1		1
Bunch, Sarah			1		
Bunch, William	1		3		1
Bunch, Ishmael	1	1	3		
Bacchus, John	1				
Bunch, Prissilla		4	5		6
Bunch, Cullin	1	3	2		1
Boyce, Leah	1		2		
Bond, James	1				
Buckley, Richard	2	1	3		3
Bacchus, Thomas	2	2	3		
Byrum, Joel	2	2	4		
Blanchard, Micajah	1	2			6
Bufkin, Sarah			1		
Byrum, Isaac	2	3	3		
Byrum, Isaac, Junr	1	1	1		
Bufkin, William	1				
Byrum, Lavina		2	1		
Bowen, George	1				
Bosworth, Obediah	1				
Crucy, Mary			2		5
Crucy, Lemuel, Esqr	1	2	1		29
Crucy, Nathan	1	1	2		6
Crucy, Frederick	1	2	3		18
Chessire, Willson	1		2		2
Charlton, Thomas	1	2	1		11
Clements, John	1	1	2		
Charlton, John	1	1	3		3
Charlton, Job	1				
Cox, John	1		1		2
Chew, Mary			4		
Coffield, Edward	2	1	3		3
Coffield, Benjamin	2		1	1	12
Coffield, John	1	3	1		19
Cox, Elisha	1		1		3
Champion, Joseph	3	3	2		1
Chambers, Thomas	1	2	3		2
Cabarrus, Stephen, Esqr	2		1	1	73
Collins, William	1				8
Cannon, Jeremiah	1	1	2		1
Coffield, Jeremiah	1	1	1		1
Coffield, Michal			3		4
Chappell, Micajah		1	1		
Chappell, Josiah	1		3		
Caruthers, William	1	1	1		
Cullen, William	1	2	1		5
Chappell, James	1		1		
Copeland, Josiah, Esqr	3		4		21
Copeland, Josiah, Junr	1	2	2		
Copeland, Joseph	3		2		
Coffield, Job	1				2
Cleyland, Rebecca			1		
Donaldson, Robert	2	1			2
Deshon, Jacob	1		1		
Deshon, Augustine	2	1	4		3
Deshon, Lewis	1	1	1		1
Deal, William	1	1	2		
Deal, Malachi	2	3	1		

NAME OF HEAD OF FAMILY.	Free white males of 16 years and upward, including heads of families.	Free white males under 16 years.	Free white females, including heads of families.	All other free persons.	Slaves.
Delany, John	1				
Elliott, Stephen	1		3		4
Evans, James	2	1	2		
Eliff, John	1	2	4		3
Elliott, Miles	1	4	3		6
Eccleston, John	2		3		1
Earl, Charity		1	2		10
Earl, Ann			1		26
Evans, John	1	1	5		
Ellis, Thomas	2		6		
Gregory, William	1	2	2		7
Gregory, Luke	1	1	4		7
Garrott, Richard	1	1	5		3
Farrow, Tinch	1				
Fife, John	1	1	2		
Fallow, William	1	1	3		1
Fullerton, John	1				
Farrow, John	1	1	1		
Ford, William	1	1	2		
Floyd, John	2	1	4		
Felton, William	2		1		6
Felton, Shadrack	1	2	1		11
Felton, Ann		1	2		2
Felton, John	1				1
Floyd, William	1	1	5		
Garrott, Everard	3	1	1		2
Garrott, George	1				
Godwin, Caleb	1	1	1		6
Goodwin, William	1	2	5		1
Garrott, James	1	1	1		3
Griffin, Willis	3	2	1		
Goodwin, Thomas	2		5		1
Goodwin, Joseph	1		1		
Goodwin, Lewis	1	1	2		
Gregory, Henry	1	1	1		7
Gregory, Benjamin	1	3	1	1	1
Hobbs, Moses	1		1		1
Haughton, Jonathan	3	4	4		8
Haughton, William	3	1	3		
Haughton, Jeremiah	1				4
Haughton, Edward	1		4		7
Haughton, Charles	1	3	3		22
Haughton, Richard	1	3	4		15
Holmes, William	1	1	3		4
Hall, Judith			2		3
Horniblow, John, Esqr	2	4	4		27
Hassell, Jesse	3	3	3		4
Hallsey, Henry	1		3		
Hoskins, Sarah		2	4		8
Howent, Nathaniel	1		1		10
Hall, Clement	2		3		5
Hinesley, Martha			3		
Hoskins, Samuel	2		2		10
Hoskins, Richard, Esqr	3	1	7		20
Holmes, Mary		1	1		3
Hoskins, John, Junr	1				
Hicks, William	1	1	2		
Hicks, Job	1	3	3		
Hicks, Patrick	1		2		
Hurdle, Josiah	1	1	4		5
Hallsey, William	1	3	4		
Hallsey, Daniel	1	3	8		
Hallsey, Malachi	2	2	4		
Hallsey, Cullen	2	2	1		1
Hallsey, Harris	1				
Hoskins, John	2		2		4
Harrell, William	1		4		
Hurdle, Martin	1	2	4		
Hollowell, Luke	1	3	3		
Hurdle, Henry	1	2	2		1
Hurdle, Harmon	1	2	2		8
Humphries, Richard	1	4	3		
Hobbs, Thomas	1	4	4		
Hurdle, Benjamin	1	1	3		5
Hobbs, John	1				
Hollowell, Abana	2	2	3		6
Harris, Abraham	2	2	1		
Humphries, William	1		4		
Johnston, Samuel, Esqr	1	2	3		96
Johnson, Charles, Esqr	2	2			35
Johnson, Joshua			1		
James, Edward	1	2	2		3
Jones, James	1	5	4		11
Jones, Thomas	6	2	4		7
Jones, William	2		5		22
Joiner, Humphry	1				
Jordan, Jacob, Esqr	2		2		11
Jordan, Demny	1		2		
Jordan, William	1		3		1
Jordan, Ichabod	1				
Jordan, Hance	1	2	1		
Jordan, Charles	2	2	6		
Jordan, Nicholas	1		3		
Jackson, Mary			3		2
Jackson, William	2	1	7		19
Jones, Josiah	1		3		

NAME OF HEAD OF FAMILY.	Free white males of 16 years and upward, including heads of families.	Free white males under 16 years.	Free white females, including heads of families.	All other free persons.	Slaves.
Jordan, Joseph	1	3	4		2
Jordan, Jacob	1	2	3		
Jordan, Caleb	2		1		1
Jordan, Nathan	1	1	2		
Jameson, Bond	1	1	3		2
Johnson, Joseph	1		3		
Johnson, Bersheba		1	3		
Jordan, Josiah	1	1	4		
Keal, James	3	1	4		
Kirby, William	1		2		
Leary, John	1		2		8
Luten, Henderson	1	2	3		3
Liles, William	2	2	3		9
Leary, Job	1	2	3		10
Lane, Samuel	1	1	1		
Lane, Abraham	1	3	5		
Lane, James	1	2	2		
Lane, Miles	1		2		
Mixon, Hannah	1		2		
Ming, Thomas, Junr	1		2		2
Moran, John	1	1	2		
Middleton, John	2	3	2		3
McNider, Thomas	2	1	2		
Ming, Richard	1	1	1		2
Ming, James	1		1		4
Ming, John	1	1	4		1
Ming, Joseph	1	1	3		5
McGuire, Philip, Junr	1	2	2		5
Miller, Ephraim	3				1
Miller, Mason	1	4	2		2
Miller, Malachi	1	3	2		4
Miller, Mary		1	1	1	2
Matthias, Thomas	1		3	1	3
Muns, Thomas	1	1	4		
Muns, William	2	2	5		
Muns, William, Junr	1	5	2		
Mitchel, John	2	6	4		
McGuire, John	2	6	5		
McGuire, Samuel	1		1		2
Meridith, John	1	2	2		
Mansfield, Zebulon	1	2	4		
Moore, Robert	1				
Moore, William	1				
Ming, Thomas	2	1	4		10
Martin, William	1	3	2		
McClenny, Ruth		1	4		
McGuire, Philip	1	3	2		
Norcom, John	3	2	3		26
Norcom, Frederick	3	3	1		15
Newbern, Nicholas	1	1	3		
Newbern, William	1				
Newbern, Willson	1	2	1		5
Norflet, Abraham	1	1	2		4
O'Neil, Peter	1	1	3		1
Pettyjoh, Abraham	1	3	1		1
Pittyjohn, John	1	2	3		3
Procter, John	2				4
Procter, Ruben	1				1
Perkins, Robert	1		4		
Price, James	2		2		6
Price, Thomas	2	2	7		9
Price, Noah	1				14
Parker, Seth	1	1			2
Parker, Isaac	2		3		3
Parker, Willis	1		3		5
Padgett, John	1		3		
Poppieston, John	1		2		
Pettyjohn, Job	1				
Privet, Elizabeth	2		2		
Parrish, James	1				
Parrish, John	3	4	3		
Parker, Nathan	1				2
Parker, Elisha	1	2	3		2
Philips, John	1				
Powell, Charles	3	3	2		8
Perry, Samuel	1	3	4		
Parker, Samuel	1	1	5		
Perry, Amos	1		4		
Paddin, Patsey			4		
Parker, Peter	1	3	3		1
Parker, Job	2	3	8		
Parker, Enoch	1	1	4		
Roberts, Thomas	1	3	1		
Righton, William	1		1		20
Rea, Samuel	1	2	2		
Rea, Thomas		2	2		3
Roberts, Willis	1	2	3		5
Robinson, John	1	1	4		
Roberts, Charles	1		2		13
Roberts, William, Esqr	2	2	3		21
Rodith, Mary			2		
Rodith, John	2	1	2		5
Rogers, Joseph	1	2	7		26
Roberts, James, Esqr	1	1	3		7
Simons, Argyle	2				
Simons, Joshua	1				

EDENTON DISTRICT, CHOWAN COUNTY (EXCLUDING EDENTON TOWN)—Continued.

Name of head of family.	Free white males of 16 years and upward, including heads of families.	Free white males under 16 years.	Free white females, including heads of families.	All other free persons.	Slaves.
Simons, John	1	2	3		2
Simons, Jacob	1	2	2		23
Simons, Charlton	1				9
Simons, William	1		1		2
Simons, Thomas	1	2	2		2
Simson, Samuel	1	4	3		2
Simson, Benjamin	1		2		
Smith, Rebecca			2		2
Swann, Rebecca			1		2
Sutton, James	1	2	3		8
Small, Benjamin	3	4	5		8
Standin, John	1	2	1	1	
Small, Josiah	3	1	5		5
Sterns, James	1		4		
Sumner, Abraham	1	2	3		7
Standin, Joseph	1		3		15
Sowell, Mary		1	4		
Stewart, Mary	1		3		1
Skinner, Evan	2		1		9
Skinner, Samuel	1	2	4		1
Skinner, William	1	3	1		2
Simson, Evan	1	2	2		
Simson, John	2		1		2
Simson, Mary	1	1	2		1
Simson, William	4	3	3		9
Simson, John, Junr	2	5	3		1
Stacey, Nathaniel	1		1		
Small, Joseph	1	1	2		3
Smith, John	1	1	4		
Stallings, Nathan	1	1	1		
Stallings, Miles	1				
Stallings, Nicholas	2	2	6		1
Stallings, Elias	1	1	3		
Scott, Joseph	2		3		
Taylor, John	1	2	3		1
Taylor, Thomas	1		2		
Taylor, John, Junr	1				
Thack, Gregory	1		1		
Thomson, Thomas W	1	2	2		12
Toppin, Samuel	1	2	5		
Trotman, Amos	1		1		7
Thurston, William	1	1	1		
Underhill, Sarah			3		16
Vail, Thomas	1	4	2		18
Whiteman, Matthew	1	2	2		2
Webb, William	1	1	3		
Wilkins, William	1		1		11
Wyatt, Joshua	1	2	2		2
Walton, Holladay	1		3		2
Wilden, John	1				2
Ward, Thomas (Yeopin)	1	3	3		
Webb, John	3	2	3		
Wedburn, Joseph	1				
Wilden, Francis	1		2		2
White, James	1				2
Woodward, Edward	1	3	4		1
Ward, John	1		2		
Ward, Solomon	1	1	2		
White, Silas	2	3	3		
White, Charles	1	1	1		
Woodward, Richard	1	2	2		3
Walton, John	1	2	4		3
Welch, Edward	1	6	3		
Ward, Lowderick	1	1	4		
Ward, Thomas	3	1	4		
Ward, Humphrey	1		1		1
Ward, Ephraim	1	1	2		
Ward, Frederick	1				
Woodward, James	1		2		
Wood, Seth	1	2	3		
Ward, William, Junr	1	1	2		
Welch, Isaac	1		3		
Welch, Margaret	1	3	3		
Ward, Jeremiah	1				
Woodward, Jane			4		
Ward, Hardy	1		4		
Wood, Judith			1		
Ward, Thomas (son of Willm)	1	1	2		
Winslow, William	1	1	2		1
Ward, Denby	1		1		1
Ward, Nathan	1		1		
Ward, Aaron	1				
White, Thomas	1	1	2		9
Ward, Nathan, Junr	1		1		
White, George	1	3	2		
White, Elizabeth	1		4		
Ward, Lewis	1	1	5		
Winslow, Job	1	2	1		1

EDENTON DISTRICT, EDENTON TOWN.

Name of head of family.	Free white males of 16 years and upward, including heads of families.	Free white males under 16 years.	Free white females, including heads of families.	All other free persons.	Slaves.
Allen, Jemima			1		2
Allen, Nathaniel, Esqr	4		5		17
Askens, Elizabeth			1		
Barker, Penelope			1		
Borritz, William, Esqr	2	1	2	1	17
Blair, William	1				2
Blount, Joseph, Esqr	1	2	5		33
Butler, Samuel	1		1		12
Bond, Henry	1	2	3		5
Bent, Thomas	1	1	2		3
Brinkley, Mary		3	3		1
Bissell, Thomas	3	4	1		3
Black, Alexander	1	1	2		6
Bennett, Sarah			4	3	1
Bruster, Lott	1		1		2
Burdick, Josiah	1	1			
Brown, James	1				
Brown, John	1				
Blount, Jacob	1		2		16
Bateman, Thomas	2	1	2		2
Brown, Ann			2		
Beasley, John	1			2	2
Barr, David	1				
Banks, Jane				2	
Cumming, William, Esqr	1	1			2
Carter, William	1	2	3		3
Collagan, William	1	1	1		
Cameron, John	2		3		3
Cooley, Penelope			1		1
Carpenter, Stephen	1	1	2		6
Cheshire, Henry	2		1		1
Carter, Leah		1	1		
Cunningham, James	1		2		1
Cotten, James	1		3		1
Cox, Thomas	1	1	5		5
Collins, Josiah	3		1		30
Collins, Allen, and Dickenson	3				113
Clark, John	1				
Clark, Abraham	(*)	(*)	(*)		1
Dickenson, Samuel, Esqr	(*)	(*)	(*)	(*)	19
Decamp, James	(*)	(*)	(*)	(*)	7
Dunscomb, James	(*)	(*)	(*)	(*)	2
Dalling, Mary	(*)	(*)	(*)	(*)	(*)
Dear, Ann	(*)	(*)	(*)	(*)	1
Demsey, Peggy					2
Eelbeck, Joseph H	1				8
Engs, Madett	3		3		13
Egan, Robert	2		2		17
Eberton, John	2	2	5	1	1
Eelbeck, Henry	1				3
Frazel, John	1	1	2		3
Farlow, Happy			2		
Forrow, James	1	1	1		2
Ferrybought, Henry	1		3		1
French, Robert	1	2	2		2
Flury, Henry	2	1	1	1	1
Felps, Sarah			1		
Finch, James	1	1	1		
Gordon, Mary	1	1	1		3
Gallop, Jeremiah	2				3
Gantz, Frederick	1	1	2		2
Gardner, Henry	1		2		1
Hardy, Robert	1				1
Hardy, Margaret			1		5
Hardy, Rachael			1		
Hopkins, Joseph	1		2		5
Hayse, Kitty			1		
Culver, Ann			5		
Churton, Joe				1	
Hines, Robert	1	1	2		
Hodge & Wills	3				
Hathaway, James	2		4		3
Hamilton, John	1	1			6
Hamilton, Alexander	1				
Hankins, Thomas	3	3	1		2
Hartford, John	1	1	2		3
Hughs, Charles	1		4		1
Henderson, Mary			1		
Jameson, Samuel	1		1		
Iredell, Thomas	1				
Janders, Charles	1				
Imes, Denten	1		1		
Jackson, Samuel	1				
Joseph, Anthony	1		1		
James, Mary				2	
Kock, Hans I	1	3	2		2
Kennedy, Henry	2	1	6		5
Kennedy, Hannah			2		
Lattemore, Samuel	1	3	4		
Litt—*, William	3	3	6		62
Ly—* Ann					3
——*, Charles	1	2	2	1	2
——*, Hen—	1	2	1		1
——*, Absa——*	1	2	1		
——*, King	1	2	2		5
Lit—*, John	1	5	3		17
Leming, John	1		4		2
Linch, Charles	1				
Miller, Robert	1	1	2		2
M'Keal, Michael	1	3			2
Mitchel, Nathaniel	1		1		2
Morgan, George	3	3	3		5
M'Donald, William	1	1	3		16
M'Donald, John	1				
Mare, John, Esqr	2		3	1	22
Miles, Jane			4		5
Montgomery, Sarah			1		2
Murray, Dominigue	1	2	4		1
Murray, William	1	2	1		2
Morris, John	1		3		1
Meridith, David	1		2		6
Norflet, Elisha	4	2	3		4
Neil, Honour	1	1			2
Neil, James			1		
O'Malley, Matthew	1				4
O'Malley, Miles	1		2		12
Overton, Jonathan	1				5
Overin, Samuel	1				
Payne, Michael, Esqr	2		3		25
Powell, Stephen	1	1	1		
Pollock, Cullen, Esqr	1		1		204
Purdy, Ivy	1	1	2		6
Parker, Thomas	1		1		
Pollidore, Phebe				1	
Person, William	1				
Pambrune, Elizabeth			1		
Philips, Fanny	1	2	3		
Pierson, John	1	1	1		
Prentice, James	1				
Rumbough, William	2	1	4		8
Reiley, Edward	1		1		
Ramsay, Allen	1				3
Ramcker, Frederick	2	1	4	2	12
Rondett, Francis	1	1	5		1
Rodney, Henry	1		1		
Reeves, Richard	1		3		2
Rud, Mary				4	
Stanton, Barbary	(*)	(*)	(*)	(*)	(*)
Swinne, Sarah					1
Spooner, John	(*)	(*)	(*)	(*)	2
Smith, James	(*)	(*)	(*)	(*)	2
Squires, Roger	(*)	(*)	(*)	(*)	2
Satterfield, James	(*)				(*)
Small, John	1	2	2		1
Satterfield, William	1		1		3
Satterfield, Thomas	1		1		1
Sinkler, Elizabeth	1	1	4		
Standin, Lemuel	2	1	3		7
Spencer, James	1				
Sinkler, Ann		1	4		1
Seaman, Thomas	1		1		
Starr, Henry	1		1		
Shaw, William	1		2		1
Udell, William	1				
Vernice, Jeremiah	1	1	5		1
Wilkenson, George	1	1	2		
Wynant, Penelope			3		1
Williamson, Rebecca	1	2	2		
Webb, Zachariah	1	3	2		1
Watkins, Deborah		1	1		
Waff, Thomas	3	1	2		5
Waff, William	1				
Wallace, Mary			1		1
White, Theresa	1	1	2		1
Whidbee, Joseph	2	1	4		5
Willson, Robert			3		
Willson, Rebecca			3		
Williams, John	1		2		
Webb, James	1	2	2		
Ward, Meriam			2		
Waters, Catharine	2		1		
Gellelty, Catharine		2	2		1
Mann, John	1	1	1		
Yeomans, James	1	3	1		1
Mustapher, Mary				2	
Mustapher, Debby				1	1
Mustapher, Patty				1	

* Illegible.

EDENTON DISTRICT, CURRITUCK COUNTY.

Name of head of family.	Free white males of 16 years and upward, including heads of families.	Free white males under 16 years.	Free white females, including heads of families.	All other free persons.	Slaves.
Ferebee, Samuel	4	2	2		10
Allcock, Solomon	1	2	1		
Etheridge, Timothy	2	2	5		2
Berry, Samuel	1	3	3		
Parr, Daniel	1		2	2	1
Gregory, Rachael		2	8		
Gregory, Mary		1	2		
Hutchins, Anice		1	3		
Midgett, William	7	6	6		4
Midgett, Samuel, Esqr	1		1		9
Midgett, Thomas	1	1	3		4
Ashby, Solomon	1	1	5		7
Beasley, Jacob	1		5		
Owings, Nathaniel	1				
Fletcher, Stephen	1				
McKinsey, Thomas	1				
Coams, Thomas	1				
Carter, William	1				
Hunt, Charles				6	
Midgett, Samuel	1	3	5		3
Midgett, Joseph	2		2		
Linton, Lazarus	1		1		8
Midgett, Maurice	1	2	2		
Daugh, Samson	2	3	4		5
Daugh, Thomas	1	2	3		
Wescutt, Stephen	5		3		6
Wescutt, John	1	4	3		
Savage, George	1		3		
Ashby, Abel	1	3	4		10
Mann, John	3	2	7		4
Etheridge, Adam	1		4		3
Etheridge, Jesse, Junr	1		1		
Brickhouse, Caleb	4	2	2		
Twifoot, Levin	1		2		
Baum, Abraham	3	4	4		7
Humphry, James	2	4	2		2
Dolby, Absalom	3				
Baum, Maurice	4	2	4		6
Etheridge, Jesse	1	2	4		6
Etheridge, William	1	5	1		
Etheridge, Tart	4	3	5		
Etheridge, James	2	4	4		
Beasley, William	1	1	4		
Beasley, Ann	3	2	3		
Montigue, Ann	1	2	2		
Etheridge, Ruben	1				
Mann, Edward	2	3	2		7
Savage, Southy	1	1	2		
Midgett, Samuel, Junr	1	2	5		
Hassell, Joseph	1	1	1		
Beasley, Stephen	1		1		
Daniel, Belcher	1	6	3		12
Daniel, William	2	3	6		1
Daniel, Gidion	2	1	2		2
Cudworth, John	1	1	1		
Daniel, David	1	2	2		
Boswell, James				8	
Bryan, Sarah				4	
Daniel, Joseph	2		6		2
Daniel, John	1	5	1		
Daniel, Samuel, Junr	2	4	3		
Daniel, William, Junr	2	1	5		
Brinston, Adam	1		3		
Brickhouse, George	1		3		
Rogers, Harding	1		2		
Midgett, Joseph, Junr	1	1	2		
Williams, John (Banks)	2	1	5		
Lurk, Elizabeth		3	2		
Tillitt, Thomas	4		3		4
Fountain, William	1		2		
Beacham, John	1		4		
Jones, Thomas	1	1	1		
Merchant, Caleb	1	1	3		
Guard, Joshua	2		3		
Johnston, Randolph	1		2		
Patterson, William	2		3		
Paddrick, Hannh	1	3	1		
Paddrick, John	1	3	2		
Caps, Lewis	1		1		
Paddrick, Ann		1	1		
Toaler, Mary	1	3	2		
Beacham, Mary		1	5		
Beacham, Thomas	1	2	2		
Garrott, Thomas	2	3	3		
Parker, James	1	1	2		
Caps, Selenian	1		5		
Gamewell, James	1	2	2		
Best, William	1		3		
Franklin, Thomas	1		3		
Williams, Absalom	1	1	1		
Caps, Moses, Junr	1	1	2		
Daugh, John	1	2	5		
Tillett, Isaac	1		1		
Gallop, Shadrach	1		3		
Merrett, Isaac	2	2	3		
Tillett, Lemuel	1	2	5		
Sikes, Henry	3	1	3		
Gallop, Demsey	1	1	2		
Humphries, Joseph	1	1	3		
Perry, John	1	2	3		
Best, Mary	2	1	3		
Lenark, John	2	1	3		
Best, Thomas, Senr	1	3	2		
Hayman, Daniel	1	1	3		
Best, Thomas, Junr	1		1		
Gamewell, Benjamin	1	1	2		
Hill, Joshua	2	1	3		
Gamewell, John, Senr	1				
Gallop, Jonas	1	5	8		
Austin, Daniel	1	2	2		
Austin, Thomas, Junr	1	1	1		1
Austin, William	1	1	2		
Austin, Thomas	1	2	4		
Stow, Joseph	4		1		
O'Neal, Sarah	1		1		
Ballance, Thomas	1		3		
Ballance, William	4	4	3		
Ballance, John	1		3		
Stow, Samuel	2	2	5		
Quidley, William	1	1	3		
Dunkin, Thomas	1			1	4
Barcham, John	1		4		
Burris, John	2	2	5		1
Payne, Thomas	2		2		7
Payne, John	1		3		
Midgett, Richard	3		1		
Midgett, Christopher	1	3	5		1
Midgett, Jesse	1		1		
Midgett, Daniel	1	3	5		3
Midgett, Banister	1	1	2		2
Neal, Christopher	2	6	6		1
Clark, William	1		3		
Neal, William	2		3		5
Badley, Frankey		2	4		
Lory, Joab	2	3	3		
Stewart, Darby	1		2		
Merchant, Catharine			6		22
Merchant, Thomas	1		1		8
Monden, Stephen	1				
Turton, Mary		1	3		5
Doughty, Edward	4		1		9
Pew, Perthena	1	3	2		1
Dohatoon, William	1	1			2
Duglas, Anthony	1		2		
Payne, Thomas, Junr	1	4	2		1
Pugh, William	4	4	2		
Flowers, John	1	4	2		
Midgett, John	1	1	2		
Midgett, Christian	1		4		
Meekins, Roger	1	4	5		4
Peal, Francis	1	1	3		
Peal, John	1	1	2		
Peal, Christopher	1		4		
Gray, William	4	1	4		
Gray, Joseph	1	1	1		
Williams, Keziah	1		4		
Price, Henry	1	1	1		
Scarborough, George, Junr	1		2		
Scarborough, Edward	2		4		
Scarborough, Ignatius	1	1	4		
Meekins, William	2	4	4		
Williams, Comfort	1		2		
Hooper, Ezekiel	2	3	2		
Williams, Joseph	1	1	5		
Williams, Jacob	1	2	6		
Miller, William	3	3	3		
Farrow, Isaac	2	1	2		
How, William	1	1	1		1
Gray, Thomas	1	2	4		
Midgett, Thomas	4	3	3		
Midgett, Timothy	1		1		
Farrow, Francis	2		6		5
Farrow, Francis, Junr	1	1	2		
Farrow, Thomas	1	3	2		3
Scarborough, Austin	2		3		2
Scarborough, George	1	1	3		
Braydy, Thomas	2		2		
Farrow, Hezekiah, Junr	1	1	3		
Robison, Francis	2	1	3		
Jinnett, Joseph	1	2	4		
Jinnett, Jesse	1	1	4		
Farrow, Hezekiah	3	2	3		
Farrow, John	1		2		
Wahab, James	2		2		
Smith, John	1	1	2		10
Adkins, William	1				
Dring, Price				1	4
Clark, Henry	3			1	
Clark, Bathiah		1	2		
Clark, Major	2	2	2		
Midgett, Matthew	1		2		
Midgett, William, Junr	1		3		
Neal, Thomas	3	1	2		
Wedby, Elizabeth		1	1		
Midgett, Christopher			4		
Neal, Christopher, Junr	1	1	3		
Scarborough, Mary		3	1		
Taylor, Caleb	1	1	3		
Holt, Taylor	1	1	2		
Scarborough, William	2	1	4		
Basnett, Mary				4	4
Basnett, Robert		1			8
Farrow, Jacob	1		2		
Farrow, Christopher	1				
Robinson, Christopher	1	2	3		
Burrows, Robert	3		4		1
Robinson, William	1	2	4		
Robinson, Elizabeth		1	1		
Scarborough, Ruth		2	1		
Tolson, Daniel	1	2	2		
Robinson, Christopher, Junr	1		1		
Quidley, Thomas	1	4	3		
Dauge, Griffith	1	6	2		2
Backster, John	2	3	6		
Backster, Joseph	1		1		
Chittam, Benjamin	1	2	4		1
Sawyer, John	1	1	2		
Bell, Brickhouse	2	1	3		10
Collins, Noah	2	1	2		
Simmons, Anthony	1	2	2		
Crab, James	1		2		
Hanners, Lydia	2		3		
Robertson, John	1		4		5
Anderson, William	1		3		1
Simmons, Jiles	2	5	4		1
Turton, Mary		1	2		5
White, Amey		1	2	1	8
Younghusband, Thomas	1	2	1		17
Jarvis, Thomas, Junr	1		1		4
Bates, Andrew	1		2		5
Beasley, William	1	3	3		1
Kennett, Brickhouse	1	2	1		
Neal, Samuel	1	2	1		1
Baxter, Joseph	1		4		
Simmons, Hilliry	2		1		7
Lee, Asa	3	1	2		6
O'Neal, Nathan	1	1	3		1
Allen, Jarvis	1		2		
Jones, Malachi	1	1	1		1
Jones, Sarah	2		2		6
Chandler, William	1	2	1	1	1
Brite, Henry	1	2	4		4
Nichols, Josiah	1	4	3		10
Whitehead, Elizabeth	1		6		
Williamson, Jonathan	2	2	3		1
Cox, Thomas	2	4	2		
Forker, George	3		1		
Perkins, Jacob	1	1	4		2
Ferebee, Thomas	1		2		12
Cruf, Gideon	1	1	3		2
Harris, William	1	2	4		
Heath, John	1	1	5		
Sanderson, Thomas	1		2		14
Ward, Jonathan	2	4	4		
Barns, Jonathan	2	3	3		3
Lindsey, Jonathan	1		1		2
Beasley, Mordecai	1	1	2		1
Beasley, Cornelius	1	2	4		
Gray, John	1		3		7
Holstead, Jesse	1	4			1
Etheridge, Samuel	1	1	2		
Etheridge, James	2	2	4		4
Parker, Thomas, Senr	2		2		
Wilber, James	1	1	4		
Beasley, Bridget	2	1	1		
Stevens, John	1		1		
Wilson, Lemuel	1		1		11
Dauge, Enoch	1		2		6
Hughs, James	1				1
Dauge, Dory	1		1		
Grimstead, John	2	3	3		
Phillips, James	1	2	6		4
Williams, Holloway	1	4	2		9
Ferebee, Joseph	4	2	7		8
Butt, Arthur	4	2	5		2
Bray, James	1	3	2		5
Burnal, Edward	1		2		
Moncrief, Thomas	1	1	4		3
Morse, Zachariah	1	1	4		1
Poyner, Nathaniel	1	1	2		2
Morse, Francis	1	3			
Lurry, William			4		9
Simmons, Jesse	1	4	4		3
Gregory, Caleb, Senr	1		1		1
Hall, Nathaniel	1	1	2		4
Ballance, Willis	2	1	3		4
Poyner, William	2	2	1		
Barnard, Thomas	1		1		5

EDENTON DISTRICT, CURRITUCK COUNTY—Continued.

NAME OF HEAD OF FAMILY.	Free white males of 16 years and upward, including heads of families.	Free white males under 16 years.	Free white females, including heads of families.	All other free persons.	Slaves.
Sanders, John Senr	1	1	3		7
Williamson, Williamson	2		3		3
McClannan, John	2	4	3		
Taylor, William	2		1		
Lindsey, Daniel	1		2		2
Simmons, John	2		2		4
Gray, Joseph	1	2	5		20
Moncrief, William	1	4	4		1
Perkins, Jeremiah	1	3	2		
Evans, Henry	1		1		
Jarvis, William	1	1	1		
Taylor, Joshua	2	1	4		
Taylor, Thomas	1	1	3		
Bray, John					
Doxey, John	3	3	5		
Moncrief, William, Junr	1	2	3		
Parker, James, Junr	1		3		
Taylor, Ebenezer, Junr	1	1	1		
Bell, Horey	1	2	2		5
Edy, Samuel	1		1		
Burton, John	1	2	3		1
White, Thomas	2	2	2		3
Gibson, Henry	2	4	5		
Ball, Ruben	1	3	4		
Brunt, James	1	3	2		
Fisher, George	2		3		
Simmons, William	1	1	5		3
Moss, Caleb	2	1	1		
Taylor, Ebenezer	1	1	2		
Dauge, James	1	3	1		4
Williams, Dorastus	1	1	3		
Miller, Thomas	1	5	4		
Ball, Joshua	1				
Poyner, Peter	1		2		
McClannan, James	1	2	2		1
Jarvis, Foster	1	1	6		
Dauge, Mitchell	1	1	3		4
Hutchings, Nathaniel	1	4	5		3
Gibson, John	1	3	6		
Wilson, Taton	1		5		23
Laton, William	1	2	3		
Taylor, Joseph, Junr	1	1	1		1
Tatom, William	2	3	3		1
Lee, Letetia	1	2	1		
Whutly, John	1	1	1		
Tatom, John	2	3	5		
Mercer, Jeremiah, Junr	1	3	2		5
Barrott, John	1	1	4		
Hall, John	1	1	1		
Hollaway, William	2	3	5		
Holstead, Jolliff	1	2	3		
Tatom, Benjamin	1		2		
Ballantine, Henry	3		2		7
Slaughter, John	3		3		2
Calm, Theophelus	1	3	3		2
Lee, Daniel	1	1	3		1
Caps, John	1	3	3		
Gibson, Jeremiah	2	3	4		
Taylor, Jonathan	1	4	3		
Walker, Caleb	4	2	2		
Campbell, Keziah		1	3		
Poiner, Joel	1		4		
Smith, William	2		2		
Jones, John	1		2		
Gregory, Enoch	1	1	3		2
Turner, Sylvanus	1	2	3		
Whutly, William	1		1		3
Berry, John	1	2	3		
Bell, John	2	1	3		
Hinnings, Zachariah	2		2		
Thomas, James				8	1
Case, Jonathan				4	
Hunt, Hyram				2	
Smith, Isaac	1	2	1		
Hunt, Demsey				2	
Holstead, Lydia		1	1		6
Purlington, Zachariah	1	1	1		2
Gregory, Griffith	2	1	3		
May, Joseph	1		4		
Simmons, Lemuel	1		2		
Smith, Laban	1	3	4		1
Taylor, Joseph	1	1	4		
Postwood, Benjamin	3		2		
Whitehouse, Godfrey	1		1		
Caves, John	2		3		
Stewart, Affiah		1	3		
Simmons, Meriam	1	2	4		
Tatom, David	1	1	1		7
Nicholls, James	1		4		4
Simmons, Elizabeth			1		
Dauge, Philip	2		2		5
White, Willoughby	2	2	4		7
Mercer, Thomas	1		3		
Thomson, Nathan	1	1	1		1
Pell, Joseph	1				
White, James	1	5	4		5
Ives, Thomas	1	4	2		

NAME OF HEAD OF FAMILY.	Free white males of 16 years and upward, including heads of families.	Free white males under 16 years.	Free white females, including heads of families.	All other free persons.	Slaves.
Poyner, Adam	2	1	5		
Holstead, John	3	2	6		
Dauge, Tulle	3	3	4		16
Burnal, Emely	2		4		
Simmons, Samuel	1	2	8		2
Sheregold, Telamaceus	1	1	2		1
Snowden, Francis	2	3	2		
Miller, Evan	2	3	2		
Stevens, William	3	1	3		
Snoden, William	1	2	2		
Poyner, Thomas	2		2		2
Poyner, Ann	2		2		5
Panderson, Ann			2		5
Poyner, Peter	1		1		
Brite, Hanson	1		3		
Dauge, Peter	1	2	3		3
Howard, George	1		2		
Gregory, Jacob	1	1	2		
Walker, Willis	2	4	2		
Thomson, Mary	1		6		
Thomson, John	1	3	5		
Mills, Thomas	1		3		
Glasgo, William	1	3	4		
Williams, John	6		6		6
Katon, John	1		2		1
Standly, Thomas	2	4	4		
Lufman, Jonathan	1	2	3		
Thomson, Malachi	1		1		
Case, Joseph	1	2	3		
Bunnett, Thomas	1	2	3		
Barnard, Robert	2	2	2		12
Barnard, Luke	1		2		
Banks, James	1	4	1		
Chittam, John	1				
Mercer, Thomas, Senr	2	2	3		4
Heath, Thomas	1	3	4		5
Nicholson, Griffith	1	2	1		
Morrice, Willoughby	1	2	2		
Ballance, Jervan	1	1	2		2
Ballance, William	1		2		
Chittim, James	1		3		1
Holstead, Levina	1	1	1		6
Dauge, Elias	1		5		1
Perkins, John	2	1	4		4
Williams, Christopher	1				
Williams, Elizabeth			3		6
Williams, Thomas Pool	3	1	2		12
Gall, William	1	1	2		
Ellis, Matthew	1		2		
Linch, Rilah	1				
Dauge, Richard	1	2	3		
Fulford, Daniel	1	3	4		
Heath, James	1	1	4		
Wheatly, Robert	2	1	4		
Ellis, Thomas	1	1	2		
Fanshaw, Henry	1	1	3		
Griffin, William	1	1	2		
Matthias, Simon	1	2	2		2
Jarvis, Mary			2		3
Piner, Joseph	1		2		
Etheridge, Amos	2	1			5
Jervis, Solomon	4	1	2		
Glasgo, Cornelius	1				
Simmons, John	1	1	3		1
Gray, Josiah	1	1	4		
Merchant, Gideon	1				5
Gibson, Thomas	1				1
Dill, Michael	1		1		
Williams, James	1	1	1		2
Williams, Samuel	1	1	2		1
Dauge, Rachael			4		
Mercer, Jeremiah	1	1	2		
Parr, Josiah	2	1	7		1
Jarvis, Willis	1		3		
Whitehouse, Samuel	2	3	4		2
Lee, Thomas	1		2		
Hutchings, James	2	2	2		4
Bell, Edy	1		2		
Leach, Edward	1	2	4		
Avery, Frederick	1	3	2		
Parr, Richard	1	1	3		
Hutchings, Richard	1				
Parr, William	2		2		
Parr, Caleb	1		2		
Poiner, Robert	1		1		10
Poiner, James	1		1		1
Poiner, John	1		2		1
Williamson, William	1		1		
Poiner, Lemuel	1	1	3		
Poiner, Benjamin	1		3		
Poiner, Benja, Junr	1		3		
Salyer, Samuel, Junr	3	1	6		7
Salyer, Samuel, Senr	2	1	2		8
Walker, Edward	1	1	2		
Brown, Letia	1		2		7
Thomson, Mason	1		1		
Taylor, Benjamin, Senr	1	2	6		7

NAME OF HEAD OF FAMILY.	Free white males of 16 years and upward, including heads of families.	Free white males under 16 years.	Free white females, including heads of families.	All other free persons.	Slaves.
Duke, Andrew	2		3		7
Hall, Spence, Junr	2		1		2
Taylor, Ruben	2	3	3		4
Perry, Jesse	1		3		3
Barrot, Richard	1	2	1		
Adderson, Elisha	1	2	1		
Parker, Peter	1	3	3		
Grigs, Charles	1	2	3		
Jarvis, Thomas (B. S.)	1	1	4		3
Sanderson, Jesse	2	2	6		20
Whitehall, Alexander	3	3	4		6
Smith, Sarah	1		4		
Rolands, Sarah	1	3	4		1
Baits, Asa	1	1	1		
Taylor, Joseph, Junr	1	1	1		1
Burnett, Elizabeth	2		4		
Burnett, Lidia		2	2		
Woodhouse, Hezekiah	1	3	2		6
Dowdy, Joseph	3		4		
Dowdy, Josiah	2		3		
Dowdy, Jacob	1		3		
Ruin, Jeremiah	1		1		
Dowdy, John	1	1	2		
Long, Bathiah	1		2		
Kenly, Lydia	1	1	2		
Overton, Maryann	1	2	1		
Vever, William				4	
Boswood, Thomas	1	3	1		
Baker, Samuel	1	3	2		
Hall, Spence	1	1			
Toaler, Matthias	3		3	1	6
Nelson, William	3	2	3		18
Lindsay, John	2		1		8
Evans, Malchia	1	3	2		
Walker, Thomas	1	3	5		
Simmons, John	1	2	2		
Aydetoll, John	1	2	2		
Walker, Samuel	1		1		
Walker, O'Neal	3	2	3		
Walker, Adley	1	2	2		
Evans, John	1	2	1		
Woodhouse, Adley	3	3	3		1
Evans, Benjamin	1				2
Walker, Michael	2		2		
Evans, Sarah			2		2
Evans, Jane		1	2		
Chaplin, James	2	4	2		4
Forbes, William	1	4	4		2
Wright, Gamial	1	2	3		1
McCoy, William	1	1	2	1	1
McCoy, John	1	1	3		
Padrick, Peter	1	3	2		
Cooke, Cullin	1	2	3		
Walker, John	1		1		
Greaves, David	1		1		
Lindsay, David	1	1	1	1	1
Evans, Joseph	1	2	2		
Lietchfield, Abraham	4	1	5		
Greaves, Matthew	1	2	3		
Adams, John	1	2	3		
Aydetoll, Caleb	1	2	3		
Dewe, Sarah	1		2		
Harrison, Zorobabel	1		2		1
Gregory, Thomas	1	1	3		
Duke, Jonathan	4		2		
Harrison, Josiah	2		1		
Aydetoll, William	1		2		
Etheridge, Samson	3	1	6		1
Etheridge, Asa	2		3		
Dowdy, Caleb	1	4	2		
Dowdy, John	1		2		
Gamewell, Joseph	1	2	2		
Grunt, John	2	3	2		
Gregory, Samuel	1		3		
Greaves, Absalom	1	2	2		
Etheridge, Samson, Senr	1		1		
Toaler, Caleb	2		3		
Saunders, Lucy		3	1		
Fuller, Edom				1	
Daugh, Richard	2	6	5		4
Daugh, Gideon	1		2		1
Barrott, Thomas	1		2		
Sikes, Benjamin	1	2	2		
Jarvis, Thomas, Senr	3	1	3	3	8
Gilbert, John	1	1	2		
Fountain, Jonathan	1		3		
Brown, Nancy		2	3		
Hitom, Elizabeth				5	
Majo, Duke	2	1	1		
Thomas, Laban	1	1	1		
Gordan, Peter				10	
Toaler, James	2		3		2
Garrott, Thomas	3	3	4		
Sikes, Mary			2		
Harris, Thomas	2	1	3		
Coffee, Jacob	1		1		

EDENTON DISTRICT, CURRITUCK COUNTY—Continued.

Name of Head of Family.	Free white males of 16 years and upward, including heads of families.	Free white males under 16 years.	Free white females, including heads of families.	All other free persons.	Slaves.
Mann, Thomas	1	1	3		
Harris, Elias	1		2		
Dunton, William	2	2	5		
Burges, George	1	1	2		
Burgess, Peter	1	1	2		
Williams, Rachael	1	2	4		
Gallop, James	2	3	2		
Caps, Moses	1	1	1		
Coffee, George	1	2	1		
Gallop, John	2	1	1		
Hill, Clement	1	2	3		
Hill, James	1	1	4		
Gregory, Jesse	2	2	5		
Gregory, Isaac (N. R.)	1		3		
Lutts, William	1	1	1		
Ferrebee, Elizabeth	2		3		10
Ferrebee, William	1	1	6		17
Spann, Thomas	1	1	1		
Standly, Richard	1	2	1		1
Humphries, John	7	7	10		23
Mann, William	1		1		4
Killegrew, John	1	1	2		
Wamsley, John	2		1		
Smith, Sarah			2		
Dissiness, Benjamin			1		4
Church, Caleb	1	2	1		6
Lindsy, Elizabeth		2	1		
Read, Malachi	1	1	1		2
Caves, Cornelius	2		2		
West, Joshua	1	1	3		
Seers, Caleb	1	1	1		2
Rogers, John	1				
Dauge, Milbry		5	2		
West, Obediah	1	1	1		1
West, Edward	2	1	5		7
Dauge, Willis	1	2	4		
Mulder, Ann		3	2		
Morse, Archelaus	1		3		2
Mulder, Kedar	3	5	3		5
Payn, Enoch	1	2	1		
Parsons, Ann			2		
Berry, Mallachi	1	3	1		
Lory, Kedar	1	2	1		1
Duglas, Charles				7	
Turner, Bellar				5	
Turner, Samson				6	
West, Mary		2	3		
Merchant, Kedar	1	1			1
Merchant, John	1		2		
Hutchings, Sinney	1	3	4		
Creckmer, Samuel	1	2	2		
Dauge, Willoughby	2	3	4		16
Gregory, Richard	1	4	2		1
Gregory, Cornelius	1		2		1
Jarvis, John	1	2	3		1
Fisher, John	1	2	6		
Gray, Griffith	1	2	2		
Matthias, Robert	1	2	2		
Evans, Caleb	1		1		
Mackey, John	1		1		8
White, Henry, Junr	1		6		3
White, Patrick	1	1	2		
Mitchell, Elizabeth			2		
Ansell, James	2	1	4		2
White, Solomon	1		2		6
Harvey, Thomas	1	1	2		
Wisher, Lovey		2	1		
Humphries, Sarah	1		5		
White, Henry, Senr	1	2	4		12
Austin, William	1	2	6		
Capps, Caleb, Senr	2	3	5		1
Capps, Junr	1	1	5		

Name of Head of Family.	Free white males of 16 years and upward, including heads of families.	Free white males under 16 years.	Free white females, including heads of families.	All other free persons.	Slaves.
Miller, Solomon	1		1		
Miller, Willis	1	1	3		
Bryan, John	1	1	3		
Rogers, William, Senr	1		1		
Wicher, Willis	3		4		
Martin, Moses	1	1	3		
Capps, Dennis	2				
Bonney, Jonathan	2	3	2		5
Williams, Jacob	1		2		
Heath, John	1	2	2		
Dunton, Daniel	2		1		3
Williams, Elias	2	3	5		4
Simson, John	1	2	3		3
Smith, Eli	1	1	3		
Capps, Malchia	1	2	2		
Dudley, William	2	1	3		
Jasper, Samuel	3		5		5
White, Winson	2	1	3		1
Waterfield, William	3		3		
Capps, William	1		5		
Waterfield, Abraham	3	3	3		
Guin, William	1	3	4		
Waterfield, John	1	3	2		
Leitchfield, John	1	2	4		1
Waterfield, Benjamin	1	1	4		
Rogers, William, Junr	1		1		
Waterfield, Michael, Senr	1	1	2		5
Holly, William	1		1		
Gordon, John	1	3	2		
Waterfield, Michael, Junr	1	6	3		
Williams, Capt John	1	2	3		3
Etheridge, Samuel	1	3	3		1
Williams, Thomas	1		2		6
Jasper, Darcas			3		5
Chappel, George	2	3	6		6
Jones, Evan	1	1	6		3
Jemmison, John	1				4
Hill, John	1	3	5		
Grigs, George	1	1	1		
Burkett, Caleb	2	1	1		
Simmons, Caleb	3	2	4		
Hill, Luke	1		3		
Jacobs, David	1	1	3		
Morse, Ruben	1	1	3		1
Morse, Arthur	1	1	1		
Morse, Arche	3	1	2		
Hewett, Benjamin	2	1	1		
Dyer, Sarah	1		1		
Wildlear James	1	1	3		
Cox, Jonathan	1	1	3		
Simpson, Joshua	1	1	2		
Lugg, Kesiah	2		1		
Leitchfield, Comfort		1	1		
Leitchfield, Jacob	1	2	1		
Swindell, Parker	1	2	1		
Sexton, William	1	2	2		
Cherry, Josiah	1	1	2		
Etheridge, Richard	2		2		
Etheridge, Richard, Junr	2	1	2		
Hayman, Isabel		1	6		
Jones, Abil				3	
Fruman, William	1		1		
Bright, Courtney			1		
Hayman, John	1	1	1		
Miller, William	1	1	2		
Garrott, Elizabeth		3	2		
Fruman, Moses	1		2		2
Mekins, Margaret			3		3
Bright, Charles	2	2	4		2
Etheridge, Josiah	1		3		1
Williamson, Henry	3	2	1		
Butt, John	2		1		

Name of Head of Family.	Free white males of 16 years and upward, including heads of families.	Free white males under 16 years.	Free white females, including heads of families.	All other free persons.	Slaves.
Etheridge, Abel	2	4	3		
Wormington, John	3	3	3		
Williamson, William	1				
Fruman, Moses	1		2		2
Bennett, Carter	2		2		
Ballentine, James	1				
Brite, Jonathan	1				
Brite, Willis	2	2	3		
Mekins, Richard					3
Borin, Maximilion	1	3	2		
Brite, Jesse	2		2		
Grannis, John	3		2		2
Ballance, Daniel	1	1	2		
Cox, Marmeduke	1		1		2
Etheridge, Henry	1	3	2		
Etheridge, Emsley	1		1		
Cason, Hillary	1	2	3		
Etheridge, Mattnias	1		2		
Etheridge, Caleb, Senr	1	3	2		
Powers, Caleb	1	2	3		
Cox, Lewis	1	1	1	1	1
Powers, Willis	1	1	1		
McPharson, Daniel	2	3	3		
Etheridge, Caleb, Junr	2	2	1		
Cox, Solomon, Junr	1	2	4		
Etheridge, Jesse (Moyok)	2	1	2		
Ives, Jesse	1	2	2		
Culpepper, Peter	2	3	4		
Lee, Linton	1	3	4		
Powers, Samuel	1		2		
Brite, Aaron	1	3	1		
Bennett, Jessu	1		4		2
Davis, Cornelius	1				
Powers, George	1	3	5		1
Linton, Benjamin	1		3		
Hubert, Isaac	1		4		
Powers, William	1		1		
Etheridge, Peter	1				
Powers, William, Junr	1		1		
Cherry, Willis	1	3	3		2
Bathouse, Mary				2	
Etheridge, Nathan	1	3	2		
Etheridge, Henry	1				
Etheridge, Richd	1				
Northern, John	3	2	3		2
Northern, Charity	1	3	4		5
McPharson, Hewes	1		2		
Cox, Javan	1		1		
Spence, Malchia		1	1		
Spence, Cary	1				
Cox, Caleb	1	2	4		2
Powers, Cunett	1				
Burnham, Samuel				4	
Ballentine, Joseph	1		4	1	4
Ballentine, Peter	1	2	3		1
Brite, Silas	1	1	1		10
Northen, William	1	2	2		2
Ballentine, Henry	3		3		9
Powers, John	1		1		
May, Joseph	1		4		
Cox, Solomon, Senr	1	1	1		
Ballentine, Mary		3	1		
Boran, Sarah	1	4	4		
Walker, Prissilla		3	3		6
Glasgo, Elizabeth		3	3		
Standley, Ufan		1	2		
Wist, Willoby	2		3		
Simmons, Mary	2	3	4		6
Thomson, Earah					
Curl, Rachael		2	4		
Palmer, Malchia	1	2	4		

EDENTON DISTRICT, GATES COUNTY.

Name of Head of Family.	Free white males of 16 years and upward, including heads of families.	Free white males under 16 years.	Free white females, including heads of families.	All other free persons.	Slaves.
Blanshard, Americas	1	1	4		1
Hobbs, Aaron	1	2	4		4
Hill, Aaron	1	2	3		5
Walton, Ann		1	5	1	
Barrot, Alse			2		1
Matthews, Andrew, Senr	1	1	2		1
Harrell, Asa	1	1	2		1
Matthews, Anthoney, Junr	1	3	2		
Harrell, Aaron, Senr	1		2		
Pierce, Abraham	1		2		
Green, Abraham	1	5	2		1
Harrell, Abraham	3	3	3		
Hurdle, Abraham	3	1	3		5
Cason, Abraham	1	2	2		8
Spivey, Abraham	1	2	3		1
Matthews, Anthoney, Senr	1	5	1		
Lasitor, Abisha	2	4	3		
Blanshard, Abner	1		2		7

Name of Head of Family.	Free white males of 16 years and upward, including heads of families.	Free white males under 16 years.	Free white females, including heads of families.	All other free persons.	Slaves.
Blanshard, Aaron	1	3	2		
Smith, Amos	2	3	3		
Lasitor, Aaron, Junr	2	1	2		
Pierce, Abner	1	1	1		
Lasitor, Amos	2	3	1		
Riddick, Abraham	2		4		
Spight, Ann		1	4		1
Lassitor, Aaron	2	1	5		1
Powell, Ann	1	1	1		4
Parker, Amos	1	4	4		1
Rude, Abraham	1		2		
Cason, Alexander	1	2	2		2
Holland, Arthur	1		2		2
Morgan, Abraham	2	2	1		9
Ellis, Aaron	2		2		
Cross, Abel	3		8		19
Bethey, Ann			2		7
Goodman, Ann		2	5	1	
Carter, Ann			1		2

Name of Head of Family.	Free white males of 16 years and upward, including heads of families.	Free white males under 16 years.	Free white females, including heads of families.	All other free persons.	Slaves.
Harrall, Aaron	1	2	2		1
Piland, Ann			1		1
Harrall, Ann	1		2		2
Ellis, Ann		1	2		
Jones, Burben					
Minehew, Bond	1	4	3		12
Williams, Benjamin	1				
Robbins, Bashford	1			2	
Gordan, Benjamin	2	1	4		22
Jones, Belson	1				
Warren, Bray	1	2	2		16
Barnes, Benjamin	2	1	2		1
parker, Benjamin	1	3	4		1
Euri, Blake	1				
Euri, Benjamin	1	3	4		
Rude, Benjamin				3	
Smith, Charles	1	1	2		1
Morriss, Charity			3		
Bennet, Christian		1	5		
perry, Chrismas	1	1	3		

EDENTON DISTRICT, GATES COUNTY—Continued.

NAME OF HEAD OF FAMILY.	Free white males of 16 years and upward, including heads of families.	Free white males under 16 years.	Free white females, including heads of families.	All other free persons.	Slaves.
Riddick, Christopher	2	2	5		12
Pierce, Christopher	1		4		2
parker, Catherine		2	4		2
Costen, Christian	1	4	3		7
Jones, Charles	1				
Polson, Caleb	1		2		1
Cross, Cyprean	1	3	5		10
Saunders, Charity	2		2		4
Ellis, Charity			2		
Gale, Christopher	2	4	4		8
Euri, Charles	2	3	4		7
Carter, Charles		1	1		
Osten, Claborn	1		2		3
phelps, Demsey	1	1	1		
Small, David	1	4	4		
Hill, David	1		1		
Harrel, David	1	1	2		7
Jones, Demsey	1	2	3		11
powell, Daniel	1		1		
Hays, Daniel	1				
parker, Demsey	1		4		1
piland, David	1				
Trotman, Demsey	1				8
Blanshard, Demsey	1	2	5		1
Jones, Demsey, Junr	2	2	2		2
Jones, Demsey, Senr	2	1	2		
Jones, David, Senr	1		1		10
Jones, David, Junr	1	1	2		
Quinn, Daniel	1	1	3		
Rue, David	1	1	1		11
Adam, Demsey	3	1	3		11
Williams, Demsey	1	3	3		8
Sumner, Demsey	3	2	2	1	
Watson, David	2		1		4
Cross, David	1	1	2		5
Barnes, Demsey	2		7		7
Williams, Demsey	2	4	3		
Sumner, Demsey (of Virgia)					6
Rooks, Demsey	1	1	1		
Lewis, David	1	1	3		
Euri, Daniel	2		3		
Umflet, David	3	1	5		
Langston, Demsey	2		3		
Ellis, Daniel	1		2		
Vann, Dorcas	1		1		1
Nobbs, Edmund	1				
Godwin, Exum	1	2	4		4
Briscoe, Edward	1	4	2	1	
Morris, Ephraim	1	3	2		
Piland, Edward	1		2		
Piland, Edward	1	1	1		2
Graham, Ebenezar	1				1
Matthews, Easter		1	1		
Beriman, Edward	2		2		1
Harrell, Emelia		1	2		3
Blanshard, Elizabeth	1	1	3		
Sivils, Elizabeth		4	3		
Harriss, Elisha	1	4	2		
Trotman, Ezekiel	3	4	2		11
Spivey, Elijah	1	1	7		
Rice, Elizabeth			2		2
Jones, Even	2		3		1
parker, Elizabeth		2	3		4
Norflet, Elizabeth		1	4		
Norflet, Elisha	1				7
Jones, Edith			3		
Benton, Elisha	1				
Brinkley, Elisha	1				
Daughter, Edward	3		1		6
parker, Elisha	2	1	4		8
Sumner, Edwin	1				10
Rogers, Enos	1	3	2		5
Cross, Elisha	2	5	3		6
potson, Edward	1				
Brinkley, Elisha	2		4		2
Sears, Eborn	1	1	4		2
Harrell, Elisha	1	2	1		1
Harrell, Demsey	1	3	3		
Ellis, Elisha	1	4	4		1
parker, Elisha				4	
parker, Edith			2		
Eason, Frederick	1				4
Brinkley, Francies	1		1		1
parker, Francies	1	2	7		1
Spight, Francies	1	2	3		19
Farrow, Frederick	2		2		1
Eason, George	1	2	5		20
Outlaw, George	1			1	
Bennet, George				1	
Allen, George	1	3	4		1
Williams, George	2	3	5		2
piland, George	1		4		
Williams, George	1	1	4		
Lassitor, George	2		3		5
Eason, George	2		4		7
Martin, Gabril	1	1	4		
Russell, George	1	3	5		1
Gatlin, George	1		1		3
Hargroves, George	1	3	1		1
Hobbs, Henry	2		4		
Hill, Henry	1		2		
Hill, Hemrick	1		2		
Forrest, Henry	1	2	6		14
Robins, Hardy				1	
Alphin, Hezekiah	1	2	1		1
Hudgins, Humphey	1	4	2		9
Watton, Henry	2	2	5		9
Jones, Hezekiah	2		3		1
Rude, Hardy				8	
Maroney, Henry	2	1	2		
Griffin, Henry	1	3	5		1
Willey, Hillory	2		1		1
Wills, Hardy	1		1		
Cross, Hardy (Virginia)					6
Spight, Henry	1	2	1		8
Lee, Henry	4	1	5		10
Saunders, Henry	3		2		9
Dilday, Henry	2		1		3
Goodman, Henry	1	3	2		15
Copeland, Henry	1	1			7
Howard, Hardy	1	3	1	1	1
Brown, Hardy	1	1	4		1
Jones, Hezekiah	1	2	2		
Spivey, Jessey	1	3	3		3
White, John	1	3	2		
White, Joshua	1	2	2		
Freeman, James	3	2	3		9
Hobs, Jacob	2	2	2		
Ward, Jesse	1		3		
Roberts, John	1	3	3		
Cullan, Jacob	1	1	3	2	
Miltear, Jethro	2	2	4	2	3
Roberts, Jonathan	2	2	5		18
Walton, James	1	1	2		4
Outlaw, James	1	1	1		8
Trevathan, James	2	1	1		
Robins, James					15
Bennet, Joseph					1
Thomas, Jacob	1	2	3		
Rountree, John	1	1	2		9
Eason, Jacob	1	2	2		10
Brinkley, Joseph	1	2	3		14
Steptoe, John	1	2	2		
Wilkeson, Joseph	1	1	1		
parker, Josiah	1	1	2		
Bauos, James	2	2	1		
Dirdon, John	1				1
Martin, Jesse				8	
parker, Isaac	3		3		
Sumner, James B.	1		1		19
Figg, Joseph	2	1	4		3
Figg, Joseph	1				
Tugwell, James	1				
Smith, James	1		1		
Smith, Jonathan	1		1	1	1
piland, James	1	2	2		
Norflet, Joseph	1				
Garret, Joseph	1				
Slavin, Jethro	1		3		
Spight, Jeremiah	2	3	9		17
Cuff, John				9	
Rice, John	2	1	2		6
Fillon, John	1	3	2		
Brown, James	1	2	5		2
Shepard, John	3	3	2		3
piland, John	1		2		
Brown, James	1				
Miller, Isaac	2	2	2		4
Baker, John	1	2	4		32
Dukes, John	2		3		1
Slavin, John	1	2	2		
Jonston, Jacob	1		2		
pierce, Jacob	1		6		
Nichols, Jonathan	1		1		
Hurdle, Joseph	1	1	2		10
parnall, John	1	3	7		
Jones, James	1	3	7		
pierce, Jacob	1	2	5		1
Holland, Jacob	1	2	1		
Wills, John	1	1	3		
Hays, Jacob	3	1	5		
Alphin, Joseph	1		2		
Foster, Joel	1	1	2		2
Hays, James	1	2	2		7
Wallon, John B	1	2	1		10
Hunter, Isaac	1	2	2		10
Lassitor, James	1	2	3	1	
Lassitor, Josiah	2	3	5		
Robbins, John	1		1		1
Briggs, John	3	1	1		
Costen, Isaac	1				6
Costen, James	1		3		12
Riddick, Jobe	1	3	5		27
Hunter, John	1	1	3		1
Eason, Isaac	1	1	2		4
Hoffler, John	1	1	2		2
Lassitor, Jonathan	2	3	5		5
Gordan, Jacob	3	3	6		8
Baker, James	2		1		3
Hare, John	1	2	3		
Riddick, Joseph	2	1	4		15
Lassitor, Jeremiah	1	1	4		
Jordan, Jeremiah	1	3	2		1
Robbins, John, Junr	1	3	2		
Granbery, Josiah	4	4	2		30
Harrell, Isaac	1	1	2		13
Jones, James (of David)	3	2	5		5
Davis, James	1		3		2
Davis, John	2		3		
Jones, Josiah	1		1		
Brinkley, John	1	1	2		3
powell, James	1	1	2		8
Jones, John (of Jo)	1		3		1
powell, John	3	1	8		17
Ellis, James	1		2		
Morgan, John	1		3		
Benton, Isaac	3	1	4		
Ellis, John	1	2	2		
Jones, James, Senr	1	1	2		3
Riddick, John	1	1	6		9
Hare, Joseph	1	1	3		1
Brinkley, Josiah	1		2		
Rude, Isaac	1		1	4	
Knight, James	1	2	4		6
Sumner, Jethro	1	1	3		20
Benton, Jethro	1		1	1	3
Small, John	1	1	1		4
powell, John, Junr	1				
Small, James	1				9
Small, Joshua	1		1		1
Sumner, Joseph J.	1				9
Jones, John (of Lewis)	1				
Ballard, Jethro	1	1	6		25
Cowper, John	1	1	1		15
Duke, John	2	3	7		1
Norflet, James	1		5		24
Darden, John	1		1		9
Lamb, Isaac	3	1	3		
Walters, Isaac	1	1	8		3
Dilday, Joseph	1	4	3		4
Garlock, John G.	1				
Benton, Jeremiah	1				
Rogers, Jonathan	2		1		6
Daughter, John	1				
parker, John	1				2
Brady, James	1	3	4		4
Arline, James	1	1	2		4
Arline, John	2		2		2
Williams, Jonathan	1	5	5		4
Benton, Josiah	1	3	3		2
parker, James	1	2	2		2
Arnold, John	1	2	4		3
Saunders, John	1	1	4		
Benton, Jesse	1		1		2
Matthews, James	1	1	1		
prenden, James	2	4	2		1
phelps, James	3	2	2		4
Bristow, James	2		3		3
potson, John	1		5		
peal, Joseph	1	2	3		
Skinner, James	1		1		
parker, Jonathan	1	2	2		
Weaver, James				6	
Sumner, Jethro (N.)					14
Adam, John (Son of Wm)	1	1	2		
Varnal, John	3	1	3		
Walters, Jacob	1	1	2		1
Goodman, Joel	1		2		11
Rooks, Joseph	2		3		3
Lang, James	1		3		1
Gregory, James	2	1	6		29
Gordan, John	2		1		15
Curle, James	1	2	3		
Vann, John	1	5	2		2
Jones, James	1	4	2		
Odam, John	1	2	2		18
platt, Joseph	1	2	2		
Brady, Joseph	1	2	2		2
Hiat, Jesse	1	2	3		
Gatling, John	3	2	2		20
Lewis, John	1	2	2		7
pipkin, Isaac	3		5		34
Boon, James				1	1
Landing, John	1	1	2		
Ransom, James	1		1		16
bann, Jesse	2	1	5		6
Jones, Jesse	1	2	2		1
parker, John	1		2		3
Saunders, Jesse	3	3	4		21

EDENTON DISTRICT, GATES COUNTY—Continued.

NAME OF HEAD OF FAMILY.	Free white males of 16 years and upward, including heads of families.	Free white males under 16 years.	Free white females, including heads of families.	All other free persons.	Slaves.
Brady, James	1	1	2		17
Bethey, John	2		4		5
Crafford, James	1	1	2		
Weatherly, John	1	3	1		5
Valintine, Joseph	1		3		8
Burges, John	1		2		1
Warren, John	1				9
Wills, James	1	1	3		
Spight, Joseph	1	3	2		25
Durden, Isaac	1		2	2	2
Langston, Jesse	1		2		1
Carter, Isaac	1	3	3		2
Thomas, James	1	2	1		
Carter, James	1	3	2		1
Stallings, John	1	1	1		
Landing, James	3	2	3		
parker, John	1	4	3		1
Langston, Isaac	1	1	3		1
Euri, John	1	1	2		
Green, Isaac	1		2		
Crellings, Jonathan	3		6		
Burman, Joval	2	3	4		1
Harrell, Josiah	1	1	3		
Stallings, Josiah	2	2	4		
Fryer, Isaac	1		2		
Carter, John	1		3		1
Euri, James	1	5	2		
Harrell, Jesse	1	2	3		
Taylor, Jesse	1	1	2		
Worrel, Jesse	2	1	6		
Stallings, Jesse	1				
Odam, Kadar	1	2	2		4
Herston, Kader	2	3	3		5
Benton, Kadar	1		3		
Ballard, Kadar	1	2	2		20
phelps, Kadar	1		1		
parker, Kadar	1	2	2		
Outlaw, Lewis	1	1	1		5
Eason, Levi	1	2	4		2
Taylor, Lamuel	2	1	4		
Walters, Lewis	2	1	4		
Baker, Lawrence	2	3	5	3	29
Brooks, Lodowick	1	1	2		1
Riddick, Leah		1	4		14
Spivey, Lidia	1	1	3		4
Dure, Levin	1		2		1
Jones, Lewis	1	4	4		2
Sumner, Luke	1		5		17
Collings, Lamuel	1	3	2		
Lewis, Luten	1	1			2
Sparkman, Lewis	2	1	5		1
Keen, Lamuel	1	1	1		
Lee, Levi	2	4	4		
Hill, Moses	1	1	6		10
Rountree, Miles	1				4
Rountree, Mary		1	2		7
perry, Mordicae	1	1	4		7
Blanshard, Moses	1				
Carter, Monc	1	1	4		1
Williams, Moses	1		2		
Reade, Micajah				4	
Lawrence, Michael	1	1	3		
Boyce, Miles	1		1		
Smith, Mary	1		4		
Riddick, Micajah, Junr	2		1		10
Spivey, Moses	2		3		
parker, Mary		1	2		
Briggs, Moses	2		2		2
Lasitor, Michael	1	1	2		1
Spight, Moses, Senr	3		3		2
Spight, Moses, Junr.	1	3	3		
Davis, Moses	1	2	5		1
Binton, Moses	4	4	3		2
Ellis, Mills	3		3		
Taylor, Mary	1		2		
Boyce, Moses	3	1	3		1
Benton, Mary	2		3		4
Hines, Moses	2		3		
Odam, Mills	1		5		
Riddick, Micajah, Senr	3	1	3		8
parker, Mills	1	2	1		
phelps, Micajah	1	3	4		
Morgan, Matthias	1	2	3		
parker, Miles	1	1	3		2
parker, Mary			1		2
Kittrits, Moses	1	3	5		7
Mitchell, Meney				2	
Sumner, Mourning	1	1	2		10
Hare, Moses, Junr	1	2	2		
Hare, Moses, Senr	2		2		7
Benton, Miles	1		3		40
phillips, Major	1	3	1		
Rogers, Milley		1	1		
Lewis, Mills	1				

NAME OF HEAD OF FAMILY.	Free white males of 16 years and upward, including heads of families.	Free white males under 16 years.	Free white females, including heads of families.	All other free persons.	Slaves.
Thomas, Matthew	1	1			
Jones, Moses, Senr	2		3		
Harrell, Milley	2	1	4		2
Euri, Mills	1	2	3		
Jones, Moses	1				
Taylor, Nathaniel	1	1	2		
Harrell, Noah	1		3		6
Riddick, Nathaniel	1		2		7
Fitton, Noah	3		3		4
Nixon, Osten	4	3	6		
Hobbs, Patience		2	2		1
Onley, Penelope	1	1	2		
Rogers, Philip	1	5	3		1
parker, Peter	1	1	4		5
Hagrity, Patrick	1	1	3		1
Lewis, Phillip	3		2		11
Dunford, Phillip	2	2	3		
Harrell, Peter	2		7		1
Mitchell, Richard	1	1	1		12
Bond, Richard	2	1	2		6
Taylor, Robert	2	1	2		1
Hobbs, Ruben	1	3	3		
Bond, Richard, Senr	2		1		10
Ward, Robert	1	4	3		
parker, Robert, Senr	1	5	4		3
parker, Robert, Junr	1				
Green, Richard	2	1	5		
Baker, Richard	2		2		6
Fitton, Richard	1		1		
Moore, Robert	1		2		
Rude, Rachel				2	
Lassitor, Ruben	1		2		
Riddick, Ruben	1	2	1	1	2
Miller, Rachel		2	1		1
Riddick, Robert	2				2
Briggs, Richard	1	1	1		2
Vann, Rachel	2	3	1		4
Osten, Richard	1	1	2		1
parker, Robert	1	3	3		2
Lasitor, Ruben	1	1	2		
Hiatt, Rebekah			1		
Sparkman, Ruben	1	1	6		1
Rountree, Seth	1	1	3		12
Hinton, Seasbrook	1			2	
Stallings, Simon	1	2	4		15
Trotman, Sarah		2	2		12
Stallings, Seth	1		3		1
Hurdle, Sarah			4		1
Ross, Solomon	1		1		
Williams, Samuel	2	3	2		
Harrell, Stephen	1	2	3		
Smith, Samuel	3	2	3		3
Euri, Samuel	1	2	4		
Fitton, Sarah	1	1	3		1
polson, Sarah	1		2		
Wilson, Seasbrook	1				
piland, Sarah			3		
parmile, Salmon	1				
Green, Samuel	1	3	3		1
Harrell, Samuel	4	3	5		6
Eason, Seth	1	2	1		12
Brown, Samuel	1	3	1		
Briggs, Solomon	3	1	3		
Brinkley, Simeon	1		2		7
Langston, Sarah			2		
Williams, Samuel	4		3		
Baker, Samuel	2	4	3		9
King, Solomon	1		3		15
Watters, Stephen	1		1		
philips, Swin	1		2		
Thomas, Samuel	2	1	2		
Harrell, Samuel	1	2	2		1
Ellis, Shadrick	1				
piland, Stephen	1	3	4		
Green, Samuel	2		4		
Taylor, Samuel	2	2	4		3
Euri, Stephen	1		2		9
Hoffler, Thomas	1	3	2		7
Marshall, Thomas	1	2	2		5
Trotmon, Thomas	3	3	4		18
White, Thomas	1	4	4		
Freeman, Timothy	1		1		2
Langston, Thomas	1	3	5		
Smith, Thomas	3	4	4		17
Robertson, Thomas	1	1	1		
Fitton, Thomas	1		1		
Fryer, Thomas	1	4	4		
Finney, Thomas	1	3	2		7
Green, Thomas	1		8		
piland, Thomas	1	1	1		
Hurdle, Thomas	2	3	4		4
Lasitor, Timothy	1	3	2		18
Hunter, Thomas	3	2	3		33
Williams, Thomas	1				

NAME OF HEAD OF FAMILY.	Free white males of 16 years and upward, including heads of families.	Free white males under 16 years.	Free white females, including heads of families.	All other free persons.	Slaves.
Travis, Thomas	1	2	2		1
parker, Thomas	1	2	9		4
Ellis, Thomas	1		3		
Hiatt, Thomas	1	3	2		
Barnes, Thomas	1	2	3		7
Vann, Thomas	2	3	4		8
Rogers, Timothy	1		1		
Smith, Thomas	1	1	2		
piland, Thomas	1		2		
Harrell, Thomas	2		3		
Horriss, Thomas	1	3	2		
piland, Thomas	1				1
Odam, Uriah	1				
Euri, Uriah	2	1	2		
Kelley, William	2	2	4		
Freeman, William	1	2	5		11
Beriman, William	1	1	2		3
Robertson, William	1	2	2		1
Hurdle, William	2	5	3		6
Henlove, William	1	3	4	2	12
King, William	2	3	4		2
Cleaves, William	1	3	3		5
Draper, William	1	2	2		
Hays, Write	1	5	5		4
Brown, William	1		1		
Brown, Willis	2	1	3		5
Brooks, William	1		3		6
Williams, William	1	2	4		
Spight, William	1				
Harriss, William	1		2		31
Boyce, William	1	2	2		
More, Willis	1	1	1		
Hays, William	1		2		1
parker, William	1				
Gren, William	2		1		
Baker, William	2	2	5		35
parker, Willis	1	2	5		
polson, William	1		1		1
Vallintine, William	1	3	3		9
pierce, William	1	3	2		
Hunten, William	2		5		3
Bond, William	1		1		1
Lewis, William	2	1	4		2
Gordan, William	1		3		2
Bristow, William	2	2	4		
Booth, William	1	1	3		3
Hinton, William	1	3	3		26
phelps, William	2		3		
parker, William	1				
Carter, William	1				
Taylor, William	1	1	2	1	
Matthews, William	1	5	1		7
Wiggins, Willis	4	3	2		
Arnold, William	1	1	2		5
Ellis, William	2	3	4		6
Ellis, Wright	1	1	2		
Daughter, William	1	2	5		6
Matthews, William	3	3	3		1
Barr, William	1	1	2		3
Guinn, William	1	1	3		
Cralters, William	1		2		11
Jenkins, William	1			1	1
Howell, Watson	1	1	3		
Odam, William	2	2	2		7
March, William	1	2	2		1
Warren, William	1	3			
Walters, William	1	2	2		
Gatling, William	2		2		20
Gatling, William, Senr	1				9
Warren, William	1		2		4
Goodman, William	1	1	3		15
Collings, William	1	3	2		
Dilday, William	1				
Rutter, William	2	1	2		
Fryer, William	1	2	4		1
Hews, Willis	1	1	1		2
Sparkman, Willis	1	2	2		
Umflet, William	1	1	2		
Ellis, William	3		3		
Crafford, William	1	4	1		3
Brown, William (of S.)	1		1		
Morriss, William	2	2	2		
Sparkman, Willis	1				
Wiggins, Willis	1				
Hinton, Zadock	1		3		2
Minchen, Zacheriah	1		1		2
parker, Zacheriah	1	2	1		
Davis, David	1	1	1		
Lassitor, Jonathan	1		1		
Garret, Richard	1	1	2		
Fanney, John	1	1	1		
Blanshard, Keziah		1	5		
Smith, Mary			1		
Tomson, Nathan	1				

EDENTON DISTRICT, HERTFORD COUNTY.

Name of head of family.	Free white males of 16 years and upward, including heads of families.	Free white males under 16 years.	Free white females, including heads of families.	All other free persons.	Slaves.
McFarlane, Walter	1	2	6		11
Hannell, Mary	1	1	3		11
Hannell, William	1				7
Jones, William	1				6
Evans, Benjamin	3	3	5		5
Brickell, Aron	1	1	7		29
Winborn, Josiah	1				3
Penney, Abner	1		4		10
Moore, James	4	5	2		39
Benthal, Joseph	1	3	4		9
Moore, James	1	3	4		23
Hill, Charles	1	1	1		2
Brown, James	1		2		
Long, John	1	1	2		
Cornelios, Mancha		1	2		
Hooks, Elisha			1		
Darden, Willis	1	3	3		5
Darden, John	2	3	2	2	5
Battle, John			2		
Battle, Martha	1	2	4		9
Goodman, David	2				3
Bolton, Thomas	2		3		
Wilkins, James	1	2			4
Williams, Charles	3		2		
Weakes, Arthur	1				1
Bell, James	2				
Willey, James	2	2	4		10
Muller, William	4	4	6		10
Gatling, James	1	2	3		2
Daughtry, Elizabeth	2	1	2		10
Darden, Elisha	1	1	4		4
Williams, Richard	2	1	1		2
Darden, David	4		1	4	8
Barnes, William	1				
Steickey, John	2	2	4		
Muller, James	1	1	3		7
Boone, Arther				6	
Weakes, William	1	1	1		
Cretchelon, Prudence		1	5		
Whitley, Ann	1	3	4		
Baley, William			1	6	
Wilkins, William	1	2	1		
Wilkins, Richard	1		4		
Carr, Robert	3	4	4		14
Wiggans, William	1	4	3		2
Halomon, Hanche	2	1	3		
Beamon, Cullen	1		1		
Darden, Elisha	1	3	6		9
Darden, Allen	1				
Hobbs, William	1				
Porter, Abram	1	4	4		18
Darden, Henry	1	1	2	2	1
Hobbs, William	1		1		2
Hobbs, Jacob	2	2	3		
Weakes, Julin	2				23
Hill, Henry	3				
Carr, Matthew	3		4		11
Vasser, Jessee	1				7
Barnes, Randolph	3	1	3		
Carr, Laurence	2	1	2		4
Haine, Joseph	1	4	4		5
Whitley, James	3		3		
Porter, Hubbird	1		3		2
Porter, Henry	1		1		1
Driver, Samuel	1	1	2		8
Jiggits, Edward	1	1	3		7
Magott, John	1	2	5		17
Johnson, Ben	1	2	3		
Calf, James	1	5	3		7
Mullen, John	1	2			1
Williams, William	1		2		6
Hobbs, Abram	1	1	1		
Drew, Richard	1				8
Britt, James	1	3	4		10
Britt, Abram	1	2	2		1
Christia, James	1		1		
Sandifer, James	1	2	1	1	1
Hutchins, William	2	1	3	1	3
Britt, Ben	1	3	2		
Story, John	1	1	5		3
Sandifer, John	1	1	2		
Cook, Charles	1	1	1		
Cooke, Ben	1				
Heart, John	1				7
Britt, Martain	1	4	3		
Boone, Niclis	1	2	3	1	4
Barden, William	2	1	2		1
Hutchins, James	2	1	3		1
Land, Bird	2		1		9
Barden, James	1		1		
Williams, Warren	1	2	1		
Jacson, Isaac	1	3	2		
Britt, Silas	1	2	2		1
Grantham, James	2	1	6		
Britt, Arther	1				
Matthews, Farmer	1				
Foster, James	1		1	1	5
Wernell, Richard	1	1	2		1
Gay, James	1	1	5	2	
Chetulow, Elizabeth		1	5		10
Fulton, Elisha	2	4	2		16
Carter, Lewis	1	3	4		6
Brown, Elizabeth	2		2		12
Howard, Luke	2	3	2		7
Teyler, Helen	1	5	2		14
Carter, Isaac	2	1	1		28
Powell, Shadrick	2				5
Nichols, William	1	3	2		1
Perrey, Simeon	2	3	4		8
White, Henderson	4	1	3		12
Mash, George	1	4	4		
Hancock, Nehemiah	1	3	3		
Howard, Mosses	2		3		3
Beley, Benjamin	1	1	5		2
Bruse, Abram	1		2		1
Williams, Nathan	1		2		2
Williams, Gilstrap	1	1	1		
Sanders, John P.	1	3	3		
Read, Hamilton	2	1			3
Caneday, John	1	1	4		
Bruse, Bennet	1	3	2		1
Davis, Luke	1		2		
Weaver, Ned					7
Teften, John B.	1	1	3		
Nichols, John	2	3	4		
Smith, James			2		6
Webb, Ben	3	4	2		2
Duning, Samuel	1	2	1		1
Williford, John	3	4	2		8
Flowed, Randolph	2		2		
Perney, Ezekel	2	1	3		10
Thomas, Isaac	1		1		
Thomas, Josiah	1		2		
Horton, Hugh	2	6	3		7
Humphry, William	2	3	5	1	1
Howard, Elisha	1	2	4		
Harnell, Elijah	3		2		
Moore, Morrice	1	2	1		4
Horton, Matthew	3		5		
Moore, Willis	2	2	4		8
Driver, Martha	1		1		7
Rynals, Thomas	1				
Powell, Anna		1	1		2
Powell, Dempsey	1	1	6		4
Smith, Abram	1	1	3		
Smith, John	1	1	2		
Hipton, William	1	3	1		
Cotten, Godwin	1		6		9
Sumner, Mary	1	4	8		15
Spires, Elisha	1				1
Spires, Absalom	2	2	1		2
Askew, James	1	2	2	1	6
Irven, Samuel	2	3	3		1
Horton, Elizabeth			3		
Hutchens, Aaron	1		1		
Burton, John	1				
Brickell, Thomas N.	1	1	3		3
Scull, Edward	1	2	3		
Lee, James	1	1	1		
Blake, Elizabeth		1	3		
Jones, Sarah			3		3
Cotten, William	2	3	3		2
Kelley, Delphia		1	2		
Brickell, Mat	2	1	2		11
Askew, Mabell		2	4		8
Brickell, William	1		2		8
Moore, Aron	3		3		13
Haine, Marmaduke	2				5
Turner, William	1	5	1		1
Rawles, William	1	2	3		12
Baker, Blake	2	2	7		3
Brantley, Ben	2	2	4		5
Weston, Jorden	1	1	2		9
Jones, James	1		2		7
Jones, Amilesent			1		2
Wiggans, Sarah		4	3		
Rivets, Mary			4		4
Brown, Fredrick	1		2		3
Rabey, Joel	1	3	2		
Peal, Edward	2	3	3		
McGlauhn, Elisha	1		2		
McGlauhn, George	1		2		1
McGlauhn, James	1		1		2
Rhods, Abram	3	1	6		6
Ward, Isaac Hill	1	1	3		9
Newson, Joel	1		4		2
Jornagan, Needham	1	3	2		7
Cherry, James	1		2		5
Peal, Dempsey	1	4	1		
Godwin, James	1	1	4		1
Rasbery, William	1		2		
Outlaw, Thomas	1	3	5		4
Peal, Ann		3	2		
Brickell, Jonathan	1	1	1		
Bird, Robt	2		2		
Horton, Williford	2		3		4
Peal, Thomas					1
Pinnen, Rachel	1	3	3		1
Sessoms, Ann	1	3	2		14
Harison, James	1	2	2		3
Askew, Cullen	1	1	4		1
Holomon, Malichi	1	4	6		1
Driver, John	2	3	3		13
Holomon, Samuel	2	2	2		
Outlaw, William	1	4	3		19
Pearce, Daniel	1	7	4		7
Holomon, Silvia	2		2		
Holomon, Aaron	3		6		
Holomon, David	1	4	4		1
Newsom, Charles	1		3		5
Rawles, Moriah	1		3		
Sumner, Moses	2	5	4		28
Williams, Ben	1		1		2
Archer, Armstrong				4	
Archer, Evans				3	
Rowals, Jessee				11	
Outlaw, Lewis	1	1	2		1
Brown, Lewis	1	1	3		1
Newsom, Heosia	4	2	7		14
Hill, Handay	1	4	1		
Hill, Michal	2		3		
Brown, Richard	1		2		2
Brown, Sarah			2		1
Brown, Stephen	1	2	4		
Breton, Benjamin	1	1	1		3
Modlin, Dempsey	1	3	3		
Newsom, John	1		3		1
Rasbery, Marget	2	2	3		
Denton, Polley		1	2		2
Weston, Jessee	2	3	2		
Ellis, Oszel	2		5		
Sanders, Nathan	1		3		
Northcutt, John	1		2		
Lewis, Eden	1	2	3		
Overton, James	1	1	2		
Overton, Nat	1	3	5		
Northcutt, John	2	1	4	1	1
Odom, Jacob	1		2	1	3
Russell, Thomas	1		1		
Brown, Sophia			3		
Spivy, Daniel	1	2	2		
Lewis, Isaac	2		2		
Simons, Joshua	2	1	3		13
Williams, George	1	3	3		
Kail, Jeremiah	1	3	1		
Host, John	1	3	2		
Green, Joseph	2	2	2		3
Hays, Ezekel	1		1		
Fainless, Handay	2	2	4		
Sowell, Dempsey	1	1			2
Williams, Whit	2	1	3	1	8
Luton, Samuel	2		3		2
Luton, Thomas	2	2	3		2
Bayer, John	1		2		2
Scull, John	1	1	6		3
Blanchard, Miles	1		4		7
Baker, Zadoc	1		4		3
Roscoe, Alexander	1		2		
Brown, Benjamin	3		1		10
Morgan, Willis	1		3		
Holland, Thos	1	2	4		21
Sharp, Jemima	1	1	4		16
Scull, Elisha	1		4		11
Dowing, William	2	3	3		3
Blich, Elisha	2	1	4		
Evans, Cornelias	2	3	4		3
Evans, William	2	1	3		3
Sessoms, Rachel	2		2		6
Sheephed, Providence	1	2	5		
Wynns, John A.	1	1	1		11
Thomas, Ben	1		1		
Cotten, Samuel	1		3		7
Cotten, Noah	1				2
Sea, William	2		3		8
Rooks, Dempsey	1	2	2		1
Rooks, Joseph	1	1	2	2	
Manley, Gabriel				2	
Fley, John	1	1	1	1	1
Deanes, Daniel	3	2	4	1	7
Porter, William	1	2	4		10
Porter, John	1				4
Winson, William	2	2	4		
Vaughn, William	1	3	3		
Gay, John	1	3	3		
Mashborn, William	1	3	3		
Winson, James	1	1	5		2
Gatling, William	1				
Winson, Peter	1	2	2		
Vaughn, William	1				
Figeuns, John	1		1		
Figeuns, William	1	3	6		11
Knight, William	1	1	3		2
Langston, Luke	1	2	4		2
Watson, Micajah	1				

EDENTON DISTRICT, HERTFORD COUNTY—Continued.

NAME OF HEAD OF FAMILY.	Free white males of 16 years and upward, including heads of families.	Free white males under 16 years.	Free white females, including heads of families.	All other free persons.	Slaves.
Yeats, Sarah	1		3		6
Banks, Benjamin		3	2		9
Banks, Alexander	3		2		11
Cuyer, James	1		1		
Munfree, William	2		1		20
Michel, William	1	2	2		
Fitt, Thos	4	2	1		13
Masongill, Daniel	3	4	5		3
Miller, John	2	2	2		1
Jiggets, William	1	4	1		
Benson, Ezekel	1	3	2		3
Denis, Litleton	2				
Christen, David	1				
Trader, Rachel	1	1	3		
Harison, Thomas	1	3	3		
Greyham, Chancey	1	2	3		2
Warren, Obediah	1	1	3		
Garvy, Patrick	5		2		6
Byrn, John	2		2		3
Frasure, John	2				2
Hichborn, John	4				2
Munfree, Handay	5	3	5		45
Rea, William	1				1
Blak, Ellis Gray	1				
Hall, Mantain	1				
West, James	1				1
Cross, Stephen	1				
Tuyler, Samuel	1		8		1
Brewer, Jessee	1	1	3		1
Skinner, James	1	2	3		35
Baley, William	2	2		1	
Stricling, Drew	1		4		1
Jacson, Low	1	2	1		1
Sandefer, Nancy	1	1	5		2
Joiner, Charles	1	2	3		
Wernell, Rhodah		1	1		1
Gatling, Edward	1				
Willison, Matthew	2	4	4		21
Boone, Allen	1	3	3		2
Britt, Thomas	2	4	3		7
Britt, Joseph	4		2	1	
Darden, Jethro	1	1	1		11
Darden, Jet	1	1			7
Goodmon, David	1	1			3
Manney, James	1	1	3		39
Thannie, Peggey		2	2		7
Glover, William	2	4	5		9
Vasser, Robert	1	1	1		7
Little, George	3		2		36
Figeurs, Thomas	1	1			19
Ridley, Timothy	2				11
Basset, Elizabeth		3	1		11
Morgan, Elizabeth		1	1		
Holoman, Christopher	2	2	5		2
Rawls, Jessee	1	3	2		
Hill, Whitmill	1	1	3		
Holomon, John	1	2	4		3
Pinner, Miley		1	1		1
Archer, William			1	5	
Archer, Peggey				2	
Harnell, Jesse	1	3	3		
Perrey, William	1		2		4
Haine, Ben	1	1	2		17
Moore, William	1	1	1		17
Winborne, Thomas	1		2		2
Peal, Daniel	1	2	2		1
Rindal, Joseph	1	1	2		1
Rutland, William	1	2	3		4
Wiggans, Wright	2		2	2	
Eley, Michal	1		4		9
Eley, Edward	1	1	2		13
Perrey, James	1	3	2		7
Deanes, James	1	1	3		
Walker, Patsey		1	5		11
Riley, William	1	1	1		
Jordan, William					
Best, Henry	1	1	1		
Deanes, William	1	1	1		4
Holoman, Cornelius	1	1	1		1
Cotten, James	1		1		2
Bremagen, John	1	3	5		
Best, Thomas	1	1	2	1	
Best, Mary			3		3
Parker, Samuel	2	2	3		
Cotten, Thomas	2	4	3		3
Wright, Henry	1	1	1		11
Benthal, Daniel	2		5		
Bass, Willis			4		
Garner, Anthony			2		
Weaver, Jessee			6		
Archer, Caleb			5		
Bowser, Thomas			9		
Nickens, Malichi			5		
Orange, Henry			3		
Shewenaft, William			8		
Read, Shadrick			6		
Haine, Jessee	1		3		7
Carter, Isaac	3	3	3		23

NAME OF HEAD OF FAMILY.	Free white males of 16 years and upward, including heads of families.	Free white males under 16 years.	Free white females, including heads of families.	All other free persons.	Slaves.
Williams, Sarah	3		3		
Lewis, Luke	1	1	8		3
West, John	1	2			3
Norvell, Dempsey	2	2	3		1
Lawed, Mauget			4		
White, Absalah	1		2		1
Haine, William	2	2	5		
Morgan, Handay	1	2	1		
Lassitor, Jeason	1		3		1
Norvell, Ben	1		5		2
Hobbs, Sarah	1	1	3		
Norvell, Mary	1	1	3		
Daws, Ann	1				
Wirtherington, Arcada		1	5		1
Vanpelt, John	1		3		1
Henson, Shadrick	2	2	5		1
Wirthington, Sarah	2	1	3		1
Sears, John	1			8	
Jinkens, Charles	1	1	4		9
Best, David R.	1	2	3		5
Copland, Mary	3	1			1
Copland, Thos	1	1	1		1
Copland, Halowell	1	4	2		1
Copland, Eley	1	1	5		2
Thomson, Elizabeth			4		3
Askew, William	1	1	2		3
Askew, Mary	1	1	2		1
Pearce, Jobe	1	1	3		
Bridgen, Joseph	3	1	4		5
Jenkins, Webb	1	1	5		4
Yeorley, George	1		2		4
Askew, Zachariah	1	5	3		2
Chalk, Stephen	1	1	1		1
Askew, Persillea	1		3		
Perney, Celia	1	1	2		21
Doughtee, Jethoro	2		1		
Askew, Shadrick	1		1		17
Vanpelt, Sarah	1		2		
Brown, Rhodrick	1		2	2	3
Daws, Mary		1	2		
Bezelle, Solomon				11	
Dildea, Joseph	1	4	4		
Clarke, Kerney	1		1		
Godwin, Barney	1		2		
Godwin, John	1				
Overton, James	1	1	2		
Willibea, John	3	1	7		
Pearce, Jobe	1	1	3		
Colemon, Thomas	1	3	2		1
Archer, Thomas				5	
Manley, Sarah				3	
Evans, Peter	1	2	3		
Rawles, Absalom	2	1	2		6
Evans, Robert	2	2	2		
Boone, Mary	1	2	2		3
Pearce, Richard	1	5	4		
Clark, William	2	1	2		
Barrow, John	2	2	4		
Northcutt, Anthony	1	1	2	1	1
Brown, Francis	1	2	2		3
Parker, Abigale			2		
Beaman, John	2		1		1
Wiggans, Sarah				8	
Alexander, Tebbs	1	1	5		
Manley, Moses				11	
Harrison, William	2	1	1		
Moore, Laurence	2	3	1		10
Winborn, James	1		2		1
Powell, Charles	3	3	1		20
Evret, James	1	2	1		6
Lintal, Joseph	2		1		
Doughte, James	1		1		
Doughte, William	1		4		
Harton, William	1	3	4		
Freeman, Josiah	1				2
Daniel, Joseph	3		2	2	
Gliston, Daniel	2				2
Mayne, Robert	2	2	5		4
Pender, Jethro	1	2	1		
Copland, Thomas	2		2		7
Copland, James	2				3
Johnson, Anna		1	2		
Beamon, Morning		1	3		1
Brown, Jeremiah	2		5		23
Nicholes, Nat	1	1	4		
Rhods, William	1		4		7
Yeats, Jessee	1	1	4		7
Askew, Charnady	1	5		1	5
Copland, Stephen	1		1	1	2
Jenkins, William	2		2		1
Fells, Edward	2	1	2		
Hale, Fereby		1	2	1	
Howell, John	1		2		5
Evans, William	1		2		5
Parker, William	1	2	2		2
Dunn, George	1	2			12

NAME OF HEAD OF FAMILY.	Free white males of 16 years and upward, including heads of families.	Free white males under 16 years.	Free white females, including heads of families.	All other free persons.	Slaves.
Spines, Thomas	3	1	3		
Rogers, Jonathan	1	2	3		15
Wiggans, Joshua	2	3	4		2
Macone, William	3	4	2		
Mashborn, Matthew	1	1	6		1
Warren, Jorden	1	1	1		
Parker, William	2		4		3
Gatling, Harday	1	6	6		
Griffith, John	1	4	2		4
Parker, John	1	4	3		8
Jinkens, Dempsey	1	1	2		4
Parker, Silas	2	2	6	1	
Rivel, Matthew	2	2	3		
Best, William	1	1	3		
Cook, Daniel	2	1	2		2
Carter, Martha	2	1	3		
Macoone, Ephraim	1		2		
Rivel, Silis	1	1	1		
Sanders, David	1	1	2		
Archer, Jacob				8	
Brown, Thomas	2		3		
Wynn, Matthew	1	1	3		1
Jinkens, Samuel	1	1	1		2
Gatling, Arther	2	2	4		5
Winson, Drury	1		2		
Parker, Peter	3	4	5		12
Langston, John	1	3	2		2
Carter, James	1	3	2		
Sanders, William	2	2	2		
Parker, Ephraim	1	1	3		1
Brown, John	1	2	2		1
Ezell, Benjamin	2	3	5		
Winborn, John	1			1	5
Tayler, Michal	1	2	4		
Matthews, Edmond	1		2		1
Bolton, John	1	2	1		
Fawn, Ann	1		1		4
Shewenaft, William	1	1	3		
Moore, Edward	1	3	3		21
Matthews, Richard	2	1	1		
Langston, Martha	1		3		12
Bushap, John	1		2		8
Hill, Joseph	2	1	4		10
Deanes, Thomas	1		1		4
Larrence, Axum	2	3	2		4
Jenkins, Winborn	1	5	4		5
Jenkins, Henry	2	1	3		17
Livermon, Edmon	1	1	4		
Bushop, Jessie	1	3	3		
Gatling, Edward	1	3	4		
Davis, Samuel	2	2	5		10
Winson, Elisha	1	4	4		
Parker, Daniel	1	1			
Denton, James	3		3		3
Vaughn, John	1				
Jinkens, Benjamin	1	1	2		3
Dickerson, John	1	2	6		
Nox, James	1		4	1	
Shewenaft, Abram	2		3		
Slade, Thomas	3		3		
Griffith, Bunnell	1		3		2
Griffith, Hirtwell	1		1		1
Knight, William	1		1		
Matthews, Giles		4	2		
Knight, Dempsey	1	3	4		
Sumter, Elizabeth	1		2		
Mashbonn, Charitey		4	3		
Gatling, Rachel			2		
Williams, Constant				1	
Manley, Letisha			4		
Gatling, David	2		2		1
Davis, Blake	2	1	2		1
Morgan, James	2	3	3		1
Brasure, Abram	1		3		
Manley, William				5	
Wright, Jane	1		3		14
Botton, John	2		3		
Porter, Edward					2
Winborn, Henry	2				43
Tayler, Winiford	1		4		4
Perrey, Elisha	1	3	4		1
Phelps, Dempsey	1	1	1		
Hays, James	1	2	1		4
Hays, William	1		2		
Perry, William	1	2	2		3
Lassitor, Zadoc	1				34
Green, Randolph	1	2	3		
Livermon, Sarah		3	3		
Wynns, George	4		4		34
Stephens, Ann		5	4		
Mountgomery, Elinder	3	1	2		
Sowell, William	1		4		
Simons, Obediah			3		
Rider, Nancey			3		
Pearce, Jaldah (for John Brikele, ded)	1	1	1		10
Bell, Frances			3		3
Wynns, Thomas	1		3	1	33

EDENTON DISTRICT, HERTFORD COUNTY—Continued.

NAME OF HEAD OF FAMILY.	Free white males of 16 years and upward, including heads of families.	Free white males under 16 years.	Free white females, including heads of families.	All other free persons.	Slaves.
Hall, Mary				6	
Wirtherington, Mary	1		3		2
Brown, Samuel	2		1		4
Boutwell, Adam	1	1	2		11
Manley, Martha				2	
Ronals, Patience				6	
Bacon, James	1	4	3	1	5
Williams, Elizabeth		3	8		2
Sorrell, James				8	
Bird, Molley		1	4		
Rogers, James	2	2	7		
Evans, Frances	2	3	5		
Moore, William	1				2
Valintine, Paul	1	1	2		
Valintine, Isaac	1		1		
Valintine, David	2	2	3		2
Boroughs, Handay	1	1	1		
Boroughs, Sarah			3		2
Morgan, James	1	2	2		
Valintine, Alexander	2	1	4		1
Baker, Bea	2	2	2		
Wiles, Joshu	1		3		26
Howard, Stephen	1				
Sander, Nat	1	1	2		
Fainless, William	2	1	2		
Fauney, William	1		3		
Bouroughs, Samuel	1	2	2		
Fainless, William	1	1	2		
Fainless, Bea	1	1	3		
Evans, Thomas	1	1	3		
Lowell, Richard	1	2	2		
Harnell, Nathan	1	2	3		11
Ditto for J. Sharp					5
Ditto for S. Sharp					5
Fainless, Zadoc	1				
Tayler, Boaz	1	1	1		
Keele, Jacob	2	1	5		
Byram, John	2	1	2		
Byram, Thomas	1	1	2		
Morgan, Jacob	1				
Lassetor, William	1			1	18
Quimley, Jessee	2	3	3		7
Rawles, Jessee	1	5	4		2
King, Jessee	1				2
Scott, John	1	2	4		18
Smith, Thomas	1	3	6		
Sorrell, William	1	2	5		
Brown, Lewis	1	3	5	5	6
Crow, Elezabeth					1
Holland, Keziah		4	2		
Wynns, William	2	1	5		29
Jordan, Elezeth	1	1	4		15
Mountgomery, Robt	1	2	5		17
Holomon, Samuel	1	3	5		2
Godwin, Kenney	3	1	5		10
Godwin, Barney	3		3		
Nickens, James				3	
Merideth, Lewis	3	1	2		19
Ireland, Grafton	2	1	1		4
Roberts, William	1	2	1		5
Hill, John	1				13
Andrews, Richard	1	1	4		
Gatling, Jethro	2	1	2		3
Benberry, Bryan	1		4		11
Rayner, Amos	3			5	
Edes, Stephen	1				
Brown, Patrick	1				

EDENTON DISTRICT, PASQUOTANK COUNTY.

NAME OF HEAD OF FAMILY.	Free white males of 16 years and upward, including heads of families.	Free white males under 16 years.	Free white females, including heads of families.	All other free persons.	Slaves.
Arnold, Joshua	2		6		1
Armour, Willis	1				
Ackis, Thomas	2	2	5		6
Albertson, Elias	1	2	3		3
Allen, Benjamin	1				
Albright, William	1		3		1
Albertson, Albert	1		3		
Allison, Henry	1		3		1
Allison, John	1	1	2		
Albertson, Samuel	1		2		
Banks, Thomas	1	2	3		19
Brosher, John	1				5
Brosher, Thomas	1				
Bundy, Demsey	1				
Blackburn, James	1				
Bailey, John, Junr	1	2	1		
Barns, Thomas	1		1		17
Bundy, John	1	2			
Bundy, David	1	1	2		1
Bundy, Ruth		1	3		
Bailey, Robert	1	1	1		13
Berry, John	1	3	2		2
Banks, Joseph	1	1	2		4
Barns, James	1	2	1		7
Boyd, William	1	2	1		3
Boyd, Roger	2				4
Bell, John	1		1		
Bright, Mary	2	1	2		
Bundy, John	1	1	3		
Benton, John	2	1	2		
Bailey, Patrick	1	4	2		
Bailey, Thomas	1				
Bailey, Benjamin	1				
Bailey, Jane			3		
Bailey, Ann	1	2	1		
Boswell, Joseph	4		5		
Bailey, John	1	1			12
Boswell, Abraham	2	2	3		1
Bundy, Josiah	1	2	3		
Bundy, Joseph	1	1	2		
Bundy, Caleb	1		4		
Bailey, David	1				15
Brothers, Levi	2				3
Brothers, Joseph	2	4	7		1
Brothers, Joshua	1				
Bailey, David, Jur	1	2	2		
Benton, Elkana	1		5		1
Brothers, Richard	3	3	3		
Bundy, Benjamin	1	1	2		
Bundy, Jeremiah	1				
Bright, Ann	2	1	3		
Brown, John				2	
Bundy, James	1				
Brown, Mary			1		2
Brewer, William	1	2	1		4
Brownrig, Thomas	3		1		15
Bailey, Sarah		1	2		
Brothers, Jonathan	1	1	3		
Bowe, Robert				5	
Bowe, Tulle				3	
Brothers, John	1		5		
Brothers, Thomas, Jur	1		5		
Bundy, Jonathan	2	2	2		4
Bowls, David	1	4	1		
Brothers, William	1	2	3		
Brothers, Andrew	5	3	3		6
Brothers, Job	1	2	3		
Brothers, Lewis	1	1	2		
Barrow, William	2		3		1
Boswell, Isaac	1	1	1		
Burges, John	1	2	2		
Brothers, Malachi	2	3	5		
Bright, Jesse	1	1	3		
Bright, Asa	1		1		
Benton, Devotion	1		2		
Bright, Willis	1	3	2		
Bright, Ephraim	1	2	4		
Brothers, David	1		1		
Burnham, John	1	2	2		
Blount, James	2	5	2		
Burnham, Ivy	1	1	4		
Burnham, Isaac	1	2	4		2
Beeks, Elizabeth		1	4		
Burnham, Timothy	2	1	3		
Best, Charles	1		5		
Bidwell, James	2	1	1		1
Benton, John	1	1	4		
Bailey, Gabriel	3	2	2		
Brooks, Jonathan	1				
Brothers, Joseph, Jur		1			
Bundy, Meriam	1	1	2		
Bundy, Jehu	1	2	5		
Bailey, Joseph	1		4		
Bailey, Joseph, Jur	1		4		
Brothers, Thomas	1	1	6		
Cartwright, Hezekiah	1	1			
Cartwright, Caleb	1	4	3		10
Cartwright, Darius	1	1	2		2
Cartwright, Robert	1	1	2		
Cory, Davidson	1	4	2		
Cox, John	1	3	2		
Cox, Jacob	1		4		
Chalk, William	1	1	4		4
Coppersmith, Micajah	1		2		
Commander, Thomas	1	1	3		3
Cartwright, Clement	1	1	1		9
Commander, John	2	2	3		2
Commander, Tukes	1				
Clary, William	1	2	3		2
Call, Charles	1	2	5		
Carman, Charity		2	2		
Cooper, Darcas		1	5		
Cartwright, Hezekiah	2				
Cartwright, Benjamin	1		1		
Cartwright, Isaac	1	2	1		
Cammeron, Mary		1	1		
Collins, John, Jur	1				
Charles, Susannah		1	1		
Caruthers, George	1		1		
Cooper, Lucretia			1		
Delon, Charles	2	2	2		1
Davis, William	1	2	2		7
Denby, Nathan	1	2	2		
Davis, Levi	1	1	1		
Denby, Benjamin	1				
Davis, Devotion, Esqr	4	1			6
Davis, Robert	1	2	3		1
Davis, David	1	3	1		2
Delon, Mark	1	5	4		
Davis, Reuben	1	4	2		6
Davis, Thomas	1	4	2		4
Duffee, Hugh	1	4	3		
Davis, Benjamin	1				1
Davis, Thomas, Jur	1				1
Duglass, Hannah			1	4	
Davis, Elizabeth			1		5
Davis, Thomas, Ser	2	3	1		
Davis, Devotion, Jur	1	1	2		8
Davis, Frederick	1	1	2		6
Dameron, Onisephorus (Living in Virginia)				8	
Davis, Archibald	1	4	2		3
Davis, Jesse	1	1	3		
Davis, Reuben, Senr	1	2	3		
Davis, John	1	3	2		
Davis, Thomas	1	2	2		
Dailey, Jesse	1	1	5		
Davis, Shadrack	1	2	4		1
Davis, Thomas, Jur	1		4		
Davis, Reuben, Jur	1				
Davis, Benjamin	2	1	5		
Davis, Sandford	1	4	2		
Davis, Dedrick	1	1	3		
Davis, Arthur	1	1	3		3
Davis, Willis	1	5	2		
Davis, Robert	1		1		
Davis, Anthony	2	1	3		1
Dresser, Joseph	1	1	4		1
Dunscomb, Edward	1	1	1		
Done, Nathan	2	3	5		3
Davis, Devotion (the young)	1	2	1		
Deshon, Christopher	1				
Dailey, John	1	1	3		
Duglas, John	1				
Darnell, William	1	3	2		
Davis, Thamer	1	3	3		
Davis, Mary			1		
Davis, Elizabeth (widow)	2	1	2		
Davis, Joseph	1	1	4		
Dammeron, Thomas	1				
Davis, Rebecca			1		
Dick (a free negro)				1	
Evoregan, Edward	1				27
Evans, Grace		2	3		
Elliott, Nathan	1	1	2		1
Elliott, Cornelius	1		1		4
Earl, Elizabeth			1		3
Emmerson, James	2	4	1		1
Easman, Benjamin	2		2		
Evans, Robert	2		2		
Early, Mary		1	4		
Commander, Joseph	1	1	4		
Commander, Joseph, Jur	2	1	2		4
Commander, Elsburg	1				
Coppersmith, Thomas	1				
Cartwright, Jesse	1	4	1		2
Cosant, Gabriel	2	3	2		
Cook, Isaac	2	1	2		1
Crookham, John	1		1		1
Crawford, Joseph	2				
Carver, Job	1	4	3		13
Cartwright, Jehu	1	3	4		
Crocker, John	2	1	2		5
Chancy, Micajah	1	3	3		
Clark, Martha			1		3
Cartwright, Martha			1		3
Clark, Isaac	1	1	4		
Cook, Josiah	1	2	4		
Casey, Prudence		2	2		
Cartwright, Thomas	1	4	2		1
Cartwright, Thomas, Jur	1	1	1		
Cartwright, John	1	2	4		1
Cartwright, James	1	1	3		
Casey, John	2		1		4

EDENTON DISTRICT, PASQUOTANK COUNTY—Continued.

NAME OF HEAD OF FAMILY.	Free white males of 16 years and upward, including heads of families.	Free white males under 16 years.	Free white females, including heads of families.	All other free persons.	Slaves.
Casey, Arthur	1		1		
Clark, Cornelius	1		1		
Clark, James	2	1	5		
Clark, Benjamin	1				
Cartwright, Ahaz	1	6	2		
Clark, Goshen	1	1	3		
Casey, Willis	1	4	3		1
Cartwright, Elizabeth			1		1
Cook, John	1	4	4		
Cannady, John	1	4	1		
Cooper, Joel	1				
Cartwright, John	1	4	4		
Cartwright, Simon	1	1	4		
Cartwright, Thomas	1		3		
Coppersmith, Thomas	3	3	2		1
Coin, Mary		3	3		2
Clarkson, Elizabeth	1	1	2		
Conner, Demsey, Esquire	1	3	4		53
Evans, Evan	1	2	3		
Elliott, Gabriel	1				2
Everton, Susannah				2	
Freswaters, Thaddeus	2	2	6		21
Fox, Joseph	1	1	3		5
Fox, William	1	1	1		2
Fletcher, Francis	2	2	4		3
Fentress, William	1	3	4		
Foster, William	1		2		
Foster, Andrew	1		2		1
Faringe, William	1				
Fennell, John	1	3	2		
Foster, John	1	3	4		
Fentress, Lemuel	1		1		
Frew, John	1	6	4		
Forbes, Peter	1	2	1		1
Forehand, David	4	4	3		
Forehand, Elizabeth	1	1	1		
Forehand, Jordan	1	1	1		
Forehand, Joseph	1				
Forehand, Lemuel	2	1	4		1
Gordan, William	1				
Gordan, Joseph	1	2	4		
Gardner, Demsey	1	2	4		
Gavin, Samuel	1		3		
George, David	1	2	4		15
Gaskins, Thomas	2		8		17
Gilbirt, Josiah	1				
Grieves, Rhoda		2	4		10
Guy, William	1	1	4		
Griffin, Joseph	2	3	6		
Gilbert, Jeremiah	2	3	3		
Griffin, James	1	2	2		1
Gordon, Abraham, Jur	1				5
Glassgow, Caleb	1	1	3		
Glassgow, Lemuel	1	1	2		
Grieves, Lydia		2	5		
Goldsmith, William	1		4		1
Gray, Joseph	1		1		
Gray, Nathaniel	1				
Gray, Robert	1		1		2
Gray, Anthony	2	2	6		
Gordon, Abraham	1	1	1		7
Gibson, Elizabeth		2	4		
Grice, Charles	2	3	1		2
Gibson, Elizabeth		3	3		
Guyer, Joseph	1		2		
Grindy, Joshua	1				
Henly, Joseph	1	4	5		6
Hall, Lemuel	1				
Howett, Rowan	1	4	1		17
Hosea, Abraham	1				
Hosea, Seth	1		1		4
Hosea, John	1	1	1		1
Harvey, Thomas, Esqr	1	4			34
Hosmer, Sylvester	1		2		13
Hollowell, Samuel	1	4	2		
Harris, Hezekiah	1		5		
Harris, Joseph	2	4	4		
Harris, Joseph, Jur	2		1		
Harris, Josiah	1	1	2		
Harris, John	2	3	1		
Henry, Rolen	1	1	3		
Holstead, John	3	3	6		10
Holstead, Edward	2	2	1		
Holstead, Jarvis	1				
Harrison, Joseph	1				
Harrison, Thomas	1	3	4		
Hankins, John	1	3	2		
Hall, Elisha	1	1	2		
Harris, John, Jur	1				
Hunt, Charles				5	
Hastings, Richard	2		1		
Jennings, John	2	2	3		
Jennings, Joseph	2		2		11
Jennings, Demsey	2	4	3		9
Jennings, Lemuel, Jur	2	1	4		
Jempson, John	1		1		1

NAME OF HEAD OF FAMILY.	Free white males of 16 years and upward, including heads of families.	Free white males under 16 years.	Free white females, including heads of families.	All other free persons.	Slaves.
Jempson, James	1		1		2
Jackson, Zachariah	4	8	5		1
Jordan, Isaac	1	3	6		
James, Solomon				1	
Jackson, Joshua	2	1	3		14
Jackson, David	1	4	3		
Jones, Henry	2		5		
Jordan, William	1	1	3		13
Jackson, Zachariah	1	1	5		
Jackson, Jehu	1	1	1		
Jordan, Thomas	2	2	5		
Jackson, Joab	1	1	2		1
Johnston, John	1		3		
Jackson, Daniel	1				
Jackson, Jesse	1	3	2		
Jackson, Mordica	1	7	4		
Jackson, Lemuel	1	2	2		
Jackson, Moses	1	1	1		
Jackson, Bailey	3		4		
Jackson, Demsey	3	3	4		1
Jennings, Isaac, Jur	1	2	2		
Jennings, Zachariah	1	1	4		
Jennings, Arthur	2	1	5		
Jennings, David	1	1	1		
Jennings, Thomas	1	3	4		
Jennings, Lemuel	2	1	4		3
Jennings, Benjamin	1	3	3		
Jennings, Hannah		3	2		
Jennings, Jessee	1	1	1		
Jennings, John, Jur	1	2	1		6
Jones, Isaac	1		1		
Jones, James	1	1	3		1
Jones, Javis	4	4	4	8	2
Jones, Joseph	1				
Jones, John	1	1	3		
Jackson, Miles	1		5		
Joes, Rhoda		1	2		
Jackson, Courtney			1		
James, William	2		1		
Jordan, Isaac	1	4	4		
Jones, Ruth		2	3		
Jackson, Asa	1	4	1		
Jennings, John	1				
Jennings, Elenezer	1				
Jackson, Sarah	2	1	3		
Jackson, Samuel	1	3	2		
Jackson, Lewis	1		2		
James, William, Ser	1	1	2		
Jennings, Jarvis	1				
Keel, Charles	1	1	5		
Keaton, Henry	1	1	5		1
Keaton, William	1	5	1		5
Keaton, John	1	3	3		
Keaton, Stephen	1				
Keaton, Ruben	1				1
Keaton, Joseph	2	4	4		17
Keaton, Patrick	1		3		
Keaton, Dorathy		2	4		
Knight, Thomas	1	1	1		3
Knox, Ambros, Esqr	3	3	2		17
Knox, Hugh	1				
Kerby, Abraham	1		3		10
Koin, John	3		3		
Keely, Abraham	1		3		12
Kinyon, John	1	1	2		
Kinyon, Joseph	4		2		4
Lassell, Othniel	2	4	4		5
Luton, Constantine	1	3	2		1
Lowry, Mary	1		5		
Lowry, John	1		2		10
Lowry, Robert	1	1	3		10
Lowry, Benjamin	1				5
Lowry, William	1				7
Luffman, William	2	1	3		3
Lowe, Thomas	1				
Lowe, John	1	3	3		3
Lowe, Aaron	1	4	3		
Lowe, Barnabee	1	1	3		
Lowe, Hannah			2		
Lister, Daniel					1
Lester, Jacob		2	1		2
Lancaster, Henry	3		1		8
Lester, Elisha	2	2	4		2
Lowry, Noah	1	2	3		
Lane, John, Esquire	1		6		5
Leonard, Benjamin	1	2	4		6
Lowe, John, Jur	1	1	2		
Lacey, Peter	1	1	3		1
Lacey, Josiah	1				
Leonard, James	1		1		6
Lancaster, Mary			1		2
Levory, Simon	1	1	2		6
Luther, Ingram	1				
Leake, Isaac	1		3		2
Leake, Jacob	1	2	3		
Linn, Aron	1	3	5		
Lane, William, Esquire	2	4	3		4

NAME OF HEAD OF FAMILY.	Free white males of 16 years and upward, including heads of families.	Free white males under 16 years.	Free white females, including heads of families.	All other free persons.	Slaves.
Markham, Charles	1	2	4		1
Markham, Thomas	1	3	4		
Markham, Lowry	1				
Markham, Joshua	1		3		3
Madux, Alexander	1	2	1		
Madux, Benjamin	1				
Madux, William	1		1		
Moore, Arthur	1				
Moore, Jesse	2	1	3		
Mudes, Thomas	1	1	2		1
Meads, Timothy	1				
McKinney, Neval	1				
Morriss, Aaron	2	1	6		10
Morriss, Mordica	1	7	3		4
Morriss, Joseph, Senr	2	1	7		
Morriss, Anthony	1	2	3		12
Moon, Hulda		2	5		5
Morriss, John	2	2	3		
Morriss, Aaron, Jur	2	3	5		18
Morris, Thomas	1				
McKeel, John	2	1	2		1
Morriss, Nathan	1	5	3		
Mundin, Simon	1	2	2		
Morgan, Seth	1	4	3		
Morgan, James	2	1	5		
Meredith, William	1		3		
Moss, Benjamin	1	1	3		
Mundin, Ruben	1				
Morriss, Aaron, Senr	4	6	6		
Morgan, Charles	3	1	5		
Morriss, Benjamin	1		3		
Morris, Melissent		3	3		
Morris, John, Jur	1		4		
Mitcalf, George	1				
Mundin, John	1	1	3		
McDonald, John	3		2		5
McMorine, Robert	3	1	1		5
Miller, Andrew	1		1		
Mundin, William	1	3	4		
Mann, Thomas	1		2		4
Martin, Zachariah	1		2		5
Moseley, Emperor	1	2	5		10
Morriss, William	1	2	1		
Madrin, John	2	2	3		
Madrin, Nathan	1	1	3		
Morriss, Thomas	1	3	2		
Madrin, Matthias	2	1	2		1
Murdin, Jeremiah	1	3	3		6
McDanil, John	1	3	4		
Morgan, Asa	1	1	5		1
Madrin, Ruben	1	4	3		
McDonald, Caleb	1		4		
McPhason, Jesse	1	1	4		
Milby, Zadock	1				
Mullen, John	1				4
Morriss, Joseph, Jur	1		2		
Miller, John	1	1	2		
Madrin, Sarah			2		
Mackey, Rebecca		2	1		
McMorine, Charles	1				
McNeal, Jane		3	2		
Meads, Benjamin	1				
McPhason, Joseph	1		3		
McDanil, Rachael			2		1
McCoy, Malachi	1	4	5		
Mires, John	1		4		
Mundin, Thomas	1	4	1		
Molben, Malachi	1		3		
Madkins, William	1				
Mundin, Robert	1	1	1		
Mitchell, Rachael				9	
Morriss, Will (free negro)				3	
Nicholson, Thomas	1				
Nicholson, John	1		1		1
Nicholson, Christopher	1				
Nixon, James	1				6
Newby, John	1		3		
Newby, James	1	1	3		
Needham, John	3	2	3	1	
Nash, Demsey	1	2	5		7
Nichols, Joseph	1	1	4		2
Nicholls, Joseph, Jur	1		2		3
Nicholls, Willibee	1		1		
Nichols, Anthony	2				1
Nicholls, Willis	1	2	3		
Nicholls, William	1	1	1		
Nichols, Benjamin	1				
Nicholls, James	1				
Norriss, Thomas	1		3		3
Norriss, Malachi	1	3	1		5
Norman, Patience		1	1		
Overman, Othnial	1	1	1		
Overman, Ohias	1				
Overman, Ozias	1				
Overman, Thomas	1		2		
Overman, Nathan	1	1	2		4

EDENTON DISTRICT, PASQUOTANK COUNTY—Continued.

NAME OF HEAD OF FAMILY.	Free white males of 16 years and upward, including heads of families.	Free white males under 16 years.	Free white females, including heads of families.	All other free persons.	Slaves.
Overman, James	2	3	5		1
Overman, William	1	2	5		8
Overman, Sarah		1	4		
Overman, James, Jur	1		4		2
Overman, Joseph	2	1	5		
Overman, Charles	2	5	3		2
Overman, Thomas, Jur	1				
Overman, John	1		4		
Overman, Enoch	1	1	3		4
Overman, Robert	1	1	1		
Overman, Benjamin	1	1	2		2
Overman, Nathan, Jur	1	2	1		1
Overman, Charity		3	2		2
Overman, Samuel	1	2	4		1
Overman, Ephraim	3	2	4		4
Overman, Charles, Jur	1	1	2		
Overman, Isaac	1				
Overton, James	1		2		
Overton, Samuel				3	
O'Bryan, Eustace	1	2	3		
Pettigrew, Charles	2	2			16
Pool, James	2	3	3		1
Palmer, Demsey	1		1		
Palmer, Joseph	1	3	4		1
Palmer, Thomas	2	2	4		
Pendleton, Lemuel	1	3	4		1
Palmer, William	1	1	1		
Pendleton, John F	1		1		1
Pool, Robert	1	3	3		1
Palmer, David	1	1	1		1
Pendleton, Robert	3	3	4		10
Pendleton, Thomas	2	1	2		
Pendleton, Caleb	2	2	2		8
Peirson, Nathan	2		3	3	
Pendleton, Joseph	2	2	3		2
Parr, Noah	1	4	1		2
Pool, Ann		1	4		1
Pritchard, Matthew	1		2		
Pendleton, Joseph, Jur	1	1	5		7
Pendleton, Joshua	1		2		
Pendleton, Zachariah	1	1	1		
Pendleton, Frederick	1	1	2		5
Pendleton, Jesse	1				
Pool, Joshua	2	2	3		4
Pritchard, Thomas	3		3		28
Pendleton, Thomas, Jur	1	1	2		
Pendleton, Ann		1	2		3
Pool, John	1		3		1
Perry, Josiah, Esquire	1	4	3		5
Price, Jonath	3		3		1
Pool, Patrick (son Patk)	1	1	3		3
Pike, John	1	4	4		
Price, Benjamin	1				
Pool, Solomon, Senr	1		1		8
Pool, Thomas	1				
Pool, Patrick (son of Jo)	1	4	4		1
Price, John	2	2	4		2
Pruno, Joshua	2	1	3		
Pritchard, Benjamin	1	5	3		2
Pritchard, Benjamin, Jur	1	1	1		3
Palmer, Willis	1	2	5		
Palin, Thomas	2		5		17
Pool, Solomon, Jur	1	4	1		
Pendleton, John	2	1	3		7
Pritchard, James	1	1	1		14
Pritchard, Samuel	1	1	3		
Pritchard, Thomas, Jur.	1	4	6		
Pritchard, Bathiah		1	2		
Proby, William	1	3	5		4
Pritchard, Richard	1				
Pritchard, John	2		4		
Pritchard, John, Jur	1	1	3		
Pritchard, David	2	4	3		4
Price, Samuel	1	1	3		
Pritchard, Joseph	1	1	3		
Pritchard, Elisha	3	2	2		
Pritchard, Elisha, Jur	1		3		
Purdy, William	1		1		
Pendleton, Timothy	1	1	1		
Pendleton, Peleg	1		1		
Pool, Henry	1				
Perkins, Noah	1	2	3		
Relse, Enoch, Esqr	3	2	2		21
Raper, Cornelius	1	3	4		1
Rankhoon, Joshua	1	4	3		
Raper, John	1	3	1		1
Robinson, John	2	2	2		1
Redding, Joseph, Esqr	3	2	3		23
Redding, Thomas, Esqr	3	3	4	1	17
Russell, Thomas	1	1	3		5
Relse, Joseph	1	1	1		2
Relse, Darcas	1	1	3		10
Redding, William	1				
Rowe, Samuel	1		3		
Relse, Benjamin	1				
Ripley, Ann		1	4		6
Richardson, William	3	1	3		5
Ratclift, John	1	1	1		
Richardson, Daniel	1	2	2		
Richardson, Labias	1	1	2		
Richardson, John	2	3	6		4
Rud, John	1	1	3		1
Richardson, Richard	1	4	3		
Richardson, Stephen	1	3	3		3
Richardson, Thomas	1		3		4
Richardson, Joseph, Esqr	2	3	5	1	3
Russell, James	1				
Ross, William	1		1		1
Jacob, Richardson	1		4		8
Reding, Samuel	1				2
Spence, Samuel	4	2	2		1
Saunders, Joseph	1	3	3		6
Saunders, Evan	1		3		
Saunders, Richard	1				
Samson, Joshua				1	
Stewart, Samuel	1		1		5
Sanders, Lovey		1	2		8
Sawyer, Frederick	3		3		12
Simons, Matthew	1		1		1
Simons, Elizabeth		1	4		
Simons, Ann		1	3		
Simons, Abraham	1				
Simons, Abraham, Jur	1				
Stevenson, John	1	1	3		16
Simons, John, Jur	1	2	2		
Stamp, Richard	1	1	3		
Small, Nathan	1		3		
Small, John	1	1	1		
Simons, Jesse	2	7	4	2	2
Symons, Jeremiah	1				5
Small, Samuel	2	2	2		1
Small, Joseph	1				
Symons, Absala		2	2		
Shakespear, Samuel	3	2	1		1
Stanton, Andrew	1		1		2
Shipperd, Smith	1				17
Simson, Elizabeth		5	4		
Scott, William	1	4	4		4
Simson, Thomas	3	1	6		
Scott, Joseph	1	2	4		16
Sawyer, Jane	2	1	3		
Scott, Joseph, Jur	1		2		23
Stafford, Samuel	1	3	1		
Simson, William	3	2	5		
Smithson, John, Jur	2	1	5		13
Sproat, John	1	2	2		
Swann, John, Esquire	1		4		60
Sikes, Levi	2	4	3		
Simson, Joab	1	3	2		
Scott, Stephen	4	3	3		
Scott, Samuel, Jur	1				
Scott Robert	1	1	2		
Scott, John	1				
Simson, Josiah	1	1	1		
Stafford, John	1	1	4		
Scott, Samuel, Senr	2		3		2
Scott, Simson	1	1	2		
Scott, Marmaduke	1		2		6
Simson, William, Jur	2	2	2		
Sawyer, Prissilla	1	1	5		
Smithson, John	4	1	3		
Sharborough, Luke	2	1	1		
Stafford, Stephen	2	2	4		
Scott, Abraham	1	1	2		
Sharborough, Joseph	1				
Sharborough, Jehu	2		2		
Smithson, Matthias	1	2	4		
Smithson, Ruben	1	3	2	1	
Smithson, Isaac	1	1	3		
Sixton, Malachi	1	2	3		
Smithson, Seth	1	2	1		
Smith, Davis	1				
Spence, David	1		2		
Sawyer, Ebenezer	2	2	4		2
Sawyer, John	1	1	4		2
Sawyer, James	1		1		
Spence, James	1	1	3		
Sawyer, Isaac, Jur	1		4		4
Sawyer, Isaac	1		3		
Stoakley, Joseph	1	2	2		12
Sawyer, Lott	1	2	3		
Spence, Lemuel	1	2	3		1
Smith, Mordica	3	1	3		5
Spence, Marke	2	1	2		1
Sexton, Mark	1		1		
Spence, Rencher	2	5	4		
Sawyer, Solomon	1		1		
Spence, Samuel	1		3		
Smith, Thomas	1	2	4		
Scott, Thomas	1	1	3		
Sexton, Willis	3	1	6		
Sawyer, John	1	1	5		
Sylvester, Thomas				4	
Shannonhouse, Susannah	1	1	2		2
Stafford, William	1		1		
Sawyer, Lemuel	1	1	1		
Stafford, Joseph	1				
Spence, Isaac	1		3		
Simons, Sarah		2	6		8
Stafford, Josiah	1	2	2		
Symons, John	1	2	5		7
Sawyer, Matthias	1				
Stone, Lemuel	2	4	2		
Thackery, Oliver	1		2		
Trublood, Samuel	1	1	2		3
Taylor, John	3		4		
Taylor, Shadrack	1		1		
Taylor, James	1		6		2
Trueblood, Caleb	2	4	3		3
Trublood, Thomas	1	2	3		10
Trublood, Timothy	2	1			2
Turner, Sylvanus (free negro)				4	
Turner, Charles				4	
Turner, Demsey				4	
Tatlock, Edward	2	5	4		
Trublood, Joseph	1	3	2		
Trublood, Daniel	2		2		18
Trublood, John	2	2	4		
Trublood, Jesse	1				
Trublood, Abell	3	1	5		
Trublood, Josiah	3	2	4		4
Trublood, Caleb, Jur	1	1	2		
Trublood, Aaron	1	4	1		
Tatlock, John	1	2	5		
Trublood, Joshua	1		1		
Tooley, Adam	1		1		
Trublood, Caleb	2	1	2		
Tatlock, James	1	1	7		1
Temple, James	1	1	2		3
Temple, Joseph	2	3	5		5
Temple, Thomas	2	1	4		7
Taylor, James	2		5		
Taylor, David	1	2	1		
Trublood, Thomas	1		1		
Tuckness, Henry	1	2	1		
Turner, Joseph	2	2	4		2
Tuttle, Joseph	1	3	1		
Trublood, Fisher	1	3	2		
Taylor, Daniel	1	2	1		
Varden, Elizabeth	1		2		
Varden, Tulle	1		3		
Varden, Moses	1	4	2		
Wootten, Charles	1				
Woodley, Hezekiah	1	3	1		
West, Charles	1	1	1		
Wootten, Samuel	1		2		
Willson, John	1	1	3		
Williams, Asa	3	1	2		1
White, James	2	1	4		
Tummigan, William	2	1	2		2
White, Anthony	1				
White, John	2	1	3		
White, James	1	4	3		1
Warner, Samuel	1	1	1		7
White, Thomas	1	1	2		1
White, Saml, Jur	1	1	4		2
White, Devotion	1	1	2		1
Wood, Thomas	1	2	5		
White, Nathan	1	2	2		2
Wood, Joseph	1		3		
White, Joshua (son of B.)	1	1	1	2	
White, Benja (s. of Z.)	1				
White, Charles	1		2		3
White, John	1		2		6
White, Arnold	1		1		
White, James	3		1		
White, Francis	1	1	4	1	1
White, Benja (son Josh).	2	1	2		2
White, Rachael	1	2	5		5
White, Benja, Jur	1				
White, Jordan	2	3	2		
Willson, John	1	1	2		
White, Abraham	1	3	2		
Williamson, Malachi	1		1		
Whorton, Willis	1	3	5		
White, Thomas	1	1	2		
Wood, Evan	1		2		1
White, Thomas, Jur	1				
Winson, John	1		2		
Wiggins, Seth	1				
Williams, Rufus	1		1		
Whidbee, Samuel	1				6
Wayman, Thomas	1	1	4		
Walden, Thomas	1	1	2		1
Wharton, Robert	1	1	5		
Wayman, Corban	1	3	2		

EDENTON DISTRICT, PASQUOTANK COUNTY—Continued.

NAME OF HEAD OF FAMILY.	Free white males of 16 years and upward, including heads of families.	Free white males under 16 years.	Free white females, including heads of families.	All other free persons.	Slaves.
Wormington, Wm	1	3	1		
Wimbery, Winifred				7	1
Wood, John	2	2	2		1
Williams, Daniel	1				3
Williams, David	1		3		5
Williams, Lauderick	1	2	1		
Williams, Owen	1	4	2		2
Williams, Zebedee	1		3		1
White, Robert	1				
Whidbee, Elizabeth	1	3	3		
Willocks, Winifred	1	2	4		
Walls, John	1				
White, Samuel, Jur	1		1	1	
Williams, Thamer			3	4	7
White, Zachariah	1	1	3		2
Wood, Margarett			2		1
White, Elizabeth			3		
White, Joseph	1				
White, Nehemiah	2		4		
Willson, Joseph	1	2	3		5

EDENTON DISTRICT, PERQUIMANS COUNTY.

NAME OF HEAD OF FAMILY.	Free white males of 16 years and upward, including heads of families.	Free white males under 16 years.	Free white females, including heads of families.	All other free persons.	Slaves.
Avery, Robert	1		1		
Avery, Ruth			2		
Albertson, Joshua	1		1		
Arrington, Richard	1	2	4		
Arrington, Ezekiel	1	6	2		3
Arrington, William	2	1	4		4
Arrington, William, Junr	1	2	2		4
Asbell, John	1	2	5		
Albertson, Benjamin	3	4	5		1
Albertson, Chaulkley	3	5	3		2
Albertson, Benjamin, Junr	2	3	3		
Albertson, Jesse	1		2		
Anderson, Samuel	1		2		
Anderson, John	2		3		1
Albertson, William	1	1	1		
Anderson, Joseph	1	3	5		1
Albertson, Josiah	1	5	4		1
Albertson, Jane	1		3		3
Arnold, William	1	2	2		2
Arkell, William	1	1	8		4
Arrington, Robert	1				
Albertson, Mary	1		3		
Ashburn, Winefred				5	
Bedgood, Joseph	1	1	6		1
Bagley, Joshua	1	1			
Bunch, Jesse	2				
Bunch, Joshua	1	2	4		
Bunch, Nazereth	2	5	2		2
Branch, Issachar	3	2	5		4
Brinkley, James	3	1	2		11
Braughton, Benjamin	1	1	1		
Braughton, Nathaniel	2	4	3		
Brinkley, Eleazer	1				5
Bateman, Jonathan	1		3		
Blaxton, Thomas	1	1	3		
Barrow, Eri	1	1	1		15
Butler, Margaret		2	3		3
Branch, Job	1		4		
Burnham, Caleb	1	1	4		1
Barrow, John	3	1			6
Boush, James	1		2		3
Barrow, Joseph	1	3	3		
Barclift, William	1	3	3		
Bateman, Thomas	1	1	2		3
Bedgood, Benjamin	1	2	2		
Barclift, Joseph	1	3	3		19
Bagley, Elisha	1	1	2		
Briggs, Charles	1		1		
Boyce, Joseph	3	6	6		
Burke, Arnold S	1		1		4
Barber, Isaac	1				10
Bagley, Thomas	2	2	1		
Brown, Alexander	1	6	2		
Bundy, Josiah	3	3	6		
Bundy, Caleb	1	1	2		
Bagley, Ephraim	1		4		1
Bagley, Nathan	1	2	6		
Boswell, George	1	1	2		
Boswell, William	1				
Boswell, Joshua	1				
Bagley, Samuel	1	1	6		2
Boyce, Joseph	2	3	4		
Boyce, John	1	2	1		
Boyce, Moses	2	2	3		
Bond, William	1	3	1		
Bond, Pritlow	1		1	1	
Bagley, John	1	1	6		4
Bunch, Joannah		1	5		
Bundy, Abraham	2	2	5		
Boyce, William	1	2	6		
Barker, William	1	2	3		
Bond, Job	1	2	2		5
Barber, Moses	1				
Barber, Joel	2	1			
Butt, David	1		2		
Bogue, Ann		1	3		
Boyce, Mourning		1	2		
Bailey, Henry	1	1	1		
Bond, Abigail		4	3		
Boyce, Benjamin	1	1	3		
Barns, Stephen	1		1		1
Bateman, Joseph	1	6	4		
Bateman, John	1		2		1
Barclift, Marwood	1		1		3
Berryman, Sarah	1	1	4		
Banks, Richard	1	1	2		
Barber, Sarah			5		
Barker, John	2	2	3		
Crucy, William, Esqr	1	1	3		14
Cale, Timothy	2	1	4		
Collins, Christopher	1	2	3		
Cale, Richard	1	2	5		
Cale, John, Junr	1				
Crucy, Levi	2	2			
Collins, Jeremiah	1		2		1
Copeland, Charles	1	3	1		
Carter, John	1	3	4	1	7
Clayton, William	1	3	3		10
Crucy, Eleazer	1				7
Cale, Joseph	1		5		
Clements, William	2	3	1		7
Crucy, Thomas	1	2	4		4
Coppage, William	1		2		
Cale, Robert	1		3		
Church, Thomas	1	1	3		
Chappell, Jemima		1	2		1
Cox, Joseph	1				
Caruthers, James	1	1	3		
Cosand, Aaron	2	3	8		
Cosand, John	1				
Chappell, Job	2	4	6		
Chappell, John, Junr	1	2	4		
Chappell, Joseph	1	1	2		
Chappell, Robert	1	1	3		
Clary, John	2		2		3
Chappell, Mark	1		3		
Chappell, Isaac	1		3		
Clyvester, James	1		1		
Clary, Charles	1	2	3		
Chappell, John	1	2	3		1
Chappell, Samuel	1				
Champion, Henry	2	2	2		
Cornwall, Ann		1	1		
Caruthers, George	1				
Dough, Jeremiah	1		3		
Deal, John	1	3	2		1
Deal, William	1	3	1		
Deerow, Sarah			3		9
Donaldson, Andrew	2	1	3		7
Deal, Elizabeth	3		2		
Draper, Thomas	1	1	2		
Draper, Joseph	1	3	2		
Draper, Silas	1	7	2		
Draper, Josiah	1		1		
Davis, John	1	2	2	1	4
Donaldson, John	1		3		4
Davis, Caleb	2	2	2		
Davis, Elizabeth	2	3	2		
Duglas, David	1		2		
Duglas, Frances			2	5	
Duglas, Elizabeth	1		2		
Edwards, Sanford	1	3	4	1	1
Evans, Joseph	1		2		
Elliott, Ephraim	2	2	1		9
Elliott, Pritlow	1		1		
Elliott, Mary	1	2	2		1
Elliott, Exum, Junr	1		1		
Elliott, Caleb	1	3	2		7
Elliott, Winslow	1	1	3		1
Elliott, Josiah	1	4	3		6
Elliott, Seth	1	3	1		
Elliott, Exum	1		2		
Elliott, Meriam	1	4	3		12
Evans, Thomas	1		2		
Elliott, Samuel	1	1	3		
Evans, Robert	4		1		1
Evans, John	5		1		3
Elliott, Nixon	2		2		
Edwards, James	1		2		
Elliott, Joseph	1	2	5		
Elliott, Demsey	1	2	3		
Elliott, Mordecai	1	3	2		1
Elliott, Hannah	1	1	2		
Elliott, Thomas	1	2	2		
Elliott, Joshua	1		2		
Elliott, Elizabeth	3		1		
Elliott, Abraham	1	2	4		1
Elliott, William	1	3			
Elliott, Hushai	1		1		
Elliott, Obediah	1				
Elliott, Job	1				
Foster, Francis	1	4	5		2
Fletcher, Joshua	1	1	1		11
Forbes, Bailey	3	2	2		3
Forehand, Benjamin	1		4		
Foster, Mary		1	2		6
Foster, James	1	1	2		1
Foulon, John B	1		1		
Fletcher, Jesse	1		1		13
Fiveash, John	1	1	2		
Forehand, Cornelius	2	1	2		
Godfrey, Joseph	1	4	5		4
Greer, Bartley	1				
Gilbert, Joseph	1	1	1		
Gray, Isaac	1	1	2		
Gordon, Nathaniel	1	1	3		5
Gilbert, William	1	1	2		12
Griffin, Eliab	1	4	5		2
Griffin, Amos	2	3	3		
Godfrey, Francis	1				
Griffin, William	1		3		
Griffin, James	1		3		
Griffin, Josiah	1	2	3		
Griffin, Josiah, Junr	1				
Gregory, Hosea	1	2	3		1
Guyer, John	2	3	4		
Guyer, Meriam	2	2	4		
Griffin, Jesse	1	1	2		
Goodwin, John	2	2	5		6
Goodwin, Richard	2		3		
Goodwin, Nathan	2	1	2		
Goodwin, Jacob	1		4		6
Gilliam, Hinchea	3	3	2		1
Godfrey, Tulle	1	1	4		5
Gurley, Frederick	1	2	3		
Hollaway, Hannah	2	2	2		8
Harvey, John	4	3	5		38
Harvey, Joseph, Esqr	1	1	3		25
Harvey, Benjamin, Esqr	1	4	3		31
Hall, Rachael	5		3		4
Hatfield, John	1				
Hollowell, Ezekiel	2	1	5		2
Howett, Abraham	1		4		14
Hinton, Noah	2	2	2		
Humphries, William	2	2			5
Hines, Ann			2		1
Hallsey, Edmund	1	1	3		
Hatfield, Richard	2	2	2		2
Hodges, Ann	—		4		
Harmon, Thomas	3		2		1
Hall, Edward, Esqr	1	3	5		9
Hallsey, Frederick	1	6	1		4
Hopkins, George	1				
Hollaway, Upharasha			1		6
Hollaway, Thomas	1	1	1		
Hopkins, William	1	1	3		6
Hobdey, Thomas	1	1	2		1
Hodges, John	2	1	4		2
Hinton, Jonas	1	1	2		
Harrell, Demsey	1		1		
Harrell, Samuel	1				
Haskett, Silas	2	5	3		
Hatfield, Richard, Junr	1				1
Harvey, Mary		2	4		21
Hollowell, James	1		4		
Henby, Thomas	1		5		
Haskett, Silas, Junr	1	4	3		
Hollowell, Henry	2	3	4		2
Hall, Isaiah	1	2	2		
Haskett, Thomas	1	2	1		5
Hinton, Demsey	1	2	2		
Haskett, Joseph	1	2	2		
Henby, Sylvanus	1				
Haskett, Joshua	1	1	1		
Hosea, Thomas	1	4	4		
Hendrick, Nathan	1		2		
Haskett, John	2	3	5		2
Haskett, Jesse	1	3	1		3
Haskett, Alice			2		
Hall, James	1	1	1		3
Hollowell, William	1	2	4		1
Hendrick, Job	1	2	3		
Hendrick, Joseph	2	1	3		
Hendrick, Nathan, Junr	1				

EDENTON DISTRICT, PERQUIMANS COUNTY—Continued.

NAME OF HEAD OF FAMILY.	Free white males of 16 years and upward, including heads of families.	Free white males under 16 years.	Free white females, including heads of families.	All other free persons.	Slaves.
Hollowell, Thomas	2	1	4		
Hollowell, Thomas, Junr	2	1	3		
Hollowell, Joel	1				
Hurdle, Christian	1	2	3		4
Hurdle, Martin	1	2	3		
Hudson, Uriah	1		4		6
Hudson, Joseph	1	1	3		
Harmon, Elizabeth		1	2		
Hendrick, Solomon	1		3		
Hartmus, John Peter	1		1		4
Hollowell, Meriam	1	5	2		1
Hosea, William	1	4	4		
Harrell, Abner	1	2	4		
Hendrick, Seth	1		3		
Hackney, Richard	1	1	3		
Jones, Margaret	1		3		
Johnson, James	1	2	1		
Ivy, Lemuel	1		2		3
Johnson, John	1	1	2		
Jackson, Moses, Junr	1		4		
Jones, William	2	2	5		3
Jones, William, Junr	1				
Joiner, William Jones	1	2	1		
Jackson, William	1	2	3		
Jones, Joseph	1	3	5		13
Jacocks, Elizabeth		1	3		13
Ives, Joshua	1	4	2		1
Jackson, Samuel	1	3	3		2
Jackson, Joseph	2		1		3
Jemston, Richard	1				1
Jessop, Thomas	2		1		
Jordan, Elizabeth		2	3		3
Jordan, Joseph	4		3		
Johnson, Willis	1				
Jackson, Rachael			1		
Jackson, William, Junr	1				
Johnson, William	1		1		
Jackson, Moses	1	2	1	3	2
Johnson, Mary	1		2		
Jordan, Thomas	1				
Kenyon, Benjamin	1				
Kelly, Jethro	1	1	2		
Knowles, William	1	1	4		5
Knowles, Abner	1	1	3		2
Kenyon, Joab	2	2	5		2
Kenyon, Levi	1				
Kenyon, John	1		3		
Lamb, John	1	1	1		1
Lilly, Ruben	1	1	1		
Long, Joshua	1	1	3		2
Long, William	1		1		8
Long, Lemuel	1	2	2		5
Leary, John	2		1		
Lamb, Joseph	1		1		1
Long, Ruben	1	1	3		
Layden, Thomas	2	2	1		4
Lane, Benjamin	1	3	3		
Long, Thomas	1	6	1		3
Long, Simeon	1		5		
Long, Nathan	1	1	3		1
Lane, Sitterson	1		1		
Layden, William	1				
Lamb, Phinehas	1	3	4		1
Lacey, John	1		1		
Lunisford, John	1	2	3		1
Lawton, Peleg	2				19
Lilly, Sarah		2	3		
Layden, Francis	1	2	2		11
Lacey, William	1		2		
Luten, Frederick	2	2	4		2
Leigh, Gilbert	3	3	1		12
Lane, Jacob	1	1	2		
Lane, William	1	2	1		
Lane, Moses	2		3		
Lemmon, Joseph	1				
Lane, John	1	2	5		
Lamb, Zachariah	1		3		
Lilly, William	2				3
Lacey, James	1	1	2		
Lacey, Joseph	1	2	4		
Moore, Charles	3	2	3		15
Murdaugh, Josiah	3	3	4		35
Moore, John	1				7
McClenny, James	1		1		
Matthias, Joseph	1	3	4		
Mullen, William	1		2		
Mullen, James	2		2		1
Matthias, Isaiah	1	1	1		
McNider, John	1		3		
Morris, Joseph	1		1		
Mullen, Joseph	3	2	2		32
Mullen, Joseph, Junr	1	1	2		
Moore, Charles, Junr	1		2		1
Maudlin, John	2	5	5		
Mullen, Isaac	1	1	1		8
Mullen, Zadock	1	2	5		1
Morgan, Lemuel	1	1	5		
Morgan, Job	1	1	5		
Morris, Jonathan	1	4	1		
Macke, Joseph	1		1		1
Moore, Joshua	3	1	2		5
Maudlin, Thomas	1	2	3		
Mundin, William	1	1	3		1
Mundin, Elisha	1				
McClanahan, Mary		1	3		7
Maudlin, Joseph	1	2	3		
Morgan, John	1	5	4		
Mundin, Nathan	1		3		4
Mundin, Levi	1		5	4	
Moore, William	1				
Moore, Samuel	2	1	3		
Moore, Thomas	1	1	2		
Miller, Charles	1				
Mullen, Richard	1	1	2		
Maudlin, Nathan	3		4		
Moore, Karonhappuck	1		1		2
Miller, Mary			4		5
McAamd, Joseph	2		3		5
Meridith, Meriam			2		2
McCulloch, Robert H	2		2		2
Mitchell, Walter	1	1	4		
Mundin, Elisha	1		2		
Newby, Francis, Esqr	1	1	4		28
Newby, Thomas	1		2		2
Newby, Exum	1	1	5		5
Newby, Francis, Junr	1	2	2		1
Nixon, Samuel	1		2		3
Nixon, John	1	1	1		
Nixon, Delight	1	2	3		7
Norcom, Joseph	1				5
Nicholson, Nicholas	2	3	4		3
Nixon, Hannah			3		2
Nixon, Zachariah	3	4	4		18
Nixon, John	2	2	6		
Newby, Enoch	1		1		
Nicholson, Samuel	1				
Newby, Robert	1	1	1		4
Newby, Jonathan	3	1	2		3
Newby, Zachariah	1	4			4
Newby, Thomas, Junr	1	3	3		1
Newby, Joseph, Junr	1	4	3		1
Nicholson, Robert	1				1
Newbould, Samuel	1	1	1		
Newby, Gabriel	1	3	1		1
Newby, Elizabeth	1		1		6
Newby, Joseph	1	2	5		2
Newbould, William	1		1		
Newby, Gideon	1	1	1		
Newby, William	1		2		
Newby, Jesse	1		1		1
Newby, Thomas (son of Nathan)	2	2	4		5
Newby, Mike	1				2
Newby, William	2				
Newby, Benjamin	1	4	1		
Overton, Thomas	1	1	4		
Overton, John	1	2	2		
Overton, Malachi	1	1	4		
Overton, Elijah	1	1	1		
Overton, Perthena					10
Overton, Rachael					7
Overton, Lemuel					2
Overton, Samuel					1
Overman, Morgan	4	1	6		
Overman, John	1	3	5		
Parks, Daniel	1	2	5		
Pierce, Nathan	2	1	2		1
Perry, Joseph	1				8
Pierson, Nathan	1	1	2		
Perry, Dwelly	1	2	2		1
Perry, Miles	1	3	3		1
Perry, Mary			5		14
Perry, Lawrence	1				2
Perry, Rewben	2	2	2		
Perry, Benjamin, Esqr	1	1	3		15
Perry, Jacob	1		1		
Perry, Philip	3	2	5		4
Parrimore, Thomas	3		4		
Penrice, Samuel	1				
Penrice, Thomas	1				
Pratt, Zebulon	1		4		
Portlock, Catharine		1	2		1
Parks, Humphrey	2	1	3		9
Parks, Nathan	1		2		
Pierce, John	1	1	2		
Pointer, Henry	4	3	4	1	10
Pierce, Thomas	1				
Pearson, Eleazor	1				4
Pierce, David	1		2		
Pearson, William	1	1	6		
Pierce, James	1				6
Perry, William	1		2		
Parker, John	2	2	5		
Peed, James	1	2	2		
Perry, Israel	1	2	2		4
Pierce, Joseph	2	4	2		11
Pritlow, Keziah	3		3		12
Perry, Jesse, Esqr	3	4	4		5
Perisho, Joseph	1	4	2		1
Peed, Lemuel	1		2		
Perry, John	1				1
Penrice, Clark		2	5		
Perry, Seth	1		2		
Pierce, Abner	1	1	2		1
Pratt, Mary			2		
Pierce, Miles	1	4	3		
Parker, Elisha	1		1		
Perry, Nathan	1	2	1		
Reddick, Robert, Esqr	1	1	2		13
Reddick, Josiah	1	2	5		
Reddick, Ruth	1		2		7
Reddick, Solomon	1	2	1		2
Reddick, Seth	1	4	4		2
Reddick, Jacob	2	1	4		3
Rountree, Jesse	1		3		5
Robinson, Thomas	1	1	4		2
Rogerson, Josiah	2	3	3		13
Rogerson, Jesse	1		2		4
Rogerson, John	1		4		
Robins, William	3	2	2		6
Raper, Elizabeth	1	1	3		
Roberts, John	1	4	1		
Russell, Nicholas	1	2	3		
Reed, Benjamin	1	1	3		21
Raper, Robinson	1		2		
Reed, William, Esqr	2	2	2		29
Reed, George	1	3	2		7
Roberts, William	1	4	1		3
Robins, John	1	1	2		9
Raper, Henry	1	1	3		1
Raper, Luke	1		2		1
Raper, Robert	1	2	4		1
Roberts, William, Junr	1				
Ray, Thomas	1	2	1		
Roberts, Benjamin	2	2	3		2
Roe, Robert	2	1	2		
Robins, Joseph	1				
Robinson, Josiah	1				
Rowan, John	1		4		
Roberts, John, Junr	2		2		1
Rogerson, Elizabeth			4		2
Ratclift, Thomas	1	4	3		
Raper, John	1	1	4		1
Raper, Joseph	1	2	1		1
Rogerson, Mary	4	2	4		6
Richards, William	2	2	3		1
Sanderson, Richardson	2		2		10
Skinner, William, Esqr	1		5		47
Skinner, Joshua, Esqr	2	3	7		20
Skinner, John, Esqr	1	1	2		38
Skillings, Sarah			3		8
Scott, Severn	1	1	3		
Stakes, Thomas	3	3	3		1
Stacey, Thomas	3	6	2		
Stevenson, Thomas, Junr	1	2	3		
Stepney, William	2	3	5		3
Smith, John	2	1	3		4
Sutton, Francis	1	1	3		
Skinner, Richard	2	2	5		5
Stevenson, Thomas	1	1	3		12
Sutton, Jeremiah	1	3	2		
Stone, Elisha	1	1	1		
Skinner, Nathan	1	2	2		2
Standin, William	1	2	5		11
Simmons, Thomas	1	3	1		
Saunders, John	1	3	4		
Skinner, Joseph	1	1	1		
Skinner, Ann			3		2
Sutton, Ashbury, Esqr	1	3	6		25
Sitterson, Isaac	1	1	5		
Sitterson, Thomas	1	3	2		
Stanton, John, Junr	1		4		4
Sitterson, Samuel	1		2		
Skinner, Stephen	1		1		7
Saunders, John	4		3		
Sutton, George	1	1	5		11
Stafford, Alexander	1	1	2		4
Stafford, Lemuel	2	4	2		
Saunders, Josiah	1	1	1		
Smith, Job	1	5	2		
Smith, Leah			4		4
Saunders, William	1		3		
Saunders, Benjamin	1	2	3		9
Saunders, Joshua	1		2		
Saunders, Joseph	1		2		
Smith, Benjamin	2		2		1
Small, Miles	2		1		
Saunders, Mary		3	3		8
Saunders, Stephen	3	1	3		2
Saunders, Richard	2	4	3		2
Sutton, Greenbury	1		2		7
Saint, Daniel	2		3		1
Saint, Thomas	2	1	3		3
Small, William	1		4		

EDENTON DISTRICT, PERQUIMANS COUNTY—Continued.

NAME OF HEAD OF FAMILY.	Free white males of 16 years and upward, including heads of families.	Free white males under 16 years.	Free white females, including heads of families.	All other free persons.	Slaves.
Stanton, Thomas	2		4		1
Sutton, Thomas	1	1	5		
Sutton, Thomas, Junr	1		2		
Small, David	1				
Smith, Samuel	1	1	4		
Sumner, James	2		3		26
Sumner, James (for Thomas Sumner)					16
Sutton, Samuel	1	2	4		9
Sawyer, William	3	1	2		
Stafford, Thomas	1	1	2		
Stafford, William	1		3		
Stafford, Thomas, Junr	1	2	4		
Stevenson, Hugh, Esqr	1	1	4		13
Sitterson, Joseph	1	1	5		
Stanton, John	2		2		
Swann, Henry	1		2		2
Swann, Willson	1		3		
Stone, Moses	1		2		3
Stone, Moses, Junr	1	1	4		
Sutton, Joseph	1	1	1		14
Stallings, Reuben	1	2	4		2
Stallings, Solomon	1				
Stallings, Henry	1	1	1		
Stallings, John	1	1	3		
Stallings, Daniel	3	3	2		7
Smith, James	1		2		
Stallings, Jesse	2		2		3
Stallings, Luke	2		2		3
Stone, Florilla		1	2		
Saunders, John	1		4		4
Scott, James	1	2	1		
Saunders, Benjamin	1	2	5		2
Snowden, Zebulon	2	1	3		
Smith, John, Junr	1	1	2		
Stone, Cornelius	1	1	3		
Smith, Jane	2	2	2		
Scarborough, Benjamin	2	2	2		
Thatch, Levan	1		4		
Thatch, Joseph	1	3	2		
Thatch, Thomas	1	1	1		
Turner, John	1	1	2		
Tow, William	1		2		4
Thatch, Spencer	1	2	1		1
Tucker, John	1	2	2		1
Turner, Joseph	2	1	2		
Turner, Joseph, Junr	2	3	6		11
Turner, Joseph (the younger)	1	1	2		2
Turner, George	1	2	2		
Turner, Joshua	1				
Turner, Elsbury	1	2	1		
Turner, Thomas	1		2		3
Turner, Benjamin	2	2	2		
Turner, Miles	1	4	2		3
Jones, Martha		2	1		16
Thornton, Joseph	1	1	1		1
Townsend, Elizabeth		3	1		2
Tuiddy, Aaron	2	3	3		
Toms, John	2	3	5		12
Toms, John, Junr	1				
Toms, Gosby	1	7	4		52
Toms, Foster	1	2	1		18
Talton, Joshua	1	2	3		
Tow, Joseph	2	4	3		2
Taylor, John, Junr	1		2		
Twine, Jesse	2		1		2
Twine, Abraham	1		3		6
Twine, Thomas	1	2	6		8
Taylor, John	2	1	3		
Tow, Deborah		1	2		
Upton, John	1	1	5		2
Versey, Joannah			1		1
White, William	2	1			
White, Sarah	1	2	4		32
Whidbee, Thomas	2	5	5		19
Webb, John	1	1	1		
Weston, Elizabeth		2	1		
Willson, Ann	1		3		
White, Luke	2	1	4		6
Wyatt, John	1	3	3		10
White, Isaac	1	1	3		10
Whidbee, Mary			2		4
White, James	1	1	4		11
Wingate, Edward	3	2	3		
White, Joseph	1	1			1
Wood, Edmund	1	2	3		
Wells, Joseph	1	1	5		5
White, Robert	1	1	2		1
Williams, Spencer	1	2	2		
Williams, Isaac	1	1	2		
White, Henry	1	3	3		
Winslow, Jesse	1	1	6		
Willson, Christopher	1	1	2		1
Wingate, Ephraim	1	1	2		
Woodley, John	1		3		3
Whitehead, David	1	2	1		
White, Gabriel	2	1	2		
White, Caleb	4	3	4		2
White, Francis	1		2		
Williams, William	1				
Williams, Mary	1	3	4		1
Wheaton, William	1				
Willson, Jacob	2		2		6
Willson, Ruben	3	2	4		1
Willson, Abraham	1		1		
Willson, Jonathan	1		2		
Williams, Nathaniel	1				
Williams, Lockhart	1	1	3		8
Whidbee, James	1	1	4		10
White, John	3	1	3		6
Weeks, Willson	1		1		11
Whidbee, Thomas, Junr	1	2	2		7
Whidbee, Seth	1	1	2		4
Whidbee, William	2	1	4		14
Weeks, Thomas, Junr	1	2	3		1
Weeks, Lemuel	1	1	2		
Wardsworth, Caleb	1	1	3		
Weeks, Samuel	2	2	2		1
Weeks, Thomas	1	2	4		4
Wright, John	1	1	1		
Wright, William	1	1	1		
Whidbee, John	1	4	3		3
Winslow, John, Junr	1	2	2		
White, Josiah	1	7	3		2
White, Joshua	1		3		3
White, John, Junr	1	1	1		
White, Edmund	2	1	2		6
Winslow, Jacob	2		3		3
White, Thomas	3		4		4
White, Benjamin	3	4	3		1
Winslow, Caleb	1	3	3		7
Wood, Joseph	2	2	4		
Woollard, Martin	3		8		
Winslow, Benjamin	3	2	2		1
Willson, Lidia	1	2	5		
Williamson, John	1	1	2		1
White, William	2	1	2		8
White, William, Junr	1		2		
White, Jesse	1	2	2		
Winslow, John	1	1	3		
Winslow, Samuel	2	1	5		1
White, Jacob	1	4	2		1
White, John	1	1	2		2
White, Samuel	1		2		2
White, Mary	2		3		2
Willson, Ann		1	3		5
White, Benjamin, Junr	2		2		
Winslow, Jesse, Junr	1	1	1		10
Willson, Isaac	2	4	5		
White, Mary, Junr	1		3		1
Wyall, William	2				1
Willson, Elizabeth			3		
White, Benjamin		1	2		
Whidbee, Robert	1		2		
Weeks, Shadrach	1	1	2		
White, Thomas, Junr	1		2		1
White, Arnold	1	1	1		
Willcocks, Prissilla			2		
Welch, Comfort			4		
Walls, Absalom	1	1	3		
Willson, Benjamin	1		2		
Willson, Mary			3		
Willson, Christopher, Junr	1	1	1		

EDENTON DISTRICT, TYRRELL COUNTY.

NAME OF HEAD OF FAMILY.	Free white males of 16 years and upward, including heads of families.	Free white males under 16 years.	Free white females, including heads of families.	All other free persons.	Slaves.
Clifton, John	1	4	1		
Davenport, Jacob	1	2			
Ambrus, James	1	2	3		
Clifton, Robert	3	1	5		
Tarkenton, Benja	1	2	4		
Phelps, Josiah	4	1	3		2
Phelps, James	1		3		
Phelps, Rosanna			2	3	
Barnes, Isaac	1		1		
Barnes, Reuben	1	4	3		
Jethro, Thomas	1	2	2		
Tarkenton, Joseph	1	1	3		
Davis, Zephaniah	2	2	7		2
Spruil, Miles	1	2	1		
Bateman, Solomon	1	1	4		1
Phelps, Josiah	1	1	2		2
Smith, Thomas	1	2	3		
Powers, Joshua	1	1	5		
Alexander, Anthony	1	2	3		
Alexander, John	1	1	2		
Oliver, Alexander	1	2	2		
Oliver, Joseph	1		4		
Hassell, Levi	1		8		
Hill, Asa	1	2	1		
Spruil, Miles	1	1	6		
Skittletharpe, Charles	1	4	3		
Ambrus, Micajah	1	1	1		
Ferlaw, John	2	3	3		
McClary, Keziah		1	3		
Ambrus, Jesse	1	1	4		
Long, James	1	3	1		
Caswell, Samuel	1	2	3		
Oliver, Andrew	1	3	2		1
Ansley, Edward	1		2		1
powers, Isaac	1	1	4		
Ansley, Solomon	1		3		1
Bateman, Stephen	1	3	4		
Ansley, Joseph, Junr	1		2		
Hagman, Henry	2		2		
Weatherly, Thomas	1	2	1		
Tellit, Avery	1	1	2		
White, Jonathan	2	3	4		
Simmons, Josiah	1		2		
Simmons, John	1	2	1		
Alcock, William	1		2		
Cahoon, Joseph	1		2		
Cahoon, Benjamin	1				
Alcock, Sarah	3	2	3		
Simmons, Willis	1	5	1		
Sawyer, Jonathan	1	5	1		
Sawyer, Bartlet	1		1		
Richason, Hannah		4	1		
Hutson, Anthony	1		2		
Hutson, Elijah	1	3	5		
Howard, Willm, Senr	1	1	1		
Howard, William, Junr	1		1		
Norriss, William	1	3	3		
Howard, Thomas	1	3	2		
Cahoon, John	1	3	3		
Cahoon, James	1	1	5		
Smith, John	1	1	3		
McGown, William	1		2		
McGown, John	1	1	2		
Ronsom, Elizabeth			2		
Liverman, John, Junr	1		2		
Mekins, John	1		2		
Gibson, John	1	1	2		5
Smith, Zebedee	1	2	1		
Gibson, Samuel	1		1		
Jarman, John	1	3	2		
Jones, Corbin	1	3	4		
Cullifer, Henry	1		2		
Cullifer, James	1		3		
Liverman, Willm	2	2	5		15
Liverman, Thomas	1	5	3		3
Liverman, John	1		4		
Hoskins, Thomas	2	3	5		37
Mekins, Isaac	1	6	4		
Cahoon, Ezekiel	1	3	5		
Bodwell, Solomon	1	1	1		
Francis, Thos	1	1	2		
Hassell, Solomon	2	1	4		
Hassell, Solomon, Junr	1		2		
Johnston, Joshua	1				
Hassell, Joshua	1	2	2		
Hassell, John (son of Solomon)	1	1	2		
Riggins, Jemimiah			2		
Armstrong, John	2	2	3		
Phelps, Edward	3	2	6		
Tarkenton, Benjamin	1	3	5		
Banks, Henry	1	1	1		
Warrington, John	2		4		6
Woodland, Samuel	2		2		1
Powers, Josiah	1	2	3		1
Davenport, Jacob	1	1	2		
Patrick, Isaac	1	4	3		1
Goddin, John	1	3	2		
Phelps, Jonathan	1	2	2		
Lewark, Anne	1	2	2		
Oliver, John	1	2	2		
Alexander, Ezekiel	1	2	3		
Craddack, Joseph	1	2	1		
Hassell, William	1	3	3		
Goddin, Ezekiel	1	1	4		
Hassell, Zebedee	2	1	2		6
Hopkins, Thomas	1		3		7
Morriss, Cornelius	2	2	3		
Alexander, Henry	2	4	2		
Alexander, Joseph	1		2		1
Alexander, John	1	1	2		

EDENTON DISTRICT, TYRRELL COUNTY—Continued.

NAME OF HEAD OF FAMILY.	Free white males of 16 years and upward, including heads of families.	Free white males under 16 years.	Free white females, including heads of families.	All other free persons.	Slaves.
Alexander, John, Senr	2	2	5		3
McClease, John	1	3	3		
Meades, Benjamin	1		2		
Trueblood, Asa	1	1	4		
Davenport, Hezekiah	1		4		
Steatman, Jeremiah	1	3	3		
Barnett, William	1	2	3		
Caroon, John	1	5	4		12
Caroon, Joseph	1		1		1
Midgett, John	1	2	3		4
Mann, Solomon	1	1	3		2
Oneal, Richard	1	2	3		
Brown, Samuel	1	1	1		
Mann, Samuel	2	1	4		3
Popperwill, George	1	2	5		
Barnett, Stephen	2	3	7		
Coffee, William	1	3	5		
Hill, David	1	1	1		
Hill, David, Senr	1		1		
Williams, James	1	2	2		
Psalter, William	1		1		1
Rascow, Daniel	2	1	5		
Payne, John	2	4	3		1
Mann, Thomas	2	2	3		1
McGlocklin, Mitchel	1		1		
Alexander, Zilpha	1	1	7		6
Warrington, Thomas	1		2		3
pierce, Miles	1	4	3		
Davenport, John	1	2	2		
phelps, Seth	3	2	4		5
Saunders, John	1		2		
Hassell, John, Senr	4	1	7		15
Tarkenton, Joseph	1	2	1		2
Brown, William	1	2	4		
Spruil, Sarah	1		2		
Dukes, Hezekiah	1	2	6		
Powers, John	1		2		
Powers, Ephraim	1	1	2		
Hassell, Stephen	1	2	3		
Vollovay, Joseph	5	2	5		
Brim, Richard	1	1	6		
Armstrong, Russell	3	4	2		4
Cullifer, John	1		2		
Cahoon, Catherine			8		
Clayton, John	1	3	4		8
Hill, Celia		3	3		
Baker, Benjamin	2	2	4		
Jones, Robert	1	2	1		
Foster, Silas	1		4		
Russ, William	1	1	2		
Williams, Josiah	1	4	2		
Sikes, John	1	2	4		
Spence, Anne		2	4		
Spence, Robert	1		3		
Sawyer, Robert	1	2	3		
Sawyer, Isaac	1	2	2		
Sawyer, James	1	5	2		
Jannett, Joseph	1	1	1		
Sawyer, Peter	1	4	2		
Smith, Jabith	1	1	3		
Sawyer, Joab	1	3	1		
Sawyer, Leven	1		2		
Sawyer, Keziah			2		
Best, Betsy		2	3		
Belanger, Elisha, Senr	1	1	3		
Belanger, Elisha	1	1	1		
Belanger, Abel	1		1		
Smith, Jesse	1		3		
Smith, John	1	2	4		
Ward, Anthony	1	1	5		
Simmons, Josiah	1				
McDewil, Mary			1		
Liverman, John, Senr	1	2	5		3
Liverman, Hezekiah	1	1	5		
Liverman, John	1		4		
Smith, Rachael		2	1		
Sawyer, Dennis	1	1	2		2
Brown, Abram	1		3		
Owens, Thomas	1	2	4		4
Owens, Peter	1		2		
Pledger, Joseph	1	4	6		9
Holloway, Moses	2	1	5		
Rhoades, Leven	2	2	3		
Hancock, William	3	1	4		
Howett, William	2	3	3		9
Chapman, Joseph	1	5	3		
Hopkins, John	1	2	3		
Brickhouse, Major	3	2	7		
Spruil, Hezekiah, Esq	2		5		12
Parsons, Asa	2	1	2		
Hopkins, Elizabeth		1	3		
Hopkins, Philip	1				
Ansley, John	2	2	7		7
Ansley, Joseph	1	1	2		1
Arnold, Joseph	3	3	6		1
Ambrus, Shimie	1		2		
Alexander, Joseph, Junr	2	3	3		3
Airs, Isaac	2	3	5		
Alexander, Sarah			2		
Alexander, Joshua	1	1	1		
Alexander, Joseph	1	4	3		3
Armistead, John	1	1	2		8
Airs, John	1		1		
Adams, Isaac	1	2	3		2
Adams, Thomas	1		2		
Allen, Henry	1	4	2		
Bateman, Jeremiah	2		2		2
Bateman, Nathan, Senr	2	3	5		3
Bateman, John	1				2
Bateman, Levi	1	1	1		1
Blount, Stevens	1	4	1		
Barnes, John	1		1		
Bateman, Godfrey	1	1	1		
Bateman, Stephen	1	2	2		
Blount, Hannah	1		3		
Brown, James	1		1		
Bateman, Simeon	1		1		
Bates, Thomas	1				
Bobbit, David	1				
Bateman, Jesse	1	1	3		
Bateman, Pethiah	1	3	2		
Bernbridge, Sarah		1	2		
Blount, Jacob	2		4		3
Blount, Levi	1	1	3		23
Bernbridge, Caleb	3	3	3		5
Blount, John	1		1		
Burns, Anne			1		2
Blount, William	1	4	3		22
Blount, Edmund, Junr	1	2	3		13
Bateman, Andrew	1	3	4		5
Bateman, Jonathan	3	5	2		4
Bateman, Isaac	1	3	6		1
Bateman, Solomon	1	2	2		
Blount, Benjamin	1	2	3		5
Bozman, John	1	2	3		
Byrd, R. Martin	1				2
Boyman, Leven	2		1		3
Bozman, Joseph	1	1	1		1
Blount, Nathan	1	1	2		
Chesson, Samuel	1	1	5		8
Cutter, Ebbin	1				
Chesson, John	1		1		1
Chesson, William	2	3	2		5
Canady, Richard	1				
Chesson, Joshua	1	1	1		
Canady, Frederick	1				
Canady, John, Senr	2		3		
Cullifer, Isaac	1	3	5		
Collins, Caleb	1	2	1		
Court, John	3	3	2		
Clifton, Mary		1	4		
Canady, John	1				
Chesson, Joseph	2	2	2		
Cotrell, Francis		1	2		3
Camel, John	1	2	2		
Crooke, Clement	1	1	5		7
Camel, Rebecca		2	2		
Corprew, Joshua	2	3	2		5
Corprew, Thomas	1	3	2		2
Corprew, Jonathan	3		2		7
Condry, William	1	3	5		
Blount, Edmund, Senr	3	3	5		3
Davenport, Mosses	1	2	3		
Dillin, John	1	3	1		
Davis, Richard	1	1	2		4
Davenport, Daniel	1		3		5
Davenport, Joseph, Junr	1	3	2		
Davenport, Frederick	1	1	2		1
Davenport, Doctr John	2	2	3		
Davis, John	1	3	3		
Davenport, Ephraim	1	3	6		
Davis, Thomas	2	4	2		
Dunston, Abram	1		4		
Davenport, James	1	2	2		3
Davenport, David	1	1	3		1
Davenport, John	1	2	2		
Dillin, James	1	4	4		1
Davenport, Joseph, Senr	2	6	2		
Davenport, Joanne		3	6		2
Davenport, Isaac	3	2	4		
Davison, Robert	1	3	4		5
Draper, Richard	2		1		1
Davis, John, Senr	2	3	3		3
Davis, Arthur	1		1		
Davis, William	1				
Davis, Matilda		1	2		
Airs, David	2	2	1		
Airs, Nathan	1		1		
Collins, Ferubah	2	1	3		
Corprew, Esther			5		
Corprew, John	1	1	2		
Adams, Martha			2		
Etheridge, Ephraim	2	2	6		1
Earl, William	1		1		10
Everitt, Joseph	1	6	5		
Everitt, Jeresiah	2	3	5		2
Ezekiel, Caleb	1	1	1		
Everitt, Thomas	2	2	4		5
Everitt, Nathaniel	1	3	1		1
Freeman, William	1		4		
Freeman, James	1		2		
Frasier, Richard	1		2		2
Ferlaw, William	1				
Frasier, Jeremiah	2	5	8		6
Floyd, Solomon	1		4		
Fagan, Thomas	1				
Fagan, Frederick	1				
Fagan, Enoch	1				
Fagan, Shadrach	1	1	2		1
Fagan, Richard	2	3	5		
Fagan, William	1	3	3		3
Freeman, Thomas	1		2		1
Goddin, Aaron	1	1	1		
Gilbert, James	1	4	4		
Girkin, Joshua	1				
Girkin, John	1				
Girkin, Anne			4		
Gray, Godfrey	1	3	4		
Gray, Henry	3		5		
Gilbert, Nicholas, Senr	1	1	2		
Gilbert, Nicholas, Junr	1		1		
George, Isaac	1		2		1
Griffin, Zilpha		2	4		
Gillikin, George Anson	1	1	1		1
Garrett, James, Junr	1	1	1		
Garrett, Thomas	1		1		
Garrett, Daniel	1		1		
Garrett, John, Junr	1	1	2		2
Garrett, Thomas, Junr	1		3		
Garrett, John, Senr	2	1	3		11
Cunningham, Timothy	1	1	1		
Garrett, Samuel	1	1	1		
Garrett, James, Senr	2		1		4
Hooker, Nathan	1	2	2		9
Hare, James	1	4	3		
Hatfield, Jesse	3	1	3		1
Harrisson, John	1	2	2		
Harrisson, Edmund	3	3	3		
Hassell, Benjamin	2	1	2		
Hays, Robert	1		4		
Howet, Edmund	1				
Hassell, Edward, Jun	1		4		
Hawkins, Thomas	2	1	4		
Hassell, Anne	1		4		
Hassell, Mary			3		
Harrisson, Joshua	1	3	1		
Hill, Jesse	1	1	2		
Hardison, Benjamin	2		2		2
Harrisson, William	2		4		3
Hollis, Armit	2	1	4		
Howard, Sarah	1	1	3		1
Harrisson, Benjamin, Junr	1	3	3		
Harrisson, Thomas, Junr	2	2	3		3
Harrisson, Thomas, Senr	2	2	3		6
Hardison, Mary	1	2	3		8
Hardison, Jasper	1	3	3		2
Hamilton, James	1		2		
Hollis, James	1	2	5		
Harrisson, Frank	1		3		
Harrisson, Susannah	1		1		
Hoff, Richard	2	1	2		3
Jones, Jones	2	3	4		
Giles, John	1		2		
Jones, Joshua	1		2		
Jones, James, Senr	1	2	1		1
Jannett, Abraham	3	1	3		2
Jones, Frileg	2	2	7		11
Jones, Margarett		1	2		
Jones, Joseph, Junr	1		2		
Jones, Joseph, Senr	1		2		
Joy, George	1		2		
Jerard, Henry	1	1	1		
Lasher, John	2				
Leary, Joshua	1	2	2		7
Long, James (son of Andrew)	1				
Long, John (son of Colo Long)	1	1	2		11
Long, John, Junr	1		2		4
Langley, James	1		1		
Long, William	1	1	2		2
Long, Isaac	2	2	1		
Long, James (son of Giles)	1		3		6
Long, Rebecca	4	2	4		
Leary, John	1		1		
Leary, Enoch	1		1		

EDENTON DISTRICT, TYRRELL COUNTY—Continued.

NAME OF HEAD OF FAMILY.	Free white males of 16 years and upward, including heads of families.	Free white males under 16 years.	Free white females, including heads of families.	All other free persons.	Slaves.
Leary, Cornelius	2	2	4		
Long, Colo James	2		1		12
Lee, Thomas	2	2	1		18
Lewis, Jesse	2	3	2		
Leggett, Daniel	1	1	5		
Leggett, Luke	1		2		
Dwight, William	1	1	2		
Jordan, John	1	1	4		2
Mariner, John, Senr.	1				
Middleton, Josiah	1				
Mires, Thomas	1	3	3		9
Mariner, John	1	1	3		
Mariner, Peter	1		1		
McDewil, Frederick	1		2		
Mackey, William	1	2	3		15
Mills, Penelope		1	2		
Mariner, Rixom	2	2	4		
Mashaw, Matthew	1	1	3		4
McDonough, Andrew	1	2	3		1
Moss, Mary			1		
Matthews, George	1				
Norman, Henry	2	1	1		8
Newberry, John	1	1	2		
Norman, Hezekiah	1	2	2		1
Norman, James	1	1	4		
Norman, Simeon	1	1	3		
Norman, Joseph, Senr.	3		2		
Norman, Joseph, Junr.	1				
Norman, Isaac	1	2	2		
Norman, John, Ser	1	2	5		
Norman, Rachael	1	2	3		6
Norman, Thomas	3		2		2
Nevins, John	1	2	1		1
Dauson, George (for estate of Harrymond)					15
Overton, Edward	1		4		
Oliver, George	1				
Orsborn, Philip	1	1	2		
Oliver, Edward	1				
Martin, Charles	1	1	2		
Phelps, John	1	1	1		
Phelps, Joseph	4	1	3		
Phelps, Urijah	1				
Phelps, Benjamin	1	2	1		
Phelps, John, Senr.	1	4	3		2
Phelps, Joseph, Senr.	1	4	2		7
Phelps, James, Senr.	1	1	4		
Pratt, Lott	3	1	5		
Phelps, Godfrey	3	2	4		
Phelps, Joseph, Junr.	1				
Phelps, Anne	2	1	5		
Padgett, Jesse	1				
Phelps, Zadock	1		2		
Phelps, Joshua	1	3	3		
Phelps, Edward	1	1	4		
Phelps, Capt. James	2		2		
Phelps, Asa	1	2	1		
Pettegrew, Charles	2	2	1		16
Patrick, Thomas	1	4	3		
Rowe, Levi	1	3	3		1
Rankhorn, Joseph	1	1	4		
Russell, Thomas	1				
Robason, Peter	1		2		3
Raby, James	4		4		
Rogers, Airs	1	1	3		
Rogers, Nathan	1	1	2		
Rogers, Anne	1		4		
Patterson, Mary		1	1		4
Spruil, William	1	3	2		
Spruil, Benjamin	2	1	4		20
Stubbs, Thomas, Junr.	2	1	4		5
Spruil, Samuel, Senr.	3	3	3		
Snell, Roger	2	4	3		
Swain, Stephen	2	2	2		
Swain, John	1	3	3		1
Spruil, Charles	2	1	1		3
Spruil, Colo Joseph	2	1	1		2
Slade, Joshua	1	1	2		6
Skinner, Evan	1	2	3		2
Swift, Joseph	1				7
Smith, Abram	1	5	6		
Snell, James	1	3	3		
Spruil, Godfrey	1		1		
Spruil, Jesse	1		4		1
Sutton, Lemuel	1	1	1		
Spruil, William	1	1	3		
Spruil, Samuel	1	3	3		
Snell, Sarah	1	2	6		
Swain, Cornelius	1	2	3		1
Spruil, Jose	1	3	3		
Spruil, Thos Hawkins	1	3	1		
Spruil, James	1	2	3		
Spruil, Simeon	2	1	4		9
Snell, Abijah	1		1		
Snell, Jesse	1		1		
Stealy, Elizabeth	1		2		
Spruil, William, Senr.	1	2	5		
Spruil, Thomas	2	2	6		
Spruil, Joseph	1		3		
Spruil, Miles	1	2	1		
Swain, Eleazer	1	3	4		2
Stealy, Jeremiah	1		1		
Sutton, William	3		3		
Stealy, Edmund	1				
Stealy, Frederick	1		1		
Smiley, William	1		2		
Stubbs, James	1	2	3		
Stubbs, Aaron	1		1		1
Stubbs, Everard	1	1	4		4
Stewart, Thomas	1		1		4
Stubbs, Samuel	2	1	4		
Stouffer, George	1	1	1		
Stubbs, Levi	1	1	3		1
Stubbs, John	1		2		4
Sevinson, John	1		1		4
Sexton, Dempsey	1	1	1		
Padgett, John	2	1	3		
Peacock, George	1	2	4		
Stubbs, Thomas, Senr.	1		1		4
Stubbs, Micajah	1		3		2
Stubbs, Richard	1	2	3		4
Stubbs, William	1				1
Snell, John	1				
Spruil, Josiah	1	2	3		
Spruil, Sammy	1	2	4		
Spruil, Evan	1	3	4		
Smith, Francis	1	4	1		
Spruil, John	1				
Tarkenton, William	2	2	7		4
Tarkenton, Isaac	3				
Tarkenton, Joseph	1		2		5
Turner, Arthur	1	2	4		7
Tetterton, William	1		2		
Tarkenton, John	1	1	3		10
Tarkenton, Zebulon	2	1	7		1
Tod, John	1	2	5		
Trotter, Thomas (for the Lake Compy)	3				113
Thomas, Elizabeth		1	2		
Tarkenton, Joseph, Junr.	1		2		1
Tetterton, Ephraim	1	2	1		
Tyrrell, Justice	1				
Ramsey, William	1		2		
Phelps, Cuthbert	1		2		
Vandal, Isaac	1		1		
Wyatt, Joseph	3		2		7
Wynne, Jesse	3				1
Wynne, Benjamin	2	2	3		
Wood, James	4	4	5		5
Wiley, Stephen	2	1	2		
Walker, John	1	2	3		
Wiley, Thomas	1	2	4		3
Wiley, James	1	1	3		
Wynne, Robert	1	1	3		3
Woodland, John	1		1		
Wynne, Andrew	1	4	2		
Walker, Thomas	2	1	6		13
Webb, Harmon, Jun.	1	1	1		1
Williams, Thomas	1	3	6		
Walker, Stewart	1	5	1		
Ward, William	1				1
Webb, Harmon, Senr.	2	2	3		17
Willett, Elizabeth			1		2
Woollard, Joseph	2	1	2		
White, William	1	2	2		
White, Thomas	1		1		
Rhoades, Nathan	1	2	3		
Vandycke, Joseph	1	1	2		
Young, Zilpha		2	6		
Swain, Joshua	2	2	4		
Walker, Edward	2	2	4		1
Simons, Margarett			2		
Revel, Eleven	1	6	2		
Buncombe, Thomas	1				31
Stubbs, Jesse	1	1	3		1
Mackey, Colo Thomas	1	3	1		25
Foster, John	1	1	3		9
Jones, David	1		1		
Hardy, Lewis (for Estate of Humphry Hardy)	1	1	4		23
Gunning, John	1	1	3		
Simpson, Reddin (free colored)	1		3		
Simpson, Jacob (free colored)	1	1	1		
Will, Elizabeth (free colored)		1	2		
Williams, Jack (free colored)	1				
Foster, William (free colored)	1	4	2		
Dempsey, John (free colored)	1				
Biffins, Philip (free colored)	1				
Vollovay, Jane (free colored)	1				
Bryan, Bridgett (free colored)			1		
Pierce, Israel (free colored)	1	2	3		
Pierce, Thomas (free colored)	1	3	4		
Alexander, John	1	4	4		
McCallister, Robert	1	1	3		
Perisher, Rufus	1	1	5		
Crane, Joseph	1		3		
Twiddy, Benjamin	1	1	2		
Twiddy, David	1	1	1		
Rowton, Daniel	1		1		1
Rowton, Richd	1	1	4		
Johnston, Jonathan	1	2	3		
Johnston, Randal	1	1	2		
Perisher, Devotion	1	1	2		
Rowton, Edward	1		4		1
Basnett, Jacob	1	2	5		
Jackson, Thomas	1		2		
Orum, George	1	2	1		
Sawyer, Griffin	1	2	4		
Bray, Isaac	1	3	4		
Hassell, Anne	2		2		5
Thorogood, Paul	1	2	1		
Demeritt, Jesse	1	2	2		
Davenport, Ezra	1	1	2		
Mann, Benjamin	1	2	2		
Twiddy, John	2		1		
Twiddy, Devotion	1		2		
Brickhouse, John	1		2		
Alexander, John	1	2	4		1
Alexander, William	1	1	1		1
Alexander, Joseph	1	1	4		
Craddack, Eleazer	1		4		
Chapman, Richd	2	3	2		
Swain, Nathal	1	3	2		1
Swain, Jeremy	1	1	4		
Alexander, Benja	1	4	3		3
Alexander, Willm	1		1		
West, William	1	4	7		
Volloway, Elisha	1				
Swain, James	1	1	3		3
Swain, Eliakim	1	3	2		
Swain, Abram	1	3	3		
Swain, Jeremiah	1	6	3		
Smith, Ebenezer	1	2	2		2
Rhoades, Henry	1	1	2		
Armstrong, Andrew	1	1	2		
Horton, William	1	1			2
Powers, Samuel	1	3	3		
Hassell, Edward	1		2		
Alexander, Edward	1	3	3		
patrick, John	1	3	3		
Tarkenton, John	1		4		
Davis, Elisha	1	3	1		
Alexander, John	2		3		
Tarkenton, John, Senr.	1	1	4		4
Phelps, Amos	2	3	3		
Barnett, Justice	1		1		
Cornel, Ezra	1				
Wynne, Joseph	1	1	5		
Hassell, Zebulon	1	2	2		1
Wynne, George	1	2	3		
Hassell, Joseph	1				
Massey, Adkins	1	1	1		1
Timmons, Elisha	1	2	4		
Hassell, John	1	1	5		
Hassell, Abram	1	1	3		1
Tarkenton, Joshua	2	1	2		6
Tarkinton, Jesse	1				
Perisher, James	1	4	2		
Alexander, Joshua	3		1		3
Hooker, John	1	1	2		
Battin, George	1		1		
Twifoot, William	2	1	6		4
Cowel, William	1	1	3		10
Smith, John	2		2		
Basnett, William	2	3	5		
Owens, Zachariah	1	1	3		
Basnett, Joseph	1	1	6		
Hooker, William	1		1		
Twiddy, Samuel	1		2		
Hooker, Nathan	1		1		
Hooker, Stephen	2	5	3		
Edwards, Jacob	1	2	1		
Owens, Isaac	1				
Owens, John	1				
Basnett, James	3	1	2		
Sawyer, Richd	1	2	1		
Crank, Levi	1	3	3		
Johnston, Joshua	1				
Alexander, Isaac	1	2	3		

EDENTON DISTRICT, TYRRELL COUNTY—Continued.

Name of head of family.	Free white males of 16 years and upward, including heads of families.	Free white males under 16 years.	Free white females, including heads of families.	All other free persons.	Slaves.	Name of head of family.	Free white males of 16 years and upward, including heads of families.	Free white males under 16 years.	Free white females, including heads of families.	All other free persons.	Slaves.	Name of head of family.	Free white males of 16 years and upward, including heads of families.	Free white males under 16 years.	Free white females, including heads of families.	All other free persons.	Slaves.
Alexander, Abram	1		2		4	Neal, William	1	4	5		1	Goddin, Joseph	1		1		
Alexander, Mary			1		4	Kelly, William	1					Davenport, Isaac, Junr	1	3	7		3
Jarvis, Foster	1	1	2			Spruil, Nehemiah	4	1	3		11	Pool, John	1		3		
Cooper, Willis	1	2	2			Banks, William	1	1	4			Hunnings, Philip	1		1		5
Ludford, Enoch	1	1	2		2	Holmes, Henry	2	2	2		3	Ethridge, Nathan	1				
Creed, Jonathan	1	2	2			Spruil, Ebenezer	1	1	5			Hooker, Anne			2		
Alexander, Abner	1	3	3		7	Phelps, James	1	2	4			Brin, Richd	1	1	3		
Snell, John	5	2	5		2	Phelps, Enoch	1	1	5			Brown, Sarah	1	1	6		
Wynne, Capt John	2	2	5		9	Hopkins, Samuel	1	2	3		1	Owens, Lucretia	1	3	2		
Hunnings, Zachariah	3	1	2		13	Hassell, Joseph, Senr	4	1	2		2	Howet, Richd	1	1	4		10
Jones, Bartlet	2	1	4		2	Rhoades, Henry	1		2			Claghorn, Shubal	1	2	2		
Cahoon, James	1	4	5		3	McDaniel, William	1	2	3		2						

FAYETTE DISTRICT, ANSON COUNTY.

Name of head of family.	Free white males of 16 years and upward, including heads of families.	Free white males under 16 years.	Free white females, including heads of families.	All other free persons.	Slaves.	Name of head of family.	Free white males of 16 years and upward, including heads of families.	Free white males under 16 years.	Free white females, including heads of families.	All other free persons.	Slaves.	Name of head of family.	Free white males of 16 years and upward, including heads of families.	Free white males under 16 years.	Free white females, including heads of families.	All other free persons.	Slaves.
Lampden, Robert	1		3			May, William, Jr	1	1	2			Hinson, Benjamin	2	4	6		2
Arthur, John	1	3	3			Lanier, Burwell	2	1	5		28	Weatherford, Charles	1	5	4		
Searcy, William	2		2			McClendon, Ezekiel	1	4	3			German, William	1	1	1		
Wood, William	1	3	2			Trull, Stephen	1					Lee, Robert	3	1	3		1
Denson, Shadrack	1					Williams, Josiah	1		1			Ganade, Martin	1	2	1		
Denson, Jesse	1					Bailey, Lydia	2	2	1			Threadgill, William	1	1	2		7
Nayes & Porter, Messrs	6				2	Isgett, Joseph	1	5	3			Pursley, Anthony	1	3	5		
Ponsey, Godfrey	1		1			McAskill, Daniel	2		2			Atkins, Lewis	1	1	5		
Barnwell, Joseph	1					Franklin, Lawrence, Jr	1		1			Lowry, John	1	3	4		1
Gilbert, Jesse	2	2	5		6	Lisles, James	1	4	3		1	Diggs, Pleasant	1	1	1		
Yarborough, Humphrey	1	1	1			Gulledge, William	1	2	4			Bittle, John	1		1		
Yarborough, William	1					Bennet, Neavel	1	1	2		2	Tatum, Jesse	1		1		
Allman, James	3	3	6			Morris, William	1	1	2		2	Plant, Williamson	1	1	3		
Williams, John	2	2	5			Smith, Edward	3	2	4			Temple, Frederick	2	3	2		
Treddiway, Daniel	1	3	4			Diggs, Marshal	5	4	3		1	Mooreman, Benjamin	1	3	1		1
Bloodworth, John	4	2	3			Kindred, Elisha	1	1	2		2	Hinson, Charles	1		1		1
Bass, Frederick	3	2	3			Ryal, John	1				1	Yarborough, James	1		3		
Lee, William	1	2	2			Colson, Joseph	1	1	2		5	Mills, John	1	2	5		
Dudney, John	1	3	4			West, John	2	3	2			Boggan, James, Sr	5	4	5		3
Bylue, Henry	1	3	5			Wynn, Zachariah					1	May, Starling	1	2	2		
Soward, Nancy		1	4			Garrot, James	1					Nichols, Isaac	1		3		
Stinson, Mary	1	2	4			Lewis, Jeremiah	1		1			Lambden, John	1	2	4		
Proctor, Linney		2	6			Booth, John	1	1	4			Harrell, James	1	1	1		
Jones, Honor		2	2			Bird, John	1	3	5		6	Davidson, Daniel	3	2	4		
Odom, Richard	1		2		9	Richeson, William	1	5	3		2	Ryal, James	1	3	1		
Ricketts, John	2	3	3			Dabbs, Nathaniel	2	3	3		1	House, Thomas	1				
Scott, Drury				4		Lewis, Thomas	1	4	7		3	Brewer, John	1		3		
Scott, Francis				1		Osborne, Nathan	1		3			Pound, Samuel	1				
Newton, John	2	1	2			Davis, Arthur	1	4	6			Baker, James	1	2	2		
Bailey, Jacob	1		1			Birmingham, Joshua	1	2	5			Falkner, Archd	1		2		
Murphy, John	3	2	3			Birmingham, Charles	2		1			Culpepper, John	1	1	3		
Benton, James	1	1	5			Ellis, Thomas	1		4			Dabbs, John	1	2	2		
Johnston, John	1	6	4			McClendon, Benjamin	1					Cox, William	1	2	2		
Wade, Thomas	5	1	2		17	Knotts, John, Jr	1	1	2			Vivion, Charles	1		2		9
Wright, John, Jr	1	1	1		8	Franklin, Laurence, Sr	1		2			Wadkins, Christo	3	1	2		
Bailey, Mathew	1	3	3			Wright, John	1		2			Boggan, James, Jr	1		1		1
Bailey, Thomas	1	2	5			Smith, John, Jr	1	1	2			Wisdom, William	2	3	5		
Arrington, James	2	5	2			Demery, Allen				7		Breler, Elisha	1	1	2		
Johnston, John, Jr	1	3	1			Grissard, Hardy	1	4	4		1	Rushing, Abraham	3	2	3		3
Ingram, John	1	5	5			Smith, John, Sr	2	4	4			Sparks, Charles	3	1	1		3
McRae, Daniel	1	3	4			White, Joseph	3		4		5	Watts, Malachia	1	1	5		6
Bylue, Abraham	1		2			Burres, Joshua	1	4	4		3	Colson, John	1	1	1		9
Duglas, James	1	1	1		8	Davis, Joshua	1	3	4			Whitlow, Henry	1		1		
German, Robert	2	2	2			Brown, Morgan	4	1	2	1	5	White, John	1		1		
Hall, Robert	1					Tarlton, Britton	1	1	1			Mullis, John	1	1	1		
Stanfill, Sampson	1	1	3			Tarlton, John	1	1	1			Winfield, Peter	1	1	4		4
Dabbs, Josiah	1		3			Knotts, John, Sr	1	1	3			Nash, Griffin	1	1	1		
May, William	2	4	5		7	Lambden, Bixley, Jno	2	1	2			Presley, Elias	1	3	1		
Threadgill, Randal	1	3	1			Nash, Michael	1	2	2			Rushing, Philip	1	3	3		
Sasser, Joseph	2	2	5			Franklin, Esom	1	2	2			Harrel, Zachariah	1				
Childs, Elizabeth	1		2		5	White, Henry	1	2	1			Hamer, Mary	3	1	4		5
Rogers, Job	3	1	3			May, William (2nd)	1	1	2		1	Leonard, Jonas	1		1		
Hilldreath, David	1	3	3			Lowe, William	1	1	2			Loyd, Edward	1		4		
Gould, Daniel	1	2	3		4	White, George	1		2			Griffin, David	2	4	4		3
Dejarnet, Mumford (minors)		2			5	Hill, John	1	4	1			Williams, Roland	1	4	5		3
Kirby, William	1	2	3		7	Baylor, John	1	3	1			Hamer, Frances	1	2	3		9
Hinson, John	3	3	5		3	Ingram, Jesse	1		2			Melton, Jesse	1				
Boggan, Patrick	1	2	8		7	Ingram, John, Jr	1	1	4			Melton, John	1		5		
Lanier, William	1	1	2		10	Stanfill, John	1		3			Huntly, Thomas, Sr	2		7		
Covington, Simon	1	1	1			White, John	1		2			Rushing, Philip, Jr	1	2	2		
Johnston, William	3	6	6			Dixon, John	1	1	2			Medows, Thomas	3	4	4		
Duncan, John	2	2	3			Rushing, Robert	2	4	4			Jackson, David	1	2	1		
Gordon, Frederick	2	2	2		1	Beachum, Jesse	1		2			Wilson, Samuel	2	2	2		3
May, Lewis	1	1	1		3	Kirby, John	1		5		17	Tison, Jehu	1	6	2		2
Taylor, Charles	2	2	4			Jackson, Isaac	1	1	3		2	Gaddy, Thomas	1	4	4		
Lindsey, George	2	2	4		1	Jackson, John	1		2		1	Dale, John	1				
Caudell, Elizabeth	1		1			Hough, Hezekiah	5		5		6	Ferrell, Charles	1	1	5		
Clinton, Thomas	1		1		5	Adams, Zadock	1					Hellems, Betty			1		
Tarlton, John	1	2	2			White, Joseph	1	4	2		6	Hellems, William	1	2	4		
Pace, Stephen	2	3	5		8	Colson, Mary		3	6		17	Hellems, John	1		2		
Threadgill, John	1	5	4			Howlet, Mary	2	1	5			Hellems, Tillman	1	3	2		
Lanier, Isaac	1		1		7	Ross, Hugh	3		4		1	Hellems, Jacob	1	5	5		
Gathings, Philip	3	3	3		1	Ledbetter, Zedekiah	1	2	5		6	Head, Olive	1	2	2		
Farr, Richard, Jr	1		1			Ratliff, James	1	1	2			Beachum, William	2	1	3		1
Rushing, William	1	4	1			Ratliff, Robt C	1		2			Beachum, Susanah	1		2		
Hammonds, George	1	4	2		9	Bylue, John	1		2			Tomkins, Thomas	1		1		
Crawford, Michael	2	4	4		12	Long, Nancy			1			Price, John	1		1		2
May, William (carpenter)	1	3	2		8	Bass, Frederick, Jr				3		Curtis, Elijah	1	2	3		
						Ratliff, Zacharius	1					Madcalf, William	1	3	3		1
						Jackson, Agnes	1		5								

FAYETTE DISTRICT, ANSON COUNTY—Continued.

NAME OF HEAD OF FAMILY.	Free white males of 16 years and upward, including heads of families.	Free white males under 16 years.	Free white females, including heads of families.	All other free persons.	Slaves.	NAME OF HEAD OF FAMILY.	Free white males of 16 years and upward, including heads of families.	Free white males under 16 years.	Free white females, including heads of families.	All other free persons.	Slaves.	NAME OF HEAD OF FAMILY.	Free white males of 16 years and upward, including heads of families.	Free white males under 16 years.	Free white females, including heads of families.	All other free persons.	Slaves.
Clark, Cornelius	1		2	4		Martin, John	1		2			Moses, Samuel	1	1	2		
Carter, Benjamin	2	2	4			Phillips, Benja	2	5	2			Moses, Joshua	1	1	4		
Gatewood, Griffin	1		1			Turner, William	3	1	2		8	Tallent, Thomas	1	1	3		
Gatewood, Thomas	1					Ashcraft, John	3	2	5			King, John	2	2	4		
Wells, Barnaby	3	2	3			Ashcraft, Thomas	2	3	3			Henry, William	2	2	2		4
Green, Joseph	2	2	2			Elliott, John	1	1	3			Booth, David	1	2	3		
Curtis, Samuel	1	4	4			Young, Daniel	1	4	4		1	Ducksworth, Joseph	2	2	2		
Morris, Jesse	1		2			Rogers, William	1		1		1	Martin, Abraham	1				
Short, Daniel, Sr	1	3	5			Meadows, Job	1	1	5			Short, Daniel, Jr	1	2	2		
Lowry, Peter	1	2	6			Howell, Stephen	1	2	4			Thomas, Joseph	1				
Griffin, John	1	1	2			Meadows, Lewis	2	3	3			Adams, William			1		
Lisles, James, Sr	3	4	1			Slay, Daniel	1	2	1			Gaddy, Thomas	2		1		
Evans, John	2					Flake, Samuel	2	3	2		1	Murphy, Daniel	1	3	5		
Rushing, Richard	1	4	4			Hutcheson, William	2	2	1			Bailey, Jacob	1		1		
Self, Vincent	3	2	5		2	Tarlton, Thomas	2		2			Cooper, Benjamin	2	2	6		
Lanier, Lewis	1		6		13	Falkner, Asa	1	3	3			Bradley, Hobbs	1		3		
Pemberton, Richard	1	2	3		3	Davidson, Daniel	3	2	4			Everat, Henry	2	1	1		1
Johnston, Grisset	1	3	7			Snugs, Richard	1	2	2			Watts, Alice		2	3		
Falkner, Francis	3	1	4			Lindsey, William	1	2	5			Bylew, Henry	1	4	4		
Loyd, Edward	1		3			Tallent, Richard	1		1			Wiggins, Betty		3	4		
Craft, Frederick	1	2	4			Smith, William	1	2	4			Hudson, William	1		2		
Turner, John	1		3			Howell, Hardy	1	3	2			Mullis, Solomon	1	3	1		
Jones, Thomas	1	3	3			Howell, Joseph	1	1	2			McMillen, Amon	1	3	4		
Smith, William	2	2	4			Baxley, Mary		4	1			Watson, William, Jr	2	1	3		
Dabbs, Nathl, Jr	1		1			Hamlet, John	1	2	1			Polk, Charles	1	2	2		4
Phillips, Rueben	1	1	3			McClendon, Dennis	1	2	1			McGehee, Thomas, Jr	1	4	3		
Hinson, Elijah	1		1			Tison, Jacob	1	4	1			McGehee, James	1	6	3		
Dotey, Isaac	1	3	5			Haney, Timothy	1	2	1		1	McGehee, Thomas, Sr	2		3		
Reddish, Willimuth	2	1	4			May, William	1	1	1			Shelby, Jacob	1	1	2		
Lisles, Rebecca	2		4			Vandeford, James, Jr	1		3			Watson, William, Sr	1	3	3		
Ingram, Isam	3	5	5			Vandeford, James, Sr	2	2	3			Leaird, James	1	1	1		
Hinson, William	1	1	2		1	Vickers, Ralph	2	1	2			Godwin, John	2	2	1		
Hinson, John	1	2	3			Trull, James	1	2	3			Shelton, Beverly	1		6		
Hinson, Henry	1		1			Griffin, Jesse	1	1	2			Langley, Noah	1				
Barnes, James	3	2	4			Austin, Michael	1	2	2			Child, John	1				
Barnes, Samuel	1	1	1			Auld, Susanah			4		3	Strong, Lewis	1	1	1		
English, James	1	3	2			Lindsey, William, Jr	1	1	1			Caudell, Absalom	1		3		
May, John	3	2	4		8	Phillips, Samuel	3	2	5			Barber, Abraham	1	3	4		
Mallaugh, Sallay		1	1			Porter, Charles	2	1	2		2	Baker, John, Sr	2		1		
Frederick, Phillip	1	5	3			Benton, William	1		2			Baker, William	1	3	4		
Wallis, John	1	1	2			Brewer, George	1	2	7			Manus, Richard	2	3	4		
Yarborough, Richard	4		2			Forehand, Nehemiah	1		2			Manus, John	1	1	2		
Ingram, Joseph	1	5	2		16	Dunham, Joseph	1		1		1	Yarborough, Davis	1	3	4		1
Wallis, Nelly	1		2			Gordan, John	2	1	2			Robbins, John	1	1	3		
Swearingen, Vann	1	2	5			Lacy, Thomas	3	2	4		3	Croswell, Richmond	1		1		
Ford, Richard	3	3	3			Farmer, James	1	1	4			Hudson, Joseph	1		7		
Fallent, Moses	2	1	5			Huntly, Thomas	1	1	4			Alston, Drury	1		4		
Bass, Frederick			1	2		Bennet, William	2	1	3		1	Costillo, Michael	2		4		
Reed, Burlingham, Sr	1	1	3			Falkner, Elizabeth		2	2			Collins, William	2	1	5		
Wade, Holden	3		3		10	Arrington, Thomas	1	2	2			Yarborough, Jonathan	1	4	6		
Vining, Thomas	1	1	5		6	Smith, Robert	2	1	2			High, Gardner	1	2	3		
Wade, Jane			1		10	Howell, Joseph	1	1	2			Yarborough, Humphrey	3	2	5		
Prout, Joshua	1	1	2		9	German, John	2	1	3		1	Johnston, Solomon	1	3	2		
King, John	2	2	3			Turner, Mathew	1	1	3			McHenry, Jesse	2				
Jamieson, James	1	3	1		1	Hyde, Stephen	1	2	3		11	Broadway, Gracy	3		7		
Morris, Nathan	1		2			Tatum, Edward	1	2	2			Plunket, James	1	4	3		
Short, John	1	1	4			Cock, Odom	1	2	7			Biven, John	1	1	1		
Nance, Buckner	1		3			Kelley, Thomas	1		5			Bevin, Nathaniel	3	3	3		3
Laine, James	1		2			Sides, Henry	1	7	5			Martin, John H.	2	2	3		
Shepherd, William	3	2	2		2	Beverley, John	1	3	1			Winfield, Edward	1	1	1		
Thomas, Edmund	1		1			Pratt, William	3	2	3		1	Meadows, Jason	1	1	2		
Spencer, Honble Samuel	1	1	2		18	Ross, Walter	1	2	1			Meadows, Edward	1		2		
Everat, Thomas	1		3			Huntley, Robert	1	2	4			Rorey, Sally		1	4		
Bylue, Katy	2	3	3		5	Gulledge, William	3	3	5			Robertson, Drury	1		2		9
Ratliff, Richard	1	4	3			Rushing, Mathew	1	2	2			Meadows, Thomas	1	1	1		
Ratliff, Thomas	1	3	2			Baker, John, Jr	2		7			McDonald, Elizabeth	1	2	3		
Bailey, Thomas, Sr	3	1	4		1	Courtney, John	2	2	4			Meanly, Richard	2	2	2		9
Briley, Joseph	1	2	1			May, Pleasant	2	2	3		2	Smith, Jeremiah	2	5	5		
Bermingham, Caleb	1	1	3			Spencer, Joseph	1	3	1		2	Ramsey, John	3	1	2		
Hand, John	1	3	4			Campbell, Charles	1	3	2			Honey, Elias	1		1		
Hand, Isaac	1		1			Faircloth, James	1					Raines, Stephen	1				
Lindsey, Edward	3	3	1			Booth, David	2	2	3			Lowe, Patty	1	1	5		
Dickson, Thomas	3		2			Booth, John	1		2			Jackson, Samuel	1	1	1		
Howell, Lewis	1		3			Austin, John	1					Lewes, Jeremiah	1	5	1		
Briley, George	1	4	3			Hemby, Dennis	1	1	2			Downer, John	1	3	6		
Threadgill, Thomas	1	4	3		9	Ricketts, William	1	1	2		4	Murphy, John	1				
Vanderford, William	2	2	3			Morris, William	2	1	4			Benson, Elizabeth					
Tallent, Aron	3	2	2			Davenport, William	1	2	5			Harry, John	1	2	5		
Gray, Benjamin	1	1	3			Rushing, Solomon	1	3	4			Curtis, Thomas	1	2	4		1
Stinson, Mary	1	2	4			Rainey, David	1	3	6			Short, James	1	2	1		
Denson, Nathaniel	1	1	3			Jennings, John	1	4	4		6	Rorey, William	2	1	5		7
May, John	2	2	4		9	Brumbelow, Isaac	2	3	3			Ottery, John	2		4		
Burr, William	1	1	2			Brumbelow, Edward	3	3	4			Lissenby, John	1	4	3		
Diggs, Judy	2		2			Bennett, James	1	3	5		1	Rorey, Sarah		1	4		
Martin, Thomas	2	1	1			Brumbelow, Isaac, Jr	1	3	1			Rorey, James	1		4		
Phillips, Samuel	2	5	2			Curlee, William	1	3	4			May, John, Jr	1		1		6
Smith, Richard	1		2		6	Davis, John	1		4			Cheek, John		5	4		
Hilldreath, William	1	2	6			Falkner, Nathan	2	5	4			Willoughby, John	1	5	4		7
Ingram, Joseph, Jr	1	1	3		1	Davis, Isam	1		4		1	Hendrick, Gustavus	3		3		
Lee, William	1	2	2			Griffin, Thomas	1	5	3			Green, Gideon	1	6	4		1
Wells, George	2	1	2		3	Parker, John	1	3	5			Shivers, William	2	3	3		
Smith, Francis	1	3	2		15	Stewart, William	1	3	3			Green, Jacob	2	4	4		
Williams, Joshua	1	3	6			Hinson, John	1		2			Hinson, John	1	2	4		
Boush, Richard	1	1	2			Hinson, William	1				1	White, John					2
Jones, William	1	1	2			Hinson, Daniel	1					Lowry, Robert	2	1	3		6
Thomas, Stephen	3	2	3			Barnes, James	5		4			Jackson, Stephen	3	1	2		
Smith, Robert	1	2	9			Martin, Kinchen	1	2	1		1	Grice, Joyner	3	1	3		

FAYETTE DISTRICT, ANSON COUNTY—Continued.

NAME OF HEAD OF FAMILY.	Free white males of 16 years and upward, including heads of families.	Free white males under 16 years.	Free white females, including heads of families.	All other free persons.	Slaves.
Presley, John	1		1		
Rushing, Noah	2	1	3		2
Carlisle, William	1		4		
Scott, Nathl	2		1		2
Stokes, Jones	1		1		
Givin, Hardy	1	2	5		
Rushing, Abraham, Jr	1		3		
Harrington, Charles	1	2	5		5
Bennet, Joseph	4	1	3		
Woods, Frame	1	4	3		5
Marshall, James	3	1	8		20
Jones, William	1	1	2		
Honey, Thomas	1		1		
German, John	2	1	3		1
Robertson, Booth	1		2		
Thomas, Evan	1	4	1		
Robertson, Drury	1		2		9
Presley, Thomas	1	2	2		
Presley, Richard	1		4		
Rushing, Jacob	1	1	3		
Presley, Thomas, Sr	1		5		
Rushing, Rowland	2		3		
Halcomb, William	1		2		
Johnston, Charles	1	1	2		
Stuckey, Lucy	2		2		
Exum, William	1		2		
Hair, Elkeny	1				
Austin, John	3	1	1		
Harrel, John	1	1	3		1
Harrel, Mills	1	1	1		
Auld, John	1	4	2		23
Lytle, James	3	2	4		
White, Josiah	1		1		1
Stewart, William	1	3	3		
Cone, John	1	2	2		
Rosser, Joseph	2	3	3		4
Rushing, Mark	2	2	3		
Rushing, Sibrina		3	4		
Yoe, William	2	1	3		
Bass, Frederick, Sr					9
Wimberly, James	1		1		
Howell, Hopkin	1	1	3		
Hogan, James	3	1	3		10
Willoughby, John	1	1	5		
Thomas, Benjamin	1	5	3		
Girley, Jacob	1	4	3		
McClendon, Dennis, Sr	1	1			
McClendon, Frederick	1				
Johnston, Timothy	1	3	3		
Scarbrough, Rebecca		1	2		
Pearce, Wright	1	4	2		
Smith, Robert	2	1	3		
Horton, Robert	1	2	2		
Mercer, Jeremiah	1	1	3		
Smith, Arthur	1	5	3		1
White, John	1				
Presley, John, Sr	1	5	5		
Presley, John, Jr	1		1		
Kimbrell, Buckner	3	3	6		1
Magby, Vardray	1	4	2		
Collins, William	2	1	5		
Gurley, William	2	1	4		3
Sykes, Arthur	1		1		
Wright, Stephen	1				
Richeson, John	1		3		
Boggan, William, Jr	2		1		
Boggan, William, Sr	1		2		
Moses, Joshua	1	1	4		
Moor, Ransom	1		2		
Abercromby, Isaac	1	3	2		
Hickman, Jesse	1				
Dabbs, William	1				
Bird, Thomas	1		2		
Bird, William	1	2	5		
Creel, Thomas	2		2		
Worley, Joseph Jno	1	4	4		
Melton, Michael	1				
Rushing, William, Jr	1		2		
White, Joseph	1		1		4
Phillips, Jacob	1				
Beachum, William	2	1	3		1
Gaddy, William	1		2		
Dickerson, Leonard	1	2	2		
Vaughn, William	1	1	6		1
Reed, Burlingham, Jr	1				
Conner, Ruth	1		3		
Falkner, Francis	3	1	4		
Milton, Isam	2	2	5		
Ricketts, John	1	2	3		
Ricketts, Moses	1	2	2		
Hews, Saml	1		3		
Elliott, Robert	1	2	2		
Grimes, Charles	2	2	2		
Howell, William	2	1	6		
Thomas, Josiah	1				
Hicks, Charles	2		1		6
Wadkins, Christopher	3	1	2		1
Evans, John	3	3	4		
Magby, Rachael			1		
Finney, Thomas	1		4		
Lee, Richard	2		3		1
Bell, William	2	4	5		
Ferrell, Sarah		1	3		
Medford, John	1	1	1		
Jamieson, David	1	3	3		6
Mullis, Margaret		1	3		
Stroud, William	2		2		
Taylor, John	1	3	3		
Burrows, Joshua	2	3	4		3
Allen, John	1				
Miller, Abraham	1	1	2		
Howard, James	1	3	2		
Tomkins, Stephen	1	5	2		8
Watts, Ealsy		2	3		
Sibly, Benjamin	1				
Tomkins, Stephen, Jr	1		1		1
Churning, Bartholomew	2	1	3		1
Bayles, Ferebe	2	3	4		
Bailey, Lydia	2		1		
Bailey, Mary		2	2		
Cruize, Armsby	1	3	3		
Prescot, Rachael		1	2		
Howell, John	1	1	1		
Paul, Sarah	2	2	2		
Perret, John	1		2		
Wagers, Drury	1	2	3		
Packer, George	1	1	2		
Stanfield, Mary	1		2		
Ross, Gustavus	1	3	4		
Paul, Philip	1	1	1		
Bluford, Henry	1	3	5		
Blackford, Rachael			2		
Jones, Elizabeth		2	4		
Martin, William	2	4	4		
Purdue, Richard	1	4	1		1
Gray, David	1				
Ross, Andrew	1	3	1		
Long, Margaret		1	1		
Williams, Josiah	1		2		
Ross, Walter	1	1	3		
Mask, Mary			4		
Davidson, John	1		2		
Moore, John	2				
McDonald, Hugh	1	1	1		
Martin, Calvine	1	2	4		3
Come, John	1	2	1		
Hooker, Hardy	1		3		
Booth, John, Jr	1	1	3		
Tallent, Joshua	1				
Yoe, Nathan	1				
Lindsey, William, Jr	1	1	1		
Scago, Joseph	1	1	2		
Tallent, Aron, Jr	1	2	1		
Lowe, Daniel	1				
Gordon, Thomas	2		1		
Lisles, Joseph	1	2	1		
Lindsey, George	3	2	2		1
Parsons, Francis	1	3	7		
Tudor, Owen	1	3	4		
Jordan, Charles	2	4	5		
Akin, John, Jr	2		1		
Akin, John	1		4		3
Everat, Thomas	1		2		
Phillips, Robert	1		2		
Phillips, Mary		3	3		
Collier, Drury	2	3	3		8
Lynch, Philip	1		2		
Ramsey, John	2	2	2		
Herrin, Anna		2	4		
Robinson, Jeremiah	1	5	3		
Dickson, Thomas	2				
Howell, Lewis	1	1	3		
Melton, John	1	1	3		
White, Elinor		1	2		
Pearce, William	1	3	4		
Pearce, Desey		1	3		
Redfern, John	1	3	2		
Renfrow, Joel	1	2	5		
Hough, Amos	1	3	3		
Deason, Enoch	1	2	6		
Causley, Michael, Sr	3		2		
Taylor, Frederick	1	2	3		
Thomas, Jacob	1	1	3		
Pearce, Moses	1	2	5		
Adams, Joseph	1	2	3		
Arlige, Caleb	1	2	2		
Price, Monsier	1	2	2		
Price, Isaac	1	3	1		
Wingate, William	1	1	4		
Wingate, Rueben	2	2	1		
Pagett, Ephraim	1		5		
Shepherd, William	3	1	2		2
Cook, Charles	1	2	1		
Causley, Edward	1	1	4		
Smith, Abraham	1		2		
Adams, Elizabeth		1	2		
Medcalf, John	1		2		
Medcalf, William, Jr	1	2			
Evans, Anna			1		
Thomas, John	2	3	4		
Tomerlinson, Moses	1	4	2		
Gillen, Rebecca		1	1		
Shelby, Thomas	1	2	3		
Harris, Rebecca		2	1		
Johnston, Elizabeth			1		
Dees, Nancy			2		
Griffin, David	2	5	5		
Lee, Richard, Sr	1	1	4		
Medford, John	1		2		
Hutson, Joakin	1		4		
Stokes, William	2	4	2		
Bennet, Joseph	4	1	4		
Hamlet, John	1	1	4		
Parnell, Mary			3		
Poll, Arthur	2	1	4		
Pool, Mary			2		
Baker, Samuel	1	3	1		
Austin, John	3				
Packer, Nicholas	1		3		
Wright, Josias	2	3	2		
Gray, John	2				
Meanly, Richard	2	2	2		6
Arnett, William	1		2		
Buse, John	1		3		
McHenry, Milley		1	1		
Jackson, Samauel	1	1	5		
Hewlet, Mary	1	2	4		
Causly, Michael, Jr	1		4		
Thomas, Thomas	2	2	4		
Jones, Abraham			2		9
Phillips, John	1		1		
Dabbs, Richard	1		1		
White, Moses	1	1	3		
Temples, Frederick	2	3	2		
Moses, David	1				
Roberds, William	1		3		8
Clark, Joseph	1			4	4
Clark, Francis	1	1	1		3
Clark, Robert	1		3		2
Pickett, James	2	3	2		12
Long, Josiah	1	2			
Moore, John	2	1	7		
Blewit, William	2	3	3		
Rogers, Humphrey	4		5		2
Rogers, Richard	1	1	1		
Rogers, William	1		1		1
Martin, Thomas	1	1	1		
Tallent, Aron, Jr	1	1	1		
Long, Rueben	1				
Clark, Beverley	1	2	3		1
Ross, Andrew	1	3	3		
Williams, William	1	2	2		
Leek, Walter	1	1	3		16
Martin, William	1	4	3		
Griffin, Richard	1	4	3		
Ponyman, Melton	1				
Faro, Richard, Senr	1		2		11
Fields, Smith	2		5		
Leggett, James	1	2	2		

FAYETTE DISTRICT, CUMBERLAND COUNTY (EXCLUDING FAYETTEVILLE TOWN).

NAME OF HEAD OF FAMILY.	Free white males of 16 years and upward, including heads of families.	Free white males under 16 years.	Free white females, including heads of families.	All other free persons.	Slaves.
Atkins, Ica	4	2	2		17
Avera, Alex	4	2	6		11
Avera, Thomas	1		2		
Armstrong, Thomas	3	2	4	1	18
Anderson, William	1	3	2		
Avera, Henry	1	3	1		
Avera, William	1	4	4		3
Adams, John	3		3		
Andrews, Alfred	1	2	5		
Anderson, William	1	3	3		
Atkins, Lewis	1	2	5		10
Anderson, William	1				
Anderson, John	1		2		
Atkinson, Henry	1		1		
Anderson, James	1				
Atkinson, Charlton	2	1	1		1
Anderson, Stephen	1				
Alford, Jacob	1	2	1		
Armour, Andrew	1		2		
Arville, Duke	1				
Anderson, George	2	2	3		
Akin, Barbara		1	4		4
Armstrong, George	1	3	4		2
Anderson, Camell	1		3		
Allsobrook, John	1		2		1
Anderson, William	1	3	6		
Andrews, Andrew	1	3	6		
Barge, Lewis	2	4	3		17
Buchanan, Hector	1	1	1		7
Bethune, Farquhard	1	1	4		
Blocker, John	1		1		8
Barnes, Amos	1	4	1		
Bolling, William	2		1		1
Black, John	1	2	1		
Blocker, George	3		2		8
Blew, John	1	2	1		
Brice, Capt Duncan	4				
Booker, Samuel	2	2	4		
Buchanan, John	3	4	3		
Blew, Daniel	1	2	7		1
Bray, Bryant	1	1	2		
Beaton, Martin	3	2	4		
Bullard, James	2	1	6		
Ballard, Katy			1		
Butler, Mary	2	2	1		
Beard, John	3	2	2		6
Boush, John	2		5		
Bristow, James	1				
Burnsides, Thomas	1	1	2		
Brice, John	3	4	4		1
Bagget, Drury	1		2		
Brewer, William	1	1	4		
Brice, Niel	2		1		
Blew, Duncan	2	1	2		2
Burt, Joseph	1		1		3
Baine, Hugh	1		1		
Beaton, Archd	1		1	1	
Brown, Josiah	1	5	2		
Brown, Benjamin	1	3	1		
Battle, Randolph	1				
Battle, James	2		3		17
Burt, Young	1	2	2		6
Black, Niel	1	2	1		1
Bedsole, John	1	2	2		
Breachley, James	1				
Butler, Zachariah	1		2		2
Bohan, David	1	3	2		
Black, Duncan	1		2		
Blew, James	1				
Baker, Archd	1	6	5		
Bristow, George, Jr	1	2	1		
Brice, Daniel	3	1	4		
Blew, Malcolm	1				
Baker, Archd	2				
Bateman, William	1				
Baker, Daniel	1				
Brown, Duncan	1				
Brasswell, Benjamin	1	1	3		
Brice, Archd	1		2		
Black, Dugal	1				
Brice, Niel	2	2	4		
Blew, Malcolm	2		1		
Black, Duncan	1		3		
Brice, Duncan	3		2		13
Bullock, James	1	2	3		
Black, Hugh	1		1		3
Bethune, Collin	1	1	5		1
Blaylock, Hardy	1	1	2		
Beard, James	1	2	6		4
Bullard, Henry	1				
Baine, Hugh	3	2	3		2
Brice, Gilbert	3	3	2		7
Black, Peggy	1		2		
Brooks, Philip	1				
Brown, John	1	1	1		
Best, Harmon	1	2	4		
Brantley, James	3		2		

NAME OF HEAD OF FAMILY.	Free white males of 16 years and upward, including heads of families.	Free white males under 16 years.	Free white females, including heads of families.	All other free persons.	Slaves.
Byrum, Jacob	1		3		
Brice, Malcom	1		2		2
Brice, Archd (Piper)	1		2		2
Brice, Archd (Gum Swamp)	3	1	4		
Cook, William	3	1	1		
Carver, Jesse	1		4		9
Champion, William	1	3	4		
Campbell, Farquhard	2	3	3		50
Cox, George	3		4		
Campbell, James	2		4	3	2
Campbell, John (son Robert)	2		6		1
Clark, Daniel	1				1
Clark, Gilbert	4		2		6
Campbell, John (surveyor)	1	4	5		4
Campbell, Daniel	1		1		
Carraway, John, Sr	1		2		14
Carraway, John, Jr	1	2	2		
Curry, John	1				
Clark, Archd	2				
Campbell, Collin	1		3		
Clark, Archd	2				
Coates, Joseph	2	3	3		
Calvin, William	3		2		12
Calvin, James	2	5	2		
Cutts, Paul	1				
Carraway, William	1	2	3		
Cutts, William	1		6		
Campbell, Edward	1	2	2		
Campbell, Dugal	1	1	6		
Clark, Malcolm	1	3	5		3
Carver, Sampson	1	3	3		7
Carter, Jesse	2	2	5		
Campbell, Duncan	1		1		3
Colbraith, Niel	1		1		4
Clark, David	1		2		2
Clark, John	2	3	2		6
Campbell, Dugal	1	2	1		
Campbell, Alex	1		1		
Clark, Malcolm	1	4	3		1
Carroth, Robert	2				
Colquhoon, Laughlan	1	2	4		
Colquhoon, Duncan	1		1		
Chasin, Benjamin	1				
Carter, Abraham	1	2	4	1	
Colbraith, John	1				
Cox, Lewis	1				
Champion, John	1	1	4		
Conley, Niel	2		5		
Cameron, Absalom	1	2	2		
Clark, James	2		4		4
Cameron, Allen	1	2	3		
Colbraith, Peter	2	2	3		1
Clark, William	1	2	2		3
Cole, John	1				
Colbraith, John	1				
Clark, John	1				
Cameron, John	4	2	5		4
Colbraith, Daniel	1	2	2		
Colbraith, Daniel	2	2	2		1
Carmichael, Daniel	2	2	4		
Cotton, Jesse	1		4		
Caisey, Abraham	1				
Campbell, Alexr	1	1	2		
Cremon, John	1	2	3		
Clark, John (Saylor)	3		3		
Cade, Elizabeth		1	1		
Colbraith, Archd	2		1		1
Creed, Cornelius	1				
Chavers, Isam				8	
Campbell, Duncan	1		3		6
Carraway, Thomas	2				
Cutts, Sherod	1		2		
Clark, John (Taylor)	2	4	2		9
Campbell, Niel	1		1		
Campbell, Katy			4		1
Campbell, John (Rock Fish)	2	1	3		
Campbell, Alexr (Rock Fish)	2	1	2		
Clark, Archd	2	2	4		9
Cameron, Allen	1	4	2		
Cameron, Kennith	1	2	3		
Campbell, Laughlan	3	3	4		
Campbell, Daniel	4	2	4		4
Cox, Davenport	1	2	3		
Coleburn, Revil	1		4		
Clements, Rueben	1	3	3		
Clark, Alexr	1		1		1
Colquhoon, Malcolm	1	1	3		
Colquhoon, John	1		3		
Colquhoon, Archd	1		3		
Campbell, Mary	1		1		
Colquhoon, Mrs			2		
Colbraith, Margaret	2		3		

NAME OF HEAD OF FAMILY.	Free white males of 16 years and upward, including heads of families.	Free white males under 16 years.	Free white females, including heads of families.	All other free persons.	Slaves.
Campbell, William	2		3		
Campbell, Daniel	2		3		
Carver, Elizabeth		3	5		11
Carver, William	1	4	5		10
Corbet, Abel	1		1		1
Carver, Robert	1		7		13
Chason, Joseph	2	2	2		
Cook, Ephrim	1				
Clark, Luke	1		3		6
Booker, Isaac	1	1	3		
Broome, Luke	1	3	3		
Blaylock, Charles	3		5		
Braser, Elijah	2	1	5		3
Brown, Barnaby	1		3		
Blaylock, Richard	1		1		4
Brice, Hector	1				
Brice, Archd	1				
Blanchet, Edward	3		1		
Bristow, George, Sr	2				
Brown, Archd	2		6		
Brown, Anguish	1		3		
Brown, Niel	1	1			
Baker, John	2	4	3		
Brayford, Mary	2	1	4		
Beard, Daniel	1	2	4		3
Bone, Archd	1	3	4		
Burges, Malachai	1	1	3		2
Duglas, Kezia	1		2		
Draughan, Robert	4	3	2		11
Dyer, James	2	2	3	1	1
Driver, John	2	3	3		
Draughan, Hardy	1				
Dickerson, Thomas M	1	1	6		
Dye, Avera	1	2	1		
Denton, William	1		2		
Duffil, James	1	2	2		
Danock, Malcolm	1				
Dukemineer, Rachael	2		2		
Dunfield, Edward	1				1
Davis, Thomas	1				4
Dobbins, James	2		3		
Dunfield, James	3				
Draughan, John	1	1	3		
Denton, William	1	1	2		
Dawry, John	1	3	2		
Durden, John	1	1	1		
Dukes, John	1	1	2		
Elliott, George	2	1	8		35
Evans, David	1		1		7
Evans, Benjamin	1	2	3		
Evans, John	1		1		
Evans, Mary			1		
Eccles, Gilbert	3	2	3		7
Elkings, John	2	1	1		
Elkings, Owen	1	1	2		
Elkings, John	1	2	4		
Evans, William	1	2	5		
Everat, Demey	1		1		
Evans, Theophilus	1	5	2		9
Evans, Josiah	1		1		
Edwards, Susanah	1		4		3
Edwards, Joel	2	5	4		2
Evans, George	1	1	4		
Elwell, John	1	1	5		6
Elwell, Elizabeth			2		
Folsome, Israel	2	2	4		7
Folsome, Nathl	5		2		9
Falkner, John	1				
Ferguson, Anguish	1	2	4		
Faircloth, Caleb	2	2	1		1
Falkner, Charles	2	1	3		
Falkner, Caleb	1				
Freelove, Timothy	1	4	4		
Failops, Mary		2	1		
Fox, Thomas	1		1		
Ferguson, John	1		1		
Fennis, John	2	1	2		
Faircloth, Robert	1	2	5		
Falkner, Ephraim	1	3	5		
Frazier, Daniel	1				
Forster, William	3		2		
Forster, David	1				
Finleyson, John	1		6		
Faircloth, Caleb	1				
Ferguson, John, Jr	1	3	5		
Fenner, Joseph	2		2		
Fort, Sherod	1				
Gellespie, David	1		1		2
Gross, James	1				5
Gibson, William	2		1	1	3
Gardner, John	1		2		4
Grimes, Alexr	4	2	2		14
Grimes, Archd	1		1		
Grimes, John	1		2		4
Grimes, Daniel	1	3	3		
Grimes, Daniel	1				
Grimes, Alexr	2	1	4		4

FAYETTE DISTRICT, CUMBERLAND COUNTY (EXCLUDING FAYETTEVILLE TOWN)—Continued.

NAME OF HEAD OF FAMILY.	Free white males of 16 years and upward, including heads of families.	Free white males under 16 years.	Free white females, including heads of families.	All other free persons.	Slaves.
Gordon, William	2	1	6		17
Griffin, John	1	4	4		3
Garrick, John	1		4		
Garner, John	1	1	4		
Gillies, John	1	2	2		
Graham, John	1				
Graham, Robert	1				
Graham, Walter	1				
Graham, Niel	1				
Gordon, Robert	1	4	1		
Gregory, Alexr	2		1		11
Godfrey, William	2		3		
Graham, Daniel	1		7		1
Graham, Alexr	2	3	6		
Greer, Robert	2		1		4
Green, John	1	1	8		
Graham, Edward	1		1		
Graham, Daniel	1	3	5		
Gilmour, Stephen	2	3	4		5
Guest, Christopher	1		2		3
Gray, William	1	2	4		
Galbraith, Niel	1	5	2		8
Gaddy, James	1	3	5		
Germany, Emery	1	1	1		
Griffin, Joseph	2	1	1		
Gurley, Sarah	2		2		
Grimes, Michael	1		3		
Guest, Joseph	2	1	5		1
Grizzard, Ambrose	1	1	3		5
Galbraith, John	1				
Grimes, John	2	2	3		
Garner, Joseph	4	1	4		
Galbraith, Tarquil	1		3		4
Galbraith, Nevin	3	1	7		1
Galbraith, Duncan	1	2	2		
Graham, Arthur	4		3		
Gillies, Archd	1	3	3		
Hodge, Philemon	1	1	3		9
Howard, Edward, Sr	2	2	2		14
Hollingsworth, Samuel	7	2	3		10
Holton, Abel	1	3	3		2
Howard, Edward, Jr	2		1		2
Hadley, John	1	1	2		9
Harrisson, James	1	1	1		
Henderson, John	1		1		
Harwell, James	1	4	2		3
Harrisson, John	1	2	1		
Howell, Barton	1	2	5		
Hadly, Thomas	1		1		7
Hadly, Simon	2	3	3		12
Hazard, Thomas	1		4		
Homes, Hamer	2		3		
Horsun, Isaac	1	2	2		
Holt, Frederick	2	1	3		8
Hicks, Howell	1				
Howell, Thomas	1	4	3		
Hughes, Walter	1	2	1		
Honey, Abner	1	3	4		
Holmes, David	1	3	2		
Hollingsworth, Stephen	3		5		1
Horn, Sihon	4	4	6		
Hammonds, Ratia	2	1	4		
Howie, Samuel	1	3	5		2
Hair, William	1		2		
Hadly, Jesse	1				11
Hodge, Joseph	2	1	2		1
Herring, Catharine			3		
Holmes, Archd	2	2	4		5
Holton, Samuel	1		4		
Holton, Nathaniel	1	2	7		
Hayle, Joel	2		3		5
Hayle, Daniel	1	1	3		1
Hayle, Hosey	1	1	2		1
Hayle, James	2	4	5		
Hailey, Hansel	1	2	1		
Hust, Jesse	1	1	1		
Hust, Hezekiah	3	1	5		
Hadly, Benjamin	1	1	2		4
Hayle, James	2		9		
Hair, Ann	1	5	2		
Haney, Lewis	2		3		
Hadly, Hannah		1	1		
Jessop, Isaac	4	2	3		
Jones, Thomas	1	1	4		
Johnston, Archd	1	5	4		
Jolly, James	1				
Johnston, Alexr	1	2	3		
Johnston, Clary	1	3	3		
Johnston, Willis	1	1	4		
Johnston, Thomas	1				
Johnston, Archd	1		1		
Johnston, Zilla			1		2
Johnston, Benjamin	1	2	5		
Johnston, Barnaby	1	4	3		
Johnston, Tapley	1	1	3		2
Johnston, Archd	1				
Jones, Solomon	1	3	2		
Johnston, Randal	1		3		2
Johnston, Samuel	4	3	5		1
Johnston, John	2	4	2		
Jordan, Mead	1	2	8		
Jackson, James	3	1	5		16
Jones, Joshua	1				
Johnston, Daniel	4	2	1		
Ingram, Simon	1				
Ingram, Alexr	1				
Ingram, Jesse	1	2	2		
Jacobs, James	1				
Johnston, George	1		2		
Innis, Raymond	1	1	1		
Johnston, Arthur	1	2	5		1
Johnston, Philip	1				
Johnston, John	1		1		
Johnston, Jacob	1	1	3		
Jones, Marshall	1	1	2		
Knight, John	4	2	6		4
Kirven, Thomas	1	1	4		
Kirven, Thomas	3	1	3		
Killen, Thomas	4		3		10
Kirven, Kaid	1		3		
Killen, Adam	1		1		2
King, Nathan	1	1	1		7
Knight, William	1				
Knight, William P.	1				
Kelly, Daniel	1		1		
Kelly, Ananias	2		3		
Kerby, John	1				
Kennedy, John	1	3	1		
Kirkpatrick, William	1	1	5		8
Kennedy, William	2		2		1
Killen, William	1	4	1		
Kile, Daniel	1	1	1		
King, Joseph	1		1		1
King, Henry	1				2
Kemp, John	1	1	1		
Leslie, Hugh	1				
Layton, William	2	3	2		
Lawhorn, Lewis	1	1	7		
Lock, Leonard	2	1	2		9
Lawhorn, Norvill	2		3		
Leslie, John	1	2	4		
Leach, John	1				
Lee, Elizabeth			3		
Leslie, Coll	1				
Leslie, Duncan	1	3	2		
Leslie, Duncan	1				
Leach, Alexr	3		2		
Lord, William	1		2		14
Lamon, Niel	1	2	3		
Livingston, Robert	1	1	1		7
Leach, Niel	1		1	1	
Love, Roger	1	2	5		
Lanier, Thomas	1	1			
Leavens, Richmond	1		1		1
Lawhorn, John	1	3	3		
Maloy, John	2		1		4
Murchison, Kennith (S.)	1	3	2		
Martinleer, George	1				2
Murphy, John	2	4	4		
Maloy, Angus	1	3	2		
Mathews, William	1	2	2		3
Moore, Abel	1	3	1		
Martinleer, John	1				3
Moore, Mathew	2	5	3		
Moore, Jordan	1	2	4		
Morgan, Jesse	1				
Morrisson, Roger	1	1	2		
Mathews, Jacob	2	3	3		
Mitchell, James	2		1		
Mathews, Arthur	1	3	6		
Morrisson, Rodorick	1		5		
Mun, Alexr	1	1	4		
Monro, Arabell	2	1	2		3
Mun, Angus	2	3	3		
Mathews, Jacob	1	3	4		2
Morrisson, Norman	2				2
Morgan, Mathew	1	4	2		1
Mathews, Hardy	2	2	4		
Murray, James	1		4		
Mathews, David	1	2	2		1
Marsh, James	2	4	4		
Massey, Jordan	1		1		
Morrisson, Hugh	2		2		
Maloy, Duncan	1		3		
Montgomery, Robert	1				
Morrisson, Daniel	2		2		
Morrison, John	1		4		
Mason, John	3	3	7		
Morrisson, Daniel	1		2		
Moore, Mary		1	3		
Mitchell, Sarah	2		2		
Murray, Katy	1		4		
Monro, Patrick	3	4	4		1
Morrisson, Cain	1	2	3		
Moore, William	1		1		
Monro, John	1	1	3		
Moore, John	1	1	3		1
Murphy, John	1		3		
Martin, Alexr	1	4	1		
Moody, Thomas	1		1		
Mun, Daniel	1		3		
Morrisson, Daniel	1		2		
Monro, Niel	1	5	3		5
Moore, Aron	1	2	5		1
Morrisson, Daniel	2		2		
Morrisson, Kean	1	2	2		
Miller, John	1	1	2		
Murchison, Alexr	1	1	3		
Maine, Mary	1		3		
Mun, Niel	1				
Martin, Alexr (Rock Fish)	1	5	1		
Murphy, James	1				
Meachum, Mark	1	2	2		
Massey, John	2	1	3		
Melton, Charles	1		1		
Moore, Thomas	1	2	4		
Murray, Leonard	1	2	4		
Mitchell, Randal	1	1			1
Monro, Patrick	1	3	4		1
Murphy, Thomas	2	4	4		5
Maloy, Daniel	2	2	3		
Mun, Malcolm	1	1	1		
Mathews, Anthony	1	3	4		
Morrisson, Norman	2	1	3		
Morrisson, Daniel	1	3	3		
McKeathen, John	1	3	3		6
McNiel, Malcolm	3	2	4		6
McMurtry, James	1	1	1		
McKay, John	3	2	4		9
McLeod, Daniel	1	3	4		
McNiel, Archd	1				
McArthur, Peter	1	1	2		
McArthur, Daniel	4		5		
McAllester, Coll	3	3	4		15
McPherson, Collin	2				1
McNiel, John (Bluff)	1	1	2		8
McRae, Farquhard	2	3	2		
McNiel, Daniel (Black River)	1	2	1		8
McNiel, Coll	1	3	2		1
McRainey, Niel	2	2	3		1
McLerran, John, Sr	2	1	2		
McAllester, Alexr	5	1	7		40
McNiel, John (son Archd)	1	1	2		14
McNiel, Niel	1	3	2		3
McLeod, John	4	2	1		
McRae, Christr	1	3	5		
McNiel, Laughlan	2				6
McLerran, John, Jr	1	1	5		1
McDugal, Daniel	1		7		
McDugal, John	1	2	2		
McDugal, John (E.)	1	2	1		
McDugal, Alexr	1				
McDugal, Daniel	1				
McKay, Hugh	1				
McNiel, Elizabeth	1	2	5		
McSwaine, Anguish	1		3		
McRae, John	1	2	4		
McPherson, Jonathan	1	4	7		
McLellan, Daniel	1	1	2		
McQueen, Norman	2		2		
McAllister, Ann			3		2
McLaine, Archd	3	3	2		2
McDugal, Anguish	1				1
McPherson, William	1		4		
McPhail, Malcolm	1	4	1		
McAllister, Alexr	1		3		
McRae, Daniel	1		3		
McNiel, Henry	2		2		3
McKay, Alexr	2		3		1
McDonald, John	1	2	4		
McDuffie, Archd	3	2	4		13
McPherson, Mary			1		
McNiel, Sarah		2	2		
McNiel, Nancy		1	2		
McNicoll, Christian		3	2		
McFarland, Jennett			1		9
McGregory, Alexr	1		1		
McLeod, Malcolm	1	3	3		
McLaine, Nancy			1		
McKinney, John	2	1	2		
McLaine, Daniel	1	1	1		
McNiel, Malcolm	1	5	3		6
McDonald, Archd	1	1	1		
McDonald, Angus			2		1
McKinnen, Hector	1	3	2		2
McKinney, Mathew	2	3	4		14
McNiel, John	1	4	4		
McMillen, Gilbert	3		3		

FAYETTE DISTRICT, CUMBERLAND COUNTY (EXCLUDING FAYETTEVILLE TOWN)—Continued.

NAME OF HEAD OF FAMILY.	Free white males of 16 years and upward, including heads of families.	Free white males under 16 years.	Free white females, including heads of families.	All other free persons.	Slaves.
McLeod, Alexr	1	5	4		2
McNiel, Niel	1	1	3		
McLeod, William	1	1	5		
McDugal, Katy			2		
McKeathen, Niel	1	6	4		
McLaine, Daniel	1		2		
McKellar, John	3	1	3		
McMillen, James	1	1	3		
McLaine, John (Dobbins Creek)	1	2	5		
McLaine, Alexr	3		2		
McLaine, Daniel	1	1	4		
McDugal, John	2		4		
McNatt, Robert	3	2	4		
McCreman, Peter	1	1	3		
McSwaine, Angus	1	1	2		
McMillen, Niel	1	3	2		
McRae, Daniel	1	2	3		
McNabb, James	3	2	1		
McIntire, Duncan	1	3	1		
McIntire, Nicholas	1	1	1		
McNicoll, James	1				2
McDugal, Hugh	1				
McIntire, Duncan	2		2		
McLeod, Rodorick	2		1		
McIntosh, Daniel	2	1	4		
McAuley, Auley	2		2		
McAuley, James	1	2	3		
McRae, Philip	1		1		
McRae, Collin	2	1	1		
McDuffie, Duncan	1		1		7
McAlpin, Niel	1	1	1		3
McDuffee, George	1		1		2
McMillen, Edward	1	5	5		
McLeod, Roderick	1	1	2		
McNiel, Laughlan	1	1	5		
McNiel, Niel	1	2	5		
McNiel, Hector	1	1	6		1
McGregor, Hector	1	1	5		
McIntire, John	1				
McColl, Daniel	1	2	3		
McKinnen, Angus	1	2	3		
McPherson, Alexr	1	1	2		1
McCaller, Archd	1	4	3		
McLeod, Niel	1				
McDonald, Randal	1				
McLeod, John	1	2	1		
McDonald, Niel	2	5	2		
McAllum, Duncan	1	3	5		
McMillen, John	4	1	2		
McLeod, Norman	2		3		1
McIntire, Duncan	1	1	3		
McKinnen, Daniel	1				
McIntire, Daniel	2	5	3		
McKellar, John	1	5	1		
McKellar, Malcolm	1				
McDuffee, Alphia			2		
McAlpin, John	1	2	4		
McRae, Malcolm	1	1	2		
McLeod, Norman	1	1	1		
McLaine, John (M.)	2	4	3		14
McLaine, Archd	3	3	2		2
McLaine, Hector	1	3	4		8
McLeod, Murdock	1				
McNiel, Laughlan	1	4	8	2	
McLeod, John	2		3		
McLeod, Norman	1		1		
McKinnen, John	2		1		
McLeod, John	1	1	2		
McLaine, Daniel	1	1	2		1
McPhail, John	2	1	2		
McKay, Duncan	1	1	4		
McRae, John	1	2	4		
McRae, Rodorick	2	1	1		
McNiel, Niel	1	2	2		
McRae, Peggy			2		
McPherson, Alexr	1		2		7
McKay, Malcolm	1				9
McKay, Niel	1				6
McKay, Archd, Sr	2	3	5		19
McGugan, Archd	1		3		
McAuley, Murdock	2		2		
McKellar, Nelly	1	2	4		
McLaine, Hugh	1				1
McLaine, Murdock	1	2	4		1
McKellar, Nelly		3	3		
McPherson, John	1	2	5		1
McIntosh, Duncan	1	2	3		
McLaine, Daniel	1	1	4		1
McIntire, John	1		3		
McMillen, Mary			2		
McKeathen, Malcolm	1		4		1
McNiel, Daniel (Little R.)	1	5	2		10
McInnis, John	1	3	2		
McKellar, Duncan	3	1	3		
McNiel, Hector (son Archd)	1	2	2		6

NAME OF HEAD OF FAMILY.	Free white males of 16 years and upward, including heads of families.	Free white males under 16 years.	Free white females, including heads of families.	All other free persons.	Slaves.
McNiel, John (Skeablin)	2	3	4		
McNiel, Archd, Sr. (L. R.)	1		1		30
McDugal, Duncan	3	2	3		
McDugal, John	1	1	2		
McColl, Niel	1		2		
McKenzie, Duncan	1	1	1		
McLeod, John	1		2		
McLeod, Malcolm	1	1	1		
McSwaine, Rorey	1	2	3		
McCremon, Sarah	1	2	3		
McDaniel, Rorey	1		3		
McLaine, John	1	1	3		
McLaine, Christian	1	2	3		
McFall, Flora	1	2	3		
McLeod, Christian			5		
McLaine, Murdock	2	2	2		2
McDonald, Duncan	2	5	3		
McMillen, Archd	1	1	5		
McQueen, Timothy	2	1	1		
McMillen, Archd	1	4	4		
McDaniel, David	1	4	2		
McAlpin, Angus	2	2	2		2
McIntire, Charles	1				
McNatt, James	1	1	4		
McKeathen, Niel	1	1	2		
McDugal, Angus (Weaver)	2				
McLeod, Roderick	1	1	2		
McLain, Daniel, Jr.	1	1	3		
McLaine, John (Indian S.)	2	1	3		
McNiel, Malcolm	1	1	3		
McRae, Alexr	1	1	4		
McNiel, Niel (ShoeM)	1	3	5		
McDugal, Daniel	1				
McDaniel, Katy	2	4	3		
McLaine, Archd	1	5	2		
McSwaine, John	1		1		
McKinney, Niel	1				
McQueen, Daniel	1	2	2		
McDugal, Daniel, Sr	1	4	3		2
McDugal, Daniel, Jr	1		5		
McGee, Duncan	1				
McKeathen, Niel	1	1	2		
McDugal, Anguish	1				
McDugal, Alexr	2		5		
McKay, Archd	2		2		1
McDuffee, Malcolm	1				
McGill, Margaret	1	2	4		
McDuffee, Niel	1	2	1		
McPhail, John (Black R.)	1	2	1		1
McDaniel, Nancy	1	2	3		1
McPhail, Dugal, Sr.	2		2		1
McQueen, Daniel	2	2	2		
McLerran, Daniel	1	1	2		1
McLerran, Archd	1	1	2		
McKeathen, Daniel	1	1	4		1
McKeathen, James, Jr.	1	1	3		
McKeathen, James, Sr.	1		1		2
McIntire, Gilbert	4	2	2		
McLeod, Daniel	1		2		
McArthur, James	1	1	1		
McLellen, John	3		1		
McGugan, John	2		2		
McLerran, Duncan, Sr.	4		2		2
McPhail, Dugal, Jr.	1	1	1		
McIntire, Archd	2	1	6		
McNiel, Duncan, esqr	2	2	3	5	7
McDaniel, William Gray	1	1	4		4
McDaniel, John	1	1	2		3
McPhadging, Stephen	1	1	1	1	
McDaniel, Archd	1	1	1		
McGugan, Archd	1		3		
McPherson, Niel	1	1	2		
McSwaine, Daniel	1	1	2		
McMillen, Alexr	1	3	1		1
McColl, Dugal	1	2	5		
McDuffee, Archd	1	3	6		
Nunnery, Amos	2	2	1		
Newberry, Jesse	2	2			17
Newberry, John	1	1	4		4
Northington, John	1		1		11
Nicolson, Niel	2	1	5		
Newberry, John, Sr	1		2		
Northington, Samuel, Jr.	1	2	3		12
Newsome, Hartwell	1				
Northington, Samuel, Sr.	2	2	1		6
Northington, Jesse	1	4	2		7
Needson, Angus	1	6	2		
Overton, Titus				11	
Ocheltree, Hugh	1	1	3		6
Osborn, William	1	1	1		
Patterson, John, Jr.	1	3	3		5
Pearle, James	1	2	2		2
Porch, Solomon	2	1	3		7

NAME OF HEAD OF FAMILY.	Free white males of 16 years and upward, including heads of families.	Free white males under 16 years.	Free white females, including heads of families.	All other free persons.	Slaves.
Phares, John	4	5	5		
Pettiford, Philip				9	
Patterson, Malcolm	1	3	4		2
Perry, Robert	1		1		
Peyton, Thomas	3		1		3
Phillips, William	4		2	4	
Parker, Jacob	1	4	3		7
Parker, David	1	1	5		
Patterson, Niel	1	1	1		
Patterson, Daniel	1	3	6		
Patterson, Duncan	1		1		
Patterson, John	1	1	3		
Patterson, Daniel	1	1	4		5
Plomer, Richard	1		1		
Parker, John	3	3	5		1
Price, Gideon	1				
Pickett, Thomas	1		1		7
Pegram, Richardson	1				4
Pegram, William	1	2	4		1
Patterson, John	2	1	3		
Phares, Samuel	1	4	2		
Phares, John, Sr	1	1	4		
Patterson, Barbara			1		1
Powell, Margaret		1	3		
Po, Elizabeth		2	4		
Peterson, John	1	2	3		
Phillips, Margaret	1	3	3		
Purcell, Niel	2	3	2		
Purcell, Daniel	1	3	4		
Porter, Philip	1		2		
Parker, William	3	3	6		
Prince, Nathan	4	4	8		6
Prince, John	1				
Pope, John	5	2	3		
Parsons, Harrison	1				
Prescot, Simon	1				
Philips, Duncan, Sr	1		3		
Patterson, Daniel	1	1	3		
Reeves, Nathaniel	2	1	2		5
Reeves, John D.	1	1	1		
Reeves, Darling	1	2	2		3
Ringstaff, Adam	1		3		
Ray, John	2	2	4		4
Russell, Mark	2	2	2		7
Roberts, Philip	1	1	4		
Ray, John	1	4	1		
Reese, Jarrott	1	1	3		
Ryal, Richard	1	1	6		
Roberson, Edward	3	2	3		1
Reeves, Jesse	1				
Rover, James	1		1		
Readen, Robert	1				
Roberts, Philip	1				
Roper, Jesse	3	2	7		
Ray, Archd	1	3	2		
Ray, John	1				
Ray, Duncan	1	2	8		2
Rogers, Shadrack	2	3	2		
Ray, Malcolm	2		1		
Richards, Morris	1		3		
Rowan, Robert	2	1	4		11
Ray, Anguish	1				
Ray, Anguish	1	2			5
Raines, Anthony	1	3	5		
Rayford, Robert	1	2	3		9
Ray, John	2		3		3
Raines, Christo	1		1		
Ritcheson, Elizabeth		1	4		
Rand, William	2		4		21
Redding, Timothy	2	1	3		12
Redding, William	2	3	3		
Roberts, John	2	2	2		
Robertson, Joel	2	5	4		
Roberson, John	2		4		
Ray, Hugh	2	3	4		
Russell, Robert	1	1	2		1
Roberson, Philip	1	3	3		9
Roberson, Mark	1	2			
Redding, Nathan	1		3		
Reeves, George	1	1	2		
Ray, Niel	2		1		
Shaw, Daniel	2	5	4		1
Shaw, Collin	2	2	4		2
Shaw, Niel	1				
Shaw, Murdock	2	3	4		
Smith, Niel	1				
Stainbeck, Francis	1		1		7
Smith, David	2	5	5		42
Stansell, Peter	2		2		
Strickland, Jesse	3		8		
Shaw, Malcolm	1	1	2		
Smith, William	3	1	5		
Smith, Morris	1		3		
Starling, Robert	1	2	4		
Smith, Archd (Capt)	1	3	2		1
Sorrell, John	1	2	6		
Sorrell, Edward	1		5		
Smith, Flora		2	3		1

FAYETTE DISTRICT, CUMBERLAND COUNTY (EXCLUDING FAYETTEVILLE TOWN)—Continued.

NAME OF HEAD OF FAMILY.	Free white males of 16 years and upward, including heads of families.	Free white males under 16 years.	Free white females, including heads of families.	All other free persons.	Slaves.
Sutton, John	2		2		
Smith, Nathan	1		2		
Strahorn, Sarah	1		1		
Shaw, Dusee	3	4	4		4
Stephenson, Henry	1	1	2		1
Smith, Stephen	2	3	3		
Shaw, Norman	1	2	1		
Shaw, Sarah	1		1		
Smiley, James	2		3		
Smith, Enus	1		1		
Shaw, Daniel	2		2		6
Smiley, Jacob	1	2	2		4
Stephens, Solomon	1		1		
Stewart, George	1	1	1		1
Screws, Benjamin	1		1		
Smith, David	1		2		
Smith, Joab	1	1	3		
Smith, Drury	1	5	2		
Small, John	1		1		
Stewart, Alexr	2	1	1		
Stewart, John	2	4	4		
Smith, John	1		1		3
Sims, Isaac	1		1		
Sims, William	1	4	5		
Smith, John	1	3	4		
Smith, Lewis	1		1		
Smith, David	1	2	2		
Smith, William	1	3	4		
Smith, James	1				
Sims, James	1		2		
Sypress, Francis	1	3	2		
Stephens, William	1	1	1		6
Smith, Alexr	1		1		
Smith, John	1				
Smith, William	1	3	4		
Smith, Archd	2		3		
Smith, Hugh	1	1	3		
Stewart, Robert	2	3	1		5
Smith, Edward	1		9		1
Smith, Archd	1	1	2		
Smith, John	3	1	2		4
Smith, Duncan	1		1		4
Sullivant, William	1	2	4		
Shaw, Patrick	1	4	2		
Shaw, John	1		2		
Stewart, Daniel	1	3	2		1
Stewart, Alexr	3	1	1		
Smith, Daniel	1	1	2		
Smith, William	1		1		
Stewart, Norman	3	4	4		
Shaw, Murdock (R. F.)	1	3	4		
Smith, Peter	1				
Smith, Margaret	2		3		
Sentor, William	1	1	3		
Sentor, Stephen	1		2		
Sorrell, Lewis		2	3		
Scoggins, Sarah		2	3		
Smith, Daniel	1	1	2		
Smith, Hugh	1		3		
Shaw, Duncan	1		5		
Stewart, John	1	4	4		
Stewart, Joseph	1	2	1		
Stewart, Charles	1	1	1		1
Stewart, George	1		2		
Smith, John	1		6		
Shaw, Angus	1	2	1		
Sikes, Lamuel	1		5		
Spiva, James	1	1			
Smith, Philip	1	3	5		
Shaw, Niel, Sr	3	4	4		5
Smith, John (Black S.)	3	2	6		
Shaw, Nancy	1	1	2		
Sims, Isaac	1		2		
Starling, Robert, Jr	1		2		
Sikes, William	1	2	2		
Sawyer, Thomas	1				
Sanders, Richard	1		1		
Stewart, Alexr (B. River)	1		2		
Stewart, Daniel (E.)	1	1	2		
Smith, Patrick	2		2		
Smith, Alexr	1	1	1		
Stone, Elias	1	1	2		
Sims, Isaac (Willis's Creek)	1	2	5		2
Sims, Benjamin	2	2	5		2
Trapnell, William	1		2		1
Taylor, John	2	1	4		
Tyler, Aron	2	3	6		
Torry, David	1	4	2		2
Thompson, Peter	3	1	5		2
Turner, James	2		5		5
Tully, John	3	1	1		
Trent, Simon	2		4		
Tedder, Jesse	1		2		
Thompson, Malcolm	5	2	2		3
Tommy, Jonathan	1		8		11
Theams, William	1	4	4		
Thams, Martha	2	1	2		3
Tedder, William	1	2	3		
Thegod, George	1		2		
Taylor, Thomas	1	1	2		1
Thomas, John	1	2	2		
Torry, James	1	5	2		1
Torry, John	1		2		
Turner, William	1	1	2		
Townsend, Thomas	1	2	4		
Torry, George	2	4	4		1
Terrell, Micajah	2	4	5		4
Thompson, Niel	2	1	1		
Todd, Joseph	1	2	2		
Thomas, Philip	3	2	3		
Teel, Sampson	1		3		
Thomas, Barnaby	1				
Tucker, George	1	4	2		
Thompson, Benjamin	1	1	1		
Tully, Allen	1				
Tully, John, Jr	1				
Tedder, Thomas	2	3	6		
Taylor, Niel	1	2	2		
Taylor, Catherine		1	1		1
Thomas, William	4	1	5		
Theams, Thomas	1	2	3		
Theams, Jesse	1	2	4		1
Theams, Joseph	1	2	3		27
Vaughn, Susanah			6		
Vreeland, Henry	1				
Vennagam, John	1		2		
Vaughn, Anna	2		2		
Urquhart, Norman	1	3	5		
Urquhart, Henry	2	3	5		
Utley, William	1	2	6		
Willson, Robert	1	1	4		4
Washburn, James	1				
Watson, William	4		1		
Walker, Benjamin	3	2	4		9
Wilkerson, Niel	2	6	2		27
Williams, Isaac	1	4	1		27
Watson, John	1	3	2		5
Williams, Joel	1				21
Williams, Isaac	1	2	5		
Walker, William L	2	4	6		
Williams, Amos	1	1	3		
Watson, James	1		2		
Williams, Thomas	1	1	2		
Watson, David	3		2		
White, William	1		2		
Willson, Samuel	1		1		
Williams, Rowland	1	1			
Warner, John	1	3	4		1
Warner, Edward	1		1		
Walker, John	1	1	2		
Walker, Solomon	1	1	2		
Warner, Hardin	1	1	3		
West, Onesiphorus	3		1		
Wilder, John	1	1	4	1	
Withersby, Joab	1				
Ward, Mary		2	2		
White, William	1		2		
Watson, Henry D	1				
Williams, Samuel	1	1	2		19
Wright, Katy	1	1	5		
Wright, Duncan	1	2	5		
Williams, William	1		1		
Williamson, Frederick	1				
Williamson, Thomas	1	3	4		
Williford, John	1	1	4		
Walker, Francis	2	1	8		
Williford, Richard	1	1	2		
Wammock, Benjamin	2	2	4		7
Wilson, John	1	1	2		4
White, Henry	1	1	2		
Willis, Sarah	1		3		1
Willis, Agerton	1		3		2
Willis, Jeremiah	1	2	5		1
Willis, Benjamin	1		3		1
Young, Thomas	4	2	6		
Yarborough, Joseph	1	2	4		1
Zachary, Jonathan	1	1	1		4
Calvert, William	1		1		
Stewart, John (Tweedside)			1		4
Mullony, Jeremiah	1				
Cameron, John	1	2	3		2
Holliway, David	2	2	4		2
Johnston, Simon	1	2	5		
Murchison, Philp	1	3	2		
McLeod, John	1	3	5		
Roberts, Thomas	4	2	6		
Campbell, Malcolm	1	1	2		
Johnston, Duncan	1	1	2		1
Kelley, Angus	2		3		
Leach, Dugal	1				
McDuffee, Allen	1				
McNiel, John (Sand Hills)	2	3	5		12
McKinnen, Kennith	1	2	3		
McKeathen, John	1				
McLaine, Niel	1	2	3		
Smith, Robert	4		4		
Smith, Daniel (Capt)	1	1	3		
Priest, Mrs		2	3		
Melton, John	1		1		
McNiel, John	1		4		7
McNiel, Mary			1		1
Ocheltree, Flora			1		
McPherson, John	2		1		
McNaughton, Alexr	1		2		
Moore, Alexr	1		1		
Hope, William	1		1		
Vaughn, Elizabeth		3	4		

FAYETTE DISTRICT, FAYETTEVILLE TOWN.

NAME OF HEAD OF FAMILY.	Free white males of 16 years and upward, including heads of families.	Free white males under 16 years.	Free white females, including heads of families.	All other free persons.	Slaves.
Porterfield, James	4		2		28
McLaine, Daniel	1	2	1		
Bowell, Lewis	7	3	3		
McDugal, Angus	2				
Moore, James	4	2	6		15
Rayford, Philip	2				11
Bloodworth, James	3	5	3		18
Cook, William (& Edwards)	4	4	4		15
McLennen, Collin	1	1	4		
Carmichael, John	2	3	2		
Mitchell, Robert	1	5	2		1
Twigg, Daniel	2	2	3		
Meadows, Ann		1	1		
Doud, Thomas	1				
McMillen, Alpha		1	1		
Tannasee, Michael	1	1			
Hero, Mrs			1		2
Morfitts, Henry P	2		1		5
Parish, John	1	1	2		
Ward, Nathan & Co	3				
McFarlane, Robert	3		2		2
Baker, James	3				1
Clark & McLeran	3				
Black, Daniel	4	1	3		
Ritchie, James	4				1
Campbell, Dugal	1				
Miles, William	2		2		1
Eccles, John	3				11
Winslow, John	2		4		2
Howie, Samuel	1				
Duke, Mark	1		2		3
Staunton, Augustine	2	2	1		2
Stiert, Sebastian	2	1			2
Leonard, James	1		2		3
Anderson, David	2				1
Fullar, Samuel	4				
Stedman, Elisha	2				3
Meng, William	2				
McRae, Findley	1	1	1		
Ellington, Joel	1		1		
Trevathen, Lewis	1	1	4		
Ferguson, Alexr	1				
Norris, Robert & William	3				4
Perry & Tarbe	3				2
Young, Alexr	2	1	2		2
Bachop & Patterson	3				13
Fenno, Samuel	2	3	2		3
Dubrutz, Gabriel	2				4
Wheaton, Daniel	1				
Sissions, Isaac	1				
Lutterloh, Henry E	1				2
Malbone, Saunders	1				
Murchison, Kinnith	3	1	2		1
McLeod, John	1				
Carrol, James	1				
McMurphy, Daniel	1	2	4		3
Burklow, Isaac	5	5	5		4
Strong, Peter	2	2	1		2
England, William	2	2	7		25
McFedran, John	1		2		1
Rearden, John	1		1		2

FAYETTE DISTRICT, FAYETTEVILLE TOWN—Continued.

NAME OF HEAD OF FAMILY.	Free white males of 16 years and upward, including heads of families.	Free white males under 16 years.	Free white females, including heads of families.	All other free persons.	Slaves.
McRae, Duncan	2	1	4		
Murley, Samuel	1				
Gee, James	3	2	4		3
Burnsides, James	1		1		
Lowry, John	2	2	1		
Howat, James	3				1
Powell & Faux	5	1	1		1
Dugan, Joseph	2				
Bebee, Asa	1				
Bland, Joseph	1	1	2		
Adam, Robert	4		3		6
Riley, William	1	2	3		
Gillespie, William	1	1	1		1
Ray, Daniel	1	2	4		
Peacock, Jesse	1	3	3		4
Simpson, John	2				3
Gerry, John	1		2		1
Cant, James	2	1	1	1	
Armour, James	1	2	1		
Walker, George	2	3	3		
Morrisson, Allen	1				
Bethune, Murdock	1	1	3		
Stradford, Sally		1	2		
Golden, Richard	1	3	3		
Lasseter, James	1	1	1		
Hammonds, Isaac				5	
Oliver, William	3		2		
Bane, Hugh	1	1	1		
Story, Patrick	1	1	6		
Belile, Mary			3		
Roling, Nancy		1	1		
Roling, Anna	1	2	1		
McLeod, Daniel	1		3		
Walsh, John	3	1	5		
McMillen, Daniel	1		6		
Henderson, Catharine			2		
Murchison, Alexr	2	1	3		4
McPherson, John	1				
Johnston, Ann			2		
Richards, Morriss	1		3		
Richey, John	1	2	5		
McDonald, Hugh	1		1		
Pevee, James				1	
Cole, Mark	2	3	2	1	
Osborne, James	1	1	3		
Lockhart, James	1				
McDonald, Philip	1				
Campbell, Charles	1	1	1		
Fletcher, Rebecca		1	2		7
Kenan, Lawrence	1	1	2		
Smith, Joseph	2				
Biggam, Alexr	1				2
Hawley, Isaac	9	1	1		1
Owens, Francis	1				
McAuslan, Duncan	4				3
Mabry, Jordan	1				
Armstrong, William	1	3	5		4
Newman, Benjamin	1				
McArthur, Peter	1	3	4		
Osgood, Christo	1				
Hallet, Richard	1				
Stewart, Archd	1	1	1		
Lamon, John	2		4		
Morrisson, James	2	1	1		2
Greenlees, Robert	1				
Alves, Andrew	1	1	3		
Ellis, John	1	2	2		2
Walker, Mary				1	
Hylan, Michael	1				
Prindle, David	3				
Prindle, Joseph	1				
Walker, Elizabeth				1	
Williamson, John (doctr)	1		1	2	1
Dick, James	4	3	4	2	1
Bryant, Kedar				4	
Martin, Margaret			1	1	
Sutherland, Ann			2	3	4
Hicks, Robert	4		1		
Chisolm, Findley	1		3		
Chavers, Mary				1	
Murphy, Thomas C.	1		3		
Boyd, Sarah		1	2		
Clide, Robert	1				
Wilson, John (constable)	2	3	3		2
Mears, James	3	3	4		4
Mumford, Robeson	1	1	4		6
Wilson, John	2	1	2		5
Swarthlander, Philip	1				
Crawford, Dennis	1				
Kiddia, The Revd Mr	1	1	1		
Thackston, James	1				9
Cutlar, Roger	3	1			
Simpson, Jane			2		13
Ingram, John	1				10
Bolitho, Benjamin	1				
Dekeyser, Lee	3		6		7
Carrol, William	1				
Branton, Thomas	2	1	2		25
English, William	1				
Cochran, Richard	4		1		25
Emmet, Margaret		1	2		7
Willis, John	2		4		14
Shaw, John	1	2	3		
Lumsden, John	2	1	1		1
Elting, James & Edward	2				
Hawkins, Abraham				1	
Bowen, Luke	1	1			2
Winslow, Mary			1		5
Grove, William B.	1				17
Currants, Rachael			3		3
Sibly, John	7	2	1	1	1
Crawford, William	1	2	2		
McMillen, Jennet			2		
McKinnen, Laxy			1		
Grimes, Aphia			2		
Craig, Adam	1	2	1		1
Ranter, Minis	1	1	1		
Dye, Mary		1	2		
Van, William	2	1	7		4
Craine, Anthony	1	1	1		
Bass, William			1	5	
Keys, William	1		1		
Moon, Peter	1		1		
Sullivant, Dennis	1	2	1		
Taylor, Jacob	1	2	1		
Lundy, James	1	2	3		
Ciccaty, Holly		1	7		
Jarrott, Richard	1	5	1		
Jacobs, William				1	
White, Thomas	1		3	2	5
Glass, Thomas	1				
Almady, Joseph	1		2		2
Carman, Joshua	1			1	13
Rainey, John	1				
Lachman, Frederick	1				
McIver, Alexr	2	3	1		6
Colbraith, Niel	1				
McMurtry, James	2	1	1		
Walker, James	1	2	5		
Hay, John	1	1	3		10
Brenan, James	2				
Kelly, John	1				
Basset, Cornelius	1				
Turner, Benjamin	1		1		1
Lee, Henry	1				
McGuire, Edward	1				
Kennedy, John	1				6
Donaldson, Robert & Co.	3				12
Pyne, Joseph	3		2		2
Pierce, Oliver & Nathan	2				
Jordan & Burke	2			1	
Taylor, John Louis	1				1
Oniel, Patrick	1				
Jackson, William	1	1	2		
Green, John	1				
Naylor, John	3	2	1		3
Dudley, Guilford	2	2	4		6
Thompson, George	1	1	4		
Read, Lucy			2		
Barge, George	1	1	3		
Hargan, David	1	1	1		
Saltonstall, Gurdon F.	1	1	2		1
Peale, John	1				
Campbell, Archd	2		2		
Young, James	1	1	2		
Smith, George	1	1	2		
Campbell, Duncan	1		1		3
Mott, Joseph	1	1	3		3
Shepherd, David	3	1	5		2
Johnston, Priscilla			1		
White, James	2	2	3		
Potts, Jesse	1		2		9
McNaughton, Walter	1				
Hall, Peter	1		2		1
Langton, John	1		3		2
Work, John	1				
Charles, John	1	1	1		1
Davis, Dolphin	2	1	3		13
Campbell, Alexr	1		5		1
Newell, Ann			2	1	
Young, John	1	2	1		
McRacking, James	2	3	2		1
Warson, Thomas	1		1		2
Cook, Edmund	3	1			
Smith, John	1				
Fabre, Peter	1				
Hogg, James (of Hillsborough)					2
Campbell, Polly			2		
Spiller, Margaret			1		5
McLeod, Norman (S. Carpr)	1	1	2		
McPhail, John	1	2	1		
McPhail, Peggy			3		
McColl, Hugh	1				
Thompson, Daniel	1				
Meeks, James	1				
Tatham, Charles	1				
McIntire, Peter	1		2		
Tibathan, Elizabeth			3	4	
McArthur, Alexr	1				
Fretts, John	1				
Bittle, John	1		2		
Russell, William	1		2		7
Lamon, Jacob	1	1	1		
McCants, William	2				1
McNaughton, John	1	2	3		
Toney, John				5	
Arintz, James	2				1
Coffey, Thomas	1	1	1		
Steeley, William	1				
Callender & Dean	2				
McCall, Archd	1				
Kerr, The Revd Mr	3	2	2		3

FAYETTE DISTRICT, MOORE COUNTY.

NAME OF HEAD OF FAMILY.	Free white males of 16 years and upward, including heads of families.	Free white males under 16 years.	Free white females, including heads of families.	All other free persons.	Slaves.
Campbell, John	1	1	2		
Mathews, Thomas	7	2	3		7
McBride, Archd	1		4		
Watts, Mary			4		
Teague, William	1	2	4		
Glascock, John Melton	1	2	2		
Caddell, James	4		2		
Fry, Nathan	1		2		
Kenney, John	2	2	4		
Glascock, Patty	3	1	6		5
Tison, Cornelius	2		2		
Tison, Benjamin	1	1	3		
Doud, Mary		3	5		3
Tison, Aron	3	3	4		
Sutton, James	1		3		
Temples, Neeham	2	1	1		
Petty, Hubbard	1	5	6		
Petty, John	1	1	6		
McDaniel, Milley	3		4		
Clark, Jabas	1	1	2		
Barret, William	1	2	3		1
Quimby, John	1		2		
Overton, Thomas	1		2		14
Brown, Joseph	1	1	2		
Jones, Lucy			3		
Fagan, Richardson	1	4	4		1
Wadsworth, Jason	3	1	2		
Bettis, Elijah	2	3	5		3
Grimes, Thomas	3		3		
Grimes, Robert	2	1	1		
Caddell, Jonathan	1		4		1
McIntosh, Alexr	1		2		
Monro, Margaret		1	4		
McRae, Mary		2	2		
McKenzie, John	1	2	1		
Murchison, Kennith	1	4	4		
Hill, James	3		5		
Richeson, William	1	2	1		
McIntosh, Alexr	1	1	3		
Richeson, Drury	1	1	3		
McIntosh, Duncan	1	1	2		
Milton, Nathl	1	3	1		
McLennan, Mary	2	2	1		
Chapman, Abner	2	2	4		17
McIntosh, John	1	3	2		
McIntosh, Daniel	1	1	2		
Sinclair, John	1	4	4		
Davis, Ralph	2		1		
Bean, Richard	2	1	5		
Humphry, William	1	1	1		
Morris, Stephen	1		2		
Muse, Jesse	1	3	1		
Muse, Charity		1	5		2
Bullock, John	5		1		
Upton, Edward	2		1		
Upton, John	1	2	4		
Bullock, Francis	1		3		

FAYETTE DISTRICT, MOORE COUNTY—Continued.

NAME OF HEAD OF FAMILY.	Free white males of 16 years and upward, including heads of families.	Free white males under 16 years.	Free white females, including heads of families.	All other free persons.	Slaves.
Seale, William	1	3	4		
Dun, William	1	2	1		1
Shepherd, John	2	1	3		3
Carrol, John	2	4	3		
Coupland, William	1		1		
Bean, Elijah	1		1		
Harrington, Sion	1	4	2		
Hews, John	1				
Buie, Gilbert	1				2
Morris, Frederick	2		1		
Bettis, Elijah	3	3	4		2
Carmichael, Graziel		3	3		
Cheek, Robert	3		3		
Caddell, William	1		2		
Baker, John	1	2	4		3
Eggleton, Thomas	3	2	4		
Johnston, Philip	1	1	4		4
McIntosh, Duncan	1	1	2		
Murchison, Duncan	1	1	3		
Campbell, Duncan	1	2	3		
Ottery, Absalom	1	5	2		
McDonald, Alexr	1				
Ottery, Mary	1	3	5		
Ottery, James	1	1	3		
Fry, Benja	1	4	2		
Pitman, Demcy	1	4	7		
Cox, William	1	3	1		
Wadsworth, John	1	4	3		
Oliver, Willis	2	1	2		
Black, Archd	2	1	2		1
Mears, William	1		2		4
Danelly, William	1		1		
McIntosh, Daniel	1		4		
Watson, Hugh	1	3	1		
Watson, Robert	2	3	2		
Davis, Vincent	1		2		
McAuley, William	1	4	1		
Cook, William	1	4	5		
Smith, Everat	2	3	3		
Tidwell, Jeany			2		
Cagle, David	1		2		
Cagle, Leonard	1	7	3		
Boals, Robert	2	2	1		
Goings, William				10	
Yow, Christopher	2	5	4		
Tidwell, Samuel	1		3		
Campbell, Duncan	1	2	3		
Melton, James	1		2		
McKenzie, William	1	1	3		
Garner, Peter	1	3	2		
Love, Daniel	1	2	6		
McIntosh, Murdock	1	1	2		
McIver, Rorey	5		2		
Campbell, Mathew	2		6		
McIver, John	1	1	7		
Cagle, Henry	3	4	4		
Cockman, Joseph	1	1	3		
Moore, Edward, Jr	1		2		
Cagle, Christian	1	1	1		
Patterson, Duncan	1	3	1		
Manus, William	4	3	9		
Ballard, James	2	2	4		
Smotherman, Thomas	2	4	1		
McDonald, Hugh	2	4	3		
McLaine, John	1		2		
Underwood, George	1	4	5		
Blew, Peter	1	3	4		2
Murchison, Murdock	1				
Grimes, Daniel	2	1	1		
McIver, Duncan	3	1	2		
Blew, Duncan	1	1	2		1
Morrison, Maurice	1		2		
Overton, John, Sr	1		1		23
Fry, Joseph	2	2	6		
Ritter, Jesse	2	2	5		
Cagle, John	2	2	3		
Stubbs, Jacob	1		1		
Ray, Archd	1		1		
McNiel, Hector	3	1	3		10
Williamson, William	1	4	4		1
Manus, James	1				
Ray, James	2	2	4		
Murchison, Barbara	1	2	2		
McSwaine, Nancy		1	3		
Smith, Zachariah	2	5	1		
Stubbs, Jacob	3	1	2		
McRae, Murdock	1	2	3		
Hannon, Thomas, Jr	2		2		
Davis, William	2	3	4		6
Smith, Thomas	2	1	2		
Wallace, Everat	1		2		
McDaniel, John	1		2		
Blew, John	1	1	1		
McNiel, John	1	2	3		
McLaine, Niel	1		5		
Patterson, Daniel	1		3		2
Baker, John	2	1	2		
McLeod, Alexr	2	1	5		
McDonald, John	4		2		
Cagle, Roger	1	1	2		
Cagle, George	1		2		
Collins, Thomas, Jr	2	3	4		
Thompson, Thomas	1	5	2		
Read, William	1	2	4		
McIntosh, John	1		1		
Manus, Daniel	1	3	2		
Williamson, John	1	2	3		
Ramage, Darius	1		1		
Bethune, John	1	2	8		
Bean, Jesse	1		3		
McCaskill, Angus	3	1	2		
Oliver, Willis	1	4	2		
Schamburger, Peter	2	3	6		1
Teague, William	2	4	5		
Griffin, Jesse	1		2		1
Davis, Robert	2		4		1
Cheek, Richard	1	2	3		
McLeod, Norman	1	2	3		
Fry, George	1	2	8		
Robeson, Daniel	1	6	4		
Records, John	1		2		9
Parsons, Samuel	1		1		6
Brady, James	1	3	5		
Furrow, Leonard	1	4	5		
Dickinson, Willis	2	2	5		
Dun, Hezekiah	1	4	3		
Dun, Richard	1	2	3		
Keys, Thomas	2	7	3		
Eddins, Theophilus	1		3		
Munro, Daniel	3		1		6
Patterson, John	3	2	4		5
Murchison, Kennith	1	3	4		
Patterson, Robert	1	3	4		
Bethune, Christo	1		1		
Thomas, Keziah			1		
Tolman, Nancy		1	2		
Campbell, Alexr	2	3	5		
Caddell, John	1	2	1		
Morgan, William	1		4		
Dickinson, Robert	1	5	4		
Smith, Nathan	1		1		
Brown, Ambrose	1		2		
McDuffee, John	3	1	3		
McDonald, Flora	1	2	3		
Ritter, Thomas	1	1	2		
Muse, James	1	4	2		
Hargrove, John	1		6		
Hannon, Thomas, Sr	1	1	3		
Murray, Duncan	1	1	3		
Richeson, David	1		5		
Morgan, John	2	4	4		
Smith, William	1	1	4		
Ritter, John	1	1	2		
Coggin, Mathew	1	2	5		
Keys, John	3	2	5		
McDonald, John	1	3	2		
McDonald, William	1		4		
Newton, William	1	1	2		
Monk, Daniel	1	2	2		
Carrender, George	3	3	4		1
Ottery, Elijah	1	3	2		
McIver, Angus	1	2	1		
McCremon, Malcolm	1	3	4		
McCremon, Norman	1	1	2		
Allen, Joseph	1	3	1		
McNiel, John	1	2	3		
Cooper, Benjamin	2	3	2		
Street, Anthony	1	3	1		1
King, William	1	2	3		
Sewell, John	1	2	2		
McIver, Alexr	2	2	2		
Wordsworth, Archd	1				
Hews, William	2	1	3		
King, Stephen	1	1	4		
McKenzie, Murdock	1	1	3		
Fry, Thomas	1	2	5		
Hodges, Edmund	1	2	4		
McLeod, John	1		2		
Johnston, Duncan	1	4	3		
Collins, James	1	2	3		2
Maples, Burwell	1	1	3		
Collins, Stephen	1		2		
Smith, William	1	1	4		
Hair, William	1	3	3		
Cox, Henry	1	1	2		
Hair, Peter	1		4		
Worthy, John	1		2		
Riddle, James	1	3	6		1
Jackson, Nelson	1				
Cox, Moses	1	1	2		
Jackson, Christian	1		1		2
Jackson, Nancy		3	2		3
Jackson, Margaret			4		
Gilmour, Thomas	1	1	2		
McAuley, John, Sr	2		2		
Wicker, Jonathan	1	1	1		
Kennedy, David	1	2	1		
Kennedy, Alexr	2	6	3		
Bryant, Michael	1		2		
Wicker, Benjamin	1	1	4		
Richeson, Stephen	1	2	3		
Copher, William	1	4	4		
Hurley, Edmund	3	3	3		
Cole, Thomas	1	2	2		
Brown, Jesse	1		4		
Johnston, John	1	2	3		
Martin, Martin	2	1	1		
Dun, Bartholomew, Jr	1		2		
Dun, William	1	3	6		
Campbell, James	1	1	1		
Dun, Thomas	1	1	3		
Williams, George	1	4	2		
Buchannan, John	2	2	2		
Dun, Bartholomew, Sr	1		2		
Manus, Ambrose	1	4	3		
Cagle, George	1	2	2		
McNiel, Hector	1	1	4		
Cox, Edward	1		3		
Morgan, William	1	1	7		
Sewell, Mary	1	3	3		
Nall, Nicholas	2	1	3		8
Davis, Hardy	1	3	4		
Davis, Thomas	1	2	1		
Garner, John	1	1	2		13
Garner, Lewis	1	1	3		2
Garner, Bradley	1	1	2		1
Dun, Samuel	1		3		
McQueen, Donald	1	1	4		
McKenzie, Murdock	1	2	3		
McDonald, Sarah	1		1		
Spiva, John	1	3	4		
McAuley, Murdock	1	3	2		
McLaine, Hector	1	1	3		
Cole, John	3	3	3		
Upton, Richard	3		5		
McDonald, Donald	1	2	4		
Shuffil, John, Jr	1	5	1		
Shuffil, John, Sr	3	1	4		
Moore, James	1		1		1
Martin, Allen	1	1	1		
McDonald, Kennith	1	3	5		
Merrett, James	2	4	6		
McLeod, Anna	2	1	1		
McIntosh, Peter	1	3	3		
Grimes, George	1	1	1		
Smith, John	1	2	2		
Smith, William	1	1	1		
Carpenter, Owen	3	3	4		
Campbell, Charles	1	1	3		
Martin, William	1	2	3		
Martin, Murdock	1	1	4		1
Morrison, Kennith	1				
Harwick, Jacob	1	2	2		
Campbell, Angus	1	1	4		
Campbell, Angus	1	2	3		
Kitchen, Kintchen	1	2	7		
Cox, George	1				
Scale, William, Jr	1	3	3		
Sheals, Benjamin	2	5	3		
Evans, John	1	2	3		
Medlin, Joel	3	3	1		
Medlin, Rebecca		1	1		
Magee, Joseph	1	3	5		7
Smith, Archd	4	3	6		
Carrol, John, Esqr	3	3	5		2
Patterson, Duncan	2	3	4		
Mathews, James	2		1		
Ragsdell, Benja	1	4	2		
Ragsdell, John	4		2		
Lancaster, Hartwell	1	4	2		
Ragsdell, Richard	1	5	2		
Cole, Andrew	1	2	6		
Buie, Archd	1	2			
Price, Lewis	1	2	2		
Phillips, Burwell	1				
Phillips, Mark	1	2	2		
Moore, Onwin	1		1		
Phillips, Lewis	1	2	1		
Phillips, John	2	1	4		
Hood, Abraham	1	1	2		
Maulding, Richard	1		1		
Hews, Niel	1	3	3		
Doud, Cornelius	1				3
Medlin, John	1	2			
Davis Mathews	3	4	3		
Tyney, Priscilla		1	1		
Davis, James	1	1	2		
Alston, James	1				3
McLeod, Niel	3	1	1		
Monk, James	1	1	2		
Jackson, James	1	1	1		
Miles, Jesse	1				
Doud, Patrick	1				1
Dalrymple, Archd	1	1	3		

FAYETTE DISTRICT, MOORE COUNTY—Continued.

NAME OF HEAD OF FAMILY.	Free white males of 16 years and upward, including heads of families.	Free white males under 16 years.	Free white females, including heads of families.	All other free persons.	Slaves.
Gastor, Henry, Sr	2	1	1		14
Gastor, Henry, Jr	1	6	2		
Dalrymple, John	4		3		5
Davis, Arthur	1		2		
Seale, Charles	1	3	3		
Street, Richard	1	2	6		15
Rogers, John	2		3		
Petty, Theophilus	1				
Maples, James	1	3	3		
Edwards, Jacob	1	2	3		
Hancock, William	1		4		
Cameron, John (Taylor)	1	1	1		
Merrett, John	1				
Cheek, Randal	3		5		1
Magee, Joseph, Sr	1		2		
Holliman, Josiah	1	3	1		
Black, John	4	2	3		
Tison, Thomas	2	4	4		
McDonald, Norman	4				1
McDonald, Mary			1		
Sheals, Rueben	1	3	7		
Muse, Thomas	1		1		
Atkinson, Thomas	1				
Collins, Thomas, Sr	1		2		1
Watson, William	1	3			
Cole, Daniel	1	1	3		
Moore, David	1	1	1		
Blanchet, Robert	1	2	1		
Comer, Adam	2	4	5		
Murchison, Elizabeth			1		
Loving, Presley	1	2	4		
Gardner, William	2	2	5		
Gardner, Peter	1	2	4		
McBride, Alexr	1	1	6		
Mashburn, Samuel	1	2	4		
Campbell, Charles	2		2		
Love, John	2	2	5		
Shepherd, John, Sr	2		1		
Goings, William	1	4	5		
Campbell, Charles, Esqr	2	1	3		
Wicker, David	2	1	3		4
Baker, Archd	4	1	5		
Morgan, John	2	4	4		
Oates, Stephen	1	2	2		
Carraway, John	3	2	2		
McCallum, Duncan	1	1	2		
McDonald, Katy			2		
Buchan, John	1	4	3		1
Stubbs, John	1	1	1		
Dun, Joseph, Sr	1	1	1		6
Dun, Joseph, Jr	1	1	4		1
McRae, Mary			2	2	
Edwards, Joshua	1	3	3		
McKenzie, Margaret	1		1		
McDonald, Allen	2	3	2		
Buie, Duncan	2	5	3		
Maples, Thomas	1	2	1		1
Wilson, Moses	2		2		
Williamson, William	2	2	4		1
Williamson, John, Sr	1	2	3		
Smith, Stephen	1	1	2		
Smith, David	1		4		
Berryman, William	2	2	6		
Barret, Patience		1	4		
Cameron, John, Sr	2	3	6		6
Purnal, James	1				
Wadsworth, John	1				
Buie, Daniel	6		4		6
Wicker, David	3	1	5		5
Thomas, Thomas	1	5	2		
Sloan, Alexr	1	2	3		
Morris, Frederick	1	1	1		
Morris, Henry, Sr	1	3	3		
Morris, Peter	1	2	1		
Morris, Henry, Jr	1		1		
Morris, Mathew	1	1	1		
McRae, Duncan	1	1	2		
McFee, John	1	5	3		
Cameron, John	1	6	1		
Monk, Asbel	1				
Monro, Malcolm	1	2			2
McLeod, Niel	3	1	3		
Temple, Lewis	1		1		
McLaine, Daniel	1	1	4	1	
Maples, Josiah	2	2	3		
Overton, John (Bigg)	1	2	2		2
Maples, Marmaduke	1	2	1		
Buie, Duncan	1	1	2		5
Hayes, James	1	1	2		
Carrol, John	3	3	5		3
Hall, Ignatius	1	1	2		?
Mills, Joshua	1	1	2		
McLeod, Charles					
Campbell, Murdock	2				
Cole, Abraham	1	2	4		
Patterson, Daniel	1		2		2
Greenhill, Joseph	1	1	2		10
Gallemore, James	1	1	5		
Morrison, Norman	1	2	4		
Morrison, Alexr	2		4		
Morrison, Malcolm	2	1	3		
Monro, Alexr	1	2	3		
McLaine, Hector	1		2		
Melton, Anseel	2	1	4		
McLeod, Norman	1		2		
McLeod, Murdock	1		2		
McLeod, Daniel	2		1		
McLeod, Nancy			3	4	
McLaine, Norman	1	1	3		
Campbell, Daniel	3		7		
McAuley, Murdock	1		1		
McLeod, Kennith	1		1		
Ducksworth, Jesse	1		5		1
Myrick, Francis	1	2	2		
McDaniel, Daniel	3	1	2		
Harding, James	1	3	4		
Harding, Gabriel	1	2			2
Clark, Kennith	5		3		6
McDonald, Findley	1	4	3		
Ruebottom, Simon	1		2		
Ruebottom, Thomas	2		6		
Cagle, Jacob	1	3	3		
Gilchrist, Malcolm	3		4		2
McLeod, Malcolm	2	1	3		
Elkings, Benjamin	1	7	1		
Elkings, James	1	1	5		
Teague, William (Black)	1	3	4		
Phillips, John	1	1	4		
Brewer, Lanier	2	4	4		
Davis, Robert	2		4		1
Morris, Stephen	1		1		
Thornton, James	1	1	1		
Teague, William (Preacher)	2	4	4		
Overton, Amos	1	3	4		
Rogers, Ruth			2		
Hancock, Elizabeth	1	3	1		
Magee, Joseph	1	1	4		5
Johnston, Hezekiah	1	3	3		
McRae, Duncan	1	1	2		
McInnis, Alexr	2	5	2		
McRae, Donald	1		2		
Buie, Duncan (Red)	2		6		
Boyd, Frances			2		
Carlisle, Thomas	1	1	1		
Whitford, William B	1	1	3		
Carlisle, Hosah	1	1	1		
Carlisle, Robert	1	2	4		
McAuley, Angus	1	2	4		
McKinnen, Norman	1	4	2		
McKinnen, John	1				
McInnis, Murdock	1				
Monro, Niel	1		2		
Blanchet, John, Sr	1	1	2		
Brewer, Ambrose	2	3	4		
Jones, Rebecca		3	2		
Oliver, Moses	1				
Moore, Edward, Jr	1		1		
Overton, John (Little)	2		3		1
Carlisle, Robert	1		6		
Kelley, Hugh	3	2	4		
Coupland, John	2				
Hayes, John	2	2	2		
Davidson, David	1	2	1		
Morgan, John, Jr	1				
Mattheson, Donald	1	3			
Sewell, Lewis, Jr	2	3	5		
Sewell, Lewis, Sr	1	3	3		
Newton, Nicholas	2	1	7		1
Runnals, Fanny		1	2		
Runnals, Sarah		3	3		
Jackson, Elijah	1	4	5		
Jackson, Elizabeth	1	1	3		
Mattheson, Niel	2	2	3		
Merritt, Mark	1				
Paine, William	1	1	2		
Furr, Joseph	1	4	3		
Graham, Benjamin	5	4	2		
Stephens, Benjamin, Sr	2		5		
Stephens, John, Jr	1		2		
McFarland, Dugal	1	1	2		
Kitchen, Mathew	2	1	3		
Buchannan, Margery		1	1		
Freeman, Rueben	1	2	2		
Hillyard, John	1	2	2		
McLaine, Niel, Sr	1		5		
Hewings, Cornelius	1	2	5		
Harding, Gabriel, Jr	1		3		
Bowzer, James		4	6	1	
Dunlap, John	1	4	6		
Purkins, Thomas H	2		2		24
Gilbert, Benjamin	1				
Gilbert, Libra		3	3		
Womble, Samuel	2	3	4		
Houghton, Littleton	1	1	1		
Buie, Archd	3	1	4		8
Fields, Susanah		1	2		
Mears, John	1		1		
Brooks, William	1	5	4		1
Street, Henry	1				
McDugal, Angus	1		1		
Buie, Malcolm (Juniper)	1	1	5		
Dey, Ann	2	2	4		
Buie, Duncan (Taylor)	1	6	3		
Honeycut, Robert	1	1	2		
Ducksworth, Joseph	1	1	4		1
McIntosh, Mary			1		
Newman, Sarah		1			
Wicker, Ann			1		
Collins, Henrietta			4		1
Darke, Samuel	3	2	3		
McNiel, John	3	2	5		11
Cox, John	1	3	7		
Billings, Jasper	1	1	1		
Barrett, Solomon	1	1	1		
Demby, Joshua	1	2	3		7
Patterson, John	3		2		
Patterson, Archd	1		2		
Patterson, Donald	1				
Johnston, Duncan	3	2	4		
Patterson, John	1	1	1		
Patterson, Archd	2		1		
McDuffee, Norman	2	3	5		
McLaine, Donald	1	1	5		
McLaine, John	1		3		
McArthur, John	1				2
McMillen, Flora		1	2		
Patterson, Duncan	1	3	2		
Clark, Katy	1	1	2		
McDonald, Hugh	1				
Cooper, Jesse	1	3	2		
McFarland, Bartley	1				
Temple, Dickson	1				
Wood, Thomas	1	2	3		
Stephens, Benjamin	1	1	3		
Blanchet, John, Jr	2	1	3		
Nelson, John	1	1	2		
Harding, William (Buck)	1	2	4		
Brewer, Drury	1	3	3		
Harding, William	1	4	4		
Davis, Sarah			1	2	3
Goldston, John	1		2		
Cheek, Philip	1				
Stinson, John	2	1	3		
Smith, James	1				
McDugal, Duncan	1	1	3		
Baker, Malcolm	1				
McIver, Daniel (B. Smith)	1		1		
McLaine, John (Gasters)	1	2	4		
Brewer, Nimrod	1				
Bird, Robert	1	2	3		
Read, William	1	3	4		
McDugal, John	2	2	3		
Baker, Mary			1		
Campbell, John	1				
Sellars, Malcolm	2		2		
Oliver, Aron	2		1		
Campbell, Daniel	1	2	4		
McKenzie, Daniel	1	2	1		
Ragsdell, Daniel	1				
Watson, John	1				
Jordan, Mead	1	1	2		
Smith, William	1	2	3		
Yarborough, Benjamin	1	1	1		
Craig, John	1				
Strauther, Laurence	1		2		
Keys, Moses	1				
McAuley, John	1		1		
Stutts, John	1		1		
McDuffee, Agnes		1	2		
Dun, Isaac	1	2	4		
McLeod, Malcolm	3	1	3		
Lax, Robert	1	2	2		
Morrison, Christian		1	3		
Gillies, Archd	1				
McLeod, Kennith	1	1	2		
McKenzie, Betsy		2	2		
Lunsford, Augustine	1				
McDonald, Donald	1		1		
Jones, Silvanus	1	3	5		
McIntosh, Duncan	1	2	2		
McLeod, Alexr	3	1	2		
Brazel, George	1	3	3		
Bulling, Thomas	1	1	2		
Minyard, John	1	2	3		
Hunsucker, John	1	3	3		
Morris, John	2				
Moore, Edward, Sr	2	1	2		
Cagle, William	1	1	2		

FAYETTE DISTRICT, RICHMOND COUNTY.

NAME OF HEAD OF FAMILY.	Free white males of 16 years and upward, including heads of families.	Free white males under 16 years.	Free white females, including heads of families.	All other free persons.	Slaves.
Chambers, Moses	1	1	3		4
James, Philip	1		2		1
Wall, John	2	2	4	3	12
Haley, Randal	2		1		
McRae, Duncan	1	4	4		
McRae, Murdock	2	1	3		
Dawkins, George	1	2	2		1
Haley, Silas	1	2	2		1
Haley, William	1	2	3	1	
Moorman, Andrew	1	1	5		
Adcock, Henry	1	3	5		
Collins, George					4
Terry, Mathew	1	3	2		
Clark, Nicholas	1	2	2		
Moorman, Thomas	1	2	3		
Terry, William	2	1	1		5
Terry, James, Jr	1		1		
Long, James	1		1		
Curry, Edward	1	4	3		
Webb, Robert	2	3	2		3
Dawkins, William	1	5	4		
Mathews, John	1	1	3		
Webb, William	1	1	2		
Webb, George	2	3	3		
McRae, Malcolm	3	2	2		
McRae, Donald	2	3	3		
McRae, Christopher	1	3	2		
McRae, Alexr	2	2	4		
Sarterfield, George	1	3	5	1	
McRae, Alexr	2	4	3		
McRae, Nelly	1	3	4		
McDonald, John	1	1	1		
McRae, John	1	2	1		
McRae, Christopher	2	4	2		
Stewart, Angus	1	2	4		
McInnis, John	1	5	3		
Moorman, Archelaus	1	2	4		
Moorman, John	2		4		
Hunter, William	1	1	3		7
Terry, James	2	2	3		7
McAskill, Findley		2	3		7
Chambers, Rachael		2	3		
Perkins, Jacob	2	4	3		
Bounds, John	2	1	2		1
Cole, John	1		2		2
Usher, Thomas	1		2		
Williamson, Isaac	2	2	1		6
Robinson, William	2		1		6
Crouch, John		1	4		
Crouch, Sarah		1	3		
Jowers, George	1				
George, Thomas	3	1	6		
Jowers, Thomas	1	4	1		
Jowers, John	1	4	3		
Covington, John	1	3	4		
Cottingham, Elisha	2	1	4		
McKenzie, Kennith	1				
McKenzie, Flora			2		
McDaniel, Daniel	3		1		
McDaniel, William	1	1	4		3
Castle, Hawkins	2	1	4		
Willoughby, Edward	1	4	1		
Wilkerson, John	1	1	3		
Powell, Nathl	1	2	1		
Burt, Isbal	1		5		3
Ussery, Richard	1	2	2		
Elkings, Nathl	1	1	1		
Bennet, Peter	1		1		
Jackson, Daniel				8	
James, Philip	1		1		
Harrington, Nathl	2	2	7		
Williams, Thomas P	1	3	3		
Mathews, John	2	2	3		
Cole, John, Sr	5	2	2		12
Cole, John, Jr	1		1	1	1
Greer, George	2		4		
Riggell, Mark	1		2		7
Bond, Ailce			2		
McMillen, Dugal	2	2	3		
McMillen, John	1		1		
McMillen, Angus	1	2	2		
Gillies, John	2	3	1		
Meacham, John	2	3	2		
Robinson, Charles	3		1		12
Tarbutton, Joseph	2	2	6	1	
Tippet, Erastus	1	5	4		
Gad, Joseph, Jr	1	3	5		
Gad, Joseph, Sr	1		1		
Bounds, John	3	5	3		
Stealy, Lovick	1				
Webb, Henry	1				
Slaughter, Walter	1	5	3		4
Bolding, Rachael	1	2	3		3
Robinson, Charles, Jr	1	2	3		3
Graham, William	2	2	6		
Covington, Samuel	1	1	5		
Graham, John	1	2	3		
Jones, John, Jr	1		2		10
Blewit, Thomas	2	1	1		10
Williams, Edward	2	3	4		7
Bowen, Alexr	1		1		
Williams, William	1	2	1		
Martin, Alexr	2	1	2		
McNiel, Hector	2		2		2
McNiel, Laughlan	1		1		
Bostick, John	1		2		
Bostick, Ezra	1				
Sutton, Jeffrey			1		
Perman, John	1	1	1		
Tarbutton, Mary			1		
Williamson, Shadrack	1				
James, Enoch	1				
Wall, William	2	1	1		7
Covington, Henry	2		5		3
Covington, John, Jr	1		1		
McDonald, Donald	1	2	3		
McDonald, John	1		1		
Campbell, Richard	1	2	2		
Gibson, Nelson	3	3	4		3
Gibson, Thomas, Jr	1		2		1
Cole, Stephen	1	4	2		3
O'Bryan, Dennis	1				
O'Bryan, Laurence	2	1	3		
Gibson, James	1	2	4		1
Curry, Angus	2		3		
Curry, Daniel	1	1	3		
Martin, Daniel	1	3	3		
McKay, John	1	3	3		
Nicholson, Roger	2	1	2		
Jones, John, Sr	3	3	4		1
Jones, William	1		1		
Smiley, James	1	3	3		
Watson, Alexr	1		2		
Blew, Dugal	1	1	2		
Williams, Benjn	1	2	2		
Slaughter, Owen, Sr	1		2		
Slaughter, Zeblon	1		2		
Powell, Benjn	1	2	5		5
Willoughby, Edward	1	4	1		
Wilkerson, Samuel	1	3	3		
Phillips, Thomas	1	3	3		
Ezell, Gilliam	1	1	2		
McAskill, Kennith	1				
McAskill, Allen	1	3	3		
McIntosh, Sweny	1	4	4		3
McNair, John	1	2	3		
McAskill, Findley	1	1	2		
Strickland, Mathew	2				
Dawkins, John, Jr	1		2		
Dawkins, John, Sr	1	1	4		
Sprawls, Solomon	2	6	2		
Snead, David	1	1	2		1
Wilson, Robert	1	4	5		1
McRae, Duncan	1	3	3		
Smith, James	1	1	2		
Thomas, William	1	1	4		
Shaw, Roderick	1	2	2		
Smith, John	1	5	6		
Campbell, James, Jr	1		3		
Campbell, James, Sr	1	3	3		
Ages, Noah	1	1	2		3
McAskill, Christian	2		8		
Gun, Alexr	1				2
Ewing, John	3		1		
Beachum, Sarah		1	1		
Allred, Phineas	1	4	1		
McKay, William	2	2	1		1
Allred, Johnathan	1	1	8		
Allred, Solomon	3	2	4		
Covington, John, Sr	2	5	4		7
Burt, John	1	1	2		
Baldwin, Jesse	2		2		
Watson, James	3	1	2		
Strickland, Lott	2	2	2		
McLeod, Niel	1		2		
Cole, George	1	3	3		
Martin, Murdock	1		2		
Hunter, William, Sr	2		3		2
McDowell, John	3		2		1
Hines, Joseph	1	1	3		4
Bostick, James	4	3	5		5
Usher, Samuel	1				
Price, Darcas		1	4		
New, William	1	3	1		3
May, Abner					
Moorman, Zachariah	3	2	7		60
Harrington, Henry W	2	3	3		60
Snead, William	1	1	2		
Thomas, Simon	1	1	3		
Crawford, John	2		2		
Thomas, William, Sr	2	2	2		
Rowe, Susanah	1	2	2		
McRae, Alexr	2	2	2		
Snead, Israel	2	2	2		1
Howard, John	1	3	1		7
Mangrum, Jacob	2	2	4		1
O'Bryen, Tillotson	1	2	3		
Gullet, George	1	2	3		
Smith, James	1	3	2		9
Slaughter, George	2	2	3		
Morehead, Joseph	3	1	4		9
Chun, Silvester	1	2	5		1
Smith, Sarah, Sr	3		3		4
Houghf, James	1				8
Mask, William	2	4	4		1
McInnis, Nancy	1	1	3		
Patterson, Alexr	1		4		
Freeman, Archd	1	1	4		
Woodel, William	2	4	3		
McDaniel, James	1	2	4		
Powell, William	1		3		
Ayer, Hartwell	1	2	4		8
Newberry, Jonathan	1	2	4		
Pankey, John	4	4	4		
Long, Mary	1		3		
Cole, James	1	2	1		3
Rye, Dunn	1	2	5		
Deerman, Solomon	1	2	5		2
Handly, William	2	4	3		
McLeod, Norman	1	2	5		
McRae, Alexr	1	2	5		
Rye, Solomon	1	3	3		
Mask, John	2	4	5		1
McDonald, Malcolm	1		1		
McDonald, John	1		2		
Stanford, Samuel	1		1		
Crowson, John	1	3	3		
McKellar, Niel	1	1	2		
McFarland, John	2	2	4		
McNair, Edward	2		3		
McNair, Archd	1	1	1		
Clark, Daniel	1		1		
McNair, Niel	1		3		
McDonald, John	1	1	4		
Nicholson, Peter	1	2	2		
Freeman, Sarah			1		
Husbands, John	2	4	4		1
James, John, Jr	2	4	2		
James, Philip, Jr	1		1		
Ingram, Benjamin	1	1	5		
Shelton, Micajah	1		2		
Robinson, Charles, Jr	1				3
Nicholson, Rory	3	1	3		
Williams, Josiah	1		1		
Curry, Duncan	3		2		
Yates, Isaac	1	2	6		
Brigman, Isaac	2	2	6		
McQuig, Duncan	1		1		
McLeod, Norman	1	1	1		
Love, William	1	4	2		14
McDowel, William	1		3		1
Pursley, Charles	1	1	3		
Webb, John Turner	1	1	1		
Everat, Laurence	1	3	1		2
McRae, Farquhard	1		1		
Robertson, James	1				
Campbell, James	2	1	2		
McLeod, Rorey	3		1		
Morrison, John	3		2		
Thomas, Stephen	1	1	3		
Snead, Solomon	1	2	2		2
Smith, William	2	3	4		
Long, Benjamin	1	1	1		
Snead, Solomon	1	1	3		
Coward, Joel	1	4	1		
James, Jeminy	1		2		
Pettit, Mark	1	1	3		
Strong, John	1	1	2		2
Dixon, Richard	2		4		
Jernigan, William	1	5	3		
Webb, William	1	2	5		
Covington, Mathew	1	1	1		
McColl, Paul	1		4		
Cameron, Duncan	1	2	4		
Collins, Elisha	1	1	4		
Hines, Absalom	1		4		
McQuig, Malcom	1	2	3		
Gunn, George	1		1		
McColl, Duncan	1				
Snead, Daniel	1	1	4		
Adams, Richard	1	1	2		4
Snead, John	1	1	3		11
Slaughter, Owen, Jr	1	2	2		
Watkins, William	1	4	2		1
Stealy, John	1	5	3		
Dawkins, Samuel	2	2	4		
McColl, John	1		2		
McCormick, Hugh	1	1	3		
McColl, Dugal	1				
McColl, Duncan	1	1	3		
McColl, Donald	1		1		

FAYETTE DISTRICT, RICHMOND COUNTY—Continued.

NAME OF HEAD OF FAMILY.	Free white males of 16 years and upward, including heads of families.	Free white males under 16 years.	Free white females, including heads of families.	All other free persons.	Slaves.
McColl, Hugh	1				
McNair, Gilbert	1	1	5		1
Findley, Duncan	3	4	4		
Cole, Peter	1		1		
Webb, John	1	2	2		
Everat, Thomas	1	3	5		
McPherson, William	1	1	2		
McDonald, Donald	1		1		
McDonald, Angus	2	1	3		
Watkins, Israel	2	1	3		1
Webb, George	1	3	3		
Bolten, Benja	1	1	2		
Pemberton, John	1	2	1		4
Hunter, James	1		4		
McNair, Niel	2		2		
Smith, Daniel	3	3	5		
Husbands, William	1		3		
Mims, Thomas	2	1	7		
Haley, Isam	3	3	3	1	
Ingram, Edwin	1	1	3		2
James, John, Sr	1		3		7
Skipper, Benjamin	2		3		
Bounds, William	1		1		
Rye, Robert	1	3	2		
McAskill, Daniel	1				
McInnis, Katy			1		
McFarland, Duncan	5	4	6		6
Long, John	2	3	2		
Fairley, Archd	1	6	2		2
McKinnen, Flora	2	1	2		
McNair, Malcolm	1	2	2		
Rogers, William	1	3	4		
Snead, Philemon	1		3		
Melson, Robert	2	1	5		
Herbert, Charles	1	2	4		
Thomas, Daniel	2	4	4		
Covington, Benjamin	1	4	6		5
Denson, John	1	1	2		
Denson, Thomas	1		2		
Cameron, Daniel	1		4		
Gibson, Thomas, Sr	2	5	4		5
Brook, Valentine	1		2		
Watkins, John	1	4	6		1
Watkins, David	1				
Allman, Edward	2		3		
Spiva, Jonas	1	3	1		
Burnes, William	1	2	3		
McCormick, Hugh	2		3		
Davis, Isaac	1		1		
Hannigan, Derby	1		1		12
Dixon, Archd	1		1		
Dixon, John	1	2	2		
Hall, John	1	3	4		
Oliver, John	1	5	2		
Leviner, John	2	3	3		
Lasseter, Micajah	2	2	6		
Mays, Mathew	1				
Strickland, Archd	1		2		
Hill, Richard	3	1	5		
Deerman, Thomas	1	2	4		
Bell, Zachariah	3	2	1		
Ezell, John	1	2	4		2
Collins, Elisha	1	1	2		
Collins, George	1	2	1		
Brazell, Nathan	1	2	4		
Peaton, Peter	1	4	1		
Adcock, Thomas	1	1	2		
Martin, John	1		2		
Johnston, Archd	1		1		
McDaniel, Daniel	3	1	5		
Johnston, Lazarus	1	3	1		
Henery, Thomas	1	1	2		
Gladis, Richard	3	3	3		
Collins, Charles	1	1	1		
McRae, Christo	3	3	2		
Pettis, Mack	1		3		
Goodson, Arthur	1	1	2		
Powell, Richard	1	3	4		
McRae, John	1		2		
Powell, John	1	2	2		
Pitcock, Stephen, Sr	1	3	3		
Rye, Absalom	1	3	5		
Newberry, William, Sr	2		1		
Coleman, John	2	1	2		7
Clements, John	1	1	2		
Pickett, William, Sr	1		1		6
Pickett, James, Jr	1		2		12
Strauther, Nancy		3	1		9
Spead, John	1	2	4		13
Watkins, Thomas	1	3	5	1	
Watkins, Keziah	2	1	4		3
Buford, Daniel	1	2	1		
Wright, Jonathan	1	2	1		
Allman, Edward	1		2		
McKinnen, John	1	1	3		
Buchannan, William	2	1	6		
McLaine, John	1	2	3		

NAME OF HEAD OF FAMILY.	Free white males of 16 years and upward, including heads of families.	Free white males under 16 years.	Free white females, including heads of families.	All other free persons.	Slaves.
Hadly, William	1	2	1		
McLeod, Alexr	2	2	1		
McLeod, James	1		2		
Stone, Nicholas	1	3	3		5
Cotter, Hannah		2	4		
Johnston, William	1	6	2		
Crew, Joseph	1		1		
Tolson, William	2	1	6		
Bass, Alexr	1	4	2		
Hooks, Daniel	2	4	2		
Goodwin, Lewis	3		3		
Barnet, Carter	1	1	1		
Mathews, Charles	1	1	2		
Johnston, Thomas	1	3	4		
Marlow, Thomas	2	2	5		
McLaughlan, Daniel	4	4	4		2
McAllester, John	1	1	4		
Cole, Francis	1	1	4		
Stealy, Isaiah	1	1	4		
Cottingham, William	1	2	6		
Cottingham, Charles	1		1		
Rogers, Sarah		1	4		
Curry, Duncan	4	1	2		2
McDuffee, John	2	3	5		
McAskill, Malcolm	1	2	5		
McAskill, John	1				
McDuffee, Angus	1		5		
McDuffee, Murdock	1		1		
Honeycut, Bolling	1	1	6		
Crawford, Rebecca	1	4	2		12
Phillips, Lamuel	1				
Everat, Benjamin	1	3	2		
Bennet, William	1	1	2		
Massey, Elias	1		1		
Chambley, Clayborne	1				
Kennelly, Rueben	1				
Coleman, James	1	1	2		2
Campbell, Archd	2	1	5		
McLeod, Archd	1	1	2		
McLerran, Hugh	4				
Murdock, John	1	1	1		2
Lewis, Zachariah	1	1	3		
Curry, Duncan	2		1		
Doud, John	3	1	3		
McKay, Archd	2	3	3		
Brigman, Isaac	3	1	4		
Luvinor, John				8	
Lasseter, Micajah	3	1	4		
Shaw, Angus	1	1	5		
Monro, John	1	3	1		1
Carter, George	1				
McLennan, Daniel	1	2	4		1
Ferguson, John	1		1		
McDugal, Niel	1				
Keachey, James	1	5	3		
Keachey, John	1	2	2		1
Keachy, George	1	1	1		2
Johnston, William	2	2	4		
McInnis, John	1	1	2		
Black, John	1		3		
McDugal, Duncan	1	1	4		
Blew, Dugal	1	3	2		
Blew, Mary		1	5		
McNair, Margaret		1	2		
Graham, John	4		3		
Shaw, Murdock	1	5	2		
McDonald, Niel	4	2			
Chavers, Richard				5	
Chavers, John				7	
McAuley, Malcolm	1	2	4		
Overstreet, Silas	1	2	8		
Strickland, Mathew	1	2	4		
Strickland, Joseph	1		5		
Brigman, Ashur		2	3		
Norton, James, Sr	1	3	3		
Norton, Isam	1	1	1		
McLaughlan, Daniel	2		1		
Smith, Easter	1		2		2
Johnston, Winifred	2	2	5		
Norton, James, Jr	1	5	3		
Norton, William	1	4	2		
Pate, Stephen	1	1	2		
Patterson, James	2	2	5		1
Dunoho, Charles	1	1	2		
Hathcock, Thomas	1	2	3		
Wallis, Charity			2		
Wallis, Patty			1		
Rachael, Starling	1	1	2		
Butler, Edward	1	3	4		
Rachael, William	1	3	5		
Buie, John	1	3	3		
Chavers, Susana				3	
McDermad, John	2	1	5		
McAskill, John	1		3		
McNair, John (Hatter)	1		2		
McNair, Niel, Jr	1	1	2		
Snead, Hendley	1	1	4		3

NAME OF HEAD OF FAMILY.	Free white males of 16 years and upward, including heads of families.	Free white males under 16 years.	Free white females, including heads of families.	All other free persons.	Slaves.
Ferguson, Aphia		2	3		
Graham, Dugal	1	1	4		1
Watson, James	1		2		
Morrison, Norman	2	1	5		
McPherson, Edward	2	2	4		
McNair, Daniel	1	2	1		1
McIver, Margaret	1	4	2		
Blew, Mary		1	5		
McRainey, Allen	1	2	2		
McNair, Margaret		1	2		
McLaine, Catharine		1	5		
McFarland, Niel	1	1	4		
McLeod, Aphia		3	2		
Murchison, Flora			3		
McDermad, Daniel					
Shaw, Norman	1	1	2		
St Clair, Nancy	1		2		
Allen, James	1				
Green, Nicholas	1	1	1		1
McInnis, Findley	2	2	3		
McFarland, Peter	1	2	1		
Morrison, Angus	3	2	2		
McAskill, Daniel	1	1	2		
Campbell, Daniel	1	1	4		
McNair, John (S. Master)	1	1	1		
McLeod, Norman	1	1	3		
McLeod, Alexr	3	3	2		
McLerran, John, Sr	4	5	5		
McLerran, Laughlan	3		1		
McLerran, Duncan, Sr	3	6	4		
McLerran, Hugh, Sr	1	1	4		
Buchannan, John	1		1		
McKenzie, Duncan	1	1	1		
McLerran, Daniel	4		3		
McLerran, Hugh, Jr	1	3	2		
McMillen, Archd	3	2	6		
McLerran, Hugh	4		1		
Dove, Daniel	3	1	3		
McLerran, Duncan, Jr	3	4	3		
McGill, Angus	2	2	5		
McGill, Allen	1	1	4		
Smith, John	1		2		
Smith, Daniel	1	2	5		
Smith, Archd	2		3		
McDaniel, Alexr	1	2	1		
McNair, Roger	3		2		
McDonald, Niel	4	2	4		
Shaw, Murdock	2	4	2		
Shaw, Daniel	2	3	3		
Shaw, Angus	1		3		
McAllum, Duncan	2		1		
Oxendine, Henry				5	
Covington, William	1	5	1		
Purmair, John	1	1	1		
McQuig, Peter	1	1	2		
Boyakin, Samuel	1	1	1		
Ferguson, John	2		1		
Thompson, Hugh	1	2	1		
Dees, James	5	2	3		
McMillen, Alexr	1	2	2		
McCarne, Daniel	3	1	1		
McInnis, Malcolm	2	1	1		
Curry, Angus	2	1	4		
Thompson, Hugh	2		1		
Duglas, Daniel	2	1	6		
McRae, John	2	1	5		
Carmichael, Archd	1	2	5		
Carmichael, Dugal	1	2	4		1
McLeod, Norman	1	1	3		
McAskill, Allen	2	1	4		1
McKay, Archd	2	3	3		
Smith, Allen	1	2	2		
McRae, William	1	1	2		
McAllester, Angus	2	1	2		1
McIntire, John	2	1	2		
McIntire, Mary		3	4		
McBride, Duncan	1	4	3		
Henderson, Archd	3	8	3		
McFarland, Duncan	1	4	3		
Grimes, George	1		3		
McNair, Edward	1		2		
McNair, Roger	3		2		
Fairley, John	2		1		
Fairley, Alexr	1				2
Carmichael, Hugh	1	2	1		1
Brown, Samuel	1	1	1		
Smith, Niel	1		1		
McAskill, Daniel	2	5	3		
Carmichael, Dugal	1	1	3		
Dees, William	1	4	2		
McNair, John	1	2	2		
Murphy, John	1	2	2		
McCasell, Daniel	2	3	5		
McLaurence, Hugh	1		3		
Campbell, Angus	1	2	1		
McCalman, John	2	1	3		2
Carmichael, Daniel	1	5	5		

FAYETTE DISTRICT, RICHMOND COUNTY—Continued.

NAME OF HEAD OF FAMILY.	Free white males of 16 years and upward, including heads of families.	Free white males under 16 years.	Free white females, including heads of families.	All other free persons.	Slaves.
Martin, John	1	3	1		
McKinnen, Daniel	1	1	4		
McLerran, John	2	4	5		
McDonald, Alexr	1	2	1		
Crowson, Sarah	2		2		
Briggs, Catharine		1	2		
Gladdis, Richard	2	4	3		
Gordon, Alexr	1	4	3		
McKay, Daniel	1	1	4		
Shaw, Donald	1	4	4		
Sellars, Sampson	1	3	3		
McKay, Alexr	1	2	3		
Grimes, Edward	1	4	4		
Grimes, Levi	1	1	1		
Shaw, Angus		1	4		
Boyakin, Mathew	2	3	3		4
Spiva, Moses	1	1	3		
McAuley, Evan	2	1			
Chears, Nath¹	2	5	5		
Campbell, Angus	1	1	4		
McKinnen, Daniel	1	1	4		
Gillies, Daniel	1	4	2		
Dees, Benjᵃ, Sr	3	4	4		
Steen, James	1	4	4		
Gardner, Elias	1		2		
Tucker, John	1	2	1		
Grimes, George, Sr	1	2	4		
Wright, William	1	1	2		
Stewart, Hardy	1	1	2		
Webb, John, Sr	1	2	1		
Pankey, William	1	1	2		
Watson, Mathew	1	1	4		4
McColl, Duncan	1	1	5		
Bowen, William	3		2		
McFarland, Dugal	1		2		3
Smith, Archd	2		2		
Watson, Alexr	1	5	2		
Smith, Daniel	1	2	5		
Campbell, Daniel	1		2		
Millsap, Mathew	2	2	2		
Jernigan, David	2		2		
Morris, Valentine	2	1	7		
Stringfellow, Robert	1	1	1		
Stringfellow, William	3		3		3
Gordon, Thomas	1	1	1		1
Beasley, Daniel	1		3		
Jones, John, Jr	1		2		
Elkings, Richard	1	3	2		
Turnage, Luke	1	2	6		1
Grimes, William	3	2	6		
Steen, James	1	2	3		
Mask, Dudley	1	3	2		10
Stringfellow, Henry	1	1	3		
Mask, Pleasant M	2		3		5
Phillips, Solomon	1	3			4
Jones, Brice	1		1		2
Stainbeck, Thomas	1	3	5		7
Davis, Jonathan	1				
Rogers, James	1				
McColl, Daniel	1	3	2		
McLennen, John	1				
Walker, Thomas	1	3	1		3
Blackwell, John	1	3	5		
Parker, Benajah	2	1	3		
Whitlow, Henry	1		1		
Bennett, John	1	4	1		
Henry, Isam	1	1	1		
McRae, Donald	1	3	3		
McRae, John	1	2	1		
Smith, Malcolm	1	4	5		1
Clements, John	1	1	2		
Shepherd, John	1				
Shepherd, Jane			2		
Barnes, John	1	2	2		
Lampley, Jacob	4		3		
Allman, William	1	2	5		
Campbell, William	1	3			
Allman, John	1				
McInnis, Murdock	1	2	4		
Thompson, Thomas	1		5		
Merrett, Stephen	1	2	2		
Hall, Joel, Sr	1	2	1		
Hall, Isaac	1		3		

NAME OF HEAD OF FAMILY.	Free white males of 16 years and upward, including heads of families.	Free white males under 16 years.	Free white females, including heads of families.	All other free persons.	Slaves.
Hall, Jacob	1	1	2		
Hall, Joel, Jr	1	1			
Shaw, Norman	1	1	2		
Hall, Sarah			4		
Hall, John	2	2	4		
Green, Nicholas	1	1	1		1
Jenkins, John	2	2	4		
Bugget, John	1		1		
Slay, Nathan	1	1	2		
Slay, Thomas	1		2		
Usher, James	1	1	1		
Phillips, James	1	1	3		
McRae, Duncan	1		2		
Sumerall, Moses	1	2	2		
Williamson, Starling	2	3	3		
Thomas, William	2	3	3		
Pate, Samuel	1	2	3		1
McLaine, Charles	1	2	3		1
Pate, Thoroughgood	1	1	4		
Yates, Abraham	1		1		
Thornton, John	1		7		
Bower, Alexr	1		1		
Barlow, James	1		2		
Brown, William	1	1	2		
McColl, Donald	1	2	5		
McLeod, Roderick	1	1	1		
McRae, Daniel	1	1	2		
Campbell, John	1		2		
Burnes, Davis	2	1	5		
Hall, Joseph	1	1	2		
Hall, Joseph, Sr	1		1		
Griffin, Joseph	1		1		
Turner, Moses				7	1
Izard, William	1		3		
McGuire, William	2	1	2		
Newberry, William	3		1		
Weeks, Shubel	1				
Spurling, John	4	4	5		
McDonald, John	1		4		
McDonald, Zachariah	2	3	5		1
McInnis, John	2	2	3		
Gillies, John	2	3	2		
McPherson, William	1	1	2		
Adams, William	1				
Brown, Thomas	2	2	1		
Gibson, Amey			3	1	
McColl, Alexr	1				
Johnston, Robert	1	1	2		
Hull, Joseph	1				
McGahee, Margaret	1		1		2
Beasley, James	1	2	5		
Moore, Jethro	1		2		
Dumas, Benjamin	3	3	4		21
Dumas, Andrew	1		5		1
Fitcock, Stephin	1		1		
Walker, Thomas	1	3	1		4
Chears, Samuel	1	1	1		
Wilkerson, Samuel	1	3	4		
Alsobrook, Jesse	1	1	3		
Roberson, John	1	3	4		2
Hicks, Adrey	2	3	3		
Dumas Jeremiah	1		2		1
Rogers, Sarah		1	2		
Balding, Jonathan	1		1		
Watts, Peter, Sr	1		3		
Watts, Peter, Jr	1	2	3		
Watts, William	1		2		
Dumas, Susanah		3	1		
Huchings James	1				
Thomison, Arnold	1	1	1		1
Cameron, Hugh	1	3	4		
Jordan River	1	1	3		
Strickland, Isaac	1	1	2		
Burnes, Darius	1	2	4		
Brown, Edmund	1	3	5		
Campbell Dugal	1	3	4		
Curry, Daniel	1	3	5		
Carmichael, Daniel	2		3		
Clark, Henry	1		6		
Cason, John	1	1	1		6
Crouch, James	1				
Cockraham, Thomas	1	1	5		
Bagget, Shadrack	2	1	3		

NAME OF HEAD OF FAMILY.	Free white males of 16 years and upward, including heads of families.	Free white males under 16 years.	Free white females, including heads of families.	All other free persons.	Slaves.
Bagget, James, Sr	1		4	3	
Bagget, James, Jr	1	4	1		
Bounds, George	1	2	6		
Brown, Daniel	2		2		
Bennet, Richard	1		4		
Douglas, John	2	4	3		
Dees, Gabriel	1				
Dorkery, Thomas	2	2	3		9
Ezell, William	1	1	5		
Graham, Archd	8		3		1
Greer, James	1		1		
Hall, William, Sr	1	4	1		
Hurley, Moses	1	3	1		
Henry, Isam	1		1		
Jones, Lurana	1	2	1		
Johnston, Thomas	1	2	4		
Johnston, John	1	3	3		
Johnston, Robert	1	2	3		
Johnston, William	1				
Jowers, William	1				
McKinnen, John	1	3	5		
McKinnen, Laughlan	2		5		1
McKay, William	2	1	2		
Martin, Niel	1		1		
McIntire, Daniel	1	2	4		
McPherson, Daniel	1		2		
Hall, William, Jr	1		1		
Morrison, Anguish	3	2	3		
McNiel, Archd	1				
McCarn, Archd	1				
McCarn, Daniel	1	2	4		
McLerran, Duncan	1		3		
McKay, Daniel	1	1	4		
McLerran, Duncan, Jr	1				
McNiel, Hector	1	1	2		2
Odom, Richard	2		2		
Watson, Mathew	1				
Woodel, Mathew	1				
Williamson, Starling	1	4	3		
Walters, John, Sr	1	2	5		
Mixon, Francis	1	1	2		1
Mooreman, William	1				
McQueen, Malcolm	1	2	4		
McKay, Duncan	1	1	4		
McAuley, Rovey	2				
Morrison, John	1		1		
Snead, Ann			2		
Skipper, Barnabas	4	1	1		
Lasseter, Joseph	2	1	5		
McKay, Christian		1	3		
McRae, Farquhard	1	2	3		
Bethune, Peter	1	3	1		
Miles, William	1	3	4		
Strickland, Jesse	1				
Shepherd, Bird	1	2	8		
Stewart, Thomas				1	
Bolton, William	1	3	4		
Bennet, Peter	1	1			
Lyon, John	1				
McLeod, Ann		1	2		
McColl, Daniel, Jr	1	1	2		
McInnis, Duncan	1		2		
McColl, Daniel, Sr	2				
Morehead, Turner	1				
McColl, Duncan	1	1	3		
McRae, Duncan	1	2	4		
McRae, John	1		2		
Norman, Henry	1	1	2		
Stephens, Hardy	1		2		
Sarterfield, William	1	1	3		
Bounds, Stephen	1				
Bennet, Letitia		2	3		
Curry, Katy		1	3		
Thomas, Lewis	1	3	8		
Womble, James	1				
McKinnen, Hugh	1	1	3		
Pearce, Rebecca		2	4		
Johnston, Moses	2	1	1		
Lipscomb, Anderson (of Virginia)					6
Yates, James	1	2	6		
Blackwell, John	2	2	4		
Howard, Hiram	1		2		

FAYETTE DISTRICT, ROBESON COUNTY.

NAME OF HEAD OF FAMILY.	Free white males of 16 years and upward, including heads of families.	Free white males under 16 years.	Free white females, including heads of families.	All other free persons.	Slaves.
Chisolm, John	1	3	1		
Lamon, John	3	1	2		
McMillen, Daniel	1		3		
Lamon, Kennith	1	1	2		
McKenzie, Gilbert	1	2	5		
McDonald, John	1	1	3		
McMillen, William	3	4	5		
Blew, John	1		5		

NAME OF HEAD OF FAMILY.	Free white males of 16 years and upward, including heads of families.	Free white males under 16 years.	Free white females, including heads of families.	All other free persons.	Slaves.
Thompson, Nepsy	2		5		
Patterson, Malcolm	1		3		
McMillen, John	1	3	3		
McAlpin, Alexr	1	4	2		
Taggy, Betsey			3		
Little, Archd	1	3	4		
Smith, James	1	2	5		
Gilchrist, John	2	4	4		4

NAME OF HEAD OF FAMILY.	Free white males of 16 years and upward, including heads of families.	Free white males under 16 years.	Free white females, including heads of families.	All other free persons.	Slaves.
Little, Robert	1		2		
McKenzie, Kennith	1	3	4		
Councill, Charles	1	5	3		
Councill, John	1	1	5		5
Sims, Robert	2	1	5		
Stogner, John	1	1	3		2
McKinley, Daniel	1	1	4		
Mercer, Henry	2	1	2		1

FAYETTE DISTRICT, ROBESON COUNTY—Continued.

NAME OF HEAD OF FAMILY.	Free white males of 16 years and upward, including heads of families.	Free white males under 16 years.	Free white females, including heads of families.	All other free persons.	Slaves.
Mercer, Peter	1	1	3		
McNair, Duncan	1	3	1		
McMillen, Archᵈ	1	2	2		
Brice, Duncan	2	1	2		1
McDonald, Margaret		2	1		
Eikner, George	1	1	1		
Kennedy, Isaac	2	2	5		2
Powell, Ambrose	3	3	4		1
Crawford, Peter	1	1	3		
McSwaine, Roger	1		5		
Moore, William	3	1	8		1
Crawford, Duncan	1	3	2		
Stephens, James	1	1	3		
Williams, John	1	2	3		
Upton, Robert	2		5		
Musslewhight, Jesse	1	1	6		
Moss, Nancy		1	2		
Johnston, John	1	2	4		1
Baxley, William	2	6	5		
Smith, John	1	2	6		
Baxley, Job	1	2	1		
Powell, Lewis	1	3	5		
Powell, Joseph	1		2		
Powell, Katy	1		2		
Musslewhite, Leonard	1	1	3		
Baxley, Edmund	2	2	5		
Musslewhite, Nathan	1	1	6		
Musslewhite, Mary			4		3
Musslewhite, Thomas	1	3	1		
Hodge, Joseph	1	3	6		
Pintleton, Hiram	1	1	3		
Herring, Mary			3		
Hammonds, John				9	
Harrell, Jesse	2	2	3		1
Calvin, Francis	1	1	3		
Sizemore, Henry	1		5		
Colly, Thomas	1		1		
Humphrey, Lucy	3	1	2	1	
Acock, William	2		2		
Edwards, James	1	2	1		
Humphrey, William	1		4	1	
Drury, Edy		2	5		
Jackson, John	1		2		
Lee, John, Sʳ	1		3		
Rozier, John	1		2		
Rozier, Briton	1	1	2		
Barlow, Mash	1	1	3		
Bullard, Elizabeth	2		4		
Jackson, Thomas	1		2		
Spears, Harris	2	2	3		1
Edwards, Frebe	1	1	3		
Sea, Nancy			4		
Musslewhite, Milby	1	4	3		
Ellis, William	1	1	3		
Thomas, Lewis	3		2		
Casa, Charity			1		2
Blount, Samuel	1	1	1		
Clyborne, John	1	1	1		1
Farro, Joshua	1	4	4		
Willis, George, Jʳ	1		1		
Baker, Sion	1	1	2		
Humphrey, John	1	1	2		
Evers, Betty			3		
Willis, George, Sʳ	3	2	2		7
Willis, Robert	1	1	2		
Willis, Agerton	1		1		2
Willis, Simon	1		1		
Miller, John	1		1		
Odom, William	3		2		1
Watson, Charles	2	4	3		
Thompson, William (B. Swamp)	1	6	1	1	5
Lockileer, Randal				10	
Kersey, America			8		
Lockileer, John				1	
Cade, John	2	2	3	5	17
Facundus, Abraham	1				
Kennedy, William	1	1	3	1	1
Cade, Stephen	1	2	3	1	3
Smith, Samuel (of Nuse)					13
Thompson, Niel	1	2	4		
McCormick, John	1	3	8		1
Murphy, Edward	3	2	3		
McAllester, Malcolm	1				
Powell, Elizabeth		3	1		
Hunt, Ferebe			2		
Braswell, Arthur	2	1	4	1	2
Brown, Solomon	2	3	5		
Pittman, Nathan	5	3	2		
Pittman, Newett	2		1	1	
Brasswell, David	1		3		
Hunt, Alexʳ	1	3	2		
Chavers, Ishmael				10	
Taylor, William	1	2	2		
Barnes, Josiah	1	2	5		7
Hedgepath, Charity		1	4		1
Hedgepath, Peter	1		1		
Barnes, Abraham	1				8
Barnes, Elias	1	2	4	6	8
Smith, Benjamin	1		1		
Rhodes, Jacob	1				2
Willis, John	5	2	4	1	14
Moore, William (L. Town)	3		2		4
Hall, Enoch	2	2	4		1
Lewis, David	3	6	7		
McMillen, Neven	2	2	3		
Ferguson, John	1		1		
Ferguson, James	3		2		
McGill, Niel	2		3	4	
Love, Alexʳ	2	2	1		
Johnston, Angus	1		1		
Gillies, Niel	2	1	2		
McFater, Donald	1	2	2		
Jones, Zachariah	1	1	6		
Patterson, Alex	1		3		
McBride, Archᵈ	2	3	4		
Hall, Instance	1	2	3		
Hall, Lewis	2	3	2		
McGill, Roger	1		1		1
Curry, John	1				
Murphy, Niel	1	3	5		
Duncan, James	3	1	5		
Brown, Hugh	1	2	1		2
Clark, Nathan	1	2	2		
Hall, Lewis, Jʳ	1	5	3		
Hodges, Jesse	1				
Wilkerson, Angus	4	2	5		
Curry, Raynald	2		4		
Smith, Archᵈ, Jʳ	2	3	4		
Murphy, Archᵈ	2	3	4		
McNiel, William	2		3		1
Watson, Jennett, Sʳ	1		3		
Watson, Jennett, Jʳ			3		
Lamon, Malcolm	1	1	1		
McLaughlan, John	3	1	4		
McMillen, Daniel	2	2	4		
Ferguson, John	2	2	2		
Ferguson, James, Jʳ	1		2		
Wilkerson, Duncan	1	3	2		
Fairley, Robert	1		1		
McEachran, Patrick	3	2	4		2
Watson, John	1	2	3		
Watson, James	2	1	5		
McPherson, Randal	1		2		
Hews, Duncan	1		1		
Smith, James	1		2		5
McMillen, Archᵈ	1	1	3		4
McLeod, Alexʳ	1		6		
Wilkerson, Robert	1		2		
McArthur, Alexʳ	1	3	5		
McFaul, Mary	2		4		3
Patterson, John	1	2	4		
McLaine, Niel	1		3		
Crawford, Niel	3				
Boyd, James	1	2	4		
McLaine, John	1	1	4		
Gillies, Angus	3	2	5		
McNiel, Malcolm	2				
Colbraith, Angus	1	2	3		
Bird, Benjamin	1	2	6		
Teaster, Nathˡ	4	1	2		
Tutor, Dread				3	
McNiel, Tarquil	2	1	3		9
Fennell, Ephraim	2	3	4		
Colley, George	2		5		
Hall, Isaac	2	1	3		
Shaw, Malcolm	1		1		
Gillies, Daniel	1		3		
Brown, Niel	2	5	2		2
Morrison, Archᵈ	1	1	5		
Morrison, Norman	1	1	5		
Grice, Robert	1	2	5		
Strickland, Abraham	1	2	3		
McNiel, Hector	1	2	5		4
McRainey, John	2		6		
McLaine, Hector	1	3	3		
McRainey, Daniel	1	2	5		
McNiel Danold	3	3	2		1
McBride, John	2		3		
McBride, Archᵈ	1				
Lockileer, John				4	
McAlpin, Malcolm	1	6	3		
Bussell, William				5	
Johnston, Emanuel	1				
Kersey, James	1				
McFater, Christian			2	3	
McArthur, John	2	2	5		1
Lockileer, Joseph				6	
Lockileer, Jacob				6	
Lockileer, Robert				9	
Lockileer, William				11	
McNiel, John	1	2	6		
Ard, Thomas	1	3	4		6
Fort, James	1				6
Smith, Patrick	1	2	2		1
McNiel, Niel	1	2	1		
McBride, Duncan	1	1	1		
Lockileer, Malcolm				6	
Brooks, Betty				4	
Kersey, Redding	1				
Baker, Niel	1	1	8		
Monro, Malcolm	3	2	3		
McMillen, John	1	6	3		1
McLaughlan, Daniel	1	2	3		
Oxendine, John				1	
Strickland, Aron	3	2	2		
Overstreet, Ferebe	2	3	2		
Ray, Angus	3		1		
Oxendine, Charles				1	2
Campbell, Hugh	2		1	2	2
Henderson, John	1		1		
Henderson, Alexʳ	1				
McLeod, Malcolm	1	2	1		
McEachran, John	2	3	4		
Campbell, Catharine	2		3		4
Wilkes, Francis	1	5	5		
McLaughlan, Duncan	1				
McFaul, Daniel	1	2	2		2
Campbell, John	1		3		4
McSwaine, Donald	1		1		
Douglas, Donald	3	2	1		
McBride, Angus	1				
McMillen, Duncan	1				
Wilkerson, Archᵈ	1				
Smith, Daniel	1				
McDugal, Archᵈ	1		5		
Gilchrist, William	1		3		
Ferguson, Angus	1		2		
Wilkes, John	1		3		
Campbell, Robert	1				
Gillies, John	1		2		
Wilkerson, Edward	1		1		
Coward, John	1				
Murphy, Duncan	1				
Lockileer, Samuel				1	
Johnston, Isaac				1	5
Valentine, Charles				5	
McPherson, Duncan	1				
McLarty, Niel	2	1	2		
Brown, Niel, Esqʳ	1	1	7		2
Harrell, Jesse	1	3	3		1
Harrell, Elisha	1	2	4		5
Braveboy, Lydia				7	
Jackson, Thomas	3		2		
Fort, Joseph	1				4
Oquin, Tarler	3	5	2		
Oquin, John	1	4	4		
Best, Bryant	1	2	4		
Best, Patience			4		
Buie, John (Farmer)	1	3	4		1
McDugal, Alexʳ	2	1	2		
Best, John	1	2	2		
Oquin, Charity	2	2	3	1	
Baker, Sion	1	1	2		
McNabb, James	2	4	4		
McKeller, Peter	1	2	5		
McNiel, Godfrey	4	5	4		
Spear, Harris	2	2	3		1
Jenkins, Benjᵃ	1		1		
Jenkins, Lewis	3		2		
Powell, Ambrose	1	3	5		
Powell, William	1	1	5		
Little, Archᵈ	1		3		
Edwards, Ferebe		2	3		
Crawford, Duncan	1	3	2		
McDuffee, Duncan	1	2	1		
McDuffee, Archᵈ	1	2	3		
Carlisle, Saunders	2	2	4		
Hammonds, Jacob				4	
Campbell, Donald	3	3	4		3
Patterson, Donald	1	1	3		1
Fort, John	1	1	1		10
Black, James	1	2	5		
Black, Mary			4		
Black, Angus	1		4		
McCorvey, Niel	4		5		
Buie, Niel	2	1	2		7
Tarver, Jacob, Sʳ	2	4	3		1
Edwards, James	1	2	1		
McDonald, Aphia		4	2		
Buchannan, Peter	2	2	2		
Oquin, Ezekiel	1				
Smith, Archᵈ	1	3	4		1
McKay, Thomas	1				
Powell, Joseph	5	4	4		1
Biggs, James, Sʳ	3	2	4		
Little, John	3	2	4		3
Grimes, Duncan	1		3		
Scott, John			3	1	
Newberry, Joseph	1	2	2		

FAYETTE DISTRICT, ROBESON COUNTY—Continued.

NAME OF HEAD OF FAMILY.	Free white males of 16 years and upward, including heads of families.	Free white males under 16 years.	Free white females, including heads of families.	All other free persons.	Slaves.
Crawford, Peter	1	1	3		
Brown, William	1	2	5		
McSwaine, Rodorick	2		6		
McSwaine, Angus	1	1	2		
McSwaine, Donald	1		3		
Little, Alexr	3		3		
McLaughlan, Dugal	1	2	6		
Biggs, Samuel	1		2		
Revil, Burwell				1	
Humphrey, John	1	1	2		
Moore, James	1		1		3
Ford, John	1		1		3
Buie, John (S. Master)	1	4	7		
McEachran, Robert	3	1	9		
Brown, Angus	3		1		1
Pitman, Hannah	1		1		
Oxendine, Charles				11	
Lowry, James				6	3
Kelly, Duncan	2	1	2		
Ray, Angus	4	5	2		
McGill, Archd	1	2	3		
Alford, Sion	1		4		4
Sellars, Archd	1	2	4		2
Brown, Angus	2	3	4		
Houston, Daniel	1	5	1		1
Strickland, Joseph	2		1		
Sled, John	1	1	2		
Smith, Angus	2	2	2		
Chavers, Richard				3	
Smith, Archd	1	2	2		
Pitman, Elizabeth	1	2	1		
Carrol, Thomas	2	1	4		
McNiel, Daniel	1	1	3		
Wilkerson, William, Jr	1	1	2		
McInnis, Donald	1	2	3		
Wilkerson, William, Sr	1		2		
Martin, Niel	1		1		
McClendon, James	2	1	6		
Moore, John	3	2	2		
Paul, Abraham	3	2	2		
Dees, Arthur	4	1	4		2
Turner, Aron	1	3	3		
McArthur, Peter	3		6		5
Paul, William	1	1	1		
McLaine, John	3	1	2		
McFarland, Daniel	1	1	3		2
McNair, Roger	2	1	2		
Atkinson, Molly		2	2		
Nicholson, Susanah	1		3		
McLaine, Niel	2	1	3		
McTyer, Robert	1	2	2		2
McKinven, John			3		
McLaine, Daniel, Jr	1				
Alford, Jacob	3	2	6	1	7
Alford, James	1	1	2		1
Little, Alexr	1	2	4		
Hall, Susanah	1	4	2		
McKenzie, Kennith	1	1	1		
Bridgers, Sampson	1		2		1
Parker, William	1		2		
McEachran, Duncan	2	2	6		
Fiveash, Elias	1				
Price, Lydia	1	2	4		
McLaine, Archd	2	1	4		
McLeod, Alexr	1				
McKinnin, John	1	1	3		
Stewart, John	1	2	2		
McLeod, Norman	1	1	3		
McLaine, Hugh	1	1	4		
Traweek, Othinel	2	4	2		3
Ramsey, Niel	2	1	3		
McLaine, John	2		3		
Clark, John	1	1	2		
Grimes, Dugal	1		4		
Cameron, Aphia	1	4			
McCremon, Archd	1		4		
McCremon, Donald	1	1	4		
McLaine, Malcolm	1		5		
Watson, John	1	3	3		
McNair, Edward	1	1	1		
McKay, Donald	1	5	4		
McGirth, John	1		1		
Dannelly, John	1	5	3		
McGirth, Archd	1	2	5		
McCormick, Duncan	1	1	4		1
McQueen, Niel	1		2		
McMillen, James	1	1	4		
Carrel, Jesse	1		1		
McInnis, Molly			3		
Stewart, John	2	1	5		
McQueen, James	3	3	8		
McAllum, Ever	2	4	4		
McRae, Christo	1	2	3		
McRae, Donald	1	1			
McRae, Philip	1	3	4		
McIntire, John	3	2	5		
McRae, Mary		2	2		

NAME OF HEAD OF FAMILY.	Free white males of 16 years and upward, including heads of families.	Free white males under 16 years.	Free white females, including heads of families.	All other free persons.	Slaves.
McColl, John	1	3	1		
Henderson, Archd	2	3	3		
Fiveash, Demcy	1	3	2		
Fiveash, John	1	3	1		
Little, Niel	1		3		2
Thompson, Trimmigen	2	4	1		
Campbell, Kennith	2		2		
McNiel, John	1	1	2		2
McCormick, Archd	1	2	3		
McCormick, Gilbert	1	2	6		
McLaine, Daniel, Sr	1		2		
Little, Robert	1		2		
McClendon, Duncan	1				
Smith, Samuel	1	2	2		
Oquin, Tarler	1	3	7		
Thompson, Charles	2		2		7
Creel, Lazarus	2		2		
Jones, Ephraim	1	3	4		
Jones, Richard		1	1	3	
Bullard, James	1	5	4		
OHerne, Elizabeth		1	4		
Coleman, William	1		1		
Bullard, John	1	2	1	1	
Teddus, John	2		2		
Evans, Richard				4	
Grice, Mary	2	2	4		
Strickland, William	1	1	2		
Thompson, Henry	1	3			5
Wilkins, William	2		2		
Martin, Sarah	2		3		
Odom, James	1	1	3		1
Barfield, Sarah	1		2		
Star, Joseph	1		2		
Harding, Betty			1		
Rush, William	1	3	2		
Powell, Ann	2		3		
Odom, Jacob	1	1	3		
Lucas, Charles	2		1		
Hunt, James				4	
Layton, Henry	1			1	
Thompson, John	1	2	2		2
Hunt, William	1	1	2		
Drake, Britton	1	1	2		1
Kitchen, Joseph	1	1	5	1	
Thompson, George	1		1		
Atkins, Silas	1		2	2	8
Townsend, Thomas	1		4		
Thompson, William (H. Swamp)	1	4	2		4
Gaddy, Lucy	2		3		
Ward, Alley		1	2		
Thompson, Lamuel	1	1	1		1
Murphy, Edward	2	3	3		
Stableton, Alexr				7	2
Bridgere, Samuel, Jr	1	1	1		
Hunt, Alexr	1	3	2		
Hunt, Richard	1	1	2		
Willis, Simon	1		1		
Ransome, Simon				6	
Moseley, Reddick	1				
Bird, John	1				
Hunt, Lewis				3	
Bridgers, Samuel, Sr	1		3		
Pitman, James	1				
Pitman, Isam	2		1		
Lowe, John			1		
Lowe, Daniel	1		1		
Lamb, Abraham	1		2		
Moore, James, Jr	1	1	1		
Rackley, John	1	1	3		
Moore, James, Sr	3	1	3		
Rowland, James	1	5	3		
Clyburn, William	2	2	6		
Bird, Isaac	3	1	6		
Britt, Samuel	1		1		
Britt, Lamuel	1	2	6		
Powell, Nicholas	1	3	1		1
Pitman, Joel	3	3	3		
Phillips, James	1		1		
Rowland, Elizabeth	2	1	4		
Rogers, James	2	4	3		
Hill, Slaughter	1	4	3		
Barfield, Charles	3	2	7		
Hill, Thomas	1		3		
Taylor, James	1	2	3		
Mitchell, Nazara	1	1	2		
Taylor, Teacle	1	1	2		
Allen, Nancy			2		
Hill, Nancy			2	2	
Lee, Stephen	1		1		
Barnes, Michael	1	2	5		
Powell, Duglas	1	4	3		
Edwards, Charles	1	1	5		
Flowers, Simon	1	1	1		1
Collins, James	1	1	2		
Davis, Thomas	1	3	4		6
Price, John	1	3	1		

NAME OF HEAD OF FAMILY.	Free white males of 16 years and upward, including heads of families.	Free white males under 16 years.	Free white females, including heads of families.	All other free persons.	Slaves.
Taylor, Willis	1		4		
Horn, Delilah	1	1	3		
Barnes, Josiah, Jr	1		3		1
Lee, Jesse, Jr	1	2	4		2
Lee, Joseph	1		4		
Pitman, Rachael	2	2	6		
Lamb, Campbell	1	4	1		
Rackley, Frederick	1	5	1		
Pope, Zedekiah	1	1	2		
Purvis, Henry	1	2	1		
Wright, Absalom	1		2		
Taylor, Jonathan	2		2		
Inman, Hardy, Sr	3	3	2		
Pitman, Isam, Jr	1	1	1		
Tholer, William	3	4	4		2
Ivey, Adam	2	3	7		
Stephens, William	1	3	3		
Lamb, Meady	1	2	6		
Atkinson, Joseph	3	1	3		
Atkinson, Samuel	1	3	5		
Pope, Henry	2	3	4		16
Pope, Jesse	1		2		
Bullock, Charles	3	5	5		
Pitman, Isam, Sr	2		1		
Bird, Isaac	3	1	6		
Wilcox, David	1	1	3		
Barfield, David			4		
Barfield, Sarah		1	2		
Maning, Hillery	1		1		
Hill, Moses	1	1	2		
Lee, Jesse, Sr	1	1	4		2
Cox, Simon	1	4	5		
Cox, John	1	2	4		
Lambs, Kinchen	1		5		
Whitley, Solomon	1	1	4		
Pitman, James, Jr	1	1	2		
Sutton, Jesse	1				
Atkinson, Howell	1		6		
Rowland, John	2	3	4		9
Lamb, Arthur	2		5		
Lamb, Barnaby	1		1		
Clyburn, Joshua	1	2	4		
Jones, Mathew	1	2	5		
Pitman, Hardy	1	1	5		
Atkinson, Jesse	1	2	3		
Perry, Philip	1	2	2		
Pitman, Thomas	1	3	8		1
Kersey, Solomon	2		2		
Drinkwater, Daniel	1	2	4		
Porter, Samuel	1	1	4		
Wingate, Cornelius	1	3	3		10
Holt, Francis	2	2	6		
James, Solomon	1		2	9	
Rackley, Joseph	1	3	2		
Whitley, Solomon	1		1		
Jernigan, Capt Jesse	2	6	3		10
Stewart, Elizabeth		1	3		1
Ivey, Francis	2	3	5		
Williamson, Ellindor	1		1		
Grimsley, George	2	3	2		
Stephens, Moab	1	4	4		2
Lewis, Richard	1		4		
Lewis, James	1	2	4		
Edwards, Samuel	3		3		
Flowers, Mary	2	1	3		
Kennedy, Samuel, Jr	1		2		1
Kennedy, Samuel, Sr	1		2		4
Grantham, Nathan	1	1	2		
Page, Joseph	1	2	3		1
Ammon, Joshua	1	1	2		
Miller, George	1	3	3		
Hill, William	1	1	2		
Grantham, James, Sr	1		1		
Grantham, James, Jr	1		1		
Page, Solomon	2		1		
Pate, Bennet	2		4		
Johnston, Absalom	1	2	2		
Horn, Ephraim	1	2	4		
Ashley, William	1		1		2
Barnes, Britton	2	3	7		1
Sealey, Tobias	2	3	4		
Grantham, Edward	2		2		
Grantham, Josiah	1	1	3		
Thompson, Reuben	1	1	1		
Fields, John	1		1		
Brumble, Elizabeth			2		
Lamb, William	2	1	2		
Ivey, Edey	1		4		
Harding, Solomon				6	
Branch, Randal				11	
Warwick, Moses	1	2	1		
Flowers, William	1	1	3		
Britt, John	1		2		
Cox, Gilbert				6	8
Hawthorn, Kedar	1	1	2		3
Inman, Hardy, Jr	2	2	5		2
Britt, Benjamin	2	2	5		

FAYETTE DISTRICT, ROBESON COUNTY—Continued.

NAME OF HEAD OF FAMILY.	Free white males of 16 years and upward, including heads of families.	Free white males under 16 years.	Free white females, including heads of families.	All other free persons.	Slaves.
Britt, William	1		1		
Ganey, Micajah	1		2		3
Mixon, Francis	1	1	2		2
Barnes, William	2	5	3		
Flowers, John	1		1		1
Barrett, John F	2	1	3		
Flowers, Edward	2		4		1
Little, John	1	1	1		
Ward, William	2		2		
Starling, William	1		1		
Lee, Everat	1		2		
Murphy William	1				
Lee, Lucy	2	1	2		
Long, Henry	1		1		
Bullard, Priscilla	1	2	4		
Ivey, Luke	1				
Phillips, Jesse	1		2		
Starling, John	1	1	2		1
Lamb, James	1		2		
Ingram, Jacob	2	2	3		
Grantham, Richard, Sr	2	1	4		
Watson, Tabitha		4	2		
Grantham, Moses	1	1	4		
Grantham, Richard, Jr	1		3		
Warren, John	1	1	4		
Legget, Wright	1	1	2		1
Barfield, Willis	1	6	2		
Bennet, William	1	1	1		
Hayle, Joseph	1	3	4		
Pitman, Thomas (Jernigans)	2	3	5		
Griffen, Andrew	1	1	3		
Hooks, Sarah		1	5		
Jones, Frederick	1		2		
Blount, Philip	3	2	5		
Hailes, Robert	2	1	1	2	
Oliver, William	3		3		
Glear, Stephen	1		3		2
Pitman, Sion	1	1	2		
Russell, James	1		4		
Irvin, Betty				2	
Travers, Patrick	1	3	2		7
Townsend, William	1	2	4		1
Coupland, James	1		1		
Coupland, John	3		3		
Thomas, Lewis	3	2	2		
Cobb, Exum	1				
Newsom, Ethelred				3	
Cumbo, John				3	
Cumbo, Cannon				11	1
Cumbo, Nathl				4	
Cumbo, Gilbert				1	
Blount, Jacob	1	3	4		1
Bryan, James	1		1		
Pate, Charles	1	2	3		1
Blount, Thomas	1		4		
Barker, Charles	2	3	1		1
Ezell, George	3		4		
Ivey, Thomas	4	2	5		
Butcher, Thomas	1	1	3		
Howell, Ralph	2	1	3		
Skeater, Joseph	1		5		
Russell, Nelly	1	1	2		
Williams, Joseph	2	4	3		
Revil, Edmund				9	
Williams, George	1	2	2		
Roberds, Ishmael				10	
Bagget, John	2	3	6		
Little, Sarah	3	2	1		
Gilbert, William	2		2		
Storm, John	1	4	3		1
Bird, John	1				
Wood, Joseph	2	2	4		11
Regan, John	3	1	3		13
Regan, Ralph	3	1	6		4
Rozier, Rueben, Sr	2	1	3		
Carter, Emanuel				5	
Regan, Anna			2		4
Thomas, Richard	1	2	6		
Powers, Samuel	1	4	3		
Mathews, Thomas	1		2		
Bodiford, James	1	1	1		
Bird, William	2		4		
Smith, John, Sr	4		3		2
Kinlaw, Benjamin	1	1	4		
Regan, Richard	1	1	5		7
Kellyhan, Martin	1		1		
Anderson, Joseph	1		2		1
McRainey, Donald	1	1	3		

NAME OF HEAD OF FAMILY.	Free white males of 16 years and upward, including heads of families.	Free white males under 16 years.	Free white females, including heads of families.	All other free persons.	Slaves.
Lee, Shadrack	2	1	4		
Regan, Daniel	1	1	1		
McNair, Robert	1	1	4		
McAlpin, Niel	1	1	4		1
Taylor, Henry	2	1	6		
Glover, William	1	1	4		
Moss, Allen	1				
Powers, John	3	1	4		
Taylor, Patty		1	3		
Taylor, Ann	2	1	1		
Drury, Nancy			2		
Terrell, Philemon	2	5	4		
Terrell, Richmond	1	1	4		
Mercer, Christo	1	4	2		
Mercer, Solomon	1		4		
Cook, John	1	3	3		
Taylor, Mills	1	2	1		
Cook, William	1	1	4		
Kersey, William				4	
Taylor, Blake	1		2		
Howell, Ralph	2	1	3		
Mills, Anthony	1	2	4		1
Rozier, Reuben, Jr	1	2	2		
Pearce, Arthur	1	2	2		3
Ivey, Isam	2	3	4		
Ivey, Austin	1		1		
Niel, David	1				
Hawthorne, William	1		2		
Bryan, Thomas	1	1	1		
Hawthorne, John	2	2	3		9
Kersey, Peter				7	
Bryan, Isaac	1	2	2		
Freeman, Benjamin	2	3	4		
Kinlaw, Thomas	5	2	3		
Kersey, Betty				3	
Stewart, John (Capt)	1	1	1		
Curry, Alex	3	1	3		
Johnston, Alex	2	2	4		
Brown, Hugh	2	1	3		6
Buie, Archd	1	2	2		1
McSwaine, Christian		1	2		
Godfrey, William	1		2		
Craft, James	2	2	3		
McMillen, Malcolm	1		1		
Buie, Archd (Capt)	1				
McLeod, Murdock	1	1	2		
McSwaine, Angus	1	1	2		
McLaine, Donald	1		2		
McSwaine, John	3	1	2		
Callyhan, Cornelius	1	3	1		
Councill, Mathew	3	2	7		
McLaine, Archd	1	2	3		1
Stewart, John, Sr	2		2		1
McGugan, Malcolm	1				
McSwaine, Alex	1				
McDermad, Farquhard	1		3		
McPhail, John	1	4	1		
Patterson, Alex	1	2	1		1
Smith, Peter	1		2		
Monro, Lewis	2	2	7		
McLaughlan, John	1	1	2		
Morrison, Norman	1	1	4		
Huneycut, Frederick	2	1	2		
Monro, Collin	2	3	2		
McMillen, Malcolm	1		1		
McMillen, John	1		1		
Malloy, John, Jr	1	3	2		
Smith, Niel	1	3	5		1
McMillen, John, Sr	2	2	4		
McMillen, Niel	2	5	4		
Patterson, Angus	2		1		
Barlow, Ralph	1	1	2		
Barlow, John	1				
Puff, Andrew	2	1	6		
Wilkerson, Richard	3	5	4		
Henderson, Duncan	1	2	3		
Kelly, Peter	1				4
McNiel, James	4		5		8
Stewart, John (L. Land)	1	1	1		
Mathews, John	1	3	2		
Murphy, John	3	1	3		
McFaul, John	1	2	3		1
McIntagart, Daniel	1	2	3		
Mathews, Daniel	1	4	7		
Stewart, John	1	2	3		
Oxendine, Benjamin				1	
Patterson, John	1	2	2		
McGugan, Hugh	1		1		

NAME OF HEAD OF FAMILY.	Free white males of 16 years and upward, including heads of families.	Free white males under 16 years.	Free white females, including heads of families.	All other free persons.	Slaves.
Mason, Moses	1				
McPherson, Daniel	1		4		21
Dorman, Elizabeth		1	1		
Witherow, Malcolm			1		
McNiel, Niel	1	2	2		
McKay, Christo	2	6	4		
McLeod, Murdock	1	1	4		
Shaw, Donald	1	1	3		
McKinnen, Donald	1		2		
Shaw, Malcolm	2		1		1
Morrison, Murdock	1	2	3		
McNiel, Hector	1	2			1
McNiel, Archd	1	1	4		1
McMillen, Duncan	1	2	7		
Strickland, Abraham	2	2	4		
Brassell, William	1		2		
McEachran, Archd	1		3		
McDonald, John	1		6		
McLaine, John	2	1	1		
McArthur, John	1	4	2		1
Jernigan, Jesse	1	4	2		6
McMillen, Daniel	1	3	1		
McMillen, Niel	1	3	3		
McSwaine, Malcolm	1		1		
McInnis, Niel	1		2		
McInnis, John	2	3	2		
McInnis, Daniel	1	3	1		
Curry, Laughlan	1	2	4		
Craig, Alexr	2		1		
Curry, Malcolm	1	4	6		
McAllum, Duncan	2	4	4		
Ferguson, Anguish	1		2		
Teaster, Samuel	1				
McMillen, John	1	3	3		
McGeshy, Alexr	1		2		
Cameron, John	1	2	7		
Watson, James	2	1	5		
Wilkerson, Edward	1		2		
McNair, Daniel	1	2	2		
Wilkerson, Daniel	1				
Wilkerson, Niel	1	2	4		
Morrison, Murdock	1	4	3		
McKinnen, John	1		2		
McRae, Alexr, Jr	1	2	3		
McRae, Alexr, Sr	1	2	3		
Ferguson, Niel	1	1	3		
McDugal, Archd	1		5		
Buie, John	1	4	7		
Kelley, Duncan	2	1	2		
Stone, James	1		3		
Johnston, John	3	3	2		
McKeathen, Daniel	3	3	3		2
McKinnen, Duncan	1		5		
Smith, Samuel	1	1	3		
McLeod, Alexr	1		5		
Beaton, David	1	3	3		
Kelly, Daniel	1	3	3		
Ray, Laughlan	4	1	2		
McGill, Angus	2	1			
Morrison, John	2		1		
Thompson, Malcolm	2		4		
Buie, Duncan	3	1	2		1
McMillen, Archd	1	2	1		
Black, Archd	1	1	2		
Black, James	1	1	4		1
McDonald, Daniel	2	2			
Callihan, Bryant	2		1		
Campbell, Duncan	4		1		
Powers, William	1				
McEachran, Daniel	3	2	3		2
McLaughlan, Robert	1				
Gilchrist, William	1	3	2		
Campbell, Daniel	4	2	4		3
Laman, Kenzie	1	1	2		
McLeod, Alexr	1		4		
McDaniel, Daniel	1	1	3		
Buie, Malcolm	3		1		
Sinclair, Colin	1	1	2		
McNiel, Archd	1	2	4		
McEachran, Archd, Jr	1				
McCollum, Duncan, Jr	1				
Pledger, Joseph	1	2	1		
Pitman, Moses	1	1	1		
Walker, Charles	1	3	3		
Baker, James	4	1			
Griffin, James	2		1		1
McDonald, Angus	2		3		
McMillen, Niel	2	4	4		

FAYETTE DISTRICT, SAMPSON COUNTY.

NAME OF HEAD OF FAMILY.	Free white males of 16 years and upward, including heads of families.	Free white males under 16 years.	Free white females, including heads of families.	All other free persons.	Slaves.
Blocker, William	2	5	3		1
Sessoms, Solomon	1	2	5		
Faircloth, Samuel	1	1	3		
Sessoms, Isaac	2	2	2		
Faircloth, Benjamin	3	4	4		
Lucas, Lewis	1	3	3		
Harwood, John	2	4	3		
Faircloth, Hardy	1	5	1		
Fisher, Southy	2	3	2	3	3
Emanuel, Ephraim				3	
Spiller, James	1		4	1	32
James, David	3	4	5		
Bryan, Bartrum	1	1	2		
Stanly, John, Sr	2	2	7		8
Stanly, Leven	2	6	6		
Stanly, Stephen	2	1	4		
Stanly, John, Jr	3	2	6		
Powers, Jesse	2	3	2		
Underwood, Thomas	2	2	4		
Cook, John	1	2	4		
Carrol, James	3	1	7		1
Wister, John	2	1	3		6
Clark, David	3	1	3		2
Kelley, Joseph	6		4		
Williford, William	2	3	4		
Bracher, John			2		
Dean, Jeremiah	1	1	3		
Bracher, Christopher	1	1	2		
Vick, Nathan, Sr	1		4		
Vick, Nathan, Jr	1		5		
Williford, Sion	1	1	2		
Brewer, James	3	4	3		
Mason, Mathew	1	1	6		3
Hollingsworth, James	2	4	4		
Gregory, Thomas	1	2	2		
Hines, Solomon	2		2		
Crumpler, John	1	3	4		10
Fisher, Bailey	1	2	2		1
Newman, Sarah	1	5	2		
Emanuel, Jesse				6	
Hayle, Joshua	1	2	4		
Purgen, Mathew	1	1	6		1
Fields, George	1	1	5		
Hall, John	3	3	3		
Bullard, Thomas	1	1	3		
Hall, Josiah	1	1	1		
Kelley, Jacob	1	2	2		
Herring, Martha	1	2	4		6
McIlewinnen, John	2	2	5		3
Bryan, David	1		3		
Bradshaw, Thomas	2	1	2		
Bradshaw, Ephraim	1	1	2		
Bradshaw, Jesse	1		3		
Stephens, Barnaby	1	1	5		6
McClendon, James	1	1	1		
Sewell, Thomas	1		3		33
Oates, Jesse	1	4	3		8
Oates, Jethro	1	1	2		2
Oates, Artesha		1	3		11
Stephens, Mildred	2	1	3		10
Ratley, Joshua	2	2	3		
Ratley, Jesse	1		1		
Butler, Jesse	2	5	2		
Ryal, Wright	1		2		2
Ryal, John	2	1	2		
Williamson, Benjamin	3	1	3		7
Pugh, Shadrack	2	2	3		
Ammonds, Joshua	1	1	2		
Treadwell, John	2	1	3		20
Herring, Richard	4		3		12
Boon, William	3		4		
Hawes, Ezekel	1		3	1	6
Dodd, David	2	3	3		
Fort, John	3	1	4	1	
Coggen, Thomas	1				3
Bell, Orson	1	2	1		
Cook, John	1	3	4		
McClam, Solomon	1	4	4		
Bell, Benjamin	1				1
Register, Thomas	2		5		2
Register, John	1	2	3		1
Ratley, Jeremiah	1		2		
Hay, Peter	1	3	1		
Boon, Stephen	1	4	5		
Lee, Henry	2	2	4		
Pope, Thomas	3	5	7		3
Butler, James	2	3	6		
Mathews, Rice	1	3	4		1
Mobley, Biggers	2	1	3		1
Robinson, William	1	1	1		5
Merritt, Absalom	2	2	3		
Wootten, William, Sr	3	1	3		
Wootten, William, Jr	1		3		
Faircloth, John	1	3	4		
Wootten, Jesse	1		2		
Howard, James	3	3	6		
Register, John	1	1	1		

NAME OF HEAD OF FAMILY.	Free white males of 16 years and upward, including heads of families.	Free white males under 16 years.	Free white females, including heads of families.	All other free persons.	Slaves.
Ryal, Thomas	1		3		
Lockerman, Jacob	1		2		
Stephens, Micajah	1	1	1		2
Wiggins, William	2	5	2		
Wiggins, Thomas	1		2		8
Robinson, Thomas	1	1	2		6
Hatcher, Timothy	1	1	2		3
Johnston, Joshua	1	2	2		
Robinson, James	1				10
Robinson, William, Jr	1				9
Rainer, David		3	3		
Ward, Jesse	1	1	5		
Ratliff, Samuel	2	1	2		1
Hill, Jean	1	2	4		
Key, Robert	2	4	5		
McClendon, Jesse	1				
Key, Charles	1	3	6		
Joyner, Benjamin	4		4		1
Lynch, Nathaniel	1	1	4		
Elmore, Thavis	2	2	4		
Hatcher, Hancob	1	1	6		
Daniel, Isaac	2	1	5		
Pipkin, Ashu	1	1	4		
Westbrook, William	1	2	3		1
Mainer, Josiah	2	3	6		
Wilson, Elisha Moore	3	3	4		4
Fraser, David	1		2		
Wiggins, William	2	1	3		
McClan, William	1	3	9		
Wiggins, George	2	2	2		
Slokum, Joseph	2	1	3		3
Roach, John	1				2
Sutton, Thomas	1	5	3		6
Smith, Noah	1	2	3		
Murphrey, Charles	1	4	7		
Strickland, Samuel, Jr	1	3	3		
Strickland, Thomas	3	2	5		
Hodgson, James	1				
Ryal, Marmaduke	2	3	2		1
Peterson, Nathan	1	2	3		
Peterson, Thomas	1				
Peterson, Cassaann		1	1		
Bryan, Kedar	3	3	4		34
Merrett, Robert	2	1	6		5
Parker, Jonathan	1	2	5		3
Register, Thomas	1	3	4		
Marsh, Thomas	1	3	4		
Edwards, William	1		3		
Sykes, Needham	2	1	3	1	
Starling, Smiley	1	2	3		
Fowler, Richard	2	1	2		
McLeod, Daniel	1	1	3		
Daughtry, Benjamin	2	3	5		
Fowler, William	1	1	4		
Fowler, Daniel	1	3	1		
Scarbrough, Benjamin	2	1	2		
Blackburn, William	2	3	3		
Kinsey, Absalom	3	3	3		
Peterson, Aron	1	5	1		
Peterson, Moses	1	4	2		
Kinsey, Daniel	1	2	1		
Van, John	1	2	1		
Whitney, Josiah	1	2	1		6
Nealy, Andrew	1	3	5		
Bryant, Sarah	2		1		1
Gauff, Thomas	1	2	6		
Carrol, Demcy	1				
Oquin, Alexander	1	1	4		
Carrol, Stephen	1	1	4		1
Kennedy, Patrick	1	3	4		
Williams, Alexander	2	3	4		
Jackson, William	3	2	4		
Register, Benjamin	1		1		
Crumpler, Jacob	1	3	4		5
Tew, Philip	1	2	1		
Webb, James	2	3	2		
Starling, Seth	2	2	6		
Fields, John	1		4		
Kean, William	1	1	4		
Runnals, Mathew	1	1	2		
McLeod, John	1		3		
Tew, Jeremiah	1	3	6		
Carrol, Alexander	1	2	3		
Cooper, Coor	2		2		
Coor, Daniel	1	3	2		6
Jones, Nathan	1	1	3		
Butler, Charles	2	2	4		
Emanuel, Nicholas				5	
Carrol, Jesse	3	4	4		5
Goodman, Jacob	1		4		
Tatum, Laban	1	1	3		3
Sessions, Richard	2	7	6		14
Averatt, William	1	2	1		
Tatum, Joshua	1		3		1
Rich, Lott	1				
Ryal, William	2	3	3		
Ryal, Ormond	1	6	2		

NAME OF HEAD OF FAMILY.	Free white males of 16 years and upward, including heads of families.	Free white males under 16 years.	Free white females, including heads of families.	All other free persons.	Slaves.
Williamson, Stephen	1		2		
Harding, David	1	4	5		
Odom, William	2	2	1		2
Daniel, Elias	1		1		
Odom, Alexander	1	3	3		
Harris, Benjamin	1	2	1		
Odom, Abraham	2	3	4		
Bell, Samuel					10
Williams, Jacob	1	1	5		
Harding, Benjamin	1	2	2		
Harding, Abraham	1	2	2		
Mainer, Benjamin	1	2	4		
Wright, John	1		2		3
Downing, Nancy		2	3		
Nelms, Edmund	1	1	2		
Pope, West	3		2		
Colbraith, Daniel	1	1	2		1
Ammon, Thomas	1		1		
Strickland, William	5	3	3		
Holder, George	1	2	2		
Robinson, William	1				7
Tayloe, Leban	1				1
Tayloe, Jonathan	1		1		4
Herrick, Jesse	1	1	4		
Cook, James	3		1		
Register, Benjamin	1	2	2		
Jones, Henry	2	1	5		
Murrell, Merrett	1		1		
Tatum, Jesse	1	1	1		
Herring, Jacob	1	1	1		
Morgan, Edward	2	2	1		
Packer, Joseph	2	1	3		
Roberson, James	1				9
Cole, William	1	1	4		1
Hobbs, George	1	1	2		
Hobbs, Simon	1	2	4		2
Watson, Ezekiel	1	4	5		
Cameron, Isaac	1	1	4		
Scott, Joseph	1	1	2		5
Drew, Josiah	1	1	1		3
Peacock, Abraham	1	2	5		
Hargrove, Arthur	2	1	4		
McLeod, Niel	3	4	5		
Emanuel, John				5	
Smith, William	1		1		
Page, Thomas	3	2	4		4
Garner, Thomas	1	1	1		
Oates, Samuel	1	2	4		3
Williams, Joseph	1	2	2		
Atwell, John	1	2	1		1
Oates, James	1	1	5		
Butler, Jethro	1	1	5		
Hillburn, Vaughn	4	5	5		
Magee, Solomon	2		3		
Boyakin, Smithick	1	1	1		
Drew, William	2	1	1		14
Godwin, Jacob	4	1	5		
Godwin, Mary					
Magee, Philip	1	2	2		
Magee, John	2		1		4
Runnals, Amos	1	4	5		
Lockerman, Jacob	1	3	2		
Runnals, Mathew	1	1	2		
Holley, John	2	3	3		
Dean, Richard	2	3	4		
Magee, Robert	1	2	3	1	
Magee, John	1	2	4		
Ammon, Howell	2	3	4		
Ammon, Vaughn	2	3	4		
Daughtry, Joshua	1		2		6
Holmes, Hardy	2		1		14
Ship, Ephraim	1	2	4		3
Terry, David				4	
Ryal, William	1		2		
Salmon, Richard	3	3	3		
King, Stephen	2	5	3		13
Carr, Jonathan	4	3	5		2
Hargrove, John	1		1		
Smith, John	1	1	4		5
Herring, Joseph	1	1	5		3
Wootten, Thomas	2	4	1		
Ryal, Owen	2	4	2		5
Scarbrough, Michael	1	1	4		
Cameron, Daniel	1		4		
Epperson, Mary			4		
Fryer, Jonathan	2	4	5	1	9
Gregory, Lott	1	4	4		3
Lee, William	2	2	4		3
Bell, Archd	1				
Cameron, Philip	1	1	2		
Atwell, Benjamin	2	2	2		
Daughtry, Abraham	1	1	2		
Snell, Charles	1				6
Hargrove, Moses	1	1	3		
Tew, John	1		2		
Wilkins, James	1	1	2		
Cook, Shadrack	1		2		

FAYETTE DISTRICT, SAMPSON COUNTY—Continued.

NAME OF HEAD OF FAMILY.	Free white males of 16 years and upward, including heads of families.	Free white males under 16 years.	Free white females, including heads of families.	All other free persons.	Slaves.
Gavin, Samuel	1	1	2		
Jernigan, Jesse	1	5	1		2
Fraser, Thomas	1		3		
Nolley, Josiah	1	2	4		
Turbevill, Joseph	2	2	4		3
Brady, John	1				
Hobbs, William	1	5	3		
Blackwell, William	1	1	4		
Chesnut, David	1		4		
Carrol, John, Sr	2	3	5		
Van, William	2	2	5		1
Scott, Joseph	1	3	4		3
Thornton, Thomas, Jr	1	2	3		1
Herring, Uzzill	1	5	1		
Lee, Isaac	1	1	7		
King, Michael	2	2	7		10
Cook, Lazarus	1	3	1		
Enzor, Sommers	1	1	3		
Merrett, Nothiel	1	2	4		2
Merritt, Frederick	1	1	4		1
Merrett, Jacob	1	1	2		
Merrett, Theophilus	1	2	4		
Merrett, David	1		2		
Lee, Noah	1	3	6		
Gavin, Lewis	1	2	1		1
Hollingsworth, Henry	1	2	4		
Merrett, Philip	1	2	4		
Chesnut, Alexander	1		1		
Tyler, Owen	1	4	1		
Bennett, John	1	4	4		
Carr, Thomas	1	8	3		2
Gavin, Charles	1	2	2		
Boyakin, John	1				
Morgan, Hamlin	1				
Turlington, Southy	4		2		
Sykes, Cornelius	1	1	3		
Jacobs, Abraham				3	
Cooper, John	1	3	5		
Carter, Moses				9	
Conner, Ishmael	1			3	
White, George	1	1	5		
White, Luke	2	1	3		8
Register, Joseph	1	3	3		
Register, Josiah	1	1	2		
Boykin, Bijus	1	2	2		2
Scott, Nehemiah	1	1	2		19
Boyt, John	1	1	3		
Carr, Patrick	1		3		
Parker, Nicholas	1		1		2
Young, Dobbs	1		6		
Oquin, Patrick	1		10		
Taylor, Henry	1		1		
Benton, Josias	4		3		
Airs, Thomas	1	1	3		
Johnston, Peregrine	2	1	3		
Givin, Josiah	1		2		
Strickland, Holly	1	1	2		
Strickland, William	2		3		
Strickland, John	1		4		
Williams, John	3	1	3		6
Jordan, William	1	2	3		
Jordan, Philip	1	2	3		
Butler, Robert	3	1	5		1
Hall, Armager	1	2	2		
Hall, William	1		4		
Gilbert, James	1	1	5		
Chesnut, Joshua	1	1	5		1
Chesnut, John, Sr	1	6	4		
Lasseter, George	2	1	6		
Murphy, William	1	2	4		1
Whitley, Elijah	1	2	4		
Fort, John	2	1	7		10
Turner, John	1		1		
Carter, Henry				8	
Thompson, William	1	1	1		8
Faison, Frances			4	1	
Holmes, Gabriel	1		2		15
Holmes, Owen	1	2	2		13
Scott, Nehemiah	1		2		4
Chesnut, Alexr, Jr	1		2		
Register, Joseph	1		2		
Butler, Isaac	1		2		
Van, King	1	3	4		
Stephens, Hardy	1	2	2		3
Sykes, Joshua, Jr	1		2		
Sykes, Joshua, Sr	2	1	5		
King, Henry	2				4
Butler, Stephen	1				
Butler, Jacob	1				1
Holland, Thomas	1	3	4		
Wiggs, Henry	1	3	3		
Blount, William	1	2	3		
Stephens, John	1	1	3		2
Hay, Charles	1	3	3		
Spiva, William	1	3	2		
Parker, William	1	3	1		
Ward, John	1	2	3		

NAME OF HEAD OF FAMILY.	Free white males of 16 years and upward, including heads of families.	Free white males under 16 years.	Free white females, including heads of families.	All other free persons.	Slaves.
Cook, Cornelius	1	2	4		
Runnals, Dredrill	1	1	3		
Magee, Jacob	1	1	3		21
Chesnut, Jacob	3	1	7		8
Darden, Jesse	3	3	3		5
Tew, Jean	1		3		4
Tew, Marmaduke	1	4	3		
Blew, Duncan	1		3		
Register, Shadrack	1	1	1		
Tucker, William	1	3	1		11
Baine, George	1	3	3		
Samford, William	1		2		
Bryant, Sarah	2		1		1
Blackmon, James	2	1	1		4
Flowers, John				1	
Fellow, William	1	2	3		20
Clinton, Richard	2	3	3		37
Murray, Leonard	1	2	4		
Pride, Josiah	1		2		
Bell, Robert	2		6		11
Bell, Felix	1				1
Bell, Micajah	1		3		1
Ryal, Isam	1	1	2		1
Ryal, Thomas	1		3		
Turner, Myal	1	1	5		
Scarbrough, John	1	2	3		
Brewer, Henry	1	1	1		1
Peterson, William	1	3	1		
Williamson, Joseph	1		1		
Magee, Solomon	1	1	1		
Bell, Jesse	3	3	6		1
Kelley, James	2	4	4		
Butler, William, Jr	1		3		
Butler, Robert, Jr	1	1	3		1
Carrol, Demey	2		3		
Ryal, Willis	1	1	3		
Wiggins, Elihu	1	3	5		
Butler, William, Sr	2	3	4		
Williamson, William	2	2	2		
Hunnicut, William	1	2	5		
Dollar, William	1	3	4		
Williams, John	1	4	4		6
Bramble, William	1	5	4		
Lee, Joseph	1	1	4		
Williams, Rachael	1	1	3		
Williamson, William, Jr	2	1	2		
Jones, Benjamin	1	3	3		
Stewart, John	2	3	2		
Peterson, Malcolm	1	2	5		1
Jackson, George	1	5	3		
Wrench, John	1	1	2		
Maxwell, Thomas	1	4	2		1
Mathews, Frederick	1	2	6		
Lockerman, James	3	3	3		
Porter, Absalom	1	2	5		
Revil, Nathaniel					13
Crumpler, Mathew	2	1	6		
Bass, William	2	3	4		
Godwin, James	3	4	4		
Godwin, Aron	1		2		
McQueen, Norman	1	1	3		
McQueen, John	1	2	3		
Godwin, Richard	3	4	4		
Godwin, Rachael	2	2	4		
Holden, Ann	1	4	8		
Godwin, Nathan	1	4	6		
Watson, John	1	1	2		
Godwin, Solomon	1	1	2		
Bullard, Thomas	1		4		
Holley, Ozburn	1		3		
Holley, Edward	1		2		
McDaniel, Malcolm	1	1	3		
Bagley, Elizabeth			2		
Smith, James	1	2	2		
Jackson, Lewis	2	5	3		
Dean, Farmer	1	2	1		
Williford, Micajah	1	3	1		
Goodman, John	1		4		
Bass, Burwell	1		6		
Hartley, James	1	2	2		
Bass, Elizabeth			2		
Carraway, Bedreddon	3	3	5		6
House, John	3	1	1		6
Dudley, Daniel	1	3	3		
Bass, Richard	1	3	6		
Holden, William	1	1	3		
Maclemore, West	1	2	4		
Creach, Simon	1	4	3		1
Dormon, William	1	1	1		
Jackson, Richard	1		2		
Warwick, Benjamin	2	5	2		
Wadkins, Isaac	1	1	1		
Odom, Demcy	1		2		
Odom, Jacob	1		2		
Williams, Joel	1	1	4		
Laighton, James	1		1		
Starling, John	1	2	2		

NAME OF HEAD OF FAMILY.	Free white males of 16 years and upward, including heads of families.	Free white males under 16 years.	Free white females, including heads of families.	All other free persons.	Slaves.
Strickland, Samuel, Sr	1	1	2		
Smith, Howell	1	5	1		
Ganey, Jacob	1		4		
Ganey, Edmund	1		1		
Thornton, John	2	4	3		
Grantham, David	1	3	2		
Smith, William	2		4		
Lee, William	1		1		
Salkeld, Isaac	1		1		
Wilson, Thomas	1	3	3		
Mihaynes, William	1	2	2		
Ingram, Pherebee	1	2	2		9
Jones, Charles	2	1	3		
Ganey, William	1		5		1
Wagers, Dawson	1	3			
Holley, John	1	2	6		
Blackmon, Esther	2	2	2		1
Ganey, Bartholomew	4		3		7
Barks, Joseph	1	3	6		
Lee, Peter	4	1	4		6
Lee, Jesse	2	1	2		3
Daniel, Jacob	1		4		
Joyner, James	1	1	3		
Bray, Benjamin	1	1	4		
Bray, Peter	1		1		
Ball, William	1				3
Ganey, Reddick	3	1	3		
Haynes, Joseph	3	1	6		
Godwin, William	1	6	4		
Peters, Ann	2	2	3		
Vick, Robert	1	1	4		3
Lee, Sampson	2	3	4		1
Holley, James	1		5		
Smith, Noah	1	2	3		
Williamson, William, Jr	1	3	2		
Blackmon, Josiah	4	1	4		9
Lee, Westbrook	1	2	4		
Thornton, Nathaniel	1	4	4		4
Thornton, Thomas, Sr	2		2		8
Lee, Bud	1				
Wood, Furnifold	1	2	2		
Blackmon, Joab	1		4		3
Colbraith, Niel	1	7	4		1
Autry, Theophilus	1		3		
Sutton, Christo	1	3	4		
Wood, Francis	1	4	3		
Jones, John Moss	2	1	6		
Porter, John	2	1	4		
Faircloth, Samuel	1	1	4		
Williams, Robert	1	4	4		5
Autry, Cornelius	1		1		
Hall, Moses	1		2		
Butler, John	2	3	5		
Daniel, John	1	4	1		
Autry, Rachael	3	1	4		
Johnston, John	1	3	4		
Carter, Josiah	1	2	2		
Sessums, Nicholas	1	1	2		
Sessums, Richard	1	2	2		
Grice, James	1		2		
Lucas, Lewis	1	3	3		
Natt (Old)				2	
Owens, William	1	1	2		2
Wiggens, John	2	2	4		
Ryal, Young	1	3	4		4
Campbell, Alexr	1	2	4		
McKinnen, Murdock	2		4		
Moore, Sarah			1	5	
Jackston, Nathan	1	1	4		
Daniel, Elias	1		1		
Porter, Samuel	2	3	5		
Dees, Hardy	2	1	6		
Williams, Timothy	2		4		
Gibbs, Sarah			2		
Williams, Nathan	1		3		
Williams, Rueben	1	1	1		
Williams, Isaac	3	5	8		
Williams, Joseph	2	6	5		2
House, George	1	1	1		1
Williams, Henry	2		3		
Brown, Arthur	2	4	3		
Brown, Therod	1	1	3		2
Smith, Luke	1		2		
Drew, Judith	1	2	4		1
Chesnut, Alexr	1		2		
Runnals, Frances			2		
Houston, Peter	2		6		
Rich, Joseph	1		2		
Rich, Joshua	1	1	2		
Bracker, Christopher	1		2		
Wright, William	1		4		
Wright, Robert	1		2		3
Hair, John	1		4		
Bullard, Jeremiah	1		2		1
Edge, Elliott	1	2	4		
Adom, John	1	1	2		
Nance, Wynn	1	1	2		3

FAYETTE DISTRICT, SAMPSON COUNTY—Continued.

NAME OF HEAD OF FAMILY.	Free white males of 16 years and upward, including heads of families.	Free white males under 16 years.	Free white females, including heads of families.	All other free persons.	Slaves.
Walker, Baker	1		3		
Chesnut, Jacob	1	1	2		
Williamson, William, Sr	6	1	4		
Pope, Jeremiah	1	5	3		
Moore, Lewis	1				8
Moore, Ann		1	4		17
Moore, Ezekiel	1	1	1		5
Myhand, Silas	1		5		1
Pope, Jacob	1		3		
Magee, Willis	1		3		
Magee, Philip	1	1	3		
Pope, Harris	1		4		
Chesnut, Charles	2		5		
Jackson, John, Jr	1	2	3		
Creeck, Simon	1	4	3		1
Jackson, John, Sr	1		2		
Jackson, Richard	1	1	1		
Snell, Mary	2	2	3		13
Snell, John	1				5
Drew, William	1		2		
Bird, Edward	3	2	5		9
King, Michael, Jr	1				1
Izard, Henry	1	2	1		
Poitivint, Isaac	2	1	3		6
Goodman, Jacob, Sr	1		3		
Goodman, Jacob, Jr	1		1		
Lee, Edward	1				
Bryant, John	1	2	3		1
Register, John, Sr	1	2	4		
Cason, Charity	3		4		1
Hollingsworth, Zebulon	1		3		
Holmes, Lewis	1	1	2		7
Brewington, Amey				4	
Williams, Crecy				3	
Williams, Hannah				2	
Faison, James	1	4	3		5
Faison, Elisha	1	1	1		1
Gregory, Lott	2	3	3		3
Fisher, Elijah	2	2	4		1
Maclemore, Drury	1		5		
Johnston, Loasbe	1	3	3		
Ivey, Curtis	1	2	3		5
Williams, Daniel	1	3	5		11
Thompson, James	1	3	5		5
Ivey, Thomas	3		4		12
Stewart, Dugal	2		2		
Porter, Tully	1				4
Crumpler, Rayford	1				
King, William	1	2	5	1	31
Gilmour, Sophia		1	2		2
Hair, William	4	4	3		
Parker, Lessum	4	1	1		2
Holley, Sherod	1	1	2		
McPhail, Alexr	1		1		2
Vick, Cooper	1	3	2		
Kean, John	2	1	4		
Jones, Shadrack	3	2	6		
Oquin, Josiah	1		2		
McPhail, Alexr	4		2		
Cullee, Polly		1	2		
Fowler, John	3	3	4		
Fowler, Joseph	1	3	4		
Simmons, Jeremiah, Sr	4	1	3		
Simmons, Jeremiah, Jr	1	1	4		
Herringdine, James	1	1	4		1
Simmons, John	2	1	4		
Morgan, John	1		7		
Morgan, Frederick	1	1	1		
Barnes, Eliazer	1	1			
Young, John Sampson	1		3		
Merril, Henry	2		3		
Watkins, David	1	2			
Martin, Paul	2	2	7		
Hutson, Miles	1		3		
Young, Winifred			4		
Willams, Joseph				4	
Jacobs, Thomas				7	
Ireland, Amey				5	
Davis, Fanny		2	3		
Whitley, William	1		1		
Mainor, Jack				1	
Hobbs, Henry	1	1	2		
Hobbs, John	1	1	1		
Bird, Edward, Jr	1	1	1		2
Lee, Christopher	1		4		
Burnet, Catharine		1	1		
Brewington, Ann				3	
Thomas, Luke	1	1	4		1
Justice, John	1	1	3		
Darden, Mary			3		
Darden, William	1	1	1		4
Blackman, Stephen	1		3		2
McClendon, Simon	1	1	2		10
Sutton, Thomas	1	4	2	1	5
Dunn, Jacob	1	2	2		
Faison, Fanny	3	1	2		1
McCullen, John, Sr	2		2		

NAME OF HEAD OF FAMILY.	Free white males of 16 years and upward, including heads of families.	Free white males under 16 years.	Free white females, including heads of families.	All other free persons.	Slaves.
McCullen, John, Jr	1	1	2		
Pipkin, Ashur	1	1	4		1
Livingston, John	1	5	3		1
McCullen, Lewis	1	1	1		
Williamson, George	1		1		1
Stephens, Bernard	1	1	5		7
McClendon, James	1	1	3		1
Bell, Benjamin	2	1	3		1
Hill, Francis	6	1	3		4
West, Willis	1	2	3		1
Jackson, Archd	1	4	4		
Darden, William	2	1	3		4
Coley, William	1	5	2		
Hodges, Joseph, Sr	1		1		
Hodges, Joseph, Jr	1	2	1		1
Hicks, Thomas	2	1	1		16
Murphy, Miles	2	2	3		2
Murphy, Richard	1	3	2		
Pope, Blackburn	1	1	1		
Pope, Jeremiah	2	2	4		
Murphy, Michael	2	3	4		
Wiggs, John	2	2	4		
Howard, Minron	1	1	1		1
Emanuel, Levi				5	
Daniel, Jacob	1		2		
King, Mike	2				3
Magee, Jacob	1	3	5		
Wright, Lessee			1		
Smith, Mary		1	2		
Jones, Rachael		1	2		
Harris, Rebecca		1	2		
Harris, John	2	1	2		
Dyer, Samuel	1				
Roach, Sarah			1		
Wiggins, Patty				5	
Clewis, Molly				3	
Wiggins, Mary				6	
Waldon, Jack				1	
Coggin, Ruth			2		
Jones, Martha			2		
Cloeraly				4	
Fields, Samuel	1				
Womble, Suky		1	2		
Bayles, Jude		1	3		
Joyner, Isam	1		1		
Hatcher, Anna		1	1		
Godwin, Priscilla		1	1		
Williams, Anna			3		
Cobb, Becky				3	
Hammonds, Miles				1	
Dawson, Gilbert	1				
Taylor, George	1				
Gilbert, John	1				
Segars, John	1	1	4		
Strickland, Alexr	1	2	2		
Sullivant, Robert	2	1	3		
Williams, Benjamin	1				
Williams, John	1				
Stanley, Elizabeth		1	1		
Duae, William	1				
Duae, Robert	1				
Goodman, Sylvia		1	3		
Caruthers, Nancy		1	2		
Page, Thomas, Jr	1		1		
Waring, Jacob	1		2		2
Elliott, Elias	1	1	2		
Davis, Solomon	1	1	2		
Price, Richard	1	2	2		
Sessons, Richard	1		3		
Sessions, Nicholas	1	1	1		
Davis, Henry	1	1	3		
Davis, Jesse	1	1	2		
Davis, John	1	1	2		
Owens, Mary		1	2		7
Edge, Elliott	1	1	2		
Hair, Jacob	1		2		
Hair, William	1	1	3		
Hair, Thomas	1	2	5		
Whitley, Amey		1	2		
Perkins, Samuel	1	1	2		
Smith, William	1	1	1		
Morgan, Frederick	1		1		
Bell, Polly			1		2
Williams, Christian		2	2		
Owens, Thomas	1	1	2		
Bullock, Benjamin	2	2	1		
Parker, Lewis	1		1		
Clinton, Thomas	1		2		4
Easom, John	1	2	3		1
Ward, Betty		1	2		
Ward, Jane			2		
Price, Josiah	1		2		
Hargrove, Bray	1		1		
Hargrove, John	1				
Whitfield, William	1	1	1		3
Clark, James	1	1	1		4
Williams, John	1	1	2		

NAME OF HEAD OF FAMILY.	Free white males of 16 years and upward, including heads of families.	Free white males under 16 years.	Free white females, including heads of families.	All other free persons.	Slaves.
Clark, Nathan	1	2	3		1
Powell, Restore	1		1		4
Holland, Henry	1	2	3		
Snell, Stephen	1	1	3		
Griggs, John	1	1			
Harris, John	1	1	3		
Brooks, John	1	2	4		
Ryal, John	2	4	2		3
Powell, Jacob	1	1	3		
Cooper, Fleet	1	3	4		1
Cooper, William	2	3	3		
Futch, Martin	1	1			
Jenkins, John	1		2		
Jenkins, Thomas	1		2		
Hatcher, Bedy			2		
Nelms, Lewis	1		3		
Nelms, George	1	3	3		
Hudson, Job	1	1	5		
Mote, Jethro	2	4	5		
Hudson, Joseph	1	2	5		
Hudson, Lewis	1	2	5		
Elkins, Charity			2		
Van, Needham	1				
Tyler, Needham	1	2	3		
Berbage, Joseph	1	1	2		
Morriss, Elisha	1		1		
Long, George	1	2	1		
Hainey, Penny			2		
Hudson, Rachael			2		
Downing, Anna		2	3		
Pridgen, Jane			1		
Butler, Peggy		1	2		
Mathews, Mary	4	1	2		16
Bardin, Ephraim	1		1		
Pope, Robert	2		4		
Roberts, Solomon	1	2	4		
Cook, Elizabeth			1		
Bagget, Elizabeth			1		
Stringfield, William	1	2	4		
Bell, Hesekiah	1	2	4		1
Sellers, Jacob	4	2	4		
Sellers, Isam	1	4	4		1
Rees, William	1		4		1
Green, Rueben	1	3	4		
Bell, Mary	1	1	2		1
Van, Elizabeth			1		
Sellers, Joseph	1	1	2		
Sellers, Jacob, Jr	1	1	2		
Blantham, Joshua	1				
Van, Stephen	1	2	4		
Clary, James	1				
Merritt, David			3		
Cook, Ann			1		
Rowel, Benjamin	1	3	4		
Register, Judith		1	5		
Benton, Matthias	3	1	2		
Rowell, Sabra			2		
Chesnut, Mourning		1	2		
Chesnut, Solomon	1		2		
Rowell, Lucrece			2		
Merrett, Frederick	1	1	4		1
Merrett, Jacob	1	1	2		20
Bell, George	1		4		
Johnson, William	1	2	4		
Merrett, Solomon	1		1		
Johnston, Joel	1	4	3		
Johnston, Jesse	1	3	3		
Fryer, Jennett	2	2	3		2
Goodwin, Willis	1	3	3		
Watkins, Lewis	1				
Hollingsworth, Henry	1	1	1		
Chesnut, Needham	1	1	2		
Chesnut, David	1	2	2		
Jones, Levi	1				
Van, Kedar	1		1		
Benton, Anna			2		
Carrol, Elizabeth		1	2		
Merritt, Michael	1		2		
Merrett, Levi	1		1		
Merrett, Nathaniel	1				
Chesnut, Elizabeth		1	3		
Sutton, Elizabeth		1	3		
Packer, Mary		1	3		
Waters, Mary		1	2		
Jones, Moses	1		1		
Jones, Augustine	1		1		
Houston, James	1				
Williams, Bersheba		3	2		
Williams, Rachael		1	2		
Burks, Esther		1	2		
Carrol, Elisha		2	2		
Baine, Mary			2		
Kelly, Mary		2			
Green, Rachael				6	
Clenny, Lewis	1				
Vick, Nathan	2	3	4		
Smith, James	1	1			

FAYETTE DISTRICT, SAMPSON COUNTY—Continued.

NAME OF HEAD OF FAMILY.	Free white males of 16 years and upward, including heads of families.	Free white males under 16 years.	Free white females, including heads of families.	All other free persons.	Slaves.
Starling, Robert	1	1	3		
Dean, William	1	2	4		
McClendon, Samford	1		1		
Buchannan, James	3		2		1
Williams, Isaac, Jr	1	2	3		
Williams, Arthur	1		3		
Williams, Brigget			2		
Bray, Bryant	1	1	2		
McClendon, Thomas	1				
Rhodes, William	1				
McClendon, Jesse	1				
Gaven, Charles	1	2	2		
Jones, Moses, Jr	1				
Hatcher, Hancock	1	1	5		
Godwin, Sally			1		
Godwin, Mary		1	2		
Wages, Submit			2		
Gainey, John	1				
Williams, Catharine		1	3		4
Chesnut, Shade	1	1	3		
McPhail, Dugal	1				
Williams, Johanna			2		
Gibbs, Thomas			2		
Sessums, Isaac	1		1		
Dudley, Rachael	1		1		
Lee, Joan			1		
Carraway, Archd	1				
Orion, Peter	1				
Hair, Joel	1		2		
Cason, Hillery	1				
Snell, Sarah	1	3	3		10
Wiggs, Lydia		1	1		
Atkinson, Thomas	1				
Chesnut, Arthur			1		
Turner, William	1	5	2		1
Livingston, John	1	1	1		1
Person, Jonathan	1		3		
Hall, Bickley	2	1	3		
McMoore, Elias	1		3		
Autry, Drury	1		3		
Autry, John	2	1	3		
Autry, Isam	1	2	5		
Bullock, Benjamin, Jr	1		1		
Dees, Sampson	1	3	2		1
Dees, William	1	1	4		
Parker, John	3	1	2		2
Faircloth, John	1	2	4		
Love, Murdock	1	2	5		
Taylor, Samuel	2	4	4		
Jones, Rachael	1	1	3		
Brady, John	1				1
Ryal, Penelope			2		
Dudley, Levi	2	3	7		
Gilbert, John	1	3	4		
Strickland, Alex	1	2	2		
Sullivant, Aggy	2	2	1		
Strickland, Harmon	1		1		
Hall, Lazarus	1	3	4		
Hall, Mary	1		3		
Hall, Barnabas	1	2	2		
Sessoms, Isaac	1	1	1		

HALIFAX DISTRICT, EDGECOMBE COUNTY.

NAME OF HEAD OF FAMILY.	Free white males of 16 years and upward, including heads of families.	Free white males under 16 years.	Free white females, including heads of families.	All other free persons.	Slaves.
Cullin, Andrew	1	1	1		7
Battle, Jethro	2	2	5		20
Deaver, Thomas	1				
Battle, Elisha, Senr	2		3		22
Hilliard, Jeremiah	1	2	2		19
Ing, Christopher	2	3	4		8
Johnston, Jesse	1	2	6		12
Battle, John	2	2	2		16
Sumner, Joseph	1	4	2		16
Sumner, Joseph	3	2	5		14
Battle, Jacob	1	1	4		24
Mainer, Aaron	3	2	3		3
Porter, Thomas	1	2	6		7
Stallings, James	1	1	3		
Philips, Hartwell	2	1	4		14
Odom, Richard	1	2	4		7
Price, Jesse	1	2	4		
Horn, Abishai	2	2	4		5
Philips, Joseph	1		4		9
Stallings, Willis	1	3	7		
Gray, William	4				18
Battle, Demsey	1	1	2		15
Battle, Elisha, Jr	1	5	3		10
Ross, Daniel	1		3		5
Pitt, Arthur	1				
Philips, Benjamin	1				10
Barnes, Williamson	1	2	4		
Sherwood, Robert	1		4		1
Faulk, William	1	1	4		
Murfree, Josiah	2	2	5		12
Pitman, Thomas	1				
Bryant, Smith	3	3	3		5
Britain, Bryant	1	1	3		9
Garner, Absalom	1	3	2		9
Deloach, Samuel, Jr	1		5		3
Knight, Peter	2	2	4		11
Bradley, Richard	1	2	9		
Bradley, Stephen	1	5	3		
Mials, Nasworthy	1	1	5		4
Elenor, Thomas	1	2	4		
O'Neal, Isom	2	1	4		
Vann, Elisha	1	1	4		
Bracewell, William, Senr	2		1		4
Williams, Thomas	1	6	4		1
Fort, John	1	1	1		2
Bracewell, William, Junr	2	3	4		
Hardy, Michael	1				
Horn, William, Junr	1		4		11
Fort, Elizabeth	1		5		9
Cavenah, Mary			1		
Bracewell, James	1				4
Bracewell, Abner	1				1
Bayley, Harrison	1	4	4		
Waller, Sterling	1	3	3		2
Patterson, George	1	1	6		1
Casna, Lewin	1	1	1		
Killibrew, Joshua	3	2	3		7
Griffin, William	5	2	5		
Fountain, James	1				
Griffin, John	2		2		
Watkins, John	2		3		2
Horn, William, Senr	1		6		
Tye, William	1		2		
Williams, Margaret			2	1	
Horn, Joel	1	3	3		10
Robertson, Abner	1				
Woodman, Job	1				
Archer, William	1		2		
Vann, Edward	1	1	1		
Bloodworth, Thomas	2	6	2		
Blount, Thomas	3	1	4		27
Gerard, Charles	2		6		27
Jones, Hardiman	3	2	2		1
Killibrew, Kinchen	1	4	5		1
Greer, Andrew	1				4
Putow, William	1				
Sugg, Noah	2	2	2		22
Barrow, Moses	1	2	2		4
Ross, John	3		4		2
Smith, Lawrance	2	3	2		2
Jones, John	1	1	1		
Hodges, Joseph	1		1		
Coleman, Dolly		1	2		
Lyons, Henry	2	1			1
Coleman, Jesse	1				
Thompson, Archibald	1	4	4		2
Nowell, Isham	1				
Bilberry, Nathaniel	1	4	2		11
Bell, William	3	2			3
Stephens, John				9	
Pender, John	1	3	3		
Dickenson, Thomas	1		2		
Fort, Jacob	1	3	3		
Dancy, William	2	2	2		22
De Loach, Jesse	1		3		8
Killibrew, Glidewell	1		3		2
Cohon, Simon	1		2		4
Cahoon, John	1	1	1		
Proctor, Aaron	1	2	5		
White, Jacob	1	3	5		
Stanley, William	1	4	4		
Vickers, Ralph	1	1	4		1
Drahon, James	3		3		
Hargrove, Unity		2	7		
Jones, Patience			4		
Williams, Benjamin	3	1	3		
White, Benjamin	1		1		
White, Mary			2		
Jordan, Thomas	1	5	5		3
Thomas, Jacob	2	2	1		3
Deloach, Samuel, Jr	3	3	2		10
Brake, Jacob	2	1	4		
Kurl, Willis	1	2	2		2
Wester, Fugham	1	4	1		
Robbins, William	2	4	4		
Molley, Jacob	1	2	3		
Burden, Joseph	1	1	2		12
Gad, William	1	4	3		
Holland, Jacob	1	5	4		
Horn, Jacob	1	4	6		4
Ricks, Isaac	1	1	3		1
Coleman, Moses	1		1		
Holliman, Jediah	1		1		
Proctor, Moses	1	2	3		2
Brake, Nathan	1	1	2		
Wester, Elizabeth		1	2		
White, George	1		2		
Brake, Benjamin	2	2	4		
Eastwood, James	1	2	3		
Bates, Fredrick	1				
Cahoon William	4	2	2		19
Proctor, Ann	2		3		
Barrett, Thomas	1	2	2		3
Griffin, Willis	1	1	3		
Jordan, Gray	1		1		
Gay, Mary	1	3	2		
Masengill, George	2	1	2		
Dowberry, Elizabeth	2		1		
Williams, Unity	2		2		
Bridges, Briton	2	2	3		13
Horn, Elijah	2	7	3		2
Misser, Thomas	1	3	1		8
Bloodworth, William	1	4	6		5
Proctor, Stephen	1	1	1		
Bloodworth, Henry	1	3	5		
Bracewell, James	1		2		
Coleman, Hardy	1		3		
Gray, Jesse	2	2	2		
Sanders, William	1		2		3
Williams, Joseph	1	2	5		
Brake, Jacob, Sr	3	1	4		
Strother, Richard	1	3	4		3
Stephens, Peter	1	3	4		
Morris, John	2	2	3		
Thomas, James	1	3	2		
Proctor, Jane	2		3		
Long, James	1	3	2		
Waller, Lucy		1	5		
Ruffin, Samuel	2	2	8		2
Ruffin, Benjamin	2		3		
Littleton, Southern	1		1		
Harrell, Edmund	1		2		
Cannada, James	1		2		
Howell, Nathaniel	1	1	4		
Bracewell, Lamon	1	2	3		
Lane, Sarah	1		3		4
Artist, Lauer				5	
Seawell, John	1				
Thomas, Theophilus	3	5	5		21
Ruffin, Lamon	2				12
Ruffin, Bartholomew	1				
De Loach, Ruffin	1	2	3		9
Parnald, John	1		2		
Thorn, Benjamin	1	2	4		
Merritt, James	3	2	4		2
Tisdall, Rehizon	2	1	3		12
Bracewell, Benjamin	4	1	3		4
Cahoon, Joel	1	2	2		1
Gardner, Mary	1	2	4		1
Pitman, Mary	1		4		
Moore, Moses	2	3	4		
Weaver, Benjamin	1	5	4		
Boyt, Jacob	1	3	3		
Weaver, Benjamin	1	1	3		
Lancaster, Benjamin, Jr	1	4	4		1
Dixon, William	2	1	2		
Boyt, Thomas	1	2	2		
Lancaster, Benjamin, Senr	2		2		2
Dehoiety, James	1		2		
Griffin, Lucy	3		2		2
Dehoiety, Abner	1				
Richards, John	2		2		
Bailey, Samuel	1	1	4		
Gay, Henry	3	4	3		
Healy, William	1		1		
Dawtridge, Benjamin	1		1		
Dawtridge, William	2	1	4		
Pitman, Jesse, Jr	1				
Watkins, Henry	1				
Lancaster, Robert	1		2		
Weaver, Absala		3	2		
Murray, Charity	1	3	5		
Weaver, Benjamin	2	2	2		
Lancaster, Henry	1	2	6		
Lancaster, Hartwell	1		3		
Lancaster, Robert, Jr	1	2	3		
Brand, Thomas	1	3	3		
Willifield, Benjamin	3	5	2		
Pitman, Jesse	1		4		
Williams, Drury	1		2		
Cobb, Edward	1	4	7		
Williams, Jesse	1		3		

HALIFAX DISTRICT, EDGECOMBE COUNTY—Continued.

NAME OF HEAD OF FAMILY.	Free white males of 16 years and upward, including heads of families.	Free white males under 16 years.	Free white females, including heads of families.	All other free persons.	Slaves.
Wilder, Michael	1		2		
Winstead, Peter	1		2		
Robbins, John	1	1	3		15
Brand, Benjamin	2				
Solomon, Isham	1	1	2		
Bryant, Gail	1	1	1		
Brand, William	1	3	2		
Williford, Jacob	1	4	1		
Williford, Thomas	1		2		
Story, Daniel	1		2		
Pitman, Edward, Jr	1	2	5		
Gay, William	1		1		
Todd, Hardy	1		1		
Coppage, Augustine	2	2	2		
Allen, Hardy	1	3	3		3
Pitman, Edward, Senr	1		2		
Granton, Jesse	2	2	6		
Pitman, Jesse	1	5	3		
Jackson, Edward	1		2		
Stone, John	1	3	4		1
Winstead, Joseph	1	1	2		
Winstead, Richard	1	2	7		
Dixon, Coffield	1	1	2		
Flowers, Hardiman	1	1	5		8
Robbins, Jacob	5	3	3		
Proctor, Sampson	1	3	3		
Watkins, Stephen	1	4	5		
Spicer, James	1	2	2		
Horn, Michael	2	3	5		4
Barnes, Sarah			2		
Pitman, John	1		2		
Price, Joseph	1	1	2		
Horn, Ann		2	4		1
Pittman, Jethro	1	2	5		
Pitman, Ann		1	5		
Adams, Briton	1	2	3		
Rose, Amos	1		3		
Trevathan, Sion	1		2		
Trevathan, Fredrick	1		2		4
Deloach, William, Jr	2*	1	3		9
Elenor, William	1	4	5		3
Pitman, Joseph	1	2	2		
Williams, John	1				2
Skinner, Samuel	1	2	2		
Williams, Henry	1				5
Emson, William	2	4	3		
Hynes, Isom	1	3	2		3
Fountaine, Mary		2	2		
Randolph, Giles	2	2	2		
Bridges, Drury	1		1		1
Spicer, William, Jr	2	1	3		
Anderson, Elizabeth			2		
Ricks, James	2	3	2		16
Ingles, John	1		4		9
O'Bryan, Francis			2		1
O'Bryan, Lawrance	2		3		14
Garner, Samuel	1		1		
Humphrey, Isham	1	5	2		
Ford, William	1				2
Batts, Joseph	1	3	3		1
Clements, William	2		2		9
Toole, Gareldus	1				26
McDade, Willis	2	1	6		
Woodard, Daniel	2	1	3		
Wimberly, George	1		2		17
Moore, Elijah	1	3	4		
Dilyard, Barnaba	1	1	1		2
Wimberly, Joseph	2	1	5		21
Gilbert, Nathan	1				
Williams, Matthew	1				
Dickenson, Jacob	1	3	4		20
Dilyard, Mary	1		2		
Dilyard, Matthew	1				
Hart, Priscilla			5		17
Hodges, Thomas	1	4	4		22
Savage, Loveless	3		1		4
Fort, Josiah	1	4	5		35
Fort, Elias	1	1	2		7
Fort, William	2	2	2		17
Ing, Sarah			2		
Odom, Absalom	2	4	3		
Odom, John	1				
Odom, Dempsey			2	1	
Odom, Jacob	1		4		
Odom, Aaron, Senr	4		1		
Pitt, James	3		3		7
Perry, Alse			3		
House, John	2	3	5		1
Trevathan, Robert, Senr	3		2		
Trevathan, Robert, Junr	1	2	1		
Rose, Robert	3	3	3		
House, Jacob	3	1	3		1
Etherege, Caleb	1	2	6		
Thompson, Robert	3	2	2		
Brown, Jesse	2	3	4		

NAME OF HEAD OF FAMILY.	Free white males of 16 years and upward, including heads of families.	Free white males under 16 years.	Free white females, including heads of families.	All other free persons.	Slaves.
Brown, Samuel	1	2	1		
Brown, James	1		1	1	8
Boykin, John	1	3	2		
Carlisle, Coleman	2		3		
Coleman, Robert	1	1	4		
Dilyard, Mary	2		3		
Evans, Abraham	1	2	2		8
Lynch, William	1	4	4		
Langley, William	1		2		4
Pitman, Abner	1	1	3		5
Pope, Benjamin	1		2		
Pritchett, William	1	1	2		2
Pope, Josiah	1	1	6		2
Philips, Etheldrid	1	2	5		11
Price, Elijah	1	3	4		
Rose, William	1		4		
Stallings, Simon	3	3	2		
Stallings, Elisha	1	3	5		2
Thorn, William	1	1	4		
Taylor, David	1	4	2		
Trevathan, William	1				
Teat, William	1	4	2		2
Whitley, Jonas	1	1	3		
Wiggins, Hardy	1	2	3		
Woodward, Noah	2				2
Pender, Wright	1				
Soary, Malakiah	1	4	4		
Rodgers, Robert	1		4		
Adams, William	1	1	1		1
Adams, James	1	2	3		5
Ayrs, Thomas	1		1		
Adams, Hopewell	2		3		2
Anderson, Henry	1	2	2		
Bonner, John	2	2	2		2
Ballard, Benjamin	1	2	2		
Billups, John	1	3	2		
Booth, James	1	2	4		14
Bell, John	1	1	1		8
Brown, John	2	2	7		1
Cherry, Levi	1	2			
Cherry, Robert	1				
Cherry, William	1		2		
Cromwell, Alexander	2	1	2		1
Cherry, Wright	1		1		
Cherry, Wily	1		2		
Cromwell, Thomas	1	4	3		1
Cobb, Edward	1	2	5		
Cobb, James	2	3	2		
Cherry, William	1		2		
Duggin, William	3	1	6		
Davis, Joseph	1	1	2		4
Dawson, John	1	1	1		20
Flood, Enoch	1	1	4		
Gaddy, Lucy		1	4		
Godfrey, Sarah		1	1		
Hawkins, Stephen	1		2		
Hacket, Michael	1	1	3		
Hines, John	1	1	2		
Henly, Jesse	1				
Hicks, James	1		1		
Hyman, John	1	3	1		1
Hardy, Robert, Sr	3		2		1
Hall, John	1		2		14
Hardy, Allen	2	2	3		
Hardy, Joseph	1	2	5		
Hodge, Miles	2	3	3		
Hodge, Abraham	1	4	1		
Hardy, Robert, Junr	2		4		
Hopkins, Elizabeth			3		
Hall, Edward	2	3	3		86
Jenkins, Thomas	1		1		
Jones, James	1	2	2		2
Johnston, Thomas	1		1		
Keal, Hardy	1	1	2		
Key, William	1	1	3		2
Knight, Jesse	1	1	5		
Knox, Robert	2	2	5		
Little, Exum	1				
Lawrence, John	1		2		
Little, John	1	1	2		5
Little, William	2		5		1
Lawrance, Solomon	2	2	4		
Lawrance, Elizabeth	2	4	6		2
Little, Gray	1		2		
Little, Jacob	1		2		5
Lawrance, Thomas	1	1	5		
Lawrance, Jesse	1		2		
Lawrance, James	1	2	1		
Lewis, Amos	1	1	5		
Lewis, Thomas	1	4	5		
Lees, Stephen	3	1	4		
Mitchell, Thomas					10
Morgan, Joseph	1		2		10
Manning, Benjamin	1		2		
Mayo, Judith	2	2	4		3
Mayo, David	1	1	2		1
Newsom, Joseph	1				

NAME OF HEAD OF FAMILY.	Free white males of 16 years and upward, including heads of families.	Free white males under 16 years.	Free white females, including heads of families.	All other free persons.	Slaves.
Newson, Hannah			5		
Newsom, Thomas	1		5		
Piper, Solomon, Jr	1	2	3		
Piper, Abraham	1	2	1		
Pippen, John	2		3		1
Pippen, Joseph, Jr	1	1	3		
Pippen, Benjamin	1	1	6		3
Pippen, Joseph, Senr	1	1	5		3
Pippen, Joseph	1		3		12
Pippen, Solomon, Senr	1	3	4		2
Pippen, Noah	1		3		
Reiner, Samuel	1	2	3		
Rogers, William	1	1	3		
Sharp, Joshua	3		9		
Scott, Israel				7	
Smith, Reuben	1	2	2		7
Scott, Isham				7	
Sharp, John	1		4		
Sessums, Solomon	1	4	3		12
Thigpen, Etheldred	1	1	1		
Thigpen, James	3		4		2
Taylor, John	1	5	2		
Thigpen, Jonathan	1				
Walker, Solomon	1	1	4		8
White, John	2	1	5		1
Wood, Ann	1	3	4		
Wiggins, William	2	2	2		
Walker, Thomas	1		1		
Summerlin, Thomas	2	3	5		
Hodge, Mary			2		
Knight, Walker	1	1	2		1
Bell, Frederick	1	5	1		7
Price, William	1	2	2		
Dozier, Peter	1		1		
Tool, Elizabeth	1	1	4		21
Kent, Thomas	1		1		
Armstrong, Joseph	1		1		
Bracewell, Jacob	1		1		3
Bracewell, Solomon, Senr	3	2	5		16
Bracewell, Solomon, Junr	1				
Burt, John	2		3		5
Bracewell, Unity		1	4		2
Bracewell, James	1	1			
Brown, Tarlton	1		2		3
Brown, Reuben	2	3	3		1
Clarke, Edmund	1	2	2		3
Davis, Joseph	1	2	2		3
Dickenson, Jane			1	2	
Dilyard, John	1	1	2		
Griffis, John	1	2	7		
Griffis, Demsey	1	1	2		1
Griffis, Francis	1	1	2		
Griffin, Edward				1	
Harrell, Simon	2	6	3		6
Howell, Joseph	1	1	3		8
Haywood, Sherwood	2		2		16
Irwin, Lewis	8				36
Jewell, Thomas	3	1	2		8
Irwin, Henry	1				12
Lodge, Lewis, Senr	1	1	1		
Lodge, Josiah	1		3		
Lodge, Lewis	2	3	4		
Leigh, John	1				27
Mace, John	1	1	1		2
Mitchell, John	1		1		
Pass, Samuel	1		2		4
Permenter, James	2	4	5		7
Petaway, Micajah	1		1		3
Pope, Philip	2		3		
Pitt, Joseph	1	1	1		4
Pender, Josiah	1		1		2
Parker, John	2		3		4
Penn, William	2	2	3		10
Sarsnett, Richard, Senr	3	2	2		3
Sarsnett, Richd	1		1		1
Sherrod, John	2		3		2
Sugg, Mary	2	2	3		13
Southerland, John, Jr	1		2		5
Sherrod, John	1	2	3		2
Southerland, John	1	1	2		12
Waller, James	2	2	3		11
Watkinson, Michael					
Wiggins, Matthew				4	
Wilson, John	2	1	1		17
Griffin, M'chael	1				8
Wilson, William	1	2	4		7
Woodward, Thomas	1	2	1		2
Wogan, Henry	1				
Teat, James	1	1	2		
Taylor, John	2	3	6		1
Allin, Roda	2				
Boazman, Britain	2	1	2		
Boazman, James	2	1	2		
Clark, Richard	2	4	3		
Dunn, John, Junr	1				
Dunn, John	3	2	3		
Davis, Emry	3	1			1

HALIFAX DISTRICT, EDGECOMBE COUNTY—Continued.

NAME OF HEAD OF FAMILY.	Free white males of 16 years and upward, including heads of families.	Free white males under 16 years.	Free white females, including heads of families.	All other free persons.	Slaves.
Dunn, Nicholson	1	2	3		
Dunn, Stephen	1	4	3		
Forehand, David	2		2		2
Griffin, Frederick	1	1	2		
Guin, Daniel	1	3	3		
Griffin, James	1	3	2		5
Holliman, Isham	1	1	4		5
Hanberry, Elizabeth			6		
Hall, John	1	3	3		
Holliman, Jesse	1	3	3		
Hanberry, Samuel	1	3	3		
Kelley, William	1				
Langley, Isaac	1	2	1		
Mace, Equilla	2	1	3		
Nasworthy, Samuel	1	1	4		
Nasworthy, Elizabeth		1	4		5
Permenter, Nathaniel	1	4	4		2
Pitt, Joseph	1		2		1
Pitt, Robert	3	2	3		3
Pitt, Henry	1	4	3		
Proctor, John	1	1	2		
Peal, John	1	4	7		
Pitt, Thomas	1	1	1		
Ruffin, John	3	5	3		
Stringer, Josiah	1	4	3		
Stringer, Charles	1	6	5		
Small, Benjamin	1		3		
Stringer, John	4	2	3		
Surgernor, John	1	2	5		2
Scarborough, Samuel	1	3	1		
Taylor, Perigrine	1		2		
Thornton, Robert	1	1	3		1
Ward, Solomon	1	2	4		
Waller, Benjamin		1	5		4
Ruth, William	2		3		4
Bullock, Martha		1	3		
Ruffin, Hannah		1	3		
Edwards, Titus	1	1	1		
Allen, Nathan	1	1	4		
Andrson, George	1	1	2		
Anderson, James	1		1		
Atkinson, Josiah	1	1	1		
Atkinson, Mary		2	1		
Anderson, Mourning	3	1	5		
Brake, William	1	2	3		
Barns, Elizabeth			1		2
Bryant, Arthur	1	4	4		
Broadribb, Thomas	1				
Bridgers, William	1		3		
Dawterry, William	1				
Gray, Charles	2		3		26
Manning, Timothy	2		1		1
Williams, Benjamin	1	3	3		
Arrington, Benjamin	3	2	2		10
Arnold, Edward	2	2	1		5
Arrington, John	2				3
Allen, Gabriel	1	3	6		7
Davis, Henry	1		1		
Blackburn, Benjamin	1	3	1		
Bolton, Richard	2	2	8		
Belsher, Bevilla	1	1	3		12
Brownrigg, George	1	1	2		17
Cartright, Hezekiah	2	1	5		7
Causey, Philip	2		3		
Causey, Philip, Junr	1	3	2		
Crairy, Hugh	1	4	6		1
Corbitt, John	1	1	2		
Crairy, Owin	4	5	5		5
Cartright, Thomas	1	2	3		2
Chitty, John	3	3	4		
Crairy, Huk, Junr	1				
Defnal, William	1				
Drake, William	1				2
Drake, Sarah			1		3
Downing, Matthew	1	4	2		
Drake, Jesse	1	1	2		
Downing, Judith	1	2	5		
Drake, David	1	2	7		2
Edwards, Nathan	2		3		2
Edwards, Simon	1	3	1		
Edwards, John	1		3		
Ellis, John	1	1	5		19
Edwards, Edmund	1		1		
Flemming, William	1	2	2		
Flemming, Sarah	1	2	2		
Flemming, Charles	1	1	1		
Holland, Henry	3	2	5		7
Hines, Richard	1				3
Hicks, John	1		4		
Harris, George	1	1	5		
Hearn, James	1		4		
Hines, Jesse	1		3		9
Hearn, Amos	1	1	3		
Holland, Daniel	2		6		
Hearn, William	2	1	5		
Holland, James	1	3	2		
Hines, Henry	2	4	3		14
Hines, Peter	1	3	4		13
Johnston, Mary			2		2
Johnston, Esther	1	1	4		12
Johnston, Amos	5	4	5		16
Kearney, Thomas	1	1	4		
Lane, James	1		2		5
Lester, Moses	1	1	4		
Mareley, Benjamin	3	1	4		
Matthews, Samuel	1		4		
Nowell, Enos	2	2	3		
Novel, Hardy	2	2	4		1
Quin, William	2	2	3		
Spell, John	1	2	3		5
Summelin, Flowers	2	1	3		
Spell, Lewis	1	1	2		13
Southerlin, Daniel	2	1	3		8
Summerlin, Henry	1	2	3		
Stokes, Demsey	1		5		2
Shirley, Richard	1	5	1		
Taylor, Teagle	2	6	5		1
Thirston, William	1	1	1		
Walker, Daniel	3	1	1		
Wootten, Joel	1	3	4		
Wootten, James	1	1	3		1
Taylor, William	1	2	2		
Andrew, Joseph	2	1	4		
Andrew, Solomon	4		2		
Barnes, James	2	2	1		
Barnes, Benjamin	1	1	2		
Brinkley, Abraham	1		2		
Balsom, Sarah			2		
Brinkley, Aaron	2	1	4		
Boazman, Jesse	1	1	4		
Corbitt, William	4		2		
Corbitt, Elias	1	1	2		
Wilson, William (Guardn of A. J. Haywood)					27
Causey, Ezekiel	1	2	2		
Cearney, John	1		2		
Copeland, Thomas	1	2	3		
Cearney, Thomas	3	2	4		
Cone, John	1		3		1
Cox, Moses	1		5		
Colwell, John	1	1	2		5
Davis, Nathan	1	3	3		
Dunford, William	4	2	2		
Doxey, Jeremiah	1	2	1		2
Drake, Sarah			1		3
Ellis, Reubin	1	1	2		
Drake, Henry	1	2	1		
Forehand, Solomon	2	4	6		3
Gardner, Joseph	1	4	2		
Gardner, Jonathan	1	4	2		3
Gay, Zerobabel	1		1		
Godwin, Mary			2		
Gay, Henry	1		2		7
Gay, John	1		2		
Hadcock, Shadrach	1		1		
Jones, Ambrose	1	1	1		
Jones, Mary		1	3		
Kellibrew, Caleb	1	2	2		
King, Henry	1	2	3		2
Langley, Shadrack	1	1	4		
Langley, Hezekiah	1		4		
Lester, Moses	1	1	4		
Lee, Jesse	1		2		
Langley, Isaiah	1		2		
Langley, Josiah	1	1	1		
Lewis, Nathan	1	4	4		
Maund, Lott	1				
Marchment, Charles	1	4	2		2
Maund, Mary	1	2	4		3
Mayo, Samuel	1	3	4		
Mittur, Thomas	1				
Nettle, John	1	3	5		3
Owen, Andrew	1				
Owen, William, Jr	1	2	2		
Owen, John, Senr	2	1	2		
Owen, William	1	1	1		
Owen, Elizabeth	1				
Owen, Selah			1		
Owen, Moses	2	1	2		4
Perry, John	1	2	3		8
Permenter, Wright	1	3	4		2
Philips, Solomon	3	4	3		
Ruffin, Joseph	2		5		2
Russel, Sarah			3		
Robertson, Archelas	2		3		
Quin, Amos	1	1	2		
Rasbury, Jesse	1				
Stokes, William	1	1	4		1
Stokes, Demsey	1		5		2
Summerlin, Edward	1	2	3		
Stokes, David	1	2	3		2
Skinner, Demsey	1	3	4		8
Summerlin, Hardy	1	2	4		
Scarbrough, James	2	5	6		5
Skinner, John	1				
Storey, James	1	2	3		
Summerlin, Nancy	2		1		
Taylor, Samuel	1	1	4		2
Thorn, Hardy	1				5
Taylor, William	1				
Tarlton, Josiah	1	1	1		
Wootten, Amos	3	4	5		
Wootten, Joshua	1	1	1		
Wootten, William	1		1		
Cearney, Thomas	2	3	3		
Whealer, Henry	1				
Amason, William	2				1
Amason, Abraham	1	2	2		
Amason, Jesse	1	1	2		
Atkinson, Sarah		1	1		
Amason, Benjamin	1	1	4		1
Amason, Eli	1				2
Amason, Benjamin, Junr	1	2	1		1
Amason, John	2	1	2		
Amason, Uriah	2	4	2		
Amason, Josiah, Jr	1		1		
Barnes, Absalom	1	2	4		
Bruin, George	4	1	4		
Barefeild, Mills	1	2	3		
Barns, Archelaus	2	2	5		2
Barns, Aziel	2	1	3		
Baggett, Blake	3	3	6		
Barnes, Ephraim	4	3	3		
Baggett, Nathan	1	2	5		
Barns, Jacob	2	2	3		2
Baggett, Joel	1	2	4		
Bartle, John	1	2	2		
Barns, Nathan	1				1
Bentley, Joshua	1	1	5		7
Bullock, John	2	2	2		
Barefield, Daniel	2	2	4		6
Bandy, Lewis	1	1	4		
Boltin, Isaac	1	1	1		4
Brantley, Malachi	1	2	4		
Boltin, Luke	1				4
Corbitt, John	1	2	2		
Chester, John	1	2	4		
Cox, Joseph	2	4	4		
Chittin, Thomas	1	3	4		
Chittin, Winifred		2	3		
Cato, Stephen	2	2	4		
Daniel, William	1	3	2		
Davis, Thomas	2	2	4		
Daniel, Asa	1		4		
Daniel, David	1	1	1		1
Daniel, Joseph		3	1		1
Dickenson, William	2		5		8
Daniel, Rebeccah	1	2	7		
Daniel, Josiah	1	1	4		
Daniel, William	1		6		
Barnes, Selah	1	2	1		
Daniel, Levi	1		2		
Davis, John	2	2	5		
Davis, James	1	3	2		
Daniel, Nathan	1	1	6		1
Daniel, Lemuel	1	2	3		
Eason, Robert	1	2	3		3
Ellis, William	2	2	4		2
Eason, Isaac	1		9		5
Eason, Shadrack	1	4	5		5
Eason, Abner	1	1	2		1
Gay, William	1	2	2		
Gay, Richard	1	3	5		
Grice, Jesse	1	2	3		
Gay, John	2		6		
Gay, James	1	2	3		
Nowell, Patience		1	1		
Galloway, Richard	1	2	3		
Harrod, Wilson	1	2	1		
Joyce, William	1	4	2		
Johnston, James	1	3	3		
Johnston, Joshua	3	2	5		
Johnston, Daniel	1				
Johnston, Benjamin	1	1	3		
Lewellin, Edmund	1	1	1		
Mayo, Cyprian	2	2	3		
Mayo, Edward	2		1		
Mairs, William	1		1		
Mayo, John	2	3	2		
Mayo, Joseph	2		3		
Mason, John	1		5		
Moore, Samuel	1		5		9
Norwood, John	1	2	4		5
Parish, Henry	1	1	2		
Poole, Robert	3	4	2		4
Potter, John	1	4	1		
Prescoat, Benjamin	1		3		
Robertson, Henry	1	1	4		
Robertson, William	1	2			

HALIFAX DISTRICT, EDGECOMBE COUNTY—Continued.

NAME OF HEAD OF FAMILY.	Free white males of 16 years and upward, including heads of families.	Free white males under 16 years.	Free white females, including heads of families.	All other free persons.	Slaves.
Rogers, Trusse	3	2	6		
Rogers, Daniel	2	1	4		
Reason, William	1	1	5		
Reason, John	1	3	4		
Rogers, Jesse	1		4		
Stuckey, Edmund	3	3	4		3
Singleton, William	1	2	2		
Simms, Simon	1	1	5		2
Shepherd, Thomas	1		2		
Bateman, Thomas	3	2	2		
Stanton, James	4	1	3		24
Tart, Catherine			2		6
Tart, Millicent			1		3
Thigpen, Gilead	3	1	3		3
Thigpen, Cyprian	1	2	5		
Wells, Thomas	2	1	4		
Ward, Messer	2	2	4		
Whitley, William	1		6		
Wells, Leonard	1	3	6		
Whitley, George	1	3	5		
Winslow, Joseph	2	2	6		
Woodard, Elisha, Jr	1	3	4		2
Winslow, Thomas	2	2	3		
Lewellin, Thomas	1	2	2		
Ward, Daniel	1	1	4		
Bateman, Phebe		2	2		
Woodard, Elisha	2	2	1		1
Daniel, Milissent	2	2	2		
Amason, Josiah	2	1	2		
Walster, Henry	1				
Amason, James	2	2	4		
Cato, William	1	2	4		
Barnet, Lamon	1	2	3		
Runnels, Lamon	2	4	2		
Smock, John	2	2	2		
Robison, Patience	2	1	3		
Barnes, Joseph	2	3	5		5
Brooks, Elizabeth			1		
Blackburn, William	1		1		1
Barnes, Demsey	3	2	6		2
Bateman, Claburn	1	3	5		
Barnes, Jesse	1		1		1
Barefoot, Jeptha	4		1		
Barefoot, Jeptha, Junr	1	1	1		
Barefoot, William	1	1	2		
Barefoot, Noah	1		2		
Coleman, Robert	1		4		
Coleman, Charles	1	4	3		7
Cahoon, John	1	2	1		
Doudy, John	2	2	7		
Dixon, Thomas	1	2	3		5
Dew, John	1	3	2		6
Dixon, Nicholas	1	3	4		
Dew, Arthur	2	2	2		16
Deloach, John	1	3	2		5
Izzell, George	1	2	3		
Izzel, Jesse	1	1	2		
Izzel, Timothy	1	1	1		
Farmer, Benjamin	1	4	4		2
Farmer, Joseph	1	2	8		2
Forehand, Solomon	1	6	6		3
Farmer, Isaac	1	4	6		3
Farmer, Jesse	1	1	1		6
Farmer, Samuel	1	3	3		
Hall, Joseph	1	4	3		
Hedgpith, John	3		3		
Jordan, Cornelius	1	2	1		1
Jordan, Cornelius, Jun	1	4	1		
Johnston, Nathan	1	2	5		
Jordan, Joshua	3	3	4		4
Joiner, Cardy	1	1	2		
Joiner, Charles	1		3		
Murborn, John, Jur	1	2	2		
Morris, John	2	2	7		
Morris, Thomas	1	1	1		
Morris, Joshua	1	1	3		
Morris, William	1	1	3		
Murborn, John	2	3	2		
Marry, John	2		1		
Robbins, Roland	1	5	4		
Robbins, Sarah	1		4		
Robbins, William	1	3	2		
Roundtree, John	1		2		2
Robertson, Hardy	2		6		
Robertson, Ezzel	2		2		6
Roundtree, Francis	1				
Roundtree, Moses	1	2	4		
Sanders, Thomas	3	1	3		
Sims, Benjamin	1	3	4		11
Stokes, William	1	1	4		1
Simms, Joseph	5		3		27
Sims, Jesse	1	2	2		
Winburn, Joseph	1		1		
Walten, John	1	4	3		19
White, William	1	4	1		1
White, Joshua	1				
Whitehead, James	1	2	2		2

NAME OF HEAD OF FAMILY.	Free white males of 16 years and upward, including heads of families.	Free white males under 16 years.	Free white females, including heads of families.	All other free persons.	Slaves.
White, William	2	2	4		1
White, John	1	2	1		
Wood, Daniel	2	2	2		
White, Luke	1	3	2		
White, Daniel	1	4	3		
Whitehead, William	1		2		7
Askew, Josiah	3	3	2		2
Askew, Uriah	1				
Barren, Barnaba	1	1	3		7
Barren, James	1	4	4		4
Barnes, James	1	4	5		4
Bell, John	1	1	1		
Brasier, John	2	4	2		1
Barnes, Jethro	1	4	4		
Barnes, William	1		2		
Barnes, Stephen	2		1		
Batts, William	2	4	2		
Barnes, Briton	1	4	4		
Barnes, Abraham	2		2		
Brown, William	1	1	3		
Cahoon, Joseph	1				
Cahoon, John	1	2	1		
Ellis, Dehorty	1	1	2		
Ellis, Jacob	1		1		
Ellis, William	1	4	1		7
Edwards, Thomas	1	1	6		
Farmer, Joseph	1	2	2		
Farmer, Joshua	1	1	3		
Farmer, Thomas	1		1		1
Gill, Taylor	1	2	2		14
Gay, Henry	2		1		
Gardner, Martin	2	6	4		
Hickman, Nathaniel	2		2		6
Haynes, John	1		3		
Hall, David	1		4		
Hickman, William	1	3	3		4
Jordan, Joseph	1	1	2		
Mills, Naman	1	4	3		
Matthews, Gilbert	1	1	1		
Muburn, Eady	1	3	3		5
Parrish, Selathiel	1		4		
Page, Thomas	1	1	4		
Pitman, Samuel	1	2	1		
Page, Jacob	2	4	6		
Permenter, John	2	3	2		9
Powell, Daniel	1	2	8		
Permenter, Margarett	1	1	3		2
Pendor, Joseph	1	3	6		17
Page, John	1				
Rogers, William	1		2		
Rogers, William, Jun	1	2	2		
Solomon, William	1	1	5		
Sanders, Christian			1		3
Sherrod, Joseph	1	3	2		
Tart, Nathan	1	1	1		18
Thorn, Nicholas	1		3		4
Todd, Hardy, Junr	1				
Todd, Lewis	1		3		1
Thorn, Martin	3		2		
Taylor, Emanuel	1	2	3		
Thomas, Mary	1		2		8
White, William	2	2	3		
Williford, Hartwell	1	1	7		
Wiggins, Noah	1	1	2		2
Williams, John	1		2		5
Webb, Richard	1	2	6		
Williford, John	1	2	2		
Webb, John	1	3	2	1	
Thomas, Jonathan	1		1		2
Lewellin, Alexander	3	3	2		
Hales, John	1	1	2		
Baker, Blake	3		2		16
Belhul, William	1				
Batts, William	4		2		
Batts, Field	1				
Broadstreet, Charles	1		2		
McCain, Ann		1	2		
Donaldson, Robert	1				
Goodwin, Tabitha	3		6		7
Gardner, Mary	1	1	3		1
Howerton, Thomas	1	2	5		
Howell, Esther	1		3		6
Jones, Frederick	1				
Knight, James	2	1	3		11
Kelley, Sarah	1		4		1
Spiers, Wright	1		2		
Schink, Joseph	2				4
Matthews, William	1		2		
Ross, Joseph	6				2
Tolestone, Mary	1	2	3		
Thigpen, Nathan	1		4		
Norris, John	2	1	6		
Pope, Jonathan	1	4	4		
pitman, Mary	1	1	4		
pender, David	1	1	5		9
Weaks, John	1	2	3		
Webb, John	1	3	2	1	

NAME OF HEAD OF FAMILY.	Free white males of 16 years and upward, including heads of families.	Free white males under 16 years.	Free white females, including heads of families.	All other free persons.	Slaves.
Frier, Mary		2	2		
Harrison, Mary Ann	1		2		15
Smock, John	1	1	1		
Runnels, Thomas	1	3	2		
Coleman, Stephen	1		2		2
Coleman, Aaron	2		3		8
price, Samuel	1	2	4		
Coker, Brumbly	1	3	3		
Lewis, Exum	3	3	3		15
Lynch, George	1	4	6		11
Lewis, Figuret	1	1	3		12
Cooper, David	1	3	4		
Cooper, Martha	2	1	4		
Freeman, John	1		2		5
Carlile, Ann			3		4
Adams, Briton	2	3	4		
Alsobrook, Joseph	2	3	3		
Atkins, John	1	2	5		
Bradley, Samuel	1	4	3		3
Bradley, William	1	2	3		
Boykin, James	1	2	2		
Brantley, Amos	1	2	3		3
Benton, Abselom	3	3	2		40
Coker, Elizabeth	1	2	2		
Cherry, James	1	2	3		
Coleman, Josiah	1	2	4		
Coker, James, Junr	1	2	2		
Cofield, David	2				16
Coker, James	2		3		3
Coker, William	2	2			
Coffield, Benjamin	2	3	3	2	8
Cooper, Malakiah	2	2	3		
Colten, William	3	2	5		3
Coker, Richard	2	2	4		
Dixon, William	2	2	2		
McDaniel, Daniel	1	2	5		4
Daniel, John	1	3	3		
Thomas, Drahon	1	2	9		
McDaniel, Campbell	1	2	4		
Durley, Horatio	1		2		6
Dixon, John	1	2	3		
Dixon, John, Junr	1	1	2		
Deal, Adam	1	3	4		
Exum, John	1	1	2		2
Edwards, John	1	1	5		3
Edwards, Joseph	1	2	3		2
Exum, William, Junr	1	2	2		
Exum, Barnaba	1	2	3		
Edwards, Benjamin	1	2	3		2
Exum, William	1		1		20
Exum, Etheldred	1		2		3
Exum, Rachael			1		1
Exum, Susannah		2	2		2
Etheridge, George	1	2	4		
Fort, John	1		2		5
Flanagan, John	2	5	4		
Fort, William, Senr	4		1		6
Foreman, Isaac	2	3	4		
Foreman, George	1	2	4		3
Floara, Lazarus	1	2	4		
George, John	1		2		2
George, Michael	1	1	3		
Goodman, John	2	4	5		15
George, Thomas	1		1		
Hammons, Shadrack				8	
Hammons, Jordan				4	
Harris, Nathan	2	2	2		14
Hare, William	3	5	3		
Hare, Nicholas	1	1	3		
Hancock, Randolph	2		3		4
Howard, John	1	2	2		2
Hails, John	1	3	3		
Kinchin, Matthw	2	4	2		23
Howell, Nathaniel	2	1	2		
Hamilton, Andrew	1	2	3		
Ing, Joseph	1	1	7		
Jackson, Frederick	1				
Knight, Spier	1	4	2		
Landingham, Thomas	1	6	4		
Morgan, Isaac	1	2	2		
Mial, John	3	3	2		
Morris, Hadley	1	3	2		3
Manning, William, Senr	2	3	7		
Nelson, James	2	1	3		
Williams, Elizabeth		1	3		12
Nicholson, Malakiah	2	3	4		4
Nicholson, John	4	3	10		25
Pitman, Elijah	3	3	4		12
Powell, William	1	3	4		10
Parker, Francis	2	5	5		4
pyland, John	1	3	2		2
Penny, Malikiah	1		2		
pitman, William	2	2	3		
Pace, John	1	2	4		
Philips, Arthur	1	2	3		15
Price, Samuel	1	2	2		
Pace, Stephen	1	2	4		

HALIFAX DISTRICT, EDGECOMBE COUNTY—Continued.

NAME OF HEAD OF FAMILY.	Free white males of 16 years and upward, including heads of families.	Free white males under 16 years.	Free white females, including heads of families.	All other free persons.	Slaves.
Penny, John	1				
Powell, Moses	1	2	3		
Smith, Reddick	1	5	3		
Spier, Philip	2	2	2		
Spier, Christian	4	1	6		5
Lynch, Wright	1	2	2		
Watkins, Daniel	1	2	2		
Williams, John	1		4		2
Williams, Matthew	1	1	4		6
Wiggins, John	2	1	3		12
Watkins, Josiah	1	2	2		
Vann, William	1	3	2		
Vick, Josiah	1	3	3		
Murphree, David	1	3	2		
Cherry, Lemuel	2	2	3		
Perry, Ann		2	4		
Banks, Thomas	2	2	3		
Pace, John	2				5
perrit, Ann		1	3		
Anderson, William	1	3	3		
Barlow, Sarah			3		3
Bryant, George	1		1		1
Bell, William	1	1	4		9
Bryant, Billey	1	1	5		
Bradley, Burwell	2	4	3	1	2
Bradley, Joseph	1		1		
Bell, Whitmil	2	1	1		8
Bellamy, John	1	1	1		9
Bell, Bythael	1	2	3		14
Bracewell, Isaac	1	2	4		1
Bashford, Alexander	2	1	4		
Bryant, Evan	1				3
Colten, Samuel	3	5	1		6
Colten, George	1	1			1
Cooper, Josiah	1		3		
Cooper, John	1	2	4		
Hall, David	1	1	4		
Ginn, Elisha	1	1	1		
Carlile, William	1	3	6		
Cofield, Thomas	1	2	3		6
Dilyard, Nicholas	2	3	4		
Dorman, John	2	1	4		2
Dancey, Archebald	2	1	6		8
Dorman, Mary	1		2		5
McDowell, John	1	3	4		
Douge, Peter	1	2	5		
Dicken, Ephraim	2				6
Dilyard, James	2	1	1		1
Foxall, Thomas	1		2		11
Foxall, John	1	1	2		3
Foxall, Thomas, Junr	2	1	1		8
Fountain, John	2	2	6	1	
Faithful, William	1	2	4		
Fountain, Henry	2	3	5		
Harrison, Henry	1		4		6
Harper, Robert	1	3	2		5
Howell, Henry	2	2	3		
Howard, Jesse	1	2	3		
Jelks, Lemuel	2	2	3		9
Lackey, John	2		3	2	15
Meals, Jethro	1		2		
May, Hardy	2	3	4		
Moore, Elizabeth	1	3	4		2
Oneal, Edmund	1	1	3		
Oneal, Lamentation	1	3	6		
Proctor, Jacob	2		2		6
Price, William	1	2	3		
Philips, Henry	1		2		1
Price, James	1	2	2		
Price, John	1		2	1	
Philips, Sarah	1	2	3		16
Perritt, Solomon	1	3	3		2
Perritt, Ann		1	2		2
Rollings, William	2				
Stogdale, Matthew	1		4		14
Savage, Absolam	2	2	4		2
Sessums, Jacob	2	3	5		23
Soary, Malakiah	1	1	3		
Sessums, Amos	1	3	3		
Sessums, Elizabeth	2	2	4		
Stogdale, Dennis	1				1
Sebral, Joshua	1	1	3	2	
Webb, John	1		2		
Williams, Uriah	2	1	2		3
Anderson, James	1		2		
Braddy, Joseph	1	1	5		6
Braddy, Job	1		3		
Beavours, Aziel	1	1	2		
Bilberry, Donel	2	2	6		
Biggs, Bathia	1	2	5		5
Bridgers, Nathan	4	2	2		
Blackburn, William	1	3	3		
Bell, Joshua	2	2	1		14
Batts, Benjamin	1	1	1		1
Bryant, John	2	2	4		
Bryant, Jesse	1		1		
Batts, John	2	3	2		2
Clerk, Jesse	1		4		
Carlile, John	1	4	4		
Calf, Lewis	2	3	5		
Champaign, Jesse	1	1	3		
Carlile, Robert	1	1	3		
Carliles, Clark	1	1	2		
Champion, Willis	1				
Wombel, John				1	
Cook, William	1	1	3		1
Dorman, Delilah	1	1	2		1
Dicken, Ephraim	1		2		11
Dicken, Benjamin	3	1	6		7
Dicken, Edmund	1	2	2		
Davis, John	1	2	2		
Davis, John, Junr	1	1	1		
Edwards, Micajah	1		5		1
Freeman, William	1	2	4		
Garrett, Thomas	1	1	4		
Glover, Parsons	2		3		
Howard, Hardy	1	2	2		
Hodges, Willis	1	1	5		
Harris, Thomas	1	1	4		
Hudnal, Robert	2	4	6		2
Haynes, Francis	1	1	3	1	
Haynes, William	2	1	5		2
Howard, James	1	1	2		
Hackney, William	3	3	9		5
Howard, John	1	2	2		
Howard, Willis	1	1	4		6
Hudnal, Willis	1	4	2		6
Hudnal, John	1				
Hart, Benjamin	3	2	3		1
Irwin, James	1	2	3		2
Jackson, James	1	3	4		
Jones, Lazarus	1	3	3		
Key, Henry	1	3	3		
Lawrance, John	1	4	4		9
Loyd, Rederick	1	2	2		1
Northern, William, Junr	1	1	3		2
Northern, William, Senr	1	1	3		2
Pope, Atkins	1		2		
Parker, Caden	2	4	3		1
Pope, Jesse	1	1	3		
Pippen, Joseph	1	3	1		
Portice, Robert				1	
Parker, Jonas	1	3	3		7
Rhodes, Joseph	1	3	4		
Scutchion, Mary		1	4		6
Soary, Andrew		2	4		
Savage, Frederick	1		1		
Swails, John	2	1	4		4
Savage, Gerrod	1	2	2		
Swails, Joseph	1	1	1		15
Swails, Mary	1	1	2		4
Spinks, Presly	2	3	6		4
Tharp, Solomon	1		1		7
Terry, Thomas	1	3	2		1
Weathers, Howel	1		5		
Weaks, Sarah			1		2
Webb, Patience	1	2	2		
Wells, Willibe	1		1		
Weaks, James	2	3	5		2
Kitchen, Booze	1	3	2		3
Champion, Benjamin	1	3	2		8
Howard, Mary		1	3		4
Weaver, Asiel	1	2	3		
Scutcheon, Samuel	2	2	3		2
Owen, John	1	1	3		
Kitchen, Jethro	1	1			2
Bell, Joshua, Junr	1				2
Bell, Write	1				1
Weaks, Archelaus	1	2	3		
Alsobrook, Pethena			3		
Shuffell, William	1	2	3		
Fitzgerrald, George	3	2	6		2
Dancy, Edwin	2	1	3		13
Smith, Ann		2	3		
Flanagin, Mary		2	3		
Coleman, Aaron	2		1		9
Coleman, Stephen	1		4		2
Davidson, David	1	1	5		
Biggs, Tully	1	1	1		

HALIFAX DISTRICT, FRANKLIN COUNTY.

NAME OF HEAD OF FAMILY.	Free white males of 16 years and upward, including heads of families.	Free white males under 16 years.	Free white females, including heads of families.	All other free persons.	Slaves.
Arrendel, Thomas	1		1		6
Arrendel, Thos, Jr	1	4	5		3
Alfred, Hinchin	1	1	5		
Alfred, John	3	5	5		2
Alfred, Ansel	3	6	4		
Ally, Roser	1	1	2		
Asene, Charles	1	3	5		
Asene, William	1	5	3		
Adams, Jesse	1	2	5		7
Alfred, Lodwick	3		2		6
Allen, James	1				
Anders, William	2	1	1		16
Arrendel, Bridges	2	1	5		6
Alfred, Job	1				6
Alfred, Lucy		2	4		
Amos, John	1	1	2		
Andrews, John	1	2	3		
Andrews, Abram	1	2	2		9
Andrews, Green	1	5	2		14
Andrews, Evan	1		3		1
Andrews, Gray	3	2	4		16
Anders, Atherton	1	1	3		6
Allen, William	1	3	3		3
Anderson, Churchville	1	3	2		2
Andrews, John	1	2	3		
Arrendal, James	1	1	2		
Alfred, James	1	1	5		1
Andrews, Peter	4	3	4		3
Bell, Robert	1	1	4		12
Brooks, Christopher	1	3	5		5
Brickell, William	3	4	2		21
Bridges, Wm	2		1		1
Boon, Raiford	1	3	1		
Boon, Phillip	1	3	1		1
Bass, Jacob	3	1	3		10
Bass, Jacob, Jr	1	1	4		3
Bass, Theophilus	1	4	6		5
Babb, Moses	2	1	2		10
Boon, William	2	4	6		4
Bowls, Benjamin	1	2	2		
Barrow, James	1	3	6		5
Bird, Jesse	2	2	6		8
Bird, Enos	1	6	1		7
Brickell, Thomas	1	3	2		7
Bird, Jesse (for Needman Bird's orphans)	2	2	5		8
Barker, James	1		2		4
Bridges, Lewis	1	3			
Baker, James	1		3		6
Bradford, Thomas	1	1	3		7
Bridges, Doral	1	1	1		
Bowers, Giles	4	1	4		9
Bowers, Jesse	1	6	3		
Bridges, Joseph	1		2		
Betts, Wyatt	1	3	4		
Betts, James	1		2		3
Bradway, Eliza				4	
Battle, Micajah	1	2	1		
Battle, John	2	1			
Brown, Thomas	2	5	3		
Bowden, William	1		4		1
Babb, John	1	1	2		
Babb, Thomas	1		3		
Babb, William	1	2	3		
Boon, James	1	1	5		2
Bachelor, Solomon	2	3	5		
Bowden, John	1	3	4		
Butler, Robert	3		1		
Bledso, Aaron	1	2	1		
Barnes, John	1				
Brantley, Joseph	1	3	4		
Bass, Riddick	1	1	2		3
Bledso, Rush	1	2	4		4
Bibba, Absolem				4	4
Bibba, William					
Bragg, Benj	1		2		6
Bell, Lucy		1	4		6
Barnes, Grace		3	3		1
Burnett, David	2	5	4		1
Bowden, Elias	1	1	4		1
Bobbit, William	1	1	2		
Bobbit, Wm	1	1	2		1
Bobbit, Turner	1	2	2		
Bobbit, John	2	1	1		12
Brown, William	1		1		
Bradley, Frank	1		3		
Baker, Henry	1	3	5		12
Brownin, William	1	1	1		
Butler, Gwynn	1	1	1		

HALIFAX DISTRICT, FRANKLIN COUNTY—Continued.

NAME OF HEAD OF FAMILY.	Free white males of 16 years and upward, including heads of families.	Free white males under 16 years.	Free white females, including heads of families.	All other free persons.	Slaves.
Bridges, Lewis	1	3	2		
Bevin, Thomas	1	1	2		
Bridges, Thomas	1		3		
Babb, John	1	1	2		
Beck, Joseph	1	4	3		
Bridges, Aaron	1		1		
Barns, Laburn	2	4	4		
Cooley, Edward	1	1	3		1
Cooley, John	2	2	5		
Chieves, Thomas	1	2	1		
Cook, Allen	1		2		
Crabb, Jarratt	1	1	1		
Crabb, John	1		1		
Crabb, Ozborne	2		2		1
Crabb, John	2		3		
Carloss, Cole	1	2	3		
Clapton, Richard	4	2	6		18
Cook, Charles	2	3	7		
Cooper, Howell	2	2	1		
Carr, Moses	1	3	6		
Collier, Doctor	2	7	3		
Cook, John	1		2		
Cary, Elisha	1	1	2		
Cook, Thomas	2	2	2		11
Carr, Eliaz	1	2	3		
Carr, Robt	3	3	5		6
Cooper, Robert	1				
Crowder, Ruth			2		5
Cunningham, Geo	1	2	3		
Chieves, John	1	4	5		5
Cook, Jacob	2	4	3		
Clifton, Thomas	3		2		
Clifton, Nathan	1				
Carpenter, John	1	2	2		
Cook, John	2	2	5		3
Campbell, Martin	1	2	4		
Catlet, Laborne	1	1	1		
Cook, William	1	3	8		
Clapton, David	1				
Cook, William	2	2	8		3
Cole, Charles	1	1	6		
Clifton, John	1	1	3		
Conyers, Ephraim	1	1	3		2
Cooper, William	1	1	6	1	7
Cook, Thomas	1	2	3		11
Conyers, Richard	1				6
Christmas, William	1		5		11
Conyers, Joel	1				1
Carr, John	3	2	5		
Craig, Roger	1	3	3		
Crowder, William	1	1	3		
Crowder, Absolem	1	1	2		
Collins, James	2	5	1		
Cook, Benjamin	1	1	7		1
Collins, William	1	3	3		
Coppage, William	1		1		
Collins, James	1	5	2		
Carlilse, Edward	1		1		6
Carlile, James	1	2	5		4
Croctor, Jacob	2	4	2		
Conyers, William	1		1		6
Curry, Thompson	2	2	7		
Colbert, Thomas	1				
Conyers, Ross	1		2		
Cook, Blanton	1		3		
Cook, Shemuel	1		3		3
Carroll, John	1	2	2		
Cruzier, John	1	1	1		
Carter, Thomas	1	3	4		
Davis, Micajah	1	1	2		
Dixon, Eliza	2	1	8		
Deviny, Jenkins	1	3	9		9
Davis, Archibd	1		2		17
Davis, Federick	1	3	4		
Dukes, Saml	2	6	2		
Drake, Ely	1	3	4		
Davis, Ransom	2	2	3		
Denby, James	2	3	3		11
Denby, Elijah	1	2	3		6
Dowdy, William	1	1	1		
Daniel, Charles	2	5	5		
Dent, Michael	1	3	5		
Denson, John	2	1	1		
Davis, William	4	1	2		1
Driver, Charles	1	4	4		1
Driver, Shaw	2	5	2		
Dunn, John	1		2		8
Dunn, William	1	2	2		4
Denton, Jesse	1	2	2		
Denson, William	1	2	3		
Denson, Witson	2	2	5		3
Denson, Edward	2	2	4		
Drake, James	3	3	4		1
Davis, Richard	1	2	3		
Dunstall, William					
Dorsey, Solomon	2	4	1		
Dorsey, William					

NAME OF HEAD OF FAMILY.	Free white males of 16 years and upward, including heads of families.	Free white males under 16 years.	Free white females, including heads of families.	All other free persons.	Slaves.
Debord, James	2	4	5		
Duke, Sally		2	1		
Dent, John	2	1	7		
Dorman, Michael	1	3	3		
Dent, Michael	1	3	5		
Drury, Harry	1	1	2		
Edwards, Daniel	1	4	5		1
Eaves, Benjamin	2		2		
Everitt, Judathan	1	3	5		2
English, Nathan	1		2		2
Edwards, William	1	2	4		
Eagerton, Hanah	1	3	4		
Ely, Josiah	3	1	5		12
Edwards, John	1	1	4		
Ely, Ely	3	3	5		8
Elliott, William	2	1	4		
Elly, Gately	1	2	2		
Fletcher, Joseph	2	4	2		
Floyd, Shadrack	2	2	6		
Fuller, Mesheck	1	3	2		
Fuller, Arthur	1	1	5		
Fitts, Jordan	1				
Finch, Edward	1	2	4		5
Frazier, Alexander	2		3		5
Foster, John	4	1	3		9
Fawn, William	2	2	1		5
Finch, Henry	1	2	2	1	
Fuller, Littleton	1	2	3		1
Fuller, Ezekiel	2	1	3		
Ferrel, John	1		5		12
Freeman, Joseph	2	5	2		1
Ferrell, Martha		2	5		7
Ferrell, William	1	2	1		2
Freeman, William	1	4	3		2
Freeman, Henry	1	2	2		
Freeman, Daniel	1	2	1		
Ferrell, Ancil	1	2	3		1
Freeman, Edward	1		4		7
Farmer, John	1	1	2		
Freeman, Rowland	1				
Green, John	1		5		7
Gill, Joseph	1	3	2		10
Glenn, Giddeon	2		1		10
Glenn, James	2	5	3		10
Gupten, Stephen	3	5	4		
Goodwin, Peter	1	3	6		5
Gant, Charles	1	5	1		6
Griggs, James	1	1	4		
Gosset, Nicholas	1	2	4		
Gupten, Abner	1				
Gupten, James	2	2	6		
Gibbs, Raborn	2	2	2		2
Gibbs, John	3	2	3		3
Goodwin, Willie	1	1	1		
Greggs, Thomas	1		1		1
Gossett, Joseph	1		1		
Green, John, Jr	1		5		7
Gay, Elias	1	1	3		
Gay, James	1	3	3		
Gay, Thomas	1	3	2		3
Griffin, Jesse	1	2	2		1
Goodlowe, Garratt	1	2	3		10
Gilliam, Marcus	1	2	4		
Greaves, Martha	1		2		2
Gilliam, Nathl	1	3	2		
Goodwin, Young	2	1	3		9
Gilliam, Ephraim	1	2	1		1
Green, William	3	1	3		35
Gordan, Isaac	1	4	3		
Gray, James	1	1	5		38
Green, Obed	1	1	4		5
Gant, James	3		5		
Goodwin, Nancy	1	1	3		6
Hammond, Jesse	2	2	4		1
Hammond, John	1		1		
Hubbard, John	1	4	3		
Harriss, Daniel	1		1		
Harriss, Brittin	4	1	4		8
Harriss, Howell	1	3	3		2
Hunt, Henry	1	2	5	1	1
Hubbard, John	1	3	3		
Hill, Thomas	1		2		4
Hill, Richard, Jr	1	1	4		3
Hamm, Jesse	1		3		
Hamm, Elisha	1	1	6		
Harrisson, William	1	3	3		
Hilsmon, Hines	1	2	3		1
Hunt, Shadrack	1	2	2		
Hill, Henry	3	2	4		28
Hunt, James	2	1			1
Hill, Jordan	2		4		7
Hall, Thomas	1		1		4
Hunt, Henry	1	2	5		2
Hornsberry, James	1	2	3		
Harriss, Harrisson	1	1	1		
High, Robert	2	4	3		4
Huckaby, James	2	2	4		8

NAME OF HEAD OF FAMILY.	Free white males of 16 years and upward, including heads of families.	Free white males under 16 years.	Free white females, including heads of families.	All other free persons.	Slaves.
Hendley, John	1	1	3		
Hester, James	2	3	5		28
Hicks, John	1	2	3		3
House, Thomas	1	1	1		7
Hill, Bennett	2	3	3	1	15
Huckaby, James	2	2	8		11
Hays, Hugh	1	2	2		35
Hightower, Rober	2	5	7		24
Hall, Durham	2	1	5		7
Hill, Thomas	1	1	7		37
Hill, Mary	1	4	3		45
Hill, Robert	1	1	1		46
Higgs, Zebulen	1		6		
Harriss, Exum	1		1		
Hogg, Charles	1	4	2		
Hogg, John	2	1	6		1
Harriss, Benj^a	1	2	1		1
Hartfield, Jacob	2		3		26
Hogwood, Henry	3	1	3		
Howell, Margret		2	4		
Hammond, Robt	2	2	2		
Hamm, Richard	1		3		1
Hayse, Thomas	1	4	1		
Hill, Richard	1	3	3		
Hall, Jonathan	1				
Hall, John	1	1	1		2
House, Isaac	1	2	1		15
Huckaby, James	1	2	2		
House, William	1		5		7
Hight, Harbert	3	3	6		2
Hight, John	1	2	1		
Hencock, John	1	1	3		1
Hight, John, Sen	1		1		10
Hight, William	1	2	4		
Huks, Miles	1	3	2		6
Hight, Robert	2	3	4	1	3
Hencock, Saml	1	2	4		
Harvey, James	4	2			4
Hayse, James	1	1	1		
Haswell, Thomas	1	1	7		
House, Edmund	1		1		3
House, William	1		5		7
House, John	1		1		4
Hill, Green	2	2	5		14
Hunt, John	2	2	4		22
Haynes, William	1	2	4		
Jackson, Josiah	2	1	4		2
Jackson, Julius	2	3	2		7
Jones, Fredk	2	5	2		
Johnson, Moses	1	5	5		
Joiner, Moses	1	2	4		
Johnson, Charles	1		2		
Jarrall, John	1	2	2		
Jarrall, Nathan	1	3	4		
Jordan, John	3	2	4		8
Journagan, David	1		1		
Jones, Joshua	1	4	4		3
Jones, Jacob	3		2		16
Jones, Counsil	1	2	2		9
Jackson, John	1	3	2		1
Ivey, Charles	4		6		7
Jones, Leullen	2	1	1		18
Johnson, Dempsey	1	1	1		3
Johnson, Jacob	1				
Jones, William	1				
Jones, John	1	2	4		
Ingram, Thomas	2		3		
Jones, John	1	2	7		
Jones, William	1	1	1		
Jones, Richard	2	3	3		
Jones, Joseph	2	2	6		6
Johnson, John	1	3	4		12
Jones, Drury	1	4	5	3	9
Jeffreys, Simon	1	5	5	1	51
Jeffrey, Orsborn	2		1	2	69
Jeffreys, David	1	3	5		35
Jones, James	1				5
Jones, Saml	1		1		6
Jones, James	1		1		
Johnson, Benj	1	4	3		
Johnson, Nedon	1	1	2		
Jones, Roger	2	2	6		19
Jones, Daniel	1	3	5		19
Jarral, Nathl	2	2	4		4
Jones, John	1		3		4
Johnson, William	1	1	4		15
Jones, Armistead W	1	1	3		11
Jones, Betty	1	1	4		5
Jackson, Eliz	1	1	3		
Judd, William	1				2
Kirny, Shemuel	2	3	4		20
Kimbell, Arch	1	1	4		2
Kimbell, Peter	1	3	3		1
Kilby, Exper	2		2		
Kilby, John	1	1	2		11
Kitchen, Jesse	1	2	4		
Lindsey, Saml	1	1	3		

HALIFAX DISTRICT, FRANKLIN COUNTY—Continued.

NAME OF HEAD OF FAMILY.	Free white males of 16 years and upward, including heads of families.	Free white males under 16 years.	Free white females, including heads of families.	All other free persons.	Slaves.
Lancaster, William	1	1	3		5
Lennard, Jones	2	2			4
Lennard, William	1	4	3		2
Liles, Jackson	1				
Liles, Mark	1	3	1		
Loyd, Thomas	1	2	2		
Loyd, Stephen	1	1	2		
Lambert, William	1	4	2		
Lambert, William S	2	1	2		
Lunsford, Seeman	1	3	5		
Long, Gabriel	1	2	4		25
Lewis, Sherode	1	2	2		
Leeman, Joseph	3	1	6		
Lashley, Howell	1	1	2		2
Liles, Charles	1	3	5		
Lemmons, John	2	2	6		
Lindsey, Betty	1	2	2		
Langley, Amy	1	1	1		
Melton, Robert	2	6	4		
Mitchell, William	1	1	1		
Meishaw, William	1	4	3		
Meishaw, John	1	3	2		
Mitchell, John	5	1	1		
Mitchell, John	1		1		
Murphy, William	1	2	8		
Morriss, William	1	3	5		
May, Thomas	1	2	2		1
Miller, George	4	3	5		
Morgan, Josiah	1		1		
Morgan, Benj	2	1	5		2
Morgan, Robert	1	2	1		
Miller, James	2	1	2		
Moody, John	1	1	4		8
Moody, Joel	1	1	1		
Milner, Jocobine	2	2	6		9
Mabry, David	1	2	5		5
Massey, Pettipol	2	3	7		
Medlong, James	1	1	2		
Mullens, Mary	2	5	4		
McMullens, Nathan	2	1	4		
Mitchell, John	2	6	1		2
Mullens, James	1	1	1		
Myrick, John	4	1	6		6
Murphy, Nicholas	1	3	6		4
Medlong, Mattw	1	2	4		
McKinnish, William	2		3		
Medlong, Bradley	1		3		
Martin, John, Sen	1	1	2		
Martin, William	1	3	1		
Massey, Ezekiah	1	4	3		
Massey, Richd	2	5	4		2
Mabry, Jesse	2	2	6		6
Mabry, John	1		4		4
McLemore, Young	2		2		22
McLemore, Young	1				3
Meton, John	2	3	5		
Martin, John	1	2	2		
McLemore, Robert	1				4
Moses, Abram	1	3	7		
Morgan, Rubin	1		4		
Murphy, James	1	2	8		
May, Benj	1	2	2		
Madlesly, William	1	2	3		
May, William	1	1	2	1	1
May, Reubin	1		2		
May, Berry	1		1		
Miller, Thomas	2	3	4		
Moregraves, John	1		1		
Murry, Titus	1	1	2		5
Merrit, John	1	3	4		
Murry, James, Jr	1	1	2		1
Mabrey, Seth	1	1	4		20
Murry, James	3		1		15
Macon, Hannah	1	1	6		1
Medlong, Nancy		3	3		
Mabley, Benjamin					2
Medlong, Joseph	1	3	3		
Murphry, Arthur	1	1			
Murphry, James	3		3		1
Myrick, Mary		2	3		
Medlong, William	1		2		
May, Rubin	1		2		
Morgan, Nathan	1	2	2		
Matthew, Ford			2		
Mitchell, Thomas	1	1	1		5
Nicholson, James	1	3	4		
Norwood, John	2	2	6		24
Nash, Joseph	1	1	2		
Nelms, Presley	2	3	3		25
Nunnery, Peter	1				
Norriss, Robert	1				
Norriss, John	1				
Norriss, Joseph	1		5	1	2
Nowland, Geo	1	3	2		3
Norwood, Jno, Jr	1	3	4		2
Norwel, James	2	3	3		
Nowland, Danl	1	1	3		6
Nowland, Budd	1	1	2		
Normon, William	1	1	2		1
Overton, Aaron	2	3	4		
Ownby, Thomas	2		5	1	4
Oden, Theo	1	3	2		
Ostwalt, Henry	1	2	3		
Privell, Thomas	4	3	5		
Pendergrass, Jesse	1	2	2		
Person, William	1				
Perry, James	1			1	
Perry, Burwell	1		1	3	3
Perry, Jeremiah	2	1	7		5
Perry, Jeremiah	1	1	1		3
Parish, Henry	1	1	2		1
Polliam, John	2	4	4		
Perry, John, Senr	1	2	1		22
Primm, John	1	3	5		
Parham, John	1				
Parker, John	2	2	1		
Pinnell, John	3	3	4		3
Person, Francis	1				5
Parker, William	3				7
Perry, Joshua	1	1	1		17
Perry, William	2	3			15
Perry, Joshua	1				
Perry, Ephraim			2		
Perry, Drury	2	2	5		4
Perry, Jeremiah	1	1	3		3
Perry, John	1		3		1
Paschael, Isaih	1	3	5		
Prarie, Lucres	2	2			
Pippin, John	1	3	4		
Perry, Ephraim	2		2		
Plummer, William	1	2	2		23
Pace, Geo	1	1	1		
Pace, Jeremiah	7		1		
Pippin, Isaac	2	2	5		
Parish, William	1		2		
Parish, Edmund	1	4	2		
Parish, Edmd	1	4	4		
Pierce, John	2		2		
Pierce, Mildred	1		5		
Pippin, Thomas	1	2	3		
Pierce, Stephen	1	3	5		
Pierce, James	1		4		1
Pierce, Stephen	1	4	3		
Pierce, Amey	1	1	2		
Pierce, John	1				
Pace, William	1	6	1		
Powell, Sion	1	1	3		
Pace, John	2	1	2		1
Park, John	2	7	1		1
Perry, Burrell	1	3	3		3
Pace, William	1		8		6
Perry, William	1	7	5		5
Patterson, Filmore	1	2	1		1
Parish, ——	1	2	7		
Perry, Nathl	1	2	3		1
Parish, Joel	1	2	5		5
Perry, Benja	2				19
Porch, James	1	1	3		
Porch, Wm	1		1		
Parker, Cornelius	2	2	2		
Perry, Simon	2		2		
Porch, John	1		2		
Primm, James	1	1	2		
Primm, Kitchin	1	2	2		5
Pasmour, Wm	1	1	2		3
Polland, Mary		1	2		
Partrick, Street	1	1	3		
Partrick, Spencer	1	2	3		
Pippin, Richd	1	2	3		
Perry, Priscilla		5	3		6
Powell, Enoch	1	3	1		
Perry, Mary		2	4		
Peterson, Salley		2	7		
Pumphry, Sylvanes	2	3	3		4
Portiss, John	1	4	3		1
Powell, Nathan	1				
Powell, Amos	1				1
Perry, Burwell	3		4		22
Rowe, Matthew	1	1	2		
Ransom, John	1	2	3		
Rainwabe, Gilliam	1	2	2		2
Richards, Benj	2	3	2		1
Read, Geo	1				3
Richard, William	2	1			10
Ratley, Macajah	1		3		
Rowland, Willie	1	2	2		
Ransom, Ruben	2	1	6		4
Rowland, William	1	3	6		
Ragsdale, Baebe	1	2	4		1
Rackley, Joshua	1	3	4		
Rush, Absolem	1	3	2	1	1
Rush, Benja	2		2		15
Rogers, Joseph	1	1	1		
Richards, Jesse	2		3		
Reaves, William	1	3	1		1
Ross, John	1	2	5		1
Richards, John	2	4	4		3
Richards, Geo	3		2		6
Richards, William	1	1	1		3
Robertson, Willoby	1				
Ross, James	1	2	6		5
Richards, Joshua	1	3	4		
Ransom, William	1	3	1		9
Rush, Benj	1				
Richards, Major	1	1	6		8
Railey, Andrew	2	1	6		
Railey, Morriss	1		1		4
Rogers, Rubin	2	1	4		
Reed, Fredk				4	
Rogers, Ruben S	1	1	3		
Rogers, Thomas	1		1		
Reeves, Richard	1	3	4		
Roods, John	1	1	4		
Roberts, Saml	1	3	4		
Rackley, John	1	5	2		
Rackley, Robt	1	2	6		6
Richardson, Wm	1	1	1		7
Ransom, Amey	1	1	1		7
Ross, Williamson	1	4	3		
Rose, William	1	3	4		8
Rose, Thomas	1	2	2		
Ricks, William	1	5	4		
Rossen, Daniel	1	2	3		1
Rackley, Mattw	1	1	1		
Rogers, Jacob	1	1	2		4
Row, Mattw	1	1	2		
Row, Patty		1	2		
Stephens, John	1	2	4		5
Stallions, Moses	1	1	1		5
Stallions, James	1	2	1		2
Stallions, John	1	1	2		2
Stiles, William	1	3	3		
Stephens, Jeremiah	2	1			11
Stallions, Wright	1	3	3		1
Sullivent, Cornelius	2		2		2
Solomons, James	1	3	5		7
Smart, Peter	1	1	3		6
Segars, David	1	3	11		6
Savage, Randolph	2	1	8		
Smart, Denton	1	2	3		
Smart, Stephen	1	2	3		1
Sandlen, John	1		1		
Sandlen, Eliza	1		4		
Smith, James	1	3	4		3
Self, Job	2	3	2		6
Sandlen, James	1	1	2		
Stallions, Elias	1	1	2		9
Stallions, Rubin	1	4	5		2
Stallions, Josiah	1	2	4		2
Simmons, Mary	4	2	2		2
Simmons, Tho	1	1	1		
Simmons, Henry	1	3	4		1
Simmons, William	2		4		6
Smith, Fredk	2	2	6		
Strickland, Jacob	1	2	2		1
Strickland, Obed	2	1	2		
Strickland, Abel	1	3	1		
Scrug, William	1				
Solomon, William	3	5	5		3
Solomon, Goodwin	1		3		
Shelton, James	1		5		
Sebrell, David	1				
Sumner, McKinne	1				
Stanton, William	1				
Sowell, Benj	4	3	1		20
Sanders, Vincent	2	1	2		3
Sanders, Kirby	1	2	4		5
Smith, John	1	2	4		
Sanders, William	2	2	5		
Smith, Richard	1	3	4		
Strother, Christo	1		3		12
Sanders, John		2	3		
Swanson, Richd	1	3	3		5
Scarbrough, Edwd	1	2	2		
Striplen, John	1	2	2		
Sherod, Thomas	3	1	6		9
Sledge, Isham	1	3	2		7
Seawell, Lucey	1		3		8
Seawell, Tho	1	1	3		7
Stone, Jonathan	1	3	5		1
Smith, James, Sen	2				8
Smith, John	2		3		
Smith, Joseph	1	1	1		3
Smith, John	1	1			2
Stone, John	1		4		3
Stone, William	2	2	3		
Seawell, Joseph	1	3	3		21
Smith, William	3		5		4
Smith, William	3		5	5	4
Strickland, Mattw	1	2	1		
Smith, Claborn	1	2	2		

HALIFAX DISTRICT, FRANKLIN COUNTY—Continued.

NAME OF HEAD OF FAMILY.	Free white males of 16 years and upward, including heads of families.	Free white males under 16 years.	Free white females, including heads of families.	All other free persons.	Slaves.
Sanders, Archur	1	1	2		
Sanders, Mary		4	3		
Stokes, Clary			2		
Smith, Patty		2	2		2
Seary, James	2	4	4		
Scarbrough, Peter	1	2	4		
Tharp, John	1	3	4		2
Taylor, Cornelius	1		1		
Taylor, Etheldred	1				5
Thomas, Eleza	1	2	2		1
Thomas, Anathas	1	3	1		1
Tharranton, Thomas	1	3	3		
Tharranton, Enoch	1	1	3		3
Thomas, Nathan	2		5		4
Tharranton, John	2	2	3		
Tant, Sion	1	10	3		
Tant, William	1	3	3		
Tant, Willis	1	2	5		1
Tharp, Timothy	1		2		
Thomas, John	1	1	2		1
Tabb, Dianah			2		28
Tabb, Sally			1		28
Terrell, Joseph	4	4	5		16
Timberlake, Frank	1	3	3		1
Thomas, Benj	1		3		
Thomas, Benj	1	3	2		1
Thomas, William	2	3	2		17
Thomas, Carter	1	3	4		8
Taylor, Frances	2	2	3		34
Carter, Thomas	1	1	2		
Upchurch, Benj	1	2	5		1
Upchurch, Richd	1	4	1		
Upchurch, Richd, Jr	1	1	1		
Upchurch, Moses	1	3	4		
Upchurch, James	1	1	2		1
Woodliff, John	1	1	2		
Woodliff, Phillip	1	1	1		
Woodliff, Tho	3	1	2		
Wright, Griffin	1	2	7		17
White, Mark	2		5		8
White, Eliz			4		4
Wiggin, Archer	1	3	1		
Wiggins, Sampson	2		4		
Willet, Dempsey	1	1	1		
Woodward, William	1	2	2		
Wood, William	1	4	4		1
Whittacar, Robt	1				2
Wilhite, Phillip	1	2	5		6
Wilhite, John	1				1
Wood, Brittin	1	4	3		1
William, Benj	2	1	3	3	6
Williams, John	1	3	5		4
Weathers, Jesse	2	3	5		12
Weathers, Mary			2		1
Wright, John	1	1	3		3
Wright, Jephtha	1		2		1
Wrenn, Elias	1	1	4		1
Wright, Benja	1	1	1		1
Winters, John	2	3	4		1
Williams, Floyd J	1	3	4		
Wheler, John	1	2	3		
Williams, Huckman	1	2	3		
Wheelor, Joseph, Jr	2	1	3		
William, Harriss	1	1	1		
Wray, Thomas	1	2	2		
Wheelor, Joseph	1	2	4		
Walker, Amos	1	2	3		
Williams, Leeman	2	3	5		5
Williams, Floyd	1	2	6		
Williams, John	1	2	4		
Winston, John	1	5	1		7
Winston, Isaac	1	1	6		5
Winston, Anthony	1	2	4		
Winston, Nathan	1	1	2		
Winston, William	3		1		3
Winston, George	1		1		3
Williams, Richa	3		2		3
White, Gardner	2	3	3		
Wright, Benj					
Winston, Moses	1		2		5
Warmouth, John	3	3	8		7
Williams, Elisha	1	3	4		13
Walker, James	1	2	7		5
White, Berry S	2	3	7		7
Watkins, John	3		1		11
Wood, James	1		3		2
Watkins, John	1	2	1		11
West, Samson	1				
Wells, Frances	2	2	4		2
Wister, Daniel	1	4	1		1
Wells, John	2		1		
Whelar, William	1	1	2		
Wister, Benj	2	4	2		8
Webb, Richd	1	1	7		
Williams, Saml	1		2		2
Webb, Jacob	1		2		3
Webb, Jesse	1	3	2		2
Webb, William	2		3		2
Wrenn, Geo	2	1	7		1
Webb, Ried	1	2	3		
West, Jesse	1	1	2		
Whelar, William	1	1	2		
Winters, Barnett	1	1	2		
Welden, Pines	1	4	2		
Walker, William	1	1			
Williams, James	2	4	3		
Wilhite, William	1	3	2		4
West, Henry	1	1	3		
Webb, John	1	1	7		2
Webb, Lewis	2	2	1		2
Williamson, Green	1				5
Wynne, Charles	2	4	5		
Welton, Agness		1	2		
Wynne, K. Wyne	1	1	1		10
Waddell, Jacob	1	5	2		1
Wynne, John	1		1		1
Wilhite, Lewis	1	2	3		
Wilhite, Ambrose	1	1	3		
Vickory, Hezekiah	1				
Vinson, David	2				3
Verrell, William	1	2	3		14
Vincent, Ezekiel	1	2	1		
Young, James	2	2	1		
Young, Stephen	2	1			
Young, Mary	1	2	4		
Young, Demetrius	1	1	1		
Young, James	2	2	2		2
Yarbrough, Henry	2	5	3		14
Young, John	2		3		7
Yarbro, Micajah	2	2	4		
Williford, Esabell	1		4		
Edwards, John	1	3	3		
Wray, James	2		1		
Davis, John	1	1	6		

HALIFAX DISTRICT, HALIFAX COUNTY.

NAME OF HEAD OF FAMILY.	Free white males of 16 years and upward, including heads of families.	Free white males under 16 years.	Free white females, including heads of families.	All other free persons.	Slaves.
Crawford, Thomas	3	2	7		31
Carstaphin, James	1	3	4		16
Sexton, John	1	4	3		9
Nunnery, Anderson	1	1	1		
Iles, William	1	2	1		
Seat, Joseph	2	4	2		
Daniel, Lewis	2	3	4		8
Portin, William	1	2	2		
Smith, Isham	1	2			1
Corbin, Mathuel	1	2	5		
Hoalt, Thomas	1	2	2		1
Powers, William	1	2	2		
Crawley, David	2	4	1		10
Corbin, William	1	3	5		6
Nevill, William	1	1	2		1
Nevill, Benjamin	1	2	2		1
Allanack, John	1		3		6
Hoalt, Thomas	2		2		11
Cox, William	1				
Read, William	1	1	3		1
Hoalt, James	1	2	3		
Green, George	1	3	4		1
Smith, Thomas, Senr	1		1		5
Burt, John	1	3	3	1	4
Winter, Joseph	2		4		
Harlow, Thomas	1	2	3		
Martin, Patrick	1		1		20
Read, Moses	2		5		1
Nevill, John	1				
Burt, William, Senr	1	1	8		12
Kearney, Thomas	1		3		32
Daniel, Archibald	1				
Daniel, William	3	2	3		12
Daniel, Willie	1				
Iles, John	2	3	7	1	3
Knight, Meradith	1		2		1
Davison, James	1	1	3		
Sullivant, William	2		2		8
Sullivant, Jesse	1	1	2		1
Thompson, John	1		2		
Coan, Winifred	1	1	3		
Burt, William	2	3	4		
Dickens, John	1				
Read, Jesse	2	7	3		11
Daverson, Jesse	3	2	3		1
Heath, William	1	1	2		1
Brewer, Moses	1	2	2		
Smith, Miles	1	5	4		2
Smith, Thomas	1		1		1
Horton, Samuel	1		4		1
Jones, Francis	1	2	9		12
Nevill, Benjamin	1	2	2		1
Jones, Henry	2		4		
Scott, Abraham					6
Green, Daniel	2		2		
Daniel, Sterling	2	2	6		1
Hawkins, Thomas	3		1	1	10
Scott, James	1				5
Cullum, Peter	3		3		1
Carter, Charles					5
Carter, Randol					1
Carter, Frederick					1
Carstaphin, Robert	2	4	4		6
Knight, Ephraim	2	3	2	4	8
Dillard, Joel	1	1	5		7
Garland, Jonathan	1	2	3		
Qualls, Peter	5	3	4	2	18
Scott, Abraham					1
Brownlow, James			1	1	17
Marshall, Alexander	1		3		
Weldon, Daniel	2		1		6
Grinstead, William	1	5	2		4
Wood, John	2		2		
Medlin, John	1		1		6
Duffey, Samuel	1	1	4		5
Powell, John	1	2			
Taylor, Jeremiah	1		1		
Powell, Benjamin	1	1	5		
Solomon, John	3	1	4		
Pugh, David	2	2	2		1
Hethcock, Isham			1	5	
Downs, William	1	1	3		1
Mitchel, Gabriel	2	1	3		6
Matthews, John	1	2	4		1
Tabb, James	1				39
Corlew, Sarah	1	2	7		
Lausate, John	2		3		8
Parsons, John	1	2			23
Mitchel, Abraham	2		5		5
Parsons, Joshua	1				19
Hawkins, Solomon					14
Dempsey, Thoroughgood				8	
Turner, Lucy	1	2	4		16
Moss, Mary		1	2		2
Gray, John	1	1	5		
Manday, Sarah	1	1	4		
Munford, Jeoffry					
Mumford, Thomas					
Moreland, Barrot	2	3	3		
Harper, Isaac	1	5	6		4
Whitfield, William	2	5	5		3
Edmundson, William	1	1	5		1
Mason, Turner	1	2	1		3
Turner, James	1	1	2		4
Perry, James	1	1	4		1
Jones, James					
Waddle, Nowell	1	3	4		
Harper, Ambrose	1		3		6
Jones, Joshua	2	3	4	1	
Harper, Henry	2	1	6		
Mumford, John	1	1	1		
Stafford, David	1	1	2		
Hethcock, Frederick				7	
Francis, Richard				1	
Demsey, James				3	
Hawkins, Jeffrey	1	1	1		
Jones, Brackett	1	1	1		
Hethcock, Ptolemy				5	
Hethcock, William				5	
Perry, Joseph	1	3	5		1
Spiers, Joseph	1	1	1		1
Wood, William					
Batley, Moses	1	4	2		
Mumford, William	1	1	2		
Edmundson, Thomas	1				
Edmundson, Elizabeth		1	4		
Vaughan, William	1	3	1	1	
Harper, Jett	1				
Harper, Vincent	1	2	1		3
Mumford, Richard	4	2	3		
Brasington, Samuel	2	1	1		3
Tabb, Thomas	2	1	1		54
Scott, Emanuel				7	
Moreland, Edward	1	1	2	1	2
Elbuk, Montfort	1	1	6		8
Ryanes, John, Senr	1	3	4		
Pugh, Eaton	2	4	5		35
Ballard, Walter	2	2	2		13
Johnston, Abraham	4	5	2	1	
Carter, Jacob	1	1			3

HALIFAX DISTRICT, HALIFAX COUNTY—Continued.

NAME OF HEAD OF FAMILY.	Free white males of 16 years and upward, including heads of families.	Free white males under 16 years.	Free white females, including heads of families.	All other free persons.	Slaves.
Carter, James	1	1	5		1
Handstred, Henry	1	2	1		
Coley, Charles	1	1	3		
Coley, Jeffry	2	1	2		
Mallard, John	1	2	1		
Carter, Robert	1	6	4		
Carter, William	2	1	4		11
Thompson, John	1	1	3		
Lee, Frederick	2	2	3		
Lee, Daniel	1				
Coley, William	1	2	1		
Morris, Philip	2	1	3		1
Coley, James	1	1	5		
Taylor, Nathaniel	1				
Carter, Joseph	1	4	2		
Yarborough, Charles	2	3	1		2
Pike, William	1	1	3		
Story, John	2		3		
Morris, William	1	1	4		1
Elms, Edward	1	2	5		1
Sledge, Archibald	2	3	6		8
Adkins, Thomas, Jun	1				
Adkins, Thomas	1	2	4		
Allen, Taylor	1				1
Carter, Charles	1	5	6		
Sledge, John	2	2	5		10
Meloney, James	1	3	1		1
Pike, William	3		2		1
Sledge, Mins	1				
Clarke, Eldred	1	2	3		9
Williams, Augustin	1	1	3		
Jinkins, William	2	3	5		6
Tony, John				7	
Bradley, Benjamin	3		1		4
Pike, Joseph	1				
Jones, William	1	1	2		
Rickman, Nathan	2		2		
Coley, David	1	1	1		
Smith, William	1	1	5		
Smith, Sarah			2		
Rickman, Mark	1	1	2		2
Price, William	2	2	1	10	5
Shine, James	2	2	6		1
Mallard, Joseph	1		1		
Dewberry, William	1	1	1		
Carter, Jesse	1	4	3		
Woodard, David	1		2		
Willis, Augustine	1		2		24
Parson, Benjamin	2	2	5		2
Baker, James	3	2	6		5
Smith, John	2	1	1		5
Newsome, Gillum	1	1	3		7
Johnston, William	1	2	4		3
Eaves, Mark	1	5	2		5
Hall, Theodorick	1	2	4	2	6
Southall, Furnith	1	1	3		1
Thompson, William	1	1	4		
Coley, Levi	1	2	2		
Willis, Lewis	2	4	5		15
Mallory, Francis	1		1		13
Groves, Thomas	1	4	5		3
Perry, Haleard	2	1	1		
Vike, George	1		2		
Marlow, John	1	2	3		
Ellis, John	1	1	5		4
Ellis, Mary			2		
Turner, James	1	2	2		5
Ingram, Ezediah	1				3
Marshall, Thomas	1		2		4
Haws, Henry	2	3	6		9
Southall, Hoalman	1		2		13
Hamblin, Wood	1				78
Carter. Benjamin	1	1	1		
Carter, James	1		2		
Smith, Howell	1		4		
Malory, William	1				
Hamblin, Martha			2		5
Smith, Richard	1				
Justiss, John	3	5	5		16
Southerland, John	3		7		
Grimmer, Thomas	1	2	4		
Southerland, William	4	2	2		
Grimmer, William, Jun	1		4		
Rogers, William	1	3	4		
Edwards, John	2		5		22
Manning, Joshua	1	3	3		
Pope, Elijah	1	3	5		1
Whitehead, William	2	3	2		12
Harrison, William	1	1			6
Brinson, Asehel	2		1		14
Barnes, Bartley	1		4		8
Champion, William	2		4		4
Edwards, Jesse	1	1	4		2
Whitehead, William	1				1
Edwards, John	2	2	4		
Dawson, Solomon	1	1	6		6
Smith, Drew	1	1	2		26

NAME OF HEAD OF FAMILY.	Free white males of 16 years and upward, including heads of families.	Free white males under 16 years.	Free white females, including heads of families.	All other free persons.	Slaves.
Williams, John	1	2	3		4
Bishop, Mercus	2	2	3		3
Bell, Shadrack	1		1		12
Bell, Elisha	1	2	3		12
Brewer, Jesse	1	2	2		1
Harrison, Jesse	1	1	3		
Lankford, William	1	2	1		
Whitaker, Lunsford	2				1
Smith, Arthur	2	1	3		20
Barns, Matthew	2		3		1
Daffin, George	1	1	4		8
Fort, Willis	1	1	2		4
Pulley, Benjamin	1	2	4		1
Merritt, Drury	1		4		1
Bailey, William	2	4	1		10
Dickson, Josiah	1	3	4		3
Josey, Robert	2		1		3
Cooper, Thomas	1		3		25
Shield, Thomas	2	1	2		5
Baker, Jordan	2	2	1		
Mangram, Henry	1		1		
Pulley, Wasdon	1	1	3		
Jones, John				6	
Vaughan, William	1	5	3		10
Merritt, Thomas	1	1	6		7
Gammon, James	1	2	2		
Whitehead, Susannah	1		1		2
Smith, James	2	1	3		57
Bell, John	1		2		6
Whitaker, Edward	2				
Jones, Joshua	1		3		
Poire, Francis	2	1	3		4
Barker, Joshua	1	2	5		
Jones, Elizabeth			2		4
Whitehead, William	1	2	1		
Grimmer, John	1	2	4		
Davis, Thomas	1	2	3		37
Grimmer, William	1		1		
Pulley, William	1	1	4		
Ditto for Robt. Ricks	2	3	6	1	28
Rutland, Shadrack (for Rockets)					
Moore, John	1		5		10
Vinson, John	1	1	1		
Tadlock, Thomas	2	4	5		
Tadlock, James	1				
Kendall, William	1		1		
Webb, George	1		2		
Tune, John	1	3	2	1	
Turner, Peter	1	1			9
Ditto for William Turner, decea^d			1		1
Turner, John	1	1	2	2	1
Hill, William	1	2	4		1
Kendal, James	1	1	1		
Mitchell, John	2	3	5		2
Dillard, William	2	1	5		3
Overstreet, Henry	2	2	4	1	13
Carson, John	2	2	2	6	3
Lowe, Thomas	2	1	4		3
Dillard, Owin	1		2		5
Branch, William Grog	1	2			5
Duncan, George, Sen	2		4		3
Lewis, Warner				3	1
Lewis, Morgan				4	
Lewis, Charles				6	
Motley, Henry	1		1		3
Wiggins, Thomas	1	3	1		
Poredice, William	1	4	7	1	1
Jones, Robert	2	1	4	1	
West, George	3	1	4		5
Denton, John	1	2	1		2
Matthws, Moses	1	3	6		1
Heptenstal, James	1	1	2		
Elliot, Elisha	1	4	2		
Goodwin, Jane		2	3		11
Haywood, Egbert	2	1	4		17
Haywood, John	1	2	2		22
Elbuk, Joseph, Sen	1				36
Rawlins, Rodham	1	2	4		14
Pullin, William	1		2		
Burgess, Lovatt	2	3	4		40
Doggett, Jeremiah	1	3	2		13
Gaskins, John, Jun	1	1	2		
Philips, John	1			1	
Rollins, Samuel	1	3	4		
Hill, Abraham	1	2	3		
West, William	1	4	2		
Merritt, William	1		1		
Hanks, Luke	1		2		
Swett, Abreham				5	
Merritt, Frederick	1	2	4		
Merritt, Shadrack	1	1	6		5
Duncan, William	2	2	4		
Gallidge, William	1		2		
Duncan, Zachariah	1		2		

NAME OF HEAD OF FAMILY.	Free white males of 16 years and upward, including heads of families.	Free white males under 16 years.	Free white females, including heads of families.	All other free persons.	Slaves.
Sturges, William	1	1	7		
Merritt, Shadrack	2	3	4		
Megee, William				9	
Crowell, Benjamin	1	3	2		10
Knight, Robert	1	4	2		
Merritt, John	1	5	2		
Knight, John	1	2	3		1
Pearce, Mary	2	1	1		7
Elbuk, William	1				12
Joiner, Benjamin	1		3		4
Merritt, William, Jun	1	1			
Merritt, William, Sen	2	3	2		
Morgan, Peter	1	1	2		8
Gaskins, John, Sen	2	1	3		
Crowell, Edward, Jun	1		2		7
Tillery, Eppy	3	3	6		
Taylor, John	1	3	1		
Turner, Winifred			1		1
Martin, James (Estate of)					25
Turner, Edwin	2	3	8		9
Rudd, William				8	
Branch, William, Sen	1	1	3		16
Pearce, Benjamin	2	4	5		7
Branch, William, Ju	1	1	3		12
Flewellin, William	1	4	3		11
Crowell, Edward, Sen	2		3		21
Clayton, John	1	4	2		9
Ditto for Jn° Dickins					5
Lewis, John			1	4	
Landman, William		1	3		
Smith, John	2	1	3		
Baker, James	1		2		2
Batchelor, William	1	2	3		9
Butt, Jesse	1	2	5		
Bradford, Henry	1	3	3		10
Branch, John	9	3	5	1	28
Banks, William	1	2	2		
Butt, Moses	3	3	6		17
Bradley, Samuel	1		2		1
Carlile, Nathaniel	1	2	6		
Counsil, Mary	1	1	3		
Crowell, Samuel	1	3	3		15
Chrisam, William	1	2	5		1
Cooper, John, Sen	3		2		4
Curlins, Thomas	1	2			
Cooper, Iles	1		1		
Daniel, Ambrose	3	3	5		
Daniel, Randol	4	4	4		7
Drummond, Thomas	3	4	2		
Drake, Tristram, Sen	4	1	2		
Everitt, Jesse	3		3		11
Edwards, Joseph, Sen	1	1	2		
Edwards, Ransome	1	1	1		
Grizell, Willie	1	3			
Hill, William	2		2		4
Harrington, Lewrancy			2		6
Hynes, Thomas	2	1	8		3
Robert, John	1		2		
Hataway, William	1		2		
Harper, James	1	1	3		
Herbert, William	2	1	3		
Ives, Dinah	1	1	3		
Izzard, Thomas	1	1	3		
Jones, John	3	2	7		30
Ditto for Benja Rosser					
Moran, William	3	2	8		
Lock, James	1		1		
Long, Littleton	1	1	2		1
Lorton, Thomas	1	2	5		
Moran, Samuel	1	3	2		
Moran, William	1		2		
Morris, Griffin	3	2	8		
Morris, Hezekiah	1	2	3		
Morris, Holloway	1	1	3		3
Morris, Hercules	1	1	2		6
Mann, Frederick	1		1		
Morris, Jesse	1	4	3		
Marshall, John, Sen	2	1	4		17
Nichols, Luke	2		4		
Nichols, James	3	1	3		
Nichols, Thomas	1		3		
Perkins, William, Jun	2		4		
Perkins, Henry, Jun	2	5	6		2
Parker, Charles	2	2	6		
Read, John	1		3		2
Reed, William	1	3	3		
Taylor, John	2	1	3		2
Troughton, Swan	1		3		7
Turner, Solomon					
Swett, George	1	2	4	3	
Suit, Richard					
Sullivant, Drury	1	1	2		2
Shelton, Ruth	1		2		6
Scoles, William	1				

HALIFAX DISTRICT, HALIFAX COUNTY—Continued.

NAME OF HEAD OF FAMILY.	Free white males of 16 years and upward, including heads of families.	Free white males under 16 years.	Free white females, including heads of families.	All other free persons.	Slaves.
Scott, Exum				9	
Wheales, Nordy	1	5	4		
Wilsey, William	1				
Wootten, William	1	3	4		14
Ditto for W. Bradford		1	1		9
Warren, Thomas	4	4	5		
Woolsey, Joel	1	2	2		4
Walker, Joel	1	1	2		6
Whealles, Joseph	1	1	2		
Willey, John	1		2		
White, Adam	1	5	2		
White, Joshua	2	1	3		2
Whitaker, Matthew	2		2		46
Ditto for Israel West					
Whitaker, Matthew (for Jno Brinkly's estate)	1	3	4		4
Hill, William	1		2		18
Alston, Joseph, Jno	2				11
Alston, Gideon	2	1	3		17
Angel, George	2	1	3		5
Angel, John	1	2	1		
Archer, John				9	
Burt, John	1	1	1		1
Bruce, William	1	2	5		
Burt, Richard	1		1		37
Burt, Elizabeth	1	3	3		10
Burt, Joseph	1		3		3
Bull, Thomas	2	1	5		2
Bull, Randolph	2	1	4		1
Brinkley, Abraham	2		2		4
Brinkley, William, Senr	3		2		9
Brinkley, William	1	2	1		7
Brinkley, Ely	1				
Brinkley, Judith	1		8		8
Brinkley, Jerry	1				
Broom, Burrell	2	5	2		
Broom, John	1		1		
Butt, Aby	1	1	5		
Bosedale, Robert	1		5		
Cleavis, John	3	3	3		1
Cavinah, Thomas	1	1	3		5
Conner, James	3	1	7		1
Conner, William	1				8
Davis, Isham	1	6	6		6
Ditto for Hopkins's Orphans					8
Doles, Jesse	2	1	5		3
Daniel, Elizabeth	1	1	7		9
Daniel, West	1	2	1		2
Davis, Merritt	3	1	4		4
Daniel, Buckner	1	2	4		1
Flewellin, Richard, Junr	2	2	3		
Flewellin, Abner	3	1	3		9
Flewellin, Taylor	1	2	3		6
Fuqua, William	1	2	2		
Fruar, Robert	1	1	2		33
Ganes, Moses	2	1	3		8
Gilbert, Matthew	1	6	3		4
Gilbert, James	1	1	3		
Gilbert, William	1	1	2		
Hart, Sinah			4		2
Harvey, Thomas, Senr	2	3	7		22
Hervey, William, Senr	1	3	3		1
Hervey, William	1	3	1		1
Hervey, John	1	4	3		1
Hervey, Thomas	1		3		1
Hall, Mary			3		5
Hawkins, Samuel				1	1
Humphris, Elijah	2		5		12
Hall, Robert	1	2	3		
Higgs, Samuel	2	3	4		
Jordan, William	2	4	4		
Jordan, Joseph	1	2	5		
Johnston, Jacob	2	1	2		3
Jordan, Edward	1	3	4		
Kirk, Isaac	2	3	5		12
Kelley, William	1	1	2		
Long, John	1	3	5		
Lee, John	2	3	6		1
Lee, Green	2		2		
Lock, Josiah	2		2		
Matthews, Richard	3	6	3		6
Matthews, Samuel	1	5	3		2
Matthews, Jerry	2	3	5		7
Moore, George	1	1	3		
Marshall, Stephen	1				
Matthews, James	3	3	4		12
McLilley, William	1	2	3		
Pritchett, Christopher	2	3	4		5
Ditto for Tho. William's Orphans			1		1
Powers, John	2	3	5		9
Porter, Samuel	1	3	4		6
Perkins, Thomas	3		2		
Perkins, William	1		1		
Perman, William	1	3	3		2
Rogers, Shadrack	1	2	2		1
Rogers, Thomas	2	2	4		1
Richardson, Benjamin				12	
Richardson, William				7	
Rams, Robert	1		2		3
Rosser, Isham	1	3	2		
Stephens, John	3		5		
Sullivant, Jerry	1	5	6		2
Smith, Samuel	2	1	2		8
Sullivant, John	2	3	4		
Sullivant, Christian	1		2		1
Vincent, Philip	1	3	4		2
Wright, Sterling	1	6	2		
Williams, Joseph John	1	2	4		66
Williams, James	2				27
Williams, Thomas	1		1		
Williams, Samuel	1	2	5		
Williams, Wood	1	1	3		1
Worley, John	1	2	4		
Worley, Lovick	1	1	3		1
Winter, Moses	1	1	4		
Weaver, James				4	
Williams, Elisha	1	5	3		1
Edwards, Peter	1	1	4		5
Rose, Thomas	1	1	2		
Perkins, William, Senr	2	2	6		1
Lee, Jesse	1		1		1
Patrick, John	1		2		3
Malton, Samuel	2	1	3		
Morris, Dunston	1	3	3		
Sikes, James	1				
Mehoney, William	2	4	3		6
Parker, William	3	1	3		6
Smith, Zachariah	2	1	2		
Adams, Philip	1	1	2		2
Sikes, Joel	4	2	5		
Harris, Asey	1		2		
Miles, Thomas	2		3		
Williams, Francis	1	3	2		7
Green, Robert	2	3	3		4
Green, John	2	3	4		
Hardy, David	1	3	3	2	6
Blanton, Charles	1		1		2
Green, Berry	1	2	6		3
Dickens, William	1	2	4		
Brown, William	1		2		
Gammon, Jesse	1	2	1		
Grissam, Oliver	1	3	3		3
Good, Edward	3	2	5		
Dawson, Larkin	1	1	2		
Mehoney, John	1		5		
Morris, George	1	2	2		
Carter, Molton	1	2	4		
Wright, James	1	2	2		3
Roper, John	1		4		3
Wilson, Joshua	1	1	2		2
Johnston, Lewis	1	2	2		
Moody, Burrell	1	2	4		1
Dameron, Tignal	1	2	4		
Harvil, Starling	1	2	3		16
Harris, Roe	1	2	3		
Tucker, Gray	1		1		1
Johnston, Abraham	3	3	2		1
Brown, Jesse	3	4	5		
King, Burrel	1	1	3		2
Williams, George	1	2	4		
Gill, James	1	1	2		
Bobbit, Sherret	1	3	1		
Allen, John	1				
Harris, Warner	3		8		12
Allen, William	1	3	1		
Williams, Samuel	1	3	4		
Sikes, Joshua	1	3	4		1
Jackson, Edward	2		2		6
McDougal, Samuel	2				7
Dennison, John	1				
Mehoney, William	1		2		5
Colley, John	2		2		2
Brown, John	2	3	4		
Yerby, Henry	1	2	4		
Stephens, Richard	1	1	2		
Stephens, Lewis	1	2	2		
Dickens, Thomas	1	2	1		
Megriggo, Anthony	1		3		4
Green, Jesse	1		2		
Newsome, Jacob	1	1	2		7
Alston, Joseph Jno	1				60
Mallory, John	1	3	4		3
Alston, Willis	2	5	5		40
Morris, George	1	2	2		
Morris, William	2	2	1		20
Lindsey, John	1	2	5		26
Harper, John	1	2	3		
Williams, William	2	3	4	3	
Carney, Richard, Junr	2	5	6		11
Carney, Stephen	1		2		24
Carney, Richard, Senr	2		5		27
Spane, Little Berry	1	2	1		2
Joiner, Theophilus	3	1	2		4
Daffin, John	1	2	3		5
Harden, James	1		1		3
Watson, Samuel	3	2	2		2
Homes, Willis	2	2			1
Howell, Matthew	1	1	1		
Moore, John	1	1	2		2
Mann, Absalom	2	2	6		9
Linton, Samuel	1	1	4		
Vaughan, Lemaston	1				5
Joyner, John	1		4		4
Corbin, Charnel	1	1	2		
Lane Gisburn	1	2	2		1
Buck, John	1	2	2		6
Langford, John	1	2	2		1
Harmon, John	1			4	
Brasill, Benjamin	1				50
Seat, Isham		2	4		
Lanturn, Joseph	1			6	
Lucas, Farnith	1		3		
Flood, Benjamin	1	1	3		
Epps, Thomas	1	3	1		3
Armstrong, John	1	1	1		
Pope, John	4				9
Pope, William	1				
Spellings, Frederick	1	2	1		
Qualls, Henry	1				
Flood, Jesse	1	3	2		
Dwyer, Patrick	1				11
Mason, Thomas	1		2		13
Fort, Micajah	2	1			4
Fort, Allen	1	1			3
Brantley, James	1	2	3		9
Harden, William	2	1	3		1
Onions, George	2	2	1		1
King, William	1		1		
Goodwin, Jesse	1				10
Lane, David	5		2		15
Shelton, Burrel	1	1	2		12
Lassiter, Jethro	4	4	2	2	51
Jallipp, Joseph	1		3		
Duke, Millia			1		1
Hardin, William, Jun	1				2
Fort, Elias	2	3	2		22
King, Edward	2	3	4		4
King, John	2				
Skinner, Thomas	1		4		
Pulley, James	1	2	3		
Steward, Joseph	1	2	2		
Hendley, James	1	1	3		
Langford, Zachariah	1	2	4		3
Pearce, William	2		5		4
Whitaker, Thomas	1		3		1
Fort, Sugar	1		2		19
Joiner, Henry	3	3	5		19
Lane, Levi	2		5		32
Joyner, Bridgman	2				16
Barnes, James	2		2		19
Ricks, Isaac	2	3	4		27
Qualls, Peter	7	2	5		24
Topp, George				4	
Sikes, Dempsey	1		1		1
Barker, Joshua	1	3	1		
Jackson, William & Edmund	2				
Undrew, Demsey	1		4		
Kelley, William	1	1	1		
Alsobrook, Edward	1	2	4		2
Emry, Edward	2	1	4		
Brantley, Lewis	2	1	5		1
Cotten, William	1	1	1		7
Sessums, Elinore	1		4		
Dew, Thomas	1		2		9
Biggs, Azeriah	1	2	2		
Biggs, Robert	1	2	2		
Drew, Joshua	1		4		
Alsobrook, Howell	5	4	4		
Wilkings, Elijah	2	2	5		1
High, Thomas	1	5	4		
Bynam, William	1	1	5		
Turner, William	1		1		
Bradley, Micajah	1				
Martin, John	1		1		1
Hogan, Lemuel	1				
Cain, Joseph	1		1		
Drew, John	1	1	4		17
Young, Marmeduke	1	4	4		21
Turner, Sarah			2		5
Fillips, John	1		1		
Spear, William	2	2	5		
Spear, William Exum	1	1	1		
Jackson, William	1	2	2		
Jones, James				3	
Alsobrook, Claburn	1	2	1		1

HALIFAX DISTRICT, HALIFAX COUNTY—Continued.

NAME OF HEAD OF FAMILY.	Free white males of 16 years and upward, including heads of families.	Free white males under 16 years.	Free white females, including heads of families.	All other free persons.	Slaves.
Taylor, Thomas	1	1	7		
Bynam, James	1		2		
Haynie, William	1	1	2		
Haynes, Thomas	1	1	2		
Harriss, Elij.	2	6	3		19
McCombs, Alexander	1	2	2		
Norfleet, Marmaduke	1	1	5		59
Alsobrook, John	1	3	3		5
Alsobrook, Thomas	3		2		1
Drew, Thomas	3	1	3		
Hobgood, Lemuel	1		7		
Hobgood, Elijah	1	1	2		
Wall, Francis	1		1		
Good, Elizabeth	2		3		
O'Daniel, Jacob	1				
Cain, James	2	4	6		6
Killebrew, Wiggan	1	2	2		
Powell, James	1	3	4		1
Alsobrook, Samuel	1	3	2		
Brazwell, Drury	1	1	2		
Bass, Solomon	1	3	2		1
Whitehead, Benjamin	2	4	5		3
Slaughter, James	4	1	7		20
Alsobrook, Drew	3		2		9
Spear, Nathan	1	1	6		
Hill, Isham	1	2	7		
High, Luke	1	1	1		
Haynie, Benjamin	2	3	5		
Dicken, Lewis	1				1
Dicken, Benjamin, Senr.	2	1	4		16
Rawls, Philip	2	3	4		
Hodges, Robert	1	1	2		1
Alsobrook, James	1	2	3		2
Hodges, James	2	1	4		1
Simmons, James	2	1	3		2
Hodges, David	1	1	3		1
Murrell, George	1				
Banks, Thomas	1				
Hail, Ogburn	1		2		
Dicken, Benjamin, Junr.	1				
Cotten, Young					3
Alsobrook, William	2	1	4		6
Ford, Elias	2	4	2		24
Merritt, James	2				
Ford, Turner	1	1	1		1
Raifield, Babel	1	2			
Murry, Mark					9
Cotten, Theophilus	1	5	3		4
Cochran, Robert	1	4	3		1
Gayner, Samuel	1	2	4		4
Mellen, Ely	4	1	1		
Mullen, Robert	1	1	2		
Bradley, Thomas	1	4	3		
Haynie, Lewis	1	1	3		
Alsobrook, David	3	3	4		1
Carter, Benjamin	1	1	2		3
Bell, George	2	1	6		6
Lain, Cardy	1		2		
Bell, Benjamin	1	2	3		
Bell, Lemuel	1	1	3		
Strickland, John	1		3		3
Pernal, John	2	4	6		2
Ditto for Andrew Mead					18
Hail, Williamson	2	1	5		2
Ubanks, George	1	1	4		7
Jones, Briton	1		2		1
Hail, Aris	1		2		
Dewberry, William	2	3	1		
Hail, Jonathan	1	7	2		1
Dicken, William	3	7	3		
Hunt, Howell	1	4	3		
Hargrove, Sarah	2		4		9
Barrott, Priscilla	2	1	3		3
Hail, Jesse	1	1	2		
Stafford, Joshua	1	2	3		
Cullum, William	1				
Wood, John	1	1	1		2
Dicken, Bennet	1	1	1		
Crosslin, Edward	1				
Browning, Levy	1	3	2		
Cullum, William, Senr	2	1	3		
Cullum, Jeremiah	1		3		
Dewberry, Daniel	1	1	1		
Peobles, Drury	2	6	1		
Hargroves, John	6	3	5		13
Crawley, Daniel	1	2	4		
Harriss, Abner	1	1	6		5
Thompson, John	1		2		
Williams, Thomas	1	2	3		1
Bagby, Davis	3		6		4
Gillum, William	1	3	3		
Smith, Zacheus					8
Bagby, William	1	1	2		
Killingsworth, Mark	1		2		
Hawkins, Henry				3	
Killingsworth Matthew	1	3	4		

NAME OF HEAD OF FAMILY.	Free white males of 16 years and upward, including heads of families.	Free white males under 16 years.	Free white females, including heads of families.	All other free persons.	Slaves.
Bloss, Henry	2	1	4		1
Waddle, C.	1	4	2		
Dicken, Joseph	2	2	2		1
Powess, Henry	1	2	1		
Smith, Josiah	1	1	3		1
Myrick, Ann					
Hawkins, Joseph				9	
Harriss, Robert	1	2	6		
Gardner, Josiah	1	2	2		1
Sherman, Matthew	1				
Roan, Jesse	1				
Corlew, Philip	3	2	5		1
Smith, Priscilla			2		
Corlew, John	2	1	4		
Potts, Mary Ann			2		
Killingsworth, William	1	1	5		
Richards, Richard	2				7
Harriss, Isaac	3	2	4	3	9
Crawley, Alice	1		1		1
Hargrove, Dudley	1		2		2
Vinson, Benjamin	1	2	2		
Roan, John	1	2	3		
Smith, Sarah	2				1
Long, Elizabeth	1	1	4		2
Crabb, Susannah			3		
Evans, Mary	1		4		1
Hawkins, Isham	2	2	3		6
Edmonds, William	1	2	2		
Bumpass, John	1				
Bishop, James	3				9
Edmonds, Elizabeth	1	1	4		9
Alston, Joseph John (for W. Alston Esta)					
Alston, Willis, Jun	2	2	4		34
Stigall, Samuel	1				
Eubanks, Joseph, Sen.	1		2		4
Thompson, Richard	1		4		
Harper, Jacob	1	4	5		
Vinson, Willis	1	1	4		
Ashe, Charles				11	
Killingsworth, John	1				
Hyde, Hartwell	2	1	7		9
Hide, Henry	1	5	3		21
Zoliofer, George	1	4	3		28
Lewis, Nicholas	1	5	2		
Pettypool, Henry	1	1	3		
Smith, William	3		2		1
Purnal, Charles	1				
Axum, Mary	1	1	1		
Griffis, Henry	1				
Ashe, John Baptist	3	1	4	2	63
Aaron, Isaac	1	3	2		
Aaron, William	1	1	1		
Aron, George	1				
Aaron, Amey	1		3		1
Barnes, Thadeus	1				
O'Neill, Thomas	1				
Bond, Hance	5	1	3	1	9
Berryman, John	1		2	3	13
Barksdale, Benjamin	1				
Barber, Joshua	1	1	2		
Barksdale, Daniel	1				
Coleman, John	3	2	6	1	
Cotten, Robert	4	1	3	1	15
Ditto Exr of J. Bass	1	2	4	2	8
Cole, Joshua	1	2	4		26
Davis, Goodorum	2		1	1	14
Davie, William R.	1	2	2		36
Elbeck, Elizabeth			2		6
Eaton, John	1	1	3		12
Easley, Benjamin	1				
Elbeck, Dorothy			2		6
Elbeck, Mary			2		4
Elbeck, Penelope			1		
Fenner, Robert	1	1	4		31
Fawcett, James	1	2	4		1
Gray, James	2				10
Gerrard, Thomas	2		1		5
Gilchrist, Martha			1		13
Gilmour, Charles (Admr of Wm Hendrie)					24
Gilmour, John & Charles	3	1	1		36
Gilchrist, John	1		2		1
Geddy, John	2		6		22
Gilmour, William	3	3	1		32
Gilmour, Charles, Junr	2	2	2		4
Garrigus, Matthew	1	5	1		
Green, John				16	
Greene, William				1	
Pasteur, Thomas					
Hall, Robert	2	1	4	2	11
Harveey, John	1	2	3	1	40
Housin, Ann			1		
Hannon, John	3	2	2		4
Hunter, Charles	1			1	
Hogg, Elizabeth					16

NAME OF HEAD OF FAMILY.	Free white males of 16 years and upward, including heads of families.	Free white males under 16 years.	Free white females, including heads of families.	All other free persons.	Slaves.
Hail, Lewis	1				
Housin, John	1				
Hendry, Michael	4	1	2		8
Harrison, Collier	1				52
Jones, Willie	2	2	6		120
Ditto for Jarrott Wallace					17
Isbell, Peter	1	1	2	1	1
Johnston, Jacob	1		1		
Jamica, Henry	1		1		
Kinchen, John	2	2	1		32
Kay, John	3				13
Kelley, William	1		4		
Kelley, John	1	3	4		
Lowe, William	2	1	3		9
Lowe, James	1	2	1		5
Long, Nicholas, Senr	5	2	8		89
Long, Nicholas, Junr	2	3	4		33
Long, Lunsford	1				1
Lyon, Richard	1				
Lynes, David	1				
Muir, William	5	1			9
Morgan, John	1	3	3		2
Miller, Christopher	1	2	2		
Ring, John	2	1	2		1
Morgan, George	1				
McCulloch, Alexander	1				60
McCulloch, Benjamin	3	6	11	9	40
Marsham, Samuel	1				
McDaniel, Patrick	1	2	2		2
Montfort, Joseph	1				2
McClanahan, John	1				4
Murry, Frances				6	
Pasteur, Charles	1	1	5		33
Perkins, William	1			2	17
Powers, Robert	1		5	2	
Pasteur, James					27
Ponns, John	3		2	5	13
Ponton, Mungo	1				3
Philips, Thomas	1		1		
Rymes, Jesse	1				
Roberts, Francis	1	1	2		1
Richardson, William	1				6
Smith, Martin	1	1	2		
Sheeter, Josiah	1	1	2		
Suttles, Matthew	1				1
Smith, Major	1	1	2		
Tillery, John	2				4
Watson, John	2	2	2	1	4
Watson, William	1	1	1		
Williamson, George	1	2	2		10
Warren, Samuel	1				
Yarborough, John	6	1	2		
Young, George	1	1	3		4
Morgan, John				16	
Drew, John					
Pulley, David	3	3	5		3
Russell, Richard	2	3	3		6
Dancey, John	2	1	2		9
Brantley, Robert	3		1		11
Powell, Benjamin	2	2	3		13
Carter, Joseph	2		5		22
Pitman, Elisha	2	4	5		11
Bird, Peter	1	1	3	1	3
Fort, Willie	1	1	3		7
Champion, John	1	1	2		9
Sands, Barham	2		2		12
Merritt, William	1	1	4		2
Wootten, John	2	1	3		4
Spier, Samuel	1		2		1
Spier, Ann		4	1		3
Brantley, William	3	1	6		13
Whitehead, Arthur	2	5	3		3
Lewis, Lewis	2	1	3		2
Bird, Allin	1	1	1		4
Applewhite, Henry	1		2		1
Applewhite, Thomas	4	1	2		
Knight, Moore	1				7
Dancey, Edwin	1	2	1		10
Ward, Robert	1	1	7		4
Pitman, Arthur	1	4	2		6
Jones, Jarvis	2	2	6		
Noblin, William	1	4	4		6
Ward, James	1	4	4		3
Jones, James, & Kindred Spier	2	4			12
Bass, Isaac	1		2		4
Barrow, Robert	2				9
Smith, Richard	1		1		1
Whitaker, Richard, Senr	2		3		17
Whitaker, Cary	2	2	1		25
Whitaker, Richard, Jun	1		2		6
Kindred, Knight	1	1	3		4
Barrow, Olive			3		45
Lain, Elizabeth			3		20
Pitman, Samuel	4	1	2		12
Haynes, Lucy	1				4

HALIFAX DISTRICT, HALIFAX COUNTY—Continued.

NAME OF HEAD OF FAMILY.	Free white males of 16 years and upward, including heads of families.	Free white males under 16 years.	Free white females, including heads of families.	All other free persons.	Slaves.
Cherry, Samuel	1	2	4		1
Foot, John	2	4			15
Hillman, Jesse	1				
Wyatt, Jesse	2	1	3		1
West, Arthur, Junr	1	4	2		6
Whitaker, John	3	5	4		28
Ditto for Wilson Carter	1				4
Howell, Thomas	2	1	3		7
Jackson, William, Senr	3	2	3		11
Jackson, William, Junr					
Jackson, Matthew					
Foreman, Samuel	2	3	4		5
Wyatt, James	1		4		
Simmons, Zadock	1		1		
Kirkley, George	1	1	2		
Pass, William	2				3
Hill, William	1	1	2		13
Whitmill, Thomas	2	3	2		18
Henderson, William	2	1	1		26
Smith, Ann	2	1	2		40
Bell, Marmaduke	1		1		8
Joyner, Joel	3		5		12
Harris, Norfleet	1	1	1		28
Hodge, Henry	1	5	2		6
Naron, Jesse	1	3	6		
Joiner, Ely	1	1	1		4
Young, Thomas	1	3	5		7
Sills, Benjamin	1	3	3		1
Sills, Isham	3	3	2		
Tippet, Erasmus	1	3	2		5
Myham, James	1	4	2		3
Atkertson, William	1	2	2		5
Joyner, Blount	1		1		11
Barber, Joshua	1	2			4
Doles, John	1	1	3		
Parks, John	1	1	2		1
Gayner, Thomas	1		3		3
Foreman, Benjamin	3	2	5		12
Young, Dolphin	1	4	5		12
Williams, John	1		3		5
James, Benjamin				6	
Winburn, Thomas				3	
Wiggins, William, Senr	2	1	1		9
Stamper, Robert	1	2	3		1
Wiggins, William	1	2	1		
Hunter, Henry	1	2	4		7
Young, Francis	1	1	2		10
Land, Sarah		1	4		3
Adams, John	1	1	4		3
Bryant, William	1	3	3		11
Baylis, John	1	2	1		4
Drew, John	4	4	3		99
Myham, Jesse	1	1	2		2
Barrow, Milla		1	6		13
Bishop, John	3	1	4		1
Baylis, Britain	1		1		2
Maclemore, Howell	2	1	3		1
Boykin, William	1		1		42
Binston, Jacob	1		2		1
Dukes, Josiah	1	2	2		5
Garner, Ann			1		4
Griffin, Priscilla			6		5
Griffin, Michael	1				
Griffin, Brinkley	1				
Bryant, Lewis	1		3		1
Bayliss, Amey	1		3		1
Armstead, Robert	1		3		5
Hines, Dempsey	1	1	1		
Cotten, Joab	2	3	5		25
Dawson, John	2	3	1		61
Jones, Phill				7	
Fair, Bythel	2	1	6		
Jones, James				4	
Davis, Thomas	1	1	3		3
James, Elisha				6	
Nelms, Jeremiah	2	1	4		22
Moore, David	3	2	1		12
Sturdevent, Jesse	3	7	4		3
Sturdevent, Charles	1		4		
Tucker, William	2	2	6		
Christie, Jesse	2	3	4		
Sampson, Stephen	1		1	3	
Garner, Valentine	2		9		
Judge, James	2	3	2		6
West, William	2	1	3		10
Heath, Richard	3	1	7		10
Hadley, Joshua	1	2	4		4
Hadley, Martha	1	2	4	1	5
Hadley, Ambrose	1	1	3		4
Coffield, Grissum	1	4	5		1
Butt, Joshua	4	1	3	1	
Sikes, William	1	1	3		
Thrower, Baxter	2	5	2		6
Davis, John	1	2	4		2
Pullin, William	2	5			6
Dean, Isaac	4	1	3		3
Passmore, Mary		1	4		
Leath, William	1				
Williams, Howell	1	1	3		1
Nicholson, Joseph	2	3	2		16
Hill, Sarah	1		2		18
Heath, Adam	2	2	6		13
Jones, Henry	2	2	5		15
Davis, William	1	2	2		3
Berryman, Balaam	1		2		8
Powell, Nathaniel	1	3	2		11
Parram, William	1				1
Hynes, Benjamin	1	2	3		5
Flewellin, James	1	1	4		13
Harden, Thomas	1				
Flewellin, Shadrach	1				
Flewellin, Elizabeth			3		9
Wright, John		2	4		16
Sikes, Willouchby	2	2	4		
Johnson, Josiah	2	1	1		3
Heath, William	2		1		8
Cox, William	1	1	1		1
Nelms, Meredith	1	1	4		
Bustion, Martha	1	2	4		16
Barksdale, William	1		1	2	12
Pitts, Ann		3	5		8
Long, Ann		3	2		18
Wood, Aron					
Ballard, Deverix	1	1	3		1
Brady, James	1	3	2		9
Wright, Roderick	2	1	4		
Pitts, Elizabeth	2	1	4		7
Wright, Joseph	1				
Lowe, William	1	1	2		2
Brady, Brasil	1	2	5		
Parrum, Rebeccah	1		5		6
Heath, John	1				
Heath, James	1	1	4		1
Williams, Joseph	1	3	3		
Matthews, Thomas	1	3	6		
Moore, Reubin	1	2	3		
Williams, Ely	2	1	6		3
Etheridge, William	2	1	3		
Cleveland, James	1	1	4		
Nicholson, Lemuel	1		3		5
Pace, Thomas	2	2	3		26
Ward, Benjamin	2	1	2		9
Williams, John	3		8		32
Ward, Joseph	1		3		1
Rhodes, David	1	2	1		
Anderson, Charles	1	3	4		2
Pitts, Henry	2	1	3		8
Williams, Jesse	1	2	1		12
Moore, James	1	3	1		7
Thrower, Mason	2	1	3		16
Davis, John (Ex^r of A. Davis, Deceas^d)	2	1	5		9
Pitts, Mark	1				1
Etheridge, Calib	4		2		5
Williams, Daniel	1	1	2		1
Murden, John	2	2	5		10
Hopkins, Joshua	2				8
Robertson, Mary	1	1	2		1
Harrison, Elisha	1	1	3		
Whitehead, Lazarus	1	1	1		
Lowe, William	2		3		
Murden, Edward & Jeremiah	2				12
Drake, Thomas	3		2		
Scoles, Peter		1	6		
Etheridge, Caleb	4		2		6
Nicholson, Lemuel	1		3		9
Moore, Charles	2	1	3		15
Harwell, Gardner	1	3	1		24
Simmons, John					
Powell, Ptolemy	3	2	2		3
Hockaday, James	1	1	1		5
Norwood, Samuel	1		1		9
Spann, Willis	1	2	2		6
Taylor, Mary	1		4		4
Turner, James	2	1	2		7
Scott, John				5	
Good, William	1	3	3		1
Smith, Moses	2	3	2		6
Smith, William	2		1		2
Kelley, Thomas	1	1	4		1
Downs, William	3	1	4		
Martin, William	3	4	4		7
Hockaday, William	1		2		1
Narsworthy, John	2		3		3
Sikes, Jacob	1	2	1		
Heath, James	1	1	4		1
Glover, Nathaniel	1	1	1		2
Norwood, Richard	1				7
Arnold, David	1	1	2	1	4
Rose, Elisha	2	2	5		8
Simms, Zachariah	2	1	6		1
Hammell, Jenny	2	5	5		1
Easley, James	1	4	1		12
Simmons, John (for David Short)	2	2	4		16
Roan, Lewis	3	3	5		1
Gill, Philip	3		5		
Powell, George	1	1	3		
Bumpass, Samuel	1	2	2		
Jones, Thomas	1	1	1		
Sikes, James	1	1	2		
Hockaday, Warwick	1	3	2		
Jones, John, Junr	1	1	6		
Martin, Jesse	1	1	3		
Sikes, Joab	1	2	2		
McCrawley, John	1	1	4		
Edmundson, Bryant	1	3	3		
Smith, Uriah	2	2	3		1
Shaw, James	2	1	1		
Allen, James	1			3	1
Powell, William, Sen	1	3	5		7
Adams, Benjamin	1		3		
Walker, Solomon	1	1	2		
Shaw, John, Thomas, & Sarah	5	6	6		10
Smith, John	1		2		2
Spann, Richard	1		1		2
Rose, Wormley	1	1	2		5
Mills, Benjamin	1	1	2		1
Rose, William	1	2	3		6
Powell, William	2	2	4		10
Green, Benjamin	1	2	4		
Green, Hannah	1	1	2		
Pearson, George	3	1	3		
Kelley, William	1	1	2		
Winter, Joseph	1	1	2	2	
Smith, Peter, Junr	1	2	4		
Jones, John, Senr	1	2	4		
Powell, William	1	1	1		6
Davis, Owen	1	1	2		
Spann, Frederick	1	1	3		6
Brasington, Joseph	1	1	4		5
Yarborough, George	1	5	3		2
Smith, Peter, Senr	2		1		12
Ivey, Robert	1	2	4		3
Adams, James	1	1	8		
Powell, Zachariah	1	2	4		3
Shaw, Elizabeth	1	3	5		
Taylor, Richard	2	2	4		7
Dulley, James	1	3	4		
Powell, William, Junr	1	2	3		1
Siris, John	1		2		
Banks, Thomas	1	2	3		
Lewis, Cullin	1		2		
Porter, Benjamin	1	3	2		
Vinson, Hannah			4		
Yarborough, Richard	1	1	6		
McCalley, Joseph	1		1		
Axum, Mary	1	2	1		
Vinson, Charles	1	3	2		
Green, William	1	1	3		
Sarasho, Robert	1	1	2	1	1
Bogas, Ann	1	1	3		
Mattox, Samuel	2	2	3		
Hilton, John	1	1	4		
Hilton, William	1	1	1		
Hilton, Willis	1	2	5		
Edwards, Anthony	1	1	6		
Williams, Sarah			3		1
Wells, Mistress		1	4		
West, Dorothy			2	3	
Abbinatha, Abby	1	1	3		
Pulley, David, Senr	1	1	3		
Pulley, David, Junr	1	1	2		
Scurlock, Thomas	1				13
Scurlock, George	1		1		2
Lewis, John	1				1
Williams, William	1	3	5		
Harris, Willie	1		2		
Edmonds, Martha				5	
Rock, John	2	1	3		
Young, Reubin	1	1	3		
Harrison, John	1	1	2		
Sledge, Hartwell	1		1	1	1
Bowler, Elizabeth		2	2		
Bowler, Sarah	1	1	2		
Carter, Jacob	1	1	3		
Armstead, Henry	1	2	2		
Stephens, Jones	2		5		
Winters, James	3	3	4	1	2
Burt, John	3	1	4		18
Cobb, Patsy			1		5
Fawcett, Mary	1	2	4		
Hogg, Rebeccah	2	2	4		
Sanders, Sarah	2		7		
Parker, Nancy					
Parker, Joshua	1				
Garland, Jonathan		1	2	1	
Davis, Nancy			1		1

HALIFAX DISTRICT, HALIFAX COUNTY—Continued.

NAME OF HEAD OF FAMILY.	Free white males of 16 years and upward, including heads of families.	Free white males under 16 years.	Free white females, including heads of families.	All other free persons.	Slaves.
Ray, William	1		2	1	3
Noble, Francis	1				
Herriman, Joseph				1	
Ring, John	2	1	2		1
Burt, Stephen	1				
Kelley, James	1	2	3		
Kelley, William	1		1		
Royall, John	1	2	2		
Bird, Polly				4	1
Bird, Peggy				3	
Bird, Richard			2		
Leach, Mary			3		
Smith, Mistress	1		3		
Harry, Nancy				2	
Coleman, Sarah			1		
Dennick, Peter	1	1	2		
Yarborough, William	1				
Scott, John			7		
Eilbeck, John	1	1	1	1	2
Navill, Thomas	5		1		8
Southall, Farnith	1		2		18
Warbutton, John	1				
Carstaphin, John	1				
Fountain, Jacob	1				
Cotten, Young	1				
Ellis, William	1				
Pope, Joseph	1				
Pope, Benjamin	1				
Hinesley, Joel	1				
Hinesley, John	1				
Cook, Francis	1				
Gain, John	1				
Clarke, Thomas	1				
Pattypool, William	1				
Garlock, George	1				
Markham, John	1				
Brickle, William	1				
Conner, William	1				
Brooks, John	1				
Chambers, David	2		2		1
Griffis, Daniel	1	2	1		
Dawson, John	1	2	3		
Smawley, Nancy			3		
Harrison, Joseph	1		3		
Harden, Richard	1	2	4		
Nairn, Sarah		1	1		
Churchwill, John	1				
Churchwill, William	1				
Peare, Jones	1				
Harrison, Gidion	1				
Landifor, Robert	1				
Broose, Abner	1				
Southintine, Nancy			2		
Doles, Sarah	1		3		1
Brasill, James	4	1	4		
Andrews, Sarah	1		4		
Gardner, Thomas	1	1	6		
Packer, Matthew	1		3		
Wall, Francis	1		1		
Cain, Jeremiah	1	2	4		
Jackson, Jesse	1	1	2		
Joyner, Jonathan	1	2	4		12
Dwyer, John	1		2		5
Jones, Thomas	2	1	2		
Blackmore, Absalom	2	1	2		
Edmunds, John	1				
Jackson, William	1		2		
Vance, John	1	1	1		1
Brown, Arthur	1				5
Morgan, James	1		1		5
Pitman, John	2	1	3		9
Hyatt, David	2		4		
Whitehead, Callin	1	1	2		
Bynum, William, Senr	2		1		2
Edwards, Benjamin	1	2	2		2
Pass, Hunt	1				
Crab, Benjamin	1	3	3		
Bird, Charity			2		2
Pitman, Lilah			3		
Pilant, John	1	2	2		
Hammons, Anthoney				4	
Ford, Issabella	2	2	3		7
West, Arthur, Senr	1				5
Pass, Nelson	1				
Lowry, Ann	1	3	2		3
Brantley, Samuel	1		2		
Waller, Mary	1	1	3		
Cobb, Simon	1		1		
Vick, Mary		1	5		
Alsobrook, Martha	1		1		
Cain, Jeremiah	1	2	4		
Cain, Thomas	2	1	2		
Merritt, Sarah	1	1	5		13
Vorden, Christian	1		3		
Drew, Solomon	1	1	3		
Brassill, James	5	1	4		
Morgan, Mary			3	1	
Ross, Jacob	1	1	2		
Brantley, Martha	1		2		1
Adkinson, Thomas	1	2	2		
Turner, Jesse	1	4	4		7
Hobgood, Francis	1		3		1
Turner, Solomon	2		3		3
Joiner, Ely	1	1	1		4
Taylor, Harris	1	4	1		
Alsobrook, James	1	2	2		
Haynes, Xpher	1	3	1		
McMullin, Ely	4	1	1		
Haynie, Catherine	1	3	3		
Hobbs, Drury	1		1		
Hogan, Lemuel	1	4	6		59
Hill, Simon	1		1		
Peete, Samuel	1				13
Walker, John	1				
King, William	1				
McClanahan, William	1				
Stafford, Sterling	1				
Moore, John	1				
Fields, Henry	1				
Daley, John	1		1		
Printon, Tapley	1				
Ives, Thomas	1				
Magee, William	1				
Mosely, George	1				
Dundelow, Henry	1				
Horton, John	1				
Elliott, Leroy	1		2		
Lucas, Francis	1				
Wood, Horton	1				
Coon, William	1				
Tuttle, Jeremiah	1				
McCartie, John	1				
Sterling, Jesse	1				
Johnston, James	1				
Lisiver, Thomas	1				
Willkings, Robert	1				
Hoalt, Michael	1				
Tuttle, Peter	1				
Boyd, John	1				
Hays, Adam	1				
Durden, Daniel	1				
Dew, John	1				
West, William	1		1		
Kelley, Archibald	1				
Hall, Randol	1				
Jinkins, Joseph	1				
Blakey, Morris	1				
Reed, John	1				
Moore, John	1				
French, John	1				
Cartist, John	1				
Thompson, Adam	1				
Robertson, Nathaniel	1				
Pride, Halcot	4	1	2		54
Short, William	3	4	3		
Kindall, Ann	1	2	3		
Sweett, George				4	

HALIFAX DISTRICT, MARTIN COUNTY.

NAME OF HEAD OF FAMILY.	Free white males of 16 years and upward, including heads of families.	Free white males under 16 years.	Free white females, including heads of families.	All other free persons.	Slaves.
Moore, Maurice	1	2	3		7
Hardison, John	1	3	2		
Mizell, James	2	4	2		
Ross, Martin	1	4	3		12
Hardison, James	1	1	1		2
Hardison, Joshua	2	1	3		6
Clarke, Henry	1	1	2		
Moore, Winifred	2	1			1
Claghorn, Haws	1	1	3		
Claghorn, Benjamin	1		2		
Claghorn, Shubal	1	2	3		
Parsons, Levi	1	1	2		
Bonner, George	1		1		2
Smithwick, John	2		3		8
Carmer, James	1	2	1		
Mizell, John	2		4		1
Mizell, Lukeson William	1				9
Smith, John	2	2	3		8
Warbutton, Francis		1	2		2
Smithy, John	1	2	2		
Stewart, John	22	3	5	4	33
Hardison, William	2	2	3		1
Cooper, Edward	1		2		1
Simpson, Archibald	1	2	2		1
Griffin, David	1	2	1		
Mizell, Edward	2	3	4		3
Morris, Esther		1	2		
Gray, Lovick	1				
Simmons, Edward	1	1	5		
Harriss, Josiah	1	2	4		
Morriss, Rebeccah	1		4		
Ange, Abigail		2	1		
Melone, Michael	1		2		
Vernatson, Mary	1		3		
Hardison, Richard	2		4		3
Hardison, Thomas	1	1	4	7	2
Collins, John	2	7	2		2
Weatherton, Joseph	2	1	4		1
Sparkman, Thomas	1	1	3		
Taylor, Richard	1		2		1
Phagan, Stephen	2		3		1
Moss, William	1		4		
Buttery, John	1	4	3		5
Hooten, Charles	1	2	5		5
Hooten, William, Senr	1				13
Hooten, Henry	1	2	3		1
Hooten, William	1		3		12
Seals, Hannah	1		6		
Milliner, Thomas	1		2		
Watson, Addison	1	1	2		
Phelps, John	1		3		
Watson, Mary	1	1	2		
Rolock, John	1	1	2		13
Ward, Francis	1		4		32
Karkect, William	2	1	3		1
Everitt, Nathaniel	3	1	4		10
Hinson, Mary	1		1		
Olivent, Henry	1	1	2		
Shields, William	1		3		
Demeritt, Aaron	1		4		
Crowley, Sarah					7
Cooper, Henry	1	2	2		
Cooper, Lauton	1	1	1		1
Cooper, Griffin	1	2	1		
Raye, Samuel	1	1	2		4
Williams, John	1	1	2		
Mizell, James, Senr	4				
Amis, Edward	1	1	1		
Mizell, Hardy	1		2		
Hassell, Caswell			3		
Smith, John, Senr	2		4		
Brown, David	1	1	1		
Hollowday, John	1	2	5		1
Hollowday, Thomas	1		3		
Flood, James	1		2		
Smith, William	1	2	3		
Everitt, Nathaniel	1	1	3		
Cooper, Edward, Junr	1	1	3		
Amis, Thomas	1		2		
Hinson, William	1		3		
Moss, Sarah	1	1	2		
Hardison, David	1	1	3		
Buttery, Silvanus	2	2	4		
Middleton, John	1	1	3	1	7
Browney, Thomas	1	2	2		
Vernation, Charles	1	2	2		
Nearn, Drury	1	1	2		
Browney, John	1	1	4		
Ange, Francis	2	2	2		
Adams, William	1	2	4		
Gierkey, Jeremiah	3		5		
Garrett, James	1	1	3		
Bingall, Nancy				3	
Stubbs, Tames	1	2	3		
Petty, Thomas	1		1		
Alexander, Gideon	3	1	2		
Alexander, Simeon	1		1		
Leggett, Mary			2		1
Soans, John	3				
Sawyer, James	1		2		
Leggett, David	1	3	2		
Caraway, Anne	1		2		2
Eason, Mary		1	5		5
Smithwick, Edmund	2	4	5		11
Smithwick, Samuel	5	2	4	2	31
Ross, William	1	3	4		5
Duggan, William	1	3	4		2
Duggan, Aaron	2	3	4		2
Swain, James	2		2		1
Hollowday, Hardy	4	1	1		
Hollowday, Jesse	1	1	2		
Reddick, Christian		1	2		6
Reddick, Elizabeth	3	3	1		3

HALIFAX DISTRICT, MARTIN COUNTY—Continued.

NAME OF HEAD OF FAMILY.	Free white males of 16 years and upward, including heads of families.	Free white males under 16 years.	Free white females, including heads of families.	All other free persons.	Slaves.
Ellis, Michael	2		2		
Reddick, John	1	2	4		
Jones, Soloman	2	4	3		
Caraway, Jonathan	1				1
Maddocks, William	1	2	3		
Carroway, David	1	1	2		
Swain, Elizabeth	1	1	3		1
Swain, William	1		2		1
Bennett, John	1	1	2		
Flood, William, Senr	1	1	4		
Condau, William	1	3	4		
Garrott, James	1	1	2		2
Godward, George	3		2		
Mizell, Luke	1	1	4		
Gardner, Samuel, Senr	1	2	2		
Brown, Thomas	2		4		1
Gardner, John	1		1		
Gardner, James	1		1		
Gardner, Samuel	2	2	3		
Gardner, Thomas	1	4	1		
Hardison, John	1	1	1		4
Mizell, Mary	1		3		1
Mizell, James	3				
Manning, John	1		2		
Robason, Joshua	1				
Daniel, James	1		2		2
Daniel, William	1	1	7		
Robason, Daniel	1	1	2		
Woollard, Richard	1	2	5		
Woollard, Benjamin	2	3	3		
Robason, James	1		11	1	
Coovey, John	5	1	3		
Reddick, David	1	3	6		7
Binnitt, William	3	2	5		7
Binnitt, Thomas, Senr	2		2		4
Binnitt, Thomas, Junr	2	1	6		
Reddick, Whitmill	2	2	1		3
Stallings, Hardy	2	2	6		1
Ring, Robert	2			2	
Moore, Levi	1	2	5		1
Robason, John, Senr	4	1	2		
Robason, James	2	3	8		1
Smithwick, Simon	1		1		
Perry, Jacob	1		1		
Reddick, Mills	1	2	1		
Smithwick, John, Junr	1	1	3		
Perry, William	1	2	5		
Robason, David	2	3	5		2
Smithwick, Luke	1	1	2		2
Lanier, Robert	1	3	4		2
Peele, John	1	3	2		1
Reddick, Josiah	1	1	1		1
Woollard, John	1		1		
Perry, Sarah	1		3		7
Lilly, Timothy	3		2		
Robason, John	4	1	1		
Robason, James	1	2	2		
Rogers, David	4	2	5		
Smithwick, Edward	2	3	4		13
Smithwick, Edward Junr	1	3	1		1
Toyce, Jacob	2	4	2		
Swain, John	1	1	2		
Sparkman, William	1		1		
Campbell, James	4		3		
Lilley, Kadar	1		4		
Lilley, Josiah	1	1	3		
Smithwick, John, Senr	2		3		9
Robason, John	1		2		
Smithwick, William	1	1	2		3
Griffin, John, Junr	3	3	5		
Griffin, Martin	1	5	4		
Griffin, Edward	1	2	2		1
Griffin, Elizabeth		1	2		
Robeson, William, Senr	5		2		1
Robason, David	1	2	3		1
Gardner, Isaac	3	3	3		1
Smith, Josiah	2	1	3		
Cushion, Isaac	2		1		
Peele, James	3		1		
Bachus, John	2	3	3		
Eason, Mills	1	2	3		
Gayner, Samuel	1	3	1		
Mizell, William	2	2	1		7
Mizell, John	1		3		
Lanier, William	1	2	3		2
Mizell, James	2	2	3		1
Swinson, Levi	1				4
Hooks, Charles	2	1	3		
Bennett, James	2	4	3		6
Lilley, Joseph	1	2	6		
Biggs, Cadar	2	3	3		
Lanier, John	1	1	5		7
Mitchell, Burrell	1	2	2		
Harrison, James	1		2		
Stallions, Joel	1	2	4		6
Chapple, Malachiah	1		5		2

NAME OF HEAD OF FAMILY.	Free white males of 16 years and upward, including heads of families.	Free white males under 16 years.	Free white females, including heads of families.	All other free persons.	Slaves.
Hollowell, Levi	3		3		
Waters, William	1		2		
Ashur, Jesse	2				
Jinkins, Osborn	1	2	1		
Jinkins, Winburn	1	3	2		
Parker, James	2		8		
Bryant, Joseph	3	3	6		22
Burroughs, Benjamin	1	2	9		8
Davis, William	1	2	3		5
Conroy, John	1				
Griffin, John	1	3	2		
Kelley, Auterson	1				
Smith, John	1				
Hyman, Thomas	1				
Haughton, William	1				
Cherry, Jeremiah	1	1	1		1
Jinkins, William	1		3		
Nicholson, John	1	4	1		1
Cherry, Job	3		3		3
Barnes, Allen	3				1
Burroughs, Anthony				1	
Cotanche, Willie				1	
Magruda, Nathaniel	1				
Burroughs, William	1				
Yellowby, Edward	1				
Pierce, John	1				
Prentice, Thomas Henry	1			1	
Foreman, Thomas	1				
Fisher, James	1		1		
Parker, John	1		1		
Lane, Joseph	1				
Detor, William	1		1	1	
Simmons, James	1	2	3		
Sowell, Hillery	1				
Canaday, Benjamin	1	3	3		
Martin, Sarah		3	3		
Hunter, Thomas	23	3	3		44
Hunter, Mary		1	2		10
Hunter, Henry, Senr	1				10
Hunter, Henry	2	3	3		14
Dashwood, John	1				
Barnes, Sarah		1	4		
Virgin, James	1		2		
Virgin, Samuel	2	1	4		
Mitchell, Suckey		2	1		
Summers, John	1	2	4		
Osbern, Rainny		2	4		
Anderson, Francis	1	1	2		
Anderson, Alexander	1		1		
Gayner, Elizabeth		1	2		
Gilbert, Nicholas	1		2		
Wilson, James Lewis	1	1	2		
Biggs, William	1	1	3		3
Powers, James	1		4	3	1
McKinzie, William	2		3	8	
Watts, John	2	2	2	1	2
Morriss, Mrs			3	2	
Martin, William	1	2	1		
Gilbert, James	2		1	3	
Lawrance, George	1		2		
Jackson, Chloe			1	3	
Price, Thomas	1	1	2	1	1
Garlinton, William	1	2	3		
Pulley, William	1	1	4		6
Collins, Margaret			2		7
Biggs, Joseph	1		2		2
Travis, Amos	1	1	4		5
Wheatley, Benjamin	2	1	4		5
Nicholson, Thomas	1		4		
Slade, William, Esqr	3	1	1		28
Slade, William	1	1	1		1
Cherry, Jesse	1		1		
Day, John	2		2	1	
Holloway, Miles	1				
Beach, Thomas, Senr	1		3	1	
Webb, Jiles	1	2	2		
Boaman, Thomas	1		3		
Garganus, Lamuel	1	4	1		
Basley, William	2	1	3		2
Ward, Spellar	4				
Wyatt, William	1	2	1		
Ward, William	2		1		
Ward, John	1	2	6	1	
Suvanner, Henry	2		2		2
Williams, Samuel	2	1	5		
Swanner, William	1	1	1		
Mitchell, Jesse	1	2	2		
Fowler, George	1		2		
Williams, Dixon	1	1	4		
Brewer, Robert	3	2	6		
Bond, William	1	1	2		
Hooks, William	1		4		
O'farrell, John	1		4		
Leigh, John	1	3	2		
Jenkins, John	1	1	2		
Kelley, Timothy	1	2	2		
Nowell, Emelia	1	3	1		

NAME OF HEAD OF FAMILY.	Free white males of 16 years and upward, including heads of families.	Free white males under 16 years.	Free white females, including heads of families.	All other free persons.	Slaves.
Sowell, Chloe		1	2		
Saunders, Zelpah		1	3		
Ward, Nancy		1	2		
Stallings, Job	1	4	3		4
Warren, Mary	2	1	6		
Warren, Joseph, Senr	1		1		
Hogan, Amey			3		
Turner, Penny			2		
Yarrell, Matthew	1	3	3		6
Pearce, William	2	1	4		3
Turlinton, William	2	1	3		
Brogdon, David	1		4		
Bowers, Silas	1				
Lanfesty, Elias	1				
Brontley, Matthew	1	2	4		
Anderson, Andrew	1	4	2		
Page, Absalom	1				
Page, William	1	2	3		
Page, John	1	1	4		
Whiters, Hillery	1	2	1		
Price, William	1		4		
Bilch, William	1	1	3		2
Matthews, Luke	1	1	3		
Balentine, Nehemiah	1	1	4		
Bryant, John	1	1	2		
Manning, Malachi	1	4	2		
Page, Ann		2	2		
Cobb, Sarah		1	1		
Edmundson, Joseph		1	3		
Brewer, Edmund	1		2		
Brewer, James	1		5		
Cogbern, Daniel	1	1	4		
Pinkett, Zackariah	1		2		
Harwood, William	1	2	3		
Coburn, George	3	1	5		2
Knowell, David	1		2		
Andrews, Warren	1		1		1
Collins, Jethro	1		1		
Ellison, William	1		1		
Glesson, James	1				
Joice, Caleb	2		3		
Bonner, Stalleton	1	2	2		1
Ross, Thomas	1	2	2		
Cone, Levi	1		2		1
Brown, Alexander	2	1	4		
Ross, Joseph	1		3		
Cobern, Abner	1	1	3		4
Joice, Martin	1	3	3		
Spivy, Nathaniel	1	3	3		
Manning, William	1	1	1		
Ross, Hugh	2	1	2		3
Nowels, James	1		1		
Brewer, Mary		1	2		
Ellison, Martha			2		
Kelley, William	2	2	2		
Brewer, Mary	1		1		
Roebuck, Rolley	1		2		
Rogers, Sterling	1		4		
Haze, Martha			1		
Glisson, Isaac	1				
Whitfield, John	1	1	4		
Cobb, David	1		2		
Taylor, Sampson	1	2	3		
Taylor, Samuel	1	1	1		
Ballentine, Edward	1	1	3		1
Carder, James	1		1		
Cobern, James	1	1	1		
Ross, Martha			3		
Cobern, Francis	3	2	3		2
Cobern, John	2		3		
Cobern, John, Junr	1	1	4		
Cobb, John	4	1	4		
Cobb, Nicholas	1		1		
Whitfield, William	1		2		
Philips, Alexander	1	1	6		
Moore, William	1	1	3		
Smith, Malakiah	1	2	2		4
Nowell, Josiah	1		4		
Cobern, Andrew	1		5		
Manning, John	2	2	1		1
Carter, George	1				
Cobern, Griffin	1				
Ross, James	1		3		
Edmundson, James	3		3		
Drake, John	2	2	3		
Joyce, Elizabeth			1		4
Edmondson, Nathan	1	1	2		
Powell, John	1	1	3		
Downing, James	2	3	5		2
Ives, James	1		3		1
Little, Micajah	1	4	6		
Southerland, James	3	3	2		1
Edmundson, John	1	4	2		
Rhoads, Benjamin	1	1	2		
Rhoads, Benjamin, Senr	2	1	4		
Awins, John	1	1	5		2

HALIFAX DISTRICT, MARTIN COUNTY—Continued.

NAME OF HEAD OF FAMILY.	Free white males of 16 years and upward, including heads of families.	Free white males under 16 years.	Free white females, including heads of families.	All other free persons.	Slaves.
Cogbern, George	1	3	4		3
Savage, Briton	1		2		2
Rainer, William	1	2	1		
Hill, Nathan	1	2	5		
Collins, Shadrach	1	2	2		
Savage, Warren & Carter	2	1	4		13
Savage, Robert	1		2		1
Savage, Sterling	1		2		3
Jackston, George	1	3	1		
Knight, Richard	1	4	3		
Gayter, Samuel	1	1	3		
Howard, Wilson	1	1	2		1
Garrot, John	1	3	3		
Staton, Nehemiah	1	1	5		
Kent, Thomas	1	1	1		
Edmondson, Thomas	1	2	2		2
Barefield, Charles	2	3	4		1
Hyman, William	1	1	3		
Hill, Isaac, & E. Wallace	1	7	7		10
Rayner, Thomas	2		2		
Davidson, David	1	1	4		1
Jones, Frederick	1	2	2		4
Jones, William	2		1		3
Edmundson, William	1	1	4		
Wiggins, Mary		1	2		
Killingsworth, Patrick	1	2	3		
Johnston, Sarah			3		
Jones, John	1	1	5		7
Staton, Arthur	1	1	3		3
Grimes, Thomas	5	2	6		9
Staton, Jesse	4	1	2		1
Staton, Ezekiel	2	2	5		7
Staton, Zadock	2	1	1		
Everitt, James	1	3	6		1
Solomon, Barnes	1	1	3		1
Raynor, John	1	3	1		
Barefield, John	4	1	2		
Jones, John, Senr	1	1	3		10
Howell, Jethro	2	4	4		8
Mays, Natha	3	3	4		15
Jackson, Edward	3	3	6		
Lewillin, John	1	2	3		20
Taylor, Thomas	1		1		
Pervice, Lewis	1	3	3		
Jackson, Mary			1		1
Wallace, William	1	6	3		6
Taylor, Richard	1	1	7		
Cross, Thomas	1		2		
Deal, James	1	2	2		
Crisp, Benjamin	1	1	4		1
Crisp, Ezekiel	2	2	1		
Bullock, Josiah	1		3		
Crisp, Samuel	1	7	2		2
Crisp, Jesse	2	1	3		2
Crisp, Francis		1	1		8
Mayo, Micajah	1		2		6
Manning, Marcus	2	1	4		2
Fillpott, Fereby	1	2	6		
Manning, William	1		2		
Scott, Jehu	1		1		
Scott, Luke	1	1	2		
Harrell, Samuel	2		6		
Freeman, Moses	1	3	5		3
Cross, John	1	2	4		
Cross, James	1	3	1		
Harrill, Ephraim	1				
Best, Thomas	2	3	3		14
Miller, Stephen	1	1	5		
Leggitt, Noel	1	1	1		
Staton, Kasiah			2		
Council, Charles	2	1	4		
Council, John	1		1		
Harris, Richard	2	3	4		
Taylor, John, Junr	1		1		
Taylor, John	1	2	4		2
Taylor, Joseph	1		2		
Taylor, David	1	2	2		2
Taylor, John	4		2		6
Taylor, Richard	1	2	5		
White, Frederick	1				
Price, John	2	4	4		1
Pennywell, Thomas	1		4		
Joyner, Thomas	2	1	8		8
Edmundson, James	2	2	4		
Purvice, William	1	3	5		
Griffin, John	1				14
Hoard, Micajah	1	3	2		
Church, William	1	2	2		
Ellison, Jesse	1	3	5		
Vance, Elijah	1	1	3		
White, James	1	2	2		
Banks, John	1	2	2		
Lawrance, Williamson	1	4	3		10
Hansill, John	1	3	4		2
Everitt, John, Junr	1		1		
Ballard, James	1	1	3		3

NAME OF HEAD OF FAMILY.	Free white males of 16 years and upward, including heads of families.	Free white males under 16 years.	Free white females, including heads of families.	All other free persons.	Slaves.
Carter, Michael	2	4	1		
Andrews, Etheldred	1	1	5		13
Ballard, Silas	1	2	2		10
Griffin, William	1		2		15
Whorton, Elisha	1	1	3		
Stricklan, Jacob	2	4	2		
Barden, Asa	1				7
Boyt, Solomon	1	3	7		
Sherrord, Robert	1	4	5		9
Sherrord, John	1				1
Griffin, Micajah	1				
Wills, Edward	1				
Griffin, Epenetus	2		4		3
Johnston, Jesse	2	2	4		
Ellis, William	2		5		1
Boyt, Isaac	1	1	3		
Cooper, David	1	4	5		
Price, Elias	1	2	3		
Wheatley, John	1	5	2		1
Whorton, David	1	3	1		
Hansill, William	1		2		
Johnston, Robert	3		1		2
Chance, Jacob	1	2	2		
Carter, Reddick	1				
Everitt, William, Senr	3	1	2		
Carter, Micajah	1				
Griffin, Benjamin	1	1	4		
Wharton, John	1	2	6		
Clarke, Nathan	1				
Sherrord, Randol	1				
Hyman, John	1				
Butler, Simon	1	1	2		8
Pearse, Jesse	1	3	3		9
Ward, Timothy	1	1	1		6
Barden, William	1				5
Bennett, John	1	2	3		11
Bennett, Robert	1		2		
Little, James	1	2	2		3
Spiller, Thomas	1	1		2	7
Sherrord, Lewis	1		1		5
Everitt, William	1	1			8
Hyman, Eleazer	1	2	5		4
Vance, John	1	1	2		
Vance, David	1	2	3		
Drake, John	1	2	1		
Hyman, William	2	1	5		5
Fortune, William				1	
James, Benjamin				4	
Stricklin, John	1	1	1		
Drake, Jonas	1				
Price, Lewis	1	1	2		
Davis, Thomas	2		3		
Everitt, John	1				22
Outerbridge, William	1		2		8
Outerbridge, John	1		1		3
Outerbridge, Burrel	1				
Cooper, Stancell	1				
Callend, John	1				
Good, John	1				
Hundley, Humphry	1	3	2		
Wood, Jonas	1	1	1		1
Rooks, Charity		1	2		
Cooper, Mourning	2		3		
Clifton, Elizabeth			2		
Vance, John, Senr	1	2	2		
Cogburn, Jesse	1	1	1		
Council, Rachael			4	1	
Marshall, Nancy		1	2		
Chiff, Chloe		3	4		
Glisson, Ann			1		
Barden, Elizabeth			2		2
Mitchell, Sarah		2	1		
Jack, Buttlers				2	
Fortune, Hannah				2	
Megaskey, Mrs	2	2	4		10
Pearce, Chloe	1		3		
Frizell, Daniel	1		3		
Braveboy, John & mother			1	7	
Day, William	1		2		
Rogers, Rebeccah		1	2		
Butler, Mrs		4	3		
Williams, William	2	4	3		94
Kindday, David	1	1	2		
Carnal, Thomas	1	2	3		17
Andrews, Thomas	1	3	2		8
Weatherly, John	1				2
Harrill, Hesther	2		3		2
Jones, Dickey	1		4		
Brown, Reubin	1				1
Bryant, Lewis	1	4	2		
Harrill, Joel	1	1	2		
Pearce, Andrew	1		2		
Baggett, Thomas	1				
Hyman, Thomas	1	3	4		
Weatherly, William	1	2	2		
Bernitt, John	1	3	3		9

NAME OF HEAD OF FAMILY.	Free white males of 16 years and upward, including heads of families.	Free white males under 16 years.	Free white females, including heads of families.	All other free persons.	Slaves.
Regerson, Daniel	1		4		
O'Cain, William	1	1	3		
Culpepper, Jeremiah	2				
Hyman, Hugh	1	1	2		1
O'Cain, John	1				
Brown, Jacob	1		4		2
Boyt, Thomas	1	1	2		1
Bland, William	1	3	5		
Medford, James	1	4	4		
Parker, Jacob	3	3	5		
Savage, Carter	1				
Price, William	1		4		1
Hyman, John	1	2	4		4
Byrnett, Matthew	2	1	6		4
Ballard, Jesse	1		4		
Price, William	1	1	1		1
Long, Equilla	1	3	2		1
Price, John	1				1
Cherry, Jonathan	2	2	5		
Bernett, James	2	4	4		
Hynes, Christopher	3	2	4		
Guy, William	2		2		10
Hynes, John	1		3		
Lynch, Henry	1	3	3		
Parker, John	1	2	3		
Ballard, Elisha	1	1	2		7
Forrest, George	1		2		4
Strawbridge, Elijah	1	4	3		10
Bernitt, Ephraim	1		5		
Pitman, Edward	1				
Cross, Stephen	1	1	4		
Hatson, Thomas	2	2	4		5
Moore, Hodges	3		4		30
Collins, Timothy	1	2	4		3
Savage, Thomas	1		3		
Weatherly, Thomas	1	1	3		7
Wiggins, Lemuel	2	4	3		24
Howell, James	1	2	4		3
Etheringane, George	2	1	2		5
Harrell, Lott	3	2	6		14
Stafford, John				5	
Bland, Thomas	1	1	3		
Brewer, Thomas	1	3	5		2
Watson, William, Junr	1		2		
Johnson, Joshua	1		3		
Harrell, Hezekiah	1	2	2		
Pierce, Thomas	1		3		2
Bryan, Hardy	1	3	4		1
Bryan, Needham	2	3	1		5
Belflower, William	1				
Bryan, Elias	2		3		7
Jackson, Gibson	1		3		
Williams, Samuel	1	5	7		104
Baggett, Thomas	1		2		
Watts, Lewis	1	3	1		
Bryan, Robert	1	2	3		2
Spivy, George	1	1	1		1
Lee, Mason	1				3
Archer, Zachariah			1	6	
Rawls, Silas	1		1		
Taylor, John	1	2	4		26
Whitney, Samuel	1				1
Taylor, Joshua	1	7	4		21
Mitchell, William	1				
Medfort, John	1	5	1		
Mitchell, James	1				
Kiff, James	1	1	4		
Culpepper, Jane					1
Pierce, Lovick	1	2	3		
Brown, James	2	4	5		5
Wiggins, John	1		2		4
Thompson, William	1		3		1
King, Michael	4		1		15
Brown, Abner	1	3	3		3
Kent, John	1	2	1		
Wiggins, Blake	2	6	3		43
Hill, Whitmill	34	4	6		140
Maning, Thomas	2	4	3	1	2
Reading, Joseph	2	2	3		6
Kent, William	1	1	5		
Vance, David	2	1	5		
Bates, Isra	1				
Parker, William	1	1	1		9
Singclair, Benjamin	2		3		
Short, William	2	1	2		
McDaniel, James	1			6	
Benbory, Miles	1		2		1
Cooper, Joseph	2	3	6		
Cross, John	1	1	4		
Cross, William	1	1	3		
Weathersley, Lucy		1	2		
Boothe, Elizabeth			3		
Jones, Richard				5	
Jackson, Mary		3	3		
Robason, Hardy	1				
Foster, William			2		
Watson, William, Senr	2		3		

HALIFAX DISTRICT, MARTIN COUNTY—Continued.

Name of head of family.	Free white males of 16 years and upward, including heads of families.	Free white males under 16 years.	Free white females, including heads of families.	All other free persons.	Slaves.
Jackson, James	1		2		
Medford, Henry	1	2	1		
Griffin, Matthew	1	2	4		
Ballard, Nancy			2		
Ballard, Betsey		1	2		
Watson, Jacob	1	1	1		
Watson, Thomas, Junr	1		1		
Lynch, Jesse	1		5		
Dickson, Thomas	1		2		
Glisson, Mary	1	2	3		
Harrell, Mourning		3	2		
Murray, Mark				9	
Mitchell, Isaac	1	4	1		
Hynes, Joseph	1		2		
Baggett, Thomas	1				
Waldon, Mary				3	
Belflower, Ann	1	3	2		
Anthony, John	1		2		33
Ross, John	2	1	5		6
Ross, James	1	2	1		
Rawls, James	1		2		1
Burrice, David	1		2		
Ross, Martin	1	2	1		
Rogers, Levy	1	2	4		
Ross, John, Junr	1	1	2		
Collins, John	3	3	5		2
Ross, William	1	1	3		
Britt, Joel	1		6		
Roebuck, George	1	2	3		
Barnihill, James	2	3	4		
Moore, Joseph, Junr	1	4	5		
Moore, Moses	1	3	1		2
Moore, Joseph	1		3		
Moore, John	1	1	1		
Carter, Benjamin	2	3	2		1
Bonner, Mary			2		2
Bonner, Stapleton	2	2	1		2
Anderson, Ann	1	1	3		3
Morriss, Jacob	2	2	5		
Moon, Priscilla	1	3	1		
Cone, William	2	4	4		
Cone, Neal	1		7		
Cone, Levi	1		3		1
Brogdone, James	2	1	5		
Barnihill, Daniel	1	1	2		
Ballard, Sarah	1		6		5
Currell, Elizabeth	1	5	2		7
Ballard, Silas	1	1	3		2
Cooper, Jesse	2		3		
Cone, Jesse	1	2	1		1
Jones, Darling	3		2		
Norfleet, Sarah	1	1	1		
Wheatley, Hardy	2	2	6		
Qualls, Judith	1		6		
Beach, Thomas	1	5	3		1
Haselip, Southy	1	3	1		
Cherry, Joab	2	2	5		
Western, Jeremiah	1	1	2		
Harrill, John	2	1	2		
Cherry, Harrill	1	1	2		
Price, Elijah	2	2	7		5
Kenaday, John	2	2	6		1
Haselip, Frederick	1		3		
Lilley, Zachariah	2		2		
Hedgpith, Josiah	1	2	3		
Leggett, Samuel	1	2	3		
Hagges, Dorcas		1	4		
Mobley, William	1		4		
Williams, John	1				
Mobley, Edward	1				1
Price, John	1		2		5
Hurst, William	1	1	1		
Collins, James	1				1
Collins, John	2	3	4		2
Keneday, Isaac	1		1		
Rawls, Jesse	1	3	4		
Wynne, John	1	1	1		4
Bland, John	1		4		
Rawls, William	2	3	4		
Rawls, Joshua	1	3	3		
Everitt, Joshua	1		1		6
Leggett, Benjamin	3		3		
Leggett, Hezekiah	1	3	3		
Bullock, Obadiah	1	2	3		
Woollard, Jesse	1	1	1		
Wynne, Watkin W	3	3	4		8
Hollowday, Thomas	2	3	7		7
Leggett, John	2	4	5		
Ward, William	2		2		
Mitchell, Jesse	1	2	2		1
Biggs, Joshua	1	2	2		
Ward, Henry	1		4		
Beach, Thomas	1		4		
Hodges, Francis	1		2		
Robason, Henry	3	3	2		9
Rolls, William	2	3	4		
Rolls, Jesse	1	3	4		
Rolls, Joshua	1	3	3		
Mizell, William	2				
Cherry, Jesse		5	5		6
Cherry, Joel	1	3	4		1
Cherry, James	2		1		
Cherry, Jonathan	1		1		
Hisk, William	1	3	2		
Bird, Edward	2	3	3		2

HALIFAX DISTRICT, NASH COUNTY.

Name of head of family.	Free white males of 16 years and upward, including heads of families.	Free white males under 16 years.	Free white females, including heads of families.	All other free persons.	Slaves.
Arranton, Arthur	1	3	5		13
Arranton, John	1				4
Arranton, Peter	1	2	1		5
Arranton, William	2	1	3		16
Arranton, Peter	1	2	4		5
Arranton, Joseph	1	3	3		10
Arranton, Joseph, Jr	3	2	3		10
Atkins, Newell	3	3	3		
Atkinson, James	1	2	4		4
Atkinson, Tho	1	3	4		
Atkinson, Henry	4	5	3		14
Allen, Thomas	1	3	3		
Allen, Arthur	1				
Andrews, Joseph	2		6		
Andrews, Wm	1		1		13
Avon, William	2	4	4	1	12
Blanton, Richard	1	4	2		1
Butts, Redford	1	1	2		
Battle, John	2				18
Battle, William	2	4	1		19
Boothe, Andrew	1	3	1	1	
Bell, Green	1	4	5	2	
Bell, Benjamin	1	1	3		
Blount, John	1		3		4
Baggel, Nicholas	1	1	3		1
Bridges, Benja	2	1	4		4
Boyd, James	1	3	4		
Biggel, David	1	3	5		
Barrow, Barnaby	2	6	5		5
Brown, James	2	2	4		
Brown, Mary	3	1	4		
Burge, Jeremiah	1	4	1		2
Bryant, Benj	1	3	2		1
Brown, James, Jr	1				12
Boothe, ——	1				
Bond, John	1	2	7		13
Butler, Christopher	2		2		
Bryant, Wm	1		4		4
Ballard, Peter	1	1	2		5
Ballard, Edward	3	1	6		
Bunn, Henry	1				4
Brewer, Hardy	2	1	3		3
Brantly, John	1	2	5		
Baker, William	3	1	6		
Baker, Allen	1		2		
Baker, William	1	1	3		1
Baker, John	1	2	4		1
Baker, James	2	2	1		
Bone, John	1	6	4		
Brantley, Jacob	3	3	4		
Boddy, William	1	1	5		21
Boon, Benjamin	1	6	5		2
Braswill, William	1	1	4		
Braswel, Jacob	1	2	3		1
Braswell, Robt	1		1		3
Bridges, William	2	5	4		8
Bunton, Jeremiah	1				
Battle, James	1	1	5		13
Bass, Abram	1	2	4		12
Bass, Jesse	2		1		2
Boddy, William (for M. Thomas)					56
Bass, Isaac	3	3	4		9
Bass, John	1				
Bass, Sion	1	3	5		4
Brasswell, Jacob	4		4		13
Boddy, Nathan	4		2		40
Braswell, Saml	2	1	6		4
Braswell, Micajah	2	2			
Braswell Dempsey	1	2	4		
Beckwith, Tho	4	2	3		7
Beckwith, Amos	2	4	5		5
Barrot, John	2	5	7		
Barrott, Nathan	1	3	3		1
Barnes, James	1	3	4		
Bone, John	1	6	4		
Brantley, Jacob	3	3	4		
Boddy, Wm	1				
Bunn, Redmon	2	1	3		4
Bunn, Benj.	1	3	4		4
Bunn, Joel	1				
Bunn, Burwell	1		1		7
Bunn, David	1	3	3		7
Bunn, Benj., Sen	3	1	6		29
Barns, Benj	2	2	6		1
Barnes, John	1	1	2		
Barns, William	1	3	6		2
Barns, Jacob	2	3	2		
Boykin, Hardy	3	2	5		
Blankenship, Jas	2	2	4		
Brown, Edmund	1				
Barns, Joseph	1		1		
Boykin, Drury	3	4	4		
Bail, William	1	1	2		
Bottoms, William	1		4		
Boykin, Drury, Jr	1	4	4		
Ballard, William	2	3	4		
Bowls, John	2	3	1		
Burge, Burwell	1	4	4		1
Bachelor, Joseph	1	4	2		
Bellle, Barnaby	1	1	1		
Bunten, William	1	5	2		
Bryant, Saml	2	6	1		19
Bachelor, Stephen	2		2		
Bachelor, Saml	2	4	4		
Braswell, William	1	3	4		1
Bryant, William	1	3	4		
Braswell, Benj	1	3	2		
Barnes, Benjamin	1	2	1		
Barns, John	2	2	6		1
Britten, Charles	1		1		
Barnes, Henry	1	3	5		
Bass, Jethro	2		2		5
Bachelor, James	1		3		4
Burge, Richard	2		1		9
Bruce, James	1	1	1		
Bryant, William	1		3		4
Basset, David	3	2	3		
Ball, Jordan	1	1	1		
Blackwell, Ferreby		2	2		
Bass, Charely		1	2		
Biggs, Efferd				3	
Bryant, Betty		1	4		
Bachelor, Daniel	1	1	1		
Barnes, John	1	2	5		5
Brantley, Lewis	1	3	3		
Bachelor, John	1		2		
Bachelor, John	1	1	2		
Bedgood, John	2	3	4		
Butts, Jacob	1				
Bass, Jesse	2				4
Bryant, William	1		1		4
Bryant, Benj	1	3	1		2
Bottons, Saml	2	2			
Barnes, Basset	1		1		
Benton, Agness		1	4		
Bass, Jethro	2	3	2		
Barrot, Reddeck	1	1	1		
Beckwith, Burwell	1		1		
Barrow, John	2	2	2		
Bottons, Saml	1		2		
Boddy, George	1		2		5
Benton, Ann	1	1	5		
Brantley, Sarah	1	1	5		
Bedgood, Jemima		1	1		
Cooper, Edward	1		2		
Cooper, Edward, Jr	2	2			6
Connel, Davis	4	3	5		2
Cox, John	1	3	4		1
Cooper, Penelope	1	3	4		2
Cain, James	1	3	4		20
Carter, Thomas	2	3	5		
Carter, Solomon	2	4	6	6	
Carter, Saml	1				
Chapman, John	2	1	6		1
Collins, Jesse	2	1	1	4	1
Collins, Abehue	1	2	1		
Chapman, William	1	1	4		1
Carigus, Job	1	1	2		
Carpenter, Tho	1	1	2		1
Carpenter, Tho., Jr	1	1	2		
Cone, Joshua	1	3	6		
Cone, James	1	3	5		
Cooper, Marcome	3	3	4		4
Currel, Lewis	1		7		4
Currel, Wilson	1	2	7		4
Clench, John	1	4	4		18
Currel, John	1	3	4		

HALIFAX DISTRICT, NASH COUNTY—Continued.

NAME OF HEAD OF FAMILY.	Free white males of 16 years and upward, including heads of families.	Free white males under 16 years.	Free white females, including heads of families.	All other free persons.	Slaves.
Currel, Joseph	1	4	2		4
Cross, Stephen	2	2	3		
Cobb, Benjamin	1	2	4		6
Carter, Charles	2	3	3	1	
Carter, Jacob	1	2	2		
Cochrell, John	1	2	2		
Cochrell, Jacob	1	2	2		
Coleson, Chester	1		2		
Carter, Toby	1				
Carter, Thomas	2	3	6		2
Coleman, Robert	1		1		8
Carter, Reese	1				7
Coleman, Theophilus	2		2		
Crowell, Martha	1	1	6	4	
Carter, William	4	7	3		
Cockrell, William	1	5	5		4
Curll, Matthew	2		3		
Cain, Currell	1	2	3		
Carter, Jacob	1	3	5		2
Creekman, Robert	1	2	5	12	2
Culpepper, James	2	2	4		
Culpepper, Christopher	1				1
Culpepper, James, Jr	1	3	3		3
Culpepper, Jeremiah	1	1	1		
Colley, Solomon	2	2	4		
Creekman, Volintine	1	1	2		
Cone, Jesse	1	2	7		
Cone, John	1	2	3		
Cone, James	1	3	5		
Cith, Iasabel		1	3		
Carter, Charles	2	2	4		1
Carter, Mary		2	4		
Council, Michael	1	1	4		
Cook, Patience		1	2		
Council, Mike	1		2		
Coleson, Jonas	1	1	2		
Cooper, John	2	1	5		3
Churchill, James	1	1	5		
Cobb, Nathan	2	1	3		24
Cooper, Benjamin	1	2	2		2
Dorch, Lewis	1	3	4		9
Dozier, John	1		1		
Davis, John	3	3	4		
Drury, Henry	1	3	7		
Denson, Jethro	1	4	5		
Drake, Thomas	1	1	3		2
Davis, Abell	1		1		3
Davis, Enoch	1				2
Drake, James	3	1	3		22
Devaughan, Saml	1	4	6		
Dyson, Mary		1	4		
Durley, Arthur	2	4	3		
Dudley, Elizabeth		1	2		
Dudley, John	1				
Dance, Etheldrede	1	2			2
Daughtridge, Benjn	1	1	3		
Denson, John	1	2	1		
Denson, Joseph	1	2	5		
Druett, James	1	1	1		1
Drake, Edmond	4	1	7	1	13
Drake, Matthew	2	2	8		16
Drake, William	3	4	4		17
David, Donald	1	4	5		4
Daniel, Federick	1	5	2		3
Drake, Hynes	1	2	3		1
Dawson, Dempsey	1		4		5
Dew, John	1				8
Dew, Duncan	1		1		20
Dickerson, William	1	3	6		
Driver, John	1	3	6		
Dunn, Richard	2		2		
Deens, Willis	1	2	4		
Deens, Mary	1	4	4		
Deens, Sherrod	1	4	3		
Deens, Thomas	3		5		8
Deens, Richard	2		2		
Denson, Benjamin	1	2	3		
Denson, Jesse	1	1	2		
Denson, John	1	3	4		
Deens, Henry	1	4	3		
Den, William	1	1	1		8
Driver, Mary			4		
Dawson, Dempsey	1	4	5		
Driver, William	1	4	6		
Drake, Delilah	2	1	4		
Dozier, William	3	1	4	9	
Evans, William	2	2	3	4	
Evans, Burrell				1	
Eason, Samuel	2	1	2		
Eason, Elizabeth		1	4		
Eason, William	1		3		
Eason, Samuel	1	1	2		
Evans, John	1	6	3		
Evans, Sherrod	1				
Evans, David	1	3	5		1
Edmundson, Ambrose	1	1	4		
Howell, Ellen	1	1	6		4
Exum, Joseph	1	3	5		5
Exum, John	1		3		4
Edward, Solomon	1	2	7		1
Eatman, Noel	2	2	6		
Eatman, John	2	5	4		8
Etheridge, Jeremiah	5		8	3	3
Etheridge, Peter	1	3	4		
Evans, Thomas	2	3	1		
Eden, Richard	1		3		
Evans, Samuel	1	1	5		
Freeman, Henry	1	3	6		3
Fore, William	1	3	1		1
Finch, Isham	2	1	3		
Floyd, Pinnuel	1		3		5
Floyd, Benjamin	1	1	3		
Flowers, Henry	3	1	4	6	6
Flowers, John	1	4	5		
Flowers, Benjamin	1	5	3		3
Flowers, John (S. of H.)	1	2	3		2
Flowers, William	1		5		
Floyd, Thomas	1	1	1		2
Finch, Isrom	2	1	4		
Finch, Allen	1	1	4		
Flowers, Martha			2		
Griffin, Hardy	2	1	4		8
Green, James	1		2		5
Green, Nathan	1	1	2		
Gardener, Pryer	1	2	5		4
Goodwyn, John	1				1
Gardener, Wm	1				1
Gardener, George	1	2	6		6
Gardener, James	1	2	8		
Goodwin, James	1	2	8		
Gains, James	2	5	3		
Gray, Edward	2	2	3		8
Gandy, Amos	1	1	2		1
Gray, John	1	4	5		3
Griffin, Pierce	1	2	2		3
Griffin, Micajah	1		4		
Griffin, Matthw	2	3	5		
Griffin, Archibald	1				2
Griffin, Thomas	1		3		
Glanding, Major	1	1	3		
Griggett, George	1	2	2		
Griggett, William	2	1	2		
Griggett, Horrod	1		2		
Griggett, Ellick	1				4
Gracie, Theophilus	2		8		8
Glover, Thomas	1	2	5		
Gay, John	1	4	4		3
Glover, Elizabeth	2	1	4		1
Grimm, George	1	2	3		
Griffin, James	1	3	2		
Goodson, Betty		1	3		
Griffin, Ann	1	1	3		
Harrison, John	1	4	4		12
Harrison, John, Jr	1				3
Hayes, Joseph	2	4	5		20
Horn, Henry	1	2	4		3
Harris, Thomas	1		2		6
Hopkins, Peter	4	5	6		9
Hicks, Solomon	1	1	3		
Hall, William	1	2	3		1
Halton, Thomas	1				
Harper, Benjamin	1	1	3		1
Horn, Elisha	1	1	1		5
Hollon, Daniel	2	2	3		
Hunt, David	1		5		
Hunt, Christn	1	3	3		
Hamilton, Thomas	1				7
Hilliard, James	2	5	4		84
Horn, Edward	1	2	4		4
Harris, Harday	2	1			22
Hynes, Lewis	2	1	7		4
Hunter, Priscilla		2	3		5
Hunter, Drury	1	1	1		2
Horn, Jacob	1	1	3		2
Harris, Randolph	1	4	6		7
Harrell, John	1		3		1
Hamilton, Francis	1	2	5		
Horn, Josiah	1	1	3		5
Hynes, Federick	1	1	3		10
Hart, Thomas	1	2	1		
Hart, Thomas	1		4		
Hunt, Jesse	1	2	6		
Horn, Joshua	1	3	2		
Horn, Michael	1	2	4		5
Horn, Wilson	1	1	4		
Horn, Thomas	1	3	5		4
Harrison, Jethro	2	5	3		3
Horn, William	1		4		
Hitchpeth, Jesse	1		1		
Horn, Richard	1		1		
Horn, Jordan	1		3		
Henry, William	2	3	6		
Hill, Zion	1	2	5		
Hobbs, Herbert	1	2	5		3
Harris, William	1	2	1		
Harris, Wm	1	2	5		
Hammon, William	2	1	2		3
Harris, John	2	2	1		
Hithford, James	4		5		1
Hale, Polly			4		
Howlings, Charles	1	2	7		
How, William	1	3	3		
How, John	1	1	8		
Hight, Joseph	1				
Horn, Jeremiah	1	3	2		2
Hicks, Ciety	1		2		
Harrison, Hanah		1	3		
Hethpeth, Abram	1	1	3		
Hendrick, Wm	2	2	5		
Horn, Patience	1	2	3	1	
Hunt, Judah		1	3		
Hight, Daniel	2				
Henry, Isaac	1				
Jones, John	2	2	6		6
Jackson, Wm	1	1	4		
Johnson, Andrew	1	1	3		
Jones, Fedrick	2	2	2		
Joiner, Nathaniel	2	2	3		
Joiner, William	1	3	6		1
Joiner, Jacob	1	5	3		
Joiner, Lewis	1	3	3		1
Joiner, Burwell	1	2	3		1
Joiner, John	2		1		
Joiner, John, Jr	1				
Joiner, Jesse	1	1	3		
Joiner, Nathl	1	1	5		
Joiner, William	1		1		
Joiner, Jordan	1	1	1		2
Jackson, George	2	1	1		11
Joiner, Celia		1	4		2
Joiner, Joseph	1	3	2		
Johnson, Josiah	3	2	3		
Jones, John	2	2	7		5
Jones, Nusom	1	2	5		1
Johnson, William	1	2	4		
Jones, Brittin	1	1	2		
Jelks, Etheldridge	3	1	3		
Jones, John	2	3	6		14
Jolley, James	2	2	6		
Jones, Barnaby	4				
Joiner, Solomon	1	4	2		
Johnson, Andrew	1	1	3		
Joiner, Cordie	1	3	3		8
Joiner, Drury	1		1		3
Jones, Cooper	2	4	3		
Joiner, Cornelius	1		1		
Jenkins, Jesse	1				5
King, Thomas	1	2	4		
Kith, James	1				
Keachen, William	2		2		2
Kent, Jesse	2	4	1		4
Knight, Kinsman	2		2		
King, Julian	1				5
Kent, Jesse, Jr	3	3	1		
Ketchen, Jesse	2		4		
Kinton, Charles	1	3	3		
Lewis, William	3	1	3		4
Lassitor, Tobias	5	5	3		
Lassitor, James	1	3	2		
Lassitor, Arthur	1	3	2		
Lee, Charles	2	3	3		
Letbetter, Rowland	1	2	4		
Lewis, Mayor	1	2	3		
Letbetter, John	2	3	3		
Locus, Frank				8	
Locus, James				6	
Lee, James	1	4	6		7
Laurance, Jesse	3		4		
Lassau, James	1	2	4		
Lemmons, Duncan	2	3	5	6	40
Lemmons, John	1				4
Lemmons, Archd	1				15
Locus, Barnaby				8	
Locus, Abner	1		1		
Locus, John				6	
Locus, Arthur				7	
Locus, Frank				8	
Lewis, Nathl	2	1	6		
Lee, Jonathan	1	2	2		
Lampkin, Lewis	1	2	5		8
Lewis, Henry	1	4	3		
Lain, Jonathan	1		4		
Locus, George				5	
Lain, Elizabeth	2	1	5		
Lindsey, William	1	5	1		
Letbetter, Holding	1	2	4		
Letbetter, John	2	3	3		
Langley, Nathan	1	1	3		
Lindsey, Billy	1	1	3		
Lee, James	1	4	5		7
Lindsey, Sion	1	1	4		
Laurance, Betty			4		
Mason, Henry	4	4	4		
Mason, Ralph	2	5	6		

HALIFAX DISTRICT, NASH COUNTY—Continued.

NAME OF HEAD OF FAMILY.	Free white males of 16 years and upward, including heads of families.	Free white males under 16 years.	Free white females, including heads of families.	All other free persons.	Slaves.
Mason, Foster	1	4	3		1
Mason, Mark	1	1	3		1
Mason, William	1		2		
Matthews, Benj	1	3	4		1
Matthews, Joel	1		3		
Musten, Joseph	1	1	3		
Musten, John	3	4	5		
Mann, Thomas	2	1			36
Mitchell, Sam¹	2	3	5		
Mason, Mark	2		3		7
Mossly, David	1		1		
Mossly, Joseph	2	3	5		
Medleng, Shadʰ	2	4	4		
Morgan, John	2	2	6		
Medleng, Bryant	2	3	5		
Morgan, Hardy	1	2	3		
Morgan, William	1				
Moore, William	1				
Moore, Wade	1	1	1		
Matthews, William	1		3		
Milton, Zach	1		2		
Milton, John	2	5	1		
Milton, Josiah	1	2	3		
Mannen, Mattʷ	1		1		
Mannen, Margret	1		7		14
Masengail, James	1		2		
Masengail, Walker	2		3		
Masengail, Joseph	1		4		
Masengail, James	1	3	6		
Masengail, Henry	4	2	2		
Moses, Smith	1	3	4		
Mann, Denton	1		4		14
Mearns, William S	1	4			14
Morriss, Thomas	1		5		
Mannen, Sam¹	2	1	3		
Merril, William	1		3		4
Morriss, Mitchel	1	2	5		
Merril, Benjamin	1		4		5
Merril, William	1		3		8
Mannen, Thomas	1	2	5		
Milton, John	1	1	6		
Moonahow, John	2	2	6		
Morriss, James	1	4	2		3
Moonahow, Tho	1	3	5		
Mannen, William	1	2	2		
Moore, James	1	2	4		3
Moore, Edward	1				4
Mannen, Benjª	1	2	3		
Mannen, Willoby	1		5		7
Morriss, William	1	1	3		
Mannen, Mattʷ	1				
Mitchell, John	1		1		
Masengail, Eliz		1	3		
Mitchell, Mary			4		
Masengail, Nancey		3	3		
Mannen, Lucy		2	5		
Mannen, Margret		1	7		
Nicholson, Joseph	1	1	3		11
Norriss, James	1	5	5		7
Navin, William	1		4		
Navin, John	2	3	4		
Nash, Joseph	1	2	2		1
Newton, Benj	2		5		
Nicholas, Job	1	2	5		
Nicholas, Jeremiah	2	4	4		
Nicholas, Jeremiah, Jr	1		3		
Nicholas, John	1	4	5		
Nicholas, Edward	2		4		8
Night, Sarah	1	2	4		
Nolleyboy, Sally		1	1		
Owens, John	1		4		
Owens, Daniel	5	2	3		3
Owins, Elias	1	2	3		
Oneal, Arthur	3	2	6		
Otham, Willis	1	1	5		
Owens, Mary		3	3		
Powell, Willoby	1	3	5		12
Powell, Danl	1	1	5		4
Portes, John	2	2	4		
Powell, John	3	1			
Powell, Allanson	1		4		
Powell, Nathan	1	1	4		10
Pritchet, John	1	2	4	6	6
Perry, William	1	4	3		
Parish, John	1	4	3		
Parker, William	1				4
Pace, George	1	2	4		
Pucket, Abraham	1		1		
Pridgen, David	2	1	4		5
Pridgen, Eliz. Allen			1		5
Pridgen, M. Mannen		1			7
Pridgen, Drury	1				
Pollon, John	1	5	5		1
Pridgen, Hardy	1	3	5		1
Pasmour, John	1	2	3		
Powell, Jesse	2	4	5		8
Pitts, John	1	1	8		10
Parker, William	3		5		
Parker, Francis	1	1	1		13
Parker, Ann		1	1		1
Pope, John	1	2	3		3
Pope, Dempsey	1	2	4		
Pope, Elisha	2	3	4		
Pope, Micajah	1	3	4		
Parker, Gabriel	1	1	2		
Phillips, Jethro	1		4		9
Phillips, Ephraim	1	3	4		4
Phillips, William	1	1	1		1
Phillips, Josiah	2	1	3		7
Poland, William	1	2	3		3
Parker, Aarn	1	3	4		
Parker, John	1	3	4		
Parker, John, Jr	2	3	6		
Pughe, William	4				
Parker, Eliza		3	1		4
Pope, Barnaby	1		3		9
Pridgen, Jesse	1	3	5		4
Pierce, Eliza			2		
Pursell, Eliza	2	3	4		
Parrott, Joseph	2	3	4		
Pierce, Joshua	2		3		1
Pace, Wm	4		3		
Parker, Mary		2	6		
Pellepet, Phillip	1	3	6		
Rose, Frances	2	1	5		4
Robertson, John	1		2		1
Rose, William	2	1	4		6
Robertson, Peter	1	1	1		
Rutherford, James	2		2		1
Rutherford, Robert	1		1		
Rutherford, James, Jr	1	1	1		
Reed, John	1	3	4		3
Richardson, Thomas	1		2		2
Rose, Burwell	2	2	4		
Rackley, Parsons	1	2	4		
Rean, Howell	1	6	4		
Rose, Burwell, Jr	2	2	4		
Rose, John	1	4	2		
Rowe, William	1	3	3	4	4
Revell, Micajah					12
Revell, Elijah					12
Russ, Randolph	1	2	5		
Ricks, Mary		2	3		
Richardson, William	2	3	2		
Richardson, Wm, Jr	3	3	2		
Rogers, Jacob	1	1	2		
Rogers, Robert	3	1	6		1
Ricks, Abram	1	3	4		
Ricks, Joel	1	2	3		
Ricks, Jacob	1	2	5		
Ricks, Wm	1	5	4		
Ricks, Sarah		1	4		
Ridley, Thomas	1		2		
Rackley, Parsons	1	2	5	3	2
Rackley, Mattʷ	1	1	1		
Rackley, Frank	1	2	1		
Ricks, Priscilla		1	2		
Ricks, William, Jr	1	5	4		
Rossin, Daniel	1	2	4		1
Rackley, Mattʷ	1	1	1		
Rogers, Jacob	1	1	3	4	
Sandiford, William	3	2	7		1
Smelly, John	1	2	4		
Scruize, Henry	3	2	5		1
Statter, James	1	3	4		1
Smith, Samuel	1	2	4		
Strickland, Henry	2		2		4
Strickland, Hardy	1		2		8
Strickland, Nash	1	3	3	2	2
Strickland, Mattʷ	1	1	1		
Strickland, Lazª	4	1	3		
Strickland, Harmon	3		5		
Smith, Clayton	1	2	3		
Sutton, Thomas	1	4	4		
Strickland, Mark	2	4	6		17
Stallions, Moses	1	3	1		
Strickland, Tho	1	2	2		
Strickland, Joseph	1	2	4		
Strickland, Lazarus	1	1	1		
Strickland, John	4	2	2		
Strickland, Simon	1	3	4		
Smith, Peter	1	2	3		
Scott, Absolem				8	
Savage, Moses	1	1		4	
Savage, Drury	1	1	2		4
Sikes, Phillip	1	1	5		
Stephens, Joshua	1	2	3		
Sutton, George	1		1		
Sanders, John	1	6	3		
Sanders, Cornelius	1		4		
Sanders, Thomas, Jr	1	1	4		
Sanders, Thomas	1	1	3		
Seary, Aquilla	1		2		
Sanders, John	1	1	1		1
Sullivent, Owen	1		2		
Sossberry, Sam¹	2		1	5	
Skinner, Emanuel	2		5		1
Skinner, William	2	2	5		4
Strickland, David	3	2	5		
Strickland, Henry	2	2	5		5
Sanders, Henry	2	2	4		5
Sketo, William	1	1	6		1
Solomons, Lazarus	1	2	5		
Selah, Joseph	2	1	6		
Smith, Benjamin	1		5		28
Selah, Joseph, Jr	1	3	6		
Sheppard, John	3	1	5		
Sellers, John	1	5	1	3	3
Sherod, Jordan	1	2	5		
Strickland, Joseph	1	1	1		
Smith, Babson	1				
Sellers, John	1	5	1		5
Sellers, Arthur	1	1	2		
Smith, Peter	1	2	5		
Strickland, Mattʷ	1	1	2		
Smith, Clayton	1	2	3		
Stallions, Moses	1	1	3		
Skinner, Samuel	3	1	3		1
Selah, Drury	1	1	1		
Sellers, William	2	4	6		
Smith, Jesse	1		2		
Turner, James	2	3	3		
Taylor, James	2	2			1
Taylor, John	1		2		1
Taylor, Burwell				6	
Taylor, Benjª	3	1	6		
Taylor, Sam¹	1	1	4		1
Taylor, William	1				
Taylor, Benj., Jr	1				3
Taylor, Demsey	1	2	2		
Tann, Benjamin				5	
Taylor, John	2	2	5		4
Tucker, Benjamin	1	3	4		4
Tucker, Jacob	1	2	5		
Tucker, Daniel	1	1	4		
Tucker, Benj	4	3	5		
Tucker, Thomas	1	3	6		
Tucker, James	1	3	6		
Tucker, James, Jr	1	3	5		
Tucker, Sarah		6	2		6
Taylor, Daniel	3	5	4		
Taylor, Drury	1	5	1		3
Taylor, Christopher	1	1	5		3
Taylor, Wilson	1	2	5		5
Tyce, Thomas	1	2	2		
Taylor, Reuben	2	3	5		15
Taylor, Milles	1	5	2		1
Thomas, Alexander	1				
Turner, William	1		5		
Turner, John	1	5	3		
Thomas, Jacob	1		4		
Thomas, Jesse	4	1	6		
Thomas, Jethro	1	2	4		1
Turlington, Elizabeth	1	2	3		
Tucker, Reubin	1				
Tucker, Jacob	2		7		
Underwood, Sam¹	3	2	4		3
Underwood, Jacob	3	1	4		3
Underwood, Howell	1	1	2		1
Vick, Robert	1	1	2		
Vick, Robert, Jr	1	2	4		
Vick, Joseph	2	5	5		
Vick, Jordan	2	3	5		
Vaughan, Dempsey	1	2			
Vaughan, Stephen	2	2	4		
Vester, William	2	2	4		
Vester, William, Jr	1	3	3		
Vaughan, Ephraim	1	3	5		
Viverett, Thomas	5	3	5		15
Vick, John	2	3	3		
Vick, Lewis	1	2	4		1
Vick, Henry	3	2	4	1	1
Vick, Nathan	1	2	3		
Vick, William	1				4
Vick, Robert	1	1	1		
Vester, Ciely	1	3	1		
Vick, Richard	2	3	4		
Vaughan, Fredk	1	2	4		
Wester, Hardy	1	3	2		2
Whitehead, Tho	3	3	3		9
Whitehead, Benj	3	3	3		9
Wright, William	3	4	5		21
Whitley, Solomon	2	1	8		
Whelas, William	3	2	5		1
Whelas, Mildred	1				
Ward, Francis	1	3			
Whitehead, Rachel	1	1	2		10
Whitehead, Lazarus	1		2		3
Whitehead, Charles	1	1	1		
Warburton, John	1				

HALIFAX DISTRICT, NASH COUNTY—Continued.

NAME OF HEAD OF FAMILY.	Free white males of 16 years and upward, including heads of families.	Free white males under 16 years.	Free white females, including heads of families.	All other free persons.	Slaves.
Williams, Benjamin	1	2	3		
Whitehead, Lazarus	3		1	7	20
Wenburn, Abram	1	2	5		
Wenburn, Josiah	1	2	4		
West, Arthur	2	1	2		
Wyatt, Dempsey	2	2	6		
West, Nathan	1	2	3		
West, Dempsey	1	1	4		
West, William	1	1	3		
Woodward, Jesse	1	5	3		5
Whelas, Jacob	1		3		8
Williams, Joel	1	5	3		
Williams, Rowland	1	1	4		10
White, Allen	1				
Williams, Benjamin	1	1	4		8
Whitfield, John	3	3	4		
Warren, Mary	1	2	3		
Williams, Philander	2	1	4		8
Whitby, Mary		2	2		
Williams, Drury	1	3	1		5
Woodward, Thomas	1	3	2		
Williams, Elkany	1	3	5		
Wright, Joseph	1				1
Williamson, Joseph	1	1	5		1
Willis, John	1		1		
Wright, Saml	2	2	1		
Winstead, Peter	1	3	4		4
Williams, Wm	1	4	4		1
Williamson, Jonas	1	5	4		15
Williams, Nathan	1	1			2
Willson, Edward	1	2	4		
Wilson, Edward	1	3	5		
Wilson, John	2	1	2		2
Wilkins, John	2	1	4		2

NAME OF HEAD OF FAMILY.	Free white males of 16 years and upward, including heads of families.	Free white males under 16 years.	Free white females, including heads of families.	All other free persons.	Slaves.
Whitehead, Arthur	2		1		
Whitehead, Bennet	1				
Williams, James	1	2	5		11
Whitley, Thomas	1		2		
Watkins, Henry	2	1	5		
Whitfield, Thomas	2	2	3		4
Whitfield, Solo	1		8		
Whitfield, Willis	1	1	1		2
Willis, William	1	1	3		
White, Joseph	1	1	3		10
Wister, Elias	1	2	4		
Whitty, Jonas	1	1	1		
Webb, Stephen	1	4	3		
Walker, Green	2		4		
Walker, Joell	2	1	4		
Woodward, David	1		1		1
Williams, James	1	2	2		1
Watkins, James	1	1	2		
Williams, Burwell	3	3	7		2
Winston, William	1	2	3		5
Whitehead, Nathan	2	1	3		
Woodward, Aaron	1	3	2		
Williams, William	1	3	6	3	
Whitfield, Ruben	2	2	4		
Wills, Joshua	1				1
Wills, Absolem	1				
Wister, Samuel	1	1	8		4
Whitten, John	1	1	4		1
Whitfield, Benja	1	1	2		2
Whitehouse, John	1		1		
Whitfield, Wm	1	2	5		
William, Charles	1	3	5		
Walker, William	1	3	3		
Walder, Robert	1				

NAME OF HEAD OF FAMILY.	Free white males of 16 years and upward, including heads of families.	Free white males under 16 years.	Free white females, including heads of families.	All other free persons.	Slaves.
Warren, John	1	2	1		
Wilder, Moses	2		3		
Williams, Edmund	2	2	4		
Willson, John	1	1	3		2
Walker, James	1	1	3		
Walker, Amos	1	3	3		
Wilder, Elenor		3	1		
Wilder, Robert		1	1	3	3
Whitfield, Benj	3	3	3	6	3
White, Joseph	1		3		
Whitehead, Henry	1		1		11
Wills, Elisha	2	1	1		
Wadkins, James	1		1		
Whitehead, Arthur	2		1		
West, Sarah		1	3		
Winstead, Joseph	1	1	6		
Whitfield, Nancy	1		6		
Whitehead, Mattw	1		2		11
Wiggins, James	1		1		
Woodward, James	3	1	4		1
Woodward, David	1		1		
Woodward, Aron	1	3			
Woodward, Nancy			2	2	
Whitfield, Mattw	1		1		
Whitehead, Tho	1	1	1		
Webb, William	1		2		
White, Olive			1		
Wall, Mark	1	3	2		
Whitby, Sion	1		1		
Williams, James	1		1		1
Willis, Stephen	2	2	2		
Young, Stephen	2	4	4		
York, Edward	1	1	2		3

HALIFAX DISTRICT, NORTHAMPTON COUNTY.

NAME OF HEAD OF FAMILY.	Free white males of 16 years and upward, including heads of families.	Free white males under 16 years.	Free white females, including heads of families.	All other free persons.	Slaves.
Edwards, Benjamin	1	2	2		25
Eaton, Thomas	1		2		51
Clanton, Mark	2		2		12
Jones, Capta William	2	5	5		22
Jones, William	1	1	6		8
King, Henry	1	2	3		3
Clemmons, William	1	2	5		10
Eaton, William A	1		1		38
Lashley, Howell	1	2	4		8
Gold, John	1		2		3
Patterson, John	1				5
Brock, Uriah	1	2	3		
Skinner, William	1	1	1		1
Cawthorn, William	1		6		
Rook, John	1	3	2		17
Scott, Saul					1
Scott, Sterling					6
Scott, Stephen					5
Peters, Gilliam	1		2		
Gilliam, Burwell	2	1	6		7
Goldson, John	1	2	3		4
Norwood, George	1	2	6		2
Jones, Lewis	2	1	5		21
Johnston, Benjamin	1	2	2		8
Day, Lewis	1	2	3		2
Dubry, Joshua	2	1	4		
Moody, Benjamin	1		7		11
King, John	2		3		3
Jones, Richard	1		3		13
Day, Thomas	1				
Woodson, Booker	3		1		38
Day, Edmund	1		2		
Ticker, Anthony	2	3	3		13
Brooker, John	1	2			1
Squire, Roger	1	2	3		
Fulks, William	2	7	5		6
Moody, Surrell	3	2	4		4
Rook, Benjamin	1	1	1		5
Crow, Robert	1	1	1		
Harris, Edward				10	
Williamson, Benjamin	2		7		54
Jenkins, Thomas	2	5	7		29
Suite, Samuel	1	4	1		1
Smalley, John	1	1	4		2
Scott, Randol				7	
Tuter, Robert	1	2	5		
Gilliam, Wyatt	1	1	3		
Ingram, William	1		3		
Groves, Ezekial				6	
Rook, Martin	1				2
Parish, Peter	1	2	2		
White, Joshua	1	1	1		
Parish, Obed	1		3		
Brown, Robert				7	
Putney, Richard	4		1		17
Scott, Mason	2				1
Moody, Burwell	1	3	2		1

NAME OF HEAD OF FAMILY.	Free white males of 16 years and upward, including heads of families.	Free white males under 16 years.	Free white females, including heads of families.	All other free persons.	Slaves.
Tucker, Curle	1	3	3		4
Jones, Mary		1	4		
Thrift, Nathaniel	1	1	2		7
Jackson, Benjamin	1	1	2		1
Etter, John	1	1	1		1
Woodard, Simon	1		2		
Rook, Sarah	2		2		2
Carter, Sewil	1	1	1		
Haynes, Eaton	2		2		50
Smith, Benjamin	1	3	3		1
Lockhart, Samuel	1	3	5		26
Lucy, Burwell	1		2		
Wilkins, Sarah		1	3		
Roy, James	1		1		1
Archer, Thomas	5		5		
Love, Elizabeth		3	4		1
Glover, William	1		2		1
Hattaway, John	1		2	1	
Kemp, William	1	2	2		
Wornum, Elizabeth		1	2		1
Love, William	1		1		
Scott, David					8
Harris, Nathan	1	4	2		2
Harris, Nathl	1	1	4		
Harris, Simon	2	3	1		6
Moody, Gilliam	1	3	2		4
Serrett, Thomas	1				
Rosser, Kinchen	1	1	2		3
Hudson, Thomas	1				8
Peebles, Seth	1		1		10
Horton, James	1		3		2
Love, Alexander	1		2		3
Narsworthy, William	2	2	4		
Horton, William	3	2	5		6
McDaniel, Jno	1		1		
Walthorpe, Michael	2	1	2		
Key, Matthew	1	4	1		
Collier, Also	1	2	3		4
Moughan, Peyton	2	1	4		
Melone, Robert	2	2	3		3
Thompson, Charles	2	2	3		1
Weaver, Peter	1	2	6		14
Johnston, Isham	3	4	3		5
Land, Lemon			1	6	
Collier, Jesse	1	4	2		
Melone, Charles	3		2		1
Collier, Joseph	1	2	3		
Glover, Jones	2	3	2		3
Brewer, George	2		1		2
Moughan, Thomas	1		1		
Edwards, Isaac	3	2	4		
Moughan, William	3	6	5		2
Collier, William	1	2	1		
Turner, Capt. Jno					7
Morgan, William				3	
Hudson, Edward	1	2			9
Crews, James	1	4	1		

NAME OF HEAD OF FAMILY.	Free white males of 16 years and upward, including heads of families.	Free white males under 16 years.	Free white females, including heads of families.	All other free persons.	Slaves.
Gary, John	1		2		3
Horton, Jesse	2				
Glover, Benjamin	1	1	2		3
Mitchell, William	1	1	5		
Crittenden, Robert	1		2		20
Barker, Nathan	1		6		1
Ladd, Thomas	1		1		
Norwood, Nathaniel	1	6	4		20
Mitchell, Jesse	1	1	1		16
Wornum, Samuel	3	4	2		3
Hodges, Thomas	2	4	3		
Poythress, Odam				9	
Weaver, Henry, Senr	1	1	5		11
Capell, Edward	2	4	4		8
Collier, Frederick	1		4		
Meacham, Henry, Senr	1	1	3		
Morgan, John				4	
McGregor, John	1	1	4		9
Mitchell, William, junr	1		5		
McGregor, William	1	3	3		2
Harden, John	3	4	2		6
Jean, William	2	1	1		4
Crew, Andrew	1	3	2		
Benford, John	1	3			1
Lee, Drury	2	1	2		1
Poythress, Hardimon				5	
Stafford, Cuthbert	1	1	2		2
Williams, Mark	1	3	2	1	1
Dancy, Francis	2	5	4		37
Rives, John	1	3	6		25
Johnston, Thomas	1				
Morgan, Mark				7	
Justis, Mark	1	1	4		
Brown, Jno				5	
Agers, Frances		2	2		
Sandifer, John	1	2	1		2
Hayle, Jonas	3	1	2		12
Hines, Kinchen	1		3		10
McDougall, James	2				1
Carr, Benjamin	2				2
Carr, William	1	3	2	1	1
Barrett, Thomas	3		1		17
Barrett, Thomas, junr	3	4	3		14
Crump, Josias	2	1	3		32
Ellis, Robert, jr	1	1	3		
Smelley, Rhody		2	2		10
Sills, Gray	2		1		
Prince, John	2		1		
Peebles, Benjamin	1	3	2		7
Peterson, Kinchen	1		5		2
Epps, William	1	2	5		3
Capel, Ann	2	4	3		
Taylor, Christopher	1	3	3		
Vinson, James	1	1	3		9
Tarver, Benjamin	1	2	2		3
Penticost, James	1	1	1		18
Peterson, John	2	3	1		26

HALIFAX DISTRICT, NORTHAMPTON COUNTY—Continued.

NAME OF HEAD OF FAMILY.	Free white males of 16 years and upward, including heads of families.	Free white males under 16 years.	Free white females, including heads of families.	All other free persons.	Slaves.
Stanton, Frederick	1		3		9
Roberson, Wyatt	1	3	4	1	
Roberson, John	1		1		
Mitchell, John	2	1	6		
Armstrong, Adam	1	1	2		
Gee, William	1	1	1		2
Williams, William	1	1	3		
Reams, William	1		1		
Collins, James	1		2		2
Moore, John	1	1	3		5
Stokes, John	2	3	5		
Smith, Arthur	1		4		1
Moore, Anthony	1	1	4		11
Gee, John	1		1		4
Hayle, James	1	3	2		7
Gee, Charles	2		2		9
Thompson, Charles	1	1	2		3
Thompson, William, junr	1	2	4		
Thompson, William	1		1		9
Thompson, William	1				
Gee, Joseph	1				1
Walden, Drury				8	2
Ellis, William	1	1	5		
Ellis, Robert	3	2	1		8
Thompson, Henry	1	1	1		
Dobey, Nathl	1	2	5		5
Peebles, Howell	1		1		4
Wren, Alexander	1	2	2		
Medling, Richard	1				
Pace, William	2		2		11
Thompson, John	1				
Richards, William	2	2	2		9
Tarver, Mary	1	3	1		
Ellis, Drury	1				
Glover, Amey	2		2		
McGregor, Flower	1				2
Williams, Buckner	1	2	3		4
Medling, Michael	1		2		
Williams, Charles	1	3	2		
Metton, John	2		4		19
Jeter, Andrew	1	3	3		9
Ellis, John	1	1	3		
Faison, Henry	1	1	2		1
Short, James	1				5
Floyd, Morris, Senr	1		1		4
Binford, John M	2	3	3		19
Patterson, John	1		3		3
Patterson, Joseph	1	3	5		1
Patterson, William, jr	1	4	5		1
Patterson, Jonathan	2	1	5		5
Patterson, David	1	2	2		
Patterson, William	3		3		
Patterson, Joseph, jr	1		4		
Patterson, Benjamin	1	2	2		1
Patterson, William	1	3	4		
Merrymoon, David	3	3	4		1
Merrymoon, Francis	1	3	2		
Merrymoon, John	1	1	1		
Merrymoon, Peter	2	1	6		
Merrymoon, Robert	1	2	3		
Merrymoon, Kiziah			2		
Reams, Margaret		2	5		
Reams, Willm, junr	1	1	2		
Binford, James	2		3		32
Peebles, Robert	2		4		8
Short, David	1		1		16
Short, John	2		1		23
Robirson, Nathaniel	1		2		2
Step, James	2	2	6		4
Edlow, David	1		2		
Webb, Cordall	1	1	1		1
Amis, William	4	3	4		74
Dupree, Jesse	1	3	2		9
Wilkinson, John	1				
Hicks, Thomas	1	1	2		
Roper, Ann		2	3		
Parker, Thomas	2		2		25
Emery, Balaam	1	2	1		
Coaker, Benjamin	3	4	6	1	
Richards, John	1	4	2		6
Epps, John	1	4	2		
Smith, Leonard	3	1	5		1
Simms, David	1		1		
Floyd, Morris, junr	1	2	2		
Floyd, Buckner	1	3	2		
Thompson, Henry, Senr	2	1	4		
Hathcock, Newmon					4
Brady, John	2	3	3		
Wall, Robert	2	3	4		
Reams, John	1		1		
Moore, Richard	1		1		2
Rhymes, William	1		2		1
Hart, Hardy	2	1	2		8
Dupree, Thomas	1	1	6		13
Jordan, Benjamin	1	3	4	1	13
Jordan, Arthur	1				10
Smith, William	1		1		8
Hailey, Holliday	2	4	4		28
Tooke, John	4	6	2		4
Evans, John	2	2	2		
Smith, Joel	1	2			4
Smith, Lewis	1		2		11
Jordan, George	2		2		17
Finnie, Robert	2	3	1		5
Grigory, Arthur	1				7
Grigory, Charles	3	1	5		11
Jordan, Batt	1		3		10
Bass, Samuel	2		2	1	3
Wall, John	2	1	2		4
Hart, Henry	1	2	3		12
Streater, Edward	1	4	1	1	2
Hollimon, Exum	2		2		11
Boyakin, Burwell	1	2	2		11
Ward, James	2	2	4		8
Pollard, Josiah	1				
Roberts, Jonathan					5
Roberts, William					1
Scott, Isaac					9
Dupree, Cordall	1		4		2
Smith, Littleberry	1		1		6
Tabon, Nathan					3
Anderson, Jeremiah					7
Spivey, Benjamin	2	2	3		1
Jordan, John	1				5
Howell, Henry, Jr	1	1	3		2
Roberts, Elias					4
Lewis, William	1	2	3		1
Howell, John	1				5
Howell, Henry	1	1	2		5
Spence, Joseph	1	2	1		
Munger, Henry	1	1	3		3
Stephens, Henry	3		2		
Boyakin, Sterling	2		1		4
Tabon, Allen					7
Roberts, James, Jr					7
Finnie, John	1	3	5	1	1
Hayley, William	1				
Warwick, Benjamin	1		1	1	
Tabon, Isaac					3
Boyakin, Jesse	1		3		11
Doles, Francis	1		2		1
Grayham, George	1		3		
Peebles, Henry	1	4	3		5
Brown, Benjamin	2	3	6		8
Smith, Nancy			1		3
Chapman, Harrisson	1				2
Bass, Matthew	1		2		
Boyakin, Robert	2	2	5		7
Homes, Henry	1				
Forster, Christopher	2	2	1		3
Sexton, Mark	1	1	3		
Roberts, John				8	2
Jordan, Over	1		2		
Cumbo, Cannon				5	
Stewart, Peter				2	5
Longbottom, Saml	1		1		2
Clarke, Leonard	1	4	2		
Clarke, James	1				
Boyakin, John	2	2	4		16
Wood, Hathorn	1	1	3		
Homes, Zebulon	1	1	3		
Clarke, Sarah	2		4		16
Cook, Giles	3	6	2		
Lewelling, Lyson	1		4		3
Roberts, James				4	2
Kay, John	1	1	1		2
Scott, Hardy				8	
Jordan, Thomas	1	5	2		5
Brantley, Etheldred	1				4
Nicholas, William	2	1	1		
Sauls, Brittain	3	2	2		1
Campbell, James	2	6	3		
Peterson, William	1	1	2		20
Bryan, John M	2		3		34
Goodrich, James	1		3		5
Bryant, Saml	1		1		26
Gumbs, Nathan	2		1		1
Gumbs, Abraham	2	1	4		1
Thompson, John	1				
Pace, Solomon	1		2		8
Pace, William	1				11
Bell, James	3				6
Jones, Frederick	1	2	8		
Parker, Samuel	2	3	3		2
Grant, Richard	2	3	3		
Griffin, Arthur	2	4	3		
Flanner, William	1		1		
Young, Thomas	1	2	3		
Taylor, Dempsey	2	3	7		11
King, Thos (Ovr for Pollock)	1				42
Grant, Absolom	1		1		
Cobb, Henry	1				
Goodwyn, Joseph	1	1	1		
Lewis, John	1	1	1		
Hays, John	3		1		
Winborne, Jesse	1				
Guthridge, Mrs		1	4		
Daughtrey, Elisha	2	4	2		1
Boon, James	2				
Howell, Dempsey	2				13
Bell, Samuel	2	1	2		5
James, Jesse		*		9	
James, Jeremiah				3	
Jones, Servant	1	2	3		3
James, David				3	2
Goodson, Mandew	1	2	2		
Revil, Lazerous	1	1	1		
Winborne, Elias	1		1		
Bridgers, Willis	1				1
Nichols, John	1		1		4
Brazil, George	1	2	3		
Vaughan, John	1	1	1		
Duke, Sherrard	1				
Dales, John	1				
Alphan, James	1	2	4		
Bridgers, John	1	2	3		7
Sherrard, John	1	1	1		3
Griggs, John	1				
Winborne, John	1	2	4		1
Lewis, Eliphas	1	1	4		
Bedingfield, Sarah		2	3	1	1
Summersett, Joseph	1	1			3
Winborne, James	5		4		4
Grant, William	1	2	3		11
Durden, Carr	1		6		
Powell, Jesse	1	1			
Nelson, James	1	2	3		
Walden, John				7	1
Grant, Port	2	3	6		
Sherrard, Patience	3		4		
Branch, Burwell	1		1		6
Hays, Solomon	1	4	3		6
Boon, Thomas	3	1			16
Boon, William	1	3	5		1
Leeke, Higlow	1		2		
Boon, Nicholas	1		2		3
Allen, Harris	1	1	2		
Hays, Elijah	1		1		
Allen, Richard	1	2	1		2
Brewer, William	1	1	3		
Hays, Elias	1	3	5		
Dempsey, Rachel	1	4	5		1
Wilkinson, James	1		1		
Atherton, Elizabeth		1	3		28
Jones, Harwood	1				37
Jones, John	1	1	1		36
Dancy, John	1	2	1		11
Webb, Jno Thos	1	3	2		2
Prichard, Swan	1	3	2		4
Buffelow, Matthew	1	1	4		1
Burke, John	1		1		
Vasser, James	1	3	1		3
Webb, Jesse	3	6	2		
Moore, Anthony, Jr	1	1	2		1
Tarver, Benjamin	1	1	2		3
Spivy, Brittain	3	3	4		
Tarver, Frederick, Jr	1		4		
Warbritton, William	1		4		9
Tarver, Frederick	2	1	3		3
Tarver, Lucy	2	1	3		3
Webb, Hill	1				3
Lewis, James	1	3	1		
Tarver, Samuel	2		4		5
Vasser, Joseph	2		2		9
Burke, William	2		2		6
Dancy, James	1				6
Dancy, Benjamin	1				11
Acols, John	1		1		
Wilkinson, William	1		1		
Smith, Etheldred	1	3			
Dancy, Sarah			2		5
Harrisson, Isham	3	2	5		22
Norton, Willie	1		1		
Thrift, Jenny		1	3		
Jubalough				2	
Wheeler, John	2	2	3		6
Underwood, Jesse	2	1	3		
Garriss, John	1	1	5	1	
Johnston, Silas	1	2	3		
Deloatch, Francis	1	3	3		10
Davis, Thomas	2		4		
Barkley, Rhodes	1	3	4		4
Bartley, Saml	1		2		
Daughtrey, Lawrence	1				8
Sumner, Richard	1	3	5		7
Underwood, Jesse	2				
Davis, John	1	4	4		
Davis, Arthur	1		2		

HALIFAX DISTRICT, NORTHAMPTON COUNTY—Continued.

NAME OF HEAD OF FAMILY.	Free white males of 16 years and upward, including heads of families.	Free white males under 16 years.	Free white females, including heads of families.	All other free persons.	Slaves.
Davis, Edward	1				
Copland, William	1	1	1		
Bridges, William	1	4	2		2
Edwards, John	1		2		1
Bridgers, Joseph	2		2		1
Wade, Elisha	1		2		
Johnston, Joseph	1	1	3		4
Bridges, Benjamin	1		3		1
Sikes, Brittain	1	2	1		2
Parkes, Robert	1	5	6		
Warren, Henry	1	1	2		
Martin, John	3	1	4		4
Robinson, Thomas	2		4		
Powell, Hardy	1	4	7		
Allen, John	2		2		7
Allen, Jesse	2	1	3		
Gay, Elisha	1	1	4		
Jones, Isham	1	1	4		
Newsom, Booth				3	
Johnston, John	1	3	3		
Gay, Solomon	1	3	1		
Garriss, James	1		1		
Gay, Prudence			4		1
Gay, Jonathan	1	3	3		1
Boon, Joseph	1	3	2	1	3
Jones, Sarah		2	4		
Edwards, John	1	5	3		
Taylor, John	1	1	4		
Sikes, Thomas	1	1	5		7
Parkes, Andrew	2		4		
Parkes, James	1	6	4		1
Parkes, William	1	2	1		
Pope, Joel	1	1	2		
Parker, John	2	1	2	1	
Rose, James	1	2	3		1
Parker, Aron	1		2		1
Taylor, Joseph	1	6	4		
Sumner, Isaac	1		1		1
Lassiter, Willie	1				1
Jackson, Daniel	1		2		6
Deloatch, Michail	1	1	8	4	
Bridgers, John	2	1	3	1	1
Underwood, John	1				
Jackson, Edmund	1				
Edwards, Isaac	1	2	2		
Grizzard, Jeremiah	1	2	3		2
Brittle, Jese	1	3	3		7
Murrill, Mark	1	1	4		
Cobb, William	1		5		
Suiter, Henry	1	3	4		4
Doles, Thomas	1		2		1
Morgan, Timothy	1	3	5		1
Westbrook, Thomas	3	1	6		
Morgan, Arnold	1	4	3		1
Maddra, Nathaniel	2	2	1		
Newsom, Moses					14
Cook, John	1	2	2		3
Ingram, John	1	2	2		
Nicholas, Edmund	1		3		
Lawrey, Henry	2	2	5		8
Newsom, Amos			6		
Newsom, Nathl			3		
Hathcock, John			4		
Tann, Drury			4		
Byrd, Arthur			5		
Artice, George			3		
Newsom, James			11		
Allen, Arthur			9		
Banks, Silas			3		
Demory, Daniel			10		
Conner, Benjamin	1		1		
Joyner, Jesse	1	2	3		8
Williams, Thomas	1	2	5		8
Joyner, Giles	1	3	3	1	4
Strickland, William	1	1			
Nicholas, Elemelitch	1		2		
Boon, Jesse	1		2		1
Deberry, Absalom	1	4	5		7
Deberry, Drury	1	3			8
Joyner, Thomas	2		4		15
Roper, James	1	1	2		11
Howell, Benjamin	1	1	2		2
Haynes, Bythal	1	2	1	1	3
Davis, John	1		1		6
Brittle, Sarah		2	1	1	3
Monger, William	3		5		
Monger, Samuel	1	1	3		13
Taylor, Ann	1		3		15
Hart, Eliza		1	3		19
Broom, Hailey	1	4	4	1	6
Williams, Mary		1	2		
Armistead, Anthony	1		4		10
Joyner, Abraham	1		1		
Dawson, Solomon	2				6
Deloach, Solomon	2	2	3		5
Inmon, Judith	2	1	3		6
Sawrey, John	1		1		2
Vaughan, James	2	2	5		16
Faison, William	1				2
Doles, Henry	1	1	2		2
Smith, Solomon	1				5
Turner, Martha	1		1		22
Turner, Edmund					11
Branch, Benjamin	2		3		31
White, Davis	1		3		4
Brittle, Mary	1		4		1
Westbrook, Benjamin	1	1	2		
Coaker, Henry	1		1		6
Penrice, Joseph	1	4	2	1	9
Deberry, Benjamin	1	2	4		13
Jones, John	1	2	2		
Pope, Jonathan	2	4	3		2
Cary, Elphinston	1	1	3		4
Harty, Saml	1	2	2		
Pierce, Jacob	1	2	4		
Drake, Jordan	1	2	2		
Hill, Spencer	2	3	2		
Lane, William	1	1	3		2
Stancil, Nathan	1		4	1	2
Davis, Josiah	1	4	1		1
Stephenson, Abram	2	4	3		4
Stephenson, Arthur	1		2		6
Burn, Owen	1	1	1	1	4
Boon, Benjamin	1	1	5		3
Stancil, John	1	3	3		1
Brittain, Jesse	1	5	4		4
Luten, Giles	2	1	5	1	3
Gay, Elisha	2	1	3		
Wall, Abram	2	3	7		
Deberry, Henry	1	1			36
Daughtrey, James	1	2	2		
Allen, James	1	2	3		1
Pierce, Elisha	3	5	3		
Wood, John	1	2	6		10
Parker, David	1		2		
Tanner, Benjamin	2	1	4		
Powell, Jacob	1	2	5		7
Bennett, William	1	2	3		15
Johnston, Elijah	1	2	3		7
Stephenson, William	1		4		
Bennett, Bowen	1	1	3		4
MacCone, Jesse	1				
Clifton, Cloyed	1	2	5		1
Watkins, John	2	1	3		7
Smith, Joseph	1	2	2	1	
Burn, William	3	1	1		
Daughtrey, Mandew	3		3		1
Boon, Jacob	1	1	1		4
Boon, Jacob, jr	1	2	6		
Faison, Elias	1		1		3
Faison, Harwood	2	2	5		9
Underwood, John	1	4	3		
Lumley, Abraham	1		1		
Burn, Etheldred	1		1		1
Wall, Elizabeth			3		
Griffin, James			3		
Bridgers, William	1	2	3		25
Baum, John	1	3	4		
Pedan, William	2	2	5		
Dawson, Henry	2	1	2		23
Combs, Robert	1		3	1	
Peele, John	3		4	8	
Hilliard, John	2		2		22
Narsworthy, John	1	1	1		5
Lawrence, Robert	1	4	3		17
Lawrence, John	2	5	8		27
Narsworthy, George	2	1	3		5
Narsworthy, Henry	1	1			8
Dickinson, Eliza			1		9
Wood, Joseph	3		1		30
Wood, Henry A	1	3	7		17
Baggett, Josiah	1	1	1		1
Cotton, James, jr	5	1	1		32
Abington, Hardimon	1	2	4		17
Randolf, William	1				6
McDonald, Isaac	1	2	2	3	12
Veal, John	1				23
Cotton, James	1		2		19
Peele, Edmund	1	3	4	3	
Randolph, Giles	3	2	4		14
Knox, John	2	4	4		3
Temples, Solomon	4		1		
Horn, William	1	1	3		
Horn, James	1	1	8		
White, John	3		4		9
Rutland, Thomas	1	2	1		2
Bittle, William					5
Peele, Thomas	1	1	4		
Bittle, Jeremiah	1		4		
Daughtrey, Jesse					
Cartright, William	1	3	4		4
Outland, Jeremiah	1	2	3		
McDonald, Peter	1	4	4		
Rutland, Reddick	1	3			4
Maddra, James	1	4	3		8
Hobday, Robert	2	4	4		5
Marshall, Isaac	1				1
Boddie, Willie	1	1	3		12
Lawrence, Robert, jr	1		2		
Garrott, Danl	1		3		2
Jordan, Benjamin	1	2	3		2
Bryan, Jane			4		
Sharrock, George	2				1
Ricks, Jacob	1		2		
Hiott, Elisha	1	1	2		
Daughtrey, Jesse, jr	1		2		
Bryan, Allen	1	4	1		1
Daughtrey, Henry	1				
Sherrard, Henry	1	2	2		
Daughtrey, Enos	1	1	2	1	2
Lamberson, James	1	3	4		1
Hall, Moses	1	1	1		
Hall, John	1				
Rutland, Blake	1	4	1		
Rutland, Charity			1		4
Outland, Josiah	2	3	4		3
Bass, Jethro				8	3
Bryan, Clarky	1	3	3		
Pinner, Joseph	1				
Lawrence, Elias	1		4		3
Burges, Robert	1	3	4		1
Josey, John	2	1	2		4
Bass, Council				7	2
Dortch, Isaac	1				21
Bryan, Jason	1	1	1		
Lightfoot, William	1	3	4		6
Temples, Daniel	1		3		
Carter, Brittain	2		4		
Temples, Jacob	1	1	4		
Temples, Thomas	1				
Bryan, James		2			1
Harpe, Alse		2	3		2
Rich, John	1	1	3		
Roads, William	1		3		
Chase, John	1	1	4		
Baum, Adam	1		5		
Daughtrey, Eliza	1	2	1		5
Rawley, Jacob	1	1	1		
West, James	1				
Nichols, Bethias		1	3		
Mitchiner, John	1	1	5		
Jordan, Richd	1		2		
Nichols, Lemuel	1	1	2		
Glisten, Thomas	1				
Bruce, Moses	1				
Vinson, Abner	2				
Tutrill, Arthur	1		3		
Darden, Abraham	1				1
Lawrence, Lemuel	2	2	4		19
Powell, Exum	1	1	1		
Ozborne, Sarah			1		2
Pipkin, Stewart	1		1		9
Fawn, John	1	1	1		1
Futrill, Martha			1		6
Futrill, William	1	1	1		1
Powell, Willie	1		1		6
Futrill, Sampson	1	1	1		4
Futrill, Sandras	3	3	4		1
Parker, Saml	2		3		
Maggett, William	1		2		5
Jenkins, Winborne, jr	1		1		8
Futrill, Henry	1	1	2		1
Odam, James	3		2		
Futrill, John	1		2		3
Futrill, Ephraim	1	3	2		7
Jenkins, Winborne	2	2	1	2	7
Nelson, Abraham	2	4	5		
Blanchard, Ephraim	2	2	3		1
Powell, Mattw	2	4	4		10
Johnston, Barnabas	1		5		6
Johnston, Barnabas, jr	1	4	1		
Fuller, Robert				4	
Lassiter, Joseph, jr	1		1		1
Lassiter, Mary	1	1	5		6
Lassiter, Joseph	1		6		6
Vinson, James	2	1	5		3
Roberts, Esther			5		10
Parker, Francis	3	1	2		
Cryer, Sam	2		5		8
Washington, Nicholson	1	6	5		7
Boon, Thomas	2	4	3		
Vinson, James, jr	1	2	2		
Conner, Burwell	1		2		
Parker, Charity			4		
Futrill, John, jr	1	1	4	1	1
Revil, Michael	1		3		
Futrill, David	2		4		4
Futrill, Thomas	2	1	4		6
Benthalt, Joseph	1		2		3
Benthalt, William	1		2		6
Bowers, Thomas	1	1	2		

HALIFAX DISTRICT, NORTHAMPTON COUNTY—Continued.

NAME OF HEAD OF FAMILY.	Free white males of 16 years and upward, including heads of families.	Free white males under 16 years.	Free white females, including heads of families.	All other free persons.	Slaves.
Futrill, Benjamin	1		2		
Long, Brittain	1		2		7
Bagby, Robert	1	6	3		
Futrill, Dempsey, jr	1		4		
Futrill, David, Jr	1	1	1		1
Sherrard, Joel	1	2	15		1
Futrill, Dempsey	1	2	5		7
Smith, Jacob					4
Lassiter, Shadrack	1	2	4		1
Futrill, John	1	4	4		5
Hall, William	1	1	3		10
Oliver, John	1	4	3		
Manly, Littleton				5	
Wood, Wynn	1		2		
Bullock, James	1		1		1
Hollowell, Saml	2		3		
Johnston, Darden	1	2	4		3
Thompson, Hudson	1		3		3
Allen, Jeremiah	1		3		
Hawley, Benjamin				3	
Sherrard, James	1		4		
Manly, William				4	
Lassiter, James	3	1	2		
Fennell, Ann	1		4		4
Shuffield, Ephraim	3	1	1		4
Williams, Arthur	3	1	4	1	1
Mabrey, Francis	3		1		
Rogers, Sarah	1		2		4
Griffin, Robert	1	1	4		
Clifton, Susannah	1		3		1
Mann, William	1	3	1		1
Futrill, Joel	2	1	5	1	1
Mann, Richard	1	2	6		
Lassiter, Jesse	1	1	4		
Futrill, Etheldred	1	5	2		1
Nelson, Jno	1	1	1		
Nelson, Jonas	1		1		
Parker, Richard	1	1	1		
Woodard, Oliver	2	2	1		6
Benns, Mourning	1		2		15
Crocker, Samuel	1		1		
Simons, Sarah			2	2	
Darden, Reddrick	1	2	1		4
Woodard, Thomas	2	3	4	1	
Woodard, Mary			2	1	
Coleson, James	1	2	2		
Smith, Robert	1	1	1		
Futrill, Lawrence	1		1		
Thomson, Etheldred	3	1	3		5
Powell, Elizabeth			1		2
Barker, River	1		2		5
Cook, Christopher	1	1	3		
Rogers, Benjamin	1				
Warren, Joshua	2				1
Strickland, Benjamin	1	3	2		
Tyner, John	4	2	3		12
Fly, Elisha, jr	1	1	2		1
Liles, Jesse	2	1	1		
Boon, John	2	3	5		10
Tyner, Nicholas	1	2	2		9
Long, Joice	2	1	4		11
Sherrod, Mary	1		2		9
Warren, Robert	2		3	1	2
Gray, Hannah		2	4		
Murrill, Benjamin	1		1		5
Fly, John	2	2	4		
Boon, Thomas	1		1		3
Judkins, Joel	1	2			1
Judkins, James	1	2	3		1
Gardner, Nathan	2	1	3	1	2
Rodgers, Joseph	1	2	2		2
Edmunds, Howell	2		1		25
Futrill, Jos	1	1	3		
Figures, Mattw	2				8
Mosson, Richd	1		1		
Figures, Batt	1	3	3		4
Coakley, Benjamin	2	1	4		15
Hotfield, Benja	2		6	3	
Hotfield, John	1	1			
Skinner, James	1				1
Judkins, Carolus	1				3
Riggen, Jonathan	1		2		
Odam, Willie	1	1	1		
Figg, Joseph	1	2	1		
Horn, William	1		2		
Lowerby, Henry	2		2		11
Atkinson, William	1		2		
Jenkins, Dew	1	1	7		
Faircloth, Newsom	1	1	2		
Boon, William	1		3	1	
Franklin, William	1		4		
Powell, Thomas	3				
Stephenson, Abraham	2		4	1	21
Ramsey, Henry	2	1	2	1	12
Edmunds, Nicholas	1				
Cobb, Absalom	2		1		10
Daughtrey, Jeremiah	2		4		13
Stoke, William	1		3		2
Washington, James	3				2
Liles, Benjamin	3	4	6		2
Warren, Eliza	1	3	2		2
McLain, Lachlan	2				1
Clarke, Hannah		2	2		1
Gatts, John	1		2		
Sherrod, Arthur	1		2	1	7
Sherrod, Benjamin	1		2		1
Woodard, Micajah	2	3	2		
Fly, William	1	3	5		
Fly, Elisha	4	2	4		
Barnes, Jane	1				2
Butler, Kader	1	1	2		
Odam, Josiah	1		1		
Hogan, James	1	2	2		
Murrill, Winborne	1	1	2		1
Futral, Stephen	1		1		
Barnes, Thomas	1	1	3		
Coan, Thomas	1		1		
Woodard, Brittain	2		1		
Maddra, William	1	2	2		2
Maddra, Randolph	1	2	5		2
Tyner, William	1		4		
Tallow, Absalom	3	2	3		
Tyner, Mary			4		
Taylor, Sarah	1		3		
Strickland, Mary	1	1	5		
Strickland, John	1				
Strickland, Joseph			2		
Slade, John	2				
Brown, Warren	1		1		
Warren, Benjamin	1		4		
Murrill, Patience			1		
Strickland, Olive			1	1	
Johnston, John, jr	1	1	1		4
Smith, Nathaniel	1				
Woodard, Joseph	2		4		
Johnston, Joseph	1	1	6		4
Strickland, Joseph	2	1	3		
Burn, Jacob	2		1		3
Saunders, Thomas	1		4		
Luter, Hardy	1	4	4		1
Smith, Jesse	2	2	2		
Morgan, Sampson	1	2	5		
Mungis, John	1	1	5		
Newsom, Nelson	1				
Massingale, Abraham	1	1	7		1
Phillips, Mark	1	1	4		
Parker, William	1	2	3		
Meacham, Henry, jun	1		5		2
Norwood, William	3	3	6		17
Millikin, James	1	3	3		
Webb, Joseph	1		4		
Seat, Gerrard	1	2	4		
Newsom, James	1	1	1		
Bradley, James	1				3
Smith, John	1	2	2		4
Young, Gerrard	1		2		
Powell, William	1		2		
Crump, Richd	1		1		8
Webb, Mary		3	2		2
Gee, James T	1	1	2		12
Jones, Robert	2				29
Hart, Warren	2	3	2		4
Snipes, John	2				
Tarver, Billison	1	3	7		
Tarver, James	1	1	6		3
Rowell, William	1		4		5
Vaughan, Fredk	1		4		
Hill, Henry	1	2	3		3
Wheeler, Henry	1	2	1		
Hart, Jno	2	4	2		12
Jones, William	1	3	1		
Barnes, Moses	1	2			
Wilkinson, James	1		1		
Seat, John, jr	1				2
Wheeler, Boon	1	1	2		
Gay, Henry	1	4	2		
Chappell, Mary			3		
Massey, John	1	1	1		1
Tarver, Andrew	2				3
Snipes, Robert	3		3		4
Thompson, Henry	1	2	1		
Carr, Jno	1				
Edwards, Isaac	1	2	2		
Revil, Mattw	1	1	1		
Smith, Jos	1				
Seat, Jno, Senr	3	1	1		
Luter, John	1				
Mac Dowell, James	2	1	3	2	2
Harris, Thomas	4		1		14
Sparks, William	1	1	1		
Coats, John	1	1	3		
Boon, John	1	3	3		
Prichard, Presley	1		3		
Elren, John	1		2		1
Spraberry, Archd	1	2	2		
Griggs, Patience		2	4		
Fulgham, Michael	2	3	4		16
Prichard, Mary	1		3		3
Revil, Humphrey	2	1	1		
Barnes, Zachariah	1	1	2		
Moose, John, jr	1		3		4
Vinson, Henry	1				1
Hill, Herman	1		1		2
Hatton, Francis	1		2		4
King, Sarah			1		4
Williams, Eliza			1		1
Tucker, Drury	1				
Moore, John	1				5
Owen, Thos	1				
Hogwood, Jno	1				8
Hays, Saml	1		1		
Hathcock, Reubin	1	1	1		
Wells, Ann				6	
Jenkins, Reubin	1		2		1
Underwood, John	1				
Sikes, Jethro	1		3		
Mann, Theodorick	2		6	2	8
Dupree, Thos	1		1		
Parker, Mills	2	3	2		
Smith, Joseph	1	1	4		
Fiveash, Jas	2	5	2		
Pope, Jonathan	2	4	3		3
Powell, John	1	2	1		
Hogwood, Hancil	1				
Hogwood, Howell	1				
Owen, David	1				
Rowalton, Elias	1				
King, Benj., Junr	1				
Ellis, Batt	1	2	2		
Collier, Joshua	2	1	2		2
Daniel, James	1		2		
Sturdivant, James	1		2		2
Garner, William	2	2	3		6
Smith, Lawrence	2		2		30
Short, William	1		3		8
Doby, Jarrot				7	
Davis, Etheldred, jr	2	2	3		25
Skinner, Kindred	1		7		
Strickland, Drury	1	1	3		1
Seat, James	1	2	4		3
Davis, Edward, jr	1	2	2		
Webb, Joseph	1	2	3		
Ricks, Dempsey	1	2	2		
Parker, Saml	1		3		
Daughtrey, Lewis	1	3	4		
Dickinson, David	1	1	1		23
Phillips, Mark	1	1	4		
Howell, Ason				6	
Clade, John	1	4	6		9
Gay, Henry	2	4	2		
Duffell, Michael	1				
Stephenson, Silas	1	1	1		
Mann, Richard	1	2	6		
Dupree, Thomas	1		1		
Cornet, Byrd				8	3
Drake, Jordan	1		2		
Smith, Joseph	1	1	4		
Massingale, Abraham	1	1	7		1
Boon, Jacob	1	2	6		
Mann, Nathan	1		3		
Edwards, Martha	2	6	1		3
Duberry, Sol	2	1	2		3
Horn, William	1		6		18
Hart, Thomas	1	1	1		12
Rutland, Wilson	1	1	2		
Cotton, Roderick	1				5
Poysland, Sabestian	1				29
Rutland, Sion	1		1		
Moore, Duke	1				
Ricks, William	1	2			4
Sumner, Sarah	1	1	4		4
Odam, Josiah	2	3	6		
Benn, George	1		1		4
Brown, William	1	1	5		
Fennell, Jno	1		4		4
Futrill, Nathan	1		1		
Mann, Nathan	1		1		
Lawrence, Elisha	1	1	2		
Parker, Lemuel	1		2		3
Parker, Susannah			3		1
Davis, James	1	2	3		2
Rodgers, Joseph	2	3	4		3
Deloatch, Thos	1		1		
Stewart, Rebecca			3		
Odam, Jacob	2	2	3		
Parker, Jos	3		3		
Benthall, Laban	1	1	1		1
Manuel, Christo				8	
Johnston, Joseph	1	1	6		4
Fryer, William	1		1		
Tadlock, Thos	1	1	2		3

HALIFAX DISTRICT, NORTHAMPTON COUNTY—Continued.

NAME OF HEAD OF FAMILY.	Free white males of 16 years and upward, including heads of families.	Free white males under 16 years.	Free white females, including heads of families.	All other free persons.	Slaves.
Sikes, Gethro	1	1	3		3
Boon, Jos	1	3	3		3
Clall, Abram	2	3	7		
Lassiter, Shad	1	3	1		1
Odam, Moses	1		3		8
Rogers, Abram	1	3	5		
Fetts, Archibald	1	1	2	1	
Medling, Mich¹, Jr	1		2		10
Norfleet, Marma	1				6
Bryan, Sarah		2	1		10
Parker, Jeremiah	1		2	1	1
Parker, Amos	1	1	5		
Scott, Stephen	1	2	1		7
Bass, Dempsey	1				
Peete, Mary			3		11
Bryan, Thomas			3		11
Ogborne, Charles	1	1	1		11
Winborne, Bryan	3		4		8
Dupree, John	1	2	7		
Flanner, Wm, Jr	1				
Winborne, Will	2		3		4
Boon, James	1				
Howell, Elisha	1				
Howell, Will	2	1			
Murfree, Margaret			1		
Byrd, Phil				5	
Walden, Michael				5	
Winborne, Will, jr	1				1
Allen, Will	1				
Duke, Sherrard	1				
Volentine, Nathl	2			1	
Sharp, James	1			2	
Griffin, Mattw	1	2	4		7
Parker, Joseph	3		3		10
Winborne, Dempsey	1				
Goodwin, Pitt	1				
Taylor, Sylvia	1		1	1	1
Bittle, Eliza		3	4		5
Luten, Henry	1	2	5		
Parker, James	1	1	1		
Parker, Jacob	3	5	4		
Brewer, Jno	1	2	4		3
Moore, Will	1				
Gibbs, Thos	1	1			1
Ezell, Isaac	1	3	2		
Pace, Hardy	2	2	3		29
Ricks, Betty			2		1
Branch, Mary		3	2		23
Dawson, John					18
McLellen, Phillip	1	2	3		28
Whitaker, Richd	1		3		6
Roe, Salley			4		
Sikes, Charity		1	3		
Atheridge, Anne		3	2		4
Sikes, Milly		1	1		
Godwin, Josiah	1				
Morgan, Humphrey	1	2	6		
Hays, Elijah	1	3			
Stewart, Christo				3	
Mitchell, Joyce				2	
Chace, Jno	1	1	3		
Byrd, Ruth				5	
Cobb, Martha			2		
Cuningham, Charity				2	
Plumbly, Obediah				7	
Mitchell, George	1		2		
Daughtrey, Mrs		3	3		
Branch, Benjamin	1		1	1	1
Byrd, Nathan				8	
Dales, William				10	
Jones, Allen, Esqr	10	5	13		177

HALIFAX DISTRICT, WARREN COUNTY.

NAME OF HEAD OF FAMILY.	Free white males of 16 years and upward, including heads of families.	Free white males under 16 years.	Free white females, including heads of families.	All other free persons.	Slaves.
Alston, James	1	3	4		31
Armistead, William	1	2	2		5
Alexander, John	1				12
Allen, Jones R	1		1		
Allen, George	1	1	4		
Allen, William	1	1	3		1
Archur, William	1		6		
Allen, George, Senr	1		2		
Adams, John	1		2		12
Anders, William	2	4	4		1
Anderson, Daniel	5	4	2		7
Allen, John	1	5	4		7
Arnold, Solomon	2	3	6		1
Allen, Vinson	1		2		4
Allen, Charles	1	3	1		
Allen, George	1	2	2		3
Allen, James	1	1	1	1	
Allen, Charles, Sen	1	4	4		8
Arranton, James	1	2	5		
Alston, Henry	2	2	4		41
Alston, Saml	1				31
Acock, John	2	3	4		
Alston, William	1	8	3		105
Phillip, A. G	2		5		42
Alston, Thomas W	2	2	2		39
Acree, Isaac	3		3		7
Allen, William	1				
Aslen, Lawrence	1	3	3		
Ballard, Jesse	1	1	2		
Balthrop, Augustin	2	1	5		10
Bell, Amey		2	6		
Bell, Mary	3	1	4		
Brown, James	1		2		
Bell, Thomas	1	1	3		
Bell, Charles	3	1	5		1
Baxter, John	1	2	4		
Balthrop, William	1	4	4		
Baxter, James	1	2	4		
Brown, John	1	6	6		8
Baxter, John	1		2		
Bell, John	1	2	1		
Bobbet, Joshua	1	1	1		2
Blanchet, Henry	1		1		
Brown, Jeremiah	2		3		10
Barrow, Daniel	2		4		13
Bartholomew, John	1	3	2		
Bilbro, Berry	1	1	5		10
Blanchard, Saml	1	2	3		
Burford, Phillip	2				21
Burchet, William	1	2	3		6
Burford, Phillip	2	3	4		3
Bush, Jeremiah	1	2	5		6
Biard, Anthony	2	3	5		
Butrel, Thomas	1	1	2		1
Ballard, William	3	3	5		
Beasley, William	1		2		
Bobbet, Stephen	1	5	3		4
Barrow, William	2	2	2		10
Burrow, Thomas	1	1	1		2
Bartholomew, Lewis	1				
Bobbet, John			2		2
Bobbet, Drury	1	1	3		9
Basford, Patty	1	3	2		
Bartholomew, Charles	2	1	3		
Bobbet, Randolph	1	2	1		
Bobbet, John	1	1	1		8
Bennet, Joseph	1	1	4		3
Ballard, William	1		2		5
Brown, James	1	1	2		
Blanch, Hezk	2	2	2		2
Bradley, James	1	2	2		5
Bobbit, Miles	2	1	6		
Bobbit, Lewis	1	4	4		1
Brehon, G. James	3		2		16
Berry, William	1		4		
Boothe, Geo	1	3	4		
Berry, William	4	1	3		1
Burchet, Isaac	1		2		
Boothe, Eppa	1		1		
Boothe, John	1		2		
Bell, John	1	2	3		
Bullock, Len H	1	2	3		51
Buckham, James	2	5	7		
Bowdown, John	1	1	7		9
Bukham, William	2		6		
Bennet, Reuben	1	1	3		
Beckham, Solomon	1	1	2		
Beckham, Jesse	1	2	3		4
Beckham, Stephen	2	4	4		
Ball, Daniel	1	1	2		1
Ball, James	1	3	3		
Beckham, William	1	2	2		
Beckham, Phillip	1	3	9		1
Brown, Archd	1	2	3		
Beckham, Benj	1	1	3		
Ballard, Lewis	1				
Beckham, Simon	1	5	1		1
Ballard, William	3	1	2		2
Bennet, Reuben, Jr	4		2		
Basket, Pleasant	4		4		8
Brogdon, William	2		3		
Bagby, William	2		2		20
Brown, John	1	4	8		9
Burt, William	2	2	3		20
Blanch, Tho	2	3	5		1
Beasley, Pitts	1	2	4		10
Betty, George	3	4	3		
Brewer, Hezekiah	1	1	2		
Bennet, Moses	1	1	2		
Blanchard, Thomas	2	5	2		
Blackburn, Elias	1		2		
Breedlove, John	1	3			7
Bennet, Nancey		1	1		1
Bradley, William				3	3
Bennet, James	1	4	5		
Boswell, Ransom	1		1		10
Bartlet, Saml	1	2	2		1
Bell, Charles	1		1		
Bell, Jesse	4	1	5		1
Clanton, Ede	1	1	1		
Cyaras	1				
Colclough, Rice				2	
Crain, Stephen	1	2	2		4
Capps, Henry	1	2	4		
Capps, John	1	2	6		1
Capps, Caleb	1	3	5		
Capps, Orasha	2	3	4		
Capps, Frances	2	1	6		
Cyress, Fredk	1	2	4		
Capps, John	1		1		
Cocke, Joseph	1	8	1	1	35
Cheek, John	1		3		7
Cheek, William	2		4		18
Cheek, Randolph	1		4		4
Capps, Joshua	3	2	4		
Capps, Frances	1	1	4		
Clark, William	2	6	4		
Cogwill, Isrom	3	2	4		
Cogwill, James	1	2	2		1
Chism, Benjamin	1				
Christmas, William	1		1		4
Clemmons, William	1		1		9
Clark, William	2	1	2		
Clark, John	1	6	4		
Cooper, William	2	2	3		3
Corsey, William	1	2	3		
Cauthron, William	1	3	2		1
Cole, Rhoda	1	2	3		1
Carten, Job	1	2	1		4
Cauthron, John	1	1	4		10
Cauthron, James	1	2	4		3
Clark, Lenn	1	1	1		
Christmas, Tho	2	1	5		23
Clark, Thomas	2		3		1
Capps, Hillery	1	1	2		
Clanton, Dudley	1				8
Clanton, Francis	3	1	2		16
Cheatham, James	1	4	2		8
Coleman, Saml	1	1	2		
Carrol, Thomas	1	4	6		6
Connell, Avery	1		1		
Croctor, Robert	1		3		
Cimp, William	1	1	2		
Colemon, Peter	2	1	2		5
Crutchfield, Saml	2	4	2		
Caller, James	1	1	1		13
Calvany, James	2		1		
Caller, Robert	2		1		36
Clack, John	1				
Clack, Sterling	1	2	3		
Cox, Peter	1	3	8		16
Crysick, Jemina	1		1		1
Christmas, Henry	2				4
Christmas, William	1		1		9
Christian, Giddion	2	1	2		8
Cannon, James	1	3	1		2
Coleman, Edward	1	2	2		1
Colclough, John	2	3	6		12
Clayborn, John	1	3	3		2
Colclough, Rice	1				2
Durham, John	2	1	7		4
Dunn, James	1	1	1		2
Duke, William	1		1		4
Davis, Jonathan	1	6	1		16
Duke, Simon	1	4	4		6
Dye, Martin	1	4	2		1
Duke, William	1	1	3		2
Daniel, Peter	1		2		3
Davis, Joshua	2	4	4		17
Dent, Susanah			2		4
Dent, William	2	2	2		
Dent, Isabell			2		
Davis, John	2	4	3		
Darden, James	1	3	2		8
Dorson, Henry	1	1	2		1
Dowden, John	1	3	2		2
Davis, Thomas	1	6	2		
Duke, Hardy	1	2	1		
Duke, Ransom	1				2
Duke, Repps	1		1		11
Duke, John	1	4	6		
Duke, Isham	1	1	1		
Davis, John	1	4	3		
Duke, Matthew	1				5

HALIFAX DISTRICT, WARREN COUNTY—Continued.

NAME OF HEAD OF FAMILY.	Free white males of 16 years and upward, including heads of families.	Free white males under 16 years.	Free white females, including heads of families.	All other free persons.	Slaves.
Davis, Mattw	1	3	9		10
Duke, William	2	4	2		53
Daniel, Sarah	2		4		16
Duke, Green	3	2	6		45
Daniel, John W	2		3		11
Drury, Charles	2	1	2		
Duncan, Blanch	1	2	3		
Duke, Saml	1		1		
Daniel, John	1	1	3		3
Daniel, Ruben	1	1	4		4
Duke, Burwell	1	4	8		4
Duke, Harrold	1	2	2		
Duke, Brittin	1	4	4		13
Dewilen, James	2		8		8
Davis, Peter	2	3	4		9
Davis, Burwill	1	1	2		1
Davis, Jiles	1	2	3		2
Davis, Saml	1	2	3		8
Elliott, William	1	2	4		
Evans, James				9	
Estes, John	3	3	4		1
Emmerson, Catron	1	1	1		3
Eaton, Thomas	1	1	3		138
Eagerton, Wilmot	1	3	3		3
Ellis, Edwd	2		4		
Ellis, Martha	1	3	4		2
Ellis, Bray	3	3	3		3
Ellis, John	2	5	3		6
Ellis, Richard	1	3	4		1
Ellis, John	1	1	2		
Ellis, William	2	2	5		1
Ellms, James	1	1	1		3
Ellenton, James	2	1	4		3
Ellenton, Dan'l	1	1	4		
Ellenton, John	1	5	6		9
Ellenton, William	2	2	5		1
Ellis, Ephraim	1	3	4		4
Ellis, William	1	1	5		
Evans, Isaac				9	
Finly, John	1	1	2		
Freeman, Arthur	2	1	3		2
Fain, William	1				
Fain, Joel	1				
Fogg, Joseph	1			6	
Freeman, Robert	1		1		22
Featherston, John	1	2	3		
Fool, Henry	2		4		6
Fool, William	1	1	3		3
Fills, Henry	2	1	3		16
Faulion, John	2	1	3		78
Fills, Nathan	2		2		
Fills, Hardy	1				
Fills, Isham	1	2	1		
Fills, Nathan	1	2	3		
Fills, John	1	2	3		
Fowler, Thomas	1		2		11
Fills, Cary	1	1	1		3
Forkner, William	2	1	1		8
Fills, Francis	2	3	6		
Flemming, John	1	2	3		
Flemming, Peter	3	1	5		
Flemming, William	1	2	3		
Flemming, Thos	1	5	1		
Fussell, Aaron	1	1	2		10
Forkner, Hardy	1		2		
Forkner, Moses	1	3	2		
Forkner, John	1	5	4		
Forkner, Emanul	2		2		
Fussell, John	1	1	1		
Fain, Ann		1	3		6
Glover, John	1	1	2		
Gressam, Oliver	1	2	4		5
Gill, John	1		1		
Goodwin, Jane		2	1		
Gardner, Mary		3	3		
Granshaw, William	1		1		
Green, Josiah	2	3	4		7
Gregory, James	1	4	1		
Garrot, Thomas	1	5	7		
Garrot, Matthew	1	3	9		4
Goodfrey, James	1	2	3		
Guthrie, William	1	2	3		5
Garrot, William	2	1	3		
Gray, Benj	1	3	4		
Green, Solomon	1	1	2		12
Green, Edmund	1		1		11
Galespe, Robert	1		1		3
Green, Tho	4	1	2		13
Green, John	1				6
Granshaw, John	2	1	2		1
Garrald, John	1	3	5		
Glover, Henry	3	2	3		
Green, William	2	1	7		61
Gray, William	1	6	4		
Gardner, Tho	1	1	3		6
Gorden, James	1	2	2		7
Groen, Josiah	1	3	4		8

NAME OF HEAD OF FAMILY.	Free white males of 16 years and upward, including heads of families.	Free white males under 16 years.	Free white females, including heads of families.	All other free persons.	Slaves.
Harriss, John				6	
Hazard, John	1	2	2		
Harriss, Billy		3	3		3
Hilton, Dianah			2		
Howard, Thomas	1				
Hamer, Brittin J	1	2	3		4
Hevlin, Benjamin	1	2	3		
Haines, John	1	3	3		
Huddleston, Robt	1	1	4		1
Harton, Howell	1	5	4		1
Harton, John	1	1	4		
Hall, Thomas	1	2	2		
Hastings, James	1				
Harton, Tho	1	2	2		
Hudson, Charles	1				
Huff, Tho	1				10
Hunter, James	1	1	1		6
Hunter, Isaac	2	2	4		33
Hicks, Charles	1	1	3		
Hastings, Jeremiah	3	1	3		
Hawks, Fredk	3	4	3		
Hasting, John	2	2	3		
Hicks, John	1	5	4		1
Hicks, Susanah		1	1		
Hawkins, Wyatt	2	2	3		5
Harriss, Jordan	2	1	7		6
Harriss, Bedford	1	1	1		
Hall, Dudley	1	2	3		5
Harriss, Rachael	1	1	3		5
Harriss, Howard	1	2	2		1
Hudson, John	1	1	3		
Holleman, William	1	4	3		2
Hazlewood, Warwick	2	1	3		1
Harriss, Edwin	1	4	2		
Holleman, Blake	1	1	2		
Harriss, Claborn	1	1	1		
Harriss, Joseph	2		5		
Hawkins, John, Sen	2		1		3
Harriss, Michael	2	1	2		
Harper, Joseph	2	2	5		16
Harriss, Simon	1	1	2		2
Harris, James	1	2	4		
Harriss, James	1	1	3		4
Harriss, Robt	1	1	1		
Harris, Sterling	1	1	5		7
Harriss, James	1	2	5		7
Harris, Fredk	1				2
Harriss, Harbert	1	1	1		1
Hazlewood, Randolph	1	1	2		9
Harriss, Mattw	1		1		9
Harriss, Edmd	1	3	4		
Hamlet, Richard	1	2	5		
Harriss, Elisha	1	1	3		
Harriss, Catron	2	3	3		4
Hogwood, William	1	1	1		1
Harper, William	1	1	2		1
Hudson, Henry	1	3	4		
Harriss, Newel	2	3	5		10
Haynes, Harbert	1		2		138
Harriss, Nelson	1				
Haethcock, John	2	4	2		2
Hilliard, Thomas	1	1	4		4
Hammock, Charles	1		3		
House, James	2	5	3		5
Harrisson, William	1		4		1
Harriss, Ransom	1	3	2		1
House, Dudley	1	2	3		
House, William	3	2	1		16
Hawkins, Philemon, H. T	1	3	3		10
Hawkins, Philemon, Esq	1	6	5		62
Harris, Isham	3	2	4		11
Harriss, Nusom	1	3	2		
Harriss, James	1	2	4		
Hawkins, Phil., Jr	2			1	5
Hawkins, Phil., Sen., Esq	2		1	1	54
Howard, William	1	4	2		
Hawkins, Benj	2				19
Jackson, Jeremiah	1				
Jones, Susanah			6		
Israel, Nancy		2	2		
Jones, Joshua	2	3	7		1
Jones, Richard	1				
Jeffreys, Peyton	1				
Jones, Martha		1	3		
Jones, Robt	1	5	5		1
Jackson, Drury	2	4	2	1	3
Johnston, William E	2				44
Johnson, Terasha	3	2	3		3
Johnson, Michl	1	4	4		
Jenkins, Jesse	1	4	6		11
John, Saint William	1	1	2		5
Johnson, Benj	2	3	4		21
Jackson, Benj	1	3	4		5
Jordan, Marcillus	2	2	7		28

NAME OF HEAD OF FAMILY.	Free white males of 16 years and upward, including heads of families.	Free white males under 16 years.	Free white females, including heads of families.	All other free persons.	Slaves.
Jenkins, Jeremiah	1	4	3		7
Jones, Leonard	1	4	7		
Johnson, Phillip	1	4	5		
Ivey, Peter	1	1	1		1
Johnson, John	1				
Johnson, Hugh	2	1	2		20
Johnson, M. Duke	4	3	5	1	35
Johnson, Joseph	1				
James, Isaac	1	3	4		3
Jones, Peter	1				5
Jones, Sugars	1	2	3		12
Johnson, James	2	3	2		23
Jones, Edward	3	3	6		32
Jones, Robert	1	2	5		16
Judkins, Thomas	4	1	1		2
James, George	1	1	1		
James, Charles	1	1	1		2
Jones, John	2	3	7		2
Johnson, William	2	1	2		39
Kindruk, Isham	1	2	1		4
Kinnemon, Philemon	2	1	3		
Kelly, Thomas	1	3	4		
Kimbell, Nathl	1	4	4		
Kimbell, David	1	3	1		1
King, Geo	1	1	2		3
Key, Luck	2	2	5		
Kimbell, James	1	3	2		6
Kimbell, Ransom	2	2	2		5
Kimbell, Benj., Sen	2	1	2		8
Kicker, John	2		7		
Knight, William	1				
Kerny, James	2		3		31
King, Anthony	1	2	3		
King, Charles	1	2	2		1
King, David	2	2	2		
Kerny, Phillip	2	2	5		88
Kelly, Benj	1	2	3		1
Kimbell, Leonard	1	2	3		1
Kimbell, Spell	1	5	2		
Kimbell, Benj	2	1	2		8
Knowls, Butler	1				
Knowles, Laurance	1	3	3		2
Knowls, William	2	3	4		
Little, Susanah	1	3	3		
Lancaster, John	1	3	2		
Lindsey, Joseph	2		2		3
Lindsey, Laborn	1	2	2		1
Lain, Jesse	1				
Lee, Joseph	2				2
Lashley, Howell	1	1	1		2
Laughter, John	1	2	5		3
Laughter, William	1		2		
Lanier, John	2	1	2		8
Lamkin, Leanah			6		
Lancaster, Lawrce	1				
Lancaster, Joel	1	5	6		
Lancaster, John	1	3	2		
Lancaster, Moses	1	3	3		
Mills, Daniel	1				
Marshall, Hezb	1	1	5		
McClannan, John	1				1
Mabry, John	1	1	5		
Malone, William	1				
Mealer, James	1	2	3		1
Mabry, Mattw	1	5	5		15
Moss, Wilkins	1	3	4		
Merret, Silvanis	1	3	5		
Meadows, Isham	3	7	2		
Moss, Richard	1	3	5		3
Myrick, Richard	1		2		5
Massey, Hezekiah	1	2	2		
Macon, G. Hunt	1	2	3		21
Mayfield, Tho	1	1	5		23
Mills, James	2		1		11
Maddra, William	2	6	1		
Morriss, William	1	2	2		
Morriss, Saml	1	3	5		1
Marshall, Stephen	1		3		2
Marshall, Saml	2	5	7		
Moore, Lewis	1	2	5		
Moody, Tho	2	2	2		15
Marshall, Richd	1	2	5		8
Musten, William	1	5	1		
Musten, Patty		5	1		
Mosely, James	2	1	2		8
Marshall, Isaac	3		2		
Malone, John	3	1	5		
Moore, Mark	1				5
Myrick, Mattw	1				20
Moore, Thomas	1	1	1		1
Mabry, Dilk	1	2	5		5
Meadows, Isham	1		4		
Mabry, Benj	1	2	4		1
Myrick, Moses	2				19
Myrick, William	1	2	2		3
Maddra, Richard	1	2	2		2
Myrick, James	2	1	3		22

HALIFAX DISTRICT, WARREN COUNTY—Continued.

NAME OF HEAD OF FAMILY.	Free white males of 16 years and upward, including heads of families.	Free white males under 16 years.	Free white females, including heads of families.	All other free persons.	Slaves.
Moore, Higdon	1	2	3		
Montford, Henry	1	1	3	2	16
Mabry, Joshua	1		2		11
Mayfield, Abram	1		1		22
Marshall, Dixon	1	1	4		
Marks, William	1	5	3		
Mabry, Repps	1	2	3		5
Mayfield, John	2	5	4		5
Moss, William	1				
Moss, David	3	4	5		21
Mabry, Charles	1	4	2		2
Milam, Drury	1	1	2		
Mosely, John	2				11
May, Enoch	1		2	1	
Milam, Rowland	1	2	2	1	
Mitchell, James	1	1	6	5	12
Mosely, Jesse	2	2	2		12
Miller, Mary			1		11
Myrick, Matthew	2	2	5		2
Malone, Miles	1				
Miller, Thomas	3	4	5		39
Milam, James	1	3	4		1
Malone, John	1				
Murrah, Charles	1	3	4		
Hawkin, John	2	3	5		56
Mayfield, Edwd	1	1	2		3
Marshal, Tibatha	1	1	3		15
McLemore, Atkins	1		3		16
Munday, Edwd	1	1	2		
Morriss, Mary	2	1	4		12
Merret, James	1	3	3		
Moss, Benj	2		2		2
Macon, John	2	3	4		36
Macon, Nathl	1	1	2		20
Mannen, Saml	1	1	3		
Macon, Saml	1	1	3		4
Marshall, Mattw	1				6
Monger, Tabitha	3	3	2		
Muckleroyah, John	1		1		1
Marcus, William	1		1		
Mabry, Gray	1	2	3		15
Nichols, Alexander	1	3	4		
Neal, Ralph	3	2	2		14
Nichols, James	1	1	2		
Nichols, Urbane	1	2	4		4
Nichols, Archd	1		5		1
Nichols, Davis	2	1	2		16
Nichols, Brittin	2	1	3		12
Newman, Tho	1		1		
Newman, Tho., Sen	1		2		1
Newman, Avery	1	2	2		
Neal, Aron	1	2	2		
Neal, Jeremiah	1		1		2
Neal, Moses	1	1	2		
Normon, William	1		2		
Normon, Saml				2	
Narsworthy, Wm N	3	3	4		3
Nichols, George	1				
Nichols, Michl	2		1		7
Newell, John	3		3		9
Nichols, James	2	1	1		13
Narsworthy, James	1	2	2		
Neal, Ralph, Jr	1	2	5		
Normon, Thomas	3	1	3		
Newmon, Daniel	1		1		
Night, Betty			2		
Newell, William	1		1		4
Newell, John	1		2		
Owens, James	1	1	2		39
Owens, John	1	1	1		
Pope, Umphrey	1	1	1		
Partrick, Rubin	1		3		
Patterson, John	1		1		
Parrish, Edwd	1	2	4		
Patterson, James	1	1	2		
Patterson, Geo	2	1	1		
Patterson, Calway	1				
Pryor, William	1	2	3		
Patterson, Lewis	1	3	2		
Price, William W	1	1	5		
Person, Thomas	3		1		58
Pegram, Edwd	1	4	3		
Pickrell, Walker	1		4		
Paschael, Saml	1	2	4		8
Partrick, Lewis	1	3	3		3
Pascheal, Tho	1	6	3		6
Partrick, John	1	2	3		3
Procter, Richd	2	1	4		5
Patterson, Peterson	2		3		3
Powell, Honorius	1	2	1		3
Person, Jesse	2	4	5		9
Powell, Wm	3	1	2		22
Powell, James	1				5
Patterson, Isham	1	2	3		
Perry, Joshua	2		3		20
Perry, William	2	1	7		4
Parrott, Nathl	1	1	4		
Paschael, Dennis	3	5	5		

NAME OF HEAD OF FAMILY.	Free white males of 16 years and upward, including heads of families.	Free white males under 16 years.	Free white females, including heads of families.	All other free persons.	Slaves.
Paschael, James	3	5	5		
Paschael, Elisha	3	5	5		
Paschael, Anderson	1				
Pegram, Danl	2	2	4		1
Pegram, Geo	2	3	5		
Pegram, William	1	4	2		
Pryor, John	1		3		4
Pegram, Giddeon	1		2		
Paine, James	1	2	8		26
Peebles, Thomas	1				1
Peebles, Nathan	2				4
Pardiew, Joseph	1	1	1		
Pardiew, William	1	1	3		2
Pardiew, John	1	5	3		
Proctor, Micajah	1	2	1		
Park, Betty	2	2	7		69
Person, William	1	1	2		22
Patterson, Eliz					3
Patterson, Patty		1	4		
Pardiew, Beverly	1	5	2		
Plummer, Kemp	1				38
Pardiew, Patram	1	4	1		
Petway, John	1	3	4		22
Riggan, William	1	4	2		
Ransome, James	1		2		24
Riggan, Jacob	2	1	5		
Riggan, John	2	3	4		1
Riggan, Joel	1	2	2		
Robbins, William	1				
Richardson, Lawrns	1	1	2		4
Rose, Ann	1	1	3		
Russell, Ann	1	3	1		17
Russell, William	3		4		5
Raibon, George	1	2	2		
Robertson, Mima	1	1	1		5
Robertson, Christo	1		2		16
Robertson, Isham	1	2	4		10
Rowland, William	3	3	4		2
Riggan, William	1	1	2		
Robertson, William	2	1	7		4
Riggan, Francis	2		5		3
Reeves, Joshua	1	2	4		
Reeves, William	1	1	1		3
Reed, William	1		5		
Riggan, Charles	1	2	7		
Redwood, James	1		1		
Riggan, Mary			1		2
Rice, John	1	4	1		
Robertson, Burwell	1	4	4		20
Roirce, William	2				1
Reed, Dempsey				8	
Redford, John	1	2	2		
Reeves, Joel	2	3	6		12
Sledge, James	1	1	4		9
Senseng, John	1	1	4		1
Senseng, Peter	1		2		
Stephens, Joseph	1	3	4		4
Stokes, Saml	1	5	1		1
Sosebery, Benj	1	1	1		5
Stokely, Jehue	1	3	2		1
Stephenson, Saml	1	1	2		2
Scott, John	2		4		9
Stiles, James	1		2		
Sheren, Isham	1	1	2		
Shearin, Lewis	1	1	4		1
Sherin, Sterling	1	2	2		5
Sherin, Fredk	1	2	1		2
Story, William	1	1	3		
Sherin, John	2		3		
Shearin, Amey			3		13
Shell, Stephen	1	4	6		3
Shell, Stephen, Sen	1	2	5		9
Sledge, Joel	1				2
Sledge, Daniel	2		2		19
Sims, Elisha	3	4	4	2	9
Smith, William	2	2	3		17
Sartin, John	1		4		4
Simms, Lennard	1	3	3		36
Simms, William	2	1	8		6
Short, John	1	3	1		
Sartin, Tho	1	2	3		
Shearin, William	1		9		19
Simms, Thomas	1	3	3		1
Sumner, E. Thomas	1				15
Sanders, John	2	4	4		5
Smith, Frank	1	2	4		
Storey, John	1	2	4		
Smelty, John	1	3	1		6
Standback, Patty		3	6		
Sherin, Aaron	1	2	6		
Shearin, William	1	1	1		
Shearin, John	2		6		
Snow, Spencer	2	1	4		4
Shers, Isham	2		1		
Swinny, Tho	1		8		
Saml, Andrew	1	1	4		5
Shearin, Major	1	3	4		

NAME OF HEAD OF FAMILY.	Free white males of 16 years and upward, including heads of families.	Free white males under 16 years.	Free white females, including heads of families.	All other free persons.	Slaves.
Sturdevent, Henry	1	3	5		
Sturdevent, Randh	1	1	5		3
Sallmon, Jonathan	1	2	3		
Shearin, Fredk	1				1
Sutton, Richd	1	1	1		4
Sutton, William	1	2	4		7
Simms, Edwd	1	1	4		2
Shearin, Moses	1	3	4		2
Tucker, John	1	3	1		
Tucker, Claibon	1				
Tucker, Henry	1	2	3		
Tucker, Claiborn	1	1	4		
Tucker, John	1		1		1
Tucker, John, Jun	2		3		9
Twetty, Peter	1	3	4		3
Turner, Edward	1	1	3		
Tucker, Henry	1				
Thornton, Francis	1			3	25
Thornton, Betty		3	4		
Thomas, William	1	3	4		1
Taylor, Howell	1				20
Tanner, John	1	3	1		25
Thompson, Drury	1	3	3		
Turner, John	2				39
Thompson, John	1		1		3
Taylor, Samuel	1	3	2		1
Tucker, Willis	1	2	3		
Tuttle, Jeremiah	1				
Thomas, David	1	2	2		
Tattey, Fredk	1	5	3		3
Towns, David	1	3	8		5
Thomas, Richd	1	3	5		11
Tunns, Richd	2	3	4		1
Thorn, Thomas	1		8		3
Tunstall, Richd	1				
Thorn, Charles	1				4
Thorn, Presley	1	2	3		3
Turner, Tirasha	1	2	2		7
Tycer, Richd	1	3	4		
Turner, Stephen	2	3	3		11
Terry, Benjamin	1	2	6		
Turner, James	1				20
Thompson, James	1	1	3		8
Thompson, William	1	3	3		
Urlls, Obed	1	2	4		
Vaulx, Daniel	1	1	5		17
Vanlandingham, Dorson	2	4	4		1
Vaughan, Vincent	1	1	4		
Virser, Wm	1	3	5		1
Willson, Richard	1		4		
Wood, Bennet	2	1	5		1
Wilson, Thomas	1	1			
White, John	4	3	6		3
White, Admeral	1	2	2		
Wilson, Tho	5	1			
Walker, Partrick	2				1
Williams, Lewis	1	2	5		
Williams, Amey			3		4
Wortham, William	2				3
Williams, Duke	1		3		2
Williams, Wyatt	1	1	9		18
Williams, Benj	1	4	1		1
Weathers, John	1				8
Wynn, John	1	2	6		1
Ward, Gilbert	1	2	1		
Wood, Misell	1				
Wright, Brittin	1		4		
White, Cajabeth	2	1	8		3
Williams, William	3	1	4		3
Waller, Robt	1		3		15
Wilson, Daniel	1	5	4		4
Wilson, William	1		1		5
Wilson, Robert	1		1		
Wilson, Unity		2	4		1
Williams, John	1	3	4		
Walden, Eaton				3	
Williford, Saml	3	3	5		
Williams, Sarah	1		2		6
Webb, George	1		2		
Williams, Henry	2				49
Ward, Elizabeth	1	1	4		15
Williams, Saml	1		2	1	40
Williams, William	1		3		42
Williams, Solo	2				2
Wilden, William	3		2		6
Williamson, Wm	3	2	4		2
Walker, William	1	2	4		8
Ward, Benjamin	1		1		8
Ward, John	2				8
Ward, Ann	1	3	4		8
West, William	1	2	2		
Williams, Simon	3	1	6		26
Williams, Parmenas	2				23
Wilson, Mary					4
Williams, John	2	1	3		6
Williams, Francis	2	2	4		7
Williams, Ashkinar	2		4		8

HALIFAX DISTRICT, WARREN COUNTY—Continued.

NAME OF HEAD OF FAMILY.	Free white males of 16 years and upward, including heads of families.	Free white males under 16 years.	Free white females, including heads of families.	All other free persons.	Slaves.	NAME OF HEAD OF FAMILY.	Free white males of 16 years and upward, including heads of families.	Free white males under 16 years.	Free white females, including heads of families.	All other free persons.	Slaves.	NAME OF HEAD OF FAMILY.	Free white males of 16 years and upward, including heads of families.	Free white males under 16 years.	Free white females, including heads of families.	All other free persons.	Slaves.
Wilson, Henry	1	5	3	....	2	White, James	3	7	3	....	7	Wamble, Josiah	1	1	5	....	
Watkins, Rich^d	2	....	2	....	2	Walker, Samuel	3	3	2	....	5	Wilson, James	2	3	3	....	5
Wortham, John	1	4	3	....	18	Watkins, Henry	1	....	....	....		Williams, Thomas	1	3	2	....	
Weaver, William	1	1	5	....		Watkins, John	1	....	2	....	1	Wood, Elizabeth	....	....	3	....	1
Williams, John	1	1	3	....	2	Worsham, Ludson	2	1	....	....	6	Yarbrough, W^m	2	2	3	....	7

HILLSBOROUGH DISTRICT, CASWELL COUNTY.[1]

CASWELL DISTRICT.

Arnet, Joseph
Allin, Davis Scarlett
Allin, Jesse
Alverson, James
Avery, Isaac
Atkins, William, Jun
Arnett, Joseph
Arnett, Thomas
Arnett, John
Allin, Davis George
Alverson, Archibald
Brockman, Major
Beaver, William
Beaver, Jerrimiah
Bullock, John
Bullock, Samuel
Bevil, Robert
Brackin, Samuel
Baxter, Thomas
Baxter, William
Beaver, Joel
Boggins, William
Bastin, Thomas
Baldwin, Henry
Boggus, Richard, Sen
Boggus, Richard, Jun
Brown, James
Baldwin, John
Black, Sarah
Burton, Jane
Chitton, John
Chitton, James
Coleman, Spillsby
Clarke, Soloman
Cobb, John
Chitton, Jacob
Chitton, Able
Cobb, Jesse
Conaway, Thomas
Coleman, John
Curtice, Henry
Chapman, James
Cooksey, Abednego
Dalton, Isham
Dickerson, Wier
Dixon, Henry
Dixon, Charles
Dixon, Martha
Dixon, Tillman
Durham, Isaac
Dickerson, Nathaniel
Dinnis, John
Durham, John
Dameron, Joseph
Dixon, Wynn
Dixon, Roger
Elmore, William
Embery, William
Embery, Robert
Elmore, Peter
Ethel, Benjamin
Ewell, Jonathan
Foster, John
Ferrill, John
Ferrill, Henry
Ford, Lem
Greenhaugh, Jonathan
Gossage, Daniel
Gossage, Robert
Gatewood, Dudly
Grant, Neeley
Gattis, Thomas
Griffith, Hillard
Gibson, John
Grant, James, Sen
Grant, James, Jun
Graham, John
Gibson, James
Gibson, Mary
Gomer, John
Gomer, William
Graham, William, Sen

CASWELL DISTRICT—con.

Graham, William, Jun
Grant, John
Howard, Henry
Humphreys, George
Hardister, Benjamin
Holloway, Obediah
Huston, Christopher
Ingram, John
Ingram, Charlton
Ingram, James
Johnston, Alexander
James, Thomas
King, Robert
Kannon, John
Kinnon, William
Kinnon, Joel
Lyon, Robert, Sen
Lanman, James
Lyon, Robert, Jun
Long, John
Lyon, William
Lutteral, Jerrimiah
Morgan, William
Martain, Bailey
Meddlebrooks, John
McWilliams, James
Mullins, Thomas
Mills, Edward
McClarney, Henry
McClarney, Paul
Martin, Joseph
Mayo, Robert
Millar, James
McGonegal, Patrick
Middlebrook, John
Miles, Abram
Miles, Thomas
Moss, William
McCollum, John
Nunnald, Alie
Nuhols, John
Norton, William
O'Neal, Thomas
O'Neal, John
O'Neal, Edward
Parr, Capt. William
Parr, John
Perkins, Abram
Perkins, Archebald
Perkins, Jesse
Payne, John
Perkins, John
Perkins, Martin
Pendergrast, David
Perkins, James
Page, William, Jun
Perkins, Jesse
Price, John
Price, William
Paul, Samuel
Paul, James
Page, Nathaniel
Porter, Capt. Alexander
Powel, James
Page, William, Sen
Powel, Margaret
Quine, Benjamin
Quine, William
Rion, Mitchel
Roland, Findel
Ransom, Benjamin
Roberts, Vinsent
Richardson, James
Richardson, Thomas
Rowark, Timothy
Rodgers, Ademiston
Rogon, Timothy
Richardson, Laurence
Smith, Peter (R. H.)
Strader, Conrad
Sammons, Edward
Sammons, John

CASWELL DISTRICT—con.

Swift, Dichard
Swan, Thomas
Strader, Lewis
Shelton, Benjamin
Sommers, James
Strader, Henry
Sawyer, Absalom
Sommers, Capt. John
Stansbery, Samuel
Smith, Thomas
Sommers, George
Smith, Peter
Stubblefield, Wyatt
Tony, Arther
Turner, Berryman
Tinnason, Ignatious
Terry, Olive
Tarply, John
Trigg, William
Tucker, Obediah
Underwood, John
Ware, William, Jun
Ware, Thomas
Whalebone, Thomas
Whitten, William
Whitton, Robert
Watlington, Armstead
Walker, James
Womack, Abram
Waters, Thomas
Ware, John
Ware, William, Sen
Weatherford, William
Waters, Ezekiel
Weatherford, Thomas
Whitton, George
Whitton, Thomas

GLOUCESTER DISTRICT.

Arnold, Richard
Azwell, Pearce
Anthony, Elijah
Allin, Clifton
Atkinson, John
Atkinson, Joseph
Anthony, Jonathan
Bruze, Robert
Bates, John
Burton, Henry
Bryant, James
Brukur, William
Butry, Abram
Bruce, Robert, Sen
Bullis, Samuel
Browning, Edmund
Bruce, John
Burton, James
Bruce, Alexander
Barnwell, William
Browning, George
Barnett, John
Bush, Joseph
Byrd, John
Bruce, Robert, Jun
Browning, Samuel
Barker, Susannah
Browning, Edmun, Jun
Bruze, William
Burford, Daniel
Burch, George
Burch, Nicholas
Cheatham, James
Culberson, James
Carrell, William
Currie, James, Jun
Currie, Hugh
Culberson, Joseph
Childes, Hezakiah
Cole, Thomas
Cook, Augustine
Corder, Lewis

[1]Names taken from county tax lists.

HILLSBOROUGH DISTRICT, CASWELL COUNTY—Continued.

NAME OF HEAD OF FAMILY.	Free white males of 16 years and upward, including heads of families.	Free white males under 16 years.	Free white females, including heads of families.	All other free persons.	Slaves.
GLOUCESTER DISTRICT—continued.					
Currie, Mary					
Cooper, Henry					
Culberson, William					
Cochran, John, Sen					
Crisp, John					
Corder, John					
Colemand, James					
Currie, John					
Dickey, John, Sen					
Dickey, David					
Donaho, William					
Dollarhide, Ezekiel					
Devenport, Samuel					
Davis, Henry, Sen					
Enock, David					
Enock, Benjamin					
Enock, Andrew					
Evanse, Thomas					
Evanse, Samuel					
Evanse, Walter					
Evanse, Lewis					
Everet Samuel					
Evanse, Zachariah					
Ford, Calvan					
Ferrill, John					
Fullar, Henry, Sen					
Florance, Obediah					
Forrest, William					
Greer, Ann					
Gooch, William, Sen					
Gooch, David					
Gooch, William, Jun					
Graves, Thomas					
Graves, Soloman					
Graves, Bazillia					
Gollerher, William					
Graves, Azariah					
Hightower, John					
Hightower, Richard					
Harks, Abram					
Hopper, Harmon					
Hays, James					
Hughes, James					
Hearndon, Larkin					
Haralson, Forbis					
Haralson, Thomas					
Huston, George					
Hughes, William					
Johnston, Richard					
Jackson, Thomas					
Jones, William, Sen					
Jones, Thomas, Jun					
Jones, Thomas, Sen					
Jones, James					
Jones, David					
King, Nathaniel					
Kimbrough, Thomas					
King, Edward					
Kitchen, James					
Kindreck, Thomas					
Kimbrough, John, Sen					
Kimbrough, James					
Kimbrough, William					
Kilgore, Thomas					
Knight, Absolam					
Knight, James					
Kerr, John					
Langly, Thomas					
Langly, John					
Love, Samuel					
Leak, William					
Lea, Gabriel					
Lea, James					
Love, Jane					
Motheral, Samuel					
Moore, Robert					
McGilvery, Daniel					
Melton, Daniel					
Melton, James					
Moore, George					
Martin, Robert					
Melton, John					
McIntosh, Alexander					
Morton, Peyton					
Morton, Masheck					
Melton, Benjamin					
Murphey, Gabriel					
Murphey, John					
Murphey, Gabriel					
Martin, Richard					
Martin, Anthorite					
McKoy, Neill					
Mason, Elijah					
McMinimy, John					
McMinimy, Alexander					
GLOUCESTER DISTRICT—continued.					
McReynolds, Joseph					
McMullin, John					
McMullin, Henry					
Muzzle, William					
McIntosh, Nimrod					
Nowel, James					
Nowel, Edward					
Pleasant, Major					
Pleasant, John					
Pleasant, William					
Phelps, Thomas					
Pendergrast, James					
Payne, John					
Parks, Solomon					
Poe, Jonathon					
Poe, Rhodin					
Paine, John					
Pearce, Moses					
Richmon, James					
Richmond, John					
Ray, James					
Rhone, Thomas					
Richmond, William					
Richmond, Mathew					
Robertson, Mark					
Rosson, Abner					
Reid, James					
Reid, John					
Rowark, Elisha					
Rainey, Isaac					
Sargent, Thomas					
Shy, Samuel					
Shy, John					
Simmons, Thomas					
Smith, William					
Siddle, Job					
Siddle, John					
Slade, William					
Smithey, Elizabeth					
Scott, ——					
Smith, James					
Smith, Moses					
Turner, John					
Turner, Henry, Sen					
Turner, Henry, Jun					
Taylor, Charles					
Thornton, Joel					
Taylor, Joshua					
Turner, James					
Whitloe, Jordon					
Wallis, John					
Wallis, Elias					
Wiley, Thomas					
Wisdom, Larkin					
Whitloe, John					
Warrin, Samuel					
Warrin, William					
Waterfield, John					
Williamson, Henry					
Wisdom, Martha					
Wisdom, Abram					
Wall, Buckner					
Woods, John					
Watkins, William					
Wiley, Alexander					
Washburn, Elizabeth					
Wallis, James					
Wallis, Elizabeth					
Yancey, John					
Yellock, William					
Yancey, Ann					
Yancey, James					
Yates, Thomas					
Zachary, John					
NASH DISTRICT.					
Allin, Charles					
Allin, Drury					
Auston, Stephen					
Archdeacon, James					
Brooks, Arther					
Brooks, Robert					
Brooks, David					
Brooks, John					
Barnett, Andrew					
Boswell, James					
Bright, Robert					
Barnett, David					
Briggs, Isaac					
Bailey, Yancey					
Brown, William					
Bright, Isaac					
Barnett, John					
Burchet, Robert					
NASH DISTRICT—con.					
Buckhanon, Andrew					
Buckhanon, James					
Baird, John					
Bozwell, Benjamin					
Coleman, Richard					
Clayton, Thomas					
Clayton, John, Jun					
Cooper, John					
Denny, Lachareah					
Denny, Clairborne					
Denny, Benjamin					
Day, John					
Donalson, Robert					
Deshazo, Richard					
Dixon, Jacob					
Davey, James					
Davey, Robert					
Davey, William					
Davey, Gabrial, Esq					
Ellis, Nimrod					
Gwin, John					
Gunn, Thomas					
Guttery, Garrott					
Grun, Major					
Gunn, Daniel					
Gill, Robert					
Gunn, Mary					
Gregory, Abraham					
Glenn, Joseph					
Harrilson, Paul, Sen					
Haliberton, John					
Haliberton, Charles					
Haliberton, Thomas					
Harrison, Ellin					
Hix, Daniel					
Huston, James					
Hix, David					
Hollway, John					
Harris, John					
Harrison, Sarah					
Huston, William					
Hudgins, William					
Johnston, Joseph					
Johnston, John					
James, Stephen					
James, Sherwood					
Jones, Stephens					
James, John					
Layton, John					
Layton, James					
Lawson, John					
Lawson, Francis					
Lord, Lord					
McFarland, Margaret					
Moore, Seth					
Mitchel, Charles					
Mitchel, James					
Morris, Zachariah					
Mann, John					
Mann, Elizabeth					
McNeill, Henry					
Neill, John					
Newton, Henry					
Owen, Edward					
Pettypool, William					
Parrish, John					
Pitman, Joseph					
Pryor, J. Henry					
Ragon, Jessie					
Ragon, Nathan					
Ragon, Owen					
Rooks, Buckner					
Rodgers, Byrd					
Stone, Hezekiah					
Sheppard, William					
Street, Moses					
Sanders, Richard					
Self, Abraham					
Turner, John					
Tatom, Joseph					
Thaxton, William					
Vanhook, Isaac					
Vass, Phillip					
Walker, Burkley					
Walker, Jesse					
Walker, Moses					
Wray, James					
Wheeler, Samuel					
Wall, Byrd					
Wood, Isaac					
Winstead, William					
Winstead, Manley					
Wilkerson, John					
Willson, James					
Willson, James					

HILLSBOROUGH DISTRICT, CASWELL COUNTY—Continued.

NAME OF HEAD OF FAMILY.	Free white males of 16 years and upward, including heads of families.	Free white males under 16 years.	Free white females, including heads of families.	All other free persons.	Slaves.
NASH DISTRICT—con.					
Winstead, Samuel					
Winstead, Cotance					
Woody, John					
Yarbrough, Samuel					
Yarbrough, John					
RICHMOND DISTRICT.					
Atkinson, Rodger and John Jones					
Atkinson, Rodger					
Adams, John					
Atkins, Thomas					
Boulton, Charles					
Bennet, Thomas					
Bennet, John					
Baxton, Peter					
Barnett, John					
Belus, Isaac					
Bradley, Judth					
Bradley, James					
Bradley, John					
Boulton, Thomas					
Boman, Royal					
Barnett, John					
Lands, Weston					
Bradley, Thomas					
Burke, James					
Boman, Robert					
Burton, John					
Carney, Joshua					
Carmon, John					
Carriol, George					
Cox, Phillip					
Carter, Jessie					
Comer, Nathaniel					
Carman, Caleb					
Cochran, David					
Camron, John					
Climer, James					
Conaldy, George					
Cooenton, Richard					
Dix, John					
Dyer, Samuel					
Dobbin, Samuel					
Dobbin, Richard					
Dobbin, Hughes					
Dobbin, John					
Draper, William					
Dameron, Joseph					
Donaho, Patrick					
Dameron, Joseph					
Dollarhide, William					
Dollarson, Mary					
Dunaway, Abram					
Dameron, Christerpher					
Dollarson, Andrew					
Dobbin, Catharine					
Donaho, Maj. Thomas					
Delone, Nicholas					
Evanse, Elisha					
Escridge, George					
Escridge, Richard					
Farley, Hesekiah					
Fowler, Israel					
Farley, Stewart					
Farley, George					
Flin, John					
Ferry, John					
Farley, J. James					
Farley, James					
Farley, Sarah					
Glaspy, Joseph					
Grimes, Travis					
Gomer, Benjamin					
Harrison, Thomas					
Harrison, Ninian					
Harwell, William					
Hipworth, John					
Holcomb, Will					
Holcomb, George, Jun.					
Harwell, Peyton					
Harney, William					
Hudson, Joshua					
Hardiwell, John					
Horton, Townsin					
Horto, George					
Harrison, Andrew					
Holt, Claiborne					
Hall, John					
Hubbard, Ralph					
Hinton, Christopher					
Hall, Darias					
Hodge, Hannah					
RICHMOND DISTRICT—continued.					
Hightower, Epiphraditus					
Henderson, Samuel					
Horton, Rawley					
Hariss, Matthew					
Haralson, Hearndon					
Ingram, James					
Ingram, Susannah					
Jane, Philip					
James, Joshua					
Jean, Jessie					
Johnston, John					
Jones, John					
Johnston, Samuel					
Johnston, John					
Jones, William					
Jeffreys, Thomas					
Kersey, John					
Kersey, Drury					
Kersey, John					
Kersey, James					
Kersey, Samuel					
Kiles, James					
Kiles, Elizabeth					
Keeling, William					
Lewis, Charles					
Lewis, John					
Lewis, Robert					
Lea, Alexander					
Lea, James					
Lea, John					
Lea, Capt. John					
Lea, John					
Law, John					
Long, Robert					
Lea, William (L. B.)					
Lea, Major					
Lewis, John (Att.)					
Long, James					
Merrit, Benjamin					
Merrit, Soloman					
Moore, James					
Miles, Jacob					
McGinnis, James					
Moore, James					
Matlock, Nicholas					
Murphy, Archibald					
Morrow, William					
Miles, Jacob					
Maden, Catharine					
Montgomery, James					
Montgomery, Michael					
Moore, William (Parson)					
McDaniel, William					
Merrit, Daniel					
Nowel, Ephraim					
Newberry, Joseph					
Oxford, Jonathan					
Ponds, John					
Pass, Hollaway					
Poteete, William					
Ponds, James					
Phelps, Mary					
Phelps, Reubin					
Pass, Nath., Jun					
Pass, Nathaniel					
Phelps, Thomas					
Parker, William					
Preston, David					
Prowel, William					
Peterson, John					
Peterson, James					
Pettet, John					
Pearson, Jacob					
Parks, Col. Robert					
Quawls, Abner					
Quine, Henry					
Roper, James					
Ralph, Lewis					
Roper, William					
Roberson, James					
Roan, James					
Roberts, Absolam					
Randolph, William					
Ragsdale, William					
Roberts, Thomas					
Robertson, Samuel					
Reed, William					
Ray, Francis					
Reid, John					
Ray, Darling					
Reed, George					
Randolph, James					
Rainey, William					
Rainey, Wesarn Waters					
RICHMOND DISTRICT—continued.					
Ragsdale, John					
Ragsdale, Montgomery					
Ragsdale, William					
Randolph, James, Jun.					
Roberts, Thomas					
Ragsdale, Peter					
Regnolds, Elijah					
Sanders, Richard					
Strother, Peter					
Smith, Robert					
Stephens, Thomas					
Stokes, Man					
Starkey, Jonathan					
Sanders, William					
Sanders, Col. James					
Samuel, Benjamin					
Stansbury, Luke					
Shelton, John					
Stafford, John					
Swan, Joseph					
Swann, Edward					
Samuel, Anne					
Samuel, Anthony					
Stephens, William					
Shelton, David					
Sherman, William					
Samuel, Archebald					
Stephens, Benjamin					
Sanders, Col. Adams					
Stansbury, Aquilla					
Sanders, Obediah					
Stafford, Labon					
Smith, Joseph					
Slade, Thomas					
Stafford, Adams					
Staphens, Charles					
Stephens, William					
Sanders, James					
Shackleford, Yonous					
Shackleford, John					
Samuel, Jeremiah					
Suite, Enos					
Sanders, William					
Tolbert, Joseph					
Thomas, Phillip					
Tarpley, James					
Thomas, David					
Travis, David					
Thomas, Rupert					
Thompson, Cuthburt					
Taylor, Reubin					
Tuning, Thomas					
Vanhook, Loyo					
Wright, Caleb					
Womble, Demsey					
Wilson, Johnston					
Willson, Thomas					
Willson, Robert					
Willson, Maj. William					
Williams, Jacob					
Wade, Edward					
Willson, Capt. James					
Willson, James					
Watson, Richard					
Welch, Samuel					
Watlington, Paul					
Wright, Abram					
Warwick, John					
Wright, Jacob					
Wright, Zachariah					
Williamson, Pulliam					
Yates, John					
Yates, William					
ST. DAVIDS DISTRICT.					
Anglin, William					
Adcock, Edmund					
Anglin, William					
Anderson, John					
Brintle, William					
Brinsfield, Thomas					
Burton, David					
Blackwell, Robert					
Beaver, John					
Barton, James					
Buchannon, John					
Brothers, John					
Brown, Leonard					
Brown, William					
Barker, David					
Barker, John					
Barton, Lewis					
Brown William					
Baldwin, John					

HILLSBOROUGH DISTRICT, CASWELL COUNTY—Continued.

ST. DAVIDS DISTRICT—continued.

NAME OF HEAD OF FAMILY.	Free white males of 16 years and upward, including heads of families.	Free white males under 16 years.	Free white females, including heads of families.	All other free persons.	Slaves.
Ballard, Dudly					
Barton, John					
Barker, George					
Boyd, Joshua					
Brooks, Jonathan					
Barker, Isreal					
Browning, James					
Brooks, Thomas					
Browning, John					
Brown, John					
Brown, Jethro					
Brooks, Richard					
Cash, Howel					
Cantril, Joseph					
Cantril, William					
Cobb, Samuel					
Cobb, Noah					
Carmical, Dunevan					
Carter, William					
Carter, Joseph					
Dickens, Henry					
Dill, Richard					
Dill, John					
Davis, Cornelius					
Duke, Samuel					
Davise, Henry, Jun					
Dickins, James					
Dorris, William					
Dabney, Cornelius					
Estic, Bartlett					
Estic, Richard					
Foste, Thomas					
Fanning, Middleton					
French, Samuel					
Gwin, Daniel					
Graves, Capt. John					
Hirriss, Tyre					
Harriss, Simpson					
Hornbuckle, Thomas					
Hews, John					
Hews, David					
Haggard, Edmund					
Humphreys, Thomas					
Hornbuckle, Solomon					
Hensely, John					
Hensely, William					
Hay, John					
Harrison, James					
Herbin, John					
Herbin, William					
Holderness, William					
Harding, Prestly					
Hart, Col. David					
Hensely, David					
Hensely, Maisfield					
Haggard, Richard					
Isuit, Mathew					
Isuit, Mary					
Johnston, James					
Johnston, Lanslotte					
Jones, John					
Jackson, George					
Jackson, Solomon					
Kean, John					
King, Kuthburt					
Kidd, Benjamin					
Kerr, Alexander					
Kimbrough, Robert					
Larrimore, Thomas					
Leath, Charles					
Leath, Freeman					
Lackey, John					
Lenox, John					
Lay, Martha					
Lay, Peter					
Mitchel, William					
Mallery, John					
Mahone, William					
McIntosh, William					
Mallary, John, Jun					
Martin, Joseph					
Mitchel, Robert					
Moore, Samuel					
McCauley, John					
Owen, William					
Ove, James					
Oldham, Moses					
Powel, Abner					
Pike, Lewis					
Payne, William					
Payne, Greenwood					
Payner, David					
Penix, John					
Pane, Joshua					
Pike, Lewis, Sen					
Pool, Mecajah					

ST. DAVIDS DISTRICT—continued.

NAME OF HEAD OF FAMILY.	Free white males of 16 years and upward, including heads of families.	Free white males under 16 years.	Free white females, including heads of families.	All other free persons.	Slaves.
Poston, Jerre					
Rice, Thomas					
Rice, William					
Rice, Nathan					
Rodgers, Armstead					
Rice, Hesekiah					
Rice, Ipsan					
Roberts, Humphrey					
Rice, John					
Rice, John					
Rice, Nathan					
Rice, H. William					
Rice, John					
Rudd, John					
Simpson, Richard					
Simpson, Mary					
Starkey, John					
Swift, Anthony					
Shannan, John					
Slade, Thomas					
Scott, Joseph					
Swift, Thomas					
Swift, William					
Staey, Malon					
Sawyear, John					
Scott, James					
Swift, John					
Sims, George					
Spence, John					
Sykes, Jonas					
Smith, Francis					
Smith, Richard					
Taylor, James					
Tate, Ann					
Williamson, Nathan					
Williams, Daniel					
Williams, Elizabeth					
Walker, William					
Wilkerson, William					
Williams, Col. John					
Watlington, John					
Williams, Jerremiah					
Windsor, Jon					
Wright, Pleasant					
Willis, Henry					
Williamson, James					
Walker, James					
Williams, John					
Walker, James					
Wright, William					
Williamson, Benj.					

ST. JAMES DISTRICT.

NAME OF HEAD OF FAMILY.	Free white males of 16 years and upward, including heads of families.	Free white males under 16 years.	Free white females, including heads of families.	All other free persons.	Slaves.
Allin, David					
Ashley, Graves					
Anderson, George					
Anderson, James					
Burton, Daniel					
Broadaway, John					
Blalock, Millington					
Blalock, William					
Bumpass, John					
Blalock, Will, Jun					
Bividin, John					
Blalock, Thomas					
Bowls, John					
Burch, Benjamin					
Bumpass, John, Jun					
Clixby, John					
Cate, Robert					
Crews, Hardy					
Coleman, Daniel					
Cochran, James					
Cozzart, Peter					
Cate, Robert					
Caughran, John					
Clayton, Daniel					
Clayton, Daniel, Jun					
Clarke, Nathaniel					
Clark, Drury					
Commins, John					
Cash, Moses					
Clayton, Colaman					
Cozzart, John					
Dickins, Robert, Esq					
Daniel, James					
Davis, Robert					
Day, Isaac					
Day, Henry					
Day, Francis					
Daniel, Mathew					
Eddy, Thomas					
Eastwood, Alexander					
Farmer, Casandra					
Farmer, Daniel					

ST. JAMES DISTRICT—continued.

NAME OF HEAD OF FAMILY.	Free white males of 16 years and upward, including heads of families.	Free white males under 16 years.	Free white females, including heads of families.	All other free persons.	Slaves.
Farmer, William					
Glenn, Beverly					
Glenn, Susannah					
Gray, Alexander					
Hicks, John					
Hicks, Robert					
Hester, Robert					
Hicks, Daniel					
Hubbard, Joseph					
Harst, John					
Hawkins, Ephram					
Harrison, Benjamin					
Jones, Benjamin					
Johnston, Joshua					
Jay, James					
Jeffrey, Paul					
Jones, Richard					
Kennady, James					
Lansford, Joseph					
Ledbetter, Daniel					
Ledbetter, Ed					
Ledbetter, Joel					
Medearest, Abram					
Miller, John					
Moore, Ann					
Mason, Thomas					
Meadows, Daniel					
Morrow, William					
Moore, Charles					
Moore, Ephram					
Neely, Samiel					
Nichols, Willis					
Oakley, John					
Oakley, Walter					
Prat, Agness					
Paine, William					
Parks, Joseph					
Parker, Powel					
Parker, Richard					
Parker, David					
Paine, Robert, Esq					
Robert, George					
Rodgers, Samuel					
Rimmer, James					
Roberts, John					
Roberts, Arther					
Roberts, Daniel					
Roberts, Duke					
Ren, Benjamin					
Satterfield, Jesse					
Swaing, John, Sen					
Satterfield, Bedwell					
Satterfield, John					
Swaing, James					
Sneed, Samuel					
Swaing, Levi					
Satterfield, Isaac					
Sneed, John					
Satterfield, John, Jun					
Scroggin, John					
Scroggin, Francis					
Taylor, Joseph					
Taylor, John					
Tapp, William					
Terry, Thomas					
Wells, James					
Williams, Bennett					
Waller, John					
Yarborough, William					

ST. LAWRENCE DISTRICT.

NAME OF HEAD OF FAMILY.	Free white males of 16 years and upward, including heads of families.	Free white males under 16 years.	Free white females, including heads of families.	All other free persons.	Slaves.
Atkinson, John					
Atkinson, John, Esq					
Allin, William					
Bostwick, Charles					
Blueford, ——					
Bradsher, John					
Black, Thomas					
Browning, Joshua					
Barnett, John					
Black, George					
Black, John					
Barnett, Thomas					
Bradsher, Moses					
Barnett, Thomas, Jun					
Barnett, Hugh, Sen					
Barnett, Joseph					
Barnett, Hugh					
Bostwick, Chestley					
Barnett, Thomas, Sen					
Barnett, Hugh, Jun					
Ball, Jacob					
Barnett, William					
Bell, James					

HILLSBOROUGH DISTRICT, CASWELL COUNTY—Continued.

NAME OF HEAD OF FAMILY.	Free white males of 16 years and upward, including heads of families.	Free white males under 16 years.	Free white females, including heads of families.	All other free persons.	Slaves.	NAME OF HEAD OF FAMILY.	Free white males of 16 years and upward, including heads of families.	Free white males under 16 years.	Free white females, including heads of families.	All other free persons.	Slaves.	NAME OF HEAD OF FAMILY.	Free white males of 16 years and upward, including heads of families.	Free white males under 16 years.	Free white females, including heads of families.	All other free persons.	Slaves.
ST. LAWRENCE DISTRICT—continued.						ST. LAWRENCE DISTRICT—continued.						ST. LUKE'S DISTRICT.					
Beedles, Joseph						Lewis, Elizabeth						Allin, Drury					
Barnett, Thomas, Esq.						McKnabb, Robert						Aldridge, Joseph					
Clay, Edward						Mitchell, Robert						Aldridge, Peter					
Carnel, Richard						McNeill, Ann						Burch, Phillip					
Carnel, Mary						Mitchel, David						Brown, John					
Clift, John						Melene, Halloy						Burch, Henry					
Chamber, James						Mitchel, John						Burch, Richard, Jun					
Carver, Josias						Mason, Patrick						Burch, Pemberton					
Chambers, John						Miles, Thomas						Burton, Benjamin					
Carver, Thomas						McNeill, Benjamin						Brown, William					
Chambers, William, Sen						McFarland, Daniel						Bryan, William					
Chambers, William						Moore, Robert						Badget, Thomas					
Campbell, John						McGhee, Muntford						Burch, Richard, Sen					
Carver, William						Moore, Joseph						Bryant, James					
Carlton, John						Mitchel, Arther						Brown, Abram					
Dickson, Josias						McFarland, John						Brooks, Aaron					
Dickson, Michael, Jun						McNeill, John						Byrd, Bayton					
Debose, Frederick						Morgan, William						Bryan, William, Sen					
Duncan, Mary						Milam, Lewis						Burton, Richard					
Darbey, George						McKain, John						Cock, William					
Darbey, Daniel						Morrison, Alexander						Cate, Thomas					
Dueast, Isaiah						Mitchell, Joshua						Cooper, Martin					
Duest, Hezekiah						Newton, Reubin						Cannady, John					
Duty, George						Neeley, Thomas						Cooper, John					
Doil, Edward						Newton, John						Cate, Joshua					
Debse, Benjamin						Newton, Benjamin						Christenbury, John					
Douglass, John, Esq						Owen, Richardson						Carney, Joseph					
Douglass, Thomas						Olliver, Douglass						Douglass, Benjamin					
Denwiddie, John						Olliver, Stephen						Davis, Aquilla					
Ellis, George						Pitman, Mathew						Durham, Daniel					
Fullar, Catherine						Parrot, Reubin						Durham, Isaac					
Ferguson, Andrew						Perryman, John						Duly, William					
Farrar, William						Phelps, William						Ellison, Hezikiah					
Farrar, Henry						Parker, John						Eubank, George					
Foley, Mason						Patterson, James						Eubank, John, Sen					
Fulcher, William, Sen						Price, Acque						Eubank, John					
Fulcher, Henry						Paschel, William						Farrar, Joseph					
Fulcher, William						Paschel, Thomas						Farmer, Joseph					
Fleps, John						Pinkerton, Ann						Farrar, John					
Farley, John						Pendergrass, Richard						Fisher, Risdorn					
Fullar, Peter						Roberson, James						Foshee, Charles					
Fullar, George						Reynolds, Hamelton						Farrer, Peter					
Fullar, John						Roberson, Thomas						Farmer, Thomas, Sen					
Fullar, James						Rodges, John						Farguhar, James					
Fullar, William						Rosch, John						Fullar, Stephen					
Fullar, William, Sen						Roberson, John						Farrar, John					
Gregory, James						Roberson, Joseph						Grayham, Alexander					
Gold, Joseph						Stuart, Stephen						Gately, Thomas					
Gold, Daniel						Scroggin, Nathan						Green, Lewis					
Golph, Thomas						Simmons, James						Gately, William					
Going, Gutridge						Sargent, William						Graves, Thomas					
Gregory, George						South, Benjamin						Green, Burwell					
Glaze, Samuel						Standfield, Harrison						Green, William					
Hix, Reubin						Standfield, John						Graves, Henry					
Hughes, Ann						Sargeant, Daniel						Gately, Joseph					
Hughes, James						Sargeant, Stephen						Gains, Edward					
Hamlet, Moore Thomas						Stokes, Sylvanus						Hall, John					
Harrys, James						Stuart, Agness						Hargiss, Abrim					
Hunt, William						Stewart, James						Hargiss, Richard					
Hemphill, Hugh						Southward, Robert						Hall, Phillip					
Howard, Henry						Southard, William						Hargiss, William					
Hopkins, William						Standfield, William						Hargiss, Thomas					
Horley, Joseph						Stuart, William						Hargiss, Shadrach					
Hamlett, James						Seymore, Robert						Holman, Chas					
Henley, Edmund						Tunks, William						Holman, Richard					
Haralson, Sarah						Tunks, Rachael						Hunt, Samuel					
Hall, George						Twiner, Abram						James, Francis					
Hamlin, William						Twiner, Joseph						Johnston, James					
Henley, D. James						Trotter, William						Jacob, Benjamin					
Hamlett, William, Jun						Trickey, Giles						Jones, Drury					
Hatcher, Benjamin						Tunks, Aisley						Jones, Goodrich					
Irvine, William						Underascon, Stephen						Jacob, Richard					
Justice, John						Vanhook, Thomas						Jones, Clayton					
Johnston, Theodoruk						Vanhook, Robert						Joblin, Benjamin					
Jamison, William						Virmillion, Wilson						Lockheart, William					
Johnston, Benjamin						Vanhook, Lawrence						Lyon, Richard					
Johnston, John						Williamson, James						Lewis, Joseph					
Johnston, George						Warrin, John						Lyon, Peter					
Lea, Zachariah						White, Thomas						Lowther, William					
Lea, James						Whitehead, Samuel						Lyon, Henry					
Lea, Abner						Warrin, Hedgman						Lyon, Jane					
Lea, George						Warrin, John, Jun						Messer, James					
Lea, John						Walters, Abraham						Malone, David					
Lea, Barnett						Warrin, Goodloe						McKissock, Thomas					
Lea, William						Warrin, Jeremiah						Moore, Abram					
Long, William						Williams, Tobias						McKissock, William					
Lewis, Edmund						Warrin, Robert						Malone, John					
Long, Reubin						Wood, John						Malone, Thomas					
Lea, Richard						Walters, Paul						McMurry, John					
Lea, William						Warrin, Samuel						Malone, George					
Long, Ambrose						Wood, Stephen						Minzy, Richard					
Long, John						Walters, Henry						McMurry, James					
Lea, Carter						Walters, John						Malone, Nathaniel					
Long, James						Warrin, William						Moore, Dempsey					
Long, James, Sen						Warrin, Hackley						Mann, David					
Long, Benjamin						Williams, Thomas						Mitchell, David, Sen					

HILLSBOROUGH DISTRICT, CASWELL COUNTY—Continued.

ST. LUKE'S DISTRICT—continued.

NAME OF HEAD OF FAMILY.	Free white males of 16 years and upward, including heads of families.	Free white males under 16 years.	Free white females, including heads of families.	All other free persons.	Slaves.
McKee, William					
Mitchel, David, Esq					
McMurry, Samuel					
Pope, Joel					
Pogue, John					
Pryar, Charles					
Price, John					
Pogue, Joseph					
Ragsdale, Thomas					
Roberts, Shadrach					
Ragsdale, Benjamin					
Rankin, James					
Robertson, Charles					
Robertson, David					
Rose, Alexander					
Surrall, John					
Sykes, John					
Step, Elizabeth					
Sherman, John					
Step, Joshua					
Surratt, Joseph					
Simms, Buckner					
Tarpley, Hosea					
Trim, Henderson					
Trim, Charles					
Vanhook, Jacob					
Vanhook, Lucy					
Wright, Jarrot					
Willingham, John					
Woods, Samuel					
Wheely, John					
Wilkerson, Thomas					
Woods, Joseph					
Williamson, James					
Womack, John					
Watkins, Phillip					
Wilson, John					
Willson, Joseph					
Watson, Jesse					
Willson, Henry					
Waite, William					

HILLSBOROUGH DISTRICT, CHATHAM COUNTY.

NAME OF HEAD OF FAMILY.	Free white males of 16 years and upward, including heads of families.	Free white males under 16 years.	Free white females, including heads of families.	All other free persons.	Slaves.
Bland, James	1	5	2		
Bland, John	1		2		
Brinkly, Thos	1	5	1		
Brewer, Nathl	2	6			
Burchard, Jeddediah	2	1	5		
Brumbe, James	2		3		
Burns, William	1	2	2		2
Burchard, Josiah	1		1		
Clark, Wm	1	1	5		17
Copeland, James	2	3	6		
Copeland, Daniel	1	2	4		
Cumbo, Jacob	1	2	1		
Campbell, John	1	2	3		
Clark, Benja	1	2	2		
Chamberlin, Elijah	1				4
Crain, Wm	1	2	2		6
Clark, Phebee		3	2		5
Copeland, James, Jr	1				
Dillard, George	2		6		
Drummer, Daniel	1				
Davis, Ellithan	3	1	4		3
Dismicks, George	2	3	3		6
Dilliard, Willis	1		2		
Ferrell, Francis	1		4		1
Fasker, Joseph, Senr	1	1	3		4
Fasker, Wm	1	4	4		
Fasker, Joseph, Jur	3		3		
Fasker, Elijah	1	1	1		3
Fasker, John, Jur	2	5	6		
Fasker, John, Ser	1				
Fike, John	2	3	2		
Fike, Elijah	1	2	3		
Fasker, Wm	1	1	2		
Griffith, Roger	2	3	3		4
Gee, George	1		1		
George, Harris	1	4	3		
Gunter, Isham	2	2	4		
George, James	4	3	2	1	3
Guthrie, Saml	2	3	4	1	5
Harmon, John	1	1	1		
Hackney, Wm	1	2	6		
Henderson, Wm	1	1	2		
Howard, Wm	3		3		9
Harmon, Zachariah	3	3	10		11
Harrington, Phillimon	1	3	4		2
Hatley, John	1	2	3		
Howard, James	2		3		6
Herndon, Stephen	1	2	4		
Hamblet, Wm	1	2	7		3
Hoget, Willis	1	2	3		
Henderson, Lewis	1		1		
Harrington, Thos	1	2	4		1
Kelley, Giles	1	3			
Lucus, George	2	2	3		68
Lucus, Wm	1		4		3
Mossey, James	3	3	5		4
Miliken, Quaintain	1				
Manley, Basil	1	1	1		6
Mckeever, James	1		1		
Mash, Robert	2	1	5		2
Mash, Wm	1	3	4		2
Morgan, Zachariah	1	1	2		
Morgan, Edmon	1	2	4		
Morgan, Joseph	1	2	3		1
Morgan, Charles	2	3	1		
Millihen, George	1	1	3		
Morphus, John	1		4		
Moyer, Peter	1				
Malton, John	1	1	2		3
Mott, Joseph	1	1	2		
Mironey, Wm	1				
Mironey, Pilliph	2	2	1		1
Paterson, James	3	1	3		3
Poe, Simon	1	4	2		
Pettey, James	1	2	1		2
Poe, Reuben	1	1	2		
Pettey, John	2	4	5		2
Pettey, Rueben	3	3	4		2
Pettey, Isaac	1	1	1		1
Paterson, Thos	1		1		5
Poe, Wm	1	2	4		
Pettey, Ambrews	4	3	5		2
Pettey, Wm	2	1	2		11
Rigbey, James	2	1	2		2
Robertson, Thos	2		1		5
Riddle, Ricd	1	2	3		
Riddle, Wm	1	2	3		3
Straughn, Stephen	1	3	3		
Sanders, George	1	1	1		
Stewart, James	2	2	3		
Straughn, Crispen	3		4		
Siurlock, Sarah	2		2	4	14
Sanders, Wm	1	3	2		
Stewart, Thos	1	1	1		
Stewart, Spencer	1		1		6
Sanders, John	1	1	3		
Straughn, Rud	1	2	1		
Steedmon, Nathan	1		1		10
Snorlock, James	1		1		6
Stewart, Elizabeth			1		3
Thomas, Even	4		6		
Thomson, Robert	1	3	4		3
West, Philliph	1				
West, Rud	1				
West, Thos	2	1	3		2
Ward, Henry	1	2	3		
Williams, John	2	1	5		6
Brown, John	1	3	3		
Stewart, Joseph	2		4		
Peake, Benja	2	1	1		
Poe, Stephen	1		5		
Johnson, Robert	2	3	6		
Gunter, Wm	1	1	1		
Gunter, Thos	1	2	5		
Minter, Margret	2	2	6		
Crofford, John	1	1	2		
Straughn, Hosea	1		3		
Riley, John	1		3		
Riston, Ricd	3				
Brown, John	1	3	3		
Henson, Charles	4	2	2		
Green, Hubbard	1	3	1		
—, Ambrous	2	5	1		1
McBune, Daniel	1	2	2		
Poe, Simon, Ser	2				3
Gorden, John	1	1	2		4
Bradsberrey	1				
Curtis, Charles	1				2
Higdon, Charles	1	1	1		
Higdon, Daniel	1		3		
Page, Nathl	3	2	4		
Stewart, James, Jr	1	1	4		1
Wilson, Joshua	1				
Burge, Robertson	1				
Abet, Wm	1	3	3		
Brown, Archebell	2	1	3		4
Bohannon, Robert	2	3	5		8
Brantley, John	3	3	3		5
Bushop, Benja	2		1		
Brewer, Thos	3		3		
Branch, Edmon	1	1	2		8
Brantley, Joseph	3	2	2		12
Collier, Henry	1	2	3		
Clark, Jesse	2	1	3		
Cark, Ricd	2		1		1
Drake, Ricd	1	1	1		
Drake, Wm	2	2	4		6
Evins, Thos	1	3	3		10
Goss, Joshua	1		1		
Gresham, James	2	2	4		
Gross, Francis	1	2	4		
Holding, Joshua	1		2		
Hesther, Robert	1		1		
Harden, Nicholas	2	1	1		
Hesther, Beveley	1	1	1		
Holden, Elizabeth	1	1	4		
Johnson, Wm	2		1		
Johnson, Joseph	1	3	5		1
Johnson, Wm	1	4	3		
Jones, S. I	1	3	1		3
Julus, Coley	1	1	2		
Lasseter, Wm	2	2	2		2
Lasseter, Abner	1	1	5		
Leopard, Wm	1	2	4		
Minter, Morgan	2	3	6		7
Matthews, Isaac	2	3	5		7
Minter, John	2	1	3		10
Minter, Joseph	3	1	2		6
Parham, Francis	1		1		1
Partridge, Thos	2	4	3		7
Parish, David	1	4	8		
Pettishall, Wm	2	3	1		1
Pritchit, Edward	1		3		
Parham, Drury	2	1	2		5
Parham, Wm	1	1	3		1
Pool, James	2	3	7		
Riddle, John	1	2	4		3
Ramsey, Ambrous & John Ramsey	4		7		11
Stephens, Ricd	2	5	5		
Stephens, James	1	2	6		
Simons, Solomon	2	2	2		1
Stokes, Thos	1	3	1		27
Tomlinson, John	2		1		4
Tomlinson, Moses	1		1		
Taylor, Simon	2		5		
Tabour, Thos			1	3	
Wicker, Thos	2	5	3		1
Wicker, James	1		2		1
Wicker, Plesant	1	2	2		
Yarbrough, Elisha	1		2		4
Yarbrough, Nathan	1		2		
Yarbrough, Joseph	2	2	2		
Minter, Margret	2		5		
Poe, David	1	2	4		
Parham, John	1	1	2		
Harris, Wm	1	1	2		3
Wormack, John	3	3	5		8
Matlock, David	2	3	5		
Parker, Elizabeth		1	5		
Lassiter, James	1		2		1
Brooks, John	1	2	3		
Motley, Robert	2	1	4		1
Simpson, Sarah		3	4		
Minter, Wm	1	1	3		10
Chatman, John	2	2	7		5
Harden, Philliph	3	2	3		7
Gunter, Isham	3		4		
Ranes, James	1	2	1		
Drake, Ricd	1	1	2		15
Anderson, James	1		2		15
Andrews, John	1	2	4		
Adkinson, Benja	2	2	4		
Andrews, Ellizair	3	2	7		
Burns, Thos	1	1	9		
Bryant, Thos	1		1		6
Brown, John	1	2	6		
Barter, Wm	2	3	3		
Bryant, John	1		1		
Burns, James	1		3		
Barns, Seth	1		1		
Beal, Thos	1	2	3		1
Burns, John	1		3		1
Burns, John	2		5		
Barns, Jonathan	2		5		1
Barter, Moses	2	1	2		
Brown, Daniel	1	5	4		1

HILLSBOROUGH DISTRICT, CHATHAM COUNTY—Continued.

NAME OF HEAD OF FAMILY.	Free white males of 16 years and upward, including heads of families.	Free white males under 16 years.	Free white females, including heads of families.	All other free persons.	Slaves.
Bryant, Aron	3	2	3		
Beal, Benjn	1	1	3		
Barber, Rud	2	3	5		
Bryan, Obediah	2	3	5		
Bryan, Aquilla	1	3	2		
Beck, James	1	1	1		
Caps, Wm, Jur	1	4	2		
Clark, Robert	1		2		
Caps, William, Sr	1	4	2		
Clark, James	1	2	3		
Clark, Nathl	1	1	3		
Campbell, Nicholas	1	2	4		
Carrot, Starling	1	2	3		
Caps, Wm, Ser	2	1	7		
Caps, Oliver	2		6		
Dowdey, John	1		3		
Duncan, Wm, Ser	3	6	3		
Dowdy, William	1				
Dowdey, Rud	1				
Dowdey, Jesse	1				
Dowdey, Benjn	1		2		
Dowdey, Joseph	2	6	2		
Dackerly, John	1	3	2		
Dodson, Wm	1	1	4		
Dowd, Judith	4		3		
Dowdey, Daniel	2	3	4		
Dodson, George	1		3		
Elliot, John	2	2	2		
Elliot, Ebenezer	1				
Gober, William	1	1	2		
Galiway, Thos	1	2	4		
Gilmore, Saml	2	4	4		
Green, Wm	1	3	4		1
Griffin, Edward	1	3	4		
Hillard, Ezechail	1	5	1		
Harley, Amos	2	4	5		
Harley, John	1		1		
Hodge, Wm	3	3	6		
Higdon, Phillip	1		2		
Hart, John	1				
Hart, Wm	2	4	3		
Jeffres, Henry	1	2	3		
Jones, Edward	1	3	4		
Kendrick, Martin	2		7		1
Kendrick, Wm	1	1	3		2
Lawton, Joel	1	1	3		
Lea, Joseph	3	2	6		13
Mckeever, Alexr, Sr	1	3	3		
Mckeever, Alexr, Jur	1	1	2		
Mckinnis, Miles	1	2	5		
McIntire, John	2	1	4		
May, Henry	1	4	5		3
Modglin, Straingmon	2	1	4		
Mckeever, John, Ser	2	4	3		
May, Joseph	1				
Modglin, Trumon	1	1	3		
Mckinsey, Cristain	1		2		
McDaniel, James	2	3	6		
Mongomery, John	1		6		18
Mckeever, John, Jr	1	1	2		
Merack, Moses	1	1	3		2
McCollum, Malcom	2	1	2		
Nall, Rud	1		4		2
Nall, John	1		4		
Oaldhum, Rud	2	2	2		
Paterson, Charles	2	5	5		
Paterson, Gilbert	2	8	6		1
Pasiel, Wm	1		2		
Poplin, George	1		4		
Powell, Confert	1	1	2		1
Paterson, Joel	1	1	3		1
Riddle, Cato	1	2	3		
Rogers, Randolph	1				
Riddle, Julus	1	1			
Roberts, Wm	1	4	4		
Riddle, Thos	1	2	6		1
Parish, Self	1	3	5		6
Smith, Daniel	1	2	6		
Smith, James	1	2	3		
Shammell, Wm	1		2		
Smith, Abner	2	3	4		
Swanson, Richardson	1	5	1		
Tison, Ricd	1	2	2		
Tayler, Willington	2	1	6		
Thomson, John	3	1	6		5
Taylor, Phillip	1	2	3		36
Taylor, John	1				10
Taylor, James	1		1		18
Temple, Saml	1		2		
Tyrrell, Simon	1	2	5		6
Tilmon, Joshua	1	4	2		
Tregle, Griffin	1	1	1		1
Temples, Benjn	2	4	2		
Wheelus, Isaac	1		1		
Wilkins, Robert	1		2		
Wilkins, John	2	2	3		7
Wade, Peter	1		3		1
Wilcox, John	1	4	3	1	11
White, Spierwood	1	2	3	1	
Wilkerson, Thos	1		2		
Williams, Jacob	1	2	5		
Caps, John	1		1		
Rivard, Lion	1		1		
May, Thos	1	2	3		
Caps, Jacob	1		1		
Hinson, Saml	1	6	3		
Molding, Claton	1	1	6		
Right, Joseph	1	2	2		
Kelley, James	1	2	2		
Kelley, Wm	1	2	2		
Linklear, John	1		2		
Weaver, Shaderick	1		1		
Lawton, Wm	1		2		
Morgan, Wm	1		2		1
Self, Bradley	1	4	2		
Barnes, Jeremiah	2	1	4		
Turner, Matter	1	2	2		
Dowdey, Wm	3	5	4		
Berry, Wm	1	1	3		
Mckeever, Edward	2	1	1		
Upton, David	2	3	6		
Bulluck, Saml	1	3	7		
Bradley, Wm	1	3	2		
Bass, Moses	1		2		
Bass, Edward	1	1	4		
Bray, Edward, Ser	3	2	2		
Bray, Edward, Jr	1		2		
Branson, Joseph	1				
Berry, John	1	4	6		1
Jones, Burrough	1	1	1		
Branson, Levi	3	2	3		
Bushop, Wm	1	2	4		
Cashatt, John	1	2	5		
Caster, Saml	3	2	2		
Caster, John	1	4	2		
Chamness, Joshua	1	1	7		
Casthat, John	4		4		
Caster, Isaac	1	6	5		
Culberson, Andrew	3	1	7		
Cox, Isaac	2	1	3		
Davis, John	2	3	6		
Doan, Thos	1	2	4		
Dowdey, Thos	2		3		
Doan, John	4	1	6		
Davis, Joseph	1	1	3		
Dickson, Thos	1	3	2		
Doan, Joseph	1	2	3		
Doan, Jacob	1	1	2		
Dickson, Benjamin	1		2		
Dickson, John	1	1	4		
Dickson, Solomon	1		1		
Esiry, Thos	1	1			
Fox, John	1		3		
Freeman, Robert	1		4		
Fox, David	2	3	5		
Fox, Nicholas	2	5	3		
Fills, Isham	1				
Hopkins, Wm	1	2	3		
Hobson, Stephon	5	3	2		
Hickman, Joseph	1	2	6		
Hobson, Charles	2	3	7		
Hornaday, Christopher	1	4	3		1
Hobson, Wm, Ser	2	1	5		
Hobson, Wm, Jr	1				
Howell, Robert	1		7		
Henshaw, Benjn	1	5	5		
Henshaw, Joseph	1	1	2		
Harper, Travis	1	1	1		3
Hornaday, John	1	3	3		
Johnson, Matha	1	2	1		
Johnson, Joseph	1	6	2		
Johnson, Joseph	1				
Johnson, David	1	2	5		
Jones, Henry	2	1	5		
Johnson, Jesse	3	4	3		
Jones, George	1	1	1		
Kemp, Joseph	1	4	4		
Kemp, Ricd	1	1	2		
Moon, John	2	4	4		
Moon, Jacob	1	1	5		
Moon, James	2	2	5		
Morley, Benjn	1	2	3		
Marshall, Wm	1	2	2		
McMarster, Wm	1	4	2		
McMaster, James	3		1		
McMaster, Jonathan	1	2	2		
Marley, John	1	3	3		
Marshall, Benjn	1	3	3		
Marley, Henry	1	3	2		
Murphy, Archabell	1	2	3		
Mosset, Adam	1	1	2		
Macklefield, Hugh	1		2		
Pew, Thos	1		2		
Pew, Jacob	1	1	2		
Peyot, John	1	5	3		
Pigmon, Lennord	2	2	3		
Ratliff, Amoss	1	1	2		
Ransey, Joel	1	3	2		
Remonton, John	1		1		
Ricard, David	1	2	2		
Ray, Thos	1	2	2		
Lamey, James	1	3	4		
Stewart, Henry	1	1	4		
Smith, John	1	5	4		
Stewart, John	1		3		
Tison, Wm	2	4	2		
Lamb, Josiah	1	1	2		
Toppin, Wm	1	1	3		
Terry, Thos	2	1	2		
Thomson, John	1	1	2		
Terry, James	1	2	3		
Thomas, Temple	2	2	3		
Ward, Thos	2	2	3		
Whitehead, Thos	1	3	5		
Williams, Ezikiel	1	3	2		
Whitehead, Joseph	1	3	6		
Whinarey, Robert	1	1	3		
Wiers, James	1	1	1		2
Youngblood, Jacob	1		1		
Vestill, Wm	1				
Vestill, Capt Wm	1		4		
Vestill, Wm, Jr	1				
Vestill, Thos	4	1	1		
Vestill, David	3		7		
Silor, Pever		2	2		
Johnson, James	3		3		
Hussey, Ann	1	4	2		
Hobson, Isaac	1		1		
Hackman, John	1	3	4		
Hobson, Joseph	1		1		
Silor, Elizabeth	2		1		
Howell, Robert, Jr	1	1	2		
Silor, Phillip	1	4	5		
McDaniel, Marey	1		4		
Stanton, Robert	1	1	4		
Berry, Henry	1		2		
Johnson, Isaac	2	2	3		
Jones, George	1	1	1		
Unstot, Catey		1	3		
Blalock, Julius	2	5	2		1
Branton, Thos	2	3	4		
Brewer, Henry	1	2	5		
Baker, John	1	6			1
Balding, Saml	1	1	5		2
Buckner, Jesse	1	5	4		
Balding, John, Sr	2	1	4		2
Berry, Isaac	1		2		
Clark, Robert	2	1	2		
Conklin, Daniel	1		1		
Clark, Yelikel	4	2	1		1
Cool, Joseph	1	3	4		
Cook, Abraham	1	1	5		2
Copeland, Rebeccah	2		3		
Crutchfield, Milley	3	1	5		15
Cook, Benjn	1	2	2		
Curle, Wm	2	3	6		
Crutchfield, Martin	1	4	4		1
Davis, Elnathan	3	3	3		2
Dickson, Solomon	2	4	3		
Duglas, Wm	1	2	4		4
Davis, James	1		2		
Fasker, Joseph	2		1		
Fasker, Elisha	1		2		1
Folden, Lewis	1	1	2		
Gillum, Wm	1	2	2		3
Henderson, James	1	3	6		
Henderson, Isaac	2	2	5		
Hadley, Simon	1	3	2		
Holliday, Saml	1	2	6		
Hadley, Thos	1	3	2		
Henderson, John	1				
Jones, Charles	2		2		
Jones, Thos	1	4	4		
Jones, John	2	6	2		
Jones, John	2		5		
Kirk, George	2		2		5
Lukes, Wm	1	2	4		
Linsey, James	1	3	3		2
Lee, Isaac	1	1	2		
Linley, Wm	1	3	1		
Linley, Aron	2		3		
Linley, Owen	2	2	3		
Litterloth, Lewis H	2	4	2		6
Moutre, James, Ser	3	2	2		
Martin, Wm	3	2	2		8
Meeham, Joseph	2		3		
Martin, John	1		4		
Meekam, Wm	3	2	1		2
Meekam, John	1		3		
Manor, John	2	7	3		
Meekam, George	1		1		

HILLSBOROUGH DISTRICT, CHATHAM COUNTY—Continued.

NAME OF HEAD OF FAMILY.	Free white males of 16 years and upward, including heads of families.	Free white males under 16 years.	Free white females, including heads of families.	All other free persons.	Slaves.
McMatt, Wm, Ser	2	3	3		1
McPherson, Othneil	1		1		
McMatt, Wm	1	1	2		1
McCracken, Wm	1	2	1		
Mashburn, Matthew	1	4	3		
Moutre, James	1	1	2		1
Nicholason, Isaac	1	3	3		
Newland, John	1	4	2		
Pickins, William	1	2	5		
Price, Lenny	1	1	2		
Pourtis, James	1	2	3		
Person, George	2	1			
Pasmore, David	1		2	1	
Quackenbush, Peter	2	1	4		
Quackenbush, John	1	1	2		
Rogers, Josiah	3	2	2		
Richardson, Isaac	1	3	4		
Loan, Thos	3	3	5		
Sinkler, John	1	2	1		2
Spurling, Wm	1	1	5		1
Steal, Thos	1	2	6		
Sinkler, Mary	4	2	2		
Simons, James	1		6		
West, William	1	3	3		5
West, Ignatus	1	2	6		1
Wilkey, George	1	3	5		
Witsman, Cannord	1		2		
White, Simon	2	1	4		
West, Thos	2	2	4		3
West, Ignatus	1	1	6		
Smith, Buckner	1	3	1		
Simmons, Thos	1	1	2		
Balding, John	1		1		
Groves, Jacob	1		1		
West, Philliph	1				
Morphus, John	1	2	4		
Cook, Henry	2	4	2		3
Tison, Wm	1	4	1		
Alwater, Justis	2	2	2		
Binom, Luke	3	1	4		15
Brigah, Cannon	2	1	1		
Baley, James	1	2	4		
Brown, Abner	1	1	5		
Allen, Elijah	1				
Beaver, Rigston	2	1	7		
Brewer, Oliver	4	2	2		3
Burnet, Daniel	2	5	3		2
Brewer, Edward	1	2	2		
Blalock, George	3	2	5		
Binom, Tapley	1	4	1		1
Cate, Rud	1	3	6		
Crow, Stephen	1	4	2		1
Crow, Isaac	1	2	2		
Crow, James	1		2		
Caudle, Beckner	1	3	1		
Crow, John	1	4	4		
Crow, Wm	1	1	1		
Clay, Thos	2	1			2
Cobb, Robert	2		4		8
Edward, John	2	2	3		
Ellis, Jesse	1	4	6		
Edwards, Wm	1	3	3		1
Edwards, Robert	2	1			3
Edwards, Hugh	1	2	2		
Edwards, Edward	1	1	3		
Duglas, John	1		2		1
Danor, Marmaduck	1	1	1		
Fan, Jesse	3	3	5		
Hathcock, Hosea	1	4			
Hearn, Howell	1	1	3		
Hearndon, John	1	2	3		
Hatley, Ricd	1	3	2		
Hackney, Joseph	1	3	5		1
Hood, Athur	1	1	3		
Gunter, James	2	3	3		
Glawson, Sarah	3	4	4		
Griffin, John	2	3	3		
Griffin, Wm	1	4	3		5
Jewell, Absalom	1	3	3		
Jolley, Jalf	1		1		
Justin, Wm	1				
Justin, John	5	2	3		12
Jolley, John	3	1	3		
Kirksey, James	1	2	1		
Kirksey, Gidian	2	1	1		1
Kirksey, Isaac	1		3		
Kirksey, Wm	1		2		3
Kirksey, Christopher	3	5	5		17
Lacey, Pillimon	1		4		4
Lacey, Pillimon, Jr	1	1	1		
Lassiter, Hezekiah	1	4	3		
Lassiter, Jacob	1	2	2		
Merack, Wm	1	6	4		3
Moutre, Joseph	1	2	3		
Man, Rowland	1	2	2		
Man, Thos	2	2	3		
Owen, Jacob	1		1		

NAME OF HEAD OF FAMILY.	Free white males of 16 years and upward, including heads of families.	Free white males under 16 years.	Free white females, including heads of families.	All other free persons.	Slaves.
Odam, Thos	1		1		3
Owin, Oliver	1	2	3		
Owin, Daniel	2		7		3
Powell, Thos	1	3	2		
Powell, Wm, Sr	1	3	1		
Powell, Wm, Jr	1		1		
Powell, James, Ser	2	2	2		
Pilkerton, Saml	1				
Powell, Nicholas	1	3	1		
Pilkerton, James	1				
Person, Lewis	1	3	2		
Poe, Robert	1		1		
Powell, James, Jur	3	2	3		
Poe, Terry	1				
Poe, James	1	1	4		
Pritchit, Thos	1	1	1		
Powell, Elizabeth	1		2		
Pilkerton, Wm	1	4	1		
Person, William	2		5		
Person, Surling	1	4	3		
Ramsey, Wm	1	1	3		3
Rosser, Josser	1		2		14
Rigdon, Beaver	2	1	6		
Smith, Isham	2	1	5		
Smith, Henry	2	3	5		
Smith, Isham	2	3	4		
Smith, Mark	1	1	1		
Snipes, John	1		3		
Snipes, Thos	1	4			4
Snipes, Thos	1	3	5		
Snipes, Wm	1	1	2		1
Smith, Absalom	1	4	2		
Stephens, John	2	3	3		
Smith, James	1	2	5		
Smith, Moses	1		6		
Straughn, Edmon	1	1	1		
Tatom, Edmond	2	1	2		4
Tatom, John	1	4	3		
Trip, John	3	2	4		
Smith, Wm	3	2	2		
Ward, Robert	1		5		
Wood, Wm	2	3	4		
Williams, David	1	6	3		
Brown, Thos	2		2		
Pilkerton, Anthony	1				
Kellum, Daniel	1				1
Smith, Frances			3		
Powell, George	1	5	1		
Powell, James	1		2		1
Owen, Wm	2	3	4		
Bellary, John	1	1	4		
Mosley, George	1	1	2		
Coal, Thos	1	3	4		
Halley, Wm	2	3	5		
Wood, Solomon	2	4	2		
Pritchit, Thos	1	1	2		
Smith, Wm	1				
Andrews, Thomas	1	2	2		
Adcock, Joshua	1	2	3		
Brown, Mordica	2	5	1		2
Brewer, John, Sr	1	3	6		
Bray, Henry	1		2		
Bray, Mathias	1	3	2		
Bray, James	1	1	2		
Bray, Wm	1		2		
Brooks, Mark	2	4	7		
Brewer, John, Jur	2	1	4		
Brewer, Amos	1	2	1		
Brewer, George	1	1	3		
Bradley, Lewis	2	5	3		
Baker, Humphrey	1	1	6		
Brooks, Isaac	2	1	5		12
Bayley, Henry	3	1	2		
Bayley, Benjn	1	1	1		3
Brewer, Wm	1		6		
Brewer, Nicholas	2	7	3		
Bright, Simon	2	1	4		
Bray, John	1	2	3		
Campbell, Wm	1	5	2		
Carvins, Ricd	1	1	4		
Cox, Solomon	3		3		
Cox, Saml	1		3		
Culberson, James	1	2	3		
Dulley, Thos	1	2	3		2
Dickson, Jesse	2	3	8		
Dickson, Joseph	1				
Dickson, Hannah	1	3	6		
Dickson, Saml	1	3	1		
Dickson, Zabulen	1				
Deaton, James	2	5	3		
Edwards, James	3	2	1		
Edwards, Joshua	1	2	2		
Elkins, Benjn	1	2	6		
Emberson, James	3	3	5		
Fismire, Martin	4		5		
Flemmings, John	1	1	1		
Flemmings, David	1	3	4		

NAME OF HEAD OF FAMILY.	Free white males of 16 years and upward, including heads of families.	Free white males under 16 years.	Free white females, including heads of families.	All other free persons.	Slaves.
Glass, Josiah	1				
Groves, Wm G	3	6	3		
Groves, Thos	1	2	4		
Glover, Thos	1	2	3		
Glass, Josiah	1		3		
Glass, Daniel	1		4		
Gass, Thos	1	2	5		
Gregory, Ricd	2	2	4		
Gillerland, Joseph	1	2	3		
Ginn, William	1	1	3		
Headen, John	1		1		
Hadley, Mary	2	1	5		
Hadley, Joshua	1	2	1		
Hart, Heath	1	4	4		
Hobson, George, Jr	1	2	6		
Dickson, Nathan	1	3	2		
Hobson, James	1	2	6		
Hobson, George	1	2	2		
Hayes, Saml	1	3	1		
Hunter, Elisha	1	3	4		
Headen, Wm	2				
Hackny, Daniel	1	2	2		
Jones, Andrew	2	1	5		
Johnson, Benja	1	3	1		
Jones, Plebius	1	1	1		
Jeffers, Henry	1	2	3		
Jones, Ricd	1	4	4		4
King, Robert	1		4		
Kelley, Wm	1	2	3		
Kirk, Joseph	1	2	4		
Lambert, John	1		3		1
Lambert, John, Ser	2		3		
Lambert, Joseph	1	2	1		
Moore, Thos	1	1	2		
McRay, Martin	1	2	1		
Moodey, Wm	3	2	7		1
McCaslin, Catey	1	1	3		
Moodey, Thos	1	1	3		
McCaslin, James	1	1	2		
McAmus, Eli	1	1	4		
McSwane, John	4	4	5		
McCaslin, James	1	1	1		
Martin, George	1	1	2		
McMannis, Laurance	3	2	2		
Asten, John	1	2	2		
Moyr, John	2	1	3		
Maffett, Hugh	5	3	3		
Martin, Zachariah	2		2		6
Moon, Thos	2	2	4		
Moon, James	2	3	3		
Martin, James	2	3	1		2
Nall, Martha	1	2	2		1
Philliphs, Dennis	1	2	1		
Philliphs, Wm	1	1	2		
Philliphs, Willis	1		3		
Philliphs, Lewis	1	2	4		
Philliphs, Joel	1	3	1		
Pervis, Robert	1	4	3		
Philliphs, Jeremiah	3	2	3		
Powers, John	2	2	3		
Parrot, Joel	1	5	2		7
Raglin, Thomas	1		3		
Rhodes, Wm	1	1	3		
Ratliff, John, Jr	1	3	4		
Ratliff, John	3	1	3		
Ramsower, Michael	2	1	1		
Ramsower, Edward	1		1		
Smith, Coley	1	2	5		
Smith, Abraham	1	3	3		
Smith, Wm, Sr	2	3	4		
Sanders, Benjn	2	3	4		
Smith, Ambrous	1	1	2		
Smith, David	1	7	2		
Stinson, Robert	1	1	4		
Stephens, Joseph	2	3	6		
Tucker, John	1	3	4		
Thomson, Saml	1	2	4		
Talley, John	1	1	2		
Tucker, Wm	1	2	2		
Thomson, Balom	2	3	7		3
Underwood, James	3	3	5		
Collins, Wm	1		2		
Hinton, Sarah			2		5
Venderver, John	2	2	6	1	
Grainger, James	1	1	1	1	2
Smith, Wm	1	2	5		
Jones, Reuben	1		1		
Brewer, Sampson	1	1	2		
Estrick, Willis	1	2	2		
Wilson, Wm	1	2	4		
Dickson, George	1	2	3		
Grainger, Thos	2	2	3		
Willit, James	3		4		
Willit, James	1	4	2		
Willit, Ricd	2		2		
White, Philliph			4		
White, Catey			4		

HILLSBOROUGH DISTRICT, CHATHAM COUNTY—Continued.

NAME OF HEAD OF FAMILY.	Free white males of 16 years and upward, including heads of families.	Free white males under 16 years.	Free white females, including heads of families.	All other free persons.	Slaves.
Stinson, Aron	1	2	5		
Rogers, George	1	2	2		
Bradus, Owin	3	2	3		
Jones, Sam¹	4	1	1		
Philliphs, Mary		2	5		
Welch, John	1	1	3		
Murry, Jane		1	3		
Ratliff, Edom	1	1	2		
Henry, Micajah	1		1		
Winter, Sam¹	1	3	2		
Ward, Job, Sr	1	1	2		
Ward, Job, Jr	1	1	2		
White, Charles	3		3		
White, Stephen	1		1		
Brantley, Wm	1	1	1		6
Wimberley, Jesse	1	1	3		
Smith, John	2		3		
Wilson, John	1		1		
Tigue, Isaac	1	3	2		
Hobson, Thos	1		1		
Hadley, Jeremiah	1		2		
Adcock, Joshua	1	2	3		
Burnet, Wm	1	1	2		
Dutey, Wm	2	1	5		
Wilkerson, John	1		2		
Collins, Wm	1		3		
Marcus, Job	2	1	3		
Gillum, John	2	3	4		
Burges, John	1		3		
Mirphit, James	1		1		
Welch, Walter	3	2	5		
Wilkerson, Robert	1	2	4		
Wilkerson, Ricd	2	4	9		
Routh, Robert	2	5	3		
Linin, James	1	3	1		
McVay, Martin	1	2	1		
Wilson, Daniel	1	1	3		
Terrell, Solomon	1		1		
Wismiland, Shadrick	1	2	1		
Wismiland, Patey	1		3		
Moody, Wm	1				
Smith, David	1		1		
Younger, John	1	2	2		
Class, Cloe			3		
Dredyard, John	1	2	5		
Harper, Sam¹	2	3	4		
Allen, Henry	2	2	8		
Brantley, John	1	2	8		8
Brooks, Thos, Ser	1		1		5
Brooks, Thos., Jr	2	1	10		6
Brantley, Wm	2	2	6		10
Burk, Millinner	1	2	4		
Brantley, Mary		1	3		10
Byant, Wm	1	3	6		
Beal, Daniel	1	2	2		
Brown, Thos	1	3	2		
Boyds, John	1	1	4		
Bullard, James	1	3	3		
Bagley, Henry	1	1	3		
Brooks, Stephen	2	4	2		
Beal, John	1		3		
Blalock, David	1	2	4		
Brooks, Sam	1	5	6		4
Copeland, Nicholas	2	2	3		
Copeland, John	1	2	1		
Copeland, Ruth			3		
Cox, Presley	1	2	4		13
Coan, John	1	1	4		
Dark, Joseph	2	4	7		6
Dark, Sam¹	1	3	3		
Evens, Ruth	2	3	5		
Edwards, Wm	2	1	3		9
Evens, Owen	1	1	1		
Fields, James	1	2	2		
Fields, James, Jr	1	3	2		
Fike, Elizabeth	1	3	2		
Green, Abell	2	5	3		
Glosston, Wm	1	1	5		10
Ginn, Elizabeth		1	5		1
Gutree, Wm	1	4	1		4
Harden, John	1				1
Hunter, Margret	1	2	5		7
Hunter, John	1	1	2		
Hill, Wm	2	3			5
Harrington, Agnes			1		5
Hart, Thos	1	2	4		
Hayes, Joseph	3	3	5		
Harris, Benjs	3	4	4		14
Henson, Lezacus	1	4	6		
Howell, Samuel	2	5	3		2
Harrington, Whitmill	1	2	2		1
Hayes, Wm	1	5	6		
Hart, John	1	1	2		
Howell, John	1	2	5		
Headen, Andrew	1	2	3		4
Jones, Matthew	4	3	3		42
Johnson, Lewis	1	2	8		

NAME OF HEAD OF FAMILY.	Free white males of 16 years and upward, including heads of families.	Free white males under 16 years.	Free white females, including heads of families.	All other free persons.	Slaves.
Kennon, Rud	1	4	5		25
Malane, John	3	1	4		22
Morphis, Joseph	1	2	3		
Matthews, Britain	1	2	1		1
McDaniel, Arthur	1		5		
Minter, John	2	3	3		8
McPherson, John	1	1	2		
McGee, Micajah	1	1	2		4
May, Joseph	1	2	5		5
Pettey, Wm	1	3	3		1
Peoples, Hugh	3	1	4		5
Roe, Solomon	2	2	5		4
Roser, John, Jr	1	3	6		
Roe, John, Sr	1		2		
Ramsey, Matthew	1	3	2		8
Robertson, Upshear	1				
Roper, John, Sr	1		3		
Todd, William	2		1		
Tomlinson, Wm	2	1	5		2
Tomison, Ricd	1	3	7		2
White, Philliph	2	2	2		
White, John	3	1	2		
White, Jacob	3	1	8		
Wilkins, Alex	1	1	1		
Womble, John	1	1	3		
Right, Simon	3	1	5		
Webster, Ricd	1	1	2		
Roper, John	1				
Dark, Wm	1	3	4		1
Jones, Edward	1	4	4		
Hart, Wm	1		1		
Landom, Abner	1	2	2		1
Standley, Danny	1	2	4		
Riley, John	1		3		
Coley, Julus	1	2	1		
Underwood, Wm	1		3		
Baker, Humphri	2	1	7		
Bennet, James	1	1	3		
Ausley, Willis	1		1		
Avin, John		1	8		5
Ausley, Jesse	1	1	4		1
Ausley, David	1	1	4		
Brinkley, Peter	2	3	4		
Butter, James	2	3	6		
Burt, Ricd	2	3	4		5
Bohannon, Joseph	1	1	2		
Bohannon, Benjs, Sr	1	2	4		14
Booker, James	1	1	8		8
Branton, Wm	1	1	2		2
Booker, John	3	3	5		
Browdey, Dorcas	1	2	2		
Branton, Thos	1	3	3		
Browder, John	1		5		
Clark, Burges	1	2	4		
Casten, Seth	2	2	5		4
Chapman, Solomon	2	3	2		8
Chapman, Henry	2	4			
Chapman, David	2		5		6
Covenah, David	1		2		1
Copeland, Wm, Sr	1		1		
Christain, John	1	3	3		
Crump, Joseph	1	2	5		2
Copeland, Ricd	1		1		
Copeland, John	1	2	3		
Caudle, Isham	1	5	3		
Caudle, Bleaker	1	2	2		
Davis, Matthew	1	4	2		
Daniel, Isham	2		2		
Dillard, Elisha	1		2		
Davis, Wm	1	1	3		
Darton, Benja	2		2		
Dillard, Wm	1	3	4		4
Daniel, Jesse	1				
Dreshill, John	1		3		
Dillard, John	1	2	1		
Dillard, Auzborn	1	2	3		
Dillard, Zacharias	1	1	2		2
Elkins, Joshua	1	1	3		
Edwards, John	1		5		
Griffis, Thos	1	5	3		10
Hamton, John	1		4		
Hales, Josiah	1		3		
Hutchins, Gabril	1	2	4		
Horn, James	1	2	3		
Hinsley, Benja	3				
Hinsley, Nathl	1	3	5		
Hogan, Wm	1	6	4		
Hudson, Wm	2		2		6
Hudson, Allen	1		4		
Haley, Robert	1		4		
Hamton, Moses	3		3		
June, Jesse		1	2		1
Jones, Lewis	3	5	4		
Jinks, Wm	1		2		
Johnson, Wm	1	1	2		
Linn, Elizabeth		1	4		1
Lankston, Jams	2	1	2		

NAME OF HEAD OF FAMILY.	Free white males of 16 years and upward, including heads of families.	Free white males under 16 years.	Free white females, including heads of families.	All other free persons.	Slaves.
Marshall, Wm	1				
Matthews, Laurance	3	4	3		
Moore, John	2	1	6		
Mason, Ricd	2	3	2		
Mims, David	2	3	3		
Matthews, Clabon	2	5	4		
Moore, Wm	2	2	2		
Nevin, John	4	4	3		
Richardson, John	1	1	3		2
Richardson, Thos	2	4	1		7
Redding, Charles	1	2	3		3
Raglin, Wm	1	2	2		7
Richardson, George	1		2		
Raglin, Sarah		1	3		17
Redding, Wm	2		1		3
Raglin, Federick	1		2		2
Rolins, John	1	5	2		2
Singlton, John	2	2	6		
Sigirs, Joshua	1		2		
Stephens, Jarrot	1	4	3		
Tedder, John	2	2	9		
Upchurch, John	1	3	4		
Wilson, Blumore	1	3	3		
Wormack, Britain	2	3	6		
Williams, Burwell	2	1	7		20
Watson, Christopher	2		3		
Winnington, James	1		2		2
Wallace, Sherrod	1	3	3		
Wilson, Stephen	1	1	1		
Wilson, Michael	1	1	2		
Weaver, Isham	1	1	3		
Wilson, Wm	1	3	2		
Wilson, Blumore	1	3	3		
Yarbrough, Lewis	1	2	5		
Bass, Aron	1		2		
Hicks, Thos	1	3	3		
Philliphs, James	1	5	2		
Stephens, Lewis	1	1	3		
Wilson, Sam¹	1				
Bodling, John	1	1	1		
Lankston, James	1		1		
Willis, Arthur	1		1		
Jinkins, John	2	1	5		
Johnson, Isham	1	3	6		1
Hogan, John	1	2	2		
Christain, James	1				
Christain, Thos	1			1	
Ozborn, Stephen	1	2	1		
Caudle, Jesse	1	1	2		
Chapman, Tabithey			1		8
Cotten, Wm	1		2		
Hatch, Alexr	1				
Warthen, James	1		4		
Whitehead, Arther	1	1	2		
Dosit, Clemment	1		2		
Chambs, Charity	1	3	5		
Tigue, David	1	3	2		1
Tigue, Edmond	1	3	1		
Stewart, Edward	1	2	1		
Reynolds, Florence	2		2		
Dosit, Francis	1	1	5		
Silley, Federick	1	1	2		
Tigue, Francis	1	1	3		
Allen, George	1				
Adwek, Henry	1		1		1
Rogers, Henry	1	1	1		
Dosia, John	1	2	1		
Webster, John	1	2	2		
Rosser, John	1	2	3		
May, John	1				
Tigue, Jacob	3	2	4		
Stewart, James	1	1	2		
Watson, James	1	3	2		
Hackney, Joseph	3		3		8
Page, John	1	3	6		
Webster, James	1	1	4		
McDaniel, Jacob	1	2	3		3
Bridges, Joseph	1	1	1		12
Hadley, Joshua	3	4	5		
Hall, John	1	3	5		
George, James	1	3	5		
Whitehead, John	2		6		
Johnson, Levi	2	2	4		1
Hart, Morgan	1		2		
McKinsey, Peter	1		2		
Laurance, Patrick S	2	3	2		7
Claton, Ricd	2	2	2		
Stewart, Sam¹	4	1	2		5
Rogers, Stephen, Ser	2	3	5		
McDaniel, Sam¹	1		7		9
Rogers, Stephen	1				
Foster, Thos, Ser	1	1	4		
Foster, Thos, Jr	1	2	3		
Craton, Thos	1	3	2		
Piles, John	2	1	3		
Holliday, Thos	1	1	5		
Adcock, Wm	1		3		

HILLSBOROUGH DISTRICT, CHATHAM COUNTY—Continued.

NAME OF HEAD OF FAMILY.	Free white males of 16 years and upward, including heads of families.	Free white males under 16 years.	Free white females, including heads of families.	All other free persons.	Slaves.
Tigue, Wm	1	1	1		
Collins, Wm	1		1		
Rogers, Wm	1	1	3		
George, Wm, Jr	1				
George, Wm, Sr	2		5		
Tigue, Mayner	1	3	2		
Forrester, Nathl	2	2	5		
Dossit, Solomon	1		1		
Tison, Francis		1	1		
Tigue, Moses, Sr	1		1	1	
Tigue, Moses, Jur	1	1	1		
Womley, John	2	2	3		
Curshalt, Jacob	1	2	5		
Hadley, Joseph	2	4	4		
Nobbit, Robert	1	2	1		
Nobbit, Wm	2	3	4		
McDaniel, John	1		1		
Greer, Charles	1	3	2		
Davis, Joseph	1	3	1		
Christain, Drewry	2	1	1		2
Gunter, Isham	2	2	4		
Williams, Wm	1	2	6		
Adams, Thos	2	2	1		
Akemon, Adam	1	2	4		3
Adams, Thos	1	5	4		
Bishop, Benja	1		1		4
Bullard, Thos	1	2	5		
Bell, Thos	2	3	2		5
Brinkley, Peter	2	1	4		
Bialock, Charles	1	1	2		1
Binom, Isaac	1	2	2		
Buzby, Jesse	2		2		1
Bishop, Ricd	1	3	4		1
Buzby, Phindul	1		1		
Buzby, Phindul	1	2	5		
Bilbary, Isham	1		2		
Barber, Gray	1	5	4		6
Boling, Wm	1	1	1		
Bishop, Henry	1	2	4		1
Buzby, Henry	1		2		9
Buzby, Isham	1	3	3		1
Buzby, Ephraim	1	3	3		2
Bilbary, Thos	1	1	2		
Binom, Wm	1	2	2		
Cain, Hardy	1	1	1		1
Cuddle, John	1		4		
Cypruss, Thos	2	1	3		
Coal, Wm	1	3	1		1
Cole, Thos	1	3	4		
Cosins, Thos	1		1		
Copeland, Josiah	2	1	3		
Carter, Benjamin	1	5	2		
Coker, Jacob	1	1	1		
Copeland, Josiah, Jr	1				
Copeland, Wm	1	2	2		
Cuddle, Benja	1	3	2		
Carter, Vincent	1	2	2		

NAME OF HEAD OF FAMILY.	Free white males of 16 years and upward, including heads of families.	Free white males under 16 years.	Free white females, including heads of families.	All other free persons.	Slaves.
Cain, Elisha	3	1	5		11
Dickson, James	1	2	2		
Durham, Charles	1		1		
Dodd, William	1	2	4		
Edwards, Hugh	1	2	5		
Foremon, Benja	2		2		2
Freeman, Howell	1	4	3		
Flowers, Jacob	1	1	6		15
Goodin, Shadrick	1	1	3		2
Goodwin, Wm	1	5	2		
Gregory, Harden	1		2		
Gregory, Thos, Ser	1	1	5		
Gregory, Wm	1		4		
Gregory, Bray	1	2	3		
Gregory, Presley	2	1	2		4
George, Isaac	1	2	1		1
George, Joseph	1				
Goodwin, Gideon	4	2	4		17
Gregory, Jeremiah	1	1	2		
Gregory, John	1	3	3		
Golson, Charles	3	2	6		
Horsey, Isaac	3		2		
Hatley, John, Ser	5	2	2		8
Hatley, John	1	1	1		
Hatley, Hardy	1	1	2		
Hatley, Jacob	1		1		
Harrod, Malakiah	1		2		
Hathcock, Wm	1	3	3		
Hathcock, James	2	1	8		
Hudson, Ricd	3	2	5		
Hanes, Robert	2	2	6		
Harndon, John	1	2	4		5
Harrod, Absalom	1	1	3		4
Holland, James	1	3	2		
Johnson, Robert	1	3	5		
Jones, Arthur	2	1	2		
Jones, Tignal	1		7		
Jones, Francis	1	1	2		13
King, Wm	1		3		1
Kelley, Henry	2	2	5		
Kirby, James, Ser	2	2	6		4
Kirby, James, Jr	1	4	2		
Lankston, Wm	1	2	4		
Lassiter, Mary	1	2	1		
Lambeth, John	2		4		
Ledbetter, Colmon	1				
Ledbetter, John	1				
Ledbetter, Wm	3	2	4		
Lambeth, Wm	1	2	1		
Moore, James	1	5	2		3
Moodey, Joel	3	3	5		
Merrot, William	2	3	2		8
Mass, John	1	1	5		
Mitchel, Allen	1	2	3		
Null, Presley	1	1	1		6
Ohiiley, William	1	1	2		1
Oaldham, John	2	2	4		1

NAME OF HEAD OF FAMILY.	Free white males of 16 years and upward, including heads of families.	Free white males under 16 years.	Free white females, including heads of families.	All other free persons.	Slaves.
Parker, Lewis	1	4	2		2
Pewet, Joel	2	4	3		7
Powell, Simon	1	2	2		
Pendergrass, John	1	1	2		
Pitts, Joseph	1	1	3		1
Pitts, John	1	4	5		1
Parker, Robert	1	2	4		
Quishingberry, John	1	4	2		3
Quishingberry, Nicholas			2		5
Ragons, Charles	1		3		
Rhodes, Elisha	1		3		
Rickmon, John	1	1	3		1
Ragons, Wm	1	4	4		
Rhodes, Wm	1	3	4		1
Rogers, Isham	1	4	4		
Rowland, Jesse	1	5	5		
Rigsbey, Luke	1	4	2		
Rowland, Jesse	1		1		
Rogers, Bias	2	1	7		
Sanders, Phillphs	2	4	2		
Sillers, James	1	3	4		
Sillers, David	1	2	4		
Sillers, Robert	1	2	3		1
Stone, Francis	1	2	4		
Stegall, Mosses	3	4	5		
Sillers, James	2	3	4		
Sillers, Isaac	1				
Suars, Barber	1		1		1
Smith, Solomon	1	5	5		
Smart, Laborn	1	2	3		
Tatom, Jesse	1	1	2		
Williams, Wm	1		2		1
Wood, John	1	3	4		
Wilson, Benja	1	1	2		
Wimberle, Jacob	2	1	1		
Wimberle, Lewis	2	2	4		
Wayster, Wm	1	3	3		
Underwood, Hamblet	2	1	4		
Yeals, William	1	1	2		
Bullard, James	2	3	4		
Medien, John	1	3	2		
Smith, Elias	2		2		
Bilbury, Laurance	1		2		
Honey, Bias	1		3		
Jenkins, Saml	1	1	1		1
Mitchel, Reuben	1	1	3		1
Harrod, Joseph	1	2	2		
Gregory, Thos	1	1	3		7
Hathcock, John	2	3	4		
Pilint, Cary			2		5
Straughn, Ricd	1	3	1		
Jones, Aquilla	1		2		
Ferrington, John	1	1	2		
Odam, Thos	1	3	2		
Brown, Thos	1		4		
Rigsbey, Luke	1	4	2		

HILLSBOROUGH DISTRICT, GRANVILLE COUNTY.[1]

ABRAHAM'S PLAINS DISTRICT.						ABRAHAM'S PLAINS DISTRICT—continued.						BEAVER DAM DISTRICT.					
Smith, Samuel						Tindal, John						Pope, John					
Smith, Samuel, Jun						Roberts, Willis						Pope, Osborn					
Downey, James						Downey, James, Jun						Pope, John, Jr.					
Howard, John						Raven, John, Jun						Moore, Major					
West, James						Graves, Ralph						Lyles, Wm					
Davis, Baxter						Montague, Latteney						Bailey, Jeremiah					
Norman, George						Melone, Robert						Bailey, John					
Leavel, Edward						Allen, Capt. Grant						Mangum, Absolom					
Pittard, John						Allen, Thomas						Mangum, James					
More, John						Lewis, Howel, Jun., Esq.						Bradford, David, Jun					
Graves, Henry						Lewis, Howel						Phillips, David					
Williamson, Thomas						Knight, Jonathan, Esq.						Jones, Frances					
Towns, Henry						Butler, Anne						Jones, Samuel					
Hart, John						Owen, Jacob						Hawley, Jacob					
Smith, John						Morgan, Elizabeth						Horn, Howel					
Frasyier, Arthur						Hendrickson, Ezekiel						Lawrence, Wm					
Mitchel, Jacob						Knight, John						Nance, Harrod					
Montague, Henry						Knight, Wm						Harris, Edward					
Burrage, Edward						Amis, Wm						Buckhannon, Wm					
Hunt, James						Smith, Anderson						Tanner, Wm					
Graves, Mary						Williams, Thomas						Nance, Richard					
Chavis, James						Crieth, Samuel						Austine, Valentine					
Fraisyier, Wm						Oliver (Widow)						Pascall, James					
Owen, Frederick						Stamper, John						Hooker, John					
Owen, Wm. (son of James)						Burch, Nicholas						Huscatt, Farthy					
Owen, John						Hawley, Nathan						Brown, John					
Siddler, Jesse						Mutter, Thos						Champion, Charles					
Hester, Wm						Love, Allen (Est. of)						Bradford, Richard					
Raven, John						Crenshaw, Abram						Wilkerson, Wm					
Montague, Young						Oliver, Mary						Weaver, Wm					
Johnston, James						Yates, Lovit						Hays, Leonard					
												Harris, Harrison					

[1] Names taken from county tax lists.

HILLSBOROUGH DISTRICT, GRANVILLE COUNTY—Continued.

NAME OF HEAD OF FAMILY.	Free white males of 16 years and upward, including heads of families.	Free white males under 16 years.	Free white females, including heads of families.	All other free persons.	Slaves.
BEAVER DAM DISTRICT—continued.					
Glasgow, Richard					
Hendley, Wm					
Allen, Robert					
Bradford, Philemon, Jr					
Winningham, John					
Wright, Hannah					
Taylor, George					
Harp, Henry					
Bradford, David					
Bailey, Rich					
Mann, Arnold					
Bradford, Philemon					
Griffin, Lawrence					
Heflin, John					
Hooker, John, Jun					
Hudson, Drury					
Cape, Williamson					
Moore, John					
Thomas, John					
Heflin, Wm					
Heflin, Fielding					
Mills, Robert					
Bradford, Booker					
Champion, Joseph					
Holt, John					
Roberts, Thomas					
Bradford, Ephraim					
Mitchel, Isom					
Champion, John, Jun					
Mitchel, Jane					
Carrell, John					
Tanner, Finnings					
Weathers, James					
Nicholson, George					
Whitfield, John					
Anderson, Frank					
Clement, Simon					
Cavenaugh, George					
Harris, Christopher					
Bridgers, John					
Harris, John					
Peet, John					
Bridgers, Drury					
Fullar, Capt. Jones					
Fullar, David					
Allen, Champion					
Goodloe, Robert					
Leathers, James					
DUTCH DISTRICT.					
Hunt, William					
Peck, John C					
Wilkerson, Wyatt					
Carver, Edmund					
Veasey, Elijah					
Clements, Thomas					
Fussel, Moses					
Walker, Nathaniel					
Jones, Thomas					
Stew, Jacob					
Cooke, Richard S					
Moore, George L					
Cash, Joseph					
Turner, Charles					
Moore, Benjamin					
Taggle, John					
Bailey, John					
Bailey, Stephen					
Walker, James					
Brasfield, Caleb					
Story, George					
Cash, Peter					
Cash, James					
Ornerry, Richard					
Byart, Mary					
Baxter, Joseph					
Bottoms, Thomas L					
Jarret, John					
Swinney, William					
Cozzort, Jesse					
Toller, John					
Wheeler, Benjamin					
Carnes, Joseph					
Farmer, John					
Emmery, Ephraim					
Brasfield, George					
Brasfield, Elizabeth					
Pizor, Matthew					
Swinney, Thomas					
Beck, Michael					
Landish, Joseph					
Tucker, Thomas					
Tucker, Frederick					

NAME OF HEAD OF FAMILY.	Free white males of 16 years and upward, including heads of families.	Free white males under 16 years.	Free white females, including heads of families.	All other free persons.	Slaves.
DUTCH DISTRICT—continued.					
McLemoore, James					
Hall, Futril					
Merreman, Malekiah					
Oakey, Joseph, Jun					
Beck, Frederick					
Culberhouse, Thomas W					
Tatom, John					
Beck, William					
Merreman, William					
Culberhouse, Jeremiah					
Hoofman, Jacob					
Jenkins, Thomas					
Adcocke, Bowling					
Harrison, Saria					
Lawrence, Abraham					
Haskins, James					
Ogilvie, Harris					
Green, William					
Bradley, James					
Claxton, James					
Potter, Lewis					
Parker, Samuel					
Willard, Augustine E					
Withus, William					
Ogilvie, Kimbro					
Freeman, Gideon					
Jones, William, Jun					
Adcocke, John					
Wade, Anna					
Bullock, Micajah, Esq					
Tippett, John					
Harris, Samuel					
Williams, John					
EPPING FOREST DISTRICT.					
Fuller, Henry, Senr					
Roberts, William					
McDaniel, James					
Hornsby, William					
Thomason, Richard					
White, Valentine					
Roberts, Isaac					
White, Thomas					
Finch, John, Jun					
Edwards, John					
Fuller, Britton					
Johnson, Benjamin					
Alley, Rosser					
White, Mark					
Finch, Williamson					
Cook, William					
Floyd, Mosses					
Rogers, William					
Lloyd, Isaiah					
Fowler, William					
Laurance, John					
Highfield, Hezekiah					
Hickman, Corbin					
Roberson, Robert					
Kittrell, Jonathan, Jun					
Hunt, John					
Fuller, Henry, Jun					
Cook, Blanton					
Smith, Thomas					
Spears, Phillip					
Spears, John					
Leeman, William					
Bobbit, William					
Ragsbill, Backster					
Rogers, Joseph					
Roberson, Nicholas					
McDaniel, Joseph					
Floyd, William					
Parrish, Brisse					
Kittrell, Jonathan, Senr					
Finch, John, Senr					
Harding, Sterling					
Askyou, John					
Crowder, Ueel					
Tedder, James					
Johnson, Joseph					
Higgs, Leonard					
Finch, George					
Lock, John					
Laurance, Deborah					
Cooper, Kannon					
Kittrell, Joshua					
Hester, Joseph					
Fuller, Samuel					
Eaton, Chas. R					
Hays, Sarah					

NAME OF HEAD OF FAMILY.	Free white males of 16 years and upward, including heads of families.	Free white males under 16 years.	Free white females, including heads of families.	All other free persons.	Slaves.
EPPING FOREST DISTRICT—continued.					
Kittrell, Samuel					
Ragsdel, David					
Harp, John					
Rowler, James					
York, Thomas					
Moore, Charles, Jnr					
Harp, Thomas					
Moore, Charles, Senr					
Evins, Burrel					
FISHING CREEK DISTRICT.					
Peace, John, Sen					
Peace, Joseph					
Brummit, Nimrod					
Hayslip, Laborn					
Smith, John, Jun					
Williams, Walter					
Carden, James					
Moore, Joel					
Inschore, Stephen					
Lankfurd, John					
Parish, Jesse					
Petyfurd, William					
Harp, Sampson					
Tyler, Bartlet					
Walker, Wm					
Snellings, Barnet					
Chavons, Wm					
Thornton, Solomon					
Harp, Thos					
Anderson, Jacob					
Bass, Nathan					
Hays, Henry, Jun					
Cooper, John					
Lankfurd, Barrish					
Dickerson, John, Jr					
Miner, Wm					
Garrott, Jesse					
Earls, Jesse					
Dickerson, William					
Thomas, Christian					
Snellings, Ann					
Walker, Samuel, Sen					
Cooper, Conealut					
Bynum, Henry					
Newby, Thomas, Sen					
Barr, James					
Inscor, Reuban, Sen					
Inscor, Reuban, Jun					
Williams, Wm					
Hunt, Wm					
Hunt, Daniel					
Lankfurd, Henry					
Parrish, Elijah					
Cork, James					
Snelling, Hugh					
Smith, John, Sen					
Priddy, Wm					
Bass, Reubin					
Peace, Jos., Sr					
Smith, James					
Harp, John					
Fowler, James					
York, Thomas					
Moore, Charles, Jun					
Harp, Thomas, Sen					
Dickerson, John					
Dickerson, John					
Ball, Eligah					
Evins, Buril					
FORT CREEK DISTRICT.					
White, Wm. (X Roads)					
Carter, Jesse					
Kittle, Christopher					
Magehee, Benjn., Sen					
Magehee, Benjn					
Peace, John, Jr					
Vincent, Alex					
Vincent, Jacob					
Rogers, Wilson					
Magehee, Josiah					
Magehee, Jesse					
Philips, Garland					
Priddey, Robert					
Magehee, Joseph					
Simmons, John, Sen					
Bowers, Philemon					
Rust, John, Sr					
Rust, George					
Rust, Samuel					

HILLSBOROUGH DISTRICT, GRANVILLE COUNTY—Continued.

NAME OF HEAD OF FAMILY.	Free white males of 16 years and upward, including heads of families.	Free white males under 16 years.	Free white females, including heads of families.	All other free persons.	Slaves.
FORT CREEK DISTRICT—continued.					
Evans, Morran					
Champion, John					
Bradford, Benjn					
Nailing, Wm					
Blackley, James					
Blackley, Charles					
Welch, John					
Magehee, Robert					
Williams, Jeremiah					
Rogers, John					
Mayfield, Valentine					
Jenkins, James					
Whitlar, Nicholas					
Priddey, George					
Priddey, Thomas					
Blackwell, James					
Magehee, Nathan					
White, George					
Carter, Thomas					
Carter, Alex					
Mayfield, Abe					
Champion, John, Sr					
Blalock, David					
Myars, Jacob					
White, John					
Taylor, Lewis					
Mills, Wm					
White, Coleman					
Jeffrys, Wm					
Huddleston, John					
Gillam, Harris					
Lewiston, James					
Knowland, Chs					
Jones, Abraham					
Gowin, Jenkin					
Simmons, James					
Homes, Sam'l					
Bradford, John					
Magehee, Nathan					
Knowland, Dan'l, Jr					
Vincent, Peter					
Vincent, Isaac					
Blalock, Jeremiah					
Jones, Jonathan					
Cooke, Claborn					
White, Searl					
Cooke, Shem, Sr					
Alison, Robert					
Norris, James					
Heflin, Chs					
Taylor, Edm					
GOSHEN DISTRICT.					
Weston, James					
Oliver, John					
Olliver, Peter					
Mitchel, Josiah					
Knott, John					
Pointer, Samuel					
Jordan, Robert					
Ligon, Thos					
Beezley, Stephen					
Parrish, John					
Barker, Ambrose, Esq					
Ragland, Stephen (Est. of)					
Loyd, William					
Hester, Robert					
Knott, David					
Pool, Thomas					
Douglass, Joseph					
Evans, John					
Chandler, James					
Wade, Robert					
Wright, Francis					
Chandler, Joseph					
Lassiter, William					
Bedford, James					
Daniel, Chesley					
Tack, John					
Sandford, Robert					
Ashman, Lewis					
Bennet, Capt. Peter					
Daniel, Martin					
Owen, John, Jun					
Williams, Gideon					
Edwards, Thomas					
Pettyford, Seth					
Blanks, Joseph					
Jones, Reuban					
Obrian, Patrick					
Harris, John					

NAME OF HEAD OF FAMILY.	Free white males of 16 years and upward, including heads of families.	Free white males under 16 years.	Free white females, including heads of families.	All other free persons.	Slaves.
GOSHEN DISTRICT—continued.					
Harris, Robert					
Glass, William					
Mitchel, James					
Webb, John					
Graves, Henry, Jun					
Milinder, William					
Wilkerson, David					
Duty, Richard					
Aplin, Thomas					
Bennet, Lewis					
Le May, Susannah (Est. of)					
Wilkerson, Francis					
Palmer, William					
Jones, Ambrose, Sen					
Harris, Charles					
Le May, Samuel					
Lewis, Nathaniel					
Kennon, John					
Winfrey, James					
Wade, Charles					
Owen, John, Sen					
Pettyford, John					
Saterwhite, Michael					
Owen, Thomas					
Grant, Thos					
Allen, Francis					
Lumsden, John					
Paterson, Andrew					
Person, Thomas, Esq					
HENDERSON DISTRICT.					
Williams, Jno., Esq					
Burton, Ro., Esq					
Sneed, Step'n					
Burdin, Jno					
Gilliam, Wm					
Stark, Jas					
Craft, Thos					
Jordan, Arth					
Cox, Charnich					
Gresham, Rich'd					
Gresham, Stephen					
Harrison, Isham					
Smith, Ransom					
Smith, Edm'd					
Morse, John					
Stringfellers, Rich'd					
Craft, John					
Daniel, Joseph					
Pollin, William					
Rainwater, John					
Morse, Reuben					
Christian, Gideon					
Crichter, Thomas					
Wiggins, Thomas					
King, George					
Wiggins, Fred					
Seears, Joseph					
Grisham, Henry					
Harris, John					
Gillpin, Henry					
Henderson, Ples't					
Weaver, Minor					
Roland, Thos					
Perdue, George					
Denton, Benj					
Brame, James					
Brame, Thos					
Reaves, Sam'l					
Brack, Sam'l					
Barnes, Mirim'c					
Hanks, William					
Mitchel, Major					
Morse, Phillis					
Williams, Sam'l					
Weaver, John					
Yancy, Sterling					
Weaver, Edw'd					
Bowden, Francis					
Mitchel, David					
Mitchel, Ely					
Mitchel, Phillis					
Henderson, Rich'd					
Satterwhite, Thos					
Kimboll, Bartho					
Reves, Samuel					
Temerson, Will					
Shullhines, John P					
Macon, John					
Chadwick, John					
Brack, Samuel, Jun					

NAME OF HEAD OF FAMILY.	Free white males of 16 years and upward, including heads of families.	Free white males under 16 years.	Free white females, including heads of families.	All other free persons.	Slaves.
ISLAND CREEK DISTRICT.					
Jones, Vinkler					
Kelley, Thomas					
Terry, Roland					
Norwood, Benj'n					
Pitchford, Daniel					
Davis, Absolom					
Davis, Solomon					
Scott, John					
Smith, Joseph					
Cardwell, Thomas					
Smith, Lenard					
Byars, William					
Perry, Peter					
Park, William					
Grizel, Harley					
Hargrove, Richard					
Fleman, Henry					
Hanks, Arguile					
Mason, David					
Akin, James, Sen					
Strome, Bartholomew					
Lewis, James					
Johnson, Henry					
Collins, John					
Akin, James					
Terry, Stephen					
Glover, Cap'n Dan'l					
Glover, Joab					
Matthews, James					
Gober, Martha					
Collins, Thomas					
Norwood, Jordan					
Scurry, Benjn					
Satterwhite, James					
Norwood, Gillum					
Akin, James					
Davis, Auguston					
Akin, Joseph					
Laniere, Lewis					
Duncan, William					
Barnett, Jesse					
Akin, Isom					
Whitlow, Jordan					
Harris, Christopher					
Lyne, Henry					
Hencock, Benj'n					
Smith, Sam'l					
Driskel, Timothy					
Smith, Henry					
Johnson, John					
Smith, James					
Gooch, Gidion					
Redd, Field					
Gober, William					
Sneed, Sam'l					
Sneed, Dudley					
Taylor, John (Br. G.)					
Barnitt, John					
Kindrick, Thomas					
Summerhill, Charles					
Bridges, Joseph					
Robertson, Benj'n					
Chapman, George					
Moor, William					
Parrish, Humphry					
Williams, Daniel					
Hargrove, John					
Robertson, John					
Dotson, Charles					
Dotson, William, Jr					
Barnett, Sarah C					
Hyde, Robert					
Harper, Jesse (Estate of)					
Hammond, Joab					
Lewis, Frances					
Suite, Dent					
Bullock, William					
Taylor, John, Esq. (Estate of)					
Bullock, James					
Goldsmith, Thomas					
Taylor, Elizabeth					
Penn, John					
Marshal, William					
Patillo, Rev. Henry					
Akin, Isom					
Hargrove, Stephen					
Butler, Reubin					
Ruth, David					
Burroughs, James					
Johnson, Benj'n					
Terry, James					

HILLSBOROUGH DISTRICT, GRANVILLE COUNTY—Continued.

NAME OF HEAD OF FAMILY.	Free white males of 16 years and upward, including heads of families.	Free white males under 16 years.	Free white females, including heads of families.	All other free persons.	Slaves.	NAME OF HEAD OF FAMILY.	Free white males of 16 years and upward, including heads of families.	Free white males under 16 years.	Free white females, including heads of families.	All other free persons.	Slaves.	NAME OF HEAD OF FAMILY.	Free white males of 16 years and upward, including heads of families.	Free white males under 16 years.	Free white females, including heads of families.	All other free persons.	Slaves.
ISLAND CREEK DISTRICT—continued.						**KNAP OF LEEDS DISTRICT—continued.**						**RAGLAND DISTRICT—continued.**					
Moor, William						Clement, John						Wright, John					
Hester, Zacheriah						Webb, Wm						Plummer, Zephaniah					
Gooch, Joseph						Merrit, Stephen						Ragland, William					
Melton, Henry						Green, Daniel						Currin, Hugh					
Burch, Nicholas						Brayleton, Jacob						Sears, John					
Crawley, Robert												Kimball, Henry					
Cocker, William						**OXFORD DISTRICT.**						Bass, Ed					
Wilson, Henry												Davis, Jos					
Hester, Abraham						Linsay, Sarah						Davis, P					
Carter, Thomas, Jun						Sniper, Nathaniel						Grisham, James					
Stubbs, William						Searcy, William Hargrove						Norman, Thos					
Lyne, James						Johnston, Saml						Parish, Charles					
Lanier, Thomas						Frasier, Jeremiah						Parrish, Wm., Sen					
Howel, John						Hicks, Thomas						Parrish, Wm., Jun					
Dodson, William						Howard, Allen						Harris, Darnin					
Robertson, Mary						Bussure, Francis						Parris, Thos					
Sumervil, John						Mitchell, Charles						Bishop, Jas					
Maron, Daniel						Upchurch, William						Williams, Nath'n					
						Cothran, William						Hays, Joshua					
KNAP OF LEEDS DISTRICT.						Gray, Morton						Hicks, Wm., Jun					
						Walker, Solomon						Earles, John, Sen					
Tims, Amos						Walker, Samuel						Pettyford, Drury					
Green, Henry						Hunt, John						Earls, John					
Addams, Samuel						Hunt, Samuel						Crews, James					
Walker, Mary						Maloney, Wm						Harris, George					
Tatum, William						Parker, Jeptha						Taylor, Will'm					
Green, Joab						Beardon, Benja						Hicks, Thos					
Oakey, Micajah						Parham, Wm						Wicker, Thos					
Ellis, Joseph						Longmin, Wm						Foups, Mat'w					
Ferrybough, Jacob						Crews, Caleb						Crews, Thos					
Mangum, Joseph						Walker, John						Wilkins, Rich					
Cozzart, Ben						Minor, John						Crews, Gidion					
Cozzart, Jacob						Hopkins, George						Alston, George					
Eastwood, Israel						Howel, Thomas						Wasff, George					
Long, George						White, Phil., Jun						Neister, Benj					
Eastes, Silvanus						Hester, Francis						Rivis, Lan					
Brissil, Francis						Butler, Isaac						Wilkins, Thos					
Ford, Absalom						Towel, James						——, Drury					
Clement, Stephen						Hilliard, James						Ridley, Bromfield					
Eastis, William						Hicks, Robert						Brodie, John					
Jones, Charles						Hester, Zachariah											
Jones, William (big)						Williams, Thos						**TABB'S CREEK DISTRICT.**					
Clement, Obediah						Butler, Thos											
Rose, Frederick						Taylor, Joseph						Shemwell, James					
Wilburn, Zachariah						White, Phil., Sen						Parrish, David					
Wright, William						Tally, Reuben						Bristow, John					
Patterson, David						White, Jonathan						Tatom, Barnard					
Wright, George						Tomason, Thos						Hays, Theophilus					
Phillips, Bennett						Harris, Charles						Johnston, Wm., Sen					
Bowlen, John, Sen						Harris, Samuel (Virga)						Sute, John					
Jones, Edward						Rose, Thos						Johnson, Gideon					
Arnold, William						Clay, Samuel						Parham, Cannon					
Perkerson, Joel						Mathews, Littlebury						Parham, Thomas, Sen					
Jonse, Moses						Harris, Robert						Johnson, Noel					
Waller, Joseph						Sample, John						Johnson, Thomas					
Clement, Samuel						Noland, Edward						Lanford, Jesse					
Mangum, Howel						Harris, Sherward						Clark, Leonard					
Partic, Ben						Parham, Thos						Hays, Joshua					
Borolen, Wm						Lock, Jona						Page, Lewis					
Cole, Wm						Pulliam, John						Hicks, Samuel					
Terry, Stephen						Robards, John						Reaves, Hardy					
Oakey, Joseph						Taylor, Edward, Sen						Reaves, William					
Harris, Claburn						Boyd, John						Hicks, William					
Ogilsvie, Smith						Hunt, George						Reaves, Frederick					
Ogilsvie, Wm						Bird, Robert						Johnson, Jonathan					
Bullock, Jeremiah						Marshell, John						Johnson, William, Jr					
Bullock, Joshua						Morris, John						Parham, Lewis					
Mauler, Jno. Wm						Hunt, George						Parham, Ephraim					
Cozzort, Ann						Critcher, James						Dunkin, John					
Meadows, Jesse						Locust, Valentine						Wright, William					
Hunt, James						Taburn, Drury						Hayes, Joseph					
Jones, Brereton						Mitchel, Arch'd						Parham, Avery					
Tims, Hollis						Anderson, Lewis						Parham, Thomas, Jun					
Eastis, Lodowick												Morriss, Henry					
Adcock, Leonard						**RAGLAND DISTRICT.**						Biram, John					
Cozzort, David												Hutchinson, Joshua					
Veasey, Zebulon						Rice, Thos						Hedgpeth, Carter					
Partee, Charles						Jetter, Sam'l						Riggs, Zachariah					
Gafford, Reuben						Ragland, Reuben						Woodall, Absolam					
Hawkins, John						Ragland, Amis						Bristow, James					
Harris, Richard						Loyd, Edw						Parham, Isham					
Parker, Amos						Driskall, Dennis						Debruler, Micajah					
Adcock, Edward						Willson, John						Allison, Robert					
Goss, Thomas						Hicks, Harris						Allison, John					
Primrose, Wm						Williams, Charles						Bryant, Rowland					
Jackson, Samuel						Parish, David						Barton, William					
Chambless, Joel						Parish, Claborn						Mathis, William					
Bullock, Charles						Bell, Josa						Fowler, Henry					
Hawkins, Matthew						Bates, John						Parham, William					
Waller, Zephaniah						Hicks, Bishop						Parham, John					
Pulliam, Barnett						Lindsey, Elijah						Whitlow, Nathan					
Gorch, Rowlen						Fordwine, Lemuel						Hicks, David					
Knott, James						Allen, Samuel						Bristow, Philemon					
Jones, Wm						Thomson, Thos						Farer, Searcy					
												Smith, Edward					

HILLSBOROUGH DISTRICT, GRANVILLE COUNTY—Continued.

NAME OF HEAD OF FAMILY.	Free white males of 16 years and upward, including heads of families.	Free white males under 16 years.	Free white females, including heads of families.	All other free persons.	Slaves.
TABB'S CREEK DISTRICT—continued.					
Parham, Isham, Jun					
Parham, John, Jun					
Hopkins, Ann					
Jett, Stephen					
Higgs, Zacharias					
TAR RIVER DISTRICT.					
Slaughter, Jacob, Sen					
Slaughter, Jacob (Taylor)					
Dunkin, Geo					
Roberts, James					
Wood, John					
Williams, Solomon					
Obryan, Dennis					
Badget, Wm					
Hill, John					
Gooch, Danl					
Forsythe, James					
Bass, Rich					
Dunkin, Harrison					
Brinkley, Peter					
Meadows, Michael					
Briggs, Richard					
TAR RIVER DISTRICT—continued.					
Hopgood, Hezekiah					
Gunter, Jesse					
Hester, Wm					
Pettyford, George					
Frazer, Ephraim					
Badget, John					
Lumpkin, Anthony					
Harris, Anthony (son of Rich.)					
Thomason, John					
Mathews, John					
Goss, Shearmon					
Brinkley, James, Sr					
Long, Charles					
Johnson, Isham					
Clark, Nathan'l					
Cock, Wm					
Meadows, James					
Meadows, Daniel					
Washington, John, Esq					
Wells, Miles					
Adcock, Robert					
Brinkley, James, Jun					
Badget, Peter					
Philpot, Wm					
TAR RIVER DISTRICT—continued.					
Oakley, Thos					
Thorp, John, Sen					
Terry, James					
Thorp, John, Jun					
Oakley, William					
Slaughter, Jacob, Jr					
Cragg, John, Jun					
Millener, James					
Gooch, Amos					
Shearman, Michael					
Fowler, Richard					
Cragg, John, Senr					
Russel, John					
Howard, Graves					
Bass, Benj., Jun					
Bass, Benj., Sen					
Putman, Benja					
Gill, William, Esq					
Bruer, Amery					
Williams, Capt. John					
Brinkley, Richard					
Jones, John					
Pulliam, Barnett					

HILLSBOROUGH DISTRICT, ORANGE COUNTY.[1]

NAME OF HEAD OF FAMILY.	Free white males of 16 years and upward, including heads of families.	Free white males under 16 years.	Free white females, including heads of families.	All other free persons.	Slaves.
CASWELL DISTRICT.					
Hunter, Robt					
Russell, Alex'r					
McDaniel, Eli					
Dill, Isaac					
Bradshaw, Thos					
Pain, Joseph					
Durham, John					
Roach, James					
Thompson, John					
McVey, James					
O'Daniel, John					
Millison, John					
Trip, John					
Taylor, Hardiman					
Peacock, Samuel					
Carter, Wm					
Moore, John					
Moore, Rich'd					
Rhodes, John					
Harsey, Isaac					
Dale, Henry					
Crawford, James					
Isel, Randall					
Pinnin, James					
Moore, John					
Mickle, Abraham					
Willis, James					
Morrow, William					
Cate, Robt					
Durham, John					
Sykes, Allen					
Sykes, John					
Cate, Richard					
Cate, Thos					
Cate, Joseph					
Cate, Robert					
Moore, William					
Davis, Benj					
Durham, Matthew					
Hunnecut, Robt					
Bates, James					
Lashley, Thos					
Lindsay, John					
Robinson, Athanarius					
Stalworth, Joseph					
Strader, John					
Kelley, Chanler					
Durham, Thos					
Leary, Benj					
Kirk, James					
Cate, John					
Workman, John					
Williams, Peter					
Cate, Stephen					
Millikan, Robt					
Millikan, James					
Ray, John					
Millikan, Charles					
Dixon, Benj					
Durham, Wm					
Buckner, Wm					
CASWELL DISTRICT—continued.					
Williams, Fred'k					
O'Daniel, Henry					
Carrigan, John					
Shy, Jesse					
Stroud, Wm					
Brewer, Henry					
Kirk, Lewis					
Horton, Abraham					
Curtins, John					
Austen, Wm					
Cate, Thos					
McDaniel, John					
Lashley, Barnet					
Edwards, Henry					
Edwards, John, Sr					
Cate, Thos., Jr					
Kirk, Wm					
Christmas, Mary					
Pratt, Janie					
King, Thos					
Gibson, James					
Nichol, Benj					
Pickett, Henry					
Holwood, Thos., Jr					
Moore, James					
Holwood, Thos					
Roberts, James					
Ray, Wm					
Thompson, Thos					
Thompson, James					
Thompson, Wm					
Thompson, Thos., Jr					
Paid, John					
McMullin, Sam'l					
Powall, John					
Clendening, Wm					
Johnston, Geo					
Johnston, James					
Pain, James					
Smith, Reuben					
Smith, David					
Smith, Wm					
Jones, Jonathan					
McCracken, Jeremiah					
Kennedy, John					
Williams, Arthur					
Howard, Thos					
Jones, Aquilla					
McDaniel, Daniel					
Pugh, Daniel					
McDaniel, James					
Gordon, Wm					
Rainey, John					
Thompson, John					
Pickard, John					
Pugh, John					
Trousdale, James					
Trousdale, John					
Ray, Wm					
Baker, Tobias					
Lewis, Henry					
CASWELL DISTRICT—continued.					
Bradford, Joseph					
Jones, Thos					
Jones, Francis					
Marshall, Jacob					
Murdock, Wm					
Morrow, Andrew					
Thompson, James					
Harvey, Eli					
Pickett, Alex'r					
Pickett, John, Jr					
Patton, Catherine					
McPherson, Wm					
Holladay, Wm					
Holladay, Robt					
Wilson, Thos					
Andrews, Robt					
Ray, Robt					
Holladay, Henry					
Thompson, James					
McDaniel, John					
Stockard, James					
McDaniel, James					
Newlin, John					
Tagart, Isaac					
Rayson, John (of Robert)					
Allen, James					
Matthews, James					
Newlin, James					
Maris, George (Est. of)					
Madden, George					
Woody, James, Jn					
Andrew, Wm					
Laughlin, Rich'd					
Ray, Wm., Sr					
Morrison, Rob't					
Brooks, John					
Powell, Jesse					
Carter, John					
Holladay, Henry, Jr					
Common, Wm					
Lindley, Mary					
Dix, Zachariah					
Dix, Nathan					
Andrew, Rob't, Jr					
Woody, John					
Woody, James					
Woody, Wm					
Grimes, John					
Lowrey, James					
Whitted, Thos					
Woody, Joseph					
Way, Nathaniel					
Patton, John					
Harvey, Nathan					
Shoridine, Geo					
Murray, John					
Cox, Moses					
Paris, Wm					
Wilkins, George					
Mann, John					

[1] Names taken from county tax lists.

HILLSBOROUGH DISTRICT, ORANGE COUNTY--Continued.

NAME OF HEAD OF FAMILY.	Free white males of 16 years and upward, including heads of families.	Free white males under 16 years.	Free white females, including heads of families.	All other free persons.	Slaves.
CASWELL DISTRICT—continued.					
Cate, Bernard					
Carters, Nathaniel					
Bradley, Enoch					
Shy, John					
Edwards, Melen					
Hackney, John					
Edwards, John					
Edwards, Rich'd (heirs of)					
Edwards, Sylvanus (heirs of)					
Edwards, Wm (Estate of)					
Christmas, Rich'd					
Holmes, John					
Armstrong, John					
Morrison, Nathaniel					
Roach, Lewis					
Partin, James					
Lindley, Jonathan					
Lindley, Wm (Estate of)					
CHATHAM DISTRICT.					
Marley, Adam					
Marley, Samuel					
Stalcup, Wm					
Holt, George, Sr					
Harden, John					
Campbell, George					
Cook, Nehemiah					
Gimlin, James					
Williams, Wm					
Bowen, James					
Fawcett, Wm					
Harvey, John					
O'Neal, Wm					
Morris, Joseph					
Crickman, Timothy					
Morten, Jacob					
Sullivan, Dan'l					
Smathers, Wm					
Cook, Ephraim					
Tate, Rob't					
Jackson, Wm					
Tate, Zacheus					
Charles, Michael					
Burch, James					
Judge, Bryant					
Barber, Allen					
Nelvin, John					
Martin, Henry					
Boyle, James, Jr					
Boyles, John					
Boyles, James, Sr					
Boyles, John, Jr					
Bracken, James					
Moore, Thos					
Boyles, Wm					
Robertson, Hugh					
Dinning, David					
Dinning, David, Jr					
McCauley, Joseph					
Smith, Sam'l					
Smith, Mary					
Garrison, Jacob					
Moore, Rob't					
Bracken, Isaac					
Simmons, Peter					
Bracken, Isaac, Sr					
Smith, Andrew					
Dinning, John					
Groin, Alex'r					
Moore, John					
Moore, James					
McLean, James					
Robe'tson John					
Sloss, John					
Rainey, Wm					
Rainey, Benj					
Litt, James					
Wishart, Absolom					
Wishart, Elias					
Wishart, Jacob					
Mickle, Andrew					
Davis, Wm					
Browing, John					
Garrison, Garret					
Smathers, Thos					
Swathers, John					
Smathers, Alex'r					
Gwin Edward					
Bracken, Wm					
Hurdle, Hardy					
Jacobs, Henry					

NAME OF HEAD OF FAMILY.	Free white males of 16 years and upward, including heads of families.	Free white males under 16 years.	Free white females, including heads of families.	All other free persons.	Slaves.
CHATHAM DISTRICT—continued.					
Straders, John					
Straders, George					
Straders, Henry					
Holston, Jacob					
Cockledress, Michael					
Haney, John					
Crowden, Jeremiah					
Garner, Lewis					
Hatchett, Wm					
Garner, Parish					
Holt, John, Jr					
Coble, John					
Holt, Jacob					
Holt, Israel					
Garrison, John					
Sellers, Thos					
Holt, George					
Thomas, Edward					
Harden, Nicholas					
Given, Wm					
Turner, Rob't					
Albright, Ludwick					
Albright, Geo					
Holt, Jeremiah					
Bowldin, Wm					
Whitesill, Adam					
Robbs, Alex'r					
Albright, Philip					
Suthard, John					
Jordan, Jonathan					
McCracken, John					
Huffine, Dan'l					
Jeffers, Garner					
Jeffers, Evan					
Jeffers, John					
Powell, John					
Powell, John, Jr					
Hatmaker, Malachi					
Hatmaker, Malachi, Jr					
Coble, Philip					
Lynbury, Jacob					
Crisman, Geo					
McClure, Henry					
Holt, Michael					
Harden, John					
Holt, John					
Albright, Jacob					
Holt, John, Sr					
Holt, Christopher					
Albright, John					
Gant, John					
Killin, John					
Hudson, Chamberlain					
Staves, John					
Long, Casper					
Cook, John					
Cook, David					
Cook, Edward					
Cook, Archibald					
Osborn, James					
Hudson, John					
James, Abner					
James, Solomon					
Philips, Jesse					
Gant, John					
Gant, John, Sr					
Dawley, John					
Pyles, James					
Cook, John					
Stark, John					
McCulloch, Robt					
Garrison, Geo					
Tickel, Peter					
Tickle, John					
Huffman, Suffah					
White, Henry					
Wallace, Miles					
Brinkley, Peter					
Brinkley, Peter, Jr					
Coble, Antony					
Pate, John					
Griffiths, Wm					
Melvin, Edmund					
Armstrong, John					
Averett, Nathan					
Campbell, Ezekiel					
Bracken, Thomas					
Murray, Jonathan					
Servir, Henry					
McCulloch, Thos					
Tate, James					
Bewswick, Caleb					
Love, Thomas					
Dunnivan, John					
Collins, John					

NAME OF HEAD OF FAMILY.	Free white males of 16 years and upward, including heads of families.	Free white males under 16 years.	Free white females, including heads of families.	All other free persons.	Slaves.
HILLSBORO DISTRICT.					
Cloud, Daniel					
Allison, John					
Thompson, Sam					
Neelson, Abraham					
Turner, Edward					
Ringstaff, Conrad					
Clark, Wm					
Thompson, Albert					
Thompson, Benja					
Hastings, James					
Collins, Andrew					
Thompson, James					
Huntingdon, Roswell					
Palmer, Martin					
Hart, Stephen					
Crabtree, Thomas					
Jamison, Wm					
Collins, Eli					
McCallum, Jonathan					
Murdock, James					
Hastings, Henry, Sr					
Aston, Wm					
Aston, Sam'l					
Watson, James					
Adams, John					
Lamb, Benj					
Crabtree, James					
Bailey, Thos					
Roberson, Michael					
Rountree, Thos					
Woods, Sam'l					
Taylor, John					
Hall, Wm					
Shannon, Wm					
McCaulis, Jane					
Ray, James					
Roberson, Michael, Jr					
Thompson, John					
Roberson, James					
Tinnin, John					
Combs, Wm					
Tarlton, James					
Breeze, John					
Johnston, Thos					
Hall, Robt					
Whealey, Benj					
McCulloch, John					
McCulloch, James					
McMahan, Dan'l					
Anderson, John					
McCaulis, John					
Collins, Enoch					
Ray, Robt					
Allison, David					
McBroom, Andrew					
Anderson, Jane					
Allison, Elizabeth					
Griffin, Andrew					
Williams, David					
Parks, Wm					
Rountree, John					
Rountree, Charles					
Smith, Robt					
Murdock, Agnes					
Donaldson, James					
Clark, James (Hiss)					
Nichols, John					
Wilson, Robt					
Wilkison, James					
Carson, James					
Clark, Thos					
Clark, Wm					
Bane, Thos					
McKee, Alex'r					
McCulloch, Robt					
Crabtree, Wm					
Anderson, Robt					
Turrentine, John					
Wood, Wm. (Bl. Smith)					
Clark, Wm. (Eno)					
Clark, James (Estate of)					
Whitehead, Wm					
Jackson, Wm., Sr					
Williams, Rich'd					
Ray, Charles					
Johns, John					
Waggoner, Catharine					
Miller, Jesse					
Strayhorn, Gilbert					
Hannah, David					
Clark, Wm. (L. R.)					
Woods, John, Sr					
Niel, Robt					
Jackson, Isaac					
Boreland, Alex'r					

HILLSBOROUGH DISTRICT, ORANGE COUNTY—Continued.

NAME OF HEAD OF FAMILY.	Free white males of 16 years and upward, including heads of families.	Free white males under 16 years.	Free white females, including heads of families.	All other free persons.	Slaves.	NAME OF HEAD OF FAMILY.	Free white males of 16 years and upward, including heads of families.	Free white males under 16 years.	Free white females, including heads of families.	All other free persons.	Slaves.	NAME OF HEAD OF FAMILY.	Free white males of 16 years and upward, including heads of families.	Free white males under 16 years.	Free white females, including heads of families.	All other free persons.	Slaves.
HILLSBORO DISTRICT— continued.						HILLSBORO TOWN.						ORANGE DISTRICT— continued.					
Clark, James (L. R.)						Allison, John						Murray, James					
Allison, John, Sr						Thompson, Henry						Estor, Samuel					
Allison, John, Jr						Stone, David						Patton, John					
Hammond, Edward						Stubbins, Joseph						Daly, Wm					
Nichols, Baldwin						Wilson, Isabel						Dorris, John					
Nichols, Jonathan, Sr						Hunter, James						Williams, Thos					
Gray, John						Kelly, Wm						Mebane, Sam'l					
Nichols, Jonathan, Jr						Finley, Hugh						McAdams, John					
Regan, Thos						Courtney, Wm						Trolinger, Henry					
Copeland, David						Brooks, Thos						Barnwell, James					
Wilson, James						McCauley, Wm						Hodge, Robt					
Wilson, John						McCauley, John						Murray, James					
Woods, Wm						Ferguson						Murray, John					
Jordan, Robt						McCollom, Harvey						Pinnix, Overton					
Andrews, James						Bevans, Thos						Crawford, Hugh					
Jordan, Enos						Newman, Wm						McAdams, Hugh					
Jackson, James						Harris, Starling						Giffy, William					
Mitchell, John						Moore, Joseph						Carswell, John					
Killin, Wm						Alves, Walter						Beasom, Jacob					
Fowler, Sam'l						Wilkerson, Vincent						Anderson, James					
Keiley, John (Eno)						Anderson, Kenneth						McAdams, James					
Riley, Jacob						Whitehead, Jehu						Stanford, William					
Allison, James						Heal, Joseph						Anderson, Alexander					
Davis, John						Phillips, James						Bradford, William					
Clark, James, Sr						Farmer, Thos						Pattison, William					
Clark, James, Jr						Whithead, Wm						Murray, James					
McKee, Wm						Brooks, Asa						Whitmore, Charles					
Bowls, Thos						Huskins, Geo						Whitmore, Jesse					
Bowls, Wm						Duncan, John						Long, Koonrad					
Wood, John (son of Hugh)						Keys, James H						Hodge, William					
Riley, John (L. R.)						Nichols, John						Hodge, Margaret					
Armstrong, Wm						Cain, Wm						Eccles, William					
Riley, Wm. (L. R.)						Taylor, John						King, Armore					
Faucett, James						Burke, Andrew						Lindsay, Ely					
Barlow, Benj						Ray, David						Lapsley, James					
Thompson, Sam'l						Childs, Francis						McCracken, Samuel					
Jordan, Thos						McQuister, William						Thomas, Jacob					
Berry, Robt, Jr						Sharp, Joseph						Elmore, Randall					
Jackson, Jacob						Croer, John						Blackard, William					
Cragston, George						Hooper, Wm						Paul, Elizabeth					
Chambers, Sam'l												Baker, Joseph					
Strayhorn, James						ORANGE DISTRICT.						Beason, Henry					
Harvey, Caleb												Justice, John					
Crabtree, Wm						Mebane, Wilson						Turner, James					
Burnside, Robt						Walker, John (Stiller)						Dorris, Robert					
Scarlett, John						Stradwick, William						Patton, Samuel					
Toulson, Thos						Nelson, Sam'l						Allen, James					
Faucett, David						Walker, John						Chance, William					
Barton, Thos						Walker, Wm						Elmore, John					
Fruit, Uriah						Walker, Peter						Elmore, Athy					
Faucett, Rich'd						Walker, Andrew						Tate, Joseph					
Berry, John						Bradford, David						Faucett, Robert					
Blake, Isham						Dobson, James						Daly, John					
Fade, Joseph						Boyd, George						Wason, Henry					
Holden, John						Douglas, David						Cantrill, Mary					
Holden, Thos						Thompson, Joseph						Allen, George					
Flinlain, John						Foust, George						Foster, Richard					
Campbell, Wm						Douglas, William						Hall, Isaac					
Faucett, Ralph						Bryan, James						Ball, Richard					
Carson, Alex'r						Pate, James (Carpenter)						Elmore, Peter					
Berry, Robt						Bird, Thos						Hall, Levy					
Baldridge, Dan'l						Fitch, William						Hall, James					
Hart, James, Jr						Bird, Emmon						Dickson, Joseph					
McVey, Patrick						Bird, Rich'd						Pinnin, Robt					
Hart, James, Sr						Fitch, Thomas						Pinnin, Carnes					
Hart, Thomas						Bradford, George						Newland, Eli					
Berry, Joshua						Mason, Henry						King, Edward					
Allison, Joseph						Hicks, Zebedy						Stalcup, Isaac					
Jackson, Wm						Griffin, John						Rony, James					
Ray, John						Whiteside, Sam'l						Wason, Daniel					
Thompson, Theophilus						Hamilton, Joseph						Martin, Obadiah					
Hastings, Wm						Rives, John						Rippy, Thos					
Hastings, Henry						Lynch, Jesse						Gott, Robt					
Armstrong, John						Hughes, John						Trousdale, John					
Armstrong, James						Lynch, Thos						McFarlan, Walker					
Armstrong, Martin						Scott, Mary						Hopkins, James					
Elliott, John						Forrest, John						Patton, Robt					
Faddis, John						Fulton, Jesse						Foust, Deborah					
Miller, James						Witty, Joshua						Beason, John					
Cooper, Wm						Nelson, John						Stanford, Chas					
Benton, Jesse						Fulton, Margaret						McAdams, Joseph					
Hart, Col. Thos						Wilson, Robt						Scott, Wm					
Baldridge, James						Carr, James						McEvoy, John					
Parks, John						Wilkerson, Francis						Millington, John					
Doherty, Antony						Bradford, Thomas						Eccles, John					
Doherty, James						Whitman, Nowell						Norvel, Wm					
Tapp, Abner						Tinnin, Robert						King, John					
Taylor, Fred'k						Lapsley, David						Gooch, Wm. G					
Pratt, James						Wilson, Edward						Pendergast, Luke					
McCool, Archibald						Rickett, Edward						McMusty, John					
Gitson, David						Redding, Thos						Dorris, William					
Morgan, Thos						Murray, Wm						Dorris, Isaac					
												Stewart, Robert					

HILLSBOROUGH DISTRICT, ORANGE COUNTY—Continued.

NAME OF HEAD OF FAMILY.	Free white males of 16 years and upward, including heads of families.	Free white males under 16 years.	Free white females, including heads of families.	All other free persons.	Slaves.	NAME OF HEAD OF FAMILY.	Free white males of 16 years and upward, including heads of families.	Free white males under 16 years.	Free white females, including heads of families.	All other free persons.	Slaves.	NAME OF HEAD OF FAMILY.	Free white males of 16 years and upward, including heads of families.	Free white males under 16 years.	Free white females, including heads of families.	All other free persons.	Slaves.
ORANGE DISTRICT—continued.						**ST. ASAPH'S DISTRICT—continued.**						**ST. ASAPH'S DISTRICT—continued.**					
Smith, Andrew						Bates, Ambrose						Spoon, Adam					
Thomas, Hannah						Woolf, Wm						Coble, David					
Dicky, Zechariah						Jones, Jacob, Jr						Nankins, Mary					
McMon, James						Holt, James						Smith, Tobias					
Lindsay, Matthew						Woolf, Peter						Shofner, Martin					
Huggins, Jacob						May, John						Counselman, Jacob					
Stalcup, Tobias						Tinnin, James						Coble, Christian					
Smith, John						Wells, John						Mason, Phillp					
McCracken, Thomas						Eulis, Philip						Sharp, John					
McClury, Andrew						Williams, Elizabeth						Albright, John (B. Creek)					
Fawsett, Robt						Ward, Stephen						Noe, John					
Lynch, John						Springer, George						Bullock, John					
Gant, William						Sugars, John						Albright, Henry					
Stanford, John						Nail, Wm						Albright, Jacob					
Hodge, Joseph						Courtney, Daniel						Asley, Philip					
Freeland, James						Pike, Samuel						Sharp, Poyston					
Freeland, James, Jr						Graves, Jacob						Shofner, Michael					
Hawly, Daniel						Pridle, George, Sr						Moser, Nicholas					
Murray, Walter						Foust, George						Williams, Shafney					
Thomas, George						Cuntz, John						Albright, Jacob, Sr					
Shaw, Samuel						Paterson, James						Calk, Conrad					
Lake, Jacob						Smith, James						Kimbrough, Fred'k					
Lake, Rich'd						Piles, Conrad, Sr						Loy, John					
Wilson, Charles						Rogers, Wm						Patterson, John					
Galbreath, John						Snothley, Philip						Loy, Henry					
Lyons, Frances						Loy, George, Jr						Cook, Henry					
Davis, William						Pore, Peter						Sharp, Aaron					
Ross, James						Clap, John						May, Daniel, Sr					
Stevens, Henry						Diason, John						Eaflet, David					
Stanford, Rich'd						Graves, John						Neace, Martin					
Allen, John						Lynn, James						Albright, John					
Jefers, Jacob						May, Daniel, Jr						Kimbrough, Paul					
Gate, William						Homes, Rob't						Homes, James					
Hastings, John						Homes, Joseph						Godfrey, James					
Stevens, Benjamin						Ward, Wm						May, Ludwick					
Holloway, Martha						Taylor, Jonathan						Boggs, James					
Rippy, Mathew						Courtner, Peter						Helton, Peter					
Pate, Thos						Ware, John						Hilton, Abraham					
Rainey, William						Kinrow, Henry						Hilton, James					
Rippy, John						Fourt, Daniel						Hilton, Peter, Sr					
Wrightsmon, Peter						Shaddy, John						Cloud, Samuel					
Thompson, Joseph						Thomas, Abraham						Whinery, Abraham					
Carroll, Robt						Fogleman, Katrina						Foust, Peter					
Carroll, Henry						Fogleman, George						Clendennin, Joseph					
McAdam, Sam'l						Sharp, Aaron, Jr						Neece, George					
Galbreath, Wm						Sharp, G. (Estate of)						Norman, Joseph					
Dickson, Thos						Hiefman, John						Kimrow, George					
Dickson, Stuart						Hiefman, Jacob (Estate of)						Holt, John					
Stanford, James						Troxler, Barney						Jackson, Colby					
Smith, William						Peter, Conrad						Lynn, John					
Forrest, James						Troxler, Jacob						Smith, Adam, Jr					
Chance, Zekiel						Roberson, Thos						Gurbs, Nicholas					
Dicky, James						Thompson, Anthony						Moyer, Philip					
Dickson, James						Houseman, Joseph						Coble, Adam					
Dickson, Robt						Kime, Henry						Smith, Adam (Red)					
Rony, Benj'n						Alexander, James						Noe, Rosanna					
Fy, Larry						Alexander, John						Springer, Uriah					
Compton, Aquila						Henseroe, John						Darknet, Jacob					
White, David						Roberson, Nathaniel						Rinehart, David					
Huchison, James						Wells, Nathan						Esley, Malichi					
Ellis, Thos						Albright, Joseph						Brown, Wm					
Holgan, Thos						May, George						Marshall, Wm					
Phillips, David						Noe, Peter						Morrow, Wm					
Kirkpatrick, Alex'r						Albright, Ludwick						Brown, Ebenezer					
White, Stephen						Shofner, Frederick						Stout, Charles					
Hugh, Wm						Rich, Thos						Stout, Peter					
McCloskey, Ed						Smith, Adam						Stout, Joseph					
Barnwell, Robt						Fogleman, Malachi						Allen, John					
Sturges, John						Garnet, Henry						Freeman, Samuel					
McCauley, And'w						Moser, Philip						Underwood, Alex'r					
Mebane, Alex., Sr						Williams, Edward						Clark, John					
Mebane, David						Williams, Joseph						Hunnicutt, Moses					
Smith, Wm						Moser, Michael						Picket, Benj					
McMon, Wm						Antony, Jacob						Picket, Joshua					
Ward, Sutton						Shofner, Michael						Dale, Isaac					
Minson, Rich'd						Price, William						Freeman, Dan'l					
Blair, John						Fogleman, Michael						Beverly, Elijah					
McCracken, Robt						Moser, Jacob						Wells, Isaac					
Collins, Brice						Shofner, George						Wells, Joseph					
Thomas, Abram						Courtner, Daniel						Wells, Joseph, Jr					
Jones, Lewis						Fogleman, John						Gifford, Levi					
Paul, John						Stoner, Jeremiah						Moser, Frederick					
Ward, John						Stoner, Peter						Pike, John					
Murdock, Andrew						Rich, Jacob						Wheeler, John					
Mebane, Alex'r, Jr						Holt, Joshua						Buckingham, Joseph					
Shepperd, Wm						Randolph, John						Moser, Abraham					
						Campbell, Nancy						Dronebarger, Ludwick					
ST. ASAPH'S DISTRICT.						Calk, Henry						Long, John					
						Smith, Henry						Neal, James					
Harden, John						Eafler, John						Holt, Nicholas					
Williams, John						Patterson, Wm						Holt, Francis					
Roberson, James						Coble, John						Dison, Wm					
Roberson, Elijah						Spoon, John						Fogleman, Peter					
Hunnicutt, Dempsey						Coble, Henry						Noe, Joseph					
Hunnicutt, Lewis																	

HILLSBOROUGH DISTRICT, ORANGE COUNTY—Continued.

NAME OF HEAD OF FAMILY.	Free white males of 16 years and upward, including heads of families.	Free white males under 16 years.	Free white females, including heads of families.	All other free persons.	Slaves.
ST. ASAPH'S DISTRICT—continued.					
Clap, Barney					
Aycock, Jesse					
Hornaday, Lewis					
Stoneman, James					
Perkins, Thos. H.					
ST. MARK'S DISTRICT.					
Sears, Rosey					
Stanford, Israel					
Horn, Thos.					
Lewis, Enoch					
Massey, Abraham					
Bennett, James					
Daniel, Christopher					
Green, John					
Marcom, Richard					
Huggins, James					
Davis, Rich'd					
Watson, Dan'l					
Holden, John					
Holden, Wm., Jr.					
Hurst, John					
Rhodes, John					
Castlebury, James					
Hayes, Leonard					
Bilbo, Joseph					
Hampton, Robt.					
Lord, Wm.					
Horn, Wm., Jr.					
Marcom, Thos.					
Burgess, Thomas					
Davis, James					
Dollar, James					
Horn, Joshua					
Edwards, Charles					
Duggen, Alexander					
Price, John					
Fennell, Joseph					
Watson, Daniel, Jr.					
Massey, Abner					
Booth, Joseph					
Booth, Daniel					
Daniel, Sam'l					
Hobson, Wm.					
Marcom, Wm.					
Vaughan, James					
Barber, John, Jr.					
Davis, John					
Hall, David					
Daniel, George					
Hutson, Wm., Jr.					
Grice, Edward, Jr.					
Price, Joseph					
Hinkley, David					
Riggen, Powell					
Daniel, John					
Collies, Charles					
Barbee, Christopher					
Herndon, Benj.					
Merritt, Sam'l					
Tudor, Harris					
Price, Thos.					
Hall, Thos.					
Price, James					
Rhodes, Wm., Jr.					
Horn, James					
Barbee, Mark					
Leigh, John					
Grice, Ezekiel					
Shepherd, William					
Price, Edward					
Moore, John					
Rhodes, Wm.					
Dezern, James					
Barbee, John, Sr					
Carlton, Leonard					
Couch, John					
Couch, Edward					
Paterson, John Barbee					
Price, Wm.					
Davis, Nicholas					
Hobson, Elizabeth					
Moreland, Francis					
Shepherd, Sam'l					
Horn, Wm.					
Daniel, Paterson					
Marcom, John					
Anderson, Abraham					
Turner, Wm.					
Holder, Wm.					
Couch, James					
Edwards, John					
Hall, John					
Couch, Thos.					

NAME OF HEAD OF FAMILY.	Free white males of 16 years and upward, including heads of families.	Free white males under 16 years.	Free white females, including heads of families.	All other free persons.	Slaves.
ST. MARK'S DISTRICT—continued.					
Pickett, Wm.					
Pickett, Wm., Jr.					
Picket, Henry					
Farmer, Othniel					
Surles, Francis					
Surles, Thos.					
Farn, Sarah					
Herndon, George					
Herndon, Jachariah					
Pool, Wm.					
Pool, Samuel					
Standifer, Joshua					
Surles, Ephraim					
Glenn, King					
Glenn, Wm.					
Glenn, Ezra					
Miles, David					
Lloyd, Thos.					
Green, Daniel					
Westmoreland, Reuben					
Mitcham, John					
Browning, Mark					
Fogarty, Cornalis					
Chandler, Dan'l					
McDaniel, Dan'l					
Leigh, Rich'd					
Allen, Joseph					
Burton, Wm.					
Andros, Richard					
Stringer, Leonard					
Daniel, John, Jr					
Magee, Daniel					
Hudson, David					
Huggins, Moses					
House, Peter					
Gwinn, Thos.					
Daniel, Roger					
Rone, Charles					
Briant, John					
Barbee, Joseph					
Barbee, John, Jr.					
Allen, Jersey					
White, Joseph					
Peeler, Benj.					
Paterson, Mark					
Booth, Gray					
Deserne, Nathaniel					
Hurst, Joseph					
Hudson, Wm.					
Barbee, Christopher					
Campbell, Rob't					
ST. MARY'S DISTRICT.					
Horton, Henry					
Harris, Edmund					
Tilley, Jahn, Sr.					
Ashley, James					
Moore, John, Sr.					
Moore, John, Jr					
Woods, Edward					
Craig, Jonathan					
McFarlin, Thos.					
Pilley, Lazarus					
Carrington, Nathaniel					
Cates, Richard					
Cole, Sam'l					
Nutt, David					
Cates, Benjamin					
Cates, Matthias					
Smith, Stephen					
Hunt, Thos.					
Grimes, Barney					
Brinkley, Eli					
Horner, Geo., Jr.					
Horner, Thos.					
Woods, Joseph (Eno.)					
Woods, Sampson					
Carrington, Geo.					
Dorsett, Thos.					
Harris, Hugh					
McFarlin, Wm., Jr.					
Horner, Geo., Sr.					
McFarlin, Keziah					
Walker, James, Jr.					
Ricketts, Anthony					
Chisenhuse, Reuben					
Mannin, Charles					
Riggs, Geo., Sr					
Nealy, John					
Montgomery, Wm., Sr.					
Britton, Joseph					
Ciower, Wm.					
Horton, Thos.					
Moore, Henry					

NAME OF HEAD OF FAMILY.	Free white males of 16 years and upward, including heads of families.	Free white males under 16 years.	Free white females, including heads of families.	All other free persons.	Slaves.
ST. MARY'S DISTRICT—continued.					
Leathers, Moses					
Roberts, Charles					
Tilley, John, Jr.					
Mize, John					
Duke, Robt.					
Carrington, Ephraim					
Mangum, William					
Roberts, Abner					
Ray, James					
Mashburn, Josh, Sr.					
Mashburn, Elisha					
Peddegwin, Wm.					
Robinson, Wm.					
McMullen, Alex'r					
Garvard, John					
Glenn, Warham					
Allen, Samuel					
Collins, Wm.					
Harris, Archer					
Clower, Dan'l					
Parish, Allen					
Roberts, Jeremiah					
Moore, James					
Watson, James, Sr.					
Bobbit, Sihon					
Watson, John, Jr					
Wilson, Samuel					
Pickle, Henry					
Cates, William					
Wilson, Thos.					
Cozart, Anthony					
Bagley, Henry					
Walker, James, Sr.					
Mashburn, James, Sr.					
Horton, Charles					
Davis, Abraham					
Wilburn, John					
Dunnegam, Wm., Sr					
Woods, Joseph					
Woods, Eli					
Lynch, John					
Guess, George					
Warren, Josiah					
Cannaday, James					
Piper, John, Sr.					
Wallace, Wm.					
Woods, James					
Grisham, George					
Woods, Thos., Sr.					
Dollar, Jonathan					
Fulton, James					
Roads, Thos.					
Cates, Lazarus					
Roads, Aquilla					
Woods, Blayton					
Dorsett, Wm.					
Dunwoody, Henry					
Holloway, Rich'd.					
Forester, Benj					
Sears, Elizabeth					
Clinton, Matthias					
Ragan, John					
Townsley, Joseph					
Johnston, Drury					
Chisenhall, John					
Forrest, Isaac					
Forrest, Edmond					
Hill, George					
Woods, Thos., Jr.					
Sutherland, Mordecai					
Curry, James					
May, Samuel					
Turner, Elias					
Bunch, Henry					
Whitacer, Abraham					
Dunning, Nicholas					
Cole, Levi					
May, John					
Curry, John					
Riley, James					
Curry, James					
Riley, Wm.					
Downs, Wm.					
Lewis, Thos.					
Leathers, Wm.					
Alston, James					
Forrest, Stephen					
Paterson, Andrew					
Forrest, Shadrack					
Roads, Wm.					
Lewis, Fielding					
Woods, Wm.					
Scarlett, John					
Cates, Rob't.					
Jolly James					

HILLSBOROUGH DISTRICT, ORANGE COUNTY—Continued.

ST. MARY'S DISTRICT—continued.

NAME OF HEAD OF FAMILY.	Free white males of 16 years and upward, including heads of families.	Free white males under 16 years.	Free white females, including heads of families.	All other free persons.	Slaves.
Nevis, John					
Grisham, Rob't					
Harris, Richmond					
Forrest, Hezekiah					
Dorsett, Wm., Jr					
Laycock, Thos.					
Chisenhall, Wm.					
Ray, Wm., Sr.					
Umstead, David					
Roberts, John					
Wilson, James					
Turrentine, Sam'l, Sr.					
Turrentine, Sam'l, Jr.					
Latta, John, Jr.					
Hopkins, Wm.					
Parker, Abraham					
Mize, Henry					
Graves, Rob't, Jr					
Robinson, Edw'd					
Mize, Zachariah					
Taylor, John					
Jamison, Wm.					
Smallwood, Wm.					
Roark, James					
Forsyth, Rob't					
Glenn, Jeremiah					
Gabley, Isham					
Wurtham, Edward					
Dunnagam, Sherrid					
Umstead, Richard					
Riggs, Sam'l					
Latta, John, Sr.					
Riggs, John					
Laycock, Wm.					
Burres, James					
Ware, Wm.					
Britton, Benj.					
Baldwin, John					
Piper, Sam'l					
Morgan, Thos.					
Walker, Rob't					
Morgan, Wm.					
Linch, Darling					
Latta, James, Sr					
Latta, Thos.					
Latta, James, Jr					
Morris, Hugh					
Redding, Thos.					
Hite, Joseph					
Woods, Hugh					
Cales, John					
Cain, James					
Scarlett, Stephen					
Popley, John					
Clenny, Sam'l					
Carrol, Stephen					
Dollar, Elijah					
Holloway, Thos.					
Cole, John					
Burton, Cuthbud					
Belvin, William					
Newton, George					
Sutton, Thos.					
Lewis, John					
Carroll, Benj.					
Browning, Thos.					
Clenny, Wm.					
Cabe, Wm.					
Roades, Richard					
Durring, James					
Horn, Thos.					
Woods, John (Sheriff)					
Clarke, Wm.					
Guess, Joseph					
Clements, Thos., Jr.					
Clements, John					
Chisenhall, Sam'l					
Wilson, Stephen					
Carrington, John, Sr.					
Dunnagan, Charles					
Tatom, Mourning					
Tatom, John					

ST. MARY'S DISTRICT—continued.

NAME OF HEAD OF FAMILY.	Free white males of 16 years and upward, including heads of families.	Free white males under 16 years.	Free white females, including heads of families.	All other free persons.	Slaves.
Critchen, James					
Carrington, John, Jr.					
Cain, John					
Bennehan, Richard					
Hurley, Wm.					
Cain, Wm.					
Riggs, James					
Jones, John					
Kilby, John					
Hunt, Henry					
Hunt, John					
Rhodes, Rich'd					
Riggs, James					
Allen, Jacob					
Walker, Wm.					
Sears, Joseph					
Douglas, John					
Redman, John					
Way, Thos.					

ST. THOMAS' DISTRICT.

NAME OF HEAD OF FAMILY.	Free white males of 16 years and upward, including heads of families.	Free white males under 16 years.	Free white females, including heads of families.	All other free persons.	Slaves.
Andrews, William					
Pendergrass, William					
King, Wm.					
Blackwood, James					
Owen, Peter					
Bradbury, John					
Partin, Leonard					
Blackwood, Wm.					
Pendergrass, Job					
Fann, John					
Strayn, Alexander					
Price, John					
Johnston, Geo.					
Burns, Wm.					
Wilson, John					
Freeland, John					
Riggans, James					
King, Nathaniel					
Rodes, Alex'r.					
Massie, Abijah					
Hogan, John					
Lloyd, Wm.					
King, Chas.					
Gaddice, James					
Gaddice, Sam'l					
Scott, John					
Lloyd, Stephen					
Connolly, John					
Lloyd, Fred'k.					
Stephens, Dan'l.					
Price, Archibald					
Howell, Benjamin					
Kirkland, Joseph					
Bevill, Zechariah					
Hogan, David					
Ivey, Henry					
Lloyd, Owen					
Caldwell, John					
Craig, James					
Lloyd, James					
Ivay, David					
Owen, John					
Moseley, Samuel					
Williss, Peter					
Yeargin, Benj.					
Patterson, Mann (orphan)					
Patterson, Charles P. (orphan)					
Reeves, Rev. George					
King, John					
McCauley, Matthew					
Walter, John					
Burrow, John					
Piper, Alex'r.					
Piper, Sam'l					
Piper, Abraham					
Moseley, John					
Rigsbee, William					
Sparrow, John					

ST. THOMAS' DISTRICT—continued.

NAME OF HEAD OF FAMILY.	Free white males of 16 years and upward, including heads of families.	Free white males under 16 years.	Free white females, including heads of families.	All other free persons.	Slaves.
Colther, Hinson					
Colther, Matthew					
Howell, Edward					
Stroud, John					
Partin, Wm.					
Conally, Thos.					
Hastings, Joseph					
Pate, John					
Jones, Edmund					
Strain, John					
Thrift, Isham					
Wemes, John					
Willis, Wm.					
Stroud, Anderson					
Mitchell, Andrew					
Weeks, Joseph					
Hunter, Samuel					
Hunter, Aaron					
Cheek, Masting					
Baker, Thomas					
Woohley, John					
Coruthers, Hugh					
Cheek, Rob't					
Forsith, Wm.					
Long, George					
Baker, John					
Mitchel, John					
King, Hannah					
Pettiford, Elias					
Stroud, Elizabeth					
Trotter, Robt.					
Haywood, Jesse					
King, Thos.					
Pendergrass, Thos.					
Bynum, John					
Brewer, Sackfield					
Honeycutt, Wike					
Fannin, John					
Rigsbee, Jesse					
Gaddice, John					
Gaddice, Alex'r.					
Hinshery, John					
Gaddice, John, Jr.					
Brewer, Ezekiel					
Brewer, Thos.					
Cooper, Mark					
Smith, James					
Morgan, Hardy					
Herndon, Comfort					
Willis, John					
Morris, Henry					
Morris, Rich'd					
Nevill, Jesse					
Caudle, David					
Cheek, James					
Allen, Abraham					
Craig, Samuel					
McCauley, Wm.					
Craig, Elinor					
Strayhorn, John					
Craig, John					
Hart, James					
Wilmoth, Thos.					
Hobbs, Wm.					
Couch, Wm.					
Carroll, Michael					
Bowls, John					
Baker, James					
Clerk, Joseph					
Hastings, Joseph					
Baker, Robt.					
Miller, Joseph					
Bolling, Baxter					
Hinkley, Ezekiel					
Strayhorn, Wm.					
Craig, James, Sr.					
Flowers, Jacob					
Morgan, John					
Hogan, Sarah					
Maron, Jacob					
King, Baxter					

HILLSBOROUGH DISTRICT, RANDOLPH COUNTY.

NAME OF HEAD OF FAMILY.	Free white males of 16 years and upward, including heads of families.	Free white males under 16 years.	Free white females, including heads of families.	All other free persons.	Slaves.
Alexander, James			1		3
Brown, Michael	4	1	4		
Brewer, John	2		2	1	1
Beason, Edward	1	2	4		
Brown, James	1	2	3		
Beason, Isaac	2	3	2		
Barton, John	1		2		
Brown, Jacob	1		2		
Barton, Elizabeth	1	1	7		
Beason, William	1	1	8		
Beason, Richard	1	4	6		
Bond, John	1	5	3		
Beason, Benjamin	1	1	2		
Barnett, Obed.	1		3		
Barnett, Uriah	1	2	3		
Buntin, Ebenezer	3		2		
Barton, Elizabeth		2	3		8
Brown, Federick	1	1	3		
Clou, Thomas	2	2	1		
Coble, Nicholas	2	1	5		
Chamness, Joseph	3	2	6		
Crawford, Eve		1	2		
Coble, John	2		2		1
Coble, John, Jur	2	1	5		

HILLSBOROUGH DISTRICT, RANDOLPH COUNTY—Continued.

NAME OF HEAD OF FAMILY.	Free white males of 16 years and upward, including heads of families.	Free white males under 16 years.	Free white females, including heads of families.	All other free persons.	Slaves.
Caucey, Isaac	1		4		5
Davidson, James	2	5	2		
Dennis, John	1	1	2		
Dennis, Thomas	1	1	2		
Elliott, William	2		1		
Elliott, Israel	1	1	3		
Elliott, Obediah	1		4		
Elliott, Peter	1	1	1		
Elliott, John	1	2	1		
Elliott, Abraham, Jur	1	2	2		
Elliott, Samuel	1	1	3		
Elliott, Abraham	1	2	2		
Elliott, Joseph	1	2	4		
Elliott, Jacob	1	2	8		
Elliott, Abraham, Senr.	3		2		
Erwin, William	3	4	4		
Field, William	2	1	5		
Ferguson, John	1		1		
Field, Roger	1		1		
Field, William, Senr	1		2		4
Field, William (of Robert)	1		5		1
Gearing, Simeon	1	1	1		
Hudson, John	1	3	4		
Hemphill, Samuel	2	5	2		
Henshaw, Jacob	2		2		
Henshaw, William	2	1	4		
Hail, Joseph	1		1		
Harmon, Leonard	3		3		
Hogget, Joseph	1	1	3		
Hogget, Stephen	1	2	2		
Haman, Ephraim	1	1	2		
Julon, Jesse	1	1	3		
Jackson, Joseph	1	3	4		
Jones, Silas	1	1	3		
Jones, Aquilla	1	2	3		
Jones, Thomas	2	5	3		1
Jenkins, John	1				
Jenkins, Thomas	3		8		
Kins, David	1	2	1		
Kirkmon, Elisha	1	3	6		
Lamb, Jacob	1	1	4		1
Love, John	1		1		
Lewis, David	3	3	5		
Lamb, Henry	1	2	3		
Lewis, Richard	1	4	2		
Lamb, John	2	1	3		
Lamb, Joseph	2	3	2		
Lewis, John, Ser	1		5		
Lewis, John	1	2	3		
Lamb, Benjamin	1	1	4		
Lamb, Nathan	1		2		
Lamb, William	1	3	2		
Morris, John	2	2	5		
McCollum, Stephen	1	1	2		
Macey, Joseph	3	1	5		
Mattuck, Samuel	1	2	4		
Mendenhall, Elisha	1	1	1		5
Morriss, Christian	1	1	3		
Morgan, Ezekiel	1		3		
Nashon, Christopher	3		3		
Osborn, Samuel	3	1	3		
Osborn, Matthew	2	1	4		
Osborn, David	1	2	1		
Osborn, William	1		2		
Person, William	2		3		
Phillips, Joel	1	3	2		
Powell, Elijah	1		3		
Pennington, Levi	1	5	2		
Pugh, Thomas	1	2	3		
Reynolds, David	1		3		
Robbins, Christopher	1	2	5		
Robbins, John	1	6	2		
Richardson, Peter	3	2	4		
Reynolds, Jaremiah	5	1	6		
Reynolds, William	1	4	2		
Swim, John	3	4	4		
Scarlett, John	1	3	2		
Staley, Coonrod	3	3	5		
Staley, Martin	4	4	3		
Smith, Federick	1	5	4		
Stanton, Samuel	2	5	4		
Suites, Jacob	1	1	1		
Tillery, George	2	2	3		
Vucory, Sampson	1	1	5		
Vucory, Christopher	2	5	3		2
Weathington, John	3	3	3		
Wood, John	1	2	3		
Webb, Joseph	1	1	2		
Wood, Clement	1		2		
Wood, Zebedee	1		2		
Wilson, Jessee	1	2	3		
Worth, Joseph	4		2		
Wilborn, John	1	3	5		2
Wood, Reuben	1	4	3		2
Wood, Zebedee, Esqr.	2	2	4		
Wilson, William	1	3	5		
Underwood, Samuel	1	5	3		
Branson, Thomas	1		5		
Jones, Aquilla	1		2		
Lamb, Elizabeth	1	3	2		2
Dennis, Rachel	3		3		
Harmon, William	1	1	1		
Wood, John	1		1		
Beason, Benjamin	1		1		
Dennis, William	1		1		
Bartin, William	1	3	1		1
Garner, Perish	1		3		
Canine, David	1	1	3		
Field, William (of William)	1	1	2		
Alred, John, Senr.	2	1	5		1
Alred, Elias	1	5	1		
Alred, John	1	1	3		
Alred, William	2	1	4		1
Alred, John (of William)	1		4		
Allin, Samuel	1	1	5		
Alred, James	1	1	8		
Alridge, Nathan	2	4	7		
Barker, Robert	2	2	7		
Barker, William	1		1		
Benson, Thomas	1	1	4		
Crabtree, John	1	6	2		
Cox, Amos	2	3	7		
Crabtree, James	2	1	4		3
Code, Timothey	2	2	4		
Code, William	1		1		
Cox, Isaac	1		1		
Cox, Thomas	1	2	4		
Cox, William	1	2	2		
Cox, Harmon	2	1	2		
Duncan, John	1	2	2		
Davis, Enuch	1		1		
Fruit, John	1	2	3		
Fruit, James	1	5	1		
Fagin, William	2	1	2		
Garner, Thomas	1		1		
Garner, Jessee	1	1	1		
Garner, Henry	1	3	3		3
Gaving, Hugh	1	1	3		
Grimes, John	1	2	1		
Hudson, Richard	2	2	4		
Hudson, John	1				
Henson, Joseph	2	2	5		
Henshaw, William	1	5	4		
Henshaw, Israel	1	2	4		
Henshaw, Thomas	1	4	2		
Henshaw, John	1	2	1		
Hardin, Mark	1	1	4		
Henshaw, William	1		3		
Henson, William	1	3	3		
Harper, John	1	2	6		
Hislop, James	1	1	1		
Juland, George	1	2	6		
Juland, Rainey	1	4	5		
Jones, John	1	1	1		
Lewis, Stephen	1	3	4		
Lane, Joseph	1	2	4		
Lamb, Cornelius	1	1	1		
Lane, Isaac	1	1	1		
Lane, Abraham	1				
Lane, John	1	3	6		4
McCollum, James	1	1	1		
Moser, Tobius	1	2	6		
McCollum, Isaac	1	1	1		
McClane, Robert	3	4	3		1
McKee, Sarah			1		
Odle, Nehemiah	1		2		
Pugh, James	2		2		
Reines, Robert	2	4	7		
Smith, William	1	1	1		
Swift, Thomas	1	1	3		
Swift, Thomas, Ser.	2		4		
Swaford, William	2	5	4		
Swift, Elias	1	2	2		
Spoon, Christopher	1	3	2		
Scott, James	1				
Trogdon, Solomon	1				
Trogdon, John	1		2		
Trogdon, John	1	1	2		
Williams, Abraham	1	1	2		
Wilburn, John	1	4	5		
White, John	3	2	5		
Wilburn, Esther	1		2		8
Walker, Samuel	2	3	5		1
Walker, Samuel	1	3	3		
Wilburn, Elijah	1		2		
Walker, Robert	1	2	3		
York, Henry	1	1	2		
York, William	1	1	3		
York, Samuel	1		5		
York, Silvana	1	2	2		1
York, Semore	1	2	4		
York, Jeremiah	1	4	5		
Yates, William	1	4	3		
Arley, Henry	1		3		
Long, Solomon	2	2	2		
Haild, Jacob	1	1	2		
Hackeb, Robert	1	2	2		
Avret, John, Jur	1		2		
Rigbey, John	1		1		
Duffey, Ann			1		
Avret, John, Ser.	1	3	5		
Duncan, John, Ser.	1	3	5		
Alred, William	3	3	4		
Dafrin, John	1	1	4		
Alred, Margret	2	1	2		
Husbands, William	1		2		
York, Eli	1		1		
Underwood, Mary		2	3		
Loller, Evan	1	2	1		
Hendrix, Edward	1	3	2		
Cox, Nathan	1		1		
Bradley, Ambrus	1	3	1		
Hamer, John	1		1		
Aldridge, Elizabeth	2	2	4		
Ammick, Nicholas	1		2		
Alred, Ezekiel	1	3	3		
Aldridge, John	1	3	1		
Alred, John	1	5	2		
Amick, John	1	5	1		
Alridge, Isaac	1	3	3		
Barker, John	2	2	4		
Borough, Dobson	4	4	4		14
Beck, Jethro	2	4	5		
Bane, James	3	2	3		
Brown, Adam	1	1	2		
Burgis, William	1		1		
Burgis, James	3		1	2	
Brown, Christopher	1	3	3		
Black, George	1	3	3		
Bradley, Laurance	2	2	1		
Blair, Hugh	1		3		
Bootrout, Joseph	2		2		
Bennett, Benjamin	1	4	2		2
Cruthers, John	1	1	7		
Chaplin, David	1		3		
Chambers, John	1	1	3		
Curtis, Samuel	1		8		
Cammell, Malcum	1	2	6		
Curtis, John	1		3		1
Cox, William	1		4		
Campbell, John	1	4	3		
Cloud, Joseph	2	4	4		
Canter, James	1				
Clap, John	1		3		
Campbell, Alexander	1	2	4		
Chaplin, David	1		1		
Dickson, William	2		1		
Evans, Solomon	2	2	4		
Frasher, Francis	2	3	1		
Frasher, Thomas	2	2	4		
Frasher, George	2	6	4		
Fox, Leonard	1	1	1		
Grandey, John	1	1	1		
Graig, Jacob	4	4	2		
Grimes, Richard	1	2	5		
Grimes, Richard, Ser.	1	2			
Hayes, Edmond	1	2	2		
Hammilton, Thomas	1	2	5		
Husbands, John	1		2		
Hammon, Elisha	1	3	4		
Harvey, William	2	3	4		
Harriss, Evan	2	4	4		
Hancock, Joshua	1	2	1		
Hamer, John	1		3		
Holder, John	1	2	1		
Jones, Leonard	2	5	3		
Jones, Charles	3	4	4		
Johnston, Henry	1				
Kivet, Peter	3		1		2
Kivet, Peter, Jur	1	2	2		
Kivet, Henry	1	4	1		
Lineberry, Jacob	3	5	3		
Langley, Allen	1	2	2		
Loller, Elie	1	2	3		
McDaniel, Abraham	1	2	6		
McGown, William	1	3	1		
Loller, John	3	1	2		
McDaniel, Isaac	1	3	6		
McDaniel, Abraham	1	3	7		
McDaniel, John	1	2	1		
Marley, William	2	3	3		
McCollum, Jonathan	1	1	2		1
McMasters, Andrew	1	2	4		
McDaniel, Amos	1		4		
Morfet, Adam	2	2	5		
Morfet, James	1		1		
Matthews, William	3	2	5		1
Neadham, Thomas	4				

HILLSBOROUGH DISTRICT, RANDOLPH COUNTY—Continued.

NAME OF HEAD OF FAMILY.	Free white males of 16 years and upward, including heads of families.	Free white males under 16 years.	Free white females, including heads of families.	All other free persons.	Slaves.
Nelson, Samuel	2		2		
Overby, John	2	2		1	1
Pugh, John	1	2	6		
Provo, Catharine	1	1	2		
Rustin, James	1	1	2		
Reines, George	3	5	2		
Ruth, Jacob	1	6	1		
Russell, George	1	5	3		
Ruth, James	1	1	4		
Reines, John	3		3		
Reines, Antoney	1	2	2		
Reines, Israel	2	1	5		
Reines, Robert	1	2	7		
Stout, Peter	1				
Scotton, John		4	3		
Souch, Jacob	1	1	1		
Staley, Christopher	1				
Staley, Jacob	1	1	4		
Stout, Samuel	3	5	6		
Sillars, Phillip	2		2		
Savage, William	1				
Savage, Thomas	1	2	2		
Sutton, Joseph	2	5	4		
Scotton, John E	1		1		
Stout, Samuel	1		1		
Wilson, William	2	3	4		
Wilson, John	1	3	3		
Williams, Benjamin	1	5	2		
Walker, John	2	2	6		
Ward, William	1	3	3		1
Williams, Daniel	1	1	4		
Warren, James	1				
Warren, Joseph	1	1	3		
Watson, Jacob	3	2	3		
Ward, Thomas	1	4	4		
White, Nicholas	2	4	1		
Worrell, William		1	2		
York, John	1	4	4		
York, Edmond	1	3	2		
York, Joseph	3	4	4		
York, Aaron	1	3	4		
York, John	2	2	5		
York, Subell	1	1	4		
Wood, Joseph	1		1		
McMasters, Solomon	1	1	1		
Rightsman, Mary	2	5	5		
Chambers, Edmond	1	4	7		
Frazer, John	1	1	1		
Nelson, Samuel	1				
Foust, Jacob	1	5	3		
Billinsley, Sarah			1		
York, Elliner			1		
Rustin, William	1				
Reines, Laurance	1	2	5		
Barker, Samuel	3	2	7		
Phillips, Edmond	1	1	1		
Davis, William	1	1	3		
Asbell, Emanuel	2	1	3		
Andrews, Charity	1	4	4		
Andrews, Adam	1	2			4
Asbell, William	1	2	3		
Argo, John	1	1	3		1
Argo, William	1	2	5		1
Andrews, David	1	4	3		
Bird, Richard	2	3	4		1
Bookout, Charles	1	1	2		
Bell, Linsey	2	2	5		
Bell, William	1				
Bland, Benjamin	1				
Bryan, William	1				
Bland, Moses	1		1		
Bland, William	3	2	4		
Bowdown, James	1	2	1		
Bowdown, William	1	3	2		5
Brewer, Howell	3		8		
Cost, Thomas	1	3	4		
Comer, Jessee	1	1	5		
Cox, Nicholas	1	1	3		
Craven, Peter	2		2		
Carnes, Mathias	1	1	1		
Cox, Samuel	3		4		
Cox, Henry	1	2	2		
Cost, Thomas, Jur	1		1		1
Car, Robert	1	3	6		
Car, Joseph	2	3	2	1	5
Dempsey, Luke	1	1	1		
Derbey, William	1	2	3		
Edwards, John	1	2	5		
George, Moses	1	4	1		
Garner, James	1	2	1		
Garner, John F	2	3	4		3
Garner, James	1	3	5		3
Hammilton, Matthew	1	4	4		
Hall, Thomas	1	2	2		
Hicks, Joseph	3	4	3		
Johnston, John	1	5	2		1
Lodermilk, Jacob	1	4	5		

NAME OF HEAD OF FAMILY.	Free white males of 16 years and upward, including heads of families.	Free white males under 16 years.	Free white females, including heads of families.	All other free persons.	Slaves.
Lawley, Christopher	1	3	3		
Lodermilk, John	1	1	2		
Laurance, William	1		3		
Latham, James	1	5	7		
Ledloe, James	1	5	6		
Laurance, John	3	3	3		6
Latham, Cornelius	1	2	5		1
Lawley, John	1	1	3		
Mullins, Nathaniel	1	2	2		
Moon, Joseph	1	6	2		
Moon, John	1	4	2		
Mullins, Jeremiah	2		2		
Mallett, William	1	2	2		
Macon, Gideon	1		2		
Needham, William	1	1	2		
Needham, John, Ser	2	4	5		8
Needham, John, Jur	1		1		
Needham, William	3	2	3		
Odle, Isaac	1		1		
Powers, Bradley	1	1	4		
Pearce, Windsor	2	1	4		
Rede, John	1	1	1		
Ruster, John	1	3	2		1
Rede, Arthur	2	1	5		
Ruth, Joseph	3	4	4		
Spinks, Lewis	3	2	5		
Spinks, Enuch	1	2	2		
Smith, Arthur	1	1	4		
Spinks, John	1	5	5		
Smitheman, William	1	3	4		
Smith, Fortunatus	1				
Searcey, William		2	5		
Reines, William	1	3	2		1
Stuart, Charles	2	2	1		7
White, James	1		4		4
Waddle, Edmond	4	4	5		22
Routh, John	1	2	2		
Pope, Richard	1				
Ruster, William, Jur	1				
Stephens, Robert	1				
Mafet, Robert	1		5		
Grove, Sarah		1	1		
Reins, Mary	1	3	2		
Harden, Robert	1	2	1		
Carrelton, George	1	2	2		
Hicks, Robert	1		1		
Lawley, Joseph	1		1		
Reins, Isaac	1				
Mallett, James	1		1		
Andrews, Michael	1		1		
Rede, Benjamin	1	2	5		
Rede, William	1		2		
Bowden, Travers	1		1		
Pitt, Jessee	1				
Bookout, Marmaduke	1	3	4		
Latham, James	2		1		
Spinks, Garrett	1		2		
Smith, William	1	1	1		
Garner, Bradley	1		3		
Putman, John	1	1	2		
Redfearn, Isaac	1	3	4		
Daten, James	1		1		
Daten, Matthew	1	1	1		
Coller, Nancey		2	4		
Call, William	1	2	1		
Grey, Charles	1	3	3		
Bookout, Joseph	1	2	1		
Norton, Sarah					3
Smith, Febey				4	
Lawley, Elisha	1	1	1		
Ruth, Jacob, Jur	2	5	3		
Call, Josana		1	1		
Johnston, Mornin	2	2	3		
Andrews, Ephraim	1	1	1		2
Avira, William	1	3	4		
Brown, Joseph	2	1	2		
Brown, Robert	2	3	5		2
Barker, Nicholas	3	3	1		
Brown, Daniel	2		1		
Brown, Samuel	1		1		
Brown, Henry	1	2	2		
Craven, Peter	2	4	2		
Car, Thomas	1	2	2		
Carr, Joshua	1	3	2		
Carr, Joseph	1	4	2		
Craven, Thomas	2	5	5		
Craven, John	1		3		
Chaney, Francis, Ser	1				
Chaney, John	1		1		
Cox, Thomas	2	1	4		
Cox, Charles	1	2	2		
Craven, Daniel	1	2	3		
Cox, Thomas	1		2		
Chaney, Francis	1	2	3		
Cox, John	1	3	3		
Craven, Joseph	1	3	3		
Carter, Edward	1	3	3		

NAME OF HEAD OF FAMILY.	Free white males of 16 years and upward, including heads of families.	Free white males under 16 years.	Free white females, including heads of families.	All other free persons.	Slaves.
Cox, John	4	1	3		
Cox, Benjamin	2	1	4		
Corner, Amos	1	2	3		
Corner, Robert	3	1	10		
Cox, Nathaniel	1	2	4		
Cox, Elie	1				
Craven, Henry	2		3		
Cox, Jeremiah	1	1	4		
Diffey, Moses	1	1	5		1
Diffey, John	1	2	1		
Duskin, Sarah	1		2		3
Edwards, Peter	1	3	5		1
Giles, Chrispen	2	4	7		
Hussey, Stephen	3	2	2		
Henson, Jessee	1		3		
Hendricks, Samul	2	1	5		
Hopkins, Josih	1	1	2		
Hopkins, Dennis	1	2	4		
Henshaw, Absolum	2		3		
Hodgins, Robert	2	2	5		
Harland, Stephen	1	1	1		
Hendricks, Joseph	1	1	1		
Hendricks, Tobias	1	2	1		
Jackson, Isaac	1		2		
Kenworthey, David	4	3	4		
Kayes, Isaac	2	1	2		
Kain, Isaac	1		1		
Kenworthey, Joshua	3	2	4		
Ledmon, Stafford	1	2	5		
Litter, Menshaw	2	2	7		
Morfit, William	3	1	4		
Moser, Jacob	1	1	3		
Morfit, James	2	6	4		
Pickett, Jeremiah	1	3	4		
Ramsower, Henry	1	2	5		
Richards, Isaac	2	2	3		
Ratliff, Moses	3	2	2		5
Shaffer, Jacob	1		2		
Stroud, Abraham	2		4		
Scott, Daniel	1	2	3		
Stroud, Jessee	1		2		
Stroud, John	1	1	2		
Stamper, Jammes	2	1	6		
Stafford, Trice	1	1	4		
Snede, William	1	1	1		
Sell, Enos	1	1	2		
Trogdon, Samuel	1	5	3		
Winniyham, Richard	1	2	6		
Williams, Onean	1	2	2		
Right, Peter	1	1	2		
Wright, George	1		2		
Mafit, Samuel	1	1	1		
Gradey, Thomas	1				
Smith, William	1	6	3		
Harriss, William	2	5	4		
Lawley, Elisha	1				
Moon, John	1				
Pugh, Rachel		1	3		
Richards, William	1	2	3		
West, Isaac	1	3	6		
Moon, Daniel	1		1		
Cox, Benjamin	1	1	5		
Alred, Thomas	2		1		
Henshaw, Absalum	1	3	3		
Goodwin, James	3	3	5		
Cantrel, Charles	2	4	3		
Anstat, George	1	1	2		
Anstat, John	1		5		
Taylor, Florance	1	2	6		
Winneham, Grace		1	1		
Askins, Richard	1	3	3		
Graves, William	2		1		
Davis, William	1	3	4		
Philps, Jonathan	1	1	2	3	
Hudson, Obediah	1	2	2		
Tucker, Sarah		1	2		
Mann, Malicah	1	4	3		
McCraney, Kason		2	1		
Buckhannon, William W	1				
Bowling, Benjamin	1	3	5		
Bean, Richard	2	6	5		
Bowling, William	2	2	5		
Branson, Thomas	1				
Branson, Henry	1	1	1		
Barnes, Burwell	1	1	4		
Coontz, Gasper	1	3	3		
Cole, Matthew	1		1		
Cole, Stephen	3	1	6		2
Cox, Caleb	1	2	2		
Cox, Richard	1	1	3		
Comer, John	1		1		
Dollihide, Asel	1		4		
Dollihide, Hezekiah	1	1	5		
Edwards, Morgan	1		2		
Edwards, Jonathan	1	2	3		
Graves, James	1	4	2		

HILLSBOROUGH DISTRICT, RANDOLPH COUNTY—Continued.

NAME OF HEAD OF FAMILY.	Free white males of 16 years and upward, including heads of families.	Free white males under 16 years.	Free white females, including heads of families.	All other free persons.	Slaves.
Graves, Samuel	1	2	2		1
Graves, Richard	1	1	2		
Harvey, William, Jur	1	4	3		1
Hudson, Joseph	1	4	2		
Hammon, John	2	1	1		
Hammon, Moses	2	2	6		
Hooker, Robert	1	3	4		
Hooker, Jacob	1	3	4		
Hobson, John	1	3	5		
Harvey, William	1		1		5
Harvey, Michael	1	2	1		
Johnston, John	1	2	2		
King, Thomas	1	4	2		
King, Peter	1	3	4		
King, Johnston, Ser	2	4	5		
King, Johnston, Jur	1	1	1		
King, William	3	1	4		1
Lewis, George	3	1	6		2
Luther, Christian	1	4	3		
Lotham, John	2	4	4		3
Graves, John	1	2	2		
Mills, Micajah	1	2	2		
Melson, Peter	1		1		
McGloughlin, Stephen	1				
Oscar, Jeremiah	1	1	3		
Page, Benjamin, Jur	1		4		
Page, Benjamin, Ser	1				
Prisnal, William	1	3	3		
Prisnal, Daniel	1	2	1		
Prisnal, Stephen	1	3	2		
Prisnal, James	2	2	2		
Rolins, David	1	1	2		
Rede, John	1	2	5		
Rede, Lamburd	1	2	3		
Richardson, John	1		3		
Rooks, Hardy	2	1	4		
Steed, John	1	5	5		
Scott, John	3	1	1		
Stanfield, John	1	3	4		
Smith, John	1	3	4		
Tucker, Nathaniel	1		1		
Tucker, George	1	1	1		
Tucker, John	1	1	5		
Tucker, George, Senr	3		8		
Tucker, William	2	6	3		
Wright, William	1	4	5		
Williams, William	1	5	2		
Williams, John	2	1	5		
Voncannon, William	1	2	3		
Voncannon, Peter	2	1	2		
Voncannon, Peter, Jur	1	1	2		
Williams, William	3	3	4		
Williams, John	2	3	5		
Williams, George	1		1		
Williams, David	1	3	6		
Winslow, Thomas	2	3	5		1
Williams, John	1	2	2		
Macey, Richard	1		2		
Crow, Nancey	1	1	3		
Prisnal, John	2	3	5		
Richardson, William	2	1	4		
Constant, William	3	3	5		
Little, Abraham	1	1	1		
Rede, William	1	2	5		
McGloughlin, Ann		3	4		
Hill, Thomas	1	1	3		1
Belford, Margaret			1		2
McGloughlin, John	1		1		
McGloughlin, Jacob	1	1	1		
Williams, Jonathan	2	2	6		
Underhill, John	2	3	4		
Hancock, Vachel	1	1	1		
Hancock, Sarah	1		2		
Carmon, John	1	3	1		
Harvey, John	1	3	1		
Luther, Michael	1	4	1		
Latham, William	1		1		
White, Joseph	1		3		
Millsaps, William	1		1		
Hamm, Nehemiah	1		3		
Keneday, Sarah			3		
Spencer, John	1				
Thompson, John	2				
Cranford, Samuel	3	1	2		
Thompson, Henry	2		1		
Savage, John	1	2	6		
Cox, Enoch	1		7		
Botsford, James	1	2	4		
Arnold, Jeremiah	1		1		
Arnold, Francis	2	3	4		2
Arnold, Fielding	1		1		
Been, John	1		2		
Bingam, Thomas	2	4	2		2
Bundey, Samuel	1	3	3		
Bundey, Christopher	2	2	3	1	1
Brookshear, Emanuel	2	3	5		
Brookshear, Thomas	1	1	2		
Bailey, William	1	2	5	1	1
Chandler, William	1	1	3		1
Carter, William	1	1	6		
Carter, Finch	1	2	5		
Cranford, Elias	1		5		
Charles, Samuel	2	2	5		
Charles, Joseph	1				
Canady, Sherwood	1	1	3		
Cranford, William	2		3		
Fuller, Isham	1	3	4		2
Fuller, Britain	1		4		
Farmer, Frederick	1		5		5
Farmer, Joseph	4	2	3		
Griffin, Lewis	1	2	3		
Hopkins, Charles	1	2	1		
Hill, Aaron	1	3	2		
Hamilton, Samuel	1	1	2		
Hardester, Thomas	1	4	3		
Hartgrove, George	1	3	3		
Hannah, William	1	1	4		
Hartgrove, Thomas	1				
Hamon, Joshua	1	1	1		
Hamon, Abraham	2		2		
Hill, Aaron	1	3	2		10
Hannah, Andrew	1	1	2		
Henley, Jessee	3	1	3		8
Jackson, Thomas	1	3	2		
Irwin, John	1	2	3		1
King Thomas	2	1	5		
Kean, Silas	1				
Kain, John	3	1	4		
Lindon, Henry	1	1	2		
Lasiter, Sarah	1		6		5
Lax, William	1	3	1		
Lassiter, Micajah	2	2	1		1
Lewis, Samuel	3	1	4		
Lacey, William	1	2	3		
Muckleroye, Andrew	1		3		3
Millsaps, Thomas	2	2	2		
McLemore, Sterling	1	3	3		
Orick, William	1	4	3		
Orick, John	2	2	6		
Patterson, Thomas	1		4		
Patterson, Alexr	3	1	5		
Rich, Samuel	2	4	5		
Randolph, Thomas	2		2		
Rogers, Randolph	1	2	1		
Robbins, Joseph	1	3	2		
Hannah, William	1	2	1		
Anderson, Thomas	1	2	3		
Steed, Nathaniel	2	4	3		8
Shaw, Guardner	2	5	1		
Stiles, John	1				
Trublood, William	1	1	3		1
Trustey, John	1	1	1		
Towery, George	1	1	7		
Wade, Joseph	3	1	6		
Webster, John	2	2	7		
Winslow, John	2	2	3		
Thornberry, Thomas	1		1		2
Chandler, Timothey	2	2	7		
Seal, Solomon	1	2	3		
Oruc, Samuel	1			1	1
Andrews, Writter		5	2		
Bean, Richard	1	1	2		
Gowin, William	2	3	4		1
Thompson, Walter	1	1	3		
Hall, William	2	1	1		
Patterson, John	1	1	1		
Randol, James	1	2	3		
Hannock, Richard	1		5		1
Albertson, Arthur	1				
Anderson, John	1	1	1		
Abertson, Joshua	1	4	6		
Arnold, John	2	2	5		1
Bell, Franciss	3	1	2		
Bassell, Barneby	1	2	2		
Bailey, John	1	1	3		
Bibbins, Joseph	1	5	1		
Bass, Jordan	2	2	3		1
Bell, John	1	1			
Bickerdick, Richard	1	4	4		
Bell, Thomas	1	2	8		
Brookshear, William	2	2	4		
Bell, William	3	3	4		
Curtis, Benjamin	1	1	4		
Curtis, John	1	2	4		
Curtis, Joshua	1	1	1		
Caps, Dempsey	1		4		
Debenport, John	1	5	1		3
Elliott, Axum	1		2		
Elliott, Jacob	1		2		
Fouts, Elizabeth	1	3	2		
Fuller, Ezekiel	1	2	1		
Fouts, Jacob	2	3	3		
Fuller, Solomon	5	3	4		10
Gibson, Thomas	1	1	1		
Green, Benjamin	3	2	5		
Gaddis, Archebald	3	4	1		
Gibson, George	1	4	4		
Hoover, Andrew	1	3	4		
Hall, Benjamin	1	1	1		
Hanley, John	4	5	3		
Hoover, Jonas	1	4	5		
Harvey, Jessee	1		3		
Hunt, Tumius	1	1	5		
Hill, Seth	1		3		1
Hall, William	1	1	2		
Hicks, Willis	1	1	2		
Hill, William	5	5	3	5	
Harvey, Michael	3		5		
Jackson, Andrew	1	3	5		
Ivey, Benjamin	1	1	6		2
Jackson, James	1	2	2		
Jackson, Robert	1	1	4		
Jackson, William	1	4	4		
Kindley, Edward	1	1	4		
King, James	2	3	7		
Ledford, John	1	1	5		
Lamb, Reuben	2	1	4		
Luvallin, William	2	4	2		
Marteal, Benjamin	2	5	2		3
Miller, Haman	3	1	5		17
Most, John	2		5		
Miller, Jacob	1	3	5		2
Masieu, Lemuel	1		3		
Miller, Peter	1		3		1
Millsaps, Thomas	2	1	2		
Mitchelner, Valentine	2	3	4		
Millsaps, Robert	4	1	3		
Nance, Hudson	1				
Newbey, Jessee	1		1		
Newbey, Joseph	1		1		
Newbey, Samuel	1	3	5		
Nance, Thomas	2	1	3		1
Overman, Epharimin	1	3	2		
Overman, Zebulun	2	2	2		
Prikit, John	1		1		
Prevo, John	1		1		
Prevo, Alexr	1				
Pool, William	1	4	3		
Ray, Ann	1		1		2
Ratliff, Cornelius	1	1	4		1
Ridge, Godfrey	1	6	2		1
Roberts, James	1	2	5		8
Robbins, Joseph	1		1		
Russell, Jeffrey	1	2	3		1
Ratliff, Richard	2	1	2		
Roberts, Riland	1		1		1
Ridge, William	1	1	1		
Small, Benjamin	1		1		
Shine, Jacob	3	1	6		
Small, Obediah	1	2	2		
Smith, Phillip	1	4	2		
Turner, Ezekiel	1		1		
Thompson, John	1				
Thompson, Robert	2		1		
Thompson, William	1		2		
Warrell, Amos	1	3	3		4
Wilemon, Elias	2	4	2		
Waymire, Federick	3	2	4		
Wright, Philburt	2	4	4		
Ward, Timothey	2	1	3		
Wood, William	1	2	6		1
Yates, Peter	1		2		
Zink, George	2	3	7		
Sandifor, Robert	1	1	2		
Gibson, David	1		2		
Gibson, Gilbert	1	1	1		
Hill, Jessee	2	3	2		
Vinters, Pharow	4	3	5		
Brookshear, Morning	1				
Bayel, William	1	1	3		
Taylor, Solomon	1		2		
McLemore, Wright	1				
Low, William	1		1		
Williams, Vinun P	1	1	3		2
Arnold, Whitlock	1	1	1		
Smith, Peter	1		1		
Ledford, George	1		2		
Bevvins, Joseph, Jur	1		2		
Dunber, James	1	2	2	1	
Fuller, Mary		1	1		1
Hobes, Elisha	2	3	5		
Albertson, John	2	4	2		
Hicks, Elizabeth	3		2		
Eades, George	1	3	3		
Lacey, Ann	1	1	2		
Gaddis, Susanna	1		2		
Roberts, Sarah			2		
Hinshavins, Robertson	1				
Draper, William	1		6		
Fuller, Britain, Ser	2	1	5		4
Wright, Philburt	1		2		

HILLSBOROUGH DISTRICT, RANDOLPH COUNTY—Continued.

NAME OF HEAD OF FAMILY.	Free white males of 16 years and upward, including heads of families.	Free white males under 16 years.	Free white females, including heads of families.	All other free persons.	Slaves.	NAME OF HEAD OF FAMILY.	Free white males of 16 years and upward, including heads of families.	Free white males under 16 years.	Free white females, including heads of families.	All other free persons.	Slaves.	NAME OF HEAD OF FAMILY.	Free white males of 16 years and upward, including heads of families.	Free white males under 16 years.	Free white females, including heads of families.	All other free persons.	Slaves.
Luvellin, Jonathan	1					Hoover, Peter	1		1			White, William	2		4		
Farmer, John	1		2			Bryan, Peter	2	2	3			Gray, William	1	1	1		
Alexander, William	1					Blair, Enos	1	4	5			Brown, Mary			2		
Alexander, William, Ser.	3	2	7			Brown, John	1		3			Hoggot, Phillip	1		3		
Alexander, Stephen	4		3			Bratton, Robert	3	3	4			Jackson, Isaac	1	2	5		
Allin, James	1	3	4			Clark, Joseph	1	1	6			Smith, David, Ser	1	1	1		
Archer, William	1	3	3			Clark, Samuel	1					Thomas, Esther			1		
Burkit, Christian	1					Clark, Samuel, Jur	2	2	6			Martin, Joseph	1				
Bearley, Phillip	1	3	6			Clark, Edward	2	1	6			Turner, Moses	1		1		
Bradley, Joseph	1	1	3			Clark, Baptist	1	3	7			Nucols, Zachariah	1		1		
Beard, John	2	3	3			Coltrain, David	1	1	4			Anderson, Robert	1		1		3
Galleymore, William	1	3	3			Coltrain, William	3	2	4			Broil, Federick	3		3		
Beaverley, Isaac	1		1			Carnes, Samuel	1					Buller, Thomas	1	6	2		3
Brothers, Miles	1	3	1	1	1	Davis, James	1	1	5			Bell, William	1		2		16
Cains, Joseph	1		2			Davis, Job	1		3			Boid, William	1	2	4		1
Curtis, Joseph	1	4	3			Wright, Amos	1	2	2			Bridgegan, Edward	1				
Curtis, James	1	3	4			Davis, Amos	1	2	3			Curtis, Thomas, Senr	2	3	1		
Curtis, Caleb	1	2	4			Davis, Jessee	1	5	3			Collier, John	1	2	7		
Darnald, William	2	4	5			Elder, James	1		1			Clark, William	1	3	3		
Elder, John	1	4	2			Ellis, William	1					Cantral, Joseph	1		7		
Everley, George	1		2			Ellis, James, Ser	1	3	3			Clark, Young	1	1	3		
Fouts, David	1	1	2			Frasher, William	1	3	2			Clark, George	2	1	2		2
Fouts, Michael	2		5			Frasher, John	3	2	2			Curtis, James, Jur	1	3	1		
Fouts, Andrew	1	4	5			Frasher, Samuel	1					Clark, John	2		2	1	2
Fouts, Jacob	1	3	5			Gosset, Elijah	1	2	3			Dougan, James	1	5	3		
Failow, Nathan	4	3	5			Gossett, William	4		2			Dougan, Robert	2	1	2		
Fouts, John	3	3	5			Grey, Robert	3	2	3			Dougan, Thomas	1	1	5		7
Fouts, Lewis	1		3			Hilton, Samuel	1	2	1			Farlow, William	1	4	2		
Fouts, John, Ser	2	1	4			Henderson, John	1	5	2			Farlow, George	1	3	3		
Fincher, Benjamin	2	1	3			Hilton, John	1	2	2		1	Green, Joseph	3	1	5		
Galleymore, John	1	1	3			Hoggot, Stephen	1	1	1			Hascot, Abraham	2		1		
Gray, John	2	5	2			Hoggot, Joseph	1					Hudson, Lemuel	1				
Galleymore, John	2	1	2			Hoggot, John	3	1	3			Hascot, Joseph	1	3	5		1
Hoover, Daniel	3	2	3			Hill, Thomas	2		2			Hopper, Archebald	1	2	2		
Hodge, John	1	2	2			Hill, John	1	2				Hencock, Benjamin	3	3	4		
Hamon, Cutlif	1	2	6			Hoggot, Jessee	1		2			Hendley, John	1		3		2
Hamon, George	1	2	2			Hoggot, Moses	1		2			Juland, Isaac	1	4	2		
Hammon, Matthew	1		5			Hill, William	1	1	1			Ledford, Federick	1		3		
Hoover, David	1	1	1			Johnston, Joseph	1	2	2			Ledford, Peter	2	2	3		
Hoover, Jacob	2	5	1			Johnston, John	1	3	2			Lytle, Thomas	1		1		7
Hoover, John	1	1	3			Kendal, Benjamin	2	3	2			Low, Samuel	3	2	7		
Harper, Jeduthan	1	1	6		14	Kendal, William	2	2	1			Millican, Benjamin	1	3	4		
Jones, Thomas	1		4			Kendal, John	1	1	4			Moore, Samuel	1	2	3		
Justice, Joseph	1	3	4			Loe, James	1	1	1			Nixon, Phinehas	1	2	5		3
Garren, Jacob	1	3	4			Loe, Thomas	2		1			Pearce, Richard	1	4	4		9
Garren, John	1	2	1			Lemare, Osborn	1	2	3			Viccory, Luke	1	1	1		
Johnston, John	2		2			Leach, Hugh	2		3			Robbins, John	1	4	6		3
King, William	1		2			Loe, Thomas	1		4			Rich, Joseph	1				
Lutford, John	1		4			Leach, William	1	3	2			Robbins, William	3		8	1	9
Merrill, Benjamin	1	3	5		1	Millican, William	1	6	1			Robbins, Moses	1	1	2		1
Most, David	1		3			McFetrick, Matthew	3		3			Rich, Benjamin	1	6	2		1
Mineas, Benjamin	1	2	1		3	McDade, John	1	1	2			Rich, Peter	1	2	1		
Merrill, John	1	4	3			McFetters, Andrew	1	1	1			Reading, Robert	1	3	3	1	
Meanes, Andrew	1	4	5			Morgan, David	1	1	3			Roddey, Phillip	1	4	6		
Merrill, Daniel	1		4		2	Morgan, Lewis	1	1	4			Robbins, Isaac	3	3	5		
Most, John	1	1	3			Moore, George	1	1	2			Rush, Mary		1	4		
Moon, Joseph	1	3	5			Milton, Samuel	2	4	4			Rich, John, Ser	2	1	2		
Mullanin, Jonathan	2	2	6			Millican, William, Sr	1		1			Sharp, Michael	1	1	6		
Newbey, William	2	3	4		1	Moore, John	2	3	5			Simmons, Job	2	4	4		
Newbey, Federick	1				3	Mullins, Charles	2	2	5			Shites, Solomon	3		2		
Newbey, Joshua	1		1			Pindry, James	1	1	3			Viccory, George	1	1	1		
Overman, Obediah	1	2	4			Ruddock, John	3		3			Alexander, Samuel	1	2	4		
Plummer, Phillimon	1	2	6			Rice, Caleb	1	2	4			Woodward, William	1		2		
Park, Samuel	3	1	2		31	Ruth, Samuel	1	5	2			Webb, Jessee	3	2	1		
Reading, Joseph	1	3	3		1	Ruddock, Joseph	1		5			Watson, Daniel	1	2	2		
Snow, Isaac	1		1			Serjant, William	1	1	4			Yount, Henry	2	2	5		
Summers, William	1	3	2			Smith, David	1	4	3			Yount, George	1	1	7		
Summers, Thomas	1	1	2			Smith, Alexander	1		9		1	Rush, John	1		1		
Smith, John	1		2			Smith, Bryan	1	1	3			Loe, Ralph	1	2	5		3
Stone, Connoway	1	2	4			Tomlinson, William	4	3	4			Rich, John, Jur	1	3	3		
Snow, Ebenezer	1	3	2			Thompson, Andrew	3	2				Morrow, James	3	2	1		
Sheppard, Peter	1	3	4			Thornberry, Martha			3			Miller, Richard	1	3	3		
Sheppard, Charles	1	3	1		2	Thornberry, George	1	1	3			Ledford, John	2		2		
Stuart, John	1		1			Thornberry, Edward	1		4			Ledford, John, Ser	1	1	2		
Snow, Martha	1		2			White, Ralph	2	5	3			Lorhard, William	1	1	1		
Stootmon, Jacob	5	1	4			White, Joseph	1		3			Ledford, Federick	1		1		
Wright, John	2	5	2			White, Thomas	1	2	6			Yount, John	1		1		
Wright, Benjamin	4	1	6			White, John	1	1	4			Robbins, James	3	2	2		
Woodward, Abraham	1	2	5			Viccory, John	3	2	6			Sanders, Joseph	1	3	5		
Wright, James	1	2	1			Viccory, Christopher	1	1	1			Curtis, John	1	1	2		
Whisenhunt, George M.	3	4	2			Ward, James	1	3	3			Randals, John	1		2		
Waymire, Randolph	1	6	1			Branson, Daniel	1		2			Robbins, Joshua	1		2		
Varner, Jacob	1	2	1			Lane, Jessee	1	3	4			Dicks, William	1	1	2	1	
Wright, Joseph	1	4	2			Croket, Eliza		1	1			Hoof, Jessee	1	1	1		
Ward, Benjamin	2	4	4		3	Thornberry, William	1		4			Laurance, James	1		2		
Muliner, Greenberry	1	1	1			Thornberry, Ann	1		3			Kelley, James	1				
Humbrie, John	1		1			Moore, Robert	2	1	1			Dickey, William	2	6	3		
Varner, John	1	3	2			Coonrod, Peter	1					Karr, Nathaniel	1	1	4		
Yount, Jacob	1	2	3			Collet, James	3	1	3		7	Dougan, John	1		5		
Bryan, John	3	2	5														

HILLSBOROUGH DISTRICT, WAKE COUNTY.

NAME OF HEAD OF FAMILY.	Free white males of 16 years and upward, including heads of families.	Free white males under 16 years.	Free white females, including heads of families.	All other free persons.	Slaves.
Sugg, Aron	2	1	3		4
Bawsom, Britain	1	1	2		
Booth, Batt	1	1	3		
Medlin, Benjn	1	4	3		
Barnabas, Lane	1	1	4		6
Vick, Burwell	2				6
Pinney, Charles	1	2	3		
Curtis, Chrstepher	2	2	2		7
Partin, Drewry	3	2	3		
Ferrell, Ephraim	1	2	7		
Buzby, Edmond	2	1	3		1
Hobson, Francis	3		3		12
Rogers, Green	1		5		
Pool, George	1	1	2		
Pool, Hardy	1	3	2		
Depray, Haley	1	3	3		
Gregory, Howell	1				
Hubbard, Henry	2	2	5		
Peters, James	1	2	4		15
Recraft, John	1	1	3		
Nicks, John	1	1	3		
Moore, John	1	4	2		
Parnold, John	1	3	6		
Pool, John	1	2	4		2
Orr, John	2	3	3		
Kelley, John	1	2	4		2
Huckins, John	1				
Green, Jemiah	1	1	2		
Hindon, James	2	1	2		6
Powell, John	1	2	1		
Lane, James, Ser	3	1	5		11
Clifton, John	2	1	3		
Bracken, James	3		3		
Bowcom, John, Sr	3	2	3		
Butler, James	1		3		
Bowcom, John, Jer	1	2	5		
Hutchins, John, Sr	2		3		
Sugg, Joshua	3		4		10
Laurance, John	1	1	3		
Sugg, Joshua	1		1		
Pool, Lewis	2				4
Sugg, Mosses	1	2	2		4
Nordan, Melchazedick	2		2		
Sugg, Mark	2	1	5		
Powell, Moses	1	2	6		
Dushin, Michael	1	3	5		1
Jordan, Nicholas	1	2	3		
Barber, Plier	1	3	2		
Smith, Ricd A	2	3	5		
King, Ricd	1	2	5		13
Hunter, Reuben	3	2	7		
Powell, Robert	1	1	3		
Johnson, Robert	1	2	3		
Proctor, Reuben	2	2	5		
Hockaday, Saml	1		2		5
Buffelow, Steel	1				
Tarver, Saml	1				
Rycraft, Thos	1	1	2		
Simpkins, Thos	1	3	1		
Buzby, Thos, Jer	1	4	4		3
Hunter, Theop, Senr	3	1	3		47
Hunter, Theop, Junr	1				
Thomas, Thos	3	1	3		
Hornby, Wm	2	1	7		
Hutchins, Wm	1				
Sugg, Wm	1	2	4		
Tipper, Wm	1	2	2		
Studefent, Wm	1	1	4		4
Nutt, Wm	1	4	4		2
Atkins, Wm	1	2	3		2
Clifton, Wm	1		3		
Jones, Wm	1	2	7		3
Hutchins, Thos	1	2	2		
Tedder, Solomon	1				
Hutchins, Moses	1		1		
Studifent, Hollum	2	2	5		8
Nordan, John	1				
Chambers, Josias	1				
Simpkins, Wm	1	1	1		
Mustin, Thos	1		3		1
Harrod, Benjn	1	7	3		1
Brown, Joseph	1				
Minten, David	1				
Jordan, Abner	1	2	5		
Smith, Needam	1	1	3		
Bawcom, Ricd	1		1		
Jordan, Amos	1	2	5		
Hiot, Asa	1	2	4		
Fowler, Bullard	4	2	4		9
Body, Bennet	1				10
Oneal, Benjn	2		3		
Robertson, Chritepher	1	1	2		2
Hobbs, David	1	1	1		
Martin, David	1	3	4		
Henley, Elmore	2	3	5		1
Earp, Edward	1	5	2		
Hocut, Edward	3	4	6		

NAME OF HEAD OF FAMILY.	Free white males of 16 years and upward, including heads of families.	Free white males under 16 years.	Free white females, including heads of families.	All other free persons.	Slaves.
Trawick, George	1	1	4		3
Warren, George			2		3
Lassiter, Hardy	2	3	1		
Bedingfield, Henry	1	4	3		
Shaw, Hugh	3	1	2		1
Earp, Henry	1	3	4		
King, Henry	1	2	4		1
Robertson, Harbert	1		1		2
Burge, Henry	1		2		
Segar, John	2	3	2		3
Earp, John	1	2	5		
Brown, John	2	1	2		
Edins, John	1	3	4		
Traywick, John	1	1	1		
Parker, John	1	1	5		1
Duck, John	1	2	4		
Edwine, John	1	1	2		
Watkins, Joseph	1				2
Watson, James	1	3	4		
Tucker, Joseph	2	1	3		20
Gilbert, James	2	2	5		
Ward, John	1				
Adams, Joshua	1	3	1		
Nicols, Josiah	1	8	2		
Moneyham, Jacob	1	2	2		
Johnson, Julius	1		3		
Brown, John	1		1		
Coal, John	1	3	7		
Johnson, James	1	2	2		
Jordan, James	1	1	4		
Snipes, John	1	1	6		
Hinton, Kimbrough	2		1		29
Alford, Lodwick	2	3	4		24
Ward, Lyda	1	1	3		
Benton, Moses	1	3	3		1
Tucker, Pashell	1	2	3		2
Benton, Robert	1	3	5		
Rabon, Ricd	1	4	3		
Hillard, Rightman	1		3		
Traywich, Robert, Ser	3	4	6		
Traywich, Robert, Jr	1		5		
Horten, Saml	2	4	2		
Hood, Thos	1	2	2		
Coal, Thos	1				
Meals, Thos	2		2		6
Cogbill, Thos	2	1	1		7
Robertson, Thos	2	2	5		8
Barron, Thos	2	2	3		
Wilder, Wm, Jer	1	1	3		
Hocut, Wm	1	1	3		
Tucker, Wm	2	1	4		2
Hobbs, Wm	3		7		3
Earp, Wm	1	1	4		
Wilder, Wm, Ser	1	1	3		
Wilder, Willis	1	3	3		
Rabon, Wm	1		4		
Abot, Sarah			3		
Earp, Susanna			1		2
Prator, Thos		1			
Curtiz, John	1		4		4
Lee, Ann			4		
Edwins, James	1	5	2		
Massey, Hezekiah	1		1		
Duck, Robert	2		2		
Hood, Jesse	1	3	1		
Bedingfield, Wm	1	3	4		
Austin, James	1		1		
Lassiter, Isaac	1		1		
Youngblood, Delilah	1	2	5		
Bell, Burwell	1	1	4		8
Horten, Amos	2	1	4		3
Carpenter, Benjamin	1	2	1		
Austin, Charles	1	2	3		
Amos, Charels	1	5	3		
King, Drewry	1	2	2		
Jones, Drewry	1	2	2		
Bunch, David	1		3		
Horten, Drewry	1	2	6		
Peoples, Elisha	1	1	5		3
Redding, Francis	1	2	4		
King, Francis	1	2	3		
Redding, Francis	1	4	1		
Philliph, Francis	1	1	1		7
Bradley, G	1				2
Hosel, Henry	1		3		2
Alford, Hudson	1	2	3		7
Througher, Henry	1	1	3		
Williams, Hubbard	1	8	5		
Temple, Henry	1		3	6	
Temple, Henry	1	2	3		
Peoples, Joseph	2	1	5		
Mitchel, John	2	3	5		2
Walker, John	1		3		
Harrison, John	2	1	3		
Kelley, John	2	1	3		
Redding, James	2	1	2		
Scarbrough, John	1	1			

NAME OF HEAD OF FAMILY.	Free white males of 16 years and upward, including heads of families.	Free white males under 16 years.	Free white females, including heads of families.	All other free persons.	Slaves.
Privet, James	1	2	1		
Boon, James	1				
Jones, James	4	4	4		5
Laurance, John, Ser	1	2	4		
Lassiter, Jonas	2	4	6		
Thrower, Jesse	1		3		
Wright, James	1	1	1		
Ellis, Jacob	3	5	4		
Lassiter, Jothram	2		3		15
Davis, Jane			1		
Laurance, John, Jr	1		2		
Robertson, John	2	1	3		3
Malaby, John	2	2	6		
Gay, James	1	2	2		
Hinton, John	3	2	3		40
Peoples, John	2		5		1
Lassiter, Luke	1	1	4		
Jordan, Liles	1		2		
Davis, Lewis	1	4	8		1
Robertson, Lott	1				
Hill, Nathl, Ser	2	2	2		1
Hill, Nathl, Jur	1	2	5		7
Verser, Nathan	1	2	2		1
Temple, Robert	3	2	2	8	9
House, Ransom	1	1	2		
Scarbrough, Saml	1		4		
Carpenter, Saml	2	3	5		1
Scarbrough, Saml, Jr	1	1	2		
Harris, Saml	2	1	5		9
Wall, Saml	1	5	8		
Davis, Thos	1	2			
Harris, Thos	1	1	3		1
Robertson, James	1	1	3		
Brown, Thos	1	4	6		
Musten, Thos	1	2	2		
Dookam, Wm	2	3	5		
Walker, Wm	2		5		3
Hill, Wm	1	3	5		
Ambrous, Wm, Ser	1	2	2		1
Jones, Wm	1				
Matthews, Wm	1	1	3		
Ambrous, Wm, Jer	2	3	2		2
Arnull, Wm	1	2	7		2
Gilbert, Wm	1		5		
House, Wm	2	1			6
Hinton, Wm	1				6
Jeffres, Wm	2	2	6		60
Davis, Amey		2	3		
Wright, John	1		5		
Jordan, Wm	2		1		
Ellis, Charles	1	1	2		
Bunch, Thos	1		1		
Waters, Thos	1		2		
Weathers, Elizabeth	1	1	4		
Bunn, John	1	3	5		
Gay, John	1	1	1		
Gay, C		2	2		
Davis, Susanna			3		
Winters, Barney	1	1	3		
Wade, Andrew	1		3		
Horten, Ann	2		3		
Fowler, Ann		1	4	2	3
Wheeler, Benjn	1				
Massey, Burwell	1		1		
Carpenter, Burwell	1	1	5		
Beaver, Benjn	1	4	2		
Flips, Boling	1				11
Bunn, Benjn	2	4	3		
Upchurch, Charles	2	4	6		
Bunn, David	2	1	3		
Philgo, David	2	2	5		
Bagwell, David	1	3	4		
Ray, Daniel	1	2	2		
Horten, David	1	2	2		3
Strickland, Elsha	1	1	4		
Bagwell, Federick	1	4	4		
Strickland, Federick	3	4	6		
Massey, Federick	1	4	3		
Bell, George	1		4		4
Fowler, Godfrey	4		4		5
Fason, Henry	1	4	5		
Dunn, Hardmon	1	3	5		
Massey, Herze	3	1	5		
Pendergrass, John	3	2	5		
Bolton, James	1	3	4		
Privit, Isarel	2		3		
Crudup, Josiah	3		6		23
Bird, Joel	1	3	4		
Pace, James	2	3	3		
Wheeler, John	1				
Stricklung, Joseph	1		2		
Chambley, Isaac	3	3	4		
Walker, John	1	3	5		2
Merrit, John	1	1	2		
Wright, Joseph	2	2	4		16
Hammon, Jesse	1	2	3		
Earp, Joseph	1		3		6

HILLSBOROUGH DISTRICT, WAKE COUNTY—Continued.

NAME OF HEAD OF FAMILY.	Free white males of 16 years and upward, including heads of families.	Free white males under 16 years.	Free white females, including heads of families.	All other free persons.	Slaves.
Perry, James	2	3	3		2
Privit, Jacob	1	2	1		1
Fowler, Joseph	1				
Burin, Jesse	1	1	2		
Morphus, James	1		2		
Rhodes, Jeremiah	1	3	1		
Lee, James B	1	1	2		2
Strickland, Joseph	1		2		
Privit, John	2		2		
Strickland, Isaac	1		1		
Butler, James	1	1	3		2
Segraves, Jacob	1	2	1		
Jilks, Kinchen	1	4	4		8
Earp, Luke	1	3	5		
Strickland, Matthew	1	2	7		13
Bird, Mosses	1	3	3		
Upchurch, Nathan	1	2	2		
Perry, Nathan	1	2	2		
Strickland, Nathan	1	4	4		
Massey, Nathan	1	2	1		
Chambley, Robert	2	3	4		
Rhodes, Radoll	3		3		
Lumlin, Stephen	1	2	2		
Strickland, Sampson	1	2	2		
Hall, Solomon	1	2	7		
Strickland, Saml	1				
Bolton, Sherrod	1	1	2		
Pulley, Thos	1	5	3		
Merrit, Thos	1	1	3		
Lewis, Thos	1	2	4		
Wheeler, Wm	2	1	5		
Ray, Wm, Senr	2	3	6		1
Bunn, James	1	2	1		
Massey, Wm	1		5		
Bagwell, Wm	1	3	1		
Reynolds, Wm	4	3	6		
Alford, Warren	2	3	2	3	11
Barham, Wm	1	3	5		13
Broadwell, Wm	1	2	4		
Nordin, Wm	1	1	4		5
Privit, Wm, Ser	1	3	2		
Privit, Miles	1	1	3		
Jarrot, Willie	1	2	3		
Privit, Wm, Jer	1	1	2		
Ray, Wm, Jer	1		2		
Merrit, Wm	2	2	1		4
Fowler, Wm	2	1	7	1	1
Bell, Zadock	1	2	5		6
Ferrell, Pall	1				
Strickland, Wm	2	4	5		
Wright, William	1				
Perry, Nathan	1	3	4		
Jordan, Dempsey	1		1		
Chamley, James	1	1	1		
Hill, Joseph	1	7	3		
Privit, Peter	1		5		
Newsom, James	1		1		15
Hogwood, George	1				
Martin, Abraham	2	3	3		13
Holding, Arther	1	1	1		
Wall, Arther	2	3	4		
High, Aborgill		1	2		
Smith, Benjn	2	3	4		11
High, Alsey	1	3	3		12
Williams, Dudley	1	3	1		
Williams, David	1	2	3		
Grimes, Dawson	1	1	4		
Powell, Dempsey	3	2	5	1	20
Perry, Francis	4		5		15
Spane, Federick	1		3		18
Perry, Francis	1		3		2
Holding, Federick	2		6		
Fort, Federick	3	4	4		7
Martin, George	1	1	1		20
Grimes, George	1		2		1
Rives, Hannah		2	2		
Meekans, Henry	1	2	2		
Dean, Hardy	2	4	3		3
Moring, Henry	1		1		2
Eazel, John	4		4		2
Holding, John	2	4	4		
Fort, John	2	1	2		8
Harris, John	1	2	2		
Kemp, Jesse	1	1	2		
Wall, Jesse	1	1	3		2
Williams, John	1	1	3		
Fort, James	1		2		6
Marlow, John	1		1	4	
Moreholland, John	2	1	4		1
Kemp, John	3		3		
Roan, John	2	3	3		
Lewis, James	1	1	3		39
Pullen, John	4	2	2		10
Moore, John	1	2	2		1
Rogers, Jacob	1				
Lowry, Matthew	1	4	3		1
Rogers, Michael	5	1	6		25

NAME OF HEAD OF FAMILY.	Free white males of 16 years and upward, including heads of families.	Free white males under 16 years.	Free white females, including heads of families.	All other free persons.	Slaves.
High, Mark	2	3	2		7
Walle, Robert	1	1	2		
Smith, Ricd	1	2	5		
Harris, Reuben	1		6		
Dean, Ricd	1	2	4		
Kemp, Ricd	1	3	2		
Rice, Ricd	1		1		
Thomson, Saml, Sr	2	1	6		3
Harris, Sherrod	2	3	2		
Thomson, Saml, Jr	1	1	1		
Tyrrell, Solomon	2	2	5		7
Holding, Saml, Sr	1		2		3
Holding, Saml, Jr	1	1	2		1
Spane, Thos, Ser	1	3	4		
Williams, Thos	1	2	2		
Boyakin, Thos	2		2		2
Young, Thos	3	2	4		4
Spane, Thos, Jr	2	4	6		4
Lee, Wm	2	5	4		6
Grimes, Wm	1	1	2		
Williams, Wm	2		2		2
Philliphs, Wm	1		2		7
Grimes, Wm, Ser	1	2	3		
Young, Wm	1		2		4
Hockaday, Wm	1		2		2
Martin, Wm	3		6		15
Thomson, Zachariah	4	2	1		2
Bledsoe, Wm	1		1		
Rice, Wm	2	2	4		
Ray, Nathan	1	1	1		
Wall, Burwell	1				
Woodward, Dempsey	1	3	1		
Matthews, John	2	6	5		
Dryars, Thos	1	4	2		
Rogers, Etheldred	4	1	5		7
Rogers, Aron	1				
Holding, Matthew	2	5	2		11
Ferris, James	1		1		
Mobley, Alexr	1				
Lowry, Arther	1	2	3		
Bruce, Arnell	1		5		1
Davis, Benjn	3	1	2		
Pace, Buckner	3		4		10
Wallace, David	1		2		1
Daniel, David	1	2	8		2
Gill, David	1				
Paterson, Francis	4				
Allen, George	2	3	5		
Davis, Glaphzoa	2	1	6		8
Brasfield, George	2	2	2	1	1
Bodine, Grbell	2	1	5		
Russell, George					11
Kennerday, Hugh	1	1	1		
Kemp, Henry	3	3	1		
Mobley, Hammon	2	1	5		
Hall, Joel	1	3	2		
Joplin, James	1	2	2		3
Shaw, John B	3	2	6		12
Weaver, James	1	5	3		
Wallace, John	2	1	7		9
Huskey, John	2	1	4		1
Ward, James	1	1	2		
Gill, Isaac	1				
Hill, Jacob	1	2	1		
Ferguson, Joel	1	4	4		
Kilgo, Isaac	1	1	5		
Pace, John	2		2		1
Lowry, Jesse	1	2	3		
Ray, Joseph	1	1	6		
Micklroy, John	1	2	2		1
Ray, John	1	2	6		
Ray, Luke	2		2		5
Guttree, Lewry	2	2	2		
Joplin, Mark	1	3	4		
Mobley, Milley	1		2		2
Forrist, Martin	2		2		4
Stewart, Mary		1	3		
Mobley, Mordica	2		6		19
Fluellin, Obediah	1	4	2		
Bruce, Peter, Ser	2	2	2		
Bruce, Peter Jr	1	3	3		
Surtherland, Ranson	1	3	4		25
Vinson, Reuben	1	3	4		
Vinson, Saml	1	2	3		
Goodwin, Theops	1	4	3		
Barlow, Thos	1	2	3		
Burnet, Thos	1	2	5		
Shaw, Wm	1	5	3		1
Hall, Wm	1	1	2		
Kennerday, Waystaff	1	7	3		
Rockill, Wm	2	3	6		
Barlow, Wm	1	4	3		
Embrew, Wm	2	4	3		
Weaver, Wm	2		6		
Hall, Wm	1	2	3		1
Jones, Wm	2	1	3		
Vinson, Wm	1		2		

NAME OF HEAD OF FAMILY.	Free white males of 16 years and upward, including heads of families.	Free white males under 16 years.	Free white females, including heads of families.	All other free persons.	Slaves.
Kittle, Wm	2	2	8		
Ferris, Jesse	1		2		
Rice, Roger	1	3	2		
Riddish, John	1	1	3		
Vinson, Joseph	1	2	1		
Tyrrell, Jeptha	3	1	2		13
Bledsoe, Wm	3	1			
Kittle, Benjn	1	2	2		
Elliot, James	1		4		
Jones, Francis			5		
Russell, James			3		
Locklear, Thos			13		
Paterson, Smith	3		3		
Turner, Sarah		1	1		1
Spencehead, Alexr	2	2	3		11
Belvin, Abraham	1		1		
Parram, Avera	1	2	3		
Bledsoe, Barnabas	2	2	7		2
Ward, Benjn	1		2		
Briggs, Charles	1	1	1		10
Dilk, David	1	4	1		4
Burton, David H	2	5	3		
Ragan, David	1		3		
Melone, David	1		3		3
Spears, Dempsey	3	1	2		2
Justice, David	1		3		4
Holderfield, Elizabeth	1	3	5		
Brasfield, Elijah	1		1		
Barker, Edmond	2	3	4		6
Brasfield, Elizabeth			2		
Rigsbey, Federick	1		4		
Wilson, George	1	2	3		1
Thomson, George	1	4	3		
Warren, Henry	2	2	4		7
Rives, Hardy	2	1	3		
Mosley, Henry	2	3	6		2
King, Henry	1	1	4		2
Humphris, John (Virga)	1	3	5		1
Kuton, John	2	1	4		
Goodwin, Isham	2	3	7		
Williot, John	1		4		
Belvin, John	1	4	4		
Moore, James	2		3		
Diol, James	1	4	5		
Brasfield, Joseph	1	1	3	1	1
Golihon, Joseph	1		1	1	
Riley, John, Ser	1	3	3		
Moore, James H	1				
Ward, John	1	1	6		
Ellis, John				3	
Rilley, John, Jr	1		1		
Yergin, John	1	1	2		
Dennis, John	1	1	1		
Goodwin, John	1	1	4		
Ward, Joseph	1		1		
Bledsoe, Jacob	3	1	2		11
Holleway, John	3	1	2		10
Bledsoe, Isaac	1	3	4		
Bledsoe, Jacob, Jr	2	1	3		2
Bodine, John	1		1		
Dilk, Joseph	1		1		
Kercum, James	2	3	7		3
Bledsoe, John	2	1	3		3
Bledsoe, Jacob	1	1	3		
Dobey, John	1	3	3		
Martin, John	1	2	4		3
Pope, Jesse	1	2	2		
Brevis, Job	1		1		
Cheavis, James	1	4	3		13
Gray, John	3	2	4		9
Canneday, Leannerday		1	2		
Bledsoe, Lewis	1	3	3	6	3
Barker, Lewis	3	2	6		7
Moore, Lewis	2	1	5	1	4
Pollard, Major	1		4		3
Marshall, Moses	1	3	1		
Evins, Morris	1	2	8		
Sexton, Obediah	1	4			
Belvin, Pricilla					3
Kilgo, Peter	1	4	3		
Rogers, Peleg	4	3	6		17
Allen, Runnell, Sr	3	1	1		3
Gradey, Robert	3	1	3		
Pollard, Ricd	1		3		
Harrell, Robert	1	1	3		
Mossey, Ricd	3		2		7
Gradey, Robert	3		4		
Holderfield, Ralph	1	2	5		
Philliph, Robert	1				
Evins, Reuben	1				
Allen, Runnell	2	4	2		1
Thomson, Swan	1	5	4		10
Jackson, Thos	1		3		11
Ship, Teller	2	1	2	1	
Goor, Thos	1	2	2		1

HILLSBOROUGH DISTRICT, WAKE COUNTY—Continued.

NAME OF HEAD OF FAMILY.	Free white males of 16 years and upward, including heads of families.	Free white males under 16 years.	Free white females, including heads of families.	All other free persons.	Slaves.
Warren, Wm	2	5	1		3
Dennis, Wm	1	2	4		
Holley, Wm	1		1		
Kelgo, Wm	2	1	2		9
Tate, Wm	1	3	7		1
Commons, Wm	2	2	4		5
Gibbs, Wm	1		4		1
Ship, Wm	2	2	4		3
Griggs, Wm	2	1	5		
Brasheld, Wm	1		2		
Moore, Wm	1				
Wilson, Whitfield	1	1	1		
Allen, Young	1	4	1		2
Shaw, Zachariah	1	2	3		5
Beaver, Zachariah	1	1	4		
Barnes, Lulley		1	4		
Raba, Elsha	1	1	3		
Thomson, Wm	1		3		
Thomas, James	3		2		
Barker, Abner	1	2	1		
Jones, Thos	2		1		4
Pollard, Wm	2	3	3		
Bullard, Joseph	1	1	2		
Robertson, James	2	1	3		
Capman, Saml	1	4	3		
Beaver, Thos	1		4		
Reynold, John	1	2	4		2
Jackson, Wm	1	3	4		
Powell, Willis	2	2	2		
Daniel, Winifred		2	2		
Harrison, Mary	1	7	2		
Evins, Thos					6
Snede, Robert	1	4	3		
Gradey, Dennis	2	1	8		12
Hayes, Jery	1	2	1		
Humphris, Thos	1	1	2		
Hartsfield, Andrew	2	3	4	1	5
Abbott, Abraham	1	1	5		
Jones, Albridgston	1	2	2		1
Sims, Adam	1	1	4		
Pulliam, Benja	2	2	7		5
Dunn, Boling	2		6		10
Card, Benson	1	3	4		
Sexton, Britain	1	1	1		
Campbell, Collin	1	1	3		3
Dunn, Drury	1	2	7		13
Lee, Daniel	1	2	3		
Spane, David	3	2	6		
Andrews David	2	2	5		7
Rains, Enuch	2	1	4		
Parsons, Ephraim	1				
Page, Edward	2	2	5		
Vandegriff, Garret	4	4	5		1
Andrews, Henry	1		1		
Buffelow, Henry	1	3	5		1
Moodey, Henry	1	2	5		
Ivey, Henry	2	2	6		
Sexton, Absalom	2	2	1		
Hunter, Jacob	2	1	6		7
Nutt, John	1	3	3		3
Butler, John	2	2	3		
Rich, Jacob	1	3	4	3	
Hindon, James	1				
Ragan, James	1	1	2		
Walker, Joseph	1	2	4		
Miller, John	1	2	2		
Andrews, Jesse	1	1	5		
Foster, John	1		2		
Little, John	1	1	1		
Harris, Jesse	1				
Spam, John	1	6	4		
Sims, Isham, Jur	1	2	3		
Fergoson, Isaac				6	2
Stephens, Joseph	1	1	2		
Brown, Joseph	1	2	2		
Allen, Joshua	3	3	3		
Sims, Isham, Sr	2		2		2
Sing, John	2	1	3		
Hindon, Isham	2		2		3
Tipper, John	1	3	3		
Proctor, John	1	1	5		
Sexton, John	2	2	6		2
Ragan, Joseph	1		2		
Hunter, Isaac, Ser	3	2	5		29
Gray, Joseph	1	4	2		
Profit, Larkin	2	2	3		
Sims, Murry	1		5		1
Wallis, Matthew	1	4	4		
Sims, Mark	1	2	3		
Rich, Mary	1		2		5
Ivey, Peter	2	2	3		2
Lee, Rowland	1	2	6		
Dodd, Ricd	1		2		
Flemming, Robert	2	1	2		5
Brewer, Rice	2	1	2		11
High, Saml	1	3	5		19
Cheavis, Thos	1	1	3		9

NAME OF HEAD OF FAMILY.	Free white males of 16 years and upward, including heads of families.	Free white males under 16 years.	Free white females, including heads of families.	All other free persons.	Slaves.
Newby, Thos	1	1	3		
Proctor, Thos	3	4	5		
Embrew, Thos	3	3	2		1
Collier, Thos	1	4	3		
Sims, Wm	3	3	7		8
Ragan, Willis	1	2	2		
Dawson, Wm	1		1		1
Campbell, Mary			2		
Sexton, Peter	1	1	2		1
Campbell, Walter	1	3	6		1
Spane, Thos	1		4		
Shorte, George	1		2		
Campbell, John	1	1	3		
King, Arthur	1	2	4		
Hartsfield, Andrew	1				2
Loyd, Ebenezer	1	1	5		
Stripten, Benja	1				
Jones, Burwell	1				
Ward, Benja	1		2		
Hicks, Benja	1				
Low, Cardrick	1	1	1		
Valentine, David	1	1	1		
Hunter, David	2				
Pride, Edward	1		5		14
Silvy, Edward	2	2	4		
Thomas, Francis	2		2		11
Jinks, George	2	1	2		
Thomas, Giles	2	2	5		2
Lane, Henry	2		2		14
Vinson, Hozias	2	2	2		
King, John	3	5	4		
Hartsfield, James	1	3	2		
Sigers, Josias	1		1		
Freman, John	1	2	8		
Terry, John	1	3	2		
Oliff, Jesse	2	1	2		
Freeman, John	2	2	2		
Keath, John	1	6	2		
Hartsfield, John	1		2		1
Jones, James	2	2	4		
Rigsby, James	1	2	2		
Morris, John	1	1	3		1
Wallace, John	2	2	1		
Dillard, Joseph	2	3	3		4
Rhodes, John	1	2	2		30
Kimbrough, John	2		4		30
Lane, Joel	2	2	5		27
Lane, James	1	1	2		16
Dillard, Josiah	1				
Smith, James	1				
Bodine, John	1	2	2		
Smith, Joseph	2	3	2		
Hambey, Mary			2		
Freeman, Needham	1	1	4		
Hicks, Nathl	1	4	1		
—, Newmon	2		4		
Duffee, Patrick	1	2	6		
Holderfield, Ralph	1	1	2		
Holiway, Reuben	1	2	6		
Hamby, Saml	1	2			
King, Sampson	1	1	2		
Hambey, Stephen	1	4	2		
Cope, Thos	3	2	5		
House, Thos	3	3	7		
Dillard, Theops	2	1	2		2
Hunter, Theops, Jur	2	2	1		10
Holliman, Thos	2	3	5		
Jinks, Thos	1	3	3		
Smith, Thos	1		4		
Brazor, Wm	3	3	4		
Brewer, Wm	1	1	4		
Cooper, Wm	1	4	5		4
Wilmouth, Wm	1		1		
Smith, Wm	2	3	6		2
King, Vinson	1	2	2		
Loyd, Ebenezer	1	1	5		
Hucks, Stephen	2	2	3		
Watson, David	1		4		
Rigsbey, Archabeli	1				
Page, Edward	2	2	4		
Humphris, Thos	1	1	2		
Simons, Wm	2	2	4		
Pinney, James	3				
Johnson, Aron	1	3	3		
Burges, Athel	3	4	5		
Bird, Bonner	1	2	4		
Lewis, Berry	1	4	2		
Hobson, James	1				
Almon, Cannada	1	1	3		3
Roberts, Curtis	1	4	3		
Surls, Coventon	1	4	3		
Pealer, Christain	1	3	4		
Blake, Dempsey	1	1	4		7
Barnes, Drewry	1	2	2		
Hobson, Daniel	1		3		
Bradley, Dennis	2	2	1		

NAME OF HEAD OF FAMILY.	Free white males of 16 years and upward, including heads of families.	Free white males under 16 years.	Free white females, including heads of families.	All other free persons.	Slaves.
Roberts, Edmon	1	3	4		3
Sorrell, Edmond	1		1		6
Barber, Going	1	1	4		1
Herndon, George	1		3		
Wardroop, George	1		1		
Motley, Harrison	1				
Surls, Henry	1	3	2		
Hill, Henry	1	2	1		
Buzby, Henry	1	3	4		
Mondaris, John	2	3	5		14
Smith, Isaac	1	3	4		
Loalan, Jesse	2	1			1
Smith, John	1	1	3		
Gatling, Jesse	1	4	2		
Humphris, John	2	3	3		3
Roberts, James	1		1		
Rigsby, John	1		4		
Rigbey, James	1	3	2		
Johnson, Isarel	1	2	2		
Wood, Jacob	1		1		
Motley, John	2	3	4		8
Marr, John	1		1		
Linn, John	1	5	2		2
Roberts, John	1	5	7		
Weatherspoon, John	1	1	2		
Harrod, James	1	2	2		
Herndon, James	1	3	4		
Laskley, Joseph	1		2		
Barber, Joseph	2	5	5		1
George, Jesse	2	2	4		
Motley, John	1	1	5		
Harrod, John	1	3	5		
Wardrop, James	1				
Lumley, Jesse	1	1	3		
King, James	2	4	4		
Brown, James	1		3		
Sicars, John	1	1	2		
Smith, John	1		1		
Blake, James	1	3	4		
Harrod, Martin	1	1	2		
Jones, Mary	2	1	4		16
Roberts, Moses	3				
Johnson, Nathan	1		1		
Perry, Nicholas	1	3	2		2
Marr, Nimrod	1	1	3		
Herring, Owing	2	4	5		
Hobson, Reuben	1		2		
Blake, James	2	4	2		4
Marcom, Saml	1	1	2		
Bradley, Sampson	1				
King, Saml	1		4		
Low, Stephen	2	2	5		
George, Solomon	2	1	3		
Roberts, Thos	1	4	4		3
Johnson, Thos	1		1		
Rich, Timothey	3	1	1		1
Brown, Thos	1	3	4		
Murry, Thos	1	3	2		2
Morris, Thos	1	4	5		
Hobson, Thos	2		4		8
Jones, Tignal	2	2	3		39
Smith, Uriah	1	1	1		
Bodine, Vinson	1		2		
Buzby, Wm	1	1	3		
Mainyard, Wm	3	5	3		7
Sorrell, Wm	1	5	2		2
Weatherspoon, Wm	3	2	2		
Thorn, Wm	2	2	4		2
Yeats, Wm	1	3	7		
Harrod, Wm	2		3		
Hill, Wm	1	1	4		
Brown, Wm	1	2	2		
Ward, Wm	1	3	5		10
Hudgins, Wm	1		2		
King, Wm	1	4	2		
Hobson, Zachariah	1		1		
Smith, Zachariah	1	1	4		2
Laulin, Moses	1	1	1		
Smith, Wm	1	1	1		
Smith, Thos	1	4	4		
Smith, Thos	1	2	1		
Holderfield, Elizabeth	1	4	3		
Jenkins, Saml	1		5		
Sorrell, Thos	2	3	4		6
Burns, John	1				
Corn, Julus					3
Roberts, Solomon	1		1		
Roberts, Aron	1		2		
Burges, Thos	1		1		
Petiford, Laurence				8	
Bodine, John	1	1	2		
Smith, Drewry	1		3		
King, James	1		2		
Morris, Thos	1	5	3		
Cook, Arther	1	1	1		18
Franks, Anthoney	1	2	3		
Sicars, Asa	1	1	3		

HILLSBOROUGH DISTRICT, WAKE COUNTY—Continued.

NAME OF HEAD OF FAMILY.	Free white males of 16 years and upward, including heads of families.	Free white males under 16 years.	Free white females, including heads of families.	All other free persons.	Slaves.
Proctor, Benja	1		4		
Whitehead, Burwell	1	2	3		
MGee, Charles	1	1	1		2
Babb, Christpher	1	6	3		
Joiner, Drewry	1	1	2		
Darnull, David	1		4		3
Hudson, Drewry	1	2	1		
Brown, Drewry	1				
Wiggins, Elijah	1	4	2		
Moore, Field	1	2	3		
Cole, George	1		3		
Utley, Hezekiah	1	1	4		2
Edwards, John	1	2	3		
Bradford, John	3	3	3		3
Linn, James, Jur	3	2	2		10
Taylor, John	4	3	6		
Stinson, Jarrot	1	3	3		
Brown, Josiah	1	2	5		
Cohoon, Jeremiah	1	1	1		
Hudson, John	2	1	6		
Turner, Jasper	1				
Hudgins, John	1	1	1		
Hunter, Isaac, Jur	2	1	1		
Yeats, John	1	1	2		
Woodall, James	1	4	3		
Lane, Joseph, Jr	1	1	3		7
Landinham, James	1	3	4		
Pulliam, James, Jr	1	4			
Streeter, John	2				5
Lane, Joseph, Ser	2				6
Smith, Lewis	1				
Shorte, Lundmon	3	2	4		
Jones, Levy	2	1	2		
Lane, Martin	1		4		5
Muckleroy, Micajah	1	2	3		1
Jones, Nathl, Ser	2		5		17
Jones, Nathl (x Road)	2	3	6		16
Pulliam, Paterson	2	1	3		
Joiner, Patience		1	4		5
Jones, Phillip	1	3	4		
Hunter, Reuben, Jr	1	2	2		1
Rench, Rebecah	1	1	2		
Edwards, Rias	1	1	2		
Bukingham, Sion	1	1	2		
Shorte, Sion	2		1		
Simmons, Solomon	2	1	3		
Behaney, Simon	3	1	1		
Philliphs, Thos	2	3	5		
Hudson, Thos	1	1	1		
Lane, Wm	2				4
Spights, Wm	1	2	2		10
Brown, Wm	1	5	4		
Utley, Wm, Sr	1		1		7
Brown, Wiles	1		3		
Self, Willibey	3	2	4		
Corder, Wm	1		2		
Cole, Shadrick	1		2		
Low, Cradrick	1	1	1		
Bledsoe, Abraham	1	1	4		
Hill, Ann		3	3		7
Piddy, Andrew, Jr	2	2	4		
Wood, Arther	1	1	2		
Oliff, Abell	1	2	3		
Beckworth, Boling	1	1	1		
Utley, Britain	2	1	3		1
Utley, Burwell	2	1	2		
Stephens, Carnaby	1	2	2		
Straight, David	2	2	5		
Barker, Daniel	1	1	2		
Barker, Drewry	1	1	2		
Oaks, Daniel	1	2	6		
Herring, Ephraim	1	2	1		
Lashley, Edmond	1	2	3		
Watson, Elijah	1	1	2		2
Talley, George	1	1	1		
William, George	1	3	2		1
Sinters, Henry	1	3	2		
Wood, George	1				
Bowers, John	1	3	1		
Holliman, James	1	2	3		
Huckabee, James	2	1	3		1
Holland, James, Sr	2		1		
Wood, James	1				
Harrison, John	1		2		
Huckabee, John	2	1	2		6
Hill, Jacob	1	1	2		
Linn, James	1	1	3		
Laurance, Joseph	4		4		
Leavins, Jacob	2		5		3
Leavins, James	1		2		
Norris, John	2	3	5		
Olive, James	2	4	3		
Oliff, John	1	3	3		2
Piddey, Jeremiah	2	3	2		
Stephens, James	1		1		
Thomas, Joseph	5	4	2		
Wood, Kenehin	1	2	1		

NAME OF HEAD OF FAMILY.	Free white males of 16 years and upward, including heads of families.	Free white males under 16 years.	Free white females, including heads of families.	All other free persons.	Slaves.
Barker, Lewis	1	1	3		
Lashley, Lewis	3	3	2		
Barker, Mark	1	2	3		
Bledsoe, Moses	1	2	2		
Hicks, Moses	2	1	4		
Wood, Moses	2		5		6
Dennis, Nathan	1	4	5		
Holland, Ricd	2	3	3	1	
Leavins, Ricd	1	2	2		
Leavins, Ritchmon	1		2		
Barker, Shaderick	1	2	5		
Holland, Sampson	1	5	3		
Hamblton, Stewart	1	3	4		
Olive, Southwood	1	2	4	1	
Rowland, Saml	1	2	2		
Wood, Sampson	2	3	4		
Holland, Thos	1		3		
Hayes, Thos	1	1	4		
Reddin, Thos	1	4	5		
Barker, Wm	2	2	4		5
Hayes, Wm	3	3	5		19
Jennings, Wm	1	5	2		
Oliff, Wm	2	3	4		1
Segraves, Wm	1	2	3		
Thrailkill, Wm	3	3	4		
Sillers, John	2	1	5		
Wood, Burges	1	1	2		
Rogers, Stephen	1		3		
Brown, Robert	1	4	3		
Brown, Barnabas	1		3		
Crain, Henry	1		1		
Thomas, Michael	1				
Hamblton, Andrew	1	2	5		
Turner, Augustus B	2	1	2		
Poe, Benja	1	2	4		
Noles, Benja	1				
Woodward, Corbell	2	1	2		1
Stinson, Clemment	1	1	2		
Segraves, Daniel	1				
Peters, Deal	1		3		
Wheeler, David	3	1	6		
Matthews, David	1	3	4		3
Smith, Ezackail	1	4	7		
Jones, Elkin	1	3	4		
Jones, Etheldred	1	4			5
Jackson, Federick	1				
Wheeler, Henry	1	2	2		
Johnson, Hardy	1		1		
Lilley, Hardy	1	3	4		
Thomas, Hillery	1			2	
Moss, James	2	1	3		
Lewis, Jesse	2	5	2		
Strickland, John, Ser	1	1	5		
Thomas, Jonathan	1	2	2		
Stinson, John	1	2	3		
Franks, Joseph	1	1	2		
Strickland, John	1		5		
Richardson, John	1	2	4		
Hodges, John	1	2	2		
Segraves, Jacob	1	4	5		
Stinson, James	2		3		
Dilk, Joseph	1		1		
Jint, Jesse	1		6		
Jint, John	2	1	3		
Segraves, John, Sr	1	2	3		
Utley, John	2	2	5		1
Woodward, Jordan	1	1	2		2
Farrar, John	3	6	3		11
Utley, Jacob	2	3	4		10
Driver, John	1				
Jones, James	1		2		
Jones, Jesse	2	3	8		2
Dorman, Keziah	2	2	2		
Caudle, Lewis	2	3	2		
Jones, Lewis	4	2	4	1	1
Stinson, Lovit	1				
Messer, Lott	2	2	4		
Yarbrough, Meredith	1	1	1		
Harvell, Moses	1	1	1		
Macklin, Matthew				6	
Rowland, Nathan	2		3		
Thomas, Nathan	2	1	5		
Powell, Nathan	1		2		
Woodward, Plesant	3	1	4	1	
Woodward, Ricd	2		4		1
Green, Silas	1	2	4		5
Driver, Thos, Ser	1	2	4		
Jint, Thos	1	2	6		
Wood, Obediah	1	4	4		
Driver, Thos, Jr	1				
Macklin, Thos				11	
Turner, Titus	1				
Strickland, Wm	1		2		
Rowland, Wm	2	2	5	1	
Harvell, Wm	3	3	3		
Love, Wm	2	2	1		
Williams, Wm	1		1	1	

NAME OF HEAD OF FAMILY.	Free white males of 16 years and upward, including heads of families.	Free white males under 16 years.	Free white females, including heads of families.	All other free persons.	Slaves.
Stewart, Wm				11	
Braswell, Valenitin	1		2		
Jones, Wm	2	2	6		7
Jones, David	3	1	5		
Jones, John	3	4	4		
Watkins, Robert	1	1	2		1
Jackson, Peggey			2		
Beaney, Thos	1	3	3		
Segraves, Wm	2	2	3		
Ren, Joseph	1	2	1		
Matthews, Redmon	2		1		
Hogan, Abraham	1	2	4		4
Griffis, Allen	1	4	1		
Collins, Andrew	5	4			9
Myat, Alexr	1		1		2
Turner, Ann	2		5		18
Ogdon, Benja	1		3		
Myat, Britain	2		2		1
Garner, Book	1		4		
Britt, Benja	1				
Wade, Benja	1		3	1	
Mills, Bethiah	2		4		4
Sanders, Britain	1	1	2		16
Peoples, Drewry	1	2	2		
Utley, David	1	1	4		
Stephens, David	1	3	3		
Turner, David	1				4
Sanders, Ellick	4				5
Buzby, Federick	1	3	2		
Sanders, Hardy	2	1	4		14
Freeman, Henry	1	2	2		
Britt, Joseph, Ser	1	2	1		
Atkins, Isaac	1		3		
Hudson, Isaac	1	2	4	1	2
Britt, Joseph, Jr	1		2		
Lewis, John	1	4	7		
Buzby, James	1	5	3		
Lewis, James (B.)	1	3	1		
Rice, John	1	2	2		
Singlton, James	2	3	7		
Boyeworth, James	2	3	4		
Fisk, Joseph, Jr	1	1	2		
Buzby, John	1		1		
Copeland, Isaac				4	
Myat, John, Ser	2	1	1		5
Utley, Isham	2	5	2		4
Liptrot, James	2	1	2		
Atkins, John	5		4		13
King, John	1	4	3		6
Whitaker, John	2	4	5		7
McCullers, Matthew	2	2	3		14
Nall, Martin	1	2	1		1
Tedrick, Michael	1	2	2		
Myat, Mark	1	4	4		5
Myat, Matthew	1	4	4		1
Nall, Nathan	1	1	3		
Atkins, Nicholas	1				
Hillard, Phillip	1	2	2		
Penney, Penul	1	3	5		3
Pearson, Parish	1	2	3		1
Britt, Ryals	1				
Nall, Ricd	1		1		3
Swanson, Ricd	2	1	7		
Fitch, Roger	1				
Britt, Wm	1				
Gawf, Starling	1	2	5		
Wright, Saml	3	1	3		
Parish, Sherrod	2	1	4		
Pearson, Saml	2	2	3		8
Parish, Thos	2	1	2		
Turner, Simon	2				6
Hill, Theops	1	1	3		
Smith, Turner	3	2	4		1
Cormack, Wm	3	2	4		
Rand, Walter	1	1	2	1	6
Bridges, Wm	2	3	7		1
Tomlinson, Wm	1	1	2		
Rivers, Wm	1		2		
Walton, Wm	3	2	5		14
Pope, Wm	2	3	5		
Stephen, Zaichariah	2	1	2		
Pau, Wm	1	6	1		
McGuffin, Elizabeth			2		
Page, Jesse	5	1	5		
Lankford, Stephen	1		1		
Myat, Wm	1	4	2		
Lewis, James, Jr	1				
Williams, John, Jr	2	4	2		
Smith, Jonathan	2	2	6		23
Fowler, Asley	1				
Sweat, Allen	1				
Jones, Benja	1	3	2		
Allen, Bartlet	1	1	5	1	
Clark, Benja	1	2	4		
Dunston, Charles	1	2	6		
Ferrell, Christain	2		4		
Tabourn, Dempsey				5	

HILLSBOROUGH DISTRICT, WAKE COUNTY—Continued.

NAME OF HEAD OF FAMILY.	Free white males of 16 years and upward, including heads of families.	Free white males under 16 years.	Free white females, including heads of families.	All other free persons.	Slaves.
Brasfield, David	2	1	2		3
Parkinson, Drewry	1	3	3		
Tucker, Daniel	1	5	3		1
Tucker, Ethel	3		2		4
Chammill, Elisha	1		1		3
Siat, Emanuel	1	1	2		
Ruth, Elizabeth			3		
Gear, Federick	2	2	6		9
Campbell, Fanney		2	2		
Evins, Gilber	2	4	3		
Ruth, Georth	2	4	6		
Brogdon, George	3		2		
Shaw, Gabell	2	1	5		2
Ellis, Hicks	2	2	2		
Dockery, Haslin	1	1	1		
Bagley, Harmon	1		4		1
Fowler, Henry	1	2	3		
Tulley, Halack	1	4	3		
Morris, Hugh	2	2	5		
Allen, Jesse	1	1	1		
Thomas, John	1		5		
Nichols, Julus	1		1		
May, John	2	4	4		
Allen, John	2		2		
Colton, John F	1		1		
Nicks, Joseph	3	2	4		
Murry, James	1		2		
Corn, Justin				3	
Jordan, John	3		5		
Shammill, Jonathan	1	1	5	1	
Phillips, John	1	4	2		
Rogers, Job	1	1			2
Sherring, John	1	5	3		1
Shammill, Isaac	1	1	2		4
Rives, Jonathan	2	5	4		
Parkinson, Joel	1	3	4		
Smith, Joshua	1		6		
Dockary, John	2	1	2		
Hicks, Isaac	3	1	4		8
Alston, John	1	7	4	5	15
Little, Joseph	1	3	2		
Little, John	1	1	1		
Carter, Jesse	1	2	5		1

NAME OF HEAD OF FAMILY.	Free white males of 16 years and upward, including heads of families.	Free white males under 16 years.	Free white females, including heads of families.	All other free persons.	Slaves.
Scoggins, John	1	2	5		
Alley, Joseph	1	1	1		
Parker, James	1	2	1		1
Tabun, James				3	
Sandey, Jarred	1	3	2		3
Conyers, John	1		1		
Freeland, Isaac	1		1		
Watts, John	1	1	1		
Reynolds, Jethro	1	1	1		
Rice, Jessee	1		1	1	3
Allen, Kinsmon	1		1		
Ragan, Larkin	1	1	2		
Ferrell, Micajah	2	2	4		6
Reynolds, Michael	3	2	1		
Patterson, Mary	1	2	6		
Holloway, Major	1	5	4		2
Jordan, Margaret	1	4	5		
Cammall, Mary		4	3		
Tomson, Maton	1	2	3		
Dempsey, Micajah				2	
Pollard, Nancey		1	3		
Hudson, Peter	1	3	5		
Hedgepith, Peter				5	
Gouch, Pumphrey	2		2		
Corn, Robert				4	
Tomlinson, Richard	1		8		
Pollard, Richard	3	2	4		
Hall, Robert	1	2	3		
Wilkins, Richard	2	1	4		4
Standley, Richard	1	1	4		
Talley, Richard	1	2	2		3
Patishall, Richard	1		1		
Gooch, Roley	1	1	2		
Griggs, Rodeyan	1	1	2		2
Banks, Richard	4	1	2	2	12
Smith, Samuel	1	2	2		
Peck, Samuel	2		2		12
Jenkins, Samuel	1	2	4		
Pitchford, Samuel	2	4	2		3
Tarrey, Starling	1	2	2		
Campbell, Sarah			1		3
Watts, Spiner	3		2		5
Alley, Samuel	1	4	3		1

NAME OF HEAD OF FAMILY.	Free white males of 16 years and upward, including heads of families.	Free white males under 16 years.	Free white females, including heads of families.	All other free persons.	Slaves.
Talley, Spencer	1		1		
Ross, John	1	2	3		
Noe, Thomas	1	4	3		
Tomlinson, Thomas	1	3	5		26
Pruit, Thomas	1		4		
Nicols, Thomas	2	3	4		
May, Thomas	1	2	2		
Dorus, Valentine				8	
Carpenter, William	1	2	4		
Rives, William, Jur	1	1	1		
Nicols, William, Jur	1		5		
Nichols, William, Ser	2	2	3		
Evans, William	2	6	5		
Burks, William	2	4	1		
Hodge, William	1	2	6		
Allin, William	1	2	4		
May, William	1		3		
Grant, William	1	1	4		
Jones, Willis	1		2		5
White, William	2	3	4		7
Bagwell, William	1				4
Watts, William	1	3	5		
Ferrell, William	3	3	6		
Little, William		1	2	2	
Rives, William	2	4	3		8
Sandey, William	1		1		
Daniel, Woodson	3	3	6		26
Ashley, William	2	2	3	2	3
Reynols, William	1	2	2		
Floyed, Amos	1	3	3		
Rowland, Federick	1	4	4		
Allen, Josiah	1				3
Griffis, John	3	2	2		
Ivey, Peter	2	1	3		6
Emborough, William	2	2	4		
Olive, James	2		1		3
Myatt, John, Jur	1	1	1		2
Buzby, William	2		4		
Hinton, James	1	4	2		36
Herrington, Samuel	1	1	8		
Burt, John	1	2	4		13

MORGAN DISTRICT, BURKE COUNTY.

FIRST COMPANY.

NAME OF HEAD OF FAMILY.	Free white males of 16 years and upward, including heads of families.	Free white males under 16 years.	Free white females, including heads of families.	All other free persons.	Slaves.
Dobson, Jos., Jr	3	3	5		1
Young, Joshua	1	5	4		
Davidson, George	1	3	1		1
Wasburn, Matthew	1	1	1		
Bradshaw, Isaiah	1	1	2		
Stroud, Peter	1	5	2		3
Stroud, Peter, Jr	1		1		
Stroud, Jesse	1	3	1		
Washburn, David	2		6		
Washburn, Drury	1	1	2		
Patten, Wm	1		2		
Patten, Sam	1	3	2		
McWilliams, Jas	1	2	5		
McCracon, Quilla	1	2	5		1
Reed, Robt	1	4	3		1
Trammell, Jno	1	3	4		
Brown, Jos	4		5		
McDowell, Jas	1	2	2		2
Cathey, Wm	3	4	5		3
McClure, Andw	3	5	5		
Durr, Wm	3	2	4		3
Welsh, Thos	1	3	1		1
Hannah, Tho H	1		1		
Dickeson, Cathrn	1	1	5		
Melony, John	1		1		
McClure, Francis	3		4		
Jones, Jno	1	3	3		
Edenten, Rhoda	2	5	2		
Collet, Wm	1	2	2		
Bibo, Thos	1	1	3		
Burchfield, Mishh	1	1	4		5
McDowell, Jno	1	1	1		1
Carol, Sterling	1		1		
Carol, George	1	1	8		
McDowell, Jos, Jun	1	2	1		9
Carson, Jno	2	5	2		12
Welsh, Jno, Senr	3	3	5		
O'Neal, Wat	2	1	3		
Webster, Moses	1	2	4		
McPeters, Jonathan	1	2	2		
McPeters, Jos	1	3	5		
Plumley, Wm	3	1	3		
Trorps, Nicholas	3	3	3		
Shuke, Jacob	1	6	3		
Davidson, Jno	3	5	6		6
Neall, Wm	4	1	4		
Patten, Elijah	1	2	6		2

FIRST COMPANY—con.

NAME OF HEAD OF FAMILY.	Free white males of 16 years and upward, including heads of families.	Free white males under 16 years.	Free white females, including heads of families.	All other free persons.	Slaves.
Hobs, Mary			2		
Mitchell, Pounce	1	2	2		
Inman, Saml	1	2	1		
Inman, Henry	1		1		
Plumly, Stephen	1	1	2		
Williams, Henry	1	1	3		
Stout, Saml	2	5	3		
Reid, Jno	1		3		
Neall, Jas	1	4	2		1
Wiggins, Abram	1	2	2		1
Brittain, Aron	1		2		
Brandon, Martin	2	4	7		
Cathey, George	2	3	4		5
Brown, Chas	1		4		
Cathey, Marget			4		
Neall, And'w	1	1	4		
Lewis, Wm	1	2	4		
Kelton, Wm	1	4	6		7
Flord, David	1	3	2		
McGonigle, Jno	1	1	3		
Posey, Francis	1	4	2		
Wilson, Thos	5		2		12
Hill, Robt	1	1	1		
Rus, Rose	1	3	5		
Davis, Ben	5	3	4		
Culberson, Davd	1	1	1		
Bright, Tobias	1	1	1		
Blakely, Robt	1	1	6		
Mashburn, David	1		2		
Jetton, Jno	1	1	4		2
Higgins, Wm	3	2	6		
Norton, Messer	1	3	5		
Templeton, Arche	4	2	4		
Martin, Jno	3	4	5		
Hix, James	1	1	2		
Atwater, Isaac	1				
Melony, Edwd	1	2	6		
Davidson, Ben	2	1	9		
McBride, David	1	2	1		
Glass, Thos	2		6		
Glass, Henry	1	2	1		
McGonigle, Wm	1	1	3		
Logan, Jane	2	1	3		
Kelly, Wm	3	5	3		
Bird, Ben, Sen	2		2		2
Bird, Ben, Jr	1	1	2		
Brevard, Zeb, Jr	1	2	3		

FIRST COMPANY—con.

NAME OF HEAD OF FAMILY.	Free white males of 16 years and upward, including heads of families.	Free white males under 16 years.	Free white females, including heads of families.	All other free persons.	Slaves.
Hemphill, Thos	2	2	7		11
Adkins, Jno	3	2	6		
Ellison, Thos	1	1	5		
Ellison, Henry	1	4	1		
Hambrick, Robt	1	2	2		
Thompson, Zach	1		1		
Penhly, Jno	1	2	2		
Regan, Thos	2	4	4		
Vickry, Luke	1	1	3		
Ellison, Ben	2	2	3		
Young, Jane			2	5	
Wilson, Jno	1	1	1		
Smith, Jared	1		1		
Gunter, Agusta	1	1	1		
McClisky, Jno	1		1		
Kelly, Alex. Ham	1	2	2		
Oneal, Charles	1		1		
Rogers, Mourning	2	3	2		
Adams, George	1	1	2		
Givins, Wilm	1	2	4		
SECOND COMPANY.					
Conally, John	1	3	5		10
Shell, Jno	2	4	4		
Martin, Isaac	1	6	3		
Hashan, Abram	1	4	3		1
Dudly, Rebekah			2		
Martin, Marget		2	1		
Wagoner, Marget			1		
Francum, Wm	1	3	3		
Francum, Jno	1		1		
Martin, Tho	1	2	4		
Moore, James	2		5		
Conally, Wm	2	2	2		
Fleming, Abram	1	3	3		8
Winkler, Conrod	1	1	3		
Spencer, Jno, Sr	1	3	5		
Smith, Zadock	1	5	3		
Murray, Jno	1		4		
Murray, David	1	2	5		
Clarke, Ben			1		
Suttlemire, Jacob	1	3	4		
Bradshaw, Wm	1		7		
Boman, Edw'd	1		3		3
Boman, Gilbert	1	2	6		
Fips, Jno	1	3	7		

MORGAN DISTRICT, BURKE COUNTY—Continued.

SECOND COMPANY—con.

NAME OF HEAD OF FAMILY.	Free white males of 16 years and upward, including heads of families.	Free white males under 16 years.	Free white females, including heads of families.	All other free persons.	Slaves.
Bellew, Jos	2		3		
Clarke, Beverly	1		3		
Bellew, Stephen	1	1	4		
Howk, George	2	2	6		
Tillotson, Ben	1	2	5		
Turner, Nathan	1	1	4		
Francum, Rebekah	1	1	1		
Conally, Jas	1	3	4		
Conally, Hugh	1	1	3		
Barnhart, Jno	1	2	3		
Dereberry, Jacob	1	4	3		
Derebery, Mich'l	1	3	4		
Pain, Wm	1	2	7		2
Perkins, Joshua	3	3	2		
Taylor, Wm	1		1		
Stoner, Henry	3	2	7		
Clarke, Wilm	1		4		
Grenstaff, Michl	1	1	4		
Whitehead, Mary			3		
Winkler, Thos, Sr	1	1	2		
Suttlenire, Adam	2	3	3		
Bellew, Willm	1	9	2		
Master, Henry	1	1	5		
Williams, Anne	1	1	2		
Baker, H. Barton	1	3	5		
Brown, Dan'l	1	2	4		
Berry, Joseph	2	3	6		
Berry, Jas	1	1	1		
Berry, Jno	1	1	4		
Berry, Lot	1	2	2		
Baldwin, Wm	1	4	4		
Giles, Saml	1	2	2		
Winkler, Joseph	1	1	2		
Wilson, Jno	1		2		
Smith, Thos	2	1	4		
Erwin, Agnes		1	1		
Martin, Jas	1	1	1		
Spencer, Jno, Jr	1		3		
King, Jas	1	1	3		
Mason, Robt	1	1	5		
Marcle, Laurenc	1	1	3		
Pack, Elisa	2		2		
Hart, Michal	1	3	7		
Winkler, Thos, Jr	1	1	2		
Gibs, Jno	1	6	3		
Baker, James	1	1	4		
Boone, Sherwood	1	1	2		
Parmer, Jno	2				
Pruett, Jno	1	2	5		
Grider, Martin	1	1	6		
Williams, Leah	1	1	2		
Pruett, Henry	1		1		
Innes, James	3	2	2		
Bradsha, Josiah	1	3	3		
Grasty, Mary		1	2		
Morgan, George	1	5	2		

THIRD COMPANY.

NAME OF HEAD OF FAMILY.	Free white males of 16 years and upward, including heads of families.	Free white males under 16 years.	Free white females, including heads of families.	All other free persons.	Slaves.
Baker, Davd	1	3	3		
Penland, Robt	1	4	6		1
Penland, George	3	2	5		
Hanson, Bartlet	3	4	3		6
White, Ben	2	3	3		
Antony, Paul, Sr	2	2	2		1
Baker, Jas	1				
Baxter, Jas	1		4	2	
Browning, Jno	3	4	5		
White, Thos, Jr	1	6	4		
Parks, Ben	1	4	4		3
Antony, Jacob, Sr	3		4		
White, Reuben	1	2	3		
Baker, Jno	1	2	3		
Mason, Elisa			4		
Beck, Jacob	3	6	5		
Rogers, James	1	1	2		
Shefela, Philip	2		1		
Penland, Wm	5	2	3		1
Baker, Charles	1		2		
Prichard, Jas	1	2	7		
Fowler, Edwd	2	1	3		
Walker, Tho	1		2		
Medly, Jos	1	1	2		
White, Thos, Sr	1		2		5
Shell, Simon	1		4		
Shell, Fred	1	3	6		
Shell, Fred, Jr	2	1	2		
Shenite, James	1	1	3		
McDonell, Dav'd	1	1	3		
Mitchenor, Thos	1	3	2		1
McGahey, Jno	1	1	2		
Erwin, Arthur	3		9		
Avery, Waight	1	1	6		24
Brown, Jno Colwill	1	3	5		7
Pruett, Jos	2	4	2		7

THIRD COMPANY—con.

NAME OF HEAD OF FAMILY.	Free white males of 16 years and upward, including heads of families.	Free white males under 16 years.	Free white females, including heads of families.	All other free persons.	Slaves.
Mosely, George	1	2	5		2
Pincy, Stephen	1	2	5		
Wright, Dan	1		1		
Fox, Titus	1	2	3		
Scott, George	1		7	7	
Baker, Henry	1	3	4		6
Gyer, Jacob	2	3	4		
Cole, Alex	1	1	3		
Fox, Jno	1	3	2		
Wakefield, Henry	1	2	4		2
Simpson, Jno	1	2	3		
Harbison, Alex	3	3	3		
Stilwell, Jno	1	3	3		
Odel, Reuben	1	1	1		
Rose, Ben	1	1	2		
Penly, Joshua	1	3	4		
Parks, Thos	2	3	6		1
Alexander, Elisa	1		2		
Antony, Paul, Jr	1				
Brasfield, Jno	1	1	1		
Antony, Philip	1		4		
Trammell, Jno	2	1	2		
Painter, Jno	2	2	3		
Alexander, James	1	5	4		
Antony, Jacob, Jr	1		1		
Fox, Allen	1	2	2		
Branch, Saml	1	2	4		
Scott, Miriah	2	1	3		
Gilmore, Robt	1	2	2		
Parks, Larkin	1		2		
Phillips, Larasus	1	3	3		
Penly, Willm., Jr	3		1		
Penly, Wm., Senr	2	3	3		
Hall, John	2	2	2		
Burkes, Rollin	4	4	4		
Church, Robt	1	2	1		
Church, Thom	1	1	1		
Tramel, Big Denis	2	2	3		
Simpson, James	1	1	1		
Wakefield, John	1	4	3		
Scott, Wiley	1		6		
Piercy, Elisa	1	3	3		
Ustam, Wm	1	1	2		
Tramele, Little Denis	1	1	3		
Allen, Jumima			2	2	
Sherrill, Ute	1	4	4		
Wagley, Jno	2		4		
Duk, Jno	1	2	2		

FOURTH COMPANY.

NAME OF HEAD OF FAMILY.	Free white males of 16 years and upward, including heads of families.	Free white males under 16 years.	Free white females, including heads of families.	All other free persons.	Slaves.
Forgayn, James	3	3	4		
Edmison, Jas	3	3	3		
Holinsworth, Sam	2	2	9		
Adams, Howell	1	1	2		
Hailey, Mark	1		5		
Raybon, Kizzi			1		
Conizo, Harison W	1	2	8		
Green, Wm	2	4	1		
Green, Elijah	1	2	5		
Morris, Wilm	2	4	3		1
Haily, Rd	2	3	4		
Williams, Thom	1	2	2		
Raybon, Hodge	1	2	1		1
Harris, Wooton	2	1	3		
Huggins, Luke	1	4	3		
Wadkins, Else		2	1		
Adams, Ben	1	1	2		1
Fleming, Jno	1	2	3		
Fleming, Peter	1	3	4		
Davis, Clem	1	4	1		
Fleming, Thom	1	3	4		
Pickeral, Ben	1	4	4		
Hailey, Wm	1	4	4		
Humphris, Jas	1		1		
Smith, Jas	1		1		
Goodbread, Philip	1	1	3		
Goodbread, Jos	1	2	4		
Huggins, Phillip	2		1		
Stoker, Jas	1	1	2		
Wheeler, Thos	1	4	2		
Janis, Thos	1		2		
Wallace, Jno	1	2	1		
Oaks, Joshua	1	2	3		
Bradsha, Obadiah	1	1	5		
Bryan, Thom	1		2		
Mendinall, Jesse	1	2	2		
Burgin, Ben	2	6	1		
Hamby, Wilm	3		2		
Cozby, John	2	2	5		
Nicols, Thos	1	3	6		
Portman, Wm	1		1		
Jax, Wm	1	1	2		
Wilson, James	1		2		
Noblet, Jno	1	2	2		

FOURTH COMPANY—con.

NAME OF HEAD OF FAMILY.	Free white males of 16 years and upward, including heads of families.	Free white males under 16 years.	Free white females, including heads of families.	All other free persons.	Slaves.
Chafen, Jos, Jr	3		3		
Petillo, Jno, Sen	2		2		3
Hodge, Robt., Sr	1		6		
Porter, Wilm., Sr	2		4		
Haws, Jacob	2	3	1		
Horrill, James	1		1		3
Chafen, Mary			2		
Hughes, Sam	2		2		
Jackson, Edward	2	5	3		
Fikes, Elisha	1		1		
Litle, Thom	1	3	1		
Petillo, Midleton	1	1	1		1
Brown, Thos	2		3		
Cornpin, Ellis	1	1	1		
Ledford, Nicholas	1		1		
Porter, Wm, Jn	1	1	3		
Strain, Henry	1	4	1		
Elliot, James	1		3		
Chaffen, Elias	1		1		
Diment, Mary	2	2	2		
Keller, Jacob	1	2	3		
Hodge, Robt., Jn	1	2	1		
Wood, Jos	1		1		
Doaty, Jno	1	2	2		
Davis, Thom	1	2	1		
Engld, William	1	2	3		
Scolds, Joseph	1		4		
Wallace, Ben	1	4	4		
Beward, Zeb., Jn	1		2		
Julin, Ben	1	1	4		
Julin, William	1	2	6		
Penkly, Michal	1	1	1		
Redick, Cornelius	1				
Chaffen, Amos	1	1	3		
Gilliland, Jno	1	4	4		
Collins, Prudence					

FIFTH COMPANY.

NAME OF HEAD OF FAMILY.	Free white males of 16 years and upward, including heads of families.	Free white males under 16 years.	Free white females, including heads of families.	All other free persons.	Slaves.
Kilpatrick, Robt	1	5	4		
Webb, Jas. Crit	4	2	1		
Murphey, Wilm	1	3	1		3
White, Joseph	1	2	4		7
Johnson, Wm	1	3	6		
Boone, Jesse	1	3	5		
Hankins, John	1	3	2		
Holliway, George	1	1	2		
Lovin, Wilm	1	1	4		
Hickman, George	3	4	5		1
Weakfield, Charles	4		3		3
Wakefield, Thom	1		3		
Ewings, Isaac	1		1		
Fletcher, Reubin	1	2	1		
Church, Jno	1	1	4		
James, Jos	1		4		
Williams, Wm	1	3	2		
Hite, Reid	2		5		7
Moore, Jno, Senr	2	2	4		
Moore, Jno	1	1	4		1
Adkins, Ben	1	5	3		
Eastress, Reubin	1	4	3		9
Harris, Lewis	2	5	3		
Haris, Edward	2	1	13		
Miller, George	1	1	3		
Waters, Deep	1		3		
Waters, Abram	1	3	5		
Coker, Leonard	1	1	1		
Coker, Charles, Sr	2	2	3		
Coker, Charles	1	1	2		
Coker, Wm	1	2	1		
Moore, Jesse, Sr	2		7		
Moore, Jesse	1		3		
Moore, Danl	1		4		2
Coffee, Reubin	1	1	4		1
Coffey, John	1	1	1		
Coffy, Jas	1	1	3		1
Holland, Jas	2	4	5		
Coker, Joseph	1		2		
Moorhead, Jas	1	2	2		
Whitlock, Matha	2	2	3		
Mullin, Danl	1	1	5		
Calleway, Ricd	1		1		1
Hicks, David	2	2	3		
Beard, Ezekiel	2	3	2		
Beard, Saml	3	2	2		
Ward, Byn	2	4	2		
Ward, Joshua	1	1	2		
Giddins, James	1	1	4		
Searsey, Robt	2	3	3		
Edmison, Wm	2	2	4		1
Hays, Thom	3	3	3		
Hays, George	1		2		
Webb, Ben	1	1	2		
Webb, Jas., Jr	1		2		
Walker, Reynard	1	5	2		

MORGAN DISTRICT, BURKE COUNTY—Continued.

NAME OF HEAD OF FAMILY.	Free white males of 16 years and upward, including heads of families.	Free white males under 16 years.	Free white females, including heads of families.	All other free persons.	Slaves.
FIFTH COMPANY—con.					
Boon, Jonathn	1	3	5		
Dowell, George	2	3	3		
Helle, Moses	2		4		
Anderson, Thos, Jr	2	2	6		1
Powers, Jessey	1	1	5		
Powers, Thom	2	1	2		
Rice, Jno	3		2		
Smith, Nathan	1	1	2		
Medecarst, Rice	1	2	5		
Staff, Moses	1	3	3		
Neely, Jas	1	4	6		
Wilson, Michal	1	3	3		
Jenell, Wm. F.	1	3	7		
Wilson, James	1		2		
James, Rollin	1		6		
Renault, Wm	1		1		
Hutchins, George	1	3	3		
Eastriss, Leonard	1		2		
Wilson, Wm	1	1	3		
Church, Thom., Sr	2	1	4		
Snead, Jacob	3		8		
Carter, George	2	4	5		
Church, Robt	1	2	1		
Eastriss, Laybon	2		2		
Brown, Jno	1	3	3		
King, Baker	1	2	2		
Whittenton, Jno	1	3	2		
Guin, Champion	1		1		
White, Wm, Senr	5		2		12
SIXTH COMPANY.					
Cowan, Joseph	2	1	3		
Reed, Jno	1		3		
Wilson, Greenberry	1	1	4		3
Bars, Caleb	1	5	4		
Sellers, James	1	1	4		
Hall, Jno	1	3	6		1
Wilkinson, Moses	1		3		3
Sellers, Jno	1	2	1		
Pearson, Michal	1		1		
O'Neal, Patrick, Jr	1		1		
Dizard, Jno	1	6	4		
Sellers, Robt., Sr	1	2	3		
Sellers, Robt	1		5		
Rutherford, Jas	1	2	3		2
Dizard, Marget	1		1		
Allen, Jno, Sr	4	2	4		
Hytle, Hezekiah	2	2	6		1
Morrison, Wm	5	1	4		
Andrews, Danl	3	4	4		
Rutherford, Wm	2		2		5
Rust, Enos	4	3	2		
Rust, Peter	1	2	3		
Moore, Wm	1	3	5		6
Gunter, Claybon	1	1	1		
Plumly, Aham	1	1	5		1
Devine, Jas	1	1	2		
Denton, Elisa	2		4		
Carely, Jas	1	1	2		
Carely, Henry	1	4	2		
Sullivan, Danl	1		2		
Grant, Isaac	1		2		
O'Neal's, Patrick	2		2		
Montgomery, Jno	2		2		
Montgomery, Jas	1	3	4		5
Blag, Jas	1		2		
Leatherwood, Edw'd	1	3	5		
Montgomery, Bridgt			2		2
Hunter, Andrew	1		4		
Justice, Jos	2	2	1		
Simmons, Rd	1	2	1		
Gray, Lydia	2	1	3		5
Bradshaw, Field	1	4	3		2
Hytle, Edwd	1	3	3		
Tenison, Jacob	1	1	1		
Chanler, Henry	1	4	3		
McDowell, Jno	2	2	4		5
Montgomery, Robt	1	4	3		7
Beall, Thos	1	4	5	1	1
Hyett, Simon		1	3	1	
Ferrile, Isaac		5	4	1	
Robison, Alex	1		3		
Barchfld, Aberilla	1	3	3		
Bellew, Robt	3	3	5		
Rust, David	2	3	3		
Mays, Jno	1	3	2		
Finley, Charles	1	6	3		
Rutherford, Jno	2	2	3		2
Gardner, Wm	2	3	7		3
Polk, Jno	2	4	3		
Downing, Jno	2	3	2		
Long, Alex	2		2		
McAdams, Jno	3	3	4		
Jones, Ben	1	3	2		
Worley, Frank	1	3	2		
Sumners, Jno	5	2	4		

NAME OF HEAD OF FAMILY.	Free white males of 16 years and upward, including heads of families.	Free white males under 16 years.	Free white females, including heads of families.	All other free persons.	Slaves.
SIXTH COMPANY—con.					
Wood, Saml	3	3	6		
Reno, Jno	1	2	5		
Morison, Wm, Jr	1		4		
Jackson, Chaswl	1	1	8		
Probit, Wm	1		1		3
Patten, Elijah, Jr	1	1	2		
Hemphill, Jas	3	4	4		
Morison, Eliza		1	6		
Lonels, Davd	1		1		
Martin, Henry	2	1	5		
Jewell, Jas	2	1	3		
Corby, Wm	3		4		
Hicks, Zacheus	1	1	2		
Greg, Wm	1	3	2		
Elder, Andrew	1	2	1		
Woods, Andw	2	1	5		
Patten, Robt	1	1	3		
Patten, Frank	3	1	6		2
Cowan, Marget			1		
Daniel, Jno	2		5		
Blankenship, Lodo	1	4	1		
Hodge, Frank	1		1		
Hodge, George	1	1	3		
Hall, Jno, Jr	1		2		
Hall, Joshua	1		3		
Hughes, Andrew	1	1	4		
Baker, Bardel	1		1		
McElwrath, David	1	5	7		
Woods, Robt	1		1		
Evits, George	1		3		
Hall, Naomi		2	2		
Walker, Jno	1	3	3		
Smith, Jno	1	3	3		
SEVENTH COMPANY.					
Coreponong, Albert	1	4	4		
Franklin, Jno, Sr	2	1	6		
Antony, Martin	2	5	2		
Sansom, Micaja	2	2	4		
Fais, Edmund	1	3	3		
Littlejohn, Eli	1	3	3		
McDowell, Col. Jos	2		5		10
McKinny, Henry	1		1		2
Tomson, Jeremiah	2	2	4		17
Erwin, Jno	1	6	3		3
Maxwell, Jno	2	1	2		
Lane, Jno	1	2	2		
McGimsey, Jno			1		3
Fleming, Robt	1	2	8		
Wilsken, Thos	1	1	6		9
Coffee, Ben	1	3	2		
Murphey, Jas	1	1	1		5
Harper, Jno	1		2		
Harper, Jno, Jr	2	3	3		
Erwin, Alex	1	3	7		11
Fonay, Jacob	1				6
Kelly, Ben	1	3	1		
Tummins, Saml	1		2		
Isom, Christn	2	3	3		
Case, Thos	1		3		
Macay, Hugh	1	2	2		
Fismire, Wm	1	1	3		
Cook, Adam	2		3		
Maxwell, Isaac	1	2	2		
Dotson, Esau	1		1		
McKinny, Elisa	1		4		1
Bradford, Bennet	1	2	4		1
Carter, Wm	1		1		
Husband, Elsa			3		
Turmire, Saml	1		1		
Goble, Jno			1		
Clarke, Nancy	2	4	5		
Clarke, Joana	1	3	3		
Clarke, Jno	1		3		
Arney, Lorane	1		3		
Wagoner, Christi	1	3	2		
Sutser, Adam	1	4	2		
Cook, George	1		5		
Dobs, Chesly	2	4	4		
Winkler, Adam	1	1	2		
Winkler, Thos, Sr	1		3		
Winkler, David	1		2		
Winkler, Jersey Conrod	1	1	2		
Winkler, Big Conrad	1	2	2		
Howk, Michl	1	3	4		
Moody, Tho	1	2	2		
Moody, Jno	1	1	2		
Sweat, Gilbert	1	2	4		
Sweat, Ephraim	1		4		
Hughes, Hana			4		
Martin, Phillip	2	1	5		
Martin, George	1	2	4		
Little, Wm	1	1	3		
Little, Jno	3	1	1		
Day, Thos	3		6		
Stallins, Abram	1	1	6		

NAME OF HEAD OF FAMILY.	Free white males of 16 years and upward, including heads of families.	Free white males under 16 years.	Free white females, including heads of families.	All other free persons.	Slaves.
SEVENTH COMPANY—continued.					
Stephens, Phil	1	3	7		
Davis, Wm	2	2	2		
Fiass, Jonathan	1	2	2		
Hobs, Nathan	1	3	2		
Lane, Thos	1	4	3		
Trible, Jno	2		2		
McDowell, Charles	1	2	5		10
Perkins, Elisha	2	2	2		9
Murphy, Silas	1	5	2		
Pilm, Wm	2	1	3		
Lorance, Wm	1		1		
Dinbery, Adam	1	3	5		
Husband, Veasy	1		2		
Tips, Jacob	1	4	3		
Franklin, John, Jr	1	1	3		
Cragg, Thos	1		2		
Crag, Saml	1		2		
Harper, Meredith	1	1	3		
Baldin, Jacob	1		1		
Crawford, Tom	1		1		
Gibson, David	1	2	4		
Gibson, William	1	3	2		
Gibson, Harmon	1		1		
Cray, Joab	2	1	2		
Stafford, Jno	1	2	2		
Barns, Rd	1	1	2		
Coffee, Cleveland	1	2	4		
Crag, Christn	1	3	2		
Hughes, Jno	1	1	2		
Bolinger, Danl	1	3	2		
Henery, John	2		2		
Little, Marget			2		
Jones, Ambrous	1		1		
Crisp, Wm	1		2		
Baldin, Jno, Senr	1		1		
Landers, Jno	1	1	4		
Prichard, Jas., Sr	2	2	2		
Gilbert, Joshua			1		
EIGHTH COMPANY.					
Reid, Henry	1	2	3		
Reid, James	1	1	3		
Mayberry, Lewis	1	2	1		2
Barns, George	1	1	6		
Gibson, Stephen		2	1		1
Rutor, Lewis	1	1	1		
Bradburn, Thos	1		1		4
Warren, Robt	2	3	6		
Warren, Wm	1	3	1		
Pane, George	3	1	3		
Reid, Wm	1	4	3		
Steel, Andw	3		2		3
Burgess, Matthew	1	5	3		
West, Alex	1	2	4		
Scott, Thos	1	4	4		
Emmit, Rd	1	2	5		
Bradford, Jno	1	2	2		
Green, Thos	4	3	6		
Russell, Ried	1	1	2		
Crisp, Bray	1	1	1		
West, Alex, Sr	1	2	6		
Horse, Jno	3	1	1		
Collier, Jas	1	1	2		
Smith, Jno	2	1	2		
Cox, Matthew	3	1	1		4
Roberts, Wm, Jun	1	1	1		
Moon, Robt	1	1	2		
Brown, George, Jr	1	2	3		
Brown, Rd	1	2	2		
Steel, Saml	1	2	2		
Winkler, Jacob	5		1		
Tuttle, Amos	2	2	2		
Sherril, Wm	1	4	5		
Headley, Jno	1	2	3		
Austin, Ben	2		6		
Hunsucker, Abrm	2		1		
Hunsucker, Abrm., Jr	1		5		
Hunsucker, Jno	1	2	4		
Pain, Barnet	1	4	3		4
Fletcher, Jas	1	2	5		
Medlock, Nicolas	2		3		
Medlock, Nicols, Jr	1	1	2		
Falls, John	1	2	4		
Bains, John	1	2	2		
Reid, Hugh	1	6	2		
Banks, Elijah	1	3	2		
Fox, Hugh	3	4	7		
Baker, Henry	1	3	4		
Keller, Jacob	1	1	2		
Keller, Martin	2	3	2		
Price, Jno Yeats	1	2	4		
White, Luke	1	3	7		
Jones, Nicholas	1	4	2		
Walker, Dailey	1	2	5		
Teague, Edwd	1	6	3		2
Teague, Jno	1	4	3		

MORGAN DISTRICT, BURKE COUNTY—Continued.

EIGHTH COMPANY—con.

NAME OF HEAD OF FAMILY.	Free white males of 16 years and upward, including heads of families.	Free white males under 16 years.	Free white females, including heads of families.	All other free persons.	Slaves.
Hadly, Joshua	1		4		
Green, Elijah	1				
Roberts, Wm, Sr	2	1	6		
Keller, Christina	1	1	1		
Tenny, James	1	3	3		
Colwell, Wm	1	1	1		
Gibson, Jos	1	1	1		
Hooker, Jno	1		2		
Dockery, Wm	1	2	2		
Conrod, Jno	2	1	1		
Roberts, Jno	1	1	4		
Cuningham, Jas	1	5	2		
Dockery, Jas	1	2	4		
Steward, Saml	1		2		
Peniton, Absalom	1		2		
McErtin, Jno	1	3	4		
White, Jonas	1	1	2		
Hood, Jno	1	1	2		
Reed, Tho	2		3		
Brown, Absalom	1	3	2		
Pain, Danl	1	1	1		
Hephaer, Phillip	1		1		
Grenstaff, Isaac	2	2	4		
Gibson, Isom	1		2		
Parmes, John	2	1	2		
Fullerton, Wm	1		1		
Clarke, James	1	5	2		
Thomas, James	1	1	4		
Grenstaff, Jane		2	2		
Walker, Charles	1	1	5		2
Walker, Simon	1	3	4		
Medlock, John	2		3		
Austin, Ben., Sr	3	1	5		
Gibson, Major	2		3		
Spradling, Jesse	1	1	2		1
Gibson, Wilburn	1	1	2		
Scott, Jno	1		2		
Dockery, Jno	1	1	2		
Banell, Jonathan	2		2		
Yokely, Jno	1		3		
Fox, Jas	1	3	2		
Graham, Aha	1	1	2		
Prisly, Jas	1		4		
Steward, James	1		4		
Davis, Uriah	3	5	3		
Green, Elizabeth			1		5
Price, Rd	1	4	3		
Prew, Phillip	2	3	4		
Dishazer, Eliza		2	2		
Irons, Wm	1	3	3		
Smith, Wm	1	1	3		
Troutman, Adam	2	2	7		
Cumming, Jno	2	1	3		
Allen, Jno	2	1	3		
Alexander, Wm	1		1		
Macay, Wm	1	1	2		
Matthewson, Alex	3	2	2		

NINTH COMPANY.

NAME OF HEAD OF FAMILY.	M16+	M<16	F	Other	Slaves
Thomson, Peter	3	4	4		1
Sumpter, Jas	1		3		
Bartley, Jno	1	4	4		
Hays, Jno	2	4	6		
Murray, Joshua	2	1	3		
Howk, Nicolas	1	4	4		
Tucker, George	1		2		
Baker, Joseph	2	1	3		
Moony, Wm	3		2		
McCrary, Jos	4	5	4		
Murray, Jno	1		1		
Murray, Jno., Jr	1	1	3		
Grider, Fred, Jr	1	5	1		
Grider, Fred, Sr	2		1		
Murry, Barbara		1	4		
Smith, Saml	1	3	3		
Prowell, Thos	1	1	2		
Angely, Peter	1	2	2		
Hartley, George	2	2	2		
Lathrum, Johnsn	1	1	2		
Fincannon, Jno	1	5	3		
Grider, Jno	1	4	2		
Grider, Jacob	1		2		
Smally, Abner	1	3	5		
Repeto, Wm	1	4	4		
Wilson, Ezekl	1		4		
Wood, Jno	1	7	4		
Garlin, Eliza			2		
Periman, Wm	1	2	4		
Shoat, Saybort	1		3		
Gilmore, Eliza	1	1	1		
Green, Rd	1	4	6		
Abshire, Christn	1	4	3		
Swaringin, Saml	1		6		

NINTH COMPANY—con.

NAME OF HEAD OF FAMILY.	M16+	M<16	F	Other	Slaves
Stilwell, Jeremy	1		2		
Smith, Solomon	1	3	4		
Penly, Jas	1	1	1		
Wilson, Edward	2	1	1		
Hines, Jno	2	4	5		
Pots, James	1		3		1
Nailor, Jas	1		1		
Coffee, Jno	1	4	4		
Amons, Mark	1		3		
Allen, Micajah	1	1	1		
Tucker, George, Sen	1	1	1		
Ramsy, Saml	1	1	1		
Davis, Wm	2		2		
Thornton, Wm	1	1	3		
Allen, Jno	2	1	2		
Hottsdaw, Henry	4		4		
Owens, Edwd	1		3		
Mayson, Isaac	1	1	4		
Streeton, Hezekiah	1		3		
Hartley, Wm	1	1	3		
Hartley, Sarah	1	3	4		
Blair, Jno	1	3	2		1
Hons, James	1		2		
Onions, Saml	1	4	5		
Day, Jno	1	3	3		
Day, Nicholas	1	3	5		
Day, James	2	1	2		
Hicks, Willis	2		8		
Green, Jacob	1		1		
Wisdom, Jos	1	3	5		
Highsaw, Fred	2	2	3		
Streetton, Susana	1	2	5		
Harris, Jno	1	2	2		
Hammons, Elijah	1	2	3		
Randolph, Thom	2	1	3		
Herrin, Wm	2	1	3		
Blair, Colvard	1	1	2		2
Sumpter, Wm	3		2		
Sumpter, Thos	2		3		
Sotherd, Abram	1	2	2		1
Neely, Jno	1	1	1		
Allen, Jonathn	1		2		
Allen, Jonthn, Sr	1		1		
Dennis, Rd	1		2		
Crisp, Jno	2	5	4		
Crisp, Wm	1		2		
Ramsey, Richd	1	3	4		
Constable, Linsy	1	3	2		
Ramsy, Eliza			2		
Hott, Peter	1	4	5		2
Hott, Jacob	2		2		2
Reily, Aron	1	1	1		
Swaringin, Check	1		2		
Powell, Ambros	2	4	5		1
Powell, Elias	1	3	3		
Townsend, Jno	4	1	2		6
Grissom, Wm	1	1	1		
McDaniel, Jno	1	3	3		
McDaniel, Saml	1		2		
Thrasher, Wm	1	3	4		
Wilson, Ginral	1	3	2		
Greenaway, Joseph	1		1		
Greenaway, Jos., Sr	2	1	3		
James, Thos	1		2		
James, Wm	1		1		
James, Mary			2		3
Taylor, Jno	4	1	3		
Miller, Robt., Jesse	1	2	2		2
McDaniel, Tempe		1	4		
Smith, Sarah		2	2		
Swaringen, Saml	1		1		
Phillips, Isaac	1	2	2		
Powell, Thos	1	1	4		
Powell, Eljas	1		1		2
Cox, Isaac	2	2	4		
Long, Edward	1	4	3		
Eashman, Isaac	1	4	4		1
Notherly, Robt	2	5	2		
Powell, Elias, Sr	1		2		1
Powell, Lewis	1		1		

TENTH COMPANY.

NAME OF HEAD OF FAMILY.	M16+	M<16	F	Other	Slaves
Young, Joseph	1		2		
Demerlin, George	1	4	2		4
Wofford, Wm	2		4		
Bolin, Amy		1	4		
Holinsworth, Jacob	1	5	1		
Wofford, Ben	1		1		
Hopper, George	1	2	7		
Holinsworth, Saml	1		3		1
Nation, Jos	2	4	4		
Nation, Wm	2	1	4		
Hancock, Joel	1		2		

TENTH COMPANY—con.

NAME OF HEAD OF FAMILY.	M16+	M<16	F	Other	Slaves
Spoons, Wm	1		2		2
Hall, Jno	1	2	5		
Burleson, Agnes	1	1	2		
Phillips, Charles	1		1		
Vann, Jno	2	1	3		
Phillips, Wm	3	5	4		
Holefield, Danl	1		3		
Rose, Isaiah	2	2	4		
Bridges, Wm	1	1	3		
McFalls, Delila		3	1		
Hopper, Charls	2	4	5		
Carson, James	2	2	6		
Robison, Jno	1	3	3		
Bell, Marget			3		
Hensly, Ben	3	3	3		
Lee, James	1	3	3		
Johnson, Louisa		1	1		
McKinny, Wm	1	3	6		
McKinny, Thom	1		2		
Medlock, Rd	1	3	4		
Gouge, Jno	1	1	2		
Rose, Jno, Senr	1	2	3		
Rose, Jno, Junr	1		2		
Wilson, Jas	2	1	4		
Harden, Jno	2	2	4		
Morron, James	1	5	3		
Ainsworth, Jas	2	4	3		8
Moody, Wm	1	5	2		
Billins, Wm	1	2	4		
Forsythe, Jacob	1	1	3		
McFalls, Jno	1	1	1		
Brown, Danl	1		1		
Turner, Robt., Sr	1		1		
Turner, Robt	1	1	3		
Moore, Wm	1	3	3		
Wilson, Jno., Jr	1	2	1		
McCracon, David	2	1	7		
Wilson, Jno	3	2	4		
Night, Thos	3	3	3		
Night, Thos, Sr	1	1	4		
Deaton, Neathn	1		2		
Moore, Thos	1		1		
Wilson, Sam	1	1	1		
Wilson, George	2	2	7		
Young, Thom	1	1	2		2
Young, Joshua	1		1		
Kensy, Abigail		2	1		
Hull, Sally		1	1		
Devenport, Martin	3	4	3		4
Bright, Saml	1	2	2		
Wiseman, Wm	4	4	5		
Wiseman, Thos	2	1	3		
Jones, Jos	1	3	4		
Price, James	1	1	5		
Bright, Wm	1	1	2		
Hill, Wm	2	1	6		
Taylor, Jas	1	1	4		
Hill, Wm., Senr	2		1		
Beckerstaff, Thos		1	1		
Loller, John	1	2	2		
Mullins, Jno	1	3	3		
McFalls, Arthur	1	3	1		
Gillespy, Henry	3		2		

ELEVENTH COMPANY.

NAME OF HEAD OF FAMILY.	M16+	M<16	F	Other	Slaves
Vance, David	2	1	5		3
Deever, Wm	6		4		
Smith, Jo	2		6		
Smith, Nat	1	1	1		
Beefle, Jacob	1	1	2		
Dunsmore, Adam	2	2	2		
Gilbert, Jno	3	2	3		
Heatly, Henry	2	1	6		
Unfrin, Sam	1	1	6		
Rogers, David	1	4	3		
Cunnigan, Jas	1		6		1
Bartlet, Nathn	2	2	3		
Bartlet, Jno	1		1		
McAfee, Wm	2	3	5		
Young, Wm	1	1	2		
Patten, Matthew	1		3		
Moore, Jno	1		3		
Graham, Wm	3	1	4		
Lacky, Jno	1		5		
Summers, Jonson	2		1		
Davidson, James	2		6		3
Davidson, Saml	1		1		
McWhorter, Ben	1		1		1
Patten, Robt., Sad	1	2	5		2
Long, Jno	1	2	3		
Patten, Thos	3	1	3		
Cunigam, Hump	1		3		
Patten, Jas	1		5		

MORGAN DISTRICT, BURKE COUNTY—Continued.

ELEVENTH COMPANY—continued.

NAME OF HEAD OF FAMILY.	Free white males of 16 years and upward, including heads of families.	Free white males under 16 years.	Free white females, including heads of families.	All other free persons.	Slaves.
Clemments, Jas.	1	1	3		
Alexander, Jno.	3		4		
Alexander, James	1	3	2		
Patten, Matthew, Sr.	3		2		1
Patten, Aron	1		3		
Patten, Matt., Jr.	1		1		
Davidson, Wm.	4	2	4		8
McMahan, Jas.	3	1	2		
Smith, Jno.	1	1	1		
Davidson, Thos.	2		2		
Ritchy, James	1	2	4		1
McNabb, Jas.	1	4	2		3
Jones, Wm.	2	1	3		
Rice, Joseph	1		3		
Cunigam, George	2	4	3		
Gudger, Ben	2		1		
Neall, Arche	2		4		
Forgay, Sam	1	2	4		4
Kow, Wm.	1		2		
Patten, Jno.	1	1	4		2
Ragsdil, Gabrl.	1	2	1		3
Lee, Eloner			5		
West, Jno.	1	1	3		
Gudger, Wm.	1	2	6		1
Randolph, Jos.	1	1	4		
Phillips, Ezra	1	1	2		
Whitson, Wm.	1	5	2		2
Smith, Phil.	1	1	2		
Killian, Danl.	1	2	1		
Phillips, Jno.	1	2	1		
Boys, James	1	1	4		1
Ryant, Wm.	1	5	3		
Case, Abram	2	4	5		
Davis, Jno.	1		6		
Bufle, Jno.	1	1	2		
Ingrum, Wm.	1	1	6		
Jenkins, Thos.	2		4		
Jenkins, Jno.	1		2		
Ramsy, George	1	3	4		
Davis, Baxter	3	6	1		
Blevins, Jnothn.	1	1	3		
Cravens, Jas.	2	3	2		
Gillahan, Jno.	1	1	3		
Gouge, Jones	2	2	4		
Kennedy, Connell	1	1	1		
Bufle, Adam	1		1		1
Roberts, Jno.	1	2	3		
Weaver, Jno.	1	1	3		1
Wagoner, Jacob	1	5	2		
Roberts Wm.	2		4		
Bound, Jno.	1	3	2		
Brittain, Wm.	1	2	2		
Dillard, Jno.	1	3	5		
Gregory, Wm.	3	4	3		
Baily, Wm.	1		3		
Guin, Jake	1	1	2		
Stanfield, Jas.	1	2	6		
Guin, Chas.	1	1	2		3
Chambers, Jno.	2	2	2		
Gregory, Jno.	1		1		

TWELFTH COMPANY.

NAME OF HEAD OF FAMILY.	Free white males of 16 years and upward, including heads of families.	Free white males under 16 years.	Free white females, including heads of families.	All other free persons.	Slaves.
Parmer, Edmund	1	3	4		
Edes, Chals.	2	1	3		
Ramsy, Jno.	1		1		
Bailey, Wm.	2		1		
Bradly, Jno.	1	1	3		
Boiler, Jacob, Sen.	5	1	3		
Killer, Jno.	1	2	5		
Treadaway, Aron	2	2	5		
Atkison, Henry	1	3	4		
Bounds, Jos.	1	3	1		
Keller, Nicolas	1	1	3		
Barnett, Tim	3	3	3		
Treadaway, Wm.	1	1	4		
Treadaway, Robt.	1	1	3		
Finley, Wm.	1		1		
Tony, Jno.	3	3	3		
Lekins, Jno.	1		1		
Shoat, Christi.	1		1		1
Shoat, Moses	1	2	1		
Devus, Henry	2	5	3		
Shoat, Christi, Jr.	1		1		
Pyburn, Jacob	3	1	5		
Pialms, James	1	4	6		
Tinker, Jno.	2	5	5		
Forsythe, Jos.	1		1		
Chanler, Josha	1	2	2		
Blacwell, Jno.	1	1	3		
Webb, Mendoth	3	4	5		5
Win, Martha			4		
Bound, Jas.	1		2		
Shoat, Austin	1	6	2		
Rice, Jno.	1	3	2		
Elkins, Gabriel	2	1	2		2
Pialms, Wm.	1	1	2		1
Pialms, Edmund	1	4	3		1

TWELFTH COMPANY—continued.

NAME OF HEAD OF FAMILY.	Free white males of 16 years and upward, including heads of families.	Free white males under 16 years.	Free white females, including heads of families.	All other free persons.	Slaves.
Street, Jno.	1	2	2		
Higins, Koland	1	3			
Bunis, Elijah	1	2	4		
Hensly, Henry	1	5	5		
Renfren, Jno.	1	2	8		
Hensly, Jno.	1		3		
Langford, James	1	1	2		
Edward, Wm.	1		2		
Hinton, David	1	1	2		
Stanton, Jno.	1	3	4		
Angling, Isaac	1	4	3		
Hoodenpye, Phil.	2	3	5		
Caleway, Charls	1	3	2		
Summers, Allen	1	2	1		
Phips, Hana			2		
Hinton, Wm.	1	1	2		4
Robison, Julius	1	4	4		
Marcum, Abner	1	5	4		
Williams, Phil.	1	3	3		
Hamons, Obadiah	1		3		
Baker, Robt., Jr.	2		2		
Hensly, Jas.	1	2	4		
Ray, Thos.	3	3	2		
Carrol, Jno.	1	2	4		
Hamons, Peter	1	3	2		
Bennett, Jas.	2	1	3		
Hensly, Hirman	1	4	3		
Baker, George	1	3	4		
Edwards, Jno.	2	4	6		
Arrington, Jas	1	1	5		
Baker, Jno.	1	5	3		
Foster, Mark	1	3	5		
Foster, Mark, Jr.	2	1	4		
Hughes, Jno.	1	4	1		
Paterson, Jane		1	2		
Hughes, Peter	1	2	1		
Dyer, Lettice		1	2		
Haeworth, Austin	1	3	4		1

THIRTEENTH COMPANY.

NAME OF HEAD OF FAMILY.	Free white males of 16 years and upward, including heads of families.	Free white males under 16 years.	Free white females, including heads of families.	All other free persons.	Slaves.
Galliard, Jno M.	1	1	6		
Eagan, Mary	2		2		
England, Danl.	1	2	6		
England, Jo.	1	2	3		
Hilterbrand, Conrod	1	2	1		2
Bellen, George	1		2		
Bradburn, Jno.	1				
Mull, Peter	3	1	3		1
Morgan, Josep.	4	2	3		
Welsh, Jno.	1	3	2		1
Direberry, Anne	2		1		
Duckworth, Jno.	1	2	4		
Walker, West	1		2		
Direberry, Andrew	1		2		
Largin, Thom	1	3	5		
Hartley, Jno.	2		1		
Lack, James	1	1	1		
Macky, John	3	2	5		
England, Jno, Sr.	2	2	7		
Hughes, Jno.	2	4	3		1
Macay, Saml.	2	1	6		
Tomson, David	2	2	3		
Beall, Danl.	2	1	5		3
Downs, Zach.	2		2		
Macay, Thos.	2		4		
Tate, Jno.	5		3		3
Nulin, Ben.	1	2	1		
May, Erasmus	2		1		
Hensy, Patrick	1	1	1		3
Jucin, Jno.	1		2		
Duckworth, Wm.	2	1	1		
Wood, Henry	2	4	3		
Dobson, Joseph, Jr.	1		1		3
Priest, Jo.	1		2		
Downs, Zach, Jr.	2	1	2		
Brittn, Phillip	1	1	5		
Cooper, Jno.	1	2	3		
Lyon, Leonard	1		5		1
West, Wm.	1	3	3		
Young, Elisa			3		
Spears, Jno.	2	2	1		
James, Wm.	2		4		
Craige, Robt.	2	2	2		
Guin, Debo	2		2		
McDowell, Wm.	1	4	4		
Skevely, Jno Henry	3		1		
Tompson, Isaac	1	1	2		
Balley, Alex	2	3	1		1
Wood, Robt.	1	1	3		1
Cumings, Alex	1		1		
Kell, Thos.	1		1		2
Smith, Thom	1		1		
Greeneu, Jas	1	2	5		24
Mackey, Jas.	1	1	1		
Worthy, Sally		1	1		
Sorrils, Walter	1	3	4		
Lowman, Lewis	1	2			

THIRTEENTH COMPANY—continued.

NAME OF HEAD OF FAMILY.	Free white males of 16 years and upward, including heads of families.	Free white males under 16 years.	Free white females, including heads of families.	All other free persons.	Slaves.
Anderson, Martha		1	3		
Pearson, Jas.	1	1	2		
Boteat, Edwd.	1	2	1		
Hawkins, Joseph	1	1	3		
Kell, Robt.	1	3	6		
Walker, George	3	2	6		
Walker, Reubin	1	3	2		
Southorlin, Wm.	2	2	7		
Howard, Ruson	1	1			
England, Thos.	1				
Hawkins, Austin	1	2	3		
Boteat, Wm.	1	1	1		
Kell, Thos, Jr.	1	1	2		
Kell, Wm.	1		2		
Hufman, Sam	1	3	3		
McTagart, Jno.	5		3		
Brown, Saml.	2	1	4		
Higden, Thos.	1	2	2		
Chapmn, Nicolas	1	2	2		
Southorlin, Tindel.	1		1		
Wise, Adam	1	2	1		
Dougherty, Ed.	1	2	6		
Hart, Josiah	1	1	2		
Burns, Nicolas	1				
Burns, Phillip	1	1	3		
Roper, James	1	2	1		
Craig, Jno.	1	2	1		
Brittu, Jumima	1	1	1		
Stilwell, Jacob.	2	1	1		1
Box, Henry	1	3	4		
Morrow, Dan.	3		3		
Ross, James	1	1	5		
England, Jno, Jr.	1	1	1		
Bortles, Christn.	1	1	1		
Jeferis, Jno.		2	4		1
Gibs, Rd.	1	2	4		
White, Jno.	1	1	3		
Hawkins, Wm.	1	1	2		
Rogers, Stepen	1	1	1		
Carol, Danl.	1		1		
Smith, Adam.	1	1	3		
Craig, Ruth		1	1		
Daily, George.	1	1	4		
Clarke, Eloner.	2		2		
Sealy, George.	1	1	4		
Oxford, Jno.	1	1	1		
Oxford, Saml.	1		1		
Elmore, Sarah.		2	4		
Howard, Robt.	1	3	2		
Mouser, Rd.	1	2	2		
Miller, Henry	1	1	3		
Overwon, Adm., Jr.	1		1		
Walker, Thom, Jr.	1	1	2		
Walker, George.	1	3	2		
Hughey, Eliza	1	2	3		
Hughey, Jos.	1		2		
Scott, George.	1	2	3		
Jones, Wm.	1	5	4		
McEntirs, Jas.	4	3	4		5
Gibs, Jno.	1	3	4		
Garison, Henry.	2	3	2		
Erwin, Jno.	1	2	1		11
Hays, Wm.	1	3	7		
Orr, Wm.	2	1	5		
Layman, Stophl.	1		2		
Adams, Mary.		2	1		
Smith, Jno.	3	3	4		
Scott, Jos.	1	4	7		1
Neall, Jno.	2	2	2		
Bailey, Wm.	2	3	6		3
McMurry, Saml	1	5	4		
Rucker, Jos.	3	5	2		
Pearson, Thos.	1		2		
Pearson, Christe.	1		2		
Hips, Jacob.	1	2	4		
Gallion, Thos.	3	3	5		1
Hips, George, Sr.	3	2	2		
Hips, George.	2		4		
Cammell, Jno.	1	1	2		
Anderson, Bartlet	1		1		
Hartly, Jas.	1	1	1		
Templeton, Jas.	2	2	3		
Scott, George.	1	2	2		
Direberry, Hana.	2		1		
Patten, Thos.	1	2	2		
Burgess, Jno.	1	2	6		
Pearson, Jno.	4	3	8		1
Burgess, Rd.	1		5		
Downs, Thos.	1	3	1		
Carswell, Jno.	2	2	2		
Good, Solomon.	1	1	6		
Boteat, Jno, Sr.	3	2	3		
Boteat, Jno, Jr.	1		1		
Camil, Anguish.	1	3	4		
Wrenshaw, Aham.	2		3		
Gunter, Jno.	2	1	2		

MORGAN DISTRICT, LINCOLN COUNTY.

NAME OF HEAD OF FAMILY.	Free white males of 16 years and upward, including heads of families.	Free white males under 16 years.	Free white females, including heads of families.	All other free persons.	Slaves.
FIRST COMPANY.					
Sherrill, Moses	2	5	2		5
Sherrill, Adam	4	2	7		4
Litten, James	1	3	3		
White, Elias	1		3		
Ward, Catharine	4	3	3		
Robison, Isaac	2	6	3		2
Alexander, Jno	3	3	6		
Brevard, Jane			3		3
Bates, Wm	1	1	1		
Brown, Wm	1	1	3		
Fikes, Mal	2	1	4		
Robison, Rebekah	1		3		
Davis, Upshire	1	2	3		
Taylor, Ben	1	2	5		
Johnson, Francis	1	2	2		
Gordon, Jane	1		3		
Loller, Henry	1	3	4		
Rail, Belser	2	1	4		
Kennedy, Wm	1		4		
Whitworth, Fendal	2	3	1		
Lyons, Jno	2	6	1		
Lyons, Wm	1	1	2		
Perkins, Rich'd	3	1	5		
Bridges, Elisha	1	2	5		
Fish, Jno, Sen	1	1	3		
Fish, Jno, Jr	1	3	4		
Fish, Wm	1	3	5		
Hamilton, Arche	1	4	5		
Snider, Jno	3	1	2		
Perkins, Augutn	1	1	2		
Freeman, Aron	1	1	3		
Wilcocks, Dav	1	2	1		
Hubbard, Richd	1	4	3		
Neall, Elizabeth	3		4		
Hamilton, Alex	1				
Bridges, Wm	1	6	3		
Bridges, Marget			2		
West, Robt	3		4		
Brown, Amos	1	1	3		
McCormic, And'w	3	4	3		
Sherrill, Jos	4	2	5		
Sherrill, Jude	4	1	5		6
Lowrance, David	1	4	1		
Sherrill, Jacob, Jr	1	3	1		2
Lowrance, Danl	1	2	1		
Lowrance, Abrm	1	1	1		
Aidon, Saml	2	1	6		
Duncan, Peter	2	1	3		
Spilman, Nathan	3		5		1
Brown, John	3		5		
Bodine, John	2		1		
Williams, Edward	1	2	4		
Litton, Sarah	2		2		
Sherrill, Wilson	1	2	2		
Allen, George	1	2	2		
Witherspoon, Eliz	1	1	3		
Jones, Jas	1		2		
Hill, Henry	1	3	5		
Wilbrooks, Jno	1	1	2		
Perkins, Jno	5	1	3		12
McDonald, David	1	1	3		
Colwell, Danl	1	2	4		
Gant, Jno	1		2		
Harwell, Saml	1	4	3		6
Litten, Thom	1	3	2		
Neall, Wm	1	2	1		2
Henyeaul, Rowell	1	1	1		
Wilson, Jas	2	1	7		
West, Thom	1	4	6		
SECOND COMPANY.					
Wilson, Matthew	1	3	5		
McKessick, Danl	2	4	3		2
Summy, Frederick	1	1	5		
Patten, Jno	1	1	3		2
Wilson, Jas., Sr	1	1	5		11
Wilson, Jas., Jr	1				7
Earwood, Jno	1		2		
Sumrow, Mich'l	1		1		
Holman, Antony	1	5	6		1
Antony, Paul	1		3		
Braniman, Chiste	1	1	3		
Blackburn, Robt	3	3	3		
Lengeyer, Henry	1	1	3		
Wilson, Wm	3		4		3
Gortner, Jacob	1	1	1		
Lochart, James	1	1	1		1
Earwood, Wm	2	2	5		
Tepong, Conrod	1		1		1
Martin, James	1		3		
Crismore, Henry	1		4		
Obrian, Patrick	1	2	4		
Gross, Henry	1	5	4		
Wilson, Joshua	1				
SECOND COMPANY—con.					
Rudeel, Phil	1	2	4		
Ramsour, Henry	1	1	1		1
Cunrod, Rudolph	1	2	2		
Keiner, Jno	1	5	4		
Keiner, Martin	1	2	4		
Gross, Christn	3	3	4		
Laurence, George	1	1	9		
Pfifer, Jacob	2		6		
Hephner, George	1	1	3		
Boyd, Jno	1	4	4		5
Byers, Jno	2	4	6		
Huyet, Lewis	1	2	1		
Earwood, Mary	1	3	3		
Stroap, Peter	1	1	1		
Cresemore, Jacob	1		1		
Kline, Valentine	2	2	5		
Killian, Adam	1	1	4		
Earwood, Thom	2	1	1		
Johnson, John	1	4	1		
Garner, Jno Burn	4	3	3		3
Padget, Ephraim	1	2	5		
Johnson, Lewis	1	2	2		
Coddle, Moses	1	1	2		
Miller, Jno	1		2		
Wason, Jno	1	4	6		
Lutes, George	1				
Reather, Conrod	1	2	1		
Sumron, Henry	2	2	2		1
Earnest, Danl	2	3	4		
Sumron, Henry, Sr	1		1		
Barns, Jno	1	1	4		
Crissell, Andw	3	3	4		
Cumins, Laurence	1		1		
Bysinger, Henry	1		3		
Snider, Wm	1	3	4		
Tropick, Adm	1	2	1		
Tropick, Jacob	1		3		
Martin, Jno	1	1	1		
Martin, Solomon	1		2		
Witheron, Jas	2	1	5		
Summy, Jacob	1	4	2		
Launce, George	2	1	4		
Wise, Frederick	3	1	2		1
Ashtruner, Arben	1		2		
Scott, James	3	1	2		
Antony, Phillip	1	1	1		
Brilhart, Jacob	1	2	3		
Lutes, Jacob	4	1			
Stocking, Andw	2	4	5		
Carpender, Henry	2	1	3		
Lear, Peter	1		1		
Clay, Nicolas	3		1		
Smith, Mary	1	4	0		
Coonrod, Peter	1		1		
Renabaugh, Adm	2		3		
Horse, Phillip	2	3	1		
Bandy, George	1	4	3		
THIRD COMPANY.					
Tipong, Elias	1	2	2		
Coons, Adam	1		2		
Killian, Saml	1	2	3		
Killian, Jno	1	3	1		
Killian, Jno, Sr	4	1	3		
Killian, Jacob	1	2	1		
Mouser, Fred	1	3	4		
Bowman, Danl	2	4	5		
Deetz, John	2	1	1		
Phillips, Peter	1	3	4		
Harbison, Wm	5	4	9		3
Bolinger, Henry	2	3	4		2
Steel, Joseph	1	1	3		6
Crismore, Jno	3		1		
Yount, Phillip	1	2	2		
Mehaffy, Joseph	1		3		
Shell, Henry	1	3	4		
Antony, Jno	2	6	3		
Ichard, Peter	2	2	6		
Ichard, Henry	1	2	4		
Ichard, Lowrance	2	2	2		
Fry, George	1	3	2		
Boovey, Matthias	2	2	2		
Kline, Michal	2		2		
Killian, Jno	3	1	2		
Cline, Jacob	1	2	3		
Vanhorn, Isaac	1	4	4		
Fry, Jacob	1		1		
Fisher, Thom	2	2	2		
Houk, Jno	1	3	5		
Sigman, Jno	1		1		
Sigman, Mary		3	4		
Minges, Conrod	3	2	3		1
Coons, Wm	1		2		
Setser, Jno	1	2	3		
THIRD COMPANY—con.					
Sigman, George	3	1	1		
Ring, Francis	1	3	3		
Bolinger, Mathias	1	1	1		
Bost, Jno	2		3		
Brown, Jas	1				
Fry, Phillip	1	3	4		
Probst, Henry	2	4	2		
Phry, Jacob	2	1			
Gyger, Phillip	1	3	4		
Menskinon, George	2	3	1		
Horse, Simon	1	1	1		
Reather, Wm	1	3	5		1
Star, Jacob	1	2	3		
Bost, Wm	2	1	4		
Reather, Adm	1	1	4		
Smire, Jno	2	3	1		
Sigman, Jno, Jr	1	2	1		1
Wagoner, Conrod	1	1	1		
Baker, Phillip	1		2		
Baker, Susana	1	3	2		
Keller, Michal	1	3	5		
White, Joshua	1		2		
Sherrill, Jacob	1	1	6		2
Farloe, Thom	1	2	3		
Perkins, Jesse	2		3		
Holman, Henry	2		4		1
Pain, Robert	1	1	7		1
Belchel, Jacob	1		1		
Bealy, Wm	1		3		
Heager, David	1	2	1		
Keller, Henry	1		2		
Hestle, Jacob	1	2	3		
Huyet, Jno	1	1	3		
Kasler, George	1	1	1		
Punch, Thos	1	5	3		
Harmon, Wm	2	1	2		
Reid, Jno	1	5	2		
Baxter, Jno	1	1	3		
Baker, Elias	1	2	4		
Sirone, Nicolas	1		5		
Sirone, Jno	1	2	1		
Deal, Jacob	2	4	4		
Kline, Jno	2	3	4		
Cline, Chiste	1	3	1		
Peirce, Charls	1				
Gorman, James	1		1		
Davis, Hugh	1				
Doron, Patrick	1				
Peirce, George	1				
Wagoner, Mary		1	1		
FOURTH COMPANY.					
Horton, Joseph	1	1	4		
Cotter, Jno	1		1		
Whitener, Henry, Sr	1		2		10
Robison, Jesse	1		1		5
Whitener, Danl	1	3	3		2
Moyer, Jno	5	1	4		
Whitenr, Henry	1	3	5		
Wilfong, George, Sr	2		3		
Shell, Gasper	3	1	3		
Mull, Jno, Sr	3	1	6		
Wilson, Jno	1	3	3		1
Robison, David	1	3	4		3
Whitener, Phillip	1	3	1		
Dillinger, Jno	1	3	3		1
Janet, Saml	1		2		
Robison, Jno	1	1	3		6
Wilfong, George	2	2	1		1
Bradly, Jno	4	2	8		
Hutson, Danl	3	3	4		
Wilfong, Jno	1		2		
Hyde, Jno	4	1	4		
Johnson, Jos	2	2	5		
Johnson, Robt	1		1		
Shuford, Jacob	1				
Canot, Wm	2	1	1		
Shuford, Daniel	1	3	4		1
Haun, John, Sr	4	1	4		
Hoover, Thomas	1	5	5		1
Gross, John	1	6	3		
Speigle, Marton	3	3	1		
Whitsil, Jacob	2	2	7		1
Clay, Abram	1		3		
Ichard, George	1	2	1		
Sigman, George	1	2	4		
Fisher, Jno	1	4	5		
Colter, Martin	1		1		1
Colter, Phillip	1	3	4		
Sigman, Barnet	1		4		
Johnson, Martha	3		1		
Staymy, Henry	1	2	2		
Miller, Jacob	3	1	2		3
Agle, Josia	1	1	2		

MORGAN DISTRICT, LINCOLN COUNTY—Continued.

FOURTH COMPANY—con.

NAME OF HEAD OF FAMILY.	Free white males of 16 years and upward, including heads of families.	Free white males under 16 years.	Free white females, including heads of families.	All other free persons.	Slaves.
Hoselbareer, Jno	2	2	6		
Whitener, Ben	2	2	5		
Whitener, Michal	1		1		
Wilson, Andrew	1	2	2		
Johnson, Elizabeth	1	3	2		
Shuford, David	2		2		1
Hampton, Jno	1	1	1		
Haun, Jno, Jr	2	4	5		
Haun, Joshua	1	2	4		
Haun, Peter	1		2		
Haun, Benedict	1	5	4		
Haun, Jacob	1		2		
Low, Thom	2		2		
Wilson, Thom	1		2		
Havner, Frederick	3	5	2		
Pilgrim, Rebekah	2	1	4		
Lynn, John	1	1	3		
Shoup, Peter	1	2	2		
Ward, Estis	4		1		
Hogshed, Waller	1	1	1		
Queen, Sam	1	1	2		
Milroy, Henry	1		2		
Moore, Jackson	1		1		
Miller, John	2	2	4		
Cook, Didrich	1	2	2		
Borland, John	1	1	5		
Robison, Jonathn	1	2	4		
Blanton, Zech	1	2	2		
Sharp, Thom	1		7		
Whitley, George	2	1	4		
Martin, Jacob	1	1	2		
Martin, Eliza		1	1		
Orr, Robt	2	2	6		
Orr, Jno	2		5		
Harris, Nathan	1		1		
Covey, Jno	2		5		
Covey, Jno, Sr	3	1	4		
Rinehart, Jacob	1		1		
Rinehart, Jacob, Jr	1	1	1		
Penugh, Jere	1	1	6		
Shugle, Saml	1	1	3		
Shugle, Michl	1	1	2		
Mull, Jno, Jr	1	1	4		1
Orr, Wm	2	1	5		
Tumbleson, Jas	2	5	6		
Martin, John	1	3	3		
Oliver, Thom	1	1	1		
Gullet, Jesse	1	3	1		
Weaver, Conrod	1	1	1		
Weaver, Catharine		1	4		
Hiltebrand, Henry	2	4	6		
Fry, Peter	1	3	4		
Fry, Nicolas	1	1	5		
Coulter, Martin	1	2	1		
Majoir, Jno	1		5		
Gortner, Jacob	1	3	4		
Goder, Catharin	4	3	2		
Ney, Chrste	2		2		
Gatner, Martin	1	1	2		
Collins, Jno	1	1	2		
Jarrett, Jno	1	1	1		
Yount, Jacob	1	3	3		
Baldasser, Andw	1	3	1		
Rider, Frederick	1	4	5		
Ashbraner, Henry	1	3	5		
Miller, Henry	1	3	4		
Baker, Peter	1	3	5		
Chester, David	1	1	2		
Smith, Danl	1	2	5		
Hart, Peter	1	2	2		
Gilbert, Michal	1	2	8		

FIFTH COMPANY.

NAME OF HEAD OF FAMILY.	Free white males of 16 years and upward, including heads of families.	Free white males under 16 years.	Free white females, including heads of families.	All other free persons.	Slaves.
Edwards, Griffa	1	2	4		
Bolick, Adam	1		4		
Sigman, Wm	1	3	2		
Erlinger, George	1	2	2		
Sigman, Balsar	1	2	3		
Grount, Peter	3	1	4		
Grount, Jno	1	1	1		
Bumfield, Jno	2	5	4		
Turr, Adam	1		2		
Sigman, Barnet	2		1		
Dawfey, Ben	1		1		
Sigman, John	1	2	1		
Dawfey, Bazil	1	2	3		
Dawfey, Jno	1		1		
Delph, Jacob	1	1	5		
Hessian, Arthur	1	2	4		
Frizzel, Wm	1	2	5		
Fulbright, Jno	2	2	2		
Fulbright, Wm	1		1		
Yount, Peter	1	3			
Yount, Abram	1	1	2		

FIFTH COMPANY—con.

NAME OF HEAD OF FAMILY.	Free white males of 16 years and upward, including heads of families.	Free white males under 16 years.	Free white females, including heads of families.	All other free persons.	Slaves.
Goforth, Geo	1	1	3		
Mass, Mathias	1		2		
Coon, John	1	2	3		
Syps, Abrm	1	1	1		
Sypes, Paul	2		2		
Woodring, Danl	1		3		
Sypes, Danl	1	3	4		
Williams, Griff	1	2	4		
Goodwin, Isaac	2	3	3		
Lowrance, Isaac	2	2	9		
Shuke, Jere	1		3		
Plunk, Peter	2	1	6		
Williams, Isaac	1	2	4		
Smith, George, Sr	3		6		
Smith, George	1	1	1		
Loutsiba, Mary		2	2		
Eher, Adam	2	1	3		
Sigman, Cloe	1		2		
Moses, Francis	1	1	2		
Moses, Jacob	1	4	3		
Johnson, Robert	1				
Frissell, W	2		5		
Cross, James	2	1	1		
Oliver, Jno	1	4	3		
Whitenberg, Wm	1	4	5		1
Eher, Martin	1	2	2		
Sigman, Barnet	1	2	3		
Crider, Cornelius	1	4	3		
Lucamore, Geo	1		1		
Killian, Jno	1	1	2		
Justice, Peter	1	3	2		
Hunsucker, Devt	3	3	8		
Bolock, Boston	1	4	4		
Bolick, Godfrey	2	3	4		
Grount, Peter	1	2	3		
Graff, Fred	3		1		
Philps, Burgess	2	5	4		
Clubb, Jacob	1		1		
Freflesstet, Fred	1	1	4		
Dell, Wm	2	4	4		
Dell, Peter	1	2	3		
Sloan, Wm	3	4	1		3
Stayway, Barnet	3		1		
Yount, George	2		4		
Drim, Phil	1	1	3		
Dell, Geo	1	2	5		
Treflestet, Mary	3		1		
Pope, Henry	2	2	5		
Fulbright, Jacob	1	6	4		
Harris, Rd	1	1	4		
Bolick, Gasper	1	1	4		
Bolick, Jacob	1	4	3		
Gobb, Jno	2	1	4		
Havner, Melcar	1		2		
Traflestet, Peter	1		1		
Null, Jno	1	2	2		
Orm, Jno	1	2	3		
Cowan, Jas	1	2	6		1
Keller, Michal	1	4	3		
Matthes, Jno	1	5	1		
Cillars, Conrod	1	1	3		
Festler, Peter	1	1	2		
Wineberger, Geo	2		2		
Bridges, David	1	2	8		
Owin, Thomas	1		3		
Baker, Phil	1		2		
Rosemond, Jacob	1	2	2		
Levaun, Isaac	1	3	4		
Ischour, Valentine	1	3	4		
Ischour, Jno	1	3	4		
Cross, Ben	1		2		
Graves, Phil	1		1		
Armstrong, Nat	1				
Jonas, Simon	1	2			2
Jonas, Jno	1				9
Oxford, Sam	3	4	4		
Graves, Wm	1	4	4		

SIXTH COMPANY.

NAME OF HEAD OF FAMILY.	Free white males of 16 years and upward, including heads of families.	Free white males under 16 years.	Free white females, including heads of families.	All other free persons.	Slaves.
Moore, Jno	2	2	3		11
Mooney, Adam	1	3	1		
Eher, Peter	2	1	2		
Hostirle, Eve	2	1	2		2
Fulweder, Jno	1	4	4		
Tecoybaugh, Phil	1	4	4		
Delinger, Henry	1	2	3		
Rinehast, Christe	2	4	2		11
Carpender, Henry	1		2		
Earn, Ben	3		3		
Morris, Jos	3		3		
Warlich, Lewis	2	1	1		
Friday, Jonas	1		1		3
Friday, Andw	1		1		4
Hedirk, Andrew	2	1	2		

SIXTH COMPANY—con.

NAME OF HEAD OF FAMILY.	Free white males of 16 years and upward, including heads of families.	Free white males under 16 years.	Free white females, including heads of families.	All other free persons.	Slaves.
Deter, Nicolas	1	1	2		
Roberts, Josh	1	1	4		
Logan, Drury	1	2	3		
Edwards, Wm	1	2	2		
Haynes, Leonard	1	3	4		
Cox, Paul	1		2		
Eaker, Christe	1		2		
Havner, Nick	1		2		
Money, Valentine	5	3	2		1
Rine, Jacob	1		3		
Hovis, Jno	1	2	1		
Hite, Henry	1	4	1		
Wallis, Jno	1		6		
Havner, Abram	1		6		
Havner, Jacob	1		3		
Eaton, Jno	1		2		
Simerman, David	2	1	1		2
Bonham, Abr	1	1	6		
Campbell, Jno	1	3	1		
Shull, Charles	1		1		
Rush, George	1	2	4		2
Givens, Saml	3	5	8		7
Dellinger, Mich	2	1	2		
Strudle, Martin	2	3	4		
Havner, Martin	1	1	1		
Lower, Jno	1	4	3		
Cook, Phillip	1	2	3		
Hoke, Henry	2	1	2		3
Barnett, Wm	1		2		
Crous, Jno	2	2	3		
Friday, Martin	1		2		2
Peiry, Jno	1		1		
Srum, Jno	1	1	1		
Aderholt, Fred	2	1	2		
Rudesel, Phil	1		3		
Ramsey, David	3	1	2		
Ramsey, Wm	4		2		
Ramsey, James	1		1		
Carpenter, Christe	2	2	3		3
Plunk, Jacob	1	1	5		
Plunk, Peter	1		2		
Eaker, Christe	2	1	2		
Seigal, Jno	4		5		
Mestellar, Peter	2	6	3		
Nerns, Ben	2		2		
Rinehot, Conrod	1	3	1		
Whiter, Rd	1	2	1		
Eaker, Michal	1		4		
McCalin, Wm	1				1
Havner, Fred	2	1	3		
Null, Phillip	2	1	7		1
Cox, John	2	1	2		
Sigman, Jno	1	2	3		1
Kline, Henry	1		3		
Refe, Mich	1		1		
Nixon, Sam	2	1	2		
Probst, S	3	1	1		
McCasland, Robt	2		4		3
Srum, Nicholas	2	2	5		1
McLurg, Nathan	1	3	5		
Carpender, John	1				
Ramsour, Amie	2	2	4		6
Brilhart, Jacob	2		3		
Stotler, Conrod	1	1	5		
Turner, Andrew	1				3
Streeker, Danl	1		1		
Carpender, Jacob	1	3	1		4
Cox, Aron	1	1	1		
Cox, Morris	1	3	3		
Black, Elizabeth		1	3		1
Black, Ephrm	1		1		
Moore, Moses	1	2	2		
Sullivan, James	1	5	2		
Sullivan, Thom	1				
Barr, Jno	1	2	1		
Plaidluler, Michal	1		1		
Cox, Elisha	1				
Horse, Jno	2	2	4		
Buff, Michal	2		5		
Horse, Frank	2		2		
Antony, Phillip	2	2	2		
Horse, Christe	2		5		
Carpenter, Jno, Jr	1	5	6		
Eaker, Peter	1		1		7
Baker, Joseph	1		1		
Englefinger, Chs	1		7		
Brown, Anne		2	8		
Moany, Jacob	1	3	7		
Cross, Jos	1	2	3		
Lee, Abrm	1	1	6		
Froniberger, Jno	1	2	2		
Froniberger, Wm	1	3	1		
Foster, Thom	2	4	5		
Hagar, Simon	2		4		
Roam, Jacob	1		3		

MORGAN DISTRICT, LINCOLN COUNTY—Continued.

NAME OF HEAD OF FAMILY.	Free white males of 16 years and upward, including heads of families.	Free white males under 16 years.	Free white females, including heads of families.	All other free persons.	Slaves.
SIXTH COMPANY—con.					
Hamilton, Wm	1	1	2		
Rudul, Phil	1		2		
Gilbert, Conrod	1		3		
Rudul, Michal	1		2		
Simon, Isaiah	1	4	3		
Ramsom, Mary		3	1		1
Ramsom, Jno	1		1		1
Warlick, Catharin	2	3	5		
Baker, Jos, Jr	1	1	2		
Conally, Neal	2	1	3		
Carpenter, Christe, Jr	1	2	6		
Welsh, Wm	1		4		
Duncan, Eljah	1	1	5		
Carpender, Jacob	1		1		
Reynolds, Jno	1		4		
Cobb, Ambrous	1	2	4		
Reip, Adm	2	1	4		
Canuller, Phil., Jr	2		1		
Carpenter, Peter	4	5	2		
Havner, Eliz	1		2		
Havner, Fred	1		2		
Reynolds, Jno	1	1	5		2
Fulks, Charles	1	2	3		
Haun, Jacob	1	1	2		
Reynolds, Thos	1		2		
Norman, Fan	1	2	5		
Tanhesly, Wm	4		6		
Probst, Lewis	2	2	4		
Cox, Jno	1	1	2		
Cyzer, George	1	6	1		
Cyzer, Adam	1	2	4		
Parker, Christ	1	2	2		
Plunk, Jacob	1		1		
Carpenter, Peter	1		1		
Penugh, Philip	1	3	2		
Bullenger, Phil	1	3	4		
Sepah, Jacob	1				
Nisenger, Jos	1	1	3		
Baker, Abrm	1		4		
Myers, Peter	1		1		
Myers, Pet, Jr	1	1	1		
Jackson, Jno	3	2	2		
Reynolds, Rd	1		2		
Reynolds, Wm	1	1	1		
Reynolds, Jno	1	2	3		
Welsh, Thom	1	1	5		
Patterson, Geo	1	4	4		
Welsh, Nei	1	2	3		
Bently, Hana			4		1
Davis, Mish	1	4	4		
Reynolds, Perry	1		2		
Tucker, Sam	1	2	4		
McNemar, Fran	1	3	3		
Reynolds, Rd., Jr	1	1	1		
Reynolds, Sarah	1	3	3		1
Sepah, Christe	2	3	3		
Buff, Martin	2	2	2		
Bullinger, Jacob	2	2	1		1
Wallaw, Jacob	1	2	3		
Boyles, Charls	2		4		
Rigdon, Enoch	1	1	1		
Whisenhunt, Adm	1		1		
Reinhart, Jacob	1	2	3		
Bently, Danl	1	3	2		
Cook, Phil	1	2	3		
Newcastle, Robt	1	4	3		
Lownrats, Andw	1	3	2		
Whails, Sam	1	1	2		
Alexander, Jno	1		4		6
Barker, Christe	1	2	2		
Whisenhunt, Phil	1	1	2		
Carver, Christe	1	1	1		
Roany, Jno	2		2		
Bruksten, Robt	1	2	2		
Snider, Jno	1		4		
Stotler, Adm	2	1	1		
Trout, Henry	1	6	3		
SEVENTH COMPANY.					
Huggins, John	4		2		2
Beard, Jas	2	4	5		6
Graham, Jas	1	2	7		
Veneble, Rd	3	5	3		1
Ferguson, Andw	3	3	2		
Blackwood, Sam	1	1	4		
Martin, James	2	1	8		2
Vernor, Wm	1	1	1		
Barber, Jno	1	2	8		3
Wilson, Jno	3	3	4		
Gilliland, Alex	2	4	5		4
Martin, Jno	1		1		5
Martin, Joseph	1	1	2		2
Witherspoon, Jas	3	3	6		1

NAME OF HEAD OF FAMILY.	Free white males of 16 years and upward, including heads of families.	Free white males under 16 years.	Free white females, including heads of families.	All other free persons.	Slaves.
SEVENTH COMPANY—continued.					
Venable, Rd	1		1		6
White, Thom	1	2	1		
Dunwiddee, Jno	1		4		1
Lewis, Jno	1	2	6		2
Nance, Sherwood	1	2	3		
Mellon, Edward	4		2		
Robinson, Jno	1	2	3		1
Nill, Jas	1	1	2		1
Finly, Robt	3	2	2		
Martin, Robt	2		7		
Neel, Jos	1	2	3		
Lewis, Isaac	4	3	3		
McClever, Jno	2	1	4		
Beard, Adam	1	2	7		3
Beard, Jno, Sr	3	2	1		1
Tiltman, Jno	2	3	3		
Berry, Jno	1	2	4		
Miller, Robt	1	2	3		
Gorden, Hugh	1		3		1
Neely, Jno	1	2	3		
Gullick, Jno	1	2	5		4
Henry, Jas	1	2	4		
Henry, Wm, Senr	1		2		
Wason, Jas	3	1	2		
Barrett, Sam	1	2	6		
Wason, Henry	1	3	1		
Oats, Jn	1	7	2		
Craigs, Jno	1	2	2		
Ferguson, Robt	3	3	4		
Patrick, Andw	2	1	6		
Gullick, Jno	1	6	4		
Clarke, Antony	2	3	3		
Falls, James	1	2	1		1
Gingles, Sam	1	3	2		1
Reynolds, Wm	1	4	3		1
Groves, Wm	2	2	2		
Carson, Jno	1	1	1		
Carson, Andw	2	3	5		1
Buccannon, Thos	1	2	4		
Falls, Andw	2	4	2		9
Robison, Joab	4	5	4		
Robison, W	3		3		
McLean, Charles	2		1		4
Wilson, Jno	1		2		
McLean, Ephm	1	1	1		5
Ford, Jno	1				
Hudson, Thos	4		2		11
Hudson, Thos, Jr	1				
McNear, Jas	1	2	4		
Rankford, Moses	1	2	1		
Dickson, Jno	1		2		
Ford, Teddy	1	2	3		3
Ford, Nathan	3	1	2		8
Husan, Mason	1				
Husan, David	1				
Wilson, George	3	3	4		
Bell, Jno	1	1	3		
Egnen, Wm	2	1	2		
Price, Thos	5	4	4		7
Ford, Jno	1	3	4		
Ferguson, Jno	2	3	2		
Mondenall, Nathn	1	1	3		1
Price, Wm	1	4	1		1
Denny, James	1	2	2		1
Henry, Jos	1	2	5		
Carson, Peter	2	1	2		
Rice, Wm	2	1	2		
Torence, Hugh	3	1	3		
Massey, Jno	1	1	3		
Massey, W	2		3		1
Daniel, Moses	1	4	3		
Berry, Wm	2	3	3		1
Berry, Robt	2		2		
Brison, W	1	1	3		
Paterson, Wilm	3		3		3
Robison, Alex	8		2		2
Glen, John	5	2	2		1
Grissom, Drewry	1	5	6		
Triplet, Joel	1		3		
Henry, Wm	1	6	2		1
Beard, Jno, Jr	1	1	2		1
EIGHTH COMPANY.					
Center, Stephen	1	4	1		
Hovis, George	3	3	4		
Best, Boston	3		1		1
Best, Jno	1		2		
Best, Jacob	1	1	1		
Gosnel, Charls	2		1		
Spencer, Nancy	3	1	2		
Gosnel, Peter	1	2	1		
Smith, Wm	1		5		

NAME OF HEAD OF FAMILY.	Free white males of 16 years and upward, including heads of families.	Free white males under 16 years.	Free white females, including heads of families.	All other free persons.	Slaves.
EIGHTH COMPANY—con.					
Jenkins, Jno	1	2	4		
White, Sam	1	2	2		
McCartey, Corni	2	1	3		
Wayett, Edwd	3	2	3		
Hoyl, Jno	4	5	5		2
Black, Robt	1				
Witheriss, Jas	1	1	2		
Jenkins, Jos	1	2	5		3
Rine, Phil	1	1	1		
Rine, Michl	1	1	3		
Hoyl, Michl	1	2	6		3
Wells, Jas	2	2	5		
Wells, Wm	1		1		
Jenkins, Jenk	2	2	3		
Jenkins, Edwd	2	4	2		
Jenkins, Jno, Jr	1	1	2		
Golden, Jas	1		3		
Siden, Thom	1	1	3		
Costner, Mary	1	1	5		
Parmer, Eliza	1	1	3		
Parmer, Jesse	1	2	3		
Holloway, Jos	1	3	5		
Wilson, Saml	4		3		
Paster, Christen	2	3	3		
Hislet, Ezekl	1	4	3		
Smith, Jos	1	4	5		
Bennet, Wm	2	1	3		
Massey, Dron	1		1		
Rodes, Jacob	1	3	3		
Rhodes, Peter	1	1	2		
Hufman, Jno	2	2	2		
Pack, Jno	1	1	1		
Fariss, Stephn	1	1	1		
Bud, Sarah		1	3		
Pinnor, Jno	2	4	5		
Wilson, Eliner	1	3	3		
Linsey, Sam	1		1		
Crago, Jno	1		2		
Knight, Sam	1	2	2		
Rhodes, George	1	1	1		
Glance, Cath	2		1		
Poston, Danl	1	1	2		
Potter, Wm	1		1		
Withers, Jno	1	3	3		
Suthard, Henry	2		2		
Withers, Elisha	1	3	2		
Posten, Eliz		2	2		
Withers, Jas	1	3	5		
Rine, Jacob	1	6	1		
Rine, Peter	1	4	4		
Hoyl, Andw	1	4	6		
Pearson, Geo	1	1	2		
Pearson, Geo., Jr	1				
Edwards, Mark	2		2		
Mason, Peter	1	3	2		
Dudrow, Jno	2	2	7		
Weyet, Jas	2	4	4		
Lineberger, Fred	2	1	2		
Kender, Conrod	5	2	9		
Hoyl, Martin	1	3	5		1
Rhodes, Jacob	1	1	4		
Hamontree, Wm	2	4	4		
Costner, Michl	2	2	2		1
Boyd, Wm	1	2	4		
Reasoner, Jno	1		2		
Collier, Francis	2		2		
Holland, Julius	1	1	2		
Hawkins, Sam	1	5	7		
Best, Peter	1	1	4		
Smith, Jno	2	4	5		
Smith, Peter	1	2	1		1
Rodes, Christe	2		1		
Rodes, Henry	1		2		
Linberger, Barb		2	4		
McFarlin, Jacob	1	3	4		
Lisly, John	1		1		
Shanler, Boston	1		1		
Hunter, Patty		3	3		
Costner, Jacob	1		1		2
Jones, Charles	1		7		
Gibson, Davd	1	4	6		
Hoyl, Peter	1	2	3		
Holland, Isaac	3	4	4		
Rosner, Jno	1	1	1		
McGill, Thos	3	3	7		1
Vandycke, Rd	3	5	4		
McCarver, Jno	1	2	2		
McCarver, Jas	4	2	5		
Spencer, Zack	2	1	3		
King, Wm	2	2	2		
Cobb, David	1	2	1		
Kikendal, Sam	1		1		1
Massey, Winney		2	4		2
Beats, Henry	1	1	5		

MORGAN DISTRICT, LINCOLN COUNTY—Continued.

NINTH COMPANY.

NAME OF HEAD OF FAMILY.	Free white males of 16 years and upward, including heads of families.	Free white males under 16 years.	Free white females, including heads of families.	All other free persons.	Slaves.
Shully, Jacob	3	2	7		
Lear, Conrod	1	2	2		
Baldridge, Alex	3		6		2
Sherman, Sam	1		3		
Reed, James	2	3	4		
Reed, Jno	3		4		1
Rudiul, Henry	1	1	4		1
Wells, Jno	1	3	2		2
Fengar, Peter	2	1	3		
Sicles, Jacob	2	1	4		
Adleman, Peter	3		3		
Davis, Jno	2	1	3		
Hinkle, Jacob	1	1	1		
Abernathy, Jno	1		5		1
Addleman, Jno	1	2	2		
Jones, Richd	4	1	4		2
Hansil, Wm	3	2	1		1
Collin, W		1	5		
Sicles, George	4	4	4		4
Baldridge, Jno	2	1	3		
Hoskins, Jno	2	1	7		7
Bradsha, Jonas	1	3	4		3
Morison, Wm	2	4	4		
Hager, Jane	1	4	4		
Womac, Abner	1	1	2		
Cooper, Mary	2	2	3		
Long, Sam	2	1	3		
Long, Reuben	1	4	15		
Cohnan, Jno	1	6	15		
Cherry, David	3	2	5		
Pucket, Ben	1	2	2		
Beaty, Marget	1	2	9		9
Fornay, Peter	8	2	3		4
Beaty, Wm	2		3		3
Wilkeson, Jas	1		3		2
Childers, Robt	1		8		
Johnson, Jas	1	4	4		8
Martin, Jos	1		3		
Nelson, Jno	2	2	2		16
Nelson, Alex	2				7
Givins, Wm	1		2		
Kinkaid, Wm	1	1	5		
McMin, Sam	1		6		
Nixon, Wm	2	1	4		1
Nixon, Jas	1		1		
Nixon, Jno	1	2	1		
Womac, Abrm	3		2		
Riggen, Chas	1	3	3		
Davis, Jno	1	1	2		
Huchison, Jonathn	1		1		
Black, Wm	1	3	3		
Long, Jno	2	2	5		7
Caruthers, Wm	2		3		
Caruthers, Robt	1	3	3		3
Beall, Rd	1	3	4		
Beall, Wm	1		1		
Cloniger, Phil	1		1		
Killian, Leond	2		1		1
Killian, David	1		1		
Brian, John	1		1		
Litle, James	3	3	3		1
Beall, Jno	1		2		5
Rankin, Jos	1		1		
Lysle, Arche	1	4	3		
Hagar, Wm	3	3	4		1
Hagar, Jno	1	1	3		
Robinson, Jno	1	1	2		
Beall, Jno, Jr	1		2		
Beall, Wm	1		1		
Thompson, Wm	1		3		
Bradsha, Charles	1	1	2		2
Sicles, Jacob	2	2	4		
Kinkaid, Thom	2				
Hager, Simon	1	2	2		
Kinkaid, Jno	1	1	2		
Kinkaid, Jno, Sr	3		3		7
Luckey, Jas	2		2		
Bonner, Wm	1	2	2		
Edwards, Jno	4		1		
Woods, Mary			3		
Reeper, Tho	1	1	3		
Abernathy, B	1	2	3		1
Robison, W		1	2		
Forney, Jacob	1	1	1		5
Bogs, Jno	3		3		
Bogs, Aron	3		3		
Williamson, Robt	3	1	1		
Wells, Conrod	3		4		
Statia, Barnet	1	3	2		
Williams, Charles	1	2	5		2
Williams, David	1		1		
Williams, Joel	1	1	2		
Williams, Wm	1		3		1
Nill, Lewis	1	3	5		2
Hariss, Arthur	1		1		3

NINTH COMPANY—con.

NAME OF HEAD OF FAMILY.	Free white males of 16 years and upward, including heads of families.	Free white males under 16 years.	Free white females, including heads of families.	All other free persons.	Slaves.
Nantz, Clemm	1	1	2		
Nantz, Wm	4		4		
Fight, Jno	1	4	2		
King, Ester			3		
Kinkaid, Robt	1	2	1		
Kinkaid, Jas	1		2		
Arnhart, Abrm	1		2		3
Airhart, Catharin			2		
Airhart, Phil	2	3	3		
Goldman, Jno	1	2	2		
Edwards, Lewis	1		2		
Asberry, Danl	1	2	1		
Maize, Wm	1	2	2		
Slinkard, Henry	1	1	2		
Slinkard, Jno	1		2		
Club, Peter	1	1	2		
Spice, Amos	1		4		
Sherman, Sam	3		3		
Club, Gasper	2	3	3		
Surat, Leonas	1		3		
Taylor, Sam	1	1	2		
Master, Jno	1	2	1		
Abernathy, Tarnul	2	2	1		2
Fortner, Wm	1	1	4		
Rominger, Geo	1	1	2		
Rominger, Geo, Sr	1		2		
Abernathy, Jos	1		7		
Reel, Geo	1	1	3		
Devault, Mathias	1	4	4		
Bowers, Jno	1	2	2		
Flat, Jno	2		5		
Cristis, David	3	2	2		
Abernathy, David	1	2	3		2
Abernathy, Jno	1		6		1
Abernathy, Sarah	5		1		11
Connuller, Phillip	3	1	4		
Walker, Jno	1	3	4		
Link, Fred	1	2	3		
Williams, Rd	1	4	5		1
Gardner, Jere	1	2	5		2
Edwards, Lewis	2		2		
Walker, Ben	1	3	2		
Bishop, Wm	3		3		
Bishop, Beal	1	1	1		
Statia, Aron	1	1	2		
Link, Jacob	2		2		
Hill, Jno, Sr	1		5		5
Hill, Jno, Jr	1	1	1		1
Hill, Thos	1	1	3		1
Maxil, Wm	1	1	2		
Sanders, Thom	1		1		
Sanders, Lemuel	3	4	5		
Goodson, Matt	1	3	3		
Abernathy, Jas	1		4		
Davis, Jno, Jr	1		2		
Snider, Christn	1	3	3		
Orm, Jno Godfry	1	1	6		1
Johnson, Robt	2	3	5		
Slinkard, George	1	2	2		
Club, George	1		3		
Ridicil, Wltr	1		1		
Rudcil, Jacob	1		1		
Rudcill, Henry	1	1	1		1
Duncan, Abs	1	2	1		1
Parr, Jno	2		3		3
Binham, Sam	1	2	5		10
Duncan, Jno	1	2	5		
Richards, Jno	1	2	3		
Abernathy, Dav, Sr	3	1	2		18
Abernathy, Robt	1	1	5		1
Abernathy, Charls	1	3	3		1
Sutton, Saml	1		1		
Myers, Elias	3	1	2		
Myers, Elias, Jr	1	2	4		
Dellinger, Geo	1	3	2		
Benham, Arthur	2	3	3		
Clifton, David	1	2	3		1
Clifton, Wm	1	4	4		
Shoup, Jacob	1	1	1		
Shoup, Adam	2	3	4		
Reis, Geo	1		3		
Master, Jacob	2		5		
Crites, Peter	2	3	4		
Willms, Charls, Sr	2		4		6
Dellinger, Wm	1	2	2		
Sadler, Henry	1	2	6		
Bradshaw, Jos	1		2		
Bradshaw, Jude			2		4
Cloniger, Adm	1	4	5		
Rominger, Geo	1	1	4		
Summet, Frank	1	5	4		
Sites, Peter	1	3	6		
Rine, Jacob	1		2		
Hovis, Jno	1	1	2		
Rhades, Fred	2		4		

NINTH COMPANY—con.

NAME OF HEAD OF FAMILY.	Free white males of 16 years and upward, including heads of families.	Free white males under 16 years.	Free white females, including heads of families.	All other free persons.	Slaves.
Abernathy, Wm	1	3	3		
Chapman, Hana		1	4		
Dellinger, Jacob	1		4		
Bomgarner, Peter	1	1	3		
Filker, Michal	1	1	2		
Bumgarner, Joel	1	2	2		
Crotz, Tilly	2	2	4		
Engle, Jno	1	9	5		
Hopper, Adm	1	1	5		
Reel, Geo	3	1	4		
Slinkard, Jacob	1		4		
Ashbean, Web	2	2	4		
Master, Michal	3		8		
Master, Jno	1	1	1		
Stoup, Jacob	3	2	2		
Stoup, Phillip	1	1	2		
Engle, Michl	1	6	4		
Eaker, Jos	1	3	2		
Butt, Michl	2	2	4		
Hufman, Jacob	1	1	5		
Goodson, Wm	1	3	3		
Kuler, David	1	4	2		
Parker, Jno	1	3	2		
Srum, Peter	1	2	1		
Finger, Jacob	1	5			

TENTH COMPANY.

NAME OF HEAD OF FAMILY.	Free white males of 16 years and upward, including heads of families.	Free white males under 16 years.	Free white females, including heads of families.	All other free persons.	Slaves.
Reid, Jno	1	1	3		
Goltny, Nathan	1	1	4		
Nox, Robt	1	2	6		1
Cunkleton, Jno	1		2		
Crunkleton, Jo	1	1	2		
Keince, Abrm	3		2		
Dillon, Jno	2	1	6		
McCorkle, Frank	2	3	4		10
Bohnger, Jno	1	5	5		
Long, Jno	1	2	2		
Riden, Jno	1	2	4		
Hutchison, David	2		2		
Jones, Jesse	1	2	4		
Richison, Jno	1		1		
Wiliford, Theo	1	2	2		
Givin, Geo	1		2		
Givin, Wm	2	1	2		
Brotherton, Mary		4	2		
Fisher, Eliz	3		2		
Cunnigan, Jno	2	1	3		
Lockman, Sarah	2		5		
Allen, Wm, Sr	2	2	4		
Thompson, Mary		1	5		
Lytle, Geo	2		4		
Rutherford, Henry	1	3	3		2
Loller, Isaac	2	3	6		
Kein, Abrm, Jr	3		3		
Perkins, R. Bigm	3	3	3		
Hunter, Rd	1	1	2		
Gabrull, Jacob	1	2	6		1
Wheeler, Jno	1	2	3		
Childers, Jno	1	1	3		
Lytle, Ellis	1	1	2		
Ballard, Jas	1	3	3		
Ballard, Lewis	1	1	3		
Ballard, Wiley	1		3		
Glen, Jno	1		1		
Newman, Michl	2		1		
Parks, Andw	1	1	3		
Wheeler, Thom	1	1	3		
Clark, Wm	2	2	4		
Thompson, Sam	2	3	4		
Bell, Thom	1	4	2		
Cornelius, Ben	1		2		
Cornelius, Wm	1	1	5		
Hill, Inez	2		3		
Stiles, Ben	2		3		
Perkins, Wm, Jr	1	1	1		1
Perkins, Wm, Sr	1	6	2		
Perkins, Ben	1	2	2		
Arrowwood, Jno	1	2	2		
Long, Danl	2	5	4		
Hughes, James	1	3	2		
Patten, Henry	1		2		
Alexander, Lidiz	3		5		
Gilliland, Thom	1	3	2		
Lee, Jas	1	1	1		
Pitts, Jas	1	1	2		
Pettilo, Littletn	1	1	4		1
Hawkins, Matt	1		2		
Hawkins, Jas	1	3	2		
Culdwell, Jas	2	3	3		
Rainey, Aron	1	3	2		
Harwell, Jackson	1	1	2		
Holdiman, Jacob	1	2	2		
Hilderman, Nick	1	2	3		
Allen, Jno	2		7		

MORGAN DISTRICT, LINCOLN COUNTY—Continued.

NAME OF HEAD OF FAMILY.	Free white males of 16 years and upward, including heads of families.	Free white males under 16 years.	Free white females, including heads of families.	All other free persons.	Slaves.
TENTH COMPANY—con.					
Petty, Reuben	2	2	2	....	....
Parten, Ben	2	3	2	....	....
Allen, Wm	1	2	5	....	....
Allen, Jos	1	4	3	....	....
McCabe, Jno	3	4	6	....	....
Turbefield, Jno	3	2	6	....	3
Edwards, Jno	2	6	3	....	....
Narwell, Sam	1	....	1	....	9
Narwell, Nasbit	2	2	1	....	5
Narwell, Francis	1	....	3	....	1
Abernathy, Nartil	1	1	1	....	2
Abernathy, Robt	1	4	3	....	7
Stiles, Jno	1	5	4	....	....
Brewer, Buckly	1	2	1	....	....
Davis, Jno	1	....	1	....	....
Slinkard, Jacob	1	1	2	....	....
Hoot, Uley	....	....	6	....	....
Jackson, Nathnl	1	3	5	....	....
Sherrill, Elisha	1	3	3	....	....
Sherrill, Agness	....	....	2	....	1
Robison, Isaac	1	3	7	....	....
Perkins, Adm	2	....	2	....	....
Narwell, Ambros	1	1	3	....	2
Berkly, Robt	1	2	4	....	1
Lineberry, Peter	3	3	4	....	....
Wagoner, Edmond	2	2	3	....	1
Arrowwood, Zach	2	1	3	....	....
Killian, Mathias	1	3	4	....	....
Cummins, Wm	1	....	3	....	....
Hugins, Henry	1	1	1	....	....
Richards, Jno	1	2	2	....	....
Ninzy, Jos	2	3	5	....	....
Lollar, Thom	1	3	2	....	....
Lynch, Anne	....	2	2	....	....
Cunigan, Frank	1	2	5	....	2
Fleming, Arche	1	3	6	....	....
Fisher, Ezek	1	4	1	....	....
Jones, Jemima	....	2	5	....	....
Cloniger, Mich	1	2	3	....	....
Wooten, Lucy	....	2	1	....	....
Loften, Jas	1	....	....	....	....
Sherrill, Josh	1	6	2	....	1
Holsclaw, Jas	1	3	3	....	....
Chapman, Mary	....	2	4	....	....
Kelly, Mary	....	....	3	....	....
ELEVENTH COMPANY.					
McLean, Alex	4	....	2	....	5
Johnson, Robt	3	2	3	....	5
Rankin, Sam	4	4	4	....	....
McGee, Thom	2	....	2	....	4
Spencer, Zach	1	1	3	....	....
Clubb, David	1	2	1	....	....
Leeper, Jno	1	2	2	....	3
Cathey, Geo	1	1	3	....	2
Moore, Alex	1	2	4	....	....
Taylor, Andw	2	1	2	....	....
McCombs, Robt	3	2	4	....	2
Alexander, Robt	1	1	3	....	14
McKee, Jas	4	4	2	....	4
Smith, Bennet	1	1	2	....	2
Dickson, Jas	1	2	3	....	2
Shannon, Robt	1	1	5	....	3
Shannon, Jas	1	2	3	....	....
Graves, Jno	1	2	2	....	5
Dickson, Thom	1	5	1	....	....
Martin, Sam	6	4	5	....	1
Tayton, Jno	2	1	5	....	1
Harbison, Jas	1	1	1	....	....
Barry, Hugh	5	....	2	....	1
Ewing, George	1	....	4	....	1
Colwell, Wm	1	....	3	....	....
Ewing, Hugh	1	1	1	....	....
Colwell, Sam	1	1	3	....	8
McKee, Jas	2	6	2	....	4
Lute, Peter	1	7	2	....	....
Clinton, Jas	2	1	2	....	....
Farris, Jas	1	....	2	....	....
Davis, Fr	2	3	5	....	....
McElvin, Jas	3	....	1	....	....
Camell, Robt	1	....	2	....	9
Newton, Ben	1	2	6	....	....
Armstrong, Robt	2	....	....	....	3
Leeper, Moses	2	....	3	....	....
Cunigam, Jas	1	....	1	....	....
Hanks, Rd	1	1	2	....	....
McCombs, Robt	4	4	6	....	1
Rhine, Thom	1	3	5	....	6
Graham, Jas	3	1	1	....	....
Dickson, Jo	4	2	2	....	14
Mayberry, Jno	1	6	2	....	2
Rudirill, Wirey	2	2	3	....	....
Cox, George	2	6	4	....	2
ELEVENTH COMPANY—continued.					
Scott, Abram	2	2	2	....	7
Hays, Moses	1	....	2	....	2
Beaty, Jas	2	4	4	....	1
Erwin, Isaac	1	2	3	....	....
Alison, Antony	1	1	3	....	....
Chitton, Wm	1	1	7	....	6
Armstrong, Matt	1	5	4	....	....
Henry, Jos	3	1	3	....	....
Henderson, Jas	3	3	3	....	2
Patterson, Jno	1	2	3	....	2
Gillispi, Jno	1	1	1	....	....
Hanks, Jas	1	2	4	....	....
Swanson, Jno	1	1	3	....	....
Davis, Wm	2	1	4	....	7
Dobins, Alex	3	1	6	....	....
Barnett, Sion	1	1	2	....	....
Cumin, Matthew	1	....	2	....	....
McLean, George	1	1	1	....	....
Lovsay, Shadrach	1	1	1	....	....
Lewis, Henry	2	3	2	....	....
Abernathy, Robt	2	....	1	....	1
Abernathy (Widow)	2	....	1	....	9
Abernathy, Jas	1	....	4	....	....
Abernathy, Smith	1	2	3	....	....
Abernathy, Robt., Jr	1	6	2	....	13
Abernathy, Betty	1	2	3	....	10
Arnold, Michal	1	1	5	....	....
Bradsha, Wm	1	....	3	....	9
Bradsha, Charles	1	2	2	....	....
Beaty, Jos	1	1	1	....	....
Bull, Edwd	2	2	4	....	....
Bealk, Jno	2	3	4	....	....
Cobb, Ambrous	1	....	1	....	6
Cobb, Joseph	1	2	1	....	....
Cox, Vincen	1	3	7	....	....
Dildenhart, Wm	1	2	2	....	2
Devenport, Geo	1	....	....	....	1
Davis, Joel	2	....	3	....	1
Pharaoh, Nat	1	2	2	....	1
Pharaoh, Jno	1	4	2	....	1
Feathernh, W	1	2	5	....	7
Fete, Leonard	1	4	2	....	....
Gillispi, W	3	1	3	....	....
Gaskins, Francis	4	....	3	....	....
Flinkil, Wd	2	3	9	....	....
Hamilton, Alex	1	1	3	....	....
Hamiller (Widow)	2	2	2	....	....
Jenkins, Moses	1	1	3	....	....
Moreland, Francis	1	....	....	....	4
Moore, Jno	1	1	2	....	1
Moore, Jas	1	....	1	....	....
Moore, Wm	2	4	5	....	2
McCalley, Jno	1	5	3	....	3
McCalister, Jas	1	3	2	....	....
McCalister (Widow)	2	3	5	....	....
Moreland, Francis	1	1	1	....	3
Newton, Ebenezer	3	....	2	....	....
Newton, Wm	1	4	2	....	....
Oliver, Jas	1	....	....	....	....
Phillips, David	2	4	5	....	....
Rutledge, Jas	1	3	4	....	4
Starit, Wm	3	1	4	....	....
Starit, Moses	1	....	....	....	....
Venatey, Peter	1	4	4	....	....
Williams, Moses	1	4	3	....	....
West, Isaac	4	2	4	....	....
West, Barny	1	....	4	....	....
West, Stephen	1	1	1	....	....
Wells, Burrell	1	2	4	....	3
Campbell, Mary	....	2	3	....	....
Abernathy, Jno	1	5	4	....	1
Drake, Jno	1	1	4	....	....
Fetherson, Jesse	2	3	2	....	10
Abernathy, David	1	4	4	....	1
Starit, Alex	1	....	2	....	....
Dumport, Abram	1	....	....	....	5
McCarver, Jas	4	2	5	....	....
Rutledge, Chas	1	1	2	....	....
Bradsha, Seth	1	1	2	....	1
TWELFTH COMPANY.					
Whishenheatt, Geor	1	2	6	....	1
Ormon, Ben	1	3	5	....	1
Weer, Robt	1	5	1	....	5
White, Jas	1	5	4	....	....
Oakly, Lebon	2	....	2	....	....
Carruth, Jno	1	2	4	....	8
Whitler, Thom	3	1	3	....	6
Magnis, Wm	2	....	....	....	12
Ferguson, Jas	1	1	1	....	....
Creator, Phineas	2	1	6	....	1
Long, Jno	3	2	5	....	7
Alexander, Jno	1	....	4	....	....
TWELFTH COMPANY—continued.					
Asby, Sam	2	1	5	....	1
Dyer, Saml	2	2	4	....	1
Rutledge, Jno	2	3	3	....	....
Pauley, Jas	3	1	2	....	....
Titterburn, Jno	3	4	4	....	....
Harmon, Henry	1	2	1	....	....
McCurey, Abrm	1	1	4	....	....
Parker, Thom	1	2	2	....	....
Lidford, Wm	1	1	1	....	....
Hinsly, Ben	1	3	1	....	....
Cortney, Jas	1	3	1	....	....
Childers, Wm	1	3	1	....	....
Hope, Saml	1	3	2	....	....
Snider, Barich	1	....	4	....	....
Parker, Nicolas	1	2	6	....	....
Ensloe, Jno	3	....	3	....	....
Parker, Thos	3	1	5	....	....
Parker, Esau	1	2	2	....	....
Tucker, Jno	3	1	5	....	....
McAfee, Jas	3	2	1	....	7
Oats, Wm	2	3	3	....	....
McCallon, Jas	2	2	6	....	1
Collins, Danl	2	3	5	....	....
Self, Wm	1	4	4	....	....
Bandis, Marget	1	3	6	....	....
Guttery, Frank	1	....	1	....	....
Smith, Danl	3	4	6	....	....
McDaniel, Jas	1	1	2	....	....
Gabby, Robert	1	3	2	....	....
Harmon, Peter	4	1	3	....	....
Harmon, Jno	2	2	1	....	....
Dickson, Jno	1	....	4	....	....
Dickson, Thom	2	1	....	....	....
Fauls, Jno	2	4	5	....	1
Elder, Wm	1	....	2	....	....
Hogan, Patrick	1	....	4	....	....
Harris, Wm	1	2	6	....	....
Patterson, Geo	1	4	4	....	....
Kughley, Sam	1	....	1	....	....
Carpenter, Michl	1	1	2	....	....
Smith, Jas	1	1	2	....	....
Dunlap, Wm	4	2	3	....	....
Thompson, Charles	1	1	2	....	....
Hederick, Thom	1	1	4	....	....
Carpenter, Jacob	1	2	4	....	....
Crous, Peter	1	2	1	....	....
Paterson, Arthur	4	1	2	....	....
Patterson, Thos	1	1	4	....	....
Patterson, Wm	1	1	3	....	1
Arthur, Jos	1	....	2	....	....
Fullinberry, Jno	2	....	4	....	....
Boman, Wm	1	1	1	....	....
Whitworth, Wm	1	....	4	....	....
Weere, Jno	2	3	5	....	....
Babtist, Jno	2	1	5	....	....
Shermsha, Jno	1	1	4	....	....
Alexander, Jno	1	....	5	....	....
Hamright, Jno	1	2	2	....	....
Hare, Jas	1	2	1	....	....
Numan, Jonathn	1	....	3	....	....
Gladdin, Jos	3	4	3	....	....
Cottins, Saml	1	3	5	....	1
Wells, Jno	2	4	4	....	....
Hamilton, Jane	1	....	3	....	....
Goforth, Eliz	....	2	3	....	....
Eldus, Mary	....	1	1	....	....
Arthur, Sam	2	2	3	....	....
Hullit, Mary	1	....	5	....	....
Collins, Jos	2	3	....	....	....
Glen, Robt	1	5	7	....	....
Davis, Winny	1	1	3	....	....
Newman, Thoc	1	1	1	....	....
Cronister, Adm	2	....	1	....	....
Landers, Felix	1	3	4	....	....
Fowler, Wm	2	1	8	....	....
McEntire, Alex	1	3	2	....	....
Collins, Abrm	2	1	2	....	1
Collins, Jacob	1	3	3	....	....
Collins, Jas	3	....	2	....	....
Hawkins, Jos	1	1	2	....	....
Waterson, Jno	2	3	5	....	....
Romine, Abel	1	1	4	....	....
Neall, Adam	1	7	1	....	....
Beaty, Deborah	1	....	1	....	....
Spurling, Jno	1	....	2	....	....
Bird, Mark	3	3	....	....	5
Miller, Thom	1	1	2	....	1
White, Wm	1	....	1	....	....
Hope, Henry	1	1	1	....	....
Edwards, Charls	1	2	4	....	....
Parker, Humphry	1	1	2	....	....
Graham, Arthur	3	1	5	....	22
Williams, Wm	1	1	3	....	....
Taylor, Jno	1	1	4	....	....

MORGAN DISTRICT, LINCOLN COUNTY—Continued.

TWELFTH COMPANY—continued.

NAME OF HEAD OF FAMILY.	Free white males of 16 years and upward, including heads of families.	Free white males under 16 years.	Free white females, including heads of families.	All other free persons.	Slaves.
Erwin, Jas	1	1	1		1
Martin, Agness	1	1	3		1
Auston, Jas	1	2	5		1
Potts, Dav	2		1		
Melton, Elisha	1	1	1		
Green, Jos	1				
Ferguson, Robt	1	3	2		
Wadle, Wm	1	1	2		
Woods, Jno	1	1	4		
Conner, Saml	2	6	3		
Mestellar, George	2	1	1		
Dicky, Alex	1		3		
Whiteside, Thom	1	1	1		
Whiteside, Jno	1	1	3		
Graham, Jas	1	4	5		
Graham, Arche	1	1	3		5
Burgan, Jno	2		1	2	
Head, Rd	2	2	2		
Ferguson, Robt	1				
Murphey, Jno	1		2		

MORGAN DISTRICT, RUTHERFORD COUNTY.

FIRST COMPANY.

NAME OF HEAD OF FAMILY.	Free white males of 16 years and upward, including heads of families.	Free white males under 16 years.	Free white females, including heads of families.	All other free persons.	Slaves.
Lewis, Rd	1	1	2		9
Adams, James	1		1		5
Lewis, Jno	1	2	1		4
Frisman, Milone	1	1	2		
Miller, Jno	1	1	3		7
Lewis, Charls	1	2	1		3
Holland, Jas	2	2	3		24
Kilpatrick, Hugh	1	2	5		
Kennedy, Jno	1	1	3		
Roland, Thos	2	1	7		2
Lewis, Henry	1				4
McFadden, Alex	1		3		4
Miller, Col. James	1	1	3		10
Scott, Jas	3	3	4		
Scott, Jno	3	2	7		9
McClure, Rd	3	3	3		
McClure, Jno	3		2		
Driskil, Jno	1	2	5		
Williams, Jno	2	3	5		
Driskil, Wm	1	4	4		
Harmon, Micajah	1	4	5		
Upkirch, Sherwood	1		1		
Price, Wm	1	1	1		
Miller, David	2		1		3
Grant, Wm	3	1	4		
Grant, Andw	1		2		
Dicky, Anthony	2	3	5		
Taylor, Robt	2		3		9
Macay, Alex	2		2		1
Macay, David	1		1		
Willis, Stephen	1		1		7
Tyrrill, Anne		1	3		2
McClure, Jno	1	3	1		1
Watson, Adam	2	1	2		
Taylor, Joshua	1	3	3		3
Dorton, Wm	1	2	2		
Swinny, Edwd	1				
Bradley, Jno	2		1		
Hutson, Moses	1	3	2		
Taylor, Wm E	1	1	1		
Tully, Michal	1	3	2		2
Corby, Wm	1		2		
Medcalf, Warner	1	2	2		
Kilpatrick, Jas	2		2		
Richardson, Chas	1	3	4		1
Wise, Ben	2		2		
Young, Mary		1	3		
Benson, Bethia	2	2	5		
Brummet, Thom	1	2	5		
Billen, Wm	1	2	7		6
Hughes, Jno	1	3	4		
Hider, Ben	2	3	8		4
Twittey, Wm	1	2	2		4
Sweany, Danl	1		3		
Young, Jo., Sr	3		2		
Fleming, Jno	2	2	2		
Twitty, Russell	1		1		2
Miller, Jas., Jr	2	2	7		3
Person, Chas	1	2	4		
Lynch, Fred	1	2	3		1
Wherry, Jno	1	4	3		1
Jones, Berry	1	2	4		
Hannah, Jno	1	4	1		
Evans, Jno	1	2	2		
Macay, Davd	1				
Morriss, Jas	1	3	4		
Hampton, Andw	2	1	5		5
Donalson, Tho'	1		1		
Dicky, James	1	1	1		
Wherry, Thos	2	1	2		
Walker, Tho'	2		3		
Bradly, Patty	1	1	3		
Griffn, Chism	1				2
Taylor, Sarah		2	4		
Kilpatrick, Jas	3	2	3		
Dickey, David	1	5	4		3

SECOND COMPANY.

NAME OF HEAD OF FAMILY.	Free white males of 16 years and upward, including heads of families.	Free white males under 16 years.	Free white females, including heads of families.	All other free persons.	Slaves.
Harvey, Danl	2		4		14
Earl, Jno	4	2	9		12

SECOND COMPANY—con.

NAME OF HEAD OF FAMILY.	Free white males of 16 years and upward, including heads of families.	Free white males under 16 years.	Free white females, including heads of families.	All other free persons.	Slaves.
Music, George	2	1	3		
Jackson, Jas	1	3	4		
Young, Cap. Sam	1	4	4		
Still, Tho	2	4	3		
Snowden, Lovel	1	2			
Matthews, Aoquilla	1	3	4		
Hogan, Edwd	1		1		1
Brigs, Gray	1	1	1		2
Jones, Jno	1		2		
Trapp, Jno	1		3		
Clarey, Wm	1		3		
Snowden, Jas	1	2	1		
Hays, Saml	1		2		
Newell, Jno	2		2		
Harper, Matt	3	4	3		
Music, Joel	1	2	1		
Cummins, Jno	2	2	6		
Brown, Speller	1	4	6		
Pullum, Marget	1	1	4		2
Vaughn, Ben	1	2	2		
Armstrong, Wm	1	4	3		
Snowden, Anne	2	2	1		
Hughes, Jno	1		2		
Tacket, Wm	2	4	3		
McMullin, Robt	2	1	4		
Music, Abram, Sr	6	1	2		6
Armstrong, Jno	1	4	4		
Jordan, Reuben	1	1	2		30
Kirkpatrick, Wm	1		2		
Alsup, Wm	1		1		
Ussery, Rd	1	3	2		
French, Moses	1	3	3		
Blackwell, Jno	1	4	4		
Hamilton, Robt	3	3	2		
Owens, Jas	1	6	3		
Martin, Lewis	1	2	2		
Martin, Adam	1	2	4		
Burgess, Wm	1	2	3		
Jones, Zacheus	1		2		
Swadly, Mark	1		3		
Jones, James	1		2		
Horton, Jno	1	3	4		
Morrow, Patrick	1	2	6		
Vaughn, Jno	1	3	1		
Hunter, Tobias	1				
Young, Saml Jr	1		2		
Kennens, Jno	2	1	4		
French, Sarah	1	1	2		
Wood, Wm	1	1	2		
Blackwell, Joel	1		2		
Price, Jno	2	3	4		
Wilky, Davis	1	5	3		
Barns, Wm	1	4	5		
Dunkin, Wm	1	2	2		
Jenkins, Tabitha					
Dipriest, Christn	1	2	4		
Ridens, James	1	3	4		
Robison, Amos	1	4	3		
Blacwell, James	2	1	5		
Lyles, Tho'	1	1	3		
Hawkins, Wm	2	2	4		11
Cooper, Wm	1	2	6		
Bailey, Mary	1		2		
Vaughn, Wm	1		2		
Caziah, Jno	1	2	2		
Swafford, Jas	4	3	2		
Moore, Jos	1	1	4		
Carson, Roger	1	1	3		
Wilson, Anne		1	4		
Redman, Saml	1	3	2		
Moore, Jno	2		2		
Jenkins, Rd	1	4	2		
Green, Rd	1	2	2		
Capshan, Wm	1	4	4		
Hunter, Peter	1		1		
Trapp, Robt	1	1	2		
Sherwood, Wm	1				
Hays, Mary			3		
Still, Richd	1		2		
Barns, Jno	1		4		
Brigs, Mary		3	7		2
Glen, Andw	3	2	3		

THIRD COMPANY.

NAME OF HEAD OF FAMILY.	Free white males of 16 years and upward, including heads of families.	Free white males under 16 years.	Free white females, including heads of families.	All other free persons.	Slaves.
Ledbetter, George	1	3	5		14
Coon, Nicholas	1	3	1		
Strayson, Henry	1	4	1		
Ledbetter, Rd	1	3	4		16
Nanny, Rice	1	3	4		2
Bradly, G. Walter	1		1		3
Ownby, Jno	3	5	3		
Morris, Thom	1	5	5		
Goodbread, Jno	3	4	4		16
Byers, Jno	2	4	4		
Pots, Mary		2	4		
McDaniels, Alex	1	1	2		
Justice, Jared	1	1	1		
Jones, Ephraim	3				
Hill, Wm	3	1	3		
Crawford, Jno	1	3	6		
Grant, Alex	1	2	3		
Yancy, Wm	1	1	1		
Dobs, Foster	1	2	1		
Morriss, Tho', Jr	1				
Jones, Jno	1	3	1		
Boils, James	1	2	4		
Hampton, Ben	1		2		1
Reeves, George	2	3	4		
Hunes, Sarah		4	2		
Kelly, Henry	1	5	3		
Bagwell, Lunsford	1	1	4		
Nanney, Tho'	1	1	3		
Elms, Jno	1				1
McDaniel, Jos	1		2		
Thomas, Abigail	2		2		
Williams, Jones	2	1	1		3
Middleton, James	1	1	3		
Williams, Austin	1		1		
Harriss, Wm	1	2	4		3
McDaniel, Alex., Jr	1	2	1		
Durnell, Eliza	1	2	5		
Curtis, Jonathn	2	2	6		
Alford, Jno	4	4	5		
Cook, Ephrm	1	3	4		
Alford, Jno, Jr	1		1		
Jones, Stephen	1		1		
Dorton, Tho'	1		2		
Dorton, Davd, Sr	1		7		
Dorton, Davd, Jr	1	3	2		
Sirce, Rd	1	3	2		
Hill, Jas	1	1	3		
Ownby, Jas	1	1	3		
Morgan, Permenter	2	6	3		
Hill, Robt	1	3	6		
Stringfield, Ezekil	1		4		
Kirkland, Jess	1	4	1		
Bradley, Richd	1	5	3		1
Kirkland, Jas	2	1	2		

FOURTH COMPANY.

NAME OF HEAD OF FAMILY.	Free white males of 16 years and upward, including heads of families.	Free white males under 16 years.	Free white females, including heads of families.	All other free persons.	Slaves.
King, Sam	3	2	2		
Davenport, Jno	1	1	2		
Briggs, Jessee	1	1	2		1
Whiteside, Jno	1	3	3		1
Medcalf, Anton	2		4		
Shateen, Joel	4	2	2		
Miller, Laurence	1	1	3		
McCasky, Thos	1	1	3		
Morgan, Elias	4	3	5		2
Latter, Jas	4		6		
Doyle, Jas	1	5	3		2
Ballard, Saml	1		2		
Hunter, Saml	3	3	2		
Corbo, Wm	1	3	1		1
Reeves, David	1	5	6		6
Rite, Moses	2	3	5		
Hill, Ephrm	1		4		
Gray, Wm	1	2	5		
Beard, Wm	1	3	1		
Robinson, Vol	1	2	2		
Dills, Peter	1	3	4		
McCane, Jno	1	3	5		
Hanes, Wm	1	2	5		
Dorton, Jno	1	3	5		
Elliot, Wm	1	3	3		

MORGAN DISTRICT, RUTHERFORD COUNTY—Continued.

FOURTH COMPANY—con.

NAME OF HEAD OF FAMILY.	Free white males of 16 years and upward, including heads of families.	Free white males under 16 years.	Free white females, including heads of families.	All other free persons.	Slaves.
Sirce, Wm	1		1		
Smithers, Garnet	1		3		
Taylor, Celia		2	4		
Taylor, Charls	1		2		
Spive, Jonas	1	1	3		
Spive, Isaac	1	2	4		
Wright, Grunby	1	5	4		
Sims, Tho'	1	1	2		
Metcalf, Wm	1		3		
Stice, Phillip	1	1	3		
Gray, Agnes	1		1		
Hill, Jno	1		2		
Nettles, Wm	2	1	3		
Haslip, Thos	1	3	4		6
Simmons, Wm	1		2		
Porter, Jane	2	1	5		
Dorton, Davd	1	3	3		
Jones, Ben	1	3	2		
Elliot, Merrill	1	2	4		
Hart, Harde	1				
Sheldon, Jno	1	6	4		
Nettle, Shadrach	1	3	4		
Latten, Ben	1	2	3		
Bryan, Isaac	1	1	1		
Covinton, Josiah	1		3		
Henson, Wm	1	4	5		
Brown, Jno	3	2	4		
Russell, Mary	1		1		5
Underwood, Jno	1		1		

FIFTH COMPANY.

NAME OF HEAD OF FAMILY.	Free white males of 16 years and upward, including heads of families.	Free white males under 16 years.	Free white females, including heads of families.	All other free persons.	Slaves.
Wilson, Mumfort	1	3	4		4
Smith, Jno	3	1	2		
Whiteside, Jno	2	2	3		
Fariss, Wm	1	5	1		1
Ross, Sarah			1	4	
Singleton, Rd	2	3	4		1
Tracy, Nathan	1	4	5		
Stocton, Saml	2	1	2		
Street, Thos	2	2	6		
Barnett, Martn	1	2	3		
Forbes, Wm	2		4		
Streets, Simon	1		1		
Money, Jacob	1	1	2		
Money, David	1	1	1		
Goforth, Zac	1	3	1		
Vinzant, Jas	1		3		
Vinzant, Jared	1	2	3		
Munroe, Anne	2		2		2
Smith, Hugh	1	1	3		1
Smith, Robt	1	1	1		
Stocton, Tho	1		4		
Munroe, Arthur	1	4	4		
Osborn, Arthur	1	2	4		
Phillips, Jno	1	1	2		
Barnett, David	2	1	2		
Barnett, Wm, Jr	1	1	1		
Barnet, Biram	2		5		
Phillips, Tho'	1		1		
Sellers, Jno	1	2	3		
Morrow, James	2		3		
Morrow, Henry	1	2	3		
Barnhill, Jno	1		2		
Barnhill, Jas	2		4		
Jones, Jno	1	1	2		1
Millon, Danl	1	1	2		1
Hall, Jno	1	5	3		
Jones, Jno, Sr	2	5	7		1
Jones, Isaac	1	2	6		1
Jones, Robt	1	4	3		
Steward, Wm	1	3	2		
Milton, Eli	1	2	1		1
Smith, Wm	1	2	6		
Munroe, Wm	1	7	3		
Black, James	1	3	4		
Stocton, David	1	3	5		
Cole, David	2	4	4		
Grissom, Jos	2	4	5		
Whiteside, Eliza	1	1	1		
Goldsmith, Jno	1	4	3		
West, Jos	1	2	8		
Megee, Rebeca		3	4		1
Laferty, Sara	1		3		
Laferty, Alex	1		1		
Walker, Jas	1	1	3		
Brown, Abram	1	3	4		
Lacefield, Jno	1		3		
Lacefield, Ben	1	2	3		
Boothe, Mary	1		3		
Lacefield, Dan	1	3	3		
Simons, Nancy	1		3		
Simons, Moses	1	1	1		
Thompson, Jno	1	3	2		
Lacefield, Wm	1		1		

FIFTH COMPANY—con.

NAME OF HEAD OF FAMILY.	Free white males of 16 years and upward, including heads of families.	Free white males under 16 years.	Free white females, including heads of families.	All other free persons.	Slaves.
Royally, Tho'	1	2	1		
Short, Chas	1		2		
Holden, Wm	1	2	3		
Hill, Burrel	1		2		
Sparnach, Jas	1	3	3		
Condor, Claybon	1	3	5		
McCracon, Jno	1	2	4		
Sheppad, Martha	1	1	5		
Gutters, Wm	1	2	2		
Webb, Tho'	1	1	3		
Rogers, Wm	1				
Chitwood, Jas	3				
Phillips, George	2	1	4		
Blantn, Claybon	1		2		
Phillips, Wm	1		1		
Latimor, Cap. Jno	2	2	3		7
Carson, Walter	1	2	3		
Carson, Danl	1	2	2		
Chambers, Alex	1	1	1		
Chambers, Jno	1	3	4		
Chambers, David	1		3		
Miller, Jno	1		2		
Mitchell, Andw	1	2	6		
Mitchell, Wm	1		2		
Latimore, Frank	1		6		5
Latimore, Danl	1	2	5		
Stocton, Jno	1	3	3		
Whiteside, Thos	1	3	3		1
Price, Jno	1	4	5		
Wilson, Wm	5		5		
Clarke, Abram	1	1	2		
Clarke, Abrm., Sr	2	2	3		
Stocton, Newbery	1	1	1		
Stocton, Davis, Jr	1	1	3		
Short, Wm	1		1		
Stocton, Danl	1	1	1		
Cogsdill, Jno	1				

SIXTH COMPANY.

NAME OF HEAD OF FAMILY.	Free white males of 16 years and upward, including heads of families.	Free white males under 16 years.	Free white females, including heads of families.	All other free persons.	Slaves.
Wilson, Jno	1	1	3		2
Rollin, Charles	1	2	1		
Vinzant, Jacob	1	3	3		
Harden, David	1		3		2
Graham, Wm	1		4		11
Collins, Isaac	1	2	2		
Bradly, Joseph	1	5	2		
Wilson, Jonathn	1	3	3		
Allen, Rahel			3	5	
Koil, Sam	1		2		
Botton, Solomon	1	1	3		
McEntire, Wm	1	1	1		
Holman, Isaac	1	7	2		
Moode, Jas	1	3	5		
Mode, Jno	1	1	1		
Mode, Wm	1	4	4		
Moore, Francis	1	2	3		
Moore, George	1		2		
Camp, Danl	1	1	3		
Curlock, Henry	1	3	5		
Parmer, Saml	2	2	6		
Ross, James	2	2	4		
Conn, Wm	1	2	4		
Coils, Alex	1	3	3		
Jones, Wm	1		3		
Fortenberry, Isaas	1	1	4		
Crane, Mayfield	1		4		
Mitchell, Mary	1	1	2		
Blackburn, David	1		1		
Parker, Jno	1	1	1		
McEntire, Jas	1	2	2		
McEntire, Anne		2	2		
Parker, Andw	1	2	3		
Blackburn, Jas	1	5	5		
Singleton, Dan	1	3	4		
McMurray, Wm	1	3	5		1
Fouch, Jonathan	1	3			
Gregory, Jas	1		4		
Cornwell, Edwd	1	3	2		
Person, Jno	1	2	2		
Portman, Ben	1	7	4		
Ridly, Wm	1	5	2		
Thomson, Jno	2	1	2		
Tomason, David	1		4		
Rice, Ben	1	2	5		
Wilson, Jno	1	1	3		2
Lusk, Sarah		2	1		
Lomac, Throp	1	2	1		
Bridges, Wm	1		2		
Hamrie, Nathan	2	2	4		
Nicols, Frank	1		1		
McGuire, Jas	1	6	6		
Earls, Frjd	1	2	2		
Wilson, Jno, Jun	1	2	3		
Downy, Patrick	1	2	4		

SIXTH COMPANY—con.

NAME OF HEAD OF FAMILY.	Free white males of 16 years and upward, including heads of families.	Free white males under 16 years.	Free white females, including heads of families.	All other free persons.	Slaves.
Magnes, Peregreen	2		2		3
Roberts, Jno	1		2		
Harden, Thomas	1		2		
Harden, Robt	1		2		
Durham, Kellis	2	2	5		
Smith, Micajah	1		2		
Lequane, John	1		5		
Constant, Edward	1	3	6		
Hamrick, Enoch	1	1	4		
Beaty, Wallace	1	2	3		
Beaty, Francis	1		2		
McBrian, Wm	3	1	3		
Collins, Jno	1	5	3		
Smith, Wm	3	2	6		
Mason, Peter	1	1	3		
Harden, Ben	1	5	3		1
Roberts, Morriss	1	3	6		7
Harden, David, Jr	1	2	1		
Harden, Jo	1	2	2		
Harden, Jonathn	5	3	5		
Weaver, Ruth	2		1		
Kinkendal, Abram, Jr	1	2	4		7
Bridges, Jno	3	3	8		
Bridges, Wm	1		1		
Bridges, Jas	1		4		
Adams, Wm	1		2		
Hambrick, Jas	1	1	7		
Stice, Andw	1	1	1		
Adams, Ben	3	3	4		
Stice, Charls	2	2	6		
Blanton, Jno	1	3	4		5
Hambrick, Jermiah	2	1	3		
Hamrick, Henry	1		4		
Cain, Wm	1	2	4		
McSwane, Wm	1	2	5		
Harris, Jno	1	3	2		
Linsey, Mary	1	3	2		
Randolph, Silas	1		1		
Hambrick, Sam	3	4	5		
Briges, Jno	1	4	2		
Kemp, Joseph	4	3	7		3
Camp, Wm	3	4	4		
McFastin, Jno	1	3			
Hogan, Michal	1	1	4		
Coleson, Robt	1	1	3		
Brookfield, George	1		1		
Hambrick, Price	1	2	1		

SEVENTH COMPANY.

NAME OF HEAD OF FAMILY.	Free white males of 16 years and upward, including heads of families.	Free white males under 16 years.	Free white females, including heads of families.	All other free persons.	Slaves.
Walker, Thom	1	1	1		1
Prince, Jos	2	6	4		
Freeman, Ben	2	3	2		
Freeman, Jesse	1	1	1		
Prince, Jno	2	3	3		1
Holland, Jno	1	2	6		
Hughey, James	1	3	6		2
Burnett, Joseph	3		5		
Watson, Patrick	1	3	6		
Inlow, Agnes	3		6		
Pell, Jonathan	1		2		
Erwin, Jno	2	1	2		1
Reives, Isom	3	5	3		2
Tomvelin, Moses	1		2		
Evis, Bartlet	2	2	2		
Burnett, Jesse	3	1	4		
Capel, Thom	1		1		2
Morris, Micajah	1		2		
Patterson, Matthew	2		3		
Baker, Wm	2	3	7		
Lewis, Abel	1	1	2		1
Price, Thom	1		1		
Dougherty, Rd	3	1	3		
Robison, Thom	3	1	4		
Andrews, Saml	3	2	2		
Long, Wm	4		3		
Turner, Michal	1	3	1		
Shunk, Henry	1		1		
Long, Gloud	3	2	4		
Robison, Wm	3	6	3		
Wickle, Peter	3		3		
Davis, Goodman	1	1	1		
Smith, Lewis	1		2		
Scott, Jno	1	3	1		
McAdams, Jno	1		3		
Goforth, Jno	1	5	4		
Tomson, Jas	2		4		
Price, Adah		2	3		
Parks, James	2	2	5		
Donaldson, Sam	1		1		
Huddleston, Wm	5	1	6		1
Cartwright, Eliza		3	3		
Patterson, Jos	1	1	1		
Smart, Mary	1		8		
Davis, Thom	1	2	3		

MORGAN DISTRICT, RUTHERFORD COUNTY—Continued.

NAME OF HEAD OF FAMILY.	Free white males of 16 years and upward, including heads of families.	Free white males under 16 years.	Free white females, including heads of families.	All other free persons.	Slaves.
SEVENTH COMPANY—continued.					
Evis, Groves	1	1	1	....	1
Davis, Simon	1	2	3	....	....
Patterson, Robt	1	2	3	....	....
Parks, Robt	1	1	1	....	....
McMurray, Sam	2	1	5	....	....
Cole, Wm	3	3	5	....	....
Huddlestone, James	1	3	3	....	1
Nix, Jno	1	2	3	....	....
Witherow, Jas., Es	1	2	2	....	9
Witherow, Jno	1	....	2	....	9
Carson, Jno	1	1	1	....	....
Milton, Reuben	1	5	7	....	2
Huddleston, Wm	4	1	4	....	1
Milton, Jesse	1	3	3	....	1
Norrill, Sam	1	2	5	....	....
Milton, John	1	3	5	....	....
Milton, Ben	1	1	2	....	....
Early, Thos	1	9	1	....	....
Moore, Wm	1	1	2	....	....
Barnett, David	1	3	3	....	....
McGahey, Danl	1	....	3	....	....
Harden, Wm	1	....	1	....	....
Garison, Richd	1	3	3	....	....
McGahey, Mary	....	2	5	....	....
Horton, Taunson	1	....	....	....	....
Sweasy, Richd	....	3	3	....	....
Ross, James	3	6	4	....	....
Welsh, Thom	1	3	2	....	....
Welsh, James	2	1	5	....	....
EIGHTH COMPANY.					
Melone, Robt	1	1	2	....	....
Geir, David	1	1	9	....	....
Gilhy, Robt	5	1	6	....	1
Bates, Jno	1	1	3	....	....
Sorrils, Jno, Jr	1	1	3	....	....
Sorrils, Jno	1	1	6	....	....
Smith, Thom	2	1	1	....	....
McFadden, Saml	2	4	4	....	....
Newton, Robt	1	1	4	....	....
Nix, Wm	2	3	4	....	....
Cook, James	1	4	4	....	....
Logan, Francis	3	3	2	....	....
Hampton, Andw., Jr	2	1	1	....	....
Johnson, Arthur	1	3	5	....	....
Hunter, Joseph	1	4	4	....	....
Black, Rachal	1	3	3	....	1
Kestor, James	1	4	2	....	....
Flack, Jno	1	3	4	....	5
Beall, James	1	3	5	....	6
Harris, Jno	2	3	5	....	....
Mitchell, George	1	2	3	....	....
Porter, Col. Wm	2	4	4	....	....
Mitchell, James	2	2	3	....	....
Campbell, Robt	2	3	7	....	....
Baldrige, Alex	1	1	3	....	....
Coxey, Wm	1	1	6	....	....
Marshall, Jno	1	1	2	....	....
Coxey, Jno	1	3	3	....	....
Guffy, Jno	4	2	4	....	....
McMurray, Thos	2	2	3	....	....
Reid, Saml	2	1	2	....	....
Watson, Hugh	1	....	1	....	....
McGahey, Alex	3	2	5	....	....
Baldridge, Jno	1	2	4	....	....
Jones, Jno W	1	2	5	....	....
Largen, Jas	1	4	3	....	....
Bates, George	2	1	3	....	....
Wren, Sarah	....	2	6	....	....
Hanes, Ephrm	1	2	4	....	....
Cherry, Robt	1	3	3	....	....
Moore, Rachal	....	2	5	....	3
Moore, Elisha	2	1	2	....	....
Fauman, Dug	1	....	1	....	....
Ransom, Ezart	1	....	....	....	....
Tanner, Michal	1	1	3	....	....
Panter, George	1	2	3	....	....
Nix, Jno	1	2	3	....	....
Harris, Lewis	1	2	4	....	....
Calihan, Henry	1	5	....	....	....
Goforth, Jno	1	6	4	....	....
Ketto, Henry	1	1	1	....	....
Johnson, Henry	2	1	3	....	....
Johnson, Martha	2	1	3	....	....
Mastril, John	1	1	2	....	....
Williams, Wm	1	1	2	....	....
Williams, Wm, Sr	1	3	1	....	....
Hamton, Jonathan	1	4	4	2	2
Johnson, Nathnl	1	3	3	....	....
Goforth, Andrew	1	3	5	....	....
Watson, Wm	1	1	3	....	....
Clements, Rachl	2	3	1	....	....
Clements, Cornelius	1	2	2	....	....
Watson, Eliz	1	1	4	....	....
Smart, Wm	3	1	1	....	....
EIGHTH COMPANY—con.					
Smart, Wm, Jr	2	1	6	....	1
Spratt, Tho'	1	3	3	....	....
Watson, Jno	1	1	2	....	....
Huddleston, David	1	1	5	....	1
Logan, Drury	1	3	3	....	....
Flack, Wm	2	....	1	....	....
Wray, Fanne	1	3	3	....	....
Jones, Jno	1	1	4	....	....
Fleming, George	1	4	4	....	....
Baldrige, Tho'	1	1	2	....	....
Bowen, Jno	1	3	4	....	....
NINTH COMPANY.					
Carpenter, Saml	1	1	5	....	1
Bedford, Jonas	2	2	1	....	....
McDaniel, Charles	1	1	2	....	2
White, Jeremiah	4	....	1	....	....
Moss, Henry	1	2	4	....	....
Chitwood, James	1	5	2	....	....
Gardner, Wm	1	1	3	....	....
McMurray, Wm	1	1	3	....	1
White, Isaac	1	1	3	....	....
Anderson, Jno	2	1	4	....	....
Woodard, Peter	4	1	6	....	....
Thompson, Nathan	1	1	3	....	....
Black, Robt	1	3	5	....	....
Black, Jno	1	3	5	....	....
Hinton, Isaac	2	1	3	....	....
Buccannon, Jas	3	....	2	....	....
Hiltebrand, Jno	2	3	5	....	1
Wolbert, Christe	1	1	4	....	....
Wolbert, Jno	1	3	1	....	....
Brown, Mark	1	1	2	....	....
Blanton, Claybon	1	....	2	....	....
Higdon, Jno	2	....	2	....	....
Craig, Jno	1	1	3	....	....
Craig, Ruth	1	1	1	....	....
Higdon, Mary	....	1	2	....	....
Sisk, Robt	1	3	3	....	....
Smally, Nancy	....	1	1	....	....
Morgan, Eliz	....	1	2	....	....
Bracket, Mary	....	1	3	....	....
Willis, Henry	1	1	4	....	....
Smith, Jno	1	3	3	....	....
Invistor, Hugh	1	2	3	....	....
Nunnery, Jno	1	1	1	....	....
Wilson, James	1	1	2	....	....
York, Wm	2	....	2	....	....
McCurdy, Abram	1	5	2	....	....
Lewis, Herculus	1	....	2	....	....
Willis, Joseph	1	3	2	....	....
Downs, Ezekiel	1	....	3	....	....
Mitchel, Andrew	2	2	7	....	....
Castion, Wm	1	3	2	....	....
Upton, Edwd	1	7	3	....	....
Francis, Edwd	1	3	7	....	....
Bracket, Ben	2	2	4	....	....
Davis, Hezekiah	1	4	1	....	....
Cline, David	1	....	3	....	....
McGlamery, Jesse	1	....	1	....	....
Johnson, Danl	1	3	6	....	....
Beaver, Ben	2	5	2	....	....
Hucaboy, Joshua	1	3	4	....	....
Mooney, Daniel	1	....	2	....	....
Willis, Wm	2	5	2	....	....
Wortman, Danl	1	3	2	....	....
Harris, David	1	2	4	....	....
Peeler, Peter	1	1	2	....	....
Robinson, David	1	....	1	....	....
Roper, Rev. David	1	1	5	....	....
Roper, Charles	1	2	5	....	....
Roper, Merideth	3	1	4	....	....
Roper, David, Jr	1	1	1	....	....
Falkner, Wm	2	1	5	....	....
Falkner, Wm, Jr	1	2	3	....	....
Falkner, Ezekl	1	....	1	....	....
Thompson, Nathan	1	1	3	....	....
Queen, Wm	1	4	6	....	4
Gardner, James	1	....	3	....	....
Carpender, Jos	1	....	3	....	....
Young, Saml	1	1	2	....	....
Bowan, Joseph	1	....	5	....	....
Hogan, Shadrach	2	3	4	....	....
Thomas, Aron	1	3	3	....	....
Chapman, Eurith	2	....	1	....	....
Silman, Jno	1	4	3	....	....
Green, Jno	1	3	3	....	....
Burlison, Thos	1	4	3	....	....
Burlison, Jo	1	....	1	....	....
White, James	1	1	3	....	....
Morris, James	1	....	2	....	....
Wilman, Wm	1	1	4	....	....
Cogsdil, Fed	1	2	4	....	....
Willis, Jno	2	1	2	....	....
Ravin, Wm	1	2	2	....	....
NINTH COMPANY—con.					
Crowder, Phillip	1	2	3	....	....
Moss, James	2	1	4	....	....
Martin, Jno	1	1	1	....	....
Hamson, Tho'	1	1	2	....	....
Johnson, John	1	1	5	....	....
Ore, Robt	2	....	1	....	....
Ally, Shadrach	1	4	4	....	2
McEntire, Jno	1	....	2	....	....
White, Elinor	....	4	4	....	....
Wilkinson, Ben	1	4	4	....	....
White, Austin	1	1	2	....	....
White, Stephen	1	1	3	....	....
McEntire, Allen	1	1	3	....	....
Arington, Sarah	....	5	4	....	....
Wells, Jno	2	....	1	....	....
Nowlen, David	1	3	3	....	....
TENTH COMPANY.					
Alexander, Elias	2	3	4	....	1
Tomason, Wm	1	....	1	....	....
Tomason, Eliza	1	2	7	....	....
Russell, Jno	1	5	4	....	....
Pain, Eliza	1	....	1	....	....
Wilmoth, Wm	1	....	1	....	....
English, James	1	....	2	....	....
Witherow, Wm	2	4	4	....	....
Mullin, Charles	1	3	4	....	....
Osborn Michal	1	1	1	....	....
Walker, Wm	1	1	2	....	2
Farmer, Nathan	1	4	4	....	....
Walker, Jno	3	....	3	....	3
Berry, Willm	1	2	3	....	....
Bedford, Raymd	1	1	2	....	....
McKinny, Jno	3	....	2	....	1
Thompson, Gideon	1	4	4	....	....
Swann, Saml	2	....	6	....	2
Lyles, Brittn	1	1	2	....	....
Sutton, Jno	3	3	6	....	1
Hedlow, Andw	1	1	1	....	....
Evis, Wm	2	3	6	....	....
Settle, Bushrod	1	5	2	....	....
Swan, Robt	1	....	3	....	....
McClane, Jno	1	2	3	....	....
Suttle, Isaac	2	2	4	....	....
Berry, Mary	1	3	3	....	....
Bias, Nathan	2	4	6	....	....
Dobins, Wm	1	4	4	....	....
Dobins, Jas	1	1	3	....	....
Scrugs, Rd	2	3	5	....	....
Davis, Jacob	1	3	5	....	....
Womack, Louisa	2	4	1	....	....
Robins, Wm	2	4	4	....	1
Scott, Moses	1	4	4	....	....
McKinny, Henry	1	2	1	....	....
Greenwood, Hugh	3	7	4	....	2
Maddin, Danl	3	....	....	....	....
Sealor, George	1	1	3	....	....
Wren, Shadrach	2	....	2	....	....
Renols, Mary	....	2	4	....	....
McLean, Jno, Sr	1	3	1	....	1
Tomason, Jno	1	....	2	....	....
Tomison, Eliza	1	2	6	....	....
Draper, James	1	....	2	....	....
Shumake, Landy	1	2	2	....	....
Morrow, Tho'	1	1	4	....	....
Roberts, Jno	1	....	1	....	....
McKinny, James	1	....	1	....	....
Dills, Henry	1	2	4	....	....
Robins, Wm	2	2	4	....	....
Davis, Abner	1	3	2	....	....
Poore, Sarah	....	1	3	....	....
Sutton, Martha	....	....	3	....	....
Cargil, Jno	2	2	5	....	....
Hall, Thom	2	....	3	....	....
Gaddis, Mary	1	2	1	....	....
Harris, Eliza	1	3	2	....	....
Paterson, Hugh	1	....	3	....	1
Morrow, Wm	1	3	3	....	....
Webb, David	1	4	6	....	....
Bicas, Sarahan	2	1	4	....	....
Phillips, James	1	4	5	....	....
Wadkins, David	1	2	3	....	....
Wadkins, Peter	4	....	3	....	....
Blackwell, Joel	2	2	7	....	....
Camp, Thom, Sr	3	3	3	....	....
Blacwell, James	1	....	3	....	....
Goode, Jos	1	2	3	....	5
Dobins, Wm	1	....	1	....	....
Cocran, Minor	1	4	5	....	....
Ashlock, Josiah	1	1	2	....	....
Ashlock, Sarah	1	1	2	....	....
Gill, Joseph	1	....	1	....	6
Goode, Richd	1	2	2	....	7
Goode, Thom	2	2	3	....	4
Hopson, Wm	1	4	2	....	10

MORGAN DISTRICT, RUTHERFORD COUNTY—Continued.

NAME OF HEAD OF FAMILY.	Free white males of 16 years and upward, including heads of families.	Free white males under 16 years.	Free white females, including heads of families.	All other free persons.	Slaves.
TENTH COMPANY—con.					
McAdams, Tho'	2	1			
Oldhane, Danl	1	4	5		
Hinson, Phillip	1	5	4		
Huddleston, Jno	1	2	4		1
Goode, Jno	1		1		5
Crawford, Saml	1	1	1		
King, Priscilla		4	4		
Johnson, Wm	2	1	2		7
ELEVENTH COMPANY.					
Harrod, Thom	1	4	9		
Moore, George	4	1	2		9
Erwin, Robt	2	4	4		8
Moore, James	2	1	1		1
Jones, John	1	6	6		
Green, Shad	1		1		
Kemp, James	1	3	4		1
Rigs, Timothy	6	1	2		
Holland, Wm	1	2	5		
Hoskins, Robt	2	2	1		
Webb, Wm	2	4	3		1
Bradlove, Charls	2	3	6		
Davidson, Jas	1	3	2		
Shipman, Danl	2	2	4		
McDow, David	2	1	6		1
Lyles, Burges	1	2	5		
Webb, Robt	1	3	5		
Webb, Thom	1	4	3		
Green, Wm	1	4	3		5
Kirkendal, Jno	1	1	5		
Cooper, Alex	1	3	5		
Hill, Abel	2	3	3		1
Collins, Wm	1	1	2		
Webb, Danl	1		5		
Hill, George	1		4		
Cooper, Alex., Jr	1	3	6		
Armstrong, Eliza		2	2		
Hill, Jno	2	1	4		
McNess, Jo	1		1		1
Bridges, Aron	3	3	5		
Hern, Denis	4		3		
Kemp, Thom	1		4		
Ellis, James	3	2	5		
Blanton, Reuben	4	2	5		2
Blanton, Burn	1	3	2		
Graham, Jno	1		2		
Williams, Britn	1	1	2		
Williams, George	1	2	1		
Bolin, Layney	1		1		
Robison, Isaac	1		3		
Brown, Jno W	1		2		
Bridges, Tho'	1		2		
Rucker, Wm	1	1	2		
Turner, Sam	1	1	1		
Turner, Sam, Jr	1		1		
Bridges, Isaac	1	1	3		
Williams, Ben	2	3	7		
Blackburn, Sam	1	4	2		
Tabor, James	4	1	3		
Dicas, Edw'd	1	1	3		
Leis, Jos	1	2	4		
Warden, Danl	1		1		
Beard, Jno, Sr	1	1	1		
Beard, Jno	1		3		
Humphris, Wm	1	4	3		
Wilkins, Charles	2	4	3		5
Willis, Peter	1	1	1		5
Brock, Reuben	1	5	1		
Walker, George	1				3
Horn, Lucy		2	2		
Night, Jno	1	2	4		
Dedham, Mark	1	2	3		
Adams, Jere	1	4	4		
Bailey, Wm	2	2	4		
Johnson, Wm	1	5	3		
Sanders, Patrick	1	2	4		
Holland, Matt	1	3	1		
Hall, Wm	1	2	2		
Williams, Geo	2	2	1		
Saterfield, Jas	2	3	7		
Green, Henry, Sr	1	1	4		
Green, H., Jr	1	1	3		
Hawkins, Tho'	1	3	6		
Dicas, Jno	1	4	2		
Southerly, Jno	1		4		
Murray, Tho'	1	1	10		
Johnson, Jno	1		2		
Sally, Eliza		2	4		
Hose, Jno	1	1	1		
Kikendall, Matt	1	1	4		
Norman, Isaac	1	2	2		
Smart, Jos	1	4	4		
Collins, Wm	2		2		

NAME OF HEAD OF FAMILY.	Free white males of 16 years and upward, including heads of families.	Free white males under 16 years.	Free white females, including heads of families.	All other free persons.	Slaves.
ELEVENTH COMPANY—continued.					
Smart, Jo, Sr	2	3	4		
Jones, Jno	2	7	6		
Green, Shad	1		1		
Green, Shad, Sr	1	2	3		
Landers, Henry	1	3	6		
Saterfield, Wm	1	1	1		
Stater, Jehu	2	1	3		
Lee, Robt	1	4	5		
Lee, Isaac	1		1		
Rolins, Prudy	1		2		3
Wilson, Jno	1		2		
Street, Antony	1	1	3		
Street, Wm	1	1	3		
Harrell, Housen	2	3	5		
Franklin, Mary	4	1	3		
Franklin, Jno	1	4	2		
Crispan, Jacob	2		1		
McMin, Robt	1	7	2		
Shipman, Jacob	1	3	4		
Shipman, Danl., Jr	1		1		
Shipman, Dan, Sr	1	1	1		2
Sunderlin, Wm	1		1		
Bridges, Moses	2	3	6		
Clarke, Jesse	1		3		
Armstrong, Martin	1	1	4		
Davidson, Alex	2	4	5		5
Davison, Jno	1	1	2		
Davison, Alex, Jr	1	2	2		
Lunn, Sam	1	2	5		
Gage, David	2	2	3		
Hill, Jno	1	1	5		
Wilson, Wm	1		5		
Gage, Lucy		3	2		
Gage, Jas	1	1	3		
McKeine, Tho	1	3	4		
McNess, Ben	1	5	3		1
McNess, Jno	1	4	2		
Gage, Reuben	1		1		
Sally, Wm	1		2		
Walker, Jno	1	4	4		
Gibs, Jesse	1	1	1		
Gage, Danl	1	2	4		
Tolly, Elias	1	2	2		
Miller, Jacob	3		1		
Shipman, Edwd	1	7	4		
Webb, James	1	3	4		
Brook, Wm	1	6	1		
Gage, David	4		3		
Davis, Vachal	1		3		
Webb, Jno	1	3	4		
Collins, Wm	1	2	2		
Webb, Bess	1	1	4		
Webb, Dan'	1		5		
Webb, Jacob	1		3		
Ashworth, Jos	1	2	1		
Cooper, Jno	1		1		
Barkster, Wm	1		2		
James, Mary		4	2		
Hetherly, Sam	1	2	1		
TWELFTH COMPANY.					
Young, Robt	3	2	3		3
Caruth, Revr. Robt	2	2	5		
Yielding, Rd	1		2		
Jeffery, James	2		2		3
Russell, Henry	1	3	1		
Young, Jno	2		4		
Garrett, Mary	1	2	4		
Mills, Jesse	1		3		
Wilson, Spencer	1	1	3		
Young, Jno	2	1	2		
McBriers, Sam	4	5	4		
Fisher, Jno	1	4	3		
Mills, Wm	1	2	6		8
Logan, Jas	1	4	2		
Neville, Yelverton	1		2		
Carter, Alex	2	2	3		
Jones, Jno	1	1	1		
Justice, Tho, Jr	1		2		
McQuin, Mich'l	1	2	2		
Taylor, Drury	1	1	5		
Lanford, Jno	1		1		
Foster, Jno	1	1	2		
Sullins, Jno	2	2	3		1
Hobs, Jno	1		3		
Twitty, Allen	1	1	1		1
Case, Tho'	1	2	2		
Caruth, Robt. Mc	2	6	3		3
Brader, Robt	1	3	6		
Terry, Eliza		4	3		
Sullins, Rd	1		2		
Butler, Jas	2	2	2		
Jones, Freeman	1		1		

NAME OF HEAD OF FAMILY.	Free white males of 16 years and upward, including heads of families.	Free white males under 16 years.	Free white females, including heads of families.	All other free persons.	Slaves.
TWELFTH COMPANY—continued.					
Waldrip, Jeconias	2	4	3		
Hawkins, Michl	3	3	6		
Butler, Mildred		3	3		
Johnson, Ben	2		3		
Cochran, Jas	1	2	12		
Jenkins, Richd	1	3	2		
Cochran, Thos	1		2		
Brown, Dan	1	4	3		2
Lyles, Robt	1		4		
Donnom, Henry	1	5	4		
Harmen, Wm	1	4	4		
Hays, Wm	1	3	1		
Rose, Bazil	1	1	3		
Wadlington, Tho'	1	2	6		11
Brown, Francis	1	2	2		
Brimer, Wm	1	3	3		
Williams, Jacob	1	1	3		
Carrick, Jno	3	1	7		6
Cochran, Tho'	1	2	5		
Turner, Jonathan	4	4	4		
Taber, Jno	1	6	3		
Waldrip, Ezekl	1	1	1		
Green, George	1	1	3		
Music, Abram, Jr	1	5	3		
Music, Abrm, Sr	1	3	2		
Music, Jonathan	1	2	0		1
Sanders, George, Jr	1	1	2		
Sanders, George	1	2	1		
Williams, Jos	1	4	1		
Langford, Robt	1	1	1		
Taylor Lewis	1	3	4		
Langford, Jno, Jr	1	1	3		
Witt, Jesse	1		2		
Witt, Hezekiah	1	2	3		
Shields, Jeremy	1	4	3		
Sawyers, Charls	1	3	3		
Hix, Wm	1	1	4		
Covran, Jonathn	1	2	2		
Larince, Jo	1	1	1		
Weaver, Tho'	1	1	3		
Bartlet, Jas	2	3	3		
Justice, Tho', Sr	1	1	3		
Conway, Jeremiah	1	1	5		
Tumins, Eliza	1	6	3		
Ducaren, Waitmn	1	1	3		
Langford, Wm	1	3	3		
Fariss, Mary	1	3	1		
Morgan, George	2	4	1		
Barkley, George	1	2	2		
Thomson, Wm	1	2	3		
Jackson, David, Jr	1		2		
Jackson, D., Sr	4		2		
Chapman, Job	1		2		
Brimer, Jesse	1		2		
Fisher, Jno	1	4	3		
Grivat, Jno	1		2		
Tunnill, Jno	2	3	6		
Conard, James	3	3	6		
Case, Jno	3	4	1		
Hall, Tho'	1		2		
Ellison, Jno	1	2	2		
Edwards, Thos	2	5	4		
Jones, Jno B. C	2		4		
Laxon, James	1	1	5		
Tabor, Jn, Jr	1		2		
Justice, Amos	1	1	3		
Carter, Lewis	1	3	2		
Junun, Antoney	1	3	2		
Cooper, Mary			1		
Blend, Jno, Lewis	3	2	2		
Kendel, Nancy			6		
Meban, Martha	1	2	7		
Butler, Jno	2	5	2		
THIRTEENTH COMPANY.					
Gash, Martin	3		1		
Randolph, Sam	1	1	5		
Randolph, Sam., Jr	1		1		
Smith, Danl	1	3	3		
Foster, Wm	2	1	6		3
Chambers, Abigail	2	1	4		
Hawkins, Ben	3	2	3		
Hitown, Oldham	1		1		
Holcom, Kinchin	1	1	4		
Davidson, Wm	4	4	4		1
Hitown, Austin	1	4	5		
Fugit, Randolph	2	4	5		
Medlock, Jas	2	2	3		
Barren, Wm	1	1	2		
Ingrm, Mourning			5		
Kizzia, Sandefer	2	1	2		
Kizzia, Jno	1	1	5		
Anditon, Tho'	2	1	5		

MORGAN DISTRICT, RUTHERFORD COUNTY—Continued.

NAME OF HEAD OF FAMILY.	Free white males of 16 years and upward, including heads of families.	Free white males under 16 years.	Free white females, including heads of families.	All other free persons.	Slaves.
THIRTEENTH COMPANY—continued.					
Bradly, Jno	1				
Hill, Wm	1	1	1		
Hill, Rd	1	2	2		
Lee, Elijah	1		3		
Williams, Edwd	1	6	3		
Hargett, Thos	1		3		
Ashworth, Jno	1	1	5		3
Bridget, Jas	1		3		
Selser, Matthias	1	4	3		
Wood, Jas., Senr	3	3	3		
Wood, Jno	1		2		
Wood, Jas., Jr	1		2		
Miller, Laurence	1	2	2		
Nanny, Nancy	1	1	2		
Hinson, Jess	1	1	3		
Wason, Wm	2	3	3		
Hinson, Jno	1	1	3		
Duncan, David	1	1	1		
Gibson, Jno	1		1		
Parks, Jno	5	1	2		
Cooper, Adm	1				
Wallace, Jno	3		3		
Yardly, Ben	3	3	6		
Johnson, Edwd	1	2	2		
Thomas, Jno	1	5	2		
Thomas, Stephn	1		2		
Fletcher, Wm	3	4	2		1
Winson, Elijah	1	1	4		1
Reed, Harmon	1	1	2		
Roberts, Mark	1	1	5		
Cody, Tho'	4		2		
Edmison, Basdel	1	2	2		
Cody, Godfry	4		2		
Johnson, Jas., Jr	1		7		
Johnson, James	1	1	1		
Warren, Jas	1	3	4		
Green, Jas	1	1	2		
Haslip, Robt	1	1	3		
Lyda, Andw	1	6	2		
THIRTEENTH COMPANY—continued.					
Case, Tho'	1	1	1		
Slipp, Jas	2	4	3		
Shelton, Wm		1	2		
Shelton, George	1	1	2		
Gray, Jno	1				
FOURTEENTH COMPANY.					
Reed, Abram	1	2	3		
Stringfeild, Jas	4	1	2		
Brittain, Jas	1	2	4		
Boidstone, Jas	3		1		
Kikendal, Simon	1	1	1		
Medcalf, Jas	2		1		
Medcalf, Norris	1	2	2		
Miller, Andw	1	1	4		1
Stringfeild, Jno	2	1	1		
Boidstone, Sam	1	2	1		
Boidstone, Jas., Jr	1	2	3		
Arnold, Tho'	1		4		1
Osborn, Jeremiah	2	1	1		
Claypole, Jno	1	1	3		
Osborn, Jno	1	1	1		
Box, Jno	1	2	4		
Osborn, Jonathn	1	1	3		
Claypole, Stephen	1		1		
Newport, Michl	3				
Woodphin, Tho'	1	2	2		
Wood, Jno	1	1	2		
Woodpin, Nicholas	2	1	6		
Wood, Henry	1		2		
Newport, Jno	1		1		
Abbs, Thom	1		4		
Gardner, Jacob	2	1	3		
Gray, Jas	1		3		
Ashbrooks, Moses	3	3	7		
Parks, George	2	2	5		
Sweiton, Robt	1		1		
Sweiton, Jno	1	1	4		
FOURTEENTH COMPANY—continued.					
Sweiton, Edwd	3	2	4		
Gage, Aron	1	2	2		
Burlison, Jno	1	1	2		
Meda, Abram	2	2	5		
Craford, Moses	1		2		
Craford, Jas	1		2		
Craford, Isaac	1		1		
Crawford, Thom	3	1	3		
James, James	5	2	2		
Graham, Thos	1		1		
Durham, Wm	2		2		
Weaver, Sam	3	1	2		
Reid, George	1	2	4		
English, Wm	2	5	4		
Steward, Jno	1	2	5		
Allen, Sam	1		6		
Denton, Sam	2		1		
Odel, Ben	2		1		
Odel, Jno	1		1		
May, Tho'	2	2	3		
English, Joshua	1	4	2		
Lamb, Jno	1	1	2		
Graham, Spencer	1	1	2		
Englsh, Jas	2	2	1		
Denton, Jonas	2	1	2		
Shateen, Abram	1	1	2		
Shateen, Edwd	1		3		
Shipman, Edwd	3	5	4		
Susco, Jacob	1	2	2		
Susco, Jno	3		4		
Davidson, Jas	1	3	2		
English, Jos	2		1		5
Still, Booze	1		4		
Jones, Stephn	1	4	4		
Robinson, Jas	1	2	3		
Vane, Jos	2	1	5		1
Roberts, Obadiah	1	2	2		
Hix, Wm	1	2	3		
Cooral, Jonathan	1	1	3		

MORGAN DISTRICT, WILKES COUNTY.

NAME OF HEAD OF FAMILY.	Free white males of 16 years and upward, including heads of families.	Free white males under 16 years.	Free white females, including heads of families.	All other free persons.	Slaves.
FIRST COMPANY.					
Ferguson, Thom	1	2	4		
Coffey, Ben	1	4	5		
Hays, George	1	1	3		
Coffey, Jane			1		7
Coffey, Eli	1		1		
Mills, Eliz		2	2		
Richardson, James	2	2	2		
Richardson, Sam	1		2		
Walters, Jno	1	2	2		
Edmison, James	1	1	2		
Israel, Michal	1	4	2		4
Coffey, Reuben	1	1	4		
Israel, Johnson	1		2		
Cox, Airess	2		2		2
Israel, Solomon	1		1		
Israel, Jesse	1		1		
Pierce, Jno	1	4	2		
Jackson, James	1	3	2		
Coffey, Thom	4	5	4		
Allen, David	1	1	2		
Jones, Joshua	1	5	4		
Coffey, Jno	1	2	4		
Alloway, Abram	1	3	7		
Gillum, Paphrodite	1	1	5		
Eperson, Robert	2	1	6		
Gordon, Charles, Jr	1		1		5
Silory, Stephen	1		3		
Elston, David	1	7	1		
Elston, Ben	1		2		
Epperson, Jas	1		1		
Long, Sam	1	4	1		
Parr, Methias	1	2	4		
Long, Robt	1	1	6		
Baird, Andw	3	3	1		5
Jacobs, Dutty	1	1	3		
Childers, Jno	1	3	3		
Runion, Jno	1	2	5		
Fields, Thom	2	1	5		
Crumton, Hezekiah	1	1	1		
Caffinder, Stephen	3	2	3		
Mills, Hardy	1	2	1		
Yarnell, Danl	3	2	1		
Reed, Thom	1	3	4		
Durham, Marshal	1	2	4		
Yarnal, Joseph	1	1	3		
Humphress, Owen	3	3	4		
Ferguson, Jos	1	3	4		
Lunn, Jno	1		2		
Hulme, Wm	1		2		
FIRST COMPANY—con.					
Hulme, Eliz	1		2		
Hulme, Geo	1	2	3		
Stacey, Geo	2		5		
Ferguson, Wm	1		2		
Horton, Zeph	1	1	1		
Ferguson, Nicolas	1	1	4		
Ferguson, Jeremiah	1	1	1		
Moore, Jno	3	3	2		
Northern, Peggy			2	3	
Baird, Zeb	3	4	5		
Steep, Thom	1	2	1		4
Demass, Jas	2	3	3		2
Demass, Lewis	2	3	3		5
Jones, Ben	1	1	6		5
Jones, Morton	3	4	2		
Wood, Elias	1	3	3		
Cody, Pierce	1		2		
Barrett, David	1	1	5		
Lenoir, Wm, Es	1	3	5		12
Munson, Moses	3		3		
Tate, Andrew	2	3	6		1
Duley, Wm	1	2	3		2
Crisp, Chesly	1	2	2		
Merrit, George	2	2	4		
Lay, Thom	1	1	3		
Coffey, Ambrous	3		2		1
Lansdown, Wm	2	2	6		
Campbell, Peter	1		1		
Cotrel, Thom	2	2	3		
Curtis, Wm	1		1		
Curtis, Sam	1		2		
Curtis, Josh	2		8		
SECOND COMPANY.					
Gordon, Nathanl	1	3	2		3
Ussory, Thom	1		2		
Carter, Edwd	1	2	1		
Keeling, Leonard	1	4	3		
Holman, Danl., Es	2	3	4		
Colvert, Wm	1		5		
Vickers, Elijah	1	2	3		
Fletcher, Spencer	1	4	2		
Russell, Buckma	1	2	5		
Williams, Jas., Sr	2		4		
Humphriss, Milley		1	5		
Dobson, Jno	1				
Souther, Mary	2	2	4		
Greenstreet, Betty		2	2		
SECOND COMPANY—con.					
Tindal, Saml	1	3	4		
Stanley, Lucy		2	5		
Stanly, Jno	1		2		
Young, James	1	1	5		
Young, Ephraim	1	2	1		
Martin, Zadock	2	6	1		
Martin, Ben	1		1		
Martin, Jas	1	2	1		
Anderson, Jno	1	2	3		
Smoot, Jas	1	1	3		
Anderson, Cornelius	1		5		
Anderson, Geo	1		2		
Anderson, Sam	1		2		
Fletcher, Wm	2	1	1		2
Shinn, Sam	2	1	7		
Parker, Henry	1				
Parker, John	1	3	2		
Johnson, Wm	1	5	4		
Shumate, John	1	5	2		
Parks, Anne	1	3	5		8
Reynolds, Jas	1		3		
Cargil, Wm	1	1	5		
Cunningham, Jno	1	5	3		2
Chandler, Timothy	1	3	4		
Chandler, Robt	1	3	2		2
Chandler, Josia	1	2	1		
Herrin, Wm	1	2	1		
Hariss, Bradock	1	1	2		
Hariss, Edward	1	4	6		
Chandler, Danl	1	4	4		
Porter, Joseph	2	2	4		
Cornwall, Elijah	1	1	3		
Curry, Wm, Sr	1		1		
Curry, Nathan	1	2	4		
Curry, Jno	1	3	5		
Curry, Wm	1	3	3		
Fletcher, James	1	1	4		
Childress, Miller	1		2		
Burke, Jno	1		1		
Chambers, Wm	1	4	1		
Hull, Danl	1		1		
Busby, Isaac	1	2	1		
Busby, Jno	1		1		
Russell, Hilloval	1	3	9		
Burke, Jno	1	4	8		
Profit, Jno	2	2	7		
Fletcher, Jas., Es	2		2		2
Wilson, Sam	1	1	2		
McDonol, Geo	1		1		

MORGAN DISTRICT, WILKES COUNTY—Continued.

SECOND COMPANY—con. / THIRD COMPANY

NAME OF HEAD OF FAMILY.	Free white males of 16 years and upward, including heads of families.	Free white males under 16 years.	Free white females, including heads of families.	All other free persons.	Slaves.
SECOND COMPANY—con.					
Keeling, Calton	2	3	6		
Underwood, Lewis	1	2	2		
Gordon, Charls, Sr	1		1		14
Hopper, Jno	1	2	2		
Bruce, Robt	1	1	2		
Gordon, Chapman	1	1	3		4
Miller, Jno	1	4	5		
Tanner, Comfort	1	2	2		
Huckerson, David	1	4	3		2
Huckerson, Charles	3		1		
Roberts, Jno	1	2	4		
Gordon, George	1	2	6		17
Cross, Asel	1	1	4		
Ray, Eliz			2		
Wilky, Mourning		1	2		
Tomkins, Silas	1	4	4		
Miller, Leonard	1	4	3		
Davis, Wm	1	1	3		
Reynolds, Elisha	1	1	3		
Estridge, Jno	1	1	2		
Herndon, Jos	1	2	3		9
Reynolds, Frank	4	3	7		6
Henry, Jno	1	1	2		
Carter, Henry	1	4	6		
Cargil, Jno	2		4		4
Cargil, Joa	1	5	2		
Vennoy, Danl	1	2	2		1
THIRD COMPANY.					
Cleveland, Robt	4	4	6		10
Hamby, Wm	1	5	4		
Jones, Henry	2	4	3		
Holeman, Thom	1	4	3		
Bushop, Roger	3	2	3		2
Bunton, Nell	1	3	3		
Brown, John, Esq	3	5	6		22
Lovelace, John	3	3	5		
Profit, Sylvester	1	1	3		
Castle, Sam	2	1	4		
Proffitt, Jno	1	1	2		
Cordwell, Prin'	1	4	5		
Jackson, Wm	1	3	5		
Fairchild, Eben	1	2	4		
Case, Isaiah	1		3		
Lips, Jno	1	3	2		
Lips, Jno, Sr	1		2		
Walters, Walter	1		5		
McLeain, Jno	3	3	6		
Minton, Meredith	2	3	2		
Webb, Ussby		1	2		
Webb, Frank	1		2		
Webb, Cutt	1	2	2		
Webb, Jno	1		5		
Flanigin, Jno	1		3		
Regins, Peter	1	4	1		
Stonecypher, Jno H	2	1	3		
Bankes, Wm	1		1		
Tomkins, Jonathn	1		1		
West, Wm	1		1		
Story, Joshua	2	5	3		
Jackson, Jas	1	4	2		
Tomkins, Moses	1	1	2		
Adams, Wm	1		1		
Elmore, Thos	1		3		
Profitt, Wm	1	1	1		
Case, Aron	1		3		
Adams, Jane		4	2		
Gullit, Danl	1	5	5		
Henson, Jno	2	2	3		
Adams, Jno	2	1	6		
Adams, Wm	1	1	8		1
Bushop, Frank	1	2	3		
Sewill, Abrm	1	2	6		
Sevell, Dawson	1		4		
Yates, Wm	1	2	5		
Hendrin, Jonathn	1	2	1		
Hendrin, Jo	1	1	4		
Fairchild, Elijah	2		2		
Wilson, Mary		1	3		
Wall, Jonathn	1	3	3		
McNeel, George	3	3			
Bingham, Robt	1		3		
Smith, Ben	1	3	3		
Givin, Peter	1	1	2		
Francis, Matt	1		1		
Yates, Jno	1	4	3		
Pincen, Elias	1		1		
Francis, Wm	1		1		
Baker, Andw	2	2	2		
Roberts, Jas	1	1	4		
Church, Phil	1		2		
Church, Amos	1	1	3		
Andrews, Jas	2		2		
Church, Jno	1	2	2		

THIRD COMPANY—con. / FOURTH COMPANY

NAME OF HEAD OF FAMILY.	Free white males of 16 years and upward, including heads of families.	Free white males under 16 years.	Free white females, including heads of families.	All other free persons.	Slaves.
THIRD COMPANY—con.					
Vancey, Nath. (E.)	3	3	7		
Baker, Philip	1		4		
Reed, Thom	1	3	2		
Harmon, Jno	1	3	3		
Carter, Jos	1	3	2		
Crane, Phil	2	3	4		1
Crane, Polly		3	4		
Yates, Jno	1		2		
Lowe, Isaac	1		1		
Sharp (Free Negro)				1	
Roberts, Sarah	2	1	2		
Paslier, Isaac	2	2	7		
Sam (A free neg.)				1	
FOURTH COMPANY.					
McNeel, Wm	1	1	3		
Smith, Wm	1	6	2		
Smith, Jno	1	3	4		
Robins, Jno	3	1	7		11
Sertain, Jas	1	1	2		
Owin, David	1	4	2		2
Tyre, Jno	2	3	5		
Colvert, Wm	2	2	5		
Tyre, Wm	1	3	4		
Tyre, George	1	1	3		
Lorance, George	1	1	2		
Querry, Wm	1		2		
Sheppard, Robt	2	1	7		
Judd, Rollin (E.)	3		1		
Judd, Rob	1	2	2		
Judd, Natt	1	3	5		
Pinion, Ben	1	1	2		
Robins, Reuben	1	1	4		
Baker, Peter	1	2	5		
Certain, Lucy			3		
Denny, Elijah	2	2	2		
Copland, Joel	1	3	4		
Vannoy, Frank	2	2	7		
Absher, Wm	1	1	1		
Owen, Wm	1	3	5		
Owen, Thom	1	2	10		
Owin, Jno	3		1		
Owin, David, Jr	1		1		
Erwin, Frank	3	1	3		
Cash, Wm	1	4	3		
Sheppard, Jno	1	1	1		
Copland, Joel, Jr	1		4		
Sheppard, John	3	1	4		
Wallers, Robt	1	2	2		
Copland, Wm	1		4		
Qurry, Jno, Sr	1		5		
Kilby, Adam	1	3	0		
Wall, Jonathn	1	3	3		
Kilby, Michl	1	1	5		
Kilby, Wm	4	4	5		
Carter, Sam	1	3	5		
Hopper, Thom	1	1	1		
Hays, Jas	1	2	3		
Sheroon, Isaiah	1		3		
Hays, Robt	2		3		
Adam, Henry	1	1	3		
Adams, Sarah			3		
Adams, Peggy		1	3		
Tinsly, Isaac	1	2	2		
Wilson, Mary		1	4		
Hockins, Jno	2	1	4		
Yates, Jas	1	1	2		
Brown, Walter	4		5		
Smith, Oswall	1	1	3		
Smith, Humphry	1		1		
Boon, Hiram	1		1		
Smith, Jarvis	1	5	2		
Forester, Fieldin	1		1		
Wooton, Eliz		1	5		
Sebastin, Lewis	1	3	2		
Sebastin, Ben	1	3	5		
Dickson, Wm	1	2	3		
Barker, George	1	2	3		
Underwood, Wm	1	2	1		
Estridge, Jno	1		1		
Barker, Hezekia	2	6	2		
McGrady, Jacob	1	5	1		
Pon, Rd	1	3	1		
Grimes, Moses	1	3	3		
Forester, Jno	1	3	4		
Hall, Owen	1	3	4		
McDowell, Mike	1	4	2		
Hall, Robt	2	4	2		
Jennins, Luke	1	3	1		
Venoy, Andw	2	5	4		
Pumphy, Henry	1	3	4		
Vears, Wm	1	3	4		
Jennins, Jno	3		2		
Atkins, Silas	1	3	1		

FOURTH COMPANY—con. / FIFTH COMPANY / SIXTH COMPANY

NAME OF HEAD OF FAMILY.	Free white males of 16 years and upward, including heads of families.	Free white males under 16 years.	Free white females, including heads of families.	All other free persons.	Slaves.
FOURTH COMPANY—con.					
Hall, Jno	1	1	3		
Hall, Jesse	1	1	7		
Ray, Dicey		2	1		
Hall, Wm	1		3		
Rhodes, Sarah		1	3		
FIFTH COMPANY.					
Harvell, Isom	1	3	2		
Norman, Jas	2	6	4		
Lican, J. Goodin	1	2	4		
Bell, Even	1	3	2		1
Love, Jno	1	2	1		2
Crabtree, Ben	1		3		
Pale, Mary	1	3	4		
Sanders, Francis	1	4	2		
Howard, Jno	2	3	4		
Bussell, Presly	1	2	4		
Reeves, Isaac	2	2	4		
Reeves, James	1	1	3		
Lewis, Wm, Jr	1	3	4		
Reeves, Jno	1				
Chambers, Nathn	1	2	2		
Mayberry, Randol	1	1	3		
Young, Vachal	1	1	6		
Longbottom, Jos	1	1	1		
Lewis, Wm	2	2	5		
Hethmon, Jonath	3	2	4		4
Roberts, Ros	3	1	2		
Wilson, Jno	1	1	3		
Wilson, Mary	1	3	4		
Roberts, Jas	1		3		
Johnson, Charles	3	2	7		
Chambers, Wm	1	4	3		
Chambers, Jno	1	1	1		
Chambers, Drury	1	2	2		
Brown, Danl	1	1	2		
Baker, Baswell	1	2	1		
Welch, Wallar	1	3	1		
Brown, Rebekah	3	3	2		
Mundy, Christopher	1	1	3		
Garrison, Jas	1	5	4		
Hughlin, Jno	1		2		
Hughlin, Ambrous	1		1		
Dickins, Wm	1	3	5		
Hendron, Jno	1	1	2		
Fitspatrick, Thom	1	3	4		
Bales, Mary		1	4		
Hooper, Wm	1	1	1		
Cole, Jobe	1	2	3		
Comps, George	1	4	2		
Combs, John	1	1	7		
Combs, Thom	2		2		
Silcox, Sarah		1	1		
Lunceford, Jack	1	1	2		
Stanley, Thom	1		2		
Nance, Wm	1	2	6		
Mills, Wm	1		1		
Stanley, Eliz		5	3		
Roberts, Eliz		2	2		
Kelly, Ben	1	1	3		
Cooks, Eliz	1	5	5		
Grant, David	1				
Lunceford, Jno	1	2	3		
Crabtree, Sam	1	3	4		
Lunceford, Ben	1	5	2		
Lunceford, Elisha	1	2	3		
Lunceford, Elijah	1	1	1		
Hendron, Nimrod	1	2	2		
Hendron, Wm	2	4	1		
Mullis, Sarah	1	2	1		
Needson, Abel	1		1		
Taylor, Chas	1	2	5		
Rush, Danl	3	4	5		4
Mitchell, Wm	1	2	4		
Nicolson, Sam	2	4	4		
Jarvis, Jas	1	3	1		
Mise, Martha			2		
McBride, Jas	1	3	10		
Mehaffy, Thom	3		3		
Hays, Henry	1	3	4		
Wooton, Patty		1	2		
Watts, Jno	1	1	4		
SIXTH COMPANY.					
Johnson, Sam	1	2	3		5
Wheatly, George	1	1	5		
Stamper, Jonathan	2		2		1
Turner, Thom	1	2	2		
Turner, Edmund	1	2	2		
Turner, John	1	2	3		
Grimsly, Thom	1	2	1		
Buttery, Timothy	1	1	4		
Sparks, Jno	1	4	3		

MORGAN DISTRICT, WILKES COUNTY—Continued.

SIXTH COMPANY—con.

NAME OF HEAD OF FAMILY.	Free white males of 16 years and upward, including heads of families.	Free white males under 16 years.	Free white females, including heads of families.	All other free persons.	Slaves.
King, Robt	1	2	1		
Love, John	1		2		
Turner, Roger	1	2	3		
Richeson, Alex	1	3	3		
Lyon, Wm	1	4	4		
Stone, Cudy	1		2		
Sparks, Reuben	1	1	3		
Gambell, Jno	2	3	4		
Holbrooks, Jno	1	2	3		
Joines, Thom	1	1	7		
Morgan, Thom	1	2	3		
Rice, Wm	1	4	4		
Billins, Gasper	1		1		
Lewis, George	2	1	10		
Townson, John	1	3	2		
Hicks, Claybon	1	1	3		
Morgan, Thom	1	2	3		
Morgan, Wm	1	1	1		
Fugate, Esom	1	2	1		
Conally, Henry	1	5	4		
Botts, Joshua	2	2	2		
Craft, Chilus	1	1	2		
Adams, Jacob	1	4	4		
Lovelace, Arche	1	1	1		
Colwell, Seth	1	2	4		
Stamper, Joel	1	3	3		1
Clarke, David	1		1		
Mulky, Jno	1		1		
Gambell, Mary	1	1	2		7
Oscar, Dan	1	3	2		
Hammon, John	1	3	8		
Hammon, Ben	1		2		
Hammon, Wm	2	1	2		
Adams, Ben	1	1	5		
Alexr, Willis	1	2	1		
Johnson, Thom	1	1	5		
Bowe, Edmund	1	2	5		
Webb, Jas	1	3	2		
Hously, Charity			4		
Warner, Winney	1		3		
Johnson, Wm, Esqr	1	3	2		
Johnson, Phillip	1	1	2		
Johnson, Rachal	2	2	3		
Thaxton, Jno	1		4		
Coddle, Stephn	1	1	4		
Coddle, Jas	2		2		
Holbrooks, Colby	1	1	1		
Holbrooks, Randol	1	5	3		
Medlin, Wm	4	1	3		
Medlin, Duk	2				
Lorance, Jas	1	1	1		
Lorance, Thom	2	1	2		
Cate, Charls	1	2	5		
Cate, Jno	1	2	2		
Fugot, Patia			2		
Adams, Jno	1	1	5	3	
Ross, Emanuel	1		5	1	
Scott, Wm	3	3	5		
Manard, Kit	1	3	3		
Lion, Wm	1		3		
Adams, John	1		2		
Boggers, Rd	1	6	2		
Hagins, Jno	1		1		
Wiatt, Abby		1	3		
Hariss, Susana			4		
Harriss, Wm	1	1	4		
Welsh, Thom	1	2	4		
Lyon, Jacob	1		4		
Holbrooks, Zach	1	2	1		
Holbrooks, Jno	1	2	1		
Holbrooks, Wm	2		1		
Hargis, Wm	2		2		
Reed, Jas	2		2		
Stamper, Jonath	2	4	4		
Billings, Thom	2		4		
Billings, Thom	1				
Prewitt, Jo	1	2	3		
Stones, Sam	1	2	2		
Minor, Jesse	1		2		
Manor, Gibson	1	2	5		
Manor, Jas	1	1	4		
Blackburn, Wm	1		3		
Manor, Drury	1		4		
Frazer, Micajah	1	3	4		
Cornelius, Wm	1	1	3		
Roberts, Edwd	1	1	3		
Hammon, Jas	1	1	1		
Sparks, Jno	1	4	3		
Scrutchfield, Art	1	2	3		
Hidden, Elisha	3	1	4		
Adams, Spencer	1	3	3		2
Hiddy, Gilbert	1				
Pruitt, Lus		1	2		
Bradberry, Wm	1	2	2		
Bradberry, Jas	2	2	2		
Donathn, Nelson	1	2	2		

SEVENTH COMPANY.

NAME OF HEAD OF FAMILY.	Free white males of 16 years and upward, including heads of families.	Free white males under 16 years.	Free white females, including heads of families.	All other free persons.	Slaves.
Gynn, Rd	1	1	1		11
Bucknall, Sam	3	2	4		1
Lewis, Jas. M.	1	1	1		8
Loving, Gabriel	1	2	7		
Parkes, Ambrous	2		2		3
Parks, Reuben	1	1	1		1
Johnson, Rachl	1		2		2
Jonson, Jelfery	1	1	1		
Jonson, Ben	1		2		1
Johnson, Jno	1	3	5		
Johnson, George	1	3	6		
Johnson, Wm	1	1	1		
Denny, Edmund	2		2		1
Baltrep, Jno	2		2		
Parks, Ruben, Jr	2	4	5		
Wheatly, Geo., Sr	3	3	4		
Sloan, Wm	1		2		
Dotson, Patty		2	2		
Allen, Rich'd, Es	3	2	4		1
Allin, Jas	1	1	1		
Borot, Abigail		3	2		
Stubblefield, Thom	3	4	6		
Garison, Isaac	2	2	4		
Watts, Rd	1	2	5		
Gray, Jno	1	2	6		
Gooch, Jos	3	3	5		
Powe, Jno	2	1	2		
Powe, Rd	1	2	3		
Kennedy, Aron	1		3		
Powe, Jno	1	2	3		
Phillips, Stephen	1	1	2		
Davis, Jas	1	3	5		
Davis, Wm	1	4	2		
Kilburn, Amos	1		1		
Kilborn, Isaac	2	2	2		
Mailia, Patric	1	6	4		
Reed, Sam	1	1	4		
Dolison, Wm	1	2			
Darnell, Nancy	3	4			
Darnell, Cornelius	1	2	2		
Carter, Simon	1	3	6		
Bonsil, Wm	1	1	1		
Wall, Jacob	2		1		
Parks, Geo	1	3	3		
Tolby, Wm	1	4	3		
Smith, Lucy		3	1		
Burke, Rd	1	2	2		
Ross, Thom	1	2	7		
Carrol, Wm	3		4		7
Parkes, Jno	1				7
Parks, Sam	1	3	4		1
Loving, Gabriel	1	2	4		
Gyn, Jos	2	1	1		3
Wall, Jno	1	2	4		
Younger, Jos	1	1	1		1
Major, Jno	2	4	8		6

EIGHTH COMPANY.

NAME OF HEAD OF FAMILY.	Free white males of 16 years and upward, including heads of families.	Free white males under 16 years.	Free white females, including heads of families.	All other free persons.	Slaves.
Greer, Ben, Esqr	3	6	1		
Council, Jesse	2	3	3		
Council, Jurdin	1				
Ingland, Aron	1	3	1		
Ingland, Ezek	1	1	1		
Moss, Jacob	1		1		
Moss, Jos	4		1		
Green, Rd	4	4	3		
Horton, Nat	1	2	1		
Chambers, Henry	2	1	4		
Ayr, Jas	1	2	3		
Ellison, Thom	1		1		
Murphy, Mary			3		
Colman, Sarah	1	2	3		
Miller, Wm	2	3	2		
Reece, Felle	1	5	4		
Brown, Jno	1	1	3		
Wood, Andw	1	1	5		
Stoncypher, Jo	1	3	2		
Egers, Danl	2	3	3		
Duncan, Josh	2	3	4		
Baker, Mary	1	3	3		
Cabel, Casper	1	4	2		
Tomkins, Jas	3	2	2		
Bailey, Ben	1	2	4		
Sewell, Jos	1	4	4		
Hampton, Thom	1	4	4		
Culberth, Ben	1	1	1		
Culberth, Dan	1	1	3		
Wilson, Sam	1	4	3		
Sheppard, Jas	1	2	1		2
Calliway, Jas	1		2		
Calliway, Elijah	1		2		
Judd, Robt	1				
Bloomer, Jeremiah	1	4	2		
Vannoy, Wm	1				
Calliway, Rd	1	1	2		1
Givin, Champn	1	1	2		

EIGHTH COMPANY—con.

NAME OF HEAD OF FAMILY.	Free white males of 16 years and upward, including heads of families.	Free white males under 16 years.	Free white females, including heads of families.	All other free persons.	Slaves.
Linvill, Thos	3	1	1		
Whitenton, Wm	2	3	5		
Estepp, Shad	2	2	5		
Whittenton, Jno	1		2		
Linvill, Thos	1	1	4		1
King, Baker	1	1	3		
Green, Jesse	2	5	2		
Hanis, Jno	1	1	3		
Beard, Ezekl	3	2	2		
Beard, Sam	4	1	1		
Hoselan, Jas	1	2	2		
Hicks, Sam	2	1	2		
Holselan, Jno	1		2		
Ward, Ben	2	4	3		1
Stephen, Lewis	1				5
Ward, Josh	1	2	2		
Smith, Bashiba		1	1		

NINTH COMPANY.

NAME OF HEAD OF FAMILY.	Free white males of 16 years and upward, including heads of families.	Free white males under 16 years.	Free white females, including heads of families.	All other free persons.	Slaves.
Witherspoon, David	3		1		10
Triplit, Danl	2	2	2		
Bailey, Edmund	2	1	5		
Bailey, Ansel	1		2		
Bradly, Jno	1	3	6		
Rucker, Colby	2		5		
Goodruch, Jno	1	5	3		
Tucker, Sam	2	2	5		1
Deir, Jno	1	3	3		
Isbell, Thom, Esqr	2	2	3		4
Ross, Jno	1		2		
Donathan, Jered	2	2	3		3
Roberts, Jno	1	2	3		1
Brown, Larcan	1	1	1		
Roberts, Jas	1	1	1		
Padjit, Jas	1	1	6		
Hodjins, Rd	1	1	2		
Cox, Thom	1	3	2		
Cox, David	1	3	2		
Ayrs, Robt	1	1	2		
Herrin, Edwd	2	1	1		
Witherspoon, Martha	2	4	5		5
Loyd, Jas	1		2		
Brumly, Jno	1	3	3		
Morris, Cloe			3		
Wallis, Jas	2		3		
Wisdom, Anne			2		6
Calton, Ambrous	1		2		
Calton, Lewis	1	3	2		
Levinston, Jno	1	2	5		
Tilley, Ben	1	3	4		
Walker, Sam	1	1	6		
Camel, Jno	1	1	1		
Nowland, Peter	1	1	2		2
Triplit, Nelly	1	1	4		4
Brown, Jas	1	5	4		
Perkins, Tho'	1	6	4		
Holman, Thom, Jr	1	2	5		
Lemon, Jno	1		5		
Welch, Andw	1	2	3		
McGee, David	2	3	7		
Land, Thom	2		1		
Ellison, Hugh	1	1	3		
Ellison, Wm	2	4	4		3
Norris, Jno	1	2	3		
Noland, Hary	1		2		
Noland, Pierce	2	3	4		
Nowland, Phil	1	1	2		
Rash, Wm	1		3		
Swanson, Wm	1	1	7		
Allen, Ananias	1	3	4		
Roberts, Rd	1	2	3		
Semkins, Jarid	1		3		
Laxton, Levy	1	1	1		
Laxton, Sarah	1		2		
Kulp, Reuben	1	2	3		
Pierce, Francis	1		4		
Parr, Jno	2		3		
Davis, Philip	1	2	4		
Stanton, Thom	1	2	7		
Stanton, Rd	1	1	6		
Lewis, Jas	1	2	4		
Coffey, Nebu	3	5	2		1
Stanly, Reuben	2	3	5		
Coffey, Cleveland	2	3	5		16
Cook, Isaac	2	2	3		
Durham, Jno	2		3		
Calton, Tho'	1	1	5		
Lewis, Geo	1	1	1		
Barton, Jno, Sr	1	2	4		
Barton, Jno	1		2		
Land, Jonathn	1	3	5		
Woodard, Sam	1	3	2		
Mooney, Patrick	1	3	1		
Suther, Michal	1	1	2		
Welsh, Jno	1	3	6		

MORGAN DISTRICT, WILKES COUNTY—Continued.

NINTH COMPANY—con.

NAME OF HEAD OF FAMILY.	Free white males of 16 years and upward, including heads of families.	Free white males under 16 years.	Free white females, including heads of families.	All other free persons.	Slaves.
Greyson, Ben	3	2	2		
Greyson, Jno	1		1		
Parker, Jno	2	2	3		
Ferguson, Jas	2	4	4		
Davis, Phil	1		2		
Roberts, Jo	1		1		
Tilly, Lazarus	1	1	2		
Tilly, Edmund	2	4	4		2
Elmore, Jas	1	2	3		
Holt, Nelly	1	1	5		
Killian, Henry	1		1		
Rash, Jos	1	3	4		
Anderson, Jno	2	1	4		
Kerby, Jno	1				
Kerby, Wm	1	5	6		
Devenport, Reuben	1	1	1		
Stanley, Eliz		2	3		
Isbell, Nancy			4		8

TENTH COMPANY.

NAME OF HEAD OF FAMILY.	Free white males of 16 years and upward, including heads of families.	Free white males under 16 years.	Free white females, including heads of families.	All other free persons.	Slaves.
Nall, Jno	1	3	3		3
Gibson, Andw	1	3	6		
Stephens, Rd	1				
Sigler, Phil	1		2		1
Gibson, Jordan	1	3	1		
Collins, Hardy	1	1	4		
Williams, Jas	3	4	8		
Colwell, Jo	1	3	6		
Richison, Danl	4		3		
Mulky, Jas	1		1		
Johnson, Alex	1	1	1		
Cole, Lenvil	1	2	3		
Hardin, Henry	1	1	3		
Collins, Vol	1		2		
Collins, Ambrous	1	1	2		
Lewis, Gideon	1	2	1		
Evans, Theop	3	2	3		
Baker, Ab	1	4	3		
Collins, Geo	1	2	4		
Smith, Jonathan	1	3	6		
Lewis, Jas	1	3	4		
Lewis, Jas	1	2	1		
Gamble, Martin	1	3	1		1
Toliver, Jesse	1		4		
Killian, Shadrach	1				
Gibson, Joel	1		1		
Gibson, Arche	1	1	9		
Gibson, Ezekl	1				
Nicols, Jo	1	2	3		
Clarke, Wm	2		2		
Parker, David	1	2	1		
Cox, Jno	2		4		11
Weaver, Wm	1	2	3		
Stiddim, Sam	1	3	4		
McDonell, Moses	1	2	3		
Jones, Sam	1	1	3		
Bolin, Jesse	1	3	3		
Sinington, Wm	1	4	4		
Richeson, Jno	1		3		
Huff, Wm	3	2	6		
Seritch, Stephen	4	2	4		
Spencer, Wm	1	1	2		
Boyd, Wm	1	4	2		
Sutherton, Enas	1	2	3		
Weaver, Mark	1		2		
Piniton, Micajah	3	3	4		
Pinniton, Ben	1	2	5		
Piniton, Elijah	1	1	3		
Angel, Nick	3	2	2		
Bodge, Jas	1	2	3		
Baker, Thom	1	1	1		
Sheppard, Jas	1		2		
Sheppard, Wm	1		2		
Sheppard, Bety		2	3		
Ruckerson, Canada	1				
McMullin, Jno	1	3	1		
Toliver, Moses	1	4	3		
Toliver, Jno	1		3		
Toliver, Chs	1	2	2		
Toliver, Wm	1	4	2		
Fips, Sam	1	2	4		
Long, Jno	1	4	4		
Perry, Wm	3	1	5		
Collins, Martin	1	3	4		
Collins, David	3	2	6		
Moore, Andw	1		2		
Gipson, Dorothy	2	2	2		
Baldin, Elisha	2	4	4		
Holsey, Wm	1	1	3		
Sanders, Wm	2	3	6		
Scott, Wm	3	3	5		
Nall, Wm	2	1	2		5
Dickson, Tho'	3	3	4		2
Bryan, Jno	2		2		
Edward, Young	1	4	3		
Supott, Adam	4		1		

ELEVENTH COMPANY.

NAME OF HEAD OF FAMILY.	Free white males of 16 years and upward, including heads of families.	Free white males under 16 years.	Free white females, including heads of families.	All other free persons.	Slaves.
Thurston, Wm	4	5	1		6
Scisk, Thom	1	3	6		
Fox, James	2	3	2		
Baker, Anne	2	6	3		
Roberts, Wm	1	1	2		
Oliver, Susana			3	5	
Filts, Wm	1		1		
Wilcox, Wm	3	4	3		1
Filts, Aron	2	2	3		
Cook, Abrm	2	5	2		1
Filts, Jno	1	1	2		
Good, Peter	1	1	4		
Lorance, Peter	1	1	1		
Brown, Wm, Sr	1	2	3		
Brown, Jas	2	1	8		
Brown, Ben	1		1		
Brown, Sam	1		1		
Brown, Wm	1	2	4		
Mathis, Slip	2	1			
Denny, Jesse	1		3		
Allen, Patty	2		5		
Denny, George	1	1	3		
Denny, Isley	1		3		
Denny, Jas	2	1	3		
Denny, Jas., Jr	1		3		
Samuel, Mordecal	1	2	1		
Jackson, Wm	1	3	3		
Bange, Thom	1	4	4		
Scisk, Live	1		2		
Smith, Nathan	1	6	2		
Scisk, Barneby	1		1		
Fox, Danl	1	2			
Sish, Timothy	1		2		
Wason, Arche	3	1	6		
Davis, Evin	1	3	4		
Lewis, Wm T., Es	1		1		5
Bange, David	1	1	1		
Boling, Abel	1		1		
Herndon, Ben., Es	4	1	6		22
Hill, Jno	1	1	1		
Coligan, Wm	1	4	2		
Upchurch, Sarah	2	1	4		
Gray, Jas	2		3		
Gray, George	1		2		
Martin, Jno	1	3	2		6
Martin, Isaac	1		1		7
Green, Thom	1	2	3		1
Bagby, Jno	1	1	2		1
Gray, Sam	1	1	6		
Martin, Robt	1	3	1		1
Reddin, Jno	1	1	4		
Martin, Henry	1	3	1		
Martin, Sarah	2		2		7
Sale, Leonard	1	2	2		
Sale, Thom	1		3		
Sale, Cornelius	2	3	6		2
Sale, Nancy	3		3		10
Kerby, Ben	1	6	2		
Grant, Jno	1	1	3		
Lycan, Hanel	1	2	2		
Armstrong, Nancy		1	2		
Turnbell, Jno	1	3	4		
Rose, Jno	1	2	7		
Rose, Sterling	1	1	5		
Rose, Ben	1	3	4		
Rose, Jno, Sr	1		1		
Camel, Theo	1				
Woodbant, Silers	1	2	2		
Walker, Howard	1	4	4		
Adams, Moses	2	6	5		
Adams, Zach	1	2	2		
Wigins, Abram	2		2		
Jones, Mary		1	2		
Wood, Allen	1		1		
Johnson, Jno	1		1		
Fife, Jno	1	2	5		
McDaniel, Wm	2		2		
McDaniel, Wm, Jr	1	2	3		
Newberry, Tho'	1	3	2		
Macay, Patrick	1	3	3		
Norton, Jno	1	1	4		
Rutledge, Wm	1	3	4		2
Rose, Opy			1		
Thurmond, Thom	1	5	3		11
Martin, Ben	2	2	6		13

TWELFTH COMPANY.

NAME OF HEAD OF FAMILY.	Free white males of 16 years and upward, including heads of families.	Free white males under 16 years.	Free white females, including heads of families.	All other free persons.	Slaves.
Jones, Russel	3	4	5		5
Howard, Ben	2	2	6		13
Howard, Joshua	1		2		1
Bates, Mathias	1	1	1		
Beaver, Thom	1		2		
Williams, Enoch	1	3	2		
Triplitt, Mason	1	2	2		
Hagler, Jno, Jr	2	2	4		2
Lay, Jesse	3		9		

TWELFTH COMPANY—continued.

NAME OF HEAD OF FAMILY.	Free white males of 16 years and upward, including heads of families.	Free white males under 16 years.	Free white females, including heads of families.	All other free persons.	Slaves.
Anderson, Thom	1	1	2		
Anderson, Thom, Sr	1		3		
Hogg, Wm	2	6	2		
Lay, Davis	1	4	7		
Lay, Thom, Sr	1	2	3		
Hall, Thom	1	1	4		
Lansdon, David	1		2		
Mill			1		2
Stanley, Nathanl	1	2	4		
Northern, Jno	4	1	3		
Stanbury, Moses	1	2	5		
Hagler, Abrm	1	2	1		
Sweeton, Dutton	1	1	4		
Tugman, Edmund	1		2		
Tugman, Thos	1	2	2		
Southerton, Danl	1	4	2		
Shearer, Jno	1	1	1		1
Shearer, Robt	1		2		
Hagler, Jacob	1	2	2		1
Lnorce, Thom	1	2	1		1
Robins, Thom	1	2	4		4
Foster, Thom	1	5	2		
Triplet, Wm	1	4	1		
Ferguson, Thom	1	2	1		1
Triplite, Thom	1	1	5		
Williams, Elijah	1	1	5		
Forbes, David	2	1	3		
Vanderpool, Jno	2		3		
Forbes, Sam	1	1	3		
Kendle, Sarah	4		2		
Corban, Jno	1	2	3		
Pitton, Charity		2	2		
Keeling, Jane	1		2		
Steid, Thom	1	4	1		
Sweeton, Robt	1		2		
Dugger, Ben	1	3	6		
Burns, Saml	1		1		
Hodge, Thos	2	3	6		
Hall, Martin	1	2	3		
Stoddil, Edwd	1		3		
Duglass, James	1	1	3		
Vest, Wm	1	3	7		
Owen, Barnet	1	3	7		
Duncan, Ben	1	4	5		
Brown, Rd	1				4
Bahs, Nat	2	2	3		
Elliott, Elis		3	4		
Walters, Jno	1		1		
Ellison, Hezekia	1	3	3		
Ferguson, Jno	1	4	4		
Ferguson, Rd	1		1		
Brown, Wm	3	2	6		
Adams, Wm	1	4	2		
Farmer, Thos	2	7	2		
Hendrix, Darby	1	1	3		
Hendrix, Ben	3	2	4		
Walters, Moses	2	3	4		
Mullin, Wm	1	2	4		
Mullin, Caty	1	1	3		

THIRTEENTH COMPANY.

NAME OF HEAD OF FAMILY.	Free white males of 16 years and upward, including heads of families.	Free white males under 16 years.	Free white females, including heads of families.	All other free persons.	Slaves.
Trible, Wm	1	3	6		
Pain, George	1	2	1		
Blackburn, Jas	2	1	2		
Jones, Peter	1	3	2		
Anderson, Geo	1		2		
Whithead, Jno	1	1	1		
Madalf, Jo	4	1	3		
Null, Jno	1	2	3		
Law, David	1	3	3		
Freeman, Peter	1	2	4		
Lowe, Thos	1	1	1		
Lowe, Sam	1		2		
Sanders, Anne	1	2	3		
Elmore, Geo	1	2	5		
Sanders, Jas	1	2	1		
Jones, Ezek	2	1	2		
Johnson, Ben	2		3		
Hamton, Nancy		2	2		
Hamton, Turner	1	1	2		
Landsdown, Jno	1	2	2		
Jones, Jno L	1	2	1		
Lowe, Mary	1	2	1		
Trible, Shad	1	2	3		
Hubbard, Ben	1	1	3		
Martin, Zac	1		3		
Wright, Solomon	1		3		
Hamton, Jacob	2		3		
Morgan, Josh, Jr	1		1		
Gray, Jno	2	3	5		
Lowe, Isaac	1	2	4		
Trible, Spil	3	7	4		
Mongomery, Eliz		1	2		
Greer, Josh	1	6	7		3
Trible, Joel	1	1	1		
Southerton, Dan	1	2	1		

MORGAN DISTRICT, WILKES COUNTY—Continued.

THIRTEENTH COMPANY—continued.

NAME OF HEAD OF FAMILY.	Free white males of 16 years and upward, including heads of families.	Free white males under 16 years.	Free white females, including heads of families.	All other free persons.	Slaves.
Donathon, Frd	1				
Walker, Isaac	1	4	2		3
Sloan, John	1		1		
Ellidge, Isaac	2		1		
Ellidge, Ben	2		2		
Greer, Jude		2	4		
Hamton, Reuben	1	2	1		
Hargram, Francis	2	3	4		4
Lowe, Wm	2	4	3		
Lowe, Rachel		2	1		
Morgan, Jno	1	1	1		
Hamton, Joel	1	2	3		
Dyer, Minoah	3		3		
Hall, Jesse	1	1	2		
Starkey, Jo	1	2	2		
Donathn, Hawkin	1	1	1		
Nicols, Jacob	3		3		1
Green, Anne	1		1	7	
Mitchell, Rachel		2	4		
Bryan, Anne	1		1	1	
Bryan, Henry	1		1		
Bray, Patrick	1	1	2		
Chanler, Jno	1				
Donathan, Wm	1	1	3		4
Donathn, Ben	1		3		
Morgan, Jos., Sr	2		6		
Poor, Betty		2	4		
Pasons, Jno	1	1	4		
Boman, Isom	1	2	5		
McGill, Wm	1	3	5		
Hines, Jonathn	1	2	2		
Stewart, Jas., Sr	3	5	4		
McCinny, Sam	1	2	9		
Holton, Alex	2	3	4		
Moore, Andw	2	5	4		
Majors, Jno	1	4	4		
Gilbreath, Wm	1	2	2		
Gilbreath, Alex	1	2	3		
Gilbreath, Jno	2	3	4		
Freeman, Jas	1	1	4		
Livinston, Jno	1	2	4		
Norman, Isaac	3	1	2		
Smither, Gabl	1	3	5		
Barber, Nat	1		2		
Barber, Rd	1	1	1		
Parkes, Aron	1	3	6		1
Preston, Isaac	1	3	2		
Lowe, Caleb	1	4	4		
Isbel, Wm	1	1	2		1
Davis, Ephrm	1		2		
Petty, Wm	3		2		
Woodforth, Jos	2	5	6		6
Hamby, Jno	1	2	3		
Choat, Seybert	1	1	2		
Slaton, Ben	1	1	1		
Mongomery, Jno	1	3	4		
Laws, Wm	1	2	5		
Boman, Amy		1	4		
Ward, Sarah			3		
Foster, George	1	3	4		2
Branham, Ben	2		3		
Ward, Jno	1	2	3		
Paterson, Agnes	2	2	4		
Patterson, Jno	1		2		
Mitchell, Wm	1	3	3		
Stephens, Jno	1	1	3		
Hill, Jas	1		3		
Ellidge, Jacob	3	4	3		
Parks, Aron	1	3	1		
Ellidge, Jos	1		2		
Allen, Sam	3	1	4		
Thomas, Notly	1	3	3		
Keller, Jno	1		3		
Walker, Patty		2	3		
Gilbert, Gideon	5		3		
Sheppard, Thom	1	4	3		
Mays, Reuben	1	2	2		
Hays, Jesse	2	2	2		1
Williams, Jot	2	2	5		
Sanders, Julius	1		1		
Williams, Jno	1		2		
Jones, Geo	3	4	4		
West, Sam	1				
Chanler, Mary			1		
Chanler, Eliz			2		
Shoat, Saybon, Jr	1		3		

FOURTEENTH COMPANY.

NAME OF HEAD OF FAMILY.	Free white males of 16 years and upward, including heads of families.	Free white males under 16 years.	Free white females, including heads of families.	All other free persons.	Slaves.
Williams, Jo	1	3	4		
Israel, Jos	1	1	7		
Roy, Jos	3	4	4		
Wilmouth, Ezekl	2		5		
Snow, Jacob	1	3	3		
Franklin, Jacob	1	3	2		

FOURTEENTH COMPANY—continued.

NAME OF HEAD OF FAMILY.	Free white males of 16 years and upward, including heads of families.	Free white males under 16 years.	Free white females, including heads of families.	All other free persons.	Slaves.
Lewis, Elias	3		2		
Franklin, Jno	1	1	4		
Umfrey, Isaac T	1	1	3		
Wolf, Danl	1	2	3		
Watts, Wm	1		4		
McCartey, Jos	1		4		
Davis, Lewis	1	2	6		
Snows, Henry	1	4	6		
Jennins, John	1	2	3		
Snow, Obed	1	1	2		
Holbrooks, Robt	1	2	2		
Snow, Wm	1		2		
Kennedy, Wm	2	2	6		
Thomson, Jo	2	2	5		
Tomson, Jo., Jr	1		1		
Tomson, Jas	1		1		
Kennedy, Saml	1	3	4		
Bench, Danl	2	2	4		
Haris, Dabney	2	3	6		
Austin, David	1	5	2		
Robison, Jno	1	1	2		
Franklin, Jesse	1		2		5
Franklin, Shad	1	1	2		
Underwood, Thom	1		1		
Underwood, Jno	1	1	1		
Underwood, Jno, Jr	2	1	1		
Watson, Jno	1	3	2		
Kirby, Henry	1		3		
Kirby, Kit	1	2	1		
McCloud, Wm	1	3	5		
Underwood, Wm	1	2	2		1
Hutson, Jno	1	2	5		
Williams, Jno	1	1	3		
Dugless, Andw	1	2	5		
Cuningham, Wm	1	3	4		
Rama, Wm	4	1	5		
Rama, Jos	1	1	4		
Rama, Ben	1	1	3		
Arnol, Thom	1	2	4		
Gallion, Jacob	2	3	2		
Gallion, Sam	1		1		
James, Abram	3	4	6		
Douglas, Edwd	1	2			
James, Jam	1	1	1		
Eldridge, Wm	1	2			
Duglass, Thom	1		1		
Franklin, Bernard	2	1	5		12
Franklin, George	1	1	6		
Johnson, Robt	1	1	1		
Canterbury, Anne		3	1		
Scott, Jno	1	1	5		
Ross, Jno	1	3	1		
Isaacs, Rachel	1	2	2		
Kenedy, Mark	1		3		

FIFTEENTH COMPANY.

NAME OF HEAD OF FAMILY.	Free white males of 16 years and upward, including heads of families.	Free white males under 16 years.	Free white females, including heads of families.	All other free persons.	Slaves.
Forester, Charles	1	4	5		
Barns, Reuben	1		3		
Sanders, Cornelius	2	4	3		
Barns, Solomon	4	2	6		
Scott, Thom	1	3	3		
Hood, Aron	1	1	2		
Philips, Wm, Jr	1				
Philips, Thos	1				
Philips, Wm	1	1	1		
Sanders, Shad	1		2		
Sanders, Wm	1	3	1		
Sanders, Wm, Jr	1		1		
Spradling, Jas	3	1	1		
Kirby, Wm	2	1	2		2
Kirby, Jno	1		2		
Scott, Rd	1		3		
Kirby, Jo	1	3	1		
Scott, Mary	1	2	1		1
Russell, Wm	1	6	4		
Monday, Wm	1	1	7		
Monday, Frank	1	1	3		
Monday, Tho	1		3		
Drew, Jesse	2	2	2		
Leech, Jno	2		3		
Chambers, Wm	1		1		
Chambers, Wm H	1	1			
Hatton, Chas	1	1	3		
Russell, Ben	1	2	3		
Hines, Eliz		1	6		
McGee, Jno	2		6		
Chambers, Jno	1	1	2		
Carson, Sam	1	4	4		
Sloan, Sam, Junyr	1	1	1		
McGee, Sally					
Boyd, Robt	2	2	1		
Boyd, Robt., Jr	1	2	2		
Boyd, Jno	1	3	1		
Boyd, Thom	1	1	3		

FIFTEENTH COMPANY—continued.

NAME OF HEAD OF FAMILY.	Free white males of 16 years and upward, including heads of families.	Free white males under 16 years.	Free white females, including heads of families.	All other free persons.	Slaves.
Hereford, Henry	2	7	2		
Vinson, Danl	1	1	2		
Meadown, James	1	1	2		
Scott, Nathan	1	4	2		
Munday, Sam	1	3	1		
Barns, John	1	2	5		
Sloan, Sam	1	5	4		
Wilson, Sam	1	5	1		
Barns, John	2	4	4		
Barns, Edwd	1	1	1		
Ellidge, Isaac	2	2	5		
Sloan, Patrick	3	2	6		
Spradin, Charles	1	2	5		
Jones, Jno M	1	2	3		
Jones, Jos	1	3	2		
Robnet, Jas			2		
Brown, Geor., Es	2	3	5		1
Adams, Thom	1	2	2		
Chapman, John	1	3	5		
Chapman, Enoch	1	2	4		
Sanders, Jno	1	2	3		
Spradling, James	1		3		
Spurlock, Wm	1		1		
Whitten, Wm	1	3	3		
Brown, Edwin	1	5	2		

SIXTEENTH COMPANY.

NAME OF HEAD OF FAMILY.	Free white males of 16 years and upward, including heads of families.	Free white males under 16 years.	Free white females, including heads of families.	All other free persons.	Slaves.
Bunyard, Jas., Es	1	5	3		
Grimes, Boston	1	2	4		
Custard, Jno	1	1	2		
Writer, Elir	1		7		
Writer, Michal	1		1		
Kisler, Olivick	3		1		
Burket, Jos	1	1	4		
Dick, Jno	1	3	5		
Reid, Jno	2	3	5		
Burket, David	1	2			
Kisler, Jos	1	3	2		
Wade, Thom	1	3	3		
Grove, Danl	1	1	1		
Jones, John	1	4	2		
Fouts, David	1	4	5		
Shirror, Christom	1	3	1		
Yonce, Laurence	1	1	2		
Carver, Jno	1	2	7		
Landers, Jacob	1	1	3		
Shirron, Christi, Sr	1	2	7		
Bowers, Jno	1	3	4		
Marsh, Aron	1		2		
Beasly, David	1		1		
Carvender, Patrick	1				
Goodman, Peter	1		3		
Crapeal, Peter	1	4	4		
Baker, Jas	1	4	1		2
Baker, Morry	1	4	5		
Smith, Alex	2		3		
Coons, Jno	1	2	5		1
Bumganer, Dan	1	1	4		
Miller, Jno	1		2		
Sheets, Jno	1	1	1		
Ray, Jesse	1	3	2		
Smith, Moses	1	5	2		
Locard, Jno	1	1	4		
King, Frank	2	1	3		
King, Jos	1		2		
King, Edwd	2	4	4		
Lewis, Gideon	2	2	5		
Reid, Stephen	3	2	5		
Vanwinkle, Jas	1	2	2		
Piniton, Micajah	1	1	2		
Little, Charls	1	1	4		
Weaver, Isaac	1	5	1		
Holinsworth, Vineon	1	5	3		
Jones, Vineon	1	2	2		
Jones, John	1	1	5		
Davis, Wm	1	3	4		
Jones, Wm	1	3	1		
May, Jacob	2	6	2		
Hubbard, Jacob	5	6	4		
Henson, Jno	2	3	7		
Munker, Jno	2	3	1		
Henson, Jas	1	1	2		
Henson, Paul	1	3	2		
Henson, Paul, Sr	1		2		
May, Abram	2	3	5		
Smith, Thom	1	2	5		
Barrier, Geo	1	3	4		
Cafinder, Matt	1	2	4		
Smith, Wm	1	4	7		
Piniton, Rd	1	2	3		
Lewis, Jas	1	3	2		
Osborn, Solomon	1	2	2		
Smith, Rd	1	3	3		
Henson, Richd	1	3	2		

MORGAN DISTRICT, WILKES COUNTY—Continued.

SIXTEENTH COMPANY—continued.

NAME OF HEAD OF FAMILY.	Free white males of 16 years and upward, including heads of families.	Free white males under 16 years.	Free white females, including heads of families.	All other free persons.	Slaves.
Smith, Randol	1	2	6		
Sweeton, Wm	1	1	2		
Jonson, Jno	1	2	3		
Flanery, Jno	1	3	4		
Elkins, Wm	1	2	5		
Nolan, Sheppe	1	1	1		
Tyre, Geo	2	1	3		
Sweeton, Chas	1	1	2		
Mitchell, Henry	2	5	4		
Bumgarner, Michal	1		1		
Mock, Fred	1	4	4		
Ellis, Peter	2	2	5		
Fouts, Jno	1	3	5		
Sturdy, Dolly		1	3		
Black, Frederick	1	1	4		
Grove, Jacob	3	2	4		
Stockerd, Michl	1				
Sheets, Henry	1		3		
Williams, Owen	1	3	5		
Reed, Robt	1	1	4		

NEWBERN DISTRICT, BEAUFORT COUNTY.

NAME OF HEAD OF FAMILY.	Free white males of 16 years and upward, including heads of families.	Free white males under 16 years.	Free white females, including heads of families.	All other free persons.	Slaves.
Jones, Josiah	1				
Sparrow, Samuel	2	2	2		3
Watson, John	1	2	2		
Campin, Thomas	1	1	4		3
Jones, William	1		1		
Tingle, Israel	1	3	2		
Harrington, John	2	4	3		
Creakmond, Edmond	1	1	3		
Harris, Judith	1		4		
Brothers, Samuel, Senr	2	1	2		
Squires, Amos, Senr	1		3		
Brothers, Joseph	1	1	2		
Muckleroy, Adam	3		5		
Curtis, John, Senr	2		3		
Holton, David	1	1	3		
Holton, James	1	4	2		1
Tingle, David	1	1	1		
Johnston, Abram, Senr				5	
Jones, James, Senr	2	3	2		
Jones, Josiah, Senr	3	3	2		4
Jackson, Anna	3		4		
Wise, Matilda	1		3		
Wise, Joseph	1	3	2		
Rigs, James	1	1	6		
Slade, Henry	1	1	3		1
Wise, Johannes	1	4	2		
Harris, William	1	5	5		
Dowdy, Thomas	1		2		
Baker, Nathan	1	1	4		
Riggs, John	2	3	1		
Linton, Lemuel	1	3	2		
Dowdy, James, junr	2	3	5		
Dowdy, James, Senr	1		1		
Mews, John	1	4	4		
Riggs, Jemima	1	1	1		
McKinsey, David	1		3		
Dowdy, Elijah	1		2		
Dowdy, Samuel	1				
Dowdy, William	1		3		
Everit, Henry	2	1	1	2	1
Jones, William, Senr	3	4	4		
Missick, Joseph	1	4	2		
Dowdy, John	2	2	5		
Baker, Henry	1		4		
Linton, Luke	1	5	4		
Linton, Daniel	1	2	3		
Slade, William	1	2	1		
Everit, Robert	2	4	4		
Everit, Hugh	1				
Campin, Joseph	1	1			3
Campin, Robert	1				3
Jasper, Jonathan	2	2	4		8
Pringle, James	1	4	4		
Everit, James	1		3		1
Rew, Mark	1		4		
Pate, Isaac	2		1		1
Equals, George	2	1	1		1
Hodge, John	1				
Hodge, Zear			1	4	
Harvey, Richard	1		2		
Harvey, James	1		2		
Jones, Robert	1				
Leath, Elizabeth	1		2		17
Watson, Burgase	1	2	3		
Fulsher, Perigaine	1	1	2		2
Everit, Thomas	1		3		
Johnston, Sarah			6		
Jones, David		1	1		
Jones, Francis	3		2		24
Curtis, Ann				6	
Dowdy, Samuel	1				
Deer, Ann		2	1		
Squires, Lydia			1		
Denny, Patsey		3	2		
Scarborough, Benjamin	1	1	4		
Rollins, John	1		3		7
Respess, Richard	1	3	3		8
Dunbar, James	1	1	2		4
Respess, John	2		1		2
Grigs, John	1	3			
Marshall, Thomas	2		1		1
Patter, Sarah		1			
Dixon, Thomas	1	2			
Moor, Samuel	1		2		
Lee, Benjamin	1	3	1		
Lee, Shadrach	1	1	1		
Banks, Lilleston	1	3	1		
Williams, Thomas	2	1			
Gregory, Samuel	1		1		
Locker, Henry	1		1		
Harrington, Joseph	1		1		
Holton, Richard	1	2	4		
Camper, Joseph	1	1	1		4
Rowe, Kitley	1	1	3		
Bennett, Josiah	1		2		1
Martindale, Henry	2		3		
Young, William	2		3		
Davis, Thomas	1	1	2		3
Everage, Jonathan	1	1	1		
Silverthorn, Bustin	2	2	3		
Wiet, Nathaniel	2		1		
Respess, Thomas	2		2		76
Collins, Timothy	1	2	1		2
Bennett, Leah	2		1	1	3
Rolls, Sarah	1	1	2		
Prescoat, John	1	1	3		
Staplefoot, Keziah	1		4		2
Peede, Henry	2	2	3		
Lewis, John	1	3	2		
Lewis, Joseph	1		3		
Keel, Ruth	1		3		
Whitus, Badson	2	2	4		2
Wainwright, Kezy		2	4		
Smiddick, David	2	5	5		
Lambert, William	1		4		
Marshal, John	1		1		1
Keel, John	1		3		
Warren, Edward	1	1	3		
Adams, Peter	1		1		
Equals, Frederick	1	1	4		
Campain, James	1		2	1	2
Pritchard, Abram	1	1	1		6
Wood, John	1	1	4		
Bennett, John	1	1	1		
Taylor, Jacob	1	1	3		
Dazer, Josiah	1		4	2	2
Equals, William	1		4		
Robinson, Luke	1	3	6		16
Tripp, Dorcas			4		
Tetterton, William	3	2	3		
Purser, James	1	2	2		
Brady, Benjamin	2	3	3		3
Lee, William	1	1	1		
Clark, John	1	2	5		
Clark, William	1	3	2		
Mayo, Thomas	2				
Campaign, Mary		2	5	3	2
Mayo, Solomon	2	3	3		
Mixon, Zedekiah	1	2	4		
Slade, Henry	1		3		
Barnett, John	2	2	2		
Davis, Arthur	1	1	2		1
Veal, David	1	1	3		1
Blount, Frederick	1	1	3		
Spring, Aaron	1	1	3		
Spring, Abram	1	1	2		
Tutterton, Kizzy					5
Pringle, Charles	1		4		
Harvey, James, junr	1		2		
Farris, William	2		5	1	7
Bond, John	1	3	3		7
Pritchard, Abram	1	4	3		8
Bond, Robert	2	1	4		4
Wallace, John	1		4	3	3
White, Solomon	2	2	2		10
Hudson, John	1		2		1
Vowse, William	1	2	1		
Pritchard, Philip	1	2	5		
Landing, Richard	1	1	6		
Harvey, Thomas	1		2		
Harvey, Richard	1		2		
Harvey, James, Senr	1		3		
Langley, Lee	1	3	3		
Pringle, George	1	1	5		
Purser, James, Senr	2	1	5		
Purser, Robert	1	2	7		1
Gainer, Samuel	2	2	3		5
Purser, David, jur	1	1	3		1
Purser, David, Senr	1	1	2		
Cotanch, Malich	1	2	3		
Broomfield, James	2	1	1		
Whitus, Simon, Senr	2		2		
Whitus, Simon, jur	1	2	2		
Capps, John	1	1	3		3
Whitus, Henry	1	3	1		
Purser, Elizabeth	1	1	2		
Hodge, Leah	1		1	4	
Turner, Rebecca			5		
Baker, John	1		1		
Jarrod, Forbes	3	1	1		8
Crawford, Charles	4		1		21
Bonner, Sarah			6		
Moor, William	1	1	1		4
Healy, Catharine				3	
Foster, Christopher	1	1	1		
Purnal, Zachariah	1		1		
Trippe, Robert	3	3	3		13
Pilly, John	1	4	4	1	1
Smith, Thomas	1	3	2		17
Adams, Isaac	1	1	1		
Orris, William	1	1	4		
Robinson, Hannah			5		
Ackley, Mary		5	4		1
Dixon, James	2	4	2		
Griffith, Edward	1	1	3		17
Stilly, John	2	1	2		
Cox, Abram	2	3	3		
Dixon, Benjamin	1	6	5		
Daw, William	1	3	1		4
Bennet, John, Senr	2	1	4		
Futon, Thomas	2	1	4		
Rowe, Joshua	1		3		1
Dowtry, Elisha	1	4	3		6
Lyons, Joseph	2	1	2		
Sermon, Thomas	1				
Fulsher, Morning		1	2		11
Blango, Sarah				5	
Blango, Dinah				6	
Conner, Merion				3	
Blango, Thomas				10	
Lee, Mary			1		
Moor, Rachel				2	
Harris, Stephen	2	1	2		
Jones, Thomas	2		1		1
Hollingsworth, Mary			4		3
Prescoat, Benjamin	2	1	5		
Hagins, Christopher	1		1		
Surls, Covinton	1	4	4		
Everit, Thomas	2	1	4		
Jones, Jesse	1	1	2		
Dowty, Elisha, junr	1	1	2		
Garrot, Benjamin	1	1	1		11
Hagins, Darby	1	2	1		
Miller, Daniel	2				5
Orrell, Asa	1		2		
Cox, Aaron	1	1	3		
Adams, Joshua	1	1	3		
Smith, Jarvis	1				
Evit, John	1	3	6		
Harrison, Jesse	1		4		
Satterthwaite, Jeremiah	1		3		
Orrill, Stephen	1	1	5		
Walker, Thomas	1	1	4		1
Gallaway, William	2	4	5		
Jones, Walter	1	2	3		
Wright, Stephan	1	1	1		9
Rowe, Robert	1	3	2		
Rowe, Jesse	1	1	3		
Hill, Joshua	1		4		1
Dunn, Francis	2	2	2		1
Shute, Giles	1	3	6		
Thomason, Matthew	3	4	2		
Taylor, John	2	2	3		
Rowe, Richard	1	2	7		
Hollywell, Irey	1				

NEWBERN DISTRICT, BEAUFORT COUNTY—Continued.

NAME OF HEAD OF FAMILY.	Free white males of 16 years and upward, including heads of families.	Free white males under 16 years.	Free white females, including heads of families.	All other free persons.	Slaves.
Hill, Lazarus	1	1	1		
Mall, Moses	1				9
Wilkinson, Aaron	1				4
Whitus, Simon	1	3	3		
Gideons, Moses	1	1	1		
Adams, Elizabeth	2	2	1		1
Pierce, Hezekiah	1		7		5
Price, Shadrach	1		1		
Moor, John P.				5	
Blango, Solomon				1	
Johnston, Joshua				6	
Carroll, William				4	
Keys, Milley				4	
Rose, John	2	1	4		1
Smith, Dolly			2		
Godley, John	1	5	3		4
Worsley, Thomas	2		4		3
Harding, Stephen	2	1	1		
Richards, Ralph	2		4		
Walls, Joseph	2		1		
Godley, Nathan, Senr.	5		2		12
Pierce, Lazarus	1	3	3		20
Laughinghouse, Thomas, Senr.	2		2		
Morris, Elisha	1	3	2	1	
Holmes, John				6	
Bartlett, Thomas	3	1	2		
Hill, Harmond	2	3	2		10
Edwards, James	2	1	3		1
Edwards, Walker	1	3	4		
Blount, Lewis	2	6	4	1	2
Blount, Nathan	1	4	6		11
Keel, Nathan	1	1	1		
Blount, Reading	1	1	2		8
Knox, Frances	2	3	2		
Summers, Rachel		1	2		3
Richards, Elizabeth			1		4
Buck, Francis	2	3	3		
Buck, Isaac, Senr.	2	1	4		
Nobles, Isaac	2	1	1		
Hardin, Israel	1	3	1		1
Owens, Stephen	1	2	4		4
Pattin, Ann		1	2		7
Blount, Abigail		3	4		8
Dunbar, Robert	2	2	2		2
Raifield, Isaac	1	3	4		
Buck, Edward	1	5	2		1
Taunt, Jesse	1		3		
Holmes, Edward				1	
Edwards, Isaac, Senr.	2	2	5		
Grey, James	1	2	3		
Bright, Elizabeth			1		
Wilkinson, John		2	1		
Caffy, Abner	1		1		
Smith, Joseph	1		1		
Barnes, Jeremiah		1	3		
Blount, Thomas	1	2	2		3
Kinson, Anthony, Senr.	1	1	2		
Buck, Isaac, junr.	1		4		
Slade, Major	2	4	4		6
Godley, Elias	1	3			
Reed, Sarah			3		1
Butler, William			3		
Long, Nathan	1	1	3		
Pierce, Joseph	1	2	6		8
Edwards, David	1	2	3		
Edwards, Isaac, junr.	1	1	2		
Richards, Thomas	1	1	5		
Nobles, John	1		2		1
Godley, Nathan	1	4	3		2
Grice, Benjamin	1		5		
Grice, Frederick	2		3		29
Vines, Samuel	1		2		3
Lewis, Jonathan	1	2	3		
Laughinghouse, Andrew	1	1	3		
Pierce, George	1	4	3		5
Laughinghouse, John	1	4	2		7
Grice, Reading	2		2		7
Creamer, James	1	3	2		
Smith, Thomas	1	2	3		
Wall, Joel	1		3		4
Smith, Benjamin	1	1	3		
Muckleroy, William	1	3	3		
Kinion, Anthony	1		1		
Palmer, James	1	2	3		
Lee, Timothy	1		2		
Blount, Bryan	1	3	3		13
Blount, Reading	1	1	2		4
Edwards, Walker	1		1		
Edwards, John	1				
Edwards, William	1	1	2		
Pollard, Jacob	1		6		
Nelson, Nathan	2	2	3		
Aicklin, Joshua	2	1	5		
Worsley, Joseph	1				
Ottery, James	1	1	1		1

NAME OF HEAD OF FAMILY.	Free white males of 16 years and upward, including heads of families.	Free white males under 16 years.	Free white females, including heads of families.	All other free persons.	Slaves.
Priggin, William	1		3		
Downs, William	1		2		
Edwards, Britton	1				
Ginn, George	1	1	4		
Edwards, Emanuel	1		2		
Palmer, George	1	2	2		
Denby, Samuel	2		2		
Bryan, Thomas	1	1	3		
Buck, William	1				
King, Harmon	1		2		
Palmer, William	1				
Stephen	1		1		
Gladson, Dempsey	1	1	2		
Gladson, John	1		2		
Gladson, George	1		2		
Lanier, William	1	3	2		9
Lathum, Agnes	2	2	4		10
Hinton, Isaac	1	1	2		2
Nowis, Philip	1		2		4
Little, Josiah	2		4		
Floyde, John	1	2	2		
Jackson, Mary		3	3		
Floyde, Griffith	1				4
Williams, Godfrey	1	2	2		2
Taylor, Lydia	1		3		
Floyde, Simeon	1	1	3		
Griffin, Amaziah	1	3	2		9
Wilson, Seth	1		3		2
Freeman, James	1	2	2		1
Crandol, James	1	2	3		
White, Daniel	1	1	3		2
Fowler, George	1		1		
Williams, Thomas	1	1	2		3
Lathum, John	1		2		4
Jackson, Josias	1	2	1		
Davis, William	1	2	3		3
McDonald, Randal	2	2	4		8
Lenier, Martha	1		2		8
Lanier, Robert	1		1		12
Jolly, Solomon	1	4	4		3
Wilson, Seth	1	2	1		3
Williams, Thomas, Senr.	1	1	4		
Williams, James	1	3	5		
Wells, John	3	1	3		
Crawford, William	1		4		2
Short, Markum	1	2	7		1
Gainer, Joseph	1	1	3		12
Little, Thomas	1	2	2		1
Brown, Ephraim	1	3	3		
Dean, Margaret			2		
White, John	3		2		
Hull, Samuel	1	1	3		
Davis, Benjamin	1	1	3		
Kiel, James	1	3	3		
Legget, Jeremiah	1	2	2		
Bowen, John	1	1	2		
Bowen, Richard	2	2	2		
Spears, James	1	5	2		
Hodges, James	1	2	2		1
Tetterton, Joseph	1	1	2		
Pinkum, James	1	2	3		
Anderson, Joseph	1	3	1		
Brown, Andrew	1	1	5		
Warren, William	1	1	3		
Jackson, Jemima	1	1	3		
Brown, Eli	1		1		
Lee, James	1		2		
Cherry, Samuel	1	2	1		1
Cherry, John, Senr.	3		2		
Cherry, John, Junr.	1		1		1
Beechum, John	1	1	3		
Merry, Ann	1		3		
Ball, James	1		3		
Ball, Mary			3		
Hodge, Thomas	1	2	2		
Hodge, Moses	1	2	3		
Brown, Jacob	1	2	3		1
Woollard, Absolam	1		2		
Fowler, Esther			2		
Tutterton, Sarah			1		
Jackson, Kizzy		2	3		
Straddle, Dorcas	1	1	3		
Barrot, Abigail			3		
Hodges, Henry	1		1		
Woollard, John, junr.	2	3	3		4
Woollard, Samuel	1	3	3		
Woollard, Jeremiah	1	5	4		
Woollard, John, Senr.	1	1	1		
Woollard, Willowby	1		1		
Hayes, Alexander	2		1		
Sparkman, Jesse	1	2	2		
Walker, Daniel	1	1	3		
Walker, Thomas	1	1	3		
Walker, William	1		3		
McKiel, Matthew	1	3	3		
Singleton, William	1		2		
Ferrill, Leah		2	1		

NAME OF HEAD OF FAMILY.	Free white males of 16 years and upward, including heads of families.	Free white males under 16 years.	Free white females, including heads of families.	All other free persons.	Slaves.
McClanny, John	1	2	1		
Timmons, Thomas	1	1	2		
Jones, James	1	3	1		
Reed, Joseph	1	3	1		
Whitacre, Abram	1	3	4		
Crawford, Elizabeth	1		2		
Jones, John R	1	1	3		
Lee, George	1				
White, Thomas	1				
Lee, Elizabeth			2		
Lanier, Hoziah	1		3		2
Carrow, Lydia			3		
Cole, Richard	1	1	3		
Singleton, Bethier		1	3		
Swanner, Jesse	1	3	3		
Holland, Philip	2	1	4		
Blount, John G.	6	4	7		74
Blackledge, Richard	1				
Arnett, Silas W.	1				1
Parker, Catherine		1	5		
Ryan, Elizabeth			2	1	
Robinson, Thomas	1		2		
Jerkins, Mary	1	2	3		
Burr, William	2	1	3		
Gardner, Letitia			3		
Miller, Henry	1		1		
Bertie, Reuben	2				4
Hatridge, Robert	1				1
French, Daniel	1		1		1
Young, John	1	2	2		8
Mullen, Thomas	1	1	2		7
Carraway, Joseph	2	1	3		1
Stewart, William	2	1	3		1
Sims, Keziah		1	1		1
Hodge, Samuel	1	3	1		3
Greenwood, Nathan	1	2	1		
Nowland, Kitty			2		
Horn, George	1	1	4		6
Osborn, John	2				1
Howard, John			2		1
Cherry, Charles	3	3	4		3
Kennedy, John	4		2		30
Floyde, Gresham	1	2	1		5
Floyde, Peter	1		1		4
Floyde, Elizabeth	2		4		12
Cooke, Charles	2		2		
Kies, Nathaniel	2	2	3	2	6
Pickett, Joseph	1	1	2		2
Groves, Daniel	2	2	2		5
Baldwin, Ann	2	1	2		3
Sheridan, Dennis	1				1
McDonald, Andrew	2		1		
Lowry, John	1		3		
Clark, George	1	1	4		
Howell, Elias	4	4	2		3
Fullington, Mary	1	1	2		1
Story, Mary			3		
Rose, Mary			3		5
Congleton, John	2				4
Congleton, Jane		2	3		2
Hilliard, Gersham	1		2		3
Worden, John			2		5
Pickett, Jane			1		2
Groves, William	1	3	2		12
Parker, Green	1	2	2		1
Jones, Roger	1				2
Lewey, John	1				2
Duso, Leonard	1				8
Symons, Hannah			2		
Melonay, Laughlin	3				2
Jones, David	1		1		5
Shoemaker, David	1	1	3		1
Eastwood, James	3		2		9
Cassoe, Peter	3		2	1	4
Peacock, Isaac	3		5		
Hurton, William	1				
White, Milly			2		
Loomiss, Jonah					7
Harvey, Augustus	1	1	1		15
Maxwell, James	1	1			3
Potts, Ralph	1				1
Hawrahan, Walter	1	1			9
Nowis, Willowby	1		1		20
Brown, Thomas	1		1		
Bonner, Henry	1				12
Bonner, James, Senr.	1	2	4		51
Bonner, Henry S.	2	1	2		6
Owins, Brannock	2	1	2		2
Roundtree, Cadir.	2				
Bonner, James, Junr.	2				2
Bonner, Joseph	1				4
Hendrixson, Salathiel	1				
Horton, James	1				
Worsley, Thomas	2	3	2		7
Lucus, Henry	2	2	2		11
Jones, William	2	1	4		6
Hair, Mary	2	2	4		26

NEWBERN DISTRICT, BEAUFORT COUNTY—Continued.

NAME OF HEAD OF FAMILY.	Free white males of 16 years and upward, including heads of families.	Free white males under 16 years.	Free white females, including heads of families.	All other free persons.	Slaves.
Smaw, Henry	1	1	3		5
Alligood, John	1		2	1	1
Smaw, John	2	2	2		9
Beezley, Thomas, Senr	4	3	4		8
Ellison, Alley	4	8	2	4	30
Vines, Thompson	1	3	4		8
Campbell, James	1		1	1	
McKeel, Edmund	2	4	3		17
Jefferson, Obadiah	1	1	4		
Cutler, Robert	3	3	5		
Elliott, Peter	1	2	5		
Tancred, George	2		2		4
Cone, Dorcas			1		
Brady, Henry	1	1	4		1
Langley, Stephen, Senr	2		2		
Jefferson, Ann		1	2		
Woollard, Michael	2	4	2		
Bryan, Mary			5		
Alligood, Jacob	1	3	5		1
Alligood, Francis	2	4	7		
Bainer, Richard, Senr	1		2		7
Bainer, John	2	1	6		5
Congleton, Thomas	2	1	3		
Congleton, James	3		2	1	
Woollard, Absalom	1	1	4		4
Chester, Martha		1	3		
Beaman, Mary			2		
Jefferson, Martha			3		
Elliot, William	1	2	5		
Ellis, Robert	1	1	1		
Brock, Elizabeth			2		
Sutton, Peter				1	
Pluto, William				2	
McKeel, James	1	4	6		4
Sivils, John	1		2		
Bright, Mary			2		
Smith, John	1		2		
Woollard, Elizabeth	1	4	2		
Brady, Rachel		1	3		
Eborn, Catherine		1	3		
Pilley, Thomas	3	2	3		2
Lewis, Archibald	1	1	2		
Hawkins, Abier			1	2	
Whitehead, Willis	1	1	1		1
Lewis, Abigail		1	3		
Bocks, John	1	2	1		2
Jones, Elizabeth			1		1
Cutler, Moses	2	1	5		
Cone, Stephen	1				
Hawkins, Major	1	3	4		
Cutler, Aaron	1		1		
Chancey, Samuel	2	2	2		7
Boyde, William	1	3	3		6
Cutler, John	2	2	4		2
Chester, Samuel	1				
Woollard, Covinton	1	1	3		
Woollard, Coleman	1		1		
Worsley, William	2		2		1
Sulivan, Richard	1		1		
Boyde, Thomas	2		2		5
Brock, Lawson	1		1		
Perkins, James	1	1	1		
Langley, Stephen	1		3		
Barrow, Thomas	1	1	2		3
North, Edward	1	2	3		
Hawkins, Benjamin	1	3	3		
Burbage, John	1	1	2		3
Little, Jesse	1	2	2	1	1
Putnall, Stephen	1	1	4		5
Tancred, John	1		1		
Groves, William	1				
Brewer, William	1	1	5		
Wallace, John	1	1	1		1
Woollard, William	1	2	2		
Congleton, William	1	1	2		
Campbell, William	1				
Lixton, William	1				
Woollard, Jasper	1		3		
Sears, Philip	1				
Bainer, Richard	1	3	1		3
Horn, Mary			2		
McKeel, Elizabeth			4		

NAME OF HEAD OF FAMILY.	Free white males of 16 years and upward, including heads of families.	Free white males under 16 years.	Free white females, including heads of families.	All other free persons.	Slaves.
Juley, Arcey				1	
Perkins, William	1	1	3	1	1
Brown, William	3		3		16
Roulhac, P. G.	2		2		19
Alderson, Thomas	1	2	3		20
Lanier, John	1	4	6		15
Smallwood, Charles	1		2		2
Woodward, Isaiah	1		1		6
Martin, Lucy			1		
Willis, Samuel	1		3		10
McAbe, Ann		4	3		
Archibald, John	2	1	5		1
Alderson, Ann		2	4		2
Thomson, Margaret		1	2		
Stewart, Robert	1	3	3		
Langley, George	1	2	4		1
Conde, Mary	1	3	2		
Tunnell, William	1	2	1		
McAbe, James	1	1	2		
Smith, Mary			2		
Few, William	1		2		
Trotaban, Mary		1	3		
Horn, Susannah			3		
Rogers, Thomas	1		4		2
Freeman, Lucy		1	1		
Dowlin, Edward			2		
Gautier, Joseph	1	1	2		1
Winley, Aaron	2		4		6
Swan, William		2	1		9
Whitley, Arthur	1	1	2		
Whitley, Arthur, Senr	4	1	5	1	
Condre, Dennis	1	1	2		2
Hammon, Hewell	1	2	3		1
Walsh, William	1	2	4		
Archibald, James	2	2	3		7
Benton, Bailey	1	2	5		
Williams, Francis	1		2		
Mixon, Elijah	2	5	2		
Condre, John	3	4	6		
Winley, Israel	4	1	3		8
Adams, Henry	1	1	3		5
Adams, Abram	1		1	1	2
Adams, James	1		1		4
Smith, James, Senr	1		3	1	
Smith, James, junr	1		3		1
Wood, John	1	3	3		1
Abell, Arthur	1	1	2		2
Hammond, Levi	1		5		
Adams, Josias	1	2	3		2
Barrow, William	1		3		5
James, William	1	1	1		
Smith, Jeremiah	1	2	3		
Brock, John	2	1	5		
Adams, Samuel	1		1	2	
Adams, Elijah	1		1		
Cordin, Thomas	2	1	3		11
Caloge, Peter	1				
Windbey, Moses	1		2		2
Fullerton, Andrew	1	1		1	1
Bount, Miles	1	1	1		
Harvey, John	2	3	3		2
Archibald, Nathaniel	1	2	2		4
Clifford, William	2		2		2
Ormond, Wyriot	2				2
Williams, Thomas	1	1	1	2	
Liscomb, John	1		3		
Moignaw, J. L.	1	1	3		3
Price, William	2	1	4		3
Lathum, James	1		2		1
Hammond, John	1				
Horn, William					1
Mason, Christopher	1	1			
Price, Enoch	2	1	2		2
Ross, Francis	1	2	4		
Foreman, Michael	1		2		1
Blount, Joshua	1				
Smith, Margaret	1	1	1		
Turner, John					3
Brayboy, John				1	6
Hammond, John	1		1		8
Jones, John	4	6	5		
Hammond, John B	2	1	2		1

NAME OF HEAD OF FAMILY.	Free white males of 16 years and upward, including heads of families.	Free white males under 16 years.	Free white females, including heads of families.	All other free persons.	Slaves.
Equals, Joseph	1	1	1		1
Hammond, Philip	1		1		1
Sanderlane, Mary		1	3		
Asbell, Whitnum	1		2		
Thomson, Elias	2		2		
Whitley, William	1	1	2		1
Lind, Dorcas			1		2
Cogdell, Richard	2	1	2		5
Thornton, William	1	1	2		
Smaw, Henry	2		2		14
Clifford, John	1				
Jackson, Eleazer	3	2	7		1
Kelly, Charles	1		3		
Hamilton, John	1	4	8		
Girkin, Benjamin	3		2		
Sinnett, Elizabeth	1	2	2		
Jones, Walter	1	2	3		
Waters, Amos	3	1	3		
Waters, John	1	1	5		
Garrott, John	2		4		
Squires, Appleton	1	2	6		
Vandannel, Edward	3	2	2		1
Ready, Peter	1	1	2		2
Risbey, Thomas	1		1		
Miller, Nathan	1	1	5		
Gergainus, Elizabeth	1	1	3		
Howren, John	1	1	3		
Garrett, Thomas	2	1	2		
Sulivan, Lambeth	1	2	4		
Martin, William	1	3	5		
Lilley, Joseph	1	2	3		
Martin, Elizabeth		1	2		
McDonough, John	1	1	3		
Ross, Benjamin	1	6	4		
Boyde, William, Esqr	3	1	3		15
Barrow, John	3	5	5		7
McDonough, Henry	1	2	2		1
Lathum, Phineas	1	3	2		
Moore, John	2	5	2		
Waters, Zachariah	1	2	3		
Waters, Jeremiah	1		4		
Waters, Winifred	1				
Lathum, Charles	1	3	3		1
Howrin, Redmond	1				
Boyde, Thomas	2	3	3		16
Boyde, William	1	2	2		3
Chester, Henry	1		5		
Harris, John	1	3	3		
Everit, Thomas	1	1	3		
Bowen, John	1	4	3		1
Kelly, Labin	1	2	3		
Risbey, Thomas	1		2		
Donnell, Arthur	1		1		
Risbey, Robert	1		1		
Risbey, Langley	1				
Ross, Elijah	1	1	7		
Gailer, Benjamin	1	1	3		
Ready, Alexander	1	1	2		7
Donnell, John	1				
Donnell, Edward	1				
Stubbs, William	1	1	3		
Odin, Charles	1	2	1		5
Odin, Richard	1				2
Donnell, James	1		3		1
Garrott, Shadrach	1	1	2		
Waters, Jesse	1	1	1		
Waters, David	1				
Waters, Frederick	1				
Waters, William	1				
Kelly, Custis	1	2	4		
Girkin, Charles	1	2	2		
Jackson, Thomas	1	2	1		
Waters, Isaac	1	3	3		2
Waters, John	1	3	2		
Hamilton, Lazarus	1				
Wallace, Thomas	1	2	3		2
Jones, Jonathan	1				
Risbey, Richard	1				
Stilley, Michael	1	1	2		
Girkin, Jeremiah	2	1	3		
Jones, William	1				
Lathum, Noah	1	2	2		

NEWBERN DISTRICT, CARTERET COUNTY.

NAME OF HEAD OF FAMILY.	Free white males of 16 years and upward, including heads of families.	Free white males under 16 years.	Free white females, including heads of families.	All other free persons.	Slaves.
Hill, Isaac	1	5	2		36
Davis, Solomon W	4	3	4		10
Hunter, Lebbeus	2	1	3		7
Stephens, Asa	1		1		
Howard, William L.	1	2	3		
West, George	1	3	4		
Picket, Oliver	3				
Brigs, John	1				
Hackell, Armstead	3		3		6

NAME OF HEAD OF FAMILY.	Free white males of 16 years and upward, including heads of families.	Free white males under 16 years.	Free white females, including heads of families.	All other free persons.	Slaves.
Ostean, John, Senr	1	1	4		
Osteen, James, junr	1	1	3		
Weeks, Theophilus	1	2	6		
Pounder, Richard	1	2	3		
Prescott, Willowby	1	2	5		
Lovick, John	2	2	6		1
Freshwater, Thomas	1	2	2		
Miller, John	1		5		
Weeks, Sarah			3		

NAME OF HEAD OF FAMILY.	Free white males of 16 years and upward, including heads of families.	Free white males under 16 years.	Free white females, including heads of families.	All other free persons.	Slaves.
Weeks, Edward	1	1	5		
Weeks, Levy	1	3	4		
Weeks, Robert	1				
Weeks, Stephen	1				
Sanders, William	1	2	4		
Stelly, Ephraim	2	2	1		
Green, Samuel	2	2	4		2
Osteen, William	1	3	2		
Smith, Richard	1	1	2		

NEWBERN DISTRICT, CARTERET COUNTY—Continued.

NAME OF HEAD OF FAMILY.	Free white males of 16 years and upward, including heads of families.	Free white males under 16 years.	Free white females, including heads of families.	All other free persons.	Slaves.
Easlick, Isaac	1	2	3		2
Wilson, Andrew	2	2	3		2
Weeks, Jabis, Senr	3		2		
Weeks, Jabis, junr	1	2	3		1
Meadows, Jacob	1	4	4		
Garvey, Thomas	1	1	1		
Brice, Ross	1		3		
Brice, James	1	1	4		1
Hatchell, Willis	1		5		1
Prescot, Aaron	2	1	1		
Smith, Jesse	1				
Hatchell, William	2	1	3		3
Prescot, Elizabeth			2		
Nelson, John	1	2	3		3
Jarman, Littleton	1	2	6		
Hatchell, Richard	1	1	4		
Hatchell, Henry	1	1	1		
Harrington, Philip	1	1			
Smith, Sarah			2		
Osteen, Samuel	2		2		
Osteen, David	1	3	2		
Ostean, Jesse	1		1		
Melson, Levin	1	1	1		
Thomson, Margaret			2		
Fearn, William	1	2	2		4
Hill, Joseph	1	2	1		22
Wiley, Sarah			2	4	
Taylor, Stephen	1		4		
Blackhouse, Allen	1				5
Philips, William	2	4	1		
Beechum, John	1	1	3		
Harris, Thomas	1	2	4		
Cowell, Butler	2	3	2		2
Culliner, William	1	1	8		
Harvey, Marcum	1	2	3		
Simson, Joshua	2	1	3		
Weeks, Abram	1				
Bourdin, William, junr	1				5
Hill, Isaac, Senr	2	1	3		10
Russell, David	2	3	6		4
Hall, Samuel, Senr	1		7		
Hall, Samuel, junr	1				
Hall, Nathaniel	1				
Hill, William			2		1
Rew, Southy	1		3		2
Taylor, Richard	1	1	1		
Lane, James	1	2	3		
Nicholson, Risder	1	1	4		
Sanders, Thomas	3	2	3		
Wallace, Reuben	1	1	1		4
Wallace, Asa	1				1
Marine, John	1	2	1		
Marine, William	1				
Taylor, Isaac	1	1	2		3
Joiner, Nathan	1		3		
Smith, Solomon	1				
Russel, William	1	3	1	1	2
Russel, Habacuck	1		1		
Brace, William	2	4	5		
Harris, Elizabeth			2		
Maginis, Jonas	1	1	3		
Bell, Winifred			2		
Black, Martin				2	
Wilson, Thomas	1		3		
Sanders, Winnifred			3		
Bell, Newell	1	6	1		3
Bell, Abner	2	3	3		2
Bell, Newell, Senr	1	3	3		1
Bell, Malicah	7	1	3		18
Peltier, Jeremiah	1	1	3		
Yates, Charles	1	2	4		
Hill, Thomas	1	1	3		
Ogilsby, Joseph	1	1	4		
Garner, William	1	4	3		1
Bell, Joseph, Senr	1	5	4		
Taylor, Levin	1	2	3		
Bell, Mary			2		1
Penevil, Price	1		2		
Temple, Thomas	3		4		
Ogilsby, Thomas	2	2	3		3
Freize, George	1	2	6		
Gardner, John	3	1	4		
Lewis, Mary	1		1		26
Simmons, William	1	3	1		1
Sanders, Samuel	3	3	4		4
Gardner, Francis, Senr	1	1	3		
Adams, Joseph	1	1	3		
Bell, Billet	2	1	1		1
Sanders, John	2	3	3		
Meadow, Joel	2		3		
Bell, Joseph	2	1	5		12
Harbert, Hilary	1		4		4
Harbert, William	1		2		
Sheppard, David	1				6
Sheppard, Jane		1	3		
Bell, George	1		3		
Adams, Nathan	1	1	3		1

NAME OF HEAD OF FAMILY.	Free white males of 16 years and upward, including heads of families.	Free white males under 16 years.	Free white females, including heads of families.	All other free persons.	Slaves.
Kennedy, Jacob	1	1	4		1
Quin, Abner	1	3	3		
Ogilsby, Gideon	2	3	2		
Sanders, Amos	1	1	1		
Yates, Bazel	1	1	3		
Brock, Elias	1	1	3		
Ogilsby, Benjamin	3	2	3		
Gardner, Francis, junr	1		4		
Meadow, Isaac	1		4		
Sanders, Philip	1				
Weeks, Seth	1		4		
Dill, George	1				
Dill, Edward	1	1	3		
Kennedy, Richard	1	2	6		3
Smith, John	1				
Kennedy, Gideon	1	2	4		
Smith, Archibald	1		3		
Ogilsby, John	1	1	2		
Stewart, Francis	1	1	5		
Kennedy, Thomas	2		3		1
McKean, John	2	4	3		
Hibs, John	1	2	3		
Sheppard, Absalom	1		3		7
Dennis, John	1				
Kennedy, Elijah	1				
Dennis, James	1				
Stewart, John	1				
Culley, Thomas	3	3	3		8
Peppers, Elijah	2		2		
Weeks, Thomas	1	1	2		
Longness, Caleb	1		4		1
Reed, Robert	4	1	3		1
Willis, Benjamin	1	3	3		
Roberts, John	2	2	4		
Dill, John	1				
Sikes, Abram	2	1	3		
Osteen, Isaac	1		2		
Russel, William	1	1	3		
Taylor, Joshua	1	1	1		
Morton, Joseph	1				
Kennedy, Willit	1		3		
Phelps, Uriah	1				
Vincent, Jesse	1	1	3		
Bell, Joseph, junr	4		3	1	
Man, Leonard	1				
Mitts, Jacob	1	1	3		
Martin, John	1				
Longness, James	1				
Tolsin, William	1	1	6		
Martin, Absalom					9
Carter, John					4
Burgase, Caesar					1
Williams, Ann	2	1	4		2
Dennis, William, Senr	3		2		23
Dennis, William, junr	1				7
Ogilsby, William	1				
Sammons, William	1	3	2		
Bell, John	2	2	2		
Adams, John	1		4		
Sanders, James	2	2	2		
Smith, Samuel	1	1	2		
Bell, Nathan	1	5	3		
Jenny				4	
Bell, Joseph, Senr	3				
Borden, William	4	3	3		43
Stanton, John	1	3	3		
Williams, William	4		4		
Bell, John	2	2	2		
Kennedy, Edward	1	3	2		
Kennedy, Willit	1		2		
Small, Benjamin	1	1	2		
Welch, James	1	1	2		
Cooke, Martin	1				
Samson (Old)				3	
Tigner, William	2	1	2		1
Riggs, Benjamin	1	1	3		
Hardister, Benjamin	2	2	3		1
Hardister, Joseph	1	2	3		2
Harris, Jesse	1	1	3		1
Willis, Elisha	1		2		1
Dickernson, John, Senr	1		1		
Dickernson, John, junr	1				
Mills, John	1	2	2		
Piner, Joab	1		1		
Peter (Free)				5	
Carolina (Free)				7	
Fisher, William	3	1	5		10
Warner, Frederic	2		4		
Dickinson, James	1	2	3		
Potter, Joshua	1	1	2		
Jones, Rebecca	2	2	4		4
Eason, John, Senr	2	1	3		7
Eason, John, junr	1		4		2
Chadwick, Gear	1	1	4		
Singletary, John	1	1	2		4
Gibble, Diderick	2	1	4		6
Piner, Charles	1	1	2		

NAME OF HEAD OF FAMILY.	Free white males of 16 years and upward, including heads of families.	Free white males under 16 years.	Free white females, including heads of families.	All other free persons.	Slaves.
Rial, Joseph	1		2		
Kennedy, Martha	1	2	5		
Piner, Unice			4		
Piner, Reuben	1	1	2		
Owens, William	1		2		
Locker, Hugh	2	2	2		1
Toby, Senr (Free)				2	
Dinah (Free)				3	
Chadwick, Zaer	1	3	3		2
Hancock, Cromwell	1	1	2		
Jones, Edward	1	1	1		
Fisher, Elizabeth			3		
Bushnell, Ann M	1		2		
Hendrixson, Sorrowful		2	4		
Lewis, Ann	1		2		
Russel, Cevil		2	1		
Noah, Letitia	1		2		
Pasquinet, Ann			2		2
Fuller, Bersheba		2	3		
Lecraft, Benjamin	1	1	4		4
Rickets, John	1		2		
Fuller, Solomon	1	2	2		3
Jones, Rier	1	2	1		4
Pasquinet, Isaiah	1		2		
Severin, John	1	1	2		1
Sheppard, John	1	1	5		
Leffuss, Samuel	2		3		
Leffuss, Asa	1		1		
Ellis, Delino	1	1	2		1
Wade, Robert	1	2	3		
Cannon, Mary	1		2		2
White, John	1		1		
Murray, John	1		1		
Warner, William	1				
Thomas, Samuel	1				
Upton, Mary		2	2		
Saviston, David	1	4	2		
Appleton, Elizabeth	1		2		4
Ward, Thomas	1	1	2		
Piver, Peter, Senr	1	1	6		
Piver, Peter, junr	1	1	2		
Piver, Johannis	1		1		
Luton, Adam	1		1		
Guthry, Jane	1	1	3		
Easlick, Francis	1	1	2		
Gorton, Bowan	1	2	3		
Wharton, Eben	1	1	1		
King, Joseph	1		2		1
Brag, Thomas	1		1		
Crandol, Elijah	1	1	2		
McDonald, Thomas	1	3	4		
Crief, John	1	1	4		
Harris, Georgeabrin	2	2	4		
Stanton, Benjamin	2	2	7		2
Mace, John	2	1	3		
Mace, James	1	2	1		
Small, Jonas	1	3	2		
Stanton, William	1	2	3		
Stanton, Owen	2	1	6		
Bundy, Josiah	1	2	2	1	
Wade, Royal	1	1	3		
Harris, Nehemiah	1	4	3		
Harris, Jesse	1	6	3		
Williston, Elisha	1		2	1	
Parisher, Samuel	1	2	2		
Gibbs, Nathan	1	1	2		
Helen, Isaac	2		3		2
Gibble, Frederic	2		5		2
Longness, Joshua	1	2	5		
Guthrey, Frederic	1	2	5		
Piver, Daniel	1	2	2		
Gabriel, Benjamin	1	2	6		
Gabriel, James	1	1	2		
Guthry, Charles	2	2	5		
Bell, James	2	2	5		
Hall, David	1	4	4		5
Moss, James	3	2	5		1
Piner, John	1	1	1		
Riggs, Isaac	1	2	1		
Moss, Joshua	3	3	3		
Dickinson, James	1	3	5		
Fodders, William	1		3		
Fodders, John, Senr	1		3		
Fodders, John, junr	1	1	4		
Davis, William	1	2	2		
Gillikin, Charles	2	3	2		
Pairtree, James	1	2	4		
Moss, Thoder	2	2	2		
Heller, Jonathan	1	1	3		
Piver, George	1		2		
Blackson, Severin	1		2		
Fulford, Stephen	1				
Moncrief, Caselton	1		1		
Fulford, Prudence		3	3		1
Simpson, Rhoster	5	2	5		3
Moss, Daniel	1		2		3
Rhease, Thomas	2	2	3	1	3

NEWBERN DISTRICT, CARTERET COUNTY—Continued.

NAME OF HEAD OF FAMILY.	Free white males of 16 years and upward, including heads of families.	Free white males under 16 years.	Free white females, including heads of families.	All other free persons.	Slaves.
Russel, John	1	1	4		
Brown, William T	1		3		
Foreman, William	1	3	2		
Riggs, Jesse	1	2	2		
Pasquinet, John	1	2	4		
Pasquinet, James	2	2	5		1
Carter, George				10	
Fodders, William	1	1	4		
Williams, William	1		2		
Parrot, James	1		3		12
Conner, George	1				
Williams, Absalom	1	1	3		
Gardner, Samuel	1				
Wallace, James	1		1		2
Cheney, Benjamin	1		2		7
Cooper, David	1	3	3		4
Fuller, Nathaniel	1	2	5		14
Gibbs, Nathaniel	1	2	4		13
Smith, Samuel	1	1	1		1
Thomson, William	1		1		14
Thomas, John	1		2		
Garrett, Ebenezer	1	1	4		
Kennedy, Elizabeth		2	3		
Henry, Joel	1	1	1		8
Watson, George	1		5		3
Love, Fanny			3		
Cooper, Peter				2	
Braddock, Peter				8	
Stanton, Joe Pie				1	
Lewis, Rosannah			1		
Jerry				3	
Ocre				5	
Lewis, Jenny			2		
Samson, junr				1	
Merrill, Arthur	1				
Picket, Cull	1	2	2		1
Chadwick, Samuel	1		1		1
Harker, Zachariah	1	3	3		5
Harker, James	1		1	1	4
Harker, Ebenezer	3		1		4
Sulivan, John	1	1	5		
Shaklefoot, James	3	1	5		2
Piner, Caleb	2		3		
Sharp, John	1	1	5		
Ellis, Freeman	2	1	5		
Brooks, John	1	3	3		
Fulford, James	1	2	1		1
Picket, Levy	1	1	2		3
Whitehouse, John	2		1		8
Whitehouse, Robert	2	2	4	1	
Gillikin, Jesse	2		4		
Gillikin, Benjamin	1	1	1		
Gillikin, George	1	1	2		
Gillikin, James	1		3		
Wade, Barney	1	1	4		
Field, Ann		1	3		
Hancock, Sarah		2	2		
White, Leah		1	4		
Lawrence, John	1	1	3		
Gillikin, Ellick	1	2	3		
Gillikin, Thomas	2	2	4		
Lawrence, Abigail	1	2	3		
Ward, David	1	1			12
Pinkum, Job	1	1	1		
Fulford, Stephen	1	3	7		5
Chadwick, James	1		3		2
Fulford, William	3	4	5		5
Pigot, Civil	2	3	3		5
Pinkum, Nathaniel	1	1	1		
Chadwick, Solomon	1	1	3		3
Rumley, Ann	1	5	2		
Arthur, Richard	1	3	3		
Arthur, Sarah			2		
Arthur, Seth	1		3		1
Simson, Joshua	1	4	3		
Simson, Robert	1	3	4		
Luster, Abel	2		3		
Waid, Toder	1		4		
Dudley, John	1	4	1		
Bell, Ross	5		2		
Waid, Abram	3		1	4	2
Picket, Culpeper	1		2		1
Hill, John	1		2		
Chadwick, Gear, Senr	3	1	4		10
Chadwick, Thomas	1	1	1		10
Chadwick, John	1	2	1		1
Chadwick, Mary			1		1
Picket, William	1	2	3		
Harris, Thomas	2		2		
Carter, John				3	
Rial, Marmaduke	1	1	2		
Jones, Adir	1	3	4		3
Jones, Ambrose	1				5
Guthry, Stephen	1	1	3		
Guthry, Samuel	2	2	4		
Guthry, Levi	1	2	4		
Hancock, Elijah	1	1	4		
Hancock, Sarah	2		3		1
Harris, John	1	1	2		
Russel, Thomas	1	1	2		
Williston, Abner	1		3		
Sipon, David	2	2	1		
Evans, John	1	2	5		
Guthry, Solomon	1	3	5		
Williston, Andrew	1	3	3		
Williston, Josiah	1	4	4		
Moor, Nathan	2	1	3		4
Pool, Matthew	2	1	5		
Waid, Valentine	5	2	6		
Davis, Isaiah	1	2	5		1
Williston, Samuel	1		4		
Harkwell, Margaret	1		2		
Moor, Thomas	2	1	5		
Williston, George	1		3		
Williston, Daniel	1	1	1		
Williston, Sophira	1	1	4		
Waid, Isaac	1	2	4		
Waid, David	1	2	4		
Fulford, Joseph	1	1	2	1	6
Fulford, John	2	1	8		7
Stewart, Alexander	1	3	3		2
Bell, Mary	1	2	2		1
Cruthers, William	1	4	3		
Davis, Joseph	3		3		
Williston, Seth	1	3	3		
Williston, Thomas	1	2	2		
Bell, George	1	2	5		16
Cratch, Richard	1	5	3		2
Ripley, William	1	2	4		
Heady, Thomas	1	2	5		
Heady, Daniel	3	2	4		
Copes, Stephen	1	1	1		
Heady, John	1	1	2		
Lewis, Thomas	2	4	3		
Bloodgood, Isaac	2	1	4		
Colbert, Matthew	2		4		
Norwood, Ann				2	
Hill, John	1	2	2		
Gillikin, Enoch	1		1		
Bell, Joseph	1	1	5		
Williston, Daniel	1	2	7		
Molbern, Samuel	1	2	1		
Howling, Christopher	1		4		
Howling, William	1		4		
Howling, Zepheniah	1	3	4		
Smith, Samuel	1		3		
Davis, William	1	1	3		
Davis, Benjamin	2	3	6		
Davis, Anthony	1		2		1
Lewis, Thomas	1		3		
Bell, Joseph	1	1	5		
Bell, Francis	1	2	4		
Nelson, Ananias	1		2		
Turner, Mary		2	3		
Morton, Ann W		1	5		
Davis, Nathan	4		1		8
Berry, Thomas	1		3		
Hill, John	1		2		
Dixon, James	2	2	2		
Roberts, John	1	2	2		
Lewis, William	1	3	3		
Huff, Richard	1	1	1		
Wallace, Robert	1	3	2		1
Willis, Joseph	1	3	4		
Robertson, William	1	1	4		
Gaskins, William	2	4	6		
Willis, Reuben	1	7	1		1
Rosemary, Joseph	1	1	1		1
Stiron, John	1		2		
Stiron, George	1	1	2		
Smith, Samuel	1	3	6		
Stiron, Samuel	2	2	5		
Stiron, John	3	2	1		
Willis, George	1	1	1		
Hill, Wise	1		1		
Mason, Joshua	2	3	5		
Bishop, Asa	3	1	5		5
Nelson, Mary			2		2
Hamilton, Robert	1	1	1		2
Hamilton, David	1		1		
Nelson, William	3	1	2		
Nelson, James	3		5		
Taylor, William	1	3	2		
Lewis, Thomas	1		3		
Gaskins, Joseph	1	7	3		3
Smith, Henry	1	1	6		
Henderson, Henry	1		5		
Barrington, John	1		2		
Salter, Richard	1	3	3		
Golding, Thomas, junr	1	2	1		
Ireland, Catherine		1	1		
Golding, Thomas, Senr	3	1	2		
Salter, Christopher	1	4	2		
Salter, Joseph	1	4	3		
Smith, Richard	1	2	4		
Salter, William	1	3	2		
Smith, William	2	2	5		
Huff, Richard, Senr	2		4		
Huff, Henry	1		1		
Smith, Thomas	3		3		
Barrington, Isaac	1		3		
Smith, Samuel	1		3		
Robinson, Allen	3	3	3		
Price, Esther			1		
Morris, Moses	2	4	2		
Fulsher, Thomas, junr	1	3	3		
Fulsher, William	1	3	2		
Fulsher, Thomas	2	2	2		
Harris, Daniel	1	2	2		
Baker, William	3	3	4		
Dannels, James	1	2	1		
Dannels, Elizabeth	1	1	2		
Ireland, David	1	2	5		
Dannels, Jacob	1	1	5		
Emery, Shadrach	1		2		
Gooding, Thomas	1	1	6		
Lupton, Christopher	2	4	3		
Philips, Manido	1	1	2		
Stiron, Samuel	2	1	5		
Stiron, Adonijah	2		1		
Stiron, Wallace	2	3	3		
Stiron, Richard	1	3	4		
Ireland, Daniel	1		3		
Tolsin, Thomas	2	3	4		
Dixon, Sylvanus	4	2	3		2
Stiron, George	1	2	5	1	
Casey, John	1	4	3		
Gaskin, John	2	2	8		3
Tolsin, Jesse	3		4		
Wallace, David, junr	3	1	1	1	1
Wallace, Robert	2	1	3		3
Wallace, David, Senr	2		3	1	16
Wallace, Joseph	1				1
Wallace, John	2				3
Williams, William	1	1	3		9
Gaskins, Adam	1	1	5		4
Salter, Henry	1		2		1
Scarborough, Thomas	1	2	1		
Scarborough, William	1	3	1		1
Gaskins, Thomas	1	3	6		3
Gaskins, John	1	2	4		1
Stiron, James	1	1	2		
Brag, Joseph	1	1	3		
Scott, James	1		2		2
Williams, John	1	1	2		1
Williams, Joseph	1		1		
Gaskins, Sarah			3		
Bragg, Jesse	1		4		
Howard, William, Senr	2	1	2		
Howard, William, Jur	2		1		
Garrish, Henry	1	1	1		
Stiron, William	1	1	7		
Stiron, Mary			2		
Howard, Cornelius	1	2	2		4
Howard, George	2	2	3		4
Neale, Francis	1	2	1		
Neale, William	1	1	4		
Neale, John	1	1	6		
Jackson, Francis, junr	1	1	2		
Jackson, Francis, Senr	4	1	4		
Dannels, Thomas	1	2	2		

NEWBERN DISTRICT, CRAVEN COUNTY.

NAME OF HEAD OF FAMILY.	Free white males of 16 years and upward, including heads of families.	Free white males under 16 years.	Free white females, including heads of families.	All other free persons.	Slaves.
Crispin, Joseph	1	2			15
Kelly, Thomas	1	1	3		11
Stiron, Wallace	1		1		6
Franklin, Joseph	2	1	2		9
Hineman, Rachel			1		
Harrington, Charles	1	1	4		
Brotin, John	1		3		
Brown, Mary		1	1		
Justice, Sylvanus	1	2	3		
Hoover, Samuel, Senr	2	2	1		
White, William	1	1	2		
Hollice, Isaac	2	2	4		1
Vendrick, Jesse	1	2	5		
Hoover, James	1	1	2		
Davis, William	2	2	4		

NEWBERN DISTRICT, CRAVEN COUNTY—Continued.

NAME OF HEAD OF FAMILY.	Free white males of 16 years and upward, including heads of families.	Free white males under 16 years.	Free white females, including heads of families.	All other free persons.	Slaves.
Jones, William	1	2	3		
Prescot, Frederic	3	3	1		
Hoover, Shadrach	6		6		
Hollice, William	3		3		
King, Thomas	1	1	3		
Broughton, Abel, Senr	1	2	2		
Broughton, Abel, junr	2	1	2		1
Atherby, Joseph	2		5		
Ackiss, Frances		1	1		
Wilson, James	1	1	1		
Harrington, James	1		2		
Franklin, Peter	1	1	2	3	8
Hudson, James	1		4		
Horseanes, Joseph	1		4		
Godfrey, Sarah	1		4		
Carpenter, George	1	1	2		2
Lawson, Samuel	1	3	3		
Stephens, Alexander	1		4		
Reed, Isaac	1		2	1	
Reed, James	1	2	3		
Vendrick, William	1		1		
Vendrick, Alice		1	4		5
Atherby, Isaac	1				1
West, Joseph	2	1	4		2
Perkins, Jonathan	1	2	3		7
Vendrick, Ann	1		5		
Bradley, Daniel	1	1			
Lewis, Nehemiah	1	1	4		
Riding, Benjamin	1	1	3		
Vendrick, Abram	1	2	2		
Franklin, Thomas	1	4	4		
Vendrick, Peter	1	1	3		
Vendrick, John	2	1	5		
Simpkins, Joseph, Senr	1	1	3		
Simpkins, Joseph, junr	1	1	1		1
Simpkins, Daniel	1	1	2		1
Ince, John	1				
Cox, William	1	1	5		
Hewkins, Hardy	1		1		1
Neale, Matthew	1	1	3		11
Hoover, Samuel, junr	1	2	1		
Hoover, Samuel, Senr	1		3		
Hollice, Hezekiah	1		1		
Whitly, William	1	3	3		
Neale, Barry	1				
Nichols, James	1	2	2		
Harper, Thomas	1		6		
Hoover, John	1	1	3		2
Miller, James	2		2		
Dixon, Joseph	1				
Hoover, Jacob	1		3		
Edgington, William	1	1	2		
Higgins, Cormick	1			2	
Hineman, Michael	3		1		7
Masters, Joseph	1	4	4	1	13
McLinn, Charles	3	2	4		63
James, Charles	2		2		5
Mason, Benjamin	1	3	2	1	4
Caraway, Francis	1	1	4		4
Young, Robert	1	1	5		12
Holley, James	1		1		
Ferguson, Mark	1				
Whitehouse, William	2	2	3		
Grover, George	1	1	2		3
Pitman, Thomas	3	2	4		2
Culley, Francis	1	2	4		
Cummins, John	2	1	1		1
Parsons, Thomas	1				
Oliver, Samuel	1	5	2	1	
Ferguson, Slocum	1	2	5		1
Cummins, Benjamin	1	2	5		
Martin, John	1		3		
Northon, John	1	1	3		
Royal, Daniel	1	4	4		
Neale, Daniel	1				
Wallace, Richard M	1	2	3		3
Nelson, Thomas	1	5	1		8
Wallace, Benjamin	1	3	5		
Mason, Joseph	1	1	1		
Masters, Thomas	1	2	3		
Holley, Richard	1	1	2		
Harper, Robert	1				
Smith, Benjamin	1				
Smith, Humphrey	1	3	1		
Messick, Hopkins	1	1	2		
Bragg, William	1	2	5		
Hamilton, John, junr	1				
Hamilton, John, Senr	2	3	2		11
Sampson, Avin	1	2	1		
Allison, William	1	2	2		3
Wallace, Robert	3	4	3		
Pitman, Joseph	1				
Wilkinson, Richard	1	1	2		
Jones, James	1	1	3		2
Wright, John	1		2		
Nelson, J. S.	1				
Tigner, Thomas	1		4		
Whitus, Elias N	1		2		
Clark, Severin	1	1	3		2
Cook, Zaphirah	1	3	4		
Smith, Daniel	1	1	2		
Biggs, William, junr	1		3		
Biggs, William, Senr	1	1	3		
Boyd, William	1	1	1		
Carraway, Edward	1	3	1	2	
Sparrow, Henry	1	2	2		4
Chance, Richard	1	2	1		
Smith, Joseph	1	1	1		
Whitus, Samuel	1		2		
Cutrall, John	1	1	2		2
Moss, Joseph	1				
Hamilton, Michael	1			1	
Godfrey, Sarah	1		3		
McHains, Stephen	3		4		
Wallace, Archibald	1		2		
Sparrow, Paul	1	3	5		9
Quinney, Stephen	1	1	2		
Gilbert, William	1		3		
Williams, Samuel	1	1	3		
Jones, John	1				
Whitus, Reuben	1				
Wallace, Benjamin, junr	1				
Cooke, Samuel	1	2	4		4
Houston, James	1				
Houston, Francis	1		4		4
Merona, J. O	1				
James, Isaac	1		1		
James, Richard	1	1	1		
Scapp, Israel	1		1		
Guard, Joshua	1	2	3		
West, Gabriel	1				
Jones, William	1				
Barnes, Thomas	2	1	3		
Ferguson, Adam	2	1	4		
Leverin, John	1				
Parsons, John	2		2	1	
James, Hovinton	1				
Burney, Joseph	1				
Day, John	1	3	3		
Walker, Mark	1				
Cullen, Nehemiah	2		1		2
Jackson, Daniel	1				
Masters, Enoch	1	1	2		1
Pitman, Southy	1				
Summons, John	2	1	2		
Hamilton, James	1		1		
Wade, Richard	3	1	3	1	
Pitman, Obadiah	1		1		
Rew, Southy I	1		2		2
Bryan, Elizabeth	1		2		7
Wilkinson, David	4	2	2		1
Lovick, Richard, Senr	3	1	4		4
Carter, Abel					7
George, William					10
Mitchel, Benjamin					3
Simmons, Samuel				5	1
Godet, Peter					1
Gregory, John				2	
Godet, John				2	
Dukes, Peter	1	3	2		
Ostean, Reuben	1	1	2		
Parsons, Thomas	2		2		
Priestley, Amy		5	3		
Stanton, John	1		4		
Cottle, William	1	2	3		
Johnston, Henry	2	2	2		2
Hill, Peter	2	1	4		
Mason, John	1		5		
Freebody, John	4				4
Cooke, Thomas	1	1	2		5
Thomas, John	1	4	2		
Thomas, Abner	1				
Collins, Alice		1	3		3
Jones, Lovick	1	3	3		13
Benners, John	3	7	7		85
Carney, John	2	2	4		13
Pritchard, Edward	1		1		6
Dew, Joseph	1	2	8		
Howard, Horton	1	1			26
Jones, Roger, Senr	3	4	1		18
Chance, Esther			2		
Rothburn, Jacob	1		2		
Carter, Joshua				4	
Wilson, Thomas	1			3	
Neale, Elizabeth	1		4	1	
Copes, Jacob					16
James, Charity		1	4		9
Jones, James, Senr	1	2	5		7
Wallace Stephen	2	3	2		1
Blair, Moses	1	1	3		
Dixon, George	2	1	3		
Pitman, James	1	1			
Finnikin, James	1		3		
Thomas	1		4		
Wallace, Robin, junr	1		5		
Thomas, Reuben	1	1	2		
Steward, Andrew	2	2	1		
Cummins, Lurenah		1	2		2
Turner, Frederick	1	1	2		
Samson, James	2	1	2		
Casey, Thomas	1	4	3		
Bragg, Solomon	1	2	3		1
Hall, Simon	2	2	5		4
Bragg, John	2	2	6		9
Godet, Ann			6		
Neale, Philip	1	2	3		6
Rew, Southy	3	4	4		13
Wilson, David	1	1	3		
Wilson, Ephraim	1		1		
Morris, Dinah		1	2		
Shapley, Mary		2	2		
Moor, Deborah				3	
Williams, John	1		1		
Crew, Thomas	1		2		2
Spaight, Richard D	1		3		71
Simpson, John	2				8
Frilick, Joseph	1				
Smith, Nathan	3		1	1	25
Lindsey, Elizabeth		1	4	1	2
Young, Richard	1				
Bartlett, William	1			1	
Ellis, Richard	1				6
Kennedy, John	1				6
Stephenson, James	1				
Tomlinson, Thomas	1		1		4
Donald, Robert	1		2		7
Simonton, Sarah		1	2		
Ellis, James	1		4		7
Scranton, John	1		1		5
McAuslan, Alexander	1		1		3
Macken, Henry	1		3		2
Jenkins, John	1	1			
Pendleton, Sylvester, Senr	2		3	1	2
Ferrill, Elizabeth	1		2	1	6
McKinley, James	6		1		6
Tinker, Stephen	1	1	4		7
Forker, John	1		2		1
Good, William	1	1	1		10
Saunders, Mary	1	1	4	1	5
Smallwood, John	2	1	1		5
Davis, Thomas	1		2	1	
Moor, Dinah				3	
Mackey, Isaac	2			2	2
Inloes, Abram	1			1	
Inloes, Anthony	4				
Low, William	1		3		
Ramsey, John	1	2	2		
Kellum, James	1				
Levingston, Henry	1	2	3		
Levingston, Samuel	1		1		
White, Cato				7	
Black, Letitia				3	
Barrington, James	2	2	4		
Ambrose, David	1	1	1		1
McQuin, Thomas	2	1	2		
Stringer, Doll				4	
Stringer, Thomas				2	
Kelly, Joseph				2	
Bryan, John C	1	2	4		8
Custis, Thomas	1	1	3		
Sealey, Martha			2		3
Hatfield, Robert	2		2		2
Dunn, Samuel	2				4
Ventures, Michael	1		2		2
Wade, Joseph	1		4		
Taylor, Mary		1	3		
Smuch, William	1		3		
Pendleton, Sylvester, Junr	1	3	1		1
Potter, Edward	2		2	1	2
Anthony, William	1	2	2		1
Gilespie, Lydia			2		1
St Leger, De	1		3		1
Goodhue, Samuel	1		4		1
Hill, Ann			3		
Little, James	2	2	3		2
West, Stephen	1	1	3		6
Gainer, William	1		3		1
Johnston, Francis	1	1	1		
Scarborough, Nathaniel					
Landmeyer, Frederick	3	1			2
Tisdale, Nathan	1				
Harris, John	1		1	6	3
Gerock, Samuel	3	1	2		7
Morrison, John	3	2	2		1
Justice, Rebecca		2	2		11
Harriot, James	1	2	2		
Turner, Philip	1	2	3		7
Chapman, Samuel	1		2		3
Durand, Ann		2	4		1
Cheek, Thomas L	1	3	2		1
McAlpin, Margaret			3		5
Halling, Solomon	1		3		1
Trippe, William	3	2	3		1

NEWBERN DISTRICT, CRAVEN COUNTY—Continued.

NAME OF HEAD OF FAMILY.	Free white males of 16 years and upward, including heads of families.	Free white males under 16 years.	Free white females, including heads of families.	All other free persons.	Slaves.
Martin, Francis Xavier.	2				1
Chaponelle, Joseph.	1			1	2
Stephens, Mary.		2	2		1
Dugnie, Alexander.	2	1	1		5
Purss, Henry.	1		3		7
Ellis, George.	1				
Thomson, Justice.	1				
Carney, James.	3	1	4	1	7
Johnston, William.	1	2	2		6
Hunley, Richard.	1		2		8
Mitchel, William.	1		1	1	2
Hawley, William.	3	1	2		7
Devereux, John.	3		1		3
Hunt, Robert.	1		2		2
Hardy, Margaret.		2	2		2
Wining, John.	1				
Creusy, Jonathan.	1				
Urquhart, John.	3	1	2		1
Tagert, Joseph.	5				1
Kean, Edward.	1				1
McMains, James.	2	3	2		4
Parker, John.	2	1	1		
Savano, Lewis.	1		1		1
Graham, Robert.	1		2		1
Terry, David.	1		4		
Gooding, Samuel.	1	1	1		
Brightman, James.	1		2		2
Steele, Thomas.	1		2		
Haslen, Elizabeth.			4		17
Stewart, Alexander.	1		1		2
Haslen, Thomas.	2	1	1		9
Stringer, Minge.				2	
Myers, Jacob.	1			1	
Moor, Jenny.				2	
McCafferty, James.	2		3		6
Barrington, John.	2		3	1	3
Dudley, William.	1		3	1	5
Bagnall, Benjamin.	1		2		
Gibbs, William.	1	1			4
Smith, John Frink.	1	2	4		16
Guion, Isaac.	2	2	5		7
Macgrath, John.	1	2	3		1
Duffy, George.	2		5		2
Henry, William.	1	1	1		17
Haines, Henry Pendergras.	1			1	1
Sears, Ann.	1	1	3		
Cooke, Jacob.	2	2	3		4
Gill, Catherine.			6	1	3
Sitgreaves, John.	1	1	1	1	23
Pasteur, Edward.	1	1	3		9
Sitgreaves, John.			3		2
Bryan, John.	1		1		1
Conner, John.	2			1	
Moor, Drucilla.				1	1
Craddock, John.	1	2	3		5
Rhodes, Malicah.	1		1		
Tisdale, William.	1	1	3		3
Powers, Jerry.				5	
Fulford, Sarah.			3		2
Coor, James.	1		2		9
Slade, William.	1	1	4		7
Dailey, Thomas.	2		1		
Burney, Sarah.		4	2		2
Cox, Thomas.	2	1	2		11
Heath, Mary.		1	4	1	10
Williams, John.	1	1	2	1	3
Russel, Ann.				1	1
McLure, William.	1	2	1		27
Cole, Jane.			1		
Coleman, Samuel.	1		2		
Palmer, Philip.	1	1	2		
Stanley, James.	1	1	3		
Turner, Thomas.	2	4	2		77
Hiet, George.	1		2		
Lewis, William.	1				
Williams, William.	1		1		1
Delonay, John.	1				
Woods, Benjamin.	1				
Bryan, Jesse.	1	3	5	1	20
Leech, Joseph.	2		1		15
McDowal, William.	2	2	2		1
Witherspoon, David.	1	1	6		113
Muckleroy, Thomas.				3	
Edgar, William.	1	2	1	2	
Teer, William.	1	1	3		
Field, Rachel.		3	1		
Alexander, Enoch.	1	3	2		5
Hyde, Luther.	1	1	4		1
Willis, Abel.	1		1		
Thomson, James.	2				
Hanson, William.	1		1	1	1
Stewart, James.	1	1			11
Grim, Philip.	1				
Allen, John.				4	2
De Bretighe, Marquis.	1		1		1
Linn, Volant.	2	1	3		
Henrion, Peter.	3				2
Thomague, —.	1				2
Rich, Rebecca.	1	1	2		1
Dorsey, Walter.	1		2	2	1
Shepard, William.	1				4
Tomlinson, Elizabeth.			1		
Manning, Pierce.	1				1
Lawrence, William.	1				
York, James.				1	
Hurley, John.	3	1	2		
Poddy, Hannah.			3		
Cupps, William.	1		2		
Harvey, John.	1	1			2
Forbes, Richard.	1	1	2	1	6
Vultius, George.	1		2		2
Chuyler, John.	1				4
Lawrence, William.	2		3		4
Gaston, Margaret.		1	3		30
Lewis, Abby.				4	
Trigler, Richard.	2	2	1		
Montague, Jane.	1	1	4		
Marshall, Mary.			3		2
Carthy, Daniel.	1				1
Tinker, Edward.	4	3	6		4
Hobday, John.	1	1	2		2
Clark, Joseph.	1	1	3		9
Pudril, Richard.	1		1		
Butler, Temperance.	1				
Biggleston, Ann C.			1		7
Webber, Ann.	2		1		
Mansfield, John.	1	3	3		
Dowdin, William.	2				
Oliver, Joseph.	1	3	2		14
McAlep, Archibald.	1				
Cain, Alexander.			2		3
Hart, Mary.		2	2		4
Adams, Mary.			3		
Johnston, Esther.	1	1	2		15
Ducksworth, Mary.			1		
Hannis, William.	1	1	4	1	7
Cohun, John.	2	2	2		
Stephenson, Stephen.	1	1	2		1
Fairfield, Reuben.	3				
Lowthorp, Francis.	6	1	3	1	11
Cogdell, Lydia.			2		4
Vail, Sarah.			3		22
Green, Margaret.			2		1
Bruce, James.	1	2	2		1
Gooding, Nancy.			1		
Calaven, Hannah.			2		
Dick, Merion.			2		
Buxton, Jarvis.	1		3	2	2
Collins, Matthew.	1	1	2		
Hudrell, Daniel.	1				
Green, John.	1	1	1		11
Paxton, William.	2		1		4
Clements, Frederick.	1		1		1
Tolman, Phobe.			1		1
Shute, Joseph.	1	1	1		7
Pearson, Thomas Wheelwright.	1				2
Tinker, Euphamy.			3		1
Cook, Silas.	1	2	1		1
Reading, Jeremiah.	1		2		1
Cutting, Leonard.	2	1	1		2
Sandy, James.	1	3	5		2
Daves, John.	1	1	4		23
Bowers, Saul.				3	
Potter, Sarah.			2		
Wrinsford, Mary.			3		1
Snead, Wilson.	1	1	2		1
Barry, John.	1				
Arnold, Margaret.			1		
Ambrose, Nancy.			1		
Cosway, Abigail.		1	1		
Cutting, James.	1				
Reed, Elizabeth.		1	2		
Almond, John.	1				
Moore, William.	1				3
Griffin, Moses.	1		2		2
Dunn, William.	3	3	2		2
Parsons, Jeremiah.	2	3	3		4
Ives, William.	1	3	5		
Dunn, Stephen.	1	1	2		2
Ives, John.	2	2	3		
Stephens, Matthew.	1	3	3		
Row, Benjamin.	1	3	3		3
Henry, David.	1	3	3		
Taylor, John.	1	1	2		
Anderson, William.	1	2	2		5
Always, Obadiah.	4	1	4	2	
Austin, Thomas.	1	1	2		1
Bailey, John.	1	1	2		4
Bishop, John.	1		2		
Bradshaw, Thomas.	3	2	3		
Booty, Nicholas.	2		3		
Blanks, John.	1	3	2		14
Binum, Arthur.	1	1	3		
Dunn, John.	1		1		
Davis, William.	1		2		12
Davis, James.	2		2		12
Ellis, Michael.	1		2		
Evans, Thomas.	1		1		4
Ervin, James.	1				
Flibus, Archibald.	1		3		1
Foye, Frederick.	2	2	1		29
Fooks, John.	1	3	1		1
Fooks, Joseph.	1		1		
Foster, Bazel.	1		3		
Foster, Philemon.	1	2	2		
Fosque, Richard.	1	1	1		
Fosque, Luke.	1	1	3		
Fulsher, Levy.	1	1	1		10
Holland, Joseph.	1				
Givin, Rolin.	1				
Knox, John.	1		2		12
Holland, Philemon.	1				
Holland, William.	1				1
Foster, William S.	1		1		10
Hampton, Thomas.	1	3	2		
Hampton, William.	1	3	1		1
Hancock, Roger.	1			1	
Hancock, Evan.	1			6	
Heath, John.	2	1	1		
Ives, Hardy.	1		5		
Ives, Thomas P.	1	1	3		1
Jones, James.	1				
Jones, Roger.	1	2	1	1	5
Johnston, Robert.	1	2	2		
Jones, Evan.	1		2	1	6
Kincey, William.	1	3	1		
Lovick, George.	1		1	1	18
Lovick, Thomas.	1				12
Murphy, Edward.	1	2	3	1	
Morgan, Edward.	2		1		
Merchant, Christopher.	1	1	1		
Potter, James.	1	1	1		2
Porter, Thomas.	2		4		
Porter, John.	1				
Parsons, Thomas.	1	1	3		2
Physic, Peter.	3	2	4		11
Moor, Margaret.				5	
Smith, Richard.	3	1	1		
Norwood, Fanny.		1	2		
Smith, Thomas.	1	2	4		
Smith, Malica.	1	1	1		
Smith, Jesse.	2		2		
Edmundson, Bryan.	1				
Tolsin, John.	1	2	3		
Tolsin, Benjamin.	1		3		
Tolsin, Thomas.	1		1		
Tolsin, George.	1				
Tolsin, Benjamin.	1		2		
Thomsin, Thomas.	1				1
Whitehead, John.	1				
Whitehead, James.	1	2	1		
Whitehead, George.	1	2	2		
Williams, Richard.	1	1	7		
Winn, William.	1	1	4		6
Upton, Major.	1		2		
Yates, John B.	4	1	3		
Jones, Moses.	1				
Collins, Shadrach.	1				
Jones, Bartholomew.	1		2		
Hancock, John.	1		2		1
Boin, William.	1	3	2		
Taylor, John.	3	2	3		1
Brittain, Catherine.		5	3		2
Turner, John.	1		1		3
Sykes, Jacob.	1	3	3		1
Cobin, Daniel.	1				
Pitman, John.	3	1	2		
Tooley, Adam.	2		1	1	9
Henry, Stephen.	1	1	1		
Caviner, Bryan.	2		1		
Dunn, Elizabeth.			1		2
Hickman, Richard.	1	2	4		
Hickman, Thomas.	1				1
Fisher, Elizabeth.		2	2		
Caviner, Sarah.			3		
Ogilsby, John.	1		1		
Fosque, Elias.			2		1
Chambers, Lavinia.		1	2		
Reasonover, Elizabeth.			2		
Carter, Isaac.				5	
Perkins, Isaac.				2	
Dove, William.				9	
Perkins, George.				4	
Dove, Pompey.				1	2
Dove, Nelly.				2	
Heath, William.	2	1	6		
Styron, Samuel.	2	1	2		
Jones, Charles.	2	4	3	1	2
Wolfe, Hannah.			1		2

NEWBERN DISTRICT, CRAVEN COUNTY—Continued.

NAME OF HEAD OF FAMILY.	Free white males of 16 years and upward, including heads of families.	Free white males under 16 years.	Free white females, including heads of families.	All other free persons.	Slaves.
Holton, Jesse	1	2	2	1	1
Moss, Joseph	1	1	1		
Hampton, Mary	1		3		
Givin, Henry	2		5		
Dowdy, Richard	1	2	6		
Rieves, Courtney	2	4	2		
Hall, Rachel			3		
Taylor, Absalom	1	1	3		
Singleton, Spyers	1	2	5		18
Lofton, Joseph	1		1		12
Bishop, James	1	1	5		
Bishop, Joseph	1	3	1		2
Jessup, Isaac					11
Hamilton, James	3	1	3	1	3
Foster, John	2	2	4		
Davis, Thomas	1				
Jones, Lewis	1	3	3		10
Bryan, Edward	1		2		12
Dubberly, Saccor	2	1	3		5
Dubberly, John	1	2	4		
Anderson, Thomas	1		1		
Oliver, Solomon	2	1	5		
James, John	1		4		
James, Charles	1				
Dubberly, William	1	2	1		
Felingims, Robert	2	3	3		
Anderson, Jonas	1	4	3		
Roundtree, Moses	1	3	2		1
Atherby, John	3	4	6		
Green, Thomas	2		4		1
Mitchel, Elizabeth	3	2	6		9
Anderson, John	2	1	2		
Phips, William	2	1	3		1
Marshal, Charles	1		7		8
King, Mary	1	4	3		2
Willis, Francis	1	3	4		2
James, Sarah	1	3	2		
Anderson, Peter	4		2		
Murphy, William	4	1	6		5
Cannon, Edward	3	1	2		
Cooper, Martha		2	8		
Jarrel, William	1	1	2		
Smith, William	1		2		
Harris, Stephen	1		2		6
Smith, John	1	1	2		
Tootle, Phoebe	2		4		
West, John	1	1	2	1	10
Duncan, Thomas	1				
Morning, William H	1		1		
Willis, John	1	1	1		2
Causway, Philip	2	1	1		1
Bull, Micaja	1		1		
Tyre, Jesse	1	1	6		
Tant, Thomas	1	1	2		
Chance, Moses	1				
Palmer, Jacob	1	2	1		
Philingim, Samuel	1	3	3		1
Mitchel, William	1	1	2		
Gwartney, John	1		1		
Cooper, James	1	4	2		
Lane, Isaac	1	1	1		
Philingim, John	3	4	3		1
Phips, Joseph	1	1	1		
Worth, Thomas	3	1	7		
Philips, Jacob	1	2	5		
Warren, Jacob	1	4	4		1
Hafford, Malicah	1	3	4		
James, Jeremiah	1	1	3		3
Palmer, Elijah	1	1	3		
Allen, John	1	1	3		27
Tyre, Major	1	1	1		
Gaskins, Harmon	2	4	3		
Taylor, Charles	1	5	4		
Taylor, Jesse	1				
Fillingim, Benjamin	1	1	5		
Charlton, George	2	1	4		
Averite, John	1	3	5		
Butler, Charles	1		4		
McIntosh, James	2		2		
Kemp, Isaac	1	2	2		
Anderson, Thomas	1	2	6		
Curtis, Thomas	1	1	5		3
Gatlin, Shadrach	1	2	3		3
Butler, Arthur	1	2	4		
Allen, John	2	3	5		1
Charlton, William	1	1	1		
Jarrell, Lewis	1		3		
Smith, William	1				
Smith, James	1		4		
Cox, Joseph	1	3	1		
Green, Thomas	1	2	1		18
Herritage, William	1	4	2		28
Lovick, William	2				13
Hollaway, John	4	2	3		6
Johnston, William	1				
Lambert, Moses	2	1	5		
Clements, Thomas	1	1	5		3

NAME OF HEAD OF FAMILY.	Free white males of 16 years and upward, including heads of families.	Free white males under 16 years.	Free white females, including heads of families.	All other free persons.	Slaves.
Swann, Evan	3		3		2
Green, John	1		3		7
Wise, Thomas	1		2		3
Heath, William	1				3
Lofton, Joseph	1	2	1		1
Lofton, Longford	1	2	2		
Lofton, Thomas	1	1	4		
Carman, William, Senr	2	1	1		3
Green, Furnifold, junr	1				12
Lane, Frederic	1	1	1		16
Prier, Samuel	1	1	2		
Gilstrap, Peter	2	1	6		
Mastin, Jeremiah	1		1		6
Gatlin, Thomas	3	5	4		11
Gooding, John	4	4	2		12
Slade, Ebenezer	2	3	4		2
Beesley, John	1	3	3		
Cormack, Lydia	1		2		
Slade, Mary		2	5		8
McKoye, Willis, Senr	3	1	3		
Beazley, Solomon	3	1	3		1
White, David	1		1		
McKoye, Edward	1				
McKoye, Willis, junr	1				
Miller, Mary	2	2	2		
Beezley, Elisha	1	1	2		
Fonvielle, Francis, Senr	2	5	1		14
Fonvielle, Francis, junr	1	2	2		
Anderson, Isaac	1	2	2		
Nucum, Edward	2		4		
Melonay, William	1	2	1		
Taylor, James	1	3	5		
White, Mary	2		1		4
Atlin, Keziah			1	3	1
Green, Furnifold, Senr	1		1		12
Daly, John	1	1	3		34
Bryan, William	2	1	7		36
Bryan, Hardy	1		1		22
Allen, Jonathan	1		2		1
Butler, Moses	2	3	3		
Bryan, George	1	4	4		5
Buchanan, William	1	3	2		
Doherty, Daniel	1	2	2		2
Doherty, Robert	1	1	2		
Fannin, John	1		2		
Gilstrap, Richard	1	1	1		
Green, Leah			2		24
Hall, Joseph, Senr	2	1	2		1
Smith, John	2		2		
Hammons, Charles	3	1	4		
Hall, Thomas	1	4	2		
Hall, Joseph, junr	1		4		(*)
Hill, William	2	3	5		
Heath, Frederic	1	5	4		
Lane, Daniel	2	2	5		
McKoye, William	2	2	2		5
McKoye, Gideon	1	1	2		1
Oliver, Thomas	1	2	2		5
Streets, Nathan	1	3	3		1
Taylor, Moses, Senr	3	3	3		
Taylor, Moses, junr	1		2		
Willis, Joel	1	3	2		
Wingit, Mary		2	3		
White, Benjamin, junr	1		3		
White, Whichc	1	3	5		
Roberts, Patience			2		
White, Agnes		1	4		
Sivils, John	1		2		
White, Benjamin, Senr	3	2	3		
Doherty, Mary			2		
Doherty, Ephraim	1	1	1		
Taylor, Susannah			2		
Spelman, Jenny					3
Newcombe, Jemima	2		4		
Fruit, William, junr	1		2		
Darby, John	1				
Prevat, Thomas	1		1		
White, Vincent	1				
Hutchins, James	1	1	2		1
Fruit, William, Senr	1		2		
Peete, Thomas	1		2		
Whitfield, Constance	1		3		25
Barney, Ashley		2	2		
Green, Elizabeth		3	2		
Cox, William	2	3	2		8
Smith, William	1	1	2		
Prior, Thomas	1		2		
Gardner, William	2	2	2		2
Lane, John	3	1	3		3
Heath, Thomas	4	1	6	1	
Randal, Nehemiah	1	4	4		
Pierce, Thomas, junr	1	2	2		
Pierce, Thomas, Senr	1	1	6		1
Doherty, Absalom	1		5		
Doherty, Richard	1	1	4		
Prescot, Austin	1	1	2		
Prescot, John	2	1	5		

NAME OF HEAD OF FAMILY.	Free white males of 16 years and upward, including heads of families.	Free white males under 16 years.	Free white females, including heads of families.	All other free persons.	Slaves.
Hawkins, Willowby	1	1	2		
West, Daniel	1	2	3		4
Cormack, John, Junr	1		2		
Fruit, Levy	1	2	5		
Jones, William	3	1	4		3
Jones, Thomas	3		1		
Carlton, Elizabeth	2	3	4		
Clark, William	1		3		
Kent, Levy	1		4		
West, William	2	2	3		
Russel, Malicah	1	2	4		3
West, Levy	1		1		1
Heath, James	1	1	2		
Heath, Christopher	2		3		3
Heath, Richard	1	1	2		
Doherty, William	1	1	2		
Heath, Stephen	2	4	2		
Heath, Rigdon	1		2		1
Moye, Elijah	1	1	3		
Griffin, William	1	3	2		
Lewis, Frederic	1	2	4		
Tyre, Ann	1	1	1		4
Prevat, Sarah	1	1	5		
Smith, Sarah		2	2		1
Carlton, Fereby		2	1		
Watson, Richard	1	2	4		
Watson, Neal, Senr	3		2		6
Rheam, Jacob	2	5	4		24
Watson, Neal, junr	1		3		
Kilpatrick, Wary	1	3	3		11
Watson, Benjamin	1	2	2		
Bryan, Isaac	2	6		1	18
Cox, Hezekiah	1		3		
Lane, William	1	2	2		
Lambert, Samuel	3	1	2		
Griffin, Benjamin	1	2	4		1
West, Elizabeth		3	3		
Prier, David	2		3	1	
Philips, Rose		1	1		
Bryan, David	2	4	4		
Cormack, John	2	3	2		
Heath, Henry	2	3	4		
Sherrod, Joseph	1		7		
Kent, Samuel	1	1	2		1
Kent, Margaret		1	2		
Lofton, Shadrach	1	1	3		8
Broadway, Jesse	1		3		
Williams, Tolbert	1	1	4		1
West, John	3		4		2
Tyre, Lewis	1	1	2		
Heath, John	1	2	4		
Broadway, James	1		3		
Cormack, Joab	1	1	3		
Arnold, James	1		3		
Doherty, Daniel	1		1		5
Carlton, Richard	1	1	2		
Cox, John	2	1	1		10
Cox, Ann			2		1
West, John	1		2		1
Gibbs, Richard	3		2		1
Heath, Henry	1		2		
Doherty, Owen	3	2	4		
Whittington, Solomon	1	1	4		
Heath, Reuben	1		1		
Wadsworth, Jonathan	1	2	2		2
Wadsworth, William	1		2		1
Mits, Frederic	1	3	3		
Rogers, William	2	1	5		4
Wise, John	1	2	3		
Cormack, Solomon	1		6		
Lambert, Ann			2		
Morris, Thomas	1	2	4		9
Jackson, Mary	1		3		
Gilstrap, James	1		1		
Ebins, Elizabeth			1		
Tyre, Thomas	1	3	1		1
Coleman, Thomas	1	2	4		7
Allen, Joseph	2	4	6		19
MacLevain, Francis	3		1		9
Fish, Thomas	3	3	7		2
Browning, Hannah			3		
Kennedy, John	1	1	4		
Davis, Brisgow	2		2		
Clark, Isaac	1	2	3		
Bentley, William	1	1	4		
Peters, Elizabeth	1		5		
Philips, Thomas, junr	1	4	5		8
Arthur, Lawson	1		3		
Blount, Reading	1		3		2
Sears, John	2		2		
Davis, John	1	2	1		
Davis, Lawson	2	4	6		
Smith, John	1	4	4		
Philips, John	2	3	3		16
Wiggins, John	1	2	4		
Moor, William	1	2	3		1
Kittrell, Jethro	1				

* Illegible.

NEWBERN DISTRICT, CRAVEN COUNTY—Continued.

NAME OF HEAD OF FAMILY.	Free white males of 16 years and upward, including heads of families.	Free white males under 16 years.	Free white females, including heads of families.	All other free persons.	Slaves.
Kittrell, Joseph	1				
Harrison, Joseph	1	3	3		
Trife, Ebenezer	1	2	3		
Hardison, James	2	1	4		
Roundtree, William	1	3	2		1
Philip, Thomas, Senr	2	2	5		
Roundtree, Francis, Senr	2		1		1
Frizzell, Jonathan	1	1	7		11
Hutchins, Edward	1	1	3		1
Clark, Edward	2		2		
Coleman, James	1	2	2		1
Dotson, Benjamin	1				
King, Brittain	1	1	5		2
Jones, Walter	2		1		2
Spiva, Moses	1	5	4		
Holland, James	1				
Dwans, John	1	3	3		
Clark, David	1				
Jones, William	1	2	4		2
Jones, Thomas	1				6
Jordan, William	3	1	2		
Pool, James	1	3	1		
Philips, Richard	1	2	1		
Coker, Hardy	1	3	2		
Roundtree, Francis, junr	1				
Warnum, John	1	3	2		
Kitrell, Jonathan	1	3	7		4
Williams, Ann		2	3		4
Philips, James	1	3	2		
Moor, James	1	1	3		
Jones, Thomas	1				
Jones, Richard	1		1		2
Wheathering, Robert	2	5	4		2
Branton, Samuel	2	2	3		1
Wheathington, Ambrose	1				
Lines, William	1		2		1
Stanley, Ephraim	1		2		1
Bryan, John	1		1		14
Bryan, William	1	1	1		11
Lewis, Elisha	1	2	4		
Lewis, Mary	1		3		
Nelson, Rebecca	1		1		
Roach, Charles	3	3	3		8
Tire, John	1		5		
Mills, Anthony	1	1	3		
Pollard, Thomas	1	1	3		
Butler, John	1	4	4		
Ottison, Malicah	1		3		
Phillingim, Jarvis	1	2	3		1
Hartley, Joseph	2	2	3		2
Nelson, George	1	4	3		
Hill, John	1	2	5		3
Nelson, William	2		3		
Pierce, David	1	1	2		6
Bryan, Lewis	1		2		19
Nelson, John	3		1		
Harrington, Jonathan	1	2	4		
Nelson, Edward	1		3		1
Nelson, Levi	1	1	2		
Chapman, Jesse	1	2	3		2
Kennedy, William	1				
Ball, Elizabeth		2	4		2
Campbell, Joseph	3	2	3		2
James, Joseph	2	3	4		
Worsley, Stephen	3	3	3		5
Johnston, Charles	1	2	2		
Bond, John	2	1	3		
Allen, Walter	1	2	2		5
Williams, William	2		1		
Williams, Solomon	1				
Lancaster, Benjamin	2	2	3		
Chapman, Freelove			1		5
Laughinghouse, Rd Ripley	1	2	1		
Clark, James	1	4	4		1
Johnston, Frederic	1		1		5
Williams, John	1		2		
James, Jeremiah	1		2		
Pollard, Frederic	1	3	1		
Bryan, Darby	1	1	4		
Winnum, Stephen	1	1	2		
Tant, William	1		2		
King, Joel	3	1	7		
Hays, William	3	3	5		
Willis, Isaac	1				
Denmark, James	1		1		
Fornes, Thomas	1	1	2		2
Mills, John	1	1	3		
Chapman, Weeks	1	3	6		6
Mills, Anthony	4	2	6		
McKinney, Isaac	1		4		8
Warren, Horsington	1	3	3		
Taylor, John	1	2	3		
Williams, Benjamin	1		4		
Otterson, Caleb	2		4		
Pierce, Benjamin	1	1	2		4
Harris, John	3	1	3		11
Hays, William	1	1	2		
Arnold, Elizabeth			1		
Mitchel, Sarah		2	2		
Hagins, Frazer		2	1		
King, Mary			2		
Gatlin, James	1	2	3		13
Lewis, William	1		4		1
Spyers, John, Junr	1	1	2		
Spyers, John, Senr	1		2		
Warren, Jeremiah	3	1	4		
Hendrix, Nathan	1	4	2		1
Lawley, William	1	2	5		
Bright, Stockl	1				13
Winnum, Sarah					3
Bright, John	1	2	1		
Warren, Henry	1	2	3		
Wiggins, Samuel	2	2	4		1
McAfity, James	2	2	2		3
Palmer, Joseph	2	3	6		24
Johnston, Jacob	4		4		12
Richardson, William	1		3		
Bryan, Danl	1				
Gatlen, Hardy	1		3		14
Arnold, Moses	1	4	2		4
Arnold, Aaron	1	1	2		54
Ives, James	1		2		
Willis, Neomy		2	3		1
Thomas, Evan	1	1	4		
Whitford, Thomas	1	2	5		1
Gatlin, John, Senr	1	3	5		
Asque, James	2		2		
Hypock, John, junr	1	1	1		
Evernton, John	1				
Evernton, Ezekiel	1	4	1		
Gatlin, John, junr	1				
Arthur, Joseph	1		3		
Evernton, William	1	2	1		
King, Harrington	1	1	6		
King, William	1				
Gaskins, John	1		2		
Hypock, Arthur	1				
Hypock, Peter	1	2	4		
Pierce, Mary	1	4	3		
Hill, Richard	1		2		1
Rowe, Elizabeth					
Rowe, John	1				
Rowe, Edmund	1				
Whitford, Richard	1	4	2		1
Stilly, Stephen	1				
Stilly, Ishmael	1	1	1		
Willis, Caleb	1	5	4		1
Willis, Richard	1	1	4		4
Willis, Joshua	1	3	7		
Hill, Francis	1				
Warren, Abram	1	1	2		1
Willis, James, Senr	1	1	4		5
Cuttrell, Amos	2	3	3		
Norton, Tomsey		2	3		
Hill, William	2	2	2		
Williams, Charles	1	1	3		8
Willis, James, junr	1	6	2		
Fruit, Henry	2	2	2		
Hellis, James	2	2	3		1
Rowe, James	1	3	5		
Parsons, Hilary	1	2	4		5
Wain, William	1	2	3		
Gatlen, William	2		4	2	
Tingle, Solomon	2	1	3		
Barrington, Richard	1	1	3		
Gaskins, William	2	3	3		4
Rowe, Thomas	1				
Gaskins, Thomas	1		1		5
Willis, Joseph	1	4	1		1
Chandler, Henry R	1				
Surles, Ann			3		1
Gatlen, Pierce	1				
Morgan, John	1		5		
Whitford, David	3	1	3		
Arthur, William	1		1		
Rigby, Thomas	1		2		
Rigby, Hugh	3		1		
Stilly, Fountain	1	3	6		
Arthur, John	1	1	2		
King, Joseph	1	1	2		
Ipock, Jacob	2	2	3		
Kerman, Michael	2	1	2	1	8
Hall, David	1		3		
Dunn, Elizabeth		2	1		
Warrin, Abram, junr	1	1	5		1
Hall, Jane		1	2		
Willis, Samuel	2	2	1		7
Carney, Elizabeth	1	1	3		
Calaway, John	1		1		
Hypock, Samuel	1	1	2		
Gaskins, James	1		3		
Willis, Thomas	2	2	4		2
Willis, Ephraim	1	1	3		1
Thomas, John, Senr	2	2	1		
Sneed, Zadiac	1	2	3		
Thomas, John	1				
Rice, James			3		
Reel, Peter	1		1		
Reel, James	3	1	3		12
Harris, Sarah		1	2		
Surles, William	1	2	2		4
Gatlen, Joshua	1	1	3		
Pierce, Ephraim	1		2		3
Toler, Caleb	1	1	2		
Gaskins, Fisher	1	3	1		1
Toler, William	1				
Rowe, Joshua	1	1	6		
Pierce, James	1	1	1		4
Barrington, Isaac	1		3		3
Toler, James	1				
Dunn, John D	2	2	5		
Whitford, John	2	2	4		3
Bexley, Simon	3	1	4		5
Gaskins, Joseph	2	3	2		
Burch, John	2	2	2		22
Smith, Samuel	4	2	1		22
Hill, Levi	1	1	2		1
Gallins, John	1	3	2		
Gatlen, Elizabeth		1	2		
Barnet, Mary			2		2
Clark, William	1	3	2		
Hill, Jane		1	2		
Werst, Daniel	2		6		3
Dixon, William	1	3	5		8
Dawson, Levi	1	2	8		13
Bedscot, John, Senr	1	1			4
Bedscot, John, junr	1	1	2		2
Edgington, William	1	1	2		
Lane, John	1	1	3		1
Brinson, Benjamin	1	2	1		1
Caton, Solomon	2	1			
Barnard, Jesse	1	1	2		3
Scot, John	2	2	5		
Daw, James	1		2		
Tingle, Hugh	1		3		
Caton, William	1	5	2		
Gatlin, William	1	1	1		1
Lee, John	1	1	2		
Rice, Evan	2		2		
Whitford, William	1	1	7		1
Holton, George	1	3	3		
Richmond, Jacob W	1				
West, David	1	2	3		
Cox, Hinson	3	2	2		
Tingle, Gideon	2		1		1
Brinson, Cason	1	5	2		
Caton, Moses	2	2	3		
Daw, William	1		2		
Gabriel, Nathaniel	2		1		
Price, James	2	2	6		
Bexley, William	1	1	2		
Tingle, James	1	1	2		
Holton, Thomas	1	1	2		
Cutrell, David	2		3		
Murphy, Sarah	1		3		2
Purify, Thomas			3		2
Rice, John	1	1	2		
Smow, James	2	1	4		
Vendrick, James	2		3		
Daw, James	2		3		
Dixon, William	2	2	1		1
Holton, Barry	1		2		
Gardner, Francis	1	1	2		
Arnold, John	1		3		7
Caton, John	1	1	1		
Holton, Jesse	1	1	2		
Simkins, John	1		3		
Vendric, Rebecca			3		
Spikes, Thomas	1	1	5		8
Brinson, James	1		2		4
Tindon, Ruel	1	2	1		
Brinson, Joseph	1	2	4		1
Dixon, Elijah	1	2	2		
Harper, Abram	1	2	5		
Simkins, James	1	1	2		
Tire, William	1	2	4		3
West, Elizabeth			3		
Wells, Samuel	1	2	4		
Harris, Sarah		2	2		
Fell, John	3		1		1
Rumley, Mary		1	2		4
Vendrick, Francis	1		5		
Daw, John, Senr	1	1	2		
Jordan, Thomas	1		2		8
Hoover, William	2	1	3		
Gabriel, John	1	1	1		
Mecans, James	2				
Mott, Abram	1				

NEWBERN DISTRICT, CRAVEN COUNTY—Continued.

NAME OF HEAD OF FAMILY.	Free white males of 16 years and upward, including heads of families.	Free white males under 16 years.	Free white females, including heads of families.	All other free persons.	Slaves.
Baker, John	1		1		
Brinson, Matthew	2	2	2		
Brothers, Mary			4		
Banks, Peter	1	3	1		
Cuttrell, Rhodes	1	2	4		
Daw, John, junr	1				
Blakey, Lawrence	3	2	3		
Price, Lucretia	1	2	2		
Brinson, Daniel	1		1		1
Brinson, James	1	2	3		
Sparrow, Samuel	3	4	2		5
Hall, Thomas	1		1	1	1
Bowdon, Avery	2	1	2		
Manley, James				1	
Gathen, David	2	1	3		
West, John	1	1	4		4
Spikes, William, Senr	2		1		9
Blakey, William	1				
Dilemar, Francis	1	3	3		5
Dilemar, Francis, Senr	1	2	2		8
Dilemar, Francis, junr	1	2	2		4
Bond, Francis	3	1	3		
Carraway, Nathan	2	4	4		2
Sparrow, Thomas	1	4	3		5
Dawson, John	1	1	1		11
Parish, John	1		2		
Hall, Oliver	1		3		5
Carraway, James	1		2		
Ives, Thomas	1	1	2		
Lewis, Mason	1		4		
Ives, William	1	4	2		
Parish, Zadiac	1		3		
Simmons, James	1	4	4		
Morris, Abram	1	1	2		
Simmons, William	1	1	3		
Clayton, William	2	3	4		
Good, Joseph	1	4	3	1	1
Moor, Jesse	2		2		8
Cary, Richard	1	1	3		
Cary, Nicholas	2	2	2		
Thomas, John	1	2	3		5
Creakman, Southy	1	1	5		2
Fulsher, Ephraim	2	2	4	1	2
Carraway, William	2	1	1		3
Carraway, Joseph	2	2	3		7
Carraway, Thomas	1		1		2
Carraway, John	1	2	2		2
Nelson, Joseph	1	2	2		10
Dilemar, Thomas	1	1	1		3
Biggs, John	2	1	5		4
Paul, Robert	1	1	1		
Green, Joseph	4	2	4		
Ballance, Benjamin	3	5	3		1
Ballance, Joshua	1		3		
Lester, Jesse	2	1	1		3
Munford, Jesse	2	2	2		
Banks, John	1		7		
Shine, William	1	2	3		8
Wallace, William	3	4	2	1	
Parish, George	2		5		
Fulsher, Joshua	1		3		16
Fulsher, Elizabeth			1		3
Carter, Jenny				1	
Waw, Amos		1	3	1	5
Carraway, Sarah	2		2		
Clayton, Mary			2		2
Good, Mary			1		2
Dawson, Elizabeth			4		5
Brothers, Robert	2		1		
Gilgo, Mary			2		
Owens, James	1	3	3		
Hudson, Sarah		1	2		
Miller, Enoch	1	1			
Holland, Spear	1	2	2		
Smith, William	1		3		1
Spelman, Asa				5	
Spelman, David				1	
Tolsin, Benjamin	1	5	5		3
Tilman, Henry	6	1	7		11
Fulsher, Jesse	1	3	4		10
Carruthers, Alexander	2				1
Brooks, William	1	1	1		3
Lewis, Nathan	2	3	5		
Morris, Nathan	1	2	1		
Brothers, David	1		3		
York, Thomas	1		2		6
Clayton, Thomas	3	1	3		6
Squires, Amos	2	4	1		
Harris, William	1		1		

NAME OF HEAD OF FAMILY.	Free white males of 16 years and upward, including heads of families.	Free white males under 16 years.	Free white females, including heads of families.	All other free persons.	Slaves.
Riggs, Shadrack	1	2	4		
Lewis, Joseph	2	3	3		
Wright, John	1	2	3		
Lewis, Joshua	1	2	3		
Harris, James	1	1	2		
Lewis, John	1		2		
Lewis, Jacob	1	1	3		3
Tilman, John	1		2		
Riggs, David	1	2	3		
Bateman, Hopkins	1	3	4		3
Driggers, Johnston				4	
Martin, John	1		1		1
Wharton, James	2		1		7
Martin, David	1	1	2		
Lewis, Major	1	2	3		
Wilcox, John	1				
Harrison, Samuel	3		3		
Rice, Gideon	2	6	3		
Slobuck, Nathaniel	1	4	3		
Morris, Aaron	1		2		
Carruthers, Clayton	1	1	2		4
McOtler, Hezekiah	4	1	6		
Wharton, William	1	1	1		2
Pitman, Joseph	2	4	2		
Wharton, David	1				1
Veal, Elijah	1	1	4		
Phips, Nathan	1	4	4		
Brooks, Joseph	1	2	4		
Morris, Thomas	1		1		
Harper, Peter	1				
Brickhouse, Jedediah	1	1	3		
Ives, John	1	5	1		
Howard, Thomas	1				
Mews, Caleb	1		1		
Dilemar, Dempson	1	1	3		2
Fulsher, Cason	1	3	1		2
Tingle, Joseph, Senr	3	1	3		5
Martin, Mary	1		2		
Willis, Jeremiah	1	3	6		
Mews, James	1	2	2		
Riggs, Mary	1		1		
Tingle, Joseph, junr	1	2	2		
Clark, John	1		1		
Kirk, Roger	1	1	2		
Hammontree, Griffin	2	3	1		
Carraway, Joshua	1	1	1		1
Muse, John	2	3	2		
Howering, Jesse	1	2	4		
Clark, John, Senr	3	4	2		
Simmons, Nathan	1		1		
Squires, Jeremiah	1		3		
Hewit, William	1				
Lindsey, Joshua, Senr				4	
Wheaton, John	1	3	4		
Sermons, Ephraim	1		2		
Willis, Thomas	1	1	3		
Holland, Martha					
Carruthers, John	2	2	1		9
Rigs, Jacob	1	2	4		
Lewis, Jacob, Senr	1		2		
Wheelton, Levin	1	1	5		
Paul, John	2	3	2		
Brooks, Elizabeth	1		1		2
Wilcocks, James	2		2		
Morris, John	1	1	2		1
Bond, Sarah			1	2	1
Macbay, Abel	1	1	4		
Paul, George	1		1		
Bryan, Needham	1	1	4		
Wilcox, William	1	2	2		1
Veal, Elizabeth		1	5		
Rice, Rebecca		1	5		
Rigs, Sarah		3	6		2
Roach, James	1				
Avery, John	1		6	1	
Hammontree, Hardy	1				
Johnston, Ann				2	
Lindsey, Mary				3	
Griggers, Elizabeth				5	
Tilman, John	2		6	1	12
Draper, Sarah			1		8
Harper, John	1		1		
Lewis, David	1		3		7
Williams, Thomas	1		1		28
Jones, Humphry	1		3		35
Fonvielle, John	1	2	2		22
McCrohon, Mary			1		16
Nixon, Richard	3		5		19
Neale, Abner	1	1	2		20

NAME OF HEAD OF FAMILY.	Free white males of 16 years and upward, including heads of families.	Free white males under 16 years.	Free white females, including heads of families.	All other free persons.	Slaves.
Blackledge, William	1		2		1
Cheney, Mary	1		3		1
Kennedy, George	1		1		2
Collier, Thomas	2	3	5		15
Saunders, Charles	2		7		4
Williams, Benjamin	1		1		92
Blount, Wilson	1		2		45
Pilchard, John	1		2		
Wilkes, Humphry	1		2		
Conner, Sarah			3		2
Jump, William	1	2	4		
Taylor, Abraham, Senr	2	2	1		
Williams, Benjamin, Senr	5	2	3		
Bradshaw, Mary		2	3		
Yates, Daniel	2	1	3		
Moor, John				12	
Hunter, Catherine	1		2		
Stephenson, Silas S	2	2	3		20
Herritage, John B	1				3
Pearson, John	3	1	2		
Bogue, Benijah	1		2		
Stanley, Wright	1	2	2		31
Carter, James	1	1		1	
Carter, Joseph	2	1	4	1	5
Carter, William	2		1	1	2
Kelleham, Barsheba		1	2		
Black, Letitia				3	
Lewis, Jesse	1	3	3		4
Gooding, Bardin	1		3		
Bogue, Dixon	1				
Sevils, William	1	1	2		
Sevils, James	1		7		
Perkins, Edmund	1	4	2	1	9
Dickinson, Edmund	1		1		
Wheathrington, James	1	3	1		
Fonvielle, Richard	1				3
Tooley, William	1	1	1	1	6
Clark, John	2	3	2		13
Hilbert, Leonard	1	1	2		
Green, William	1	1	2		2
Stafford, Mary	1		2		
Lambert, John	1	1	5		1
Keef, Edmund	1	2	3		
Fonvielle, William B	2		2		11
Charlot, John	1	2	4		4
Green, Joseph	1	3	2		
Richardson, Andrew	2		1		3
Taylor, Abram, junr	1	2	6		
Bogey, Alexander	1		1		
Johnston, Richard	1				
Wilks, Matthew	1				
Smith, Arthur	1	1	7		1
Williams, Stephen	1		2		1
Harrison, James	1		1		
Grenade, Benjamin	1				2
Davis, Thomas	1	1	6		
Smith, John	1	1	2	1	1
McKubbins, Samuel	1				
Sanders, James	2	2	3		2
Fonvielle, Thomas G	1				5
Lane, George	1	2	1	1	15
Moor, John	1	1	1		5
Wheathrington, Thomas	1	1	1		
Barnet, Ashley	1	2	2		
Mitchell, Alexander	1		1		1
Moor, Jesse				3	
Sanderson, Esther		1	2		
Ranson, Isaac				7	
Moor, Simeon				11	
Ranson, George				5	
Moor, John				2	
Brown, Samuel				4	
Harris, Thomas				10	
Moor, Abraham				1	
Morgan, James				1	
Spelman, Aaron				3	
Mosley, Caty				3	
Davis, Michael				1	
Moor, Susannah				3	
Dickinson, Levin	1		1	1	1
Copeland, Cato				1	
Jack (Old)				2	
Lewis, Thomas				7	
Wilson, Thomas					
Wilson, James	1	1	1		13
Stafford, Lodon	1		1		

NEWBERN DISTRICT, DOBBS COUNTY.

NAME OF HEAD OF FAMILY.	Free white males of 16 years and upward, including heads of families.	Free white males under 16 years.	Free white females, including heads of families.	All other free persons.	Slaves.
Edwards, Thomas	1				8
Holms, Moses	1	2	2		1
Barrow, Micajah	1				
Sheppard, Abram, Senr	3	1	1		18
Ward, Darling	3	5	2		3
Faircloth, William, Senr	4		4		15
Faircloth, William, Junr	1		3		1
Martin, William, Senr	1	1	1		
Wall, John	1	1	4		
Shepherd, William	1		4	4	5
Glasgow, James	5		3		50
Wright, James	1		3		
Holmes, James	1	1	4	1	2
Williams, John	1	1	3		4
Andrews, William	2	2	4	1	
Holms, Jesse	2		5		
Holms, Timothy	1		3		4
Holms, John	3	1	4		
Downing, Elisha	1	3	1		
Downing, Joseph	1		3		3
Pope, Poole	1		7		
Aycock, William	1	2			
Cannon, James, Senr	3		3		
Cannon, James, junr	1	2	3		
Cannon, John	1	4	3		
Taylor, William	1	1	4		4
Taylor, John	1	1	3		1
Butcher, Thomas	4	5	6		3
Price, John	1	5	1		1
Edmondson, John	3	2	5		3
Sheppard, John	1	1	1		9
Ruffin, Etheldred	1	5	3		19
Brown, Mary		3	2		7
Salls, James	2	3	2		
Price, Redick	1	2	1		1
Barrow, Harold	2	3	4		
Barrow, Sherrard	1	3	6		3
Smith, David	1	2	2		
Barrow, Jeremiah	1	2	6		
Smith, Nicholas	1		3		
Smith, Mark	1	6	5		
Hinson, Jesse	1		2		
Hinson, William	1	1	1		
Hinson, Joseph	1		4		
Smith, Henry	1	3	2		1
Jordan, Evan	1	2	4		4
Jordan, Frederick	2	2	5		15
Smith, Richard	2	3	3		10
Smith, Thomas	1	2	2		2
Smith, Etheldred	1	1	1		2
Spann, John	2		1		2
Parker, John, Senr	1		4		
Parker, John, junr	1	1	1		
Taylor, Robert	1		2		1
Smith, James	2		5		
Warters, William	2	4	5		
Barfield, Ane		2	3		
Henby, John	1	2	3		
Tiddor, George, Senr	2		2		
Tiddor, George, junr	1		1		
Tiddor, Thomas	1	2	4		
Brown, Samuel	1		2		
Glasgow, Mary		3	1		12
Reynolds, Mary		2	3		
Thornton, James	1	1	1		
Faircloth, Frederick	1		3		
Faircloth, Thomas	1	5	2		1
Sibert, John Dan	1		2		
Stephenson, Mary	1		2		
Long, Jesse		4	1		
Ward, Dierdamer		1	3		
Newby, Matthew	1				
McAlpin, Robert	1				
Brumley, Thomas	1	2	4		
Jordan, Thomas	2	5	5		2
Grainger, John	2		4		5
Harper, Francis, Senr	1		1		1
Harper, Francis, junr	1	3	2		1
Sheppard, Benjamin	8	12	19		71
Harrel, Benjamin	1	2	3		5
Pridgeon, Ruffin	1				2
Tindale, Samuel	1		3		
Tindale, John	2	4	4		1
Best, Benjamin	5	1	2		18
Best, Henry	1		2		8
Wood, James	2	5	5		9
Garland, John	1	1	2		8
Garland, Josiah	1		1		3
Edwards, William	1	4	3		7
Harper, Blaney	1	1	3		4
Hall, Poole	2	1	1		
Hall, Dempsey	1		2		
Sugg, Absalom	4	2	3		
Sugg, John, Senr	2	1	3		5
Sugg, John, junr	1	1	1		1
Sugg, Josiah	1		1		2
Oliver, Anne			4		
McNeale, Isaac	1	1	3		
Dixon, Frederick	1		4		3
Dixon, Shadrack	1		1		1
Dixon, Murfree	2	1	5		1
Harper, William	1		1		3
Kilpatrick, William	3	1	2		2
Fitzpatrick, John	1	1	2		6
Moore, Samuel	3	3	2		1
Wilson, John	2		1		
Wilson, William	1	1	1		
Lassiter, Jesse	1		2	2	7
Caswell, Benjamin	2	2	1		4
Hooker, William	1		2		11
Hooker, Nathan	1	1	2		3
Hooker, Samuel	1		7		5
Haile, John	1	3	3		4
Cale, John	3	2	4		1
Hill, Robert	1		3		
Hill, Michael	1		2		
Hill, Richard	1		2		
Aldridge, Jesse	1	1	4	1	
Aldridge, Drury	1	2	2		8
Whitley, Josiah	1		2		1
Whitley, William	1		1		
Rowe, Jesse	1	1	2		
Stanley, Isaac	3	2	1		7
Bright, Graves	1	1	1		7
Hill, Zilpha			3		
Hall, Celia			2		
Ludwell, Richard	2		1		
Freeman, John	3	2	7		3
Jones, John	1	3	2		
Jones, Frederick	2	1	3		
Jones, James	1		2		
Lassiter, Jacob, Senr	2				20
Lassiter, Jacob, junr	1		1		4
Pridgeon, Thomas	2	2	4		20
Edwards, Mary	1		2		13
Ward, David	1		4		
Johnston, James	1	2	4		
Ward, Daniel	1	1	2		
Ward, Thomas	1		3		
Edwards, Henry	1		2		3
Wade, James	2		2		2
Wade, Joseph	1		1		
Reynolds, Christopher	1	5	4		
Morris, Charles	1		2		
Reeves, William	1		1		
Rieves, Joseph	1		2		
Combe, Ebenezer	1	1	2		1
Kenney, William	1		1		
Mitchell, William	1	4	4		
Kenney, Jane			3		
Madens, John	1	1	4		
Lane, Thomas	1	3	4		2
Kilpatrick, William	1		1		1
Davis, Icabod	1		6		
Davis, Lewis	1		2		7
Sugg, William	1	2	4		
Sugg, John	1		1		
Sugg, Michael	1	1	1		
Sugg, James	1		1		
Bailey, Lewis	1				4
Denny, Mary			5		
Denny, Abram	1		2		
White, John	1	1	1		
Bush, Abram	3	1	4		6
Corwell, Spencer	1		4		4
Patrick, John			2		
Harold, Ann			2		
Williams, Jonathan	1		4		
Broom, Mason	1	1	4		
Stewart, James	1	2	5		1
Wilson, Acquiton	1	1	3		
Lewis, Cadir	1	1	2		
Lewis, James	1		3		
Lewis, Stephen	1	1	2		
Harris, William	1		5		
Lohorn, Sarah			1		
Wosdon, Austin	1	1	3		2
Hinson, Elizabeth			5		
Mezings, Ann			3		5
Spright, Samuel	1	2	5		3
Elliott, Zachariah	1	1	2		2
Hart, Moses	1		2		
Hart, Zachariah	1	1	3		5
Pate, Joseph	2	4	4		
Sparkman, John	1	2	2		
Scarborough, Nathan	1	2	2		
Ellis, Enos	1		2	2	
Matthews, Alexander	1		2		1
Williams, Jonas	1		4		8
Field, Moses	1		4		13
Shepherd, Abram	1		4		14
Brann, John B	3	4	5	1	12
Matthews, William	3	1	3		
Matthews, Richard	1		3		
Wilson, Mary	1	2	4		5
McCarthy, Timothy	2	1	4		
Carter, Jesse	2		1		1
Bryan, John	2		3		
Britt, Margaret	1		3		
Britt, William	1	1	1		
Hardy, Dorothy			2		4
Hollwell, Mary			1		1
Grimsley, John	2		3		4
Deale, William	2	2	4		
Smith, John	3		2		4
Morris, Charles	1		2		
Chalcraft, David	1	2	1		1
Henby, Joseph	1	4	3		
Rasberry, Francis	1	3	4		5
Williams, John	3	3	5		9
Jones, Jesse	2		3		8
Garner, Speedham	1	2	3		
Minshew, Isaac	1	2	5		1
Garner, Simeon	1		1		
Rasberry, John	3	1	3		8
Jordan, Richard	1	3	2		
Ellis, Hyperion	1		3		
Ellis, John	4		3		
Taylor, Robert	1	1	3		
Hallows, Josiah	1		3		
Taylor, Stephen	1		3		
Grear, John	1	4	3		
Grizzard, Lucy			4		
Minshew, Jacob	1		2		
Minshew, Keziah		2	1		4
Minshew, John	1	1	1		
Grizzard, Thomas	1	1	1		
Pipkin, Lewis	1	2	3		
Hart, William	1	1	5		
Pipkin, John	2	3	3		
Pipkin, Sarah			3		1
McKeel, John	1	1	1		
Moore, William	7		4		
Conner, Jonathan	2	4	3		
Williams, Willowby	1	1	1		8
Carrin, Robert	2	1	3		
Henby, James	3	3	3		
Spight, Stephen	2		3		
Spight, John	2	1	3		
Spight, John, junr	1	1	1		
Hall, Thomas	1		1		
Anneson, Abram	1		2		
Cuter, Stephen	1	2	1		
Hays, Isaac	1	3	5		
Butler, Elisha	1		4		1
Scarborough, Benjamin	2	3	5		
Riff, Daniel	3	3	4		
Sorrow, William	1	4	1		
Barrow, James	4	3	5		
Price, Nathan	1		1		
Price, Absalom	2	1	1		4
Hays, Mary		2	3		
Ellis, Edwin	4	1	2		13
Dannels, Delijah	1	4	4		1
Price, Thomas	1		2		
Moor, Britton	3	1	4		
Eason, Stephen	1	4	3		3
Beaman, Edmond	2	1	4		
Beaman, Jeremiah	1	3	4		
Mercer, Shadrach	1	4	4		
Paul, Jacob	2	3	4		
Minshew, Nathan	4	3	5		5
Sharp, Thomas	1	2	3		
Shacklefoot, John	1	2	1		
Spight, Alice	2	2	4		
Spight, William	2	5	6		
Hays, Ann			3		
Ward, John	1	1	3		19
Ward, Needham	1	1	2		5
Spight, Sarah			2		1
Lewis, John	1		1		
Ellis, Joseph	3	1	3		10
Davis, Joshua	1	3	2		7
Peal, David	2	2	2		3
Barzarum, Abier	1		5		
Walston, John	2		5		
Scarborough, Martha			4		
Walston, William	2	3	5		
Garris, John	1	1	3		
Barzarum, John	1	2	2		
Rasberry, Daniel	1		1		
Carter, William	2		1		1
Price, John		1	3		1
Thigpin, Margaret	1	1	2		
Walston, Philip	1	1	2		
Moor, William, junr	1		3		2
Vicks, Robert	1	1	3		
Price, Thomas	1		5		
Spight, William	2	2	2		23
Spight, Seth	1	3	3		11

NEWBERN DISTRICT, DOBBS COUNTY—Continued.

NAME OF HEAD OF FAMILY.	Free white males of 16 years and upward, including heads of families.	Free white males under 16 years.	Free white females, including heads of families.	All other free persons.	Slaves.
Barfield, William	2		2		
Barfield, Mills	2	3	5		
Barfield, John	2	2	3		
Barfield, James	3	3	6		
Hooke, Roger	2	3	2		
Hays, Susannah	3	3	3		
Shacklefoot, Willowby	1	2	3		
Ormond, William	2	3	3		12
Barfield, Thomas	1	1		1	
Murfree, William	1	1	4		4
Murfree, John	1	4	4	1	5
Murfree, Jethro	2	1	4		9
Young, James	1		5		
Jones, Joseph	1	1	4		
Wade, Samuel	1	3	3		
Sanderson, John	1		2		
Hicks, Jesse	1	1	4		
Grunsley, Sherod	1	1	2		
House, Joseph	1	1	2		
Turnage, Luke	1	1	1		
Turnage, James	2	1	1		
Magee, Daniel	1		4		
Edwards, Benjamin	1	1	5		
Butts, Elizabeth	2	1	1		
Butts, George	1		1		
Butts, Aaron	1		1		
Butts, James	1				
Tunnage, Daniel	1	1	4		
Deale, Abel	2		1		
Tunnage, George	1	2	3		
Jones, David	1		5		
Mayers, Timothy	1	3	3		
Readick, William	3	2	4		
Deal, Thomas	1	2	5		
Mayers, Mark	4	1	2		
Goodson, William	1	2	3		
Mayers, James	1	1	3		
Mayers, John	1	4	3		
Tonnage, Jesse	1	2	2		
Chalcraft, Levi	1	2	5		
McGee, John	1		1		
Taylor, Hillary, Senr	3	2	4		
Taylor, Hilary, Junr	1		2		
Davis, Martin	1		3		
Davis, James, Senr	1	1	1		1
Davis, James	1	3	3		
Griffin, William	1	2	2		
Griffin, Drew	1	1	3		
Hooker, Hymerick	1	4	2		5
Jones, John	1	2	8		2
Holliday, Samuel	1	1	4		8
Jones, William, Senr	1	1	3		
Jones, Sylvanus	2	1	5		
Lassiter, Nathan	2	1	4		14
Jones, William	1	1	2		
Pope, John	1	4	5		15
Harper, John	1	2	3		1
Tindale, Joshua	1	2	1		
Barfield, James	1	3	3		
Bryant, Benjamin	1	1	4		9
Roberts, Roger	1	4	3		
Olds, Arthur	3	5	1		5
Readick, John	1	2	4	1	
Hamilton, John	1		2		
Hort, Robin	1	4	4		18
Carr, Titus	2	3	4		29
Durdin, William	2	1	1	1	11
Tunnage, William	2	2	2		
Broom, Melius	1	4	6		4
Taylor, Henry	1		5		7
Taylor, John	1	2	2		
Rolls, Cornelius	1	2	2		
Spiva, Ephraim	1	1	1		
Spiva, Caleb	1	1	2		3
Hart, Lucretia	2	2	3	1	
Smith, William	1	4	2		
Farris, William	2	1	5		5
Parrymore, Benjamin	1	1	2		
Dukes, John	1	3	2		
Hardison, James	2	1	4		
Van Pelt, Anthony	3	2	4		
Menter, James	1	6	2		
Butler, William	1	1	1		
Griffin, Joshua	1	3	3		
Coward, Edward	2	2	4		2
Coward, James	2	2	6		
Coward, Needham	1	5	5	1	
Miller, George	2	1	6		
Miller, William	1				
Holliday, John	2				2
Jones, Daniel	1				
Ormond, William	1	1	2		
Musick, John	2		3		
McCoye, William	1				
Harrell, John	1				
Griffin, Benjamin	1				
Miller, John	1		1		
Jones, John	2	3	4	2	1
Vance, David	1	2	2		
Coward, John	1	1	5		2
Coward, Elisha	2	2	3		
Howard, Frederick	1		6		
Coward, James	1	2	2		
Coward, Ann			1		1
Philips, James	1	1	2		
Putnell, Stephen	1	1	2		
Kilpatrick, Israel	1		2		
Wade, John	1	2	4		
Moore, John	1	2	4		
Pate, John, junr	1	1	3		
Pate, John, Senr	2		2		3
Pate, Sarah		2	3		
Owens, Ann Pelia			2		
Pate, William, Senr	2	2	2		2
Pate, William, Junr	1	2	3		
Philips, Mark, junr	1	2	1		
Moseley, Elizabeth		2	3		8
Moseley, Tully	1	1	1		5
Patrick, Martha			2		5
Partridge, John	1	3	5		
Voss, Ephraim	2	2	4		
Parker, Joseph	1		2		
Withrington, Robert	1	2	3		2
Johnston, Isaiah	1	1	1		1
Bond, Isband	1		3		
Jones, William	1	1	2		2
Jones, John	1	2	3		1
Jones, John	1	1	1		3
Jones, Richard	1	4	7		
Harvey, Matthias	2	1	4		4
Philips, Mason	3	1	2		
Philips, Benjamin	1		1		
Voss, William	1	2	5		
Moore, Ephraim	1		1		
Fortner, William	1	2	2		
Sulivan, John	1		4		
Johnston, Mary	2		5		
Johnston, Elijah	1	4	2		1
Cole, Thomas	1	2	2		
Tull, Charles	1	2	3		4
Ward, Hugh	2	4	7		
Peters, William	1	2	4		
Britton, Joseph	1	1	6		4
Withrington, Willis	1	1	2		
Withrington, Nathan	1		2		6
Patrick, Manning	2	1	3		9
Smith, Isum	1	1	1		
Pope, William	1	1	4		3
Dannel, Josiah	1		2		4
Bright, James	1	2	6		8
Bell, George	2	1	8		7
Ingram, Charles	2	1	4		
Williams, Job	1	4	3		
Baker, Elijah	1	2	2		2
Baker, Frederick	1	2	2		2
Adams, Willowby	1		1		
Powell, John	1		2		
Micks, Jacob	1		2		
Grant, Isaac	1		2		
Grant, Mary		3	2		
Fortner, James	3		1		
Powell, Daniel	1	1	4		2
Fortner, Emanuel	2	3	3		
Moore, William, Senr	2	2	3		
Moore, William, junr	1	3	6		
Moore, John	1	2	2		
Moore, Isaiah	1	5	3		
Moore, Ephraim	1		2		
Moore, Amaziah	1	3	2		
Taylor, Christopher	2		2		
Taylor, James	1		4		
Hamilton, James	1	4	2		
Hutchins, Elijah	1		2		
Hamilton, Sarah			4		
Budd, Thomas	3		1		
Smith, Job	1	2	2		
Jones, William	1	2	2		1
Withrington, Stephen	1	3	3		
Withrington, Daniel	1		2		2
Dismal, John	1		2		
Philips, Thomas	2	1	2		
Dismal, Daniel	1		3		
Dismal, Jeremiah	1	5	2		
Ingram, James, Senr	2	1	5		
Ingram, James, junr	2		5		2
Jackson, Sarah			2		
Alexander, Frances			1		
Falconer, Olive	1		2		
Wootus, Merkland	1		1		
Wootus, John	2		1		
Bruton, Simon	2		2		
Cunningham, Jester	1	2	3		1
Withrington, Cleaverly	2	4	4		
Turner, Reuben	1		2		
Abbot, Elizabeth	1	3	3		6
Bond, William	1		2		6
Wilson, John	3	2	3		2
Collier, Mary	1		3		
Withrington, William	1	2	3		
Griffin, Simon	1	1	6		
Ramsay, Thomas	2	1	4		
Moore, Thomas	1	1	4		
Philips, Mark, Senr	2	7	7		
Browning, George	1	4	4		
Croom, Joshua	1	2	2		9
Parrot, John, junr	1	4	2		
Parrot, John, Sen	3	1	4		3
Parrot, Jacob	2	2	3		4
Hartsfield, John, Senr	2		1	2	2
Hartsfield, David	1	1	2		
Hodges, John	1	1	3		
Hodges, Richard	2	2	5		
Creach, Benjamin	2	2	4		
Creach, Ezekiel	1	3	4		
Bird, Richard, Senr	1		1		2
Bird, Richard, junr	1		1		
Mewborn, Parrot	1		2		
Bird, Eleanor		1	3		1
Tull, John	1	3	3		15
Tull, William	1	1	5		5
Bright, Mary			3		8
Baker, Abram	2	2	4		9
Thomas, Ratio	1	3	5		
Williams, Joseph	1		1		
Arnet, Peter	1		1		
Hutchins, Miles	1	4	7		2
Hartsfield, Paul	2	1	3		4
Williams, Joseph	2	1	1		
Williams, Joshua	2	2	7		
Wilson, James	2		2		
Frizell, John	1		1		
Hill, Mary	1	2	3		
Birton, Benjamin	1		1		
Brown, Richard	1				
Brown, John	1	4	3		
Robinson, Benjamin	2	3	1		
Bush, Sanders	1	2	1		
Cox, John	2		1		
Scean, Elijah	1	1	3		
Freeman, John	1	1	2		
Tillman, John	1	2	2		
Sutton, William	1	1	1		
Hardy, Major	1	1	2		1
Kennedy, Mary		1	1		1
Lewis, Benjamin	1	1	3		
Kennedy, Walter	1		4		1
Kennedy, John	1	1	2		
Morris, Jonathan	1	1	3		2
Arundell, William	1	1	6		3
Pool, Aaron	1	3	3		3
Pool, Joseph	1	1	3		
Caswell, James	1	1	3		
Caswell, Ann	1	1	2		3
Westbrooke, Moses	2	4	5		6
Wiggins, John	1	3	2		
Wiggins, Gersham	3		2		3
Hartsfield, John, junr	1	1	2		
Hartsfield, Shadrach	1		4		3
Pool, Josiah	1		1		
Pool, Samuel	1	2	5		
Lovick, Moses	3	2	3		
Bush, Abram	1				
Difnall, David	2	1	4		
Pool, William	1		3		
Dannels, Mary			3		
Iler, Nelly			2		
Thomson, John	1		3		
Smith, Elizabeth			3		
Smith, Joshua	1	1	3		
Smith, Nathan	1	2	1		
Smith, Jesse	1		2		
Iler, William, Senr	1		4		
Iler, William, junr	1	1	4		
McCoye, Ann			2		
Barwick, Margaret			2		
Wine, Claret	1		3		
Bars, John	2	1	8		
Garret, Ann			5		
Harrison, Thomas	1	1	4		
Martin, William	1		4		
Templer, Rachel		2	2		
Paradise, John	1		4		
Arnett, John			4		
Aldridge, John	1	1	3		2
Aldridge, Jesse	1		2		
Aldridge, William, Senr	2	1	2		2
Taylor, Isaac	2				
Aldridge, William, Jur	1		2		
Aldridge, Thomas	1		3		1
Hardy, Sarah	1	1	3		5
Croom, Hardy	1		1		17

NEWBERN DISTRICT, DOBBS COUNTY—Continued.

NAME OF HEAD OF FAMILY.	Free white males of 16 years and upward, including heads of families.	Free white males under 16 years.	Free white females, including heads of families.	All other free persons.	Slaves.
Farmer, Jesse	1		2		
Bird, Nathan	1	1	4		1
Bird, Richard	2	4	2		
Shine, Francis	1	1	4		1
Creach, John	1				
Caswell, Lany		1	3		1
Potts, Stringe	1	2	2		
Ingram, Isaac	1	2	4		
Linton, Tabitha			2		
Clark, John	1				
Freeman, Francis L.	1	1	3		
Glover, Elizabeth			3		
Philips, Thomas	2	1	2		
Langston, Abram	2	2	6		
Christophers, Christopher	1	1			3
Smith, John	1	2	5		1
Grace, William	1		1		
Richardson, Richard	2	1	2		1
Lord, William	1				1
Tilman, Ann			2		
Totwine, Simon	2		1		7
Spencer, Elizabeth		1	1		2
Markland, Charles	1			1	2
White, William	1		3		11
Hill, John	2	4	3		4
Bryn, Matthew	1				
Cobb, Jesse	1	3	4		42
Caswell, Winston	1	1	1		6
Caswell, Sarah	2	2	3		21
Crooms, William	1				23
Uzzell, Thomas	1	3	2		2
Sutton, Benjamin	1	3	6		
Stanley, Jonathan	1	3	2		
Hunter, Job	3	4	3		
Stanley, William	1	3	1		
Maxwell, Arthur	1	1	2		
Seamore, John	4	1	2		
Elmore, Francis	1	3	4		
Titterton, Isaac	1	2	1		
Henry, Robert	1		4		
Mitchel, Hardy	1		1		
Mitchel, Ezekiel	1	2	2		
Heron, John	1	4	5		7
Ellis, Jacob	1		4		
Waters, Sarah	1	2	2		3
Ellis, John	1		2		1
Scipper, Jacob	1	6	2		
Rouse, Jesse, junr	1		3		
Mezingo, Pierse	1	2	8		
Sutton, James	1				1
Sutton, John	2		2		2
Gray, John	1	3	5	1	
Stephens, Absalom	1	7	2		
Smith, Martin	1	3	2		
Elmore, Morgan	1		6		
Crooms, Major, Senr	1	1	1		14
Lassiter, Stephen	1	6	3		
Hinson, Aaron	1	6	3		
Benton, Jonathan	1	3	3		
Heron, Elisha	1	3	2		1
Langley, John	2	1	5		
Hardy, Samuel	2	2	4		20
Hardy, Benjamin	1		1		2
Rouse, Jesse, Senr	1	2	3		
Rouse, Simon	2	3	7		
Surles, Edward	3	2	2		
Potter, William	2	2	7		
Mosley, Matthew	1	4	2		11
Rouse, John, Senr	1	3	1		5
Rouse, John, junr	1	3	1		3
Woostin, John	2	3	1		2
Hughes, Thomas	2	1	1		9
Waters, John	1	7	4		
Waters, Moses	2	3	6		
Waters, Abimelech	1	2	5		4
Waters, John	1	6	4		
Bird, Joshua, Senr	3	4	2		1
Bird, Joshua, junr	1		2		
Creel, Charles	1	2	3		
Lovit, Patience	2	4	1		
Dannel, James	1	1	2		
Lawson, John	3	1	3		10
Dannel, Owen	1		4		
Dannel, John	1	2	5		
Heron, Mitchel	1	3	2		8
Taylor, William	1	1	5		12
Taylor, Robert	2	4	6		3
Taylor, Daniel	1	3	6		3
Uzzell, Isum	4	1	2		14
Totwine, Simon	1		1		
Elmore, Randolph	1		1		
Creel, John	1		2		7
Creel, Thomas	1	3	4		
Creel, Nathan	1		4		
Creel, Willowby	1	1	4		
Totwine, Isaac	1				

NAME OF HEAD OF FAMILY.	Free white males of 16 years and upward, including heads of families.	Free white males under 16 years.	Free white females, including heads of families.	All other free persons.	Slaves.
Mezingo, Booth	1	4	2		
Elmore, William	1	3	3		
Tucker, William	2		1		
Tucker, John	1	1	5		
Field, Brittle	2	4	8		
Wilson, Thomas	2	1	1		
Wilson, Joseph	1	2	1		1
Hanks, Epaphroditus	1	1	2		
Hanks, Moot	1	2	4		
Aldridge, William	1	2	2		12
Aldridge, Thomas	1	1	2		2
Dawson, Thomas	1	6	1		2
Surles, Robert	1	2	1		
Gatlen, Lazarus	1	4	6		
Gatlen, Jesse	1		2		
Rouse, Solomon	1	1	3		
Whitman, Jeremiah	1	2	3		
Crooms, Isaac	1		5		32
Crooms, Richard	1	2	2		26
Martins, Higalty	1	1	5		1
Martin, John	1		1		
Tutterton, Sarah			5		
Whitfield, Bryan	4	4	4		58
Lovit, Edward	1	2	3		
Kennedy, Henry	1	3	2		
Smith, Booky	2		2		
Perdue, Dennis	2	1	3		1
Waters, Winifred			2		
Rouse, Joseph	1		1	2	2
Dawson, John	2			1	
Joe				1	
Walker				1	
Whood, Robert	1				1
Lovit, David	1		2		
Creamer, George	1	2	3		
Ellis, Ebenezer	1	2	1		
Wilson, Obadiah	1		2		
Tucker, Delilah	1	2	3		
Cotton, Lucy			1	2	
Glohorn, Edmond	1				
Scipper, James	1	1	5		
Woodland, Robert	1		2		
Lovitt, Joseph	1		1		
Priest, David	1	2	1		
Crooms, Major, jur	1	5	4		13
Wilder, Ann		1	4		
Anders, Drury	1	2	5		
Burnet, William				5	
Henry, Burrel	1	1	1		
Lawson, John	1		1		
Aldrigde, William, jur	1				
Westbrooke, Grey	1	2	2		5
Waters, John, Senr	1	1	2		
Hardy, John	2	3	5		
Smith, Martin	1	3	2		
Dawson, Joel	1		5		2
Goodman, Henry	1		3	2	8
Tetterton, Thomas	1		3		
Tetterton, John	1		2		
Pipkin, Jesse	1	4	3		6
Pipkin, John	1	2	1		1
Hines, Isaac	2	3	3		1
Bush, Beby	1	1	4		10
Benton, Francis	3	2	7		
Carter, Edward			1	8	20
Carter, John		2	3	1	2
Hunter, Thomas	2	2	1		3
Waterman, William	1	2		1	1
Whitfield, James	1				9
Jones, Peter	1	4	2		
Smith, David	1	1	4		9
Davis, Windol	1	1	4		9
Davis, Cato	1		2		6
Whitfield, John	1	3	2		10
Grady, John	2	3	3		7
Smith, John	1	1	1		
Grady, William	1	2	3		2
Hines, Prudence	2		3		
Calley, Roger	1	6	2		4
Borin, William	1	3	3		
Pickle, Michael	1		3		
Spence, John	3		3		
Whitfield, Luke	1		3		8
Jones, Sukey			3		
Jones, Ezekiel	1	2	3		
Parker, Sarah			1	1	1
Thomas, John	1		1		
McMuller, Thomas	1	3	1		
Thomson, John	2	3	3		
Harper, John	1	1	4		
Johnston, Reuben	1		2		
Cox, John	1	2	2		
Jones, Jesse	1		1		2
Jackson, Jacob	2	4	2		1
Loiton, Leonard	2	2	6		
Delahunta, John	1		2		8
Jones, Frederic	1		2		9

NAME OF HEAD OF FAMILY.	Free white males of 16 years and upward, including heads of families.	Free white males under 16 years.	Free white females, including heads of families.	All other free persons.	Slaves.
Tilman, Joseph	3	3	3		7
Goodman, William	2	2	2		9
Jones, Thomas	1		4		
Burne, William	1		1		
Fisher, George	1		2		
Croom, Lott	1	1	4		8
Taylor, James	1	1	4		
Taylor, Isaac	1	3	5	5	7
Jones, Thomas	1				
Jones, John	2		7		
Gibbs, John	3	3	4		8
Goodman, Henry	1		2		9
Jackson, James	1		2		
Moye, Joseph	1	1	3		
Jump, John	1		2		
Wootin, Shadrach	2	6	3		6
McBearn, William	1	1	2		
Goodman, Timothy	1		2		6
Wright, Grove	1				
Wootin, William	1				
Law, Jonathan	1		1		
Williamson, James	1		1		
Easterling, William, Senr	2	1	6		
Ingram, Isaac	1	2	4		
Herritage, John	2		4		38
Spence, Charles	2		1		
Taylor, Joseph	1	2	2		9
Tilman, Mary		1	4		
Thomas, Jesse	1	3	4		
Cox, Harmon	4	1	4		
Cox, Tobias	1		3		7
Marklund, John	1				1
Lankston, Mace	1	1	6		
Edgley, John	1	1	3		
Wilson, James	1	3	3		
Coleman, Benja	3	2	5		25
Nunn, Francis	2	1	1		3
Nunn, William	1	1			
Nunn, Joshua	1	1	1		6
Lofton, Samuel	1	2	2		2
Nunn, Stephen	2		1		
Tardwel, Rebecca		1	3		
Lofton, Jeremiah	2	2	4		20
Mew, William	1	2	2		
Benson, William	1	2	6		1
Benson, Richard	1				
Heron, Nelly		3	4		
Griffin, Samuel	2		4		1
Parker, Lydia	4		2		
Griffin, Evan	1	3	5		
Griffin, James	1	2	3		
Griffin, Jacob, Senr	1		4		
Nobles, Philpenny	2	3	4		
Ivy, Robert	3	1	1		3
Trueit, Thomas	1				
Gray, Lodovick	2	2	3		
Gray, Nathan	1	1	2		
Miller, John	1				
Taylor, John	1	3	4		
Heron, Michael	1	1	2		1
Harper, Nathan	1	3	2		
Harper, Jesse	1	3	2		
Goodman, James	1		2		1
Gray, Billimillender	1		4		
Irvin, Edward	1	1	4		
Irvin, Francis	1	1	4		
Munn, Richard	3		4		
Carter, Margaret		2	2		
Hudler, John	1	2	1		
Harper, George	1	2	1		
Williams, Wm	2	3	3		
Howard, Barnet	1	2	4		
Williams, John	2	2	4		
Nobles, George	2	3	3		
George, David	1	2			3
Gray, Sylvanus	1	1	3		
Ventures, George	1	2	5		
Ivy, John	1	3	2		
Leary, Ciby	1		3		5
Barnet, Joshua	1		3		
Davis, James	1		2		
Brady, Stephen	1	1	4		
Garriss, John	1	1	5		4
Jarmin, Joseph	2	2	4		
Boyde, Applum	2	1	4		
Irvin, William	3	7	4		
Dotch, Walter	1	5	4		2
Mauldin, Tucker	1	1	4		
Cooke, Jesse	1	3	2		
Perry, John	1	2	4		
Dinkins, Joshua	1	1	3		
Williams, Edward	1		3		
Grey, Joseph	1		1		
Whaley, Ezekiel	1		3		
Mainer, Jacob	1		2		
Taylor, Jesse	1	1	2		
Taylor, William	1	1	2		

NEWBERN DISTRICT, DOBBS COUNTY—Continued.

NAME OF HEAD OF FAMILY.	Free white males of 16 years and upward, including heads of families.	Free white males under 16 years.	Free white females, including heads of families.	All other free persons.	Slaves.
Ratcliff, Aaron	1	1	2		
Jermin, William	1		2		1
Jermin, Thomas	1		1		
Hart, John	1		3		
Brown, James	1	3	2		1
Miller, Philip	1	2	4		2
Nobles, Richard	1		1		
Williams, Mark	1				
Blackman, Arthur	1	1	2		6
Mainor, Henry	1	2	4		
Ives, Job	1				
Barnet, Matthew	1				
Brown, Philip	1		2		
Howard, John	1		1		
Baker, Job	1	1	1		
White, Robert	4		2		17
Goodin, Moses	1	2	1		2
Goodin, Daniel	1	3	4		
McClain, Grace			1		3
Nots, Tabitha	1				2
Davis, Mary			2		3
Heron, Sarah	1	2	4		
Sanders, Catherine	1				3
Williams, Catherine			1		1
Howard, Penelope			3		8
Howard, Esther					2
Benson, Joseph	1				3
Stroud, Lapson	1	2			3
Quiney, Ann			2		3
Taylor, Ann			2		3
Wilson, Thomas	1	1	1		1
Tootle, William	1	1	6		1
Tootle, John	1	1	4		
Tootle, Edward	1				
Lofton, Elkaner	3	2	1		11
Lofton, Francis	2	1	4		3
Prier, Ephraim	2	1	2		
Griffin, Jacob, junr	1	1	4		
Sheppard, John M	1				
Pierce, Lazarus	1	1	3		2
Taylor, William, Senr	3	1	8		
Ball, Moses	1	3	9		1
Ball, Elizabeth		2	3		

NEWBERN DISTRICT, HYDE COUNTY.

NAME OF HEAD OF FAMILY.	Free white males of 16 years and upward, including heads of families.	Free white males under 16 years.	Free white females, including heads of families.	All other free persons.	Slaves.
Sanders, Andrew	1		2		
Money, Charles	3	2	4		
Williams, Joseph	1		2		
Swindall, Wade	1		1		
Cutrall, Peter	2		2		
Carteret, Bazel	1	1	2		
Windley, Elijah	1		3		
Williams, George	1	2	7		
Porter, William	2				
Carpenter, James	1	1	1		
Cutrill. Jacob	3		1		
Davison, James	1	1	1		
Hopkins, George	1	2	2		
Swindall, Caleb, junr	1	1	1		
Davidson, William	1		2		
Cutrill, Joseph	1	3	2		
Dunbar, James	1	1	3		
Eastwood, Israel	1	1	7		
Williamson, Samuel	2	2	3		
Blake, Elizabeth	1		1		
Howard, William	3		2		2
Turner, John	1	1	2		
West, Samuel	1	1	2		
Brinn, Richard	1	1			
Adams, William	2	4	3		5
Sanders, William	1	1	1		
Berry, James	1		3		
Hall, James	2	1	6		
Morris, David	1		1		
Dannels, Joab	2	4	3		
Sawyer, Zepheniah	3	3	6		
Swindall, Benjamin	1	1	3		
Davis, John	1	2	4		
Brin, Nicholas	1	1	2		
Mason, Thomas	1	1	3		
Swindal Joseph	1		5		
Carpenter. John	1		4		
Sadler, Richard	1	2	4		
Sadler, Samuel	1	1	5		
Swindall, Zedekiah	1	1	2		
Swindall, Parky	1		1		
Swindall, Sarah		3	2		
Boomer, Nathan	2		1		
Swindall, Isaac	2	4	4		
Thornton, Thomas	1	2	4		
Lary, Lother	1	1	1		
Lary, Joseph	2		3		
Bridgeman, Thomas	2		4		
Mason, James	2	5	2		
McGown, Joseph	3	3	3		
Sadler, John	2	3	3		
Sermon, Joseph	1		3		
Bray, John	3	2	4		
Cutrill, David	1	2	2		
Rowe, Edward	1	2	5		
Turner, Benjamin	1		1	1	
Binston, Reuben	1		2		
Harris, Elisha	1	1	2		
Hodges, James	1	2	2		3
Carter, Peter	1	2	1		
Carter, David	1		3		
Carraway, William	1	2	6		1
Green, David	1	2	4		
English, James	1		2		
Rowe, Mitchel	1	1	2		
English, Joseph	1		2		
English, Thomas	1		4		
McGown, William	1	2	3		
Binston, John	1		5		
Swindill, Caleb	2	1	1		
Harris, Jesse, Senr	1	4	3		
Swindill, Christopher	1	3	5		
White, Caleb	2	2	5		9
Tunnell, Warrington	1	2	2		
Watson, James	1	1	4		
Murray, Daniel	3	1	3		
White, Lydia	1	1	4		2
Sermon, Ann	1	1	1		
Sermon, Peter	1		3		
Carraway, John	2	3	3		
McCloud, Reuben	1	3	2		
Harris, Jesse	1	1	1		
Swindill, Joel	2	1	2		
Benson, Massey	1	2	4		
Gibbs, Cason	1	4	5		13
Jones, Abram	2	1	3		5
Dudley, George	1	1	3		2
Gibbs, Robert	2	2	5		4
Carter, George	1	3	4		
Peters, Michael	1	2	4		11
Kingsborough, Jabis	1				
Jennett, Robert	1	3	3		13
Jennett, Sarah			1		6
Jennett, Joseph	1	3	3		
Gibbs, Benjamin, Senr	1	1	6		10
Henry, Robert	1	4	2		
Henry, Samuel	2	4	4		
Insley, John	4	1	5		1
Thornton, William	1		3		
Neale, William	1	1	3		
Boomer, William	1	1	4		
Neale, William	2		3		1
Migget, Neale	1		1		
Jones, Solomon	2		3		2
Mann, Thomas	1	2	3		7
Jones, Morris	1	2	3		4
Gibbs, Benjamin, junr	1	5	2		4
Cohun, William	1	3	3		5
Gibbs, William, junr	1	2	2		4
Gibbs, John, Senr	1	2	3		3
Gibbs, Joseph, junr	2	2	2		9
Brinson, John	1	2	5		
Walls, Joshua	3		2		
Spencer, Edward	2		3		22
Spencer, Elizabeth		1	3		2
Spencer, William, Senr	3	3	5		8
Gibbs, Robert, Senr	2	2	2		31
Gibbs, Joseph	1	1	4		7
Williamson, Henry	2	1	3		
Gibbs, Selby	1		5		8
Gibbs, Jeremiah	1	1	2		3
Gaskill, Jacob	1	4	3		4
Gibbs, Robert, junr	1		2		4
Selby, Burrage	1				
Selby, Hutchins	1				7
Spencer, Benjamin	1	3	5		1
Harris, Thomas	3	1	1		
Carew, Henry	1				
Spencer, Nathan	1	3	5		1
Gibbs, William	1		1		
Hopkins, William	1		1		
Swindall, Josiah	3		5		
Spencer, Tucker	1		1		
Spring, Samuel	1		1		
Gibbs, Thomas	1		1		15
Sermon, Job	1	1	4		
Harris, Stephen	1	2	3		
Swindall, Joshua	1	1	2		
Swindall, John	1		2	1	
Cox, Jesse	1		2		1
Neale, Benjamin	1	1	6		
Spencer, Nathan, junr	1		1		
Gibbs, Benjamin	1	2	4		2
Clayton, Jemima		3	2		1
Swindall, Solomon	1		3		
Neale, John	1		3		
Harris, William	2	3	3		
Jones, Henry	1	1	2		1
Jones, Rebecca			1		4
Western, Samuel	1				
Harris, Ezekial, Senr	3	2	3		4
Selby, Samuel, junr	1	2	3		5
Selby, Samuel, Senr	1				4
Gibbs, Joseph, Senr	1		1		7
Gibbs, Jesse	1	1	2		3
Smith, William, Senr	3	3	3		
Harris, Ezekial, junr	1	1	3		
Gibbs, Thomas	1	2	1		2
Spencer, Richard	2	6	3		6
Kincey, Solomon	1	2	3		
Dier, Michael	1				
Neale, Ephraim	1	1	4		
Cutrill, Stephen	1				
Harbert, Ignatius	1	3	2		
Brooks, Thomas	1	2	3		1
Farrow, John	2	2	3		2
Caroon, Levi	1	2	2		
Swindall, Willis	1	1	2		
Sibley, Elizabeth	6	1	3		10
Spring, Abner	1	2	2		
Spencer, David	2	1	4		2
Gaskins, Jane	1	2	3		2
Gibbs, Henry	1	1	2		1
Gibbs, John	2	3	3		6
Carron, John	1	1	1		1
Boomer, Matthew	1				
Gibbs, Daniel	2	1	3		2
Spencer, Elizabeth			3		8
Reed, Ezekiel	1				
Henry, Robert	3	1	3		
Reed, Margaret	2	4	1		
Cutrill, John	1				
Cutrill, Charles	1	1			
Moor, John	1	1	3		
Isdall, George	1	1	2		
Selbey, Nathan	1	1	4		3
Spencer, Christopher	3	2	5		
Jones, Richard	1	2	5		
Coffee, Benjamin C	1	1	1		3
Cox, Winnifred	1		1		
Smith, Lucretia	1	1	4		1
Sanders, Elizabeth	1	4	3		8
Wormington, Mary	1		7		14
Mason, Caleb	1	3	2		
Wilson, Willis	1				3
Carron, Thomas	2	1	2		
Hopkins, Margaret	2		1		
Harris, William	2				
Watson, William	3	1	3		1
Duke, Francis	2	1	3		
Brooks, Stephen	2		3		4
Brooks, William	1	1	4		1
Brooks, Isaac	1	3	3		
Adams, Absalom	2	3	2		
Rascal, John	1	1	1		
Gibbs, Uriah	1		1		1
Hall, William	1		1		
Williams, Elizabeth	1	2	4		
Dixon, Elizabeth	1		4		4
Selbey, Samuel	1		4		
Spring, Aaron	2	2	4		2
Jones, Thomas	1		4		
Spencer, Thomas	1	1	3		
Brinn, John	2		3		
Evans, Caleb	1				
Swindall, Thomas	1				
Jones, David	1		1		1
Gaskell, Zerobabel	1	1	3		5
Jarvis, Josiah	3	1	7		
Caffey, John	2		3		
Jarvis, Elizabeth	2	1	3		
Jarvis, Zachariah	1		2		
Jarvis, Foster	1	1	4		
Mason, Jeremiah	1		4		
Creedle, Francis	2	6	2		
Hudson, Abel	1	1	3		
Tooley, Abel	3		3		
Fodrea, Thomas	1	2	3		

NEWBERN DISTRICT, HYDE COUNTY—Continued.

NAME OF HEAD OF FAMILY.	Free white males of 16 years and upward, including heads of families.	Free white males under 16 years.	Free white females, including heads of families.	All other free persons.	Slaves.
Creedle, James	1	1	2		
Harris, Jesse, junr	1		2		2
Tooley, Thomas, Senr	2	1	3		2
Tooley, Thomas, junr	1		2		1
Tooley, Jacob	2	1	1		11
Esther, Dorcas	1	1	2		
Slade, Benjamin	1				
Slade, Furniford	1				
Richards, Adam	1	3	1		
Richards, Richard	1	1	2		
Bell, Watson	1	2	1		
Slade, Nathanl	1	2	3		
Fortescue, John	1	1	6		5
Alderson, Simon	1	1	4		6
Jewell, Ebenezer	1	2	2		2
Banks, Ann	1		3		1
Banks, Ann	1	2	4		
Jewell, Mary		1	2		1
Slade, Ann	1	2	5		1
Whitehead, Kelan	1	4	2		
Fortescue, Moses	1	2	3		1
Slade, Ebenezer	1	2	1		1
Jasper, Elizabeth	1		2		15
Bell, Sena		1	4		
Slade, Ann			1		3
Fortescue, Simon	1				2
Tyson, Rebecca	2	2	4		10
Russel, Benjamin	1	2	5		9
Winfield, John	1				
Allen, Jesse	1	1	4		1
Allen, Josiah	1	1	2		
Allen, Jacob	1		3		
Allen, James	1	1			
Allen, Isaac	1	2	3		
Esther, James	1	2	7		
Thomas, Ross				1	
Booty, Richard	5	1	1		
Allen, Jeremiah	1	1	5		
McCarthy, Archibald	1	1	3		1
Fortescue, John	3				4
Morris, Francis	1	1	3		
Whitehead, Willis	1		1		
Allen, Raphael	1	3	3		
Allen, Hannah			2		1
Robinson, William		1	1	1	1
Huston, Hugh	1	1	2		7
Whitney, Sarah	2		2		23
Tyson, John	1	3	4		3
Buchum, William	3	4	3		
Satathwaight, Abram	1	1	1		2
Cleaves, James	2	1	4		
Jordan, Richard	2	1	3		8
Burgose, Malica	1	1	4		3
Ellis, Benjamin	5		3	1	
Swindall, Jacob	2	1	2		
Russel, John	1		2		5
Russel, William	2		8		8
Palmer, Samuel	2	1	3		2
Smith, Thomas	1	3	4		3
Davis, Samuel	2	1	3		
Parmerle, Benjamin	3	3	2		14
Brittal, James	4		2		
Tooley, Henry	1		3		8
Hasseys, Thomas	1	1	1		
Davis, David	1	1	1		4
Bernard, German	1	1	2		
Alderson, John	1	2	5	1	10
Mallison, Francis	1		8		
Tooley, Nathan	2	3	4		3
Tooley, Levi	1	2	3		1
Jasper, James	1	1	2		7
Jasper, Selden	1		1		5
Henderson, Thomas	2	1	2		1
Dennison, George	1		3		
Leary, Mary	2		1		
Seabrook, Daniel	2	1	1		
Campbell, John	2	5	1		
Fortescue, Richard	1	1			
Slade, John	1		3		1
Silverthorn, Robert	1		1		
Carter, Stephen	1	1	3		
Cutrill, Solomon	3	2	4		
Rew, Thomas	2	1	3		
Mason, Christopher	2	3	4		1
Grey, Elisha	1	3	2		
Richard, Mary	1	1	3		
Tooley, Cornelius	2		1		1
Jordan, John	1	2	1		21
Rew, Southy	2		2		
Mason, Samuel	1	1	4		4
Jasper, Richard	1	1	2		2
Mason, John, Senr	1		5		
Tooley, Richard	1	2	2		
Rew, Mary			4		
Mason, Thomas	2	1	2		
Rew, Southy, junr	1	2	2		

NAME OF HEAD OF FAMILY.	Free white males of 16 years and upward, including heads of families.	Free white males under 16 years.	Free white females, including heads of families.	All other free persons.	Slaves.
Mason, John, junr	1	1	2		
Tooley, Jeremiah	1	2	1		1
Silverthorn, John S	2		2	1	2
Bell, Joshua	2	2	4		7
Bell, Morris	3		1		2
Slade, Elijah	1	1	1		
Bell, Dixon	4		6		5
Cleaves, John	2	2	3		1
Esther, John	1		3		1
Wickerson, Shadrach	1				
Inloes, James	1				
Bell, Jonathan	1		1		3
Bell, John	1	4	4		6
Esther, Thomas	1		2		
Richard, Jacob	1		3		1
Powers, Elizabeth				3	
Tooley, Rachel	3	1	3		
Bell, George	2	2	4		1
Bell, Lyttleton	1	3	4		
Bell, Jaconias	2		1		
Bell, Cornelius	1	1	4		
Rew, Reuben	1	2	2		1
Rew, Frederick	1	3	2		1
Clark, Thomas	1		3		
Kipps, Francis M	1		1		
Davis, John	1		1		
Davis, William, Senr	1		2		
Davis, William, Junr	1	1	2		
Warner, James	1	2	1		
Tooley, Rhodes		2	2		
Whitehead, Nathaniel	1		3		
Whitehead, John	2		1		
Lacy, Isaac	1	2	1		
Lacy, John	1	1	1		
Jasper, William R	4		4		8
Potter, John	2	1	7		7
Fortescue, Elijah	1		4		
Mason, Morris	1				
Richard, John	1	1	3		
Richard, Henry	1		2		
Tooley, Major	2	4	3		
White, Church	1				
Arthur, Wilson	1				
Lacy, Adam	1				
Richard, Thomas	1				
Esther, William	1				
Alberd, Richard	1		2		
Dixon, George	1	1	2		2
Boston					2
Pairtree, Noah	1		4		
Pairtree, Wilson	1	1	4		
Pairtree, Holmes, Senr	2	4	4		
Webster, John	1	1	3		4
Cording, William	1		3		
Jordan, Rothers	3		5		6
Spruell, Stephen	2	1	3		
Jordan, Abram	1	2	3		1
Seabrook, Daniel	1	1	1		
Wright, Sarah		1	5		
Wright, Thomas	4	2	3		
Moor, Henry	3	3	4		
Fair, John	2		5		
Capps, James	1	2	4		
Harrington, Charles	1	3	3		
Burgase, Sarah			3		
Chambers, John	3		2		3
Wilkins, Patrick	1	1	2		6
Foreman, Lazarus, Senr	1	2	7		5
Bailey, James	1	2	4		
Linton, John	1	2	4		3
Foreman, Benjamin	1		2		6
Wilkins, Thomas	2	1	4		6
Barrow, Elizabeth		4	2		4
Cordan, Sarah	3	2	1		3
Eagleton, John	1	2	2		
Wilkins, Benjamin	1	1			5
Cordan, Benjamin	1		3		
Equals, Joseph	2		1		
Collins, Henry	1		2		
Harvey, John	2	2	3		1
Gergainus, Joel	2	2	4		
Capps, Richard	1	2	2	2	1
Capps, Marmaduke	1	1	1		2
Capps, Thomas	1		1		
Keach, Jasper	1	4	3		
Wilkinson, Abraham	1		3		1
Winfield, James	1		2		
Kepps, Seth	1	3	3		1
Bailey, Jesse N	1	2	6		2
Bailey, Joshua	1	2	3		1
Daley, William	3		1		6
Winley, Thomas	1		1		
Ebern, Lyttleton	2		1		1
Foreman, Lazarus G	1		4		
Chambers, John	3		4	3	
Harvey, Nathan	2	1	4		

NAME OF HEAD OF FAMILY.	Free white males of 16 years and upward, including heads of families.	Free white males under 16 years.	Free white females, including heads of families.	All other free persons.	Slaves.
Bailey, Joshua	1		2		3
Bailey, David	2	1	3		
Foreman, Joshua	1	3	2		2
Hardison, Charles	2		2		1
Hardison, Samuel	1		2		
Wright, John	1	1	2		
Eagleton, Noah	1		5		
Abrams, Robert	1		2		
Conner, Jacob	1	1	3	1	1
Booty, Rainal	1	2	3		
Hammon, Rose	1		4		
Bailey, William	1	1	2		
Bailey, Simon	1		1		1
Keach, Joseph	1	2	1		1
Fulsher, Joseph	1		3		2
Bailey, Samuel	1		5		
Hamilton, James	1		3		
Highth, Thomas	1	1	4		2
Webster, Richard	1				
Foreman, Uriah	1				
Wilkins, John	2				11
Simons, Gideon	1	3	2		
Selbey, Henry	1				
Harris, Gibson	1	1	1		1
Pairtree, Holmes, junr	1				
Pairtree, Major	1				
Slaughter, Richard	1			2	
Williams, Thomas	1				
Abrams, John	2	1	1		
Abrams, William	1	1	1		
Hardison, Isaac	1		3		
Mallison, Thomas	1		2		1
Mallison, John	1				
Elsbrey, Ormond	1	1	1		3
Jordan, Zachariah	1				1
Jordan, James	1				
Gordon, William	3		2		9
Harris, Ebenezer	1				
Martin, Hosiah	1	3	4		12
Adams, William	1				
Smith, Duncan	1	2	2		1
Harris, Sarah			3		6
Lathum, Jesse		1	3		8
Jordan, Abram	1	2	3		
Robins, James	1	4	1		(*)
Cordin, Thomas, junr	1		1		1
Selbey, Burridge H	1	2	4		8
Capps, Cason	2	3	3		
Barrow, George	2	1	1		11
Barrow, Zachariah	2		6		21
Hovey, Seth	1	1	3		5
Webster, James	1			3	1
Harvey, Wheriet	1	1	4		
Foreman, Elizabeth		1	2		7
Thorogood, Esther		2	3		2
Chance, Sarah				9	
Jordan, Thomas	1	1	1		9
Wilkinson, Elizabeth			2		9
Gailerd, Mary		3	4		1
Eborn, James	3	2	3		13
Flinn, Rebeccah		3	3		
Hobbs, Edward	1	2	1		
Gailard, Rosanna		1	2		
Winley, Thomas, Senr	2	1	1		
Sachwell, John	1	2	5		9
Scott, Henry, Senr	2	2	3		8
Gergainus, William, Senr	1		1		
Gergainus, William, Junr	1	2	4		
Lloyd, Susannah		6	3		
Lathum, Fennus	2	4	2		8
Eagleton, Mary		2	2		
Graidless, John	1				
Scot, Henry, junr	1	2	2		
Foreman, Rebecca			1		8
Eborn, Isaac	2	2	4		17
Eborn, Rebecca	1	1	1		
Gergainus, Jesse	1		1		
Winley, Maple			1		4
Winley, Sarah		4	1		2
Gergainus, Lydia			3		
Eborn, Mary	2	1	3		5
Flinn, Benjamin	2	1	1		6
Winley, James	1				
Gailerd, Jeremiah	2		7		2
Manderwell, Samuel	1		2		
Eborn, Zenus	1		2		2
Wilkinson, Isaac	1	1	3		3
Wilkinson, Jacob	1	2	4		4
Barnett, Robert	1	2	5		
Flinn, Enoch	2				
Manderwell, Samuel, Junr	1		1		
Slow, Alexander	1	1	3		
Toppin, Thomas	2	1	2		2

* Illegible.

NEWBERN DISTRICT, HYDE COUNTY—Continued.

NAME OF HEAD OF FAMILY.	Free white males of 16 years and upward, including heads of families.	Free white males under 16 years.	Free white females, including heads of families.	All other free persons.	Slaves.	NAME OF HEAD OF FAMILY.	Free white males of 16 years and upward, including heads of families.	Free white males under 16 years.	Free white females, including heads of families.	All other free persons.	Slaves.	NAME OF HEAD OF FAMILY.	Free white males of 16 years and upward, including heads of families.	Free white males under 16 years.	Free white females, including heads of families.	All other free persons.	Slaves.
Philips, John	1	1	2			Gailard, Winfield	1				1	Harvey, Richard, Senr	1		5		
Eborn, Jehu	1	2	1		3	Satterthwaite, William	1	2	4		6	Winfield, Robert	1	1	2		1
Gergainus, Jonathan	2	1	6		2	Clark, William	1	3	3		13	Davis, John	1		2		
Durdin, Jacob	1		2		7	Clark, Henry	1		3		8	Davis, William	1		4		
Gailard, James	1	4	5		2	Arthur, John	1		1			Winfield, Bryan	1	1	2		3
Winley, Michael	1	1	3		1	Winfield, John	2	1	5		10	Gallaway, Francis	1	1	1		
Winley, Churchill	1		1		1	Harvey, Richard, Senr	2		1		8	Banks, Charles	1				
Smith, James	1	2	4			Winfield, Obadiah	1	1	2			Davenport, Edmond	1	1	2		
Davenport, Joel	1	2	1			Davis, Samuel	1	3	3		1	Satterthwaite, William, Senr	1	2	3		
Howard, William, Senr	2	1	4			McWilliams, John	2	1	3		4	Stilley, Ezekiel	1	3	2		
Davenport, George	2	3	4			Gergainus, Ellen	1	2	3			Wilkinson, Thomas	2				
Ratcliff, James	1	1	1			Johnston, Jeremiah				5		Morris, William	1		2		
Eborn, William	1	3	2		2	Davis, William	2	1	5		6	Rogers, Benjamin	1		2		
Howard, William, junr	1		2			Paul, Jacob	4		4			Wilkinson, John	1	2	3		
Hollawell, Benjamin	1	1	1			Bishop, William	1		5			Banks, Moses	1	1	3		
Bilberry, William	1	1	1			Smith, Stephen	2	2	2			Smith, James	1		4		
Hollawell, Zadiac	1		1			Winfield, Withy		1	3		3	Jones, Christopher	1	1	2		
Spruell, Michael	1	1	2			Wilkinson, Abram	1	4	2		7	Ryan, William	1		1		
Gailerd, John	1					Arthur, Abram	1	2	6		1	Satterthwaite, Samuel	1		1		
Gailerd, William	1	1	1			Arthur, John	1		1			Harvey, David	1		2		1
Hollawell, Margaret	1	1	3		7	Satterthwaite, Abram	2	3	2			Gergainus, Aaron	1	3	5		1
Manderwell, John	1					Banks, Dorcas			4			Wilkinson, James	1	2	5		3
Eborn, Nathan	1		2		1	Kimmey, Ann			2		1	Winfield, Richard, Senr	1		7		7
Winley, Levi	1		1		1	Adams, Mary		3	3			Satterthwaite, Jonathan	3	4	5		5
Eborn, Samuel	1	1			3	Mason, Mary			2			Winfield, Jesse	1		6		
Simons, Elias	1					Smith, Solomon	2	2	3			Davis, John	1	5	2		
Winley, James	1					Chambers, James	2	1	2			Grey, Jeptha	1		5		
Jermin, Henry	1		3			Maynard, William	1					Satterthwaite, Isaac	1		3		
McSwain, Edward	1	1			1	Smith, Thomas	1		2			Davis, James	1	3	2		
Craig, James	1		1		2	Elsbre, Ephraim	1		2		4	Bishop, John	1	1	2		
McSwain, Zachariah	1	1	2		7	Winfield, Richard, junr	1	2				Johnston, David	1		1		
Harvey, Wherry	1	2	5			Slade, William	1		2			Slade, John	1				
Smith, Joseph	1	3	5			Rogers, Stephen	1		3			Spady, Peter	1		2		
Hollaway, William	1	2	2			Wilkinson, Frederic	1	3	2		1	Winfield, Obadiah	1	1	2		
Gaiber, Stephen	1	2	2		2	Wilkinson, Robert	1		2			Stokesberry, John	1		1		
Ratcliff, James	1	3	1			Wilson, John	1		2			Brown, Nathan				1	
Blount, Reading	2				36	Bishop, George	1	1	2								
Galaway, Francis	1	1	1			Slade, Major	1										

NEWBERN DISTRICT, JOHNSTON COUNTY.

NAME OF HEAD OF FAMILY.	Free white males of 16 years and upward, including heads of families.	Free white males under 16 years.	Free white females, including heads of families.	All other free persons.	Slaves.	NAME OF HEAD OF FAMILY.	Free white males of 16 years and upward, including heads of families.	Free white males under 16 years.	Free white females, including heads of families.	All other free persons.	Slaves.	NAME OF HEAD OF FAMILY.	Free white males of 16 years and upward, including heads of families.	Free white males under 16 years.	Free white females, including heads of families.	All other free persons.	Slaves.
Boon, Joseph, junr	3	3	3	3	24	Hill, William	1	1	2			Guein, Thomas	1	3	4		5
Gurley, John	2		2			Woodard, Benjamin	1	4	2			Powell, Benjamin	1				5
Tiner, Nicholas	1		2			Edwards, Joseph	3	2	4		1	Dees, Daniel	3	2	1		7
Musslewhite, Leonard	1		2			Strickland, Benjamin	1	2	3			Allen, John	2	2	4		15
Capps, William	1		1			Battin, Joshua	2	4	6			Davis, Jacob	1	1	3		
Boon, Joseph, Senr	1		1	2	10	Runnell, Michael	2	2	2			Davis, Arthur	1	2	3		1
Raiford, Philip	1	4	4		11	Peedin, James	1	1	4			Creech, Joshua	2	6	2		
Lynch, Elizabeth			1		1	Overbay, David	2		4			Collins, Deal	2	1	3		
Gurley, Mary, Senr			2			Oliver, John, junr		2	3			Phillips, John	1	3	2		
Gurley, Ann	2	2	2		3	Oliver, Thomas	1		1			Blackman, William	2	2	5		20
Bulls, Rachel	1		4			Tiner, Benjamin	2	1	3			Wiggins, Willis	4		4		13
Davis, Milly	1	2	3			Edwards, Micajah, junr	1	1	1			Camelion, Abram	6	4	2		22
Hughes, John	3	3	4			Bassingale, George	1		2			Adkinson, Nathan	1	2	3		12
Gurley, Mary, junr	1	2	4			Stattons, Isaac	1				1	Adkinson, John	2		1		15
Edwards, Elizabeth	1	1	2			Edwards, William	1	1	2		1	Stephens, William	1				7
Brazil, Jacob	2	1	4			Edwards, Benjamin	1		2			Jernigan, Jacob	2	2	3		13
Rains, Ann			1		1	Vincent, Levin	1	5	3			Lyttleton, Charles	1		1		1
Talton, William, Senr	2	1	2			Musslewhite, William	1	4	4			Craddock, Thomas	1	2	5		6
Oliver, John, Senr	2	1	2			Wilson, John	1	1	4			Jernigan, Lewis	3	1	5		6
Woodall, John	4		3			Whurley, Winifred			1			Lyttleton, William	2		5		
Burnet, Doll				5		Sims, Patience	2	3	1		1	Williams, Benjamin	1		1		
Bulls, William	2	2	4		2	Worrin, Elijah	2	1	4	1	4	Pervis, Jesse	1	3	4		
Holt, James	1	3	1			Prance, Solomon	1	3	2			Thomson, Elijah	1	3	2		1
Whitley, Needham	1	3	2		10	Pervis, James	1		1			Thomson, Jarret	1	2			1
Rains, Oliver	1	3	4		1	Hughes, Josiah	1	1	1			Prance, John	1		1		
Pierce, Philip	1	2	4		2	Rains, Ambrose	1	2	1		2	Adkins, Raimond	1	4	3		
Watkins, Jesse	2	3	5		1	Brewer, David	1	2	3			Pilkington, Richard	4				
Hays, John	1	1	2		7	Brewer, Martha		3	2			Burnet, Sander					12
Davis, William	1	3	1			Edwards, Micajah, Senr	2	1	4			Tiner, Jesse, junr	1	1	5		
Sims, Benjamin	1		2			Spencer, Jesse	1	1	2			Patterson, John H	1	4	3		
Gurley, Isum	1	3	2			Holt, Etheldred	1	1	2			Strickland, Jeremiah	1		4		
Wellings, Charles	2	1	3			Musselwhite, Uriah	1	1	3			Musslewhite, Drew	1	1	4		
Talton, John	1	1	3			Brady, James	1					Brady, William	1	5	4		
Capps, William	1		2		1	Oliver, James	1		1			Lankford, James	1	1	2		
Hays, Jesse	2	2	6		6	Warrin, Elijah	1	2	3		7	Tiner, Jesse, Senr	3	3	2		7
Howell, Elisha	1		3			Daughtry, Jacob	1	1	2			Parnal, Benjamin	1	5	2		
Wise, Thomas	1		3			Bryan, Lovit	1				20	Piner, Thomas	1		1		
Capps, Matthew	1	1	2			Ingram, Joseph	1	3	2		12	Harold, Samuel	2				5
Bridges, Benjamin	1	4	2		2	Roberts, William, Junr	1	3	3			Collins, George	2		4		
Gurley, Joseph	1		1			Powell, Nathan	1		2		10	Adkins, Joseph	1	3	2		
Oliver, Needham	1		1			Howard, Thomas	1	1	1			Bailey, Margaret			2		
Pedin, William	1	1	1			Strickland, David	1	2	3			Davis, John	1	3	3		
Stephens, Bethany	1	1	2	2	1	Strickland, Uriah	1		3			Turley, Richard	1		7		
Stephens, Benjamin	1		2		2	Roberts, William	1	1	2		9	Warren, Isaiah	1	4	4	2	1
Bulls, Barnaby	2	2	3		4	Warren, Richard	1		2		9	Isler, John	1	2	4		9
Bulls, Jethro	1					Bridges, Jane			2		7	Crawford, Hardy	2		1		
Edwards, Jacob	1		1			Whitley, John	1	1			10	Scott, Olive				8	
Barwick, John	1	3	1			Langford, James	1	1	2			Armstrong, Clement	1	1	6		
Gurley, Edward	3	3	3			Gray, Thomas	3	4	5		26	Stephens, Rebecca			1		
Pierce, Shadrach	1		1			Williams, John	1				4	Simpson, Thomas	2	2	2		
Massey, Ralph	1	1	2			Powell, Needham	1	3	2		7	Mitchel, Henry	2				
Whood, Charles	1					Thomson, Nicholas	1	3	4			Harold, Samuel					5
Lynch, Cornelius	1	3	3			Farmer, William	1	4	3		10	Credle, William	1	7	2		
Jernigan, Arthur	1	4	4		3	Powell, Isaac	2	1	5		7	Bryan, Benjamin	1				24

NEWBERN DISTRICT, JOHNSTON COUNTY—Continued.

NAME OF HEAD OF FAMILY.	Free white males of 16 years and upward, including heads of families.	Free white males under 16 years.	Free white females, including heads of families.	All other free persons.	Slaves.
Taylor, William	1	1	2		1
Duck, Jacob	1	1	6		3
Goodwin, Samuel	2	3	2		
Hinnant, William	2	1	7		2
Odum, John	3		3		11
Keen, Alice	2		3		
Saucer, William	1	2	5		
Brassil, Richard	1	2	4		1
Boyte, Sarah	3		3		
Watson, Elizabeth	2		2		
Watson, Mary		3	4		
Brown, William	4		3		
Langley, James	2	1	5		
Horn, William	1		2		
Durdin, Judith	2	2	2		
Pierce, Arthur	1	1	2		7
Brewer, Martha			1		
Garrell, John	2	1	2		
Godin, Thomas	2	4	4		
Wadkins, James	2	2	4		
Peacock, Uriah	1	2	2		
Peacock, Archibald	1		3		
Richardson, John	1	5	4		
Pierce, Sarah			2		6
Kirby, Jesse	2		3		1
Neusum, Patience			3		4
Bailey, William	3	1	2		1
Bailey, Micajah	1	2	2		
Brown, Jesse	1	2	1		
Brown, William	1		1		
Bateman, Jonathan	2	1	2		
Gulley, George	1	1	3		2
Bateman, William	1	1	3		
Boyekin, Judith		1	4		
Barnes, Archilaus	1		2		
Boyte, Thomas	1		4		
Bateman, Jesse	1	5	3		
Corbit, Joshua	1	2	3		
Cockroll, Thomas	3	4	5		
Folk, James	1		1		
Folk, Thomas	2	2	2		
Folk, John	1	1	3		
Folk, Henry	1				
Garrell, Isaac	1	1	3		1
Grice, Lewis	1			1	1
Grice, Stephen	1		1		1
Horn, Joel	1	1	6		
Hinniant, James	1	3	6		1
Hollimon, John	1		4		
Horn, Caleb	1		1		
Johnston, William	1		3		
Kerby, James	1				
Keen, John		1	3		
Kerby, Absalom	2	1	2		
Pierce, Everit	1	1	4		11
Pierce, Theophilus	1	3	3		1
Pierce, Richard, jun	1	1	1		1
Pierce, Simon	1	1	2		2
Pugh, Tignal	2				
Pierce, Ephraim	1		5		2
Pierce, John	1	1	1	3	4
Rentfrow, Noel	1	4	4		
Register, Jesse	1	2	3		
Ramsay, Anderson	1	1	1		
Saucer, Arthur	1		3		
Saucer, Abel	1	1	2		
Smith, Nathan	2		1		
Spiva, Aaron, jun	1	3	3		
Saucer, Joseph	1		1		
Spiva, John	1	1	3		
Spiva, Aaron, Sen	1		2		
Thorn, John	1	3	5		
Talton, Hardy	1	2	2		
Woodard, Thomas	2	4	7		1
Watson, Levin	1	3	3		
Watson, James	1		3		
Woodard, Luke	1	2	3		
Watson, Obadiah	1	1	2		
Williamson, Hardy	1		3		
Watson, Ephraim	1	2	3		
Wadkins, Kinchen	1		3		
Watson, Solomon	1		3		
Wilkinson, Alacnor	1		5		
Waddle, Edward	1	4	2		
Pierce, Jesse	2	4	3		4
Oneale, Patrick	1	1	6		
Neusum, Joel	1		1		2
Sims, Shadrack	1		6		3
Bass, William	1	4	3		
Hackney, William	1	3	1		13
Ponder, Thomas	1	2	3		4
Holder, Elizabeth	2	1	2		10
Broughton, Jesse	2		3		
Stancil, John, Sen	3	3	4		5
Johnston, Solomon	2	3	4		
Hocket, Sophia	2	1	3		
Oneales, Alice	1	2	3		1

NAME OF HEAD OF FAMILY.	Free white males of 16 years and upward, including heads of families.	Free white males under 16 years.	Free white females, including heads of families.	All other free persons.	Slaves.
Hinton, Mary	1	1	6		
Bailey, David	1	3	1		
Hollimon, Frederick	2		2		2
Richardson, William	2	4	2		6
Richardson, Applewhite	1	3	5		7
Holliman, William	4		6		1
Stephens, Ann		1	2		
Bailey, Tamsey		1	2		3
Price, John	1		6		
Bailey, William	1	4	6		
Crumple, Benjamin	2	1	4		
Gilmore, Harbert	1	1	2		1
Price, Dixon	1	1	4		
Onailes, Moses	1	4	4		
Price, Richard	2	2	2		
Jourdin, Henry	1	4	4		
Price, Etheldred	1	1	3		
Price, Rice, Senr	2	4	3		
Price, Nathan	1		6		
Woodard, Jethro	2	2	5		
Price, Micajah	2	2	3		
Oneales, Isum	1	4	1		1
Johnston, Arthur B	1		2		
Oneales, Zachariah	2	4	2		1
Bailey, Arthur	1		2		1
Pope, Arthur	2	3	5		
Johnston, Burrel	1	2	2		
Hinton, Jesse	1	2	1		
Parker, Matthew, Senr	3	3	4		
Holmes, Frederick	1	2	3		
Moore, Randal	1	3	1		
Thomas, John	1	1	3		
Wilkinson, Benjamin	1	3	3		
Eatman, Thomas	1	1	3		
Onailes, William, junr	3	3	3		2
Price, Rice, junr	1		1		
Bailey, Isum	1	1	1		
Price, James, junr	1	2	2		
Onailes, Samuel	1	2	2		
Naron, Acquilon	1		4		
Price, Simon	1	2	3		1
Pope, Richard	2		5		
Johnston, Lewis	1		1		
Cobb, John P	1	1	5		
Hall, Martin	1	3	2		
Duck, John	1	1	2		2
Boyekin, Francis	1		2		
Bailey, John	1		3		2
Joiner, Hardy	1	4	2		
Bailey, Judith		1	3		2
Joiner, Nathan	1	1	2		
Lyles, Lewis	4		2		
Crumpler, West	1	3	3		
Barber, John	1	1	2		
Barber, Henry	2	2	4		
Joiner, Thomas	1	2	2		
Starlin, William	3		7		
Stephens, William	1				
Strickland, Samuel	1		1		
Tolbert, Samuel	1	3	4		2
Onailes, Amos	1	1	2		1
Vincent, John	2	1	2		3
Godin, Edmond	3	1	2		
Hatcher, Mary			1		4
Wilkinson, Charles	3		2		
Onailes, William, Senr	1	4	2		
Parker, Gabriel	1		2		1
Gardner, Joseph	1	1	6		
Gardner, John	2	2	3		
Watson, Jesse	2	2	4		1
Watson, David	4	2	5		
Johnston, Sampson	2	7	6		
Batten, Nathan	2	7	8		
Hailes, John, Senr	2	1	5		7
Spicer, Joseph	2	3	5		
Parnal, Jeremiah	1	4	2		
Thomas, Elisha	2	2	4		15
Rairies, Anthony	1				
Walker, Major	1	1	1		
Eason, Moses, Senr	4		6		
Siercey, William	1		1		
Horn, Milley			4		
Adkinson, Milkey		2	4		
Pool, John	2	1	3		
Hill, Shadrach	2	3	1		
Smith, Samuel	2	4	7		53
Blurton, Edward	1	3	3		4
Hinnant, William	1	3	3		5
Moore, John	1	4	4		
Hearn, Mason	2	1	4		
Eason, Sanders	1	3	2		
Jones, Thomas	1	3	5		
Searcey, George	1	4	1		
Eason, Moses, junr	1	1	2		
Spicer, James	1	1	1		4
Hailes, Chapman	1		4		
Hill, Thomas	1	5	2		

NAME OF HEAD OF FAMILY.	Free white males of 16 years and upward, including heads of families.	Free white males under 16 years.	Free white females, including heads of families.	All other free persons.	Slaves.
Battin, John	2	1	4		
Walker, Jacob	1		1		
Smith, William	1		4		
Elvinton, Shadrach	1	3	2		2
Wilkinson, Charles, junr	1	1	4		
Elvinton, Gideon	2		4		1
Gardner, William		1	2		
Starling, Adam	2	4	7		
Monk, Willis	1		2		
Watson, Silas	1				
Hatcher, Benjamin	1	1	2		
Adkinson, Amos	1	2	3		
Cooper, George	1	2	5		2
Hailes, John	1	2	1		3
Watson, Jacob	1		1		
Bullard, James	1				
Johnston, James	1	4	1		
Lynch, Joshua	1	3	3		
Price, Jeremiah	1	3	3		
Watson, Ezekiel	2	3	4		
Adkinson, Micajah	1				
Hatcher, William	1	1	6		1
Parker, Hardy	1	3	3		2
Raines, Frederick	1	1	2		
Johnston, Robert	1	1	2		
Searcey, Daniel	2	3	3		
Price, Rice	1	1	3		
Spiva, William	1		1		
Onailes, Ross	1		1		
Stancil, John	1		1		1
Killingsworth, John	1	2	1		1
Stallens, Jacob	1	1	1		
Jones, Ambrose	1	1	2		
Bankum, James	1	2	3		
Watson, Simon	1	1	1		
Sessions, Ferreley					
Oliver, William	1				
Wilkinson, Reuben	1	3	3		
Searcy, John	1	2	4		6
Shaw, James	2	2	5		1
Lee, John	3		2		6
Hinton, Malichi	1	3	3		17
Hinton, Sarah		1	1		4
Parry, Dempsey	1	2	5		
Gale, Patience			2		
Muniham, Judith		1	1		
Lee, William			3		
Woodard, Elizabeth	1	1	2		2
Brenan, Thomas	2		2		
Nowell, John	2	1	5		
Owtin, Jesse	4	1	1		4
Delk, Jacob	2	3	2		
Wimberly, Malicah	1	2	5		1
Green, Elizabeth		2	2		
High, Joseph	1	3	3		
Walker, Elijah	1	1	1		
Gulley, Robert	2		4		4
Green, Jesse	3	4	5		
Walls, William	1		2		
Taylor, Josiah	1	3	5		
Irvin, Joseph	2		3		
Hill, Benjamin	2		4		
Holliman, Seth	1	1	4		
Snipes, John	1	1	2		
Walker, William	1	2	4		
Wilder, Samuel	2	4	7		3
Green, John	2	1	4		
Wall, Jesse	2	2	4		
Gulley, Meed	2	4	3		
Lee, Edward	2	2	3		
Killingsworth, Freeman	2	2	2		
Wilder, Matthew	2	3	5		2
Bryan, Lewis	2		2		
Langley, Miles	2	4	2		
Hinton, George	2				1
Watson, John	2	4	2		12
Brenan, William	1	3	3		
Wilder, William	2	1	2		
Williams, Harold	1				
Walls, John	1	1	1		
Newell, James	1	1	1		
Brenan, Joseph	1		2		
Killingsworth, Freeman, Jr	1				
Hailer, Henry	1	1	4		
Duck, Timothy	1	5	2		
Nelson, Wilson	1		3		
Hinton, William	2	1			10
Earpe, William	1	4	2		5
Welbern, Lewis	1				
Brenan, Cason	1	5	6		
Hinton, Isaac	1	6	4		13
Parcy, Reuben	1				
Lee, John	2	1	3		
King, Ilse	2	2	4		2
Earpe, William, jr	2		3		
Finch, Henry	2	2	3		

NEWBERN DISTRICT, JOHNSTON COUNTY—Continued.

NAME OF HEAD OF FAMILY.	Free white males of 16 years and upward, including heads of families.	Free white males under 16 years.	Free white females, including heads of families.	All other free persons.	Slaves.
Lysle, George	1		3		
Oneales, William	1		2		
Bryan, William	3	1	1		2
Reading, Francis	1	1	1		
Jones, Isaac	3	2	2		5
Chesser, Mary			4		
Rollins, Drury	1	1	3		
Rogers, Daniel	2	2	1		
Lockhart, James	1	4	4		11
Killingsworth, John	3	2	3		1
Turner, John	1	3	5		
Gulley, John	2	2	3		
Rivers, Richard	1	1	5		
Sauls, Abner	4		3		12
Philips, Benjamin	1				
Ferrill, Cornelius	1				
Dodd, John	1	4	5	1	
Carter, Evan	1		1	1	1
Ellis, John	1				
Bryan, Arthur	1	1			11
Gregory, Etheldred	3	3	1		8
Price, John	2		3		
Hinton, John	1	3	3		6
Averit, Daniel	1	5	2		3
Penny, Edward	2	1	3		
Price, Edward	1	1	1		2
Price, Thomas	1	4	2		
Hardcastle, James	1	4	1		
Massey, Drury	1	4	3		1
Johnston, Sylvanus	1	2	3		
Penney, Caleb	2	2	5		3
Penney, Alexander	2		2		
Copeland, Charles	1	1	5		
Luper, William	2	2	7		
Rogers, Daniel	1				
Ferrill, Jacob	1	2	6		
Ferrill, Nicholas	1	3	2		
Gulley, John	1		5		
Carter, Matthew	2	4	3		8
Bendinfield, John	2	3	3		
Willowby, Solomon	1	1	3		4
Price, James	1		2		
Jordan, Abner	1	3	2		
Kelly, John	2	1	3		
Johnston, William	2	3	3		
Brite, John	1	3	4		
Lockhart, Stephen	1				
Johnston, Joel	1	1	1		
Snipes, William	2	2	2		
Stallions, Zadik	1	3	4		5
Smith, Benjamin	1	2			5
Hinton, Hardy	1	2	1		1
Copeland, William	1	1	2		
Prince, David	2	4	4		
Lockhart, Osborn	1				
Holt, Richard	3	2	4		
Smith, Jesse	1	2	3		
Harvey, Jane			1		
Kelly, Charles	1	3	5		
Duncan, John	1	1	4		
Bryan, Needham	1		2		6
Nordin, Thomas	1	1	1		
Franklin, William	1	5	3		
James, Thomas	1		1		2
Price, Rial	1		1		
Cheshire, John	1				
Cheshire, Zachariah	1				
Blurtin, Henry	2	2	2		1
Gurlin, Mary	1		3		
Sanders, Reuben	1		3		8
Smith, Margaret		1	2		
Johnston, Moses	2		4		1
Youngblood, Thomas	2	1	2		2
Austin, John	2	3	3		
Stephenson, Solomon	2		4		
Messer, William	2	1	1		
Perry, Abram	2	3	3		
Fluellin, Sarah			4		
Johnston, Amos	3	1	2		
Barber, Plye	3	1	4		
Johnston, Martin	2	2	5		
Stephens, Edward	3	3	4		9
Johnston, Henry	2	2	3		5
Pate, Traverse	3	1	2		
Fish, Sarah		1	2		3
Leech, Thomas	2	1	5		7
Jones, Matthew	4	3	4		12
McCuller, John	1	1	4		
Johnston, Sarah	1	1	2		
Taylor, William	2	1	5		7
Gower, John	2	1	2		
Wood, John	2		2		
Smith, John	3	1	4		16
Blount, William	1	3	4		
Smith, Etheldred	1				6
Carrol, John	1	3	4	1	
Lowell, Clayton	1		2		

NAME OF HEAD OF FAMILY.	Free white males of 16 years and upward, including heads of families.	Free white males under 16 years.	Free white females, including heads of families.	All other free persons.	Slaves.
Johnston, Isum	1	1	1		
Langdon, James	1	1	5		1
Lankford, Henry	1	1	1		
Alston, Asa	1	1	2		
Stephenson, John	1	2	4		
Whittington, Richard	1	5	4		
Gower, William	1	3	5		
Johnston, Starlin	3		3		
Johnston, Amos, jr	3		3		
Williams, John	1	2	4		1
Messer, William	1		4		
Flowers, Jacob	2	7	4		
Johnston, Simon	1	2	1		1
Sanders, William	1	1	3		3
Right, Josiah	1	2	2		
Young, John	1	3	4		
Coats, Solomon	1	1	3		
Parish, Jabis	1	3	7		
Carr, Samuel	2		1		
Wren, Martha			2		
Coats, William	1	1	7		
Carrol, William	1	1	3		
Johnston, Abel	1	4	4		
Smith, Benjamin	1	2	3		
Barber, George	1	2	1		
Johnston, Philip	2				
Stephens, William	1	1	2		3
Carrol, James	1				
Munihan, John	1				
Bryan, Clement	1				13
Ivy, David	2	4	3		
Jennings, Hezekiah	1		2		
Barnes, Mirac	1		3		14
Johnston, Isaac	1		1		
Coats, John	1	2	5		
Flowers, Needham	1				
Lowell, Mary			2		
Honeycutt, Drury		3	4		
Williams, Ephraim	1		3		
Powers, Jesse	1	2	3		
Thorpe, Thomas	1		6		7
Woodall, James	1		3		
Dodd, Robert	1	3	2		
Rials, William	1		1		
Stephens, Zachariah	1		1		
Utley, Allen	1		1		1
Stephenson, James	1	1	5		
Bryan, Blake	2	2	2		9
Eason, John	2	1	3	1	9
Pool, John	2	4	3		3
Norris, Noah	1		5		1
Youngblood, William	1		3		1
Dorham, William	1		2		1
Holston, Selathial	1	2	1		
Averite, Alexander	2	1	4		5
Adams, Howell	1	2	4		
Avery, Lewis	2	1	1		
Avery, Jacob	4	2	6		
Brite, Jesse	1	2	6		
Dodd, Samuel	2	5	4		2
Dodd, William	3	4	5	1	3
Dodd, John	2	1	2		
Bell, David	1	7	4		12
Bridges, Young	2	1	1		1
Peoples, Abner	1	1	3	1	
Orr, Samuel	1	1	4		
Pool, William	2	2	3		2
Lassiter, Elizabeth	1		3		3
Rainwater, William	1	2	2		
Johnston, Obadiah	1	4	3	2	
McCullers, John	2	4	4		
Starboard, Solomon	1	1	3		
Smith, Nehemiah	1	1	2		1
Vincent, Drew	2	2	4		14
Whittington, Phady	1		3		
Hobby, William	1		2		
Rainwater, Moses, Sr	2	2	4		
Smith, John	1		2		1
Rails, Charles	1		1		
Whittington, Robert	1	3	4		
Norris, James	3		6		2
Thomlinson, Edmond	1				
Smith, Alexander	1		2		6
Kindal, Isaac	1	1	1		
Clark, Harris	1	1	1		2
Rosser, John	1		2		1
Peoples, Archibald	1		1		
Parish, Charles	1	1	4		1
Shehorn, Henry	1		5		
Stallons, Ezekiel	1		1		
Roberts, Britton	1	1			
Bankum, Alexander	1		1		
Parsons, Harris	1				
Woodall, Absalom	1	2	2	1	5
Giles, William	2	1	4	1	
Avery, Thomas	1	1	4		
Staton, Bathier	2	2	2		

NAME OF HEAD OF FAMILY.	Free white males of 16 years and upward, including heads of families.	Free white males under 16 years.	Free white females, including heads of families.	All other free persons.	Slaves.
Rosser, James, Sen	2	5	4		3
Norris, Ann	1	1	5		
Sanders, Mary	1		2		19
Thomlinson, Thomas	1	2	4		6
Avery, William	3		5		11
Avery, Alexander, Sr	4	2	5		
Brady, John	2		2		2
Bryan, Hardy	1	6	2		14
Bryan, John	2		2		22
Hewit, Goldsmith	1				
Hundy, Matthias	1				
Gillis, Malcolm	1				
Hobby, Alexander	4	3	3		
Osborn, James	1				
Hobby, Lucy		1	2		
Wren, James	2		1		
Willowby, Richard	1	4	3		
Gale, Solomon	1	2	2		
Lohorn, Rebecca			2		
Oncale, Isum	1	1	2		
Bridges, Etheldred	2	1	1		
Powell, Stephen					11
Holland, William	1		2		
Vincent, Aaron	1	3	4		12
Vincent, Amelia			1		3
Lynch, Martha			1		
Avery, Mary	1	1	4		
Bryan, Asa	1	2	3		1
Ottman, Thomas	2		3		3
Barfoot, Noah, Senr	1		2	1	1
Jackson, John	1		3		
Blackman, John	3	3	7	1	
Lynch, Milberry		1	2		
Lynch, Sarah			2		
Williams, Miles	2		2		
Ivy, James	3	3	2		2
McClenny, James	1	4	3		1
Bryan, Lewis	1		1		
Adkins, Moses	1		4		
Seats, Nathan	2		5		
Lee, Mary	1		3		6
Kean, George	1	5	1		
Johnston, Etheldred	1	3	3		
Blackman, Icabod	1	2	2		2
Langston, Joseph, Senr	1	1	2		
Lankton, Joseph, jr	1	1	1		
Williams, Nathan	2	1	2		41
Smith, Samuel	2	1	2		21
Baker, James	2	3	5		
Harold, Francis	2	4	2		
Harold, Edward	3	4	2		1
Ballanger, Mary		1	1		2
Webb, David	1		5		
Diamond, Margaret			3		
Diamond, Frances	1		4		
Barfoot, Noah, jr	1	2	3		
Morgan, John	2	1	3		
Johnston, Moses	1	3	6		1
Ballinger, John	1	1	3		3
Collins, Andrew	1	1	1		1
Rhoads, John	3	4	4		
Ingram, Shadrach	1	3	8		4
Lee, William	2	2	6		
Harris, Sharrod	1		2		
Hobby, Reuben	2	4	5		
Flewellin, Archibald	1		2		
Lee, David, Senr	2	1	3		5
Blackman, Barzella	1	3	4		1
Bryan, John	1	2	6		2
Blackman, John	3	3	7		1
Blackman, Arthur	1		4		
Shepard, Valentine	2		4		
Bridges, Joseph	1	3	5		
Lee, Samuel	1	2	2		1
Lee, Cato	1	3	2		
Woodal, Jacob	1	2	2		
Lee, David, Junr	2	3	4		
Jones, William	1	1	1		
Proctor, John	1	2	4		
Barber, Reuben	1	2	4		
Woodall, Jacob	1	3	1		
Lee, Stephen	1	3	1		1
Brewer, Hubbard	1	2	3		
Baldwin, Samuel	1	2	4		1
Connolly, Michael	2	1	6		
Bryan, William	1	2	3		2
Lee, John	1	2	3		
Guein, John	1	1	2		
Allen, Nathan	3	2	8		10
Ballinger, William	1	3	2		1
Fail, John	1	2	4		13
Adams, Bryan	1	5	1		
Aithcock, Holiday				6	
Harrell, Etheldred	1	2	5		
Sellers, Samson	1	3	4		
Farmer, Nicholas	1	3	4		4
Lee, James, junr	3	2	3		

NEWBERN DISTRICT, JOHNSTON COUNTY—Continued.

NAME OF HEAD OF FAMILY.	Free white males of 16 years and upward, including heads of families.	Free white males under 16 years.	Free white females, including heads of families.	All other free persons.	Slaves.
Lee, Lemuel	1	3	5		
Johnston, Joshua	2	3	3		
Russels, Charles	2	2	2		
Lee, Jeremiah	1		1		4
Ingram, Isaac	1	3	2		
Hairgroves, William	2		3		
Dement, John	1		2		
Fail, Dixon	1	4	4		3
Eldridge, Samuel	1	1	2		6
Lee, James, Senr	1		4		2
Baker, Dempsey	3	2	6		
Rials, William	1	6	2		
Keen, George	1	6	1		
Ward, Elijah	1	3	2		
Adkinson, Thomas	1				
Smith, Abram	1	1	2		
Smith, John	1		1		
Attman, Joel	1				
Dees, Edmond	1		1		
Powell, William	1		1		
Billington, Ezekiel	2	3	1		
Smith, Isaac	1	2	2		
Mott, Benjamin	1	2	2		
Binum, Drury	1	2	2		
Harold, Theophilus	1		1		
McGlohon, William	1	2	3		
Brown, Richard	1	2	4		
Barnes, Abram	1		2		
Ellis, Elisha	1	2	2		
Moore, Thomas	1		3		
Collins, Thomas	1				
Lankston, Charity	1	3	3		
Ellis, Elijah	1				

NEWBERN DISTRICT, JONES COUNTY.

NAME OF HEAD OF FAMILY.	Free white males of 16 years and upward, including heads of families.	Free white males under 16 years.	Free white females, including heads of families.	All other free persons.	Slaves.
Hatch, Charles	1	2	1		9
Hatch, Mary		4	3		10
Bryan, James	1	1	1		11
Hatch, Samuel, Junr	1	2	3		27
Steel, Peter	2	1	5		
Steel, Benjamin	1	1	1		
Gregory, William	1		1		3
Simmons, Emanuel	3	1	1		12
Grimes, Robert	1	2	6		8
Grenade, Joseph	1	1	5		3
Simmons, Daniel	1	2	3		16
Whitly, Edward	1	6	5	1	3
Lipsey, William	2	3	3		1
Lipsey, Arthur	1	1	3		1
Hatch, John	1	2	2		20
Gregory, Matthew	2	1	3		6
Simmons, James	1				7
Simmons, Benjamin	1	1	1		10
Hatch, Joseph	1		2		6
Hatch, Durant	1	1	4		18
Ubank, John	1	4	6		
Hatch, Edmund	1	2	1		24
Lavender, Benjamin	1		4		6
Simmons, John	3		3		8
Simmons, George	1	1	2		6
Smith, Bazel	3	1	4	2	16
Johnston, Collinson	2	2	5		
Prentice, Solomon	1				
Reed, George	1		1		1
Kincey, Stephen	1				24
Gardner, William	1	2	4		1
Lee, Burton	3	2	5		
Phelps, Jacob	1		2		2
Ramsay, Esther			2		
Littleton, Thomas	1		1		
Waters, Margaret	1		1		1
Dulin, Sugar	1	2	5		1
Taylor, John	1	1	3		36
Sanderson, Elijah	1				46
Knight, Kadir	1	2	2		
Andrews, Ruth	1	2	4		
Sanderson, Shadrach	1		2		
Foscue, Frederic	1	1	2		25
Sanderson, Thomas	2	2	5		2
Brinkley, Comfort		1	2		
Sanderson, Jesse	2	1	2		2
Sanderson, John	1	2	3		1
Sanderson, James	1	2	3		1
Griffin, William	2	3	3		
Grenade, John	3	1	4		3
Hall, John	1	2	3		
Smith, Peter	2	1	3		
Cohun, Dudley	1	1	5		
Sanderson, Levy	1	1	2		
Kincey, Joseph	1	1	5		
Mosley, John	1		3		
Dunn, William	1				
Andrews, Dorcas	1		2		
Hall, James	2				
Binum, Lewis	1		1		
Smith, Thomas	1				
Kincey, John	2	2	3		1
Hancock, James	1	5	3	3	2
Bumpus, Jabis	1		1		
Taylor, William	1	3	2		4
Lepsy, Timothy	1		1		4
Bray, Nicholas A	1		2		9
Market, John	1		1		
Market, Frederic	1				
Harrell, Enos	1		3		
Brocket, Benjamin	1	1	2		32
Lyttleton, John	1	4	2		
Lyttleton, Thomas, Senr	1		3		
Lee, Thomas	1	2	5		52
Wallace, Stephen	1	1	2		
Hatch, Samuel	1	3	4		7
Boyd, Coleman	1	2	5		
Mace, William	1		2		
Ross, Reuben	2	1	4		
Foye, James	1				31
George, William	1	4	1		1
Mundine, Francis	1	1	3		7
Jones, Brigger	1	2	2		7
Jones, John	1	2	4		
Jones, James	1	1	4		
Mundine, Benjamin	1				
Mundine, Thomas	1		1		
Reynolds, Ephraim	1	1	2		
Eubank, Elijah	1	2	4		
Gibson, Isaac	1	2	1		3
Yates, Stephen	1	2	2		
Barry, David	1	3	3		1
Watson, Moses	1	3	2		9
West, John	1	1	2		2
Mundine, John	1		1		9
Taylor, William	1		1		2
Morgan, John	2	4	4		
Taylor, James	1		4		
Dolly, Esther			2		
Mundine, Kittrel	2	1	6		13
Kellum, William	1		3		
West, Andrew	1	1	4		
Dixon, Joel	1	2	3		
Dudley, Elijah	1	1	1		1
Collins, John	1	2	3		4
Meadows, Abraham	1	2	2		
Meadows, Thomas	1	3	3		
Meadows, Job, Junior	1	3	3		
Meadows, Job, Senior	3	2	4		
Houston, James	1	1	4		
Gray, William	1	2	3		
Starkey, Edward	2		1		61
Key, Jonathan	1	1	3		5
Meadows, Bartholomew	1	1	2		6
Frazer, Ellen		1	3		
Hay, Thomas	1	5	3		2
Howard, Titus	2	1	7		12
Arnold, Mablin	1		3		2
Collins, Joseph	1		1		
Stephenson, Samuel	1	1	2		
Tilman, John	2	3	3		
Tilman, Isaac	1		3		
Jones, Josiah	1	1	3		
Prescot, Mary	1		3		
Godwin, Joseph	1	2	4		
West, Eli	1	1	4		34
Herrington, James	1		1		
Dudley, Abraham	1	3	6		27
Dudley, Thomas	1	2	5		5
Modes, Thomas, Jur	1	1	3		
Modes, Thomas, Senr	1		3		
Watson, James	2	2	2		21
Dudley, Susannah	2		2		1
Dudley, Stephen	2	2	7		16
Collins, Benjamin	1	2	1		6
Timmons, Mary			2		
Williamson, David	2	3	3		1
Jones, Richard	1	1	3		(*)
Watson, Jeremiah	2		2		(*)
Frazer, Micajah	2	2	4	7	21
Stephens, George	2	3	2	1	
Bender, John	2	3	2		
Morris, John	1	1	1		
Watson, Jeremiah	1	4	4		
Amyst, Vincent	1	5	4		
Amyst, Enoch	2		1		
Ventures, Mary	1		3		
Williamson, John	1		5		
Bradshaw, Samuel	2	2	2		
Wilcocks, Benjamin	1	3	3		
Mackay, Samuel	1		4		
Lipsey, Roscoe	3	1	4		
Stokes, Arthur	2	4	4		
McDonald, James	3	4	6		
Pybus, John	1		3		
Pybus, Mary		2	3		
Hicks, Alexander	1		3		2
Weeks, Dixon	1	1	2		
Pybus, James	1				
Ubank, George	1	6	3		
Morris, Thomas	1		5		2
Oliver, William	3	2	2		2
Williamson, Joseph	1		3		
Williamson, Richard	1	4	2		
Wood, Gasham	3	3	6		
Critchfield, Uribius	1	3	3		
Taylor, Cornelius	1				
Critchfield, Ann	1	1	2		
Goslin, John	2		7		1
Andrews, Adam	2	3	5		
Edwards, Robert	1	1	3		
Andrews, John, Senr	2	1	3		
Pollock, James	1	1	1		1
Harrison, John	1		2		
Critchfield, Philip	1	1	3		
Critchfield, Richard	1	2	1		
Bailey, J. Ag	1	2	1		
Thomas, Jesse	3		3		
Amyst, Shadrack	1				
McJay, James	1		1		
Simmons, Abram B	3	3	7		3
Hill, Mary		2	2		
Perry, Maxwell	1		2		
Perry, Robert	2		1		
Perry, Daniel, Junr	1	1	3		
Perry, William	1	1	1		
Harris, Zemeriah	1	1	2		
Pickeron, Benjamin	2	4	3		
Pickeron, Jemima		3	7		
Thornton, Thomas	1	1	4		
Busick, James	2	1	2		2
Harrison, Susannah		2	4		7
Perry, Daniel, Senr	3	2	1		7
Thornton, Thomas	1	1	3		
Busick, Michael	1		1		
Amyst, Daniel	1				
Witton, Thomas	1				
Conner, Abram				1	
Stokes, George	1				
Pritchard, William					
Slaughter, Sarah			2		
Mackay, Jane			1		
Williamson, Margaret	1		4		
Runnels, Penelope		1	2		7
Bradshaw, Reuben	1		1		
Wood, Aaron	1	2	4		
Green, Samuel	1	2	1		
Busick, William, Junr	1	3	3		
Sanders, Solomon	1	1	2		
Sanders, Southy	1		4		
Brown, James	1		3		
Busick, William	2		2		
Hill, Ann	1	1	2		
Clark, John	1				
Robinson, David				3	
Taylor, Edmond	1	3	2		
McDonald, John	2	4	3		1
Mallard, Adam	1	1	1		
Edwards, Rebecca	1	1	3		
Ross, Reuben	1	1	3		
Perry, John	3		4		
Small, Reuben	1	3	2		
Perry, William	1	1	1		
Jermis, William	1	2	4		2
Boxon, Adkin	1	5	3		
McKinsey, Alexander	3	2	2		3
Bryan, Lewis	3	5	2		24
Brown, John	2	1	3		2
Downs, Michael	2	1	2		4
Waring, Joseph	1		2		1
Allgood, Darcal	1	1	4		
Koonce, Daniel	1	5	2		
Green, James	2	4	3		8
Gilbert, John, Senior	1	2	2		1
Gilbert, Jesse	1	1	1		
Jones, Henry	2		1		
Stephenson, Matthew	2	2	3		

*Illegible.

NEWBERN DISTRICT, JONES COUNTY—Continued.

NAME OF HEAD OF FAMILY.	Free white males of 16 years and upward, including heads of families.	Free white males under 16 years.	Free white females, including heads of families.	All other free persons.	Slaves.
Miller, Mary	2	2	2	2	
Bryan, John	2		3		31
Bryan, Frederick	1		1		6
Murry, Tobias	1		1		
Gilbert, John, Senr	2	2	2		5
Tippet, John	2	1	1		1
Tippet, Joseph	1	1	3		
Blacksher, Agnes			3		2
Blacksher, Abram	2		4		
Bryan, William	1	1	3		10
Bryan, John Hill	1	2	3		14
Harrison, William	2	1	5		29
Gilbert, John, Junior	1	1	2		2
Hypock, Christopher	1	2	2		
Wade, Peter	1	1	1		
Bryan, Edward	1	2	2		18
Witton, Robert	1	1	2		3
Spencer, Benjamin	1		4		
Still, John	1	1	2		1
Lavender, John, Senr	1	2	3		2
Lavender, William	1	3	1		
Shine, John	1	3	5		8
Pitman, Ann	1		1		
Paradice, William	1	2	4		
Carlisle, Robert	1	2	1		
Johnston, John	1	3	4		
Tippet, William	1	2	3		
Potter, James	2	1	1		
Shine, Daniel	3		3		12
Tippet, James	1	5	1		
Pitman, Jeremiah	1	1	1		
Dulin, Thomas	2		3		
Turner, Smith	1	3	2		
Dulin, Rice	1	1	4		9
Blacksher, Edward	3	1			33
Messer, Noah	2	1	3		
Washburn, James	2	3	4		
Philyan, James	3	1	4		5
Whaley, John	2	2	3		2
Randall, William	1		2		19
Stanley, Elizabeth	1	2	2		
Morris, William	2		2		
Sanders, Joseph	1	1	4		
Sanders, Benjamin	1	5	1		
Freeman, Jesse	1	1	2		
Westbrook, John	1		2		
Brown, Samuel	1		4		
Brown, William, Junr	1	1	3		
Brown, William, Senr	1	1	2		1
Freeman, John	1	1	2		
Sanders, John	2		5		
Sauls, John	1	4	7		1
Gooding, James	1	1	2		
Bowers, Giles	2		3		
Conner, John	1				
Miller, Tobias	1		2		
Farrow, Lurah	1	1	2		
Smith, Michael	1	1	3		3
Killegrove, Hinch	1	2	4		4
Frank, Edward	1		3		8
Frank, John	1	2	4		5
Sanders, John	2		5		
Kincey, William	1	2	4		4
Pollard, William	2		3		
Pollock, Jesse	1	1	2		
Brown, John	1		3		
Kincey, Elany			2	4	4
Winsit, Joseph	1	2	6		1
Dinkins, Joshua	1	1	4		
Price, John	2	1	3		1
Cocks, Andrew	1	1	6		4
Cocks, Charles	2		2		1
King, Samuel	1		2		
Cocks, Aaron	1	2	1		
Winsit, Robert	2	4	2		2
Brock, William	2	5	3		
Alfin, David	1	2	4		
Whitlidge, Ambrose	1	1	3		
Alfin, Thomas	1	1	2		
Baggs, Marianne			2		
Cox, Mary			2		
Rhodes, Jacob	1	2	3		1
Johnston, Jacob	3	4	5		13
Turner, Jacob	3	4	4		
Jarmin, John	1	3	3		
Jelks, Richard	1		3		2
Pate, William	2	5	1		1
Stephens, William	1		3		
Simson, Peter	1	3	1		
Williams, Chap	1	1	1		2
Rhodes, James	2	1	3		
Alfin, William	1	1	4		
Jones, Frederic	1	1	2		1
Barnet, William	3	2	5		
Barnet, John	2	2	2		
Stewart, John	3	3	3		
Taylor, Jesse	1	1	1		
Jones, Hardy	2		2		5
Jones, William	2	2	2		9
Killegro, Mary			1	3	
Jones, James	1	3	4		2
Winsit, Hannah			3		4
Jermin, Rachel		1	1		4
Jermin, Hall	1	1	1		3
Simson, Peter	2	2	1		
Sanders, Moses	1	3	3		
Branson, Vincent	1		2		
Blacksher, Moses	1	3	3		
King, Samuel, Senr	2	1	6		
Moor, John	2	1	4		
Wamble, Nathan	2	1	2		
King, Charles	1	2	3		
King, Samuel, Junr	1		2		
Strickland, Harman	1	2	4		
Croft, Samuel C	2	1	6		
Brown, Edward	3	3	2		
Blacksher, Elis S	2		5		1
Blacksher, Jesse	1		2		
Brown, Howel	1	3	4		
King, John	1	3	6		
Kincey, Joseph	2	2	4		
Kincey, Edward	1		2		1
Kincey, Samuel	1	1	3		
Westbrook, James	1				
Lee, Jacob	2	1	5		
Everit, Hannah		1	4		13
Fordom, Benjamin	2	1	7		
Davis, Benjamin	3	1	6		
Morgan, William	1	2	2		
Stanton, Benjamin	1	2	3		2
Packer, Holiday	2	2	2		
Pickeron, Aaron	2	2	5		
Westbrooke, Benjamin	2	4	1		
Ives, Isaac				1	1
Morgan, Elisha					4
Jones, James					11
Jones, Hardy					5
Jones, Jacob					2
Connor, Mark					9
Connor, John					13
Stanley, James	1	1	7		1
Batts, William	1	1	2		
Atkinson, Elisha	2	3	2		
Blackman, Arthur	1	1	3		6
Quince, George, junr	1	5	6		7
Quince, John, Senr	1		3		9
Pritchard, Bazel	1		1		17
Pritchard, Clement	1				14
Brown, Richard	1	3	3		
Quilling, Daniel	1	2	2		
Quince, John, Junr	1	3	2		5
Bush, William	2	2	1	1	15
Gregory, Amy		1	2		5
Lavender, Samuel	1	1	6		1
Jermin, Robert	1	3	3		1
Khuince, Christopher	2	1	5		4
Perry, Adonijah	1	2	1		1
Williamson, Francis	2	1	1		
Small, Benjamin	2	2	3		
Stanley, Martin	1	2	5		
Little, John	1	2	4		
Stanley, Ann	2	1	7		
Stanley, Benjamin	2		1		
Stanley, William	1	1	3		
Pickeron, John	1		3		1
Hypock, Felton	2		3		
Khuince, George, Senior	1	3	4		
Khuince, Philip	1	1	3		3
Khuince, John, junr	1	2	2		
Pate, Philip	1		2		3
Khuince, George, junr	1		2		1
Hargate, Daniel	1	4	3		8
Maldin, Henry	1	1	2	1	1
Gergainus, Wiley	1	3	2		
Miller, Thomas	1	6	1		
Hall, Samuel	1	1	4		11
Dean, William	1	1	4		
Godwin, Aaron	2		1	1	
Gilbert, Joseph	1	2	1		1
Runnels, Richard	2	2	6		8
Cooms, Sarah			3		
Isler, John	2	3	3		47
Pate, Richard	2	3	3		
Asque, Benjamin	1	4	3		
Shute, Thomas	1	1	3		
Cox, Benjamin	1	1	2		
Mets, George	1		2		
Men, Philip	1	3	3		
Mets, William	1	2	3		
Moye, John	2	2	3		
Simmons, Daniel	1	2	3		11
Pierce, Seth	1	2	3		
Jones, William	1		3	1	
Sanders, John	1	2	1		
Huggins, Isaac	2	1	3		
Cox, Solomon	1		4		
Spikes, Simon	4	2	4		20
Becton, Michael	1	3	4		14
Becton, John	2	2	4		34
Becton, George	1	2	4		10
Asque, Thomas	1	2	7		
Bryan, Nathan	2	4	4		15
Jackson, John	2	2	4		
Delahunta, John, Senr	2		2		2
Delahunta, Thomas	1		1		1
Bailey, James	1	1	4		
Cox, John H	1	1	2		
Mets, George	1	3	4		
Truel, Joseph	1	1	2		
Taylor, John	1		1		
Cox, Abner	1	2	3		
Herbert, William	1		1		
Stanley, Benjamin	1	2	3		
Caviner, Sylvester	1	2	2		
Williams, Huggins	1	2	6		
Shetfer, John	1	4	6		1
Gilstrap, Idolet	1	3	2		5
Fearn, Mary	1		5		7
Antwince, Andrew	1	3	1		
Huggins, James	1		3		
Brice, Margaret	1		3		1
Williams, Benjamin	1	2	3		
Kelly, John	1	1	1		
Isler, William	1		1		6
Delahunta, Samuel	3	2	2		1
Bailey, Abram	1	1	3		
Taylor, Mary		2	1	2	
Runnels, Robin	1	1	2		
Scean, John	1	3	1		
Scean, Alexander	1	2	1		
Scean, Sarah	1		4		
Kent, Margaret		1	2		
Green, Stephen	1				
Jones, Mary			2		
Conolly, William	3	2	5		4
Cox, Marmaduke	1	2	6		
Macafee, John	1	1	4		
Gilstrap, Isaac			1	3	
Kellum, Elijah	1	1	4		
Gilstrap, Henry	1				
Allen, Thomas	1	1	3		
Green, William	1	2	3		
Swilley, Zeno	1	1	6		
Scean, Jesse	1				
Little, Abram	4	1	4		
Khuince, Jesse	1				
Macfashion, Daniel	2	3	2		
Hunter, Ezekiel	1				
Runnels, Sharp	1	3	4		1
Bratcher, James	1				
Normon, John	1	1	3		
Men, William	1				
Knox, William	1	3	2		
Fearn, Sarah			2		
Gilbert, Priscilla			2		
Hynes, Masten	1	3	3		
Stiller, Sarah			1		
Hargat, Peter	1	3	6		12
Brock, Joseph	3	2	5		10
White, Benjamin	1	1	2		7
McDonald, Reddick	1	2	6		
Morris, Philip	3	2	2		
Alcock, Richard Nelson	3	3	1		5
Alcock, Gatlin		2	3		
Shepherd, Rachel	2	1	1		
Stephenson, Charles	2	3	2		5
Collins, Joshua	2	1	1		1
Dunn, Thomas	2	1	1		
Foscue, Arthur	1	1	3		1
Alcock, Lemuel	1		3		1
Bogue, Josiah	1		5		
Perisher, Josiah	1		3		
Bogue, Mark	1		3	1	
Stanton, Bindon	1	3	1		
Smith, Henry	1	2	3		1
Harrison, James	1	1	3		1
Tice, William	1	1	1		1
Harrison, Edward	1	1	1		
Merritt, Hezekiah	2	2	7		5
Gray, Cox	1	1	2		
Gray, Israel			1		1
Richards, John	1		5		
Chance, Oldfield	2	4	3		
Smith, John	2	4	4		3
Sheppard, Elijah	2	2	2		
Gray, Israel	2	5	3		2
Roberts, Zachariah	1		2		2
Johnston, Edmund	1		2		
Grenade, Jacob	1	1	3		
Harrison, Stephen	1		2		
Harrison, James, Senr	3	1	2		

NEWBERN DISTRICT, JONES COUNTY—Continued.

NAME OF HEAD OF FAMILY.	Free white males of 16 years and upward, including heads of families.	Free white males under 16 years.	Free white females, including heads of families.	All other free persons.	Slaves.
Grenade, William	1	2	3		1
Hackburn, Joseph	1		2		4
Harrison, William	1				
Simons, Fella	1	2	2		
Yates, David	2	2	1		
Baker, William	1		2		
Oram, William	1	4	1		3
Cornegie, Daniel	1				
Grace, William	1	1	1		
Gregory, John	1	1	1		4
Kernegy, John	3	1	5		10
Colbert, Tamer	1	3	6		
Dollard, Jacob	1				
Hudler, David	1				
Frost, James	1				
Andrews, Francis	1		1		
Hudley, Henry	1				
Moze, George	1		1		
Moze, Isaac	1				
Clifton, Ezekiel	3	1	6		3
Colway, John	1		2		
Tracky, John	1		5		
Mercer, Robert	4	2	4		
Peters, John	1	1	3		
Griffin, Richard	1	1	3		
Hudley, Joseph	1	2	1		
Moor, Levy	2	1	1	1	2
Hudler, John	1		1		
Nelson, Sarah			3		
Gray, Gilbert	1	5	3		1
Sanderson, Benjamin	1	2	1		2
Andrews, John	2	2	7		4
Andrews, Daniel	1	1	3		
Rickerson, Jesse	1	1	3		
Murphy, John	1	2	2		
Alcock, Gatsy	1	1	3		
Mallard, Lawson	1		4		1
Mallard, Daniel	3		3	1	
Foscue, Simon	1	2	3		14
Kennedy, Elizabeth			2		
Mallard, John	2	3	6		
Kornegay, Abram	1	1			15
Burnet, John	1	2	3		1
Sanderson, Joseph	1		7		14
Lambert, Aaron	1	5	4		1
Lambert, Abner	2	4	3		
Mercer, Benjamin	1		2		
Harrison, Daniel	1	3	2		2
Stephenson, James	1		2		
Harrison, Joseph	1	1	1		4
Miller, Daniel	1		3		2
Harget, Frederic	3	2	3		16
Jones, Henry	2		1		
Busick, James	2	1	2		2
Wamble, John	1	6	3		

NEWBERN DISTRICT, PITT COUNTY.

NAME OF HEAD OF FAMILY.	Free white males of 16 years and upward, including heads of families.	Free white males under 16 years.	Free white females, including heads of families.	All other free persons.	Slaves.
Rix, Edmund	1	3	1		4
Hodges, Benjamin	1	1	4	1	5
Barrow, James	1	1	1		8
Cason, Hilary	6	3	2		7
Cucksaul, Abier	1	2	2		
Whichard, Anthony	1		3		
Moore, John	1		4		
Carmean, James	1				
Davis, Thomas	2	1	5		1
Moore, Obadiah	1	1	5		11
Fowler, Abram	1	1	1		
Hodges, Robert	2		1		17
Hodges, Henry	3	1	4		12
Hodges, Margaret	2	2	3		5
Hodges, Elizabeth	1	1	3		5
Smith, Elizabeth	1		3		
Jordan, John	5	4	3		15
Wallace, John	2		2		3
Dudley, James, Senr.	2	2	3		
Guilford, Joseph, Senr.	1	2	3		
James, Thomas	2	2	5		
Lloyd, Benjamin	1	2	2		
Morris, Mary	1		3		1
Griffin, John	1		1		1
Congleton, William	1	2	3		
Smith, David	3	2	5		21
Guilford, Joseph, Junr.	1	3	2		1
Jones, John	2	4	4		4
Spear, John	1	3	4		
Keel, Simon	1		2		1
Keel, William	1		1		
Langley, William	1		3		
Biggs, John	1	1	4		
Evans, Michael C	3		3		4
Brinkley, John	3		9		
Hinton, Dempsey	2	1	2		8
White, Francis	1	1	1		1
Little, George	1	3	4		2
Little, James	1		1		3
Little, Josiah	1	3	4		3
Piercy, John	2		1		
Langley, James	1	3	3		1
Hodges, William	1	2	3		9
Kingsall, John	2	1	3		
Little, William	1	6	4		6
Smith, William	2	3	6		
Hodges, Edmond	3	1	3		8
Spears, James	1	1	5		
Nichols, Mary		1	3		
Dean, Anthony	1	1	2		
Dean, Moses	1	1	3		
James, Daniel	1	3	1		
James, Thomas	1	1	1		
James, John, Junr.	1	2	2		
Wallace, Richard	1	3	2		
Wilson, William	1	1	2		
Whitehead, John	1	4	2		4
Shepherd, Jordan	2		5		15
Pinkett, William	2		1		7
Patrick, Solomon	2		2		3
Crandol, Christopher	1	1	3		
Daniel, Joseph	1		3		4
Whitehead, Charles	1				
Griffin, James	1	3	2		
Dudley, James, junr.	1	2	4		1
Knox, Robert	1		5		
Whitacre, John	1	3	1		
Harris, William	1				
Ames, Thomas	1	2	2		
Hewbanks, John	1				
James, Joshua	2	2	5		
McDugal, Ducan	1	1	5		
Rodgers, Shadrach	1	1	1		
Congleton, David	1		1		
Jolly, Jesse	1	1	1		
Ivey, John	1		2		
Brown, Charles	1	3	5		
Stewart, William S	1			1	16
Stewart, Alexander	1	1			12
Stewart, James	1				20
Piercy, John, Junr.	1	2	1		
Spears, John	1		1		54
Bryant, William	1	1	1		
Ewell, James	1		1		
Bryerly, Abram	1	3	3		
Parrymore, John	1	1	3		
Pressey, William	1		1		
Davis, Daniel, Junr.	1				
Davis, Daniel, Senr.	1		3		
James, John	3	2	3		
Parrimore, Ezekiel	1				
Albritton, James	3	2	1		8
Knox, Josiah	1	2	2		
Barrow, Samuel	2	1	3		15
Barrow, James	1	1	1		9
Adams, Archibald	1				2
Jones, John	1		3		5
James, Lemuel	1		3		
Leggett, Sarah	1	2	6		1
Harris, William, Senr.	3	1	3		
Salter, Clarissa			4		11
Nelmes, Thomas	1	3	2		1
Mooreing, William	1	1	4		3
Ewell, Catherine			2		
Proctor, Abner	1	1	8		
Dudley, Samuel	1	4	6		2
Albritton, James	1	1	4		4
Baldwin, William	1	1	7		1
Moore, Matthias	3	2	3		10
Moore, Jesse	1				1
Moore, Richard	1	4	1		3
Moore, Kennedy	1	1	2		1
Bryerly, William	2	1	5		
Shivers, Ann		1	1		
Ewell, Elizabeth		1	3		
Barber, William	1	1	1		
Barber, Charles	1	2	2		
Harris, Major, Senr.	1	2	3		
Harris, William	1	1	1		
Harris, Major, junr.	1		1		
Spear, William	1	1	4		
Harris, Jacob	1		1		
Robertson, James	2	3	5		
Mooreing, William	1	1	3		3
Flake, Arthur	1		1		
Flake, John	3		3		
Tucker, Wright	1	1	2		1
Herrington, Henry	1				
Herrington, Joshua	1	1	2		
Barber, John, Junr.	2	1	4	1	3
Barber, John, Senr.	2	1	2		4
Tucker, Joshua	1				
Hatten, John	1	4	2		2
James, William	1		1		
James, Matthew	1	1	3		1
Cason, John	1	4	4		12
Balderee, William	1	2	4		
Perry, Shardach	1	3	3	3	1
Tucker, Kealy	1	3	4		
Moze, Gardner	1	1	3	2	1
Daniel, Thomas	1	1			2
Daniel, Lanier	1		1		1
Daniel, Robert	2	1	1		15
Adams, Calston	1	3	3		5
Cason, Henry, Senr.	2		3		7
Shivers, Jesse	1	3	4		
Cherry, Nathan	2		3		1
Fleming, David	1	2	3		
Cason, William	1				
Little, Joseph	2	3	7		1
Cason, Joseph	1				
Stokes, Sarah	1		1		
Halton, Robert	3		1	2	1
Robertson, James	2	3	6		
Norcutt, Nicholas	2		1		2
Norcutt, William, Jur.	1		3		3
Norcutt, William, Senr.	2		1		2
Ewell, Solomon	1		2		
Ewell, John	1				
Shivers, Jonas	2	3	2		
McCoffee, James	1				
Flake, Arthur, Senr.	1		2		
Little, Jacob	1		3		
Cherry, John	1	1	3		
Whicherel, John	1	2	2		
Albritton, Adam	1				
Proctor, Henry	1	1	2		
Proctor, Nee	1		3		
Davis, Thomas	1	2	1		
Braley, Solomon	1	1	2		
McGowns, John	1	1	2		
Fleming, John	1	1	4		
Powell, Thomas	2	1	3		
Bedford, Levin	1				
Moore, Henry	2		4		4
Porter, George	3		1		4
Moore, Thomas	1		2		1
Moore, Edward	3		3		
Nobles, Nathaniel	2	3	7		1
Moore, John	1		4		
Hysmith, John	1		4		
Barnhill, Henry	3		1		
Bowers, Benjamin, Senr.	1		1		10
Moore, Sarah	2	2	2		
James, Henry	2	1	3		
Mac Dearman, John	1	3	3		
Whitacre, William	2	4	3		
Clements, George	1	2	2		
Knox, David	1	4	3		
Ward, John, Senr.	3	1	5		
Jolly, Jesse	2	1	2		2
Anders, Edmond	2	2	3		11
Sessions, Walter	1		3		
Jolly, John	3	1	7		
Levi, Alexander	1	1	1		
James, Lance	2		3		
Hubanks, Richard	3	2	4		
Gray, Joseph, Senr.	2		3		
Keel, Ezekiel	1	2	3		
Hubanks, Elizabeth		2	1		
Clements, William	3	4	5		1
Tarr, Nehemiah	1	2	2		
Dannels, George	1	1	3		3
Cooper, William	1	1	2		
Cooper, George	2		1		
Knox, William	1		1		
Knox, Archibald	1	2	1		
Hewbanks, George	1	2	4		
Moore, Caleb	1	1	3		
Moore, Moses	1	2	3		
Bullock, Edward	1		1		
Moore, Edmond	1		1		1
Moore, Reading	1	1	2		
Roye, Darling	1		2		
Collins, Josiah	1		2		
Harvey, Joshua	1	2	2		

NEWBERN DISTRICT, PITT COUNTY—Continued.

NAME OF HEAD OF FAMILY.	Free white males of 16 years and upward, including heads of families.	Free white males under 16 years.	Free white females, including heads of families.	All other free persons.	Slaves.
Harvey, John	1	2	2		
Bowers, William	1	2	4		4
Moore, Jacob	1		1		
Bowers, Benjamin	1	3	4		
Grimmer, Robert	2	1	2		2
Mayo, Peter	1	3	3		4
Highsmith, John, junr	1				1
Barnhill, Hervey, junr	1	1	2		
Ward, James	1		1		
Everite, James	1	1	2		
Levi, Henry	1	2	1		
Chance, Thomas	2	1	5		
Ward, John, junr	1		1		
Everite, Simon	1	1	2		
Mobley, Eleazer	2	3	6		
Porter, Frederic	1	3	1		1
McDearman, Michael	1				
Barnhill, Jesse	1		1		
Taylor, James	1		2		
Gilbert, John	2	2	4		
Rollins, Charles	1	2	5		
Nobles, Drew	1		2		1
Highsmith, Jacob	1	1	3		
Knox, William, Senr	2	2	2		
Barnhill, William	1		1		
Ward, William	1	2	3		
Pilgreen, William			3		
Stancell, Noble	1				3
Kelly, Jeremiah	1		3		
Jolly, Peter	3	5	4		
Perkins, David	1	2	2		9
Dannels, Robert	2	1	1		10
James, Lemuel	1		3		
Cason, Henry	4		3		6
Congleton, William	2	2	4		
Lock, John	1		3		
Page, Joseph	3	1	6		6
Manning, Reuben	3	3	7		6
Windom, John	3	1	3		
Thomas, Abel	1	3	5		1
Brown, Mourning			1		
Mayo, Mary			2		
Osborn, Luke	1	1	4		11
Stancill, Sarah	3	4	4		14
Jenkins, Henry	2	1	1		2
Williams, Robert	1	1	2		
Anders, Levi	2	2	5		9
Whitus, Badson	4	1	2		
Bowers, John	2	1	7		1
Rogers, Isaac	1	1	5		
Martin, Peter	1	3	5		
Gatlen, Edward	1	2	2		2
Keel, Rachel		2	4		
Hopkins, William	1	4	3		7
Cherry, Samuel	2	3	5		8
Luter, Matthew	2	2	5		4
Windall, Benjamin	2		5		
Bonner, William	3	3	4		13
Brown, Isaac	1	2	2		
Mayo, Peter	3	1	5		1
Mayo, William	1		3		4
Bullock, Drury	1	4	3		
Downs, Nehemiah	2	3	3		
Waldron, Charles	1	3	4		5
Windom, Green	2		3		
Mayo, Shadrack	1	1	5		
Windon, Solomon	2	3	5		
Coggin, William	1	2	5		
Meeks, Robert	1		4		
Nichols, Jane	1	2	3		
Taylor, John	2	3	6		
Taylor, William		1	1	2	
Taylor, Frances		2	1	3	
Lewis, Willis	1	1	3		
Wilkinson, William	1				2
Wilkinson, Benjamin, Senr	2	2	3		4
Cobb, James	1	4	5		
Wilkinson, Benjamin, junr	1				
Bryant, Frederick	1	5	2		8
Horeso, William	1	5	2		11
Cherry, Solomon	4		4		5
Summerland, James	1		4		
Etherage, Malicah	3	1	2		
Rogers, Isaac	2	1	5		
Anders, Whitten	1		2		
Batton, Thomas	1	3	3		
Ross, Thomas	1	1	1		
Whitus, Richard	1	1	4		
Whitus, Arthur	1	2	3		
Page, John	2		1		5
Buntin, Daniel	1	1	5		
Buntin, John	1		1		
Wilkinson, Joshua	1	2	4		4
Cearson, Thomas	1	4	2		
Whitley, Samuel	2	5	5		8
Nichols, Elizabeth			3		
Carter, Robert	1	1	2		

NAME OF HEAD OF FAMILY.	Free white males of 16 years and upward, including heads of families.	Free white males under 16 years.	Free white females, including heads of families.	All other free persons.	Slaves.
Williams, George	1		1		
Buntin, Mary	1		2		
Williams, Margaret		3	2		
Whitus, Samuel	1	2	1		
Strawbridge, William	2	2	4		
Adkerson, Benjamin	4		2		23
Bryant, Nicholas	2		5		5
Evans, Moses	1	4	1		1
Evans, Ephraim	1	3	1		1
Evans, Amos	1				
Clark, Samuel	1	1	4		5
Harris, William	1	1	1		
Harris, George, Senr	3		5		
Harris, Hood	1	2	4		
Williams, George	1	2	1		
Williams, Harris	1	1	5		
Harris, Henry	1	1	3		
Mourning, John, junr	1		1		1
Mourning, John, Senr	2	1	4		14
Mourning, James	1				
Gwartney, Thomas	2	4	2		7
Sherod, William	1		3		14
Rieves, Peter	1		1		20
Brady, James	2	5	5		
Brady, Susannah	2		3		
Teale, Emanuel, Senr	2	2	3		1
Teal, Jacob	1	2	1		
Teal, Moses	1	1	3		1
Savage, Joseph	1				
Pollard, John, Senr	3	1	5		
Pollard, John, junr	1	2	3		1
Pollard, Everit	1	3	3		
Brown, Samuel	1	1	2		1
Brown, James	1		3		
Brown, James, junr	1	3	3		
Teal, Emanuel, junr	1	2	1		
Brown, Benjamin	1	1	4		1
Bryerly, Jacob	1				
Williams, Joel	1	2	4		1
Brierly, Joseph	1	2	5		1
Brierly, Isaac	1		1		
Brierly, Richard	2	4	3		
Teal, Lodovick	1		2		
Teal, Richard	1				
Adams, Levi	2	7	7		
Parrimore, Amos	1		1		
Mills, Henry	1		2		
Williams, John	1	3	2		
Little, Isaac	2		4		
Little, Pleasant	1	1	2		
Womble, Benjamin, junr	1	1	1		
Womble, Simon	1		2		
Stokes, James	1				
Pennington, William	1				
Brown, Sophira			2		1
Anderson, John	1	2	3		
May, John	1	2	5		
Teal, William	1	1	4		
Spain, William	1				
Robertson, Severin	2	4	8		
Anderson, William	2	1	3		1
Anderson, Lawrence	1	2	4		2
Bell, Benjamin	2	5	3		16
Spain, Fetherston	1		1		
Griffin, Samuel	1	1	1		
Griffin, Caleb	1				
Mayo, Jacob	1		3		
Mitchel, Thomas	1	1	4		
Fulford, Joseph	1				
Herrington, Isaac	1	1	2		
Lewis, Winnifred	1	2	2		
Avery, Bridget		1	2		
Wyett, Keziah		2	2		
Love, Thomas	1		2		
Robertson, William	1		7		
Venters, Lancaster	3	1	2		3
Spain, Augustus	1	2	4		
Spain, Drury	2	1	1		
Mayo, Nathan	2	2	3		
Meeks, James	1	2	5		
Harris, Ann	1		1		
Ewell, Elizabeth		1	3		
Teal, Bradbury	1	4	2		
Teal, William	1	1	1		
Ward, Isaac	1	1	3		
Lewis, Willis	1	1	3		
Ward, William	1	3	2		
Reeves, Richard	1	3	2		9
Hickman, Joseph	1				
Little, James	1	4	4		5
Stokes, Markus	3	1	2		12
Adkinson, Amos	2		5		14
Hathaway, Edmond	1		2		
Hathaway, David	3	1	2		11
Hathaway, Thomas, Senr	1		4		
Hall, Thomas	3	2	3		16
Perry, Sarah			5		
Hearn, Benjamin	1	1	3		3

NAME OF HEAD OF FAMILY.	Free white males of 16 years and upward, including heads of families.	Free white males under 16 years.	Free white females, including heads of families.	All other free persons.	Slaves.
Averit, David	1		1		
Summerland, Thomas	1		1		
Meeks, Uranah	1	3	3		
Church, Isaac	1	2	7		
Church, Cornelius	1	2	2		
Church, John	2	1	4		
Mayo, Richard	2		2		
Robinson, John	2	1	6		
Hall, Charles	1				2
Adkins, Allen	1		1		6
Mayo, John	3	2	2		
Cobb, David, Senr	2	2	5		2
Cobb, Keziah	1	3	2		
Whitley, Mary			2		11
Moseley, William	3	1	1		
Milbern, John	1	2	3		1
Drake, Elizabeth	1		3		
Clark, John	1	2	3		
Whitley, William	1	2	2		7
Lewis, Nathan	1	2	2		
Meeks, Francis, junr	1	1	1		
Right, Isaac	1	2	3		
Randal, Latimer	1				
Everit, David, junr	1	2	6		
Coggin, John	2	1	6		
Hix, David	1				
Rix, Lucy	1		1		4
Cobb, Edward	3	2	5		
Jones, Henry	1	3	4		14
Cobb, Briton	1	3	4		
Swearinggame, Mary			5		
Taylor, John	1	5	2		
Avery, James	1		3		
Asbel, Joseph	2	2	2		
Grimmon, Jacob	1		4		
Womble, Benjamin, Senr	2	4	3		
Dupree, Bird	2	2	2		20
Dupree, Starling	2	3	5		8
Williams, Roderick	1	2	6		
Dupree, Benjamin	2	2	4		11
Proctor, Richard	1		2		9
Williamson, Henry	1		1		6
Duffil, Thomas, Senr	2	1	4		
Wallace, Thomas, Senr	2	1	6		2
Williams, John, Senr	3		1		13
Williams, John, Junr	1	2	2		3
Williams, James	1	4	2		5
Johnston, James	2	3	5		4
Wootin, John	2	1	2		7
Allen, Richard, Senr	2		3		7
Trust, Samuel	2	1	2		1
Peal, James	3	2	5		
Harrill, Reuben	1		5		
Buxton, William	1		3		4
Ross, William	1	1	3		
Tyson, Thomas	2		2		8
Foreman, Jesse	1		5		1
Evans, George	1				6
Lester, Jeremiah	1	1	3		
Sturdivant, Henry	1	1	4		8
Williams, Robert	1		3		
Sturdivant, Matthew	1		1		6
Sturdivant, Sarah		1	2		4
Moye, George	2	3	6		3
Lawrence, Josiah	1	1	2		9
Lawrence, Jesse	1				4
Foreman, John	1	2	2		12
Harris, Henry	2	3	2		4
Allen, Merryman	2	2	4		
Blann, John	1		3		
Browne, Arthur	1	1	2		1
Hathaway, Nathan	3	1	3		
Hathaway, James	1	1	4		
Harris, William	1	1	1		1
Sugg, Elizabeth	2		3		6
Eason, Ann		1	2	1	
Hathaway, Francis, Jur	2	1	9		
Trust, Joel	1	1	3		1
Bell, William	1		1		
King, John	3	2	2		2
Peedin, Patrick	1	1	5		4
Taunton, Henry	1	2	7		
Powers, David	2		5		
Powers, Ephraim	1	2	3		
Wadford, Joseph	2	4	3		
Moore, John	4	3	3		3
Williams, Edward	1		1		5
Williams, Abram	1	2	3		
Philips, Mary		1	2		
Corbett, Merida	2	3	2		
Allen, Paul	1	2	4		4
Mourning, Christopher	1	2	2		
Jordan, Richard	1	1	2		
Rogers, Absalom	1				
Spaniard, Pumbererer	1	1	2		
Cobb, James	2		6		
Rogers, Joseph	1	2	3		

NEWBERN DISTRICT, PITT COUNTY—Continued.

NAME OF HEAD OF FAMILY.	Free white males of 16 years and upward, including heads of families.	Free white males under 16 years.	Free white females, including heads of families.	All other free persons.	Slaves.
Hodges, Portlock	1	3	4		
Rogers, Drew	3	1	5		1
Cobb, Moses	1	1	2		
Harris, James	1		1		
Duffel, Thomas, junr	1	2	2		
Allen, Richard, junr	1		2		2
Anders, Catherine			3		
Peeples, Baldwin	1		2		
Bullock, Samuel	1		1		2
Dilde, Jesse	1	1	2		
Rigging, Darbey	1		3		
Pastern, Elizabeth	1	1	4		
Little, Noam	2		1		
Matthews, Joseph	1	1	3		
Tidder, Martha			1		
Williams, Josiah	1		2		2
Edwards, Elizabeth	1	2	4		
Lester, Jeremiah	1	2	3		1
Leggott, James	2	4	6		10
Barnes, Joshua	1		1		3
Francis, John	1		1		
Langley, Azaniah	2	1	4		
Page, William	3	2	3		1
Page, Joseph	1	3	2		
Turnage, Emanuel	1	1	2		1
Jolly, Jonathan	2	2	3		
Turnage, Abram	1		1		
Tyer, George	2		1		
Baker, Richard	2	1	3		
Jones, John	2	3	3		
May, Benjamin	1	2	8		29
Tyson, Job	1	3	2		9
Pope, John	1		1		6
Nicholas, Benjamin	1	1	1		
Joyner, Abraham	3	2	6		
Messer, John	1	4	1		
Baker, James	1	3	4		
Moore, John	1	3	2		
Baker, Asa	1		1		2
Flanagan, Edward	1	4	5		
Jordan, Jesse	1	5	7		
Dew, Arthur	1	2	3		
Forbes, Joseph	2	3	2		3
Forbes, Henry	1		2		
Johnston, William	2	1	3		
May, Benjamin	1				2
Smithe, William	1	1	4		
Sulivan, Joseph	2				
Grizzard, Hardy	2	4	4		
Davis, Samuel, junr	1	1	5		
Scoggins, Jeremiah		1	2		
Davis, Samuel, Senr	3	1	6		1
Davis, Lewis, Senr	1	3	3		
Davis, Lewis, Jur	1	2	1		1
Moye, William	1		4		3
Easton, John	1		4		21
Tison, Bethany			2		5
Tison, Sabra			1		4
Walston, Thomas	2		5		
Walston, George	1	1	5		
Moore, John	3				
Moore, Nathaniel	2	4	3		
Moore, William	2	1	9		
Moore, James	1	3	3		
Beazley, William	1	3	2		
Nicholas, Joel	1	2	1		
Dunning, Ezekiel	1	1	2		
Dunning, Jesse	3	1	3		
Lockhost, Merinah			4		
Bunday, Sabra		1	3		
Cartwright, Matthew	1	1	5		3
Alberson, Solomon	1	2	1		
Pipkin, Jesse	3		3		2
Rogers, Drury	2	2	5		1
Davis, Thomas	1	1	3		3
Moze, Joel	1		1	1	5
Deberry, Lemuel	3	3	6		18
Ashen, David	1	1	2		2
Bynum, Benja	1	3	1		5
Jordan, Benja	1	5	5		
Tyson, Frederick	1	5	4		
Senders, Abram	2				2
Wincles, William	1	4	1		
Oberry, Thomas	1				3
Smith, Stephen	3	1	2		
Ellis, Henry	4	6	6		12
Rix, Benjamin	1	3	3		
Lacy, Parker	1	3	1		
Joiner, Abram	1	4	3		1
Joiner, Isaac	1		3		1
Goff, Henry	1	2	2		
Hort, Barrom	1	1	3		
Wallace, George	1		2		
Goff, Thomas	1		1		3
Moore, Arthur	1		1		
Murray, Gardner	1		1		
Ivy, Samuel	1		5		
Narris, John, Senr	1	1	5		
Sanders, Robert	1	2	2		2
Hervey, James	1	2	2		
Moye, George	1		1		5
Numans, John	1		2		6
Tison, Richard L	1	1	1		1
Moye, Richard	1	3	3		3
Moore, Levi	1	3	2		4
Smith, Benjamin	1	3	3		
Allen, Charles	1	2	3		
Tyson, Joab	1		1		
Jones, Zadiac	1	3	3		
Baldwin, William	1	3	5		5
Moore, Elisha	1	2	5		
Tison, George, Senr	2	1	2		2
Tison, Cornelius	2		1		
Tyson, Icabod	1	4	2		2
Ryland, Benona	1		2		
Tyson, Cornelius	2		3		12
Forbes, Arthur	1		5		18
Moore, Jesse	2	3	6		13
Moore, John	1	1	2		1
Williams, John, Esqr	3	1			13
Joiner, Elizabeth		2	3		6
Bland, George	2		2		3
Barney, Lucy	1	1	1		2
Tison, Moses, junr	1	2	3		4
Joiner, Rebecca	1		2		
Coward, John	1	2	3		2
Tison, Edmond	2		1		
Moore, Arthur	1	2	6		
Bunday, Gideon	1	2	2		
Otterey, William	1	3	2		
Barrow, Benjamin	1	3	3		8
Ellis, John	1		4		3
Moye, George	1	2	5		
Dixon, Jeremiah	1	1	2		3
Ellis, Shadrack	1	2	3		
Forbes, Clement	1	5	4		5
Allen, Roger	2	3	5		
Allen, Peter	1	2	6		
Robeson, John	1	2	1		
Vines, John	1	2	6		5
Tison, Hezekiah	1	1	2		
Randolph, James	1	1	3		5
Tison, Henry	1	3	1		
Vines, Samuel			1		2
Moye, James	1		1		3
Tison, Moses, Senr	3	1	2		6
Allen, Zachariah	1	3	6		
Dilday, Charles	1	4	2		
Moor, Shadrach	3	3	3		
Forbes, John	2	1	1		9
Moore, Anna		3	3		
Norris, John	1				
Tison, George, junr	2		2		
Tison, Abraham	1	1	7	3	
Tison, Moses	1	2	3		4
Bryant, John	1	4	3		
Rogers, Dewey	1		5		
Randolph, Jesse	1		2		4
Ewell, Stephen	1	1	2		
Smith, Lazarus	2	3	2		
Smith, William	1	1	2		
White, Richard	1	1	1		
Harris, Mary		1	3		
Lester, Martha		1	1		
Wiscaney, Elizabeth	1	1	1		
Coleman, Isaac	2		1		1
Sutton, Abimeleck	1		2		
Powell, John	1	3	4		
Granby, George	1	3	4		
Jenkins, Zadiac	1		2		
Harrington, Paul	2	2	5		
Slaughter, Elizabeth	1		2	1	
White, Rachel	1	1	1		
Powell, James	1		2		
Barber, John	1		4		
Joiner, William	1		2		
Powell, Reuben, junr	2	3	4		
Ringold, Sarah		3	2		6
Powell, John	1	2	3		
Blount, Isaac	1	3	2		
Blount, Benjamin	1	1	2		2
Roundtree, Jesse	1		2		2
McGlahon, Adams	1	2	3		
Jackson, John	2	3	4		4
Jackson, Joseph	1	4	4		3
Cannon, William	2		2		
Manning, Elijah	1	1	2		
Bell, Balaam	1		1		
Sutton, Solomon	3	3	4		
Garret, Thomas	2	1	3		
Sirman, Eli	2	1	3		
Dennis, Lucy	2	1	3		
Powell, Reuben, Sr	1		1		
Wingate, Jeremiah	1				
Williams, Willis	1	5	3		
Moss, Dempsey	1	2	4		
Hardy, Thomas	1		8		
Calcraft, Mary	1		1		
Mariner, John	1				
Banod, Boaz	1		2		
Peels, Josiah	1		1		
Peels, Reuben	2	2	4		
Bentley, Thomas	1	3	3		
Windom, Micajah	2	1	2		
Wilson, John	1		2		
Bentley, Tapley	1	1	1		
Braxton, James, junr	1	1	4		
Branton, William	1	1	2		
Bowden, May	1		2		
Hamilton, Lucius	1	4	3		
Wingate, Joel	1		1		1
Harris, Joseph	1	2	3		
Sutton, Jacob	1	2	2		
Dewe, John	1	2	2		
Trueluck, George	1		1		
Trippe, Caleb, junr	1		1		
Powell, James	1		3		
Loving, Frederick	1	1	2		
English, Samuel	1	4	3		
Smith, Edmond	1				
Smith, Joseph	2		2		
Jackson, Joseph, Senr	1		2		
Wingate, Isaac	1		1		1
Falconer, George	1	3	6		1
Surman, Thomas	2	1	5		
Turner, William, Senr	2	4	6		
Turner, William, jur	1	1	2		
Alaster, Jacob	1	1	5		
Slatter, John	2	2	3		
Trippe, Caleb	3	4	3		
Ringold, James	1	3	4		
Fulford, James	3	5	4		
Blackston, John	4		3		
Blackston, Thomas	1	5	4		
Blackston, James, Senr	2	3	4		
Deale, Paul	1	3	3		
Whitfield, William	2	3	5		1
Powell, Simpson	1	1	4		
Trizell, John	3		6		1
Kitrall, John	1	2	1		3
Blount, Jacob	1	2	1		12
Williams, Dennis	1	1	1		
Williams, Ephraim	1		3		
Manning, Samuel	2	1	5		
McGlohon, Jeremiah	1				
McGlohon, George	1		3		
Castle, John Innis	1	1			
Vincent, John	1		3		
Smith, Joseph	3		2		
Smith, Jesse	1	1	1		
Hardison, Joseph	1	1	4		
Hardison, Joshua	1	3	2		
Sirman, John	1	2	4		
McClain, Daniel	1	2	3		
Clark, Jethro	1	1	3		
Barber, Elizabeth		1	3		
Bowen, Abraham	1		3		
Holland, John	2	1	3		5
Johnston, Holland	2	1	2		10
Brooks, Stephen	6	2	3		31
Blackledge, Thomas	2		3		24
Wright, Josiah	1	3	3		2
Cambriling, Stephen	2	1	3		4
Bullard, Daniel	1	1	2		2
Smith, Oliver	1		2		6
Blount, Benjamin	1	1			4
Patrick, Cornelius	2		8		1
Manning, Hilary	1	1	2		8
Wilcox, Stephen	1		2		1
Moye, John	1	2	2		14
Green, George	1	1			
Easton, James	2		3		12
Simpson, John	1		2		10
Crawford, Andrew			3		
Simpson, Elizabeth	1		3		30
Adams, Abram	3	5	6		5
McKean, Edy	1				
Hall, James	1		2		
Nobles, Winifred		2	3		2
Gwartney, William	1				7
Tyron, Elisabeth	1		3		
Blount, William	2	3	2		30
Simpson, Samuel	1		3		10
Hilling, William	1	3	5		5
Hardy, Abram	2	4	2		9
Smith, David	3	2	4		21
Tyron, William	1	1	5		
Badard, William	1		2		
English, Thomas	1	1	3		2
Richards, Solomon	1		3		
Cherry, Lemuel	1	5	5		2
Hannis, Jesse	2	3	4		2
Slatter, Sampson	1	1			
Slatter, Absalom	1		7		
Eastwood, William	1	1	6		1
King, John	1	2	3		1
Smith, Abner C	1	1	1		

NEWBERN DISTRICT, PITT COUNTY—Continued.

NAME OF HEAD OF FAMILY.	Free white males of 16 years and upward, including heads of families.	Free white males under 16 years.	Free white females, including heads of families.	All other free persons.	Slaves.
Corry, Joseph	1		2		
Corry, Elizabeth		1	1	1	
Bell, Starkey	1	4	4		
Hardy, Elizabeth	1	2	4		21
Hardy, Robert	1				
Williams, George	3	1	1		3
Williams, David	1				
Williams, Simon	1				
Williams, Anne	2	2	1		1
English, Peter	1				
Tyron, Noah	2	5	1		1
Nobles, Margaret			2		
Lasley, John	1	2	4		1
Harris, Elijah	1		2		
Scotfield, William	2	1	2		1
Patrick, Benjamin	1				
Tyron, Jonathan	2	1	8		
Balderee, Isaac	1		3		
Driding, John	1	1	2		
Gordon, Stewart	2	2	4		
Moye, John, Senr	1		1		1
McGowns, William	2	1	5		
McGowns, George, Senr	1	1	4		
Moss, Peter	2	4	3		
Leadom, Christopher	1		1		2
King, William	1	1	3		3
Moore, David	1		1		
Diggins, Joseph	1				
Phaling, Edward	1				
Barnhill, John	2				
Davis, John	2				
Kennedy, Bartholomew	1				
McNeale, Hopestill	2				
Cobb, William	1	2	4		2
Bullock, John	1	2	3		
Roads, William	1				
Everit, Reuben	1				
Blount, Benjamin H	1				
Moore, David	1				
Salter, Cloe	1		2		
Adams, Archibald	3	1	5		5
Cannon, Lewis	1	1	2		13
Brooks, James, Senr	2	1	5		6
Cannon, Henry	1	2	3		16
Cannon, Nathaniel	1	4	5		9
Moss, Michael	1	3	7		
Mills, Nasby, Senr	2	4	6		
Williams, George	2	1	1		3
Haddock, John	2	4	5		
Mills, John	2	3	5		
Mills, Isaac, Senr	3	1	6		
Stock, Isaac	1		6		8
Stock, John	2	5	5		9
Kite, Samuel	2	1	2		
Muckleroy, William	4		1		
Moss, Peter	2	4	3		
Cannon, William	2		2		
Moye, John, Senr	2		2		
Hancock, James	4	4	6		1
Deale, Abel, junr	1	1	4		
Cannon, Mary			1		7
Brooks, John	1	5	2		
Brooks, William, Junr	1	3	4		
Mills, Nesby, junr	1		1		
Hardy, Thomas, Senr	2	1	4		1
Moore, Newton	1	3			
Tucker, Readick	1				
Moye, Gideon	1	1			
Brooks, William, Senr	1	2	4		
Adams, William	1		2		1
Cox, Aaron	1	1	3		
Stocks, William	1	2	2		
Pettite, Gideon	1	2	3		
Mills, Isaac, junr	1		4		
Tootle, William	1	1	4		
Roach, James	1	1	1		
Haddock, Charles	1	1	3		
Deale, Abel, Senr	2	4	5		
Cox, Abram	1	3	2		
Stocks, Sarah	1	2	4		
Cannon, Thomas	2	5	4		2
Cannon, Furney	2		1		2
Tuten, John	1	2	5		
Wilson, Daniel	1		4		
Wilson, Willis	1	2	5		
Kite, Henry	1	1	3		
Kite, John	1	1	2		
Adams, William	1	2	3		
Carrill, Isaac	3				
Corben, Esther		1	2		
Haddock, William	1	4	5		3
Haddock, Admiral	1	2	3		
Simmons, Mary		2	3		
Mills, William, junr	1	4	3		2
Mills, William, Senr	1	2	3		
Putnall, Joshua	1		2		
Mills, Frederick	1	4	9		4
Slatter, Thomas	1	1	5		
Slatter, John, Senr	2	2	3		
Slatter, Samuel	1	1	1		
Curlee, John	1	2	3		
Randal, William	1	1	2		1
Deale, Thomas	1	4	1		
Brooks, Ephraim	1	3	3		
Smith, Joseph	1	4	5		
Dudley, Hannah			2		
Smith, William	1	2	3		
Smith, Charles	1	3	6		
Smith, Henry	1	4	3		
Smith, Francis	1	1	2		
Golding, Lemuel	1	2	3		
Wilson, William	1	4	4		1
Barber, Elizabeth		1	3		
Deale, Abel, junr	1	1	4		
Mills, Henry	1	2	4		
Buck, William	2	4	3		3
Armstrong, James	3	2	3		10
Salter, Ann, Senr	1	1	3		11
Salter, Ann, jur	1		4		22
Salter, John, Senr	1	3	3		8
Wade, Joseph	1		1		
Moore, James		2	1		
Hall, William	1	2	2		
Arnold, Elizabeth			3		
Jones, Thomas	2	1	2		15
Boyde, Robert, Senr	3	2	4		12
Boyde, Isaac	3		2		8
Watkins, Thomas	2	1	3		
Walkins, Janet		1	4		1
Mayo, John	2		2		
Mayo, Benjamin	1		1		
Ward, George	3		3	1	
Boyde, Joseph, Senr	3		4		4
Boyde, William	1	1	1		1
Boyde, Robert, junr	1	2	1		1
Taylor, Mary		1	3		1
Buck, Benjamin	3	4	3		2
Grimes, William	1	1	2		15
Buck, James	1	3	5		4
Dixon, Ann	2		3		7
Dixon, John	1				
Gorham, James	2	8	4		50
Noble, Levi	1	4	4		2
Nelson, Giles	1	2	2		
Nelson, James	1	2	3		
Nelson, Martin, Senr	2	3	5		5
Nelson, Martin, junr	1	1	1		1
Bates, James	3		2		
Tuten, Shadrach	2	3	8		1
Edwards, William	1	1	2		
Elks, William	1	1	2		5
Elks, Uriah	1		1		1
Robeson, Amy			1		1
Dixon, Edward	4		4		
Dixon, Abraham	1	2	3		
Dixon, William, Senr	3	3	3		
Dixon, Frances			3		
Dixon, Absalom	1	1	2		
Dixon, William, junr	1	1	3		
Albritton, Peter	4	1	1		4
Albritton, James	1		3		3
Albritton, William	1	1	3		
Kemp, Joshua	1	1	4		
Moore, Moses	2	1	6		10
Newman, James	1		2		2
Moore, Jacob	1	1	1		
Brooks, Isaac	2	1	3		
Edwards, Daniel	1	1	3		
Whitfield, Alexander	1	1	2		
Edwards, Israel	1		5		
Nelson, Samuel	1	2	2		
Buck, John	1				10
Tildsley, Charles	1	3	1		
Tildsley, Thomas	1		1	1	
Nelson, John	2	2	5		
Rochel, Jacob V	1		2		2
Salter, John, junr	1		4		9
Watkins, Ann	2		4		9
Stewart, Elizabeth			2		
Angel, Sarah		1	2		
Moore, Obadiah	1	1	1		
Crafton, Ambrose	2		5		
Campbell, Archibald	2	3	5		
Fleming, George	1	2	6		
King, Priscilla		1	2		
Buck, James, Junr	1		1		
Stevens, William	1		3		
Brooks, John	1		3		
Buck, Appollos	1	2	2		
Albritton, Henry	1	3	2		
Savage, Joseph	1		1		
Arnold, William	1	5	2		
Tindale, John	1				
Judkins, Thomas	2		2		
Judkins, Charles	1		1		
Elks, Samuel	2	2	2		
Mills, Nasby	3	3	6		
Allen, Shadrach	2	2	4		15
Smith, Samuel	1	3	4		5
Avery, David	1		3		
Cadeaduff, Mary	2	2	3		
Blount, Sharp	2		1		47
Harvey, Ann			1		18
Mills, James	1	1	4		
Jarrell, Henry, Senr	2		1		6
Jarrell, Henry, junr	1	3	7		1
Murphy, Thomas	1	3	6		
Pugh, Hugh, Senr	1	1	1		26
Cabell, James	2	2	5		4
Pelt, Henry	3		3		
Ventis, Benjamin	1	1	2		
Sutton, David	5	3	4		
Gardner, Isaac	1	4	2		3
Gatlin, Stephen	1	1	1		3
Gatlin, Elizabeth	1		4		7
Gatlin, John	1	1	1		3
Gatlin, Levi	1	3	2		1
Pugh, Hugh, junr	1		2		12
Smith, Henry, junr	1	2	3		2
Smith, Henry, junr	1		2		5
Shipp, Mary	1		1		4
Shipp, William	1		1		
Clark, Osborn	1	1	1		
Burney, Simon	1	3	2		5
Wherry, William	1	2	4		12
Pollard, John	1	5	2		
Jarrell, Jacob	1	6	4		
Smith, Abram	1		4		
Smith, John	5	2	3		1
Browning, William	1	2	8		
Pugh, Stephen	1		1		7
Adams, Ezekiel	3	6	2		
Ventis, Patience	2		2		
Rice, John	1		2		
Cox, Aaron	3		2		
Nelson, Peter	1	3	5		
Hickman, Jacob	1	1	1		
Smith, Cannon	1	3	3		3
Roys, Charles	1		2		
Stafford, William	1		2		
Dunn, Walter	1	3	1		1
Kight, Samuel	1	5	6		
Pelt, John	1	2		1	
Gwartney, Benjamin	1	1	1		
Roys, Edward	1		1		1
Roys, Leaven	1	1	1		
Jarrel, Shadrach	1	6	1		1
Peters, Joseph	3	6	3		2
Patrick, Joel	2	1	5		2
Patrick, Micajah	1	1	2		
Coart, John	2	2	4		18
Forms, Ruth		1	2		
Dunn, Walter	1	3	2		2
Kennedy, David	1	1	2		
Kennedy, David, junr	1		2		1
Quinlow, Patrick	1		1		
Quinlow, Edward	1		1		
Gardner, Edward	2	2	2		5
Patrick, Micajah	1	1	2		
Browning, Peregrine	1	5	4		
Cannon, Radford	1	2	3		
Carmaday, Jonathan	1		3		
Wingat, John	1	2	1		4
Davenport, William	1	2	2		1
Branch, James	1	2	2		
Branch, Simon	1	3	1		
Cannon, Edward	3	2	2		2
Kite, Stephen	1	2	1		
Kite, David	1		1		
Cox, Daniel	1		1		
Stokes, John	1		1		
Stokes, James	1				
Conner, John	1		1		
Smith, Platt	1	3	1		
Peters, William	1	1	1		1
Everit, William	3	2	6		
Nichols, William	3	2	3		
Cobb, David, junr	1		1		
Tolsin, James	1		1		
Edwards, Britton	2	4	4		8
Alford, Jesse	1	1	1		
May, Allen	1				
Ayres, Thomas	1		1		
Thigpin, Dennis	1		1		
Hatway, John	2	2	1		
Hatway, Edmond, Junr	1		1		
Hatway, Francis	1	1	3		
Peebles, William	1	1	2		
Meeks, Matthew	1		2		
Lewis, Joshua	1				

NEWBERN DISTRICT, WAYNE COUNTY.

NAME OF HEAD OF FAMILY.	Free white males of 16 years and upward, including heads of families.	Free white males under 16 years.	Free white females, including heads of families.	All other free persons.	Slaves.
Slocum, Ezekiel	1	1	2		1
Whitfield, Needham	2	2	4		27
Whitfield, William, Sr	1		2		27
Heron, William	2	3	2		
Whitfield, William, Jr	2	3	3		36
Winkfield, Joseph	1				5
Casey, Micajah	1	4	4		1
Heron, Samuel	1	4	4		
Hines, Reuben	1	5	2		
Carraway, John	1	2	3		1
Holmes, Charles	3	1	2		16
Heron, Jane	1	1	6		2
Martin, Paul	1	2	4		
Davis, Hugh	1	2	2		
Bass, Rice	1	3	1		
Bass, Aley, Senr	1	2	7		
Lane, William	1	3	2		
Rieves, Jesse	1	1	1		
Rieves, William	2	2	4		4
Gideons, John	1	2	3		
Bass, Thomas	3	1	4		4
Jones, John	2	2	2		
Rieves, John	1				
Carraway, Adam	1	2	5		12
Hines, Willis	1		1		1
Hines, Owen	1				3
Griffin, Dempsey	3	2	4		
Brown, John	1	2	3		
Brow, Noah	1		2		
Brown, Ann		1	3		
Brown, Christopher	1		1		
Boyekin, Thomas	1	2	2		1
Langston, Isaac	1		1		
Bass, Joshua	1	1	4		1
Husk, Mary			2		
Drew, George	2	1	7		2
Turner, Joseph	1	2	6		3
Bass, Alice, junr			3		24
Bass, Andrew	1	1	5		
Falconer, Robert	1	3	3		
Edwards, John	2	3	5		1
Edwards, David	1	1	2		
Edwards, Sampson	1	2	1		
Newell, Peter	1		2		
Newell, John	2	2	8		
Birquit, Moses	2	1	1		
Starling, Robert	1	2	1		
Starling, Abram, Jr	3	1	4		
Beard, John	3	3	3		
Everit, Amy	2		3		2
Norris, Jesse	1		1		
Flowers, John	1	4	3		2
Lane, William, Senr	1				
Lane, Samuel	1	2	3		
Hill, John	1	1	2		
Taylor, Jonathan	2	1	4		
Jennett, Thomas	1	1	2		
Jernigan, David	3	1	3		26
Frazer, George	3	1	5		4
Carraway, Elizabeth		1	3		5
Smith, John	1		2		
McKinney, Richard	2	6	3	1	16
Linton, George	1		3		1
Frazer, James	1	1	1		
Neusam, David	1				
Jennett, Joseph	1	3	4		
Starlin, Elijah	1		4		
Starlin, Abram, Senr	1	2	5		
Boyte, Stephen	1				
Hudson, Ann			2		
McCullen, Bryan	1	3	4		2
Bradley, James	1	1	3		
Bryan, William	2	3	5		
Flowers, Simon	2	1	1		
Flowers, Jesse	2	1	6		
Harrell, Samuel	2		3		2
Martin, Aaron	3	4	3		2
Flowers, Jacob	1	2	1		1
Harrell, Daniel	2	2	5		
Harrell, Hazel	1		1		
Barfield, Blake	2	1	4		1
Killit, Sarah			1		1
Barfield, Solomon	1	1	3		
Wolfe, Charles, Senr	4	2	5		10
Adkinson, John	1		1		10
Adkinson, Samuel	1	1	3		
Goodman, William	1	3	5		
Elmore, Reuben	1	2	2		
Crow, Sarah	2	1	1		4
Crow, Isaac	1	3	1		
Dannel, John	1	2	4		
Benson, Benjamin	1	4	5		
Benson, John	1		1		
Wolfe, Charles, junr	1		1		
Killit, John	1	2	3		
Dannels, Alice	1	1	4		4
Odum, Jethro	1	1	4		
Ingram, William	1	1	1		
Rhodes, William	1		3		15
Wolfe, George	4		1		5
Manley, James	3	2	2		8
Pipkin, Arthur	2	2	5		
Pipkin, Philip	1	1	2		
Thomas, William	1	2	2		
Thomas, Thomas	3	1	5		2
Odum, Jacob	2	3	2		
Dennin, Robert	4	1	6		
Howell, John	2	3	3		
Cole, James	2	2	3		
Joiner, Joel	2	1	9		
Vick, Benjamin	1		4		
Parker, Arthur	1	3	2		
Rhodes, James	1	3	2		
Raifield, Southy	1	3	2		
Pipkins, Elisha	2	3	5		14
Crawford, William	3	1	2		
Whood, Nathan	2	3	4		
Pipkin, Luke	3	2	1		1
Pipkin, Jesse	1	3	3		
Fulgum, Raiford	2	2	5		7
Cogdell, David		4	5		21
Heron, Frederick	2				5
Buck, Caleb	3	2	3		1
Dannel, Hardy	1	1	1		
Holliman, Jeremiah	1		1		
Holliman, Ezekiel	1	3	3		1
Mayhon, Dixon	1	2	4		
Carraway, Willis	1	1	6		
Carraway, Elijah	2		4		3
Carraway, Thomas	1	1			12
Brown, Amy	1	3	1		
Thomas, Solomon	1	2	3		
Lloyd, John	1		3		
Holliman, Christopher	1	3	5		
Wallace, Aaron	1	1	3		
Barbary, William	2	2	5		
Dannels, Shadrach	1	3	3		
Dannels, John	1	2	4		
Mayhon, William	1	2	3		
Pipkin, Stephen	1	3	6		
Rhodes, William, Jur	1	2	2		9
Sharp, Groves	1	2	5		1
Bizzel, John, Senr	2		1		2
Jourdin, William	2	1	3		
Bradbury, James	1		4		1
McKinney, Mary	3	2	5		16
Cox, Micajah	1	5	3		1
Cox, Mary	2	2	3		
Kennedy, John	2	1	2		
Cox, Phoebe	2		3		
Cox, Smithson	1	1	2		
Cox, Richard	1		3		
Cox, Josiah	1	1	6		1
Grantum, Mary	1	2	2		1
Bennett, Sarah	2	3	2	1	
Pellis, Dinah			1		
Lee, Christopher	1		4		
Musgrove, Thomas	4	2	3		
Musgrove, Moses	1	4	4		
Grantum, Joel	1	2	3		
Grantum, Jacob	1	1	3		
Lohorn, James	1	2	2		2
Miles, James	1	2	3		
Salmon, Vincent	1		3		
Wigs, Joel	1	1	2		
Bizzel, William, Senr	1				
Bizzel, William, junr	1		1		1
Grantum, Jesse	1	1	3		
Grantum, James	1		4		
Bizzel, Jesse	1		3		
Pettite, David	1		2		
Dunn, Benjamin	1	4	5		
Brogdon, Thomas	1		4		
Westbrooke, John	2	3	4		
Flowers, Humphrey	1	1	3		
Dunn, Thomas	2	2	4		
Dinkins, James	2		2		
Westbrook, James	2	5	3		4
Brogdon, John	1	2	6		
Salmon, Zachariah	1		2		
Linch, Bryant	1	2	2		
Dunn, Richard	2	3	3		
Grantum, Solomon	1				
Shaw, Joseph	1		2	1	1
Bizzell, Thomas	1	1	5		2
Pipkin, Willis	3	5	3		6
Bizzell, David	1				
Strickland, John	1	1	1		
Holmes, William	1	1	1		
Harper, John	2		2		
Sohorn, Benjamin	1	2	3		
Johnston, William	1		5		
Hull, Nathaniel	1		2		
Westbrooke, Burrel	2	2	4		9
Scull, Alexander	1				
Brown, Khelan	1	1	3		
Harp, Richard	1	3	4		
Bizzell, John, junr	1	3	3		
Pike, John	1	4	3		
Quimby, Jonas	1	3	6		10
Moore, Luke	1	3	5		1
Bass, Edward	1	4	3		16
Musgrove, John	1		1		
Musgrove, Joel	2	1	4		
Shaw, Hugh	1	1	2		1
Pierce, Elizabeth			1		
Benton, Charity			1		
Hamm, Resters	1	1	3		1
Mourning, Burrel	3	4	6		9
Mourning, William	2	1	5		
Shadding, James	2	2	2		
Grace, James	2	2	2		6
Lane, Isum, Senr	2	3	5		5
Taylor, William	1	5	10		2
Howell, William, Junr	1		1		1
Bell, William, junr	1	3	3		2
Bell, John	1	3	1		1
Bell, William, Senr	1	1	2		1
Howell, William, Senr	5	2	4		13
Packer, Micajah	2	3	4		6
Parker, Samuel	1	2	2		
Page, Ephraim	1	1	1		
Sauls, Raimond	1	4	3		1
Warrick, Jacob	1	1	1		
Gardner, Olive			3		
Wells, Micajah	1	3	3		
Hanley, James	1	2	6		8
Cato, George	1		1		7
Hollawell, Thomas	3	1	3		
Wosdon, Jonathan	1	2	6		12
Flitcher, Sarah	1	3	3		
Flitcher, Ralph	1	1	2		
Howell, Etheldred	1	1	5		10
Bell, James	1	1	5		
Malliby, William	1	1	6		
Nixon, Henry	3	1	3		
Nixon, John	2	2	4		
Outland, Thomas	2		2		7
Britts, Henry	2	3	3		
Hamm, William, Senr	1		3		
Hamm, William, junr	2	3	6		
Lancaster, William	1	1	6		
Gin, Hardy	1		2		
Lane, Isum, junr	1	2	1		
Johnston, Henry	2	1	1		
Mitchel, Isum	1	2	3		
Lanch, Linum	1		1		
Donnels, William	1	2	4		
Smith, Simon	1	2	4		
Dannels, Margaret		2	2		
Packer, Marmaduke	1				
Outland, Jonathan	1	2	1		1
Dawson, William	3	3	7		3
Smith, Arthur	5	1	3		
Peele, Willis	1	1	3		
Smith, John	1		1		
Ham, Henry	1	3	4		
Ham, Zachariah	1	2	1		1
Ham, Richard	1	5	1		
Monday				4	
Beamon, Uzias	1	1	3	4	
Luke				1	
Revil, Edmond	1				
Revil, Micajah	1				
Dawson, Isaac	1	2	1		
Hollawel, John	1	2	1		
Peacock, Peter	1	1	3		2
Wradford, William	3		1		6
Best, Robin	1				
Sherrod, Benjamin	1	1	3		2
Parker, Isaac	1	2	4		
Fort, William	1		2		10
Robinson, Thomas	1		3		
Radford, Noah	1	1	4		
Parsons, Solomon	2	3	3		4
Bundy, Jane		1	2		
Beaman, Francis	3		4		
Beaman, James	2		1		
Warwick, Wiat	1	4	2		
Wilson, John	1	3	2		
Wilson, Robert	1	2	2		
Aicock, Simon	1	2	6		
Beaman, David	1	1	2		
Joiner, Matthew	1	1	6		
Handley, John, junr	1	1	1		
Williams, William	3	1	2	2	
Bundy, Mark	1		3		
Burdin, John	2	2	1		1
Bordin, Woodard	1				
Smith, Benjamin	1	2	1		
Amey				4	

NEWBERN DISTRICT, WAYNE COUNTY—Continued.

NAME OF HEAD OF FAMILY.	Free white males of 16 years and upward, including heads of families.	Free white males under 16 years.	Free white females, including heads of families.	All other free persons.	Slaves.
Pate, Shadrack	1	3	1		
Bundy, William	1	3	2		
Coley, Gabriel	1	5	5		
Branch, Edy	1		2		
Combs, John	1		2		
Powel, Eli	2		2		
Fort, Benjamin	1	1	6	3	24
Sherrard, William	2				
Morris, Milley			1		
Bogue, Jesse	3	1	2		
Lancaster, Wright	2		1		
Lancaster, Levi	1	1	5		
Edmundson, James	1	5	5		19
Johnston, Abram	1	2	2		
Sherrord, John	2		3		16
Bryan, Willis	1	2	2		5
Bryan, Joel	2	1	1		
Perkins, Jeremiah	1	3	4		
Coleman, Elijah	1		1		
Parker, Isaac	1	2	1		
Sanders, Dicy		2	4		9
Sandiford, John	3		1		
Sandiford, James	1	1	3		
Bundy, Dempsey	1	4	2		
Hall, Caleb	1	1	2		1
Elvinton, Noah	1		4		1
Johnston, Abram	1	2	2		
Brassil, Sampson	1	2	2		2
Elvinton, John	1		2		7
Brassil, Richard	1	2	3		1
Brassil, Shadrach	1	2	1		3
Brassil, Elizabeth		1	2		2
Sauls, John	1		3		3
Martin, William	1	3	2		
Lane, John	1				2
Sauls, Henry	1	1	3		
Sauls, Cord	1				
Elvinton, Hardy	1	5	2		2
Downing, George	1		4		
Hasty, William	1	1	3		
Hasty, Joseph	1		1		
Hasty, Edwin	1	1	1		
Hagins, Mary				1	
Stanton, John	2	2	7		7
Minshew, John	2	3	2		10
Bartlett, Samuel	2	4	7		
Bridger, James	2	2	3		
Deal, William	1	1	3		2
Sceater, John	2		1		
Hasty, John	1	1	3		
Outlaw, Cornelius	1	2	4		
Woodward, Isaac	2		1		19
Hollawell, Joseph	3	4	5		
Overman, John	3		2		
Morris, Zachariah, Senr.	1		1		
Cooke, Margaret		1	2		2
Cooke, Thomas	1	3	4		
Cooke, Arthur	1	1	4	1	
Cooke, Stephen	1	1	2		5
Stephenson, Lemuel	1		2		
Brassil, David	1				1
Blow, Priscilla	2	3	3		
Green, James	1		4		
Morris, Thomas	1		2		
Woodard, John	1	1	2		1
Morris, Zachariah, Junr.	1		1		1
Morris, Isaac	1	1	1		
Morris, Jeremiah	1		2		
Parker, Elisha	3	1	2		
Wootin, William	1	1	3		
Overman, Aaron	1	2	4		
Overman, Thomas	1	1	1		
Arnold, Benjamin	1	4	4		
Cooke, Jacob	1		2		3
Davis, Richard	1	1	1		
Morris, Benjamin	1	3	2	1	
Arnold, Joseph	1	2	3		
Bailey, Henry	1	1	2		
Talton, Josiah	1	1	3		
Davis, Huldy			2		
Davis, John	1	3	2		
Davis, Joshua	1	1	1		
Hollawell, Silas	3	1	4		
Pervis, John	1				
Lovin, William	1	1	2		
Lovin, Isum	1		2		
Nusum, David	2	3	5		
Alberson, Joseph	1		2		
Casey, Jeremiah	1	3	4		
Gilbert, Joel	1	2	2		
Nusum, William	2	3	4		1
Dodd, Aaron	1	4	3		
Brookins, Bridgman	3	1	5		
King, John	1	2	5		5
Peel, Jesse	2	3	1		
Dannels, Isaac	2	1	2		
Dannels, Ephraim	1		2		11

NAME OF HEAD OF FAMILY.	Free white males of 16 years and upward, including heads of families.	Free white males under 16 years.	Free white females, including heads of families.	All other free persons.	Slaves.
Merritt, Sarah			1		
Lovin, Reddick	1	2	1		
Parisher, James	1				
Rogers, Jonathan	1	1	2		3
Martin, Joseph	1		2		1
Ellis, John	1	1	3		
Downing, Mary			3		
Boswell, Simpson	2	2	2		
Brookins, Hannah		1	1		
Brookins, Absalom	1		1		
Peale, Pasco	1		5		
Nousum, Joel	3	2	3		
Peter				1	
Aicock, Jesse	2	4	2		3
Watkins, William	2	3	3	3	
Watkins, John	1	3	5		1
Maddocks, Robeson	1	2	2		
Holland, James	2		1		
Holland, Elisha	2	1	1		
Tucker, Robert	1	2	5		
Smiddick, Samuel	2	2	2		
Pender, Hardy	3	4	3		
Peacock, Samuel, Senr.	1	2	3		4
Peacock, Samuel, junr.	3	3	2		
Sims, Robert	1	2	3	1	4
Love, Edmond	1	3	5		
Davis, Thomas	3	2	4		
Dickinson, David	1				
Sims, Abram			2		11
Cooke, Benjamin	2	3	3		1
Dannels, Isaac			1		
Chance, Stephen	1	2	1		
Dickinson, Shadrach	1	2	7		14
Dickinson, Joel	3	1	3		13
Dickinson, Daniel	2	6	1		3
Sims, Barnes	1	6	1		2
Tomberlinson, William	1	2	4	1	
Coleman, Elias	1	3	4		
Dickinson, Henry	1		2		
Dickinson, Jacob	1		1		
Dickinson, William	1		3		
Powell, Jacob	1		3		
Fooks, Solomon	1	3	1		
Sandiford, John	1	1	2		
Ferrill, William	1	3	1		
Pope, Henry	2	2	4		
Sullivan, Owen	1		2		
Simmons, Jesse	1	1	2		
Rose, Theophilus	1		2		
Evans, John	1	3	2	1	
Evans, Isum	3	2	2		
Evans, Joel	1	5	3		
Woodard, Joshua	1	3	4		
Dannels, Elias	1	2	3		
Hay, Reuben	2		4	1	
Love, George	1		1		1
Brookins, Thomas	1	1	1		1
Turner, Matthew	2		5		28
Whood, Edward	1	3	3		4
Whood, Edward, junr.	1	2	2		
Hilliard, Francis	1	1	1		
Hilliard, Francis, Senr.	3		3		
Fooks, William	1	2	5		1
Boswel, Thomas	2	2	1		
Barnes, William	1		2		1
Boswel, Zadik	1	3	3		
Lucus, John	1	3	4		
Watson, Samuel	2	2	1		
Evans, David	2	4	5		
Spiva, Joab	3	1	4		
Rentfrow, Jacob	1	3	5		
Bass, Abram	1		2		
Ridgin, Frederick	1	2	4		
Ridgin, William	1				
Lamb, Merion		8	5		
Rogers, Jesse	1				
Roundtree, Francis	1				
Whood, William	4	3	6		
Barnes, Samuel	1	4	5		8
Barnes, Simon	3	4	6		6
Watson, Isum	1	4	3		4
Barnes, Jesse	2	2	2		9
Barnes, James	1	1	3		
Barnes, Jacob	1	1	1		
Whitley, Drury	1		4		
Whitley, Micajah	1	1	4		
Rose, Thomas	1		3		
Wiggins, Thomas	1		1		
Hatchel, Morris	1	6	3		
Horn, Thomas	1	3	7	1	
Horn, Henry	1	2	5		5
Horn, Jeremiah	1	2	2		
Cobb, James	3	2	1	2	14
Cobb, Patience		4	7		5
Cobb, Bridget		1	3		13
Barefoot, John	1		2		25
Lee, John	3	1	5		

NAME OF HEAD OF FAMILY.	Free white males of 16 years and upward, including heads of families.	Free white males under 16 years.	Free white females, including heads of families.	All other free persons.	Slaves.
Lee, Jonathan	1	1	1		
Arthurs, Sarah				2	
Lamb, Jacob, Senr.	2	2	2		2
Lamb, Hardy	1	3	4		
Lamb, Abram	1	3	4		
Lamb, Joshua	1		2		
Rentfrow, James	2	2	3		
Brown, Jesse	1	1	1		
Holland, John	1	4	2		1
Nichols, John M	1		3		
Ellis, Sampson	1	1	1		
Durdens, William	2		3		
Ellis, Josiah	1	1	2		
Ellis, Joel	3	2	3		
Lamb, Isaac	1		5		
Pearson, Christopher	2	4	6		
Cobb, Stephen	2				5
Cobb, Nathan	2	2	3	1	21
Horn, Damaris		1	2	2	1
Lamb, Reddick	1		2		
Lamb, Jacob, junr.	1	2	4		
Lucus, Joseph	1	2	4		
Simmons, Jesse	1	2	3		
Barnes, John	1		2		7
Peacock, Levi	1	3	3		1
Thomson, William	1	1	3		5
Powell, Peter	2	1	3		1
Powell, Enos	1		2		
Powell, William	1		3		
Sanders, William	1	4	3		
Price, Rice	1	1	4		
Copeland, Joshua	2	3	5		
Edgington, Joseph	1	1	3		
Edginton, Thomas	1	4	3		
Rogers, Willowby	1	4	1		
Peacock, Kate		1	1		
Mitchell, Reuben	1	3	2		
Biggs, Elijah	1	1	2		
Baggott, Every	1	1	5		
Boyd, Josiah	1	2	1		
Morrison, Alexander	1	2	2		
Sears, David	1	1	2		
Buntin, James	1	1	2		
Bradbury, George	2	1	4		
Howell, John	2	1	3		10
Hooks, William	2	3	5		14
Pike, Nathan	2	3	4		
Hall, Isaac	2	3	4		
Collier, Samuel	1	4	2		
Gibson, Charles	1	2	3		
Worrell, Richard	1	2	3		1
Worrell, Priscilla		2	1		
Worrell, Benjamin	2	1	4		
Worrell, William	3		5		
Cithum, Sabry		2	3		
Alford, Benjamin	1	2	3		
Afley, Daniel	1	4	6		
Howell, Joshua	3	1	4		5
Worrell, John	1	1	2		
Modlin, Edmond	3	2	1		
Langley, Oswell	1	2	1		
Price, Kinchin	1		4		
Howell, Admiral	1	2	2		3
Heron, John	1		1		3
Hanley, John	2		2		11
Applewight, John	1	1	2		4
Saint, Samuel	1	1	2		
Brown, Jesse	1		6		
Modlin, Thomas	1	2	2		
Scott, Thomas	1	5	2		
Worrell, Elizabeth			3		
Worrell, James		3	1		
Langley, Miles	1		2		
Tilton, Elizabeth	1	1	2		
Wilson, Henry	1	2	2		
Pate, James	1	3	4		1
Pate, Isum	1	3	2		
Pate, Elias	1		2		
Pate, Daniel	1	2	2		
Pate, Martha			1		
Thomson, Peter	1	2	1		
Thomson, Jethro	1		1		
Thomson, Zadik	1				1
Howell, Archilaus	4	4	2		12
Davis, James	3	1	4		1
Deanes, Dempsey	1	1	4		2
Deanes, James	1	2	1		
Boyekin, William	1		2		13
Thomson, Thomas	1	3	4		
Boyt, Joseph	1		3		
Boyt, Amos	1	4	2		
Boyt, Thomas	1	2	3		
Deanes, Elizabeth		2	6		
Alford, William	5	2	9		11
Rhodes, James	1				
Thomson, Rachel	1	1	1		2
Pope, Charles	2		4		1

NEWBERN DISTRICT, WAYNE COUNTY—Continued.

NAME OF HEAD OF FAMILY.	Free white males of 16 years and upward, including heads of families.	Free white males under 16 years.	Free white females, including heads of families.	All other free persons.	Slaves.
Pope, Winfield	2	1	4		
Pope, Hardy	1	2	2		
Pope, John	1		1		
Howell, Daniel	2	5	4		
Whitney, Ebenezer	1	3	2		
Peacock, John	1	4	4		1
Langley, Jacob	1	1	2		
Scott, Andrew	2	2	3		4
Hopton, Charles	2		2		10
Howell, William	2	1	4		
Howell, Noel	1	1	1		
Thompson, John	1	4	4		2
Vincent, Sarah	1	3	2		
Thomson, James	1	1	4		1
Lane, John Thomson	1	2	4		
Langston, Uriah	1	2	3		
Heron, John, Senr	3		6		20
Windum, Jesse	1	1	2		
Boyt, Shadrack	1	1	5		
Holleman, Silas	1	3	3		
Daughtery, Martha	1	1	4		
Hix, Micajah	1	2	1		
Musgrove, James	2	2	3	1	
Langston, Ann	1	2	4		
Ward, Sarah	1	2	1		12
Heron, George	1				3
Howell, Hopton	1				
Wilson, John	1	1	4		
Blanchet, James	1		1		
Humphries, John	1	1	2		
Jonerkin, Josiah	1	4	3		2
Jonerkin, David	3		2		6
Pope, Sarah		1	5		16
Jones, Elizabeth		2	4		
Jones, Arthur	1	2	4		1
Barnet, William	1	1	2		
Jones, James	1	1	1		
Jones, Sarah	1		5		
Ammons, Jesse	1	2	3		1
Bicard, Edmond	2		3		
Waldin, Benjamin	2		3		
Waldin, Samuel	1		1		
Holland, Matthew	1		3		
Jonerkin, Miles	2	1	2		2
Jonerkin, George, Senr	2		4	1	
Coor, Thomas	3	2	2		
Howell, Benjamin	1	2	4		2
Howell, Rachel	2	1	1		2
Jonerkin, George, junr	2		4	1	
Robertson, John	1		2		
Alford, Theophilus	2	2	3		1
Hetchpeth, Daniel	1	1	2		
Howell, Mills	1	1	4		
Hetchpeth, John	1	4	2		
Hetchpeth, Ezekiel	1	1	3		
Hines, Joshua	1		3		
Howell, Major	1	1	3		
Howell, Abram	1	5	2		
Jones, William	1	2	1		
Jonerkin, William	1	1	2		
Wise, Josiah	1	1	3		8
Saucer, Ruth		1	5		1
Hooks, Robert	1	3	1		14
Saucer, Stephen	1	3	5		
Coorpender, John	1	2	3		11
Fellows, Robert	2	1	4		1
Wiggs, Jordan	2		2		
Corbitt, John	1	3	3		
Corbitt, Samuel	1	1	4		
Daughtery, Arthur	1	1	6		
Wiggs, Ralph	1	2	4		
Slaughter, Samuel	1	3	4		
Wiggs, John	2	3	6		4
Boyt, Edward	2		2		
Boyt, Benjamin	1	4	2		
Wiggs, Benjamin	2	3	6		
Fulgum, Miles	1	3	5		
Brewer, Moses	2	2	1		
Crawford, Lazarus	2	2	6		6
Page, John	1		3		6
Raiford, William	3	5	4		5
Davis, David	1		3		5
Boyt, Etheldred	1	3	6		2
Wiggs, William	1		3		
Crawford, Robert	2	4	8		4
Rogers, Isum	2	2	1		5
Hamilton, Aaron	1	1	3		
Shehorn, Joseph	1	1	5		
Saucer, John	1	3	2		
Gurley, Lewis	1	2	4		2
Howell, Ralph	1		1		
Pitman, Noah	1		1		6
Hines, Peter	1	1	3		
Coor, Thomas, Senr	3	5	5		7
Massey, William	1	1	2		
Wiggs, Henry	3	1	3		
Holland, John, Senr	1		2		
Holland, John, junr	1	2	2		
Howell, John	1	3	5		
Toler, Robert	2	2	7		5
Moore, John	2		3		1
Toler, Nehemiah	1	3	5		1
Edginton, James	1	2	2		
Smith, John	1	2	2		7
Toler, John	2	5	2		6
Gurley, Joel	2	2	7		4
Wise, John	1	2	4		
Wise, Isaac	2	2	6		
Wise, James	1	3	3		1
Oliver, Henry	1	3	3		2
Tiner, William	2	1	6		
Coggell, Celia			3		8
Bass, Richard	2	1	1		28
Toler, Stephen	1		1		
Toler, Thomas, Senr	1				1
Blanchet, Jesse	1	1	2		1
Rogers, James	1		1		
Whurley, William	2	1	4		2
Massey, Pelick	1	2	1		3
Baggot, Allen	1	3	2		
Toler, John, junr	1	1	1		
Boyte, Josiah	1	1	1		
Tiner, James	1	2	4		
Gurley, George	1	1	2		
Bridges, John	2	3	5		
Lupsey, Bolin	1	1	2		
Jones, Willis	1	3	3		
Jones, Hardy	1	4	4		2
Howell, Arthur	1	2	1		
Potts, Daniel	1				
Linton, John	1				
Heron, Jesse	2	1	4		4
Jernigan, Stephen	1	1	4		24
Green, Joseph	8	2	4		70
Daughtery, Lawrence	1	1	4		
Grooms, Jesse, Senr	1	1	5		4
Vincent, Benjamin	1	3	3		
Pope, Henry	1		5		2
Heron, David	1		3		16
Burn, James	4	2	7		
Heron, Bridget		1	3		6
Bradberry, Chambers	1	2	5		
Wests, John	2	2	3		
Grooms, Jesse, jr	1		2		
Grooms, Charles	1	2	3		2
Grooms, Daniel	1				
Rosser, Burrel	1	1	1		
West, Charles	1	1	2		4
Wallace, Mary					5
Windom, Jesse	1	1	2		
Cummins, Elizabeth			2		
Edwards, Absalom	1	3	5		
Smith, John	1	2	2		
Douglass, Rhody		2	3		
Roberts, John	1	5	5		5
George, David	2	4	7		9
Thomson, Thomas	1	3	1		1
Langston, William	1	2	2		
Jones, Traverse	1		3		1
Williams, Absalom	2		2		7
Garland, John	1				8
Wood, William	3	3	2		
Smith, Benjamin, Senr	1	3	4		
Smith, Benjamin, jr	1	1			
Smith, William	1		2		
Williams, Arthur	1	1	1		
Smith, Josiah, Senr	1	4	3		
Smith, Josiah, junr	1		1		
Smith, John	2	2	1		
Smith, Drew	1		2		
Smith, John	2		4		8
Lohorn, Nathan	1	2	1		
Lohorn, William	1	2	3		
Uzzell, Elisha, Sr	2	1	3		5
Uzzell, Elisha, Jur	1	3	3		
Grant, William	2	3	2		
Grant, Michael	1	2	2		
Grant, Elisha	1	2	2		
Anderson, John	1	1	1		
Ballard, Robert	1		2		
Anderson, Jesse	1	1	2		
Stuckley, James	2		3		
Colton, Ephraim	2	4	4		1
Wilson, William	1	1	3		
Smith, John	1		2		
Hart, Richard	2	1	6		
Davis, William	1		3		
Medlin, Nicholas	1	3	5		
Dannels, Nathaniel	2	1	1		
Hinson, James	3	3	5		
Hinson, Elijah	1	1	4		
Scrivins, James	1	1	3		1
Dawson, Patience	1	2	3		
Heron, Henry	1	1	3		
McArtney, Michael	1	2	1		
Bachelor, Unity		1	10		
Benton, Jemima	1	1	2		
Heron, Anthony	1	1	5		
Heron, Joel	1	1			7
Saucer, Benjamin	1	5	3		
Heron, Simon	1	2	6		
Hines, Hardy	1	2	4		
Heron, Jacob	2	1	4		
Keethly, John	2		1		6
Homes, John	1		2		2
Anderson, Mills	1	1	5		
Anderson, Thomas	1	1	2		
Heron, Michael	1	2	3		10
McKinney, William	1		2		8
McKinney, Barnaby	1		2		11
Whitfield, Lewis	1	1	2		32
Stanley, Moses	3	4	5		12
Ivy, John	2	3	3		
Forehand, William	1	3	3		
Henderson, Robert	1		4		
Surles, William, Senr	1		3		
Roach, Sarcenet	2	2	7		
Hanks, John	2	2	5		
Roach, Solomon	1	1	3		
Garris, Joshua, Senr	2	1	2		
Garris, Joshua, junr	1	1	2		
Burley, John	1	1	2		
Thomas, James	1	2	4		

SALISBURY DISTRICT, GUILFORD COUNTY.

NAME OF HEAD OF FAMILY.	Free white males of 16 years and upward, including heads of families.	Free white males under 16 years.	Free white females, including heads of families.	All other free persons.	Slaves.
Dent, William	2		3		7
Graham, William	1	1	2		
Smith, Samuel	1		5		1
Nicholson, Elisha	1	1	2		
Wilson, Richd	2	1	3		
Benbow, Thomas	3	2	1		
Buchanan, James	2		3		
White, Benja	2	2	4		
Lambert, William	1		3		
Foster, John	1		2		
Foster, Saml	1	1	2		
Reed, William	2	4	3		
Johnstone, Andrew	1		1		
Touchstone, Jonas	1		3		
Dent, William, Junr	1	5	3		
McNary, Frances	1	3	2		1
Stuart, George	2		2		
Shaw, Patrick	4	1	4		
Moreland, William	2	5	3		14
Briges, William	1	2	3		
Laurence, Augustus	1	1	1		
Burney, Adam	1		1		
Massey, Joab	1	5	1		
Johnston, Benja	1	2	1		
Maxwell, Thomas	3	3	4		
Strickland, Jacob	3	3	6		9
Holen, Laban	5				
Wheler, Saml	1	2	1		
Fruer, Isaac	1	2	1		
Brown, John	1	3	6		
Hart, Henry	1	3	2		1
Winegarden, Joseph	1	3	2		
Cob, Henry	2	3	3		
Gardner, Caston	2		2		
Islig, Philip	1	2	2		2
Shoemaker, Suzanah	2	3	5		2
Goodner, Mary		3	3		
Montgomery, Willm	1	1	3		
Canaday, Charles	1	2	7		
Sweet, John	3	2	6		
Doherty, John	3	1	5		
Finley, Michael	2	1	3		
Peyatt, James	1				
Coffield, John	1		1		
Findley, Josiah	1	2	3		
Kerr, Davd	1	3	2		
Lackey, Adam	1	1	4	4	
Gawdy, William	5	1	4		
Stephens, Even	2	5	2		
Howlet, William	2	3	5		
Hunt, Thomas	1				

SALISBURY DISTRICT, GUILFORD COUNTY—Continued.

NAME OF HEAD OF FAMILY.	Free white males of 16 years and upward, including heads of families.	Free white males under 16 years.	Free white females, including heads of families.	All other free persons.	Slaves.
Hunt, Jacob	1	3	3		
Night, Abel	2	2	6		
Hiatt, George	1		1		
Stephens, Davd	1		3		
Porter, James	3	1	2		
Cook, Abraham	4	1	2		
Weatherley, Jesse	4	2	5		
Thompson, John	2		1		
Thompson, Willm F	1	2	1		
Learkin, John	1	4	3	1	
Clement, Peter	2	3	8		
McBride, Isaiah	2	2	6	1	
Land, Reubin	2		2		
Cansbey, James	2		2		
Holloday, John	1	2	5		
Tharp, Joseph	1		3		
Masey, Nathl	3	1	3		
Clagg, William	1	1	1		
Murphey, Jonathan	1	2	2		
Dick, William	2		2		
Rankin, Robt	2		2	2	
Dick, James	1	2	1	1	
Rankin, John	1	3	3	1	
Hunt, William	1	2	2		
Sisney, Joseph	1	2	3		
Cain, Jerediah	1	4	4		
Mongomery, William	2	3	4		
Wilson, James	1	3	6		
Hiatt, William	2	2	5		
Hiatt, George	2		3		
McClain, Moses	3	1	2		
Pegg, Martin	2		1		
Roberson, Jacob	1	5	4	1	
Hunt, Eleazor	1	4	1		
Donnal, John	1	4	6	1	
Donnal, Andw	1	3	3	1	
Donnal, James	1	2	5		
Driskel, George	1	2	2		
Unthank, Allen	1	4	4		
Cuningham, James	3		1		
Rogers, Jacob	1		1		
Hiatt, Christopher, Junr	1	4	4		
Night, Thomas	5	2	9		
Pegg, Isaac	1	1	1		
Conner, James	1	2	5		
Briket, Isarel	1	2	3		
Britton, James	2	2	6		
Wicker, William	1	1	2		
Hardgrove, Frederik	1		1		
Brown, George L	2	1	2		
Brown, William	2	2	3		
Whicker, Thomas	1	1	1		
Brown, William	1	3	1		
Larkin, Saml	1	2	1		
Carney, Arthur	1	1	2		
Gray, Isaac	1	1	2		
Gray, James	1	4	4		
Gray, William	4		2		
Wolfenton, John	3	5	6		
Britton, Saml	1	3	5		
Bingerman, Thomas	2		4		
Raper, William	3	1	1		1
Bingerman, John	1	3	3		
Gray, William, Junr	1		3		
McNight, Robt	1	1	2		
Russel, John	1	4	1		
Russel, Robert	1	3	4		
Akin, William	2	1	6		
Denney, George	1	5	3		
Starratt, John	1	2	6		
Starratt, James	1	1	1		
Mitchel, Adam	1		2		2
Simmons, John	1				
Stuart, John	1	1	5		
Cross, Jonathan	5	2	3		7
Tharp, William	1		4		
Owen, Mathew	1	1	3		
Jackson, Joseph	1	1	3		
Climer, John	2	4	4		
Tomlinson, James	1	1	1		
Cross, William	1	1	3		
Sisney, Stephen	1	1	3		
Downey, William	1	3	3		
Williams, William	1	3	3		
Calhoon, Robert	1	1	3		
Persons, George	4	4	4		
Calhoon, James	2		3		
Green, Robert	2	1	3		
Arnet, Valentine	1	5	2		
Williams, Leven	1	1	2		
Wright, Willis	1		3		
Mendenhall, Aron	1	3	4		
Waid, Thomas	2	4	4		
Armfield, William	3	2	3		
Sisney, John	1	1	1		
Hunt, Isaiah	1	3	5		
Stuart, John	1		1		2

NAME OF HEAD OF FAMILY.	Free white males of 16 years and upward, including heads of families.	Free white males under 16 years.	Free white females, including heads of families.	All other free persons.	Slaves.
Endsly, Abraham	2	1	5		
Goff, Stephen	1	4	3		
McCuiston, Walter	3	1	3		
Wilson, James	3		2		2
Willis, Joel	1	1	3		
Denney, James	1		1		
Denney, William	2	1	4		1
Pierce, Robert	2	5	4		
Hunt, Abner	2	2	6		
Mendenhall, Richd	1	2	1		
Maxwell, Saml	2	3	5		2
Peasly, Robert	2	4	5		
Masey, Timothy	1		5		
Widows, Isaac	4	1	3		
Worth, Francis	2		3		
Gardner, Stephen	1	4	5		
Peasley, John	3	2	7		12
Albright, William	1	1	8		
McGrady, James	4	3	2		
Jester, Nimrod	1	2	1		
Smith, Richd	1		3		
Masey, Thomas	1		2		
White, Isaac	2	1	5		
Smith, Ralph	2	1	5		
Loakey, John	2	2	3		
Jones, Jesse	1	1	2		
Millis, James	1	1	1		
Sherwood, Hugh	1	1	4		
Jones, Davd	1	1	4		
Ford, Henry	1	3	4		
Scott, Absolem	1		2		
Philips, Ezekeal	1	1	1		
Williams, Jesse	1	2	2		
Masey, Enoch	2	2	4		
Hoggatt, Philip	1	1	4		
Osburn, Saml	1	4	5		
Sullaven, Flurance	3	2	2		
Osburn, Richd, Senr	1	1	2		
Sullaven, Joel	1		1		
Covey, George	1	1	3		
Osment, John	1	1	4		
Valiant, Ansel	1		2		
Craner, Moses	1		1		
Masey, Paul	1	2	7		
Rankin, Robert, Jun	1	2	3		
Miller, William	1				
Toney, Dennis	1	1	4		
Russel, Andrew	1	2	3		
Armfield, John	1	2	1		
Egle, William	1		2		
Holland, William	1	1	1		
Osburn, James	1	1	1		
Sullaven, Wm	1	2	4		
Jestor, Thomas	1	1	1		
McGrady, William	1		3		
Lester, Nathan	1		2		
Sullaven, Flurance	1	1	1		
Wheler, William	1	1	3		1
Gardner, Richd	2		5		
Macy, David	1	3	2		
Knott, James	1	2	7		3
Baldwin, Uriah	1	3	1		
Kenman, James	1	1	3		
Perkins, Isaac	1		2		
McClintock, John	1		1		
Poore, Jeremiah	1		1		
Tatom, Edward	2	3	1		6
Hunt, Atha	1		3		
Terrel, Micajah	2		2		2
Dicks, Joshua	1		4		
Knott, James	1	2	4		1
Poore, David	1	1	4		
Thompson, Robert	1		6		
Gray, Leven	1	3	2		
Idelot, Benjamin	1	3	5		
Nix, George	1	3	4		11
Nelson, Alexander	1	2	5		
Mortemore, William	3		2		
Hays, James	2	2	3		4
Idelot, Jedediah	1	1	1		
Pope, George	1	6	2		
Peggot, Saml	1	3	3		
Nelson, George	1		3		
Idelott, Rhody			3	4	
Perry, Richd	2	2	5		
Kirkpatrick, Hugh	1		5		
Tharp, Laben	1	1	2		
Stokes, Thomas	1		2		
Wilcots, Thomas	1	2	1		
Everet, Saml	5		2		
Maxwell, James	1	1	3		
Keene, Richd	1	2	3		
Bell, Francis	1	2	6		
Tindle, Jeremiah	1	5	3		
Dixson, John	1	2	3		
McKamie, Nathl	1				

NAME OF HEAD OF FAMILY.	Free white males of 16 years and upward, including heads of families.	Free white males under 16 years.	Free white females, including heads of families.	All other free persons.	Slaves.
Stafford, William	1	4	3		
Braden, Alexander	2	1	2		
Underwood, Joshua	1	4	2		2
Saxton, Thomas	1		1		
Rumbly, Smith	1	2	1		
Smith, William	4		1		
Weatherly, William	1		1		
McCuestion, Moses	2	1	5		2
Given, Robert	2		1		6
Weatherly, Abner	3		1		
Witt, Michal	1	1	10		
Flack, Andw	5		3		1
Mathews, William	1	3	3		
McNight, William	2		3		
Dawson, Elijah	2		1		
Campble, Thomas	1	2	1		
Caldwell, David	3	5	3		8
Fulton, Samuel	2	5	2		
Coats, James	1		5		1
Casey, Samuel	1	1	3		
Gardner, Isaac	1	4	2		
Springer, Stephen	1	1	2		
Russel, William	1		2		
Werick, Martin	1	2	5		
Morgan, Thomas	1		1		
Ramsey, James	1	1	3		
Bell, James	3	1	8		
Shelkott, Kain	1		2		
Holland, John	1				
Werick, Jacob	2	3	4		
Roberson, William	2	2	3		
Roberson, Abner	1		1		
Roberson, Nicholas	1		3		
Hester, James	1				
Greeson, Jacob	1	1	1		
Jessop, Caleb	1	1	4		
Mills, Reuben, Junr	1		4		
Pegg, Valentine	3	3	5		
Morrow, Robert	1	2	4		
Dean, Joshua	2	3	4		
Hodgson, Thomas	1	3	3		
Baldwin, Danl	1	3	4		
McClaig, John	1	1	1		
Pullen, John	1		4		
Allum, Saml	1		1		
Wright, John	1				
Wright, Frances	2		2		1
Warren, John	1	5	4		1
Covey, William	2	4	5		1
Fields, Robert	1	1	1		
McGlamery, Edwd	1	1	6		2
Peasley, William	5	1	2		
Blizard, Purnel	1	2	3		
Bishop, Robert	4	2	4		
Stuart, Findlay	4		4		2
Wright, James	2		1		5
Thomas, John	3	4	4		
Mitchel, Saml	1				
Stack, Elisha	1		3		
Drury, Saml	1	4	1		
Haskins, Moses	1	3	1		
Hussey, Thomas	2	2	6		
Tatom, Edward	1		1		3
Tatom, John	2	3	5		6
Allum, Robert	2	1	3		
Moore, Camm	1	3	3		1
Cummins, Joseph	1	2	5		
Burney, Robert	1	1	2		
Trotter, Benjn	1				
Hughey, James	1	2	4		
Nix, Quinton	1		1		12
Cannaday, William	1	1	7		
McCaddin, Wm	1				
Lownsbury, Wm	1	2	2		
Trotter, Josiah	1	3	4		2
Moore, Smith	2	2	5		7
Moore, Mary	2		3		1
Alexander, George	1	5	3		
Doherty, Danl	1		3		
Gulbreath, Robt	1	3	4		
Thompson, Benjn	1	1	6		
Sullaven, Saml	1	3	3		
Britton, Wm	3	1	3		1
Donnal, Danl	1	3	3		3
Donnal, Robt	3		1		4
Evians, Warrenton	1	2	3		
Callaway, Obediah	1	1	3		1
Dennis, William	1	2	3		
Callaway, Jonathan	1	2	3		
Hannah, Roddy	1	4	5		
Hannah, Robert	1	5	2		8
Doak, John	1	2	3		4
Brown, Arther	1		2		
Bliar, John	1	2	4		
Coulk, Leven	1	3	4		
Donnal, William	1	4	1		2
Coulk, John	1	1	2		

SALISBURY DISTRICT, GUILFORD COUNTY—Continued.

NAME OF HEAD OF FAMILY.	Free white males of 16 years and upward, including heads of families.	Free white males under 16 years.	Free white females, including heads of families.	All other free persons.	Slaves.
Anderson, Robert	1		3		
Kerr, William	1	1	3		
Kerr, David, Senr	1		1		5
Doak, William	2	4	3		2
Ross, Reuben	1	4	3		
Hardin, Charles	2	2	4		
Barr, James	1	1	2		2
Macy, Mathew	1		3		
Russel, Timothy	2	3	3		
Leventon, John	2	4	5		1
Nilson, George	1	3	4		
Kimman, James	1	1	3		
Coine, Lias	1	1	5		
Fields, Jeremiah	4	2	6		1
James, John	1		1		
Loyd, Humphrey	3	3	5		7
McClintock, John	4	1	2		7
Haskins, Joseph	1	2	4		1
White, Thomas	1	2	3		
Gamble, William	1	2	1		
Gamble, Andrew	1		3		
Brasel, Jacob	1	3	3		
Night, Jonathan	1	2	3		
Guite, William	2	2	5		
Sullaven, Andrew	1		2		
McCuiston, James	2				1
McAdaw, James	3		1		7
Loman, Adam	1		1		
McCuistion, Ann	1		1		
Shaw, Benjn	3	5	2		
Mullin, John	1		3		
Osborn, Joseph	3	1	2		
Shepard, Isrel	1		1		
Philips, Nancy		2	3		
Spruce, Robert	3	2	3		
Archer, Thomas	1	3	3		3
Rogers, William	1		1		
Archer, John	1		3		
Sampson, James				4	
Britton, Benjn	2		2		1
McCain, Hanie	1	1	1		
McGlauheny, Wm	1				
Donnal, Latham	1		2		2
Perkins, John	1		4		
Perkins, Joseph	1	2	2		
Johnston, Joshua	1	2	5		
Johnston, James	1				
Johnston, Caleb	1	1	2		
McDowel, Joseph	1	2	3		1
Duck, Saml	3		2		
Johnston, Jere	1	2	3		
McAdow, James	1	2	3		1
Parker, Howel	1		2		
Parker, Jesse	2	1	6		
McGee, William	1				
Stone, Barton	1				
Mcrunnels, Benjn	1				
Dodson, Richd	1	2	2		
Hartgrove, Saml	2	6	5		
Peeples, Nathl	1	1	1		8
McGee, Andw	1	2			4
Dillon, Danl	1	3	4		
Chapple, Ambros	1	1	3		
Dillon, Isaac	1		2		
Hilton, Alex	1				
Hilton, James	2	1	4		
Farrington, Willm	1		2		
Perry, John	1	3	2		
Perry, Ebenezor	1	2	5		
Gilbert, William	1	3	2		2
Plafield, Willm	1				
Martin, Rhodeham	1	3	4		
Walker, John	2	3	3		
Gilbert, John	1		2		8
McMurry, John	1	1	1		1
Dillon, William	2	3	3		
Black, George	2		3		
Williams, Prudence	2		5		
Williams, Richard	1	3	2		
McCuistion, Thomas	1		2		
McMurry, James	1	3	6		
Billingsley, James	3	3	2		2
Rale, George	4	2	4		
Billingsley, Henry	1	3	3		
Harris, Hannah		3	7		
Hunt, Nathan	1				
Findley, Andw	2	1	8		
Smith, William	1	2	5		
Hiatt, Joseph	1				
Hiatt, John	4		3		
Hiatt, Even	2	4	4		
Hiatt, John, Junr	2	3	4		
Hiatt, Enos	1	1	4		
Hiatt, Isaac	2	4	6		
Brown, Thomas	1	4	2		
Coffin, Bathewel	1	3	3		
Edwards, Wm	1	3	3		
Erwin Saml	1	3	3		
Erwin, James	1	2	2		
Erwin, Robert	1		1		
Nowland, Paul	1				
Lane, Danl	1	6	3		
Lane, William	1	5	5		
Stuart, Sampson	1	4	4		2
Armfield, William	1	2	3		
Ryann, Edwd	2	1	2		
Guin, John	1		4		
Thornbury, Joseph	1	5	1		
Mordack, John	1	1	2		
Lain, Mordica	1				
Lamb, Saml	1	2	4		
Wilson, Allin	1				
Brown, James	1		1		
Mongomery, James	1	2	5		
Macy, Matthew	1	1	5		
Fraisor, Isaac	1	1	4		
Osburn, William	1	4	2		
Gosset, Thomas	1	2	4		
Swain, Joseph	1	4	2		
Leonard, William	1	2	7		
Hodgings, William	1		2		
Osburn, Davd	1	1	2		
Clearwaters, Jacob	1	3	2		
Fraizer, Solomon	1	2	2		
Walker, Richd	1	1	2		
Rice, Thomas	1	4	4		
Hiatt, Isaac	1	5	6		
Hodgings, Joseph	3	2	7		
Brown, John	1	2	3		
Hodgings, John	1	1	2		
Brown, Saml	1		1		
Edwards, Anecal	1	2	1		
Young, William	1	1	6		
McCrackin, Jane	1		2		
Edwards, James	1	2	2		
Hodgings, Heer	1		2		
Gamble, James	1		1		
Idilot, Obid	1	3	1		
Hodgings, Robert	5		6		
Hodgings, Richd	1		2		
Hogings, Jonathan	1	1	1		
Hodgings, David	1		2		
Hignut, John	1	2	3		
Richards, Annanias	1	1	1		
Hodgings, George	2	3	6		
Hubbard, John	1	1	5		
Dillon, Leven	1		1		
Sanders, James	1	2	1		
Ballard, William	3	1	6		
Osburn, John, Senr	4		3		
Osburn, John, Junr	1	2	5		
Coffin, Barnabas	2	2	5		
Coffin, Sermon	1	4	4		
Johnston, Margret	1	2	2		
Lowder, John	1	1	1		
Bruce, Edward	5	3	3		
Book, Thomas	1	6	4		
Jessop, Jacob	1	4	3		
Moon, Simon	2	3	5		
Moon, James	1		1		
Sesney, John	1	1	1		
Sesney, Stephen	1	1	3		
Forbus, John	4	2	4		
McMin, Danl	2	3	8		
Hacket, Oliver	1	5	1		
Hendrick, Henry	2	1	2		1
Causy, Nehemiah	1	4	3		
Kirkman, James	3		1		10
Cook, Jesse	1	1	2		
McImma, William	1		1		
Iddings, Joseph	1	4	3		
Howel, John	1	1	3		
Mountain, John	1	1	4		
Doake, Robert	2	4	6		5
Coffin, William	2		1		
Woodburn, Thomas	2	4	3		
Coffin, Peter	1	2	2		
Coffin, Peter, Senr	1		2		
Hilton, Peter	1	2	3		
Heath, Smith	1	4	5		
Hamilton, George	2		1		2
Harris, John	1	3	2		
Smith, Robert	1	3	5		3
Stanfield, William	4		2		
Charles, Leven	3	3	4		
Deay, Richd	1	2	2		
Martin, James	1	1	2		
Stuart, James	3	2	4		
Thornbury, Joseph, Senr	2	1	3		
Ham, Philip	3		2		
Way, Henry	1	4	7		
Gardner, William	1	4	7		
Bunker, Reuben	1	4	6		
Balwin, John	1	4	3		
Harris, Obediah	2	1	5		
Thornbury, Thos	1		3		
Thornbury, James	2	2	6		
Thornbury, Marthey		2	5		
Stanly, Micajah	3	3	4		
Stanly, William	2	1	5		
Hunt, Azor	2	1	2		
Burny, John	1		4		1
Donnal, William	1		1		1
Blear, James	1	1	1		
Stuart, James	1		1		
Crouch, Thomas	1	3	1		
Thompson, James	1		7		
Lovet, Joseph	1	2	3		
Stanly, Shadrack	2	3	5		
Evins, Jesse	1	3	2		
Jestor, Jacob	1		1		
Rice, William	1	1	1		
Hady, Saml	1	5	4		
McAdow, James	1	2	3		
McAdow, Davd	1	2	2		
Blear, Thomas	1	2	2		7
Gladson, Nathan	1	3	3		
Hunter, John	1	3	1		
Mabin, David	1		1		
Ballenger, John	2	4	6		
Craner, Thomas	1	3	3		
Jackson, Joseph	1	2	1		
Jackson, William	2		5		
Tharp, James	2	1	6		1
Hawrin, Windsmore	1	3	1		
Jackson, Willm, Junr	1	2	3		
Knolt, Justin	2	1	2		4
Clark, Nathl	1	3	2		1
Dillon, Danl, Senr	1		1		
Donnal, Robert	1	2	4		
Allison, Alex	2	4	1		
Frazor, Solomon	2	1	1		
Dillon, Nathan	1	1	4	1	
Mulloy, Edward	1	4	2		
Bullock, Edwd	2	3	5		
Bell, Saml	4	4	6		
Slown, William	1				
Harvey, William	1		3		
Wilson, Michal	1		2		
Masey, George	1	1	3		
Moore, John	3	1	3		
Jean, Philip	1	2	1		4
Madaris, Charles	3	3	4		
Wright, Leven	1	4	2		
Bruce, Charles	3	1	6		10
Garrel, Ralph	2	2	6	1	5
Archer, James	1	1	4		5
Mitchel, Adam, Senr	1				5
Thompson, Saml	1	1	4		5
May, Martin	1		4		
Fisher, Danl	2	4	3		
Lomax, William	2	2	3		
Eliott, Moses	1	2	2		
Perdue, James	1	6	2		
Wiley, Davd	1	4	4		1
Wiley, Hugh	1	3	4		1
Donnel, George	1	2	2		3
Owens, Edward?	1		2		
Rawly, Elisha	1	3	4		
Knuitt, Jacob	3	1	4		
Brawly, Prier	1	1	2		
Dun, Solomon	1		3		
Gibson, Jacob	1	2	1		
Dunn, Federick	1	2	9		
Stanly, Joseph	1	4	4		
Foster, James	2	2	1		
Brasher, Asa	3	4	3		7
Hayley, John	3	1	3		2
Parks, George	1	3	3		2
Erwin, Joseph	1	4	3		
Gillaspie, John	2	1	3		7
Holland, Edward	3	2	3		
McCuestion, Thomas	1		3		
Lewis, Aron	1	1	3		1
Wilson, Andrew	1	5	2		2
Chambers, John	1		2		2
Jeans, Edward	1	5	5		1
Hill, Nathan	1	1	3		
Jean, William	1	1	3		2
Jean, William, Senr	2	1	1		3
Brown, Thomas	1	1	1		
McCain, Alexander	1				
Perry, Cornellas	1				
Millis, Edward	3	1	3		
McBride, John	1	1	2		
Hiatt, Ashor	1	1	2		
Smith, Henry	2		2		
Hiatt, Christopher	2	3	3		
Hamilton, John	1		4		6
McNary, Robert	1		1		
Hamilton, Thomas	1		1		

SALISBURY DISTRICT, GUILFORD COUNTY—Continued.

NAME OF HEAD OF FAMILY.	Free white males of 16 years and upward, including heads of families.	Free white males under 16 years.	Free white females, including heads of families.	All other free persons.	Slaves.
Hamilton, Hance	3	1	2		14
Stanley, Strangeman	3	1	4		
Dunlap, John	2		1		
Prichard, Alexander	1				
Bunch, William	1	2	5		
Dunlap, Robert	1		1		
Gorden, Moses	1	2	5		
Wheatly, Thomas	1	1	1		
Copper, James	1	3	4		
Fleming, John	2	3	4		
Smith, John	2		3		
Smith, John, Junr	1	1	2		
Shilcut, John	1	3	6		
Tate (Widow)	1	2	4		9
Underwood, Abraham	3	2	4		
Isely (Widow)	1	4	2		
Dausen, Daniel	2	3	2		5
Gibson, Andrew	1	5	2		11
Elmore, John	1	3	2		
Tate, Zepheniah	1	2	8		11
Brumfield, Philip	1				
Isely, Christan	2	1	4		
Isely, Philip	1		2		
Isely, Elizabeth		4	3	1	
Loman, Adam	1	1	4		
Waggoner, Peter	1		2		
Whitsel, Ludwick	1	1	2		
Cook, Henry	1	2	2		26
Fall, Christian	3	3	6		
Shaver, William	2	2	3		1
Shaver, Jacob	1		2		
Shaver, William	1		2		
Loakey, William	1	3	5		
Sullinger, Peter	3				5
Dunlap, Robert	3	3	3		
Boon, John	1	3	4		4
Summers, Peter	1	2	3		1
Summers, Filty	1	4	4		1
Diclenger, John	4	1	6		
McKamie, Robert	4		1		1
Woodside, John	1		1		
Ross, Henry	2	4	4		
McAdow, John	2	2	2		2
Gilchrust, John	3	2	4		
Gorsil, William	1				
Nicks, John	4	3	5		5
McClain, Joseph	2	3	2		
Alexander, James	1		4		1
McCollister, James	1	3	2		
McClain, John	1				
Leak, William	1	1	2		
Gillaspie, Danl	3	4	4		6
Williams, Roland	1		1		
Williams, William	3		3		
Williams, Wm, Junr	1		2		
Hughs, Thomas	1	1	2		
Morgan, Lewis	1	2	4		
Harry, Even	1		2		
Cork, John	1	1	2		
Coffin, William	1	2	1		1
Wright, Isaac	2	3	3		7
Cannon, Minas	1	3	3		
McDauman, Michal	2	5	3		
Charles, Elisha	1	4	2		
Chipman, John	1	3	2		
Peeples, Hubbard	3		3		14
Barham, Charles	2	3	3		4
McGibbony, Patrck	2	2	6		5
Dickson, William	1	2	5		
Knight, Archd	1	2	3		
Barrom, Newsom & John	2				
Dick, James	1	2	1		1
Hoskins, Arnol	1	3	3		
Landreth, Thomas	3	3	1		
Dicks, James	1		6		
Thompson, John	1	2	2		
Duck, Samuel	3		2		
Starbuck, William	1	2	7		
Parker, Jonathan	1	2	1		
Widdop, William	1	1	2		
Calhoon, Saml	1		1		
Calhoon, James	2		5		
Clark, Nathl	1	2	3		1
Stuart, Saml	1				
Shannon, William	2		2		
Stephenson, John	1	3	3		
Armfield, Nathan	1				
Sherwood, Danl	1	2	4		
Linthacum, Richd	1	1	1		
Swain, William	1		1		
Sherwood, Hungh	1		1		
Kirkman, Leven	1	2	3		1
Stanly, Saml	1	3	3		
Wheatly, James	2	5	4		
Madaris, Oliver	1	3	2		
Love, John	1		2		1
Coffin, Leve	1		4		
Stuart, George	1	3	2		
Young, Davd	1	3	3		
Mathews, Hugh	1		2		
Wiley, John	2	5	3		
Forbus (Widow)	2		3		
Mills, James	1	4	5		
Shear, Jacob	1	4	4		
Shear, Jacob, Senr	3	1	2		
Shaver, William	1	2	3		1
Isely, Christian	2	1	6		
Isely (Widow)	1	4	4		
Shaver, Frederick	1	4	1		
Whitemon, Mathias	1	1	3		
Low, David	2	3	4		4
Clapp, Jacob	4	2	4		3
Clapp, Tobias	1		2		
Wakes, Danl	1	2	5		
Fifer, Valentine	1	1	1		
Clapp, George	2	3	3		5
Clapp, Lodwick, Senr	2	2	3		1
Clapp, Jacob	1		1		
Clapp, Lodwick, Junr	1		2		
Neace, George	3	3	5		
Albright, William	1	2	3		
Denney, William	3	3	5		
Allison, Saml	3	1	4		
Stuart, Findly	4		4		3
Causbey, James	2		2		
Dun, Shadrick	1	5	4		
Waggoner, Peter	1		2		
Waggoner, John	1	3	4		
White, Edward	1	4	7		
Isely, Balser	1	3	4		
Wiley, William	1	2	1		1
Wiley, Alexander	1				3
Forbus, George	1	4	5		
Ross, Reuben	1	5	3		
Tomb, John	2	5	4		
Buzard, David	1		4		
Tingle, George	2	5	11		
Paterson, Michal	1	4	2		
Coble, George	3	2	2		
McDill, Saml	1	1	7		
Causby, Hance	2		4		
McBride, John	2		5		
McBride, Jno, Senr	2	3	2		
Coble, George	3		6		
Clap, Philip	2		2		5
Cooper, David	3	2	1		1
Coan, Elias	1	1	5		
Clark, Hance	2		5		
Coble, Nicholas	1		3		
Shatterlin, Michal	1	1	7		
Clapp, Valentine	1	1	3		
Prowel, Sampson	2	2	4		
Crowel, Mary			2		
Swing, Lodwick	2	1	2		
Swing, Mathias	1	3	3		1
Eamicks, Mathias	3		6		
Eamicks, Nicholas	1	1	2		
Coble, Anthony	2	1	4		
Coble, Lodwick	1	2	3		
Coble, George, Junr	1	3	6		
Foust, Christian	2	2	4		
Heags, Coonrod	1	2	2		
Low, Davd, Senr	2		2		1
Oneal, James	1	3	4		
Low, Peter	2	1	8		
Low, Thomas	1		3		
Low (Widow)			3		
Deveney, Samuel	1	3	7		2
Wilkerson, Thomas	2		8		
Walker, George			8		
Glass (Widow)		1	2		
Harman, Jacob	1	1	1		
Shatterlin, Andrew	1	1	5		
Glass, George	1	3	4		
Borow, Charles	4	2	3		
Coble, Peter	1	1	1		
Kime, Philip	1	1	1		
Camick, Philip	1	2	1		
Plunket, William	1	1	3		
Wing, John	1	2	2		
Cortner, Danl	1	2	3		
Smith, Peter	4	1	3		
Sullavent, Fletcher	3	4	5		
Evins, Davd	3	2	8		
Brown, Adam	1		4		
Walker, James	1	1	5		
Tingold, Peter	1	3	2		
Bennet, Elisha	1	4	4		
Shoe, Philip	1	4	4		
Whitsel, Adam	1	3	4		
Limebary, George	1	2	8		
Burrow, Philip	2	2	3		
Burrow, Starling	1		2		
Greenson, Isaiah	2	1	2		
Shockman, Christopher	1	2	1		
Low, Samuel	1	2	3		1
Burrow, Ishmal	1	1	2		
McClain, John, Senr	3	1	2		
McClain, Thomas	1		3		
McClain, Joseph	1	2	3		
McClain, John, Junr	1	3	4		
Greer, Mathew	2		3		
Greer, Thomas	1		3		
Smith, Thomas	1	2	3		
Lesly, Peter	1	2	2		
Holland (Widow)		2	3		
Barnhil, William	1	3	4		
Forbus, John	1		3		
Shaw, Hugh	4	1	3		
Morrow, Robert	1	2	5		
Jobb, John	4	5	4		
Cartright, Wm	3	4	2		
Wright, Willis	1		4		
Miner, Leven	1	1	3		
Dickson, Thomas				1	
Wright, Charles	1		1		
Mead, John	1	3	3		
Dwiggins, John	2	4	4		1
Thornbury, Edwd	1	2	5		
Cain, Danl	1	1	4		
Cusick, William	2		3		3
Anderson, John	3	1	4		
Garner, William	1		1		
Morgan, Thomas	1		3		
Warton, Watson	4	3	4		2
Shelly, James	1	3	3		
Rian, John	1	2	4		1
Lindsey, Robt	2	4	4		11
Whealer, James	1				
Findley, James	1		5		
Price, Zacariah	1	1	2		
Hamilton, Thomas	1	3	3		1
Burton, Richd, Senr	3		5		
Heath, William	1	1	1		
Burton, Richd, Junr	1		1		
Simpson, Peter	1	1	1		
Heath, Jacob	1	1	1		
Boyd, James	1	3	3		
Houlton, Isaac	3	1	3		
Kersey, Eleazor	1	1	3		
Kersey, Thomas	1	1	4		
Ballard, Joseph	1	4	2		
Hiatt, Joseph	1	1	3		
Way, William	1	3	3		
McKeen, Alex	3				
Rittey, James	1	2	3		
Langril, Curtis	1		2		
Fitzgeral, Wm	1	1	2		
Coe, John	1	4	4		
Unthank, Joseph	1	4	4		
McCallock, Thos	2	1	1		
Clapp, Jacob	1	4	4		
McBride, John, Senr	2		5		
McBride, John	2	3	2		
Donnal, Lathan	1		2		2
Huston, Richd	1	1	1		
Evins, David	2		2		
Blisset, William	1		1		
Dewese, Ezekel	1	2	3		
Simpson, Nathl	2	3	3		
Simpson, Richd	1				
Carrel, Elizabeth		1	5		
Cuningham, John	1	1	2		3
Criswell, James	2		2		1
Maxwell, John	1		2		
Bussell, James	1	3	2		1
Minner, Leven	1	1	4		
Hardin, Thomas	1		4		
Weatherley, Jobb	1	1	5		
Barnhill, William	1		4		
Cartright, William	2	3	2		
Wheeler, Charles	1		4		
Kirkman, George	2	4	6		1
Mabin, John	1		6		
Kirkman, Levin	1	1			
Rankin, William	1	3	4		
Rankin, John	2	2	9		
Russell, Robert	1	3	2		2
Cummins, Robt	1	1	2		
Summers, Joseph	1	2	7		
Cummins, Thomas	2		6		
Fitchee, Saml	1	2	2		
Hopkins, Erle	1	3	3		
Hancok, Maiga	5	2	4		
Buckingham, Levi	1		4		
Williams, Celas	1	4	6		
Charlscroft, Thos	2		6		
Hilton, James	1	2	2		
Hilton, Peter	1	1	4		
Hilton, William	1		4		

SALISBURY DISTRICT, GUILFORD COUNTY—Continued.

NAME OF HEAD OF FAMILY.	Free white males of 16 years and upward, including heads of families.	Free white males under 16 years.	Free white females, including heads of families.	All other free persons.	Slaves.
Walker, James	1		6		
White, James	2	2	1		3
McMurry, John	3		2		
Scott, William	3	2	5		4
Henderson, Betty			1		
Ructman, Joseph	1	2	3		
Waddle, Davd	1	1	2		
Lamb, Simon	1	1	3		
Wilson, Michal	1	5	6		
Newman, John	1	2	3		
Lamb, Robt	1	1	3		
Linard, Joseph	1	1	2		
Davis, John	1	1	3		
Davis, Tristan	1	1	2		
Anderson, Thos	1	5	4		
Reeves, Thomas	1	2	1		
Wilson, John	1				
Stone, Salathial	1	3	5		
Wiley, Robert	1	2	6		
Davis, Epsebi	2	1	2		
Barr, James, Senr	2		1		4
Chambers, John	1		1		1
Wright, Thomas	1	1	1		1
Law, Andrew	3		3		
Simpson, Richard	3	1	4		
Simpson, Richd, Senr	1		1		
Reeves, William	1	3	5		1
Lambert, Saml	1	2	2		
Jones, Isaac	1		4		
Jones, Isaac, Senr	1	1	2		
Linard, John	3	1	7		
Jester, Jacob	2	3	4		
Gray, Alexander	4		6		
Mendingall, George	2	5	5		
Hines, Saml	1		2		
Mabin, Davd	1		1		
Cannaday, John	5	2	3		
Wilson, George	3	4	4		
Simpson, Thomas	3	2	7		
Knight, Davd	1	3	2		
Taylor, John	1	1	2		
Mendingall, Mordica	1		2		
Charles, William	3	1	5		
Hoggat, Joseph	3	2	3		
Mendingall, Richd	1	2	1		
Harbin, Enoch	3	6	3		
Mendingall, Mordica, Senr	1	2	1		
Mendingall, Jesse	2	4	2		
Carsey, Jesse	1	2			
Mendingall, Seth	1	1	7		
Mendingall, John	1	2	1		
Mendingall, Moses, Senr	1	1	2		
Mendingall, Stephen, Senr	1		3		
Rix, James	2	3	5		
Mendingall, Benjn	3	1	4		
Mendingall, Moses, Junr	3		4		
Mendingall, Stephen	3	4	6		
Stephen (Negro)					11
Lay, John	2	2	3		
Rice, William	1	1	1		
McGuire, John	1	1	4		
Leonard, George	1		2		
Dicks, Peter	1		3		
Beals, John	1	1	3		
Wilson, Abbigal	1		5		
Swain, Marthey			3		
Worth, Danl	2	2	4		
Stone, John	1	1	2		
Coffin, Aaron	1	2	4		
Osburn, Danl	2	3	3		
Swaim, William	3	2	5		
Swaim, Michal	1	4	6		
Coffin, Adam	1		2		
Armond, Jacob	1	1	6		
Osburn, Peter	1		2		
Edwards, Henry	1	1	5		
Wilson, George	1	1	5		
Wilson, Thomas	1		1		
Buller, Moses	2	1	4		
Worth, Jobb	1	1	2		
Hoggat, William	1	1	1		
Frazier, Isaac	1	2	4		
Macy, Henry	2	2	3		
Osburn, John	2		2		
Hodson, John	1	4	4		
Mash, William	2	4			
Scott, Thomas	1		1		
Barr, Davd, Junr	1	3	3		
Barr, Davd, Senr	1		1		4
Hester, Francis	1				
Bishop, Aron	1				
Smith, Henry	3	1	2		
Dennis, Mathias	1		2		
Tharp, Isaac	2		2		
Scott, Margret			2	5	
Barham, Hartwell	1	7	3		
Harris, Joel	1	4	3		3
Tharp, Laben	1	1	1		
Tharp, Joseph	1		2		
Cairy, Hezekiah	1			1	
Peeples, Drewry	1	1	3		3
Schrader, John I	1		2		
Hester, Robert	3	4	2		
Small, Knight	1		1		
Starbuck, Hezekiah	1	5	3		
Wheeler, John	3	1	5		
McCairny, Francis	1	3	2		
Hunt, William	1	3	2		
Coggeshall, Job	2		5		
Mendingall, Phinias	3		2		
Melrainy, Joseph	1	1	2		
Mendingall, John	3	1	3		
Stanford, John	1		1		
Gifford, Jonathan	2	1	5		
Beason, Isaac	4	1	3		
Tolbert, John	2	1	3		
Beason, Benjn	2	3	5		
Hains, Joshua	1	6	3		
Beason, Saml	3	2	3		
Beason, Edwd	1		1		
Beard, Richd	1				
Sanders, Joel	3	3	5		2
Sanders, David	1	2	3		
Hunt, John	1	4	1		
Sanders, John	2		2		
Mills, Reuben, Senr	1	2	4		
Johnston, Tarlton	2	2	9		
Whickershem, Jehu	1	3	4		
Gardner, Sylvenus	5	3	3		
Hayworth, Stephen	3		5		
Stuart, Jehu	3	2	4		
Mills, Joseph	1	2	3		
Mills, Amos	1	2	6		
Beard, William	2	2	3		
Huddleston, Seth	1	1	9		
Mendingall, James	1	2	2		
Mills, John	1		1		
Beard, Reuben	2	2	2		
Wheeler, Manlov	1	4	3		
Ball, Thomas	1	1	1		
Sanders, Marthey	1		6		2
Hoggat, Jonathan	1				
Crew, William	1				
Barr, Davd	1		2		1
Barr, James	2		3		4
Bellingsley, Brasel	1	1	1		
Reeves, Thomas	1	2	1		
Reeves, Jonathan	1				
Reeves, Jesse	1	2	1		
Hogans, John	1	1	5		
Dearens, John	1	2	3		3
Mileham, Saml	1	2	4		
Mileham, Welter	3	3	2		
Pealt, Jacob	1	1	2		1
Williamson, Lewis	1	1	2		
Callum, Henry	1	3	4		
Cannady, William	1	1	7		
Johnston, Andrew	1		1		
Barham, James	1	4	5		3
Williamson, Upton	3	4	3		1
Love, John	1		2		1
Tharp, James	2	2	6		1
Goslin, Wm	1		1		
McDannil, Isaah	1		4		
Coffin, Mathew	1	1	6		
Persons, Thos	2	2	4		
Thornbury, Joseph	1	3	8		
Carsey, Daniel	1	4	1		
Raduck, William	1	1	5		
Beall, Thadeous	1	4	6		12
Whitsel, Henry	2	2	3		
Cortner, George	2	3	4		

SALISBURY DISTRICT, IREDELL COUNTY.

NAME OF HEAD OF FAMILY.	Free white males of 16 years and upward, including heads of families.	Free white males under 16 years.	Free white females, including heads of families.	All other free persons.	Slaves.
Auton, Thomas	1	1	3		
Almery, Benjamin	1		3		
Anderson, John	1		3		
Batey, Thomas	3	3	4		7
Brown, William	1	2	3		
Brevard, Benjamin	1		3		5
Baker, John	1	3	2		
Braley, Neil	2	5	4		1
Baird, Margret		2			
Biars, James	2	5	4	1	6
Baird, John	1	2	5		4
Biars, Joseph	1				21
Bowman, William	1	2	3		
Brown, Robert	1		4		
Brown, John	1	1	3		8
Bowman, James	3	4	2		
Brevard, Adam	1	2	3		5
Brevard, Robert	2		4		8
Brevard, John	1	2	3		5
Brevard, Alexr	2	2	3		12
Cooke, John	3	1	8		11
Creswell, William	1		4		
Creswell, David	2		2		
Cupples, Elizabeth	3		2		
Cooke, Thomas, Senr	1		1		4
Cooke, Thomas, Junr	1	2	4		1
Carruth, John	2	3	3		1
Cooke, James	1		2		
Davidson, George	5		3	1	11
Davidson, William	1	2	4		3
Duncan, Thomas	3		2		
Durham, Joseph	1	2	4		
Dickey, John	2				3
Dickey, Samuel	1		2		5
Douney, Charles	1	1	3		
Gracey, Patrick	1	2	4		
Gracey, William	1	2	2		
Ewing, Nathaniel	1	3	4		6
Gray, Hugh	2	2	3		
Gray, Robert	4	1	2		
Gray, Thomas	1	1	1		1
Huston, James	1	3	5		2
Henderson, Mary	2	3	3		
Hains, James	1	2	3		2
Hains, John	1	2	3		
Huggins, Robert	1	1	6		4
Huggins, John	1	2	5		3
Hart, James	1		3		2
Hughes, Alexander	2		2		2
Hughes, Thomas	1		1		
Hart, Mathew	1	1	1		1
Hughey, John	1	1	2		
Hains, Joseph	1	4	4		
Huggins, James	2	1	3		9
Hughes, James	3	3	2		
Hannah, Samuel	1	2	3		11
Kelton, Robert	1	1	2		
Kerr, Nathaniel	1		2		3
Kerr, Revd David	3	1	2		3
Kitchen, John	1	3	1		
Lindsay, John	2		2		
Lair, John	1		2		
Logan, George	2		3		
McCrery, Samuel	3	3	2		
McferSion, Robert	4		3		
McConnell, John, Ser	1		1		8
McConnell, John, Jur	2	1	7		1
McEwin, John	1	3	4		
McEwin, Joseph	2	2	3		
Milholland, James	1	2	2		
Moore, Abraham	2	2	2		
Moore, Adam	2		2		
McEwin, James	1	1	2		
McGee, Patrick	1	1	3		
McKnight, Hugh	4	2	5		6
McKnight, James	3	3	5		2
McNeely, Robert	1	1	1		
McConnell, Benjamin	2		1		1
Moss, Benjamin	1	4	2		
Nelson, Joshua	1	4	4		4
Norad, John	2	2	4		
Osborn, Adlai	2	5	5		19
Porter, James	1	2	2		
Porter, John	1		6		
Porter, Robert	1	1	7		
Reese, William	2		2		
Rankin, Robert	1	3	6		1
Redman, John	2	2	2		
Scott, Robert	2	2	4		
Strain, Andrew	1	4	2		
Sloan, Robert	1	2	3		2
Thompson, John	3		2		6
Templeton, Robert	3	1	3		
Templeton (Widow)	2	4	5		
Templeton, George	1	2	3		
Templeton, Joseph	2	3	4		
Torrence, Hugh	4		3		5
Torrence, George	2	1	2		1
Thompson, Benjamin	1		2		1

SALISBURY DISTRICT, IREDELL COUNTY—Continued.

NAME OF HEAD OF FAMILY.	Free white males of 16 years and upward, including heads of families.	Free white males under 16 years.	Free white females, including heads of families.	All other free persons.	Slaves.
White, Robert	3		1		
Wingfield, Thomas	1	1	7		
Work, Alexander	1		2		25
Work, John	2	4	5		10
Wilson, James	3		5		
White, Mary	1	2	3		3
Williamson, Richard	1	3	4		
Winslow, Moses	1		4		7
Walker, Robert	1	1	1		
Wallice, William	1	2	4		
Young, Alexr	1	1	4		
Young, James	1	2	2		
Andrew, James	1	3	4		
Anderson, James	1	3	6		
Allison, Theophilus	1	1	3		4
Armstrong, John	1	1	1		
Brown, William	5		2		
Barr (Widow)	1	2	3		2
Bell, Walter	2	2	6		
Berringer, John Henry	1		2		
Brown, Valentine	1	1	3		
Crawford, John Miller	1	2	3		
Clendennin, Mathew	2		3		1
Clayton, George	1	2	3		1
Cammins, Gasper	1		1		
Crawford, James	1	2	1		3
Clayton, Lambert	1	4	2		1
Crawford, John	1	1	2		
Cavan (Widow)	3		4		
Cavan, John	1		3		
Cooke, Thomas	2	3	6		
Chambers, James	1	2	3		
Chambers, John	1	1	1		
Campbell, Allen	1	3	4		
Christey, Andrew	1	3	3		
Christey, Joseph	1	1	3		
Christey (Widow)	1		1		
Davidson, Joseph	1		1		2
Davidson, Alexander	1	3	5		
Duglas, Solomon	2	1	6		
Erwin, John	1	1	3		1
Erwin, William	1	2	1		
Erwin, Thomas	4	1	4		
Erwin, Abraham	2		6		1
Erwin, John, Ser	2	4	3		
Flemming, James	1	5	1		
Foley, Thomas	1	1	3		
Flemming, John	4	2	4		9
Flemming, Samuel	1	3	3		
Flemming, Samuel, Jur	1	2	4		
Gamble, Thomas	1	2	1		
Hibath, James	2		1		
Hendry, James	4	1	1		1
Herrald, John	1	3	4		
Huston, James	1		1		1
Huston, Samuel	1	3	5		
Henner, Levi	1	3	1		
Justice, Hance	2	1	2		
Kerr, James	1		2		6
Kerr, Andrew	1	3	5		2
Kerr, William	1	4	1		2
Kerr, William, Jur	2	2	1		
Knox, Mary	1	4	4		6
Knox, Joseph	1	4	4		4
Koyle, William	1		3		
Kitchen, Stephen	1	2	2		
Knox, John	2	3	4		3
King, Thomas	1	2	5		4
Mclaud, William	1		4		
McCoy, (Widow)	1	1	3		
Lawrance, Adam	1	1	2		
McCoy, Alexander	1	1	3		
McCoy, Daniel	1	1	2		
McDaniel (Widow)		2	3		
McKisick, Robert	3		2		
McCoy, George (S. M.)	1	1	2		
McCoy, Alexander	1	2	5		
Morton, John, Jur	1	1	1		1
McCoy, William	1	3	3		
Morton, John	2		4		
McLoud, William	2	1	2		
Mcbride, William	1	4	4		
McLoud, Anguish	1				
McCoy, Daniel, Jur	2		4		
Moore, Robert	2	2	7		
McClain, James	2	1	5		
Miller, John	1	3	3		
McEwen, James	1	5	5		1
Murdock, William	2	3	5		1
McHenry, Isaac	1	1	1		
Mares, William	1	1			
McCoy, Robert	2		3		
McCoy, Daniel (S. M.)	3		4		
McCoy, George	1	2	4		
McKinsey, Robert	1		4		
McRavey, John	1	3	2		
Moffet, William	1		2		

NAME OF HEAD OF FAMILY.	Free white males of 16 years and upward, including heads of families.	Free white males under 16 years.	Free white females, including heads of families.	All other free persons.	Slaves.
Nail, Andrew	1		1		5
Nail, Gilbraith	2	6	2		2
Nail, Samuel	2		1		
Nail, William	2	1	4		
Nail, Robert	1	1	3		
Nislett (Widow)		1	1		
Nail, James	2		1		
Nail, James, Jur	1		3		
Orbison, James	1	1	2		
Oliphant (Widow)	2	1	1		5
Oliphant, John	2	1	1		3
Orton, James	1	2	6		
Patterson, James	3		4		1
Phillips, Thomas	1	4	2		
Baker, Peter	2	2	4		
Pustle, Henry	2		2		
Patten, Robert	1	3	5		
Patten, John	1				
Ramsey, James	3	2	2		
Ramsey, David	1	2	3		
Ramsey, Robert	1		2		2
Ramsey, Andrew	1	2	2		1
Raynolds, William	1	1	4		
Scroggs, John	1		2		
Smith, Robert	1	3	2		
Simenton, Theophilus	1	2	1		1
Troutman (Widow)	1		2		
Thomas, James	1	1	3		
Torrence, James	1	3	1		
Troutman, Jacob	1	1	1		
Thompson, John	1		1		
Wetherspoone, John	2	1	3		
Walker, Arthur	4	2	4		1
Wetherspoon, William	1	1	3		
Wilson, John	2	1	4		
Samuel, Wilson	1	1	3		
Wilson, Samuel, Jur	1		2		
Young, William	2		3		1
Alexander, Gabriel	2	3	5		
Andrews, John	1	1	6		
Alexander, James	2	2	6		
Alexander, Ebenezer	1		3		2
Allen, Moses	3		6		
Adams, James	2	2	3		5
Black, David	2		3		
Brady, Archabald	1	2	4		
Boyd, Robert	1	3	4		
Davis, Patrick	1	1	5		
Erwin, William	1	1	2		1
Eslinger, Gasper	1	1	3		
Flemming, Peter	1	4	2		
Femster, William	2	1	3		3
Harris, Samuel	1	2	3		7
Guy, James	2	3	4		7
Hill, Abraham	1	1	4		
Hannon, William	1				
Hill, John	3	1	5		
Hill, Robert	1		1		
Hill, James	1		1		
Huston, James	2		2		
Hogland, Tunis	1		2		
Ireland, William	1	1	2		3
Ireland, John	2		1		2
Ireland, William, Jur	1			1	
Johnston, Andrew	3	1	5		
Johnston, Adam	1	3	6		
Lewis, Richard	2		4		4
Landen, Robert	1	1	3		
Massey, Jacob	1		3		
Massey, Nicholas	1		3		2
Morrison, James	1	4	2		
Morris, Samuel	2	3	4		
McKee, John	2	1	4		
McClelland, William	1	1	3		5
McKnight, James	1	3	4		1
Morrison, James, Jua	1		1		1
Morrison, Andrew	3	2	4		5
McKnight, William	1	1	5		
Morrison, William	2	3	6		1
Milligan, Alexander	1	2	4		
McKnight, David	1	2	4		
Murdock, Robert	2	5	2		
Moore, Alexander	1	1	3		
McFarlin, James	4	3	4		
Moore, Robert	1		1		
Morrison, Thomas	1		4		4
Morrison, William (Miller)	4	3	5		1
Murphey, Samuel	1	3	4		
McClathey, John	1		1		
McAdoe, William	1				4
McCulloch, James	2	2	2		1
McClathey, Hamilton	2		6		
McCollum, James	1		2		4
McClachey, John	1	1	1		1
Nesbitt, John	2	4	5		6
Olliphant, Mathew	3	1	5		

NAME OF HEAD OF FAMILY.	Free white males of 16 years and upward, including heads of families.	Free white males under 16 years.	Free white females, including heads of families.	All other free persons.	Slaves.
Purviance, David	1	1	2		
Reed, Abraham	1	2	4		
Potts, James, Jur	1		3		
Purviance, James	2	3	7		7
Potts, William, Jur	1	1	2		1
Potts, James, Senr	4		5		
Potts, William, Ser	2	3	3		3
Purviance, John, Ser	2	1	9		2
Rodman, Francis	1				
Roberts, Moses	1				
Ramsey, John	1	3	2		
Stephenson, Robert	3	2	6		
Stuart, John	3	5	4		
Scroggs, John	1	5	3		
Scroggs, David	1	1	2		
Stephenson, William, Ser	3	1	2		4
Stephenson, John, Jur	1	2	4		
Stephenson, James	1				
Scroggs, Jeremiah	1	1	3		
Stephen, William, Jur	1	1	3		1
Henry, Thomas	1	2	2		
Thomas, John	1	4	3		1
Thomas, Jacob	1	4	3		3
Thompson, John	2	4	4		
Wallis, John	4	2	4		1
Whealy, John	1				
Woodside, John	1		2		
White, Andrew	1	1	2		
Wetherspoone, Alexander	1	4	4		
Woodside, Hannah	2		3		
White, Samuel	1				
Whealey, Joseph, Senr	1	1	10		
Waugh, William	2	2	4		
Watt, James	3		6		4
Watt, William	1	4	4		4
Whealey, Joseph, Jur	1	1	3		
William, Woodside	1	3			
Woodside, John	2	1	1		
Alexander, Allen	3	4	1		9
Alexander, William	1	5	3		
Barns, Elijah	1	5	3		
Campbell, Colin	2	4	1		3
Draxin, John	2	3	2		
Gordan, John	1				
Gordon, Gilbert	1	3	5		
Gordon, George	1		1		
Galleher, James	1	3	2		
Hood, Solomon	1	2	3		
Huston, Joseph	2	1	4		1
McCoy, Robert	1		1		
McCoy, Nail	1		3		
McCoy, Daniel	2	3	3		
Morrison, Murdock	2		2		
McCloud, William, Jur	1	1	1		
McClain, Donald	1	2	1		
McClain, John	1	2	3		
McIntosh, Anguish	1				
McCloud, Robert	1		3		
McIntosh, John	1	1	2		
McCoy, Alexander	1	3	4		
McIntosh, Alexander	1	1	1		
Milligan, James	1	1	1		
Milligan, Fergus	1	1	6		
McCloud, William	2	1	4		
McCoy, George	1		5		
McCoy, Alexander	1	2	3		
McKinsey, Kenith	1	5	4		
McDonald, Alexander	1	2	1		
McCoy, Thomas	1		1		
Rice, John	1	1	3		
Rounsevall, John	1	1	3		
Rector, Benjamin	1	1	3		
Ramsey, James	1	2	3		
Stuart, James, Ser	4	2	7		
Snodey, Samuel	2		1		6
Wallace, Robert	1	2	3		
Wallace, John	2	4	3		2
McIntosh, George	2	2	3		
Matison, George	1	2			
McCaskey, Daniel	4		4		
McCoy, James	1		2		
McCoy, William	2		2		
McCoy, George	2	1	3		
McKinsey, Kenith	1	2	4		
McKinsey, George	1	2	3		
Arington, John	1	2	3		
Black, John	1	2	4		
Black, Gavin	1	1	2		
Buteram, William	1	3	3		
Bogle, Samuel	1	3	5		
Barnes, John	1	1	2		
Brown, Isach	1	2	2		
Baker, Howell	1	3	5		
Bentley, Benjamin	2	1	4		
Bell, William	2	1	4		

SALISBURY DISTRICT, IREDELL COUNTY—Continued.

NAME OF HEAD OF FAMILY.	Free white males of 16 years and upward, including heads of families.	Free white males under 16 years.	Free white females, including heads of families.	All other free persons.	Slaves.
Barkley, James	2	2	5		
Baker, Isaac	1	1	1		
Bogle, Robert	1	1	3		2
Baker, Howell	1	4	4		1
Couden, William	1		1		
Caeton, Peter	1	5	4		
Carson, Robert, Jur	1	1	3		
Caeton, William	3	1	2		
Cooke, Richard	1		1		6
Cathey, James	1	1	5		
Carson, Robert, Senr	1		4		
Davis, James	1	2	4		
Davis, Solomon	1	4	3		
Davis, Joshua	1	1	3		
Durham, James	2	2	5		
Freemon, Aron	1	2	3		
Fortune, Aron	1	5	4		
Griffith, John	1	1	2		1
Griffith, Robert	1		2		
Griffith, Edward	1	4	1		5
Graham, John	2		2		
Hughes, William	1	5	1		
Harrison, Joseph	3	3	3		
Harrison, Nathaniel	1				
Harrison, Jeremiah	1				
Hartness, Nathaniel	1	1	2		
Hall, Adam	2	2	6		
Hogston, Archabeld	1	1	2		
Kelley, Solomon	2	2	5		
King, James	2	2	4		8
Lackey, William, Jur	1	3	2		
Lackey, Thomas	1	2	4		
Lackey, George	1	1	4		
Lackey, William, Ser	1		3		
Lackey, George, Ser	2	1	2		
Leach, William	1	1	2		
Montgomery, John	1		1		2
Milsaps, Joseph	2		3		
Meadows, Daniel	1	1	3		
Meadows, Daniel, Jur	1	1	2		
Meadows, John	1	1	6		
Milsaps, Thomas	1	2	3		
McHenry, Archabeld	1	1	3		
McEwin, Daniel	1	2	5		
McHargue, William	1	4	1		
Madows, John, Jur	1				
McCurdey, John	1	2	7		
Madows, Randolph	1				
McClelland, John	3		2		2
Melsaps, William	1		2		
Nesbitt, John Maxwell	2	1	2		
Poin, Thomas	1	1	1		
Patterson, James	1	2	1		
Queene, Francis	1	3	4		
Robison, William	1		1		
Reavs, Henry	1	2	4		
Shaw, John	2	3	7		
Sloan, Archabeld	1		2		
Stephenson, James	2		2		2
Smith, John (Miller)	2	3	5		
Smith, John, Ser	3		3		
Stephenson, James, Jur	1	5	2		2
Sharpe, Joseph	1	4	2		3
Taylor, Thomas	1	1	2		
Upchurch, George	1	4	2		
Willis, James	1	2	2		
Wableton, Joseph	1	1	4		
Whitaker, Mark	2	2	4		
Baker, Wonsley	1	2	1		
Ball, Daniel	1	1	1		
Ball, William	1	2	1		
Cast, James	1	3	5		
Cast, Elijah	1	1	1		
Camp, John	1	4	3		
Campbell, William	1	1	1		
Crabtree, Samuel	1	1	4		
Campbell, Elizabeth		1	2		
Campbell, Pennifull	1	1	1		
Dumbush, John	1	2	2		
Felps, John	2	2	2		
Felps, William	1		2		
Fletcher, Reuben	1	3	3		2
Gipson, James	1	1	2		
Gipson, Joseph	1	1	3		
Hunt, John	3	1	4		
Henderson, Samuel	2	4	4		
Hughes, John	1	3	4		
Hughey, Lewis	1	1	4		
Johnston, William	1	5	2		
Jolley, Charles	1	1	1		
Jolley, William	1	2	2		
Lunsford, Normond	1	1	2		
Luper, Daniel	1	1	2		
Morgan, Theophilus, Ser	1	2	2		
Morgan, Martin	1	1	3		
Morgan, Reuben	1	2	3		2
Morgan, Theophilus, Jur	1	2	3		1

NAME OF HEAD OF FAMILY.	Free white males of 16 years and upward, including heads of families.	Free white males under 16 years.	Free white females, including heads of families.	All other free persons.	Slaves.
Matison, George	1	3	4		
Marlow, Mark	1				
Marlow, James	1	2	2		
Mules, George	1	1	1		
Owens, Barsheba	1		1		1
Weslock, James	1		1		
Pickett, Henry	1	3	3		
Roberts, John	1	2	3		
Roberts, Humphrey	1	5	3		
Redman, Thomas	2	3	4		
Simenton, Adam	3		5		
Speaks, Luke	1	2	3		
Speaks, Thomas	1	2	3		
Sanders, Aron	1	1	1		
Sanders, Moses	1	4	4		5
Shoemaker, John	2	3	3		
Shoemaker, Tarlton	1	2	2		
Shoemaker, Randol	1	1	2		
Thomas, Smith	1	3	3		
Sanders, Jacob	1	2	2		
Taylor, William	1	3	4		
Williams, James	2	2	4		1
Williams, Samuel	1	4	3		6
Williams, Phillip	1	2	5		
Wots, Valentine	1		1		
Andrew, Hugh	3	2	3		1
Andrew, John	1	2	2		5
Black, William	1		2		2
Brotherton, John		2	4		
Bones, William	1	2	2		
Beaty, Thomas	1	2	2		2
Beatey, James	1				
Burten, Edward	1	1	5		
Bailey, Thomas	1	2	3		5
Boone, Thomas	2	3	2		
Belt, Benjamin	1	1	2		
Bell, Thomas	2	1	5		
Boone, John	2	3	3		
Boone, Hezekiah	1	1	1		
Cooper, John	1		2		
Callihan, James	1	1	2		
Campbell, Collin	2		6		
Callihan, John	2		6		
Curent, John	1	3	1		
Clegit, Henry	1	3	4		
Carney, David	1	1	2		
Decker, George	1	3	2		
Dobson, Benjamin	4	3	7		
Dobbins, John	2				6
Dobson, Robert	1		1		
Allison, Wm	1	4	3		
Ellis, Samuel	1		2		
Ellis, Joshua	1	8	5		
Ellis, Zepheniah	1	3	6		
Ellis, Samuel	1	3	3		
Grigory, James	1	3	4		
Greene, John	2		2		
Greene, Isaac	1	3	2		
Holms, Hubbart	1		2		
Holms, Francis	1	1	4		
Hardin, William	1		6		5
Hantsman, John	1		1		
Hoy, Marcis	2		2		2
Holms, Robert	1	1	5		
Henry, David	1	3	4		1
Holms, James	1	1	1		
Harris, Aron	1	2	2		
Hardin, Jeane	2		5		5
Hendly, John	1		3		
Kerney, David	1	2	2		
King, John	2	3	7		2
King, Richard	1		2		6
Larde, John	1		2		
Lochrey, William	1	2	2		
Lock, George, Jur	1	1	1		
Lard, Nathaniel	1	2	2		
Lock, George	2	2	3		
McGuire, Thomas	2	5	7		1
McCrary, James	3	1	7		
McHarge, James	1	4	3		
Morris, Thomas	1	1	2		
McConnell, William	3	2	4		
McConnell, Alexander	1	3	2		1
McConnell, John	1		2		1
Means, Alexander	1		2		
Nichols, Jacob	3		4		12
Nichols, Joseph	2	3	4		1
Nichols, Joshua	1		1		1
Nichols, John	1	1	1		
Praither, Bazil	3	4	4		
Peeler, Richard	2		4		
Peeler, Jeremiah	1		4		
Praither, William	1		4		
Reed, John	4	1	4		1
Kinsay, Rodger	1		1		
Reaves, Edmond	2	3	3		
Remington, Richard	1	2	3		

NAME OF HEAD OF FAMILY.	Free white males of 16 years and upward, including heads of families.	Free white males under 16 years.	Free white females, including heads of families.	All other free persons.	Slaves.
Reed, John, Jur	1		1		1
Reed, Abner	1		1		
Stuart, James	4	3	4		1
Scott, James	4	1	1		
Summers, William	1	1	1		9
Sutfin, Jacob	1	1	2		
Sharpe, John	2	2	3		5
Sharpe, James	2	2	7		11
Sharpe, William	3	5	3		8
Shelley, Richard	2		3		
Swingford, Elijah	1	1	3		
Shelly, James	1	1	1		
Shelly, Benjamin	1	1	2		
Swingford, James	2		2		
Summers, Bazil	1	1	1		2
Slavin, William	1	1	4		
Simenton, John	1	1	3		
Grour, Tomlin	1				
Tomlin, John	1	1	1		
Templeton, John	1	2	5		
Templeton, Robert	1	1	1		
Templeton, Thomas	1				
Travis, Mary		1	4		
Todd, Nathan	2		4		
Tomlin, Humphry B	1	4	5		5
Wasson, James	3		3		
Welch, John	1	1	3		2
Wiselock, James	1		1		
Wasson, Robert	1		1		
Wilson, Lewis	1		3		2
Butten, John	5		3		
Clampet, Moses	1	2	3		
Carson, Andw	1	1	2		1
Caiton, Stephen	3	2	4		
Duncan, Isaac	2	2	4		
Donaldson, William	2	2	4		
Dyson, Barton	1	1	6		
Erwin, Robert	1	4	3		
Erwin, Samuel	1	2	2		
Erwin, William	2		2		
Evans, James	1				
Evans, Zacheriah	1	2	2		1
Evans, Ann	1		6		
Gipson, James	1	1	1		
Gaither, Jeremiah	1		2		
Gaither, John	2	1	5		
Gaither, Burges	2		2		3
Holeman, Isaac	1	2	4		
Holeman, James	1	1	2		1
Hays, Solomon	2	3	1		
Huston, Christopher	2	3	4		6
Jacobs, Zacheriah	1	3	3		
Jacobs, Edward	1	2	2		
Lovlace, Charles	2	2	3		5
Mitchell, Andrew	1	2	5		9
Marlow, Thomas	2		5		7
McCord, James	1	3	6		
Maddin, James	1		1		
Martin, William	1	1	3		20
Nelson, Jeremiah	1	7	3		
Nichols, Becket	2	1	4		
Patrick, Jeremiah	1	1	2		
Pugh, John	1	3	2		
Riley, James	1		1		
Riers, David	1	1	4		
Read, James	1	2	1		2
Sergeler, Jacob	2		1		
Sergelar, Phillip	1				
Swann, Zepheniah	1	1	5		
Smith, John	1	1	1		
Summers, Thomas	1	2	2		
Speaks, Charles	1	3	2		
Tucker, Rubey	1	6	2		
Tagard, Andw	2	4	6		
Wooton, George	2	2	5		
Willis, George	2	1	6		
Webb, Caleb	2	3	4		
Webb, George	1	2	3		
Young, Thomas	2	3	2		13
Young, William	2	1	1		1
Archabeld, Thomas	2		7		3
Archabeld, Mathew	2		4		
Armstrong, John	2		4		1
Allen, Drury	1	3	8		
Bell, Zadock	1		3		1
Beggarly, Thomas	1		4		
Beggarly, David	1	2	2		
Bell, David	2	4	3		1
Bell, Thomas	1		2		
Beggarly, Benj	1	1	2		1
Bowman, Hugh	2	1	4		1
Baird, Thomas	1	4	4		2
Bone, William	1		4		
Baird, David	1	2	4		
Baird, William	1		1		7
Bowman, John	1		2		3

SALISBURY DISTRICT, IREDELL COUNTY—Continued.

NAME OF HEAD OF FAMILY.	Free white males of 16 years and upward, including heads of families.	Free white males under 16 years.	Free white females, including heads of families.	All other free persons.	Slaves.
Caldwell, David	2	4	2		14
Caldwell, Andrew	1	1	1		1
Chambers, Arthur	2	5	3		1
Chambers, Henry	1	3	3		9
Erwin, Stephen	1	1	2		
Campbell, Mathew	2		1	2	
Erwin, James	1		5		
Allison, Adam	2	3	4		6
Allison (Widow)	1	1	3		2
Allison, Richard	1	2	3		5
Allison, Theophilus	1	2	2		4
Allison, Thomas	2	2	2		6
Erwin, John	1	1	3		1
Erwin, William	4	3	3		
Freeland, Andrew	3	5	3		1
Ferril, John	1	1	5		4
Gidions, Bosle	1	4	4		
Gordon, Robert	1	3	3		
Gaither, Nicholas	1	4	1		1
Gay, James	2	1	3		
Gipson, Margret	2	1	3		
Houpt (Widow)	1	3			
Hall, William	1		4		
Hogshead, David	4		7		
Hall, William, Jur	1		3		
Hair, Robert	1	1	3		
Hall, Revd Jas	2		4		9
Hall, Alexander	1	1	2		4
Hall, John	1		3		1
Hall, Thomas	4	3	7		5
Hall, James, Senr	1		1	2	
Hawill, Jerard	1		1		
Hall, Hugh	2	2	6		2
Hall, James, Jur	1	4	2		3
Hall, Andw	1		2		
Eston, Henry		1	4		
Hair, Daniel	5		2		
Kilpatrick, Joseph	2	4	4		
Kilpatrick, Andw	1	4	5		
Lesenbey, Joshua	1	2	1		1
Lesenbey, Henry	1	1	3		1
Love, Samuel	1	1	4		
Long, Samuel	2	2	2		
Lewis, Daniel	1	2	4		
Lesenbey, Thomas	1	2	5		
Mathews, Musentine	1	4	3		3
McKinzey, Andrew	3	1	5		
McKee, William	1	3	3		4
McWhorter, John	3		3		
Murdock, John	3	3	3		5
McGuire, Patrick	2	5	3		
Morrison, Andw	4	3	5		1
Murdock, James	1		3		2
McHenry, John	1	1	6		1
McClelland, John	1	3	4		1
Morrison, John	2	6	3		1
McKee, Alexander	1		1	1	
Murdock, John, Jur	1		1		
Mathews, Robert	2	2	8		
Nesbitt, John	2	4	5		3
Perter, Thomas	2		8		1
Pithey, John H	1		1		
Baker, Jeremiah	1	1	3		
Rosbrough (Widow)	3	1	1		4
Roby (Widow)			5		
Robison, George	1		3		
Stuart, James	2		1		4
Steele, Nenien	2	5			1
Summers, John	1	3	3		4
Simenton, William	4	3	4		15
Scott, John	1	2	6		
Simenton, John	1	1	2		
Sloan, Fergus	2		3		3
Stephenson, Joseph	1	1	2		
Sawyers, Edward	1				
Sloan, Fergus, Jur	1		2		2
Thornton, Theophilus	1		3		
Tucker, David	1	3	6		
Taylor, James	1	1	5		
Vandever, Mathew	1	2	4		
Vickers, John	1	3	1		
Wasson, Joseph	2		1		
Wasson, Samuel	1	3		2	
Wilson, James	1	1	1		
Wilson, Thomas	1	1	1		1
Wilson, James, Jur	1		1		
Watt, William	3		4		5
Wilson, John	3		3		1
Wilson, Alexander	1	1	1		1
Johnston, Francis	1		2		

SALISBURY DISTRICT, MECKLENBURG COUNTY.

NAME OF HEAD OF FAMILY.	Free white males of 16 years and upward, including heads of families.	Free white males under 16 years.	Free white females, including heads of families.	All other free persons.	Slaves.
Allison, Robert	1	3	4		3
Allison, Archabeld	3	1	3		
Allison, David	1				
Alexander, Wm, Jr	2	1	3		
Alexander, Ezra, Senr	3	1	3		
Elga, Francis	1	2	1		
Allison, Joseph	1		3		
Allen, John	3	3	4		
Alexander, Able	2	2	2		
Alexander, Phenias	1	3	4		
Berryhill, Wm	1		4		1
Barnet, Robert, Jur	1	1	1		2
Bryan, Mathew	2	5	4		
Brown, Patrick	4		4		
Beaty, John, Jur	1	2	4		9
Beaty, John, Senr	2	3	5		
Baker, George	1	4	3		
Buam, James	1	3	2		
Brown, David	3	1	3		
Berryhill, John	3	3	3		
Clark, Jessey	2	3	2		2
Davis, George	1	2	2		
Cooper, Doctor	1	1	2		
Clarke, Robert R	1	3	3		
Clarke, William	3		3		3
Campbell, Robert	1	1	6		
Cathey, George, Senr	3	1	3		5
Cathey, Esther	2	1	5		
Cathey, Alexander	2	1	3		
Cummins, John	1		2		
Cooper, John	2		2		
Carson, John	1				
Castillo, Miles	1	2	4		
Carroll, Joseph	3	2	2		3
Cathren, Robert	1	4	5		
Corcham, William	1	3	3		
Clayton, James				1	
Carroll, James	1		2		
Cattor, George	1		1		
Currethers, Edmond	1	1	1		
Coreham, Robert	2	1	3		
Freemon, Michael	1		4		1
Freemon, David	3	2	5		
Freemon, Reuben	1		1		
Griffey, Aron	1		3		
Gibbeney, Nicholas	1	2	4		6
Greene, John	2	2	4		2
Graham, Majr Joseph	1	1	2		8
Graham, George	1	2	2		
Graham, James				1	
Hucheson, John	1		1		
Hern, Jesse	1	3	4		
Hucheson, George	2	1	1		1
Hargrove, Thompson	1	2	5		
Hargrove, John	2	1	3		
Hunter, John, Ser	2	1	2		6
Hunter, Robert	1	3	2		3
Hogden, Nehemiah	1		3		
Haynes, David	3	2	3		2
Hepworth, John	1		5		
Hann, Margret & Son				2	
Hanks, Thomas	1	1	1		
Isler, Nicholas	2	1	2		
Jackson, Shadrick	2	7	1		
Kirkes, Thomas	1	2	1		
Kerr (Widow)		1	3		1
Kithcart, John	1	2	1		
Love, John	2	1	2		
Love, Samuel	1		1		
McCord, Able	4	1	4		1
McCord, Robert	2	1	4		
McClarey, Wm	2				
McDowell, John	1	3	4		5
McClarey, Michael	2	2	1		3
McDowell, Esther	1		3		
McKinley, William	1	4	7		
McKnight, Robert	2	1	8		
McKnight, James	1	1	1		
McNeely, James	1	4	3		
Moore, Joseph, Ser	3	1	5		
Montgomery, James	1	4	3		
McNeely, Andw	1		1		
McClure, John, Jur	4	1	2		
McClure (Widw)	1	1	2		
Cleffland (Widow)			4		
McKee, Andw	1		2		6
McKee, John	1	2	5		
McGee (Widow)	3	1	3		
McCormack, William	1	1	2		
Mariner, John	1		1		
McClure, Moses, Jur				1	
McClure, Thomas, Jur	1		1		
McDonald, David				1	
Nation, Thomas	1	3	4		
Null, James, Ser	1	2	6		
Nicholson, John, Senr	2	1	5		2
Nicholson, George	1				
Owens, James	1	4	5		
Van Pelt, Simon	2	5	5		
Pierson, Henry	3		4		
Parks, Hugh	1	2	4		2
Porter, John	1	3	4		
Plummer, Zepheniah	1		4		
Plummer, Thomas				1	
Reed, James, Senr	3	2	2		
Reed, James, Jur	1	1	2		1
Reed, James (middee)	1	4	4		1
Reed, Robert	2	1	2		
Reed, Thomas	1		2		1
Reed, John	1	4	4		
Sloan, John	1	1	3		
Sloan, James	1	2	3		1
Sumter, John	2	1	1		5
Spratt, James	1	1	4		3
Stinson, John			3		2
Stinson, Michael					1
Shields, David				1	
Tagert, James	2		2		
Wilson, John	3	2	4		5
Walker, John	2	3	4		
Walker, William	1	2	4		
Wilkeson, George	1		2		
Verner, John	1		5		
McFalls, John				1	
Alexander, Judith	1	1	1		
Alexander, James	1		3		
Bigham, John	2	3	3		4
Bigham, James, Sr	1	1	3		
Bigham, Robert	1	1	2		
Bigham, Samuel, Sr	2		1		
Bigham, Samuel, Jur	1	4	4		
Bigham, William, Jur	2	1	4		
Bigham, James, Jur	2	2	2		
Bigham, Hugh	1		1		
Barnet, Robert, Senr	1	3	4		
Barnet, John, Ser	1		3		1
Barnet, John, Jur	1		3		
Blackwood, James	2	2	4		1
Brownfield, Robert	1		1		
Brownfield, William	1	3	3		
Brown, Richard				1	
Cathey, Andw	1		1		
Cathey, George	2		3		5
Carruthers, James	2	3	2		2
Carruthers, Robert	1	2	5		1
Carruthers, John	1	3	2		
Calhoone, Charles	1	1	5		3
Calhoon, Samuel	1	3	5		
Cheek, Silas	1		3		9
Calhoon, George	1		1		
Davis, Walter	3	4	5		8
Davis, John L	3	1	2		
Dunn, William	1	2	2		
Darnell, William	1	5	4		
Darnell, Joseph	1	3	5		6
Dinkins, John	2	3	3		12
Ferguson, Thomas	1		1		1
Ferguson, William	1				
Gilmore, William	1		3		
Gilmore, Margret	1	2	3		
Gillan, John	1		3		
Greer, Thomas	1	2	3		5
Greer, James	2	2	3		2
Herron, Andw	1		2		
Hart, James	1		2		
Hart, Joseph	1	1	1		
Hart, David	1		2		
Harris, Hugh	1	2	3		
Herron, Hugh	1	2	4		5
Herren, Allen	1	2	3		
Herron, Samuel				1	
Erwin, Robert	2	2	6		3
Knox, James	2		1		
Knox, Samuel, Jur	1		1		2
Knox, Mathew	2		2		5
Knox, Samuel, Senr	2	3	3		9
Knox, John	1		2		
Kindrick, John	1	3	1		2
Kindrick, William	1		2		1
McClarey, Robert	2	2	5		2
McCormick, Robert	2		4		
McCrum, Rachel		3	3		6
McKee, Robert	3	3	6		1

SALISBURY DISTRICT, MECKLENBURG COUNTY—Continued.

NAME OF HEAD OF FAMILY.	Free white males of 16 years and upward, including heads of families.	Free white males under 16 years.	Free white females, including heads of families.	All other free persons.	Slaves.
McKee, James	1	3	2		8
McGill, Thomas				1	
McKee (Widow)	1	4	7		
Maxwell (Widow)	2	4	4		1
Null (Widow)	1	1	4		3
Neely, John	2	3	7		6
Neely, Thomas, Jur	1	4	2		2
Null, James, Jur	1		2		1
Neely, Samuel	2		2		2
Neely, Moses	2	1	4		3
Nicholson, John, Jur				1	
Porter, William	1	4	5		4
Porter, Alexander	1	1	7		
Porter, Joseph	1	1	4		
Porter, Hugh	1	1	1		
Porter, James	1	2	4		4
Patterson, William	2	2	2		
Price, Isaac	4	4	3		7
Howe, Joseph				1	
Price, John	2	1	3		13
Reed, Joseph	1				
Ramey, Thomas	1		4		
Robison, Richard	1		2		1
Robison, David	1	2	1		
Robison, Mathew	1	4	5		
Ramey, William	1		2		
Ramey, William, Senr	2	1	2		
Smart, George	2		1		4
Smart, Littleberry	1				
Smart, Elijah	2	1	2		9
Smart, Francis	2	1	2		9
Swann, Joseph	1	4	3		
Speers, James	1	3	6		
Scott, James	1	1	4		
Shepperd, William				1	
Thomas, Benja	2		2		9
Taylor, John	2	4	2		4
Vance, David	3	3	3		
Whitsitt, John	2	4	3		2
West, Martin	1	5	2		
Walker, John	1	2	4		
Wilson, Robert	6		4		
Wilson, Zachias	2		4		
Wilson, Isaac	1	1	1		2
Wilson, William	1	1	1		
Wilson, Joseph	1	3	3		
Wilson, James					
Withers, Reuben	2	1	5		4
Yurce, Francis	1	3	2		
Alexander, Isaac, Esqr	1				1
Bigham, John	1	5	2		
Barnhart, Henry	1	2	3		
Cook, Isaac	2	2	3		8
Cooper, Joseph				1	
Emerson, Henry	1	1	1		
Elliott, Samuel	2	3	4		1
Elliott, Thomas	3		2		
Henderson, Dor Thomas	1	1	6		2
Hutcheson, William	2	4	2		3
Isham, John	1		3		
Holt, William			1		
Kennaday, James	2	1	4		
Kennaday, Esther	3		1		1
Kennaday, Samuel				1	
Lefeever, Joseph	2		2		
Luckey, William	1	3	3		1
Mason, Richard	2	4	2		5
McCombs, Samuel	1	1	1		3
McCulloch, William	2				1
McClary (Widow)	1	1	2		
Martin, Thomas	1	2	1		
McNabb, Duncan	1	1	3		
McKee, David	2	5	3		3
Martin, Ephraim	1	1	2		
Cliver, George	1	2	3		
Polk, William	1		1		21
Polk, Thomas	5		4		47
Polk, Charles	2	2	1		9
Pattison, William	2	1	3		5
Riley, John	1	3	4		
Rice, George	1	1	1		
Robison, James	1	1	6		
Stuart (Widow)			2		
Springs, John	3	3	5		50
Wisehart, Joseph	1		2		1
Wright, William				1	8
Alexander, Darkus	3	1	3		8
Alexander, Wm, Ser	3		2		11
Alexander, Ezekiel, Senr	3	2	6		
Alexander, David	1				
Alexander, Ezekel, Jur	1		1		
Alexander, Daniel	1	2	2		
Alexander, Elijah	1	2	3		
Alexander, Elias, Jur	1		3		
Alexander, CaptThomas	1	3	3		6
Alexander, Dor James	1		1		
Alexander, John	1		4		
Alexander, Capt (B) William	2	4	2		9
Alexander, Charles	1	4	3		
Alexander, Benjamin	2		1		
Alexander, George, Jur	1	1	1		
Allen, Agnes		1	2		6
Allen, George, Senr		1			1
Alexander, Ezekieh, Esqr	4	2	3		13
Alexander, Capt Andrew	2				9
Bailey, Richard	1	3	3		4
Batey, Samuel	1	3	4		4
Barlow, Amrose	1	2	4		
Braley, Thos C				1	
Batey, William	1	1	1		
Balch, Thomas	1	3	3		
Campbell, Alexander	1	1	2		2
Carney, Patrick				1	
Davis, Samuel	1		1		4
Fipps (Widow)			7		
Daker, Christopher	3	2	4		
Goforth, William	2	2	6		
Graham, Samuel	1				1
Gipson (Widow)	2	2	4		
Houston, Henry	1		2		1
Henderson, Cairns	3		1		1
Houston, William	2	2	2		
Henderson, Andrew	1	1	3		
Johnston, William	3	3	5		2
Johnston, David	2	1	3		
Kennaday, David	2	2	2		
Kewer, Henry	1	2	2		
Lemons, Robert	1	3	2		
Luckey, Robert	1	3	3		
Mitchell, John	1		1		
McGee, John	2	2	1		
Mitchell, Robert	3		3		2
McCulloch (Widow)		1	2		
McGintey, Alexander	1		1		2
Montgomery, John	1		1	5	
Montgomery, Robert	1	3	5		
McClure, Thos Senr	2	1	1		
McKee, Wm, Junr	1		1		1
McDowell, Archabeld				1	
Miller, Samuel				1	
Neely, Hugh	2	3	3		
Neely, Thomas				1	
McCall, James	2	2	4		
Orr, Nathan, Senr	3	1	6		
Orr, Wm	1	1	7		9
Orr, James (Jockey)	1	4	3		6
Orr, Nathan, Jur	1	3	1		1
Orr, James (white)	1	2	2		
Parks, John, Senr	3	3	4		3
Parks, David	4	2	3		
Parks, John, Junr	1		2		3
Parks, Samuel	1		1	2	
Reed, George	1	4	2		
Richey, David	2	1	5		
Richey, John	1		3		
Ross, George	2		3		
Robison, John	1	1	2		1
Robison, Robert, Senr	1		2		
Robison, Robert, Jur	1	2	7		
Robison, Moses	1		1		
Robison, David	3	1	1		
Robison, James, Senr	1		1		2
Robison, Wm & Richard	2		3		
Rogers, David	1		2		
Shields, William	1		3		
Stuart, David	1	3	4		
Strachback, Daniel	1		1		
Sample, Samuel	2	1	3		
Starling, James				1	
Tasey, Alexander	1	1	2		
Wise, Thomas	2	2	5		
Wallace, Ezekel	2		3		4
Wallace, Mathew	1	1	3		
Wallace, William	1	1	1		
Wallace, George	1	1	3		
Wallace, Alexander	3		1		
Wiley, William	3		3		2
Wiley, John	1	4	3		
Williamson, Benjamin	1	1	3		
Watson, William	1	1	4		
Wiley, Joseph	1		1		
Alexander, Col George	3	1	5		11
Archabeld, Rev. Robert	1	1	4		
Alexander, Abraham	1	1	2		
Alexander, William	2	3	5		1
Alexander, Moses	3	7	2		1
Alexander, Benjamin, Jur	2	2	5		
Alexander, Moses, Jur	1		3		
Alexander, Andw	1	3			6
Alexander, Hezekiah	1		2		1
Alexander, Abijah	2	1	5		
Bouchfriend, George	1		2		
Brown, James	1	2	3		1
Black, William	2	1	3		7
Buckhanon, Robert	3	2	4		
Cowden (Widow)	1		2		
Caldwell, Charles	1		1		2
Caldwell, Capt David	1				
Craighead, Robert	2	4	3		4
Clark, Eliner	1		1		
Doherty, James	2	3	1		1
Edmiston, John	1	2	4		
Giles, Edward, Esqr	4	2	4		
Gardner, James	1	1	6		2
Gilmore (Widow)	1	3	3		2
Gilmore, Nathaniel	2	1	5		
Gardner, William	2		2		
Gardner, John	1	1	2		
Galliway, Thomas	1	5	2		
Garrison, David	1	3	5		
Giles, Nathaniel	1	1	3		
Hunter, Henry	2	7	3		2
Hunter, John	1		3		1
Hope, Robert	3	5	4		6
Irwin, Robert	1	2	2		1
Kelugh, Samuel	2	3	4		3
Meek, Adam	2		2		3
Meek, Moses	1	2	5		
McClain, Joseph	2		2		
McCandeless, John	1	1	2		3
McCay, Michael	1		3		
McCallister, John	1	2	4		
Meek, Robert	1		2		
Newman, John	1	3	4		
Query, Alexander	3	2	4		
Reed, John	1	3	4		
Robison, Alexander	2		2		
Russell, James	1	1	3		
Pickens, William	1		1		2
Smith, Col Robert	1	1	3		15
Sharpe, Ezekel	2		7		3
Smith, James	1	1	2		
Sloan, John	1	3	2		
Sloan, James, Senr	1	1	2		
Sloan, James, Jur	1	1	2		
Sloan, Thomas	1	2	2		
Simmons, William	1	2	4		
Shelby, Evan	1	1	6		4
Strain, Dor Wm	1		1		
Simmons, Thomas	1	3	5		
Wallace, James	2		3		6
Wilson, Zachias, Senr	1	1	1		
Wallace, John	1	2	2		1
Woods, John	1		1		
Young, Joseph	2		7		5
Young, William	1	3	8		2
Montgomery, David	1	3	3		
Winings, Peteter	1	1	2		1
Alexander, John Mnt, Esqr	3		1		16
Alexander, William, Senr	3	1	3		
Atkins, Samuel	1	2	5		
Alexander, Ezekel	1	3	4		2
Abernathey, Miles	1	2	4		
Aldridg, Isham	1				
Aldridg, William	1	3			
Bradshaw, Josiah	2	1	5		1
Beach, Justice	1	2	5		
Blackwood, William	1	1	2		2
Bradley (Widow)	1		3		
Blackwood, Thomas	3	1	3		1
Cannon, John	3		1		
Clark, James	1	1	3		
Cannon, Margret	1	1	2		
Cannon, Joseph	1	1	5		
Cannon, James, Senr	1	1	7		
Crocket, Robert	2		2		2
Dunn, Andrew, Senr	2	1	2		
Dunn, Robert	1		2		
Dunn, James	1		4		
Dunn, John	1		4		
Doherty (Widow)	1		4		2
Davidson, John (Mercht)	2	1	2		9
Ewart, Joseph	2	3	4		
Elliot, George	3	3	3		3
Elliot, William				1	
Frazer, Joseph	1	4	3		
Frazer, Samuel	1		2		
Frazer, James	1				
Ferrill, John	1	2	1		
Ferrill, Gabriel	1	1	2		
Flenniker, Charles	1		1		
Gailbraith, Martha	1	3	2		
Garrison, John	1	1	2		1
Gibson, John	1		4		2
Henderson (Widow)			2	4	

SALISBURY DISTRICT, MECKLENBURG COUNTY—Continued.

NAME OF HEAD OF FAMILY.	Free white males of 16 years and upward, including heads of families.	Free white males under 16 years.	Free white females, including heads of families.	All other free persons.	Slaves.
Henry, James	1	4	3		
Hudson, Richard	1	2	5		
Hammond, Mathias	1	1	4		
Hipp, Stephen	2	1	3		
Hipp, Valentine	1	2	1		
Jimeson, Robert	1	1	2		
Johnston, Nathaniel	1	3	5		
Jemison, Arthur	1	4	4		
Jemison, Thomas	1		2		
Erwin, Edward	1	1	5		
Johnston, Isaac	1	4	4		1
Johnston, John	1	2	4		1
Kerr, Joseph	1	2	6		
Knox, Capt James	2	1	3		15
Kerr, Robert	1	3	4		
Kerr (Wid)	1	2	3		3
Lewing, William	3	1	5		
Lewing, Andrew	1		4		
Lather, Robert				1	
Long, Capt John	3	2	3		1
McClennahan, Reuben	1	2	2		
McClure, Capt Mathew	3		2		6
McIntire, James	1		2		1
McCoy, Beaty	4	5	3		5
Moore, Joseph	2	3	5		2
McClure, John, Junr	1	2	4		
McCracken, James	2	2	7		
Maxwell, Ann	1		4		
Montieth, Jane	3		4		2
Montieth, Nathaniel	1				
Moore, James	1	3	6		
McClure, William	3	2	3		
Moore (Widow)	2		3		3
Mullen, Harris	1	1	3		
McGinn (Widow)	3		2		
McClure, Moses (Thos Son)	1	2	3		
Moffitt, William	1		1		
Nation, John	2	2	6		
Nighten, John	1	1	3		
Patten, Charles	2		1		1
Parker, Isaiah	1	4	6		
Peoples, John	1	2	1		
Robison, Mathew	1	2	3		
Robison, George	1	1	2		
Robison, Alexander	1	2	2		
Russell, David	1	2	6		3
Ramsey, William	2	3	4		
Raphil, John	1	1	2		
Stephenson, Richard	3		1		
Sharpe, James	1	1	1		3
Sharpe, John	5	3	2		1
Steele, Peter	1	1	2		
Sample (Widow)	1	1	6		
Sullivan, Patrick	1	1	3		1
Sullivan, Jeremiah	1		1		
Thompson, John	1	1	6		
Thompson, Gideion	2		2		2
Thompson (Widow)	4	1	3		
Todd, William	3		4		
Todd, Adam	1	2	1		
Todd, Joseph	2		2		1
Todd, John	2	1	6		
Williams, Billy	1	2	2		
Woods, Robert	1	2	3		
Woods, Mathew	2	1	1		
Watkins, James	1	2	2		
Alexander, Amos	1	4	3		6
Alexander, Moses	2		1		
Alexander, Aron	2	3	4		1
Alexander, David	5		4		2
Alexander, Daniel	1	1	2		
Alexander, Joel	1		1		
Alexander, Isaac				1	
Bryson, Hugh	2	4	4		
Bell, John	1				
Black, Thomas	1	4	5		
Berry, Capt Richard	4		6		
Bailey, Francis	1	1	5		2
Blythe, Samuel		2		1	1
Blythe, Richard	1		2		
Bell, Walter	1				
Brodinax, John	1	3	3		16
Currey, James	1	3	4		
Caldwell, William	1	4	2		4
Cathey, Capt Archabeld	1	1	3		11
Cochran, Benjamin	1		1		
Conner, James	3		4		
Cooke, James	2	5	4		6
Carson, Jane			2		
Conner, William	1	2	1		
Doherty, David	2	1	5		
Davidson, Thomas	1				
Davidson, Samuel	1	2	2		
Davidson, Majr John	2	2	6		26
Duck, John	1	1	3		
Duck, Simon	1	2	3		

NAME OF HEAD OF FAMILY.	Free white males of 16 years and upward, including heads of families.	Free white males under 16 years.	Free white females, including heads of families.	All other free persons.	Slaves.
Duck, George	1	4	2		
Duck, Abel	1	2	3		
Duck, Absalom	1	3	1		
Duck, George, Jur				1	
Davis, David	1	1	5		
Davis, Daniel				1	
Evitts, William	2	1	3		
Forsyth, Robert	3	3	4		
Gillaspie, Joseph	3		2		1
Gillaspie, James	1	2	2		2
Gilmore, Patrick	1	7	1		
Givvins, John, Senr	2		1		
Givvins, John, Junr	1	2	2		
Givvins, Edward	2		2		11
Givvins, Jno Ruther	1	4	3		
Garrison, Samuel	1	1	2		4
Graham, William	3	7	1		4
Harper, William	1	2	3		3
Henderson, John	1	1	1		3
Henderson, John, Jur	1	1	6		
Henderson, William, Senr	2	2	2		3
Henderson, William, Jur	2	4	4		6
Hill, William	1	4	6		
Hansill, John	1	3	2		
Hampton, Patrick	3	1	4		9
Henry, Capt Henry	2	4	6		
Harris, Majr Thos	2		5		7
Hunt, Turner	1	1	6		15
Hunneycut, Howell	1	1	1		
Hamilton, William				1	
Jetton (Widow)			1		1
Jetton, Lewis	1	4	5		3
Johnston, John	3	4	1		
Irwin, Samuel	1	1	1		1
Kelly, Thomas				1	
Knox, Allison	2		6		
Latta, Joseph	1	1	5		
Lucas, Hugh	1	3	5		
Lowrance, Michael	1	1	2		
Jetton, Abraham	1	1	1		2
Morrow, John	2	2	2		
Morrow, Robert	2	2	3		
Morrow, John, Jur	1	2	2		
Maxwell, James	1	4	2		
Maxwell, Benjamin	2	1	3		
McDugal, Thomas	1				
McCorkle, Thomas	2		2		6
Meek, James, Esqr	1		3		
Meek, James, Jur	1	1	2		
Montieth, Henry	2		2		
Montieth, Samuel	1	1	4		
Martin, Thomas	1	1	2		
McNair, James	1	2	2		
Osborn, John	1		4		
peele, James, Ser	2		1		5
peele, James, Jur	1	1	2		
Potts, Robert	1	5	3		10
Potts, Jonathan	2	1	7		1
price, James	1	3	5		
price, John	1		4		
price, Robert	1		1		
Sloan, David	1	4	2		
Sloan, John	1	1	3		
Clark, Benjamin	1	1	4		
Hutchison, David	1	1	2		
Shelds, Robert	1		1		
Clark, Joseph	1		2		
Wilson, Samuel, Senr	1	1	3		
Sloan, Robert	2		2		
Stanford, Samuel	1		4		
Stanford, Isaac	1		1		
Smith, David	1		1		5
Smith, James				1	
Torrence, Hugh	1	1	5		12
Tucker, William	2	1	1		
Taylor, Elijah	1	3	3		
Wilson, David	1	4	2		1
Wilson, Benja	1	1			3
Wilson, Samuel, Jur	1		2		9
Wilson, John	1		1		
Wilson, Joseph	1				
Wise, John	2	4	4		
Wise, William	1		1		
Walls, Abin				1	
McCong, Thomas				1	
Wilie, John	1		4		
Wilie, William	1	2	3		
Wilson, William	1				
Waddle, William	1	3	4		1
Wilson (Widow)	1	1	3		
Williams, Jas L			1		4
Emmerson, James	1	1	4		
Christenberry, Nicholas	2	1	3		
Christenberry, Moses	1		1		
Wilson, John, Junr	1		1		
Andrews, Moses	1	1	2		

NAME OF HEAD OF FAMILY.	Free white males of 16 years and upward, including heads of families.	Free white males under 16 years.	Free white females, including heads of families.	All other free persons.	Slaves.
Andrews, Robert	2	2	7		
Anderson, Robert	2		5		
Alexander, Capt Stephen	2	1	7		2
Alexander, Josiah	1	3	2		2
Brown, Benjn	2	2	3		1
Brown, Samuel	1	2	2		
Bradford, Mary	2	1	3		
Benson, Thomas	1	2	2		
Benson, Robert	1		2		
Bell, James	2	2	2		
Bradford, James			2	1	
Bowman, Samuel	1	1	5		3
Bartley, Daniel	1	1	6		
Carrigan, James	2		4		2
Cooper, John	1	2	2		
Copeland, Dennis	1	2	3		
Casey, Mary	1		1		
Carruthers, John	3	3	3		
Davis, Isaac	1		2		
Davis, John, Senr	2		2		
Davis, David	1		2		
Flemming, Mitchell	1	2	2		
Farr, Margt	2		2		6
Gilleland, John	2		4		
Gilmore, Archabeld	1		1		
Gillaspie, James	1	1	4		
Houstin, John	1	3	4		1
Houstin, Capt Archabeld	2		1		3
Houstin, David	1		2		2
Hamilton, Hugh	1	1	2		
Harris, Robert, Esqr	2	1	4		11
Henderson, John	2		2		
Harris, Oliver	1		2		1
Harris, Robert	1	1	6		1
Harris, James	2	1	4		1
Irwin, Thomas	1	2	4		
Lewis, Benjamin	1	2	1		4
Moffit, Martha	3		3		2
McCulloch, John	1	2	6		
Morton, Samuel	4		1		
Martin, Robert	2	1	3		
McCown, Margt	1	3	3		
McCabb, James	1	3	3		1
Null, John	1	1	1		
Null, James	2	4	6		
Pruie, Reese	1		1		13
Penney, John	2	1	2		
Penney, William	1	3	4		
Pickens, Capt Samuel	1	4	4		5
Ross, William	1	4	3		
Ross, John	1	1	2		2
Ross, George	1	2	1		
Stevenson, Jas	1	2	5		
Steele, John	1		2		2
Templeton, David	1	4	3		
Tanner, James	1	3	3		
Wells, William	1	2	1		
Wilson, John	1	1	5		
Allison, John, Esqr	3	1	3		5
Armstrong, John	1		1	1	
Armstrong, John, Jur			1	1	
Alexander, Francis	1	1	2		
Baker, John	1	5	4		3
Berry, George	1	2	2		
Baker, Christopher	2	3	3		3
Baker, Joshua	1	1	3		
Biggers, Robert	1		2		
Barns, William	1	5	4		
Booker, Joseph	1	2	5		
Campbell, Thomas	1				
Carruthers, Andw	3	1	8		1
Creaton, James	1		1		1
Cannon, James	1		1		3
Doherty, James			1		
Frazer, William	1	3	6		
Glover, Ezekel	1		2		
Glover, John				1	
Glover, William	1		1		
Gaseway, John	1	4	2		
Houston, Capt William	2	2	3		4
Holbrook, John	2		4		
Holbrooks, Caleb	1	2	2		
Holbrooks, William	1	3	5		
Houston, David	1	1	2		
Hall, Morgan	1		2		
Hosey, Jonathan	1		2		
Holbrook, Vaitch	1	2	2		
Kyles, John	1				
Lock, Francis	1	2	4		5
Lingo, Daniel	1	2	4		
McClartey, Archabeld	1		4		
McClartey, Alexander	2	1	2		
Means, John	3	2	2		4
Martin, Robert	2	3	2		
Martin (Widow)	1		2		
Morrison, William	1	1	3		1

SALISBURY DISTRICT, MECKLENBURG COUNTY—Continued.

Name of head of family	Free white males of 16 years and upward, including heads of families	Free white males under 16 years	Free white females, including heads of families	All other free persons	Slaves
McCray, William	1	2	5		1
Martin, Richard	1	4	5		
McKinley, David	1	2	3		
McKinley, John	2	1	2		
Murphey, John	1	1	5		
McRea, Arthur	1		3		
Martin, William	1	2	2		
Phifer, Col Caleb	1	1	6		19
Phifer, Capt Martin	1	2	4		16
Patton, Benjamin	2		2		
Patton, Samuel	2		3		
Patton, Joseph	1	3	1		
Patterson, Samuel	5	2	3		
Patterson, Alexander	2		4		3
Patterson, Robert	1		1		1
Phifer, Henry	1		2		
Pasinger, Thomas	1	2	2		1
Reese, Solomon	1		4		
Rogers, Joseph	1	3	4		3
Rogers, Moses	1	1	3		
Rogers, Thomas	1	2	1		
Rogers, James, Junr	1		2		
Rogers, Seth	1	3	1		
Ross, Francis	2	5	2		
Russell, David	1	2	1		1
Rogers, John	1	1	1		
Scannell, John	1		1		
Scales, John				1	
Skitleton (Widow)	1	2	4		
Taylor, John	1	3	2		
Wallace, Ludwick	1	1	9		
Wallace, Jediah	1	1	1		
Wallace, John	1		1		
Wodington, John	1	1	2		
Goodman, Jacob	1	2	4		
Blackwelder, Charles	1	2	3		
Blackwelder, John	1	1	6		
Black, Thomas	1	2	2		
Bawyers, Adam	2		3		
Bryance, Henry, Senr	1				
Bryance, Henry, Junr	1	2	3		
Bryance, William	1	2	2		
Barnhart, Mathias	1	2	1		
Barnhart, George	1		2		
Barbrick, Leonard	1	1	5		
Barnhart, Christian	1		1		
Barnhart, Christian, Junr	1	1	3		
Blackwelder, Jno Adam	1	1	1		
Coleman, Mark	1	6	5		
Cerlaugh, George	1	1	4		
Campbell, James	1	1	5		
Cook, Nicholas	3		2		
Chamberlain, John	1	1	7		
Clerice, George	1	2	2		
Corzine, George, Senr	3	1	5		
Corzine, Levil	1	3	4		
Corzine, Nicholas	1	1	4		
Corzine, George, Jur	1	2	4		
Corzine, Samuel	1	1	3		
Caster, John	1		2		
Kerlock, Fredrick	1		1		
Cook, Nicholas, Jur	1	1	1		
Deaton, Mathew	1		2		
Eagley, Phillip	1	2	3		
Farr, Walter	2	5	4		1
Farr, John	1	5	6		
Ferguson (Widow)			2		5
Furr, Henry	1	1	3		
Faggenwinter, Christian	1		4	1	
Goodnight, Christian	1	4	6		
Groner, Jacob	3	1	2		
Gonder, George	2	4	4		
Haddock, James	1	1	2		
Hadley, Joshua	3	1	4		
Hartman, George	1	1	6		
Hobley, John	1	3	2		
Townsand, Dudley	1	2	2		
Townsand, George	1	4	3		
Long, John	1	1	5		
Lewis, Jacob	1	2	5		
Lewis, Christor	2		1		
Lewis (Widow)	1	1	6		
Mitchell, Mathias, Senr	2	2	2		
Miller, William	2	1	4		
Minster, Frederick	2	2	3		
Misenhimer, Jacob	1	3	4		
Mock, Thomas	2	2	3		
Masters, George	2	3			1
Morgadine, John	1	1	1		
Mitchell, Jacob	1		1		
Mitchell, Mathias, Junr	1	2	2		
Moyer, Elias	1	2	4		
Murph, Jacob	1	2	3		
Nichler, John	3	4	4		
Phifer, Martin, Senr	2		1		14

Name of head of family	Free white males of 16 years and upward, including heads of families	Free white males under 16 years	Free white females, including heads of families	All other free persons	Slaves
Phifer, Jacob	2	1	2		
Plott, George	3	3	3		
Phifer, George	1	1	2		
Rogers, George	2	1	6		
Russell, James	2		5		7
Russell, Robert	1	3	3		7
Russell, John	1	3	5		
Rogers, Nat	1		3		
Shinn, Capt Joseph	3	3	5		6
Shinn, Benjamin	1	5	5		1
Shive, Phillip	1	2	3		
Smith, John	1	2	1		1
Shaver, John	2	6	4		
Scott, James	1	5	4		
Siminer, John	1		1		6
Shelhoas, John	1		2		
Shank, Manas	1	4	1		
Tedford, James				1	
Slowgh, Martin	1	3	3		
Voyls, William	2	5	2		
Voyls, James	1	3	2		
Walter, Paul	1	2	3		
Walter, Nicholas	1		3		
Winesaugh, Michael	1		1		3
Winesaugh, Michael, Junr	1	4	3		
Wiley, John	2	1	1		
White, William	1	2	3		1
Young, John	1		3		
Young, Martin	1	1	3		
Yewman, John	1		2		
Townsand, Henry	1	2	1		
Townsand, William	1	1	4		
McGraw, William	1	1	1		
Bless (Widow)	2	2	3		
Boger, Daniel	1	2	3		
Boger, Peter	1	2	5		
Best, John	1	1	2		
Bussard, John	2		3		1
Berger, John	1	3	3		
Beck, Fredrick	1	3	8		
Baringer, Mathias	3	3	6		2
Cottiser, Henry	1		1		
Cruse, Andrew	1	1	1		
Cruse, Adam	1	1	2		
Clonts, Jeremiah	1	3	2		
Clonts, George	1	1	3		
Closian, Jacob	2		3		
Christman, George	1	1	1		
Caple, Peter	2	1	2		
Culp, John	2	2	4		
Cox, Moses	1		2		
Cox, John	1		3		
Cox, William	1		1		
Coble, Peter	1		4		
Dolin, Henry	1	2	3		
Dry, Martin	2	2	2		
Evalt, Michael	1	4	2		
Adelman, George	1		2		
Evalt, Jacob	2	2	2		
Easenhart, George	1	1	3		
Fesperman, Fredrick	1		4		
Fesperman, Michael	1	4	5		
Festerman, Henry	1		1		
Festerman, John	1	1	2		
Goodman, George	1		4		
Goodman, Michael	1		1		
Goodman, Elizabeth	2		2		
Gregory, Christian	1	3	3		
Goodman, Christopher	2	2	2		
Goodman, Michael, Jur	1	2	4		
Goodman, Christopher, Jur	1	2	4		
Hese, Conrad	1	3	5		
Herron, Elijah	2	3	3		1
Herron, Jesse	1	3	6		3
Harris, Ephraim D	2	1	6		
Juke, John	1	3	5		
Creps, Tobias	1		3		
Creps, Phillip	1	2	4		1
Lippard, John	3	4	5		5
Lippard, William	1	2	2		
Long, Henry	3	2	4		
Lingle, Jacob	1		4		
Lingle, Conrad	1		4		
Lingle, Casper	1	2	3		
Misenhimer, John	1	1	5		
Moyer, Adam	2		1		
Misenhimer, Abraham	2	1	5		
McMahan, James	1	3	4		
Minsinger, William	1	1	3		
Netterhever, Paul				1	
Ovenshine, Rinholt	1	1	2		
Ovenshine, Christian	1		1		
Aurcy, Martin	1	2	3		
Pence, Jacob	1	2	6		
Props, Henry	1	3	1		1

Name of head of family	Free white males of 16 years and upward, including heads of families	Free white males under 16 years	Free white females, including heads of families	All other free persons	Slaves
Perry, Jacob	3		1		
Brineger, Erasmus	2	1	1		
Slaugh, Jacob	1	2	4		
Seferit, Barnhart	1	1	4		
Seferit, Charles	1		4		
Semions, John	1	1	6		
Stierwalt, Adam	1	1	1		
Speck (Widow)	3		3		
Sides, Michael	1	4	5		
Isenhaker, Nicholas				1	
Rigey, George	2		2		
Richey, Jacob	2		3		
Richey, Henry	1	5	2		
Rogers, Benjamin	1	3	4		
Wolf, Phillip	3	5	3		
Wisel, Michael	2	1	3		
Walker, Fredrick	1	1	2		
Foil, George	3	2	1		
Goodman, Jacob	1	2	4		
Rosberry, Benjamin	1	3	2		
Clemments, Samuel				1	
Allen, Thomas	2	1	2		
Christman, George	1	1	1		
Hartis, John	2	2	4		
Ashley, John	1	2	4		
Brown, William	1	3	3		
Cresco, William	1	3	3		
Barringer, Paul	1	4	4		13
Barenhart, Charles	3	5	4		
Bost, George	2	3	1		
Bost, Jacob	1	1	5		
Blackwelder, Caleb	1	1	4		
Blackwelder, Isaac	1	4	2		
Bost, Elias	1	3	3		
Bostion, Jonas	1		5		
Blaster, Abraham	2		1		
Barringer, John	1	5	4		2
Blackwelder, Martin	1	1	1		
Blackwelder, Jacob	1	1	1		
Bever, Daniel	1	2	1		
Caigle, Charles	2	3	5		
Casey, Jacob	1	1	5		
Carriger, George	1	3	4		
Carriger, Andrew	1	3	3		
Carriger, Phillip, Senr	1	2	1		
Carriger, Phillip, Junr	2		1		
Coile, John	1	2	3		
Clots, Tobias	1		2		
Croul, Peter	2		2		
Cline, Michael	1		5		
Coan, Lewis	1		3		
Caigle, Charles, Junr	1		3		
Dry, Charles		2	3		
Dry, Owen	1	3	3		
Dry, Phillip	1		1		
Dove, Caleb	1	1	4		
Gruff, William	1		2		
Eafrit, Jacob	1	2	2		
Clain, George	1	2	4		
Furr, John	2	6	2		3
Furr, Paul	1	3	4		1
Fogleman, Melcher	3	2	3		
Fisher, Lewis	1		4		
Fink, David	1	2	4		
Faggett, Jacob	2	2	3		
Foil, John	1		4		
Folk, William	1		1		
Fink, George	1		1		
Fruseland, George	1	1	3		
Faggott, Valentine	1		2		
Briges, James	4	1	4		
Hagler, John	2	3	6		
Hartwick, Conrad	1	3	2		
Hardman, George	1		1		
House, John	2	2	1		
House, Elias	2		3		
Hagler, James	1	4	4		
Huber, Jacob	1	3	4		
Hardwick, George	1		3		
Hennager, Michael	1	3	3		
Hise, George	1	2	5		
Hurlaugher, Christor	3		3		
Hargey, Martin	1	3	3		
Hoan, Henry	1		5		
Hineman, William	1	1	4		
House (Widow)			6		
Hartsel, John	2	2	4		
Jarret, Daniel	2	2	5		
Little, James	1	1	1		
Honeycut, Thomas	2	1	2		
Kerlock, Fredrick	2		1		
Kerlock, George	1	1	4		
Krepps, John	1	3	2		
Little, Daniel	1	2	4		
Kneese, Bolser	2	2	2		
Lidaker, Conrad	1		2		
Linker, Henry	1	2	2		

SALISBURY DISTRICT, MECKLENBURG COUNTY—Continued.

NAME OF HEAD OF FAMILY.	Free white males of 16 years and upward, including heads of families.	Free white males under 16 years.	Free white females, including heads of families.	All other free persons.	Slaves.
Loften, Isaac	1	3	2		
Lidaker, Phillip	2	2	5		1
Lierly, Christopher	1	2	3		
Lype, Jonas	1		5		
Lype, Godfryt, Senr				1	
Lype, Godfryt, Junr	1	1	1		
Lierly, Zamah	1	3	1		
Mathews, Andrew	1	4	3		
McGraw, James	3	4	1		
Moyer, Mathias	1		2		
Melcher, John	3	1	6		
Misenhimer, George	1	2	3		
Misenhimer, Peter	1	2	3		
Miller, Jacob	1	3	3		
Neusman, Revd Mr	1	2	4		
Oudy, Conrad	1	4	3		
Ourey, George	1	3	3		
Ourey, Godfryt	1		1		
Ourey, Barenhard	1	1	3		
Price, Henry	1		4		
Pliler, Fredrick	1	2	2		
Pliler, Henry	1		5		
Starns (Widow)	1	2	3		
Quilman, Peter	1	2	2		
Rape, Agustian	1	2	2		
Reed, John	1	3	3		
Ridenaur, Nicholas	1	3	7		
Redland, Geo M	2		8		
Rinhart (Widow)		2	2		
Rigsbey, Thomas	1		2		
Sell, Phillip	2	1	2		
Smith, George	1		2		
Smith, Henry	2	2	3		
Stough, Andw	1	1	1		
Sides, Andw	4		4		
Sides, Henry	1	1	1		
Smith, Henry	2	2	3		
Starns, Conrad	1	3	5		
Stucker, Daniel	1	1	2		
Sides, Christian	2		1		
Sell, Peter	1		3		
Starns, Charles	1	1	1		
Tucker, George, Sr	3	3	5		
Tucker, George, Jur	1	1	3		
Teem, Jacob	2		1		
Teem, Adam	1	4	2		
Voyls, Thomas	2	2	3		
Wilhelm, George	1	4	6		
Witenhouse, Martin			2	1	
Wiser, Phillip, Jur	1		2		
Wiser, Phillip, Senr	3		1		
Wagginor, William	1	5	2		
Weaver, Jacob	1	1	1		
Weaver, Henry	1	3	4		
Weaver, Peter	1		2		
Walker, Michael	1		10		
Walker, Adam	2	1	2		
Cook, Jacob	1	3	3		
Suther, David	1		2		
Suther, John	1	3	2		
Miller, George	1	2	3		
Winchester, William	2	2	4		
Caigle, John	2	3	6		
Winchester, Dugles	2	3	3		
Andrews, William	1		2		
Armstrong (Widow)		1	4		
Alexander, William S.	1	3	2		4
Allen, Alexander, Jur	1	4	2		
Allen, Alexr, Senr	1	3	2		
Burns, James	2	1	6		
Bradshaw, James	2	4	6		
Biggers, Joseph	3	1	5		
Bean, Robert	3	4	1		
Black, James	2		2		
Black, Wm	1	3	2		
Black, John	1		3		
McClain, Allen	2	2	4		
Carruthers, Hugh	1	3	2		
Carruthers, James	1	1	1		
Colland, William	3	1	1		2
Crumel, James	1	1	2		
Crumell, John	2	2	5		
Coldwell, Daniel	1	4	1		
Coldwell, Robt	1		2		
Cochran, Benjn		4	2		
Cochran, Robert	1	2	6		
Campbell, Andw	1	2	2		
Cochran, Wm	2		1		
Cochran, Paul	2	4	2		
Cochran, John	1	2	1		1
Corruthers, Robert	3	3	6		
Davis, Robt	1	6	5		
Dunn, Simon				1	
Davis, Thomas	2	4	4		
Davis, Andrew	3		6		
Davis, William			1	1	
Ferguson, Alexander	1	4	2		3

NAME OF HEAD OF FAMILY.	Free white males of 16 years and upward, including heads of families.	Free white males under 16 years.	Free white females, including heads of families.	All other free persons.	Slaves.
Harris, William, Jur	1	4	1		
Hays, Patrick	1	2	5		1
Harris, John	1	1	2		1
Harris, Capt James	6		4		6
Harris, Robert, Junr	1	2	1		
Harris, Samuel	2	1	6		11
Harris, William, Senr	1	3	5		2
Gingles, John	1		1		
Harris, Capt Robert	1		1		8
Howell, Joseph	3	3	2		
Howell, John	1		2		
Kirkpatrick, Valentine	1	3	3		
Kimmins, Hugh	1	2	5		
Kimmins, Alexander				1	
McClelland, Rebeca		1	3		
McCinley, David	1		7		
McCinley, Charles	1	3	2		
McKentire, Capt William	2	4	3		
McMurray, Francis	1		2		
McMurray, Robert	1		6		3
McCahern (Widow)	1		6		
Mcfadian, Thomas	1	1	1		
Morrison, James	3	2	2		2
Morgan, Enoch	1	2	1		
McCammon, Charles	2		2		
Morrison, Robert	4	1	5		
Morrison, William	2	1	3		1
Morris, Griffin	1	4	5		
McClelland, John	1	3	3		
Mash, Ebenezer	2		2		
McGinnis, Charles	3		3		
McCurdey, Capt Archabeld	1	4	5		6
Maxwell, James	2	4	1		
Newill, Francis	1	1	4		
Newill, William	3		3		
Newill, David	1		3		
Plunket, James, Senr	1	1	1		6
Plunket, James, Junr	1	4	1		
Purviance, David	3	1	4		1
Purviance, Joseph	1	1	2		
Purviance, James	1	4	1		1
Purviance, John	1	1	3		
Russell, James	1		1		3
Ross, William	2	2	5		3
Ross, James	1				1
Scott, James	2		2		
Scott, Alexander	1	2	4		
Simons, John	1	5	2		
Stuart, Samuel	1	3	5		
Spears, James	4	2	4		
Stafford, James, Senr	2				1
Stafford, James, Junr	1	4	3		
Scott, William, Esqr	3		2		1
Stuart, William	1	2	4		
Stuart (Widow)	1		4		
Taylor, William	1	2	3		
Taylor, David	1		1		
Wite, John	2	4	3		2
White, Thomas	1	3	2		1
White, William	1	3	5		
Wiley, Oliver	1	4	6		4
Widington, Samuel	1	4	2		
Wallace, Aron	1		2		
White, Archabeld	3	1	2		
White, David	1	2	3		4
White, James	2		1		
Watson, Thomas	4	2	3		
White, Joseph	1		3		
Wallace, Moses	1	1	3		
Dorton, Charles	1	6	2		
Davis, George	1	6	4		1
Morgan, Robert	1		1		
Stuart, John	1		3		
Harris, Samuel, Junr	1		2		1
Welch, Joseph	1	4	4		
Eager, Adam	2	1	3		3
Eager, Hugh	1	2	4		
Alexander, Col Adam	3	1	3		5
Alexander, Evan	1		3		
Bean, William	3	1	4		
Bugg, William	1	2	3		
Bean, Daniel	1	1	2		
Barnhill, Robert	1	1	2		
Bailey, Joseph	1	1	2		
Brandon, John	1	3	2		
Brown, James	1	4	1		
Bryan, Kiah	1		1		
Cuthbertson, John	1	1	3		
Crowle, Samuel	2	2	2		
Cuthbertson, David	1	1	2		
Crowle, Samuel, Junr	1		2		
Carruthers, John	1		2		7
Clay, Isham	1		3		
College, Henry	1		3		
Freemon (Widow)		3	4		
Dickson, James	1	1	2		

NAME OF HEAD OF FAMILY.	Free white males of 16 years and upward, including heads of families.	Free white males under 16 years.	Free white females, including heads of families.	All other free persons.	Slaves.
Davis, James	1	3	2		
Freeman, Allen, Junr	1		2		
Freemon, Allen, Senr	1	3	3		12
Freemon, Gidion	1	1	4		1
Flaugh, David	2	3	5		
Ford (Widow)	1	1	4		
Freemon, William	1	1	4		
Freemon, Elyburn	1		2		
Garmon, Michael	1	1	7		9
Garmon (Widow)	1	1	1		8
Guliams, Travis	1		2		
Harkey (Widow)	1		3		
Hall, James	1	2	3		
Harbison, William	1	1	3		
Hall, Thomas	1	3	4		
Harris, Majr James	4		1		13
Hall, John	2	3	3		
Johnston, William	1	2	2		
Johnston (Widow)	1	2	3		
Kiser, Fredrick	1	3	3		
Kiser, George	1	4	3		
Kyger, George A	1	2			
Long, James	1		2		
Mulls, John	1	1	2		
McMurray, James	1	4	5		1
Miney, Martin	1	3	2		
McCracken, John	3	3	4		
McClartey, Alexr	1		2		
Murphey, John	2	1	1		
McCoy, John	1	1	5		2
Miller, Phillip	2		1		
Mitchell, William	1		2		
McGuist, John	2	4	3		
Masser, George	1	1	1		
McGehey, Amos	1		1		
Nelson, John	1	1	2		
McCummons, John	2	3	4		1
Pickens, William	1	2	3		
Pyron, William	2	2	5		
Powell, David	1	2	2		
Pyron, John	1	2	2		
Powell, John	3		2		
Polk, William, Jur	1	4	2		
Polk, William, Senr	1		1		2
Polk, Capt Charles	2	3	3		4
Powell, Abel	1		2		
Purser, John	2	2	5		
Polk, John, Junr	1	1	3		
Polk, Thomas, Junr	1	1	2		
Rabb, Capt William	2	4	3		3
Rogers, James	3		3		5
Rogers, Hugh	1	1	3		2
Ramsay, William	1	3	6		
Rodgers, Joseph	1	1	7		
Simpson, William	1	3	2		
Snell, Francis	1	3	4		
Smith, Thomas	1		1		
Smith, William	1		1		
Shelley, Capt Thomas	1	1	3		6
Stansill, John	1	2	3		
Smith, Samuel, Senr	2		2		4
Self, Jacob	1		1		
Smith, Samuel, Junr	1		1		
Smith, Saml (son of Saml)	1		1		
Talley, Priar	1		3		
Townsand, William	1	1	2		
Warden, Samuel	3	3	2		
Witherford, Wilka	3	3	2		
Witherford, William	1	1	3		
Wise, Benjamin				1	
Watts, Andrew	2		2		
Reed, John	2	3	2		
Tetter, George	1	3	2		
Crawford, John	1		6		
Miller (Widow)	1		6		
Miller, Mathew		2	1		1
Miller (Widow) Senr			1		
Clay, James	1	1	1		
Caegle, Henry	1	4	1		
Blair, William	3	3	5		
Buckhannon, Samuel	3		2		
Black, John	2	1	6		2
Black, Ezekel	1	1	2		2
Black, Samuel	1		1		
Black, William, Sr	1		2		1
Carragan, Thomas	1		1		
Charles, Henry	1		1		
Crum, Conrad	1	1	3		
Contz, Lewis	1	2	4		
Donaldson, John	1		2		
Ford, Zeblin	1	2	5		
Fisher, George	1		2		
Ford, John, Esqr	1		2		7
Glass, Robert	1		1		
Glass, Francis	2	4	5		
Grubble, Thomas	1	2	5		

SALISBURY DISTRICT, MECKLENBURG COUNTY—Continued.

NAME OF HEAD OF FAMILY.	Free white males of 16 years and upward, including heads of families.	Free white males under 16 years.	Free white females, including heads of families.	All other free persons.	Slaves.
Gonder, Lewis	2				7
Hood, Tunis, Senr	1				7
Hood, Capt Tunis	1	4	4		4
Hood, Reuben	1	2	3		
Harrisson, Nehemiah	1	3	5		2
Hartwick, Conrad	1		2		
Harkey, John, Senr	2	1	2		
Hartis, Lewis	1	2	4		
Irwin, William, Senr	3		3		
Irwin, Thomas	1	1	2		
Kenneday, William	1	3	2		
Kidwell, William	1	2	5		
Leagh, Henry	1		6		
Lippe, Leonard	1	1	2		
Lalgh, Jacob	1	1	4		
Lemmonds, John	2	3	3		
Mcfersion, John				1	
McIntire, William	1		4		
McGinnis, Peter	3	1	3		
Morris, William	3	3	3		1
Montgomery, John	1	3	3		
McCall, William	1	3	2		
Moore, Hugh	2	4	4		
McCombs, James	2		5		5
Miller, Abraham	3	1	1		
McCollum, Malcom	1	3	2		
McCraven, John, Jur	1		3		
McGintey, James	1	2	4		
Moore, Andw	1	2	3		
Moore, David, Jur	1	1	4		
Nail, John	1	2	4		
Orr, James (whistling)	2	5	3		
Orr, James	1	2	3		
Phillips, Adam	1	1	1		
Query, William, Senr	1		1		
Quary, John	3		1		
Quary, William, Jur	1	2	4		
Ray, Isaac	1	1	5		
Routh, Edward	1		1		
Stansill, Jesse	1		4		
Stansill, John	1	1	2		
Shaver, Fredrick	2	5	4		1
Stuart, Mathew	2	1	2		
Stevens, Emmanuel	1	4	3		
Stains, James				1	
Stilwell, Jesse	1		3		
Walker, William	2		2		
Wilson, James	3	1	4		
Wilson, Thomas	1	4	3		
Walker, Capt Archabeld	2	1	1		
Walker, Mathew, Senr	1	2			
Vance, Andw	1		6		
Irwin, William, Jur	1	1	1		
Ormond, James	1	1	2		
Carrigan, William				1	
Walker, Moses	1		1		
Wilson, Thomas, Senr	1		1		
Coul, James				1	
Vance, Valentine	1		1		
Culbertson, William	2	3	5		
Darbey, Charles	1		1		
Dunn, James	2	1	2		
Dunn, Andrew	1	2	6		
Demsey, John	1	1	6		
Duglass, James, Esqr	1	3	3		1
Dunbarr, Nathaniel				1	
Craig, John	1		2		
Elkins, Shadrick	1	1	3		
Eakins, John	1		4		
Bradshaw, Samuel	1		2		
Bradshaw (Widow)	1	2	1		
Crye, William	1	3	2		
Appleton, William	2	2	2		
Adams, Charles	3	2	5		
Blythe, James	1	6	3		
Basdill, Reuben	1	3	3		3
Barnet, Robert	1	3	3		
Bonds, George	2	3	2		
Bickett (Widow)	3		3		
Crye, John	2	1	2		
Craige, Moses	2	2	4		
Cochran, Thomas, Senr	2	2	1		1
Cochran, Thomas, Junr	1	5	7		
Crye, James	3		2		
Courtney, William	2		1		
Cochran, John	1		3		
Chainey, William	1	4	2		
Fincher, James	1	4	2		
Fincher, Richard	1	2	4		
Finley, James	1		2		
Fincher, Jonathan	2	3	6		
Fowler, John	2	1	2		
Forsythe, Hugh	1	2	3		
Finley, William				1	
Finley, Charles				1	
Forbers, Hugh	1		3		
Givvins, William	1	1	4		
Gibbens, John	1	4	2		
Givvins, Samuel	1	2	1		
Gray, Jacob	3	1	1		
Gray, Sherrod	1	2	2		2
Gordin, John	3	2	3		
Gillaspie, Jacob	1		1		
Hargitt, James	1	1	1		
Hellums, George	1	3	3		
Hellums, John	1	2	4		
Hellums, George, Senr	1		1		1
Houston, Hugh	3		1		4
Hargitt, Henry	1	1	2		
Helms, Jacob	1	1	4		
Houston, William, Senr	1		3		1
Houston, William, Junr	1		3		
Howey, George	1	2	2		
Howard, William	1	1	3		
Helms, Tilmon	1	2	2		
Hargitt, Henry, Junr	1	6	2		
Hise, Leonard	1	3	3		
Howey, William	2	1	1		1
Henninger, Dennis	2	3	6		
Howey, John	1		3		5
Houston, James	3	1	2		5
Heggins (Widow)	2	1	2		4
Harris, John	1		5		
Hellums, Isaac	1		2		
Izel, Fredrick	2	1	3		
Queban, John	1		2		
King, Robert	1	3	2		
Lawson, John	1		2		
Lewis, William	1	2	4		
Lewis, Martha			1		1
Lewis, James	1	5	3		
Lawson, Moses	1		1		
Leggit, Esther	2	3	4		2
Lawson, Thomas	2		2		
Leggit, William	2	2	2		1
Linn (Widow)	2	1	3		
McNeely, John	2				1
McCall, Francis	1		3		
McCorkle, John	1	1	3		
McCallum, John	1		1		
McCablum, Thomas	1	2	2		
McCabben, Mightry	1	1	5		
McCain, Hance	1		2		
McWhorter, Aron	2	1	4		
McCauslin, James	1		3		
Mcquistion, Joseph	1		2		
Morrison, Dr William	1		1		2
McCrorey, Hugh	1	1	2		
McCain, John					1
Newton, Robert	1	2	5		
Orr, George	1	1	5		1
Osborn, William	3	1	7		
Ormond, James	1	2	2		
Orr, David	1	4	4		
Osborn (Widow)	2	1	4		
Ormond, Jacob	1	2	4		1
Porter, William	1		1		
Paxton, Moses	1	2	2		
Potts, John	1	1	5		3
Potts, William	1	1	3		14
Porter, Capt Robert	2	3	5		
Richardson, Edward	3	2	4		
Rape, Peter	1	2	4		
Ramsay, Robert	1	3	2		
Rich, James	1	2	2		
Rape, Henry	1	2	2		
Rederick, Shadrick	1	2	3		
Redford, John	4	2	4		
Rogers, John, Senr	1		2		
Ramsay, Alexander	1	1	1		
Rich, John, Junr	1		1		
Shepperd, John	1	2	3		
Shepperd, James	1	1	3		
Shepperd, Edward	1	2	1		
Secrist, Michael	1	2	3		2
Secrist, John	1		3		
Rich, James, Senr	2	3	5		
Stuart, Joseph	1	1	2		
Storey, James	4	1	2		1
Secrist, Jacob	2	4	2		
Stevenson, James	1	4	4		
Thompson, Elijah	3	1	4		
Tanner, Thomas	1		2		
Thompson, John	1	2	5		
Spratt, Andw	1	2	5		
Williamson, James	1	1	2		
White, Thomas	1	2	1		
West, Benjamin	1		2		
Yarbrough, Joshua	3	3	1		
Uans, Robert	1		1		
Avent, James	1	1	6		5
Abbott (Widow)			4		
Allen, Andw	1	3	2		
Allen, Thomas					1
Blue, Stephen	1	2	3		
Broom, John	3		2		
Belk, John, Esqr	1		1		8
Belk, Darling	1	3	2		
Cairns, Alexander	1	4	5		3
Coak, Robert	1		2		
Coak, Charles	1		6		3
Cairns, Daniel	2	1	4		
Davis, James	1	2	6		1
Dosber, James	2	1	5		
Davis, Capt Robert	2	3	6		4
Findly, John	1		1		
Forster, Capt Joseph	1		1		4
Fisher, Paul	1	1	1		
Fisher, William	1	1	2		
Fisher, John	1	2	2		
Fisher, Charles	1		1		
Fisher, Fredrick	1	2	2		
Gantt, William	1		4		
Gillaspie, Andw	1		1		
Gantt, Thomas	1		5		
McCain, William	1	1	4		
Yerbey, Avent	1	3	2		
McCammon, John	3	3	5		
McCorkle, Archabeld	1		2		
McWhorter, James	1	1	2		
Odum, May	1		2		
Orr (Widow)		3	7		
Potts, Joshua	1	1	1		
Rogers, Hugh	1	5	3		
Rogers, Mathew	1	3	4		
Ramsay, John	1	3	2		
Rogers, John	1	3	2		
Rowan, Henry	1		2		
Faggett, Moses	1	2	4		1
Rogers, William	2	4	3		
Starns, Fredrick	1		3		
Starns, David	1	3	1		1
Stevenson, John	1	4	3		
Sibley, John	1	2	3		
Shannon, James	1	1	1		
Titus, Dennis	1	1	7		
Thompson, Alexander	1		5		
Thompson, Obediah	1	1	3		
Vinan, Thomas	1	5	3		
Vinan, William	1		3		
Gillaspie, Charles	1	1	1		
Haggins, John	1	1	2		
Gillaspie, John	1	4	4		
Kendrick, Philand	1		3		
Hughey, John	1		6		
Lathlin, Samuel	1		2		
Lathlin, John	1		3		
Lasley, James	1	2	3		1
Lackey, Robert	1		2		
Lackey, Thomas	1	3	3		1
Lesley (Widow)	2	1	1		
Lanley, George	1	2	4		1
McWhorter, John	1		1		
Myars, Hermon	1	1	1		
McElroy, John	4	2	2		
McElroy, James	1	3	3		1
McWhorter, Moses	1	2	5		
McCorkle, James	1	4	2		
McWhorter, George	3		2		
McCorkle, Owen	1		2		
McCain, Andw	1	1			
Meller, Buie	1	3	4		
McCain, John	1	1	4		
McCain, Hugh	3	1			3
McCain, Thomas, Junr	1	3	1		
Vinen, Drury	1	5	3		4
Washam, Jeremiah	2	1	3		
Walker, Capt Andw	1	1	6		3
Williams, John	1	2	1		
Wahaub, James	3	2	3		9
Williams, Ishmael	1	2	1		
Walker, John	3		1		
Walker, Thomas	1	1	1		
Griffin, Richard	1	3	1		
Redick, Barnabas	1	4	1		
Oats, Michel	1	1	3		
Bruster, James	2	2	3		5
Barnet, Hugh	3	1	5		
Black, James	2		5		
Black, William, Junr	1		3		
Batey, Walter	2	1	2		2
Chambers, James	1	1	1		
Crocket, Archabeld	4	1	5		2
Coningham, Roger	2	1	2		
Currey, William	1	4	3		
Dawns, Henry	2				3
Dawns, Samuel	1		2		1
Dawns, Thomas	1		1		1
Donaldson, Robert	1		2		
Greer, John	1	1	3		
Guire, John	1		3		

SALISBURY DISTRICT, MECKLENBURG COUNTY—Continued.

NAME OF HEAD OF FAMILY	Free white males of 16 years and upward, including heads of families.	Free white males under 16 years.	Free white females, including heads of families.	All other free persons.	Slaves.
Hoge, Francis	2		4		
Harkness, George	1	3	6		
Hadden, George	1	2	1		
Hodge, John	1	1	2		
Housten, David	1		1	1	
Harrison, Isaiah	1	3	3		2
John, Daniel	1	1	3	1	
McSparren, James	1		1		
Means, William	1	3	5		1
McKee, William	1	3	2		6
Miller, John	1	2	2		
McCauley, Daniel	1		3		
McKee, Alexander	1	3	4		
Moore, Phillip	2	1	4		
Montgomery, George	1	4	1		
Moore, David, Senr	4	4	6		1
Miller, George	1		2		
McGoughen, James				1	1
Morrison, Alexander	2		2		1
Mathews, William, Esqr	1	3	1		1
Null, Jesse	1	1	1		1
Null, Andw	1		2		
Osborn, Robert	1	2	2		
Osborn, Alexander	1	1	3		
Ormond, Adam	1		1	1	
Osborn Able	1		1		
Parks, Moses	3	3	3		
Patson, Simon	2		3		
Potter, Gordon	3	3	4		
Patterson, John				1	
Ray, Andrew, Senr	2	2	4		
Reed, James	1	2	4		
Ray, John	1	1	1		
Reed, Joseph	2	3	2		2
Robison, John	1	5	3		2
Ray, David	1	3	4		
Robison, Thomas	1	2	5		
Stuart, William	2		2		
Slitt, William	2	5	2		
Simeson, Capt John	1	1	1		4
Shanks, James	1	1	6		4
Sharpe, John	1	2	2		
Stevenson, John				1	
Stuart, John	2	3	4		
Springs, John, Senr	1		2		2
Stevenson, David	1			1	
Tawns, Elijha	2		2		
Wyatt, Sylvester	1	2	2		
Wylie, James	1		2		1
Vaich, William	1	4	3		
McBoyd, Patrick	1	2	3		
Smith, John	1	2	2		1
Gailbraith, Robert	2		5		
Rendricks, William	1		2		1
Cleymon, Simon	1	1	4		
Cleymon, Richard	1	1	6		
Alexander, Capt Charles	3	1	4		6
Alexander, Abner	1	1	3		
Alexander, George	1	1	2		
Alexander, Levine	3		2		
Alexander, Samuel	2		2		
Bigham (Widow)	3		2		
Bays, James	3	2	3		
Benham, Daniel	1	3	4		1
Brown, James	2	1	1		
Brown, William	1	2	6		
Barnett, John	1	1	3		
Baxter, James	1		4		1
Cuningham, William	1	2	3		
Cuningham, Nathaniel	1	1	2		1
Cook, Joseph	1		5		2
Dermond, James	1	2	3		
Esselman, James	1	2	2		
Flemmekan, David	1	8	3		
Graham, William	1		2		
Gaston, Thomas	1	2			
Hays, Robert	2	1	4		
Kirkpatrick, John	3		3		3
Knox, David					1
Erwin, Christor	1		6		
McCulloch, John	5	2	4		3
Menson, William	1		3		
Mulwee, John	2	2	6		
Merchant, William	1	2	7		
Osborn, Capt James	1	4	6		
Osborn, John	2	2	2		
Phillips, Robert	1	1	2		3
Page, Nicholas				1	
Rogers, John	1	3	2		
Reed (Widow)	2	2	5		
Sturgeon, John	2	2	2		
Smith, John	1	1	3		
King, John	2	3	4		
Sharpe, Edward, Senr	1		2		
Swann, John	4		2		1
Sharpe, James	2	2	5		
Sharpe, Edward, Junr	1		2		
Walker, Robert	1	1	2		
Weeks, Phillip	2		3		
Wilson, William, Esqr	2	2	3		1
Wilson, Robert	1	2	2		
Wilson, John	1	2	2		
Washingtown, John				1	
Wetherspoon, William	1	1	1		
Walker, John	1	1	1		
Yandell, James	1	3	4		
Yandel, William	4	4	7		
Yandel, Andrew	1	4	3		
Jinkins, John	3	2	3		
Smith, James	1	3	3		
Robison (Widow)		3	4		
Lindsey, Walter			3		
Wilson (Widow)	1		2		4
Alexander, Eli	1	2	3		1
Wallace, George	1		2		
Wallace, Mathew	1	2	2		
Wallace, William	1	2	3		
Miller (Widow)	1		1		

SALISBURY DISTRICT, MONTGOMERY COUNTY.

NAME OF HEAD OF FAMILY	Free white males of 16 years and upward, including heads of families.	Free white males under 16 years.	Free white females, including heads of families.	All other free persons.	Slaves.
Earles, William	4	3	5		1
Frazier, William	3	1	2		
Frazier, Henry	1				
Frazier, William	2	3	1		
Fowler, David	1		1		
Faircloth, Mary			5		4
Frazier, John	1	2	3		
Frazier, Alexander	2	4	3		
Fry, James	2		7		
Fridle, Gasper	1	1	3		
Fry, Thomas	1		3		
Freeman, Hartwell	2	3	5		1
Fisher, Littleton	1	1	2		
Fox, Lawrance	1	2	3		
Fox, Gates	1		1		
Fincher, Benjamin	1	2	3		
Fletcher, James	2	3	3		2
Fisher, George	1		1		1
Forrist, Abraham	3	1	5		18
Forrist, Nathan	1	1	1		1
Gowers, Thomas	1	1	5		
Gowers, Mathew	1	2	2		
Gibson, James	1		4		
Gibson, William	2	1	2		
Grifith, Isham	1				
Gross, Solomon	2		1		
Garratt, Presley	1		2		
Green, Richard	2	2	5		
Gibbs, William	1				
Gillam, Jordan	1	3	2		
Gorden, Alexander	1		5		
Garratt, William	1				
Golahorn, Asa	1	1	2		
Gain, Thomas	1		5		
Green, Richard	3	3	3		
Gray, James	3	2	1		1
Gilbart, John	2	1	3		
Gray, David	1	2	1		
Gusley, James	2	3	3		
Gilbart, Jesse	1	3	3		
Gilbart, John	1				
Gilbart, Nathan	1				
Green, Nathum	1		1		
Gurly, James	1	1	1		
Harris, Joshua	2	2	7		8
Hogan, Zakeriah	2	2	7		
Horn, Nathan	1	2	3		4
Harriss, Arthur	1	1	3		4
Haygood, Bird	1	5	4		
Haygood, Griffin	1	2	4		
Hill, John	2	2	2		
Harriss, John	2	1	3		
Henry, Benjamin	2	2	5		
Hix, Littleberry	1	2	3		
Haygood, Elizabeth	1		1		
Hix, Daniel	2		2		
Hix, Robert	1	1	1		
Hix, William	1		1		
Hays, Saley		1	2		
Heldness, Reuban	1	2	5		
Haltom, Joseph	1				
Heltom, Spencer	1				
Hurt, Jesse	1	1	2		
Harrison, Andrew	1				
Howard, John	1	1	2		
Harril, Mathew	1	2	3		3
Haltom, William	1	1	3		2
Humble, Jacob	2	3	3		1
Hurt, Joseph	2		3		
Humble, John	1		3		
Hardin, John	1	2	3		
Humble, Henry	1	1	1		5
Hix, John	1	1	2		
Hix, Demcy	1	2	2		
Hearn, Thomas	1	1	1		1
Harris, Jesse	3		5		6
Hearn, Ebenazer	1	1	4		
Harris, John	2	6	4		4
Hendcock, Samuel	2	4	3		9
Hearn, Pernal	2	3	5		
Harris, Arthur	1	4	4		9
Harris, Brantly	1	3	3		
Harris, Atheldred	1	3	4		2
Hearn, Stephen	1	3	4		
Hall, William	1	3	7		
Harris, West, Junr	2	4	4		7
Harris, West, Senr	2		3		13
Harris, Turner	1	3	5		1
Hurley, Joshua	1	1	3		
Harris, James	1	2	3		2
Handcock, Martin	2		5		2
Hurley, Joseph	1	2	2		
Harris, John, Senr	2	2	3		
Hall, Joseph	1	4	1		1
Hopkins, Benjamin	1	3	5		
Hambleton, Walter	1	1	2		2
Harris, Wilby	1	3	2		
Hopkins, Richard	1	2	1		
Hall, Anthony	1				
Hopkins, John	2	3	5		
Huckoby, Thomas	1	4	4		
Harris, Rowland	1	3	1		3
Hearn, James	1	5	2		
Hamblett, John	1		2		
Hatchcock, Banjimen	1	2	5		
Howal, James	1		8		
Hamblett, Peter	1	1	4		
Horton, William	1	3	5		
Hosty, James	2	2	4		
Holland, Anthony	2		3		
Hearn, Fenlary		1	3		
Handcossle, William	1		4		
Hopkins, Alexander	1				
Jordan, John	1	1	4		
Jordan, Francis	3	1	5		6
Jones, Jesse	2		2		3
Jinnings, John	1		2		
Jordan, John	1				
Jackson, Henry	1	4	6		
Jinkins, Thomas	1	2	5		
Steel, Robert J	2	1	8		1
Jordan, William	3	3	3		
Jordan, Ruban	1		4		
Jones, Thomas	1	2	2		
Jones, Charles	1	4	3		5
Johnston, William	3	3	5		16
Irby, James	1	4	3		
Johnston, Thomas	2	1	7		9
Irby, William	1	2	4		
Johnston, James	1		1		
Johnston, James, Junr	1		1		
Johnston, William	1	2	2		
Jordan, John	1				
Kimbrough, John	1	4	2		5
Kelly, Thomas	1				
Kelly, Samuel	2	2	5		1
Keller, George	2	2	4		
Keller, Jacob	1	2	2		
Keller, Thomas	1	1	1		
Key, Eligah	1		2		
Kirk, George	1	2	2		9
Kirk, Thomas	1	1	3		1
Kindal, William	3	3	1		5
Kirk, John	1	3	1		1
Kindal, Samuel	1	2	1		
Lucas, Thomas	1	4	5		
Leverett, Robert	1	2	2		
Leverett, Richard	1	2	4		1
Leverett, William	1		4		
Lethercut, William	1	2	5		
Lesrand, William	2	1	1		14
Langin, William	1	2	2		
Lilly, Elizabeth	1	1	1		6

SALISBURY DISTRICT, MONTGOMERY COUNTY—Continued.

NAME OF HEAD OF FAMILY.	Free white males of 16 years and upward, including heads of families.	Free white males under 16 years.	Free white females, including heads of families.	All other free persons.	Slaves.
Lightfoot, John	1	4	4		1
Lilly, Edmond	1				5
Loe, James	1		3		
Lunsford, Auguston	1	1	1		
Lunsford, James	1	3	4		
Landron, Timothy	2		1		
Lomsey, Thomas	1	1	4		
Loftin, William	2	3	5		10
Leathers, James	2	2	4		
Loftin, Moses	2	1	7		6
Lynch, Phillip	1		2		
Lilly, John	1	5	2		6
Lee, John	1	3	5		
Lilly, Edmond	1	1	1		28
Aldred, Mary		2	1		
Allen, Joseph	3		2		
Armstrong, Isaac	3	2	5		2
Andress, John, Junr	1	2	6		
Andress, John, Senr	1	2	1		
Andress, David	1	2	1		
Allen, Reuban	1	1	2		
Allen, John	1		4		
Ashford, William	2	3	4		1
Archen, George	2	4	4		
Atkins, James	2	4	7		4
Arnold, Peter	1	1	1		
Atkins, John	1	3	5		4
Almond, Richard	1	4	4		
Austin, Bryant	1	1	3		
Aldman, Nathan	1		1		
Aldman, Thomas	1	1	2		
Aldman, Edmond	1		5		
Avitt, Elijah	1				
Allen, John	3	3	1		1
Allen, William	1	3	3		
Atkins, Hezekiah	1				
Arldurth, Reuban	1	1	5		
Bruton, William	1	2	2		
Baton, Peter	1		2		
Bruton, George	1	1	4		
Blake, Randle	1		4		
Beard, Alexander	4	6	1		10
Blake, Thomas	1	5	2		1
Boyd, John	2	2	2		
Barlow, William	1	1	1		
Bolin, John	1	4	1		
Bolin, Jessee	1		2		
Bowlin, John	2		1		5
Bray, Peter	1	2	5		
Butler, John	1	3	2		
Butler, Joshua	1	1	5		1
Butler, Elias	1	3	2		1
Butler, Thomas	1	2	3		
Benton, Job	1	2	4		
Bowling, William					
Ballard, John	2	2	6		
Belinsly, Sias	2	6	4		
Berry, Enoch	1		1		1
Avit, James	1	3	1		
Buckler, John	1		1		
Barlow, William	1	1	1		
Bennett, Mark	1	2	1		
Bennett, Solomon	1	1	5		
Barman, John	1	1	4		
Bell, Joseph	1	1	4		
Bean, Walter	1	1	3		
Bond, Elisabeth	3	1	5		4
Bennett, Drury	1	2	2		
Benton, Joseph	1	3	3		
Bell, Richard	1		2		1
Bell, David	1		2		
Bell, John	1	3	3		
Bell, Benjamin	1	2	1		1
Barnet, William	1				
Bolland, Walter	1		2		
Boyd, Samuel	3	2	3		
Boycom, Nicholas	1	1	3		
Burns, Samson	1				
Bankston, Andrew	1	3	3		1
Brooks, John	3	2	4		8
Brookes, William	3	2	4		6
Burlison, David	2	2	5		
Burrows, Solomon	1	3	3		
Burnett, Elijah	1				
Burlison, Isaac	1	2	3		
Brown, Isaac	2	6	4		
Barnet, Elijah	3		4		
Barnet, John	1				
Patton, Daniel	1	2	7		
Allen, Isaac	4	4	3		
Chiles, Thomas, Jur	1		3		11
Chambers, Edward	3		4		2
Cox, Robert	2	4	2		
Chisom, Maliom	4	1	2		
Chambers, Edward	1	2	4		
Chambers, John	1				
Carpenter, Jonethen	1	1	2		

NAME OF HEAD OF FAMILY.	Free white males of 16 years and upward, including heads of families.	Free white males under 16 years.	Free white females, including heads of families.	All other free persons.	Slaves.
Cotton, Thomas	1	2	1		1
Cotton, James	1		1		1
Chiles, Thomas, Senr	2		1		10
Choppel, Christopher	2	3	5		2
Cathole, Josiah	1		3		1
Clark, George	4		7		
Carpenter, Soloman	1				
Cockran, Abraham	1	1	2		2
Downs, Richard	1	3	4		
Delamp, Joseph	1	1	3		
Deaton, Joseph	1	3	3		
Connel, Francis	1	1	3		
Cannon, Laurana		2	4		
Cammel, John		3	1		
Cockran, Jacob	1	5	3		
Carpenter, Temple	1		2		
Camel, John	1	3	2		
Clark, Evan	3		2		4
Carpenter, Owen	2	2	1		
Chance, Daniel	1	1	2		
Chisom, Alexander	1		2		
Cheek, Randle	1	3	2		
Caudle, David	1	2	2		
Crosswell, Nimrod	1	1	4		
Christian, Nicholas	3	2	4		2
Christian, John	1		1		2
Couples, Ama	1		2		7
Crump, John	1	6	3		5
Clemmons, Thomson	1	5	4		
Clifton, William	1	2	3		5
Coltharp, Henry	1		4		2
Crump, James	1	1	6		12
Clifton, Pricilla		4	5		1
Coggin, Simon	1	2	1		
Curtis, Moses	1	4			
Curtis, Russell	1		4		
Cranford, Lenord	1	6	6		
Case, James	1	4	4		1
Carnes, Joseph	1	4	1		
Carrill, William	1	4	2		
Carrill, Jane			3		
Carnes, Edward	2	1	2		
Cranford, William	1	2	2		
Cato, Daniel	1	4	2		4
Carter, Ephraim	1	1	4		
Carter, Charles	1				
Carter, Samuel	2	1	9		
Carter, Joshua	2	2	4		3
Cox, William	2	3	1		
Cumins, Banjemin	2	2	4		
Calloway, Isaac	1	4	5		
Carter, Samuel	1	1	2		
Cox, James	1		2		
Cooper, Isaac	1	2	3		
Carpenter, Jonathan	3	2	5		
Cretentor, William	1	1	2		
Cooper, John	1	1	3		
Coley, George	1	1	5		
Cose, Valentine	1	3	4		
Coley, William	1	1	1		
Cooper, James	1	1	2		
Couples, William	1	2	2		4
Cheek, Siles	1				
Carter, Jacob	3	3	3		
Codee, Richard	1		1		
Cooper, John	3	2	3		
Coley, Joyce	2		2		
Cato, Judith	1		2		
Codee, Richard	1		1		
Casle, George	1	3	3		
Clanton, Reuben	1				
Dafford, Rhody		1	3		
Deberry, Henry	1	4	5		2
Dumas, David, Senr	1	5	2		15
Dumas, David, Junr	1		1		3
Davison, Josiah	1	2	5		
Davis, Robert	1	4	4		1
Dennis, Aandrew	1	1	6		
Davis, John	1	4	4		
Dennis, Nathaniel	1	6	4		
Dunn, Barnaba	1		4		13
Davis, John	1	5	4		
Davison, George	3	3	4		14
Durham, Thomas	1	4	3		2
Davis, Gabriel	1	4	4		
Daniel, Barton	1	1	5		
Davis, Isaac	1		2		
Dotson, Hightower	1	1	8		
Davis, Nathaniel	1		4		
Duke, James	1				
Denson, Edmond	2	2	4		
Durgin, William	1	1	1		3
Davis, Abraham	1	2	2		
Edins, William	1		5		
Edwards, Nathaniel	2	5	1		1
Lee, James	1				
Lee, William	2	1	3		

NAME OF HEAD OF FAMILY.	Free white males of 16 years and upward, including heads of families.	Free white males under 16 years.	Free white females, including heads of families.	All other free persons.	Slaves.
Lathran, William	1	1	4		
Lee, Sarah		2	6		1
Lesby, Christopher	1	1	3		
Lewis, Charles	1	2	1		
McClain, Duncan	1	1	1		2
Munroe, Cathrine	1		2		2
Martain, John	1	4	3		
Macafee, Malcom	1		4		
Mask, William	3	2	3		10
Mathews, Daniel	1	5	1		
Mecauly, John	2	4	5		
Mecoskell, John	1	4	1		
McCloud, Duncan	1		3		
Mecoskill, John	3		3		
McClannon, Alexander	1	1	3		1
McCloud, Norman	3	1	4		
Megill, Hactor	1	3	2		
McCoskill, Mary	1	1	5		
McClannon, Edward	1	2	3		
McCloud, Elizabeth	1	2	3		
Mein, Donold	1	5	2		
McCinnan, Christopher	1	2	1		
Meckintush, Swain	1	3	4		
Murkinson, Donold	3		4		
Morgan, Thomas	1	4	4		1
Menosko, Jeremiah	1	3	5	1	
McCaskill, Hurdly	1				
McClandon, Isbal		2	4		
McDuffe, Donold	1	4	2		
McDonnold, Allen	1		3		
Munn, James	4	2	4		
Morton, William F	1		2		
Mathews, Martha	1		4		2
McCloud, Norman	1	1	4		
Moore, Micajah	2	4	3		
McCloud, Mary		1	3		
Mumford, Henry	2	1	1		4
McCloud, Christian	2	2	3		
McCallum, Edward	2	3	4		
McCallum, John	1	1	2		
Monroe, Daniel	2	1	1		4
McKinnon, Alexander	1	3	1		
Morris, Mary	1	2	3		
Minard, Thomas	2		3		
Morris, Thomas	1	1	4		
More, John	1	1	5		
McDonold, James	3	1	1		10
More, Jesse	2	2	7		
More, Thomas	3	3	3		
McClay, Colin	1	5	3		1
Mason, Thomas	1	3	4		2
Megginson, Thomas	1	3	4		6
McClendon, Jesse	2	5	3		8
Morris, John	2		6		
Morris, Haton	2	2	4		
More, Nathan	2	1	2		
Morris, Thomas	1	2	3		
More, Thomas	1		3		
McKeshon, Nehemiah	2	4	3		5
Morris, Haton, Senr	1		4		
More, James	1	1	2		
McCray, Alexander	2		1		
More, Morris	1		1		
Mercer, Christopher	2	2	2		
Morton, George	2	3	3		
Mabry, Phillip	1		1		
More, William	1	5	4		1
McClemore, John	1	3	3		
Morgan, Garrat	1	3	1		4
Morgan, William	1	1	4		1
Monday, Mary	2		3		
Monday, William	1		3		
McClemore, Stamley	1	3	3		
Morris, William	1	1	2		
Morris, William, Senr	1	1	1		
Morris, John	1	1	1		
Morris, John, Senr	2	4	3		
Morris, John, Junr	3	1	4		
Miller, Conrodhush	1				
Mabry, Sarah	1	3	4		1
McClisten, Daniel	1	2	3		
Moss, Robert	1	5	6		9
Merienan, Nicholas	1		3		
Megrigler, William	3	2	3		4
Morris, John	1				
Megrigler, Bartlett	1	1	2		
Meniman, Charles	2		3		
Miller, John	1	1	3		
Megche, Charles	1	1	3		
Megche, William	1	1	3		
McClendon, Thomas	1	3	2		
Mothary, William	1	3	2		
Mariman, Abraham	2	1	1		
Mariman, Isham	1	1	1		
Motley, Thomas	1	3	1		
Morgan, Jonathan	1	1	2		
Miller, William	2	1	5		

SALISBURY DISTRICT, MONTGOMERY COUNTY—Continued.

NAME OF HEAD OF FAMILY.	Free white males of 16 years and upward, including heads of families.	Free white males under 16 years.	Free white females, including heads of families.	All other free persons.	Slaves.
McKentire, William	1		1		
Mainer, John	1	2	1		
Mathews, Anthony	3	5	6		
McKentire, William, Ser	1		1		
Meriman, Stephen	1	1	2		
Morgan, William	1	1	7		
Chub, John				1	
Nickols, Edmond	1	3	3		
Nickols, Joseph	1	2	3		
Nickols, Edmond, Senr	1		2		
Nickols, William	1	3	1		
Nickols, John	2	2	4		
Nesbit, Jane		2	2		22
Noble, David	1	5	3		
Noble, Samson	1		3		
Noble, William	2	1			
Noble, Mary			6		
Naran, Sarah	1	2	1		7
Ozier, William	3		2		
Orie, Samuel	1		1		
Obrian, James	2	3	5		
Onsby, Walter	1	4	4		
Pemberton, Stith	1	1	4		3
Persons, John	1	2	4	1	
Persons, Joseph	1	1	2	1	
Persons, Samuel	2		5		2
Pemberton, Richard	1			5	
Poore, David	4	4	2		5
Pierce, Sion	2	1	3		
Pritchard, Cary	2	4	3		4
Pitcock, Stephen	1				
Pritchard, Thomas	2		2		
Pierce, Gadwell	1	6	2		
Pennington, Neddy	1				
Pennington, Nelson	1				
Parker, Howel	1	3	4		3
Pennington, David	3	3	8		9
Palmore, John	3	3	4		
Pennington, Kinchin	1		4		
Pistole, Charles	1				
Pool, Sanders	1	2	1		
Pool, Alexander	2	4	3		
Philips, James	3	2	3		
Pistole, Charles	2	1	3		2
Pilcher, Robert	1	2	2		
Polland, Thomas	1	3	3		
Poplin, John	1	3	6		
Philips, William	1	3	3		
Pierce, Philip	1	1	2		
Poplin, Richard	1		1		
Queen, Henson	2	2	3		1
Lusk, William	3	3	5		10
Raynolds, Anderson	2		2		
Robertson, Cornelius	3	1	3		13
Robertson, Charles	1			3	
Robertson, John	1	4	4		1
Randled, John	2		4		8
Right, Edward	1	3	3		
Randle, Johnson	1	4	1		
Randle, Benajah	1	1	5		
Raiford, Mathew	1	3	4		1
Raiford, James	1		2		2
Russell, Mathew				3	
Randle, Colby		3	5		2
Raynolds, James	2	4	3		
Redwine, Michael	1		3		
Russel, John	1	4	2		
Redwine, Jacob	1	2	7		
Russel, William	1	3	4		
Russel, Tames	1	3	1		
Russel, Thomas	1		1		1
Reaves, Josias	1		1		
Reaves, Samuel	1	3	4		
Russel, Lenard	1		2		
Redwine, Fredrick	1	1	1		
Reaves, William	1		1		
Rowland, Thomas	1	3	2		
Robins, John	2	1	5		2
Rowland, Hosea	1	2	3		
Rumage, George	1		1		
Rumage, George	1	5	4		
Rice, William	1	5	4		
Randle, James	2	3	2		16
Randle, Edmond	1	3	5		
Randle, John	2	2	7		8
Rogers, James	2	1	4		
Rogers, Fredrick	1				

NAME OF HEAD OF FAMILY.	Free white males of 16 years and upward, including heads of families.	Free white males under 16 years.	Free white females, including heads of families.	All other free persons.	Slaves.
Ransby, Isaac	2	2.	4		
Rowland, Agustine	2		4		
Roberson, Tyry	1	3	5		1
Randle, Peter	2	3	4		14
Randle, Paton	1		3		4
Roland, Sherwood	1	4	6		
Loland, Isaac	1	3	1		
Roland, Ausburn	1				
Rusby, Unslis		1	2		
Martin, John	1		1		
Sanders, Joshua	1	4	1		
Spencer, William	2	2	5		6
Spencer, Johnson	1		1		
Simons, John	1	5	1		
Smith, Alexander	1	1	2		
Simons, Benjemin	1		1		
Smith, John	1	1	1		
Smith, Joseph	1	2	4		
Swon, John	2	3	6		1
Sumner, Benjemin	1	1	5		3
Smith, John	1		3		
Story, James	2	2	2		
Singleton, Edmund	1	3	2		
Singleton, Robert	2	1	2		
Stringfallow, William	2	1	2		
Singleton, Robert	2	3	3		
Simmons, Elizabeth			2		2
Simmons, Jesse	1		1		
Sawel, John	1	2	3		
Smith, Nathan	2	3	6		
Sawel, John, Senr	1	1	2		
Smith, Isham	1	2	6		
Suggs, Jasse	1	1	2		
Sanders, Aaron	1		2		
Stogner, George	1	2	2		
Smith, John	1		2		
Scarber, John	2	2	3		7
Stephens, Henry	1	1	4		
Stephens, James	1	5	4		
Suggs, Harbert	2		4		
Stephens, John	2	2	1		
Spirey, Charles	1	1	4		1
Stephens, Francis	1	1	3		
Stephens, Robert	1		3		
Stavy, Joseph	2	2	4		
Smith, James	1	2	2		1
Scarber, James	1	4	2		
Shephard, John	1	3	3		
Suggs, Thomas	1	3	2		
Stagner, John	1	2	1		
Stagner, Benjamin	1	4	3		
Sanders, James	3	2	2		
Sanders, Joshua	1	3	4		
Sanders, Jeffrey	1		4		
Steed, Moses	2	3	5		5
Sanders, Jacob	1	4	3		
Stewart, William	1		4		
Sanders, James	1	4	2		
Stewart, John	1	1	4		
Suggs, John	2	3	3		
Suggs, George	2	1	2		
Seratt, Joseph	1	1	1		
Seratt, Joseph, Senr	1	1	1		
Sworngance, John	1	4	4		
Suggs, John Henry	2	2	3		
Suggs, Thomas	2		2		
Stokes, Robert	3	4	6		3
Simpson, Thomas	2	1	2		
Shankle, Jacob	1	3	2		
Smith, Richard	1				
Shankle, George	1		4		4
Shankle, John	1	3	4		
Smith, John	2	1	6		11
Styles, William	1		4		
Suggs, William	1				
Smith, Joseph	1	3	3		
Smith John	1		5		8
Stokes, Young	2	3	1		
Self, Spencer	1	5	3		
Self, Francis	1		6		
Stokes, William	1	1	4		
Self, Isaac	1	1	2		
Smith, Asa	1	1	2		
Shankle, Valentine	1	1	1		
Smith, Josep	1		5		
Shinpock, Lawrance	1	1	2		

NAME OF HEAD OF FAMILY.	Free white males of 16 years and upward, including heads of families.	Free white males under 16 years.	Free white females, including heads of families.	All other free persons.	Slaves.
Smith, Sherwood	1	1	2		
Self, Presley	1	2	3		
Still, Banjamin	1	1	2		
Turner, James	2	2	2		25
Travers, Charles	3	2	1		3
Touchstone, Stephen	2	1	2		7
Trent, William	1		3		
Thomas, John	3	7	5		1
Touchstone, Caleb	2	2	5		1
Thorn, Robert	3	2	5		
Turner, Susanah		1	2		
Taylor, George	1	1	2		
Turner, Brehabuck		1	2		4
Tedder, Benjamin	1	1	1		1
Tilman, Richard	1	2	4		3
Thomson, John	1	2	2		
Thompson, Elisha	1	4	4		
Tucker, George	1	2	7		
Taylor, John	1	1	3		
Taylor, Cannon	1	1	3		1
Thompson, Walter	2	1	3		
Thompson, John	1	3	2		
Tredwell, Stephen	3	3	5		
Tankisby, John	1		4		
Tindle, James	3	4	5		24
Truct, Parnel	1	2	3		
Tindle, Richard	1		2		3
Telby, Thornton	1		1		
Telby, Henry	1	3	5		
Taylor, Edmond	1	6	2		
Taylor, Hudson	1	1	5		3
Taylor, William	1	2	5		
Turner, James	3	1	8		
Turner, Thomas	1	1	2		
Thomison, Richard	2	2	4		
Tresby, David	1	2	1		
Tresby, Sarah		1	6		
Taylor, Robert	1	2	1		
Tredwell, Samuel	1		2		
Usseroy, Wilcon	1	1	6		
Usseroy, Thomas	1	5	7		4
Usseroy, Peter	1	2	2		
Usseroy, John	1	1	3		
Usseroy, Joshua	1	2	3		
Usseroy, David	1	1	4		
Usseroy, Elijah	1		3		
Usseroy, John	1		7		
Upenurch, Thomas	1	3	5		
Vickry, Joseph	1	2	4		
Vanhooser, Valentine	3	3	1		
Vanhooser, John	1		1		
Vandike, Thomas	1	1	6		
Walice, Jesse	1		3		
Ward, Thomas, Senr	1	2	2		
Williams, Thomas	2	1	11		
Williams, Solomon	1	1	10		
Wilson, Martha	1		2		5
Williams, Stephen	1	2	3		
Williams, Isham	3	2	4		2
Williams, James	2	2	4		1
Williams, Roger	2	3	3		
Williams, Seth	3	5	1		3
Wilson, Joseph	1		2		
Williams, Samuel	4	4	4		
Ware, Thomas	1	2	6		4
Watts, Peter	1	2	3		
Williams, Amos	1	2	2		
Williams, Benjamin	1	4	2		
Wolby, William	1		2		19
Williams, William	1		2		12
Brooks, Jacob West	1	3	4		
Wester, Axem	1	2	6		
Wallis, William	1				
Ward, Philip	1	3	4		
Wall, John	1	6	3		
Weaver, Michael	1	5	2		
Wardrupt, Edward	2	3	4		
Whitby, George	2	4	3		
Whitby, Exedus	2	2	4		
Wimberly, Moses	1	1	3		
Whitby, George	1	2	5		
Weaver, William	1	3	3		2
Yeoman, Stokes	1	2	1		
Young, James	2	3	2		
Yarborough, John	2		4		

SALISBURY DISTRICT, ROCKINGHAM COUNTY.

NAME OF HEAD OF FAMILY.	Free white males of 16 years and upward, including heads of families.	Free white males under 16 years.	Free white females, including heads of families.	All other free persons.	Slaves.
Stublefield, Richard	6		4		5
Bethel, Samuel	1	3	4		
Lewis, Peter	1	3	2		
Mullin, Thomas	3		2		3
Mullin, William	1		1		

NAME OF HEAD OF FAMILY.	Free white males of 16 years and upward, including heads of families.	Free white males under 16 years.	Free white females, including heads of families.	All other free persons.	Slaves.
Adair, Stephen	2	2	3		
McClain, Joseph	1	3	2		
Hainey, Reuben	1		1		
Samuel, Andrew	1	2	3		
Dixon, Berry	2	3	1		

NAME OF HEAD OF FAMILY.	Free white males of 16 years and upward, including heads of families.	Free white males under 16 years.	Free white females, including heads of families.	All other free persons.	Slaves.
Harris, Robert	1	3	3		
Bentin, David	1	2	3		
Humphris, John	1		2		1
Johnston, Henry	1	3	5		
Owen, Joseph	1	1	1		

SALISBURY DISTRICT, ROCKINGHAM COUNTY—Continued.

NAME OF HEAD OF FAMILY.	Free white males of 16 years and upward, including heads of families.	Free white males under 16 years.	Free white females, including heads of families.	All other free persons.	Slaves.
Burton, John	1	1	1		2
Caldwell, William	1	6	1		2
Hainey, Spencer	1		2		
McClain, Thomas	1		1		
Watt, Samuel	3	5	3		8
McCallum, Jas	1	3	8		8
Horseford, John	1	4	4		
Jones, Ezekiel	1	2	4		
Dean, James	2	2	1		8
Loftis, William	1	3	4		
Dean, Elisha	1	2	2		1
Dean, Charles	1	1	2		
Dean, Charles, Jur	2		2		
McCallister, William	1	3	2		
Carrot, Henry	2	4	4		
Watt, John	1	1	2		
Mills, Mathew	2	5	4		13
Chandlor, John	1	3	4		
Marr, Richard	2	3	4		23
Challis, John	2	2	2		7
Thrasher, Pleasant	1	1	3		
Hoverton, Obediah	1		1		
Knight, John	1	1	2		
Russil, William	1	2	3		
Smith, Drewry	1	1	2		
Pipkin, Isaac	1				
Davis, John	2		2		
Newcomb, Joseph	1	3	2		
McCubbin, Jas	1	2	1		
McCubbin, John	1	1	4		
Smith, John, Jur	1		4		
Aldedair, Alexander	1		4		
Smith, Samuel	1	3	2		1
Wright, John	1	2	3		
Harris, William	1	4	1		
Smith, John	2		2		4
Wright, Francis	1	4	3		
Cantril, Aron	1	1	5		
Porter, Lawrence	1	2	5		
Sparks, Thomas	1		2		
McCubbin, Nicholas	1	6	3		4
Dill, John	4	3	2		
Allen, Thomas	1	3	3		
Hopkins, Jonathan	1	2	3		
Bishop, Joseph	1		4		
Moore, William	1		2		
Ratchford, Luke	1		2		
Williams, Nathaniel	3	1	6		13
Reagon, John	1		2		4
Hornbuckle, William	1	3	6		1
Barnet, David	1	1	2		
Lowe, Thomas	2	1	4		2
Ewes, William	1	1	4		
Lowe, Nancy			3		1
Martin, Andrew		2	2		
Todd, William	2	4	3		2
Miller, William	1	2	3		
Lowe, John	1	2	7		6
Procter, William	1	1	3		
Patrick, Hugh	1	1	4		
Patrick, Mary	3		4		2
Gray, Thomas	1		1		
Appleton, Jas	2	2	3		2
Patrick, Jas	1	1	2		1
Moore, Samuel	1		2		
Hanby, David	1	3	2		12
Nelson, Levina	1	2	6		6
Johnston, Jos Pair	1	4	5		
Brown, Samuel	1	1	3		
Russel, William	1		5		
Vaughan, David	1		2		4
Cockran, Wm	2		1		1
Hubbard, William					
Hubbard, William	1	3	4		
Martin, Andw	1	2	2		
Hall, Andrew	1	2	5		
Matear, Jas	2				
Roberson, Andrew	2	2		3	
Wardlow, John	2		3		
Blockus, John	2		3		
Stratton, William	1				
Hopper, Thomas	1	2	2		
Thomas, Lewis	1	3	4		
Key, Thomas	4	1	6		4
Martin, John	1	2	3		
Mitchel, Levin	2	1	3		
Moore, Benjamin	1	5	2		2
Jones, William	1	3	3		
Curry, John	1	1	2		
Seales, David	1		2		
Denny, Joseph	2		2		
Denny, Walter	1		1		
Harris, Robert	1	3	3		
Mount, Thomas	1	1	1		
Vincent, Moses	2	2	3		6
Burton, Robert	1		3		
Morgan, Orson	1	2	2		

NAME OF HEAD OF FAMILY.	Free white males of 16 years and upward, including heads of families.	Free white males under 16 years.	Free white females, including heads of families.	All other free persons.	Slaves.
Norman, Courtney	1	1	9		
Curry, Ezekiel	1		1		
Roberts, Elizabeth		1	7		3
Lefew, Stephen	2		6		
Lefew, Mary		3	2		
Lord, James	1	3	4		
Burrll, John	1	1	4		
McBride, Francis	2	2	4		
McBride, Isaiah	1	3	2		
Moore, John	1	6	3		
Dobbins, James	3	1	4		
Lanier, Sampson	1	2	4		
Paris, Samuel	3	2	2		4
King, Thomas	2	4	4		
Frost, James	1	6	3		
Daily, Patrick	1	1	3		
Jones, Benjamin	1	4	2		
Ditto for Iron Works	2				35
Hayes, James	1		3		3
Purtle, John	3	4	1		
Hunter, John	2		6		9
Peeples, Burwell	1	2	3		3
Mobley, William	2	2	6		
Elliott, William	2	1	2		
Lyrus, Jas, Sen	1	2	5		
Walker, David	1	1	4		4
Sanders, Jas, Jur	2		1		
French, Mason					
Fits, Conny		2	5		
Martin, Spencer	1		3		
Overton, Moses	1	4	1		
Brown, Margaret	3	1	1		
Allen, John	1	4	1		
Grogan, Henry	2	3	6		
Terry, Peter	2	1	7		7
Herring, Saml	1	1	5		1
Hendricks, Abraham	1	1	5		
Williams, Robt	1		2		7
Stublefield, Richd	6		2		2
Amberson, Mathew	3		6		
Conner, John	1		2		
Conner, Thomas	1		2		
Wall, Peter	1	1	2		
Wall, David, Sen	1	1	2		1
Grady, Reuben	1	3	2		
King, Wiat	1		1		
Carter, Thomas	1	2	8		
Guttery, Thos	2	5	4		1
Hinton, Jesse	1		2		
Larkin, Thos	1	1	3		
Bernard, Thos	1	4	4		
Chance, Thomas	1	2	1		
Curry, John, Senr	3		2		
Jones, William, Senr	2	1	5		
Walker, William, Jur	1		2		
Loftis, William, Sen	1	3	2		
Taylor, Hartford	1		2		
Akins, John	2	1	3		
Thomas, George	1		1		
Prewit, Joshua	1	1	3		
North, Thomas	1		3		
Cornelious, George	1		3		
Bellingsly, Henry	2	2	3		
Wall, Rebecca	3	1	1		
Lord, Aaron, Senr	1	1	3		
Dollerhide, Aquilla	1	1	3		
Jones, William (R. S.)	2	2	4		
Conn, John	1	2	3		
Wallace, William	1	2	3		
Nickles, Jas, Senr	3	5	2		1
Jones, John	1		3		
Fleming, Robert	1	5	2		
Bethel, Duncan	1		1		
Dimond, Stewart	1	1	3		
Philips, Joseph	1		3		
Carman, Hezekiah	2		4		
Spencer, Benjamin	1	4	4		2
Spencer, Thomas	1		3		1
Hodge, Francis	1	2	2		
Donaky, Jas	3		4		
Garner, Joseph	1	2	2		2
Linder, John	1	4	5		3
Mabry, Cornelius	2	1	2		
Sealy, John	2	3	3		
Glenn, John	1	2	2		4
Todd, William, Senr	3	4	4		3
Walker, Elmore	1	2	3		
Walker, Jesse	1	2	1		
Scurry, Susannah	1		6		
Lewis, Shadrack	1	3	4		
Deatherege, Elizabeth	2		2		2
Joyce, John	2	1	2		
Morton, Jehu	2	2	6		1
Nelson, John	1		4		
Nelson, Samuel	1	2	1		
Main, Henry	1	1	4		

NAME OF HEAD OF FAMILY.	Free white males of 16 years and upward, including heads of families.	Free white males under 16 years.	Free white females, including heads of families.	All other free persons.	Slaves.
Walker, John	1	1	4		
Covington, Mary		1	3		
Moceat, Matthias	1	3	5		
Brown, John	1	2	4		
Brown, Hubbard	1		1		
Williams, David	1	4	5		
Shelton, John	1	2	3		
Knight, Robert	1	2	3		
Stone, Burgis	1	2	2		
Short, Moses, Senr	3	1	2		1
Warner, John	1	2	5		
Simpson, Thomas	1	2	4		
McCarty, Timothy	1	1	3		
Campbell, Rebecca	1	1	5		
Massy, Machner	1	1	3		
Murphy, Archibald	1	2	3		
Mack, John	2	4	3		
Mack, James	1	2	2		
Wilson, Aquilla	3	3	2		5
Wilson, James	2	2	6		2
Wilson, Thomas	2		4		4
Murphy, Miles	4	5	7		
Murphy, William	1		3		
Fitzgerald, James	1	4	5		2
Brim, Richins	1	2	1		
Cantril, Charles	1	2	1		
Brim, Keziah		3	3		
Compton, Ebenezer	1		1		
Nighton, William	1	3	2		
Smith, William	1	3	4		
Challis, Martha	1		3		10
Ward, William	2	1	5		
Bents, Abraham	2	3	3		
Garrison, Aron	1	1	2		
Huckman, William	1	2	6		
Adcock, Edward	1	3	4		
Wilson, Andrew	1	1	5		2
Humphries, John	2		2		
Wilson, William	1	5	2		1
Wilson, William, Jur	1	1	2		
Williams, James	1		2		2
Taylor, James	1		3		4
Adams, Thomas	1	1	3		
Wiseman, Martin	1	5	3		
Wiseman, Henry	1	1	1		
Burk, John	2	1	1		
Burk, Henson	1	1	2		
Jackson, John	1		2		
Roberson, William	3	1	2		
Wilson, James	1	1	2		
Roberson, William, Jur	3		2		
Vandegrift, Christo	3	1	4		1
Traynum, William	1	1	3		
Walker, Robert	1	1	2		
Dodd, John	1		2		
Curtier, Peter	1	1	1		
Howel, John	2	3	4		
Witty, Elijah	1	3	3		
Tharp, William	1		6		
Cunningham, Jno, Jur	1		1		
Stockard, John	3	5	4		
Heath, John	3		4		
Young, Samuel	2	4	3		2
Kirkpatrick, Sarah	1	1	3		1
King, Levi	1		4		
Peeples Lewis	1		5		4
Brown, George	1		5		
McPeck, John	1	1	4		
Lemore, Thomas	2	1	3		
Blagg, William	1	1	1		
Bennet, Joseph	1	4	3		
Moore, Thomas	2	4	5		
Knight, Thomas	1	2	7		
Lovel, William	1		1		
Lovel, Syrus	1		2		
Toney, Sherwood		3	1		
Traynum, Reuben	1	1	4		
Simmons, Isham	1	4	5		
Spencer, Abraham	2	3	2		1
Simmons, John	1	4	5		
Armstrong, John	1		5		
Patterson, William	2		5		
Thompson, Edward	1	2	1		
Patterson, Francis	1		2		
Farley, Benjamin	1	1	2		
Akin, Jas	1	2	3		2
Leachman, John	1		3		
Stephens, William	2	4	2		3
Toney, Charles	1	2	6		
Nichol, Thomas	1		6		
Howerton, John	1		3		
Norris, Ann		1	6		
Pritchet, William	1	4	3		
Parrott, Abner	3	2	5		21
Connelly, William	3	2	5		
Jones, William, Senr (H.)	3		6		
Mussely, Peter	1	1	6		

SALISBURY DISTRICT, ROCKINGHAM COUNTY—Continued.

NAME OF HEAD OF FAMILY.	Free white males of 16 years and upward, including heads of families.	Free white males under 16 years.	Free white females, including heads of families.	All other free persons.	Slaves.
Jones, William, Jur	1	3	3		
Denny, Walter, Jur	3		2		
Norris, William	1	3	4		
Curry, Ezekiel	3	2	6		
Cox, Joseph	1	1	1		
Brannock, Henry	1	1	2		1
Wright, Ann	2		5		
Waford, John	2	3	6		
Cox, Jas	1	2	1		
Cox, Joseph, Senr	2	2	3		
Buckanon, Wm	2	4	4		
Gill, William	2	3	4		
Mason, William	1		5		
Bean, John	1	1	3		
Conner, Andrew	3	1	1		
Philips, Abraham	1	2	3		3
Nance, Peter	1	1	5		
Mullin, Patrick	1		1		
Sheppard, John	1	2	5		
Carner, John D	1		1		
Gorman, Joseph	1	1	1		
Purnel, Samuel	2	2	4		
Case, William	1	3	2		
Webster, Solomon	2	3	5		
King, Thomas, Senr	3	2	2		
Young, William	2	3	4		
McCollister, Sutton	1	1	2		
Gray, Thomas, Jur	1		1		
Crowel, Zenas	1	2	3		
Tatom, Nathl	3	2	3		6
Conger, Benjamin	1	2	2		
Harris, George	1	2	4		
Cunningham, John	1	1	2		
Duncan, Peter	1	2	4		
Linder, Joseph	1	2	1		
Falling, Agnis	1	2	3		
Harrison, William	2	5	4		
Purtle, George	1	1	2		
Kirkman, Thomas	1	1	1		
Jones, David	2	4	3		
West, Charles	1	3	2		
Scott, Thomas	1		2		
Reesers, Leven	1	2	3		
Lowe, Thomas (T. C.)	1	3	4		
Lowe, Isaac, Senr	1		2		
Lowe, Isaac	1	2	3		
Edmondson, John	1	2	2		
Pearson, John	1	2	3		
Hodge, Sarah	1		3		
Allison, John	1	3	5		
Fields, Ansil	2	3	4		
Gowing, Jas	1	3	3		
Colson, George	2	4	4		
Pratt, Richard	1		2		1
Wright, William	1	2	7		
Bowers, Henry	1	4	4		
Watson, William	1		3		
Smith, Polly		2	1		
Barns, Terbefield	2	4	3		1
Grogan, Francis	3				
Thompson, John	1	2	5		
Fleming, William	2	3	3		2
Strange, Jas	1	2	5		
Farguson, John	1	6	5		
Reagan, James	2	2	2		3
Wright, Prudence	2		3		
Timmons, Nathl	1	2	1		
Vernon, Richard	2	1	1		
Axton, Robert	2	5	4		
Irion, Henry	1	2	3		
Smith, Zachariah	1	5	3		
Reed, John	1	4	2		
Smith, Drewry	3	3	7		
Russil, Enoch	1	1	5		
Brooks, Humphry	1	2	3		
Smith, Fanny	1	1	3		
Smith, Thomas, Senr	1	4	2		
Motby, William	1	1	2		
Hunter, George	1		1		
Hunter, Peter	1	1	1		
Roach, William	1	1	2		
Shropshire, Winkfield	4		1		
Perry, Thomas	1	2	7		
Frost, Jonas	2	3	2		2
Russil, Richard	3	3	3		
Haynes, Daniel	2	3	3		
Led, Aron, Jur	1	1	1		
Haynes, Elijah	1	1	1		
McCollister, John	2	5	2		
Geiren, Nathan	1	1	2		
McElroy, Jas, Jur	1		1		
Blackburn, John	1	5	4		
Patrick, Jas	2	1	2		1
Wright, Jas	2	3	2		
Haynes, Jonathan	2	3	4		
Morris, Nancy		2	2		
Russil, James	1	2	2		
Lord, Andrew	1	2	4		

NAME OF HEAD OF FAMILY.	Free white males of 16 years and upward, including heads of families.	Free white males under 16 years.	Free white females, including heads of families.	All other free persons.	Slaves.
Bartie, George	1	3	4		
Barns, James	2	3	4		
Periman, Joseph	1	1	2		
Baker, William	1	3	2		
Smith, Saml	1	2	2		
Brown, Saml	1	3	2		
Grogan, Bartholomew	1	3	3		
Moxley, Nathl	3	2	5		
Pratt, Thomas	1	3	4		
Pratt, John	1	3	2		
Fanning, William	1		1		
Allen, Wm Hunt	2	3	4		7
Cooper, William	2	1	1		
Kennon, William	1		2		
Gains, Robert	2	2	3		4
Gilleland, Robert	1	3	5		
Whitworth, Jacob	2		3		
Whitworth, Isaac, Jur	1		1		
Bailey, William	1	2	4		
Gates, Philip	2	2	5		
Burns, John	1	3	3		
Mathews, William	1		2		
Poindexter, David	1		8		1
Fore, Francis	1	1	9		2
Stephens (Widow)			3		
Stephens, William	1	2	3		
Cotteril, Edward	2	5	1		
Alexander, Daniel	1	2	4		
Grogan, Thomas	1	1	2		
Harris, John	3	2	5		
Grogan, Mary			2		
Alexander, Alexander	1		2		
Sams, Joseph	1	2	4		
Oliver, Williams	1	1	1		
Watson, David	1	4	7		
Fields, Mary	1		1		
Fields, Nelson	1		1		
Pratt, Jas	1	3	4		
Dearing, William	1	1	3		3
Parker, Elisha	1	3	3		
Hardin, William	1	1	1		
Warren, Robert	2	4	5		
Settle, Benjamin	1		2		1
Yell, Moses	1	2	2		5
Hallums, John	1	5	3		2
Odell, John	2	1	6		
Thrasher, Richard	1		2		1
McCollom, William	1	1	3		
Prichard, Rachael	2	1	4		3
Pearson, Sullivan	1	2	6		
McCalib, Jas	1	2	1		
Hallums, George	1	1	1		
Terrant, Henry	1		3		
Barton, John	1	1	1		
Dudley, Christo	2	1	4		
Williams, James	1		2		
Williams, Edward	1	4	3		
Brown, Samuel	1	1	3		
Simmons, John	2	4	4		
McCarrol, John	2	2	7		
Morris, Nancy		2	1		
McCarrol, James	1		2		
Forkner, Thos	1	1	4		
Tyler, Reuben	1		1		
Chambers, Thomas	1		2		
Brown, Joshua	1	1	2		
Martin, Andrew	1	1	1		
Walker, William, Jur	1		3		
Thrasher, John	1	1	3		
Short, Samuel	1	3	4		
Thrasher, John	1	1	3		
Kelly, Jas	1	5	3		
Oakley, Richard	1	1	3		
Seales, Henry	2	3	5		13
McBride, John	1		2		
Young, John	4	2	4		
Massey, Thomas	1	3	6		9
Moceat, John	1	4	6		
Oakley, Jas	1	3			
Adkinson, John	1		4		
Williams, John	1		4		
Hamlin, George	1	3	1		
Haynes, Daniel	1	3	2		
Barnet, Elisha	1	1	3		
Winchester, Coleman	1		1		
Barnet, Luke	2	3	2		
Blear, John	1		3		
Kinman, George	1	4	3		
Winchester, John	1		1		
Duncan, Peter	1				
Winchester, John, Senr	2		1		
Adkinson, John	1		4		
Cunningham, John	1	1	2		
Herron, John	1		1		
Hardiman, Thomas	3	2			7
Walker, William, Jur	1	1	3		
Lacy, Bats Cock	1				7
Philips, Thomas	1	2	2		1

NAME OF HEAD OF FAMILY.	Free white males of 16 years and upward, including heads of families.	Free white males under 16 years.	Free white females, including heads of families.	All other free persons.	Slaves.
Lacy, Martha	2	1	3		18
Menzin, John	1	3	6		11
Clark, Joseph	1		1		
Peay, George, Sen	6		1		3
Clark, William, Ju	3		3		7
Rose, Philip	5	3	5		4
Gibson, John	1		1		
Bradberry, William	1	2	2		
Cunningham, Joseph	3		3		
Haynes, John	2	3	5		
McDaniel, Jas S.	1	1	3		2
Medlock, John	1	1	3		
Hayes, Henry	1		1		
Hodge, Sarah	1		1		
Walker, Elmore	1	1	1		
Garrison, Samuel	1		1		
Dines, William	1		1		
Cunningham, Wm	1		2		
Spurier, Theophilus	1		1		
Short, Samuel, Sen	1	3	4		
Lancir, Nathl	1	5	4		
Jones, William	1	2	5		
Short, Oldham	1	4	2		
Bradley, John	1				8
Peeples, Henry	1	1	3		3
Peggs, Mathew	1	1	1		
Jones, John	1	1	4		
Moore, Thos	1	6	4		
Gwin, Hugh	2	3	4		
Brasher, Zaza	1	4	3		
Brown, Robert	1		3		
Allen, Aron	1	3	2		
Philips, Jacob	1		2		
Moore, David	1	2	2		
Lovuss, Michael	3	2	3		
Short, Moses	1	1	1		1
Simpson, Nathl	1		1		
Boyd, Andw	1		2		
Williams, William	1	5	5		
Lewis, Shadrack	1	3	3		
Owen, John	2	2	1		2
McKinney, John	1	2	4		1
Akin, James	1	2	5		
Murphy, John	1	2	1		
Hand, Christo	1	4	2		
Patterson, William	2	1	5		
Lillard, Moses	2	5	2		
Yeoman, Drewry	4		3		18
Mackie, John	1	2	4		
Hopper, Joseph	3	1	7		
Cantril, Jacob	2	4	3		
Oneal, Peter	4	5	5		11
Walker, Alexander	1	1	5		
Lynch, Hugh	1	2	6		
Barr, Robert	1	3	3		
Martin, John	1	4	4		
Martin, Walter	1		1		2
Spout, William	3	1	3		
Hill, John	3	2	3		
Dilworth, George	1	2	2		
Boyd, William	1	2	3		
Walker, William	1	2	4		1
Walker, Joel	1	2	2		1
Scurry (Widow)	1	2	5		1
Walker, Allen	1	1	2		
Roach, James	1	2	4		
Barnet, Jacob	2		7		
Stanford, John	2	1	2		
Coffer, Joshua	2		2		24
Henderson, Samuel	1	2	6		10
Dodd, Allen	3		4		
Thomas, Michael	1	2	6		1
Odell, Joseph	3	5	7		
Pain, Thomas	1	3	4		
Sutherland, William	1	1	3		3
McElroy, Jas	1	1	3		
Wardlow, Patrick	1	1	3		
Dunlap, Henry	3	5	3		
Caffey, Michael	1	2	3		
McElroy, Wm	1	1	1		
McElroy, Agnis			2		
Sheppard, John	1	2	1		
Richardson, Edward	2	1	1		
McCallister, Ezekeil	1		1		
Bright, James	1	2	3		
Covington, John	1	2	3		
Brigs, Elisha	1		3		
Thrasher, Joseph Cloud	2	2	2		5
Hendricks, Henry	1				
Chisolm, John	1	2	2		2
Williams, Drewry	1	3	3		7
Roland, George	3		3		
Hill, Walter	1	2	2		
Langham, Jas	1	1	1		
Hodge, John C.	1	1	7		
Brown, Alexander	1	3	1		1
Williams, Edward	1	3	2		
Strong, John	3		3		

SALISBURY DISTRICT, ROCKINGHAM COUNTY—Continued.

NAME OF HEAD OF FAMILY.	Free white males of 16 years and upward, including heads of families.	Free white males under 16 years.	Free white females, including heads of families.	All other free persons.	Slaves.
Richer, Jaˢ	1	1	1		
Deaver, Mary		3	1		
Strong, Mary		4	6		
McAllister, Jesse	1	1	1		
Vanlandingham, Richd	1	3	3		
Tate, Adam	2		1		11
Cox, John	1		3		2
Adkins, Daniel	1	1	6		
May, Peter	1	3	1		7
Larimore, Nicholas	4	3	5		
Grady, William	1	1	5		
Prichard, John	1	1	3		
Walker, Elmore	2	2	3		
Gustrer, Absalom	1		3		
Haggard, Benjamin	1		1		
Young, Samuel	1		5		
Wall, John	1	2	5		3
Reed, Hugh	1	5	3		
Hill, Samˡ	1		3		
Corry, Samˡ	1				
Dilworth, Thomas	1	1	2		
Dilworth, John	3	4	3		
Philips, Joseph	1		3		
Scarboro, Jaˢ	1	2	1		
Smith, Edward	1				
Dilworth, Benjamin	2	6	3		
Allen, Joseph	3		1		
Jones, Edward	1	4	4		
Allen, Daniel	1	5	5		1
Johnston, Gideon, Jur	4		8		2
Massy, Mackness	1	1	3		
Johnston, William	2	2	4		1
Fields, John	2	3	4		1
Wray, Jaˢ	2	3	4		
Walker, David, Sen	1	1	3		4
Abbott, John	1	2	5		
Hayes, James, Senr	4	2	7		1
Bailey, Thomas	2	1	1		
Martin, Robert	1				2
Henderson, Thomas	4	3	4		14
Calhoon, James	1	2	5		
Whitworth, John	1	4	2		
Whitworth, Isaac	1	1	4		1
Bevers, Abigail	1	1	2	1	
Overton, Ann Booker	3	3	3		7
Lemmon, John	3	2	5		7
Fields, William	1		2		
French, William	2		1		
Barker, Leonard	1	2	4		1
McClellan, William	1	3	3		
Barker, Mary		2	4		
Holderness, Jaˢ	2		1		5
Linder, Nathˡ	1		5		
Allison, John	2	1	4		1
Hosford, John	1	4	4		
Nance, William	1	4	4		
Williams, David	1	4	5		
May, John	1	3	1		8
Odeneal, John	1	1	6		7
Hardin, Henry	1	1	4		3
Oliver, John	1	2	3		
Thrasher, Ruth			1		
Newcom, Joseph	1	2	2		
Bishop, Joseph	1		4		
Thacher, Nathan	1		2		
Larimer, Philip	2	1	3		
Williams, Aron	1		2		10
Roberts, Naman	1	1	2		5
Rhodes, Hezekiah	2	2	2		1
Richey, John	1	3	3		
Fowler, William	1	2	3		
Norris, John	1	1	4		
Johnston, John	1	1	2		4
Hardin, Thomas	3		2		7
Allen, Benjamin	1		4		
Allen, John	2	1	4		
Small, Robert	1	6	1		1
Henderson, Richard	2	4	5		
Henderson, Jno	1	1	1		
Trolender, Michael	4	2	4		
Trolender, Adam	1	1	1		
Jones, John	1	1	1		
Lovel, David	2	1	2		
Lovel, David, Juˢ	1	2	5		
Lovel, Zachariah	1				
Lovel, William	1				
Lovel, Syrus	1				
Cummins, John	2		5		2
Cummins, Robert	1	1	2		
Jones, David	1	1	2		
Rhodes, Jaˢ	1	1	2		
Lemmons, Alexander	1	2	2		
Winston, William	2	2	3		
Triplit, Catharine	1		2		
Conner, Jaˢ	2		1		
Jennings, William	1	2	1	1	1
McClellan, Robert	1		4		
Martin, Govˢ Alexander	3	1	2		47
Allen, Valentine	3	1	1		28
Wall, David, Jur	1	1	3		
Chadwell, John	2	4	8		9
Irish, Philip Jacob	4	2	5		5
Peay, George, Jur	1	2	2		3
Gunn, Elisha	1	2	3		
Jenkins, William	1	4	1		
Wright, William	1		2		
Corry, Robert	1	1	2		1
Vermillon, Guy	1	1	2		
Cobbler, Thomas	1	1	2		
Asten, William	1		1		11
Odell, Lewis	1	1	4		
Bloyd, John	1	3	4		
Norman, Cortney	1	1	10		
Sanders, Robert	4	1	3		
Price, John	1		2		
Coleman, Robert	1	5	5		8
Harris, Nathˡ	4	2	5		10
Leak, John	3	1	6		4
Scales, Joseph	1		4		7
Clifton, Nancy	1		1		
Scales, Nathˡ	2	2	5		16
Scales, Mary	1				2
Davis, John	1	3	5		
Compton, Ebenezer	1				
Cobler, Harvey	1	3	2		
Strong, Sneed	1		4		
Roberts, Syrus L	1	2	3		3
Cook, Benjamin	1	1	3		10
Burch, Wm S	1	1	2		2
Smith, Joshua	3	2	4		3
Peggs, Mathew	1	3	3		
Gentry, Watson	1	2	4		9
Joyce, James	1	3	4		7
Whitworth, Jno	9	2	3		8
Sanders, James, Senr	2	3	6		
Harrison, William	1		5		
Harrison, Nathˡ	3	1	3		
Odell, William	1	4	6		
McReynolds, Thomas	2	3	4		10
Pounds, Thomas	2	2	6		
Wall, Daniel	1		5		
Dabney, John	1	3	5		9
Sims, Edward	1	2	2		
Suttle, Josiah	2		1		6
Lemmons, William	3	4	2		
Settle, David	1	1	2		2
Flack, Jaˢ	1	1	5		
Mabry, Cornelius	1	3	2		
Work, Henry (&c.)	1	2	5		6
Taylor, Jaˢ (for self & Farleys Estate)	2		4		32
Peay, William	3	2	13		
Gallaway, Robert	3				3
May, William	1				
Seales, Thomas	2	1	5		
Sharp, Richard	2	3	3		2
Smith, William	1		1		
Seales, John	2	2	1		3
Rogers, Samuel	3	3	4	4	4
Sharp, Samˡ	1		1		
Vernon, Mary			4		
Morgan, Milley		1	2		
Oliver, Jaˢ	1	2	2		
Bundrant, Richard	2	2	3		
Camplin, Jacob	1		3		1
Crawford, Adam	1		3		
McClaran, Alexander	1	3	3		3
Smothers, Elizabeth		1	1		
Lister, Biddy		1	1		
Rickles, John	1	1	1		
Odell, Uriah	1	5	4		
Chandlor, Joseph	1	5	4		
Gibson, Elizabeth	1	3	4		
Shropshire, Winkfield	2	2	1		
Garrott, Henry	1	4	1		
Chandlor, Joseph	1		3		4
Hill, John	1	1	2		2
Hill, Elizabeth	1	2	5		13
Joyce, Elijah	1	4	5		8
Joyce, Robert	1		1		2
Colson, Henry	1	2	3		
Joyce, John	3	4	5		2
Deatherigs, George	2	1	3		2
Oliver, Martha	1	4	5		
Bethel, William	1	3	4		5
Martin, Walter	1				
Boak, Robert	2	1	3		
George, Mathew	2		1		
Granger, John	1	2	3		
Williams, Allen	2	1	5		
Young, John	2	1	5		
Herdson, Robert	2	3	3		
Lovel, David	1	2	5		
McCulloch, Joseph	1	1	4		
Crump, William	1		3		4
Joyce, John (P.)	1	2	3		7
Jones, John	1	1	5		
Irwin, George	1	4	2		
Walker, Jaˢ	3		2		5
Joyce, Thomas	3	4	6		4
Gordon, Charles	1		2		
Gordon, Mary	1		3		
Scales, James	1	1	4		11
Philips, John	1	1	5		
Gann, John	1		1		
Vaughn, John	1	4	2		
Sharp, James	2	1	2		2
Sharp, Catharine			1		2
Hunter, James	3	3	4		11
Dalton, Charlotte	3	2	6		9
Burton, Edward	1		1		
Glenn, John, Jur	1				
Davis, James	2	3	5	4	3
Glenn, William	1		2		1
Shropshire, Dr John	1	4	4		
Osten, Richard	1	3	4		1
Curtin, Joshua	1	3	5		
Curtin, Reuben	1	3	2		4
Colley, Maynard	2	2	4		
Cruak, Richard	1	1	2		4
Roberson, James	3	2	5		
Martin, James	3	2	5		
Walker, James	2	2	4		
Roland, George	2	3	4		
Grear, Ananias	2	4	3		
Stewart, John	1		1		2
Stewart, Jaˢ	1	3	4		
Bundrant, Richd	2	3	4		
Childers, Stephen	2		2		
Brim Joseph	2	1	2		7
Scales, Absalom	2	1	2		
Garne, Thomas	1	2	4		
Philips, Irby	1				
Syrus, James	1	2	4		
Means, Robert	1	3	4		
Philips, John	1	1	5		
Pratt, Thomas	1	3	5		
Sharp, Samuel	1		1		
Sharp, Catharine	1		1		2
Dalton, Samˡ	2		1		17
Gallaway, Charles	6	1	5		14
Gallaway, James	2		2		12
French, William, Ju	2	1	1		
Main, Henry	1	1	4		

SALISBURY DISTRICT, ROWAN COUNTY.

NAME OF HEAD OF FAMILY.	Free white males of 16 years and upward, including heads of families.	Free white males under 16 years.	Free white females, including heads of families.	All other free persons.	Slaves.
Dickey, James	5	1	2	1	
Niblock, George	2	4	3		
Steller, Richard Graham	2	3	2		3
Graham, James	1	2	1		6
Graham, John, Senr	1	5	4		2
Carrigan, John	1	2	2		3
Kerr, John	1				
Young, Samuel	4	1		1	11
Young, William	1	1	3		1
Erwin, Christopher	3	3	4		8
Cowin, Isaac	1	3	2		1
Lowrey, William	1	1	2		2
Anderson, Isaac	2	4	5	1	8
Graham, Richard	1	1	5		4
Gray, James	2	2	3		
Cowin, William	1	3	1		
Wilkinson, Samuel	1	1	3		
Foy, William	1		2		
Hemphill, William	1		1		3
Luckey, Richard	1		3		
Hughell, Thomas	1	3	4		
Porter, Robert	4	2	5		
Steele, James	1	1	2		
Byers, William	2	3	5		
Trott, James	3	3	2		2
Barkley, John	1	3	1		
Kerr, James	1				
Armstrong, Able	1	2	4	1	2
Ensley, Alexr	1		1	1	
McCracken, Samuel	1		1		

SALISBURY DISTRICT, ROWAN COUNTY—Continued.

NAME OF HEAD OF FAMILY.	Free white males of 16 years and upward, including heads of families.	Free white males under 16 years.	Free white females, including heads of families.	All other free persons.	Slaves.
Morrison, David	1	2	3		
Love, Robert	1	1	6		
Smith, Samuel	1		1		
Cannaday, John	1	2	4		
Graham, Jean		3	1		2
Hall, Joseph		1	2		
Garwood, Joseph	1	1	4		
Johnston, William	2	4	3	1	5
Lowrey, John	1	2	2		
Lowrey, James	1		1		
Brandon, Benjamin	1	1	2		1
Brandon, Robert	1	1	1		5
Johnston, Elizabeth			1	1	1
Brandon, William			1	1	2
Hughey, Jacob	1	1	4		1
Hughey, Henry, Ser	1				6
Hughey, Henry, Jur	1	3	4		
Hall, Walter	3	1	1	1	
Brown, William	1	1	3	1	
Cowin, Henry	5	1	3		
Hall, George	1	1	1	1	
Steele, Nemin	1	2	2	2	1
Morgan, John	1	1	6		
Tate, John	1		1		1
Graham, Elizabeth			3		2
Graham, Agness			1		4
Steele Robert	2		3		
Brandon, John	1		1	1	2
Luckey, Samuel	5		2		2
Bunten, Robert	1	2	3	1	
Short, Peter	1	2	4	1	2
Clarke, Thomas	1	1	2		
Clarke, John	1				
Hughey, Robert	1	2	1		
Renshaw, William	1	1	3		
Smith, William	1	1	2		
Lewrance, John	2	2	3		1
Fitzpatrick, James	3	1	1		
Fitzpatrick, John	1		3		
Bailey, William, Ser	1	4	3		
Smith, Samuel	1		2		
Horton, John	2	2	3		
Horton, Joseph	1	3	3		
Law, William	2	3	4		
Steele, Samuel	1	1	3		
Salisbury, John	2	2	4		
Parker, Robert	1	2	3		
Dickey, Thomas	1	3	5		6
Dickey, Joel	1				
Campbell, Joseph	3	2	4		
Cooke, John	1		1	1	
Holdman, John	1	2	1		
Parker, Thomas	3	4	3		
Patrick, Jeremiah	1	2	1		
Johnston, Henry	1	3	4		
Steeleman, William	1	1	2		2
Steeleman, George	1	1	4		2
Bedwell, Elijah	1	2	5		
Herin, Shadrick	1	1	2		
Speaks, Richard	2	3	4		
Hendricks, David	1	2	2		
Stogdale, Sarah	1		3		
Stogdale, Vachel	1	1	2		
Beach, Aquillah	1	2	4		
Parson, John	1	1	1		
Renolds, Henry	1	2			
Patrick, William	3		2		
Stogdale, Zebediah	1	3	4		
Madden, Jonathan	1	4	3		
West, Isaac	1	1	3		
West, Hezekiah	1	1	1		
West, Elizabeth	1	2	2		
Roach, Thomas	1	1	1		
Stogdale, Thomas	1	2	1		
Blackwood, John	2	3	6		
Holms, Robert	1	2	5		
Brooks, Robert	1	4	3		
Stogdale, Warnel	1		3		
Patrick, Hezekiah	1	1	1		
Beal, Joseph	1	2	5		
Renolds, Richard	1	1	2		
Busey, Mathew	1	3	5		
Speaks, Martin	1	3	4		
Hadox, William	1	1	3		
Manon, Christopher	1	2	3		
Pinchback, John	2	1	5		6
Garther, Lydia			4		
Bucey, Samuel	1		1		
Speaks, Charles	1	4	3		
Whitaker, Thomas	1	4	5		
Casey, Samuel	2	2	2		
Trevlt, John	1				
Wilkins, George	2	2	5		
Wilkins, Abraham	1		1		
Whitley, Ebenezer	1		1		
Owen, Lawrance	2	4	3	1	
Cherry, Benja	1	1	10		

NAME OF HEAD OF FAMILY.	Free white males of 16 years and upward, including heads of families.	Free white males under 16 years.	Free white females, including heads of families.	All other free persons.	Slaves.
Brewer, William	2	2	4		
Bryan, John	1		1		
Bryan, James	1		1		
Little, John	2	2	5		
Luckey, Robert	1	1	2		
Boone, Benjamin	1	3	3		
Bryan, Samuel	1	1	5		
Boone, John	1	1	4	1	3
Leach, James	1	3	4		1
Leach, Richard	1	2	5		
Welman, Thomas	1	1	1		
Pennery, Thomas	1	3	4		
Watkins, John	1	1	2		
Huff, Valentine	3		2		1
Helper, Jacob	3	1	4		
Black, James	1		2		
Jones, Isaac	1	2	3		3
Cain, Thomas	1	2	4		
Holdman, William	1	4	5		
Jones, Solomon	2		8		
Seny, Owen	1	3	2		1
Bartey, Thomas	1	2	2		
Edwards, Enoch	2	2	6		
Holeman, Isaac	2	5	2		4
Beamon, John	2	5	4	1	1
Bucy, John	1		1		
Clark, William	1	1	3		
Beck, Sam'l Elija	1	3	3		
Eaton, Isaac	4	4	6		
English, Alexander	1	2	1		1
Wolket, Barney	1	1	2		
Clifford, Jacob	1	1	6		
Brown, William	1		2		
Hall, Abm	1	1	1		
Cherry, Peterson	1	1	1		
Whitehead, Lazarus	1	2	4	1	1
Glascock, Peter	3	4	5		
Brooks, George	2	5	3		
Luckey, Samuel, Ser	1	1	3		2
Luckey, Samuel, Jr	1	2	2		1
Andrew, James	2	1	5	1	3
Guffey, Henry	3		3		2
Erwin, John	2	3	5		
Morrow, John	3	3	4		
Lovlace, Elias	1	2	6		
Bean, Thomas	2	2	6		1
Prather, Thomas	2	2	6		2
Summers, William	2	3	3		
Freeman, Moses	1				
Ratlage, James	1	1	4		3
Teneson, Thomas	1	2	4		
Ratledge, Daniel	1	1	2		
Miller, Henry	1	2	2		1
Hudson, Isaac	1	1	1		
Hudson, Daniel	1	1	1		
Hudson, Absalom	2		1		
Brown, Bazil	1	3	1		
Howell, Joseph	1	2			
Brandon, John	1		3	1	1
Hurley, James	1	1	3		
Nichols, William	1	1	1		
Brandon, Christopher	2		5		1
Renshaw, Thomas	1	3	5		
Davis, John	1	1	2		
Evans, John	1	2	2		1
Stanley, Thomas	1	1	2		
Hardin, Alexr	1	3	4		
Brandon, Abraham	2	3	4		1
Taylor, William	2		2		
Veach, Richard	2		3		1
Brandon, Mary				4	
Maguire, John	1	2	4	1	
Bell, William	1	2	4		2
Neely, Richard	4	1	2		1
Sharbert, Samuel	3	2	6		
Davis, Sarah	1	2	1		
Smith, Jonathan	1	4	2		
Bailey, William	1				1
Harper, William	1	2	3		
Hudson, John	1	2	3	1	
Mott, Simmons	1	2	3		
Lard, John	1	2	2		
Howard, William	3	3	5		1
Hurley, Nehemiah	1	2	3		
Robison, Joseph	1	3	2		
Tegart, Andrew	1	3	5	1	
Webb, Daniel	1	5	2	1	2
Teneson, Abraham	3	2	4		
Maguire, James	1	2	4		
McMurrey, James	1	3	2		
Hughes, John	1	2			
Coleman, Peter	1	2	4		
Garther, Bazil	3	2	2	1	4
Garther, Benjamin	1	5	6		1
Eckles, John	1		2		
Johnston, Jacob	1	2	4		
Jams, Vachel	1				1

NAME OF HEAD OF FAMILY.	Free white males of 16 years and upward, including heads of families.	Free white males under 16 years.	Free white females, including heads of families.	All other free persons.	Slaves.
Jams, Beal	1		1		
Nichols, John	2	1	2		5
Clifford, John	1	1	5		
Eaton, Ebenezer	1	4	2		
Johnston, John	2	4	4		
Smith, James	1		1		
Eaton, Daniel	1		2		
Ellis, Evan	5		3		
Smith, Joseph	3		1		
Stockdale, Elizabeth			2		
Ellis, John	5	2	4	1	1
Holderfield, Valentine	2	1	4		
Call, Daniel	1		1		
Stockdale, Masheck	1		2		
Glascock, Spencer	2	2	2		10
Hendren, Oliver	1	2	2		1
Hendron, John	1	1			2
Dulin, Phillip	2	2	3		2
Harris, Isaac	1	1	1		
Williams, George	1	5			
Williams, Benjamin	1		2		
James, James	2		2		
Hays, Samuel	1		1		
Welman, Jeremiah	1	5	2		
Welman, John	1		2		
Dedmond, Edmond	1		2		
Noland, Ledston	1	4	6		
Allen, John	3		2		
Noland, James	2	2	4		
Penenton, Charles	1	1	3		
Thompson, Thomas	1		3		
Noland, Stephen	2	2	4		
Turley, Benjamin	1	2	2		
Whitaker, William, Ser	2	1	7		
Whitaker, John	1	4	1		
Whitaker, Wm, Jur	1	1	3		
Biles, John	1		1		
McMahan, Samuel	2	4	4		
McMahan, James	3		3		
Penington, James	1		3		
Shaw, Michael	1	1	2		
Williams, Simon	1	3	6	1	
Etcherson, Walter	1		4		
Glascock, Harmon	2	1	7		1
Keffer, Frederick	1	2	2		
Johnston, David	2	3	4	1	
Call, Henry	1	2	3		
Lane, Gallent	1	3	4		
Dial, Joseph	1	4	1		
Humphrey, John	2		1		1
Etcherson, Henry	1		2		
Baker, George	2		1		
Eaton, George	2		2		
Jones, David	3	5	2		
Noland, Daniel	1		3		
Johnston, Majr John	3	1	5		6
Williamson, Francis	1				
Rich, Henry	1	1	1	1	
Read, James	1	2	6	1	
Hall, George	1		2	2	
Hall, Samuel	1		1		
Deaver, Samuel	1	1	1		
Boland, James	2		3		
Venable, Sarah	1		7		
Alexander, John	2	1	2		
Wood, Cornelius	1	1	2		
Ralisbeck, Henry	2	1	5		
McKnight, Lidia	2	1	4		
Hughes, Jeremiah	1		5		
Sain, John	1		4		
Mills, David	1		4		
Mills, William	1	1	3		
Easburne, John	1	1	2		
Malon, Jeremiah	1	4	1		
Graham, Edward	1		4		
Rector, Jessey	1	1	5		
Ball, John	1		2		
Adams, Abraham	3		2		5
Call, John	1	4	5		
Frost, Ebenezer	3	5	6		
Hunter, Margret		2	4		
Sites, Jacob	1	2	2	1	
Peck, Ludwick	1		2		
Manas, Sephes	1	4	2		
Wells, Thomas	1		5		
Hunter, Charles	4	3	4		
Howard, Cornelius	4	2	3		
Garner, Henry	1	2	3		
Rupert, Peter	1	1	3		
Howard, Christopher	4		3		
Hanley, Christopher	2	3	6		
Stuart, Edward	1	1			
King, Jeremiah	1	1	3		
Stinnet, William	1	1	3		
Kenatzer, Catherina			3		
Stinnet, John	1	1	3		
Williams, Elizabeth			3		

SALISBURY DISTRICT, ROWAN COUNTY—Continued.

NAME OF HEAD OF FAMILY.	Free white males of 16 years and upward, including heads of families.	Free white males under 16 years.	Free white females, including heads of families.	All other free persons.	Slaves.
Henkle, Benjamin	2	3	7		
Williams, Edward	2	1	5		
Forster, James	1	5	3		2
Harper, William	1		3		
Hawkins, Abraham	2	1	4		
Forster, Hezekiah	1	2	2		
Forster, Robert	1	2	2		
Evans, David	3	3	5		
Hurley, Moses	1	3	1		
Ford, Ralph	1	1	3		
Aniwood, James	1		5		
Brenneger, Adam	1	3	3		
Bracken, Thomas	1		1		
Bryan, Joseph, Juʳ	1	1	3		1
Bryan, Joseph, Seʳ	2		2		4
Moler, John	1	2	1		
Gentle, George	1	1	4		
Higden, Joseph	1	3	2		
Dowell, John	1	4	5		1
Felps, James	1	2	2		
Hardisty, Henry	1	1	3		
McDaniel, Allin	1	3	3		
Berryman, Benjᵃ	1	4	5		2
Pain, Richard	1	3	2		
Shecks, Christian	2	1	2		
Smith, Michael	1		3		
White, William	2		4		3
Cooper, Phillip	1	1	5		
Snow, William	3		3		
Lafey, James	2		4		
Carender, Ezekiel	2	3	2		
Harper, Zepheniah	1	3	3		
Obriant, John	1		1		
Dowell, Phillip	1	2	2		
Robison, Demsellah		1	3		
Dowell, Peter, Seʳ	1		1		5
Tennesy, Abraham	1	1	5		
Dowell, Peter, Juʳ	1		2		3
Dowell, William	1	3	5		1
Sparks, Jonas	2	3	3		
Wiatt, John	1	1	4		
Bryan, Francis	1		2		
Gilpin, Benjamin	1	1	1		
Felps, Samuel	1		2		
Felps, Sarah	1	2	3		
Sidden, John	1	2	2		
Felps, Thomas	1	1	3		
Sheets, Jacob	1	2	1		
Blackheart, Willibee	1		3		
Caiton, Charles	3	1	4		
Caiton, George	1	1	1		
Hill, Jacob	1		1		
Tinneson, Thomas	1		3		
Martin, Asa	1	3	3		
Speaks, Ann		2	3		
Harris, Zepheniah	2	1	4		
Harper, William	1		5		1
Sparks, David	1	2	1		
Sparks, William	1	2	3		
Enochs, Mary	3		3		
Moler, Henry	1		2		
Rumbly, Edger	2	1	2		
Wesh, John	1		3		
Smith, Michael	2		4		1
Oirel, Daniel	1	1	3		
Adams, Ephriaim	1	1	1		2
Sidden, Joseph	2		2		
Holden, Edmond	1	1	2		
Enochs, Enoch	1	1	1		
Speaks, Adam	1	2	3		
Penn, Richard	1	3	3		
Hendricks, Abraham	1		2		
Wetty, Jacob	3	1	3		
Hendricks, John	1	1	3		
Watkins, David	2	4	3		2
Hendricks, Frederick	1	1	3		
Black, Jacob	1	2	2		
Black, Frederick	1	1	4		
Enochs, Isaac	2	4	9		1
Enochs, Gabriel	3	3	5		
Bryan, Samuel	1	2	6	1	1
West, Thomas	1		4		
Job, Thomas	2		1		
Sheets, Martin	2	1	7		
Crankfield, Lewis	2	2	3		
Karns, Alexander	1	3	5		
Dial, Robert	1		2		
Hutson, Thomas	1		1		
Williams, Joseph	2	1	6		
Hendricks, James	1	3	3		
Bryan, James	1	1	1		
Wearen, Conrad	1	3	1		
Dagley, James	1	3	2		
Dailey, Lawrence	1				
Maxwell, Thomas	3		1		
Renshaw, Joseph	3	3	6		
Renshaw, Elijah	1	3	4		
Renshaw, Abraham	1		1		
Warren, James	1		1		
Roland, Joseph	2	1	5	1	
Roland, John	2	3	4		
Hendricks, Phillip	1	2	1		
Hendricks, John	1	1	3		
Lewis, Daniel, Sʳ	2		4		
Lewis, Daniel, Juʳ	1		2		
Roland, Gasper	1	1	3		
Person, Stephen	1	2	2		
Beam, Michael	1		1		8
Welch, Thomas	1	1	1		
Welch, Jean	1	3	2		
Johour, James	1		2		
Doyale, Gregory	1	1	2		
Ridle, James	1	2	2		
Doyale, Samuel	2	3	2		
Spilman, George	2		1		
Sims, Elizabeth	1		2		
Beaman, Abraham	3	1	2		1
Beam, Jacob	1		3		
Wilcoxon, William	3	2	2		2
Wilcoxon, John, Seʳ	1	1	1		
Wilcoxon, John, Juʳ	1	4	6		
Nalson, Elizabeth		1	1		
Miller, Rachel		2	2		
McDaniel, James	1		3		
Hall, William	1	3	4		4
Keller, Jacob	1	4	5		
Wattar, William	1	1	6		
Dutero, Bolser	1	2	3		
Hinkle, Henry	1	1	3		
Nail, Caleb	2		1		
Sain, Casper	2	2	2		
Sprigg, Reason	1	1	2		
Nelson, William	2	3	4		
Donner, George	1	2	5		
Stokes, Elizabeth		1	1	1	9
Neat, Rudolph, Senʳ	1		1		
Neat, Rudolph, Juʳ	1	2	4		1
Tatom, Jean	1	3	4		
Tatom, Laurance		1	6		
Buckner, John	1	1	2		
Lastep, Samuel	1	6	4		
March, John	1	3	6		
March, George	1	4	5		
Henline, Jacob	1	4	2		1
Banks, John	1	3	5		
Buckner, David	1		2		
Hendricks, Isaac	2		3		
Defi, James	2		4		
Wallis, Samuel	1	1	1		
Roberts, Carnie	1		2		
Johnston, Joseph	1	1	2		
Allin, John	2	1	3		
Bracken, Samuel	1		1		
Bracken, Samuel	1		1		
McCulloch, James	1	1	2		1
Bird, Thomas	1	2	4		
White, Thomas	1	4	3		
Dobbin, Samuel	1		1		
Bailey, Samuel	2	4	3		31
Hails, Mary		1	1		
Mock, Andrew	2	1	6		1
Kenatzer, Jacob	1		2		
Booe, Jacob	1	2	3	2	
Booe, George	1	1	1		
Bartlison, William	1		4		
Coone, Jacob	2	1	3		
Nail, John	2	3	5		
Bartlison, Zacriah	1	2	4	1	
Langford, John	1	2	2	1	
Trout, Jacob	1		5		
Forster, Lucy	2		3		5
Foster, Robert	2	1	6		3
Giles, William	1		1		28
Rogers, Richard	1	3	3		
Owens, Elijah	1	1	6		
Owens, John	1	1	1		
Owens, Normon	1		1		
Roberts, Lazarus	1		1		
Walker, William	1	3	1		
Wood, John	1	2	1		
Potts, Jeremiah	1	2	3		1
Buckner, Henry	2	3	2		
Johnston, James	1	2	4		2
Dedmon, Ezekel	1	1	2		
Dedmon, Sarah	2		6		
Hudson, Peter	1		3		
Johnston, Joseph	1		3		
Smart, Thomas	1	1	3		
Bailey, John	1	2	1		2
Arriwood, Ann		1	3		
Williams, Charles	1		4		
Srock, Henry	1	3	5		
Marshal, Humphry	2	1	4		
Williams, George	2	5	1		7
Linster, Moses	2	4	6		8
Howell, John	1	1	3		2
Andrew, Joseph	1	2	2		
Williams, James	2		4		1
Daniel, Josiah	1	2	4		
Click, Nicholas	1	4	4		
Person, Richmond	1	5		5	101
Person, John	2	5	2		6
King, William	1	3	6		
Isbale, John	1	1	2		
Gentle, George	1	3	3		
Little, Jacob	2	2	4		
Koon, John	1	3	4		
Jones, Benjᵃ	1		2		
Harry, Isaac	1	1	2		
Barlow, John	1		2		
Williams, George	1	3	2		
Haggins, William	1	1	2		
Graham, Edward	1	1	3		
Adams, Abraham	1		1		
Adams, Isaac	3	2	3		
Williams, Ralph	1		1		
Adams, Silvenus	1		2		
Philips, John	2	2	5		
Brothers, Robert	2	1	3		
Thomas, John	1	1	3		
Clifton, Thomas	1	1	2		
Etchison, James	2		2		
Etchison, Edmond	1	2	6		
Wesh, Jeremiah	1	1	1		
Cummins, Thomas	1	3	4		
Bridgfarmer, Martin	2	1	3		
Mock, Henry	2	1	2		
Mock, Peter, Seʳ	1	1	2		
Mock, Peter, Juʳ	2	1	3		
Harris, Joseph	1		2		
Harris, John	1	4	2		
Martin, Allin	1	1	2		
Walker, Burch	1		1		
Mock, John	1		1	1	
Little, Lewis	1	1	3		
Stonestreet, Edward	2	2	4	1	1
Harben, Edwᵈ Villers	2		2	1	4
Bryan, Sarah	2	2	3		15
Shepperd, Nathen	1	4	7		5
Harben, Reason	1	3	2		
Literal, Richard	1	1	4		
Adams, Elisha	1	4	3		
Bailey, Henry	1	1	2		1
Easters, Thomas	2	6	6		4
McCathe, Ebednego	2	1	3		
McBryan, John	1	2	5		
Spilmon, Harmon	2		5		
Johnston, Robert	1	5	5		
Jinkins, Rodrick	2	2	5	1	
Phillips, Elijah	1	1	4		
Cowman, Thomas	2	1	4		
Phillips, John	2	1	1		
Phillips, Mary			1		
Updegrove, Isaac	1		3		
Hunt, Charles	4	4	6		
Dagley, Jonathan	1	2	2		
Hoges, William	1				
Easteb, Thomas	3	2	4		
Howell, Stephen	1	3	3	1	
Horn, Thoˢ, Juʳ	1	3	2		
Humphreys, John	1	1	1		
Tuches, Tobias	1		4		1
Brian, Samuel	1	2	4		
Wilsen, James	1		3		
Deposter, John	1	4	2		3
Chafin, Nathen	2	1	6		11
Griffith, William	1	2	1		
Eaton, Peter	1		7		5
Horn, Thomas, Sʳ	1		7		
Eaton, Thomas	1	7	6		
Wilson, Michael	1	3	1		5
McCartey, Zacheriah	1	1	4		
Hunt, Margret	3		5		1
Keen, Nicholas	1	3	4		
Griffin, Ezekel	1	2	2		
Haiden, Unity	1		2		11
Haiden, Dugles	1	2	1		9
McDermon, Michael	1	1	4		
Smith, Obediah	2	3	6		5
Butler, William	1	5	2		1
Cornwell, Elijah	1	1	4		
Adams, Jacob	1		2		
Buck, Charles	1	3	4		
Bennet, Jacob	1	1	2		
Braley, William	1		1		
Braley, John, Juʳ	1		1		4
Braley, Walter	1	2	1		1
Bradley, Josiah	1	1	2		
Braley, John, Sʳ	2	1	4		6
Backley, Samuel	3		2		
Baker, Harate	1	1	5		

SALISBURY DISTRICT, ROWAN COUNTY—Continued.

NAME OF HEAD OF FAMILY.	Free white males of 16 years and upward, including heads of families.	Free white males under 16 years.	Free white females, including heads of families.	All other free persons.	Slaves.
Batey, Charles	1	1	2		
Coleman, Phillip	1	2	4		
Kennaday, Andrew	2		6		
Cochran, Robert	4	2	3		
Donaldson, Alexr	3	2	4		
Flemming, Allison	1		3		1
Grove, Abraham	1	2	5		
Goose, George	3	1	2		
Graham, John	1	1	2		
Graham, Garret	3		2		
Hart, William	1	2	3		3
Holland, Zacheriah	1	4	3		
Hobbis, John	1	3	1		
Hart, William, Jur	3	1	3		1
Hart, James	2		3		
Jemeson, William	3		3		
Kerr, David	2		4	1	6
Laser, John	1	4	5		
Mellen, Charles	2	2			
McRea, Thos	2		1		
McClain, John	1	1	2		
McKnight, William	3		3		1
McClain, William	2	2	5		2
McGlaughlin, James	1	2	1		
Parks, John	1		4		3
Slaugh, Phillip	1	2	4		
Swann, Thomas	2	4	7		
Thompson, William	1		3		3
Tolbert, Samuel	1	2	3		
Voras, Aron	1	1	2		
Woods, David	2	2	4		2
Wodside, Archabeld	1	2	4		
Woods, Mathew	2	2	4		2
Burket, James	1		1		
Burket, Elazarus	1	3	4		
Bradford, Richard	1	2	3		
Baget, John	1		1		
Bradey, Joseph	1	1	2		
Briggs, Nathan	1	2	2		
Baget, William	2	4	3		
Briggs, James	1	3	4		
Black, Mathew	1	2	5		
Black, John	1	2	2		
Caps, Thomas	1	3	3		
Cole, William	3	1	5		10
Coggin, Burrel	1	2	3		
Crook, John	1	1	3		2
Coggin, John	1	1	2		
Cox, David	2	1	1		1
Codey, James	2	2	5		
Cotten, Alexander	1				
Cameron, John	1		1	1	
Cameron, Absalom	1	1	2		
Cotten, Abner	2	3	4		1
Cole, Stephen	1	1	1		
Davis, Henry	1				
Davis (Widow)	2	2	4		
Davis, Benjamin	2	5	5		1
Davis, John	1				
Daniel, James	2	4	3	1	9
Davis, Edward	1	2	2		
Davis, Hardy	1	2	4		
Devenport, Agustian	4	3	7		
Eps, Plesent	1	3	4		
Ellis, John	3	1	2	1	
Ellis, James	1	1	1		
Fry, Daniel	1		2		
Fry, Joseph	1	1	2		
Fisher, Michael	1	2	3		1
Giles, Richard	1	1	2		
Golsbey, Wade	1	2	1		
Gainer, John	1	2	1		
Grist, William	3	2	6		
Giles, Absalom	1	1	2		
Gess, Jacob	1	1	2		
Golsbey, Drury	1	1	1		
Gillim, Conrad	1	1	3		
Henly, William	2	1	4		
Hoges, Joseph	1	2	3		
Harris, Jesse, Ser	2	1	2		1
Harris, Jesse, Jur	1	2	3		1
Johnston, John (B. D.)	1	4	5		
Johnston, John	1	2	4		
Jones, Else	1	2	3		
Kinney, William	1	5	4		
Lofland, Daniel	1	2	7		
Lofland, Richard	1	4	4		
Loften, Lewis	1	3	5		8
Lenair, Clemment, Jur	1	1	1		
Lenair, Clement, Sr	3	5	2		3
Low, Frederick	2	1	6		
Lofland, John	1	3	4		
Ledwell, William	1	2	4		
Mills, Jonathan	1	3	7		
Mash, Joseph	1	2	3		
Mills, George	2	4	6		
Morgan, James	1	1	2		
Morris, John	1		3		
Maraum, Sarah		1	3		2
Newson, Lewis	1	3	4		
Parks, Charles	3	3	6		
Parks, Timothy	2	3	5		
Parks, Ebenezer	2	6	3		
Parks, Allen	2	3	4		
Parks, John	1		4		3
Penney, William	1		4		4
Peeler, Anthony	1	4	4		
Quick, Tunis	1	3	5		
Quick, Benjamin	1	1	2		
Riley, Ann	2	2	1		
Riley, James	1		2		3
Reed, John	1	2	3		
Roberts, Samuel, Jur	1		2		
Russell, Nathan	1	2	3		
Runyen, Joseph	1	1	3		
Runyen, Phineas	3	4	3		
Riley, George	1		2		
Runyen, Belford	1	1	3		
Roe, John	1	3	3		
Stevens, Martha		3	5		
Sarrat, Thomas	3	2	5		
Seeret, Simon	2	3	4		
Stokes, Christopher	1	2	2		3
Smith, James	1	1	3		
Smith, Alexander	1	1	4		
Silvers, John	2	1	2		
Skeans, Mathew	3	2	4		4
Shipton, Robert	1	3	4		
Stilwell, David	1	3	6		
Serrat, Allen	2	4	6		
Stilwell, John	1				
Thompson, William	1	7	5		
Tenpenney, Nathaniel	1	2	5		
Vonner, John	1	2	3		
Vonner, Henry	1	1	3		
Wallis, William	1	1	2		
Wyatt, John	2	3	5		
Wyatt, Nathan	2	3	3		
Ward, John	1	1	4		
Ward, James Jordon	1				
Williams, Thomas	2		4		
Wyatt, John, Jur	1		1		
Yont, John	2	2	9		
Daywalt, Beck	1		1		
Buckhart, John	2	1	1		
Boss, Phillip	2	1	4		
Beger, Henry	1	1	3		
Buckhart, Daniel	1	2	3		
Billing, Dr John	2		5		2
Belling, Frederick	1				
Belling, Bessima	1				
Belling, John, Jur	1				3
Beck, John	1	4	3		
Buckhart, George	2	6	4		
Buckhart, George, Jur	1	1	2		
Blaze, George	1	1	2		
Bierly, David	1	1	4		
Bierly, Martin	3	3	4		
Bierly, Jacob	2	4	5		
Brooks, Humphry			5		15
Brookshire, Manering	1				
Billings, David	1				
Billings, Henry	1				
Conger, Jonathon	2		5		
Cross, Jacob	2		3		
Cross, Peter	1		3		
Cross, Jacob, Jur	1	3	5		
Claver, Frederick	1	1	1		
Claver, John	3		4		
Kimball, Caleb	2	3	3		
Crotts, Jacob	1	3	6		
Carn, Phillip	1	2	3		
Carn, Leonard	1	2	6		
Christopher, Thomas	1	3	1		
Charles, George	1	1	2		
Capely, John	1				
Carn, Peter	1				
Derr, Melcher	1	3	3		
Duice, Thomas	1	1	4		
Davis, Merick	3	2	2		
Elston, William	2	2	2		
Floyd, John	1	2	2		
Frank, William	2	1	6	2	
Feazer, George	1	1	3		3
Frank, John	1	1	3		
Frank, Martin	1	2	2		
Fry, Henry	1	1	3		
Floyd, Francis	1	1	6		
Gallimore, James	1	2	3		
Gallimore, John	1	2	1		
Gallimore, William	1	2	6		
Gibbens, Peter A	2	3	2		
Garner, Phillip	2	2	5		
Goss, Ephraim	3	3	7		
Goss, Frederick	3	4	5		1
Goss, Frederick, Jur	1	1	2		
Huffman, Daniel	2	3	4		
Hedrick, Francis	1	6	3		
Homes, Reuben	1	1	4		1
Hinkle, Jacob	1				
Hedrick, Peter	4	3	4		
Hinkle, George	1				
Hlshouser, Michael	1	2	1		2
Holliway, William	1	1	4		
Jackson, Thomas	1	1	2		
Jones, John	1				
Lain, William	1	1	4		
Lucy, Frederick	1	2	3		
Lucy, John	1	1	3		
Lucy, Michael	1		2		
Lockebey, Henry	1	3	4		
Merrill, Samuel	1	2	3		1
Merrill, Elijah	1		1	1	3
Michael, Barnet	1		3		
Myars, Michael	1	3	3		
Miller, Frederick	1				
Miller, George	1		1		8
Marbrough, Leonard	1	3	5		
Miller, John	1		5	1	
McKaren, Michael	1	5	5		
Merrill, William	1	2	5		2
Madewell, John	1	3	2		
Madewell, James	1		2		
Martin, George	1		2		
Miller, Jacob	1	1	3		1
Miller, David	1		1		
Notheren, Samuel	1	1	1		
Notheren, Joseph	2	2	3		
Owen, James	2	1	4		8
Owen, Richard	1	1	3		
Owen, William	1				
Owen, Benjamin	1	1	1		
Owen, Ambrose	2	1	2		1
Owen, Henry	1				
Tisinger, Adam	1	2	2		
Rich, John	2	2	5		
Rickard, John	1	4	5		
Rickard, Leonard	2	1	2		
Rickard, Casper	2		2		
Roblin, Lewis	1		1		
Rickard, Jacob	1				
Rider, Adam	1	2	3		
Rich, Thomas	1		1		
Shepperd, John, Jur	1		1		
Sumey, Peter	2	5	1		
Sims, John	1	1	1		
Shepperd, John	3	2	5		
Sumey, Michael	2	1	4		
Smith, Lucy	2		1		
Smith, Leonard	1	3	5		
Senoner, Benjamin	1	2	4		
Smith, Peter	1		3		1
Smith, Casper	1	2	1		
Smith, Margret	1	1	2		4
Smith, David	1	2	4		3
Strange, William	1	2	6		3
Smith, Frederick	1	1	1		
Smith, John	1	1	1		
Shults, George	2	3	4		
Thomas, Jessey	1		1		
Thomas, Elisha	1		2		
Wolf, Jacob	1				
Wortman, Henry	3	2	5		
Womack, Archabeld	1		2		
Wolf, Michael	1	1	3		
Womack, Abraham	5	1	1		
Welch, Mathew	1	2	2		
Womack, Richard	1	1	4		
Wyman, Henry	1	2	5		
Young, Jacob	1	2	2		
Young, Frederick	1		2		
Young, Francis	1	3	3		
Avery, John	3	3	2		1
Adinger, Christopher	2	3	6		
Blessing, Jacob	1		1		
Berger, Charles		3	5		
Buck, Daniel	1	3	2		
Berger, George	1	3	2		
Clotfalder, George	1	3	2		
Clotfalder, John	1	4	6		
Coonse, John	1	3	3		
Conrad, Adam	3	2	3		
Conrad, Henry	1	1	2		
Clotfalder, Felix	2	1	2		
Cook, John	1	3	4		
Conrad, Henry	1	1	2		
Clotfalder, Peter	1	2	1		
Derr, Henry	1	3	5		
Day, Michael	1	2	2		
Day, Valentine	2		2		
Easter, Peter	1	2	3		
Easter, Michael	1		1		
Everhart, Peter	1	3	3		
Everhart, Chetian					
Eller, George	1	1	4		

SALISBURY DISTRICT, ROWAN COUNTY—Continued.

NAME OF HEAD OF FAMILY.	Free white males of 16 years and upward, including heads of families.	Free white males under 16 years.	Free white females, including heads of families.	All other free persons.	Slaves.
Frits, George	1	3	5		
Freidle, John	1		4		
Grub, Conrad	1	3	2		
Grub, George	2	2	4		
Grimes, John	2		3		
Grimes, Christian	1		3		
Grimes, Charles	1	2	2		
Hesley, Jacob, Jur	1		1		
Harmon, Adam	1	2	2		1
Hesely, Jacob	2	2	2		
Hamm, Melcher	2		2		
Hamm, Jacob	3		2		
Hagey, George	2	4	5		
Hedrick, Adam	3	4	3		
Hagey, Henry	3	2	6		
Hoppis, Henry	1		4		
Knipe, Christian	1	2	4		
Kain, Peter	3		3		
Lenard, Phillip	2	1	4		2
Livengood, Christian	4		5		
Lowrey, Lucy		3	4		
Livengood, Henry	1		2		
Lenard, Jacob	1	1	4		1
Lenard, Michael	1	4	4		
Lenard, Valentine	3	4	3		
Lopp, John, Sr	3	2	5		4
Lopp, John, Jur	1		1		
Lopp, Jacob	1	1	5		
Myars, Christian	1				
Michel, Barney	2	2	5		
Myars, Peter	1	4	1		
Myars, Michael	1	2	5		
Magines, Alexander	1	4	3		1
Myars, David	1	4	1		
Michel, Peter	1		2		
Myars, Peter	1	2	1		
Michel, Nicholas	1	2	2		
Nifong, George	1	2	4		
Pew, Reuben	2	2	1		
Picket, Ralph	3		4		
Parnell, Edward	1	4	2		
Rake, Frederick	1	3	5		
Repperd, Melcher	1		1		
Sappenfield, John	1	1	2		
Sauer, John	1		2		
Sauer, Phillip	1		3		
Shofe, Henry	2	2	5		
Slagle, Charles	1		6		
Slagle, Frederick	1				
Sappenfield, Michael	1	2	2		
Sink, Michael	1	3	2		
Sink, John	2	4	5		
Sink, Phillip	1	2	3		1
Spraker, George	1	3	1		
Shofe, Henry, Jur	1	4	1		
Snider, Jacob	2		2		
Snider, George	1	1	1		
Unger, Laurence	1				
Weaver, George	1	4	5		
Weavil, Stephen	2	3	5		
Wacley, Peter	1	2	2		
Wagginor, Joseph	2	1	2		4
Wagginor, Daniel	3	1	4		17
Wagginor, Jacob	2	3	6		7
Wagginor, Mary		1	1		
Yonce, William	1	4	4		
Yokley, Hugh	1	2	2		1
Yonce, Rudolph	1	3	5		
Blaze, Lewis	2		1		
Blaze, John	2	3	1		
Beck, Phillip	1	1	1		
Blaze, Daywalt	1		2		
Beard, Michael	1	3	3		1
Coningham, Joseph	3	3	5		
Coningham, William	1		1		
Cummins, Samuel	2	3	1	1	4
Coyl, Patrick	1	2	2		
Coningham, Hugh, Jur	1		2		
Cope, Jacob	1				
Dancy, John	2		1		
Davis, Joseph	1	1	3		
Dancy, William	1	1	2		
Dancy, John, Jur	1	2	3		
Agers, Landrine	1	1	5	1	
Greene, John	1	1	2		
Huff, Jacob	1		1		
Hollis, John	2	3	6		
Hunt, Daniel	2	1	4		
Hunt, Gasham	1	4			
Harper, Thomas	2		3		
Hannah, Joseph	3	2	4		
Harper, Samuel	1		4		
Hilton, Beachem	3	2	5		
Hunt, Jonathan	1	2	2		
Helmstatler, Peter	1		3		
Helmstatler, Adam	1		2		
Hunt, John	2	4	4		
Hollis, William	1	1	1		
Lanning, Joseph	2		5		
Lanning, John	1	3	2		
Loyd, John	1	2	4		
McCrary, Boyd	2	6	4		
McCrary, Hugh	1	1	3		
McCrary, John	1	1	4		
Morefield, John B	1	4	4		
Milsaps, William	1	2	2		2
Michel, Frederick	1	2	2		
McCrary (Widow)		1	3		5
Kelly, William	1		1		
Owen, John					
Owen, Samuel	1				
Owen, Robert	1	2	3		
Parks, Joseph	2		2		
Reed, Eldad	3	2	4		
Reed, George	1	1	3		
Rushen, Arnold	1	1	3		
Silvers, John	1	3	2		
Tracey, Michael	1	2	1		
Thompson, George	1				
Whitaker, Joshua	3	1	3		
Wilson, John	1	5	3		
Winkler, Henry	2	3	1		
Winkler, Peter	1		1		
Wiseman, William	1	4	4		
Wallen, Carhart	1	4	3		
Whitaker, Peter	1	5	5		
Wilson, Richard	2	3	3		
Wilson, Boyd	1		2		
Whitaker, John	1		1		
Wilson, Charles	1		3		
Yarbrough, Alexander	4		2		
Yarbrough, Henry	1		2		
Arenhart, Killian	1	1	2		
Arenhart, George	2	4	3		
Arenhart, Phillip	1	3	2		1
Arenhart, John	2	3	1		
Bird, Valentine	1		3		
Beam, Jacob	2	3	5		
Bullen, George	3	2	5		3
Brougher, Jacob	2		3		
Basinger, John	1	2	3		
Bradey, John	1	2	5		
Parks, Noah	2	4	5		
Bullen, Phillip	1	3	5		
Brooner, Henry	1	1	4		1
Basinger, Jacob	1		3		
Krite, Michael	1	4	2		
Koble, Adam	2	1	5		
Cason, Samuel	1	2	1		
Davis, Richard	2	4	1		
Derr, Valentine	2		1		
Dillo, Michael	1	2	4		
Derr, George	1	2	3		
Derr, Andrew	1	1	5		
Draxler, Peter	1	1	5		
Davis, Solomon	1	1	2		
Frick, Jacob	1	2	1		
Frick, Henry	2	4	2		
Frock, Conrad	1	2	3		
Fisher (Widow)	1	1	2		5
Fulwider, Henry	2	1	4	1	2
Fenil, Frederick	1	2	5		
Frick, Mathias	1				
Gatts, Joseph	2		1		
Crison, Nicholas	2	1	5		
Hollar, John	1	2	3		
Hess, John	4	2	5		
Hartline, George	2		2		
Huffman, Francis	1	3	3		
Holshouser, Jacob	1	1	3		
Hartline, Peter	1		3		
Hess, John, Jur	1		1		
Jarret, Phillip	3		2		
Kelley, William	1		1		
Kyger, Conrad	1	4	3		
Caylor, Lewis	1	2	5		
Kenup, William	1	2	2		
Klots, David	1	2	6		
Klingleman, Alexander	3	4	4		
Kyger, Christian	2		1		
Lembley, Phillip	1		3		
Lembley, John	1		1		
Lambley, Joseph	1	1	1		
Lentz, Henry	1	1	5		
Messemer, John	1	2	3		
Morgan, Nathan	1	4	2		
Miller, Peter	1		3		
Moyer, Semion	4		5		
Morgan, Hugh	2	2	3		
Miller, Christian	1	3	2		
Miller, Michael	1	4	4		
Messer, Serget	1	1	3		
Miller, Jacob	1		3		
Miller, George	2		1		
Parker, Richard	1	1	4		2
Pool, Jacob	2	1	4		
Pool, David	2	3	4		
Pitman, Michael	1	5	4		
Reedwine, John	1	4	4		
Rough, John	1	1	3		
Reed, John	2	1	1		
Reed, Madad	3		2		
Shooeman, Christian	1	3	4		
Smethers, William	2	2	5		
Shueman, George	1	3	4		
Stoner, Michael	1		5		
Shuman, John	1	1	9		
Walker, William	1		7		
Woliever, Joseph	1	1	2		
Walker, Leonard	2	4	3		
Youst, Jacob	1	1	5		
Anderson, John	1	2	4		
Albright, Frederick	2	2	3		
Benson, Leven	2		5		1
Brummel, Jacob, Jur	1	2	2		
Bodenhimer, John	2	3	4		
Bodenhimer, Peter	1		1		
Bodenhimer, Christian	1		2		
Brummell, Jacob	1	1	3		
Beene, Nicholas	1	1	1		
Burke, Edward	1	1	5		
Bodenhimer, Charity	2		1		
Billingsly, Ruth	1	1	6		
Connely, William	1	2	2		
Cormon, Joseph	1	1	1		
Coppis, Peter	1		2		
Credlespaugh, Thomas	1		2		
Chadewick, Joshua	2		4		
Chainey, John	2	2	3		
Covey, Noble	1	2	4		
Credlespaugh, William	1		2		
Craver, Phillip	3	2	3		
Clinard, Jacob	2	2	5		
Conrad, Peter	1				
Craver, Michael	1	1	1		
Cooper, James	1	3	3		
Dills, William	2		4		
Dial, Shadrick	1		6		
Davis, Hannah			3		
Davis, Jacob	2	3	4		
Davis, Henry, Jur	1	1	2		
Davis, Jacob, Jur	1	2	2		
Davis, John	1	2	3		
Davis, Samuel	1	1	2		1
Davis, William	2	2	3		
Davis, James	1	1	2		
Davis, Henry	2		4		
Danil, Peter	2		3		
Danil, Paul	1		1		
Danil, Lyon	1	1	2		
Derr, Andrew	3	1	8		
Danil, Randal	2	2	7		6
Evans, James	2		5		
Ensley, David	1	1	4		
Fox, John	4	3	7		
Fleshman, Ferdinand	1		1		
Grove, John	1	2	2		
Grimes, Jacob	1	2	6		
Howard, Stephen	1		2		
Hinkle, John, Jur	1		2		
Howard, Mikajah	4	3	4		
Harris, John	1	2	4		
Howard, John	1	2	1		
Hinkle, Nathan	1	1	3		1
Hinkle, Anthony	1	1	3		
Hinkle, Wendle	1	2	4		1
Harmon, Adam	2		7		
Houk, Jacob	1	1	2		
Hinkle, Casper	2	2	4		
Heneger, Conrad	1	5	4		
Harron, Richard	2				
Hinkle, John	1	2	1		
Harmon, Valentine	1		1		
Johnston, Archabeld	3	2	3		
Idle, George	2	2	3		
Idle, Elizabeth	1	4	2		
Jones, Ebenezer	1	2	1		1
Jones, Isaac	1	2	5		
Jones, Joseph	1	3	3		
Kestler, Jacob	3	2	3		
Klinart, Phillip	2		1		4
Kimbrough, Thomas	1	1	5		2
Klinart, Peter	1	1	2		
Klinart, Daniel	2		2		
Kamp, Abraham	1		1		
Ledford, William	2	1	1		11
Ledford, Thomas	1	2	5		2
Lewis, Walter	1		1		
Lewis, Thomas	1		1		
Livengood, Hartman	5		4		
Long, Thomas	2	4	4		
Long, Jacob	2	3	5		

FIRST CENSUS OF THE UNITED STATES.

SALISBURY DISTRICT, ROWAN COUNTY—Continued.

NAME OF HEAD OF FAMILY.	Free white males of 16 years and upward, including heads of families.	Free white males under 16 years.	Free white females, including heads of families.	All other free persons.	Slaves.
Ledford, John	1	2	4		5
Lechner, Michael	1				
Long, Felix	2				
Miller, Fredrick, Jur	1	1	1		
McCurrey, John	1	1	2		
Moore, Nathaniel	2	1	3		
Mock, Phillip	6	4	5		
Manlove, William	3		2		
Moore, Joseph	1	1	5		
Monrow, John	2	4	3		2
Molrainey, Joseph	1	1	6		
Motzinger, Daniel	1	2	3		
Motzinger, Felix	2	3	3		
Mauk, Daywalt	1	2	3	3	2
Miller, Fredrick (Sadler)	2		5		11
Miller, Fredrick, Ser	1	1	2		
Motzinger, Jacob	1	2	4		
Motzinger, Elizabeth		3	1		
Odle, John	2	1	2		
Osborn, Stephen	1	4	1		
Osborn, Nathaniel	1	2	3		
Pain, Barnabas	2	2	5		
Pain, James	1	1	4	1	1
Parsons, Robert	1				
Pope, Nathan	1		1		
Perkins, Thomas	1	2	2		
Perkins, Moses	1	1	3		
Passons, William	2	2	3		
Ross, Jean		3	4		
Russem, William	1	3	6		
Rosax, William	2	3	4		
Reese, Enoch	1	1	3		
Robison, Hugh	2	2	4		
Raper, Jacob	1		4		
Richards, Ulerigh	1	2	3		
Richards, Catherina		1	4		
Rosenbam, Alexander	2	2	3		
Ripple, Henry	1	3	3		
Salisbury, John	2	2	5		
Smith, William	2	3	6		
Sapp, Nowell	1	1	2	1	
Smith, Isaac	1	2	6		
Smith, Josiah	1	2	1		
Spurgin, Jean	1	2	3		
Simmons, William	1	1	2		1
Spurgin, William	2	1	6		
Sercker, John	3		3		
Stanley, William	2		1		
Sitzloch, Airhart	5	1	5		
Stanley, Joseph	2		3		
Tharpe, Thos	2	3	1		
Tharpe, James	1	1	2		
Teague, Moses, Jur	1		2		
Teague, Isaac	1	3	6		
Teague, Abraham	3	4	3		
Teague, Jacob	1		2		
Teague, Mathias	1	1	3		
Tice, Jacob	1	3	5		
Turner, Adam	1	4	2		
Teague, Moses	2	1	5		3
Vitteto, Stephen	1		2		
Vail, Joseph	1		1		
Wilborn, Isaac, Jur	1	1	1		
Wilborn, William	1	2	3		
Wilborn, James	2	3	4		
Willborn, William, Sr	1	3	2		
Wilborn, Isaac	1	1	1		
Waitman, George	2		4		
Wire, Barnabas	3		5		
Wilson, Christena	2	1	4		
Wilson, Jacob	1	4	1		
Watson, William	1	3	4		
Wire, William	1	5	1		
Wilborn, Isaac, Sr	4	2	5		
Wilson, Judith	1	4	4		
Wilborn, Gidion	1	1	1		
Albright, Peter	1	1	6		
Albright, John	1	1	4		
Albright, Jacob	1	2	2		
Albright, Christian	1	2	5		
Beasley, William	1	1	3		
Boston, Andw	2	2	3		
Baighel, Andw	1		2		
Bever, Nicholas	3	2	3		
Bever, Henry	2	1	8		
Boston, Phillip	1	2	3		
Boston, Mathias	1	3	2		
Baker, Jacob	1	2	2		
Boston, Stofel	1	2	2		
Bace, Henry	2	1	6		
Campbell, John, Jur	1	6	1		
Campbell, John	1	1	1		4
Freeze, Jacob	3	1	4		
Freeze, John	1	2	3		
Freeze, Peter, Jur	1	1	2		
Freeze, Peter, Senr	2	4	5		

NAME OF HEAD OF FAMILY.	Free white males of 16 years and upward, including heads of families.	Free white males under 16 years.	Free white females, including heads of families.	All other free persons.	Slaves.
Ferrill, John	1		1		2
Gibson, George	1	3	2		2
Gibson, James	1	4	3		2
Gilbraith, Thomas	1		2		
Gougher, Henry	1	2	2		
Gibson, William	2		1		
Galliher, Hugh	1	3	6		
Graham, John	4	2	4		5
Goose, John	3	1	3		
Graham, Richard	3		5		7
Hough, Henry	1	1	5		
Hough, David	2	2	4		
Hays, Andrew	1		1		
Hileman, John	2	1	3		
Kertner, William	1	1	3		
Ketner, Peter	1		2		
Kenneday, Alexander	2	1	1		5
Long, Fredrick	1	1	2		
Laymon, Fredrick	1	4	5		
Linch, John	1	2	4		
McClennahan, Andrew	3	5	4		
Miller, David	3	3	3		
Miller, William	1	3	3		
McFersion, Joseph	1		2		
McCulloch, James	3	2	6		9
Nixon, William	2		3		
Plink, John	2		2		
Penney, Alexander	2	1	2		1
Penney, John	1				2
Ross, Joseph	1		1		
Reed, John	1	2	5		
Rutherford, Griffith	4	1	3		8
Ross, John	1	2	4		
Sewill, Joseph	1		1	1	
Sigler, Fredrick	2	2	4		
Sloop, Conrad	1	2	6		
Sewill, Elizabeth		3	3		1
Savits, George, Jur	1	3	1	1	7
Savits, George, Senr	1		2	1	
Smith, Everhart	2	3	4		
Upright, Samuel	1	3	1		
Crider, Jacob	1	3	5		
Woods, William	1	4	2		
Correll, Jacob	1	1	4		
Dule, Jacob	1	2	2		
Craglo, William	1	1	1		
Anderson, William	3	3	3		
Alexander, William	2	1	4		9
Albright, Michael	1	3	4		
Atwood, James	1				1
Brandon, Mathew	1	2	5		4
Brandon, Elizabeth		2	2		4
Brandon, William	1	1	7		4
Boston, Mathias, Sr	1		1		
Blue, John	4		1		
Boston, Jacob	1	2	2		3
Brandon, John	1	3	4		9
Boston, Andw	1	1	4		
Brougher, John	1	3	2		
Bellah, Moses	2				4
Bellah, Samuel	1	6	2		
Brown, Timothey	3	2	6		
Boston, Jonas	2		3		
Bird, John	2	1	12		
Cathey, William	2				6
Cathey, John	2	3	5		5
Cathey, Jean		2	3		4
Correll, John		5	2		
Cooper, Samuel	1	2	1		
Cooper, Thomas	3	1	4		
Cooper, William	1	1	4		
Dobbins, David	1	2	2		1
Dunnevan, Mathew	1	1	1		
Eagle, George	1	1	4		
Frazer, John	1	1	3		
Finten, John	1		1		
Graham, Fergus	1	1	6		
Hill, Thomas	2		2		
Hill, Abraham	4	1	3		
Hays, Joseph	3		2		
Hays, John	1		2		
Hays, David	1	1	2		
Hartman, Michael	1	3	5		
Johnston, Nathaniel	2	3	2		2
Letaker, John	1	3	2		
Lock, Mathew	3	2	2		27
Lock, Richard	2	1	1		3
Lock, Mathew, Jur	1	3	2		1
Lock, John	1	1	1		8
Lock, Alexander	1	3	2		
Lock, Francis	3	1	2		14
Lamb, James	1	3	1		
Lamb, John	1	4	2		
Laughren, Lawrence	3	1	2		
Meanes, Frederick	1	1	1		
May, John	1				

NAME OF HEAD OF FAMILY.	Free white males of 16 years and upward, including heads of families.	Free white males under 16 years.	Free white females, including heads of families.	All other free persons.	Slaves.
Mahon, Dennis	1	6	4		
Marshall, Thomas	1				
McFeeters, Daniel	3		2		1
McConnell, Daniel	2	1	4		
Martin, Martin	1				
Phillips, John	2	4	4		
Phillips, Reuben	1	2	7		
Plummer, William	1		1		
Robison, Benjamin		1	2		1
Robison, Moses	1		1		
Rian, William	1				
Sawyers, Joseph	1	3	2		1
Stuart, Robert	3	2	1		
Stuart, John	1		2		
Smith, John	2	4	4		2
Savets, Henry	1	1	2		3
Stiller, Peter	1	2	1		
Sever, Fredrick	1		4		
Wallace, John	1	3	4		
Woods, Robert	1				
Amborn, William	1		5		
Akle, John	1	2	2	1	1
Aplin, Lewis	1	1	5		
Akle, Henry	1	2	2		2
Brown, Michael, Jur	1	1	4		
Boyer, Jacob	1		1		
Bedwell, Caleb	2	2	4		
Barier, Catherina		2	5		
Butner, Sarah		2	4		
Bumgardner, Leonard	1	2	4		
Benket, John	2	2	4		
Brindle, John, Jur	1	1	1		
Bolevar, Thomas	1		4		
Brookshier, Jesse	1	2	5		
Bolevar, Stark	1	4	3		5
Butner, William	1				
Brindle, John	2	4	6		1
Boyer, Henry	3	2	6		
Kimoroe, Leonard	1	2	3		
Cooper, Thomas	1	2	1		
Cresey, Nicholas	1		1		
Cox, James	1	4	1		
Cressema, Conrad	1	2	2		
Davis, David	1	2	1		2
Donner, Jacob	1		1		
Douthet, Thomas	1	2	4		
Douthet, William	3	5	3	2	5
Douthet, Jacob	1	1	2	1	6
Douthet, Abraham	1	2	2		
Davis, John	1	4	3		
Davis, James	2	4	3		
Dunnahoe, Ann	1	2	2		1
Elrod, Adam	3	1	9		1
Elrod, John	1	1	3		
Elrod, Christopher	1	3	2		
Elrod, Abraham	1	1	2		
Ellis, Stephen	2	5	2		
Ellis, William	1	2	3		
Felps, John	2	2	2		
Felps, Thomas	2	4	2		7
Fletcher, Mary	2		4		
Felps, Avengton	1	2	2		
Fry, Valentine	1				3
Fry, Peter	3	1	3		
Fry, Christian	1		3		
Fry, John	1	3	3		
Folts, John	1		4		
Fletcher, James, Jr	1	1	1		
Folts, Fredrick	1		3		
Fry, George	2	2	4		
Farley, Archabeld	1		2		
Farley, Stephen	1		2		
Farley, Francis	2		6		
Griffith, Andrew	3	1	5		1
Griggs, Minus	1	5	4		
George, Andw	1	3	3		
Gallion, Thomas	1	2	3		
Greenwood, Joseph	1	3	5		
Hall, William	1				
House, Archabeld	1	3	2		
Harrald, Hugh	1	1	3		
Hains, Phillip	1	5	1	1	
Hawkins, Henry	1	2	1		
Huffman, Jacob	1	1	2		
Hartman, Jacob	1	1	1		
Haye, Lazarus	1	1	1		
Hampton, Ephraim	3	5	7		7
Hopper, Thomas, Sr	1		2		
Hopper, Charles	1	2	2		
Hoozer, Jacob	1		1		
Hickman, William	1		1		
Hopper, Thomas, Jur	1				
Hill, James	1		5		
Hallin, William	1	3	2		
Hartman, Adam	2		3		
Hartman, James	1	1	2		
Hartman, Mary	1			4	

SALISBURY DISTRICT, ROWAN COUNTY—Continued.

NAME OF HEAD OF FAMILY.	Free white males of 16 years and upward, including heads of families.	Free white males under 16 years.	Free white females, including heads of families.	All other free persons.	Slaves.
Harington, Jonathan	1	2	4		
James, Nicholas	1	3	2		
Jarvis, Elijah	1	1	3		
Johnston, James	1	2	3	1	
Jarvis, Zadock	1	3	4		
Jarvis, James	1		2		
Koons, George	1	1	1		1
Kent, John	1	1	2		
Kent, James	1				
Kehely, Christopher	1	2	3		
Knows, Joseph	1	2	6		
Latherman, Jonas	1	1	2		1
Link, William	1	3	4		
Lynn, Alexander	1	1	2		
Latherman, John	1	4	1		
McKnight, George, Jur	1	2	1		
Miller, John	1	2	3		
Miller, Valentine	1	2	3		
Markland, Jonathan	1	1	2		
Miller, Michael	1	3	3		
Miller, Nicholas	1	2	1		
Monrow, Thomas	1		2		5
McKnight, Roger	1	1	1		
Miller, Mary	2	1	1		
Michael, William	1	4	3		
Milligan, Lewis	1	4	1		
McKnight, George	3	1	4		3
Miller, Henry	1	3	4		
Matherly, John	1	2	5		
Miller, Martin	1	4	1		
Mock, Jacob	1	2	4		
Murrey, John	1	3	1		
Nock, George	1		3		
Pain, Zacheriah	1	5	7		
Perryman, Isaac	2	3	5		
Petrey, Adam	1	2	6		
Peck, Samuel	1		4		
Peck, Nathan	1	1	3		
Pelley, James	2	1	4		3
Pool, William	3	1	4		
Jacobs, John	1	3	6		
Pool, William, Jur	1	1	1		
Pickel, Fredrick	2	3	3		1
Petrey, Henry	2	3	2		
Riddle, John	1		1		
Richardson, Robison	1	2	2		
Riddle, Stephen	2	1	5		4
Rys, John	1	1	7		
Spaugh, Joseph	1		1		
Stuart, Daniel	1		1		
Stuart, John, Jur	1		2		
Shoars, John	1	2	4		
Stuart, John, Ser	1	3	2		
Sluder, Henry	1		2	2	
Sluder, Isaac	1	2	2		
Simermon, Christian, Jur	1		1		
Spaugh, Adam	1		2		
Starr, Gasper	3	2	6		4
Simmermon, John	1		1		
Deele, Henry	1	4	5		
Taylor, Isaac	1	1	2		
Taylor, Rachell	1	3	3		
Tish, Henry	3	2	2		
Turnage, Michael	1		4		
Vanuver, Cornelius	1	3	5		
Vanuver, Cornelius, Jur	1	2	2		
Walk, Martin	2	5	7		
Wood, Vinsen	1		2		
Waitman, Adam	4	1	4		
Wells, Thomas	1	1	1		
White, David	1	1	2		
Wilkison, William	2	3	7		2
Warner, William	2		4		
Wasner, Mathias	1		2		
Wesner, Jacob, Jur	1	2	1		
Williams, Francis	1	1	4		2
Welch, Samuel	2	3	1		
Welch, John	1	2	3		
Winskot, John	2	4	4		
White, James	1		3		
White, Isaac	1	1	2		
Wosley, William	1	4	1		
Wood, Thomas	1		2		1
Wilson, James	1	1	1		
Weaver, Jacob	2	2	2		
Wilson, Robert	1		4	1	
Oings, Thomas	1	3	3		
Jones, Michael	1	2	1		
Johnston, James	2	2	2		
Cross, Asel	3	2	5		
Michael, Barney	1	1	1		
Helsley, Jacob	1	5	4		
Hartman, Mary		1	2		
Fisher, Michael	1		2		
Elrod, Samuel	1	2	1		
Elrod, Peter	1	1	3		
Elrod, Jeremiah	1	1	3		
Creaseman, Adam	2	2	5		
Shull, Joseph	1	3	3		
Stuart, Josiah	1		3		
Stuart, Joseph	1		3		
Hickman, John	2	3	3		
Huffman, Jacob	1	6	4		
Ruckman, Josiah	1	1	5		
Morris, John	1	3	2		
Simerman, Christian, Sr	1	2	5		
Simerman, John, Sr	1	2	1		
Michel, William, Jur	1	2	1		
Aldridg, William	3	1	2		
Atkison, James	1	2	3		2
Bates, William	1	2	1		
Baxter, Charles	2	1	7		
Borders, John	3	2	6		
Barkhiser (Widow)		1	1		
Barns, Richard	1	5	3		
Boothe, John	2		5		
Chainey, Judith		1	6		1
Chambers, Mary		2	2		
Cline, Simpson	1		2		
Cline, Peter	1	4	2		
Croswell, Andrew	1	1	3		
Croswell, Elener			1		
Club, Jean		2	2		
Croswell, Thomas	2	2	3		
Chainey, James	1	1	3		
Chapman, William	1	2	3		1
Champaign, William	1	2	2		
Dotey, Moses	1		3		
Davis, John	1	3	4		
Jones, Wise		2	4		
Earnest, George	4	3	1		
Earnest, Henry	1	1	3		
Fisher, Michael	1		2		
Farley, Stuart	1	2	2		
Farley, Daniel	1		1		1
freemon, Agnes		2	4		
German, Thomas	1	1	1		
Greer, John	1	4	2		
Gobble, John	1	4	3		
Gobble, Jacob	1				
Fitzgerrald, Garret	2	3	2		
Goss, Margaret	1				2
Garret, John	2	5	3		
Gardnor, David	1	2	1		
Harrell, Hugh	1	3	2		
Helsley, Michael	1	4	3		
Harmon, Phillip	1	3	5		
Harrawood, Zaniah	1	1	2		
Hartley, Labon	1		5		
Hartley, Benja	1	2	2		
Hill, Isaac	1	2	3		
Hise, George	1	1	4		
Hicks, Thomas	1	1	2		
Jinnings, Robert	1	2	2		
James, Peter	1	3	4		
Jinnings, William	1	2	3		
Jinnings, John	1		3		
Latherman, Christian	1	3	5		
Latherman, Daniel	1				
Lynn, William F	1	2	4		
Leach, Richard	2	1	3		
Lyons, William	1	1	3		
Lee, Andw	1	2	3		
Long, Alexander	3	3	2		26
Loyd, John	1	2	4		
McKatee, Edmond	3	2	1		
Moore, William	1	1	6		
Metsler, John	1	2	1		
Morris, John	1	2	3		
Myrick, John	2	2	2	1	
Michael, Christian	2	4	2		
Moralney, Joseph	1	1	2		
Nicholson, Lucy	1	3	3		
Patterson, James	2	4	3		
Beck, Jacob	3	3	6		1
Beck, George	1	2	1		
Pain, Joshua	1		2		
Beck, Phillip	2	5	3		
Pain, Charles	1		1		
Pain, Enoch	1	2	1		
Parreck, Thomas	1	1	2		
Reed, Avington	2	5	4		
Simpson, Ross	1	1	1		
Reess, John	1	2	2		
Ridgway, Phillip	4	4	9		1
Rinkard, George	1	5	5		
Roberts, Henry	1		6		
Reed, George	2	2	3		
Robertson, John	1		3		
Stallings, Jacob	1	1	4	1	1
Stanfild, Thomas	1	2	3		
Simpson, Benjamin	2	4	6		
Swisgood, Phillip	1		4	1	
Swisgood, Adam	1	2	3		
Slagle, Peter	1				
Smith, Landers	1	1	3		
Smith, Nathan	3	1	4		
Smith, Jacob	3		2		
Stuart, William	1	1	4		
Zevely, Henry	1	4	4		
Trentham, Jeptha	2	1	3		
Young, Michael	1	2	5		
Vaun, Fredrick	1	1	4	1	
Wotton, William	1	5	2		
Wood, Archabeld	1	1	2		
Werlau, Elizabeth	3		4		
Williams, James	2		4		1
Wood, Daniel	2	1	2		1
Wood, Joshua	1	2	1		
Wood, Jarret	1	6	4		
Walsor, Martin	1	1	3		
Walsor, Fredrick	2	1	2		
Williams, Ezekel	2		3		
Williams, Henry	1		1		
Watkins, Ambrose	1	2	2		
Winkler, Adam	1	2	4		
Wood, Mary			1		
Wood, Isham	3	4	2		
Wood, William	1	1	4		
Watkins, David	1	1	3		
Wood, Elizabeth, Jur	1	2	1		
Wood, William, Ser	1	1	1		
Wood, James	1	2	3		
Winkler, Francis	1	5	5		
Anderson, Thomas	1	2	2		
Allemang, Fredrick	3	1	1		
Allemang, Daniel	1		3	3	
Atkeson, James	1	2	2		2
Allison, Andw	1	1	3		3
Brandon, John	1		1		
Beard, Christina			3		2
Betts, Andrew	3	2	2		1
Beroth, Henry	1	2	3		
Biles, Joseph	2	1	8		2
Biles, Thomas	1	4	2		
Biles, Jonathan	3		5		
Biles, John	1				
Bues, John	2	1	2		8
Brinkle, Nicholas	2	2	2		
Beard, John	3				1
Blake, John	2	1	7		6
Brown, Peter	1	1	5		4
Bream, Conrad	2	2	2		7
Brown, John	2	3	3		
Beard, Lewis	1	1	1		5
Belfore, Elizabeth		1	2		3
Busley, John	2	2	4		
Coyl, George	1				
Coughenam, Christian	1		3		
Cowin, David	1	2	4		
Coughenam, Jacob	1	3	4		
Erwin, John	2		1		
Crosser, Leonard	2	1	2		
Cross, John	3	5	3		
Casey, William	1		2		
Clary, John	2	5	4		1
Clary, Daniel	2	5	6		11
Carson, Henry	1	1	4		1
Chambers, Maxwell	4	4	3	1	35
Carson, John	2		6	1	
Carson, Hugh	1				
Carson, William	2				5
Carson, James	1				1
Craige, James	1	3	2		13
Cross, Henry	1	1	1		
Craige, Mary	1		3		
Cotten, Isaac	1				
Dunn, Silas	1	1	2		
Dickson, Richard	1	1			
Dunn, Charles	1				
Dayton, Samuel	1		2		1
Easton, Zadock	1	1	3		
Ellis, Radford	1	2	3		4
Furr, Tobias	2				
Frazer, James	1		2		2
Frohook, Thomas	1				52
Frohook, Isham	1				
Frazer, Peter	1				
Ford, Wiatt	1	2	2		
Fisher, John	1		2		
Gay, Robert	1	2	4		
Gardner, Robert	1	2	2		1
Gardner, John, Jur	1	2	3		
Gardner, James	1				
Gardner, John, Ser	1				
Giles, Henry	1	1	3		7
Horah (Widow)		1	2		
Howard, Gidion	1	1	3		
Hamton, William	1		2		
Hoover, George	1	1	3		2

SALISBURY DISTRICT, ROWAN COUNTY—Continued.

NAME OF HEAD OF FAMILY.	Free white males of 16 years and upward, including heads of families.	Free white males under 16 years.	Free white females, including heads of families.	All other free persons.	Slaves.
Holland, Richard	1		4		
Hulin, Arther	1	6	2		
Hunt, Charles	4		2	1	6
Hendricks, Daniel	1	4	6		
Hughes, Joseph	5	3	4		20
Horah, Hugh	1		3		2
Jacobs, Abraham	4	2	4		
Kinder, George	1		1		
Leaf, John	1		2		
Harris, Charles	3		1		5
Lauman, George	1		3		1
Moore, Samuel	1	1			
Moore, Audlen	1	1	2		
Moore, John	2	1	6		
Macay, Spence	1	1	4		19
Murr, George	1		3		
Montfort, Absalom			1	1	2
Mealy, Owen			1		2
Miller, Casper	3	1	5		
Mull, John	2	3	2		
Miller, David	1	1	1		
Newman, Anthony	3	3	4		22
Pinkstone, William	2		2		
Patton, John	2	2	3		1
Pinkstone, Thomas	1	3	3		
Pasinger, Martin	2	2	1		
Pinkstone, Mashick	1				2
Rice, Isham	2	4	3		
Robison, Joseph	1	1	1		
Swink, George	1		2		
Steele, John	2		5		16
Strain, William	1				
Shrode, Christian	1	3	3		
Shuls, Jacob	1				
Swink, Leonard	1	2	3		
Swink, John, Jur	1				
Swink, Henry	2	2	2		
Story, Benjamin	1	2	2		
Silverthorne, George	1	3	4		
Swink, John, Ser	1	1	3		
Stocke, Charles	1		1		2
Shrode, Adam	1		2		
Shafer, John	2	2	3		
Stokes, Montfort	1		1		15
Taylor, Absalom	1	2	3		3
Trotter, Richard	1	1	1		7
Troy, Jean		2	4		7
Turner, Benjamin	1	3	1		
Torrence, Albert	1				1
Townsly, James	2		1		
Troy, Michael	2	4	3		2
Veal, Edward	1		2		
Vickers, William	1		2		
Vickers, Thos	2	1	2		
Utzman, Jacob	2	3	3		2
Woodson, David	2	2	4		2
Williams, Thos	4	2	4		
Wood, Charles	1	5	2		
Yarbrough, Edward	1	1	2		3
Young, Henry	1	3	2		3
Adler, Francis	1		3		
Aginder, Henry, Senr	1				
Aginder, Henry, Jur	1	3	5		
Adams, John					
Aginder, David	1	1	3		
Arenhart, Henry	4		4		
Arenhart, Jacob	1		2		
Arenhart, Abraham	1		1		
Biven, Randal	1		2		
Brown, Phillip, Jur	3	1	1		
Brown, Andrew	1	4	3		
Brown, Abraham	2	3	1		
Brown, David	1	2	3		
Brooner, George	1		2		5
Brown, Jacob	6	1	3		
Butner, Harmon	1		1		
Butner, David	3	2	3		1
Bartley, John	1		1		
Brooner, Phillip	1	2	1		
Brown, Phillip	2	3	4		
Brown, Michael	5		2		15
Biven, Corbin	1	1	2		
Beard, Valentine	1	1	4		3
Basinger, George	1	2	4		
Biven, Leonard	1	2	5		4
Crider, Michael	1	1	1		
Coldiron, George	2	1	5		
Coble, Peter	1		2		
Coldiron, Conrad	1	3	2		
Crider, Christian	2		3		
Crider, Barnet					
Crider, Leonard	1	2	4		
Doremire Andrew	1		4		
Dahenhart, Henry	1		2		
Eller, John (son of Chª)	1	1	1		
Eary, John	1	1	1		
Eary, Abraham	1	3	2		

NAME OF HEAD OF FAMILY.	Free white males of 16 years and upward, including heads of families.	Free white males under 16 years.	Free white females, including heads of families.	All other free persons.	Slaves.
Eller, Christian	3	1	4		
Eller, Melcher	1	4	2		
Eller, Henry	1	2	2		
Eller, John	1	2	3		
Eller, John Milker	1	3			
Eary, Zacriah	1		4		
Eller, Jacob	1	1	1		
Eller, Fredk	1		2		
Eller, Jno (son of Melker)	1		2		
Fisher, Fredrick	3	1	4		13
Fite, Peter	4		5		
Fraley, Henry	1		2		
Fraley, George	2	2	4		
Fite, Conrad	1		4		
Fraley, Jacob	1	4	1		
Fredrick, Christian	1	2	1		
Folts, Peter	1		1		
Fisher, Jacob	2	1	4	1	
Fults, Henry	1		2		
Getchey, John	1	3	7		
Getchey, Fredrick	1		1		
Grub, Elizabeth	1	1	5		
Hartman, John	1				
Hendricks, Daniel	1	4	5		
Holobaugh, George	1	2	3		
Hendricks, Peter	1	1	4		
Hill, John	3	3	2		
Hildebrand, John	1	2	2		
Caren, Adam	1	1	3		
Kesler, John	1	2	2		
Karen, John	2	2	6		
Coble, John	1	2	1		
Karen, Conrad	3	2	5		
Kroul, William	1	1	4		
Krotser, Phillip	2	2	3		
Kobble, Peter, Senr	1	1	4	1	
Kobble, Peter, Jur	1		3		
Kobble, Michael	1		2		
Kroul, Peter	1		2		
Lance, John, Ser	1	3	4		
Lance, Peter	1	3	5		
Lance, Benjamin	1		3		
Moyer, Henry	1		2		
Marbery, Francis	4	3	2		6
M'Cann, John	1		2		
Popst, Henry	1		2		
Rusher, Jacob	1	2	2		
Ribley, Martin	2	1	6		
Swink, Michael	1	1	2		3
Slighter, Henry	1		3		
Smith, George	1				
Sasaman, Henry		2	1		1
Shriver, John	1	4	2		
Shooman, George	1		2		
Smithell, Joseph		1	3		
Truse, Adam	1	2	3		
Truse, Michael	1	2	4		
Wervel, Jacob	2	2	3		
Walton, Richard	5	1	2		
Waller, Elizabeth	1		2		
Wise (Widow)	1	2	2		
Weighant, John	1	2	3		
Williams, John	1	3	4		
Wetheraw, Aywalt	1	2	4		
West, William	2	2	2		
Biles, Charles	1	2	3		3
Biles, Daniel	1	7	3		
Burris, Jonathan	5	2	5		5
Culbertson, John	2	4	6		
Clary, Conner	1	2	1		
Cotten (Widow)			5		
Cowen, Phebey			5		
Duglass, Mary			3		
Eanis, William	1		3		
Ghean, James, Ser	4		6		
Ghean, James, Jur	1		3		
Ghean, Thomas	2		2		
Hightower, Messener		1	3		
Hunter, John	1		1	1	
Heathman, James	1	3	4		
Howard, John	2	3	4		1
Hains, Ralph	1	2	1		
Howard, Mathew	1	1	1		
Jones, James	1	4	3		
Kenhard, James, Ser	4	3	3		
Kerr, Stephen	1	2	1		2
Kinkade, John	1		2		
Lowrey, John	2	1	2		
Leach, Benjamin	1	3	3		
Lewis, Peter, Ser	1	1	3		
Lewis, Peter, Jur	1	1	1		
Lewis, Samuel	1	1	2		
Link, Jacob	3	1	8		
M'Crakin, James	1	2	6		
Montgomery, John	1	3	1		2

NAME OF HEAD OF FAMILY.	Free white males of 16 years and upward, including heads of families.	Free white males under 16 years.	Free white females, including heads of families.	All other free persons.	Slaves.
Marlin, James	2	2	2		
Marlin, John	1	1	2		
Marlin, Thomas	1	2	3		
Marlin, Jaˢ, Esqr	1	1	3		
Marlin, John, Jur	1	1	1		
M'Coy, William	1	2	1		
Pinkston, Peter	3	1	3		
Palmer, Edmond	3	1	3		
Raimond, Wm	1	3			
Robley, John	1		1		
Robison, Richard	3		1		1
Rainey, William	1				
Robison, Henry, Jr	1				
Robison, Henry	2		4		5
Robison, Hugh	1				
Robison, George	1	1	4	1	
Robison, Henry, Esqr	4		6		
Robison, William	1	2	2		
Reary, George	2		1		
Smith, Martha			3		
Spring, Albert	1	3	5		
Sanders, Robert	1	2	3		
Tomison, George	2	3	1		3
Todd, John, Jur	1	2	4		1
Tomison, Richard	1	3	2		
Trott, Henry	3	3	4	1	
Todd, John	1		1		
Todd, James	1	2	2		
Turner, William	1	3	5		
Williamson, William	1	3	5		2
Wallace, Samuel	1	1	6		
Wilson, Samuel, Sr	2		4		
Wilson, Samuel, Jur	1		2		
Wilson, William	1	3	1		
Abbott, Benjamin	1	2	3		2
Bartley, Robert	3		3		
Blair, James	1	4	4		1
Beard, Hannah	1	3	3		
Barkley, David	1				
Bowen, Joseph	2	1	4		
Band, Brezilla	1	2	3		
Barkley, Samuel	1	1	2		
Cathey, Richard	1	1	6		2
Carson, Thomas	1	3	4		11
Cox, John	2		3		
Cox, Charles	1	2	5		
Clemmens, Henry	2	3	7		
Coningham, George	2	1	6		
Conger, John	2	3	6		
Conger, Jonathan, Jr	1	1	1		
Davis, Conrad	1	3	1		
Daily, William	1	3	4		
Dusenbery, Samuel	2	2	2		
Elston, Jonathan	2	2	2		
Ellis, Thomas	3	3	2		9
Elliot, John	1	2	2		
Elliot, William	1	1	6		
Ford, John	2		2		1
Gadbery, Nathaniel	1	4	4		
Giles, John	1	3	4		
Greene, Jeremiah	1	5	2		
Haiden, Joseph	1		3		2
Hudgins, William	2				14
Hunt, Gasham	2	2	4		
Hunt, Able	1	2	1		
Lewis, Abraham	1	3	5		
Lynn, Isarel	1	1	1	1	
M'Cartney, Lewis	1	3	4		1
M'Cartney, Thomas	2	3	5		
Mills, Samuel	1	4	4		
M'Kee, Robert	1		2		3
Merrill, Andrew	2		5		
Morlin, Vinsent	1		2		
Merrill, Jonathan	1	1	2		
Moore, William, Ser	3	2	5		
Macay, James	4		3		8
Moore, William, Jur	2	1	3		1
M'Kee, Robert, Jur	1		1		1
Maguire, Zebilla			4		
M'Kee, Dorsay	1		1		
Maguire, Daniel	2	1	3		2
Owen, Raph	1	1	3		
Patton, John (O. R.)	2	1	3		
pippinger, Abraham	1	1	2		
Pew, Joseph	1	2	1		
Quick, Richard	1				
Williams, Reese	1	2	2		
Rounseval, David	1	1	3		
Ross, John	1	2	3		
Rodsmith, Paul	2	1	2		
Rats, Godferry	1	2	2		3
Richardson, Charles	2	2	4		
Smith, Thomas	1	2	4		
Smith, Andrew	2		2		
Smith, Joseph	1				
Sloan, John, Ser	2	1	3		1
Sloan, John, Jur	1	1	4		5

SALISBURY DISTRICT, ROWAN COUNTY—Continued.

NAME OF HEAD OF FAMILY.	Free white males of 16 years and upward, including heads of families.	Free white males under 16 years.	Free white females, including heads of families.	All other free persons.	Slaves.
Smith, Benjamin	1	1	3		1
Smith, George	2		1		1
Smith, Barbara	1		2		6
Scrivner, James	1	3	6		
Stoner, John Abm	1	2	1		
Simpson, Robert	2		1		
Smith, Cornelius	2	2	3		
Scudder, Mathias	1		5		
Scudder, Abner	1	1	1		
Scudder, Isaac	1	1	1		
Smith, Clara	2		2		1
Strange, Owen	1	1	2		
Todd, Caleb, Senr	3	1	4		
Todd, Thomas	1	3	3		
Todd, Peter	1	3	4		
Todd, Benja, Jur	1	3	3		
Todd, William	1	1	3		
Todd, Joseph	1	3	2		
Todd, Benja, Ser	2	2			
Todd, Caleb, Jur	1	1	3		
Tensey, John	1		1		
Willis, Thomas, Senr	1		1		
Wiseman, Jacob	2	3	2		
Warford, Joseph	2	1	3		
Wilson, John	2		1		1
Wiseman, Isaac	1	2	3		
Wilson, John, Jur	1	2	3		
Willis, Thomas, Jur	1	3	3		
Willis, George	1	5	3		
Wiseman, Jacob, Jur	1		1		
Wiseman, James	1	1	3		
Aldeman, Peter, Jur	1	4	2		
Aldeman, Peter	1		2		
Overkersh, Francis	1	3	3		
Overkersh, George	1	2	1		
Overkarsh, Jacob	1		1		
Berger, George H.	2	2	6		3
Bullen, John	3	3	2		
Bever, Peter	4	5	3		
Brown, Thomas	1	3	5		
Baringer, Peter	3	1	4		
Berger, John	1	1	1		
Casper, Henry	1	2	2		
Cummins (Widow)		1	1		
Corl, Peter	1	2	4		
Correll, Adam	1	1	4		
Cruse, Phillip	1	1	5		
Casper, John	1	1	5		
Casper, Adam	1		3		
Crouel, George	2	3	5		
Deele, Youst	1		4		
Deele, Peter	1				
Dillo, Jacob	1				
Dillo, Michael	1	1	4		
Akle, John	1	1	5		
Fisher, John	1	1	2		
Freeze, Jacob	3	1	4		
Fisher, Jacob	1	2	4		
Garner, Mathias	1	3	6		
Helms, George	1		2		
Hofner, Martin	1	4	1		
Hampton, John	3	2	4		
Hornbarier, Valentine	4	1	3		
Hampton, William	3	1	4		
Hofner, George	1		1		
Hiley, Michael	1	4	1		
Josey, John	4	1	3		
Klotts, Jacob	1		2		
Klotts, Wendle	1	1	2		
Klotts, Jacob, Jur	1				
Klotts, Leonard	1				
Koone, Anthony	1	2	6		
Kenup, John	2	2	4		
Kaster, Jacob	2	2	4		
Kenup, Jacob	1	2	2		
Klotts (Widow)	1	2	1		
Lance, David	2	1	2		
Lance, Peter	1		3		
Lierly, Peter	1	1	2		
Lierly, Jacob	1	2	2		
Lance, Bostion	2	2	4		
Lance, Bostion, Jur	1		2		
Lingle, Anthony	1				
Lenard, Henry	1	2	5		
Lynn, Robert	1	4	1		
Lingle, Francis	1	4	2		
Miller, Nicholas	2	2	2		
Miller, Fredrick	1	5	2	1	
Morer, Fredrick	2	1	4		
Miller, Wendle	2	4	4		
Messemer, Peter	2		2		
Miller, Martin	3	1	6		
Miller, Daniel	1	4	1		
Mourer, Rudy	2	4	2		
Miller, Phillip	2	4	2		
Morer, Jacob	1				

NAME OF HEAD OF FAMILY.	Free white males of 16 years and upward, including heads of families.	Free white males under 16 years.	Free white females, including heads of families.	All other free persons.	Slaves.
Pool, John	1	4	3		
Peeler, Michael	2	2	4		
Phillips, Jessey	1		1		
Poules, Adam	1	2	2		
Randleman, John	3	3	4		2
Rimer, Nicholas	3	4	4		
Roseman, George	1	4	3		
Rebley, Peter	1		3		
Siffard (Widow)	1	1	3		
Shuppin, Nicholas	2	2	2		
Siffard, Leonard	1	7	2		
Stierwalt, John	3	2	2		
Stierwalt, Fredrick	1		3		
Troutman, Peter, Jur	1	2	2		
Troutman, Peter	2		1		
Troutman, Adam	3	1	6		
Troutman, Melcher	2	5	3		
Wensel (Widow)		3	4		
Walker, Henry	1	1	2		
Youst, Phillip	1	4	6		
Byrns, Charles (B. O.)	3	1	2		
Byrns, Thomas	2	2	2		
Bodenhimer, William	4	2	3		
Bettis, William	2	3	4		
Bowers, Jacob	1	3	5		
Butrem, William	2	3	6		
Blessing, John	1		1		
Benblossom, Jacob	1	2	1		
Brown, Daniel	1	1	4		
Benblosom, Abraham	1	2	2		
Barkshier, Henry	2	3	3		
Bowers, Adam	1	2	3		
Black, Jacob	2	2	6		
Bierly, Jacob	2		2		
Brown, James	1	3	5		
Benton, Isaac	2	5	5		
Bradburn, John	1	2	1		
Bowers, George	2		1		
Bringle, Casper	2	3	5		
Byrel, Martin	3	6	4		
Boen, John	1	1	1		
Benson, Reuben	1	1	2		
Crum, Godferry	1	1	3		
Cooper, Job	1		3		
Cooper, Charles	1		1		
Cooper, Jonathen	1	2	4		
Clotfalder, George	1		1		
Clotfalder, Rudolph	2	3	4		
Crum, Christian	1		1		
Cobble, Jacob	1	4	4		
Delap, Daniel	1	4	3		
Delp, Peter	2	4	6		
Highat, John	1	3	5		
Embler, William	3	2	5		
Eller, Leonard	1	3	4		
Ledford, Obediah	1		3		
Frisbey, Abraham	3	5	4		
Fox, Thomas	1	5	3		
Fouts, Nicholas	3		3		
Fouts, Peter	1		2		
Fouts, John	1		3		
Ferguson, William	1		1		
Tenneson, James	1		2		
Garren, Andrew	1	5	2		
Gordon, James	1	2	3		
Garren, James	1	1	6		
Grimes, George	1	3	3		
Gillim, Jesse	1		1		
Gillim, John	1	4	2		
Gillim, Drury	1				
Pigen, Samuel	1		3		
Henson, Samuel	2	2	6		
Haun, Fredrick	3		4		
Helms, John	1	3	1		
Hilton, Thomas	1	1	3		
Hichcock, Isaac	2	1	3		
Hilton, Jonathan	1	2	3		
Hughes, James	2	2	6		
Heplor, Christopher	2	3	2		
Herner, Christian	1	3	2		
Hucheson, Thomas	1	1	2		
Hilton, James	1	1	5		
Jones, Thomas	1	1	8		
Isaacks, John	1				
Kiddle, Elenor		2	1		
Kenoy, Phillip	1	2	5		
Kenut, William	1	2	5		
Krudle, John	2		3		
Pendrey, George	2	1	3		
Luckebey, John, Jur	1	2	2		
Luckbey, David	1	1	3		
Lusk, William	1	2	1		
Lusk, Hugh	1		1		
Luvin, John	1	3	1		
Lusk, Samuel	1		1		
Stiff, Moses	1	5	3		

NAME OF HEAD OF FAMILY.	Free white males of 16 years and upward, including heads of families.	Free white males under 16 years.	Free white females, including heads of families.	All other free persons.	Slaves.
Secrist, Fredrick	3	1	5		
Miller, John	1		2		
McCrary, William	1	5	7		
Morris, Isaac	1		1		
Morgan, James	2	1	2		
Mings, Joseph	1				
Morgan, James, Jur	1		3		
Manering, Andrew	1	3	2		
Miars, David	1	1	3		
Miars, John	1	2	4		
Miars, George	1	1	3		
Miars, Jacob	1	1	5		
Miars, Christian	1	3	2		
Miller, Fredrick	1	1	1		
Morris, William	1				
Odle, Isaac	1	1	2		
Owens, Andw	2	3	1		
Pair, Arthur	1	2	4		
Plummer, John	1		2		
Roberts, John	1	6	3		
Ring, Michael	1		2		
Reggins, James	1	3	2		
Ring, Martin	2	2	4		
Rimer, David	1	1	3		
Ragan, Eli	2	2	3		
Rodes, Mary	2	2	2		
Snider, Jacob	3		2		
Sears, Christian	3	2	8		
Seacrist, Jacob	1	1	2		
Shuler, Peter	1		2		
Shuler, Michael	2	4	3		
Shults, Mark	1	1	1		
Shutz, Andrew	1	2	3		
Seeley, Joseph	1	2	2		
Snider, George	2	2	1		
Summers, Thomas	2	3	5		
Sayrs, Richard	1				12
Spoolman, Fredrick	1		4		
Sears, John	1	4	3		
Sacrist, George	1	1	1		
Tacker, James	1	2	3		
Tharpe, John	1	2	3		
Tacker, Seaborn	4		4		
Tacker, Robert	2	1	3		
Tumbleson, Saml	2	2	4		1
Tumbleson, Josiah	2	2	3		
Wortman, Peter	1	1	1		
Wright, Richard	1	2	5		
Wright, Evan	1		2		
Wright, Phillimon	2	1	5		
Williams, Joshua	1		1		
Wakasor, Jacob	2	2	3		
Wright, William	1	1	2		
Williams, Postem	1				
Waller, Benja	2		3	1	4
Wright, Eassaw	1	1	2		
Veach, John	1	2	4		2
Shuts, Mark, Sr	1	3	5		
Yokley, William	1				
Yarbrough, Joab	1	2	4		
Tacker, William	1	2	2		
Andrew, James	3	2	8		1
Bartley, James	1	1	2		
Barr, Hugh	1				4
Barr, Patrick	1	4	3		1
Barr, John	2	2	3		2
Barkley, Henry	2		1		2
Bunten, John	1	3	8		6
Cowen, Thomas	1	3	8		6
Cowen, William	1	2	3		
Cowen, John	1	1	4		1
Crawford, David	1	2	4		2
Cowen, David	1		1		
Cook, Alexr	2	1	3		1
Erwin, Joseph	2		2		3
Erwin, William	1	2	3		2
Forster, David	2	2	5		2
Forster, Robert	1	4	6		
Forster, William	1	2	4	1	
Gillaspie, Thomas	1	1	4		3
Harvey, John	1		2		3
Huston, Thomas	2	4	2		
Hartsaugh, Paul	2	5	2		
Huston, James	1		2		
Huston (Widow)	1		3		
Kestler, George	2		3		
Kilpatrick, John	3		4		1
Kerr, Margret	2		2		
Kerr, John	1	1	3	1	1
Knox, Benja	3		3		1
Kerr, James	1	1	5		
Lowrance, Josiah	1		5		
Lowrance, Ann	1		2		
Lowrance, Andrew	1	3	3		
Lowrance, Abraham	1		1		1
Moffit, William	1	1	1		

SALISBURY DISTRICT, ROWAN COUNTY—Continued.

Name of head of family.	Free white males of 16 years and upward, including heads of families.	Free white males under 16 years.	Free white females, including heads of families.	All other free persons.	Slaves.
McCorkle, Alexander, Sr	2				6
McCorkle, John	2		2		
McCorkle, Alexander, Jur	1	2	3		
McClain, John	1	2	3		
McKrakin, John	3	5	3		
Gillaspie, Thomas, Sr	4		1		7
Gillaspie, David	1		1		1
Gillaspie, Richard	1		6		8
Gillaspie, Thomas, Jur	1	2	3		4
Wasson, John	3	1	3		1
Philwoward, Nicholas	1		1	1	
Price, Charles	1	1	3		
Patterson, James	1	1	1	1	
Patton, John	1				
Yarwood, Benjamin	1		1		
Rutledg, John	2		4		
Auton, Richard	1	3	5		
Bell, Thomas	3	1	2		
Bell, William	1		6		
Bowman, William	4		4		2
Baxter, Daniel	2	2	7		
Brandon, James	1	1	7		9
Baringer, Jacob	1	1	2		
Cathey, Jean			1		
Carson, Thomas	1	1	2		2
Cowin, William, Senr	3	4	3		1

Name of head of family.	Free white males of 16 years and upward, including heads of families.	Free white males under 16 years.	Free white females, including heads of families.	All other free persons.	Slaves.
Cowin, William, Jur	1	1	2		
Cowin, Benjamin	1	3	6		5
Cadihan, James	1	2	2		1
Dobbins, Alexander, Sr	5	1	5		5
Dobbins, Hugh	1	3	3		
Devenport, William	1	3	6		
Dobbins, Alexr, Jur	1		2		
Dobbins, John, Jur	1				
Dobbins, John	1		4		
Forster, Joseph	1	4	3		1
Fisher, James	1	2	4		
Fergison, Andrew	2	1	1		
Gellihan, Abraham	2	1	3		4
Gillaspie, George	3	3	4		4
Haggins, John	1		5		10
Hamilton (Widow)			2		
Jinkins, Hugh	3	1	3		3
Jinkins, Samuel	1	1	4		
Kerr, Joseph	1	2	2		5
Kerr, Samuel	2		1		6
Lock, Mathew	1	3	5	1	2
McCorkle, Samuel	1	1	4		6
McNeely, John, Senr	3		2		
McNeely, John, Junr	1	3	5	1	2
McNeely, James	1	1	2		
McConnahey, Sampson	2	1	1		
McNeely, David	3	3	3		

Name of head of family.	Free white males of 16 years and upward, including heads of families.	Free white males under 16 years.	Free white females, including heads of families.	All other free persons.	Slaves.
McGlochland, John	1	2	1		
McGlochland, Samuel	1	1	1		
McCollum, Andw	1		5		
McConnahey, Joseph	2		2		2
McConnahey, James	1				1
McConnahey, Hugh	1				
McBroom, James	1	4	2		
McNeely, Archabeld	4	3	7		
Miller, Samuel	3	4	4		2
Miller, Jean	1		4		2
Mathewson, Daniel	1		2		
Nevins, William	1	1	5		
Steele, Martin	1	1	1		
Sillimon, John	2	5	1		
Skiles, John	2		4		3
Stuart, Mathew	1	2	4		
Sloan, Joseph	2	1	4		
Thompson, Thomas	2	2	6		7
Thompson, Joseph	1	3	6		3
Tygart, John	2	4	6		
Nesbitt, William	1	1	2		13
Job, Samuel	2	1	5		
Cox, Edward	1	2	7		
King, Jeremiah	1	1	3		
Morris, Benjamin	1	2	1		

SALISBURY DISTRICT, STOKES COUNTY.

Name of head of family.	Free white males of 16 years and upward, including heads of families.	Free white males under 16 years.	Free white females, including heads of families.	All other free persons.	Slaves.
Deatherage, George	2	4	1		5
Tilly, Lazarus	2	1	7		4
Simmons, Jesse	3	1	4		
Fenley, James	2	2	3		
Tilly, Edmund	2	4	2		1
Tilly, David	1	1	1		
Cox, Joshua	2	3	3		6
Nelson, Joshua	2	6	6		2
Sprouse, David	1	1	2		
Bohannan, James	3	5	6		1
Hickman, Edwin	2	2	4		
Hickman, William	1	1	1		
Cloud, Joseph	2	2	6		1
Edgmond, Samuel	1		3		1
Lawson, John	1		3		1
Davison, David	1	3	3		
Sherry, William	1	3	4		
Wilson, John	1		3		
Faukner, Jonas	1		2		
Cloud, William	2	5	4		
Bohannan, Philemon	1		1		1
Lawson, John	1	2	1		
Collins, Jeremiah	1	3	4		
Mitchel, Ralph	1	1	4		
Collins, Roger	1	1	4		
Fields, Davis	1		4		
Gains, James	2	3	7		3
Pruitt, Peter	1	1	4		
Bailey, William	1	1	4		
Urillis, Moses	1	2	2		
Beasley, Richard	2	2	4		
Collins, Watson	1	4	2		
Hall, Randoph	1	2	4		
Fields, Lansford	1	1	7		
Beasley, William	1	1	3		
McHone, Arche	1	3	4		
Fly, John	1	1	3		
Burge, Allen	1		1		
Lawson, Patmon	1	1	5		
Shelton, Mary	2	1	4		1
Ship, Josias	2		2		2
Isbel, Hickman	1				
Garner, John	1		2		
Coomer, William	1		2		
Bullin, Isaac	1	2	1		
Lawson, David	3		8		
Bridgman, William	2	1	3		
Coomer, Richard	1	3	3		
Ship, Josias	1	2	2		1
Fields, John	1				
Fields, Davis	2		3		
Holt, Fetherston	1	2	4		
Harris, Mathew	2	2	6		
Deatherage, John	3		1		3
Moore, Mathew	6	3	4		15
Goans, Joseph	1	3	3		2
Isbel, Jason	1	2	4		5
Pierce, Jacob	1	1	1		
Nudson, Peter	1		6		
Childress, David	1	1	2		
Isbel, Thomas	1	1	3		
Gains, Thomas	1	5	4		3
Floyd, Caleb	1	3	3		1
Smith, John	1		2		
Carroll, Benjamin	1		1		

Name of head of family.	Free white males of 16 years and upward, including heads of families.	Free white males under 16 years.	Free white females, including heads of families.	All other free persons.	Slaves.
Baker, Sylvester	1	4	4		
Skeef, William	2	1	4		
Jessop, Joseph	2	3	3		
Jessop, William	2	4	4		
Jessop, Timothy	2	2	5		1
Bailey, David	1	3	1		
Jessop, Thomas	1	4	5		
Clark, James	1	1	5		
Lawson, John	1	1	4		
Lawson, Jonas	2	3	3		
Langford, William	1	2	4		
Harris, Mathew	1	2	5		
Bailey, David	1	3	2		
Lyon, James	1				8
Cook, James	2	2			4
Harriss, John	1				
Grig, Moses	2	4	5		
Jessop, Joseph	1		1		
Horton, Daniel	1	3	3		
Garrott, Welcom	1	5	4		
Stevens, William	3		4		
Bates, William	1	4	3		
Hancock, John	1		3		
Miller, Randolph	1	5	3		
Wordly, Henry	2	1	3		
Jackson, John	4	2	4		
Bellow, Peter	2	3	4		
Harold, Jonathan	1	2	6		
Southerlin, Daniel	1		4		
Gibson, John	1	2	3		
Cooper, Thomas	1	3	5		
Gibson, Valentine	2	1	3		
White, William	1	3	3		
Gibson, Garrott	1	2	4		
Sumner, Caleb	2	2	4		
Carson, John	1	2	2		
Sumner, Thomas	1	5	4		
Gibson, Archelus	1	1	2		
Nunn, Richard	2	1	2		
Nunn, William	1	3	1		
Bartlett, William	1				
Riddle, Tyre	1	1	1		
Watson, Alex	1	2	1		
Jackson, Samuel	1	3	3		
Harison, Jonathan	2	4	2		
Easley, Joseph	1	1	3		
Price, Elisha	1	2	8		
Wordly, Jacob	1	1	1		
Ballard, German	1				
Ballard, Byrum	1			1	
Beasley, Richard	1	1	1		
Lockhart, Thomas	1	1	2		
Cox, Richard	1	2	8		3
King, Peter	2	3	4		
Gibson, James	1	5	4		
Beasley, Robert	1		1		
Ship, Thomas	1	1	2		5
Shinalt, John	1	2	4		
Blanchett, Peter	1		1		
Martin, John	1	1	3		
Burrus, William	1	1	2		
Hort, Joseph	2	2	5		
King, Benajah	3	1	3		
Stevens, William	2	2	7		
Sizemore, George	1	1	1		

Name of head of family.	Free white males of 16 years and upward, including heads of families.	Free white males under 16 years.	Free white females, including heads of families.	All other free persons.	Slaves.
Harold, Elisha	1	1	1		
Gordan, John	1		1		
Shelton, John	3	3	8		
Fields, Josias	1		1		1
Witt, Ann		3	3		
Love, Thomas	1	1	3		
Harold, John	1		4		
Freeman, James		5	3		
Eaton, Christopher	1	2	2		
Bails, William	2	3	3		
Cantwell, John	1	2	3		
Deatherage, William	1	2	4		
Goodman, Ansylem	1	2	4		
Harold, Richard	1	3	4		
Low, Thomas	1	2	3		
Harold, Jacob	1				
Landers, Moses	1	2	3		
Roark, Timothy	1		1		
Safford, Richard	1	3	1		
McGinnis, Michael	1	2	4		
Parker, Jeff	1	1	3		
Price, Charles	1		1		
Scott, George	1	1	2		
Lanes, Thomas	1	2	2		
Rabe, Jacob	1				
Ransom, Joseph	1	3	1		
Teage, John	1	1	3		
Hunter, John	3	1	3		
Hunter, David	1				
Jackson, John	1	2	5		
Ballard, Archelus	1		1		
Bates, William	1	4	4		
Oglesby, Asea	1	1	2		
Bond, Samuel	1	3	5		
Horton, Margaret		2	3		
Jessop, Joseph	1		1		1
Jackson, Samuel	4	1	7		
McArter, Aaron	1		1		
Martin, George	1		3		
Isbel, Richard	1		3		
Cardwell, Thomas	1	2	3		8
Ketchum, Joel	1		2		
Lester, Archebald	1	3	4		
Mullens, William	1	2	4		
Hickman, Edwin	1	2	4		
Lawson, Mirymon	1	1	1		
Johnson, Thomas	1	1	4		
Ballard, Thomas	2	3	4		
Burge, Alex	2	2	7		1
Beasley, Benjamin	1				
Angill, Charles	1	3	5		1
Angill, Laurance	1	1	1		
Angill, James	1	1	1		
Atwood, William	1	1	1		
Bradley, George	1	2	1		1
Bair, Patrick	1	3	3		
Bair, John	1				
Brooks, William	1	1	1		
Crump, Robert	3	4	5		1
Cliburn, Thomas	1	5	3		
Dunlap, John	2	1	5		
Dunlap, James	1		2		
Dearing, Anthony	2	1	2		7
Flint, Roderick	1	2	3		
Grinder, Joshua	1	2	3		

SALISBURY DISTRICT, STOKES COUNTY—Continued.

NAME OF HEAD OF FAMILY.	Free white males of 16 years and upward, including heads of families.	Free white males under 16 years.	Free white females, including heads of families.	All other free persons.	Slaves.
Grinder, Mary	1		3		
George, Jesse	2	4	6		
Guin, Alman	1	1	3		10
Hazle, Moses	3	1	4		
Hazle, Robert	1	4	3		
Hazle, Kindler	1		3		
Harston, Peter	3	1	3		58
Kimmins, William	1	3	3		
Vest, Charles	2	2	2		
Briggs, Robert	1	3	3		
Hess, Jacob	1	1	2		
Corder, Joseph	1	4	2		
Gymon, Isaac	1	3	6		
Martin, John	1	3	1		
Hillsebeck, Jacob	1	3	4		
Flint, Leonard	1	2	1		
Flinn, Thomas	1	2	1		
Armstrong, John	1	1	4		16
Carr, John	1	2	5		
Burch, William	1	4	4		
Randalman, John	1	1	2		2
Kerby, Edmund	3	2	4		
Lester, Jesse	2	1	5		8
Martin, Valentine	2	3	4		
Hughlitt, William	1	1	5		2
Thomlinson, Alex	1	2	1		
Franklin, Malekiah	1	1	1		
Waller, Jacob	1	2	1		
Waller, Sarah	2		4		
Franklin, John	2	1	2		
Bostick, Absalem	3	1	4		21
Legrand, Abraham	1	2	2		
Ladd, Noble	1	4	3		1
Ladd, William	1	1	1		3
Lewis, William	2	4	5		
Lewis, James	1		3		
Ladd, Joseph	1	1	4		2
Moore, James	1		1		
Majors, John	2		4		
Majors, Robert	1	2	2		
Morgan, John	1	5	5		
Morgan, Valentine	1		6		
Newcam, Thomas	2	5	3		
Roberts, Bob	1	4	1		
Read, Joseph	2	4	3		
Ray, George	2	1	5		
Syrus, Jesse	1	5	2		
Southern, William	2		3		
Southern, Rubin	1	4	4		
Southern, Ford	1		1		
Southern, Boas	1	1	2		
Smith, Lemuel	1	2	4		14
Southerlin, Jesse	2	3	6		
Childress, Mathew	1	1	3		
Scott, John	3	4	5		
Franklin, Walter	1	1	1		
Spanehaur, Henry	1	2	1		
Arnal, Henry	1	3	6		
Short, James	1	2	4		
Hunter, Thomas	1	1	1		
Hunter, David	1	1	1		
Hunter, Benjamin	1		1		
Gatewood, Gabriel	1	1	4		
Doss, Mathew	1	3	6		2
Overby, Freeman	1	1	2		
Stone, John	1	2	1		
Craiger, George	1	2	4		
Edwards, Edward	1	4	2		
Fulk, Adam	1	7	1		
Fiskus, Adam	1	2	4		
Arnal, Henry	2		5		
Boyls, William	1	3	4		
Boyls, William	2	1	2		
Speace, John	1	3	1		
Thomson, James	1		1		
Terrill, Hary	4	3	3		27
Taylor, Richard	1	3	6		
Vernon, Jonathan	1	2	4		
Vernon, Jonathan	2		1		
Vaughn, Joseph	1	3	6		
Webster, John	1	3	5		
Warnock, Samuel	2				
Warnock, Mathew	1				
Ward, John	1	3	4		
Walker, William	1	8			1
Wiljohn, Abraham	1	2	1		
Nelson, Joseph	2		2		8
Nelson, Alex	1	1	2		
Angill, Sabour	1				
Wilson, Richard	2	1	6		
Ladd, Judath		1	3		2
Syrus, Alec	1	1	3		
Banks, Samuel	1	1	3		
Langham, James	1	1	7		
Chrissolm, John	1	2	2		2
Reighly, Charles	1		1		
Darnal, Joseph	1	1	5		
Gordan, John	1		1		
Childress, Armajah	1	7	5		
Tate, Arthur	1	2	2		
Oliver, Ahijah	2	5	4		
Venable, William	1	2	3		
Hampton, John	1	1	1		
Boyls, John	1	1	1		
Boatright, Daniel	2	2	5		5
Christman, George	1	1	4		
Horne, Jesse	1	1	4		
Carr, John	1	2	2		
Edwards, Abel	1	2	2		
Spanehaur, Jacob	1	6	6		
Kerby, Jesse	1		1		1
Brown, Samuel	1		3		
Vest, Samuel	1	2	3		
Sprinkle, George	2	3	7		1
Shifford, Jacob	2	5	1		
Curry, Malcom	1		4		
East, Thomas	1	2	2		8
Armstrong, Martin	3	2	3		10
Martin, Job	3	3	5		1
Pettitt, George	1	2	1		
Poindexter, Thomas	2	1	5		13
Reynolds, Justice	1	3	2		
Kelly, John	1	2	4		
East, Joseph	2	1	6		
Wright, Hezekiah	1		1		
Connel, John	1		2		
Wright, Elizabeth		1	1		
Fearer, Christian	1	4	2		
East, Isham	2	4	1		1
East, William	4	1	6		
Johnson, David	1	1	4		
Fitzpatrick, John	1	1	5		
Venable, John	1	2	2		
Vest, Isham	1		1		
Prater, William	1	2	2		1
Quiller, James	1	2	3		
Steele, William	1	3	3		
Arny, Henry	1	3	7		
Arnold, William	1	4	4		
Briggs, John	1				
Dillard, James	1	1	2		
Martin, William	2	2	5		9
Ridle, John	1	2	4		
Hutcherson, Richard	1	4	6		
Cox, Isham	2	1	1		1
Elliott, Charles	2	5	6		1
Gibson, John	1	1	2		
Ridle, Randolph	1	3	3		
Woode, Robert	1	4	3		
Newman, Payton	1	1	3		
Johns, Arther	1	4	3		
Tilly, Bennett	1	3	1		
Dean, Mathew	1		5		
Calahan, Josias	1	1	2		
Calahan, William	2	1	3		
Woode, Richard	1	3	4		
Hutcherson, Daniel	2	2	1		2
Nelson, Jacob	1	4	4		
Gains, Robert	2		6		4
Sergant, John	4		1		
Joyce, Alex	3	1	5		3
Smith, William	1				
Banister, Nancy		4	3		
Childress, Abraham	1	1	4		
Davis, Sarah	1	3	3		
Eavans, Elijah	1	1	3		
Eaton, Christian	1	1	3		
Eads, Thomas	1	3	4		
Flinn, Leoflin	1	4	5		
Franklin, Owen	1				
Hunter, John	1				
London, William	1	4	4		
Melton, John	1	1	3		
Menakey, Joseph	1	2			
Melton, David	1				
Philips, Richard	1	2	2		
Philips, Joseph	1	3	4		
Ransom, Joseph	1	4	3		
Duncan, Thomas	2	2	8		
Nichols, John	2	4	4		
Ward, William	2	2	4		
Kerns, William	1		4		
Kerns, James	1	2	1		
Kerns, Hubbard	1		1		
Steward, Charles	1	5	4		
Meridith, James	4	1	5		
Newman, John	2	5	2		
Joyce, Isaac	1		3		2
Gill, William	2	2	2		
Gill, Thomas	1		4		
Whitlock, James	1	3	3		
Gill, Young	1		3		
Radford, William	1	2	5		
Shelton, John	1		2		
Hutcherson, Daniel	1		3		
Hutcherson, William	1	7	2		
Brown, John	1		1		
Linkhorn, John	1	1	4		
Gillaton, Nicholas	1	1	3		
Young, James	3	3	5		
Musick, Elexious	1	2	7		
Leysle, Alex	1	4	4		
Gibson, John	1		1		
Wilkins, John	1	3	5		
Shelton, John	1	2	3		1
Shelton, William	1	4	2		
Shelton, Daniel	1	2	2		
Watkins, Zewel	1	1	4		
Read, Joseph	2	3	5		
Hail, John	2	5	2		
Joyce, George	2	3	2		
Robison, John	2	1	6		
Manu-l, Phyle	3	4	4		
Watkins, Thomas	1		3		
Hunter, Mathew	1	3	4		
Banks, John	1		3		
Davis, William	2	1	3		1
Mayab, John	1	2	4		
Mayab, John	3	1	4		
Childress, Mary	2		3		1
Beasley, Charles	2	1	3		1
Childress, William	1	1	1		1
Walker, James	1	3	1		4
Farmer, John	3	1	2		5
Chandler, William	2		3		
Hawkins, Benjamin	1	3	5		
Hawkins, Benjamin	1	3	5		
Dodson, Rubin	5	2	3		
Southern, William	1		3		1
Hammet, Robert	1	1	3		
Whaler, Richard	1		2		
Shelton, Sarah		3	3		
Cameron, Jarne	1	1	2		
Certain, Levi	1		2		
Duncan, James	1	3	6		
Millwoode, James	1	3	4		
Whitlock, Charles	4		3		
Martin, James	2	2	4		15
Neal, Thomas	2	5	3		
Nelson, William	1	4	7		
Nelson, John	1	1	2		
Nelson, William	1		1		
Perker, Charles	1		1		
Hughs, John	1	2	3		6
Lovin, Thomas	2	3	4		
Hughs, Archelus	1	1	1		2
Vanters, John	1	4	4		
Easley, John	2	3	8		
Aynett, Sam	2		1		
Hawkins, William	1	1	4		3
Taylor, Joseph	1	1	3		
Mayab, Robert	6	1	3		
Welch, Joseph	1	1	2		
Austen, Nathaniel	1	1	3		
Dolton, David	3	2	3		14
Tilly, Hary	1	6	4		
Webb, William	2	1	6		4
Hilton, John	1	3	9		
Musick, George	1		2		
Oliver, Gilson	1	2	4		
Angill, Elizabeth		1	3		
Asbury, Calup	1		3		
Cox, Mildred		1	5		7
Foster, Joel	1	1	1		
Holt, William	3	2	3		
Holt, Ambrose	1		3		
Richeson, Benjamin	1		1		
Vernon, James	3	2	6		
Lane, James	1	2	4		
Pafford, William	1	2	5		
Dickerson, William	2	1	3		
Baker, Henry	1	2	3		
Warden, William	1	2	2		
Pruitt, Micajah	1	1	1		
Mesinger, Coonrod	1		4		
Hedgspeth, William	1	2	2		
Rennolds, John	2	2	2		
Smith, Martha	1		6		
Okey, Nathan	1		2		
Hart, John	2	2	3		3
Davison, John	2	2	3		
Davison, Richard	1		2		
Fulton, Francis	1		1		
Davis, James	3		6		5
Mannan, John	1	1	3		
Duggans, John	1		1		
Huckby, Robert	1	2	2		
Bailey, Edward	1		1		
Nixon, Absalem	1	2	4		
Fearell, John	1	1	4		
Stanley, Jesse	1	1	4		

SALISBURY DISTRICT, STOKES COUNTY—Continued.

NAME OF HEAD OF FAMILY.	Free white males of 16 years and upward, including heads of families.	Free white males under 16 years.	Free white females, including heads of families.	All other free persons.	Slaves.
Boales, John	1	2	5		2
Rutledge, Johnson	1	3	2		
Clayton, Jesse	1		2		1
Bayse, Nathaniel	2	1	4		
Boales, Alex	2	3	2		
Spears, William	1		1		
Spears, Joseph	1	1	3		
Carter, Edward	2	2	4		
Mirritt, Thomas	1		1		
Brown, Jahue	3	2	3		
Cook, William	2		6		
Davis, John	1	2	3		
McInley, John	1	2	1		
Branum, Benjamin	1	4	6		
Sizemore, Newman	1	2	1		
Moore, Alex	4		3		
Fancher, Richard	1	2	2		
Bennett, Benjamin	2	5	3		
Ward, Elizabeth	1	1	5		
Barns, Sarah		3	3		
Mitchel, Adam	3	3	4		
Clayton, Stephen	1		3		1
Clayton, Stephen	1		2		
Cummins, Stephen	1	2	3		
McMillon, Andrew	2		1		
Blackbern, Younger	1	3	5		1
Heath, Richard	1		3		2
Childress, William	2	1	5		5
Childress, William	1		1		
Cook, Thomas	3		4		
Coffey, James	3		4		
Boales, James	1	4	3		
Vest, William	1	2	4		
Fitzpatrick, Sam	2	2	5		
Fulton, Robert	1		1		
Southerlin, Philip	2	4	3		
Fox, Samuel	1	4	1		
Merrett, John	1	2	3		
Wadkins, Henry	4	1	8		
Ward, James	1	1	3		
Halbert, Joel	1	3	3		1
Hover, Gasper	1	2	2		
Davis, Margan	2	3	4		
Hill, Mathew	4	1	3		
George, Travis	1		1		1
Duggans, Sarah		1	5		
Bailey, John	1	2	4		
Boales, William	1	3	2		
Branum, Malekia	1	4	3		
Clayton, William	1	1	2		
Brown, John	1	1	1		
Rhedick, Hardy	2	4	6		
Messor, Christian	1	4	5		
Jones, Samuel	1		2		
Moore, John	1	1	1		
Sizemore, William	1	2	4		
Sizemore, Elizabeth	1		2		
Eavans, John	1	2			
Martin, Mathew	1		3		
Moore, David	1	2	2		
Gallaway, John	1		5		
Mcanally, Jesse	3	3	5		
Campell, William	2	2	6		2
Mcanally, John	1	4	3		
Hampton, Thomas	3	1	7		
Eason, Joseph	2	6	3		
Wilson, Philip	1	4	4		1
Smith, John	4	3	2		
Smith, Philip	1	2	2		
Smith, Daniel	1		2		
Fergason, Stephen	2		2		
Fergason, Rebecca	2		4		
Branum, John	1	6	6		
Davis, Daniel	2	1	3		
Dodson, Nancy		2	2		
Heath, William	1	1	2		
Martin, Moses	1	2	4		
Mellon, William	1				
Rutledge, William	1	3	4		
Smith, Meridith	1	2	4		
Mcanally, Charles	3	1	3		5
Moore, James	1	2	4		
Burnes, Tarence	1	2	1		
Cook, Abel	1				
Kizor, John	1	3	2		
Sulavan, George	1	1	3		
Cooley, John	1	5	3		
Cooley, Edward	1	2	1		
Cooley, Joseph	1		3		
Hill, Robert	2	3	4		4
Linn, John	1				
Cook, John	1		1		
Banner, Joseph	2	1	5		5
Martin, Abraham	1		2		12
Young, Benjamin	1	1	3		
Banner, David	2	1	8		2
Wells, John	2	3	2		

NAME OF HEAD OF FAMILY.	Free white males of 16 years and upward, including heads of families.	Free white males under 16 years.	Free white females, including heads of families.	All other free persons.	Slaves.
Samwell, Edmund	1	2	2		4
Ham, Mordicai	1	1	5		
Mathews, James	1	1	2		10
James, Wm	1		4		
Prat, Thomas	1		1		
Morriss, Thomas	1	1	2		
Flint, John	1	3	8		
Hampton, Samuel	1	2	1		5
James, David	1	2	6		
Flint, Thomas	1	5	4		7
Hill, Jesse	2	2	3		5
Petree, Jacob	1		3		
Flint, Richard	2		4		7
Hampton, James	1		2		2
Peniker, William	1	1	4		
Peniker, Peter	1		2		
Peniker, Mathias	1	2	2		
Smith, Peter	1	4	4		
Zygar, Leonard	1	1	3		
Halbert, John	3	4	3		3
Goode, George	1				
Young, Nathaniel	1	1	1		
James, William	2		2		3
Waggoner, Joseph	2		4		1
Morriss, John	1	2	2		
Fry, Henry	1	4	4		3
Adams, John	1		2		1
Clayton, John	1	3	4		6
Denton, Arther	2	4	4		
Day, James	1	3	3		
Goode, Richard	2	2	4		8
Martin, Robert	1		2		
Moriss, Hammond	1	1	1		
Ray, Andrew	1	1	2		
Ring, Martin	1		3		
Sims, Pariss	1	2	3		
Ham, John	1	2	2		
Ham, Joseph	4		1		
Ham, Thomas	1	3	1		
Fountain, Stephen	1	1	5		
Merritt, William	1	3	2		
Ring, Thomas	1	2	5		
Eavans, Thomas	1		3		
Branson, John	4		3		
Davis, Letitia	2	2	5		
Gazaway, Thomas	1	3	4		
Branum, Barny	1	2	2		
Winston, Joseph	2	5	2		18
Banner, Ephraim	2	4	3		4
Mcknown, James	1		1		
Rutledge, William	1	3	3		
George, Rubin	3	5	4		
Waggoner, Samuel	1		2		1
Heath, Johnson	1	1	6		
Mounts, Jacob	1	2	3		
Petree, Jacob	1	1	2		
Merritt, Edward	3		1		
Cox, Joseph	1	2	1		
Fry, Michael	1	2	7		2
Fry, Valentine	2	7	2		
Waggoner, Gabriel	1	2	5		1
Waggoner, William	2	3	6		1
Follis, William	1	3	3		
Goode, Thomas	1	2	4		
Adams, George	1	1	2		
King, Henry	2	2	6		
Gibson, William	2	3	3		
Ring, John	2	3	5		
Ring, James	1		1		
Davis, William	1	2	5		
Raper, Thomas	1		1		
Davis, George	1	2	3		
Smith, Lias	1		4		
Petree, Doherty		5	3		
Morriss, Hammond	2	1	1		1
Morriss, William	1	2	4		
Samwell, Percilla	4		4		
Vittatoe, Thomas	1	2	1		
Wells, Anthony	1		1		
Welch, Dosha	1	2	2		
Woolf, Gottleib	1	2	4		
Pinkston, Peter	3		2		
Young, Benjamin	1	2	3		
Young, William	1	1	4		
Young, Joshua	1		2		
Young, Samuel	1	1	3		
Goode, Richard	2		2		8
Martin, William	1	4	2		2
Banner, Benjamin	1	5	3		6
Blackbern, Elizabeth	2		2		2
Ray, Usly	1		1		1
Wolf, Calup	1	2	2		
Adams, John	1	1	3		
Hartgrove, Howel	1	2	1		
Tutle, Peter	2	1	1		
Appleton, John	1	3	7		1
Adams, William	1	2	4		

NAME OF HEAD OF FAMILY.	Free white males of 16 years and upward, including heads of families.	Free white males under 16 years.	Free white females, including heads of families.	All other free persons.	Slaves.
Earnest, Gottleib	1	4	1		
Bynum, Gray	2	2	4		8
Rutledge, William	2	2	1		
Eavans, Daniel	1	1	1		
Eavans, Edward	1	1	5		
Clark, Samuel	2		3		
Southerlin, Charles	1		1		
Hall, John	1	2	4		
Fergason, John	1		1		
Tanner, James	2	4	4		
Heath, Thomas	3		1		
Cook, William	1	1	3		
Tutle, John	1	2	3		
Garison, Isaac	1	3	5		
Blackbern, John	1	4	4		3
Bolcem, Thomas	1	1	1		1
Branson, Zakariah	1		1		
Blackbern, William	1				5
Clark, Francis	1	1			
Davis, David	1				
Day, Thomas	1	2	4		
Davis, Charles	1	2	6		
Ham, Thomas	1	3	1		
Hampton, Henry	1	2	5		5
Holebrook, John	1	5	4		
Owens, Thomas	1	1	4		
Watson, Joel	1	1	2		
Watson, William	2	1	1		
Sell, Jonathan	1		4		
Mills, Aaron	1	5	4		
Sanders, John	1	4	4		
Sell, Thomas	1	1	2		
Melton, Jesse	1	2	3		
Campell, Arche	1	2	4		
Ralph, Isaac	1	2	3		
Close, John	1	1	1		
Robbins, Daniel	1	1	3		
Dobson, William	3	3	2		
Crew, David	1	2	6		
Sanders, Jesse	1	2	4		
Graham, Thomas	2	3	4		1
Walker, William	1	1	4		1
Sapp, John	2		1		
Sapp, Benjamin	1		2		
Jones, Richard	3	1	2		
Boyd, Phenehas	1	1	2		
Smith, Thomson	1	4	5		
Swallow, John	1	6	2		
Wright, William	1	4	5		
Jones, Cadwallader	2	1	3		
Jones, Quiller	1	2	1		
Mendenall, Joseph	2	1	4		
Willitts, Henry	2	1	9		
Cooper, Michael	1	2	2		
Macy, Gayer	1	1	4		
Jones, Philip	1		2		
Nations, John	2	2	5		
Nations, Christopher	1	1	1		
Jones, Robert	4	2	4		
Johnson, Ashly	1	1	2		
Dolin, John	1	1	4		
Paterson, Joseph	1				
Perry, James	2		1		
Vanhoy, John	2	6	3		
Beasley, William	1		2		
Culver, John	1	2	2		
Fore, Peter	3		5		5
Fulp, Peter	1	1	4		
Fair, Michael	1	2	2		1
Fair, John	1	1	4		
Fulp, Michael	1	4	5		
Hutchings, John	2	1	10		2
Ludwick, Daniel	1				
Lane, William			1		1
Leverton, John	1		1		
Linville, David	2	1	3		
Lowry, James	1	1	5		
Ludwick, Peter	2	3	3		
Linvill, Aaron	2	2	5		2
Linvill, Mary		3	4		
Snipes, Mathew	1	1	3		
Sapp, Jesse	1		3		
Wadkins, James	1	2	6		1
Jones, Benjamin	1		1		
Swim, William	3	5	6		
Coffin, Seth	3	2	5		
Barnhard, Francis	2	5	5		
Swain, Judath		2	2		
Hester, John	2	2	3		
Green, William	1	2	4		
Mealup, Andrew	2	2	5		
McPhesson, Joseph	1	4	6		
Teague, John	2		7		3
Willis, Garvis	1	2	5		
Paterson, Simmons	1	4	2		
Paterson, Joseph	3	1	3		1
Stogdan, Daniel	3				

SALISBURY DISTRICT, STOKES COUNTY—Continued.

NAME OF HEAD OF FAMILY.	Free white males of 16 years and upward, including heads of families.	Free white males under 16 years.	Free white females, including heads of families.	All other free persons.	Slaves.
Story, Calup	1	2	2		
Bowman, Edmund	3	2	1		
Thomason, John	2	2	7		5
Walker, David	1	3	2		
Smith, Moses	2	2	3		
Lundy, Richard	1	3	3		
Ladd, Constant	1	1	3		7
Majors, Alexander	1	1	2		
McAlup, Hugh	1		1		
Brooks, David	2		4	1	
Elmore, Thomas	3	2	5		
Drawn, Jacob	1	4	2		
Idle, Jacob	2	1	4		
Willert, George	1	3	8		
Elmore, Austan	1		2		
Watson, Claburn	1	2	2		
Paterson, Jurdan	1		2		
Pique, Nathan	2	2	6		
Estes, Lyddle	1		2		
Pitts, Samuel	1	3	4		
Pitts, John	1		1		
Pitts, Andrew	1	1	2		
Brooks, John	1	1	1		
Stogdan, Joseph	1	2	2		
Roose, Aaron	1	1	2		
Pitts, Martha	3	2	3		
Clampett, Richard	1	2	2		
Shields, Abel	1	2	6		
Frazer, William	1		1		
Green, Thomas	1	2	1		
Wortman, William	1	2	5		
Mills, Jacob	3	1	2		
Swim, John	1	1	1		
Fields, Robert	1	2	1		
Vance, Alee	1	1	3		
Williams, Owan	2	4	1		
Jurdan, John	2		2		
Thomason, George	1		1		
Tucker, Thomas	1	4	3		
Folger, Lathem	2	1	6		
Long, Israel	2	2	3		
Barnhard, Trustam	3	2	5		
Brown, James	2	3	5		
Coffin, Libni	2	2	6		
Hasket, John	1	1	2		
Huff, Daniel	2		3		
Mills, Thomas	1	2	4		
Marshal, Thomas	1	3	3		
Love, James	1	1	7		7
Hester, William	1		1		
Howel, William	2	1	4		
Lowry, John	1	1	4		
Long, Charles	1		2		
Clasby, George	1		2		
Hinshaw, John	1	4	2		
Waisnar, Micajah	1	2	1		
Scooley, Samuel	1	5	3		
Bratin, William	1	1	2		
Johnson, Thomas	2	1	3		
Green, Thomas	2	1	3		2
Piper, James	1				
Cummins, Asea	1		1		
Dillard, Katy			2		
Mastin, John	1		2		
Adamson, Jesse	1	4	3		
Adamson, Enos	1	2	3		
Starbrick, Paul	3	5	4		
Beason, Richard	1	3	3		
Whicker, James	1	3	3		
McInsy, William	2		1		
Davis, Samson	1	1	3		
Garland, James	1		1		
Suns, Casander		1	1		
Knight, John	1	1	2		
Whicker, William	1	2	2		
Quillin, John	1	2	3		
Robison, Andrew	1	3	4		
Shaw, Ralph	1	1	5		
Towmey, Patrick	1	3	4		
Watson, William	1	1			
Ward, Leavan	1	3	5		
McOwn, Sarah			4		
Long, John	1		1		
Crew, Thomas	1		1		
Tatem, Barny	1	3	3		
Anthony, William	1		3		
Angill, John	1	4	3		
Aynett, Andrew	1	4	4		
Anderson, Daniel	3		6		
Allday, Seth	1	1	1		
Brim, John	1	5	5		
Bennett, Jesse	1	1			
Burns, James	1		2		
Barrow, Moses	1				
Cook, Henry	2	1	4		3
Cook, Stephen	1				
Billeton, Alexander	2		4		

NAME OF HEAD OF FAMILY.	Free white males of 16 years and upward, including heads of families.	Free white males under 16 years.	Free white females, including heads of families.	All other free persons.	Slaves.
Cline, Stoful	1	1	1		
Doubt, John	2	5	3		
Fortney, Henry	1		1		
Fokel, Samuel	1	1	3		
Huff, Daniel	2		2		
Hartgrove, James	2	2	3		
Hoegest, John	1	4	3		
Reigh, John	1				
Rasel, John	1		2		
Smith, Robert	1	1	1		11
Segler, George	1	2	4		
Seinard, Samuel	1	1	1		
Shamell, John	1	4	2		
Marshal, Frederick W	1		3		
Benzun, Christian	1		3		
Kohler, John	1	1	2		
Usley, Sarah			1		
Koster, Adam	1				
Snepf, Daniel	1				
Holland, John	1	3	1		
Schulz, Samuel	2		1		
Cummins, John	2	3	3		5
Crew, David	1	1	2		
Clifton, Elizabeth			2		
Clasby, Charles	1		3		
Dwigings, John	2	3	3		
Elmore, Joel	1				
Easter, John	1	2	3		
Endsley, Hugh	1				
Freeman, John	1	1	1		
Gamell, John	3	1	4		
Holebrook, James	1	2	4		1
Herron, Delany	2	2	2		
Hoole, John	1				
Jones, Aquilla	2	1	3		
Jones, William	1		1		
Jones, Gabriel	1	2	3		
Jones, Joshua	1	1	4		
Johnson, Robert	4	2	4		
Johnson, James	1	1	1		
Johnson, Henry	1	3	3		
Knott, William	1				
Ledford, Nicholas	1	1	2		
Love, James	1		2		
Christ, Rudoph	3	3	3		
Hauser, Hannah			3		
Holder, Charles	1		3		
Hester, Abraham	1		2		
Curling, Samuel	1		2		
Meinung, Ludwick	1	1	5		
Kushke, John	1		1		
Yerrell, Peter	2	2	3		1
Christman, Daniel	1	1	4		
Lick, Martin	3	1	2		
Rights, John	1	4	3		
Vogler, Philip	1		3		
Micksch, Mathew	1	1	3		
Kramch, Samuel	2				
Vogler, Christopher	1				
Herbst, John H	4		2		2
Stolz, Samuel	2				
Merkle, Christopher	1				
Paterson, Nitts	3				
Landman, John	4				
Reigh, Christopher	2				
Buttner, John F	2				
Lawton, John	1				
Linvill, Richard	2	2	3		2
Linvill, Moses	1				
Low, John	1	1	4		
Miller, Jacob	1	1	2		
Mills, Asea	1				
Meningall, Mordecai	2	1	6		
McAlup, Hugh	1	2	3		
Meridith, James	3	2	4		
Nelson, Isaac	1				
Perkins, Joseph	1	1	1		
Perry, William	1	1	1		
Paterson, Turner	1				
Palmore, John	1	1	2		
Quillin, Teague	1	2	3		
Shields, Rubin	1	2	5		
Sanders, Naman	1	5	2		
Stokely, Sturd	1				
Styers, Samuel	1	1	3		
Sapp, Robert	1	3	2		
Stiles, John	1				
Wilburn, Martha			3		
Bartley, Edward	2	1	3		
Kraus, John	2	1			
Schnepf, Jeremias	2				
Schmidt, George	2		1		
Schroser, Charles	3	1			
Hanke, John	5				
Triebit, Christian	1				
Bagge, Traugott	1	2	2		
Meyer, Jacob	1		2		

NAME OF HEAD OF FAMILY.	Free white males of 16 years and upward, including heads of families.	Free white males under 16 years.	Free white females, including heads of families.	All other free persons.	Slaves.
Blum, Jacob	2	2	2		5
Loech, Abraham	2		2		
Kaske, Renatus	1		1		
Transu, Philip	2		3		
Bewighouse, George	1		3		
Praezel, Mary			3		
Schober, Gottleib	4	2	3		
Nissen, Salome		2	4		
Buttner, Sarah			1		
Aust, Mary			2		
Green, Ann			8		
Colver, Elizabeth			6		
Quest, Ann			3		
Ebert, John		1	5		
Blum, Henry	1	4	1		
Steiner, Jacob	2	1	2		
Beroth, Jacob	2	2	5		
Schulz, Gottfrey	1	3	1		1
Reigh, Mathew	1				
Hauser, Abraham	1	1	2		
Spach, Gottlieb	1	2	2		
Baumgerten, John	1				
Claus, Philip	1	1	4		
Sam (free negro)				6	
Scott (free negro)				3	
Earnst, Jacob	1		3		
Krouse, Gottlieb	2	2	1		2
Stehr, Henry	1	1	2		
Micky, John	1	1	3		1
Kinast, Christopher	1		2		4
Wageman, John	1	2	2		1
Renner, Hans	2				
Shope, John		2	2		
Christman, Balthaser	1	1	2		
Esterline, Mathew	1	1	2		
Stauber, Christian	1		2		
Schmidt, Christopher	1				
Hillsebeck, Jacob	1		3		
Pfaff, Peter	1		1		
Kruger, Henry	1		2		
Pfaff, Isaac	2		3		
Kraus, John		3	7		
Folk, Johanes	1	1	2		
Stols, Jacob	1	1	2		
Pfaff, Samuel	2		2		
Binkele, Peter	3		2		
Feisser, Peter	3	5	4		
Spanehaur, Henry	2	3	5		
Binkele, John	1		1		
Miller, Johanes	2	2	3		
Philips, Richard	1		1		
Miller, Jacob	2				1
Clayton, Briton	1	5	3		7
Brinkele, Peter	1	2	4		
Shouse, Henry	3	1	1		
Spanehaur, John	2		1		
Billetor, Alexander	2		4		
Binkele, Jacob	1	1	1		
Loggins, Majors	1		3		
Steiner, Abraham	2		1		1
Kapp, Jacob	3	1	3		
Shelhorne, John	1	2	4		
Ranke, John	2		3		
Brising, Andrew	1	2	3		
Limeback, Lewis	1	2	2		
Holder, George	2	1	2		
Akkerman, Barbara		1	1		
Wernley, Henry	1	1	1		
Aust, George	1				
Hauser, George	3	1	4		8
Hauser, Peter	3	2	3		
Strooper, Samuel	1	2	4		
Lash, Christian	1		3		1
Coonrod, John	1	3	1		1
Buttner, Adam	2	1	1		
Hauser, Michael	1	2			
Shore, Henry	2		3		
Hauser, Peter	2	2	6		1
Hauser, George	2	2	2		2
Hauser, Joseph	2		2		1
Lash, Jacob	1		1		
Beck, Valentine	1	1	1		
Stults, Abraham	1		1		
Binkele, Frederick	1	1	2		
Cornelus, West	3	1	5		
Fiskus, Fredrick	2		2		
Teague, Michael	1	2	4		
Binkele, Peter	1		3		
Shore, Henry	2		5		
Shouse, Daniel	1	3	3		
Spanehaur, Michael	2	1	3		
Strube, Adam	1				
Shore, Jacob	1	1			
Boose, George	1		2		
Clayton, Charles	1	3	3		1
Shouse, Philip	1				
Shouse, Frederick	3	1	1		

SALISBURY DISTRICT, STOKES COUNTY—Continued.

NAME OF HEAD OF FAMILY.	Free white males of 16 years and upward, including heads of families.	Free white males under 16 years.	Free white females, including heads of families.	All other free persons.	Slaves.
Smith, Christian	1	2	2		
Giles, John	1	1	2		1
Woolf, Lewis	1	1	5		
Martin, Moses	2	3	3		
Lucas, Thomas	1	1	2		
Stanton, Christopher	2	1	7		
Markland, Robert	1	1	1		1
Grabs, William	3		2		1
Seids, Michael	1		4		
Ranke, Michael	3		9		1
Cramer, Gottlieb	2	2	1		
Transu, Philip	3	2	2		
Berod, John	2		2		
Opitts, John	1	2	2		
Schnert, Samuel	1		2		
Transu, Philip	2		2		
Stols, Gasper	1	2	4		
Folk, Andrew	1		3		
Hauser, Christian	1		1		
Coonrod, Christian	2	2	4		
Limeback, Benjn	3	1	10		
Miller, Jacob	3		1		1
Hauser, Martin	2	1	2		
Hauser, Martin	1		2		
Politshek, Joseph	4	1	4		
Limeback, Abraham	4	3	5		
Saler, John	1	3	5		
Hillsebeck, Frederick	2		4		
Kreiger, Jacob	1	3	3		
Miller, Joseph	2	3	4		
Dobb, David	1	1	3		
Davis, Josse	1	4	4		
Padgett, John	2		3		
Markland, Joseph	1		2		1
Taylor, Josias	2	2	4		
Westmoreland, Alex	2	4	3		
Gordan, William	1	4	4		
Chitty, Benjamin	1	2	3		
Chitty, John	1				
Hill, Isaac	1	1	4		
Slator, Henry	2	2	5		1
Null, John	2	4	3		
Stults, Philip	2	3	2		
Hollowman, William	3	5	3		
Ruck, Christopher	1	7	5		
Williams, Reason	1	2	4		
Lasmutt, Elias	1		1		
Pedycort, Thomas	1		1		
Blake, Jacob	1				
Craig, William	1				
Andrews, David	1	4	4		
Mayse, Henry	2	1	3		1
Pedycort, Basil	2	2	3		
Cooper, John	2	1	6		
Williams, William	2	1	4		
Padgett, Thomas	1	1	4		
Markland, Mathew	2		2		
Padgett, Benjamin	1	2	2		
Markland, Mathew	1	3	1		
Blake, John	1	2	5		
Spears, William	1	2	2		
Hill, Joshua	1		1		
Boger, John	1				
Olspough, Henry	1		4		
Pedycort, William B	1	3	2		1
Pedycort, John	1				1
Hamilton, Oratis	1	2	5		
Martin, James	1	1	7		1
Crook, William	1		1		4
Bennet, Richard	1	2	4		7
Hillsebeck, Frederick	1		3		
Binkele, John	4	4	4		2
Lynch, John	3		2		9
Woolf, Adam	3	1	1		4
Moser, Peter	1	5	2		
Busy, Charles	1	1	6		
Shadock, John	1		1		
Yeats, William	1	1	2		
Ridge, Thomas	1	2	4		
Lynch, John	1		1		1
Mathews, Rubin	1	1	4		
Green, Peter	1		1		
Rominger, Michael	1	2	6		
Read, John	1	1	2		
Kersner, Anthony	3		7		
Hines, Jacob	1				
Miller, Jacob	1	1	2		1

NAME OF HEAD OF FAMILY.	Free white males of 16 years and upward, including heads of families.	Free white males under 16 years.	Free white females, including heads of families.	All other free persons.	Slaves.
Schruzfeser, Henry	1				
Kimble, Henry	1	1	2		
Snyder, Martin	1		2		
Alverd, William	1	4	6		1
Albert, Martin	1	4	5		
Weaver, Christian	1	2	1		
Fansler, Sovene	1	1	2		
Shadock, William	1		1		
Forester, James	1				
Stults, Adam	1		3		
Limeback, Ann	2	3	4		
Holder, George	1	3	4		
Deits, Jacob	1		1		
Watson, James	1	1	2		
Huffman, George	3		3		
James, John	3	3	3		6
Bitting, Anthony	3	2	3		4
Miller, John	2	2	3		
Billetor, Zebdiah	1	2	1		
Fiddler, Gottfry	1	2	4		
Miller, Frederick	2	2	3		
McBride, John	1	4	5		
Hasket, John	3	4	4		
Bolingjack, John	2	1	2		
Holder, Herny	1	5			
Fields, William	1		2		
Hall, Joseph	1	3	5		
Forester, John	1	1	1		
Murphy, Stephen	1	1	3		
Carver, George	1		3		
Krouse, John	1	1	4		
Shamlin, William	3	1	3		
Tull, Nicholas	5	1	2		
Fishell, John	1	1	2		
Fults, Peter	1	2	5		
Brady, Charles	1	1	3		
Windle, Henry	1	1	1		
Woolf, Larance	1	2	2		
Weisner, John	1	1	2		
Green, Philip	1	3	3		
Trewett, John	1	2	3		1
Tull, Frederick	1		1		
Thomson, Jonathan	1				
Snyder, Philip	1	2	3		
Seward, Samuel	1	1	1		
Steward, David	2		3		5
Stulz, Henry	1	2	4		
Snyder, Philip	2	3	4		
Smith, Daniel	2	3	4		
Stevens, William	1	1	1		
Spach, John	1	1	2		
Spach, Jacob	1		1		
Spach, Adam	1	3	4		
Seaner, Peter	1	4	2		
Shutt, Jacob	2	3	2		
Black, Andrew	1	1	5		
Hauser, Martin	1	1	1		
Lyon, John	1	3	5		
Curd, James	1	2	1		
Kitner, Francis	3	2	3		1
Carver, Christian	2	3	1		
Steward, Samuel	1		2		
Steward, Rubin	1	1	2		
Runyan, Adam	1	1	2		
Purdon, John	2	7	3		
Fair, Elizabeth	1		3		
Davis, Jonathan	1				
Jones, Jehue	1				
Fogler, Samuel	1	1	3		
Adaman, Thomas	2	1	2		
Black, Jacob	1		1		
Logans, John	1	3	5		
Philips, Joseph	3	2	6		
Robison, Jacob	1		2		
Gentry, Lucy			2		
Tull, William	1	2	4		
Grace, Allen	1	2	3		
Hauser, Martin	2	1	1		
Snyder, David	1	2	2		
Snyder, Henry	1	2	5		
Sitz, Michael	3	1	3		
Shoarwood, Thomas	2		2		
Snyder, Cornelus	1	4	2		
Riech, Mathew	1				
Robison, William	1	2	3		
Read, Jacob	2	5	2		
Rominger, Michael	2	1	3		

NAME OF HEAD OF FAMILY.	Free white males of 16 years and upward, including heads of families.	Free white males under 16 years.	Free white females, including heads of families.	All other free persons.	Slaves.
Rominger, Jacob	2	3	5		
Rodrick, Valentine	1	3	2		
Rodrick, Philip	3	6	2		
Rotrock, Peter	2	2	7		
Philpott, William	1	2	2		
Pickel, John	1	2	4		
Philips, John	1	4	4		
Nathing, Mathias	1	3	1		
Null, Michael	1	1	1		
Null, Jacob	3		3		
Miller, Joseph	2	3	1		
Miller, Monis	1	2	1		
Mock, Henry	2	2	1		
Miller, Henry	1	4	2		
Miller, Stephen	1		1		
Limeback, Joseph	1	1	6		
Leonard, Abner	1	1	4		
Lash, Nathaniel	1		1		3
Loghanhore, George	1		4		
Loghanhore, Jacob	1	4	1		
Lanouse, John	2	2	5		
Krouse, Henry	1		2		
Krouse, Andrew	1				
Krouse, John	2	3	4		
Krouse, Windle	3	1	4		
Garner, Francis	2	5	3		
Kichnast, Christopher	1		2		4
Kleinart, Laurance	1		1	3	1
Kelly, Benjamin	1	2			
Kerby, Samuel	1		4		3
Kerby, Pleasant	1				3
James, Ebenezer	2	3	3		1
Harvey, William	3	2	6		
Huffines, Daniel	1	2	5		
Harvey, John	1	1	2		1
Holder, Joseph	4		2		
Fesler, Andrew	2	4	3		
Fentor, Baston	1		1		
Fentor, Christian	1				
Fokel, Samuel	1	1	3		
Fisher, George	1	4	2		
Fogler, Michael	1	2	4		
Fiddler, Peter	2	2	4		
Faw, Jacob	3	1	2		
Engrim, David	1	1	1		
Elrod, Adam	2		2		
Elrod, Jeremiah	1		1		3
Elrod, Robert	1	2	3		
Douthard, Isaac	1	2	2		
Dull, Nicholas	4	1	2		
Cinsil, Frederick	2		2		
Crator, Jacob	1		4		
Croom, John	2	1	3		
Bonn, Jacob	1		1		
Boger, Henry	1		3		
Burton, Henry	1	3	1		
Billetor, Edward	3	1	3		
Bruner, Daniel	1	3	5		
Stevens, John	2	1	2		
Seward, Samuel	1		5		
Hauser, Jacob	3	5	3		
Hines, Jacob	1	2	3		
Hill, John	3	2	3		
Hancock, William	1				
Hill, Thomas	1	1	1		
Hartman, John	1	3	2		
Hines, John	1	2	4		
Hines, Christopher	1		1		
Hines, John	2	1	6		
Hanke, John	5				
Higher, Rody	2	4	6		
Humel, Christian	1	1	5		
Grace, James	2	2			
Gentry, Claburn	1	1	3		
Garner, George	1				
Geiger, Adam	2	4	4		
Glenn, Thomson	1	1	3		3
Glenn, Jeremiah	2		1		1
Gault, David	1	2	4		1
Green, Coonrod	1	1	2		
Fishell, Adam	2	4	3		
Brooks, Mathew	3	4	5		
Bolingjack, Joseph	3	1	2		
Binkele, Joseph	1		1		
Duggans, Agnus	1		3		
Cyrus, Nimrod	1		1	3	
Wauters, John	1	2	4		

SALISBURY DISTRICT, SURRY COUNTY.

NAME OF HEAD OF FAMILY.	Free white males of 16 years and upward.	Free white males under 16.	Free white females.	All other free persons.	Slaves.
Adams, Patrick	1	3	5		
Alberty, Frederick	1	2	1		
Ballard, Thomas	1	2	4		
Brock, Sherod	1	2	5		
Brannum, John	1	4	4		

NAME OF HEAD OF FAMILY.	Free white males of 16 years and upward.	Free white males under 16.	Free white females.	All other free persons.	Slaves.
Barras, Martin	1	2	4		1
Bean, William	1		2		
Barker, William	2		3		
Cockram, Moses	3	2	4		1
Chamberlin, Thomas	1	4	3		9

NAME OF HEAD OF FAMILY.	Free white males of 16 years and upward.	Free white males under 16.	Free white females.	All other free persons.	Slaves.
Clarke, John	1	2	2		
Carty, John	1	3	3		
Craigg, Edward	1	2	2		
Barrs, Leonard	1				
Brock, Alexander	1	1	2		

SALISBURY DISTRICT, SURRY COUNTY—Continued.

NAME OF HEAD OF FAMILY.	Free white males of 16 years and upward, including heads of families.	Free white males under 16 years.	Free white females, including heads of families.	All other free persons.	Slaves.	NAME OF HEAD OF FAMILY.	Free white males of 16 years and upward, including heads of families.	Free white males under 16 years.	Free white females, including heads of families.	All other free persons.	Slaves.	NAME OF HEAD OF FAMILY.	Free white males of 16 years and upward, including heads of families.	Free white males under 16 years.	Free white females, including heads of families.	All other free persons.	Slaves.
Cadle, Thomas	1	1	1			Blackman, John	1	1	5			Logan, Patrick	1	2			6
McAffee, William	3	4	5			Hicks, Thomas	8		2			McDaniel, William	1	2	6		
Norman, Henry	1	3	4			Gray, Biddicks	1	3	1			Matthew, James	1	6	3		
Norman, Thomas	1	1	2			Shote, Edward	1		4			Matthis, Aaron	1		6		
Norman, William	1	2	4			Martin, Thomas	2	1	4			Matthis, Matthew	1	4	4		
Oglesby, Micajah	2	1	2		5	Cornelius, Andrew	1	3	1			Martin, William	1	1	5		
Phillips, Ephraim	1		1			Ballinger, John	1		2			Miller, John	1		2		
Phillips, Cornelius	1					Vestal, Daniel						Finney, Joseph	1	1	3		
Phillips, Robert	1		1			Lindville, Andrew	2	1	4			Moore, William	3		3		
Douglas, John	1	3	1			Rutledge, Mary	2	2	4			Morphew, James	1	5	3		
Sisk, Timothy	1	1	4			Adams, Moses	1	1	1			Nerdicke, Adin	1		2		
Pritchett, Phillip	2	2	2			Vestal, James	3	2	2			Pollock, Joseph	1		2		
Pigg, William	1		2			Finney, Joseph	1	1	3			Passwaters, Samuel	1	3	4		
Porter, Joseph	1	5	3			York, James	2	3	4			Price, John	1	3	5		
Rion, Derby	1	5	4		1	Barnes, John	1		1			Phillips, Solomon	1	1	2		1
Riggs, David	2	5	6			Reynolds, Sophia	1	2	1			Phillips, William	3	4	3		
Riggs, Samuel	3		1			Willard, Augustin	1	4	2			Martin, John	1		3		
Riggs, Zadock	1	4	3			Hoott, Jacob, Junr	1		1			Robinson, John	1				
Rainwater, James	1	2	4			Woolfe, Daniel	1	3	2			Renolds, Ezekiel	1	1	5		
Ramey, Joseph	2	2	8			Franklin, John	1	1	4			Roch, John	1	1	2		1
Raybourn, Thomas	1	2	3			Hannah, John Doak	1		3		2	Ridins, John	1	3	5		
Rayborn, Silvanus	1	1	3			Benson, Benjamin	1	2	6		1	Reach, William	1	5	1		
Ross, Thomas, Junr	1	1	3			Lawrence, James	1	1	4		3	Robinson, William	1	1	1		
Davis, William	2	3	5			McLarver, Joshua	1	1	2			Scudder, Moses	1	1	1		
Davis, Jonathan	1					Jinkins, John	5	1	5		4	Stow, Abram	1	2	2		
Doan, John	1	2	4			Harris, Moses	1	2	4			Scott, Daniel	2	3	4		
Dean, Job	1					Chamberling, Charles	1	2	1			Spur, Levi	1		8		
Edwards, Gideon	1	2	2		19	Lawrence, Randolph	1		2			Spur, Leven	3	1	6		
Fruman, Aaron	1	4	4		2	Dollasson, Jane		1	3			Spur, Joshua	3	1	3		
Fletcher, John	3		5			Reed, George	1	1	6			Spur, Andrew	2	1	4		
Gentry, Joseph	2		4		3	Harris, Nathaniel	2	1	3			Spur, Shadrack	1	1	2		
Gentry, Shelton	1	2	3			Puckett, Thomas	2	2	1			Spur, Aaron, Junr	1		2		
Galaspy, Elijah	1	2	5		1	Puckett, Richard	1	1	1			Scott, James	1	3	4		
Holt, John	2		2			Puckett, Benja	1	1	1			Standley, Archilaus	2		3		
Hughs, John	1	2	3		8	Creed, John	1				8	Standley, Jesse	1		3		
Hill, Thomas	1	4	1			Humphries, Samuel	1	2	2			Smith, George	1	3	6		
Hill, William	4		5			Brison, Alexander	1	2	1			Scott, Jesse	1		7		
Hill, James	1	1	1			Stow, William	2		1			Savage, Leven	2	4	3		
Hill, John	1		2			Sheppard, Jacob	2	1	5			Thompson, Frederick	1	3	3		
Hodges, Edmund	3	3	2			Filer, Ruth	1	2	4			Taylour, Matthew	1	2	3		
Hudson, William	1		1			Finn, Daniel	2	4	5			Vandever, Charles	2	1	3		1
Hodge, Bartholomew	1	1	4			Bridgman, Solomon	1		1			Vandever, George	1		3		
Hodge, Ambrose	1		3			Maine, Presley	1		2			Vaughn, Abram	1		1		
Hodge, William	1	1	2			Askew, James	1	1	3			Williams, John	2	3	3		1
Riggs, Hiram	1	3	3			Appesson, William	1	6	1		1	Wheatherford, John	1	1	3		
Rutu, Isham	1	2	4			Pettite, Thomas	1	4	3			Williams, Thomas	1	4	2		2
Ross, Thomas	1		5			Badgett, James	1	3	3		7	Wood, Obediah	1	1	3		
Stewart, Hambleton	1	2	3			Brown, Josiah	1	3	2			Spur, John	1	1	2		
Senter, Zachariah	1	1	2			Brown, James	1	1	4			Spur, William	1		1		
Stottz, John	1		2			Brown, Samuel	1		1			Allen, John	1	4	5		4
Scott, Benjamin	1	2	4			Brown, Jesse	1		2			Brooks, George	2	6	3		
Stewart, James	1		3			Brown, John	1					Brown, Thomas	2	2	2		
Sims, Mathew	1	2	5			Bevenders, John	1					Bruce, John	2	3	5		3
Stewart, William	2	4	1			Hargrave, James	1	4	1			Baker, Moses	1	3	1		
Stewart, Nathaniel	1	5	3			Kerr, Alexander	2	1	3			Brown, John	1	1	5		
Tucker, James	3		2		1	Chanley, William	1	3	2			Brown, William	1	2	3		
Tucker, William	1	2	3			Cockburn, Henry	1	4	3			Brown, Joseph	1	2	3		
Tucker, Garner	1	1	4		1	Childress, Thomas	1	1	3			Brown, Joshua	1	2	3		
Taylor, Edward	1			1		Carson, James	1	1	2			Bates, George	1	1	1		
Tallifarro, John	1			6	3	Carson, Thomas	1					Burns, Patrick	1		2		
Talifarro, Charles	1		2			Cox, Isaiah	1	2	3		1	Carter, John	1	3	3		2
William, Moses	1	3	2			Kerr, John	1	2	5			Crochett, Samuel	1	1	7		
Straughn, Larkin	1	2	4			Dooling, John	2	2	4		2	Orison, Abram	1	1			8
Snead, Benjamin	1	3	2			Dooling, John, Junr	1					Creson, Joshua	1	3	5		2
Williams, John	1		3			Dooling, William	1	1	2		2	Clarke, Robert	1		4		
Cohone, William	1		3			Poindexter, David	1	4	5			Cambell, James	1		1		
Hall, Hudson	2		2			Davis, George	1	2	3			Coe, John	1	3	7		7
Hudson, Sterling	1	2	2			Devenport, William	2	3	5			Colverd, John B	2	1	5		
Hayes, John	2	2	5			England, Joseph	3	3	9			Colverd, William	1				
Jervis, Eliphalett	1	4	4			England, William	1		3			Douglas, Alexander	2		5		
Kirby, Joseph	1		2			England, Samuel	1					Danner, Frederick	1	4	2		
Kirby, Philip	1	2				Hynn, Jacob	1	1	2			Dinkins, Stephen	1	2	1		
Kirby, Josiah	1		3			Hynn, William	1	2	3			Donnalay, John	2		4		
Kirby, Henry	2	2	4			Hynn, George	1	2	2			Dicke, Stephen	1	2	4		
Keith, William	1		2			Hynn, Hezekiah	1	4	3			Douden, Zephaniah	1	4	3		
Lanthrop, John	2	2	4			Floyd, Thomas	2	1	3			Daniel, James	1	2	4		
McCloud, Wm	1	3	5			Pu, James	1	1	1			Dennis, John	1	1	1		
Standfield, Thomas	1	1	1			Garrett, Blunt	3	2	4			Edleman, Margarate	1	1	1		
Love, Steven	1		2			Grayham, James	2	4	5			Enjard, Silas	1	2	3		
Laffoon, Stephen	1	3	2			Gentry, Samuel	2	5	3		1	Garner, Whiatt	1	2	4		
Laufield, Joseph	1	2	6			Gentry, Atha	1	2	3			Grose, Simon, Junr	2	3	8		
McCarow, Archer	2	2	5		5	Halcomb, Lawrence	1	5	5			Grose, Devall	1	4	4		
Munkur, William	2	4	5			Huchins, Nicholas	2	3	3		2	Grose, William	1		4		
Mackey, Joseph	2	2	5		5	Hammons, John	1	1	4			Grose, John	2	6	1		
Murphy, Richard	1		2		4	Huchins, Strangman	1		3		2	Grose, Simon	1	1	1		
Moore, Samuel	1	1	2		1	Hugguman, Joseph	2		6			Gutry, Charles	1		3		
Murphy, Joseph	1	1	1			Harvey, John	1	1	5			Gibbons, Winnifred			3		
Cohone, Wm, Junr	1	1	1			Head, William	1	3	5			Spur, Richard	1		2		
Haddock, Henry	1		2			Hutchins, John	2	3				Spur, Henry	2	3	4	2	13
Clifton, Job	1	1	2			Johnson, Archibald	1		2			Spear, Jacob, Junr	1	2	1		
Frewett, Jesse	1	1	1			Lakey, Francis	3		1			Spur, John, Junr	1	4	1		
Ross, Patrick	1		1			Longino, John	1		2			Spur, Andrew, Junr	1	1	1		
Bridgman, Matthew	1		3			Longino, Thomas	1	1	2			Stielman, Matthias	2		1		
Ferguson, Robt	3	1	1			Laws, Moses	1		1			Shore, Frederick	2	2	2		
Porter, Dudley	1		2			Logan, James	1	1	1		1	Skidmore, John	2	3	5		
Pettijohn, Job	1		3			Logan, John	1					Shermer, Peter	2	1	3		
Ashley, William	1	4	4			Longino, John Thos	2	3	6		7	Steelman, Charles	1	2	4		2

SALISBURY DISTRICT, SURRY COUNTY—Continued.

NAME OF HEAD OF FAMILY.	Free white males of 16 years and upward, including heads of families.	Free white males under 16 years.	Free white females, including heads of families.	All other free persons.	Slaves.
Skidmore, Abram	1		4		
Steelman, John	1	2	3		
Soter, John	1	2	5		
Sweat, William	2	4	3		2
Summers, Manning	2		4		
Steward, David	1	2	3		
Spoon, Adam	1	3	10		
Standfield, John	2	2	3		
Thornton, William	1	4	5		2
Turner, Rodah	2	1	3		
Thompson, Catharine	1	2	4		1
Hiet, Joseph, Junr	1		3		
Horton, John	2		3		
Harrel, William	1	2	3		
Horn, Nicolas	1		2		2
Hill, William	3	3	5		
Holtsclaw, Josep	1		3		
Gibbons, James	1	5	1		
Hudspith, Thomas	1	2	1		1
Hudspith, George	1	2	3		
Hudspith, Jiles	2		3		14
Hudspith, Charles	1	1	2		2
Hudspith, Benja	1	2	2		
Haggins, William	1	4	4		
Hudspith, Joseph	1	2	2		
Head, George	1	1	3		
Halliman, Mark	1		1		1
Hawell, David	1	1	2		3
Halke, James	1	1	3		
Howard, Phillip	3	3	3		
Hootts, Jacob	3	5	3		
Hootts, John	1	1	2		
Humphries, John, Junr	1	1	1		
Humphries, John	2		3		
Hawell, James	2		2		
Humphries, Samuel	1		1		
Hawell, David	2	1	2		1
Joiner, John	5	3	3		3
Kimbrough, George	2	2	1		5
Kimbrough, Ormond	3				4
Kitchen, John, Junr	1	1	1		
Kitchen, John	2		4		
Harber, Adonajah	4	2	7		19
Herd, John	3	2	2		1
Holder, James	1	2	2		
Harper, Martha		1	3		
Hiett, George	1				
Jackson, Reuben	1	3	6		
Jackson, Curtis	1	2	7		
Jessop, Jacob	1	1	2		
Lockheart, Robert	1		2		
Hill, Bartlett	1		1		
Critchfield, Joshua	3	1	3		
Jones, Isaac	1				
Jackson, John	1	1	2		
Jackson, Joseph	2		4		
Isan, Nathaniel	1	2	2		
Kirby, Joel	4	2	7		
Kirby, Richard	3	3	4		5
Lovell, Edward	2	2	3		4
Love, William	1	3	3		
Lisby, Aaron	1	4	4		
Lane, John	1	2	1		
Linvill, Moses	2	5	5		
Lane, William	2	1	5		
Louder, John	1				
Pinnions, Thomas	3	2	4		
Thomson, John	1	1	3		
King, Mason	1	3	2		
Lash, George	3	2	5		
Mosby, Samuel	1	3	6		15
Marsh, John, Junr	1	1	1		
Marsh, John	2		2		
McCallum, John	1		3		
McCallum, Thomas	1	1	3		
McCallum, James	1		3		
Martin, James	2	3	4		
Mayes, William	2	1	5		7
Miller, John	2	1	2		
Murphy, Joseph	1	2	4		
Poindexter, Francis	3		4		
Pilcher, Daniel	1		3		
Pilcher, James	3	1	3		
Prough, Christian	1		1		
Rineger, George	2	2	2		
Rineger, George, Junr	1		2		
Richards, Leonard	1	2	6		
Rutledge, Joseph	2	3	3		
Reavis, James	1	2	2		
Rogers, Hezekiel	1				
Stockdell, Thomas	1		4		
Spur, William	1	2	3		
Spear, Benjamin	1	2	6		
Thompson, Samuel	2	4	1		
Langley, John	1	1	4		
McKinney, James	1	7	1		
Morton, Richard	1	2	1		
Morton, Patrick	1		5		
Morton, James	1				
Meeks, William	2		2		
Powell, William	1		3		
Pinson, Richard	1	5	3		
Pinson, Reuben	2	2	5		
Parker, Samuel	2	1	4		
Reter, James	1	1	2		
Reter, Aaron	1	1	1		
Reynolds, William	1	6	1		
Scott, Arthur	1	4	3		
Studdard, William	2	1	2		
Summers, Boster	2	1	4		
Stephens, John	2	3	4		
Stone, Enoch	1	3	2		
Smallwood, John	1	1	2		
Stone, John	3	1	3		1
Simmons, Peter	4		2		6
Simmons, Charles	1	2	2		
Sheppard, Jacob	2	2	5		8
Stone, William	3	3	4		
Tansey, William	1	1	5		
Tilley, John	2	3	2		
Vanderpool, Abram	1	3	3		
Watkins, George	1	2	6		
Whitehead, Robert	1	2	2		
Wheeler, Benjamin	1		6		
Watkins, Joseph	1	2	5		
Waldrop, Joseph	1	1	4		
Langford, Mary		2	3		
Simmons, Rial	1	2	3		
Chandler, Daniel	1	4	2		
Austill, Major	1		1		
Allen, Thomas	1	4	5		
Austill, Isaac	3	2	5		
Baldwin, Zenus	3	2	8		
Blackledge, Acabud	2	2	4		
Blackmon, Solomon	1				
Binge, Obediah	2	3	3		
Cobb, Clisby	3	2	6		
Cochram, Daniel	1		4		
Coock, William, Junr	1	4	3		
Crawley, Samuel	1	1	1		
Carter, Samuel	2	2	5		2
Cochram, William	1	3	4		
Cook, William H	2	2	1		
Collins, Obediah	1	3	3		
Cochram, Humphrey	1	2	5		
Downey, Samuel	1	2	3		
Whinrey, John	1	1	4		
Johnson, John	2		1		
Turner, Ezekiel	1		1		
Rose, John	1				
Jervis, John	1	5	4		
Adams, Moses	1		1		
Ashley, Joseph	1	4	7		
Ballard, Iram	2	1			
Bales, John Bostor	1	1	3		
Bales, Jacob	3		5		
Ballard, Jerman	1				
Ball, Thomas	1		1		5
Bohannan, William	3	1	1		
Barrow, Daniel	1	3	2		
Brown, George	1	1	1		
Brown, Randolph	3	1	3		
Reynolds, Nathanial	1	1	3		
Bohannan, Elliott	3	2	4		
Bursham, John	2	2	4		
Carr, Benjamin	1	2	2		
Curry, Joseph	1	2	5		
Cooper, Samuel	1		1		
Carn, Russel	1	1	5		
Cooper, Jonathan	1		1		
Critchfield, John	1		2		
Coleman, William	1		4		
Dunningham, Thos	2		10		
Downey, Abram	1	4	4		
Downey, Peter	1		2		1
Etheridge, Abner	1	2	1		
Fillden, John	3		2		2
Faircloth, Thomas	1		3		
Fariner, Nathan	2	2	3		
Greenwood, Samuel	2	5	5		1
Hide, Stephen	1	4	5		
Hill, John	1	2	5		
Hudgins, John	1	1	1		
Hurst, George	1	2	3		
Hide, James	1				
Ginnings, James	1	2	1		
Johnson, John, Junr	1		1		
Cadle, Thomas	1	1	2		
Daniel, James	1	2	3		
Jervis, Jabez	2		2		
Jervis, William	1				
Jervis, Stephen	3		1		
Jones, James, senr	1		1		1
Johnson, Isaac	1				
Anderson, James	4	5	3	1	
Jervis, Keziah	1	2	6		
Jiles, Samuel	1	3	2		
Keaton, Francis	1				
Meredith, William	3	3	6		2
Dunningham, Thomas, Junr	1	1	3		
Dudley, Charles	2		2		
Denney, Hezekiah	1	4	6		
Denney, William	2	2	5		
Donaly, John	1	1	3		
Dunningham, John	2	2	3		
Hiett, William	4	4	3		
Dunningham, James	1				
Dunningham, Jesse	1				
Evans, Daniel	1	3	2		
Early, Jeremiah	6				
Freeman, William	4	2	3		3
Gunston, James	1		3		
Haines, Jonathan	1		1		6
Hiett, Benjamin	1	2	1		
Hiett, John	1	3	1		
Hiett, Joseph	5	2	4		
Reavis, Joseph	1	1	3		1
Ryley, Gerard	1	2	2		
Riley, Jeremiah	1	1	1		6
Reavis, John	1	2	1		
Roark, John	1				
Rutor, John	2		2		
Reavis, Jesse	2		2		
Roton, Jacob	1		1		
Roark, John, Junr	1	1	1		
Russell, Charles	1	2	3		
Marsh, William	2	3	2		
Moseley, West	1	3	2		
Moore, Moses	1	1	1		
Marsh, John, Junr	1		1		
Marsh, Minor	2	3	2		
Marsh, John	3	3	3		
Meredith, John	1	4	6		
Meredith, Samuel	1	2	2		
Monaham, Shadrack	1	2	4		
McMickle, John	2	2	5		
Meredeth, Daniel	1	1	2		1
Martin, Andrew	3	1	2		
Pace, Sarah					
Pettite, Rachel	3	1	4		
Richards, John	1		3		
Richards, William	1	1	2		
Robertson, John	1	2	4		
Suedder, John	1	3	1		
Shores, John	1		3		10
Sutton, John	1	2	2		
Spur, Aaron	1	1	4		
Shores, Reuben, Junr	1	1	8		4
Sugart, John	2	1	2		
Sugart, Zachariah	3	1	4		
Thompson, George	1	3	4		
Whitlock, William	1	3	2		
Halcomb, Drury	1				
Phillips, Jonathan	1		2		
Reavis, James	1		1		4
Masters, William	1		1		
Miller, Christian	1		1		
Debord, George	2		6		
Debord, Jacob	1	1	2		
Grace, George	1				
Chappel, James	1	1	1		
Hudspith, Mary		1	1		
Spurling, Zachariah	1	4	7		
Sparks, Matthew	1	3	4		
Stubbs, Isaac	1	1	2		
Scoffield, Joseph	1				
Swim, Moses	1	3	3		
Shaw, James	1	2	2		
Stephens, John	1	3	3		
Standley, John	1	1	1		
Stephens, Edward	1	3	2		
Smith, Bennett	2	2	2		
Sanders, James	1				9
Talberd, Joshua	1	1	3		
Vestal, Thomas	1		4		
Whitfield, William	1		1		
Waggoner, Henry	3	2	7		
Waddle, Noil	1	2	4		
Wheatherman, Christian	2	4	5		
Wright, Thomas	1	3	4		
Whalen, John	1	1	1		
Wooldridge, Edward	1				3
Whootton, Richard	1	4	5		
Wiggfield, Benjamin	1		5		
Whitehead, Ann	4		5		
Williams, John	1		5		6
Whiles, Thomas	1	2	3		1
Whiles, Thomas, Junr	1	1	3		
Whiles, John	1	4	1		

SALISBURY DISTRICT, SURRY COUNTY—Continued.

NAME OF HEAD OF FAMILY.	Free white males of 16 years and upward, including heads of families.	Free white males under 16 years.	Free white females, including heads of families.	All other free persons.	Slaves.
Whiles, Luke	1		2		
Windsor, Isaac	1	2	3		
Wilson, Alexander	1	1	6		
Wright, Ann	1	3	6		
Wright, John	1				
Wilson, Samuel	1	1	1		
Whiles, Pinson	1		2		
Wagoner, Adam	1				
Weatherman, Christa	1	1	2		
Wood, Stephen	2	1	7		
Zachary, William	1	4	2		
Colton, John	4	1	3		
Bitticks, Francis	1	3	3		
Pilcher, Phebe	1		2		
Philips, Mark	2	1	2		
Inshaw, Jacob	1	4	1		
Hoppes, John	1		4		
Husband, Robert	2	2	6		
Hoppes, Daniel	1	1	2		
Johnson, Isaac	2	2	5		4
Jacks, Thomas	1		1		
Jacks, Richard	2	3	7		
Johnson, Elisha	1		3		
Jones, James	3	1	3		
Jeffrey, William	1		4		
Johnson, John	4	1	4		
Johnson, Benja	1	2	1		
Kell, John	1		1		
Keys, Joseph	2		2	1	
Kell, John, Junr	1		2		
Lackham, Robert	1	1	2		
Lacham, Aaron	1	1	4		
Long, Frederick	1	5	4		
Lacham, Alexander	1	1	1		
Liverton, Daniel	1		3		1
Moore, George	1	2	2		
Miller, Jacob	1	3	6		
Messick, Richard	1		2		
McLemore, Wright	1				
Masters, Nicholas	1		2		
Masters, James	1				
Ayers, Samuel	1		2		
Lambert, Sterling	1		4		
Thomas, George	1	1	1		
Hains, Elis	2	1	5		
Debord, John	3	6	3		
Elsbery, William	1		1		
Ayers, Eliue	1	1	2		
Ayers, Thomas	3		7		
Adkins, William	1	1	1		
Allen, Isaac	1	1	2		1
Ayers, Nathaniel	1		5		
Ayers, Moses	3	6	8		
Bills, William	1	1	2		
Broughton, Job	1	3	1		
Bills, Daniel	1	5	4		
Bray, Little Barry	1	7	4		
Colman, William	1		3		
Colman, Isaac	2	2	4		
Conner, John	1	1	2		
Davis, Isham	1	1	4		
Durham, James	1	1	3		
Denney, Samuel	1	1	1		
Ayers, John	2	1	2		
Anderson, George	1	1	3		
Devern, Frederick	2	4	3		
Messick, George	1	2	2		1
Martin, John	1	1	4		
Marshal, William	1		1		
Marshal, Joseph	1		1		
Marshal, John	1	2	1		
Meirs, Peter	2		4		
Marshal, Ruanah	1	2	3		
Moore, John	2	3	7		
Mannering, Jordan	1	3	6		
Mannering, Andrew	1	1	2		
McLemore, Ephraim	1	3	5		
McHand, Matthew	2	2	4		1
Maxfield, Sidney	1				
Mackey, John	1	2	3		
Murphy, James	1		1		
Mehaffey, Thos	1	4	5		
Mires, Joseph	1	4	5		
Sprinkle, Peter	4	2	3		
Masters, William	1		1		
Moler, Valentine	1	3	3		
Noblett, John	1	3	3		
Parker, Jonathan	2	3	6		
Petty, Zachariah	1		5		
Patterson, Greenbery	4	4	4		
Pettijohn, Henry	1	2	3		
Pettijohn, Job	3	1	2		
Dunningham, Joseph	1	1	2		
Evans, James	1	1	2		
Edward, Andrew	1	3	3		
Hoppes, George	1	4	4		
Hoppes, George, senr	1	2	1		

NAME OF HEAD OF FAMILY.	Free white males of 16 years and upward, including heads of families.	Free white males under 16 years.	Free white females, including heads of families.	All other free persons.	Slaves.
Halcomb, John	1	2	6	3	
Halcomb, May	1	2	1		
Hudspeth, John	1	3	3		
Hudspeth, Airs	1	3	6		
Hough, Daniel	3	2	7		
Inkshaw, Joseph	1	2	5		
Hall, William	1		5		
Hagin, Peter	1	2	1		
Hadley, Simon, Junr	1		4		
Halcomb, Thomas	2	3	1		
Hadley, Thomas	1		6		
Hobson, Stephen	1	2	1		
Hutchings, Thomas	1	1	3		
Hutchings, Benja	2	6	4	4	
Inshaw, Thomas	1	1	1		
Hadley, Simon	1		4		
Hudspith, Airs, Junr	1	1	4	3	
Halcomb, Grimes	2	4	2		
Harding, William	2	2	4	13	
Halcomb, George	2	2	4		
Petty, Randsall	1		1		
Poe, William	1	3	5		
Parson, Richard	1	2	2		
Petty, William	2	3	3	1	
Penright, John	2	2			
Rutledge, William	1		3		
Roton, Josiah	1	2	2		1
Riley, Edward	1	1	3	3	
Riley, James	1		3	4	
Reese, Abram	2	6	4		
Reynolds, Jonas	1	2	3		
Revis, John	1	1	3		
Ray, William	1		1		
Roton, David	1		3		
Roton, James	1	4	5		
Riley, Nincan	2		1		
Riley, Nincan, Junr	1		1		
Forester, James	1		4		
Freeman, Jacob	1	3	3		
Freeman, Samuel	1	2	3		5
Freeman, Joshua	1	1	5		8
Fanning, Thomas	1	1	3		
Greenly, James	2	3	4		
Green, George	1	4	5		
Hammons, Ambrose	1	1	6		
Howard, Jane	1	1	4		
Horn, Richard	1	2	7	2	
Haggard, Samuel	3	3	7	1	
Hicks, Nathaniel	1	1	5		
Harrisson, William	1	1	2		
Hughs, Thomas	2		1		
Hammons, John	1	4	4		
Holyfield, Valentine	1	2	4		
Henderson, George	1		3		
Hopperoumes, John	1	2	3		
Horn, John	3		3		
Hatton, John	1	4	2		
Johnson, William	2	5	3		
Jones, John	1	3	4		
Johnson, Jeffrey	2	2	3		
Johnson, Moses	1	2	5		
Johnson, Joseph	1	4	6		
Kelley, Barnabas	2		1		
Knight, Reuben	1		6		
Knight, William	1	4	3		
London, Amos	1	1	2		
Lay, Charles	1	3	1		
Lucas, John	1	1	2		
Lucas, William	1	1	3		
Mears, Thomas	2		1		
Mears, Moses	4	3	2	1	
Vindever, John	1	2	6		
Vindever, Charles	1	2	4		
Woolridge, William	1	2	5	2	
Wall, William	1	3	4		
Winston, John	2	1	2	4	
Whoshon, Philip	1	1	1		
Whoshon, Leonard	1	3	6		
Wells, James	2	1	4		
Wright, William	1	3	3		
Witasker, Johnson	1	1	2		
Welch, David	2	2	1		
Williams, Joseph	2	6	2	20	
Shelton, Jeremiah	2	1	3		
Spear, Thomas	1	4	4		
Robinson, William	1	2	3		
Adam, William, Junr	1				
Aldridge, Joseph	2		2		
Anthony, David	1	1	4		
Aldridge, Nathl	1		1		
Andersons, John N	1	2	4		
Adams, William	2	1	5		
Adams, Jonathan	1	1	2		
Alnutt, William	1		3		
Arnold, Samuel	2	4	4		3
Aldridge, Joshua	1				

NAME OF HEAD OF FAMILY.	Free white males of 16 years and upward, including heads of families.	Free white males under 16 years.	Free white females, including heads of families.	All other free persons.	Slaves.
Brown, Thomas	1	1	2		
Barrett, Joseph	2		3		
Bowen, Thomas	2		2		
Meriam, Bartholomew	1	2	4		
Meriam, John	1		8		
Manis, Henry	2		6		
Oversby, William	1		4		
Parnell, Joshua	1		5		
Pace, Edmund	1	1	3		
Ray, Benjamin	1	1	3		
Summers, John	2	3	3		
Critchfield, Joshua	1	2	3		
Smith, Edward	1	2	1		
Silvie, William	1	3	5		
Summers, Johnson	1		1		
Wheeluss, Lewis	2	1	4		
Whitaker, William	1	5	3		
Whootton, Thomas	1		1		
Whootton, Thos, Junr	1	1	1		
Weaver, William	3		2		
Weaver, Thomas	1	1	3		
Wheeluss, Reuben	1	1	2		1
Watson, John	2	1	3		
Whitacker, Jonathan	1	3	2		
Walker, Joseph	1		1		
Wright, James	1		1		
York, James	1		5		
Jones, Samuel	1		1		
Melton, Richard	2	4	1		
Brown, John	1	4	1		
Bailie, James	1	1	6		
Blacklock, Richard	1	2	4		
Brown, Christian	2				
Burnsides, James	1	1	5		
Brown, Richard	1	1	4		
Brown, William	1	3	3		
Bills, Gersham	1	1	1		
Bond, Stephen	1	4	8		
Biddicks, John	1	1	4		
Blackman, Jeremiah	1	1	5		
Brown, Jacob	1	3	3		
Bramblet, Ambrose	1	4	3		2
Clinton, Edward	2	3	4		1
Colton, Elijah	1	5	1		
Colton, Lindsey	1	2	1		
Carpenter, Matthias	1	3	3		
Callaway, Samuel	1	3	3		
Copeland, John	2	4	3		
Castevin, John	1	2	3		
Coleman, Charles	1				
Chappel, Ambrose	1	2	3		
Clanton, Thomas	1	2	1		3
Clanton, Benjamin	4	1	3		
Keer, William	1	3	3		
Davis, Andrew	2	3	5		
Dillard, John	1	4	3		
Debord, Isaac	1		2		
Hall, Joshua	1	2	2		
Bray, Hannon	5	1	5		
Burch, John	1	2	2		3
Burch, William	1	2	4		1
Burch, Thomas C	1		2		
Critchfield, William	1		5		
Blackburn, Susanna		2	3		
Bledsoe, Benjamin	3	2	5		
Bray, Stogner	1	1	2		
Burch, Thomas	1		4		
Biddicks, John	1	2	6		
Cook, William	3		5		10
Critchfield, Nathl	1	1	5		
Critchfield, Wm	1		5		
Cockran, David	1	1	2		
Crawley, Thomas	1	1	1		
Bledsoe, Learking	1	1	2		
Allen, John	1	1	2		
Owens, George	1	3	3		
Davis, William	1	1	3		
Critchfield, John	1	1	3		
Cooper, James	2	2	5		
Coons, Francis	3		5		
Emanuel, Isaac	1				
Fretwell, William	1				
Todd, James	1		5		
Davis, Gabriel	1	1	2		
Dobbins, Jacob	2	3	6		
Davis, William	1	3	3		
Dibord, Reuben	1	3	1		
Day, William	1	5	3		
Elsberry, Isaac	1	5	3		
Elsbery, John	1	3	1		
Elmore, Abijah	3	4	1		
Eastwood, Joseph	1		3		
Elsbery, Jacob	1		2		
Elliott, Lewis	2	2	3		6
Elliott, William	1	2	6		1
Elis, William	1	4	3		
Everton, Thomas	1	2	5		

SALISBURY DISTRICT, SURRY COUNTY—Continued.

NAME OF HEAD OF FAMILY.	Free white males of 16 years and upward, including heads of families.	Free white males under 16 years.	Free white females, including heads of families.	All other free persons.	Slaves.
Fender, Nimrod	1	1	1		
Fender, Gabriel	1		1		
Felton, Amoriah	1	2	5		
Fender, Christian	1	3	3		
Farris, James	1	2	2		
Frazier, Robert	1	3	2		2
Frazier, William	1	2	4		
Gentry, Nicholas	2		2		
Gentry, Richard	4		2		
Gentry, Allen	1	3	5		
Gallion, Thomas	1	3	2		1
Gallion, Jacob	1	2	2		
Garner, John	3	3	4		
Garner, William	1		3		
Garrish, Benjamin	1	1	3		
Gentry, Richard, Junr	2	1	3		
Hambrick, Henry	1	4	1		
Hill, Joseph	3	1	5		
Hurt, John	6	2	4		
Harvil, David	1	7	3		
Harris, John	1	1	8		4
Edwards, James	1		1		
Downey, James	1		2		2
Gordon, Thomas	1	5	2		
Johnson, Charles	1	4	2		
Kirby, Francis	1	2	7	1	
Lewis, Joel	1	2	2		18
Lewis, William Terrel	3	2	6		58
Moore, Aaron	1	1	3		
Morris, Nathl	3	3	3		
Morris, James, Junr	1		4		
Morris, Nathl, Junr	1				
Martin, Obediah	1		4		5
Martin, Salathiel	1	4	2		3
McBride, William	1	4	4		
McBride, Minassith	2		6		
McLaine, William	1		2		
McLaine, Laughly	2		2		
Morris, Daniel, Junr	1	1	2		
Morris, Daniel	2	1	2		4
Burris, William	5	4	7		1
Bledsoe, Moses	2	1	7		
Blanchett, Joel	1		3		
Bruce, William	3	2	3		1
Brison, James	3	6	4		
Burras, John	1	2	1		1
Burras, Jacob	1	1	4		1
Burch, William	1	1	2		
Baker, Obediah	4	2	5		
Bryant, Thomas	1		3		
Cadle, Benjamin	2		3		
Cox, John	1	5	2		
Crud, Matthew	2		2		1
Crud, Bartlett	1	1	2		
Cook, William	5	2	7		
Crud, Bennet	4	2	4		
Clarke, David	1				
Crud, Colsby	1				
Doak, Alexander	1	1	4		
Davis, John	2		2		
Davis, Matthew	3	2	5		1
Dickerson, James	2	1	5		5
Davis, John	3	4	6		

NAME OF HEAD OF FAMILY.	Free white males of 16 years and upward, including heads of families.	Free white males under 16 years.	Free white females, including heads of families.	All other free persons.	Slaves.
Conrod, Elrod	1	2	4		
Fleming, John	4	5	6		12
Faulkner, William	2	6	3		5
Griffith, Edward	1	2	3		
Griffith, Benjamin	1	4	1		4
Morrisson, William	1				
Parsons, John	1	4	3		
Parsons, James	1	2	3		
Phipps, Matthew	1	2	2		
Phillips, Abner	2	3	3		
Pipes, John	3	1	6		
Wray, Zachariah	2	4	5		
Roberds, Oliver	3	3	9		
Sparks, William, Junr	2	1	5		
Sparks, George	1	1	1		
Sparks, Joseph	1	4	4		
Spence, Thomas	1	1	1		
Suthard, Isaac	1	1	7		
Suthard, Henry	1	4	5		
Sparks, Thomas	1	1	2		
Sparks, William	1	1	2		
Spence, John	1	1	2		
Spence, David	1	2	3		
Salle, Peter	2	4	5		
Shores, Reuben	1	1	4		4
Swim, Michael	1	1	4		
Sisk, James	1	2	3		
Spurling, Zachariah	2	1	2		
Sisk, Thomas	1		1		
Swim, John	2		2		
Sisk, John	1		1		
Gittins, John	3	2	3		
Gittins, Richard	1		3		6
Golden, William	1	4	2		4
Griffith, Daniel	1		1		
Green, Thomas	2	3	4		1
Harris, Robert, Junr	1	1	2		
Harris, Tyre	1	2	2		
Hooper, Richard	3	4	6		11
Hill, Richard	3	2	3		
Harris, Robert	1				
Holder, Joseph	4	2	5		
Holder, John	1	4	2		
Hampton, Collins	4		5		
Harvey, Joseph	1	2	3		
Humphries, Benja	3		5		
Hannah, John	3	2	5		
Herren, Henry	1	1	6		
Harris, Jonathan	1	1	4		
Holder, Solomon	1		1		
Laurence, Claibourn	1	1	3		1
McCraw, Francis	1		2		
Humphries, David	1		2		3
Hammock, Robert	1	2	3		
Hammons, John	3	1	5		5
Hammons, William	1	1	2		
Harris, Robert	2	2	3		9
Hicks, John	2	3	1		
Jones, Levi	1	5	5		
Shores, Simon	2	1	5		3
Snow, Frost	2	8	2		
Van vinkle, Abram	1	2	1		1
Wilbourn, Richard	4		3		1

NAME OF HEAD OF FAMILY.	Free white males of 16 years and upward, including heads of families.	Free white males under 16 years.	Free white females, including heads of families.	All other free persons.	Slaves.
Woodruff, Gideon	1	3	2		
Woodroff, Moses	3		2		
Turner, Thomas	1		1		
Morrisson, James	1		4		
McKinney, Matthew	1	2	2		
Findley, James	3	1	3		3
Cochran, David	1	1	1		
Cooper, Nathaniel	1		3		
Bench, Christa	1	2	2		
Johnson, John	1	5	4		
Benson, Benjamin	1	2	6		1
Ahart, Michael	2	6			
Aplin, Joel	1	4	4		
Aplin, Thomas	1	1	2		2
Armstrong, William	1	1	3		4
Armstrong, Hugh	2	1	3		9
Adams, James	1				
Ballard, Thomas	1	3	5		
Brison, John, Junr	1	2	5		2
Burris, Thomas	2	2	4		8
Blackwell, David	1	1	3		1
Brison, John	1		5		2
Keith, Cornelius	3	3	2		
McCarver, John	1		4		
Morris, Daniel	1	2	1		
McKenney, Jesse	1		2		
McKenney, John	2		4		
McGee, Drury	1		1		
Spur, John	1	1	3		
McCraw, William	1	2	1		4
McCraw, Benjamin	2	3	4		
McKenny, John, Junr	1	2	2		1
McCraw, Jacob	3	5	2		7
Parkes, James	1	2	3		
Birke, John	2		3		
Patterson, Thomas	1	1	5		
Rowles, Christopher	1	3	4		
Roberts, James	1		4		
Rosinover, Joseph	4		1		4
Robertson, William	1				
Roberds, John	4	2	6		4
Ross, William	1	2	8		
Ramsey, William	2		7		
Ross, Charles	1		2		
McCarver, Joshua	1	1	2		
Steward, John	1	1	1		
Spain, Benjamin	1	1	5		
Smallwood, Elijah	2	1	5		
Studdyman, John	1	3	3		
Snow, Frost, Junr	1	3	1		
Smith, William	3		4		
Frost, Snow	3	3	6		10
Steward, Edward	1		3		
Smith, Stephen	1	3	5		1
Smith, Charles	2		5		9
Nap, Justus	1				
Brown, Samuel	1	6	2		
Guinn, Nathl	1				
Muckleyea, Hugh	1	1	2		
Wittaker, Mary		1	3		
Chambling, William	2	3	4		
Sessions, Isaac	1				

WILMINGTON DISTRICT, BLADEN COUNTY.

NAME OF HEAD OF FAMILY.	Free white males of 16 years and upward, including heads of families.	Free white males under 16 years.	Free white females, including heads of families.	All other free persons.	Slaves.
Watson, William J	1		3		19
Singletary, Joseph	3	1	3	1	12
McCree, Mrs. Margiret	1	1	1		16
Nance, Daniel	3		2		7
Handen, Josiah	1	3	3		8
Handin, Lydia			2		1
Hill, Phillip	2	1	1		
Bryant, William	2	4	2		1
Ashford, Street	3	2	1		6
Butlar, Henry	1				
Colvete, Henry	1				1
Lennon, John	1		4		
Kemp, Joseph	3	1	2		3
Lemmon, Anguish	1	1	3		
Fetzrandolf, Benja	2	1	5		10
Shaw, Neal	4	3	1		10
Harvey, John	1				
Harvey, Travis	1				
McCree, Samuel	2	2	3		1
Jones, Isaac	1	2	2		5
Moess, Elisha	1				
Hayns, Elizabeth		2	6	1	12
Guthre, William	1		1		
Owen, Thomas, Esq	1	2	3		37
McConkey, Robert	1	1	3		6
Elkins, John	1		2		
Redding, Rehun	1		2		
Bradley, James	5	1	3		20
White, David	4	2	6		4

NAME OF HEAD OF FAMILY.	Free white males of 16 years and upward, including heads of families.	Free white males under 16 years.	Free white females, including heads of families.	All other free persons.	Slaves.
Elkins, Saml, Junr	1		1		
Gaylor, James	1	5	2		
Alston, Peter	2	5	3		11
Sanderson, William	1		1		2
Bryant, John	1		3		2
Odair, Frances		1	3		1
Morehead, James	1	2	4		26
White, John	6	1	4		14
Elkins, Samuel	1	5	2		1
Elkins, Evan	1		1		
McClennan, Thomas	2	4	3		2
Pointer, Argulus	2	2	4		1
Ervan, James	1				
Noles, George	1	2	4		
Cake, Phillip	1		2		
Hesters, John	2	2	5		
Baker, Samuel	2		3		
White, Mathew Rowan	1		4		
Salter, Richard	1	4	2		
Plummer, Aron	1		3		
Singletary, William	1	1	3		2
Wair, George	1		4		
Chessur, William	1	1	2		
Chessur, Richard	1	3	3	1	5
McMillin, John	3		1		
Shaw, Anguish	2	1	4		
Singletary, Josiah	1	2	2		3
Hesters, Jesper	1	2	4		
Hesters, Tho	1		2		

NAME OF HEAD OF FAMILY.	Free white males of 16 years and upward, including heads of families.	Free white males under 16 years.	Free white females, including heads of families.	All other free persons.	Slaves.
Hesters, Joseph	1	1	2		
Guyton, James	1	2	1		
Dowlas, William	2	2	1		
Evers, James	1	3	4		
Russ, Will, Senr	2	4	5		
Russ, Will, Junr	1	4	1		1
Fason, James	2	1	3		
Bryan, Stephen	2	1	1		
Chesshar, Randolph	1	1	4		
Whetty, Joseph	1	4	4		
Wiley, Will	1	2			
Harisson, Mrs. Margerit	1		3		
Turner, Samuel	1		3		
Hesters, William	1		3		1
Smith, Lucy	1	2	4		3
Singletary, Mary	1	2	3		3
Morris, Thomas	1	3	3		
Bryant, Pheliman	1	1	3		
Gaylor, James	1	2	2		
Guyton, Priscilla	1	2	2		
Clifton, Boasman	1	1	2		
McDonald, George	1				
Olifant, Jesse A	1	5	3		1
Rowan, Pollice	1	3			
Raford, Robt	1				3
Fosters, Margarit	1		1		
White, Hannah		1	5		
Ellis, John	1	1			
Hilliard, John	1		5		

WILMINGTON DISTRICT, BLADEN COUNTY—Continued.

NAME OF HEAD OF FAMILY.	Free white males of 16 years and upward, including heads of families.	Free white males under 16 years.	Free white females, including heads of families.	All other free persons.	Slaves.
Curray, Samuel	1		1		
Allen, Tobitha		1	3		
Months, Mathew	1	3	3		
Hesters, Stephen	3	4	5		
Russ, Mary		1	2		
Stevens, Isoom	1	1	2		
Wisher, Elizabeth	1	2	2		5
Russ, John	1		3		
Carter, John	1	2	4		
Gray, William	1	2	1		
Bryant, Stephen, Jur	1		2		
Green, Betty		1		3	2
Russ, James	1	2	6		
Taylor, George	1		2		
Ervan, Jarod	1				6
Latestead, Erick, Esq	1		1		16
Singletary, Whamon	1	2	2		1
Spears, Robert	1				6
Robinson, Batrum	2	2	3		24
White, Mary		3	1		4
Lock, John	1	2	5		2
Lock, Joseph	1	1	2		10
Stanton, John	2	1			5
Purdy, James	1	2	1		28
McCree, William	1	2	4		1
Plummer, Zackeriah	1				1
Johnston, Rachel		1	2		
Cain, Joseph, Esquire	1	1	1		9
Serwin, Thomas	1	1	4		
Walker, John	1	1	2		
Counsel, Mrs. Mary		2	4		17
Singletary, John	2	1	2		8
Wilkins, John	1	3	1		11
Millar, Frederick	2	1	3		6
Wood, Lucy		1	3		
Evans, Elizabeth	2		1		
Stone, David	1	2	3		
Lock, Thomas	2		5		5
Wills, Daniel	1	4	2		1
Gause, Nedam	1		1		11
Wills, Jacob	1		2		7
Plummer, Jeremiah	1		4		
Moore, John	3	1	5		1
Singletary, Richard	2	1	4		5
Singletary, James	1	4	3		1
Yancey, Charles	1	4	1		
Jones, Edward	2				6
Plummer, John	1	3	1		
Plummer, Moses	2	1	3		
Rogeson, Elizabeth			2		7
Singletary, James, Jur	1	2	4		5
Singletary, Joseph	1		3		2
Butlar, Joseph	1	1	3		
Oveler, Amelia			2		9
Ellis, James	1	3	4		3
Storm, Mary			2		
Gales, Mary			4		
Gales, Jane			2		
Gales, John	1	3	4		
Langdel, Benja	1	3	1		
Cain, John	2	4	3		6
Parnel, John	1	3	3		
Counsil, Robt	1	2	2		3
Bennet, John	1	1	2		
Cain, Samuel	2		2		13
Robinson, Jonathan	1				
Cain, Mrs. Olive			2		4
Cain, James	1	3	5		5
Messer, Mary			2		
Landzdel, John	1	1	4		
Avery, Thomas	2		1		
Pricket, Josiah	1		2		
Pricket, Eley		1	2		
Brown, Tho	1	1	3		
Brown, John	1				
Gibbs, James	1	1	1		7
Wilkerson, William	1		7		1
Powell, Isaac	1	1	2		2
Powell, Elizabeth			4		2
Powell, Barney	1	2	2		1
White, William		1	3		1
Chanchey, Keziah	2		1		
White, Mary	2	1	4		6
King, Duncan	5	4	4		3
Begford, Jeremiah	2	2	5		
Smith, Eley	1	1	2	1	
Counsil, James	2	1	3		
Smith, Anne		2	2		5
Brown, Gerorge	1	1	5		1
Linnen, Dennis	1	3	2		7
Griffin, Joseph	1				
Buzby, Ezekel	2		5	1	
Jones, Augustus	1		1		
Hodges, James	1	1	5		
Camble, John	1	2	4		
McMillin, Dugal	2	1	5		1
McKee, George	3		2		
Camble, James	1	3	1		2
Camble, Daniel	2		1		
McColom, Daniel	1	4	6		
Taylor, Daniel	1	3	2		
Blew, John	1	2	5		
Lemmon, Duncan	2	2	3		
McKay, John	1		3		
Kelley, Archabald	3		3		1
Camble, Archabald	1		2		
Taylor, Daniel	1		2		
McCown, Robert	1	4	2		
McCown, William	1	3	1		
McCown, Mathew	2		1		
Lesley, Joseph	2		4		
Kelley, Methew	2	4	5		22
Kelley, John	1	1	2		3
Adams, Benja	1	3	1		
Bradley, Mary	1	3	2		
Munk, Jacob	1	1	2		3
Turner, Lazarus	1	1	1		
Luois, Aron	1	2	2		
Turner, Ester	2	4	5		
Bryant, John	1	1	3		
Fitzgarald, Thomas	1	1	3		2
Lewis, Josiah	2	1	7		3
Simpson, Tho., Senr	1		2		5
Simpson, Tho., Junr	1		4		5
Simpson, Edward	1		1		1
Lewis, Richard M	1		3		7
Shipman, James	1	3	4		4
Lee, Jacob	1		2		1
Hawkins, Gideon	2	1	3		
Lee, Joshua	4	2	4		3
Lewis, Moses	1		3		
Robinson, John	1	3	2		
Wiggins, Joseph	2	2	8		
Hardcastle, William	1		2		
Browden, Thomas	1	5	5		
Brown, William	4	3	5		
Stevens, Eley	1	2	2		2
Ferrel, William	1	2	3		
Ferrel, Cornelus	1		1		
Taylor, Philip	2		3		
Hays, Joshua	1		5		4
Burney, William	1	4	3		5
Chan, Moran		1	2		
Wiggins, Isoom	1				
McNeal, William	2		3		14
Pockerpine, John	1	2	2		
Begford, William	1		1		11
Lewis, Josiah	1	1	4		3
Mooney, John	1		4		
McKethen, John	1	1	2		
McColskee, Neal	2		3		6
McKay, John	1	3	4		
McClaren, John	2		1		2
Shaw, Archabald	2		1		
Shaw, Macum	1				4
McNaughton, Charles	3		3		
Chesnut, Arthur	1		3		
Folks, William	1	3	4		
Folks, Joney		1	1		
Mills, Roley	2	2	2		
Baldwin, John	1	2	4		
Green, Simon	1	2	5		
Stricklen, David	2		1		
Bright, James	2	3	3		
Folks, Josiah	1	1	1		
Folks, John	1	1	1		
Melican, Andrew	1	1	2		
Wall, Edward	2		2		
Paget, John	3	2	4		
Johnston, Thomas	2	1	1		
Johnston, William	1	2	1		
Carterite, Richard	1	1	1		
Carterite, John	1	1	2		
Williams, Joshua	3		1		
Smith, Sol	1	1	4		
Hardewick, Lenville	1	1	2		
Sanders, Thomas	2		3		
Flen, James	1	1	1		
Adkins, John	1	1	1		1
Best, John	1	1	2		
Bright, Simon	2	2	3		
Powers, Joseph	2	2	5		
Powers, Charles	2	1	1		
Register, William	3	4	4		
McColski, James	1		2		1
Lawson, Francis	2	3	4		
Parker, Ezekeil	2	3	1		
Powell, Thomas	2	2	2		
Spivey, Edmond	1	2	3		
Risen, James	2		3		
Camble, Elexander	3	2	4		
Shaw, John	1	1	2		
Talom, Richard	1		5		
Sebbet, William	1	1	3		
Wells, Joel	1	2	4		
Godden, Stephen	1	2	2		
Williamson, Lewis	2	5	3		
Hilbourn, Hamilton	2	2	2		
Nobles, Joseph	3	7	6		
Hill, Mekijah	3	1	6		
Flowers, Indignation	2	2	6		4
Flowers, Goldsbury	1		1		2
Stevens, Abraham	1	2	3		
Powell, Absolom	1	4	3		3
Sanderson, Thomas	1	2	2		
Wilson, John	1	1	2		
Nobles, Tenesser	1	2	1		
Branton, Mathew	1	1	2		
Peters, William	1		2		
Niles, Coalman	2	1	2		1
Niles, Averit	1		3		
Godden, Pearce	1	1	4		
Herring, Priscilla			1		
Hays, Mary			1		
Yales, John, Esq	2	1	4		4
Coalsman, John	2		5		
Coalsman, Moses	3	2	4		
Eason, Benjn	1	3	6		
Hollyman, Saml	1	1	4		
Folks, Richard	1	1	6		1
Gibbs, Heman	1	1	3		
Pope, Saml	1	2	2		
Hall, Burrel	1	3	3		1
Gobson, Charles	2				2
Rols, Marmaduke	1	1	2		
Hollyman, James	1	4	3		
Coalsman, Theophelas	1	1	2		
Pate, Samuel	2	2	3		
Summerset, Frances		3	4		
Tyler, Moran	1	2	4		
Stricklen, Philip	1	1	2		
Coalsman, John	1		2		
Godden, Alexander	1	1	4		
Barfield, Stephen	1				6
Folks, William	1	2	3		
Folks, Wright	2	1	4		
Folks, Simon	1	3	4		
Folks, Philip	1	2	5		
Tyler, Moses	1	1	2		
Riggen, John	2		2		
Simons, John	1	2	2		
Smith, Simon	1	2	3		
Wilson, Edward	3		6		
Green, John	1	2	5		2
Yeates, Luke	1		3		
Runnels, Ann	2	1	3		3
Wadkins, Mathew	1		7		1
Cannon, Archabald	3	3	4		
Stricklen, Mary		1	4		
Loften, Mark	1		3		
Loften, Frederick	2	1	1		
Hays, Sothy	3		3		4
Clark, George	3	1	3		
Mems, Thomas	1	2	4		4
Winget, John	1	1	1		6
Winget, Walter	1	1	3		2
Robbins, Jethro	1	1	5		
Wilson, Edward	1	1	3	1	
Young, John	1	1	3		1
Desin, Leonard	1	1	3		
Fling, Elizabeth		1	3		2
Fling, Mary			4		
Hodge, Robert	1				
Bozzell, Elizabeth	2	2	4		
Bozzell, Tho	1	1	3		
Sessions, Thomas	4	4	2		7
Bozzell, William	1	1	2		
Mooney, John	1	2	3		
Hardwick, Allen	1	2	4		
Bright, Simon, Jur	1	1	3		
Folks, John	1		2		
Chairday, James	2	2	6		20
Hairgroves, Briton	1		1		8
Column, Richard		1	1		
Busley, Robert	1	2	4		
Clark, David	1	1	1		
Hobbs, Isaac	1	1	3		
Pitman, Moses	2	1	2		2
Richardson, Thomas	3		2		2
Baldwin, William	1	2	2		4
Green, Calop	1		1		1
Baldwin, John	1		1		27
Baldwin, Charles	1	1	4		10
Green, William	1	1	2		1
Green, Robert	1		1		3
Pope, Briton	1		1		
Edwards, Newet	1	1	3		
Sols, Abraham	1		2		
Swendel, Samuel	2	2	2		11
Warren, Archabald	4	1	3		

FIRST CENSUS OF THE UNITED STATES.

WILMINGTON DISTRICT, BLADEN COUNTY—Continued.

NAME OF HEAD OF FAMILY.	Free white males of 16 years and upward, including heads of families.	Free white males under 16 years.	Free white females, including heads of families.	All other free persons.	Slaves.
Lewis Hanson	2	4	5		2
Ellis, John	1	1	7		2
Hobbs, Joseph	1		1		
Ellis, James	1	2	4		7
Folks, John	1	1	3		1
Bryan, William	3	2	3		4
Folks, Jacob	2		2		
Door, John	1	2	2		4
Jones, Thomas	1		2		
Fetchet, Christian	1		1		
Shipman, Daniel	3		2		19
Baldwin, Warren	1	1	4		
Broom, Elps	2	2	6		2
Simpson, Scarimore	1	1	2		
Stubs, George	1	1	2		
Folks, James	1	1	3		
Baldwin, Joseph	1	5	4		7
Wilson, James	1		2		2
Lewis, James	1	3	3		
Simpson, Simon	2	1	1		
Simpson, Jacob	1		4		
Stubs, Richard	1	3	3		
Stubs, John	1	1	1		3
Lambert, Richard	1	2	5		1
Simpson, Robert	2		4		
Clark, John	1	5	3		3
Simpson, John	2	2	4		
Ray, Jemina	2		2		
Baldwin, Anne		2	4		
Holms, Edmund	2				10
Johnston, Hugh	1	3	3		15
Bryant, Will, Junr	1		4		3
McCalop, Catherine		2	2		
McMullen, Runnel	1	3	2		
Robeson, Charles	1	3	4		
Richardson, Robert	2		1		
Haddesk, Drury	1	1	3		
Parker, William	1	3	3		
Edwards, Charles	1	2	3		
Richardson, John	1		1		
Council, David	2	1	3		
Murrel, Zachariah	1	4	2		
Peebody, John	2	1	3		
Green, James	2				
Banefoot, James	1	1	5		
Mems, David	1	1	4		10
Carman, Samuel	1	3	3		
Mems, James	1	2	2		2
Mems, Shadarach	1	1	2		
Mems, Volentine	1		1		1
Port, Peter	1	1	4		2
Penny, Thomas	1	3	3		
Runnels, Demsey	1	2	2		1
Runnels, Richard	1	1	2		
Runnels, Richard	1		1		
Lamberson, John	1		2		1
Lamberson, Courtney			3		3
Smith, John	1	1	4		
Lamb, John	1	2	5		3
Chansey, Demsey	1		1		
Whitehead, Jacob	1		2		
Davis, Thomas	1				
Runnels, Elijah	1	1	2		3
Wolf, Isaac	1		2		
Hairgroves, Burrel	1	1	5		
Murrel, Barnabas	1		1		
Morrison, Mrs. Margret	1	2	2		20
Dupree, James	5				22
Brown, Richard	1				2
Smith, Thomas	2	1	3		20
Singletary, Mary			2		4
Brown, John	1		2		5
Egleson, James	1				4
Doway, James	1	1	1		5
Taylor, Harbot	1	3	1		
Davis, Turner	1				20
Davis, Ezekiel	3	1	4		4
Murrel, Barney	2	2	2		3
Clayton, Benom	3	1	5		
Smith, William	1	1	1		
Smith, William	1	1	4		4
Smith, Simon	1	1	4		
McViker, John	2		2		
McKethen, Duncan	1		2		1
McFater, Daniel	1		3		
McKethen, Daniel	2	1	4		
Baine, Donald	1		1		13
Malsby, Anthoney	1		2		2
Blew, Dugal	3		1		
Downey, Daniel	3	1	4		
McEwen, Daniel	1	2	2		
McMillen, John	3		3		1
Meshaw, Peter	3		3		
McKay, John	2	2	3		15
Malsby, Thomas	1	1	2		2
Davis, William	1	3	2		3
McKethen, Archabald	2	1	1		
Darrow, John	2	1	3		
Camble, John	1		6		
Malsby, James	1	2	2		2
Kellyham, Pearce	1	1	1		
Camble, Neal	1	1	1		
Kellyham, Cornelias	1	2	2		
Cousnel, Robert	1	1	2		4
Landzdel, Benja	1	3	1		
Millar, Ralph	1	2	7		14
Lock, Benja	1		3		7
Spendlove, Jenot	3	1	2		78
Daniel, Margaret		1	4		35
Johnston, Robert	1		2		
Holmes, Moses	5	1	3		
Lucus, George (of Chatam)					20
How, Arthur	1	2	1		50
Grange, John	2	1	5		18
Russ, Jonadab	2	3	3		2
Perry, John	1	3	4		
Brown, Thomas, Esq	1	3	3		30
Oliphant, Uphemia		5	2		2
Dewry, Uphemia			3		12
O'Neal, Charles	1	5	2		
Dafford, Jeremiah	1	2	2		
Lucus, Elizabeth		3	1		12
Willis, Ann			2		2
Jones, William	2				7
Pointer, John	1	4	4		
Pemberton, Margaret	1		1		8
Pemberton, John	1	1	1		
Singletary, Richard	2				4
Slingsby, Arabella		1	3		
Taylor, John	1	3	4		
Seamore, Sarah			1		
Gantur, Joseph R	3				30
Due, Seth	1	4	5		
Johnston, Robert	1		2		
Ray, Jane	3	1	3		
Mulford, Ephram	3	5	9		15
Thomas, George	1	2	4		5
Lock, Mary	3		3		11
Salter, James	1		1		8
Lock, Agnis		3	2		5
Russ, Joseph	2		6		
Loyd, David	2	2	5		4
Thomas, John	1	2	2		1
Gavan, John	2	1	4		
Davis, Joseph	1	3	2		1
White, Will	1	1	4		3
Parnell, Elizabeth		1	2		
Singletary, John	1		1		1
Taylor, Sarah			4		
Statter, William	3	1	4		30
Parker, John	1	2	3		
Wilson, George	1		3		
Yerby, Henry	1	1	3		
Sutton, Beman	1	1	2		
Sutton, Beman	2		6		11
Larkins, James	3	5	7		11
Anderson, Catherine	4	1	4	1	12
Andres, John	3		2		21
Sikes, John	3	2	4		
Prigion, Peter	3		4		
Baity, William	2	2	2		21
Prigion, Mathew	3	1	2		
McMasters, Felex	2		3		1
McCalister, Hutor	1	1	3		
Strayhorn, Alexand	1	1	3		5
Coock, Daniel	1	3	4		
Henry, James	1	1	3		
Dane, Jeremiah	1	2	5		
Prigion, John	1		4		
Ennis, William	2	1	2		4
Cain, James	1	3	1		
Johnston, Samuel	1	1	4		
Johnston, Charles	1				
Averit, William	1	1	5		1
Sikes, Isarel	1		2		
Sikes, Jonathan	1	2	4		
Singletary, Richard	1	1	3		1
Cathwell, John	1		2		1
Bedson, Thomas	2	1	7		
Melom, John	1	1	2		
Parker, John	1	3	3		
Simmons, Jeremiah	1	2	3		
Clark, Hardy	1	1	3		
Davis, Henry	1		3		
Smith, Thomas	1	2	4		
Edge, John	1	2	4		
Edge, William	1	4	2		
Sellars, John	1	4	4		
Cain, John	1	1	5		
Gardens, James	4	3	2		
Boasman, Samuel	3	3	4		
Witherby, Kade	2	3	3		13
Cashwell, Thomas	1	5	5		
McClain, Peter	1		6		
Sellars, Duncan	1		4		
Clark, Henry	1	2	3		
Carr, James	1		2		
Curray, Edward	1	5	3		
Smith, William	1	4	3		
Davis, John	2	2	5		
Sessions, Saml	1	3	3		
Jones, Ezekiah	1	3	3		
Sessions, Culmore	1		2		
Daniel, Archabald	1	2	5		
Grim, William	1	1	3		
McColm, Rachel		1	3		
Davis, Balster	5		4		
Suggs, Will	1	1	4		
Sugs, Aligood	1	2	3		
West, James	1	4	6		
Cashwell, James	1				
Davis, Samson	3	3	3		
Thomas, Micheal	2	2	5		
Simmons, Sandrs	1		3		
Smith, John	2		3		
Cain, Neal	1				
Cain, Samuel	1	1	1		
Smith, William	1	2	4		
Valentine, Hardy	1		1		
Maclemore, Drury	3		2		
Bryant, Nedam	1	3	10		
Bryant, Bartum	1		2		1
Roan, Saml	1	3	5		
Bryant, David	1		3		
Edge, John	1	1	1		
Morehead, William	1	1	3		
Sikes, James	1	3	1		
Meloins, Daniel	1		1		
Sessions, Mary		3	4		
Avery, John	1	2	2		
Blackwell, Jesse	3	4	3		
Melvin, George	1	1	1		
Feston, Stephen	1		2		
McGee, James	1		3		
Carrol, John	1		1		
Carrol, Thomas, Junr	1	2	4		
Carrol, Thomas	1		2		
Picket, Gideon	1	1	1		
Hale, Nathan	4	4	4		
Bryant, Barney	4		1		
Edwards, Cloe			4		
Reaves, Edward	2	5	5		
Marafield, Daniel	1	1	3		
Devam, John, Senr	1	1	3		29
Devam, John, Junr	1	2	2		11
Brym, Mathew	1		1		14
Davis, Francis	1	1	5		7
Robinson, Peter	1	2	3		12
Blanks, John				8	
West, Will				3	
Cavers, John				4	
Cavers, Rasmus				3	
Cavers, Gilley				7	
Moon, James				6	
Demery, John				9	
Cavers, Mary				6	
Melchel, William				4	

WILMINGTON DISTRICT, BRUNSWICK COUNTY.

NAME OF HEAD OF FAMILY.	Free white males of 16 years and upward, including heads of families.	Free white males under 16 years.	Free white females, including heads of families.	All other free persons.	Slaves.
Neal, Thomas	1	2		1	20
Vernon, Elinor		1	3		13
Rundleson, Archibald	1	3	1		
Betts, William	2	3	2		5
Richardson, Elizabeth			2		2
Watters, Sarah		1	3		26
Vines, Samuel	1	2	4		
Turner, Amy	1		2		12
Graves, Benjamin	1		5		
Holms, Moses	3	1	1		1
Hall, John, Esq	2	1	4		43
Grange, John	2				39
Taylor, Solomon	1	3	3		
Keator, Sarah		1	3		
Boon, John	1	3	5		

WILMINGTON DISTRICT, BRUNSWICK COUNTY—Continued.

NAME OF HEAD OF FAMILY.	Free white males of 16 years and upward, including heads of families.	Free white males under 16 years.	Free white females, including heads of families.	All other free persons.	Slaves.	NAME OF HEAD OF FAMILY.	Free white males of 16 years and upward, including heads of families.	Free white males under 16 years.	Free white females, including heads of families.	All other free persons.	Slaves.	NAME OF HEAD OF FAMILY.	Free white males of 16 years and upward, including heads of families.	Free white males under 16 years.	Free white females, including heads of families.	All other free persons.	Slaves.
Freeman, James	2		7		1	Goodman, William	1		3		1	Aderson, James	1	1	4		2
Curray, Daniel	2		2			Parker, William	1	2	3		11	Taylor, Benjamin	2	2	7		
Cain, Allen, Junr	1				8	Clemmings, Timothy	1		2		5	Gressel, William	1	3	5		12
Roots, John	1	2	6		16	Chains, James	1	1	2		3	Taylor, Benjamin	1	1	2		
Smith, James	1	1	4			Rooks, John	1		1			Hargroves, Samuel	1	1	5		
Keater, Nehemiah	1		2		1	Balloon, Daniel	1	1	4		16	Wengate, William	1	1	4		7
Keater, William	1					Bell, Robert	1		6		23	Simmons, Benjamin	1	3	1		
Norris, Thomas	1		2			Russ, Thomas	3	3	4		8	Simmons, John	1	1	3		
Morris, Robert	1		1			Holdan, Sarah	1	1	3			Russ, John	2	3	1		1
Morris, Thomas	1	1	3			Swain, Levi	1	2	2			Floyd, Morris	1	2	4		
Jeanots, Benjamin	1		1			Swain, James	1	2	3			Sellars, William	1	3	4		
Jeanots, Winey			2			Gause, Susanna	1	1	2		19	Sellars, Jordan	1		2		
Jeanots, John	1		1			Hewit, Philip	1	4	4			Floyd, Bits	1	1	2		
Pounds, John, Senr	1					Hewit, William	1	2	1			Roach, James	1		4		
Pounds, John, Junr	1		2			Hewit, Ebenezar	1	2	2			Ward, Milly	3	3	7		
Pounds, Isaac	1		2			Clark, Jonah	1	3	2		5	Dugger, John	1	4	2		
Skipper, John	1		3			Clark, Henry	1		1		8	Edwards, Thomas	1	4	4		
Skipper, Moses	1	3	2			Hewit, Joseph, Senr	2	1			1	Stevens, Mekajah	1		1		
Skipper, Abraham	1	2	3			Hewit, Joseph, Junr	1		1		1	Soles, Timothy	1		2		
Flours, James	3		2		20	Sharp, William	1		1			Soles, Nathaniel	1	1	2		
Rowan, John	1		2		21	Holden, Job	1	2	3			Goodman, Luke	1	1	5		
Allen, Drury	2		2		12	Holden, James	1					Soles, Joseph	2	1	7		
Newell, Thomas	2		4			Holden, Famus					4	Imrit, Elnis	1	1	4		
Liles, Benjamin	1	2	5			Hines, Betsey					4	Carter, William	1		2		
Clark, Thomas	1		1		56	Singletary, Benjn	2		1			Alford, Amy	1	2	3		7
Mills, Jane		1	1		3	Willis, Henry	1	1	1			Moony, William	1		8		
Skipper, James	1		2			Hewit, Ezekiah	3		2			Beck, John	1	2	4		
Wheeler, William	1		2			Hewit, Robert	1		1			Reaves, Solomon	1	5	3		
Heghemeth, John	3		3			Hewit, Samuel	1		1			Hickman, Samuel	1	1	3		
Potter, James	1	3	3			Gause, Bryant	1		3		18	Sugs, Ezekel	2	2	3		
Potter, Mills	1	3	1		2	Stanley, Thomas	1	4	2			Gooden, Jonas	3		2		
Leonard, Samuel	2	1	2		2	Stanley, Samuel	1	2	3		1	Arnold, Elinor		1	3		
Carrol, John	1	1	3			Tharp, Charles	1		5			Simmons, Ann	2	2	2		
Simpson, Elisha	1	3	4			Hewit, Reuben	1		2			Simmons, John	1		2		
Leonard, Henry	1	1	3			Robinson, John	1	3	3			Norris, Frederick	1		2		
Sparksman, William	1		1			Hewit, David	1	3	3			Norris, William	1		2		
Williams, Margaret	2		2			Dudley, Jeremiah	1	1	1		3	Norris, Jerutia			2		
Barrow, Huzzy	1		3			Ivey, Lewis	1	1	6			Benson, Nathan	1	1	2		
Mills, Benjamin	1	1	3		9	Jones, William	1		1			Marlow, Nathan	1	1	5		
Leonard, Elinor	3	1	5		10	Holden, Benjamin	1		3			Simmons, Thomas	3	1	2		
Gause, Benjamin	1	2	3		4	Hawkins, Dennis	1	2	3		46	Sims, William	1	3	3		
Aderson, John	3		7		2	Daniel, Robert	1	2	3		14	Duncan, Elias	1	3	3		
Mills, William	1	2	3			Tharp, Samuel	2	1	3			Mooney, John	2	3	2		3
Sulivan, Edward	1	3	2		4	Smith, Jeremiah	2		1		1	Stevens, Alexander	1	1	6		3
Holms, John	1					Gause, John	1	1	1		7	Counsel, Hardy	1	1	3		
Sillars, James	2	5	3			Fosters, Electus Medus	1	3	1		15	Simmons, John	1				
Potter, Miles	1					Sulivan, Martha	2	3	2		2	Smith, Simon	1	2	2		
Harris, Richard	1	3	2			Craig, Benjamin	1	3	3			Clark, Benjamin, Jur	1	3	1		
Sparksman, Levi	1	3	1		1	Craig, Lewis	1	2	3			Hardy, Andrew	1	2	2		
Sparksman, Richard	1		1			Jones, John	1	2	2			Soles, Mackinne	1	3	1		
Johnson, John	1	2	1			McCree, Griffeth	1	2	2		8	Powel, Abraham	1	1	2		
Young, William	1					McKensee, George	1	1	3		30	Powel, Jacob	1	1	2		
Holms, Joseph	1					Clark, James	1	2	2		19	Cox, John	1	2	3		2
Hays, John	1	3	4			Drew, John	1	2	1			Connel, Edward	2	3	2		4
Taylor, John William	1					Gause, Nedam	2	4	1		5	Williams, Benjamin	1	1	1		
Robbins, Benjamin	1	1	1			Goodman, Henry	1	2	1			Soles, Benjamin	1		2		
Robbins, Arthur	3	2	3			Franks, Sarah					18	Williams, Moses	1	1	2		
McMurray, William	1	1	2			Roberts, Patty	1	2	1		16	Mills, John	1	2	3		
Greer, John	1	2	3			Gause, William	2	3	3		37	Grissel, John	1	2	2		17
Moore, Mary		3	3		5	Clark, Henry	3	3	3		19	Simmons, Moses	1	2	4		1
Bell, James, Senr	1		2		9	Taylor, Mary			2		3	Russ, Francis	1	2	2		
Daniel, Stephen	2	3	3		8	Corneers, John	1		4			Simmons, Isaac	1	2	1		5
Woodside, Robert	1	1	5		1	Wills, Henry	1		2			Stevens, Joshua	2		2		
Grissel, Reauben	1	1	3		5	Sillars, Mathew	1	2	2			Abbot, William	1		1		
Gause, Charles	1	1	4		15	Sillars, Elisha	1	3	1			Canniday, John	1		7		
Swain, David	1		1		1	Malsby, Samuel	1		2			Gore, Jonathan	1	3	5		
Bell, James, Junr	1	2	4		3	Quince, Richard	1		2		40	Wingate, Sarah	2	2	4		7
Folks, Shadrick	1	2	3			Weathers, Thomas	1		3		23	Stevens, Mathew	1		3		
Wescut, John	1	1	1			Lord, William	1	1	3		15	Rhoads, John	1	2	3		
Galloway, Nathaniel	1	1	3		3	Rulks, Samuel	3	1	3		6	Reaves, Mark	1	2	1		
Umphry, Joseph	1		2		3	McAlester, Archibald	1				70	Rhoads, Mary	1		1		
Galloway, Sarah		2	3		1	McAlester, James	1				13	Rogers, John	1	1	7		
Long, Henry	1	2	3		1	Wear, George	1				21	Smith, James	1	1	3		2
Cains, John	1	1	5		9	Davis, Thomas	3	3	3		35	Thomas, John	3	1	2		
Goodman, Henry	1	4	1		1	Supper, Isaac	1	2				Lay, John	2	3	2		
Sellars, Siman	1	1	2		1	Supper, Clemon	1	2	3			Gore, James	1	1	2		
How, Sarah		2	2		20	Elkson, Samuel	2		2			Ellis, Mary		1	2		
Goodman, William	2	1	3		3	Elkson, Benjamin	2		6			Smith, John	1		3		
Bell, Samuel	1	2	3		1	Supper, Jesse	1	1	1			Cox, Elijah	3	2	5		
Gibberd, Rebeca	1	2	4			Rutterland, Reddon	2				2	McKeather, Alexander	1		1		
Felps, Martha		1	1		1	McKethern, Gillard	1	1	2			Cox, Elisha	2	1	2		
Wescut, Jeremiah	2	1	1			Howard, George	1	1	6			Norris, Thomas	1		2		
Price, Solomon	1	1	3			Ward, John	3	2	4			Smithart, John	1	3	3		
Sellars, Mathew	2	1	5		2	Hickman, Thomas	1	1	1			Jordan, Thomas	1		2		
Hammer, Solomon	1		1			Hickman, Samuel	1		2			Smith, John	3	3	3		2
Bell, Nathaniel	1	1	2			Runneles, William	1		3		3	Simmons, Benjamin	1	1	3		
Beesley, Oxford	1		2		1	Solio, Silvenus	1		1			Simmons, John	1	1	3		
Morgan, William	1	2	2			Mansfield, William	2	2	3			Sellars, Mathew	1		3		
Alexander, James	1		3			Sellars, James	1		1			Cleus, George	1	1	3		
Sparksman, William	1		4			Little, Thomas	3					Outlaw, Palatiah	1	2	2		
Williams, Benjamin	1	2	3			Bennet, Joseph	1	1	2			Benton, Hardey	1	2	4		
McDugal, Runnel	2	1	3			Bousman, Etherland	1	2	3			Benton, Joab	1	3	2		
Bennet, Daniel	1	1	3			Hill, Joel	1	2	3			Lay, Joseph	1		3		
Swain, Joseph	2		3		2	Hill, Ezekel	1	3	4			Stanley, Hugh	1	2	3		
Dozur, Richard	1	3	3		2	Colbert, James	1		2		2	Mooney, James	1	2	2		
Boatright, William	1		1			Conniel, Redy	1		1			Stanley, Nedam	1	1	1		
Gibbs, William	1	1	1		1	Newel, Peter	1	1	4			Beasant, Abraham	1	2	3		4

WILMINGTON DISTRICT, BRUNSWICK COUNTY—Continued.

NAME OF HEAD OF FAMILY.	Free white males of 16 years and upward, including heads of families.	Free white males under 16 years.	Free white females, including heads of families.	All other free persons.	Slaves.
Stanley, Margret			2		2
Minks, Lucretia		5	2		2
Murrel, William	1	1	3		
Gore, William, Esq	1	3	2		2
Deupree, Lewis, Esq	1	2	2		34
Alston, Francis	2	2	2		60
Howel, James	1				
Egle, Joseph	1	3	1		29
Moore, Alfred					48
Flanican, William	1		5		
Dry, William	1				2
Ward, Frederick	2				6
Smith, Benjamin, Esq	2	2	14	2	221
Richards, Nicholas	1	3	1		

WILMINGTON DISTRICT, DUPLIN COUNTY.

NAME OF HEAD OF FAMILY.	Free white males of 16 years and upward, including heads of families.	Free white males under 16 years.	Free white females, including heads of families.	All other free persons.	Slaves.
Rutledge, Thomas, Esq	3	1	2		9
Pearsell, James, Esq	1	2	4		15
Beck, William, Esq	1	3	6		12
Hurst, William Broad	1	2	1		
Beck, Elizabeth			2		10
Glisson, Daniel, Esq	3	2	3		7
Kornagy, George	3	2	2		12
Herring, Steven	3	2	2		13
Herring, Samuel	1	1	2		1
Stevens, William	2	6	5		6
Phillips, Samuel	1		2		
Stevens, Loammy	1		2		7
Dickson, Monice	3	1	3		
Kinard, Nathaniel	1	1	1		
O'Daniel, Alexander	1		3		2
Whitfield, Joseph	1		2		
Carr, Archibald	1	3	4		2
King, Charles	2		4		8
Southerland, William	1	3	1		1
Lowell, Samuel	1	4	3		
Blizzard, Hezekiah	1		5		
Cox, John	1	2	3		
Smith, Joseph	1	1	1		3
Waller, Alexander	1	2	3		
Moshburn, Benjª	2		3		
Federick, Andrew	1	3	2		
Pearsall, Edward	1		3		7
Armstrong, John	1	7	4		
Johnson, Benjª	1		1		1
Thomas, Lewis	2	1	3		16
Carrell, Hardy	1	1	3		
Johnston, Thomas	4	5	2		
Morris, James	2	1	1		16
Houston, William Ann	1		3		
Middleton, James, Senr	2	1	5		12
Brown, Charles	1	1	2		6
Patterson, James	1	1	1		
Murrow, James	2	2	3		1
Pearsall, Jeremiah	1	2	2		4
Southerland, John	1	1	2		
Cooper, John	1	1	2		
Hunter, William	1	6	2		3
Pelcher, Richard	1	1	3		
Waller, Nathan	1		2		1
Hooks, Charles	1	1	1		1
Quinn, David	1		4		1
Williams, Joseph	2		1		
Barfield, Lewis	2	3	7		2
Hooks, Hillery	1	3	3		1
Sanderland, Samuel	1	1	3		
Johnston, Joseph	4	3	4		
Rigsby, William	2	3	3		2
Thomas, Philp	1				
Linear, John	6	1	6		1
Garison, Thomas	1	1	2		3
Newton, Patrick	2	3	4		8
Stoks, William	2	4	4		
Brook, Joseph	1	2	9		
Sunderland, Nicholas	2	1	4		1
Oliver, Francis	1	3	5		3
Sulivan, Samuel	1	3	3		
Murdock, David	4	3	6		13
Wilkinson, William	2	1	1		10
Hines, Lewis	1	2	2		1
Jones, Elisha	1	1	3		
Houston, Henry	2	2	7		5
Millar, Anthony	1	1	4		2
Wilkinson, William	1	1	1		4
Guy, William	3	3	4		4
Reardon, James	1	2	2		
Wright, James	1	3	2		7
Gillispie, James, Esq	3	1	6		30
Maxwell, James	3	3	2		2
Beck, John	1	2	2		13
Orsburn, Joseph	2	1	2		
Rouse, Andrew	2	3	1		
Williams, Theophilas, Esq	1	2	5		7
Hooks, Thomas, Esq	1	3	3		16
Beorn, Joseph	3	1	4		
Wright, John	3		4		9
Beorn, William	1	2	4		
Sutwan, Humphrey	1				1
Evers, John	1	1	2		
Grady, Alexander	2	3	6		6
Dawson, Isaac	1	3	6		2
Grady, Frederick	1	6	5		2
Grady, James	1				
Wester, Rheuben	1	1	1		
Sholders, Moses	2		2		
Merritt, William	1	5	7		
Picket, Solomon	1	1	4		1
Hollard, James	1	3	5		
Sholders, John	2	2	1		
Glisson, John	1	4	2		
Smith, George	1	5	3		1
Gulley, William	2	2	6		1
Worsley, John	1		2		4
Whitehead, John	2	4	2		
Westbrook, Demsey	1	1	3		
Taylor, Jacob	1	4	5		
Houston, Edward	1	4	1		6
Sutwan, John	1	4	5		
Sanders, Alexander	1	1	5		
Jurnigan, Elisha	2	2	2		1
Richards, John	3		2		
Hodgeson, Aron	2	2	3		
Keelley, Jonathan	1	2	6		
Lenear, Benjamin	1	2	3		
Hodgeson, Joseph	1		2		
Best, Benjamin	1	1	1		
Best, John, Junr	1	3	2		
Best, John, Senr	2	1	1		
Best, Abraham	1	1	1		
Williams, John	1	1	3		
Million, John	1	1	2		
Mumford, Zedekiah	1		4		
Strowd, Arthur	1	1	1		
Smith, Lewis	3	2	2		1
Parker, John	2	3	3		
Gibbons, George	1	2	4		
Housman, John	1	5	2		
Branch, Archibald	1	3			
Gufford, Andrew	2		3		7
Heath, James	1	2	5		1
Heath, Thomas	1	5	3		
Grimes, Sampson	1	2	3		2
Getstrap, Benjamin	1	1	2		
Taylor, Samuel	1	1	2		
Midleton, Isaac	1	1	2		2
Bearfield, Frederick	1	2	4		6
Beck, William	1		2		2
Swinson, John A	1				
Duncan, Edmund	1	1	2		1
Bryan, John	1	2	1		
Boyt, William	2	2	3		
Rodgers, James	2		2		
Motlen, Abraham	1	2	2		7
Williamson, James, Senr	2	1	4		
Outlaw, James	2	5	5		8
Grady, William	3	2	5		4
Roberts, Richard	2	1	2		
James, Thomas, Esq	3	1	5		21
Allen, Lewis	1		2		
Millar, Robert	1	2	5		
Gore, John	1	5	7		
Midleton, James	1	2	3		
Rogers, Pelick	1	1	3		
Midleton, Stephen	1	2	4		
Rogers, Job	1		1		
Delaney, Benjamin	1	3	3		
Carr, William	1	2	3		3
Beaman, Francis	2	4	4		
Cramtop, Thomas	1	1	3		
Thalley, Andrew	1	3	4		1
Wills, Jacob	1	1	3		11
Southerland, Robert	1	3	5		1
Wills, Jacob, Senr	1	1	3		
Rogers, Samuel	2		3		1
Herring, Stephen	1	1	4		6
Johnston, John	3				
Herring, Benjamin	1	3	3		1
Carter, Silus	1	4	3		
Korneagy, William	3	3	4		4
Worley, Loftus	1				
Worley, Ann		1	1		
Millar, Charles	1	1	2		1
Neal, John	2		1		1
Swenson, Theophilus	1	3	4		
Alberson, Samuel	3	1	5		5
Herring, Arthur	1	1	2		
Gauff, Samuel	1		1		
Garrin, Bedford	1	1	3		
Sulivan, William	2	4	2		6
Linear, James	3	1	5		
Williams, Labin	2	2	2		
Connor, Dennis	4	3	6		3
Bryan, Auston	1		2		7
Garisson, Adonazab	1	4	1		
Rodes, Benjamin	2		5		7
Turlington, John	1	2	4		
Branch, Archibald	1	3	1		
Brown, Jacob	2	4	4		6
Daniel, William	1		2		2
Bray, Joseph	1		1		
Bray, Joseph, Junr	1	2	5		
Money, Wumlark	2	4	2		7
Boney, John	1		1		2
Boney, Daniel	1	2	4		1
Dickson, Joseph, Esq	2	6	3		13
Savage, William	1	1	2		
Savage, Jacob	1		1		
Tearley, Jacob	1	4	1		1
Bearfield, Stephen	2		2		6
Woodward, John	2		6		2
Wilson, Alexander	1		3		1
Bradley, John	2	4	4		
Midleton, James	1		9		5
Ward, Charles, Esq	1		2		12
Houston, Samuel, Esq	2	1	4		18
Blount, Benjamin	2	1	3		
Dickson, Alexander	1				7
Woodward, John	1				
Woodward, Elisha	1	2	3		
Murrah, Adam	2	1	4		
Harris, Jesse	1	4	1		
Everit, John	1	3	1		
Rutledge, Thomas	1				1
Blount, Warren	1	5	2		1
Bunting, David	2		2		7
Wright, Thomas	1				1
Bostick, Charles	2	2	5		1
Gulley, Nathan	1				
Millard, Joseph	1	1	4		
Gauff, Charles	1	1	3		
Millard, George	2		2		
Burton, Watson	2		2		1
Strickland, Absolam	1	4	2		
Stone, John	1	1	2		
Taylor, Elizabeth			2		
Outlaw, Martha			2		6
Ward, Philip	2	3	8		
Motten, Michial	2	1	6		11
Herring, Stephen	3	1	5		14
McCollah, John	1	1	2		
Peacock, Theophilas	1		1		
Joiner, James	1	4	2		
Marsey, Berthea			3		
Jernigan, Jane	1		3		3
James, James	2	1	7		17
Glisson, Michial	1	2	1		
Hill, Thomas	2		3		24
Boyt, Arthur	1	1	3		
Carr, John	1	3	3		1
Boyt, Ephram	1	3	3		
Matchett, John	1	3	4		7
Gray, William M	1		4		
Haycraft, John	3		2		
Gray, Nathan	1	1	2		
Chambers, John	3	2	4		5
Rhodes, John	1	2	2		9
Stone, David	2	1	2		6
Carlton, John	4	2	3		
Carlton, Thomas	2	2	3		2
Stone, Robert	2	1	4		3
Strafford, Josiah	1	2	4		
Dobbson, Mary			3		
Robert, William	1		1		
Taylor, Jacob	1	1	1		
Forehead, James	1	3	2		
Benton, Joshua	3	2	4		
Glisson, Jacob	2	5	2		
Brock, Jesse	1		2		
Brock, Seven	1	2	2		
Becks, Benjamin	1		2		
Carter, Edward	1	1	1		
Carter, Solomon	1	1	1		3

WILMINGTON DISTRICT, DUPLIN COUNTY—Continued.

NAME OF HEAD OF FAMILY.	Free white males of 16 years and upward, including heads of families.	Free white males under 16 years.	Free white females, including heads of families.	All other free persons.	Slaves.
Blizzard, Hezzekiah....		1	1		
Carter, David....	1	4	1		
Deaver, Rheuben....	1				
Sumerland, Mary....	1		2		
Jones, Anthony....	1				
Snipes, Benjamin....	1	2	6		
Pepkin, Lewis....	2	2	3		1
Carter, Man....	1		1		
Mainer, John....	2	1	2		
Flemming, Alexander..	1		1	1	
Branch, Jesse....	2	2	3		
Sumerland, Jacob....	5	4	3		
Thomson, Isaac....	1				
Moody, James....	1	2	1		
Bowan, Elijah....	1	4	1		
Gray, Eloderick....	1	1	3		
Herring, Isaac....	1	3	4		
Johnston, Henry....	1		1		
Garione, Likes....	1				
Thompson, John....	1	1	1		
Thompson, Elizabeth..	2	1	2		
Carlton, David....	1	1	3		
Brock, Bizon....	1	1	3		
Carter, Walker....			1		
Thompson, Bersheba....			2		
Ellison, Jesse....	1	3	5		
Ward, Mathew....	1				
Smith, George....	3	3	5		
Smith, Frederick....	1	5	2		
Moore, William....	1	3	2		
Strond, Ludson....	1	1	3		
Herring, James....	1	4	2		7
Ray, William....	1	1	3		
Mainer, Mary....		2	2		
Mathews, James....	2	3	4		
Dawson, James....	1				
Duff, William....	4		4		
Fussell, Elizabeth....	1	3	4		
Rivenback, Simon....	1	5	3		
Smith, Stephen....	1	2	3		
Whetfield, William....	1	1	3		4
Slocum, Samuel....	1		2		1
Pickett, James....	2	3	5		1
Pickett, Henry....	1	1	2		
Fleming, John....	1	1	2		
Beaman, Abraham....	2	3	2		
Aron, John....	1	1	2		
Federick, William....	1	4	4		4
Parker, John....	2	2	4		
Alberson, William....	2		2		2
Gufford, Stephen....	1		1		
Rhodes, Joseph T., Esq.	1				8
Casson, Ame....	2	2	2		
Fooley, Flood....	1	2	3		
McIntire, James....	2	1	2		13
Hunter, Priscilla....		3	5		4
Gaylor, George....	1		2		
Walkins, Leban....	4	4	2		9
Martin, Christopher....	2	1	4		
Rutley, John....	2		3		2
Winders, John....	1		5		
Rogers, John, Senr....	5	1	4		
Blanchard, Jediah....	1	1	2		
Parker, Daniel....	1	3	4		
Rogers, John....	1	2	5		
Spince, Timothy....	2	1	3		
Salmon, William....	1		3		
Wilkins, Michial....	1	2	3		1
Stokes, Rading....	2		2		2
Taylor, John....	1	1	4		
Deaver, John....	2	3	1		
Taylor, Demsey....	1	1	5		
Bowdin, Samuel....	1	3	2		
Parker, Peter....	1		2		
Bennet, Thomas....	2	3	3		1
Durell, John....	1	3	4		
Sauser, Joel....	1	2	3		
Vick, Joseph....	1	1	2		
Korneagy, John....	1	2	1		1
Jones, Lewis....	1	1	3		
Jones, Anthony....	2	2	2		
Tanner, Samuel....	1	1	5		
Sevinson, Jesse....	1	4	2		
Ward, Andrew....	1		3		
Herring, Lewis....	1	2	2		1
Vick, John....	1	1	2		
Parker, Jonathan....	1	4	3		
Wilkerson, William....	1	3	4		
Sollus, James....	2	1	2		
Chalmbers, Joshua....	2	2	4		
Wilkins, John....	1		2		
Killbrue, Buckner....	1	2	2		5
Bennett, William....	1				
Bennett, Samuel....	1		2		
Taylor, Elef....			3		
Harris, Edward....	1	1	1		
Taylor, Catharine....	1	1	3		8
Bowden, Baker....	1	2	2		
Walkins, Peter....	1	1	1		1
Tunnage, Ezekiel....	1		1		1
Duncan, William....	2	4	4		3
Millard, Zedekiah....	1		2		
Gancy, Mathew....	1	3	4		
Duncan, Edmand....	2		3		
Duncan, Isaac....	1		2		
Johnston, Reubin....	4	3	6		
Hicks, Daniel....	1	6	4		19
Reaves, Hardy....	2	3	5		
Reaves, Adam....	1		4		
Rogers, Mark....	1	2	3		2
Ratleff, Samuel....	1	5	1		
McCann, Hugh....	1	3	5		
McCann, William....	1		1		
Gilman, John....	1		2		
Federick, Felen....	1	4	3		
Chason, Richard....	1				
Floyd, James....	1	3	2		
James, Isaac....	1		2		
Murrow, Daniel....	1	2	2		1
Bowser, Luke....	1	1	2		
Hall, William....	3		4		
Coock, Daniel....	1		4		
Allen, Ezekiel....	1	4	6		
Allen, William....	3	6	2		
Jones, Henry....	1	3	2		
Jorge, Jesse....	1	3	3		
Parker, Hardy....	1	1	2		
Bowser, Emanuel....	1	1	2		
Fussell, Benjamin....	1	1	1		
Bryan, Nicholas....	1	1	1		
Cummings, Thomas....	2	5	4		
Hedgeman, Lewis....	1		2		
Cook, John....	1	3	2		1
Cook, Mary....	1		2		2
Bryan, Walter....	2				
Boney, John....	1	4	4		
Knowls, James....	2	4	4		
Blanton, John....	4	3	4		
Williams, Joseph....	1		1		4
Williams, Aron....	1	1	2		2
Newton, Lewis....	1		3		
Green, John....	1	3	6		
Bowan, Elisha....	1	1	4		
Cook, Thomas....	1	4	1		
Knowls, John....	1	2	3		
Green, Thomas....	1		3		
Newton, Isaac....	1	2	5		
Edwards, Nathan....	1		3		
Waters, John....	1	3	3		
Brown, Aron....	1	2	1		
Alderman, David....	1	3	9		
Wallice, Robert....	1	1	7		
Wills, Federick....	3	2	5		1
Tucker, David....	1	3	3		
Wood, Simon....	1	1	5		
Mathews, Jacob....	1	2	3		
Smith, James....	2	3	1		
Davis, David....	1		4		
Thompson, Benjamin..	1	4	2		
Duff, John....	1		2		
Ezzell, Michial....	2		2		1
Ezzell, Reuben....	1		3		
Ezzell, Benjamin....	1	1	1		
Revenback, Simon....	1	3	4		
Young, John....	2		2		
Brown, John....	1	1	2		
Williams, Joseph....	2	1	5		4
Hall, David....	1		4		
Mathews, Ezekiel....	1	1	2		
Green, Lott....	1	1	6		
Wilson, John....	1	1	2		
Blake, Joshua....	1	1	1		
Mathews, John....	1	1	2		1
Wilson, John....	2		2		3
Roney, Hugh....	1				
Shuffield, Amos....	1	1	4		
Merett, Charles....	1		2		
Mathews, Arthur....	1	2	1		
Williams, Stephen....	3		4		
Knowls, Robert....	1	3	2		
Williams, Byrd....	1	2	3		1
Coock, Nathan....	1	2	3		
Williams, John....	2	3	1		
Williams, Federick....	1	6	4		2
Holiway, Taylor....	1		4		
Gauff, John, Senr....	1	2	4		2
Singleton, David....	1	3	4		
James, Elias....	2	4	3		3
Ensor, Ambrose....	1		5		
Murphry, William....	2	4	5		7
Bowan, Dann....	2	2	4		
Cook, John....	2	2	3		
Blanton, James....	1	3	1		
Daniel, John....	1	2	6		
Holms, Hardy....	1	1	3		
Holms, Key....	2	3	6		
Daniel, Aron....	1	2	2		
Burnham, William....	3	6	2	1	2
Hunt, John....	2	1	2		10
Kennard, Michial....	5	3	3		5
Dickson, Moses....	2	2	2		
Taylor, William....	1		1		
Bradley, Thomas....	1	2	1		
Ward, Luke....	3		4		3
Harris, William....	3	3	6		
Duncan, Edmand....	2		3		
Bezzell, Lewis....	2	2	5		
Gauff, John....	1		3		5
Bezzell, William....	3		4		2
Bezzell, Arthur....	1	1	1		
Cherry, Willis....	1	3	4		4
Duncan, Isaac....	1		2		3
Byrd, Robert....	6		3		3
Ward, William....	2	3	6		
Henes, William....	2	5	3		
Bezzell, James....	2	2	3		3
Flowers, Thomas....	2	2	3		1
Penelton, Noah....	2	3	6		
Underhill, William....	2	3	6		
Beck, Stephen....	1		4		1
Reaves, Hardy....	4	4	5		
Quinn, James....	1		1		
Grimes, Joseph....	1		1		
Cooper, Benjamin....	1		3		1
Farrior, John....	1	4	3	1	4
Burgel, Edmand....	1		1		
Millard, Jacob....	3		1		
McCollah, Thomas....	1	3	1		
Daniel, Jeptha....	1	1	2		
Jones, Stephen....	1	1	1		
Cannon, David....	2	4	5		
Odum, George Jurnigan.	1	6	4		2
Winders, John....	2		4		9
Grimes, James....	1	6	2		
Kenan, Michael I....	2	5	3		21
Ward, William....	1	2	2		5
Guy, Lemuel....	2	3	4		
Beesley, Auston....	1	2	2		
Guy, James....	1	2	3		
Jones, Abe....	3		5		
Wood, Peter....	2	1	6		
Coventon, Levan....	1	1	2		
Connerley, Cullen....	2	2	6		3
Cook, John, Senr....	1	2	4		1
Brown, Jesse....	1	1	4		2
Harrel, Kedar....	1	4	2		
Evans, James....	2	4	5		1
Caniday, Joseph....	1	1	4		
Williams, Jacob....	1		3		3
Adams, Robert....	1	2	2		
Ward, John....	5		1		2
Hawkins, Uzzell....	1	2	2		
Stuckey, Lewes....	1				
Carter, Zack....	1	1	5		
Branch, John....	1	3	3		
Newton, William....	1	2	2		
Mobley, Burwell....	2	2			
Ivey, John....	1		1		8
Linear, Benjamin....	2	1			
Linear, Jesse....	1	3	2		2
Murrow, James....	1	2	4		
Wood, John....	2		3		
Halso, John....	1	2	3		
Sirews, Joseph....	1	5	2		
Woodward, Elisha....	1	2			1
Murrow, James....	2	2	1		5
McGee, John....	2	3	2		
Land, Benatus....	1	1	7		
Ward, Samuel....	1	1	1		1
Castul, Lydia....	1	4	3		
Hancock, Stephen....	1		3		1
Farrior, William....	1		6		4
Ellis, James....	1	2	4		
Hines, Daniel....	1	2	3		
Flowers, William....	1	2	4		
Fountain, Nathan....	1		4		
Myrell, Jo....	1				
Hall, William....	2	6	2		11
Bachelor, Mary....	1	1	3		
Lenear, John....	2		2		
Cannon, Abraham....	1				
Dobbson, Mary....			3		
Haws, James....	1	1	1		
Shelton, Thomas....	1		1		
Shuffield, Elizabeth....		6	3		
Johnston, Amus....	2	1	3		8
Mashbourn, Christopher....	1	1	6		
Shoulders, Lewis....	1	1	1		
Sanders, Ezekiel....	1				
Baker, Isaac....	1		2		

WILMINGTON DISTRICT, DUPLIN COUNTY—Continued.

NAME OF HEAD OF FAMILY.	Free white males of 16 years and upward, including heads of families.	Free white males under 16 years.	Free white females, including heads of families.	All other free persons.	Slaves.
Harp, William	2		2		
Garisson, Epharam	1	2	2		
Rains, Daniel	1	3	2		
Quinn, Calop	1		4		
Simpson, Enoch	1	1	1		
Winders, James	1	1	6		1
Millar, Heck	1		3		1
Pu, Jonathan	1	1	2		
Craford, John	1	3	5		
Halso, Stephen	2	2	4		
Lenear, Jesse	1		4		
Brinson, Henry	1	4	3		
Holingsworth, William	1	1	2		1
Andrews, Abraham	1	2	4		3
Wallace, James	1	4	3		
Collings, William	1	4	3		
Wallace, Jacob	1	1	3		
Tuelling, Robert	3		4		2
Newkirk, Henry	1	2	3		1
James, William	5		3		2
Bryan, Timothy	1	2	3		
Powell, Brittian	1	2	4		
Meritt, Robert	1	3	4		
Sutton, Elius	2	1	1		
Powell, Hardy	1		4		
Bland, Mary	1		5		
Wills, William	2	1	2		
Willise, Jonathan	1		3		
Gitstraf, Harly	1		3		
Stallings, Shadock	2	2	4		6
Cook, James	1	1	2		
Hall, Isaac	1				
Filman, William	1	4	5		
Hennesey, David	1		2		
Beven, Joseph	1	2	4		
Leigh, Josiah	1	4	4		
Bland, William	1		2		
Stallings, Meshack	1	4	7		1
Hill, Mary			6		
Blanton, Joshua	1	1	2		
Harwell, William	2	4	5		
Coock, John	1	1	2		
Rawlings, John	1	1	5		
Newton, Abraham	2	3	5		
Newton, Jacob	1				
Rogers, Reuben	1		1		
Sweetman, William	1	1	1		
Mathews, John	1		4		
Dickson, Barbara	3	2	5		21
Martin, Paul	1	3	3		
Ward, Joseph	1	2	6		
Jones, Mary		1	7		
Walker, David	1		3		
Taylor, Thomas	2		3		
Bradley, Richard	1	3	1		
Shuffield, Ephram	1	1	2		
Serews, Joseph	1		3		
Spence, Isaac	1	1	2		
Bowden, Nicholas	3	2	1		
Korneagy, George	1		5		1
Branch, Dred	1	1	1		
Korneagy, Jacob	2	4	3		19
Durele, Roby			3		
Chandlor, Sarah			4		
Peas, Jonathan	1	1	2		
Rogers, William	1				
Cannon, Mary		1	3		3
Dickson, William	3	2	6		31
Dickson, James	4	1	6		3
Millar, Anthony	1	1	4		2
Southerland, Daniel	2	4	3		1
Norment, Thomas	2	1	2		43
Hill, John	2	3	3		26
Page, Silus	1		2		
Gibbs, John	5	1	6		4
Simplor, Christopher			3		
Walker, John	2	4	3		
Olat, Adam	2	1	3		
Stocks, Henry	2	1	2		
Newell, Joshua	2	1	2		
Pheps, Thomas	2	1	3		
Cooper, Richard	1	2	2		
Rouse, George	2	4	1		
Allen, Henry	2	3	1		
Jones, Samuel	1	2	1		
Pearce, Mikajah	1	1	3		
Southerland, Phil	2		3		
McGees, William	3	1	8		
McCann, William	3		3		5
Sanderland, Samuel	3		3		
Rigsby, John	1	1	2		
Grimes, Charles	1	2	1	1	
Cooper, George	1	2	6		6
Carr, James	1		2		6
Stuckey, John	2	2	5		7
Wetts, Joseph	1		1		7
Johnston, John	1		1		3
Odaniel, Owen	1	1	3		7
Moore, Auston	2	2	1		
Gauff, William	2	2	3		2
Williams, David	1		2		2
Facon, Susanna	2	2	5		8
Blanchard, Uriah	4	2	3		1
Best, William	1	5	3		4
Dickson, Edward	2	2	6		12
James, Charles	1		2		
Mares, Richard	1	1	3		2
Waller, John	2	2	5		1
Waller, Nathaniel	1	1	1		
Streets, Mary			3		
Cox, Moses	1		5		
Edwards, Mathew	1		6		9
Williams, Christan	1	2	3		
Umphreys, John	1	2	4		
Williams, Syvea			1		
Houston, Edward	1	3	1		6
Housten, Doctr William	1				10
Smith, Joseph	1		1		3
Millar, George	2		2		14
Housten, Griffeth	2	2	5		
Jones, Jesse	1	1	2		
Serews, Joseph	1				
Hubbard, James	1				
Smith, Ivey	2		2		6
Southerland, John	3	2	2		
Lowell, Shadrach	1	2	4		
Toomer, Thomas	1	1	3		
Fountain, Henry	1		2		
Manner, Lydia	1	1	3		1
Cottle, Robert	2	3	2		
Parker, Amiss	2	3	7		
Pickett, Margaret	2	1	2		
Batts, Sarah	2	2	3		2
Paget, Joab	2	4	3		
Paget, James	1		1		
Paget, Cornelar	1	1			
Thigpen, Joab	1	4	5		
Pickett, James	2	1	2		3
Thomas, William	4	3	2		5
Parker, Abigal		2	3		
Parker, John	2		3		
Thomas, Isaac	1	1	4		3
Williams, Stephen	1		4		2
Williams, Jeremiah	1		1		2
Williams, Jacob	2		3		6
Henderson, Anne		2	2		
Hubbard, William	1	1	3		8
Moresey, George, Esq	6	3	3		35
Teachey, Daniel	2		1		17
Tonans, Thomas	4	2	6		10
Kenan, James	3	2	6		37
Young, Peter	1	2	2		
Hodgeson, Joseph	1		2		
Ostean, Calop	1	2	2		
Balley, John	1	1	2		
Pickett, William	2	1	1		3
Pickett, William, Senr	1		1		2
Meaks, Reuben	1	2	6		
Sholders, Thomas	2		1		
Burton, William	1	5	1		1
Evans, James	1	5	3		
Lenear, Benjamin	1	1	4		
Batchelor, William	2	1	2		
Jones, Edward	2		2		
Martindal, Stephen	1	4	4		
Martindal, Samuel	1	2	4		
Whaley, Francis	1		4		
Medford, Jeptha	2	4	6		
Thigpin, John	1	5	4		
Thomas, John	1	1	2		
Bracher, Edward	1		2		1
Whaley, James	1	5	5		
Whaley, Samuel	2	3	5		
Whaley, William	2	3	7		
Millar, Stephen	2		1		4
Chambers, James	2	3	4		5
Bass, Jerediah	1		1		

WILMINGTON DISTRICT, NEW HANOVER COUNTY.

NAME OF HEAD OF FAMILY.	Free white males of 16 years and upward, including heads of families.	Free white males under 16 years.	Free white females, including heads of families.	All other free persons.	Slaves.
Long, William	1	5	1		
Carr, Daniel	2		2		1
Treadaway, Moses	1	1	7		2
Jones, Isabella			2		2
Taylor, Henry	1	2	4		3
Herring, Joshua	1	2	1		9
Holley, Henry	1	2	4		
Snell, Samuel	1		2		
White, John	1	3	3		3
Portervin, Samuel	1				2
Larkins, Roger	1	1	4		2
Boyling, John	1				
Busley, Abraham	3	2	4		1
Richards, Nicholas	1	3	2		
Molpass, John	2	1	7		
Parker, Hardy	2	3	5		
Stanley, James	1	2	1		1
Stanley, James, Senr	4		2		5
Eakins, Joseph	1				
Murphey, Fenla	3	1	4		
Sloan, William	2	5	5		1
Bannerman, George	1	1	2		3
Bennerman, Elizabeth	1	1	4		1
Loban, Micheal	3		2		
Dowd, John	1	3	4		
Lewis, John	1	1	1		
Wood, Willis	1	1	3		
Spearman, Edward	3		2		12
Bourdiant, Isaac	1	2	2		
Fellows, John	2	1	3		15
Busley, Thomas	1	1	2		
Moore, Pettigrew	2	4	5		9
Deburgue, Isaac	1	1	1		
Hale, Mathew	1	4	2		
Corbet, Thomas	3	1	3		16
Rettor, Moses	1	3	7		
Rossor, John	2	2	3		
Mason, Richard	1	2	4		
Malpass, Hardy	1	4	1		3
Evans, Edward	1		2		1
Rogers, Thomas	1	1	2		5
Taylor, John	2	1	5		
Sellars, John	1	2	4		2
Larkins, Samuel	1	1	2		3
Carr, Mary			3		
Lee, James	1	2	1		2
Burns, Bartholemew	1	3	5		1
Devane, William	1	1	2		8
Devane, Thomas	1	2	4		18
Devane, Thomas	1	2	3		28
Lamb, William	1	4	1		4
Bond, Scruting	1		3		
Bowden, John	1	1	4		
Corbet, John	1		4		
Lamb, Isaac	1	2	2		1
Savage, Arthur	1	2	4		
Rivenbark, John	3	2	5		
Devane, George	2	1	3		6
Button, Henry	1	1	3		
Porbus, James	1	4	4		1
Pigford, William	3	1	5		
Collins, John	1		3		
Larkins, Benjamin	1		3		4
Geddans, Thomas	2	1	5		
Wright, James	2	2	3		3
Marshall, John	2	3	6		
Rooks, Jesse	1	3	4		1
Smith, John	2	1	3		
Kernear, James	1		3		5
Moore, Jacob	1	2			
Moore, Moses	1		4		
Malpass, James	1		3		
Herring, Bright	1	3	1		
Corbet, Thomas	1	3	3		1
Baker, Arthur	1	4	2		
Jones, John	2	1	8		2
Johnston, Jesse	1	3	2		
Harper, James	2	1	1		13
James, John, Junr	1		1		
Larkins, James	1	2	3		10
Scull, John G., Esq	1	1	5	1	8
Colide, John	2				15
McKensie, John	1		1		
Oliver, John	1	1	4		10
Taylor, William	1	4	3		2
Morgan, Abel	1		2		
Morgan, Daniel	1		1		
Prigeon, William	2	1	3		
Lee, Solomon	1	4	7		1
Plair, Thomas	2	2	5		4
Wright, James	3		4		
Wright, John	3	1	3		
Moore, James	1	2	3		1

WILMINGTON DISTRICT, NEW HANOVER COUNTY—Continued.

NAME OF HEAD OF FAMILY.	Free white males of 16 years and upward, including heads of families	Free white males under 16 years	Free white females, including heads of families	All other free persons	Slaves
Ramsey, Thomas	1	3	5		
Savage, Francis	1	1	3		
Lewis, Thomas	1	2	7		16
Anderson, Elizabeth	1	4	3		4
Herring, Mary			2		
Wilson, James	2	3	7		4
Ennis, Daniel	1	3	1		
Walters, William	3	5	6		7
Rogers, James	1		2		4
Shaw, Mary	4		2		
Henry, Mary	1	1	3		
Simpson, Federick	2	5	3		14
Simpson, Charles	1	2	3		11
Grau, William	1	1	2		
Herring, Samuel	2	3	4		
Prooby, Richard	1		3		
McGuilford, James	2		2		12
Strong, David	1	1	6		8
Howard, Paramas	1				4
Bourdeaut, Daniel	1	3	3		5
Buxon, Bryan	5	1	3		
Lewis, Penelope	1	3	2		
Fennel, Morrice	1	2	4	1	3
Newton, Samuel	1		1	1	
Jones, David, Senr	2	5	5	2	12
Harvey, John	1	2	3		4
Brook, Lewis	1	2	4		4
Decoine, Edward	1				
Jones, Mrs. Sarah	2	1	4		55
Williams, John Pugh, Esq	1		4		39
Ashe, Samuel, Junr	2				20
Row, John	1	3	2		3
Herring, Samuel	1	3	4		
Ramsey, William	2	1	6		
Ashford, John Stonestreet	1	1	4		
McGowen, George	1				7
Hale, David	1	2	1		
Johnston, Mathew	2	1	2		1
Bird, Agnis	1		4		
Hamilton, Malakiah	1	1	1		
English, Margaret			4		
Orgood, Priscilla			4		
Bloodworth, Thomas	3	1	3		8
Wilson, Timothy	1	2	8		1
Leddon, Benjamin	1	2	2		7
Bloodworth, Timothy	2	1	5		9
Bloodworth, John	1	2	4		4
Jones, David	1	2	1		15
Corbet, Daniel	1		1		
Blake, Henry	2		1	1	
Croom, Jesse	2	3	3		
Fullard, Plen	1	1	2		2
Blake, John	1		1		
Fullard, Barney	2	1	4		
Norvet, Solomon	2		2		
Stone, Allen	1		1		1
Wills, Marten	1	2	3		10
Williams, David	1	1	1		3
Highsmith, Solomon	4		4		1
Evans, Thomas	1	2	6		
Powell, Jacob	4	1	5		
Newkirk, Abraham	3	1	3		5
Highsmith, David	4		4		1
Herring, Enoch	1	2	2		
Fennell, Nicholas	1	1	3		6
Fennell, Nicholas	1	2	3	1	
Johnston, Jacob	1	1	1		
Portervim, Peter	1				4
Rackford, Patrick	1				
Highsmith, Daniel	1	2	3		
Page, Thomas	1				
Newton, Ann	3	1	6		
Powell, Elisha	1		1		
Bland, William	2		3		
Alderman, Daniel	1	3	5		
Herrington, William	1	3	2		
Penny, Joshua	2	2			
Beardeaux, John	1	2	3		1
Bourdeaux, Isreal	1	2	2		
Turner, Nedam	1	1	2		
Woodside, Thomas	1		4		
Larkins, William	2				12
Stokely, John	2	4	4		
Lamb, Gibbs	1	1	3		
Lamb, Thomas	1	3	4		4
Jones, Federick, Esq.	1		3		77
Johnston, Thomas	1	2	3		3
Ward, Mary Ann	1		3		5
Larkins, John	2	2	5		
Portervine, Jann		2	4		7
Kernier, James	1				2
Moore, John	2		3		42
Moore, James	1		1		16
Smith, James	1	2	1		
Moseley, William	1		2		16

NAME OF HEAD OF FAMILY.	Free white males of 16 years and upward, including heads of families	Free white males under 16 years	Free white females, including heads of families	All other free persons	Slaves
Lambert, Elizabeth		2	4		2
Leguiwl, Mathew	1	4	3		5
Moore, George, Esq	1		3		34
Macnaughton, Archd	4				4
Johnston, Mathew	1	2	2		5
Heartwell, Daniel	1				
Cook, William	1	2	5		1
Furgus, John	5		2		33
Joslin, Amasiah	2	2	3		6
Machain, John	1		1		
Reardan, Dennis	1				
Wills, Robert	2	2	1		3
Talfair, John	4	2	4		9
Springs, Sedgewick	1	1	1		3
Claypoole, William	1		2		4
Walker, John	4	1	3		61
Cunningham, Thomas	2				9
McNeal, Daniel	1	3	1		2
Wilkins, Mar R	1	2	1		2
Wright, Thomas	1	1	1		31
London, Samuel	5	2	3		8
Nicles, John	2	1	5		16
Quigley, Easter		1	1		
Huntington, Jonathan	1			1	2
Martin, John	1	1	1		8
Johnston, Betty			2	3	
Lefong, Mary			2		
Harisson, Joseph	1	1	3		
Black, Sarah		1	2		
White, Darios			3		
Plain, Nancy		1			
Rooks, Henry	1		3		4
Rundle, Richard	4	1	3		4
Bemes, Patty		1	1		
Ceater, Sarah			2		
Lard, Elizabeth			1		
Potts, Joshua	2		2		6
Hoskins, Henry	1	1	1		4
Duffey, Daniel	1		2		
Millar, James	1	1	2		
Maxwell, Peter	1		1		18
Wooton, Nathan	2	4	1	1	1
Wooton, Thomas	2		3		
Blakely, John	2				2
Wooten, Robert	1	1	2		6
Dodge, Joseph	1	1	2		
Camble, John	2		1		3
Watson, Richard	1		2		5
Tompkins, Jonathan	2				
Golden, Thomas	2				
Johnson, John	3		2		2
Meaks, Mary	8	1	3		6
Routledge, William	1		3	1	2
Erutson, Severin	2				1
Hooper, George	3		2		14
Jones, Edward	1		1		2
Maclain, Thomas	1		2		10
Doty, Elizabeth		1	2		
Styles, Joseph	2				
McCollah, George	2	2	3		1
Levi, Jacob	2				
Nicles, Calop	1				1
Levi, Eleager	3	1	4		3
Bransby, John	1		1		
Younger, Thomas	1	1	2		2
Jennings, Jonathan	2		2		5
Bradley, John	2		3		5
Maclilling, John	2				3
Lord, John	1		3		10
White, James	2	1			2
Henderson, John	1		7		2
Davis, Mrs. Hariot	1		3		3
Davis, Roger	1				
Read, James	2				32
Toomer, Henry	1	2	3		51
Mabron, Arthur	1		4		8
Mabron, William	1				14
Mabron, Mary			2		25
Mabron, Samuel	1	3	1		30
Dorsey, Sal	1	2			11
Cropton, Charles	1	1	2		1
Cunnings, Henry	1		1		
Patterson, Elizabeth			3		
Welch, Margaret	1	1	4		
Stevens, James McCoy	2		2		6
Davis, Joseph	1		2		2
Carpinter, Peter	1		1		13
Furgesson, Daniel	2	1	1		2
Mooran, James	1		3		6
Bowdish, Else	3		2		
London, John	1	1			8
How, Robert	1				6
Tucker, Henry	1	1	1		4
Rundelson, Margaret			2		2
Burnard, Isaac	2		3	1	3
Herring, Mrs. Else		1	1		12
Darlington, Meredith	1		1		

NAME OF HEAD OF FAMILY.	Free white males of 16 years and upward, including heads of families	Free white males under 16 years	Free white females, including heads of families	All other free persons	Slaves
Harris, Peter	2		2		1
Keenan, Mecheal	6		4		3
Plair, Comfort			2		4
Dunlap, Elizabeth			1		
Martelhaney, John	4	1	2		2
Glisser, Abraham	2	1	2		4
James, David	3	1	2		4
Germillion, Henry	1	1	3		1
Allger, James	1		1		1
Cooper, Nathan	1	2	1		
Jecoks, Charles	2		1		13
Blith, George			3		3
Balloat, Cesar A	1		1		17
Dry, Mrs. Mary Jane			1		4
Camble, Mrs. Sarah			1		1
Fryat, Mrs. Sarah		1	3		8
Ward, Anthony	1				1
Geckee, James	1		2		12
Hostler, Mrs. Mary	1	1	2		35
Everet, Elizabeth		1	1		
McCloud, Daniel	3	1	1		
Herbe, Henry D	1				1
Nutt, William	1		1		2
Nutt, John	1	2	3		8
Camble, Hugh	1	1	1		5
Murprey, John	3				
Swann, Mrs. Lameret		1	3		8
Myter, John	1		1		
Gordon, William	1	1	2		1
Beeryman, Robert	2	1	1		1
Halsey, Henry	2	2	2		
Ross, Wity	1				44
Hanson, Mary			2		2
Cathorda, John	2		2		2
Nance, Samuel	1	1	1		3
Robenson, Sarah	1	2			
Moon, Thomas	1	1	2		14
Davis, William	1		2		
Moon, Mrs. Sarah			2		76
Duncan, Joseph	2				
Brice, Francis	1		2	1	5
Major, John	2		1		4
Millar, Mary			1		2
Huske, John	3			1	7
Hooper, William	1				10
Flemming, James	1	2	6		47
Mackenzie, John	1	1	2		31
Mackenzie, Mrs. Catharine				1	16
Simpson, Mrs. Ann		1	5		4
Mallet, Peter	1	1	5		105
Burguin, John	4	1	1		81
Walker, James	1		3		96
Qunce, Mrs. Ann			1		21
James, John	2	3	2		26
Barrow, Josiah	1		3		
Walters, Henry	2		2		27
Bloodworth, David	2	2	7		2
Quince, Richard	1				5
Duront, Amond I	2		1		14
Hill, William H	1		2		45
Hill, John	1	2	1		52
Hill, Nathan	1		2		25
Scott, Robert	1	2			16
Waddle, Hugh	1		2		85
How, Jane	2		4		24
Wheton, Daniel	1		2		1
Lestor, Robert	1		1		1
Downing, James	2	1	2		4
Vann, William	1		3		
Grout, Daniel	1				
Ervan, Daniel	1		4		9
Ervan, Jane			1		12
Bunting, Samuel	1	5	2		18
Meris, Jane		1	1		18
Waddle, John	1				70
Moseley, Samson	1		2		64
Ervan, James	1	2	2		3
Ramsey, James	1				
Beaufort, Frederick	1	1	4		4
Hill, Henry	1	3	2		34
Sampson, Michael	1	1	3		5
Martin, Clem	1	2	1		
Fish, Stephen	1	1			
Frances, Anthony	1	2	1		
Wiggon, John	1	1	1		
Moore, James	1		2		7
Shadwick, Joseph	1	5	1		
Erle, James	1				
Toomer, Anthony	1	1	1		11
Jones, Thomas	1		1		7
Swann, John	1	2	2		56
Jones, Federick	1		1		23
Green, William	2	1	1		31
Mallett, James	1		2		45
Cracke, Thomas	2	1			26
Huffum, Richard	2	2	3	1	1

WILMINGTON DISTRICT, NEW HANOVER COUNTY—Continued.

NAME OF HEAD OF FAMILY.	Free white males of 16 years and upward, including heads of families.	Free white males under 16 years.	Free white females, including heads of families.	All other free persons.	Slaves.
Johnston, Jesse	1	3	4		
Rollens, James	4		2		
Cowen, John	1	1	9		
Bowden, Martha	1	3	3		
Rivenbark, Philip	4	1	7		1
Millar, John	1	1	4		7
Strudwick, Samuel					45
Millar, Bushrod	2				
Parish, Mary	2	1	3		13
Millar, Richard	2				
Lewis, Jacob	1		2		
Henry, William	1	2	2		1
Curray, John	1		1	1	
Jones, William	1		4		9
Osbourn, William	1				4
McAllester, Charles	1		2		
Evans, William	2	3	4		21
Green, David	3		3		14
Howard, Nathan	1	1	1		
Howard, Ezekiah	1	3	5		
Henry, Catharine	1		1		2
Cowen, Magnus	1	7	2		
Huzzey, John	1	4	2		
Robinson, William	2		5		3
McCalop, Archibald	2	1	2		1
Busley, Solomon	2	2	4		2
Cook, Robert	1	2	2		
Sharpless, William	1	3	2		
Cogdale, Charles	1	3	2		10
Devane, Thomas	1	1	4		24
Robinson, Benjamin	1	4	4		34
Devane, James	1	3	3		10
Sulivan, John	1	3	1		
Felyau, Stephen	2		1	1	
Felyau, John	1	1	3		
Doty, James	1	1	3		2
Murray, Thomas	1	4	3		1
Calender, Thomas	1	2	3		8
Kingburg, Henry	1		1		
Smith, Nathan	2				
Oldfield, Nathan	1				1
Allen, John	2		1		10
Ashe, Samuel	1		1		40
Sellars, John	1	1	4		2
Sloan, William	1	5	5		
Camble, Alexander	1	1	1		
Walker, James	1		1		
Wood, Willis	1	1	3		
Evans, David	2	2	2		
Squires, Thomas	1		1		
New, William	1	2	2		
Hanchey, Martin	1	1	5		
Armstrong, Thomas	1	2	1		
Ramsey, David	1				
Shadwick, James	2		2		1
Turner, David	1		3		
Tyler, Nicholas	1	1	1		
Jeneft, James	1		2		1
Hines, John	1	1	4		
Collins, John	1	2	3		
Messer, Swan	3	2	5		
Night, Miler	1	2	3		
Hews, Thomas	3				
Carter, Ann			3		
St. George, Elisha	1	2	1		11
Nedes, Cathrine		2	2		3
Walls, Joseph	1	2	2		
Perkins, David	4	1	3		2
Green, Rebecca	1	1	2		
Wood, Edward	1		1		
Bishop, James	1		1		
Bowan, Mary			1		
Bowan, Elisha	1	1	3		
Fuch, John	1	1	1		
Hambleton, James	1		1		
Barwick, White	1		2		
Barwick, Drucilla	1		2		
Nicles, Robert	1	1	1		
Messet, Aron	2	2	6		
Edens, John	2	1	6		3
Nixon, Robert	2	1	7		27
Nixon, Nicholas	1	1	1		10
Towning, James	1	1	3		1

NAME OF HEAD OF FAMILY.	Free white males of 16 years and upward, including heads of families.	Free white males under 16 years.	Free white females, including heads of families.	All other free persons.	Slaves.
Collings, Joseph	2		2		
Edens, Jacob	1		2		
Balston, Peter	3	2	3		1
Blak, John Flemming	1	1	1		
Howard, Christopher	1	2	2		2
Townley, William	1	3	2		
Turnigan, Alexander	1	3	1		
Nixon, Thomas	1	4	3		10
Coston, Isaac	1		4		
Howard, James	2	1	7		7
Coston, John, Senr	1		4		
Coston, John, Junr	1		1		
Hedgman, George	1	1	2		
Smith, James	2		1		
Byard, Ann			1		
Bishop, Thomas	1	2	2		7
McClammy, Luke	2	2	5		9
McClammy, Mark	1	2	5		11
Nioles, John	1		2		
Adkinson, Daniel	4	2	4		3
Sadbury, Stokley	5	1	5		
Barlow, Thomas	2	2	4		2
Camble, John A	1	2	6		36
Doty, Edward	1				31
Read, Arthur	1	2	3		
Cowen, Thomas	1	1	1		1
Merrick, George	1				87
Fewell, Thomas	2		3		
Routledge, Ester			2		
Ashe, Samuel, Esquire	3	1	2		62
Harp, Mrs		3	2		
Stevens, Zelphia		1	3		
Williams, Henry	2	3	5		4
Craft, Charles	1	2	2		1
Garrell, William	1		4		
Bloodworth, Rebeca		1	5		17
Garrell, Jacob	1		3		
Alexander, Benjamin	1	2	2		
Mathews, John	1	2	3		
Pickett, Thomas	3	2	3		2
Nicles, William	3	1	4		2
Jones, Mrs. Monice			3		17
Henry, Jane			2		
McCollah, Alexander	1		2		8
Henry, James	1		3		
Celson, Daniel	1	1	1		
Beauford, Yarington	2				
Simpson, William	1		1		4
Mott, Benjamin	2	4	4		9
Messam, Patsey	1	1	3		
Young, Catharine		1	2		4
Nicles, John	1		3		
Riley, John	1		2		
McKinney, Charles	1		1		
Logan, George	6	1	3		9
Holden, John	1				
Russell, Edwar	1	2	2		5
Wane, John	2	2	4		
Hewlet, Jeremiah	2	1	3		1
Wilson, John	1	1	2		1
Chester, Nixon	1		2		4
Surs, John	1		4		
Rebenson, Thomas	4	2	6		
Steremeri, George	2		2		
Pervines, Elinor			2		2
Johnston, William	1				
Hunt, John	1		2		
Henderson, Daniel	1	2	2		
Solders, Ephram	1	1	3		
Simmons, Thomas	1	2	3		7
Deal, Adam	1	4	6		
Venters, James	1	2	3		2
James, Sarah	1	1	5		
James, Isaac	2	2	5		
James, Thomas	1	1	1		
Deal, Isaac	1		2		
Scarborough, Thomas	1		1		
Sutten, Joshua	2	2	5		13
Shepherd, Jacob	1	2	2		
Rochel, Etherington	1	2	6		
Rochel, Amos	1	4	5		
Burton, Thomas	2		1		12
Henderson, John	1	2	4		

NAME OF HEAD OF FAMILY.	Free white males of 16 years and upward, including heads of families.	Free white males under 16 years.	Free white females, including heads of families.	All other free persons.	Slaves.
Howard, John	1	1	2		
Livington, George	1	1	3		22
Blanks, William	2	2	4		13
Shadwick, Benja	1	2	2		
Shadwick, Minite	1	2	3		
Morris, John	2	4	2		
Looper, Thomas	1		2		4
Rouse, Sander	2	2	5		4
Sell, Oswell	1	2	3		7
Smith, Peter	2	1	5		
Howard, Thomas	1		4		5
Cook, Archabald	2	2	5		
Hazzell, Sophia			1		14
Roach, William	2		1	1	
Jones, John	2	1	2		
Little, Robert	1				
Adkins, Jesse	1	2	2		
Newton, Edward	1	4	3		
Henry, Francis	1	2	1		
Hines, Lewis	3	4	6		
Canble, Edward	1				
Millinder, Mrs			2		
Robinson, Calop	1		2		
Cutter, William	1		2		5
Henry, Robert	1	6	3		
Murpry, Robert	1		3		4
Henry, William	1		1		1
Pages				5	2
Hannah				1	1
Hesse				1	3
Johnston, Abram				4	
Martin, John				4	
Martin, Robert				6	
Jacob, John				9	
Freeman, William				2	
Jacobs, Mathew				2	
Jacobs, Primus				4	
Jacobs, Zachariah				6	
Jacobs, Mathew				8	
Benson, James	1		1		
Wilson, Ambrose	2		4		
Kelley, William	1		1		
Murpry, Hugh	1	1	4		4
Russ, Thomas, Senr	2	2	5		6
Russ, Thomas, Junr	1	2	1		
Berry, Elizabeth		1	3		
Singlary, Mary	1	2	2		
Benson, Elizabeth	3	2	3		
Davis, Ezekiah	1				21
Fogetu, Edmand	1				7
Singlary, Brate	2	3	2		6
Struley, William	1	3	2		
Huffum, Patty	2		7		2
Russ, Eley	1	2	2		
Satter, Richard	1	2	3		8
Lock, Unus			1		
Lock, Isaac	1	1	1		1
Larkins, John	1				
Burdaux, Peter	1	3	4		
Edwell, Benja	1	3	3		
Daves, John	1	3	5		
Parker, William	2	4	3		
Andrews, John, Junr	1	6	1		1
Meridith, Nathan	2	4	6		
Smith, Drury	1	1	2		
Henry, Alexander	1	1	3		1
Robinson, John	1	2	2		
Smith, Benja	1	2	2		
McMellens, Robert	1	1	5		
Sutten, John	1	1	1		1
Smith, James	1	2	4		
Maclemon, William	1		2		
Camon, Lucrescia	1	2	2		
Crumertree, William	3	2	8		5
Barry, William	1	1	2		
Stewart, Duncan, Esq	3		6		30
Sekes, Josiah	4	2	8		
Sekes, John	1		1		
Row, Frederick	1				
Fisher, Thomas	1	3	3		
Sutten, William	1	3	3		

WILMINGTON DISTRICT, ONSLOW COUNTY.

NAME OF HEAD OF FAMILY.	Free white males of 16 years and upward, including heads of families.	Free white males under 16 years.	Free white females, including heads of families.	All other free persons.	Slaves.
Shaw, William	1	1	2		7
Barono, Arthur	5	5	5		
Williams, Ann Mary	1		3		16
Williams, Obed	1		2		5
Shackelford, George	1	2	1		12
Sumner, Francis	1		2		
Askew, Nathan	1	3	3	1	
Williams, James	1		1		8

NAME OF HEAD OF FAMILY.	Free white males of 16 years and upward, including heads of families.	Free white males under 16 years.	Free white females, including heads of families.	All other free persons.	Slaves.
Wood, Jacob	1	1	1		3
Sanders, Robert	1	1	3		3
Battle, Ephram	2	4	4		17
Snead, Robert W., Esq	2				24
German, Lawrence	1	3	4		
Wood, Jesse	3	1	3		11
Hufman, Christopher	1	3	3		
Elles, John	1	1	1		1

NAME OF HEAD OF FAMILY.	Free white males of 16 years and upward, including heads of families.	Free white males under 16 years.	Free white females, including heads of families.	All other free persons.	Slaves.
Lillebridge, Joseph	1		5		13
Barrow, Zachariah	1	2	5		6
Barrow, Abraham	1		2		3
Barrow, Abraham, Senr	2	1	4		5
Pitman, Jordan	1		3		
Bell, William	1				
Shaw, Stephen	1	1	1		
Mills, James	1	1	3		

WILMINGTON DISTRICT, ONSLOW COUNTY—Continued.

NAME OF HEAD OF FAMILY.	Free white males of 16 years and upward, including heads of families.	Free white males under 16 years.	Free white females, including heads of families.	All other free persons.	Slaves.
Mills, Joshua	1	4	2		
Mills, William	1	5	2		5
Mills, George	1		3		5
White, Edward	1	1	3		
Wiley, Hardy	1	1	4		
White, George	1	3	3		
Thigpin, Jonas	1				
Thigpin, Joshua	1	2	2		
Wiley, Hardy	1	3	2		
Dudley, Christopher, Esq.	1	3	1		17
Dudley, Rebecca		2	2		17
Roan, William	1				
Snead, Robert, Senr	2	1	2		11
Waldron, Mary	1	2	4		4
Waldron, William	2	3	3		
Barono, James	1	2	2		
Gland, Thomas	2	2	4		
Parker, John	2	6			
Hufman, Jacob	1		3		
Sumner, Phibia			2		
Pennywell, John	1		2		
Ramsey, Jeremiah	1		2		
Ramsey, David	2	1	2		
Mills, Sarah	1		2		
Laws, Wilson	1		1		
Shingleton, Polly	2		2		
Umphrys, Mary		1	1		
Shingleton, Lurana		1	1		
Umphrys, Eustace	2	1	2		
Umphrys, Eustace, Junr	1	2	3		
Umphrys, Josiah	1	1	4		
Umphrys, Francis	1		2		
Umphrys, Jacob	2		2		
Parker, Thomas	1	3	1		
Mashbourn, James	1		2		
Rose, Betty			3		
Langston, James	1	1	1		
Foster, William	1	5	3		
Brown, Demsey	1	2	2		
Cox, Aron	2	5	5		
Cox, Jesse	1		1		
Cox, Charles	1	3	5		
German, Susanna		3	1		
Shackleford, Elizabeth	1	1	3		
Gland, John	1	3	2		
Parker, Francis	1		5		
Britton, Benjamin	1	2	1		
Ward, Patty	3	1	1		
Horn, Thomas	1	3	2		
Petuway, Peton	1	1	1		3
Turner, Mabry	1		1		7
Averet, John	1	2	4		2
Williams, Benjamin	1		1		2
Wilder, Jonathan	1		1		2
Yates, Benjamin	1	3	3		4
Williams, Samuel	1	3	4		
Averet, Jenken	1	2	1		12
Brady, Samuel	1		2		4
Smith, John	1		2		4
Young, Edward	2	2	2		13
Williams, Jesse	2	3	3		13
Grant, Rubean, Esq	2	1	5		32
Grant, Bazel	1	1	2		6
Horn, Henry	1	2	3		
Grant, Alexander	1	2	3		4
Greer, John	1	2	5		
Mumford, James	1	1	4		32
Brady, Joshua	1				
Williams, Benjamin	2		2		7
House, Mary	2		2		8
Davis, Jeremiah	1	1	3		7
Murrel, William	1	1	4		8
Ballard, James	1	5	2		1
Ballard, Joshua	1		1		
Ballard, Joshua, Junr	2		2		
Umphrys, David	1	3	3		7
Oliver, Benjamin	1		3		10
Hopkins, Neal	1	2	2		5
Seles, John, Senr	2	1	5		
Henderson, Thomas	1	4	2		2
Williams, Uzzey	2	2	8		18
Yates, Daniel	2	3	4		27
Averet, Arthur	2	2	3		2
Gregory, Hardy	1	2	2		17
Mumford, Lewis	1	2	2		17
Wilder, Joel	1	1	7		1
Wilder, Hopkins	1	1	1		2
Williams, Thomas	1	1	2		
Jones, John	2	4	4		7
Baczdon, Jesse	1	3	3		5
Williams, Nathan	1	1	3		
King, James	1		1		1
Jones, William	2	1	3		4
Barber, Thomas	2	1	2		
Manor, Henry	1	4	2		
Manor, Jacob	1	1	1		
Stiles, John, Junr	1		1		
King, William	2	5	1		
Daves, Mathew	1	2	1		
Brown, Jacob	2	3	3		
Hall, Mary	1		4		
Gurganus, Nicholas	2	1	7		2
King, John	1	1	4		1
Feutral, Moore	1	2	1		
Nixon, Robert, Senr	2		3		6
Fields, Zachariah	1	2	3		
Cox, William	2	4	1		
Barfield, Moses	2		4		1
Barfield, Aron	1	3	1		
Screws, Joseph	3	2	9		
Jordon, John	1	1	2		
Bachelor, Lydia			2		
Manor, Elizabeth	1	2	1		
Calvert, Ruth	1		2		
Brown, Nancy			2		
Mashbourn, Mary	2	1	2		
Daves, Aron	2	3	5		
Rainor, Molley	1	1	5		
Fox, Moses	1	1	1		2
Cummings, Susannah		1	2		2
File, James	2	3	5		2
Dunn, James	1	1	8		1
Jones, John	1	2	3		
Brenson, John	1	1	1		
Bond, John	1	3	2		
Mason, Richard	1	2	1		1
Cason, James	1				
Jones, Benjamin	1				
Turner, James	2	2	2		3
Shepherd, Sipian	1	1	2		
Evans, John	1	1	1		
Evans, Samuel	1		2		
Shepherd, Stephen	1		1		
Hall, Benjamin	1	1	4		4
Bryan, Jonathan	1	4	4		2
Heidelburg, Catharine	1	1	3		3
Heidelburg, John	1	1	1		1
Dickson, Jonathan	3	2	3		
Burnson, Adam	1	1	2		
Mabees, Charles	1	1	2		
Bennett, William	3		2		1
Mashbourn, Joseph	1	1	6		7
Dunn, Drury	1	1	1	1	1
Brinson, George	2				5
Shepherd, Daniel	1		4		3
Love, Amos	1	2	7		9
Rhodes, Woodhouse	2	3	3		19
Hatch, John	1	2	2		10
Rundles, William	1	4	4		
Gurganus, Zachariah	1	2	3		4
Hadnot, Lebins	1		1		2
Whitehead, Ebenezar	1	2	3		
Lee, David	1	3	5		
Ennet, John	1				
Haney, Priscilla		1	4		
Fisher, John	1	3	4		
Aman, Jacob	1	1	3	1	1
Grant, John	1	1	4		
Wadkins, John	1	2	2		
Smith, John	1				
Jenkings, Liuis, Junr	1	2	3		
Wilson, James	1		4		
Wood, Mark	1	1	3		
Kemmy, Thomas	2	2	3		
Green, Benjamin	1	3	1		1
Sanders, Elizabeth		3	2		
Loyed, Thomas, Junr	1	3	1		1
Dunn, Henry	1		3		1
Miles, Sarah		1	1		
Umphrys, William	1	1	4		
Simpson, Richard	2	1	3		7
Wheler, William	1	1	2		6
Mellon, Jonathan	1		3		
Ellis, Ely	1		1		
Butler, Jesse	1	1			
Butler, Robert	1		5		
Pescot, William	1		1		
Pitts, Thomas	1		2		1
Lee, Charles	1		1		
Butler, John	1	1	4		
Ward, Solomon	1	4	3		9
Jarrott, Isaac	1	1	2		10
Lairy, Darby	2	3	4		
Murray, Nathan	1	2			
Jenkings, William	1		3		1
Jenkings, George	1		1		2
Craft, Charles	1	1	1		9
Orrel, John	5	1	4		
Brinson, John	2		3		
Thomas, Richard	2		2		4
Fullar, John	1	2	3		
Haus, Joseph	1	1	1		
Whitus, Thomas	1		2		
Parish, Stephen	1		2		
Williams, Stephen	1	2	1		3
Whitus, Mary	3		3		6
Flay, Thomas, Junr	2	4	3		12
Landing, Stephen	1	1	3		
Johnston, Isaac	1	1	3		
Pollock, William	1	2	3		
Roach, John	1		1		
Grissom, John	2	3	4		2
Wilson, James	1		3		
Fullard, Thomas	1	4	3		
Thomson, Margaret			4		
Thomson, Thomas	1				
Hall, Edmund	1		2		
Penalton, Mrs			4		
Butt, John	1		4		4
Mannon, Lydia	1	1	3		1
Fullard, Mary			3		
Gibson, John	1		1		
Thompson, James	1		2		
Thompson, Enoch	1	2	1		
Meirrah, Hannah		1	2		
Mills, David	1	2	5		
Spicer, Elzey	1	1	3		24
Gill, Benjamin	1		2		
Gun, Alexander	2	2	2		
Perry, Thomas	1	1	2		
Burnet, John	1	1	4		
Averet, John	1		1		
King, Priscilla	1		2		13
German, Moses	2	3	4		
Malsby, Thomas	1		2	2	
Edins, James	1	1	3		
Walton, James	1		1		
Hobs, Simon	2	1	1		
Henderson, Nancy		3	2		
Howard, Thomas	1	3	4		18
Devawl, Joshua	1	1	2		
Barber, Richard	1		1		
Fengsenger, William	1		3		
Edins, Thomas	1	2	4		
Harrison, John	1	2	5		
Hatch, Asa	1		1		24
Avert, Benjamin	3	2	3		1
Goodeem, Abner	1	2	4		
Ennet, Joseph	3	1	2		5
Norman, Elijah	1	2	3		
Camble, Sarah	1		2		2
Hardeson, Gabriel	2	1	2		
Hardeson, Jesse	1		2		
Devawl, George	1	3	3		
Rhodes, Solomon, Senr	1	1	3		
Rhodes, Solomon, Junr	1		2		
King, John	1	1	1		2
Busby, Benjamin	2	1	3		
Spicer, John, Esq.	2	5	3		22
King, Benjamin	1	2	1		5
Williams, Robert	1	3			2
Read, William	1	3	2		
Russel, Linton	1	2	1		
Caston, Thomas	1		2	1	
Jones, Peter	1	2	2		
Harris, David	1	1	3		
Lain, James	1	2	3		1
Adamson, George	1	1	3		
Fumviel, Jeremiah	2	3	3		30
Wilkins, John	1	1	3		3
Fumveil, Lucy	2		2		15
Hunt, Onsipharus	2	2	5		
Hardison, Charles	1	1	2		
Singluf, Aron	1		1		1
Hall, Winey		1	3		1
Dickson, John	2	3	1		
Hobs, James	1		1		
Jenkings, Joshua	1	1	1		
Collear, John	1		2		3
Hansley, John	3	3	2		3
Austin, Francis	1		2		
Brice, Cornelias	1	1	1		
Cranford, Mary			1		
Hansley, William	1	2	1		4
York, John	3		1		5
Ennet, Nathaniel	1	3	1		
Curtis, George	1	2	4		
Williams, Richard	1		2		
Parker, Ann		2	5		1
Rows, Dedemiah	1		2	2	2
Ketchum, Jonathan	1	1	2		2
Badock, Jonathan	1	1	2		
Owens, Whitton	1		2		
Wills, William	1	1	3		
Hawkins, Stephen	1	1	2		1
Hawkins, Ezeriah	1	4	4		1
Hawkins, William	2	2	3		2
Burne, Francis	1		3		5
Taylor, Isaac	2	1	4		
Milton, Joseph	2	4	4		

WILMINGTON DISTRICT, ONSLOW COUNTY—Continued.

NAME OF HEAD OF FAMILY.	Free white males of 16 years and upward, including heads of families.	Free white males under 16 years.	Free white females, including heads of families.	All other free persons.	Slaves.
Hawkins, John	1	1	2		
Perry, William	2		3		1
Cullay, Edward	1	1	2		
Gray, Sarah		1	3		
Scott, Lucin	3	1			
Price, Benjamin	1	1	2		
Howard, William	2	1	3		1
Rows, Martha			2		
Spooner, Susanna		2	5		
Smith, Calop	2		3		
Smith, William	1		4		
Sanders, John	2	1	4		5
Scott, Lurina			3		
Hazzard, George	1	2	3		6
Rows, Elizabeth		1	2		
Cranford, James	3				
Lain, James	2	1	2		
Clark, William	2		1		1
Burns, Federick	3	3	4		8
Gregory, Jesse	4	2	4		8
Williams, Benjamin	3	3	4		9
Murrell, John	1		1		
Dudley, Edward	1		2		4
Godfree, William	1	3	1		2
Lyster, Banister	2	1	4		6
Hicks, Lewis	1		1		3
Noble, Samuel	3	2	2		7
Orrel, James	1		2		1
Johnston, Thomas, Junr	1	1	2		
Eagerston, John	2	1			1
Edmandson, James	1	1	5		
Johnston, John	2	1			1
Fair, Richard	1	3	6		5
Willey, Alexander	2	1	2		1
Murrell, Kemp	1	3	2		1
Murrell, William	1	1	3		7
Johnston, Thomas, Senr	2	4	4		9
Loyed, William	1	3	4		
Godfrey, Enoch	1	2	5		1
Ward, Richard	1		3		5
Godfrey, Francis	1		2		
Orrel, Thomas	1	2	1		1
Edmandson, William	1	1	3		
Hammond, Edward	3	4	3		8
Jarman, Thomas	1		4		
Willey, John	1		3		3
Howard, Edmand	1	3	3		2
Godfree, Francis	1		1		
Thompson, Charles	1	2	5		5
Weeks, John	1	1	3		
Bryant, Thomas	2		3		1
Eagerton, William	2	3	5		
Hazelip, Abner	1	1	3		
Marshall, Joseph	1	1	3		
Littleton, Lurry, Junr	1	3	2		
Littleton, Lurry, Senr	3		3		
Taylor, William Wilkins	1	3	2		7
Marshall, Pernal	1		2		
Huggans, Francis		2	2		
Huggins, Jacob	1		1		
Eagerton, James	1	1	2		5
West, Mary	1	2	2		
Hicks, Solomon	1	2	4		
Ball, Nancy	2	1	2		
Marshall, Umphry	1	2	2		
Row, James	1		1		
Farnell, Benjamin	1	2	1		2
Farnell, Mikajah	1	1	1		5
Morton, William	1		1		
Heart, Absolom	1		3		
Simons, Nancy			2		3
Simmons, Benjamin	1	1	1		2
Farnell, Elizabeth	1	1	2		
Ward, Joseph	1		3		3
Dudley, Stephen	1	1	1		2
Roberts, Holster	2	3	3		30
Newton, Elijah	1		2		4
Newton, Mrs		1	3		
Ball, James	1		2		
Barns, Ezikiah	1	1	4		
Milton, Edward	1	1	6		
Yewell, William	5	1	4		1
Milton, Benjamin	1	2	2		
Milton, James	3	4	4		
Edwards, Henry		2	2		3
Todd, John	1	3	1		
Todd, Aron	1		2		
Todd, Moses	1		3		
Erixson, Jonathan	1	1	1		
Yewell, John	2	2			
Jarrott, John, Junr	1	1	5		
Erixson, Samuel	1		1		
Farrow, Benjamin	1	4	2		
Collens, Richard, Senr	4	1	2		
Thomas, Betsey			2		
Collens, Richard, Junr	1		6		

NAME OF HEAD OF FAMILY.	Free white males of 16 years and upward, including heads of families.	Free white males under 16 years.	Free white females, including heads of families.	All other free persons.	Slaves.
Taylor, John	1	2	3		
Heart, John	1	2	2		
Hicks, Robert	1	2	2		3
Hadnot, Aldridge	2	1	2		15
Pearson, Thomas	1	1	2		2
Pearson, John	1	1	5		1
Edge, John	1	3	4		
Hadnot, Stephen	1	2	3		
Robenson, Mr	1	2	3		
Hancock, Enoch	3	1	3		2
Snead Thomas	1	1			
Cary, Nathan	1	1	3		1
Mumford, William	1	4	3		16
Weeks, John	3	3	3		
Venturs, Arthur	2	3	4		
Erexon, Andrew	1	2	2		
Jarrott, John	1		1		
Craeg, Elias	1	3	1		
Hancock, Nathaniel	3	2	4		1
Howard, Josiah	1		5		19
Simmons, Henry	1		5		
Mitchell, George, Esq	3	7	3		29
Gibbs, William	1	1	2		2
Cary, Miles	1				
Ward, David	1	2	7		15
Ward, Carl	1	4	4		22
Delany, Thomas	1	5	3		4
Ward, Benjamin	1	1	1		4
Ward, Edward, Esq	1	1	1		30
Fumviel, Brice	1		2		8
Felyau, James	1	1	4		4
Davis, James	1	1	3		3
Ross, David	1	2	2		
Wilson, Josiah	1	1	5		
Wilson, James	1	3	4		
Nixon, Charles	1	3	4		3
Hadnot, Joseph	1	1	2		
Strange, James	1		3		
Ryals, Nancy		1	2		
Tow, Abigail		2	5		
Burns, Otway	2	1	5		4
Jones, Kibby	1		3		17
Pastures, John	1	1	3		
Burnett, Abraham	1	2	5		7
Jones, Hull	1	4	3		7
Marcy, Edward	1	2	3		3
Mumford, Jehue	1		2		1
Fulcher, Benjamin	1	3	1		6
Sanders, Jesse	1	1	4		3
Mumford, Leark		3	1		7
Woodman, John	2		3		
Newtout, Elizabeth			3		
Whaley, Eogdal	1	1	2		
Conneway, John	2		3		1
Hewitt, John	2	1	2		1
Moss, John	2	2	5		
Rodgers, Daniel	1		3		
Wire, Thomas	1	1	3		
Wren, Catherine			1		5
Sharard, Amy		1	2		
Bell, George	1	1	2		
Farior, Benjamin	1		2		
Trott, Richard	1	1	2		
Dodd, George	1	1	2		
Burnett, John	1	3	1		1
Lovett, John	1	1	1		7
Snead, John	1		1		
Gibson, Richard		1	1		3
Newbowl, Levi	1	2	6		1
Martek, John	1		1		4
Burnett, Isaac		1	1		2
Newbowl, Sarah		1	3		
Taylor, Moses	1	2	5		
Truman, Elijah	2	3	5		1
Arnold, Peter	4	3	1		
Starkey, John	2	1	5		50
Hicks, David	1				6
Horton, Abraham	1		3		
Dudley, Betsey	1		2		1
Hewbanks, John	1		1		
Hewbanks, Elijah	1		1		4
Hewbanks, Thomas	3	1	6		4
Hewbanks, Ezekiel	1	1	1		
Simpson, Adra	2		2		
Bedale, Elijah	2		3		
Trott, Adam	1	2	1		
Trott, John	1	2	1		
Tolman, John	1		1		
Starkey, Elizabeth		2	3		35
Fields, Samuel	4		4		6
Fields, Jacob	1	2	4		5
Fields, James	2		2		2
Fields, Moses	3		2		
Keys, Joseph	1	2	1		6
Smith, Calop	3	3	11		
Sparman, George	1	2	2		10
Gibson, Thomas	3	3	3		

NAME OF HEAD OF FAMILY.	Free white males of 16 years and upward, including heads of families.	Free white males under 16 years.	Free white females, including heads of families.	All other free persons.	Slaves.
Gibson, Abraham	1		2		5
Perry, Waxwell	1		2		
Owens, Edmund	2				1
Williams, Stephen	1		3		
Wood, James	2	1	5		
Gibson, Archibald	2				8
Jones, William	1		1		8
Marshall, Leark		1	1		
Newton, Daniel	1		5		3
Willey, Susanna	2	1	5		
Godley, John	1	1	2		2
Willey, John Alexr	1		2		7
Chalcraft, Isaac	1		2		5
Cray, Joseph Scott, Esq.	1	1	2		30
Chalcraft, Stephen	1	3	2		2
Chalcraft, Anthony	1	1	3		9
Johnson, Rachel		2	6		
French, James	1				
West, Levi	1	1	3		
Hawkins, Obediah			1		
Melton, Mary Ann	2	2	2		
Eagerton, James	1	2	2		5
Eagerton, Charles	1		4		4
Hawkins, White Huck	1				
Averit, John	1				
Godley, Ann		1	1		
Linger, Elizabeth		1	3		
Hall, Doratha		3	2		13
Brinson, Mathew	1	1	3		
Serews, William	1	1	1		
Burton, Charles	1	1	1		
Shepherd, Benjamin	1	1	3		
Walton, James	1	1	3		
Garnton, Daniel	1	1	3		
Aman, Philip	1	5	6		
Brinson, Gause	1	4	1		4
Pitman, Arthur	1	1	2		
Fisher, John	1	3	3		
Cray, William	1	3	3		13
Fair, John	1	2	2		7
Lee, Rachael		1	4		6
Walker, Samuel	1		2		6
Ambruse, Daniel	1	3	4		5
Farnell, Thomas	3	1	1		3
Marshall, Jonathan	1	1	2		
Marshall, Isaac	1				
Marshall, John	1				
Morton, Peter	3	2	3		7
Morton, Richard	1		1		
Wood, Penelope	3		3		
McKenney, John	4	2	5		
Morton, Joseph	1	1	3		
Morton, Joseph	2		3		
Askins, William	3	2	4		
Melton, Richard	1	1	3		
Yates, James	2	2	2		
Chambers, Sarah	3	1	3		
Gairy, George	3	3	3		
Wood, Frederick	1	1	1		
Bowen, John	1	4	2		
Bowen, Joshua	1	1			
Jackson, Bazzell	1		2		
Wood, Joseph					
Carver, Henry	1	1	1		
Smublage, John	1	1	7		
Strange, Seth	2	3	3		
Kelly, Betsy		2	2		
Williams, William	1	3	4		
Teachy, John	1	2	3		
Williams, Stephen	1	4	2		
Skipper, Nathan	1	2	3		
Brown, Stephen	1	2	5		
Skipper, Joseph	1	4	2		
Baizdon, Patience		1	1		
Baizdon, Josiah	1	4	6		
Sumner, Mathew	1	1	1		
Petteway, Amy		1	1		
Cermott, Alexander	3				1
Mason, Abraham	3	2	5		2
Boardsman, Jonathan	2	1	3		1
Adams, Penelope			2		
Hopson, Horatia	1	1	2		
Adkinson, Harisson	1	2	5		
Bennet, James	1	1	3		
Pierce, Benjamin	1		5		
Weeks, Cornelas	2	3	1	1	1
Mason, William	1				
Wright, Elizabeth		2	2		
Scott, Adam	2		3		2
McCollah, John	1	1	3	1	5
Murray, James	1		2		
Dudley, Thomas	3	2	3		9
Javanson, Andrew	1	1	1		4
Pitts, Mary			2		8
Parks, William	1	1	2		4
Nalms, Martha	1	1	1		9
Swift, Epram	3		4		9

WILMINGTON DISTRICT, ONSLOW COUNTY—Continued.

NAME OF HEAD OF FAMILY.	Free white males of 16 years and upward, including heads of families.	Free white males under 16 years.	Free white females, including heads of families.	All other free persons.	Slaves.
Hott, Elizabeth	1		1		5
Gabriel, Nathaniel	1	1	3		
Bell, Eden	3	2	2		
Villard, Gabriel	1				1
Newbowl, John	1	1	4		
Hellen, William	2		2		1
Noble, William	1		1		
Hewit, Polley		1	3		
Newbowl, Polley			1		
Pew, Robert	1	1	2		
Gibson, Thomas	2	6	3		
Pitts, Rigdon	1	1	2		9
Taylor, Moses	1	2	5		
Gillet, John	1				
Chancy, Abel	2	3	4		
Lord, Peggy		2	2		
Cummings, Sarah			1		
Jones, Ezekiah	1	2	4		
Row, Christopher	1	1	1		
Ward, John	3	3	3		
Rigs, John	1	4	3		
Burk, Rebeca		2	4		
Morris, Thomas	2		2		
Tewday, Jesse	1		3		
Chelley, Joseph	1		2		
Thomson, John	1	3	4		2
Wood, James	1	1	2		
Baety, Mrs	2	1	3		
Shaw, Francis	1	1	2		
Williams, John	1	2	2		
Simmons, Daniel	1	1	2		
Williams, Jacob	1				4
Baety, Benjamin	1		3		
Knights, Mr	1	4	4		7
Gage, Robert	1		6		
Gellet, Phillana		4	3		5
James, Thomas	1	2	3		
Gibson, William	2	4	3		
Smith, Thomas	2	1	3		3

NAME OF HEAD OF FAMILY.	Free white males of 16 years and upward, including heads of families.	Free white males under 16 years.	Free white females, including heads of families.	All other free persons.	Slaves.
Venters, Malaka	1	1	3		
Venters, Francis	1	2	3		
Morris, Sylvia			1	1	
Justice, Laban		3	4		
Perry, John	1	1	4		
Walton, Thomas	2	2	2		
Sinclair, Robert	1		2		
Coston, Francis	2		1		
Walton, John	1	1	5		
Howard, John	3		2		
Coston, John	1	4	3		
Hunt, Nesse	2	2	5		
King, Elizabeth			3		8
Fulward, Andrew	3		1		3
Hammons, Martha	1	2	4		
Hanket, John	1	1	4		
Hibs, Wilkin	1	2	3		4
Mitchel, Barsheba			5		
Caroch, John Henry	1	2	1		
Scott, Obed	1	2	2		
Ward, Edward	1		3		4
Heart, Absolom	1		2		
Howard, William	1	4	2		
Colomn, George	1	4	3		
Colomn, William	1	3	2		
Edwards, Josiah	1	3	5		8
Dewral, Mary			2		
Proctor, Shadarick	1	3	3		
Gerganus, Jesse	2	3	7		
Shepherd, Wiliby	1		1		
Hecks, John	1	4	1		7
Murray, Jonathan	2	1	3		7
Landing, James	1	1	3		
Landing, William	4	1	3		
Haws, John, Senr	1	1	2		1
Gurganus, Barbary	1	2	3		
Loyed, Thomas	1		2		
Heidleburg, Samuel	1	1	1		2
Loyed, Susanna	1		3		

NAME OF HEAD OF FAMILY.	Free white males of 16 years and upward, including heads of families.	Free white males under 16 years.	Free white females, including heads of families.	All other free persons.	Slaves.
Loyed, Daniel	1		1		
Shepherd, John, Senr	1	2	3		4
Shepherd, George, Junr	4	4	3		5
Shepherd, John, Junr	1	1	1		1
Shepherd, Smith	1	1	2		
Loyed, Nancy			2		
Thomson, Mary	2		2		
Thomson, Absolom	1		2		
Johnson, Sarah			5		
Haws, John, Junr	1		1		
Giddins, Abraham	1	1	4		1
Boardsman, Jonathan	1	1	3		5
Aman, John	1	2	4		
Hedgepeth, Dude	1	1	2		
Bell, William	1				
Ross, Rheuben	1	1	4		
Farrah, Benjamin	1	2	1		
Clark, John	2		1		1
Britton, John	1		1		
Bender, Daniel	1	1	3		15
Askins, Joseph	1	4	1		
Costen, Robert	1	2	2		
Venters, Mrs			5		
Howard, William	2	2	5		
Clark, Rheuben	1				
Jemboy				1	6
Dry, Virgil				1	5
Freeman, Samuel				8	
Freeman, Roger				7	
Perry, Colop				4	
Perry, Charles				11	
Davis, Deck				7	
Milley				4	
Sweet, James				6	
Hays, Jacob				6	
Cumbo, Rheuben				4	
Cumbo, Stephen				4	
Cumbo, Solomon				6	
Jones, Stephen				5	

INDEX.[1]

[1] No attempt has been made in this publication to correct mistakes in spelling made by the assistant marshals, and the names have been reproduced as they appear upon the census schedules.

Gunter, Isham, 84.
Gunter, Isham, 88.
Gunter, James, 86.
Gunter, Jesse, 92.
Gunter, Jnº, 110.
Gunter, Thoˢ, 84.
Gunter, Wᵐ, 84.
Gupten, Abner. 59.
Gupten, James, 59.
Gupten, Stephen, 59.
Gurbs, Nicholas, 95.
Gurganus, Barbary, 197.
Gurganus, Nicholas, 195.
Gurganus, Zachariah, 195.
Gurley, Ann, 140.
Gurley, Edward, 140.
Gurley, Frederick, 30.
Gurley, George, 151.
Gurley, Isum, 140.
Gurley, Joel, 151.
Gurley, John, 140.
Gurley, Joseph, 140.
Gurley, Lewis, 151.
Gurley, Mary, junʳ, 140.
Gurley, Mary, Senʳ, 140.
Gurley, Sarah, 39.
Gurley, William, 37.
Gurlin, Mary, 142.
Gurly, James, 164.
Gusley, James, 164.
Gustrer, Absalom, 169.
Guthre, William, 186.
Guthrey, Frederic, 128.
Guthridge, Mrs., 73.
Guthrie, Samˡ, 84.
Guthrie, William, 77.
Guthry, Charles, 128.
Guthry, Jane, 128.
Guthry, Levi, 129.
Guthry, Samuel, 129.
Guthry, Solomon, 129.
Guthry, Stephen, 129.
Gutree, Wᵐ, 87.
Gutry, Charles, 183.
Gutters, Wᵐ, 117.
Guttery, Frank, 115.
Guttery, Garrott, 80.
Guttery, Thoˢ, 167.
Guttree, Lewry, 103.
Guy, James, 156.
Guy, James, 191.
Guy, Lemuel, 191.
Guy, William, 28.
Guy, William, 68.
Guy, William, 190.
Guyer, John, 30.
Guyer, Joseph, 28.
Guyer, Meriam, 30.
Guyton, James, 186.
Guyton, Priscilla, 186.
Gwartney, Benjamin, 148.
Gwartney, John, 132.
Gwartney, Thomas, 146.
Gwartney, William, 147.
Gwin, Daniel, 82.
Gwin, Edward, 93.
Gwin, Hugh, 168.
Gwin, John, 80.
Gwinn, Thos., 96.
Gyer, Jacob, 107.
Gyger, Phillip, 111.
Gymon, Isaac, 179.
Gyn, Jos., 122.
Gynn, Rd., 122.

Hackburn, Joseph, 145.
Hackeb, Robert, 98.
Hackell, Armstead, 127.
Hacket, Michael, 55.
Hacket, Oliver. 153.
Hackman, John, 85.
Hackney, John, 93.
Hackney, Joseph, 86.
Hackney, Joseph, 87.
Hackney, Richard, 31.
Hackney, William, 58.
Hackney, Wᵐ, 84.
Hackney, William, 141.
Hackny, Daniel, 86.
Hadcock, Shadrach, 56.
Hadden, George, 164.
Haddesk, Drury, 188.
Haddock, Admiral, 148.
Haddock, Charles, 148.
Haddock, Henry, 183.
Haddock, James, 161.
Haddock, John, 148.
Haddock, William, 148.
Hadley, Ambrose, 65.
Hadley, Jeremiah, 87.
Hadley, John, 39.
Hadley, Joseph, 88.
Hadley, Joshua, 65.
Hadley, Joshua, 86.
Hadley, Joshua, 87.
Hadley, Joshua, 161.
Hadley, Martha, 65.
Hadley, Mary, 86.
Hadley, Simon, 85.
Hadley, Simon, 185.
Hadley, Simon, Junʳ, 185.
Hadley, Thoˢ, 85.
Hadley, Thomas, 185.

Hadly, Benjamin, 39.
Hadly, Jesse, 39.
Hadly, Hannah, 39.
Hadly, Joshua, 109.
Hadly, Simon, 39.
Hadly, Thomas, 39.
Hadly, William, 46.
Hadnot, Aldridge, 196.
Hadnot, Joseph, 196.
Hadnot, Lebins, 195.
Hadnot, Stephen, 196.
Hadox, William, 170.
Hady, Samˡ, 153.
Haethcock, John, 77.
Haeworth, Austin, 110.
Hafford, Malicah, 132.
Hagar, Jnº, 114.
Hagar, Simon, 112.
Hagar, Wᵐ, 114.
Hager, Jane, 114.
Hager, Simon, 114.
Hagey, George, 173.
Hagey, Henry, 173.
Haggard, Benjamin, 169.
Haggard, Edmund, 82.
Haggard, John, 185.
Haggard, Richard, 82.
Haggard, Samuel, 185.
Hagges, Dorcas, 69.
Haggins, John, 163.
Haggins, John, 178.
Haggins, William, 171.
Haggins, William, 184.
Hagin, Peter, 185.
Hagins, Christopher, 125.
Hagins, Darby, 125.
Hagins, Frazer, 133.
Hagins, Jnº, 122.
Hagins, Mary, 150.
Hagler, Abrin., 123.
Hagler, Jacob, 123.
Hagler, Jacob, 161.
Hagler, John, 161.
Hagler, Jnº, Jʳ, 123.
Hagman, Henry, 32.
Hagrity, Patrick, 24.
Haiden, Dugles, 171.
Haiden, Joseph, 176.
Haiden, Unity, 171.
Hail, Aris, 64.
Hail, Dudley, 77.
Hail, Jesse, 64.
Hail, John, 179.
Hail, Jonathan, 64.
Hail, Lewis, 64.
Hail, Ogburn, 64.
Hail, Williamson, 64.
Haild, Jacob, 98.
Haile, John, 135.
Hailer, Henry, 141.
Hailes, Chapman, 141.
Hailes, John, 141.
Hailes, John, Senʳ, 141.
Hailes, Robert, 50.
Hailey, Hansel, 39.
Hailey, Holliday, 73.
Hailey, Mark, 107.
Hailey, Wᵐ, 107.
Hails, John, 57.
Hails, Mary, 171.
Haily, Rd., 107.
Haine, Beˢ, 26.
Haine, Jessee, 26.
Haine, Joseph, 25.
Haine, Marmaduke, 25.
Haine, William, 26.
Haines, Henry Pendergras, 131.
Haines, John, 77.
Haines, Jonathan, 184.
Hainey, Penny, 53.
Hainey, Reuben, 166.
Hainey, Spencer, 167.
Hains, Elis, 185.
Hains, James, 155.
Hains, John, 155.
Hains, Joseph, 155.
Hains, Joshua, 155.
Hains, Phillip, 174.
Hains, Ralph, 176.
Hair, Ann, 39.
Hair, Daniel, 158.
Hair, Elkeny, 37.
Hair, Jacob, 53.
Hair, Joel, 54.
Hair, John, 43.
Hair, John, 52.
Hair, Mary, 126.
Hair, Peter, 43.
Hair, Robert, 158.
Hair, Thomas, 53.
Hair, William, 39.
Hair, William, 53.
Hair, William, 53.
Hairgroves, Briton, 187.
Hairgroves, Burrel, 188.
Hairgroves, William, 143.
Halbert, Joel, 180.
Halbert, John, 180.
Halcomb, Drury, 184.
Halcomb, George, 185.
Halcomb, Grimes, 185.
Halcomb, John, 185.
Halcomb, Lawrence, 183.

Halcomb, May, 185.
Halcomb, Thomas, 185.
Halcomb, William, 37.
Hale, David, 193.
Hale, Fereby, 26.
Hale, Jessee, 12.
Hale, John, 12.
Hale, Jonas, 13.
Hale, Mathew, 192.
Hale, Nathan, 188.
Hale, Polly, 70.
Hales, John, 57.
Hales, Josiah, 87.
Haley, Isam, 46.
Haley, Randal, 45.
Haley, Robert, 87.
Haley, Silas, 45.
Haley, William, 45.
Haliberton, Charles, 80.
Haliberton, John, 80.
Haliberton, Thomas, 80.
Halke, James, 184.
Hall, Abᵐ, 170.
Hall, Adam, 157.
Hall, Alexander, 158.
Hall, Andʷ, 158.
Hall, Andrew, 167.
Hall, Anthony, 164.
Hall, Armager, 52.
Hall, Barnabas, 54.
Hall, Benjamin, 100.
Hall, Benjamin, 195.
Hall, Bickley, 54.
Hall, Burrel, 187.
Hall, Caleb, 150.
Hall, Celia, 135.
Hall, Charles, 146.
Hall, Clement, 18.
Hall, Darias, 81.
Hall, David, 16.
Hall, David, 57.
Hall, David, 58.
Hall, David, 96.
Hall, David, 128.
Hall, David, 133.
Hall, David, 191.
Hall, Dempsey, 135.
Hall, Doratha, 196.
Hall, Durham, 59.
Hall, Edmund, 195.
Hall, Edward, 55.
Hall, Edward, 64.
Hall, Edward, Esqʳ, 30.
Hall, Elisha, 28.
Hall, Enoch, 48.
Hall, Futril, 89.
Hall, George, 83.
Hall, George, 170.
Hall, George, 170.
Hall, Hudson, 183.
Hall, Hugh, 158.
Hall, Ignatius, 44.
Hall, Instance, 48.
Hall, Isaac, 47.
Hall, Isaac, 48.
Hall, Isaac, 94.
Hall, Isaac, 150.
Hall, Isaac, 192.
Hall, Isaiah, 30.
Hall, Jacob, 47.
Hall, James, 30.
Hall, James, 94.
Hall, James, 138.
Hall, James, 143.
Hall, James, 147.
Hall, James, 162.
Hall, James, Jurʳ, 158.
Hall, James, Senʳ, 158.
Hall, Revᵈ Jaˢ, 158.
Hall, Jane, 133.
Hall, Jesse, 121.
Hall, Jesse, 124.
Hall, Joel, 103.
Hall, Joel, Jʳ, 47.
Hall, Joel, Sʳ, 47.
Hall, John, 21.
Hall, John, 46.
Hall, John, 47.
Hall, John, 51.
Hall, John, 55.
Hall, John, 56.
Hall, John, 59.
Hall, John, 74.
Hall, John, 81.
Hall, John, 83.
Hall, John, 87.
Hall, John, 96.
Hall, John, 107.
Hall, Jnº, 108.
Hall, Jnº, 109.
Hall, Jnº, 117.
Hall, Jnº, 121.
Hall, John, 143.
Hall, John, 158.
Hall, John, 162.
Hall, John, 180.
Hall, John, Esq., 188.
Hall, Jnº, Jʳ, 108.
Hall, Jonathan, 59.
Hall, Joseph, 47.
Hall, Joseph, 57.
Hall, Joseph, 98.
Hall, Joseph, 164.
Hall, Joseph, 170.

Hall, Joseph, 182.
Hall, Joseph, junʳ, 132.
Hall, Joseph, Sʳ, 47.
Hall, Joseph, Senʳ, 132.
Hall, Joshua, 108.
Hall, Joshua, 185.
Hall, Josiah, 51.
Hall, Judith, 18.
Hall, Lazarus, 54.
Hall, Lemuel, 28.
Hall, Levy, 94.
Hall, Lewis, 48.
Hall, Lewis, Jʳ, 48.
Hall, Mantain, 26.
Hall, Martin, 123.
Hall, Martin, 141.
Hall, Mary, 27.
Hall, Mary, 54.
Hall, Mary, 63.
Hall, Mary, 195.
Hall, Morgan, 160.
Hall, Moses, 52.
Hall, Moses, 74.
Hall, Naomi, 108.
Hall, Nathaniel, 20.
Hall, Nathaniel, 128.
Hall, Oliver, 134.
Hall, Owen, 121.
Hall, Peter, 42.
Hall, Phillip, 83.
Hall, Poole, 135.
Hall, Rachael, 30.
Hall, Rachel, 132.
Hall, Randol, 66.
Hall, Randoph, 178.
Hall, Robert, 35.
Hall, Robert, 63.
Hall, Robert, 64.
Hall, Robert, 106.
Hall, Robt., 121.
Hall, Samuel, 144.
Hall, Samuel, 170.
Hall, Samuel, junʳ, 128.
Hall, Samuel, Senʳ, 128.
Hall, Sarah, 47.
Hall, Simon, 130.
Hall, Solomon, 103.
Hall, Spence, Junʳ, 21.
Hall, Spence, 21.
Hall, Susanah, 29.
Hall, Theodorick, 62.
Hall, Thomas, 59.
Hall, Thomas, 77.
Hall, Thomas, 99.
Hall, Thom., 118.
Hall, Tho', 119.
Hall, Thom., 123.
Hall, Thomas, 132.
Hall, Thomas, 134.
Hall, Thomas, 135.
Hall, Thomas, 146.
Hall, Thomas, 158.
Hall, Thomas, 162.
Hall, Walter, 170.
Hall, William, 52.
Hall, William, 70.
Hall, William, 75.
Hall, Wm., 93.
Hall, William, 100.
Hall, William, 100.
Hall, Wᵐ, 103.
Hall, Wᵐ, 103.
Hall, Wᵐ, 119.
Hall, William, 138.
Hall, William, 148.
Hall, William, 158.
Hall, William, 164.
Hall, William, 171.
Hall, William, 174.
Hall, William, 185.
Hall, William, 191.
Hall, William, 191.
Hall, William, Jʳ, 47.
Hall, William, Jurʳ, 158.
Hall, William, Sʳ, 47.
Hall, Winey, 195.
Hallet, Richard, 42.
Halley, Wᵐ, 86.
Halliman, Mark, 184.
Hallin, William, 174.
Halling, Solomon, 130.
Hallows, Josiah, 135.
Hallsey, Cullen, 18.
Hallsey, Daniel, 18.
Hallsey, Edmund, 30.
Hallsey, Frederick, 30.
Hallsey, Harris, 18.
Hallsey, Henry, 18.
Hallsey, Malachi, 18.
Hallsey, William, 18.
Hallum, Judah, 13.
Hallums, George, 168.
Hallums, John, 168.
Halomon, Hanche, 25.
Halsey, Henry, 193.
Halso, John, 191.
Halso, Stephen, 192.
Haltom, Joseph, 164.
Haltom, William, 164.
Halton, Robert, 145.

Halton, Thomas, 70.
Ham, Henry, 149.
Ham, John, 180.
Ham, Joseph, 180.
Ham, Mordicai, 180.
Ham, Philip, 153.
Ham, Richard, 149.
Ham, Thomas, 180.
Ham, Thomas, 180.
Ham, Zachariah, 149.
Haman, Ephraim, 98.
Hambey, Mary, 104.
Hambey, Stephen, 104.
Hamblet, Wᵐ, 84.
Hambleton, James, 194.
Hambleton, Pharobee, 13.
Hambleton, Walter, 164.
Hamblett, John, 164.
Hamblett, Peter, 164.
Hamblin, Martha, 62.
Hamblin, Wood, 62.
Hamblton, Andrew, 105.
Hamblton, Stewart, 105.
Hambrick, Henry, 186.
Hambrick, Jas., 117.
Hambrick, Jeremiah, 117.
Hambrick, Price, 117.
Hambrick, Robt., 106.
Hambrick, Sam., 117.
Hamby, Jnº, 124.
Hamby, Samˡ, 104.
Hamby, Wilm., 107.
Hamby, Wᵐ, 121.
Hamer, Brittin J., 77.
Hamer, Frances, 35.
Hamer, John, 98.
Hamer, John, 98.
Hamer, Mary, 35.
Hamiller (Widow), 115.
Hamilton, Aaron, 151.
Hamilton, Alexander, 19.
Hamilton, Alex., 111.
Hamilton, Alex., 115.
Hamilton, Andrew, 57.
Hamilton, Arche, 111.
Hamilton, David, 129.
Hamilton, Francis, 70.
Hamilton, George, 153.
Hamilton, Hance, 154.
Hamilton, Hugh, 160.
Hamilton, James, 33.
Hamilton, James, 130.
Hamilton, James, 132.
Hamilton, James, 139.
Hamilton, Jane, 115.
Hamilton, John, 19.
Hamilton, John, 127.
Hamilton, John, 136.
Hamilton, John, 136.
Hamilton, John, 153.
Hamilton, John, junʳ, 130.
Hamilton, John, Senʳ, 130.
Hamilton, Joseph, 94.
Hamilton, Lazarus, 127.
Hamilton, Lucius, 147.
Hamilton, Malakiah, 193.
Hamilton, Michael, 130.
Hamilton, Oratis, 182.
Hamilton, Robt., 116.
Hamilton, Robert, 129.
Hamilton, Samuel, 100.
Hamilton, Sarah, 136.
Hamilton, Thomas, 70.
Hamilton, Thomas, 153.
Hamilton, Thomas, 154.
Hamilton (Widow), 178.
Hamilton, Wᵐ, 113.
Hamilton, William, 160.
Hamlet, John, 36.
Hamlet, John, 37.
Hamlet, Moore Thomas, 83.
Hamlet, Richard, 77.
Hamlett, James, 83.
Hamlett, William, Jun., 83.
Hamlin, George, 168.
Hamlin, William, 83.
Hamm, Elisha, 59.
Hamm, Jacob, 173.
Hamm, Jesse, 59.
Hamm, Melcher, 173.
Hamm, Nehemiah, 100.
Hamm, Resters, 149.
Hamm, Richard, 59.
Hamm, William, junʳ, 148.
Hamm, William, Senʳ, 149.
Hammell, Jenny, 65.
Hammer, Solomon, 189.
Hammet, Robert, 179.
Hammilton, Matthew, 99.
Hammilton, Thomas, 98.
Hammock, Charles, 77.
Hammock, Robert, 186.
Hammon, Ben., 122.
Hammon, Elisha, 98.
Hammon, Hewell, 127.
Hammon, Jas., 122.
Hammon, Jesse, 102.
Hammon, John, 100.
Hammon, John, 122.
Hammon, Matthew, 101.
Hammon, Moses, 100.
Hammon, Rose, 139.
Hammon, William, 70.

9 7 8 1 6 3 9 1 4 1 7 5 3